Concise Reformed Dogmatics

Concise Reformed Dogmatics

J. van Genderen
W. H. Velema

TRANSLATED BY
Gerrit Bilkes
and
Ed M. van der Maas

P&R
PUBLISHING
P.O. BOX 817 • PHILLIPSBURG • NEW JERSEY 08865-0817

Originally published in the Netherlands under the title *Beknopte Gereformeerde dogmatiek* © 1992 by Uitgeversmaatschappij J. H. Kok at Kampen

Page design by Lakeside Design Plus

Printed in the United States of America

Library of Congress Cataloging-in-Publication Data

Genderen, J. van.
[Beknopte Gereformeerde dogmatiek. English]
Concise Reformed dogmatics / J. van Genderen, W. H. Velema ; translated by Gerrit Bilkes and Ed M. van der Maas.
p. cm.
Includes bibliographical references and indexes.
ISBN 978-0-87552-577-8 (cloth)
1. Theology, Doctrinal. 2. Reformed Church—Doctrines. I. Velema, W. H. II. Title.
BT75.3.G4613 2008
230'.42—dc22

2008035836

Contents

Publisher's Preface to the English Edition

This English edition of *Concise Reformed Dogmatics* is the merger of two translations, one by Ed van der Maas and the other by Gerrit Bilkes for the John Calvin Foundation. It is the product of a multistep process of comparing the two translations and combining their strengths. With an eye for clarity and theological integrity, a team of readers—including W. H. Velema, the lone surviving author, together with Lawrence W. Bilkes and Gerald M. Bilkes—checked the entire work.

The resulting translation reflects a preference for economy of words and closeness to the original text, including its paragraph breaks and headings. Only slight adjustments in formatting have been made to clarify organization. Importantly, this translation retains the original distinction in text-font sizes, which gives readers the option of delving into or forgoing weightier discussions.

Readers will find help for translating foreign-language titles in the list of abbreviations, the notes, and the literature lists at the ends of chapters. Throughout the text, many quotations have been conformed to published translations in English, most notably Herman Bavinck's four-volume *Reformed Dogmatics*, ed. John Bolt, trans. John Vriend (Grand Rapids: Baker, 2003–8); Karl Barth's *Church Dogmatics*, ed. G. W. Bromiley and T. F. Torrance, trans. G. T. Thomson and Harold Knight (Edinburgh: T & T Clark, 1956–75); and H. Berkhof's

The Christian Faith, trans. S. Woudstra (Grand Rapids: Eerdmans, 1979).

Finally, this edition has two indexes instead of three, one for Scripture references and the other a combined index of subjects and names.

P&R Publishing Company presents this work, a standard among Dutch theological literature, as a crystallization of the best confessionally Reformed Dutch thought in a single, manageable English-language volume.

Preface

The principle underlying this *Concise Reformed Dogmatics* is spelled out in the opening chapter, which serves as its introduction. It is therefore not necessary at this point to present a detailed account of our position. But this is indeed the place to say something about the plan of this book.

A book on dogmatics deals with the doctrine of the church. What is to be believed and confessed in the church of Christ? Various statements have been made in this regard from the perspective of the Word of God. Theologians and other Christians raise questions about these matters—adding new queries to old issues. But aside from such discussions, it is continually necessary to hold up the dogmas of the church to the light of Scripture. For this reason this book pays close attention indeed to the biblical foundation of the doctrine of the church.

The designation "Reformed" in the title does not merely imply that this work distinguishes itself from Roman Catholic or Lutheran dogmatics. Since the question as to what "Reformed" means has been answered in very different ways, a further clarification is not redundant. We interpret "Reformed" to mean confessionally Reformed, which implies that we hold that the Reformed confession must be allowed to speak for itself. It would not be right to listen to the voices of theologians of earlier and later periods and not to heed the voice of the confession of the churches of the Reformation.

In many cases we have been able to agree with the Reformed tradition of dogmatics of which J. Calvin and H. Bavinck are classic representatives. Our own dogmatics indeed carries a Reformed signature, but this does not imply that it is only meant for those of the Reformed persuasion. The current situation in the church and in theology calls for a broader presentation of information and argumentation.

In presenting this dogmatic material, the authors imposed numerous constraints upon themselves in order to limit the scope of this work. It not only constitutes a handbook for Reformed dogmatics, focusing on key issues, but can also be used as a reference work equipped with a table of contents, indexes of subjects, names, and Scripture references, and cross-references to sections and subsections.

The need for conciseness may not impede a discussion of contemporary issues. A new dogmatics must be relevant to its own time. It is for this reason that the views of theologians such as Barth and Moltmann, Berkhof and Kuitert—to list only a few names—keep turning up.

When views diverge, key differences may not be ignored. When rejecting opposing views as unbiblical, one should never fail to present them fairly and to appreciate what is good in them.

Neither should conciseness be pursued at the expense of clarity. It is important to take a clear stand in the midst of the confusing multiplicity of views that are encountered in contemporary theology. This is all the more essential since dogmatic insights have implications for preaching, instruction, and pastoral work.

As in comparable books, both a larger and a smaller font have been employed. The ongoing argumentation in larger print should be accessible to all those who think about questions of faith, while the additional details presented in finer print could well be skipped. Although the finer print is primarily aimed at theologians, this dogmatics has definitely not been written for them alone.

The number of footnotes is comparatively small, but the text itself also contains brief references to the literature. A distinction has been made between general literature and literature specific to each topic. The general literature is referred to by means of the abbreviations presented immediately following the table of contents. The specific literature is provided at the end of each chapter, including authors' names and dates of publication. In the case of several publications by the same author, the titles have been arranged in chronological order. For example, *BSLK* is the abbreviation for a book that appears in the list preceding the first chapter, and "(1977, 173ff.)"—which appears in a paragraph in Chapter 1 dealing with H. M. Kuitert—refers to a book of his that appears in the literature listed at the end of that chapter.

This list contains three books by the hand of G. C. Berkouwer, with the dates of publication determining their sequence.

No attempt was made to provide a comprehensive list of the literature. We only selected items that appeared relevant to us.

This dogmatics owes its existence to the initiative of the publisher and the collaboration between its two authors, who are both associated with the Theological University of Apeldoorn, the Netherlands, and took note of each other's work and took each other's comments into account. Each retained responsibility for his own chapters: W. H. Velema for chapters 8, 9, and 12 and J. van Genderen for the remaining chapters.

One of our students, Mr. C. J. Droger, did us a great service by proofreading most of the text and by assembling the indexes of subjects, names, and Scripture references; Mrs. G. van der Laan-de Boer typed three chapters, while Mrs. J. W. van der Zande-de Roo, our university secretary, did a great deal for the publication of this volume by typing the remaining material and preparing everything for publication. We are most grateful to them.

It is our heartfelt wish that this dogmatics, in which we, in keeping with our confession, recognize Holy Scripture to be the sole binding standard, may help readers to understand what is believed in the church on the basis of the Bible. Dogmatics is focused on the knowledge and service of God. The highest purpose to which we set ourselves in articulating Christian doctrine is the glorification of the name of the God and Father of our Lord Jesus Christ.

J. van Genderen
W. H. Velema
Apeldoorn, January 1992

List of Abbreviations

Althaus, *C.W.*	P. Althaus, *Die christliche Wahrheit* (the Christian truth), 1952^{3}
Andresen, *Handbuch*	C. Andresen, ed., *Handbuch der Dogmen- und Theologiegeschichte* (handbook on the history of dogma and theology), 1–3, 1980–84
Barth, *C.D.*	K. Barth, *Church Dogmatics*, 1–4 (Edinburgh: T & T Clark, 1956–75)
Bavinck, *R.D.*	H. Bavinck, *Reformed Dogmatics*, 1–4 (Grand Rapids: Baker, 2003–8)
Beker/Hasselaar, *Wegen*	E. J. Beker/J. M. Hasselaar, *Wegen en kruispunten in de dogmatiek* (ways and crossroads in dogmatics), 1–5, 1978–90
BSLK	*Die Bekenntnisschriften der evangelisch-lutherischen Kirche* (the confession documents of the Evangelical-Lutheran Church), 1956^{3}
Berkhof, *C.F.*	H. Berkhof, *The Christian Faith* (Grand Rapids: Eerdmans, 1979)
Brakel, *R.G.*	W. à Brakel, *Redelijke godsdienst* (reasonable service of God), 1–3 (reprint), 1881–82
Brakel, *R.S.*	W. à Brakel, *The Christian's Reasonable Service*, 1–4, (Grand Rapids: Reformation Heritage Books, 1992–95)
Brunner, *Dogmatics*	E. Brunner, *Dogmatics*, 1–3 (Philadelphia: Westminster Press, 1949–60)
Calvin, *Inst.*	J. Calvin, *Institutes of the Christian Religion*, mostly cited (in the Dutch original of *Concise Reformed Dogmatics*) from the publication by A. Sizoo (1949^{2}), sometimes as translated by W. van 't Spijker, *Teksten uit de INSTITUTIE*

	van Johannes Calvijn, 1987, and occasionally in our own translation.
Chr. Enc.	*Christelijke encyclopedie*[2], 1–6, 1956–61
C.O.	*Ioannis Calvini Opera quae supersunt omnia (Corpus Reformatorum)*
C.Th.J.	*Calvin Theological Journal*
Dijk, *K.D.*	K. Dijk, *Korte dogmatiek* (short dogmatics), no date.
D.L.	*Dordtse Leerregels*
DS	H. Denzinger-A. Schönmetzer, *Enchiridion symbolorum definitionum et declarationum de rebus fidei et morum*, 1967[34]
Ebeling	G. Ebeling, *Dogmatik des christlichen Glaubens* (dogmatics of the Christian faith), 1–3, 1979
E.K.L.	*Evangelisches Kirchenlexikon*[3], 1986–
E.Q.	*The Evangelical Quarterly*
Erickson, *Chr. Th.*	M. J. Erickson, *Christian Theology*, 1987[3]
Ev. Th.	*Evangelische Theologie*
G.T.T.	*Gereformeerd theologisch tijdschrift*
Guthrie, *N.T. Theol.*	D. Guthrie, *New Testament Theology*, 1981
H.C.	Heidelbergse Catechismus
Heppe, *Dogm.*	H. Heppe, *Die Dogmatik der evangelisch-reformierten Kirche* (ed. von E. Bizer), 1935
Heyns, *Dogm.*	J. A. Heyns, *Dogmatiek*, 1978
Honig, *Handboek*	A. G. Honig, *Handboek van de Gereformeerde dogmatiek* (handbook of Reformed dogmatics), 1938
Ten Hoor, *Comp.*	F. M. ten Hoor, *Compendium der Gereformeerde dogmatiek*, no date
Kamphuis, *Aant.*	J. Kamphuis, *Aantekeningen bij J. A. Heyns, Dogmatiek*[1,2] (notes to accompany J. A. Heyns, dogmatics), 1982
K. en Th.	*Kerk en theologie*
Kersten, *R.D.*	G. H. Kersten, *Reformed Dogmatics: A Systematic Treatment of Reformed Doctrine* (Grand Rapids: Eerdmans, 1983)
Kraus, *Syst. Th.*	H.-J. Kraus, *Systematische Theologie im Kontext biblischer Geschichte und Eschatologie*, 1983
Kreck, *Grundfragen*	W. Kreck, *Grundfragen der Dogmatik* (basic questions of dogmatics), 1977[2]
K.V.	*Korte verklaring der Heilige Schrift*
Miskotte, *V.W.*	K. H. Miskotte, *Verzameld werk* (collected works), 1–11, 1982–89
M.S.	*Mysterium salutis* (ed. von J. Feiner und M. Löhrer), 1–6, 1965–81

Müller, *Bek.*	E. F. K. Müller, *Die Bekenntnisschriften der reformierten Kirche* (the confession documents of the Reformed church), 1903
Neues Handbuch	P. Eicher, ed., *Neues Handbuch theologischer Grundbegriffe* (new handbook on basic theological concepts), 1–4, 1984–85
Van Niftrik, *Kl.D.*	G. C. van Niftrik, *Kleine dogmatiek* (short dogmatics), 1961[5]
Noordmans, *V.W.*	O. Noordmans, *Verzamelde werken* (collected works), 1–9, 1978–
N.T.	*Nieuwe Testament*
O.S.	J. Calvini *Opera selecta* (ed. P. Barth-G. Niesel), 1–5, 1926–52
O.T.	*Oude Testament*
Ott, *Grundriss*	L. Ott, *Grundriss der katholischen Dogmatik* (outline for a Catholic dogmatics), 1981[10]
Polman, *Ned. Gel.*	A. D. R. Polman, *Onze Nederlandsche geloofsbelijdenis* (our Netherlands confession of faith), 1–4, no date
Pop, *Bijbelse woorden*	F. J. Pop, *Bijbelse woorden en hun geheim* (biblical words and their secret), 1972[3]
PRE	*Realenzyklopädie für protestantische Theologie und Kirche*[3], 1–24, 1896–1913
Ridderbos, *Paul*	H. Ridderbos, *Paul: An Outline of His Theology* (Grand Rapids: Eerdmans, 1975)
Van Ruler, *Ik geloof*	A. A. van Ruler, *Ik geloof* (I believe), 1968
Van Ruler, *T.W.*	A. A. van Ruler, *Theologisch werk*, 1–6, 1969–73
Schilder, *H.C.*	K. Schilder, *Heidelbergsche Catechismus*, 1–4, 1947–51
Schlink, *Ök. Dogm.*	E. Schlink, *Ökumenische Dogmatik*, 1983
Seeberg, *Lehrbuch*	R. Seeberg, *Lehrbuch der Dogmengeschichte* (textbook of dogmatic history), 1–4, 1953–55[4, 5]
Synopsis	*Synopsis purioris theologiae* (1625), ed. H. Bavinck, 1881
THAT	*Theologisches Handwörterbuch zum Alten Testament*, 1–2, 1971–76
Thielicke, *Ev. Glaube*	H. Thielicke, *Der evangelische Glaube* (evangelical faith), 1–3, 1968–78
Th. Ref.	*Theologia Reformata*
TRE	*Theologische Realenzyklopädie*, 1977–
TWAT	*Theologisches Wörterbuch zum Alten Testament* (theological dictionary for the Old Testament), 1973–
TWNT	*Theologisches Wörterbuch zum Neuen Testament* (theological dictionary for the New Testament), 1–10, 1933–79

Vriezen, *Hoofdlijnen*	Th. C. Vriezen, *Hoofdlijnen der theologie van het Oude Testament* (main perspectives of the theology of the Old Testament), 1974[4]
Weber, *Foundations*	O. Weber, *Foundations of Dogmatics*, 1–2 (Grand Rapids: Eerdmans 1982–83)
Wentsel, *Dogm.*	B. Wentsel, *Dogmatiek*, 1981–
WA	M. Luther, *Werke* (Weimarer Ausgabe [Weimar edition])
WAT	M. Luther, *Werke*, Tischreden (table speeches, Weimarer Ausgabe [Weimar edition])

In the original Dutch edition of *Concise Reformed Dogmatics*, the Dutch confession documents were mostly quoted from the following edition: De Nederlandse belijdenisgeschriften uitgegeven in opdracht van de Generale Synode van de Nederlandse Hervormde Kerken in Nederland, de Generale Synode van de Gereformeerde Kerken in Nederland, 1983 (the Dutch confession documents published as commissioned by the General Synod of the Dutch Reformed Churches in the Netherlands, the General Synod of the Gereformeerde Kerken in Nederland, 1983).

Chapter 1

Introduction

§ 1. Dogma and dogmatics

1.1. *The role of dogmas*

There are times when dogmatics is in demand, and there are periods when this discipline is not highly regarded. Within a faculty of theology, biblical and practical courses are sometimes much more popular.

Yet as the discipline that studies dogmas, systematic theology is indispensable. This is why we first call attention to the significance of dogma. We define "dogma" as *doctrine that the church, under appeal to the Word of God, holds to be normative.*

The Greek word from which we get "dogma" turns up in the New Testament. It may signify a decree of an emperor (Luke 2:1) or the commandments of the Law of Moses (Eph. 2:15; Col. 2:14). Among the Greeks a philosophical concept could also be called a dogma, although we do not encounter it in that sense in the New Testament. In Acts 16:4 the word "dogma" signifies decisions reached by the apostles and elders in Jerusalem. This went far beyond mere human judgment, because the council was convinced that it was led by the

Holy Spirit whom Christ had promised to his church. When they announced those decisions, therefore, they could say, "It seemed good to the Holy Spirit and to us" (Acts 15:28). A decree of the emperor of Rome reflected imperial authority, but ecclesiastical decisions reflect a different and higher authority.

From the third century in the East and later also in the West the word "dogma" signified the doctrine of the church, although it was not yet an established concept. The *Ecclesiastical Institutes* is the title of an influential work by Gennadius (ca. 500) in which the term is used in the sense of an ecclesiastically adopted or authoritative teaching.[1]

The Reformers knew the word in this sense, but did not make it their term of choice. Like Luther, Calvin often spoke of doctrine (*doctrina*), a term he preferred to dogma. For him dogma was often the "new dogma" of Rome, over against which he placed the doctrine of Scripture, which is sound, pure, and spiritual.[2]

As for the councils of Nicea (325) through Chalcedon (451), Calvin said that he regarded them as holy insofar as they concerned the doctrines (*dogmata)* of the faith. When someone brings the church into confusion with his teaching and it looks as though serious discord will ensue, the churches must convene and make a pronouncement that is derived from Scripture (*definitio ex Scriptura sumpta*). Thus the Council of Nicea upheld the eternal divinity of Christ over against Arius (*Institutes*, 4.9.8, 13).

According to Rome, when the church makes a definitive pronouncement, there can be no appeal to a higher authority. For us, however, doctrine accepted by the church does not constitute the highest authority because the church does not have the final say. As Luther put it, "God's Word shall establish the articles of faith and no one else, not even an angel" (Gottes Wort soll Artikel des Glaubens stellen und sonst niemand, auch kein Engel, *BSLK*, 421).

What the church has pronounced on the basis of God's Word, and has not retracted, constitutes dogma from a formal point of view. As far as substance is concerned, however, dogma is completely contingent on revelation. The fact that dogma has derivative authority does not detract from the fact that the church accepts it as normative. In its dogmatic pronouncements, the church of Christ does not so much say what *is* being believed within its community as what *should* be believed on the basis of the Word of God.

1. Cf. G. Söll, *Dogma und Dogmenentwicklung* (dogmas and their development), 1971 (Handbuch der Dogmengeschichte = handbook of the history of dogmas. 1/5); *TRE* 9:26–41; E. A. de Boer, "Geloof onder woorden (faith expressed in words)," *Radix* 10 (1984): 68–76.

2. Cf. W. van 't Spijker, "Doctrina naar reformatorische opvatting (Reformational doctrines)," *Th. Ref.* 20 (1977): 263–80; 21 (1978): 7–25.

There are various forms of authority. The authority of the government must be recognized. Scientific theses have authority for us when they are convincing. But what the church teaches in accordance with the Word of God demands acceptance. It is a matter of the heart.

Among those who are of an entirely different view in this regard is Kuitert, who does not consider "acceptance" to be a felicitous term when it comes to truth. According to him, many view believing as being equivalent to accepting a number of clearly delineated doctrinal truths about God, Jesus, man, and the future. He advocates a radically different approach, one that requires neither "swallowing nor choking." A radical revision is required for the way in which churches tie themselves to the past. Actually, the notion of "being tied to" is not appropriate in connection with faith. Christian symbols provide food for thought, but do not prescribe what should be thought.[3]

To Kuitert, the content of the Christian faith (*fides quae creditur*) is an orientation scheme or heuristic model, a concept of God and his salvation that did not arise apart from human experience and which cannot endure without affirmation based on human experience. The Christian heuristic model soon takes on the form of ecclesiastical dogma, which brings with it the risk that it will end up as church discipline and coercion in doctrinal matters. The truth of a heuristic model is, however, not confirmed by preserving it inalterably, but only by an appeal to human experience. Is this not how it is with scientific hypotheses also? The heuristic model can and must be adjusted continually. So it is with theological research, whereby admittedly the Bible plays the key role, but not as a simple criterion. Without the first witnesses of Jesus with whom the Bible confronts us, we would not exist as the Christian church. But the church, which enters into dialogue with the first witnesses, can and may distance itself from their testimony if it believes that there are valid reasons for doing so. The Christian church is an independent entity, which *also* possesses the Spirit.

It is striking that Kuitert, who does not think that he can view Scripture as a norm or criterion, introduces another norm. Not all that the Bible authors say about God meets this norm for the truth concerning God, his salvation, and his will, namely, "that it gives people freedom and opens up the future" (1977, 173ff.).

Aside from the difficulty that this kind of norm presents as far as its content is concerned, its vagueness makes it a choice that is very subjectively determined and can never rise above subjectivism.

Theology always has a starting point. For us, this is the position that the churches subscribing to the Reformed confession in the Netherlands have traditionally held, jointly with the other churches of the Reformation. This means that the canonical books of the Scriptures constitute the sole rule of faith (Belgic Confession of Faith, Articles 5 and 7). As far as the foundation of and norm for the Christian faith

3. H. M. Kuitert, *Wat heet geloven?* (what is believing?), 1977, 185, 27; idem, *Zonder geloof vaart niemand wel* (without faith no one fares well), 1974, 54.

are concerned, nothing may be put on a par with Holy Scripture. Only the Bible has inherent credibility in itself (for the necessary substantiation, see especially chapter 3).

Kuitert's clearly articulated striving for freedom in matters of faith enjoys widespread support. Doctrinal pronouncements by the church are depicted by his followers as a law to which the faithful must submit themselves. Furthermore, they are of the opinion that such submission is tantamount to being shackled to the past, or at least to being obligated to abide by the insights of previous generations.

We point out that the form in which the dogmas of the church are transmitted to us is the confessional form. This is not the case with most of the dogmatic pronouncements of Rome, but is true of the churches of the Reformation, for their dogmas are embedded in the confessions. In this way their unequivocal character as reflection of the truth and defense against error is preserved. As decisive pronouncements that the church was constrained to make in the past, they are of lasting significance. They have been incorporated into the confessional documents in texts that not only call for consent but also can be used for believing reflection.

The ancient church dogma of the Trinity of God comes to us in the Nicea-Constantinople Creed. The words of this dogma are part of a creed that is doxological in tone.

The doctrine of justification does not merely say what is and what is not the biblical message. In Article 23 of the Belgic Confession and in Lord's Day 23 of the Heidelberg Catechism, it functions in a context in which personal faith is confessed.

The Canons of Dort give some the impression that they constitute a massive exposition of Calvinistic doctrine. But how movingly this confessional document speaks of election, the atonement, conversion, and perseverance (see 1.13, 14; 2.9; 3/4.17; 5.8–15).

Is not the main objection to continuing to attribute normative authority to the ecclesiastical doctrines and confessional statements, that they tie us to the past? Yes indeed, if we were to view these dogmas and confessional formulations in isolation. However, in a church of the Reformation, dogmas and confessions function only in conjunction with the authority of the Word of God. Every human document and every ecclesiastical decision may be appealed to Holy Scripture, which is the final arbiter in cases of disagreement.

Today a great deal of fuss is made about being bound to dated ecclesiastical pronouncements that were in part determined by their historical context. But actually this is not the most fundamental issue. A parting of ways occurs at the questions as to how we interpret the authority of the Bible and how we deal with the teaching of Scripture.

It is the task of the church and theology to understand dogmas in the light of the Scriptures and to test their validity against the Scriptures. Although this is not exclusively the domain of dogmatics, it does constitute its special concern.

1.2. *The nature of dogmatics*

"Dogmatics" is an abbreviation of "dogmatic theology." This term occurs in the title of a work by L. F. Reinhart, *Synopsis theologiae dogmaticae* (1659), and conveys more than older titles such as *Sententiae* (Pronouncements), *Summa* (Summation), *Loci, Loci communes* (Essentials), or *Synopsis* (Survey). See also H. Berkhof, 1982, 11.

In the nineteenth century, preference was given to such names as "Doctrine of Faith," or "Christian Doctrine," but especially under the influence of Karl Barth the term "dogmatics" has come to the fore again (*Church Dogmatics*). "Dogmatics" has regained its rightful place in the theological encyclopedia (Runia, 1957, 3).

Theology, however, is in constant flux, and Barth's position did not fail to elicit reaction. The new wave is characterized by the demand that dogmatics be linked to human experience and be relevant to it. These are critical, experience-based theologies that are described by a noun (e.g., theology of hope, theology of revolution) or by an adjective (e.g., black theology, feminist theology). This profusion of theologies threatens to crowd out dogmatics in which the dogma of the church has a voice.

Those who are under the spell of hermeneutics are even of the opinion that dogmatics as a theological discipline is impossible, impermissible, irrelevant, and inexpedient (Polman, 1969, 7–10).

Regardless of changes in Zeitgeist and mode of thought, an important argument for dogmatics is that the relationship to dogma finds clear expression.

Dogma expresses succinctly what the church views as central and essential in the biblical message. Dogmatics analyzes, presents arguments, and elucidates.

We will now consider what we believe to be the characteristic features of dogmatics.

1. *Its ecclesiastical character.* Without the church there would be no dogma. Actually there could be no dogmatics either, but only strictly personal statements of doctrine.

Dogmatics is a ministry that the church demands or at least should demand. We deliberately speak of ministry, for neither dogmatics nor any other theological discipline should ever seek to rule. It needs indeed to be reminded from time to time that its function is to minister. Only then can it assume a ministry of its own in the church "with exegesis as its foundation and preaching as its goal" (Noordmans, *V.W.*, 2:174ff.). This does not mean that the task of dogmatics should always be viewed in such a narrow ecclesiastical sense that all questions not directly affecting the church should be ignored by it. Such issues might not directly affect the church today, but could in the future. It is precisely dogmatics that is equipped with the necessary antennae.

2. *Its confessional character.* In our view this aspect of dogmatics is directly implied by the preceding one. We are dealing with the church and her confession. Dogmatic works reveal the confessional standpoint of their authors. Thus Bavinck's standard work is appropriately titled *Reformed Dogmatics*, and the well-known concise dogmatics of Ott is called *Grundriss der katholischen Dogmatik* (Fundamentals of Catholic Dogmatics).

For us, confession means more than tradition. We appreciate the Reformed tradition, but we are in agreement with the Reformed confession. Tradition points us in a particular direction and the confession provides us with a clear vision as to the paths to be followed, but the confession also alerts us to bypaths and ways that would lead us astray. Dogmatics must go beyond the confession. It must go to Scripture itself in order to "bring forth" out of that "treasure things new and old" (Matt. 13:52).

3. *Its systematic character.* Bavinck calls dogmatics the scientific system of the knowledge of God (*R.D.*, 1:83); H. Berkhof calls it the systematic thinking through of the relationship that God in Christ has established with us (1982, 13).

Those who strive to establish a coherent system must be on guard for formulations that are detrimental to faith. There is the danger that we will regard as secondary whatever does not fit into the system or that an a priori principle leads to one-sided conceptions.

Even if the theologian has a desire for ever-increasing knowledge and an ever-deepening grasp of the issues, he must nevertheless make the following words of the psalmist his own: "Such knowledge is too wonderful for me; it is high, I cannot attain unto it" (Ps. 139:6). Our knowledge is in part (1 Cor. 13:9), our insight limited. Of old, reference was made to a *theologia viatorum* (pilgrim theology), i.e., that we are still on the way. We discover connections and are impressed by the great deeds of God. We speak about these acts in amazement while we realize that we do not see everything and do not have a comprehensive view.

Even if we take a systematic approach, a scientific system of the knowledge of God does not lie within our reach. When we study dogmatics, we do see more and more connections and perspectives. Van Ruler calls it the poignant beauty of theology that it teaches us to speak of God in an orderly fashion (*T.W.*, 1:39).

What the apostle Paul impressed on the church certainly also applies to the theologians in her midst: "every thought" must be brought "into captivity to the obedience of Christ" (2 Cor. 10:5). Dogmatics involves faith that seeks understanding (*fides quaerit intellectum*) as well as scholarly reflection that seeks to serve faith: in short, believing scholarly reflection. However, believing reflection that is not scholarly in nature has its own value, and there is no reason to look down on it. We can also learn from it!

4. *Its critical character*. The critical task of dogmatics flows directly from the nature of dogmas. As Reformed Christians we view it with critical sympathy—as Schilder put it (cf. Kamphuis, 1980, 9ff.). Dogmatics must raise the question whether the teaching of the church is in all respects in harmony with the Word of God. That Word is the sole criterion for a dogmatics that is critical in a responsible way.

With Rome this is different, because there the church's teachings do not stand under the authority of Scripture. A dogma is considered infallible there, even though one can attempt to make a distinction between the teaching itself, which is fixed forever, and its formulation, which can be adapted to a different time or culture. Some argue that not only should it be stated differently, but also that today something different should be said from before.[4]

Besides, dogmatics must remain critical because in addition to ecumenical dogmas there are also ecclesiastical tenets that differ from each

4. We are thinking of a figure such as H. Küng, especially his book *Infallible?* 1971, in which the dogma of infallibility is in fact rejected.

other and even contradict each other, as is the case for instance with a comparison of Reformed confessional documents with the decisions and canons of the Council of Trent.

Furthermore, there are numerous *theologoumena* or opinions of theologians that also have a certain influence. It goes without saying that we have to severely restrict ourselves in this regard. Two theologians whose views we often pay attention to in this book are K. Barth and H. Berkhof. Those who are familiar with the field of theology know that this is no arbitrary selection. A critical approach to the work of others, however, does not preclude finding elements of truth that must be recognized.

5. *Its timely character*. This too is an important aspect, although it is not the primary demand made of dogmatics, for continuity must take precedence over currency. Before opening our own mouths we must listen to the answers that the church of all ages has given to the great questions of the faith. With a variation of the words of Van Ruler (*T.W.*, 2:41), we can say that studying dogmatics also definitely involves studying the history of dogmas.

However, new questions have arisen, and old answers must be reevaluated in the face of current problems. There are possibilities for restatement that does not constitute mere reiteration. The theses and antitheses that are implicit in a dogma need to be explained in terms of the past, but also confronted with the present. Reservations of various kinds encourage us to engage in a more thorough investigation of the cause that we defend.

Moreover, the ongoing task of exegesis requires that we assimilate all that is found in Scripture, including a dogmatic processing of biblical data. Exegesis repeatedly confronts dogmatics with questions and continually opens up new perspectives. Dogmatics does, however, place certain accents on exegetical material. This is to be expected in light of the current situation and contemporary problems, although the latter should never predominate in discussion.

Sometimes dogmatics must lay the groundwork for the refinement or development of the teaching of the church. Thus at the time of the Synod of Dort (1618–19), a great deal of dogmatic work was done. It is also possible that as a result of new theological reflection, old antitheses are overcome. An illustration of this may be seen in the consensus that was reached in 1956 between the Dutch Reformed

Church and the Evangelical Lutheran Church in the Netherlands with respect to the doctrine of the Lord's Supper.[5]

In our dogmatics we try to formulate what Scripture teaches us and the church confesses in such a way that it is intelligible to our contemporaries. It is tempting to add to or subtract from Scripture in order to make things easy for people to understand, but this results in accommodation theology against which we must caution.[6] Those who go in this direction are often motivated by the conviction that the Christian faith must be acceptable in every cultural context. History teaches that in doing so, new philosophical concepts are often used that give the resultant theological presentation a modern flavor. Dogmatic theology is always in communication with the thought patterns of its time, but by simply taking over a philosophical way of thinking one runs the great risk that the biblical content loses in significance. Examples abound: from the influence of neo-Platonism, Aristotelianism, Cartesianism, Hegelianism, Neo-Kantianism, and right up to existentialism!

6. *Its practical character.* In answer to the question whether theology is theoretical or practical, the Leiden *Synopsis* (1625) states that it is both theoretical and practical because it concerns the knowledge and service of God. Theory and praxis therefore are not antithetical (1:22–23). We do not apply the term "theory" to the knowledge of God, but we can say that dogmatics has a theoretical aspect because it is a scholarly pursuit. It is also highly practical because its raison d'être is to serve the church and the life of faith. It is concerned with the truth, but this truth is also truth for us personally. We may never lose sight of the connection between doctrine and life. The quest for truth and the quest for salvation cannot be separated. Calvin says: "We have given the first place to the doctrine in which our religion is contained, since our salvation begins with it. But it must enter into our heart and pass into our daily conduct, and so transform us into itself so as not to prove unfruitful" (*Institutes*, 3.6.4).

Here we must, however, oppose the notion of *the primacy of praxis* that has a large number of proponents in newer theology. As Molt-

5. Cf. C. W. Monnich and G. C. van Niftrik, *Hervormd-Luthers gesprek over het Avondmaal* (Reformed-Lutheran discussion of the Lord's Supper), 1958 (see the text of the consensus on 5–7).

6. See W. H. Velema, *Aangepaste theologie* (adapted theology), 1971 (concerning the theology of H. M. Kuitert).

mann has observed, this is related to radical changes in the modern world. Kant judged that only that which is acceptable and useful from a practical point of view can be considered to be appropriate for faith in modern times. In our era, the praxis of life itself has acquired a cognitive character and has become both source and criterion for theology. The particular kind of praxis may vary from political decisions to mystical experiences.[7] Kraus, taking his cue from Moltmann, writes, "The new principle of theology and faith lies in praxis" (*Syst. Th.*, 107).

In the Netherlands, Kuitert, in a study about truth and verification in dogmatics, defends the thesis that "Dogmatic pronouncements must prove their truth-value on the basis of what we—empowered to do so by revelation itself—may call their meaning, i.e., whether they open a future for humanity and the world."[8] Here Kuitert is in agreement with Pannenberg who states that what is at stake here is the "Bewährung an der Wirklichkeitserfahrung der jeweiligen Gegenwart" (confirmation by the experience of reality of every successive present) (Pannenberg, 1971, 178).

Like other scholarly hypotheses, dogmatic pronouncements also need verification as to their truth content. There must be a workable criterion for doing so. As we saw already (§ 1.1), Kuitert is of the opinion that Scripture can no longer serve as a criterion for doctrine. The principium of Scripture (*sola scriptura*}, with which the Reformation believed it stood on solid ground, now finds itself in a crisis situation, according to Pannenberg and Kuitert. The truth of Christianity is not served well when couched in authoritarian pronouncements that do not allow any questions to be asked.

Those who like Kuitert want to put theological pronouncements about God and his work to the test of external verification should realize what they are doing. One insurmountable objection to Kuitert's position is that for him the touchstone of truth is to be found in anthropology and sociology, which raises more problems than it solves. What opens the future for man and the world? Everyone may decide this for himself. In a later publication the criterion becomes how durable such experiences of God will turn out to be in reality.[9] Here again this theology continues to resemble a circle in which man stands at the center.

Even if in this way truth could be found that is as controllable and verifiable as possible, it still would not be the truth with which the church and theology are concerned. To know truth in the biblical sense of the word, so as to receive assurance of our salvation, we need the revelation of God and the illumination of his Spirit. Then we

7. J. Moltmann, *Wat is theologie?* 1989, 103–5. See also D. Sölle, *Gott denken*, 1990, 15.
8. H. M. Kuitert, *Om en om* (around and around), 1972, 213.
9. H. M. Kuitert, *Filosofie van de theologie*, 1988, 85–95.

are convinced by the truth itself (cf. Bavinck, *R.D.*, 1:573, 593–95). This does not mean, of course, that the experience of faith and the function that faith has in everyday life are of no importance. Statements of faith can be confirmed by such experiences, but cannot be proven by them.

The fact that dogmatics has a practical side does not mean that therefore ethics should be subsumed under dogmatics. Yet this has been done, not only in the *Synopsis* and other older works, but also in Barth who wrote, "Dogmatics itself is ethics; and ethics is dogmatics" (*C.D.*, 1.2.793). There are in principle no objections to an interweaving of dogmatics and ethics. Calvin gave an example of this when he included a few chapters on the Christian life in his exposition of doctrine (*Institutes*, 3.6–10). In practice a good case can be made for covering the *credenda* (what must be believed) in dogmatics and the *agenda* (what needs to be done) in ethics.[10] With this division one should never lose sight of the close connection between these two disciplines. Faith and works do belong together. Both doctrine and dogmatics deal with faith that works through love (cf. Gal. 5:6). There is no such thing as nondogmatic ethics, or ethics without a definite doctrinal content. Neither is there nonethical dogmatics or dogmatics without a certain ethical import.

We conclude this section with a definition. Dogmatics is the theological discipline that speaks in a systematic manner about what God has revealed in his Word, and that must test the teachings of the church against Holy Scripture, basing them on it and interpreting them in its light.

A broader description, which is also useful, is that by Kamphuis: "Dogmatics presents the systematic treatment of Christian teaching that has been formulated by the church in its dogmas in obedience to the faith and that has been made known in Scripture with the authority of the self-revelation of the triune God. Dogmatics must perform this task in solidarity with the faith confessed by the Christian church in subjection to Scripture. It also has to deal with the problems that

10. In his *Orientatie in de christelijke ethiek*, 1990, 17, W. H. Velema defines Christian ethics as "the scientific reflection on God's commandments which are normative for man's actions as image bearer of God in his relation to God and his neighbour."

have arisen in earlier and later times in the exposition of Christian doctrine."[11]

§ 2. The method

1. In every discipline one needs to give an account of one's methodology. There is no general scientific methodology, and not even a single method for all theological disciplines, because the diversity is too great. Exegesis takes its own approach as does church history, and dogmatics also treats its subject matter in its own way. It sometimes seems as though everyone follows his own preferences; there are so many trends, schools of thought, and new theologies!

It is instructive to study the various principles and methods, for they put us in touch with characteristic ways of thinking. We must, however, refer the reader to the work of others since we do not have space for this in a concise dogmatics. See Bavinck for a discussion of the traditionalistic, biblical or biblicist, and subjective method, as well as the historic-apologetic, speculative, religious-empirical, and ethical-psychological method (*R.D.*, 1:59–76, 507–59).

Of significance in our time are the dialectic method, which we associate especially with the thinking of Karl Barth, and the method of existential theology, which we associate with such figures as R. Bultmann, F. Gogarten, G. Ebeling, H. Ott, and F. Buri. But there is also a theology in which the correlative method (of Paul Tillich) is used, and various contextual theologies are developing.

Polman (1969) gives a concise overview of the assumptions or a prioris as they are sometimes called, while Wentsel (*Dogm.*, 2) presents a detailed picture.

Although we are of necessity limited in the amount of detail that can be presented in this book, something must be said about our methodology. As is apparent from the perspective presented in section 1, we stand in continuity with what has been called the Reformational thrust of dogmatics (Polman, 1950).

Whatever their differences in other areas, all Reformers considered Scripture to be the only source and the only norm. The Word is the foundation of faith (Calvin, *Institutes*, 3.2.6). Faith interacts with the Word. Without faith we will not be able to understand the Word of God: *sola Scriptura, sola fide.*

11. We refer with approval to the complete article in which this definition occupies a central place: J. Kamphuis, "Dogmatiek," in J. Douma (ed.) *Orientatie in de theologie*, 1987, 102–22. For the definition see 112ff.

Theology's concern must be a sound interpretation of the Word of God. Preference should be given to the local method or the method of the *loci*, of which Melanchthon gave an example in his *Loci communes* (1521) and which Calvin in his *Institutes* linked to a Trinitarian arrangement. In this way classic Reformed dogmatics covers the themes in a particular sequence, chapter after chapter, section after section.

Formally this method has few if any pretensions. A theological system that is dominated by a single underlying idea may appear more impressive, but the danger of one-sidedness and speculation is not insignificant. There are enough systematic theologians who have allowed themselves the liberty of dealing very selectively with Scripture! The division into *loci* provides the greatest possible openness with respect to the Word of God.

Scriptural proof constitutes the heart of Reformational theology. Behind this stands the conviction that Scripture is the Word of God and that no tradition whatever may be placed on a par with it, that it is a unity and that it is clear—a conviction that many do not share[12] but that we shall elucidate below (see chapter 3).

Of Calvin's *Institutes* it has been said correctly: "In section after section God's voice in his Word is listened to in humility. With great faithfulness and rare balance the revealed doctrines are here described and any a priori scheme is avoided." This is why there is also no room for reflections such as we all too often encounter in medieval scholasticism. The causes of such derailments are human curiosity (*curiositas*), which leads to overstepping of the boundaries that God has set in his Word, and mixing theology with philosophy, which causes much mischief (Polman, 1950, 18–23).

The vision of the Reformation implies: 1. that we may and must speak with a confident tone. Luther formulated this in his characteristic manner: take away the confident statements (*assertiones*) and you have taken away Christendom (*WA*, 18:604); 2. that critical use is made of tradition. Calvin wrote: all things are ours, to serve us and not to rule over us (*Institutes*, To the King); 3. that it is the task of theology to strengthen consciences by means of the teaching of true, certain, and

12. See W. Pannenberg, *Grundfragen systematischer Theologie* (basic issues in systematic theology), 1971, 159–80.

profitable things. For this we must be students of Christ and follow the method he himself has prescribed for us (*Institutes*, 1.14.4).

2. In many chapters of this dogmatics we consider first the biblical data that are immediately relevant on the topic under consideration. Sometimes there is an introductory section or subsection, but then also the decisive question is: what does Scripture say?

When we let ourselves be guided by what God says to us in his Word, we will constantly keep before us that the main purpose is the knowledge of God. "For of him, and through him, and to him are all things" (Rom. 11:36). An example is a dogmatics such as that of Bavinck, which is intended as a doxology to all God's virtues and perfections, a hymn of adoration and thanksgiving (*R.D.*, 1:112).

We still face the question whether dogmatics—after a shorter or longer introduction—should begin with a chapter about God or with the doctrine of revelation and Holy Scripture.

On this point the Reformed confession documents differ. In the Belgic Confession, faith in God is confessed first, but the Westminster Confession deals first with Holy Scripture.

As far as dogmatics is concerned, a case can be made for the former as well as the latter sequence (cf. Kamphuis, 1987, 147ff.). Following the lead of several Reformed theologians from earlier and later times (cf. the Leiden *Synopsis*; Bavinck, *R.D.*; Heyns, *Dogm.*), we choose the latter option. Reflection on revelation and Scripture compels us not to go beyond what is written when considering what further can be said about God and his work (cf. 1 Cor. 4:6). If our speaking about God is not determined by what he has revealed about himself in his Word, it becomes abstract and speculative.

When in the fourth chapter of this book we speak more directly about God than earlier, we maintain the position that we know him from the revelation of salvation in which he has made himself known to us in Christ. The same applies to what is said in the subsequent chapters about God's counsel, about God as the Creator, and about his providence.

§ 3. From the History of Dogmatics

1. "The history of dogmatics" would be far too broad a title for what is presented here. For this, see Bavinck, *R.D.*, 1:113–204; Weber, *Foundations*, 1:73–166; and Wentsel, *Dogm.*, 2:407–624.

As in the preceding sections, we are faced with the need for conciseness. Yet we cannot entirely bypass the considerable history of dogmatics. It would appear to us to be more helpful to look at a few highlights than to give a list of names and titles.

The history of the development of dogmatics shows that in the first place it is concerned with upholding the truth, in the second place with reflecting on the truth, and in the third place with providing a perspective on truth as a whole. With Brunner we can identify three roots of dogmatics (cf. *Dogmatics*, 1:9–11).

a. *The first root is the battle against heresy.* Since man's sinful willfulness makes itself master of the gospel, it is necessary to distinguish between truth and appearance. The subtler the falsifications are, the greater the need for reflection becomes. When biblical words are filled with alien content, an appeal to those words is no longer sufficient. When entire systems threaten the church's proclamation, truth in its entirety must be placed in opposition to them and the systematic coherence fully considered. Thus heresy calls for a conceptual formulation and a systematic approach.

b. *The second root is baptismal instruction, catechesis.* The church must instruct its members in the truth. But a person cannot appropriate the truth without running into questions. It is of great importance that answers be given to those questions seeking knowledge, insight, and certainty. The Christian message wants to rule not only man's heart, but also his mind. This leads to believing reflection on what has been revealed to us. Catechesis, especially instruction of more-educated individuals, expands into dogmatics.

c. *The third root is biblical-exegetical in nature.* Where a genuine life of faith is found, the riches of the biblical message are grasped more and more. As Scripture is compared with Scripture, its internal coherence becomes increasingly apparent. In the process, questions arise to which dogmatics wants to provide answers. This leads to the development of the "biblical dictionary" and also of dogmatics.

The first motif, i.e., apologetics or polemics, played a major role in the early church. We think of *Adversus haereses* by Irenaeus (ca. 200). This motif resurfaced in the time of the Reformation. Zwingli's *Commentarius de vera et falsa religione* (1525) belongs to this genre. As long as errors persist, dogmatics will be essential.

During the time of the church fathers *the second motif* was also present. An example is *De principiis* by Origen (d. 254). In the Middle Ages this impulse became quite prominent. A monumental work that aimed at the synthesis of faith and knowledge was the *Summa theo-*

logica of Thomas Aquinas (1225–74). Calvin's *Institutes* was initially an extensive catechism, which first appeared in 1536 as *Christianae religionis institutio (Instruction of the Christian religion)*. Calvin, who specialized in the exposition of Scripture and was in continuous dialogue with pastors and other contemporaries, continually incorporated new material. The form he gave to the *Institutes* in 1559 is not only his magnum opus but also one of the classics of Protestantism.[13]

The third motif was little in evidence prior to the Reformation, but it manifested itself immediately in the *Loci communes* (1521) of Melanchthon. Noteworthy is his attempt to follow the method of Paul's epistle to the Romans. Melanchthon hoped that his work would be an aid to the study of Scripture, and if it did not serve this purpose, he preferred to see it destroyed.

2. In the dogmatic works of the seventeenth century, the influence of scholasticism is often noticeable in the use of rational argumentation in matters of faith. The well-known Leiden academic textbook, the *Synopsis purioris theologiae* (1625), which is actually a collection of disputations, is not free from it either.

After a period of decline, Reformed dogmatics in the Netherlands was revitalized during the era of Kuyper and Bavinck. The *Reformed Dogmatics* of Bavinck (1854–1921) is a work of enduring value to which we shall refer repeatedly.[14] When we see Scripture as the source of and norm for dogmatics, there will be much, not only in Calvin but also in Bavinck, with which we find ourselves in agreement.

In the preface to the first edition of his dogmatics (1895–1901), we read what Bavinck envisioned.

a. His dogmatics is historically oriented. He points out the significance of the communion of saints within which we learn to understand dogma. When dogma and dogmatics are out of favor in a given period, it is gratifying to be able to appeal to the spiritual community of previous generations. It is also incumbent upon a Protestant to be able to give an account of his relationship to Rome.

b. His dogmatics is explicitly Reformed. This type of religion and theology is, relatively speaking, the purest expression of the truth. He

13. Cf. J. van Genderen, "Calvijns dogmatisch werk," in *Zicht op Calvijn* (focus on Calvin), 1978, 9–46.

14. Others do likewise, e.g., A. G. Honig, K. Schilder, G. C. Berkouwer, and B. Wentsel. See for Bavinck's dogmatic work especially R H. Bremmer, *Herman Bavinck als dogmaticus*, 1961.

was of the opinion that the older generations far surpassed subsequent generations in freshness and originality.

c. His dogmatics was characterized by its relevance when it was published. His work bears the imprint of his knowledge of his own era. He says: "To praise the old solely because it is old is neither Reformed nor Christian. Dogmatics does not describe what was once valid, but what must be valid. It is rooted in the past, but labours for the future."

d. His dogmatics is a classic example of caution in making judgments. "Attention is paid to the various trends that intersect each other in the theological arena. In the midst of all those a place has been sought and a position chosen. We give an account for any situation where it was our duty to deviate. But then also we sought to appreciate the good insights wherever they could be found." Bavinck's caution does not betray an inner uncertainty, but is related to his scholarly disposition, to his awareness that our knowing is in part, and to his modesty. In subsequent editions of his work, in which this preface was omitted, it is noted that the first duty of every practitioner of science, and particularly of any theologian, is to be humble and modest. He may not think himself to be wiser than he ought to think (*R.D.*, 2:239).

3. It is indeed impossible to avoid mentioning more names. A concise survey of Dutch theology in the nineteenth and part of the twentieth centuries can be found in K. Dijk (*K.D.*, 41–62, 70ff.). There are summaries of the newer theology, of which that by F. W. Kantzenbach, *Programme der Theologie* (1978), is one of the most useful. A great theologian such as K. Barth, who stimulated the thinking of many by his opposition to neo-Protestantism and his highly systematic magnum opus (*Church Dogmatics*, [1932–67] 1956–75), receives in books of this nature of course a prominent place.[15]

Roman Catholic dogmatic theology of our time has found a representative interpretation in the great work published under the title *Mysterium salutis* (1965–81). A standard dogmatics from a Roman Catholic perspective is L. Ott's *Grundriss* (fundamentals) *der katholischen Dogmatik* (1981).

15. The literature on the theology of Barth represents an entire library. G. C. Berkouwer, *De triomf der genade in de theologie van Karl Barth*, 1954, remains important. For more recent literature see *Zeitschrift für dialektische Theologie* (from 1985).

A dogmatician whose influence extends beyond the Netherlands is H. Berkhof. Whether or not one agrees with his *Christelijk geloof* (Christian Faith, 1973, 1990), it is impossible to ignore it.[16] Berkouwer did not produce a complete dogmatics but he did write a series of *Studies In Dogmatics* (1952–76) which must be taken into account.[17]

The dogmatics of E. J. Beker and J. M. Hasselaar, which may be characterized as center-orthodox (the term *middenorthodox* originating with Berkhof), has been completed (1978–90). That by B. Wentsel (begun in 1981) is not yet complete as of this writing (early 1990s). Wentsel, who occupies a confessional-Reformed standpoint, provides a broad orientation.

An older Reformed dogmatics is that of G. H. Kersten (1950); a more recent one by J. A. Heyns (1978) comes from South Africa.

Finally, we mention dogmatic work being done by Dutch theologians that may well be of significance for a long time to come: that of O. Noordmans,[18] especially *Herschepping* (re-creation, 1934, also in *V.W.*, 2); that of K. Schilder,[19] specifically his *Heidelbergsche Catechismus* (1947–51); and that by A. A. van Ruler,[20] *Ik geloof* (I believe, 1968).

Some Literature

C. Andresen (Hg.), *Handbuch der Dogmen- und Theologiegeschichte* (history), 1–3, 1980–84.

H. Berkhof, *Inleiding* (introduction) *tot de studie van de dogmatiek*, 1982.

H. Berkhof, *Two Hundred Years of Theology*, 1989.

G. C. Berkouwer, *De triomf der genade* (grace) *in de theologie van Karl Barth*, 1954.

G. C. Berkouwer, *Een halve eeuw* (half century) *theologie*, 1974.

16. For reactions to this work see: *Weerwoord* (reply), 1974.

17. For a brief review of the discussion on Berkouwer's dogmatic method see the dissertation of J. C. de Moor, *Towards a Biblically Theological Method*, 1980, 5–66. See also H. M. Kuitert, "De theologie van G. C. Berkouwer," in M. P. van der Marel, *Registers op de Dogmatische Studiën van Dr. G. C. Berkouwer*, 1988, 9–18.

18. See on Noordmans, among others, G. W. Neven, *In de speelruimte van de Geest* (within the scope of the Spirit), 1979; and *Tijdgenoot en getuige*, 1980.

19. For literature on Schilder see J. J. C. Dee, *K. Schilder. Zijn leven en werk*, 1990, 1:410–21. See also J. Douma et al., *K. Schilder. Aspecten van zijn werk*, 1990.

20. For Van Ruler, consult among others A. N. Hendriks, *Kerk en ambt* (church and office) in *De theologie van A. A. van Ruler*, 1977 (with a brief biography of Van Ruler and a survey of the literature).

R. H. Bremmer, *In gesprek met oudere en nieuwere theologen* (discussions with older and newer theologians), 1991.

A. Ganoczy, *Einfuhrung* (introduction) *in die Dogmatik*, 1983.

R. H. Grutzmacher/G. C. Muras, *Textbuch zur deutschen systematischen Theologie*, 1, 1955, 2, 1961.

H. Heppe, *Die Dogmatik der evangelisch-reformierten Kirche* (hg. von E. Bizer), 1958.

W. Joest, *Fundamentaltheologie*, 1974.

J. Kamphuis, "Dogmatiek," in J. Douma (ed.), *Orientatie in de theologie*, 1987, 102–22.

J. Kamphuis, *In dienst van de vrede* (in service to peace), 1980.

F. W. Kantzenbach, *Programme der Theologie*, 1978.

J. Koopmans, *Het oudkerkelijk dogma in de Reformatie, bepaaldelijk bij Calvijn*, 1938.

H. M. Kuitert, *Wat heet geloven?* (what is believing?), 1977.

W. Pannenberg, *Grundfragen* (fundamental issues) *systematischer Theologie*, 1971.

A. D. R. Polman, *De reformatorische inzet der dogmatiek*, 1950.

A. D. R. Polman, *Gereformeerd katholieke dogmatiek*, 1, 1969.

K. Runia, *Reformed Dogmatics*, 1957.

K. G. Steck, *Lehre und Kirche bei Luther*, 1963.

J. Urban, *Bekenntnis, Dogma, kirchliches Lehramt*, 1972.

Chapter 2

Revelation

§ 4. God reveals himself

4.1. *Starting point*

Beginning with God's revelation means beginning with God himself. Conversely: God stands at the beginning and therefore his revelation stands at the beginning. Thinking and speaking about God and his deeds must be preceded by listening to what God says about himself. We do not determine how and where we can find God, but he does. Not only because of our own limitations as human beings but also because of our alienation from God, it is impossible for us to approach God if he does not first come to us. It is already a miracle that he reveals himself to us. It has been said correctly that there is no more significant question for the whole of dogmatics and for the whole of human life than that of the reality and the nature of God's revelation (G. C. Berkouwer, 1955, 17).

We cannot avoid the term "revelation," for it lends itself better than words such as "proclamation" or "communication" to indicate the distinction from what human beings themselves conceive of. Something further needs to be said about this, because there is also a more general interpretation of this word. Revelation as referred to here is something entirely different from what in common parlance is referred to as a revelation: a surprising insight that would appear to be of great importance to someone. A revelation is then more like a discovery. But this is not the way to discern God and to get to know him. If he did not reveal himself to us, he would remain a stranger to us.

We cannot start out from the phenomenon of religion and conclude from it that religion must be based on something, and that therefore there must be a God who can be known and worshiped by humans. There are many religions that appeal to some revelation, but such a "revelation" does not necessarily come from God.

Neither can nor may we take a philosophical concept of revelation as our point of departure. According to R. Bultmann (1884–1976), we first need to form a concept of revelation before we can ask ourselves what the New Testament means by revelation. With our preconception (Vorverständnis), we would have to determine what revelation means to us and what it does not. Bultmann then posits that the meaning of revelation consists herein: that it helps us to achieve our authenticity (Eigentlichkeit), which we cannot attain by ourselves. Bultmann asks: what then has been revealed? He replies: nothing, to the extent that the quest for revelation asks for a doctrine that we would not have arrived at on our own, or mysteries which—once they have been disclosed—would be known once for all, but everything, to the extent that our eyes are opened to our own situation and we can understand ourselves.[1] In this theology God's revelation must fit into a human scheme, which in turn is derived from M. Heidegger's philosophy of existentialism. It is obvious that in this way we do not start from Holy Scripture or faith. According to Bultmann, God's revelation as we know it from Holy Scripture can no longer speak for itself.

It is understandable that repeated attempts have been made to approach God's revelation from the perspective of human thought. In various ways attempts have been made to build a bridge. But how could it be proven that God—speaking and acting—enters this realm? For those who are not open to this possibility, it is an annoyance or

1. R. Bultmann, *Glauben und Verstehen* (believing and understanding), 1960, 3:1–34.

foolishness. They will be inclined to call it unacceptable and at the very least problematic to their way of thinking.

Linking revelation and experience appears to offer a new perspective. But combining revelation with religious or moral experience as such is not particularly new. We are reminded of prominent theologians of the nineteenth century such as F. D. E. Schleiermacher (1768–1834) and A. Ritschl (1822–89).

By interpreting revelation as signifying the original foundation of a religious community, Schleiermacher takes an anthropocentric approach. God's revelation is made dependent on human experience instead of the other way around. Such a relationship between revelation and experience detracts from revelation to the extent that it does not appear to be relevant to experience. And then to think how much our experience is determined by time, culture, and personal factors! Despite numerous objections raised, not only by Reformed but also by dialectic theology, it remains attractive to many to view experience and revelation as one and the same thing.

H. Berkhof describes revelation as an event in which God makes himself known to people, because God tells them something that goes beyond their capacity to exist and understand, and that nevertheless affects the core of their being and insight; but, at the same time, Berkhof views revelation as a specific type of experience, although he would not think of interpreting all types of religious experience as revelation on the basis of their own claims.

The price that is paid for qualifying revelation as experience is quite high. Berkhof believes that apart from the Christian stream of worldwide and centuries-long revelation events, characterized by great differences and great similarities, there are additional streams of divine experience that have flowed through the centuries that have a right to scholarly thematization. This then leads to Jewish and Islamic theology being taught at our universities. There is supposedly no risk of religious confusion and theological syncretism. Berkhof concludes with a quotation from Paul: "For we can do nothing against the truth, but for the truth" (2 Cor. 13:8).[2]

But who will still be able to say what truth is when revelation and experience in religions merge into a "source experience" and when God's revelation is not placed as norm over against all experience?

2. H. Berkhof, "God voorwerp van wetenschap? II," in *Bruggen en bruggehoofden* (bridges and bridgeheads), 1981, 208–16.

Revelation is generally approached phenomenologically in the field of religious studies. This provides scope for varying conceptions of revelation[3] and precludes unanimity. Dogmatic theology is not provided with any criteria. It becomes a matter of choice. A deliberately chosen fundamental orientation is to allow ourselves to be guided by what Scripture says. Thus Bavinck argues at the conclusion of his reflections on the nature and concept of revelation in favor of a method based on faith: not a priori establishing what revelation is, but seeking the answer to that question in the words and facts that in Christianity present themselves as constituents of revelation and are recorded in Holy Scripture; not dictating to God whether and how he may reveal himself but listening to what God himself has to say to us on that matter (Bavinck, *R.D.*, 1:300).

4.2. *What does Scripture say?*

The Old Testament word for revealing is "gala," which frequently means to disclose, but in a number of places indicates God's revelation. He reveals himself. He says to Eli: "Did I plainly appear unto the house of thy father, when they were in Egypt in Pharaoh's house?" (1 Sam. 2:27). "He revealeth the deep and secret things" (Dan. 2:22). In the Old Testament there are also other words that can be interpreted as "reveal," such as in Genesis 12:7: "The LORD appeared unto Abram," and in Numbers 12:6: "If there be a prophet among you, I the LORD will make myself known to him in a vision." Quite frequently it simply says "speak," as in Exodus 20:1. The noun "revelation" does not appear in the Old Testament as such, but the following expressions come close: the word of the LORD (*debar YHWH*), the utterance of the LORD (*neoem YHWH*), and God's speech (*massa*).

In the New Testament the verbs *apokaluptein* and *phaneroun* together with the corresponding nouns are especially important. The former actually refers to the removal of a covering; the latter means disclosing what is hidden or unknown. There are additional words for the communication of what needs to be known about God (cf. John 17:26 and Heb. 9:8).

In the case of *apokaluptein* and *phaneroun* it would be too artificial a distinction to say that the former indicates subjective and the latter objective revelation, or the former special and the latter universal

3. Cf. Th. P. van Baaren, *Voorstellingen van openbaring phaenomenologisch beschouwd* (representations of revelation considered phenomenologically), 1951.

revelation, respectively revelation and manifestation. In a passage such as Romans 16:25–27 these two terms are interchangeable. Nevertheless in the case of the former the emphasis is on the removal of a hindrance to knowing, and in the case of the latter term on making public what was hidden before.

In summary, on the basis of Scripture, we can say the following about the origin, content, manner, progression, and aim of God's revelation:

1. *Revelation originates with God.* It is an act of God, which depends on nothing and no one. Thus God's revelation of which we read in Exodus 20 begins with the sovereign word: "I am the LORD thy God" (cf. also Gen. 17:1; 28:13; Isa. 45:5). God reveals himself because he desires to, and he reveals himself to whomever he wills. The encounter with God, experienced by the one to whom he reveals himself, can be very surprising (cf. Ex. 3:1–6; 1 Sam. 3:1–10). In his revelation the Lord presents himself, and he is precisely as he reveals himself to be. The Old Testament already indicates with great clarity that God's revelation is theocentric: he acts for the sake of the glorification of his holy name (Ezek. 36:22–23). It is not otherwise in the New Testament. The praise for the revelation of the mystery that was kept secret since the world began, but now is made manifest in Christ, will be accorded to God to all eternity (cf. Rom. 16:25–27).

2. *God reveals himself.* He mentions his name when he appears to Abram, Isaac, Jacob, and Moses. Revelation is God communicating himself, "Selbstdarbietung zur Gemeinschaft" (his self-offering for fellowship, *TDNT*, 3:573). The content of God's revelation is variously described. The Old Testament uses the word *tora* (word of revelation, instruction). God enunciates his Word, he makes known his ways, he reveals his counsel to his servants (Amos 3:7). "The LORD has made known his salvation: his righteousness hath he openly shewed in the sight of the heathen" (Ps. 98:2). In the New Testament we hear about *mysterion*, the secret or mystery of salvation that God has revealed (Rom. 16:25–26). A mystery is not the same thing as a secret. As soon as a secret has been told, it ceases to be a secret. But here the focus is a mystery or secret of salvation which, once revealed, does not cease to be a mystery to us. When Peter confesses that Jesus is the Christ, the Son of the living God, the Father has revealed this to him (Matt.

16:16–17), but it nevertheless remains a mystery. The mystery of God is Christ, in whom all the treasures of wisdom and knowledge are hidden (Col. 2:2–3). The "mystery of godliness" implies first of all that "God was manifest in the flesh" (1 Tim. 3:16). At the center of revelation stands Christ, who can say that he has revealed the name of the Father to those who have been given to him (John 17:6). And the Holy Spirit is the Spirit of revelation (1 Cor. 2:10; Eph. 1:17).

3. *God reveals himself in his words and actions.* As a means of revelation *the word* "corresponds the most with the spirit of the entire revealed religion of the Old Testament, which emphasizes both the fellowship and distance between God and man; it is therefore no wonder that it occupies the most central place in intercourse between God and man in the Old Testament" (Vriezen, *Hoofdlijnen* = main perspectives, 242). That God makes himself known to people by means of his word is no less prominent in the New Testament. His word cannot be compared with human communication. It is full of dynamics and power and is effectual. "God's word is an act and his activity is speech" (Bavinck, *R.D.*, 1:336). The revelation of salvation that comes to us through words and the redeeming acts of God in history can be distinguished, but at the same time form a unity. *Dabar* has both verbal and action-oriented aspects. These can flow into each other. God makes himself known and at the same time he asserts himself. Wherever he is present in word/deed, he presents himself as both speaking and acting, and his people may meet him in this way. The main idea is that we rely on his Word and obey his Word. The New Testament at times speaks of God's revelation in the past tense (perfectum): his righteousness has been manifested (Rom. 3:21), while at other times the present tense (praesens) is employed: God's righteousness is revealed in the gospel (Rom. 1:17). This is no contradiction.

4. *There is a history of revelation.* Since God has not said and done everything at once, revelation progresses through history in phases. A sequence of revelations was given to the patriarchs, to Moses, and to the people of Israel (cf. Ex. 6:2; 3:13–15; Num. 12:6–7). During the days of the prophets there was a progression in revelation. Holy Scripture itself refers already to a history of revelation, and this expression is therefore biblically sound (see Heb. 1:1). Revelation in the person and work of Christ is the absolute zenith. In him the revelation

of God is *perfect and definitive*, for God has fully expressed himself in him. Jesus said: "All things are delivered unto me of my Father: and no man knoweth the Son, but the Father; neither knoweth any man the Father, save the Son, and he to whomever the Son will reveal him" (Matt. 11:27). "No man hath seen God at any time; the only begotten Son, which is in the bosom of the Father, he hath declared him" (John 1:18). The fact that God expressed himself in Christ does not imply that he has already spoken his final word. Revelation focuses on the future and extends to the consummation of all things. For this reason believers look forward to the revelation of the Lord Jesus Christ, which they can still expect (1 Cor. 1:7). Then they will see God "face to face" (1 Cor. 13:12).

5. *The purpose of God's revelation is that we shall know him*. The key idea is knowledge of God in the full biblical sense of the word, as expressed in the words of Jesus: "And this is life eternal, that they might know thee the only true God, and Jesus Christ, whom thou hast sent" (John 17:3). This knowledge of God is the same as life in communion with God. Knowing God means acknowledging God; acknowledging and serving him; serving and glorifying him. Revelation is *communicative*. By revealing himself to human beings, God desires to establish and maintain communion with us and to make this communion between him and us steadily richer.

4.3. *The concept of revelation in theology*

One could say that every theological trend reflects a certain concept of revelation. In reviewing the history of systematic theology one only needs to note the main features and highlights to see this clearly.

Apologists defended the thesis that true wisdom rests on revelation. This was also true of any truth and wisdom encountered among those who were no Christians and had never even heard of the Christian faith. Also beyond Christianity there were seeds and traces of the Logos. In the Alexandrian school, revelation did require faith (*pistis*), but even more insight (*gnosis*), for this was deemed to be of greater value. In the theology of Augustine the biblical element increasingly won out over philosophical inclination. The history of salvation and the facts of salvation moved into center stage.

Scholasticism started out from revealed doctrine, which had been captured in the dogmas and traditions of the church. The role of theology was to make doctrine transparent and plausible. But the problem of the relationship between reason and revelation was variously approached (Anselm, Duns Scotus, Occam). To Thomas Aquinas, revelation was absolutely necessary for everything that went beyond human understanding, and served as preparation for faith. The truths of reason and revelation were sharply delineated, but they were in harmony, because God was viewed as the source of all truth.

The Vatican Council of 1869–70 closely followed Thomas Aquinas (cf. Wentsel, 1970, 18–20). Under the influence of scholasticism and neo-scholasticism, this council described faith as holding for true what God has revealed. The church is the guardian and instructor of the revealed word. The dogmatic constitution that defined the infallibility of the pope taught that the successors of Peter, sustained by the Holy Spirit, were to guard and faithfully interpret the revelation transmitted by the apostles or the content of the church's faith (*depositum fidei*). To Roman Catholicism, being entirely dependent on the revelation implies being totally dependent on the intermediation of the church. As recently as the middle of the twentieth century, an official catechism of dioceses in the Netherlands said with respect to faith that as a virtue it is a supernatural gift of God through which we accept as true all that God has revealed. To the question as to how we can know with certainty what we must believe, the answer was: what we need to believe we know with certainty through the Holy Church.[4]

The Reformational view of revelation is quite different. Luther used the term "revelation" comparatively infrequently, but spoke all the more about the Word of God as the foundation of faith. God reveals himself in Christ, the Word incarnate. He does so in order to reconcile people with himself and to grant them eternal life in communion with him. Revelation is not merely the communication of truths about God, people, and the world. In his revelation God speaks to man to enlighten him about his real situation. Man needs to discover how he relates to God and who God is to him. We would not know from ourselves that we are sinners before God if God did not specifically reveal that to us. God has revealed to us in Christ what his intention for us is. The Word of God comes to us in Holy Scripture, which Luther interpreted strongly christocentrically. In his *Large Catechism*, he explained: "For we could never attain to the knowledge of the grace and favour of the Father except through the Lord Jesus Christ who is a mirror of the paternal heart, outside of whom we see nothing but an angry and

4. *Katechismus ten gebruike van de Nederlandse bisdommen* (catechism for use in the dioceses of the Netherlands), 1957, 71.

terrible Judge. But of Christ we could know nothing either, unless it had been revealed by the Holy Ghost" (*BSLK*, 660).

As far as God's revelation is concerned, the Holy Spirit is much more implicated in it according to Calvin than he is according to Luther. It is the work of the Holy Spirit to reveal to us what is hidden. Calvin also points more to the progression of revelation in the Word of God. God has fully revealed himself in Christ. He is referred to as "the Image of the invisible God" (Col. 1:15), because in a certain sense he makes God visible to us. In himself God is invisible, not only to our eyes but also to our human spirit. He is revealed to us only in Christ. We should therefore be on our guard not to look for him elsewhere!

In Christ God has revealed to us his gracious disposition toward us (*benevolentia Dei erga nos*), and Christ comes to us in the cloak of the gospel. The Word is the foundation on which faith leans and by which it is supported. The foundation on which faith actually rests is the gracious promise in Christ.

Characteristic of Calvin is the idea that in his revelation God adapts himself to our ability to comprehend (*accommodatio*). He speaks with us as nannies do with small children. In his Word, therefore, God comes down to our level.

With respect to orthodoxy of the time following the Reformation it is said—not entirely without justification—that the center of gravity in the doctrine of revelation lay in the inspiration of Holy Scripture. This is frequently interpreted as intellectualistic petrifaction. Yet the orthodox Lutheran and Reformed theologians did not carry the rational concept of revelation to an extreme. This was done by Socinians to whom revelation was a certain doctrine found in the Bible—especially in the New Testament—and assimilated by sound reason.

When rationalism and deism emerged, it was believed that one could know a priori what revelation was, and it was expected that reason would investigate its credentials. To the thinking person it had to be sufficiently evident. If revelation met the criteria, its content was tentatively considered to be acceptable. It concerned something new or something higher that one would otherwise not get to know. But subsequently it came to the point that something was considered to be acceptable only if it did not appear to be in conflict with common sense. In the time of the Enlightenment, the entire concept of revelation became problematic. An especially weighty argument for G. E. Lessing (1729–81) was that accidental truths from history could never become proof of the "necessary truths of reason." The Christian faith spoke of a revelation of God in history. But what this implied could never be considered to be absolutely certain, however probable it seemed.

This is the time when the problem of the relationship between faith and history emerged, which, coupled with the principle of autonomy, was characteristic of the newer way of thinking.

With his contrast between faith based on revelation grounded in some Holy Scripture and the religion of reason, I. Kant (1724–1804) did not go beyond the Enlightenment (Aufklärung). Instead of what God reveals to us in his Word, many in the eighteenth century accepted the triad: God, virtue, immortality: i.e., the existence of God, freedom, and immortality, respectively.

With respect to the concept of revelation dominated by ideas of the Enlightenment, one can say that it is anthropocentric. The starting point is human thinking and autonomy.

Also, F. D. E. Schleiermacher considered human subjectivity to be also paramount, but in his case this implied "pious emotions." Religion is in essence an absolute feeling of dependence. The underlying revelation is a vague concept: the origin of the foundation of religious community. In Christianity the person of Jesus of Nazareth has this original significance. He is the highest revelation. God-being-revealed is a reality only via our pious immediate self-consciousness. The analysis of certain religious experiences is crucial here. Experience displaces revelation. Here is no relationship between revelation and faith as a direct relationship between the Word that God speaks and the response given in faith.

While acknowledging the relativity of all that is historical, there was no shortage of attempts in the nineteenth century to adhere to a decisive revelation of God in Christ (cf. Berkouwer, 1932). More radical than others, E. Troeltsch applied his historical method and posited it over against what he referred to as the dogmatic method. The three basic principles of historical thinking (criticism, analogy, and correlation) leave neither room for a supernatural or authoritarian revelation, nor a unique place for Jesus. The concept of revelation has changed and signifies a new Protestantism![5] Troeltsch was left with little more than the Christian idea, which cannot live without a religious community and a cult in which Christ is at the center.

We now throw a glance at a few important movements that emerged in the Netherlands in the nineteenth century: the modernist and ethical movements. In modernism we encounter a great variety of ideas. Theologians such as J. H. Scholten

5. Cf. E. Troeltsch, *Die Bedeutung der Geschichlichkeit Jesu für den Glauben* (the meaning of the historicity of Jesus for faith), 1911; idem, *Die Absolutheit des Christentums und die Religionsgeschichte* (the absoluteness of Christianity and the history of religion), 1912².

and H. T. de Graaf still employed the term "revelation," but not in a Christian sense, as G. J. Heering—himself a rightist-modernist theologian—has said of Scholten.[6]

To Heering (1897–1956), Christian revelation is an act of God's saving love. There is a correlation between faith and revelation and especially between the truth of revelation and the knowledge of faith, between revelation and divination. Yet it is no coincidence that Heering's chief dogmatic opus did not appear under the title "Openbaring en geloof (revelation and faith)," but *Geloof en openbaring* (faith and revelation). To Heering this correlation implies that there is autonomy in personal faith, "autonomy of self-recognition." This implies that we determine for ourselves what the gospel is, that we determine our own credo. "When one presents as revelation, as God's word, something that is not part of the revelation that has occurred to us, we set it aside reverently, whether it is contained in Scripture or Confession; it does not form part of our own Gospel (either for the time being or permanently)."[7]

Whereas liberal theology emphasizes man's autonomy, sometimes in the guise of correlation, this is not true of ethical theology. A conviction that unites ethical theologians across the spectrum from right to left is the idea that truth should not be intellectualistically but ethically interpreted. It addresses man as existential being, not as reflective being. This places a great deal of weight on man's personal experience. A favorite expression of J. H. Gunning (1829–1905) is "the faith of the church." This faith does not rest in itself, for it is dependent on revelation. The great assumption of the faith of the church is the instruction of the Holy Spirit, who has been given to the church and continues to be given to the church.[8] One must adopt as starting point the reality of things spiritual, in other words life as revealed by God (J. J. P. Valeton). Some ethical theologians have a tendency to contrast doctrine and life. Revelation is not the proclamation of a certain doctrine but the communication of life (cf. Veenhof, 1968, 90ff.).

Given the development of the concept of revelation in more recent theology, it is surprising that Karl Barth wished to start with God again and not man with his religious experience (Schleiermacher), his ethical values (Ritschl), or his religion-historical relativism (Troeltsch). Going against the views that were current in his day, he began his dogmatics with the doctrine of the Word of God (*The Doctrine of the Word of God* [*C.D.*, 1.1–2]—first published in 1932 and 1938). It contains the

6. G. J. Heering, *Geloof en openbaring* (faith and revelation), 1944[2], 85, 148–81.
7. Ibid., 317ff., 329.
8. E. J. Beker/M. G. L. den Boer, *J. H. Gunning Jr.*, 113–20.

important section on the Word of God in its threefold manifestation: the proclaimed, the written, and the revealed Word of God.

The Word of God is the prerequisite that makes proclamation into proclamation, and therefore the church into church. Church proclamation must be undertaken in the recollection of God's past revelation and in expectation of revelation that is yet to come. In the Bible the church does not address itself, but is addressed. The prophetic-apostolic word is word, testimony, proclamation, and preaching of Jesus Christ.

It is true of both church proclamation and the Bible that "it must from time to time become God's Word." When God, who is free, avails himself of them, the Bible and proclamation are God's Word (*C.D.*, 1.1.132).

The third form of the Word of God, which really ought to be mentioned first, is the revealed Word. It truly and definitively occurred once and for all. The incarnation of the eternal Word is God's revelation. And conversely: "To say revelation is to say, The Word became flesh" (134). It subsequently says: "The word reconciliation is another for the same thing" (468). In all three of its forms the Word of God represents both God speaking and God acting. God's speaking is always God's mystery. This is especially evident in its "worldliness" [in the sense of belonging to the world]. We only possess it in the mystery of its "worldliness." This means that we always have it in a form that as such is not the Word of God. The form does not correspond with the essence, but contradicts it. It does not disclose it, but conceals it. This is also true with respect to God's revelation in Jesus of Nazareth. The Bible is also the document for the history of a pre–Near Eastern tribal religion and of its Hellenistic offshoot. Jesus Christ is also the founder of religion, historically so difficult to get information about. Theology is indeed also a philosophy or a conglomeration of all sorts of philosophy (187ff.). We are ourselves thoroughly worldly. If God did not speak to us in this manner, he would not be speaking to us at all. God veils himself and in the very process unveils himself (192).

In his doctrine of the Word of God, Barth also focuses on the Trinity. The doctrine of the Word of God in its threefold form is an analogy, albeit the one and only analogy of the doctrine of the triunity of God. For revelation, Scripture, and proclamation one can substitute the names of Father, Son, and Holy Spirit and vice versa (135ff.). The revelation presented in Scripture is the revelation of the God who, as the Lord, is the Father, from whom it proceeds; the Son, who fulfills it objectively (for us); and the Holy Spirit, who fulfills it subjectively (in us), and who is the one God in each of these modes of being and action, which are quite distinct and never to be identified with each other (*C.D.*, 1.2.1).

Serious objections have been raised against this doctrine of revelation. As is well known, Bonhoeffer reproached Barth for his "revelation positivism," and many have echoed this reproach.[9] This sharp criticism pertains particularly to consciously starting out from the fact (*Faktum*) of revelation. "The Word takes the word and this is all there is to it" (H. M. Kuitert). There is no access from without, let alone an external criterion. "Barth's way out" has nevertheless dominated the theological terrain, but can best be viewed as a solution of last resort. According to the norms and standards of our culture this means: not being prepared to present proof and yet wishing to be right.[10]

We have other reservations about Barth's concept of revelation. A main theme in this doctrine of the Word of God is God's freedom in revealing himself. People do not have the Word of God freely at their disposal. But according to Barth, revelation has an actualistic character (*je und je, immer wieder fallende göttliche Entscheidung* = divine decision being made continuously, again and again). Revelation is also paradoxical in nature, because revelation constitutes simultaneously concealment, and in Barth's view its form always contradicts its essence. Could the word "mystery" in the New Testament support this view, as he thought? We must not read into this that God can and will not reveal himself other than by concealing himself.[11] Neither are there biblical grounds to equate revelation with the incarnation of the Word and atonement. Furthermore, it really is questionable whether in the threefold manifestation of the Word of God one can see an analogy with the Trinity.

Barth did indeed start out again with God and his Word. But he did not permit Holy Scripture itself to say what revelation is. He

9. D. Bonhoeffer, *Widerstand und Ergebung* (resistance and surrender), Neuausgabe (newly published) 1970, 306, 312. Cf. M. Storch, *Exegesen und Meditationen zu Karl Barths Kirchlicher Dogmatik*, 1964, 11–35.

10. Cf. H. M. Kuitert, *Zonder geloof vaart niemand wel* (without faith no one fares well), 1974, 29; idem, *Wat heet geloven?* (what is believing?), 1977, 210–32; idem, *Filosofische theologie*, 1988, 32ff.

11. On *mysterion* see *TWNT*, 4:802–28.

approached it with his own concept of revelation. This also has implications for the doctrine of Scripture and its authority.

The doctrine of the Word of God, as presented by K. Barth, has had tremendous influence. He was supported by E. Brunner, although the latter differed on some points from Barth.[12]

In the Netherlands, K. H. Miskotte, G. C. van Niftrik, and many other authors have propagated Barth's views. According to Van Niftrik, God is and remains the Hidden One even in his revelation. Under the old doctrine of inspiration we do not receive God's Word—we *have* it! This means that we do not want to live by grace, the grace through which God himself speaks his Word to us, when it pleases him (Van Niftrik, *Kl.D.*, 43, 293).

It would lead too far afield to dwell on all important views that we encounter in the more recent theology. Otherwise we would still have to discuss separately P. Tillich and W. Pannenberg.[13] In the context of the Netherlands we do need to focus on the theology of H. M. Kuitert and that of H. Berkhof—the former has written already since 1962 about the issues that occupy us here, and the latter approached it systematically in *Christian Faith* (1979). Following this, something still needs to be said about the more recent developments in Roman Catholicism.

Revelation is an important theme in the theology of H. M. Kuitert. This is apparent not only from his dissertation (*De mensvormigheid Gods* = the anthropomorphy of God, 1962) but also from works such as *Wat heet geloven?* (what is believing? 1977) and *Filosofie van de theologie* (philosophy of theology, 1988). The question has become increasingly important to him how theology can be practiced as a scientific enterprise if the revelation to which it refers, and to which Christian faith appeals, cannot be verified. The origin of its knowledge (God's revelation, special revelation) must guarantee its truth, which is unacceptable to every branch of scientific endeavor (Kuitert, 1988, 18).

We shall not be able to follow Kuitert in every respect. He posits, as a fundamental thesis, that God's disclosure coupled with human awareness constitutes what we biblically refer to as God's self-revelation. To put it differently: "revelation (being God's partner in words and actions) is only relevant through knowledge (in the sense of fellow-

12. Cf. E. Brunner, *Nature and Grace*, 1934[2]; idem, *Revelation and Reason*, 1944; idem, *Dogmatics*, 1949, 1:14–72.

13. P. Tillich's discussion of reason and revelation in *Systematic Theology*, I, 1953, 77–177, is particularly relevant. Cf. A. J. McKelway, *The Systematic Theology of Paul Tillich*, 1964. For W. Pannenberg see especially W. Pannenberg (ed.), *Offenbarung als Geschichte* (revelation as history), 1961; ibid., *Systematische Theologie*, I, 1988. One of the last studies of his theology is S. Greiner, *Die Theologie Wolfhart Pannenbergs*, 1988.

ship)" (Kuitert, 1962, 287). Kuitert consciously conflates revelation and knowledge. This has implications. When we have God's self-revelation in the form of Israel's knowledge of it, it is inextricably intertwined with a specific cultural-historical context. Then there are extraneous elements in the form of "wrapping material." God's self-revelation is not "complete" without our knowledge of him. This is not a sufficient reason to encapsulate God in his past self-revelation. The Spirit is the way in which Israel's God wants to interact with us today in a renewing and liberating manner. In this context, reference is made to time-boundedness. This has far-reaching implications. Kuitert can write: "Today we boldly interpret Jesus' work of salvation employing the words that are put into our mouths today, i.e. in terms of being-human together with and for others (Man for Others), in terms of political and societal wellbeing (The Secular City) etc.," although we run the risk of a certain—time-bound—truncation of the gospel of salvation.

Another aspect of Kuitert's theology is that he seeks to arrive at a nonauthoritarian concept of revelation. This means that no appeal is made to the authority of the Word of God, but that revelation must authenticate itself. Various verification procedures are possible.[14]

Characteristic of the development of Kuitert's thinking is *Zonder geloof vaart niemand wel* (without faith no one fares well, 1974), which stresses that we only know God's revelation in the form of human ideas and words about God's revelation. "When—in the Christian faith—we speak of revelation, we mean that God is discussed in terms of our language" (105). Life requires doctrine to be adjusted continually. We continue to speak about God, but differently from yesterday. God speaks through the (changing) speech of people (107).

When God's speaking is interpreted as God-turning-up-in-discussion, we must indeed raise the question to what extent God remains the author of revelation.[15]

It appears to be a correction when Kuitert says in a subsequent work: "Under revelation I understand, with the Christian tradition, that act of God whereby he makes himself known to people; our knowledge of God comes 'from the other side' or if you will: 'from above'" (Kuitert, 1977, 230). However, when we trace the underpinnings for this pronouncement, we find ourselves referred to the cumulative experience that people have acquired over the course of their history: "On the basis of traces of God in their world of experience, people form an image of God, which is not only based

14. Cf. H. M. Kuitert, *De realiteit van het geloof* (the reality of faith), 1966, 166, 174, 195; idem, *Verstaat gij wat gij leest?* (do you understand what you are reading?), 1986, 20; idem, *Anders gezegd* (put differently), 1970, 134; idem, *Om en om* (around and around), 1972, 187, 192.

15. Cf. W. H. Velema, *De zaak waarvoor wij staan* (the issue that we defend), 1976, 79.

on experience but is also confirmed or contradicted by experience. Christian religion also has its image of God, based on the experience of Israel, and of the evangelists and the apostles when they bear witness to Jesus" (Kuitert, 1977, 230).

The answer to the quest for truth is a referral to human experience: Christians speak about God, which refers back to the experience of former generations and calls for confirmation of their understanding through relevant, new experience.

In reflecting on this, one can agree with Kuitert that thus there is scope for communication between Christians and non-Christians. But is there scope for confirmation? And can there be certainty? How can past and future experience confirm the truth of the Christian faith? According to Kuitert it comes down to waiting for confirmation from experience: time will tell, and in the end God has the final word (146, 232).[16]

What could dogmatics possibly do with the implications of all of these deliberations of Kuitert? Human experiences, although they are cumulative, are no solid foundation for the Christian faith. There are indeed experiences that are the outcome of faith, but outcome is not the same thing as foundation.

A serious risk is—and Kuitert admits that this possibility exists—that with this depiction of affairs God becomes entirely the predicate of our experience (229).

Behind this entire train of thought we find what Kuitert already early in his career identified as the role of man in the event of divine revelation.[17] To him this implied that revelation and the historical process of the formation of human opinion about God and his salvation actually coincide.[18] Velema correctly observes: "His concept has been constructed from the ground up with the help of the indispensable contribution of man as partner in the covenant with God. Kuitert has safeguarded man's contribution via the construct of God as covenantal partner. This is our fundamental objection to the starting point of his theology."[19]

16. Compare also what H. M. Kuitert says about "profiles of God," which are (must be) tested, so that they can be exposed to reality—experience! *Filosofische theologie*, 1988, 94.

17. H. M. Kuitert, *De realiteit van het geloof* (the reality of faith), 1966, 168.

18. This is especially apparent in the book *Wat heet geloven?* (what is believing?), 1977. Cf. J. A. Heyns, *Dogmatiek*, 1978, 16.

19. W. H. Velema, *Aangepaste theologie* (adapted theology), 1971, 48.

Berkhof takes a different approach than Kuitert,[20] and also qua content there are clear differences with the latter's view of revelation (cf. Berkhof, *C.F.*, 62). Nevertheless there are significant points of agreement. Kuitert is quite comfortable with Berkhof's definition—revelation comprises a cumulative process of events and their interpretations—although according to him these interpretations include more, because he assigns a role to all of human culture (Kuitert, 1977, 231).

In the new section dealing with revelation and experience added by Berkhof to his doctrine of revelation in 1985, there are concepts that would just as well fit into Kuitert's theology. There Berkhof says that man brings his experiences with him, which partially color and determine the encounter with God. "The Spirit's sovereign freedom, who blows where he wills, entails that all experiences, ranging from the very intimate to the very universal and from the extremely negative to the extremely positive, can become entrance gates to salvation." He does add that the experiences that we ourselves bring along can have only a preparatory input. "We are dependent on the miracle that comes from the other side, forcing us to make the jump that antedates all our experiences" (*C.F.*, 58ff.).

Just as Kuitert's views revolve around the role of man in the event of divine revelation and has to do with man as partner in the covenant with God, his covenant partner, in Berkhof's case it is also the focus on the relationship between God and man in the covenant that crucially influences the concept of revelation—at the cost of the biblical element. According to Berkhof, from our own perspective, everything in the covenant between God and man depends on God. At the same time God is presented in the Bible as being dependent on us (*C.F.*, 59).

To Berkhof, revelation is an event of encounter. In an encounter the approach must always come from two sides. "By entering in a hidden form into our reality" God makes the encounter possible. Quite deliberately, Berkhof does not say that God effects the encounter. According to him God cannot effect this encounter if his partner, man, from his side does not respond to the revelation. "In fact, revelation is not even revelation, if it is not perceived and acknowledged as such by the other side. Viewed in that light, the revelation event structurally hardly differs from our encounters, even though in this case initiative to it is strictly unilateral" (*C.F.*, 63ff.).

If in the second-last sentence quoted here one were to replace "revelation" by "the Word of God" or "God's speaking in words and deeds," one would imply that the Word of God is no Word of God if it is not acknowledged as such. This is entirely in conflict with what Holy

20. See especially the wide-ranging discussion of Kuitert's point of view in H. Berkhof, *Two Hundred Years of Theology*, 1989, 212–28.

Scripture says with respect to the Word of God. It does not become the Word of God through our acknowledgement. In this connection we need to use two words to which Berkhof also refers: "revelation" and "illumination," with God being the subject. He makes himself known to us in his revelation. He is known by the opening of our eyes and hearts to his self-revelation.

Berkhof seeks to avoid saying that the "event of encounter" is viewed as solely divine or solely human. The former would be objectivistic and the latter subjectivistic. In his *Christian Faith* he employs the term "inter-subjectivity" to indicate the direction that he takes. This harmonizes with his concept of revelation. But in our view this does not avoid subjectivism: revelation requires our recognition in order to be revelation!

There is no doubt that the arguments with which he seeks to avoid objectivism and subjectivism are of interest, and that his explanations with respect to revelation and concealment and revelation as history deserve attention. Numerous opinions are explored. But even there the stumbling block is that Berkhof has his own view of revelation in which the idea of progress is an important factor. God "started out small." On the basis of both the Old and New Testaments one also needs to assess the revelatory content of the intertestamental period. Christ is the central revelation, the norm for all revelational events after him. These continue, and according to Berkhof Christ is not exclusive, but normative (*C.F.*, 50, 70–72, 82).

For his biblical-theological argumentation, Berkhof refers to his study "Openbaring als gebeuren" (revelation as event) in *Geloven in God* (believing in God, 1970). It says that the God in whom we believe began small, "disguised as one of the many tribal and national deities, with which the Near East was rife. The revelatory event focused on Jesus is called definitive and universal. It is the criterion for gauging new revelations, which are not unthinkable. But that Christ is *the* way does not mean that God cannot meet people in a thousand ways, but only that in his light the significance and limitation of all of these ways are revealed. This makes it highly probable to Berkhof that in the case of Mohammed a new revelatory breakthrough occurred (152, 166–69).

The dogmatic constitution dealing with divine revelation (*Dei Verbum*) adopted by the Second Vatican Council in 1965, and which in recognition of no minor differences of opinion was formulated with utmost care, does indeed maintain the traditionally revealed truths, but does open with a new description of revelation: it has pleased God in his wisdom and goodness to reveal himself and to make known the mystery of the decree of his will (cf. Eph. 1:9), whereby people have access to the Father and are made partakers of divine nature through Christ, the Word incarnate, in the Holy Spirit (cf. Eph. 2:18; 2 Peter 1:4). God addresses people as his friends, and he associates with them, in order to invite them to communion with him and to admit them to it. Revelation occurs through deeds and words that are inwardly interconnected. Through this revelation the most inner truth concerning God as well as man's salvation appears to us in Christ. Christ is the Mediator, the fullness, and the Finisher of revelation.

When we compare this with the earlier doctrine, what strikes us is that the concept of revelation is less intellectualistic and more personal and christocentric. In the rest of the document somewhat of a redemption-historical approach is discernable. Whereas Rome's intellectualistic concepts of revelation and faith used to go hand in hand—as was still clearly the case in Vatican I—in this constitution an attempt was made to speak also about faith in a more personal fashion, although it is obvious from the section on the acceptance of revelation in faith that this attempt was only partly successful. In addition, there are elements in the chapter dealing with divine revelation against which serious objections must be raised. But this concerns the topic of Scripture and tradition (see § 8.4).

We cannot end this subsection without taking a clear position. In dogmatic theology, views appear to diverge already concerning the concept of revelation. This is clear from varying interpretations of revelation, which necessitates making a choice.

Bavinck ends his review of nineteenth-century developments with the remark that there is great confusion in determining the nature and concept of revelation. In the modern concept of revelation, revelation and religion are viewed as two aspects of the same thing. Revelation only has reality and only is knowable and intelligible to the religious person (Bavinck, *R.D.*, 1:292–94). And does a revised concept of revelation not signify a new Protestantism, as E. Troeltsch has pointed out already?

Toward the end of the twentieth century we must be more nuanced in speaking about the modern concept of revelation. There are various tendencies.

1. There is an intellectualistic view—especially developed in the Roman Catholic Church and officially codified in 1870: revelation as the proclamation of truths.
2. There is an actualistic view—encountered most clearly in the work of K. Barth.
3. There is a correlative view: faith and revelation determine each other reciprocally (G. J. Heering).[21] The concept of revelation of H. Berkhof, who describes revelation as an encounter, is somewhat related to this.
4. There is an anti-authoritarian view, which is not based on the authority of God's revelation once given, but refers to human knowledge of God in which revelation becomes relevant, and to human experience which must serve as confirmation. This is reminiscent of Kuitert's approach to revelation.

In addition to what has already been said with respect to Scripture, we maintain in the face of all of these varying views that revelation is *a sovereign act of God*. He takes the initiative because it pleases him to reveal himself. People do not have God's revelation at their disposal. In Barth's theology this theme of God's freedom in his revelation is recognizable, but in our view this does not mean that God is neutral with respect to his word once spoken. Neither do we support the idea that God conceals himself in his revelation. When God enters into this world and employs earthly forms of speech, this is not intended to be concealment. He chooses this way to meet us partway.

God's revelation has a personal character. Therefore revelation must not become an abstract concept in theology. When we refer to God's revelation, we speak about God who sought to reveal himself in words and actions. Making his salvation and his will known to us is also self-revelation. God reveals himself when his Word throws light on man's situation and his relationship with God, for he shows what he thinks of man. God's revelation is not just a disclosure of facts that we must accept, of truths that we must adopt, or of norms to which we must adhere. In that case it would appeal to our reason or our conscience. But when God reveals himself in word and action, he addresses us in such a way that people respond with what Holy Scripture refers to as the heart, where the deepest decisions are made.

21. This is much more strongly the case with P. Tillich. Cf. A. D. R. Polman, *Gereformeerd katholieke dogmatiek*, 1969, 1:61–65.

However, it is not the case that in view of the personal character of God's revelation we must reject the concept of revealed truth, even though this is the current view in the more recent theology, which in its aversion to the intellectualistic concept of revelation (the teaching of religious and moral truths) frequently grossly exaggerates the situation. Behind Peter's confession, which has a very clear content, stands God's revelation (Matt. 16:15–17). There is a cognitive element in the full truth, to which the Spirit will guide us (John 16:13). With Paul we can tell what God has revealed to us (1 Cor. 2:10). Berkhof has correctly pointed out that one can also speak of truths in the plural. There are truths of creation, sin, atonement, consummation, and so on. "As long as it is realized that this plural can be compared with the many segments into which the one circle can be divided, which all radiate from one central point and point back to it" (Berkhof, *C.F.*, 80).

God's revelation enters into history without becoming submerged in it. When revelation makes history, it does not turn history into revelation. We can definitely not say that all of history is revelatory and that the language of its facts can be seen by all who have an eye for them, with *the* revelation being expected at the end of time.[22] The Word that God makes us hear and the faith that comes from hearing (Rom. 10:17) are not done justice by this "turning to history," while all the more scope is given to our interpretations of history and our experiences in history. The latter can also be observed in Kuitert.

The communicative nature of revelation does not turn revelation and faith into a correlation marked by mutual dependence.[23] It does permit us to say that revelation presupposes an encounter, but it is not true that in the absence of an encounter there is no revelation. God's revelation implies that he comes to us and speaks to us in order to be known and acknowledged, believed, and obeyed by us. When we have the right relationship with him and live in communion with him, he is indeed glorified.

When Bavinck seeks to summarize everything that Holy Scripture teaches about revelation, he first of all interprets revelation as being

22. Cf. W. Pannenberg, in *Offenbarung als Geschichte* (revelation as history), 1961, 95–98.

23. In this connection it needs to be pointed out that the term "correlation" is used differently by G. C. Berkouwer. A critical treatment of this concept is called for. This is also lacking in G. W. de Jong, *De theologie van Dr. G. C. Berkouwer*, 1971.

"quite generally" that deliberate and free act of God by which he makes himself known to man, in order that he may come to stand in the right relationship to God. Corresponding to the revelation of God on the human side is religion, the knowledge and service of God. In Scripture the two are closely connected; knowledge and service of God are possible only because God reveals himself (Bavinck, *R.D.*, 1:349ff.). In his revelation God turns to man, and in religion man turns himself to God. This is an essential difference that in the modern concept of revelation, however, frequently becomes vague and sometimes disappears altogether.

On biblical grounds Reformed theology ascribes to the Holy Spirit the task of bringing people to faith and obedience. Can this work of God be referred to as revelation in the broader sense of the term? This is the view of Bavinck, who thereby thought of Bible passages such as Matthew 16:17 and Galatians 1:15. This in turn leads to a distinction between objective and subjective revelation. But it is objectionable to refer to God's revelation as objective revelation or to his speaking as objective speaking. Hence the word "illumination" (*illuminatio*) is more appropriate here, especially since it is used in the New Testament. It is the Holy Spirit who gives this illumination (cf. 2 Cor. 4:6; Eph. 1:17, 18). There is also a tradition in which this illumination is pointed out. Calvin says: the Word cannot penetrate our hearts unless the Spirit, as the inner teacher, provides entrance to it through his illumination (*Institutes*, 3.2.34).[24]

It is noteworthy that in his description of revelation Bavinck did not mention Christ, while in Holy Scripture he is indeed the center of God's revelation. This is entirely different in the case of Barth, because the latter's concept of revelation is indeed christologically determined and might even be called exclusively christological. But Bavinck agrees with numerous other theologians that God's revelation cannot be a priori equated with the revelation in Christ or the revelation of salvation. He speaks first and foremost about revelation in general.

It will be necessary to ascertain whether and how a distinction can be made between one type of revelation and another, or—to put it tentatively into current terminology—between general and particular revelation. This is the next topic of the doctrine of revelation that requires our attention.

24. Cf. E. A. Dowey Jr., *The Knowledge of God in Calvin's Theology*, 1952, 173–80.

§ 5. General and Special Revelation

5.1. *General revelation*

In Reformed theology it is no longer as straightforward as it once was to distinguish between general and special revelation. Terminological or formal objections have been raised against this distinction, but there are especially serious reservations about what has been labeled as "double bookkeeping" (Barth). Does Scripture itself say that apart from God's revelation of salvation in Christ, to which it refers, there is also revelation of God in creation, history, and our conscience, i.e., the concept of "general revelation"? Is this general revelation also the initial means of acquiring knowledge with respect to God?

In starting out from general revelation, there are at least two possibilities to detract from the significance of the revelation of salvation. From revelation in nature—one aspect of general revelation—one could infer that there would have to be a natural knowledge of God for which Holy Scripture would not be required, and one could imagine general revelations or manifestations of God to mankind to explain the multiplicity of religions and relativize the significance of the revelation in Christ.

But before we address an inappropriate interpretation of general revelation, we consider what biblical and theological grounds can be marshaled to support the concept of general revelation. To use Bavinck's words: the creation is the first revelation of God, the beginning and foundation of all subsequent revelation. The biblical concept of revelation is rooted in that of creation. God first appeared outwardly before his creatures in the creation and revealed himself to them. But immediately linking up with creation is providence. This, too, is an omnipotent and everywhere-present power and act of God. Creation, preservation, and governance constitute one single, mighty, ongoing revelation of God (Bavinck, *R.D.*, 1:307). Unless one interprets creation as already constituting the revelation of salvation, God's revelation in Jesus Christ—Barth's view—the question as to whether the distinction between general and special revelation is well founded and makes sense has in principle been answered.

We find the *loci classici*, i.e., the most important proof texts in Holy Scripture, especially in the New Testament: Romans 1:19–20;

2:14–16; Acts 14:15–17; 17:22–31. In addition there are the "psalms of nature" of which it has been said that there is no nature poetry that surpasses or equals that of Israel: Psalm 19, 29, and 104. The most eloquent words of Scripture are, "The heavens declare the glory of God; and the firmament sheweth his handywork" (Ps. 19:1), and, "For the invisible things of him from the creation of the world are clearly seen, being understood by the things that are made, even his eternal power and Godhead; so that they are without excuse" (Rom. 1:20).

Up to the twentieth century this proof from Scripture appeared more than clear. But the radical theses of Barth—"Barth's offensive" (Berkouwer)—have engendered a great deal of discussion.

According to him, what is said in Psalm 19:2 has been read into the text of the cosmos, which itself is mute. In the view of the world of Psalm 104 the image of the future world becomes transparent. One cannot understand this psalm properly for one moment without the commentary of Revelation 21:1–5. In Romans 1 Paul speaks about the Gentiles in the light of the revelation in Christ, in the light of the cross and the resurrection. As a result their relationship with God has changed objectively: they know God. From the perspective of Golgotha it is clear that they cannot be excused (*C.D.*, 2.1.110–23).

The background of these unusual explanations of the words of Scripture is Barth's abhorrence of all forms of natural theology, which he equates with the doctrine of general revelation. General revelation then stands and falls with natural theology, and to Barth this means that it falls. This is indeed also a consequence of his christologically determined concept of revelation, his focus on Christology, which has been called by some "Christomonism." The revelation of God is Jesus Christ. According to Barth, this destroys any representation of revelation as coming to man through nature, history, and the awareness of his own existence.

It appears from a subsequent part of his magnum opus that questions with respect to general revelation kept occupying him. His reflections became more refined. We think of the section dealing with the glory of the Mediator, which is introduced by the thesis: Jesus Christ, as he is presented to us in Holy Scripture, is the one Word of God that we must hear, that we must trust and must obey in life and death. This is the first thesis of the Theological Declaration of Barmen (1934), whose formulation originated with Barth himself. He gave an explanation of it, and in the process went into the relationship between the Light and the lights. Jesus Christ is the Light. There are also "lights": words, truths, "revelations." The created world, the cosmos, also as such has its own lights and truths and, to the extent of its language, its own words. Its lights have not been extinguished by man's sins.

Barth was comfortable in speaking about the bright glow (*Helligkeit*) of the created world, but sought to avoid the use of the term "revelation" in this connection. Although a creature has its own revelation, this is no self-revelation of God. Compared with his earlier pronouncements concerning the text of the cosmos being mute, it sounds different when he refers to the created world as a legible and comprehensible text. Also in this connection he is reluctant to use the word "revelation," because the observability of these lights does not require faith, but only the use of common sense. Just as a reflector is illuminated by a beaming light, so the lights of the cosmos reflect the eternal Light of God, i.e., Jesus Christ, the Light of Life. In this way the lights of creation take on significance through him. The witness of a creature may and can now speak of God himself and bring him praise. The heavens declare God's glory and the firmament proclaims the work of his hands without language, without words, with an inaudible voice. And this is how their proclamation goes out over the entire earth and their language to the ends of the earth (*C.D.*, 4.3.86–165).[25]

Even now there is no room for general revelation in Barth's theological system. Jesus Christ is the one and only Word of God. Yet a creature can speak a language and praise God. This is the reflection of the glory of Jesus Christ through the existing lights, which according to Barth is implied by creation and atonement, because he sees creation as founded in Christ. He explained this in great detail in his doctrine of creation (*C.D.*, 3).

How should we interpret Romans 1:18–21? Paul says there that since the beginning of the world God's eternal power and Godhead are understood by the mind through his work, but that people suppress this truth in unrighteousness. He also says: although they knew God, they have not glorified or acknowledged him as such. What can be known of God has been revealed to them. This means at the very least that it touches them in their inner being. The explanation of this is not that it is known and transparent in and of itself, but that God has revealed it to them. It has to do with his eternal power and Godhead on which man depends and which make him aware of his responsibility.

It remains a question whether the translation "discerned by the mind" (1956 translation of the Netherlands Bible Society) is the most appropriate rendition. We come closer to the original text with: they are understood and discerned (KJV: "clearly seen, being understood"). This is to say that people come to see it and start to reflect on it. God

25. Cf. H. Berkhof/H.-J. Kraus, *Karl Barths Lichterlehre* (Karl Barth's doctrine of lights), 1978; G. Kraus, *Gotteserkentniss* (recognition of God), 1987, 120–35.

revealing his eternal power and Godhead has such an effect. Does it not go so far as to say that this revelation of God leads to knowledge of God (Rom. 1:21)?

We must indeed compare this with other pronouncements of Paul, such as the words about the world that did not know God through its wisdom (1 Cor. 1:21) and about Gentiles who do not know God (1 Thess. 4:5; cf. Gal. 4:8). The Old Testament also refers to Gentiles who are ignorant of God (Ps. 79:6). The situation of Gentiles is pictured as being rather bleak, as they "walk in the vanity of their mind, having the understanding darkened, being alienated from the life of God through the ignorance that is in them, because of the blindness of their heart" (Eph. 4:17–18). For this reason alone it is highly unlikely that the knowledge of God in Romans 1 refers to true knowledge of God. In Greek it is not a strong expression (*gnontes ton theon*). Furthermore, it is immediately added that the Gentiles have not glorified God as God or thanked him, and further on it says that they consider it objectionable to acknowledge God (Rom. 1:28). The Bible does not consider knowledge of God without acknowledgement of God to be true knowledge of God!

In this connection Calvin points out that we should note the level of knowledge with which they ended up. When we take the context into account, we see that their reaction to God's revelation is described in two ways: people suppress the truth in unrighteousness and they replace God's truth with lies (Rom. 1:18, 25). What God has to say collides with man's sinful self-assertion and is suppressed. It is consciously or subconsciously rejected, although it does not disappear. In addition to this rejection there is the replacement of truth with its antithesis. Then the creature is glorified and served instead of the Creator (Rom. 1:25), a phenomenon that we know in the form of deification of the forces of nature (see J. H. Bavinck, 1949, 171–80).

Man who turns away from God who reveals himself to man cannot be excused (Rom. 1:20). He brings judgment upon himself. "The wrath of God is revealed from heaven against all ungodliness and unrighteousness" (Rom. 1:18).

In Romans 2:14–16 Paul speaks about Gentiles who by nature do what the law commands. They demonstrate that the law is written inside their hearts. Doing naturally what the law commands is not the same thing as acting according to a natural or inner law. This is taught by the Stoa, but not Paul! "By nature" means on the basis of one's own nature, in line with natural existence (Eph. 2:3). This pericope contains the notion: knowing in the absence of God's law. In this respect Jews and Gentiles are contrasted by the apostle (Rom. 2:12). Even without knowledge of God's law, Gentiles obey norms: their own norms. They are inwardly compelled to do what the law commands, because the work of the law is written inside their hearts—which does not imply that the law of God is written inside their hearts, as the Old and New Testaments describe it (Jer. 31:33; Heb. 8:10; 10:16). This doing of what the law commands cannot be equated with fulfillment of the law, which is the ultimate objective according to the apostle Paul. When two people do the very same thing, it is not necessarily the same thing, for the question is what their motives and goals are. What is added with reference to the conscience, which testifies at the same time, and the thoughts that accuse or excuse man, indicates that he is taken to task by his own conscience. He knows that he is dealing with a norm.

Acts 14:15–17 is a noteworthy passage of Scripture. There Paul calls the Gentiles of Lystra to repentance to the living God, the Creator of the universe, who has not left himself without testimony to the people. Does he not continually grant them benefits: rain and periods of fruitfulness, food and joy in abundance? In the contact that the apostle seeks with these Gentiles his starting point is not their religion, but God's dealings with them. They could be addressed with respect to these kind providences.

A pericope that has stirred up much debate is Acts 17:15–34. The apostle appears to approach the Greeks with great understanding and to recognize the value of pagan thinking. One could ask oneself where the antithesis is, which Paul otherwise does not ignore. It has been called the riddle of Paul's speech on the Areopagus and it has even been suggested that it is a Hellenistic speech, with only the final sentence being Christian! This sermon, however, is also a call to repentance (Acts 17:30). Paul does seek to attract interest to his message by speaking a language that the Greeks can understand, by addressing Athens' religiosity, and by citing a statement of a Stoic poet. His aim is not to acknowledge elements of truth in it. The Greeks were also aware of the truth that God is "not far from every one of us" (Acts 17:27). That we are God's "offspring" is truth in the sense that we have been created in God's image. In pagan thought this degenerated into being related to the Godhead. Paul therefore associates a different content with these words than do Greek thinkers and poets. The apostle makes clear God's purpose with what he does. He wants people to seek him (Acts 17:24–27). The God who created the world and gave people places to live is the God who one day will judge everyone justly. It is he who raised Jesus from the dead (Acts 17:18, 30–32).

What the New Testament says about the revelation of God in his works and his dealings with people is in line with what is said in the Old Testament. We learn one aspect especially from the Old Testament: God's glory in nature is sung in the "nature psalms." Israel's poets were deeply impressed by God's majesty. "The heavens declare the glory of God; and the firmament sheweth his handywork" (Ps. 19:1). These psalms tell us how God reveals himself in his work. This aspect of revelation may not be viewed as secondary, for it is no mere sideline. But neither should it be isolated, for it deals with the mighty works of him who has made himself known to his people and from whom they expect their salvation. Thus Psalm 19 is a single unit in which the cosmological and soteriological aspects are intertwined (see also Pss. 65 and 147). God speaks to us in the work of his creation and we hear his Word in his law. The poets of these psalms were devout Israelites who knew their God from his revelation of salvation and recognized his work everywhere, for it bore the imprint of his greatness and goodness.

When Barth rejects general revelation, he does not do justice to Holy Scripture, which shows us the reality of the revelation of God in his works. There are not only "lights" as reflections of Christ as the Light of the World. His criticism of the Belgic Confession of Faith (article 2) is therefore not justified either. There it says that we know God "by two means" (the Latin has: in a twofold manner): "First, by the creation, preservation, and government of the universe; . . . second, he makes himself more clearly and fully known to us by his holy and divine Word."

The comparatives "more clearly" and "more fully" have come under criticism. But in reflecting on the content of the revelation of the Word of God, one must indeed agree with their validity. One could only ask whether revelation in the Word should have been more appropriately placed first. Do we not first of all learn to know God from his Word? But the sequence in this article does not indicate that in our knowledge of God the latter follows upon the former. The Bible shows us a theological sequence related to the progression from creation to re-creation. This is also the basis for the sequence in the Reformed confession.

General revelation does not imply general knowledge of God. This is not the intention of the Belgic Confession of Faith in employing the word "we." It should not be read as "we human beings," but "we who believe." As in all other articles of the confession, "believers living in the Netherlands" are speaking here (as stated in the original heading of the Belgic Confession of Faith). And it has nothing to do with "double bookkeeping," whereby knowledge of the Creator and his creatures would be actually or even solely derived from the book of nature.

Knowledge of God requires more than realizing that he reveals himself in his creation and providence, and more than rational reflection or reasoning. Calvin, who certainly does not denigrate the significance of this revelation, says: "It is therefore in vain that so many burning lamps shine for us in the workmanship of the universe to show forth the glory of its Author" (*Institutes*, 1.5.14). It is our own fault that this happens in vain. "The manifestation of God, by which he makes his glory known in his creatures, is, with regard to the light itself, sufficiently clear; but that on account of our blindness, it is not found to be sufficient" (Calvin on Rom. 1:20). To come to God the Creator we need Scripture as guide and teacher (*Institutes*, 1.6.1). Furthermore, it is true of every revelation that comes to people as they are that he must grant them his illumination and open their eyes to it. In short, we require the eyeglasses of Scripture and the eyes of faith.

It is a fact that frequently a natural knowledge of God has been inferred from general revelation, also referred to as natural revelation. Barth and many with him are right in shying away from the theories of natural theology of which we have examples in Roman Catholicism and in the ideas of "German Christians."[26] Yet we must continue to keep in mind that general revelation and natural theology are not equivalent from a structural point of view. This is indeed the case in Roman Catholicism, but emphatically not in Reformational theology—although it must be admitted that the older Reformed theology, generally speaking, expected more from natural theology than Calvin did (see § 10.2).

26. More on this in J. van Genderen, in A. G. Knevel (ed.), *Visie op Karl Barth*, 1987, 17–24.

An important phenomenon in the realm of theology is the idea of revelational universalism, which gained strength as early as the second half of the twentieth century. It advocates the idea that revelation comprises more than the revelation of salvation in Jesus Christ. Abstract natural knowledge of God or natural religion has receded to the background, and world religions have come to the fore in all their concreteness. One has begun to search for elements of truth or aspects of the one truth in order to establish points of connection for the preaching of the gospel (International Missions Conference of Jerusalem, 1928). In *Tambaram* (1938), H. Kraemer and others have emphasized discontinuity, but ever since the third Assembly of the World Council of Churches (New Delhi, 1961), revelational universalism has gained momentum. All religions are considered to be avenues that lead to God. Christ is at work everywhere as the cosmic Christ.

Similar thoughts have emerged in more recent Roman Catholic theology. Well-known names in this connection are K. Rahner, H. R. Schlette, R. Panikkar, and A. Camps. It has been said of Rahner that according to him, general revelation conceptually is achieved explicitly in Christianity and implicitly in non-Christian religions, and that general revelation finds its unique, irrevocable, and absolute culmination in God's self-expression in Christ (Wentsel, 1970, 166). Significant is a passage in the dogmatic constitution of the Second Vatican Council dealing with the church (*Lumen Gentium*, 1964): "Everything good and true that is to be found in them (i.e. non-Christians), is viewed by the Church as preparation for the Gospel and constitutes a gift from God to illuminate every person, enabling him to ultimately gain eternal life." The New Catechism expresses the conviction that in the wisdom of religions the eternal Word of God, our Lord Jesus Christ, has been at work through his Holy Spirit.[27] Yet there is a measure of ambivalence in the official Roman Catholic position. There is also salvation outside the church—which was not accepted in the past—but this does not mean that non-Christian religions are recognized as paths to salvation.

There are a growing number of documents coming out of circles of the ecumenical movement that have a bearing on the idea of revelational universalism. There appear to be quite divergent approaches in the dialogue. In Vancouver in 1973, agreement was reached with respect to the statement: we recognize the creative work of God in seeking religious truth on the part of adherents of other religions.

There is a growing minority who go so far as to say that they are prepared to give up the decisive and normative significance of Christ in a pluralistic society. They do this for the sake of a genuine, open dialogue, which is enriching to its participants, because there is a mutual give-and-take. P. F. Knitter mentions in this connection figures such as J. Hick, R. Panikkar, P. van Buren, R. Ruether, and A. Pieris, and he emphatically includes himself among them. Thus a "theocentric model" is devised with Christ no longer being viewed as being at the center. In this dialogue collabora-

27. *The Newer Catechism*, 1966, 35ff.

tion for well-being and salvation is the overall goal, and the uniqueness of God's revelation in Christ is sacrificed. Characteristic is the question mark in the title of P. F. Knitter's work: *No Other Name?* (1989^3).

This "theocentric approach" is presented as a new model for a theology of religions, and is defended with the hypothesis that creation and the history of mankind represent the place of God's acts of salvation to redeem and judge. God has not exhaustively revealed himself in Jesus Christ. Nor has he done so exclusively in him.[28]

But nowhere does the Bible give us the right to give such a generalized interpretation of revelation, God's creative work in other religions, and salvation as its outcome. "There is none other name under heaven given among men" (Acts 4:12). Jesus is not a way that does not preclude other ways. He says: "I am the way, the truth, and the life: no man cometh unto the Father but by me" (John 14:6). In the various religions there is indeed a reaction to God's revelation. It could be referred to as a seeking in order to find him gropingly (cf. Acts 17:27). But the religions of humanity react to the revelation of God's eternal power and Godhead in an obstinate and arbitrary way. The truth is shut out and replaced with something else (Rom. 1).

With J. H. Bavinck we can view man's innate religious sense, which is manifested in various ways, as the consequence of understanding and discernment (Rom. 1:20), and of rejection and replacement (Rom. 1:18, 25). This realization crystallizes around a number of specific nuclei such as holistic awareness, normativity, relationship with a higher power, the concept of redemption, and the sense that one's life is being guided (J. H. Bavinck, 1949, 187ff.).

Here we are not only dealing with forms of universalism that are in direct opposition to what the biblical message says about the one name by which we must be saved, but also a broad movement in more recent Protestantism that refers to non-Christian religions more or less positively. Thus to P. Althaus, religion is the conscious relationship of man with respect to the God who makes himself knowable to man in his "Ur-revelation" [*Uroffenbarung* = "original revelation"], which contains both truth and falsehood. Paganism can be viewed as a preliminary stage of the gospel, although at the same time it runs counter to it. According to W. Pannenberg, the history of religion must be interpreted as the appearance of the divine mystery that is presupposed in the structure of human existence, although non-Christian

28. J. van Lin, in F. J. Verstraelen (chief ed.), *Oecumenische inleiding in de missiologie* (ecumenical introduction to missiology), 1988, 196.

religions have observed the appearance of the divine mystery only in a fragmentary manner.[29]

Partly because modern universalism of revelation tends toward a general redemption history and a universalism of salvation that has a paralyzing effect on the fulfillment of the missionary call of the church as well as the Christian (Wentsel, *Dogm.* 2:94–102), it is necessary to cling to confessional statements regarding the insufficiency of general revelation. It can indeed no longer be stated that Christian theologians are unanimous in this regard (Bavinck, *R.D.*, 1:312). The term "insufficiency" implies no criticism of God's revelation, but of man who does not know God from his works. The Westminster Confession of Faith declares that "the light of nature, and the works of creation and providence . . . are not sufficient to give that knowledge of God, and his will which is necessary unto salvation" (1.1). That God can be known from his works is indeed "sufficient to convince men and to leave them without excuse" (Belgic Confession of Faith, article 2). What must be said about the insufficiency of general revelation and the absence of any excuse (Rom. 1:20), however, does not detract from the significance it has for believers. They can speak of a splendid book in which everything points to God (cf. Belgic Confession of Faith, article 2).

To them general revelation is no independent source for the knowledge of God. The two means or forms of revelation must not be turned into two separate sources. The light of Scripture must also shine on creation, and without faith we do not understand that the world was established through the Word of God (Heb. 11:3).

In the first place, the significance of general revelation consists in the belief that we learn to know and glorify God in his works. "O LORD our Lord, how excellent is thy name in all the earth!" (Ps. 8:1, 9). "O LORD, how manifold are thy works! in wisdom thou hast made them all: the earth is full of thy riches" (Ps. 104:24). We do not face the power of nature or a blind march of events, but the majesty of God. This revelation of God brings Job in the light of God's greatness and wisdom to confess his insignificance and foolishness and to humble himself before God (Job 38–42).

29. P. Althaus, *Die christliche Wahrheit* (the Christian truth), 1952[3], 93, 137ff.; W. Pannenberg, *Grundfragen systematischer Theologie* (basic questions in systematic theology), 1971[2], 289–95; idem, *Systematische Theologie*, 1988, 1:184–205. Cf. P. F. Knitter, *No Other Name?* 1989[3], 97ff.

In the second place, God's general revelation shows us clearly that there is no contrast between nature and grace. Dualism is not biblical. Nature and grace, creation and re-creation, are inextricably intertwined. It is one and the same God who in general revelation does not leave himself without a witness to anyone and who in special revelation makes himself known as a God of grace (Bavinck, *R.D.*, 1:322).

In the third place, in encounters with those of different persuasions we can start out from what binds us together. They cannot say that they have never been aware of God. Elements of truth in non-Christian religions or worldviews, which can serve as a point of departure, should not be interpreted as such, but religious awareness, which reflects man's creation in the image of God coupled with the fact that God does not ignore him, is crucial for establishing contact. There is a basis for dialogue. But dialogue must remain a tool for witness.

"General revelation" is also a current concept in Reformed theology, although one may ask whether the term "general" is the most appropriate one. "Special" is definitely not meant as qualification of "general." At any rate it is preferable not to speak of natural revelation or revelation in nature, for much more is involved. We also prefer to avoid the terms "ur-revelation" ([*Uroffenbarung* = "original revelation"] P. Althaus) or "revelation in creation" (E. Brunner), although they need not be labeled as "fatal modern expressions" (K. Barth). Descriptions such as God's acting in the world as distinguished from God's acting for salvation (C. H. Ratschow) and labels such as fundamental revelation or revelation in God's works do not entirely satisfy, let alone: partial, dim, or unfulfilled revelation. For lack of a better term we retain "general revelation." This revelation was already embedded in creation and is inextricably intertwined with sustaining and governing the providential acting of God with its general scope, implying that he does not fail to reveal himself to anyone (cf. Berkouwer. 1951, 242).

Bavinck provides a definition that is worth citing here: "General revelation is that conscious and free act of God by which, by means of nature and history (in the broadest sense, hence including one's personal life experience) he makes himself known—particularly in his attributes of omnipotence and wisdom, wrath and goodness—to fallen man in order that they should turn to him and keep his law or, in the absence of such repentance, be inexcusable" (*R.D.*, 1:350).

5.2. *Special revelation*

When a distinction is made between general and special revelation, a description or definition of special revelation is in order. Bavinck provided the following one: It "is that conscious and free act of God by which, he, in the way of a historical complex of special means (theophany, prophecy, miracle) that are concentrated in the person of Christ, makes himself known—specifically in the attributes of his justice and grace, in the proclamation of law and gospel—to those human beings who live in the light of this special revelation in order that they may accept the grace of God by faith in Christ or, in case of impenitence, receive a more severe judgment" (*R.D.*, 1:350). One might opt for a shorter formulation: it is that revelation of God through which, by special means which have their focus and climax in Christ, he has disclosed the way of life to sinners, whom he grants to live in this light. In the Old Testament there is a sharp demarcation of the circle of light cast by special revelation (cf. Ps. 147:19–20), but it was not God's intention to limit himself to a single nation. The special nature of special revelation applies particularly to its content. It is the revelation of salvation in Christ. "For God so loved the world, that he gave his only begotten Son, that whoever believeth in him should not perish, but have everlasting life" (John 3:16).

Following man's fall into sin, God did not withdraw himself. His revelation in time and history—which consists in his involvement in the world, which he created and ever since sustains and governs—continues. His revelation becomes richer still, for he confronts sin with the superior power of his grace.

The first characteristic of special revelation is that it is not only theocentric but also *Trinitarian.* God makes himself known to us as the triune God, as Father, Son, and Holy Spirit. Through the great events of salvation—the incarnation of the Word and the outpouring of the Holy Spirit—this Trinitarian character is much more pronounced in the New Testament than in the revelation of the Old Testament. Now baptism is administered in the name of the Father, the Son, and the Holy Spirit, and the church is blessed in the name of the triune God (Matt. 28:19; 2 Cor. 13:14).

The second characteristic of this revelation is that it is *soteriological.* It is the revelation of salvation: the revelation of what is needful for us to know in this life to God's glory and our salvation (cf. Belgic Confession of Faith, article 2). With the Heidelberg Catechism (Lord's Day 6) we can say that God himself first revealed the gospel in Paradise, whereby we think of the mother promise (Gen. 3:15). In the prophecies, God states who he is and how he acts: "For I am the LORD thy God, the Holy One of Israel, thy Saviour" (Isa. 43:3). At the beginning of the gospel rings the song of praise: "Blessed be the LORD God of Israel; for he hath visited and redeemed his people" (Luke 1:68). The apostle Paul proclaims salvation in Christ: "who of God is made unto us wisdom, and righteousness, and sanctification, and redemption" (1 Cor. 1:30). It has been correctly pointed out that the intention of God's revelation is the salvation and restoration of the whole person and the whole cosmos (Bavinck, *R.D.*, 1:346).

A third characteristic of special revelation is that it is *progressive*. There is a history of God's revelation. "God, who at sundry times and in divers manners spake in time past unto the fathers by the prophets, hath in these last days spoken unto us by his Son" (Heb. 1:1–2). Christ's coming and his work on earth are indeed the focus and the climax, but not yet the culmination of special revelation. Christ promises his Spirit to the apostles: "Howbeit when he, the Spirit of truth is come, he will guide you into all truth" (John 16:13).

God has employed means to reveal himself: theophany, prophecy, and miracle.

1. *Theophany*. In the Old Testament the manifestation of God to Israel, descending on Sinai (Ex. 19:18–20; Deut. 4:11–15), has a central place. Sometimes the manner of his appearance is not further specified, and sometimes reference is made to signs of his presence (Gen. 15:1; 1 Kings 8:10).

The Old Testament speaks in various places of the appearance of the Angel of the Lord (*malak YHWH*). Theology moves between two extreme views. This angel is sometimes identified as the preexistent Word of God or an Old Testament revelation of Christ; sometimes it is believed that this is an ordinary angel who represents God. It is noteworthy that this angel had no equal in the world of angels. He always appears by himself. Wherever he appears, God is among his people (cf. Ex. 3:2, 4; Judg. 6:11–24). The Angel of the Lord is the most direct form of theophany before Christ came to earth, "a true personal revelation and appearance of God" (Bavinck, *R.D.*, 1:329). When the theophany as such already says that it pleases God to reveal himself to people, we may recognize in the appearance of the Angel of the Lord a reference to the still richer revelation consisting in the fact that "God was [made] manifest in the flesh" (1 Tim. 3:16).

2. *Prophecy* is a unique phenomenon in the history of Israel itself and in the history of mankind. It has been the subject of a great deal of

thought. It is entirely in conflict with what we know of the prophets of Israel to suppose that they interpreted their own insights to be God's revelation, although there were false prophets who did so. But how they were warned against! In the case of a figure such as Jeremiah one can sense the tension between his own thoughts and the inspiration that God gave him: "O LORD, thou hast deceived me, and I was deceived: thou art stronger than I, and hast prevailed" (Jer. 20:7–18). Not only of Amos but of other prophets as well it is true: "The LORD God hath spoken, who can but prophesy?" "He revealeth his secret unto his servants the prophets" (Amos 3:8, 7). The deepest essence of the manner in which God revealed himself to his prophets remains a mystery to us (Oosterhoff, 1987, 17). In every instance it is a matter of inspiration or afflatus from the Lord. The prophets declare that the Word of God came to them or that the hand of the Lord came upon them. This implies being seized and controlled by a higher power to be entirely opened up to the word that God speaks (Oosterhoff, 1987, 10). Ezekiel had to eat a scroll, which is to say that he had to absorb the Word of God and become one with it. Jeremiah 23:18 states: "For who hath stood in the counsel of the LORD, and hath perceived and heard his word?" The true prophet—for he is the one discussed here in contrast with the false prophet—is aware of his bond with God, i.e., intimate communion with him. In this way the prophet can act as God's mouth (Jer. 15:19) and transmit God's words to his people. He is certain that it is God's message that he proclaims: thus says the Lord.

Prophecy need not only relate to the future. What God reveals through the medium of prophecy pertains to the present, the past, and the future. Prophets appeared in particular situations at specific times, but their words have largely been preserved. These words had far-reaching significance, as their interpretation confirms. The prophetic perspective encompasses the past, the present, and the future.

In proclaiming their interpretation of God's counsel and will, promises of salvation and announcements of judgment, prophets do not stand alone. There is a continuing connection with the words that God spoke earlier, and especially with the revelation that he gave to Israel through Moses' ministry. With respect to Moses and the prophets after him the Lord can say: "I will put my words in his mouth; and he shall speak unto them all that I shall command him" (Deut. 18:18). Prophecy also finds its culmination in Christ, "our chief

Prophet and Teacher, who has fully revealed to us the secret counsel and will of God concerning our redemption" (Heidelberg Catechism, Lord's Day 12).

3. A third means of revelation is the *miracle*. The first thing to be noted is that it is only God who performs miracles (Ps. 72:18). As acts of God, miracles are essentially revelations. It is said of them: "Who is unto thee, glorious in holiness, fearful in praises, doing wonders?" (Ex. 15:11). By means of them God's omnipotence is revealed in a special way, but then they must indeed be seen in the context of the entirety of his revelation. They play a role in the history of salvation. The Lord establishes his covenant, he performs marvels, and all of Israel will see his work (cf. Ex. 34:10). There are at least three periods in which miracles play an important role, so that one can speak of a cycle of miracles and signs: the time of the exodus from Egypt, the time of Elijah and Elisha, and the time when Christ was on earth and the apostles proclaimed his gospel.

Sometimes miracles serve to confirm the spoken word (John 5:36; Acts 14:3). However significant biblical miracles are (cf. John 20:30–31), they are not proofs, in the usual sense of the word, that convince everyone. They call for faith, and only in faith are they seen as miracles of God and signs of the coming of his kingdom.

This mode of revelation also has a future aspect. We are moving toward the consummation, and in accordance with God's promises, we may expect mighty wonders. The pivotal miracle in the history of divine revelation became reality when the Word became flesh. Christ is the center of the entire cycle of God's miracles.

Some Literature

Th. van Baaren, *Voorstellingen van openbaring phaenomenologisch beschouwd* (concepts of revelation considered from a phenomenological point of view), 1951.

J. H. Bavinck, *Religieus besef en christelijk geloof* (religious awareness and Christian faith), 1949.

G. C. Berkouwer, *Geloof en openbaring in de niewere Duitse theologie* (faith and revelation in more recent German theology), 1932.

G. C. Berkouwer, *General Revelation*, 1955.

E. Brunner, *Revelation and Reason*, 1944.

G. D'Costa (ed.), *Christian Uniqueness Reconsidered*, 1990.

E. A. Dowey Jr., *The Knowledge of God in Calvin's Theology*, 1952.

A. G. Honig Jr., *De kosmische betekenis van Christus* (the cosmic significance of Christ), 1968.

W. Joest, *Fundamentaltheologie*, 1974.

P. F. Knitter, *No Other Name?* 1989[3].

F. W. A. Korff, *Het christelijk geloof en de niet-christelijke godsdiensten* (the Christian faith and non-Christian religions), 1946.

H. Kraemer, *The Christian Message in a non-Christian World*, 1938.

G. Kraus, *Gotteserkentnis ohne Offenbaring und Glaube?* (recognition of God without revelation and faith?), 1987.

H. M. Kuitert, *Filosofische theologie* (philosophical theology), 1988.

H. M. Kuitert, *Wat heet geloven?* (what is believing?), 1977.

C. Link, *Die Welt als Gleichnis* (the world as a parable), 1976.

B. J. Oosterhoff, *Israels profeten*, 1962.

B. J. Oosterhoff, *Jeremia en het Woord van God*, 1987.

W. Pannenberg (ed.), *Offenbarung als Geschichte* (revelation as history), 1961.

T. H. L. Parker, *Calvin's Doctrine of the Knowledge of God*, 1969[2].

A. D. R. Polman, *Gereformeerd katholieke dogmatiek*, 1, 1969.

J. Riemens Jr., *Het begrip der openbaring in het Christendom* (the concept of revelation in Christianity), 1905.

K. Runia, *Het evangelie en de vele religies* (the gospel and the many religions), 1990.

J. Veenhof, *Revelatie en inspiratie*, 1968.

J. Verkuyl, *Zijn alle godsdiensten gelijk?* (are all religions the same?), 1984[5].

W. A. Visser 't Hooft, *No Other Name*, 1963.

J. M. Vlijm, *Het religie-begrip van Karl Barth* (Karl Barth's concept of religion), 1956.

H. M. Vroom, *Religies en de waarheid* (religions and truth), 1988.

B. Wentsel, *Natuur en genade* (nature and grace), 1970.

L. van der Zanden, *Christelijke religie en historische openbaring* (Christian religion and historical revelation), 1928.

Chapter 3

Holy Scripture

§ 6. Holy Scripture as the Word of God

6.1. *Revelation and Holy Scripture*
6.2. *The Old and the New Testaments*

6.1. *Revelation and Holy Scripture*

The revelation of God and Holy Scripture are not the same thing; neither are the revelation of salvation and Holy Scripture. Special revelation comprises more than what is contained in the Bible, for not everything that has been revealed has been written down (cf. John 21:25). Furthermore, revelation does not coincide with its written record. For example, the revelation received by the prophets was frequently not recorded until a later date. An example of this can be found in Jeremiah 36. Scripture is therefore that portion of special revelation that God has planned to safeguard for all times and for all people.

The *distinction* that we make between the Word of God that has come to people from the beginning and the books of the Bible implies no *separation* between the two. But how can we further delineate the relationship between revelation and Holy Scripture?

In Bavinck's work we come across ideas that have a strong appeal. He refers to Holy Scripture as the servant form of revelation, and thereby makes a connection between the incarnation of the Word and the recording of the word, i.e., between incarnation and inscripturation. Did Christ not take on the form of a servant? The Son of God came to us in history, and similarly revelation entered into history. The Word became Scripture, and as Scripture subjected itself to the fate of all scripture. But just as Christ's human nature remained free from sin, so also Scripture was conceived without defect. Scripture is Christ's servant and also shares in his ignominy (*R.D.*, 1:434ff.).

Just as Christ is both God and man, the Bible contains both divine and human elements. This seems like a parallel, but is not. The incarnation is an absolutely unique event. Our reception of God's revelation in human language is essentially different from adoption of human nature by the Son of God.

It is not incorrect to follow Bavinck in saying that Holy Scripture is at the service of revelation. Nevertheless, this image does not do full justice to the revelatory character of Scripture. Scripture could be at the service of revelation without being itself revelation. But the church believes that Scripture is the Word of God. We are dealing here with the divine Word, the holy and divine Scriptures, the holy and canonical books of God (Belgic Confession of Faith, articles 2–7).

The basis of the confession that Holy Scripture is the Word of God is found in Scripture itself, although it requires the testimony of the Holy Spirit to recognize this (see § 9).

The church says nothing of Scripture that is not said by Scripture itself. Only by confirming this completely and absolutely can the church do full justice to Holy Scripture.

Jesus continuously appeals to Scripture: "It is written" (Matt. 4:4, 6, 7, 10). He declares that what is written of him is bound to be fulfilled (Mark 9:12; Luke 22:37). The Holy Scripture of the Old Testament is to him the authoritative Word of God. The apostles are so convinced that Scripture is the Word of God that from time to time they directly ascribe to God what has been spoken by the prophets or the psalmists and has been recorded in Scripture. Psalm 95:7–11 is quoted as words of the Spirit (Heb. 3:7). What is said by the poet of Psalm 16 is ascribed to God (Acts 13:35). The Spirit of God speaks through the last words of David (2 Sam. 23:2).

How human writings can be the Word of God is discussed when we contemplate theopneusty or the inspiration of Holy Scripture (see § 7).

This topic presents us with the fact that we are faced with radically divergent opinions. In theology there are schools of thought that *deny any revelatory character* to the books of the Bible: *the Bible is not the Word of God.*

There are also theologians who seek to establish a connection between the Scriptures and revelation with the notion that the Bible is a *record of revelation.* It has frequently been said: *the Bible is not God's Word, but it contains God's Word.*

More so than in the past, Holy Scripture is viewed as a *testimony to revelation.* Many prefer this concept over that of a record of revelation. The Bible is not a dead protocol, but a living witness (L. Ihmels). M. Kähler (1835–1912) especially came to emphasize the view of Scripture as testimony, and many followed in his footsteps. Subsequently the characterization of Scripture as testimony gained popularity especially under the influence of dialectic theology. According to Barth, the Bible is God's Word so far as God lets it be, so far as God speaks through it (*C.D.*, 1.1.123). *The Bible becomes the Word of God* whenever it pleases God.

J. H. Scholten, one of the fathers of modernism in the Netherlands, does consider the Bible to be a source of knowledge for Christian religion, but not revelation. Holy Scripture provides information about God's revelation, but is not revelation itself and therefore cannot be called the Word of God. G. J. Heering, an important representative of rightist modernism, reproaches the Reformation for creating a heteronomous, legalistic biblicism. God does not reveal himself in a book with such a variegated content, a voluminous book representing God's own Word from Genesis 1 through Revelation 22. According to Heering, the New Testament contains many images that we could not possibly consider to be part of God's revelation, and therefore neither as being inherent to the Christian faith.[1] A critical treatment of the books of the Bible and especially those of the Old Testament leads to a rejection of Holy Scripture as the Word of God. The Old Testament scholar C. J. Labuschagne honestly believes that the Bible is no longer the Word of God. To him the Bible is a truly human book, "a deep human testimony to insights of faith concerning God and his acts."[2]

Ethical theology generously employs the term "record." Its proponents believe that the Bible is a collection of proclamations concerning the revelation of salvation.

1. G. J. Heering, *Geloof en openbaring* (faith and revelation), 1944[2], 428, 314.

2. C. J. Labuschagne, *Wat zegt de Bijbel in Gods naam?* (what does the Bible say for God's sake?), 1977[2], 100.

Like other records or early valuable documents, they deserve to be analyzed from a historical-critical perspective (J. J. P. Valeton). Ethical theologians have no problem with scriptural criticism, believing that it cannot harm God's revelation, since it is supra-historical (a term suggested by H. M. van Nes) and we may conceivably learn something from it.[3]

According to Barth, the proclamation of the Word by the church can become the Word of God to us. The same is thought with respect to the Bible as a whole. It is God's prerogative to speak through human words. It is in this sense that the Bible is God's Word. In this view the Bible reflects human attempts to restate and reproduce the Word of God in terms of human thoughts and words in certain human situations. God spoke and Paul spoke. These are two entirely different things. But when the Word of God is an event ("im Ereignis des Wortes Gottes") it is one fact. Revelation and the Bible are then word-for-word one at that (*C.D.*, 1.1.127). When viewing Holy Scripture as testifying to revelation, Barth implies a separation of revelation and Scripture. The absolute identity between the human words of Holy Scripture and the Word of God is precluded. Qua content, the Bible is testimony to the revelation in Jesus Christ; qua form, it is the testimony of the immediate witnesses. The Bible is not a book of oracles, no means of direct communication. Prophets and apostles could fall short with every word and did fall short with every word. The disputability of biblical testimony also has implications for its religious and theological content. There are parallels in the history of religion and there are mutual contradictions among authors. But it is precisely by grace alone that they have spoken the Word of God in their fallible and erring human word (*C.D.*, 1.2.530).

Barth's motives differ from those of Heering. There is a clear difference between the view that the Bible as such is not the Word of God and that through faith man must use his own judgment to determine what constitutes the gospel for him,[4] and the view that the Bible, however contestable, can through God's sovereign grace become the Word of God to us. But neither Heering nor Barth does justice to the view that is rejected by them. The church's Reformers do not teach a heteronomous, legalistic biblicism (Heering's reproach), and orthodoxy does not support a paper pope (Barth's reproach). More serious is the accusation that orthodoxy appears to refuse to live by grace and thus seeks certainties of its own. The Reformational doctrine that the Bible is God's Word does not threaten God's freedom. Is God not free to provide us with his revelation in a reliable form by human means?

It is now necessary to focus on the concept of "testimony." According to Barth, it refers to or points to Christ who is the Word of God. By distinguishing between revelation and Scripture, Barth's terminology also implies the relativity of Scripture as human testimony.

The testimony of the Bible is not subjective or fallible testimony advocated by man, but reliable testimony employed by God.

3. Cf. A. de Willigen, "Geloof en geschiedenis bij (faith and history according to) J. J. P. Valeton, H. M. van Nes en G. van der Leeuw," in *Ernst en vrede* (sincerity and peace), 1951, 193–213.

4. G. J. Heering, *Geloof en openbaring* (faith and revelation), 1944^2, 317–18, 329.

Jesus' statement that the Scriptures testify of him (John 5:39) implies something entirely different from the usual interpretation given by the more recent theology. It is a judicial term and reflects a process in which witnesses are employed to establish the truth to such a degree that no doubt can remain (cf. Deut. 19:15; Heb. 10:28). The apostles are referred to as witnesses to the resurrection (Acts 1:22). They have seen the risen Lord with their own eyes and heard him speak. He, who made his followers to be his witnesses, stands behind their testimony that goes out into the world to win men over to his cause. The apostolic testimony demands from us that we allow ourselves to be convinced and won over.

Biblical testimony does not involve facts only but also their significance. We are not at liberty to depart from either. We can say with Trimp: witnesses are those ministers of God who "are authorized by Christ and equipped by his Spirit to proclaim the factual truth and the true factuality of the salvation brought about by Christ and to hold it up to the lie that rules the world, in order to put unbelief to shame and encourage repentance" (Trimp, 1970, 26).

The Spirit of Christ already testified in the words of the prophets to "the sufferings of Christ and the glory that would follow" (1 Peter 1:11). In the conflict with unbelieving Jews, Jesus says: "And the Father himself, which hath sent me, hath borne witness of me." In this context we find the words: Ye "search the scriptures; for in them ye think ye have eternal life: and they are they which testify of me" (John 5:37–39). This implies that the testimony of the Scriptures concerning Christ is the testimony of the Father himself.

Biblical testimony is not merely a human approximation or interpretation of the mystery of revelation. It is God's testimony that is for ever sure.

As far as the concept "testimony" is concerned, the following literature is relevant: R. Schippers, *Getuigen van Jezus Christus in het Niewe Testament* (witnessing to Jesus Christ in the New Testament), 1938; H. Strahtmann in *TDNT*, 4:474–514; H. N. Ridderbos, *Heilsgeschiedenis en Heilige Schrift* (redemption history and Holy Scripture), 1955, 116–34); C. Trimp, *Betwist Schriftgezag* (disputed scriptural authority), 1970, 7–35).

Schippers concludes that bearing witness to Jesus Christ in the New Testament is speaking about him either by himself or by the Father and the Holy Spirit, or by eye- and ear-witnesses concerning his life and actions—in order to persuade people through this speaking to make their great decision with respect to faith. This testimony in terms of knowledge and representation of the facts thus serves God's justice. The New

Testament knows only of witnesses who are bound to the facts (199, 198). Especially Luke employs the concept of "testimony" in order to place the entire emphasis on the historical foundation of kerygma. Apostolic testimony, which occupies a unique place in the history of redemption, represents the link established by the Holy Spirit between the great event of redemption in the fullness of time and the emerging church. Therefore it is not merely testimony to revelation, but itself also forms part of this revelation. We do not have the right to oppose it. This testimony is not given by a single authority, but by many. This constitutes not only a reinforcement of this testimony but also a declaration of its multiplicity (Ridderbos, 117, 120, 126).

6.2. *The Old and the New Testaments*

The distinction between the Old Testament and the New Testament dates back to the beginning of the third century AD. Those who wonder why we make this distinction can find its origin in what Paul says about the Jews of his day: "For until this day remaineth the same veil untaken away in the reading of the old testament; which veil is done away in Christ" (2 Cor. 3:14). The reading of the old covenant here must be the reading of the scrolls during worship service in the synagogue. The old covenant stands in contrast with the new covenant. A Latin word for covenant is "testamentum," hence the names Old Testament and New Testament.

To Jews the *Tanach*—law, prophets, and scriptures (cf. also Luke 24:44)—represents the content of what we refer to as the Old Testament.

The distinction between the Old Testament and the New Testament does not at all detract from the unity of Holy Scripture as the Word of God. The church of Christ believes that the entire Old Testament testifies to Christ and finds its fulfillment in him. For that reason it has held to the unity of Scripture right from the beginning.

There have been those who turned this distinction into a contrast. In the second century, Marcion declared that the Old Testament came from the God of the Jews who was at the same time the Creator and the Lawgiver, but that it no longer had any value if on the basis of the gospel one believed in the God of love who had revealed himself in Christ. The New Testament came—at least in part—from the good God, the Father of Jesus Christ.

There were also those who had trouble accepting the Old Testament, e.g., Augustine, who at first could not understand that in early times different laws of God prevailed than those in his own days. He subsequently discovered that ceremonial laws belonged to shadows that had passed. Over against the Manichaeans, under whose influence he had lived for years, Augustine very clearly held on to the lasting significance of the Old Testament and the unity of Holy Scripture. Faustus attacked the Old Testament for supposedly not containing any prophecies regarding Christ. He saw it as carnally oriented and as containing a great deal that was improper. In view of the teaching of Christ, the old and the new would not go together. Those who are so critical of the Old Testament do not leave the New Testament unscathed either. We see this happen to Marcion and his followers, but also to Manichaeans such as Faustus who thought that the promised Paraclete would teach Christians what in the New Testament they should accept and reject.

Whether the Old Testament has always been properly interpreted by the church is a secondary matter. From the beginning there were chiefly two different interpretations: the typological and the allegorical. Typology clung to the primary significance of the text, but not exclusively so. The main thing was the perspective of what was to come, i.e., the "Vorausdarstellung des Kommenden" (the representation of what comes, L. Goppelt). The allegorical approach sought a truth beyond the truth. To Origen, not the literal but the spiritual meaning was important. But at any rate, the Old Testament passages were linked with Christ or with Christ and his church (Augustine).

The revelatory character of the Old Testament must be maintained over against all views that reject the Old Testament as God's revelation.

Rationalism has not spared the Bible and certainly not the Old Testament. At the beginning of the nineteenth century we encounter Schleiermacher, who viewed the Old Testament as a legalistic book. The church did inherit it, and at least at first could not avoid it. But this historical perspective is no theological justification for the recognition of the Old Testament as Christianity's Holy Scripture. Christianity does not require Jewish support.

Terms frequently employed during the nineteenth century include: Israelitic literature (the official reference in Dutch Legislation concerning Higher Education of 1876) and the record of the religion of Israel.

The twentieth century witnessed a fierce attack on the Old Testament. It was viewed as a Jewish book. The prominent German theologian A. von Harnack (1851–1930) wrote the frequently quoted statement: in the second century the church correctly avoided the mistake of rejecting the Old Testament; in the sixteenth century the Reformation could not avoid the fate of its retention; but preserving it as canonical proclamation following the nineteenth century constitutes religious and ecclesiastical paralysis.

It became worse when the Old Testament came to be referred to as the document of another religion. It was felt that it had been canceled and invalidated by the New Testament. "The New Testament concept of the kingdom of God and the Redeemer radically eliminates the Old Testament Jewish representation" (E. Hirsch).

The wave of anti-Semitism that swept through Germany during the time of National Socialism also influenced certain theologians and the German church to some extent. The slogan became: away with the Old Testament. The ideology of A. Rosenberg reflected the position that the Old Testament as religious book needed to be discarded once and for all. The aversion to the Old Testament had far-reaching consequences and also affected the New Testament. According to Rosenberg, there were clearly mutilated and superstitious messages in the New Testament, which needed to be eliminated. But this time has fortunately passed.

There is also another side. We have in mind the position that W. Vischer took in his work *Das Christuszeugnis des Alten Testaments* (the testimony to Christ in the Old Testament, 1934–42). His treatment of the Old Testament does not do justice to the historical aspect of this portion of the Word of God (cf. Oosterhoff, 1954, 16ff.).

There is indeed anti-Semitism. But there is also philo-Semitism, which views the Old Testament as preeminently a Jewish book. One can be so enthusiastic about the *Tanach* that one wants to hear of little else.

This is not the case with Van Ruler. But it goes too far to treat the Old Testament as the real Bible, also from the point of view of the Christian church, while "the New Testament is so to speak nothing but a glossary appended to explain uncommon terms."[5] One can here take into account that Van Ruler had a tendency to stimulate discussion by making extreme statements. But it is typical that in this connection he rejected the notion of an ongoing revelation that presents a linear interpretation of history. According to him the nature of the Bible is much more circular (prophetic and apostolic testimony around history proper, in the "fullness of time" of the impact of revelation).[6] This is reminiscent of Barth.

The image of a continuous line is much more consistent with the history of God's revelation. It is indeed a matter of progression (see Heb. 1:1; cf. also Rom. 16:25–26; Eph. 3:4–6). We encounter a similar line of thought in the Heidelberg Catechism (response 19).

Without schematically fixing the relationship between the Old Testament and the New Testament, we can say that there is a progression from promise to fulfillment (cf. Baker, 1976, 373). This is only an approximation, for it is not true that the Old Testament is purely a collection of promises and that the New Testament merely represents their fulfillment. Promises of God were repeatedly fulfilled in Old Testament times, and in the new dispensation by no means all of God's

5. A. A. van Ruler, *Religie en politiek*, 1945, 123.

6. Ibid., 128. Subsequently Van Ruler expressed it somewhat differently, although he kept saying that the Old Testament was the real Bible (*Die christliche Kirche und das Alte Testament* = the Christian church and the Old Testament, 1955).

promises have yet been fulfilled. Fulfillment in the New Testament does not yet constitute the final consummation of all things.

God's promises are not predictions or prognostications that cease to have relevance once they have come true. In that case part of the Old Testament would only be of historical significance to us! The church of Christ sees the coming of God to his people described in all of the Old Testament, and hears in it the announcement of salvation. Therefore the church still loves the Old Testament as the Word of God, just as it was the book of life and the book of prayer to the Son of Man.[7] Passages from the Psalms became words from the cross. Jesus said of the Scriptures of the Old Testament: "They are they which testify of me" (John 5:39). "To him give all the prophets witness" (Acts 10:43). It says in the gospel "that all things must be fulfilled, which were written in the law of Moses, and in the prophets, and in the psalms, concerning [him]" (Luke 24:44). We must keep in mind that when God's promises become true, this does not necessarily mean that they have been completely fulfilled. The Old Testament promises of salvation open mighty perspectives pertaining to consummation and God's eternal kingdom. It says that "the earth shall be full of the knowledge of the LORD, as the waters cover the sea" (Isa. 11:9). This is not yet the case. We can indeed see more of it than could those who first heard the words of this prophecy. At one time the knowledge of the God of the covenant remained practically limited to a single nation, while today the Word of God reaches around the globe. But the full realization of these promises remains outstanding. Their realization in the new dispensation will be superseded by their ultimate fulfillment in the coming kingdom of God.

The Old and New Testaments are so inextricably intertwined that we cannot accept the one as the Word of God without the other. They are so interrelated that we cannot understand the New Testament in the absence of the Old Testament and vice versa.[8] The former statement speaks for itself. Anyone engaged in Bible study discovers this. But the latter statement is equally true, although it is vehemently denied by Jews. The synagogue is of the opinion that the church reads into

7. G. C. Berkouwer, *The Person of Christ*, 1954, 137.

8. Cf. A. A. van Ruler, *Verwachting en voltooiing* (anticipation and fulfillment), 1978, 46: "One can and may not only interpret the Old Testament from the perspective of the New Testament, but must also interpret the New Testament from the perspective of the Old Testament."

the *Tanach* things that are not there, while the church says with Paul that in the synagogue there is a veil over the reading of the old covenant and that the locus of this veil is the heart. What is read does not penetrate to the heart; it remains closed to it (cf. 2 Cor. 3:14–15).

We reiterate that the New Testament is hidden in the Old Testament and that the Old Testament is revealed in the New Testament. These are the classic words of Augustine. But we are aware that what remains hidden is not altogether unknown!

Reformed Protestantism has learned a great deal from Calvin's insights, and it is in part because of this that the Old Testament plays a greater role in its confession, preaching, liturgy, and life of the church than elsewhere. Since Calvin, Reformed theology has appreciated the Old Testament the most positively and has treated it the most literally (Van Ruler). Calvin was preceded in this by Zwingli, Bullinger, and Bucer. His commentaries and his *Institutes* demonstrate that he does not accord less authority to the Old Testament than to the New Testament. Both of these testaments belong together and are essentially one. Calvin does not place the Old and New Testaments over against each other. However, neither does he place them on a par. When considering the relationship between the Old and New Testaments he keeps in mind both their unity and their differences, although their unity has priority, reflecting the unity of the covenant of God with his people, which is essentially always the same covenant, although its administration differs (*Institutes*, 2.10.2). A distinction is that "under the law" the people stood from afar in the forecourt of the sanctuary, while today nothing hinders their entry into it, because the veil has been rent. The veil—the reference is to 2 Corinthians 3—has been removed and we now see God face to face in Christ. In him the light of God shines more brightly than through the law and the prophets. The Old Testament points to him. He was present in the Old Testament, albeit in a veiled manner. He was indeed present with his power and grace, so that the significance of his coming predated his incarnation (cf. De Greef, 1984, 116ff., 214ff., 257). Referring to various Scripture passages (such as John 1:18; 2 Cor. 4:6; Heb. 1:1), Calvin says that God, when he appeared in the image of Jesus Christ—his own image—made himself to some extent visible, whereas his appearance had been indistinct and shadowed in the Old Testament (*Institutes*, 2.9.1).

Much of this we recognize in the Belgic Confession of Faith. It clearly differentiates between what is transitory and what is permanent: "We believe that the ceremonies and symbols of the law ceased at the coming of Christ, and that all the shadows are accomplished; so that the use of them must be abolished among Christians; yet the truth and substance of them remain with us in Jesus Christ, in whom they have their completion. In the meantime we still use the testimonies taken out of the law and the prophets to confirm us in the doctrine of the gospel, and to regulate our life in all honorableness to the glory of God, according to his will" (article 25).

One can speak of a double confrontation: with Rome and with the Anabaptists (cf. Polman, *Ned. Gel.*, 1:200–205; 3:168–79; Graafland, 1978, 21–24). In the Reformed view, Rome has relapsed into a new Judaism. But the rejection of the Anabaptist views is equally forceful. Just as Augustine had to defend the unity of the Old and

New Testaments over against the Manichaeans, Calvin and his co-religionists had to deal with "Anabaptist Radicals" to whom the Old Testament was of secondary significance.[9] In his commentary on Luke 24:27 Calvin combats those who hold that Christ started with first principles with the intent that the disciples would gradually progress to the full gospel and would no longer be interested in the prophecies. He points out that Christ did not open the minds of the apostles so that they would understand the law on their own, but so that they would understand the Scriptures. Thus the Old Testament is indispensable for the correct insight into God's entire revelation.

Although the books of both the Old and New Testaments are characterized by diversity, we can nevertheless speak of a single message from God. It indeed reflects the richness of his revelation that the message of salvation comes to us in such a varied form.

The unity of the Old and New Testaments does not constitute identity, for each Testament has its own character. The central message of the New Testament is what God does in Christ, in his person and in his work, and what he does through the outpouring of the Holy Spirit. This is of crucial importance for our personal relationship with God and for the life of the church of Christ. But salvation in Christ could be distorted in an individualistic or spiritualistic manner by ignoring prominent Old Testament perspectives, i.e., God's creation and his guidance through history. "Man's daily life, his interaction with others and questions with respect to marriage and the family are not exclusively human but have a direct bearing on the relationship between man and God."[10] For this reason, one report on the relationship between the Old and New Testaments concludes: "Precisely in our time with its macro-ethical and structural questions we require the breadth and depth of the Old Testament more than ever."[11]

It has sometimes been thought that there is a contrast between the Old and New Testaments as far as God is concerned. An expression such as "God, to whom vengeance belongeth" (Ps. 94:1) is referred to in order to underline the contrast between the two Testaments, because according to the New Testament "God is love" (1 John 4:8).

9. Cf. W. Balke, *Calvin and the Anabaptist Radicals*, trans. William J. Heynen (Grand Rapids, Eerdmans, 1981), 98–99, 309–13.

10. J. de Groot and A. R. Hulst, *Macht en wil* (power and will), no date, 348.

11. "De verhouding van Oud en Nieuw Testament," Rapport, opgenomen in *Kerk en theologie*, 25e jrg. ("the relationship between the Old and New Testaments," report, published in *Church and Theology*, vol. 25): 1974, 323.

The Old Testament is seen as the book of retribution. The Old Testament would present the religion of holiness and the New Testament faith in God's love. But this view is not really tenable. It is indeed the case that in the Old Testament we encounter God in his exaltation and holiness. But he is also "merciful and gracious, long-suffering, and abundant in goodness and truth." This is how the announcement of his name begins in Exodus 34:67. Thus the LORD manifests his compassion, his gracious benevolence, and his covenantal faithfulness. The New Testament testifies to God's love as manifested in Christ, but also refers to his wrath (John 3:36). "Our God is a consuming fire" (Heb. 12:29). "It is a fearful thing to fall into the hands of the living God" (Heb. 10:31).

Already the first few chapters of the book of Genesis are of fundamental significance for self-knowledge. Man, created in God's image, fell away from him, but God considered his state and sought him out. Thus man stands there as creature of God and sinner before God. God, who is his creator, also seeks to be his redeemer. God both demands and grants the atonement for sin (Lev. 17:11). Via the subsequent preaching of atonement through sacrificial ministry and through prophecy, all lines lead to Christ, of whom the New Testament says: "Behold the Lamb of God, which taketh away the sin of the world" (John 1:29). When Paul refers to Christ as the last Adam, the unity of the Old and New Testaments is underscored (cf. 1 Cor. 15:45; Rom. 5:12–21).

There is a distinction between the message of the coming of Christ and the message of the Mediator who has come, between the Old Testament messianic expectation and the New Testament knowledge of the person and the work of our Lord Jesus Christ, but it concerns the same Mediator, the same covenant, the same faith, and the same salvation (cf. Calvin, *Institutes*, 2.10.2).

Although in the Old Testament, salvation is depicted in earthly colors and national tints to a greater extent than is the case in the New Testament, life in communion with God is there also a reality for all who fear the Lord. The New Testament focuses more on the spiritual and heavenly character of what God grants in Christ, but not at the expense of what believers already receive during their lives on earth. Both testaments teach us to look forward to the new heaven and the new earth, where righteousness dwells (Isa. 65:17; 66:22; 2 Peter 3:13).

§ 7. The theopneusty of Holy Scripture

7.1. *The doctrine of inspiration and its critics*
7.2. *Scripture proof for theopneusty*
7.3. *Various views and theories*

7.1. *The doctrine of inspiration and its critics*

The conviction that Holy Scripture is the Word of God brings with it that we address the question as to how this is possible. The history of this doctrine shows that for centuries this was not considered to be an issue.

Beginning with Clemens Romanus, who refers to the Scriptures as being true through the Holy Spirit, we can find various references to the views held by Justin, Irenaeus, Origen, Hieronymus, and especially Augustine. Augustine sometimes refers to Scripture as God's handwriting or as a letter from heaven. Christ gave us Scripture by first speaking through the prophets, then through himself, and subsequently through the apostles, as much as he saw fit. This constitutes the Word of God. Aside from the term "inspiration," Augustine also uses words such as "dictation" and "direction." He gives preference to "inspiration" (perhaps as a consequence of the translation into Latin of 2 Tim. 3:16). But Augustine does not fix this term dogmatically, because he also refers to the inspiration of faith and love. His monograph on the harmony of the gospels (*De consensu evangelistarum*) attests to a deeper reflection on the nature of inspiration. This church father recognizes the fact that each of the evangelists recorded Christ's words and deeds in his own way. In this connection Polman points out that in Augustine's mind the following two hypotheses go hand in hand: to him the Bible is entirely the work of the Holy Spirit and at the same time entirely the work of the Bible authors. To Augustine, Scripture constitutes the last word in all debate: we believe that Christ was born of the Virgin Mary because it says so in Scripture, and those who do not believe this cannot be Christians and cannot be saved. Inspiration implies the reliability and the divine authority of Scripture (cf. Bavinck, *R.D.*, 1:402–5; Polman, 1955, 37–74).

In medieval theology the doctrine of Holy Scripture was hardly developed any further. However, an important pronouncement of a council deserves to be mentioned: it refers to God as the Author of the Old and New Testaments. The saints of both testaments spoke through the inspiration of the same Holy Spirit (Florence, 1439).

What changed in the time of the Reformation was described in *Klare wijn* (clear wine, 1967) as follows: Luther and Calvin are suddenly enflamed with passion. To them the Bible is not in the first instance a source of information from which they obtain truths and precepts, but in Scripture they encounter the living God and his message (27).

To Luther the Bible is a personal document of the Spirit. The Holy Spirit makes the authors of the various books speak the truth, although he accommodates himself to human understanding. The Spirit knows things better than we, who do not naturally understand and accept the Word. But Luther concurs with Augustine: the authority of the Word of God exceeds our capacity to fathom it.

This is blended, however, with the idea of a christological focus. Christ is at the heart of all of Scripture. This core sheds light on all books of the Old and New Testaments. For each book of the Bible the question is whether it clearly proclaims Christ ("ob sie Christum treiben oder nicht"). The gospel of John and the epistles of Paul and 1 Peter constitute the true core and marrow of the New Testament. Every Christian ought to read these books first and foremost. But, in Luther's opinion, James lacks the full essence of the gospel: it is but a straw epistle. This "Scripture criticism" is not the type of biblical criticism that subsequently gained momentum. Luther does not view a book of the Bible as a literary document or as a religious document from the past, and it would have been unacceptable to him for a scholarly discipline to make value judgments about what the Bible says. He considers the message of the Bible itself to be the standard for judgment. In this context it may be pointed out that he applies this standard too subjectively and one-sidedly. Comparing James only with Paul does not do justice to the former (on Luther, see: Locher, 1903; Kooiman, 1977[3]; Klug, 1971).

For the Reformed view we must commence with Calvin. To him, God is the Author of what Scripture teaches (*Institutes*, 1.7.4). God has spoken through the mouths of Moses, David, and Peter. Expressions such as "inspiration" and "dictation" were also employed by Calvin, and he felt comfortable with calling the writers of the books of the Bible "secretaries" of the Holy Spirit. With this he meant that they did not invent anything, but that they were led and controlled by the Holy Spirit. They recorded obediently and faithfully what he inspired in them. The prophets whom the Holy Spirit engaged were organs of his.

There was an important difference in interpretation between J. A. Cramer and D. J. de Groot with respect to Calvin. The former believed he could not detect any belief in the verbal inspiration of Scripture on Calvin's part. In his investigation of Calvin's view, the latter came to the conclusion that to him inspiration was not limited to the content of Scripture with respect to salvation, but affected everything that was spoken and written, including the form, the words, the language, and the style.[12]

However, a term such as "dictation" does not imply that the books of the Bible were dictated from heaven word for word. Calvin repeatedly refers to the personal activity and freedom of the authors. For

12. It has been said in this connection: "Sachgemäße Wiedergabe des Mitgeteilten heißt für CALVIN auch wortgetreue Wiedergabe" (to Calvin the accuracy of the recorded text reflected faithfulness in terms of both the message and the words), Krusche, 1957, 173.

example, with respect to the way in which Scripture is quoted in Romans 3:4, he says: "We know indeed that in quoting words of Scripture the apostles frequently took a great deal of liberty, since they considered it acceptable to merely quote what was relevant to the subject at hand."

In referring to the concept of revelation in theology, we saw that it was typical of Calvin to believe that God adapts himself to our capacity to understand (*accommodatio*). God can speak to us in a thoroughly human manner. It resembles the teaching of small children. He is like a king whose majesty we must not take lightly, but who wants to have an intimate conversation with us. When he communicates his Word to us through human mouths, in human language, he thereby takes our needs into consideration (cf. Cramer, 1926; De Groot, 1931; Krusche, 1957).

The prominence that Reformed confessions assign to Holy Scripture as the Word of God and the thoroughness with which it is treated are striking in comparison with Lutheran confessions. A good example is the Belgic Confession of Faith, articles 2 to 7. At times Luther's view is dismissed with a few words (Confession of Zürich: the books of the New Testament contain no straw), but differences with Rome receive much more attention in what the confession says about Scripture. In the context of this controversy the emphasis is placed in the testimony of Scripture itself, which we believe to be beyond any doubt; the testimony of the Holy Spirit, by means of which we accept Scripture as sacred and canonical; the distinction between the canonical and apocryphal books; and the priority of Scripture over tradition. A number of confessions refer explicitly to the inspiration of Holy Scripture.[13] *Formula Consensus* (1675) went the farthest by stating that the books of the Old Testament were inspired by God (theopneustic) in terms of both their content and their words, including consonants, vowels, punctuation marks, or at least their effect. Thus they sought to protect themselves from the type of text criticism practised by L. Capellus (d. 1658), a well-known theologian of the School of Saumur.

A useful summary of the history of inspiration is given by Bavinck: up to the seventeenth century inspiration was steadily expanded to include vowels and punctuation (*inspiratio punctualis*), and subsequently progressively reduced and restricted, i.e., from punctuation to words (*inspiratio verbalis*), from words to concepts, from words

13. *Confessio Helvetica Prior, Confessio Helvetica Posterior*, Bohemian Confession, Irish Articles, Westminster Confession; cf. also Canons of Dort, 3–4:12.

as concepts to facts (*inspiratio realis*), and from facts to religious-ethical content, to the very object of saving faith (*inspiratio fundamentalis*), from these facts to persons (*inspiratio personalis*), and finally to the denial of all inspiration as a supernatural gift (*R.D.*, 1:435).

More recent developments have been triggered by biblical criticism, which emerged at the time of the Enlightenment. The Bible was no longer considered to be divine, but came to be treated as an ordinary human book. J. S. Semler wrote a book about the free study of the canon and G. E. Lessing submitted his new hypothesis concerning the evangelists, treating them as purely human authors of history. In the nineteenth century, Bible criticism became more radical. It has been said: "A great deal of historical-critical analysis left little intact of the books of the Bible, the events related in them, and the message proclaimed by them" (*God met ons* = God with us, 1981, 33).

When we take stock after two centuries of biblical criticism, we cannot say that the progress of textual analysis, literary-critical research, historical-critical research, research in the history of religion, and the investigation of tradition and form have not produced any positive results at all (cf. B. J. Oosterhoff, "Schriftgezag en modern bijbelonderzoek" = the authority of Scripture and modern Bible research, in *Het hoge Woord* = the lofty Word, 1976, 93–114). This does not mean that those "scholarly men" deserve the unqualified thanks of the church of Jesus Christ (*Klare wijn* = clear wine, 1967, 87), for one does have to take into account the forces that biblical criticism has unleashed. A distinction needs to be made between scholarly endeavor in search of solutions to numerous problems with respect to the books of the Old and New Testaments, which apart from certain results also leads to the most divergent hypotheses and theories, and the fundamental underpinnings of the criticism that judges Holy Scripture with standards that do not do justice to it. Bavinck, who was well informed with respect to biblical criticism, pointed out the latter when he called attention to the underlying mindset. Assaults on Scripture, which have been encountered from the beginning, have an ethical dimension. These continual attacks reflect the spiritual climate of our times and reveal in the first instance the enmity of the human heart, which is not only manifested in criticism of Scripture but also in dead orthodoxy! Scripture does not subject itself to man's criticism, but judges him with respect to his thoughts and desires. Although ordinary Christians may not be aware of the stumbling blocks that scholarship puts in the way of reliance on Scripture, they are more or less aware of the battle that is fought against Scripture in the head as well as the heart. "It is one and the same battle, an ever-continuing battle, which has to be waged by all Christians, learned or unlearned, to take every thought captive to the obedience of Christ" (*R.D.*, 1:439–42; cf. Veenhof, 1968, 527–30).

In 1881 Kuyper referred to the worrisome implications of biblical criticism for the church of the living God. More than half a century later, Berkouwer considered it an indisputable fact that the questioning of Holy Scripture as a result of theology that is critical of Scripture has significantly contributed toward the secularization of life (Berkouwer, 1938, 386). Since these critical views are no longer restricted to the professional literature, but have in various ways become common knowledge, and since there is a tendency in our time to accept criticism quite readily, we should keep those words of warning in mind.

A concrete example of current popularized biblical scholarship is the work of C. J. Labuschagne, *Wat zegt de Bijbel in Gods naam?* (what does the Bible say for God's sake? 1977). The author traces to what extent and in what regard modern biblical scholarship has changed our view with respect to the Bible. He sees a fundamental difference between the idea that human beings are inspired by God's Spirit, and the notion that an entire book is inspired by God. In the latter case the authors are "nothing more than God's typewriters and their writings retain nothing human." Labuschagne holds instead that Holy Scripture is in its entirety a human book. He is deeply convinced that we can only then really understand the authors of the biblical writings and recognize something of ourselves in them, when we cease to accord them a special place. They are fellow men who even in their insights in faith remain time-bound human beings. Jesus was a child of his time, not only in his language and way of life, but also in his theological thinking and in the way in which he concurred with the biblical interpretation of his day. According to Labuschagne, the "speaking" of God that we continually encounter is one of the ways in which we speak about God and on his behalf. Although the prophets did present God as speaking, these words of God remained their own words. "Strictly speaking, these words of God do not exist."

According to this view, only human beings speak in the Bible.[14] We can learn from their writings what they have to say about God as long as we permit ourselves to be

14. A modern reader of the Bible must, at least for the time being, avoid the expression: the Bible is the Word of God. "For in the Bible only human beings do the speaking" (L. Grollenberg, *Modern bijbellezen* = modern reading of the Bible, 1971, 136ff.). Labuschagne's statement, "In God's speaking we have nothing but the speaking of the prophet who speaks on His behalf and about Him" (ibid., 99), may be compared to what H. M. Kuitert wrote: we know God's revelation only in the form of human thoughts and words *regarding* God's revelation (*Zonder geloof vaart niemand wel* = no one prospers without faith, 1974, 29).

guided by modern biblical scholarship. Labuschagne's view says: "The Bible is not a divine book that can only be unlocked by the divine Spirit, but a human, history-bound, literary document that can only be made accessible to the mind through the human occupation of serious scholarly study." Note that it says: only! Furthermore, it applies to the Bible a modern literary method according to which the interpretation of a text is related to the recognition of oneself or of something of oneself. Along with an "antiquated view of the Bible," certain biblical representations of God are now considered to be obsolete.

In the concluding chapter, one can read in summary form what remains of the message of the Bible. The objective is to believe in God in a different and superior way. This is no minor presumption! "By removing the obstacle and vexation of an antiquated interpretation of the Bible, the church will once again make itself accessible to modern man." A key aspect of the new conception is that God and man together participate in what happens in the world in partnership.

We conclude that a better title for Labuschagne's book would have been: What does the Bible say according to modern biblical scholarship?

7.2. *Scripture proof for theopneusty*

There is no dearth of attempts in the name of modern scholarship or thought to do away with the belief that the Bible is the Word of God. In contrast, the Reformed confession and Reformed theology appeal to Holy Scripture itself for the doctrine that Scripture is the completely reliable Word of God, inspired by the Holy Spirit. Confessions and dogmatic treatises refer to Bible passages such as 2 Timothy 3:16 and 2 Peter 1:21, which the more recent theology rarely discusses in any depth.

For those to whom a single Bible proof suffices, and who read 2 Timothy 3:16 in an older translation, the issue appears decided by what it says: "All scripture is given by inspiration of God." The entire Holy Scripture has been inspired by God's Spirit. But we prefer to leave this Scripture passage aside for the time being. Otherwise it might appear that the church's doctrine of Scripture depends on a single verse. There is more to it.

We have already contemplated that Scripture itself gives us grounds for the confession that it is the Word of God (§ 6.1). This is sometimes referred to as the testimony of Scripture to itself.

In quoting the Old Testament, one can say equivalently, "The Lord speaks," and, "The prophet speaks." It is noteworthy that these two expressions can be linked: "All this was done, that it might be fulfilled which was spoken of the Lord by (*dia*) the prophet" (Matt. 1:22; cf. Matt. 2:15). "God hath spoken by the mouth of all his holy prophets" (Acts 3:21). The Holy Spirit "by the mouth of thy servant David" said what is contained in Psalm 2 (Acts 4:25). "God, who at sundry times and in divers manners spake in time past unto the fathers by the prophets . . ." (Heb. 1:1). In 1 Peter 1:11 we read that "the Spirit of Christ which was in [the prophets] did signify [a definite time], when it testified beforehand [to] the sufferings of Christ, and the glory that should follow." We also think of Zechariah 7:12–13, where it says that no one listened to "the words which the LORD of hosts hath sent in his spirit by the former prophets." He called, although they did not listen.

The Word of God thus comes to people in and through the words of his servants. The relationship between God's speaking and the human words is too close and too real that only mere functionality or a mediating role of people could be implied. This connection is not exaggerated by describing it as an "identity" (cf. Berkouwer, 1975, 145). It is in this way that the Bible is the Word of God.

Those who delve more deeply into the mystery of Holy Scripture definitely cannot ignore verses such as 2 Timothy 3:16 and 2 Peter 1:21. In the former apostolic reference there is scope for varying interpretations. What is meant by "theopneutos": "breathed by God," "inspired by God," or "God breathing," "divine breathing"? On the basis of the Greek of the New Testament, the former is definitely preferable. The Vulgate says: "inspired by God" (*divinitus inspirata*). A more difficult question is whether "*theopneustos*" is part of the predicate or an attributive adjunct to Scripture. Both of these possibilities exist from a grammatical point of view. Support for treating the word in question as part of the predicate is found in what follows. Otherwise, it would say: "is also useful," and then the word "also" is actually redundant. When in the predicate Scripture is called "theopneustos," the small word "*kai*" has a pregnant meaning: "therefore." Another point is whether one can translate: "the entire Scripture" or "all of Scripture" (Authorized Version) or whether it ought to be: "every Scripture passage," "every word of Scripture" (new translation of the Netherlands Bible Society). It is best to go with an additional function of the Greek word *pas* and to give preference to: "all that is Scripture." This is why the Willibrord translation reads: "all that is in the Bible." It points at any rate to "the Holy Scriptures" that Timothy knew from childhood, "which are able to make thee wise unto salvation through faith which is in Christ Jesus" (2 Tim. 3:15). The translation of the frequently discussed text then becomes: "All *that is* Scripture is given by inspiration of God, and is profitable for doctrine, for reproof, for correction and for instruction in righteousness." The latter is indeed part of this, for the apostle does not wish to say only that Scripture is inspired by God, but also what God means by this: "that the man of God may be perfect, thoroughly furnished unto all good works" (2 Tim. 3:17).

The second epistle of Peter 1:21 deals with the origin of the prophecy of Scripture. It is no human fabrication, for men spoke on God's behalf. With respect to the verb "spoke," it has been correctly pointed out that writing is understood to be included, because the addressees know the prophecy only in written form. "The word of prophecy" (2 Peter 1:19) refers to the Old Testament in its entirety.[15] The speakers and writers were people with their own dispositions and talents, but they spoke on God's behalf (according to another interpretation: they spoke as holy men of God, i.e., as men taken into service by God). In this regard they were driven by the Holy Spirit and thus could speak in the service to God and on God's behalf. The reliability of the prophetic word is therefore secure. It is reliability itself!

The interpretation of prophecy must agree with its origin (cf. the connection between vv. 20 and 21). The first characteristic of this interpretation is then: "Continually confirming its meaning with the Holy Spirit who was its driving force, and with God who took people into his employ. He retains the right of authorship."

Also important is what is said with respect to the epistles of Paul (2 Peter 3:15–16, cf. 2 Peter 3:2). It appears that a collection of these epistles already existed. There are good grounds for agreeing with Van Houwelingen: like all of Scripture, Paul's epistles are normative for faith and give directions for the way of truth. "The gospels and the apostolic writings have been given a place in close relationship with the Scriptures of the Old Testament" (Van Houwelingen, 1988, 141–43, 150–52, 276).

So far the terms "theopneusty" and "inspiration" have been used interchangeably. The word "theopneusty" is to be preferred over the word "inspiration," because it says literally that Scripture is imparted or inspired by God, while in the case of the other word one always needs to add that this inspiration is the work of God and his Spirit. Furthermore, the meaning of the word "theopneusty" is unambiguous, while "inspiration" can also be employed in a different sense. It is said that an artist is inspired by something; or that someone had an inspiration. In the case of inspiration

15. Cf. Van Houwelingen, 1988, 141.

one can lose sight of the difference between what is inspired and what works inspirationally. However, the word "inspiration" has become so common in the doctrine of Holy Scripture that in practice it is difficult to replace it with another term.

7.3. *Various views and theories*

We distinguish mainly five views: the mechanistic, dualistic, dynamic, actualistic, and organic views of inspiration or theopneusty. This proves that a great deal of thought has been given to the way in which Scripture has come down to us.

1. *The mechanistic theory of inspiration*

This view became popular in Lutheran and Reformed orthodoxy of the seventeenth century, which is not to say that it is the classical Lutheran or Reformed view. The Bible was viewed as heavenly dictation. The authors of its books were referred to as secretaries or even living pens of the Holy Spirit. It has sometimes been thought that differences in language and style reflected a desire on the part of the Spirit to vary the way in which he spoke. Voetius also believed that no preparatory research was involved.

In this manner the authors of the books of the Bible were detached from their historical context and merely functioned as instruments in the hands of the Holy Spirit without a will of their own (Bavinck, *R.D.*, 1:431). It was forgotten that the Holy Spirit does not leave those whom he employs passive, but precisely active.

Virtually no one any longer espouses the mechanical view today. Even at the time when this view was popular, attempts were made to represent inspiration as less mechanistic. In *Synopsis* (1625), Thysius points to the personal activity of the writers. They used their minds and memories, their organizational skills and varying styles—which explains the varied manner of writing—but under the continuing direction of the Holy Spirit.

2. *The dualistic theory of inspiration*

According to this theory, inspiration remains limited to part of the Bible (partial inspiration). As a rule it is applied to the Bible's religious-ethical content. The remainder is viewed as being entirely the product of the writers of the various books. In the latter material various shortcomings can be detected, which does not affect the religious-ethical content of those books. Sometimes certain books are considered to be inspired and others not. Thus in J. S. Semler's reduction, various books are dropped out as not being inspired, such as Ezra, Nehemiah, Esther, Ruth, Chronicles, Song of Solomon, and Revelation.

Broadly speaking, Socinians, Remonstrants, and rationalists defended such dualism (cf. Du Preez, 1933). It may be objected that such a distinction destroys the unity of Scripture. Christ and the apostles never divided Scripture in this way. With this view man decides for himself what he considers to be the Word of God, on the basis of his own insights, his own religious experience, or whatever.

3. *The dynamic theory of inspiration*
This view has had a great deal of influence. Bavinck even noted that few theologians had not substantially adopted it (*R.D.*, 1:418).

This view places more of the onus of the inspiration of Scripture on the authors (*personal inspiration*). These writers lived close to God, and therefore their work exhibited a godly and noble character. They experienced the dynamics, the stimulating and sanctifying power of the Spirit, to a far greater degree than others. There is a difference only in degree and not in essence between this type of inspiration and the illumination shared by every Christian.

The great proponent of the dynamic theory of inspiration was Schleiermacher. To him New Testament writers were not the only inspired authors in the church, but indeed the first ones. The prerogative of the New Testament is not its inspired nature, but its originality. The Old Testament was not inspired by the "Gemeingeist der christlichen Kirche" (collective spirit of the Christian church) and therefore ranks far below the New Testament.

In the Netherlands, the dynamic view has been advocated especially in ethical theology. Thus, Daubanton could not see why a distinction should be made between the poet king David and the eminent Dutch poet Da Costa. To him Da Costa's poems were equally the Word of God as the Psalms of David. "Why is it not God's word wherever it is sought, found, believed, praised and obeyed? Has the Spirit of God departed from the faithful?" Even if Holy Scripture were to be lost, we would not be completely without the Word of life, for there are still other channels between God's revelation and us, such as the writings of Augustine, Luther, Calvin and others.[16]

This dynamic view is in conflict with what Scripture says about itself. The key is the theopneusty or inspired Scripture (2 Tim. 3:16). We need to distinguish between the guidance that all of God's children receive from the Holy Spirit and the inspiration of those who have spoken on God's behalf. The *agesthai* of Romans 8:14 cannot be equated with the *pheresthai* of 2 Peter 1:21. According to the dynamic theory there is no essential difference between Holy Scripture and all other types of religious literature. Those who with Daubanton assign equal value to David and Da Costa give too much credit to Da Costa's poetry and fail to do justice to the unique value of the Psalms.

4. *The actualistic theory of inspiration*
Barth sharply criticizes the view of Scripture that he encounters in the early church and in orthodoxy. There the word of man is treated as God's own Word. This turns the statement that the Bible is the Word of God into a pronouncement regarding the nature of the Bible instead of God's free grace. We do not have the right to interpret this statement as a pronouncement regarding the Bible as such.

Barth never employs inspiration in the perfect tense, but always in the present tense, not in the *perfectum* but the *praesens*. The Holy Spirit, who brought about the testimony of the witnesses, also testifies as to its truth to the people who hear and read it. "This self-disclosure in its totality is *theopneustia*, inspiration of the words of prophets and apostles" (*C.D.*, 1.2.516).

16. F. E. Daubanton, *De Theopneustie der Heilige Schrift*, 1882, 91–93.

The inspiration of the Bible is a recurrent divine decree in the life of the church and in the life of its members (*C.D.*, 1.2.504–37).

This is an actualistic reinterpretation of the doctrine of inspiration. Here theopneusty or inspiration is a miracle that happens to the text of Scripture, which of itself is a fallible and failing word of man, whenever it pleases God to speak to someone through it. At that very moment Scripture is the Word of God.

Barth's ideas have found acceptance. Van Niftrik agreed with them. According to him the hidden motivation behind the orthodox doctrine is the determination and desire to control and manipulate the truth. Placing one's hand on the Bible, one says, here is the truth. According to the old doctrine of inspiration one does not receive the Word of God, but one has it. This implies that one refuses to live by grace. Like Barth, Van Niftrik views inspiration as an act of God rather than a condition of the Bible. "Those who confess the inspiration of the Bible believe and expect that God the Holy Spirit will turn the human word of the Bible into the Word of God for us." "In the moment of his pleasure, when he speaks—, then the Bible *is* God's Word" (Van Niftrik, *Kl.D.*, 289–306).

We have serious objections to this view.

- The doctrine of inspiration is caricatured when one looks for a hidden motive in it, i.e., the desire to have the truth at our disposal and not to live by grace.
- The inspiration of the moment comes at the expense of the inspired nature of Scripture. The actualistic view of inspiration in the sense of a recurrent divine decree does not reflect what Scripture itself says, but is a consequence of Barth's actualistic concept of revelation (see § 4.3).
- When Barth refers to God's "self-disclosure" in its totality as theopneusty or inspiration, he loses sight of the distinction between the theopneusty of Scripture and the testimony of the Holy Spirit with respect to Scripture.

5. *The organic theory of inspiration*

This concerns a view for which one can appeal to Calvin, not so much because he called the writers organs of the Holy Spirit (commentary on 2 Tim. 3:16), but because he made allowances for the individuality and the personal activity of each of the authors of the books of the Old and New Testaments. But we actually owe the doctrine of organic inspiration to Kuyper and Bavinck, who maintained the unity and reliability of the Word of God in the face of criticism that considered it to be an ordinary human book and who at the same time recognized the historical character of the revelation of salvation (cf. *God met ons* = God with us, 1981, 41–46).

Bavinck says with respect to the work of the Holy Spirit in the creation of the Bible: "Having prepared the human consciousness of the authors in various ways (by birth, upbringing, natural gifts, research, memory, reflection, experience of life, revelation, etc.), he now, in and through the writing process itself, made *those* thoughts and words, *that* language and style, rise to the surface of that consciousness, which could best interpret the divine ideas for persons of all sorts of rank and class, from every nation and age" (*R.D.*, 1:438). The Holy Spirit did not spurn anything human to serve as an organ of the divine. God's revelation has entered into the human fabric, into persons and states of beings, into forms and usages, into history and life (1:442).

There are plenty of indications in the Bible to support the accuracy of this view. The books of the Bible bear the imprint of their emergence at a specific time and in a specific culture. The writers had at times been prepared for their tasks through descent and education. "Moses was learned in all the wisdom of the Egyptians" (Acts 7:22). Paul had been taught by rabbis. The choice of words and manner of expression of these writers reveal an enormous variety. In the original languages this is even more apparent than in the various translations. Differences among the four gospels naturally raise a number of questions. They combined words of Jesus that had not all been spoken on the same occasion. In comparing Matthew and Luke, one can see how an evangelist's overall objective influenced the entire structure and composition of his book. The authors delved deeply into their subject matter. In the historical books of the Old Testament there are frequent references to various sources. Luke explains that he first carefully investigated everything (1:1–4).

We also see personal experience reflected in the books of the Bible. This is especially true in the case of the Psalms. But we also see the personal side in Paul's writings.

The entire Bible contains the same message. However, this message is expressed in numerous ways. There are striking differences among the prophetic books of the Old Testament. There is also variation in emphasis among the apostolic epistles. Not without justification, Paul is called the apostle of faith, Peter the apostle of hope, and John the apostle of love. Through Scripture study we gain a better appreciation for the broader perspectives and the finer nuances. These in turn enrich our understanding of Scripture.

In various respects, this view of Scripture strengthens our defense against biblical criticism. We appreciate that historical description in the Bible differs from the work of subsequent historians. The focus of the Bible is not a description of the past but God's dealings with his people.

Organic inspiration is not a theory that can answer all possible questions with respect to the Bible. Difficulties remain. There are cruces (intellectual problems) in Scripture that will probably never be resolved (Bavinck, *R.D.*, 1:442).

Our knowledge is partial and our theories cannot explain the miracle of theopneusty. But this does not shake our belief that Holy Scripture is the Word of God and not just an ancient collection of human writings.

Objections can be raised to the term "organic" (cf. Kamphuis, 1980, 61–65), and we would be glad to have a more accurate one. We do not claim that this word adequately describes the relationship between God and man. However, it does imply that the authors of the books of the Bible were no senseless tools, but people who were totally employed by God with all of their functionalities and potentialities, because he chose to give us his Word through them.

In this context it must be kept in mind that the term "organic" should not detract from the concept of inspiration. This would be the case if writers were treated primarily as children of their own epoch or if thought processes and representations of a certain age were considered to be limited to the ideas of those days. This is reminiscent of the doctrine of accommodation of rationalism (cf. Berkouwer, 1938, 317–27).

With respect to organic inspiration it can be said that human intermediation or the human element, which was suppressed in the mechanistic view, has regained prominence. This has a parallel in more recent Roman Catholic theology (Wentsel, *Dogm.*, 2:308–17). The dogmatic constitution dealing with divine revelation, which was adopted by the Second Vatican Council (1965), contains passages that suggest that Rome feels threatened. What we refer to as human mediation is captured by this constitution when it is said that God chose people for the creation of the holy books and that he employed them together with all their capacities and powers. To this was added that it must be confessed that the books of Scripture teach reliably, faithfully, and inerrantly the truth that God has sought to have recorded for the sake of our salvation (chapter 3). When Roman Catholic biblical scholarship emphasized the human element in the development of Holy Scripture, Romeo complained that while one used to speak almost exclusively of Holy Scripture as the Word of God, in his time it was almost exclusively referred to as the word of man. That was in 1960. Berkouwer, who records this matter, finds this general complaint somewhat unreasonable, but nevertheless points out that it is always good to listen to warnings of possible threats. We agree with him that there is an acute danger that as a result of the humanization of Scripture the Word of God is no longer heard and understood (Berkouwer, 1975, 152).

Much has changed even in the *Gereformeerde Kerken in Nederland* (Reformed denomination in the Netherlands), in which organic inspiration appeared so well entrenched that a pronouncement was made in this regard in the form of a number of articles regarding Scripture and its authority (the Arnhem articles of 1930). In the report *God met ons* (God with us, 1981), this was referred to as a reorientation. What Berkouwer says of Scripture in his dogmatic studies (1975) differs considerably from what he wrote in his book on biblical criticism. A process of development of nearly 30 years had intervened.[17] A number of *Cahiers voor de gemeente* (notebooks for the church) caused a sensation because of the new view that they advocated.[18] Hartvelt does not go as far as Kuitert, but he is of the view that organic inspiration has led to

17. G. C. Berkouwer, *Holy Scripture*, 1975, compared with *Het probleem der Schriftkritiek* (the problem of Scripture criticism), 1938. Cf. also G. C. Berkouwer, *Verontrusting en verantwoordelijkheid* (disquiet and responsibility), 1969, and *Een halve eeuw theologie* (half a century of theology), 1974. Regarding Berkouwer's theology see G. W. de Jong, *De theologie van Dr. G. C. Berkouwer*, 1971.

18. G. P. Hartvelt, *Over Schrift en inspiratie* (on Scripture and inspiration), 1967; *idem*, *Goed voor Gods Woord* (Good for God's Word), 1969; H. M. Kuitert, *Verstaat gij wat gij leest?* (do you understand what you are reading?), 1968; Tj. Baarda, *De betrouwbaarheid van de Evangeliën* (the reliability of the Gospels), 1969.

a collection of numerous unresolved problems. His interpretation of theopneusty is that Holy Scripture is "good for God's Word." But Scripture being good for God's Word does not automatically turn it into God's Word. It is more of a functional and actualistic view, which implies that the difference between Scripture and proclamation becomes obscured.

The report *God met ons* (God with us) was considered to be confessionally sound by the synod of the *Gereformeerde Kerken*. It is disconcerting that this report interpreted inspiration to mean "something that inspires," in the sense that it stimulates us to think and act. Although the starting point, i.e., the creative idea, does come from outside us, it persuades us to put it to work ourselves and to apply it to our own situation. This assigns more room to "the human, time-bound aspect of Scripture" (*God met ons*, 1981, 57).

The doctrine of organic inspiration is an attempt to do justice to the Bible as the Word of God in human language. The words spoken and written by human beings were employed by the Holy Spirit in such a way that through them we received the trustworthy Word of God, the revelation of salvation, with Christ as its focal point. Its ultimate purpose is knowledge of God in Christ.

What would be the benefit of a correct understanding of the books of the Bible and the miracle of theopneusty if we did not listen to its message? We need to keep in mind that inspiration is not an isolated event. We agree with Bavinck that Scripture not only *was* inspired but is still "God-breathed" and "God-breathing." The Holy Spirit does, after the act of inspiration, not withdraw from Holy Scripture and abandon it to its fate but sustains and animates it and in many ways brings its content to humanity, to its heart and conscience (*R.D.*, 1:449ff.).

§ 8. The attributes of Holy Scripture

8.1. *Introduction*
8.2. *The authority of Holy Scripture*
8.3. *The clarity of Holy Scripture*
8.4. *The sufficiency or perfection of Holy Scripture*
8.5. *The necessity of Holy Scripture*

8.1. *Introduction*

The doctrine of the attributes of Holy Scripture (*proprietates, affectiones*) was developed in the conflicts with Rome on the one hand and spiritualism on the other hand. As far as Rome is concerned, we have in mind the relationship between Scripture and the church; and Reformed theology rejects spiritualism because its adherents are of the view that those who have the Spirit can manage without Scripture.

Although these opposing views remain in the background, antithesis does not tell the entire story. In this chapter we require a variety of terms to express how much Scripture means to us. This is one more reason for devoting a separate section to the attributes of Scripture.

Some Reformed theologians limit themselves to the authority, perfection, and clarity of Scripture, but there are others who expand this list. In Bavinck's work we encounter in addition to these three attributes the necessity of Scripture, which in *Synopsis* (1625) even ranked first. Berkouwer, Heyns, and Wentsel devote a separate chapter or section to the reliability of Holy Scripture. But this is not really necessary, for one cannot focus on the authority of Scripture without considering its reliability and vice versa.

We discuss in succession the authority, clarity, sufficiency or perfection, and necessity of Holy Scripture.

8.2. *The authority of Holy Scripture*

1. *The autopisty of Scripture*

With respect to the authority (*auctoritas*) of Holy Scripture, we are in conflict with Rome, a conflict which already came to the fore at the time of the Reformation. The Roman Catholic Church declared: All authority that Scripture has among us depends on the authority of the church. Faith stands or falls, not with Scripture, but with the church. Did Scripture not originate in the church and is it not preserved and interpreted by the church? Without the church there would be no Scripture, but without Scripture there would still be a church.

Instead of making the authority of Scripture subject to that of the church, the Reformation believed in the *autopisty* of Holy Scripture. Its trustworthiness speaks for itself and proves itself. A church that would first have to authenticate Scripture's trustworthiness would place itself above or at least on a par with it.

It is true that Scripture did come to us via Israel and the church, but this does not make it the word of Israel or the church. Otherwise the church would have the final say. It is of fundamental importance what God says to us in Holy Scripture. Not the church but Scripture is to us "the highest judge in disputes." The church's authority is derivative and limited, whereas the authority of Scripture is direct and absolute.

In the twentieth century the Bible indeed acquired greater significance in Roman Catholicism than earlier. Bible reading, Bible research, and Bible distribution have all been encouraged by Rome. But this does not necessarily imply acceptance of the principle of "*sola Scriptura.*" Moreover, more recent Roman Catholic theology is frequently rather critical of Scripture as such. The resulting problems are managed by the authority charged with ecclesiastical doctrine. Concessions can be made to modern Scripture criticism while leaving ecclesiastical doctrine intact. Whenever the authority of the church itself becomes problematic—which is not infrequently the case—Scripture is no longer seen to provide adequate support, and the result is a crisis of faith.

The autopisty of Scripture needs to be maintained not only over against Rome, which does esteem the Bible as the church's book, but also over against all those who consider the Bible to be an ordinary human book, a collection of human documents originating in a certain period of history. As a consequence of developments over the last few centuries, many no longer ascribe any special authority to Holy Scripture.

Scripture criticism has also had its impact by raising doubts with respect to the reliability of the books of the Old and New Testaments. Acquaintance with other religions has frequently resulted in treating the Bible in principle as being equivalent to the authoritative holy books of those religions. In addition, modern man has an aversion to believing anything on the basis of authority. In his days Noordmans already pointed out that when a synthesis is sought between ecclesiastical Christianity and culture, people tend to resent to be told to believe on the basis of authority "so that the concept of authority has relevance only in Roman Catholic circles where the church exercises it and in conservative Protestant circles where Scripture exercises it."

Noordmans then argues that knowledge of faith always originates externally. He stretches the concept of "believing on the basis of authority" to biblical dimensions and finds this extended form in Romans 10. Paul says that to be able to believe, one first has to hear. Hearing comes by the word. And there is no word without a preacher. Finally, there is no preacher without a Sender, i.e., without authority (Noordmans in *V.W.*, 2:135, 140). Bavinck speaks even more clearly about this. There is nothing humiliating, nor anything that in any way detracts from a person's freedom, in listening to the Word of God like a child and in obeying it. "Believing God at his Word, i.e. on his authority, is in no way inconsistent with human dignity, anymore than that it dishonors a child to rely with unlimited trust on the word of her or his father." Christian believers comes to rely more and more on God's Word. To the degree that they increase in faith, they cling all the more firmly to the authority of God in his Word (*R.D.*, 1:464ff.).

2. *What does Scripture itself say?*

The autopisty of Scripture implies that we appeal to Scripture itself to establish its authority. As in the case of theopneusty, it is not a matter of a single text, but of the entire Scripture as we have received it. As the Word of God inspired by the Spirit, Scripture speaks to us with authority. In it God addresses us with his absolute authority.

The Old Testament was to our Lord Jesus Christ not merely a collection of human writings. What authority would it have had for Him, who himself spoke with authority (Matt. 7:29), and could say that his words in no wise would pass away (Matt. 24:35)? He accepted the authority of Scripture without reservation: "It is written" (Matt. 4:4, 7, 10). To him this was the end of any dispute. "Scripture cannot be broken" (John 10:35). He saw his path of suffering spelled out in Scripture: "But how then shall the scriptures be fulfilled, that thus it must be?" (Matt. 26:54).

It is incorrect to suppose that Jesus' appeal to Scripture would reflect no more than an acceptance of Jewish tradition or an uncritical adoption of a contemporary opinion with respect to the authority of the sacred books, and in particular the books of Moses. This would be hard to believe, because he invariably opposed the views of his contemporaries whenever this was called for.

When Jesus declares in the Sermon on the Mount: "But I say unto you," this may not be viewed as undermining the authority of the law of Moses. In contrast with the scribes, he demonstrates its deeper meaning. He has not "come to destroy the law or the prophets . . . but to fulfill" them. "One jot or one tittle shall in no wise pass from the law, till all be fulfilled" (Matt. 5:17–48).

Also in the apostolic epistles we read repeatedly: "It is written." There is no room for bargaining, for Scripture has a normative character to its authors and to its hearers or readers. While introducing a quotation from the Old Testament, Paul can write: "as God hath said" (2 Cor. 6:16). The testimony of Scripture is the testimony of the Spirit (Heb. 10:15–17).

It is of great importance that in the short summary of faith in Christ, which was delivered to Paul and which he passed on to the church, the words "according to the Scriptures" occur twice. Yet no specific Scripture passage is mentioned. The apostle implies that the facts of redemption are in agreement with all of Holy Scripture (1 Cor. 15:3–4).

The authority of the writings of the apostles rests on the fact that Jesus gave them the mandate to be his representatives. When Paul and Peter address the church as apostles of Christ, this implies that they know that he employs them in his service to prosper his work. They are expected to testify to the nature and truth of salvation in an authoritative and exclusive manner and safeguard it (Ridderbos, 1955, 37). New Testament "salvation . . . which at the first began to be spoken by the Lord . . . was confirmed unto us by them that heard him" in a reliable manner (Heb. 2:3). The apostles have been endowed and equipped by the Holy Spirit for their task. Paul is convinced that he speaks with words taught by the Spirit (1 Cor. 2:13).

The apostolic authority shines through clearly in several places. What Paul preached was indeed received as the Word of God in Thessalonica (1 Thess. 2:13). Paul appeared to have confidence that what he commanded as an apostle would actually be done (2 Thess. 3:4).

Whether in 2 Peter 3:2 we should read: the commandment of your apostles, i.e., of the Lord and Savior, or: the commandment of the Lord and Savior delivered through your apostles, at any rate, the apostles are placed on a par with the prophets, which are mentioned first. Their word is authoritative. "Since *their* commandment is the commandment of *Christ*, to the church it has the same authority as the words of the prophets" (Van Houwelingen, 1988, 218).

The words that John had to record were "faithful and true" (Rev. 22:6). Nothing may be added to or taken away from the words that are contained in the book of this prophecy (Rev. 22:18–19). We agree with Ridderbos that here is revealed very explicitly a reality that is of very great significance for the entire history of redemption of the New Testament, namely that God's authority also applies to the communication of the great works of God in Jesus Christ in the writings of the specially designated qualified bearers and instruments of divine revelation (Ridderbos, 1955, 57ff.).

The conclusion is that the church may not treat the Bible any differently than Jesus—and in imitation of him the apostles and evangelists—treated the Old Testament. Therefore we accept all the books of the Bible to direct, support, and confirm our faith (Belgic Confession of

Faith, article 5). What is confessed here regarding all books of the Bible is repeated in article 25 with respect to the Old Testament.

3. *Extent and nature of the authority of Scripture*

The authority of Scripture cannot be limited to only a portion. When we confess that only Scripture has authority (*sola Scriptura*), we mean that Scripture in its entirety (*tota Scriptura*) is to us the authoritative Word of God.

In applying this rule, questions arose quite early on, especially concerning the Old Testament. Should we take everything that is written there literally and obey it to the letter? When we think of the laws that were given to Israel, it is obvious that somewhat more needs to be said than this is what the Bible says (cf. J. Hoek, in *Het gezag van de Bijbel* = the authority of Scripture, 1987, 144–69).

To give a well-known example: keeping the Sabbath Day holy is wrongly interpreted if it is viewed as a commandment to celebrate Saturday as the seventh day of the week or if the regulations of the Sabbath law (cf. Ex. 31:12–17; 35:1–3) are imposed on the church of the New Testament. Then it is overlooked that the Sabbath was a "sign" (Ex. 31:17) and a shadow of things to come, while the reality is found in Christ (Col. 2:16–17). Yet our celebration of the Lord's Day does go back to the fourth commandment of the Decalogue. This is what the Synod of Dordrecht (1618–19) meant with its pronouncement that the fourth commandment is in part moral and in part ceremonial.

Part of the recognition of the authority of Scripture is the insight that Scripture must be properly understood and correctly interpreted. In this connection we have in mind the hermeneutical principle that Holy Scripture is its own interpreter (*sacra Scriptura sui ipsius interpres*), which is reminiscent of 2 Peter 1:19 (cf. Berkouwer, 1975, 126–28). One of the implications of this is that exegesis is of the greatest importance for the church and theology as long as it seeks to bring out the true sense of Scripture. This does not mean that exegetes should have the final say. No single theological discipline, including exegesis, may predominate.[19]

19. Therefore it is quite pretentious that Labuschagne sought to employ Bible science to modify our view of the Bible. He considered the Bible as a human, historically bound, literary document that can only be made accessible to understanding through the application of serious scientific study (C. J. Labuschagne, *Wat zegt de Bijbel in Gods name?* = what does the Bible say for God's sake? 1977, 40, 43).

If we cannot accept the monopoly of modern biblical scholarship and reject all attempts to let theology—or whatever discipline—determine how Holy Scripture can show the way at this time, we cannot accept the following statement either: authority is authority and scriptural authority is scriptural authority. Do questions not arise with respect to the nature of this authority?

Bavinck points out that Scripture has a purpose that is religious-ethical through and through. It offers to us everything we need for the saving knowledge of God. The statement by Baronius—that Scripture does not say how the heavens move but how we move to heaven—has been misused. Yet it contains a grain of truth. Scripture does not speak the exact language of science and the academy, but the language of observation and daily life. It speaks of "land approaching" (Acts 27:27), of the sun "rising" and "standing still," and the heart as the source of thought. But the language of everyday experience is and remains always true. It is intelligible to the most simple person and clear to the learned (Bavinck, *R.D.*, 1:444–46).

The fact that the Old and New Testaments contain human images that we consider to be antiquated, but which the Bible employs without correction, and that its writers' concept of the world is no longer our own, does not diminish the authority of their message. The authority of Scripture should not be interpreted legalistically.

Here something needs to be said with respect to *fundamentalism*. The term itself is not unequivocal. It can refer to original fundamentalism, which represented the defense of a series of fundamental doctrines of the Christian faith. This took place in the United States in a series of documents called *The Fundamentals* (1910–15), which in the battle against the emerging modernist views did not remain without influence. The doctrine of inspiration and the authority of Holy Scripture definitely occupied a prominent place among these fundamentals.

Fundamentalism has frequently come to describe a view in which the Bible is interpreted as literally as possible. The Mount of Olives would then be the location for the return of Christ (cf. Zech. 14:4). First Corinthians 14:5 would imply that the apostle wanted every Christian to speak or prophesy in tongues. At some time in the future Satan would be bound and believers would join Christ in governing the world over a period of one thousand years (cf. Rev. 20:1–5). Infant baptism would not be biblical, because it is not specifically mentioned. There exists a fundamentalism with sectarian tendencies (cf. Wentsel, *Dogm.*, 2:573).

A second element is the conviction that the Bible does not contain any errors. This is referred to as inerrancy. As presented by H. Lindsell and others, inerrancy has something spasmodic. To be the reliable Word of God and the inerrant rule for faith and life (cf. Belgic Confession of Faith, article 5), the revelation that God gave to us by means of human beings, the Bible does not need to be free of all unevenness. W. J. Ouweneel said: "To the Christian the reliability of Scripture is not a matter of logic and theory, but a matter of faithful confidence through which he relies on the Word of God by the power of the Holy Spirit" (W. J. Ouweneel in *Het gezag van de bijbel* = the authority of the Bible, 1987, 87). The Word never misleads us!

We do have reservations about the teachings of certain fundamentalist circles, but one needs to be careful in judging these, for fundamentalism is a complex phenomenon[20] and deserves respect and appreciation for being prepared to forcefully defend the authority of Scripture.

In our own time entirely opposite tendencies can be detected in theology and in churches. By means of various distinctions and new approaches the authority of Scripture is undermined.

4. *Modern tendencies*

a. *Formal and substantive authority.* According to a report discussed by the synod of the *Gereformeerde Kerken in Nederland* (1969–70), these churches today place great emphasis on substantive authority, i.e., that the authority of Scripture is determined by its substance. The authority of Scripture is approached from the perspective of the message of salvation. The entire focus is on the core of the gospel. What Berkouwer says in his dogmatic studies with respect to Holy Scripture also points in this direction.[21]

An outright rejection of the authority of Scripture as Scripture is encountered in the work of Kuitert, who views it as empty authority. According to him the packaging must be distinguished from the message of salvation itself. But this ends in a complete separation (Kuitert, 1968, 43ff.). The result is that it is left to the subjective insight or the discretion of the interpreter or reader of the Bible to determine what the message of the Word is and what its form or packaging material is. The implication is that any appeal to Scrip-

20. Cf. "The Chicago Statement on Biblical Hermeneutics" (1982), incorporated in *Het gezag van de Bijbel* (the authority of the Bible), 1987, 185–91; H. Lindsell, *The Battle for the Bible*, 1978; N. Geisler (ed.), *Inerrancy*, 1979; M. J. Erickson, *Christian Theology*, 1987[3], 221–40; Wentsel, *Dogm.*, 2:572–90; De Vries, 1991, 283–98.

21. Cf. W. H. Velema, "Hermeneutische overwegingen rond het Schriftgezag" (hermeneutic considerations with respect to the authority of Scripture), *Th. Ref.* 13 (1970): 131–46; S. Meijers, *Objectiviteit en existentialiteit*, 1979, 149–223.

ture loses its effect,[22] while pluralism increases by leaps and bounds and consequently everyone's freedom to decide what he or she will accept from the Bible.

We may not set the content of Scripture over against its form, as though the latter is of secondary importance. If one wants to use words such as "formal" and "substantive," which in any case need to be treated with care, one could say that the authority of Scripture has both a substantive and a formal aspect. The Bible brings us the message of salvation, but this message comes to us in a certain way, in a certain form, and through the use of certain words. It is a form that is consistent with this content. One cannot ignore the three participants: the Speaker, the messenger, and the addressee, and the fact that behind the messenger the Speaker declares his love, gives his promises, and demands a reply. This ultimately defines the authority of Scripture, however much the "substance" of our salvation is important to us.[23]

b. *Distinct circles.* In a brief discussion of the authority of Scripture, Berkhof stresses that authority is a concept associated with encounter and that it only exists if the other party agrees to respect it. Furthermore, the authority of Scripture is indirect, because the Bible is not revelation itself. First, Scripture calls our attention to revelation with authority; next, we determine what revelation tells us, i.e., the testimonies of Scripture; and finally, an interaction between the two emerges.

According to Berkhof, four levels can be identified with respect to the testimony of Scripture. Its core contains stories such as that of the exodus and that of Jesus and his resurrection. The virgin birth belongs to the third level and therefore lies near the periphery. A determining factor is that it shows up only in Matthew 1 and Luke 1. The confession of eternal life, as a consequence of the immediate testimony concerning God and his words and actions, does not belong to the first but the second level. Images with respect to the eschaton

22. Subsequently H. M. Kuitert wrote: "The ultimate authority of Scripture is a thing of the past; the ultimate authority of the pope is also a thing of the past," in "Kerk en waarheid: een Gereformeerd antwoord" (church and truth: a Reformed response), *Concilium* (1981): 38. This pronouncement is reminiscent of Lessing!

23. Cf. H. G. Geertsema, "Rationele waarheidsopvatting en Schriftgezag" (rational view with respect to truth and the authority of Scripture), *Th. Ref.* 31 (1988): 133, 149.

are relegated to the third level together with views about heaven, angels, and the devil.

According to this theory of four levels of authority, appeals to the Bible become much more speculative and selective than in the past, and therefore also much more indirect and global. The work in which Berkhof proposes this view (*Christian Faith*) is an example of this approach! He proceeds not only selectively but also skeptically. The announcements of Christ's suffering are treated as fictitious and John 21 is referred to as a legend (Berkhof, *C.F.*, 94–98, 280–83).

c. *Synodical documents*. There are two important synodical documents that advocate the new approach with respect to the authority of Scripture: *Klare wijn* (clear wine, 1967) and *God met ons* (God with us, 1981). The former was unanimously adopted by the synod of the Netherlands Reformed Church and the latter was regarded by the Gereformeerde Synod of Delft as a confessionally sound explanation of the way in which Scripture wants to be understood.

Klare wijn deals with the history, mystery, and authority of the Bible. There are two extreme positions. On the one hand there are those who accept the Bible as the Word of God with great certainty. They say: I accept it as it stands written. On the other hand there are those according to whom the authority of the Bible has been irretrievably lost. They no longer believe the Bible. It is impossible to reject either position out of hand. A compromise is not likely to be accepted. A new attitude is called for. In this situation the synod believes it can pour out "clear wine," i.e., speak plainly.

The Bible should not be treated in a fundamentalist fashion as the book that contains the truths of God. The authority with which the words of Scripture come to us is not legalistic but spiritual. It appeals to our ability to make decisions instead of providing us with ready-made answers. The Bible exerts its authority in conversation with us. *Klare wijn* advocates a "dialogical authority of Scripture" (Trimp), in line with modern views regarding authority. Authority becomes authority to us only when we agree with it (cf. *Klare wijn*, 1967, 77ff., 171–204; Trimp, 1970, 155–91).

There has been much to do about *God met ons* (God with us), the report concerning the nature of scriptural authority, which was put together by a committee of synod. It represents a dated document in the process of theological and ecclesiastical reorientation, which has been in progress for some time already.[24]

24. Cf. J. Plomp, *Een kerk in beweging* (a church on the move), 1987; A. M. Lindeboom, *De theologen gingen voorop* (the theologians were in the lead), 1987.

It is therefore not surprising that the first chapter deals with changes in the concept of truth and that subsequently—when the implications for the life of the church are explored—it encourages readiness to change.

Truth is truth pertaining to man personally, i.e., relational truth and therefore no objective facts or subjective views, period.[25] Biblical truth is viewed and described in terms of faith. What matters here is what truth is for us. Writers and readers of the books of the Bible need to be allies of God. "God with us" is therefore of fundamental significance.

In the introduction, assurance is given that the concept of relational truth is not intended to be a concept of relative truth. It nevertheless encourages relativism and sanctions pluralism.

According to Vroom, the most characteristic aspect of these new insights is that all emphasis is placed on the connectivity between Scripture and its reader, God and man, fact and interpretation, object and subject. The groundwork for this emphasis was laid by Berkouwer, for whom the correlation between faith and revelation is one of the foundations of his dogmatic studies. The view of the report *God met ons* "relativizes the church's doctrine to some extent: doctrine per se is not the truth, but points to reality."[26]

The report says of miracles that their truth is strongly relationally determined. The historical form of biblical commandments would not be *without* significance, but the question is: how can we, in our own situation, live in a comparable manner from the perspective of the salvation that is revealed in these passages? Numerous critical questions could be asked about this part of the report. It focuses on the great commandment to love, but is Christian life not cut loose from the concrete commandments of God, which are clearly relativized?

Also in the case of *God met ons* one would be able to speak of a dialogical authority of Scripture. One cannot and may not resort to an "unabridged" clinging to certain biblical commandments. This would be false security. As Christians we must dare to accept our responsibility and choose over and over again what we can only perform in a responsible manner in a continuing dialogue with the Spirit of the Scriptures and openness toward each other.

In reaction to criticism, a sequel to this report was released in 1986, once again in the form of a report submitted to synod. *God met ons* contains the statement that

25. This is not a new approach in every respect! Faith and Order accepted a report in 1971 regarding the authority of Scripture (the Van Leuven report), which sought to interpret authority as a rational concept. An important passage was: "Authority is only then a present reality when people experience it as authority; at the same time it surpasses human experience. Special and explicit emphasis must be placed on this supra-individual character of authority." Cf. Flesseman-van Leer, 1982, 75, 114.

26. H. M. Vroom, "Het Schriftgezag ter diskussie in protestante kring" (the authority of Scripture in Protestant circles), *Praktische theologie* 13 (1986): 436ff.

God's truth does not exist without the endorsement of people who testify to God's supremacy and grace. One could say that in the first chapter of the sequel this idea is elaborated not with an appeal to modern philosophy and its concept of truth, but with an appeal to a new pneumatology. Relational truth is retained: "The authority of Scripture with respect to our faith originates in the clarity with which Scripture speaks about us and our world" (§ 2.4). The question, raised toward the end of this document, whether the confession does not view Scripture as a much more self-contained, divine authority than is admitted by the more relational view sketched in this document, is answered evasively. There is no doubt, however, that this question must be answered affirmatively!

5. *Time-bound or time-oriented?*

There are therefore various interpretations and perspectives that imply a circumscription of the authority of the Bible. This is not the case with the old distinction between historical and normative authority, which means that not every passage of Scripture is normative for our faith and lives. Has the Bible not also recorded sinful actions and words? Bavinck did point out in this connection that historical and normative authority cannot be so abstractly separated. Even in the deceptive words of Satan and the evil deeds of the ungodly, God still has something to say to us. Scripture also serves for warning and reproof (Bavinck, *R.D.*, 1:459–60). Furthermore, the passages in question play a role in a larger whole whose normativity cannot be denied.

When historical authority is ascribed to Scripture, this implies more than that everything in the Bible has actually taken place. It is the history of God's revelation. This does not mean that everything needs to have been recorded with historic exactness. But we do need to confess that the Bible is historically reliable.

Biblical historiography has a character of its own. Everything is presented from the perspective of God, his interaction with mankind and with Israel, his acts of redemption in Jesus Christ. This means that many details may have been left out that would have been mandatory for historical documentation of a different kind—but also that everything came to be seen in a special light, so that seemingly unimportant events became significant and centuries of time could be glossed over (Y. Feenstra, *Chr. Enc.*, 1961[2], 6:115).

In other words, the Bible is not an ordinary history book. But one needs to be very careful with the concept of "time-boundedness," which turns up regularly in the work of Kuitert and the report *God met ons*, because elements of the text supposedly reflect the time-bound background and character of Bible writers as well as the intellectual baggage of those days. Time-bound elements can be set aside as interesting material that has ceased to be relevant to us. In this way the Bible is treated quite selectively and one-sidedly. Time-boundedness automatically brings with it a reduction in authority.

The situation changes when "time-bound" is the antonym of "timeless." In that case the former term may be employed to indicate images of the world that have become antiquated (without forgetting that the more scientific, modern image of the world is also time-bound and not timeless). This "time-boundedness" then implies that what was said at a particular time in a particular situation cannot be simply applied to our time and situation. The following examples come to mind: commandments that applied to Israel as a theocracy, ceremonial laws that ceased to apply in the new dispensation because they were fulfilled in Christ, or prophetic pronouncements that had a particular historical connotation such as what Jeremiah said about the subjugation of his people to Babylon.

What is meant here might be better referred to as pertaining to a particular time and situation. The speaking of the eternal God pertains to time and is focused on concrete historical situations.

What is tied to a time that is past actually no longer has relevance for today. But words of Scripture that pertain to a particular time turn out to have surprising relevance when we listen to them with an open mind.

In connection with various misunderstandings that can arise when the divine authority of Scripture is recognized, it is necessary to reject the view that the Bible is a book of law with clauses for all possible eventualities. Neither is the Bible a reference work from which isolated quotes can be selected without having to pay any attention to their context. Frequent citation from Scripture is in and of itself no proof of being faithful to the Bible. Whenever we refer to Scripture passages, we need to take into account their meaning, purpose, and context. The authority of Scripture is not the authority of a list of truths or pronouncements, but the authority of the entire Word of God, of which Christ is the center, and that as the reliable Word of God calls for faith.

What is written in the gospel was written so that we "might believe that Jesus is the Christ, the Son of God; and that believing [we] might have life through his name" (John 20:31). "Scripture, given by inspiration of God . . . is profitable for doctrine, for reproof, for correction, for instruction in righteousness" (2 Tim. 3:16–17). Paul also said: "For whatever things were written aforetime were written for our learning, that we through patience and comfort of the scriptures might have hope" (Rom. 15:4). The words "for" and "that" express the purpose (*scopus*) of Holy Scripture, which we continuously need to keep in mind.

The authority of the Scriptures is the authority of the revelation of God. This is why we believe "without any doubt all things contained in them" (Belgic Confession of Faith, article 5). But relativization of the authority of Scripture is bound to give faith a staggering blow.

The Bible comes to us with God's authority. This is how the Word of God addresses us. We need to listen to it with an attitude of faithful reverence: "Speak LORD; for thy servant heareth" (1 Sam. 3:9). To really accept the authority of Scripture means to obey it continually.

8.3. *The clarity of Holy Scripture*

A second property of Scripture is its clarity, sometimes also referred to as transparency or perspicuity (*claritas, perspicuitas*). As Reformational Christians we appeal to the Bible so as to respect its authority. But it may be objected that among those who base themselves on the authority of Scripture, varying views are held. Does not every heretic base himself on some passage of Scripture? Is the Bible clear enough?

Roman Catholic theologians infer from the Bible itself that it is insufficiently clear. The response to Philip's question (Acts 8:30): "Understandest thou what thou readest?" is "How can I, except some man should guide me?" (8:31). With respect to Paul's epistles it is said that there "are some things hard to be understood" (2 Peter 3:16). In addition to prophecies that are not easy to understand for readers of the Bible, are there not some contradictions in the Scriptures as well? In connection with what God has revealed about the Trinity, the incarnation, and the sacraments, is the danger of error not great? (cf. Bijlsma, 1959, 308ff.).

Rome has not dared to call Scripture outright unclear or obscure. In the encyclical titled *Providentissimus Deus* (1893), Pope Leo XIII declared that the sacred books are somewhat wrapped in obscurity. This makes it plausible to depend on the church for the interpretation of Scripture. The church can play this role because it is guided by the Holy Spirit in all truth. Within the church there is a special office that is assisted in this regard by the Holy Spirit. It is for this reason that an official doctrinal pronouncement assigns the task of authentic interpretation of the Word of God to the teaching office of the church (*Dei Verbum*, 1965). No one is permitted to interpret Scripture differently from the holy mother church (Trent, 1546).

There was a time when the Roman Catholic Church preferred not to see the Bible in every hand. As recently as 1902 the pope recommended that Scripture study be restricted to the clergy. In an infamous encyclical of 1864 Protestant Bible societies were treated in the same way as socialist and communist societies. They were considered to be depraved, and those who cooperated with them were said to make themselves guilty of the most heinous sin against God and the church.

However, the Second Vatican Council recommended the reading of the Bible, especially the gospels. But the stipulation was: by means of translations provided with necessary and indeed adequate explanations, so that the children of the church may safely and profitably become conversant with the sacred Scriptures. The interpretation of the church is provided at the same time! Therefore the question still remains whether or not the Bible is truly permitted to speak for itself (cf. Sevenster, 1956).

We confess that the Word of God "is a lamp unto [our] feet, and a light unto [our] path" and that the opening of the Word of God spreads light (Ps. 119:105, 130). The "word of prophecy . . . [is] a light that shineth in a dark place" (2 Peter 1:19).

The church of the Reformation maintains that Scripture is clear. When someone says that Scripture is obscure, one needs to reply: this is not true! On earth no clearer book has been written than Holy Scripture (Luther). How important this was to the Reformer! In *De servo arbitrio* (1525) he challenged Erasmus, who employed numerous arguments that appeared to contradict the clarity of Scripture, pointed to conflicting interpretations and opinions, and considered it desirable to take Christian love seriously (cf. Beisser, 1966, 75–79). But according to Luther it needs to be completely clear to all Christians that Holy Scripture is a spiritual light that surpasses the very sun in brightness, especially in matters pertaining to salvation (*WA*, 18:653). Luther, who himself was enlightened by Scripture, employs superlatives to describe the brightness of this light. Scripture is in and of itself completely sure, completely accessible, and completely clear. It interprets itself (*sui ipsius interpres*) and it proves, judges, and enlightens everything by itself (*WA*, 7:97).

Like the Reformers, we are conscious of the fact that not everything in the Bible is immediately clear. There are difficult passages and exegetical problems (*cruces*). The Word of God reveals mysteries that surpass our understanding. Even the most capable interpreters of Scripture are not always unanimous, and there can be passages that are difficult to us.

The clarity of Scripture does not mean that everyone finds it equally transparent. Difficulties may be due to personal limitations and horizons determined by contemporary culture. But there is more. We are reminded of the apostolic words: "The natural man receiveth not the things of the Spirit of God: for they are foolishness unto him: neither can he know them" (1 Cor. 2:14). Those words are still as valid as when Paul wrote them. Christ once explained why he spoke in parables: "Because it is given unto you to know the mysteries of the kingdom of heaven, but to them it is not given" (Matt. 13:11). The Word that is light itself must also shine in our hearts (cf. 2 Peter 1:19). Paul prayed for the enlightenment of the eyes of the heart (Eph. 1:18). Enlightenment by the Holy Spirit is crucial for the understanding of the Word of God. Luther referred to this as inner clarity, lucidity (*claritas interna*).[27] In the absence of the testimony of Scripture itself, we would have no sure conviction.

The study of Scripture is not obviated by its clarity. To those who are familiar with all of Scripture, the message of the Word will be sooner clear than for those who only have limited knowledge of the Bible.

The Westminster Confession expresses the declaration of the clarity of Scripture as follows: "All things are not alike plain in themselves, nor alike clear unto all: yet those things which are necessary to be known, believed, and observed for salvation, are so clearly propounded, and opened in some place of Scripture or other, that not only the learned, but the unlearned, in a due use of the ordinary means, may attain unto a sufficient understanding of them" (1.7).

It occurs to us that the clarity of Scripture does not always come through in Reformed theology (cf. Kamphuis, 1988, 15–21). Do the risks associated with this doctrine perhaps play a role? Although it is one of the soundest bulwarks of the Reformation, free access to Scripture and its study is and has been abused by all sorts of groups and schools of thought (Bavinck, *R.D.*, 1:479). Berkouwer points out that the numerous interpretations of the words of Scripture indicate the perpetual danger of being influenced by one's own presuppositions and frames of reference, enabling one to escape from the thrust of the Word of God and causing the light of Scripture to be obscured (1972, 297). Yet—in the words of Bavinck—the freedom that is hereby given to the Christian is far preferable to tyranny that suppresses all liberty. Over against both Rome, which constrains the interpretation of Scripture, and all arbitrary treatment of Scripture in Protestant circles, we must keep in mind that Scripture is its own interpreter and that it is the highest judge in all disputes.

27. Cf. Rossouw, 1963, 181–89, 229–36; Beisser, 1966, 82–97.

Following in the footsteps of B. Kamphuis, who in 1988 devoted an entire study to this topic (*Klare taal* = clear language), we can identify various elements.

1. God speaks to us in "clear language." "The word is nigh thee, even in thy mouth, and in thy heart" (Rom. 10:8; cf. Deut. 30:14). The clarity of the revelation and the transparency of Scripture cannot be separated.

2. Theology has a ministering role in maintaining the clarity of Scripture, but when clarity is neglected, the discipline of theology comes to control the church. The general tendency in modern Protestant theology is the problematization of the clarity of Scripture in favor of the importance of theology. If it depended on Labuschagne, no Bible would be published without the necessary directions provided by scholarship![28] Just as in Roman Catholicism the church has the responsibility for authentic interpretation, in this particular case the same thing is expected from theological scholarship, as though theology could assist us to the extent that the Bible is unclear!

3. But does the clarity of Scripture not diminish with time? Does the historical remoteness of the Bible not cause its words—which at one time were clear enough—to become gradually more difficult to understand?

Those who believe that the Bible reflects the religious experience of earlier generations will gradually become estranged from it, as man always becomes estranged from his past. But here we are dealing with the living and enduring Word of God (cf. 1 Peter 1:23), which is intended for God's people of all places and all times. The Lord also had us in mind (cf. 1 Cor. 10:11). Following a history of centuries, the "today" of Psalm 95:7 remains "today" as we continue to be addressed by God (Heb. 3:7–13).

4. Scripture is "a light that shineth in a dark place" (2 Peter 1:19). It is so, because it is full of him, who is the Light of the World. This is an element that Luther emphasized in his polemics with Erasmus. The greatest mystery has been revealed: Christ, the Son of God, having become man; the triune God nevertheless being one; Christ having suffered for us and yet being Lord forever. "Remove Christ from the Scriptures and what wilt thou have left?" (*WA*, 18:606). When Christians have come to know the core content of Holy Scripture,

28. C. J. Labuschagne, *Wat zegt the Bijbel in Gods naam?* (what does the Bible say for God's sake?), 1977, 24ff.

i.e., Christ, the Son of God, everything else takes on significance and becomes entirely transparent (cf. *WA*, 44:510).

As is well known, Luther also used the criterion "was Christum treibt" (whatever conveys Christ). But it makes a big difference whether one employs it to identify what matters most, or to distinguish between "essence" and paraphernalia. The newer theology only too frequently employs a similar selection device, although not "ob sie Christum treiben oder nicht" (whether it conveys Christ or not).

5. The clarity and unity of Scripture are interconnected. Pannenberg says: the clarity of Scripture as presupposition of dogmatic pronouncements—from a Protestant point of view—cannot be separated from the unity of Scripture. He believes, however, that the unity of Scripture has been lost as a result of modern Scripture research. Not only do the various testimonies contradict each other in terms of details, but there are considerable differences and even contradictions among theological concepts within Scripture.[29] The question whether the canon of the New Testament is the foundation of the unity of the church must be answered in the negative because of the variability of proclamation in the New Testament, according to Käsemann.[30]

But the diversity of the Old and New Testaments does not threaten their internal unity. It is a unity in diversity. There is a doctrine concerning godliness (1 Tim. 6:3), a doctrine concerning Christ by which we must abide (2 John 9). The unity of faith and the unity of the church are based on the unity of Scripture as the Word of God.

6. Scripture is clear enough to be its own interpreter. This implies a rejection of the teaching of Rome that the church is to supply and guarantee the correct interpretation. In view of more recent developments, we add that we should not permit ourselves to be guided by preconceived notions, domineering theological views, or contemporary experiences.

In practice this means that we must compare Scripture with Scripture and—as advocated by Luther—interpret relatively unclear passages of Scripture in the light of the "clear and understandable portions" and not vice versa.

This approach is also very important because in this way we can take a position over against the one so bluntly expressed by Kuitert:

29. W. Pannenberg, *Grundfragen systematischer Theologie* (basic questions of systematic theology), 1971², 166ff.

30. E. Käsemann (ed.), *Das Neue Testament als Kanon* (the New Testament as canon), 1970, 124–33.

"We ourselves must decide whether something should be believed to have happened or not." "This is done in all liberty before God and men, to some extent supported by scholarly historical research" (Kuitert, 1968, 76ff.).

7. Scripture is therefore its own interpreter. At the same time it is true that the Holy Spirit is the only Interpreter of himself (*unicus sui interpres*, Calvin on 2 Peter 1:20). This is indeed not contradictory, just as in the case of Luther the external clarity (*claritas exterior)* and the internal clarity (*claritas interior*) do not contradict each other. They go hand in hand as two aspects of the same thing. However clear Scripture itself is, the Spirit is needed to understand Scripture in whole or in part, not because Scripture is not clear enough, but because the darkness of our hearts needs to be overcome. The Holy Spirit opens our eyes to the clarity of the light of Scripture and ensures that we prefer its light to darkness. Following in Luther's footsteps, Reformational theology emphasizes that the Word comes first and that the Spirit does not operate without the Word, but by means of the Word, or as Luther also expressed it: with and through the Word.

8. When it comes to broadcasting the light, the Holy Spirit shows us our mandate in all clarity. For this purpose the Holy Spirit employs people who are called to a responsible task, in interpreting and proclaiming the Word of God as well as in the translation and dissemination of Holy Scripture. They depend on the guidance of the Holy Spirit in everything. The psalm with the confession, "Thy word is a lamp unto my feet, and a light unto my path" (Ps. 119:105), is also the psalm of the prayer, "Open thou mine eyes, that I may behold wondrous things out of thy law" (Ps. 119:18).

The clarity of Scripture has provided the church with the opportunity and the obligation to summarize in confessions what the Lord says in his Word. That is what Luther and Calvin referred to as *doctrina* (instruction, teaching). Scripture proclaims to the confessing church the decisive word. It is for this reason that Reformed confessions continually appeal to the Bible. This would be useless if Scripture were not clear! It is based on the clarity of Holy Scripture itself that ecclesiastical gatherings, lay members, and office bearers of the church can express the conviction that what they confess corresponds with the Word of God in every sense.

8.4. *The sufficiency or perfection of Holy Scripture*

Just as the clarity of Holy Scripture goes hand in hand with its authority, so does its sufficiency (*sufficientia*). If it lacked perfection (*perfectio*), its authority would not be absolute.

We interpret the sufficiency or perfection of Scripture to mean that everything that man needs to believe to be saved is sufficiently taught in it. People therefore are not permitted anything else (cf. Gal. 1:8). No human documents should be considered to be equivalent to it. "We reject with all our hearts whatsoever does not agree with this infallible rule" (Belgic Confession of Faith, article 7). In essence here is confessed the Reformational *sola Scriptura* together with its consequences.

The core of this doctrine is directed at Rome, which bases itself on both "Scripture and tradition." Rome's response to Reformational doctrine at the Council of Trent (1546) was antithetical: synod accepts and adores with equal pious love and reverence (*pari pietatis affectu ac reverentia*) all books of the Old and New Testaments as well as traditions pertaining to faith and morals. With respect to Scripture it was said that God is its Author; with respect to traditions, that they were received by the apostles from the mouth of Christ himself or were inspired through the Holy Spirit and have been preserved by the Catholic Church through uninterrupted succession. It is a matter of discussion, but Scripture and tradition were indeed considered to be two distinct and consciously coordinated sources.

It is curious that it has never been precisely defined what constitutes tradition. For centuries the definition of the great traditionalist Vincentius of Lerinum held sway. In his *Commonitorium* (434), he posits that there are two ways to defend the faith: by the authority of the divine law—i.e., Holy Scripture—and through the tradition of the Christian church. But Scripture is variously interpreted. Therefore a second authority is required: "the catholic authority." According to Vincentius this is what has been believed everywhere, always, and by everyone.

It turns out that in subsequent doctrinal developments, in which tradition played an important role and sometimes was indeed a decisive factor—we have in mind the dogmas pertaining to Mary (1854, 1950)—more was inferred from tradition than was earlier supposed. The ecclesiastical teaching office, which determines what Scripture teaches, also establishes what valid tradition is. The pope could say: "I decide what tradition is!" Pope Pius IX is reported to have said: "I am the tradition!"

According to the Second Vatican Council, sacred tradition and Holy Scripture are interrelated and blended together. "Consequently the church does not draw its assurance with respect to revelation by means of Scripture alone." This is a categorical rejection of the Reformational view with respect to the role of Scripture. It is further declared that sacred tradition, Holy Scripture, and the church's teaching office appear to be so interrelated and joined together that one cannot maintain itself without the others. What can this mean other than that tradition cannot prevail without Scripture, that Scripture cannot exist without tradition, and that neither can function without the involvement of the ecclesiastical teaching authority, which in turn needs both tradition and Scripture?

Keeping in mind the history of the emergence of this dogmatic constitution (1965) and especially the fact that this council did not accept the initial recommendation, one needs to ask oneself what the relationship between tradition and Scripture really is. Is tradition required because of its complementary or its interpretative function? In the latter case the old controversy reemerges in a new guise.[31]

The contrast (between Protestantism and Roman Catholicism) is less pronounced within ecumenically oriented Protestant circles that underwrite the report of Montreal (1963), which makes a distinction between Tradition and tradition. "By *Tradition* we mean the Gospel, passed on from generation to generation within and by the Church, Christ Himself, present in the life of the Church. We take *tradition* to mean the process of transmittal." Traditions are characterized by a diversity of forms of expression, and there are confessional as well as cultural traditions. Scripture and Tradition are thus intertwined. It has been said with respect to this formulation that it bridges one of the most far-reaching differences between the "Protestant" and "Catholic" views (Flesseman-van Leer, 1982, 34–50, cf. 14).

Tradition and Scripture have the same theological significance, according to Berkhof. To him Scripture is also "an anthology of models of interpretation, usually formed close to the source," and tradition is the continuing process of translation. The Spirit proceeds from Christ to continue and interpret his saving work worldwide. "It is one continuous revelational event."

When Scripture and tradition are blended together into a higher unity, the question as to where true tradition can be found becomes problematic. There is a multiplicity of traditions and directions. According to Berkhof, Scripture does not readily lend itself to be employed in a direct and simple manner as judge of controversies with respect to tradition. "The whole church of Christ is in these cross-currents of tradition upheld by the confidence that the Spirit regularly makes the necessary corrections as well as the final decision, because he knows and points the way" (*C.F.*, 99–108).

The notion of the Holy Spirit's continuing ministry of revelation does not do justice to the principle of *sola Scriptura* and the role of Scripture as canon for faith and life, also referred to as the role of Scripture as a critical judge "over against us." The reverse of this relativization of Scripture's authority, which like tradition has a historical dimension, is the growing power of various traditions. They represent indispensable interpretations, and Berkhof's work (*Christian Faith*) is meant to be a small element in the process of tradition (*C.F.*, 101).

31. Cf. G. C. Berkouwer, *Vaticaans concilie en nieuwe theologie* (Vatican council and the new theology), 1964, 105–33; *idem*, *De Heilige Schrift* (Holy Scripture), 1967, 2:337–47. Wentsel concluded correctly that the substantive sufficiency of Scripture was not proclaimed. Neither did the council support the view that tradition is of a complementary nature as taught by the theory of twin sources. Neither was it said that tradition plays an exclusively interpretive role (Wentsel, *Dogm.*, 2:231).

Rome believes its position to be well-founded in view of Christ's promise that the Spirit will guide us in all truth (John 16:13). Berkhof, Kuitert, and numerous representatives of modern theology all appeal to this verse (cf. Kamphuis, 1988, 42–45). But Calvin already recognized the danger that lurked in isolated appeals to the Holy Spirit. In the name of the Spirit, teachings are advocated that ignore the Word of God and are alien to it. The Spirit, however, wills to be conjoined with the Word of God by an indissoluble bond (*Institutes*, 4.8.13).

The Word of God can be robbed of its force for the sake of traditions and human commandments (cf. Matt. 15:6). By ascribing authority to ecclesiastical tradition, which is considered to be a continuation of the apostolic tradition, one can sanction all kinds of ideas that arise in the human heart.[32]

Although the constitution *Dei Verbum* (1965) does say good things about Scripture and the study of Scripture, the importance assigned to Roman Catholic tradition—whether complementary or merely interpretive—appears to have played a conclusive role in the deliberations of the Second Vatican Council in numerous respects (cf. Wentsel, *Dogm.*, 2:323ff.).

This ignored the fact, clearly pointed out by Cullmann, that the canonization of Scripture implies that the church itself drew a clear and pure line of demarcation between the time of the apostles and the era of the church. The fixing of the canon implied that in the future other traditions, not documented by the apostles, would not be made normative.[33] It may be added that this also implies that varying traditions must be assessed against the norm of Holy Scripture.

We need to take a position not only over against Rome, but also over against sects and groups that maintain companion bibles. It says in the Mormon confession: we believe the Bible to be the Word of God to the extent that it has been correctly translated; we also believe the book of Mormon to be the Word of God. The Seventh-Day Adventists possess a complementary source of revelation in the writings and visions of Ellen G. White. Reasons for maintaining these additions would appear to be the incompleteness of the Bible and the

32. Cf. G. C. Berkouwer, *De strijd om het Roomsch-Katholieke dogma* (the struggle for Roman Catholic doctrine, 1940, 205).

33. O. Cullmann, *La tradition*, 1953, 43–45.

continuation of the Holy Spirit's ministry of revelation. But the result of all of these additions is that they overshadow and crowd out the truth of Scripture.[34]

Nevertheless, the confession of the sufficiency of Scripture does not imply that all traditions must be considered useless. The churches of the Reformation also recognize elements of tradition. But these are not norms for faith and life, although they can be expressions of faith, ways in which people portray their response to the Word of God. In this sense traditions are both useful and necessary. We agree with Bavinck that tradition is the means by which all the treasures and possessions of our ancestors are transmitted to present and future (cf. *R.D.*, 1:492–94). There is indeed a variegated Reformed tradition. There is tradition in our confession, in our worship service, in preaching, in theology, in devotional literature that is nurtured by Scripture. But we may never absolutize this tradition, no matter how familiar and dear to us. The stream of tradition must always lead us back to the source that is normative: Holy Scripture. Traditions become dangerous whenever they are translated from forms into norms. That can happen with established opinions as well as modern provocative views.

The Reformation only recognizes *a tradition that is based on Scripture and derives from Scripture* (Bavinck). We accept what was decided by the first four councils and we accept the three ecumenical creeds (cf. Belgic Confession of Faith, article 9), as long as traditions are in accordance with Scripture and are not placed on the same level! We can study the writings of the church fathers, keeping in mind—as Calvin put it in the preface to his *Institutes*—all things are ours to serve us, not to lord over us, and that we all belong to the one Christ, whom we must obey in all things (1 Cor. 3:21–23).

Tradition cannot determine what is true and good. Only Scripture can! It does not require or tolerate anything additional. The truth of God surpasses everything (Belgic Confession of Faith, article 7).

This means that we do not only defend the authority of Scripture (*sola Scriptura*), but also put it into practice by always asking as churches and as Christians what God has to say to us in his Word. Whether something is old or new, whether it is the opinion of the majority or not, everything must always be tested against Scripture.

34. See K. Hutten, *Geloof en sekte* (faith and sects), no date, 109–15.

8.5. *The necessity of Holy Scripture*

With respect to the necessity (*necessitas*) of Scripture, we can be brief. Among all of the attributes of Scripture, this aspect is not always treated separately.

According to Rome, Scripture is indeed useful, but not strictly necessary. Whereas the church is necessary for faith, Scripture is not.

It frequently strikes us that spiritualistic movements and groups contrast Spirit with text. Scripture is then seen to be merely dead or deadening text. The latter is at most a temporary means to an end, which the spiritual person no longer requires. The Word of God in the true sense of the word is the word that the Spirit speaks in people's hearts. Bavinck points out that the elevation of the internal word over the external word always led to the identification of the teaching of the Spirit with the natural light of reason and conscience (*R.D.*, 1:467).

To a figure such as Lessing, a typical representative of the Enlightenment, Scripture was definitely not essential. Otherwise he would not have spoken of a "paper pope" from which Luther unfortunately failed to deliver Protestantism. The relationship between Scripture and the church, as the Reformation viewed it, was inverted by Schleiermacher. Although he held that Scripture emerged in the church, he did not accept that the church was built on Scripture. Such ideas have become common currency in more recent theology.

Over against Rome and various fanatics, we maintain that we depend on Scripture. The Spirit binds us to the Word, which is his own Word. Believers will never be able to avoid this. They never become emancipated from the Word of God, but rather become ever more dependent on it!

Since God has considered it necessary to grant us the revelation of his salvation in the form of the books of the Bible, no one can say that Holy Scripture is not really necessary. Who wants to be wiser than God? The prophetic word, which according to 2 Peter 1:19 must refer to the entire Old Testament, is for us who are en route a lamp in the midst of the darkness of this world (cf. Van Houwelingen, 1988, 141–47).

To this we may add considerations of theologians such as Calvin, a number of earlier Reformed theologians, and Bavinck.[35] No one can get even the slightest taste of right and sound doctrine unless he be a

35. For theologians such as Polanus, Coccejus, and Turretinus see: Heppe, *Dogmatik*, 27ff. Cf. Bavinck, *R.D.*, 1:469–74.

pupil of Scripture. How slippery is the fall of the human mind, and how great the tendency to every kind of error. Then we may perceive how necessary Scripture is to us. We must come, I say, to the Word, where God is truly and vividly described to us from his works (Calvin, *Institutes*, 1.6.2–3).

The Dutch confessional writings do not teach explicitly but indeed implicitly that we require Scripture. The Westminster Confession does say emphatically that Scripture is highly necessary (1.1). To us the necessity of Scripture means that we need it in its entirety, not only the New Testament but also the Old Testament. "Scripture implies the indispensability of all of its components (cf. Bijlsma, 1959, 301–7).

We reject Rome's thesis that we can do without Scripture because the church is there. Under the old dispensation, God's people had to manage without Scripture for centuries, but not without the Word of God. Although Christ's church did not immediately possess the entire New Testament canon, it did have the Old Testament, and quite soon there were already a number of apostolic writings.

If Scripture were not necessary, it would lose its central position. Something else would move into the center: the church (Rome), spiritual man (spiritualism), the religious community (Schleiermacher), or man's personal opinion.

In practice, the necessity of Scripture means that one must apply oneself diligently to the reading and hearing of Scripture, if one seeks to receive any gain and benefit and any fruit from the Spirit of God (Calvin, *Institutes*, 1.9.2). To say it with Polanus: in this life we need Scripture for our daily bread!

§ 9. The testimony of the Holy Spirit and Holy Scripture

9.1. *The Holy Spirit testifies in, through, and with the Word*

When we think of the testimony of the Holy Spirit, we think in the first place of his testimony that has been recorded in Holy Scripture. In Hebrews 3:7 we read: "Wherefore, as the Holy Ghost saith . . ." followed by a Scripture passage. The Spirit stands behind the testimony of Scripture, and he maintains it right across all criticism and opposition.

The Holy Spirit has not only given us Holy Scripture, but also gives us the assurance that Scripture is the Word of God. The Belgic Confession of Faith (articles 3 and 5) confesses not only the theopneusty or inspiration of Scripture by the Holy Spirit but also the testimony of the Holy Spirit in our hearts.

The confession combats the traditional Roman Catholic point of view that the authority of Holy Scripture rests on the authority of the church since we receive Scripture from the mother church. We are not saying that it makes no difference to us that the church—which represents to us in the first instance the ecclesiastical community of which we are members—considers the Bible as the Word of God. But the Word needs no authorization on the part of the church. This would place it above Scripture, which is not the case.

We owe the doctrine of the testimony of the Holy Spirit (*testimonium Spiritus Sancti*) especially to Calvin, although we already encounter related ideas in the work of Augustine, Luther, and other Reformers.[36] Calvin says: "For as God alone is a fit witness of himself in his Word, so also the Word will find acceptance in men's hearts before it is sealed by the internal witness of the Spirit." "The same Spirit, therefore, who has spoken by the mouths of the prophets must penetrate into our hearts to persuade us that they faithfully proclaimed what had been divinely commanded them" (*Institutes*, 1.7.4).

It is noteworthy that the testimony of the Holy Spirit is also discussed elsewhere in our confessional documents, namely in the Canons of Dort, 5.10, which deals with the assurance of salvation. It refers to Romans 8:16: "The Spirit itself beareth witness with our spirit, that we are the children of God."

From these words of Paul it may not be inferred that first our own spirit would testify independently and that separately or subsequently the testimony of the Holy Spirit would come to confirm that. The translation, "God's Spirit joins himself to our spirits" (*Good News for Modern Man*, 1972), is therefore problematic. One may not read into it that the Spirit of God would so cooperate with our spirits that the actual decision would be ours. According to Scripture the Holy Spirit is directly involved in the testimony of our own spirit. He is the Spirit who testifies to the salvation in Christ, the Spirit of sonship, through whom we, if we believe, let ourselves be guided, and who causes us to pray: "Abba, Father" (Rom. 8:14–15). "The Spirit of God gives us such a testimony, that when he is our guide and teacher, our spirit is assured of the

36. Cf. J. Pannier, *Le témoinage du Saint-Esprit* (the testimony of the Holy Spirit), 1893; J. van Genderen, *Het getuigenis van de Heilige Geest* (the testimony of the Holy Spirit), 1961.

adoption of God" (Calvin on Rom. 8:16). It is not a cooperation of the Spirit with our spirit so that the testimony is in part his and in part ours, but the influence of the Spirit on our spirit so that a single testimony results.

As far as the assurance of salvation is concerned, it is of the utmost importance that we realize that it is a certainty or assurance that has its foundation and origin outside us. The foundation of this certainty lies in the mediating work that Christ has accomplished for us, while its origin is the work of the Holy Spirit in us.

Is the testimony of the Holy Spirit, to which article 5 of the Belgic Confession of Faith refers, in essence nothing but the testimony of the Spirit in Rom. 8:16? It is sometimes imagined that the Spirit provides a twofold testimony: first the testimony that the Bible is the Word of God, and next the testimony that we are God's children. There are those who go still further and speak of a general testimony of the Spirit that proclaims the truth that can also be received in the absence of saving faith, and a special testimony that says that this salvation is ours.

But according to the Reformational view, the testimony of the Holy Spirit with respect to both the Word and salvation is a privilege of God's children. The Spirit brings them to a believing acceptance of the Word of God and a believing confidence in it.

There are people who respect the Bible as a book or acknowledge that it contains truth. But not every conviction or even every religious conviction rests on an internal testimony of the Spirit. Calvin says of this: "For even if Scripture wins reverence for itself by its intrinsic majesty, it seriously affects us only when it is sealed upon our hearts through the Spirit." It is only then that "we affirm with utter certainty . . . that it has flowed to us from the very mouth of God by the ministry of men" (*Institutes*, 1.7.5).

There are undoubtedly signs that the Bible is not an ordinary book with religious-ethical content. From early days, in discussions with unbelievers, it has been pointed out that there are indeed arguments that support the believability of Scripture. The Belgic Confession of Faith refers to this when it says in article 5 that "the very blind are able to perceive that the things foretold in them are being fulfilled."

These arguments have apologetic value. However, faith is not based on intellectual considerations—it is indeed not a matter of intellectual acceptance. If reason had to have the first word, it might also wish to have the last word!

Calvin is of the opinion that unbelievers—unless they have hardened themselves—could also by means of the arguments that he provides be persuaded to acknowledge that there is clear evidence in Scripture that God is speaking. But that does not turn these unbelievers into believers. It is the Holy Spirit who works true faith in our hearts and strengthens it. According to this Reformer, the testimony of the Holy Spirit is stronger than all proof (*Institutes*, 1.7.4).

The testimony of the Spirit with respect to the Word of God, and that with respect to God's gracious disposition toward us, can indeed be distinguished but not separated from each other. According to Calvin the key is the believers' conviction with respect to the Word of God, their own salvation, and religion in general (commentary on Eph. 1:13). Our faith depends on the testimony of the Word and that of the Spirit. But how does the Holy Spirit testify in our hearts?

This cannot be identified with the testimony of personal spiritual experience. Those who hold this view focus on the impact that Scripture has on people. People receive new life, share in the joy of the forgiveness of sins, and are comforted and strengthened by grace. When these experiences become powerful enough, there is an overwhelming conviction with respect to the truth and the authority of the Bible. These experiences, which are formed and nourished by the Word of God, are then—as the work of the Spirit—a direct testimony of the Spirit to the Bible.

There is indeed spiritual experience that is fruit of the Spirit (Gal. 5:22) and which points to the Word as bearing this fruit. But fruit of the Spirit is not the same thing as the testimony of the Spirit in our hearts, just as the fruit of the Word in our lives is not the same thing as the testimony of the Word. The view in question, which is associated with ethical theology, makes experience the criterion for Scripture instead of the other way around. In the relationship between Scripture and experience, personal experience cannot be our starting point, but Scripture is.

The testimony of the Holy Spirit is no separate revelation outside the Word, like a voice from heaven. The Spirit does not add a separate message to the Word. This would be in conflict with the perfection of Scripture, which has been inspired by the Spirit himself. We say with Calvin: it is not the role of the Spirit promised to us to invent new and unheard-of revelations, but to seal in our hearts the very doctrine that is commended to us by the gospel (*Institutes*, 1.9.1). We should therefore not expect that he will whisper in our ears that the Bible is the Word of God.

It is a testimony through and with the Word (cf. Westminster Confession, 1.5). When the Holy Spirit works in our hearts, he employs the testimony of Scripture as a tool. He accompanies the words of Scripture with his convincing power to such an extent that they resonate and are effectual. Through this testimony of the Holy Spirit the Word has an irresistible power for us. Then there are burning hearts, as in the case of the disciples of Emmaus (Luke 24:32). Luther says that the Word opened to him became to him the gate to paradise, and that he then came to see everything in the Bible with different eyes.

God speaks to us in his Word. Therefore we can never contrast the testimony of the Holy Spirit in our hearts with the testimony of the Spirit in Scripture, as is the case in spiritualism, which can treat the Bible as a dead letter, while the Spirit is believed to give life. Neither are there grounds for replacing the principle of Scripture with a Scripture-Spirit principle, as proposed by Brunner. People would then not be bound by the letter that kills, because the Spirit, who opens the Word of God to them, does bind them to Scripture to the extent that they proclaim Christ, but liberates them from the letter of the Bible as a law for faith.[37]

On the contrary, we must hold on to the fact that the testimony of the Holy Spirit in Scripture does not only precede but also is foundational to the witness the Spirit bears in the hearts of believers (cf. Bavinck, *R.D.*, 1:588).

The work of the Holy Spirit is characterized by continuity. It is ongoing. Faith will always depend on it. Since the Spirit works through and with the Word, our faith depends permanently on Holy Scripture, and it is crucial to continually listen to what God has to say to us in his Word. Calvin says that those who have been taught inwardly by the Holy Spirit truly rest upon Scripture and that Scripture indeed is self-authenticated (*autopisty*); hence it is not right to subject it to proof and reasoning. And the certainty that it deserves with us, it attains by the testimony of the Holy Spirit (*Institutes*, 1.7.5).

The French Confession of Faith (1559) refers to this as the testimony and the inner conviction of the Holy Spirit. Whatever terms we may use in imitation of Calvin—testimony, affirmation, conviction, enlightenment, confirmation, or authentication—the implication is that the divine origin of Scripture is owed to the convincing work of the Spirit.

Is it still necessary to refer to certain pronouncements of Scripture? We are reminded of what it says with respect to the opening of Lydia's heart (Acts 16:14), the understanding and acceptance of the things of the Spirit of God (1 Cor. 2:14–15), and the testimony of the Spirit, who is the truth, which the believer has within himself (1 John 5:6, 10).

37. E. Brunner, *Offenbarung und Venunft* (revelation and reason), 1941, 161–80.

9.2. *The testimony of the Holy Spirit and the adoption of the canon*

In article 5 of the Belgic Confession of Faith the church confesses that it holds Scripture to be holy and canonical. It does not canonize the Bible, but accepts it as canonical. The word *canon* means measuring rod or guide. The church has no justification whatsoever to pride itself in its own insights or decisions, for from early on it has been *receptive* to the books of the Bible. Scripture is not a product of the church, but has been given to it by the Lord.

According to article 5 the canon is fixed: "these books and these only." The context (articles 4 and 6) indicates that here there is a difference with Rome, which at the Council of Trent also declared to be canonical a number of books that did not belong to the Hebrew canon, but formed part of the Septuagint and the Vulgate. Why is there no open canon, but a closed canon formed by the 39 books of the Old Testament and the 27 books of the New Testament? Many have devoted themselves intensively to the historical questions that theology must address in canonics.[38] One can say that the church took over the Old Testament canon or that it inherited it. This is not the place to go into details, but we can also let the matter rest, because it is a fact that Scripture or the Scriptures, whose authority was accepted by the Lord Jesus and his apostles, represented no other books but "the Law, the Prophets, and the Writings" that were authoritative to the Jews in the New Testament era. The authority of the Old Testament itself is affirmed by the New Testament.

But was the New Testament canon not determined by the church itself? The high-handed action of Marcion, who maintained a "canon" of his own, may have played a role; there is information, such as the *Canon Muratori* and documentation by early church fathers, which constitutes evidence of a developmental process; certain books were discussed, while the complete listing of the New Testament writings did not turn up until 367 (the Easter epistle by Athanasius of that year).

Although the church did distinguish between canonical and apocryphal, the canon does not appear to be the result of an ecclesiastical

38. Cf. among others H. von Campenhausen, *Die Entstehung der christlichen Bibel* (the emergence of the Christian Bible), 1968; J. L. Koole, "Het Oude Testament als Heilige Schrift," in *Bijbels handboek*, 1983, 2b:192–246; R. Beckwith, *The Old Testament Canon of the New Testament Church*, 1985.

selection process. The church did not maintain lists of Bible books with the intention to elevate certain books to the status of "Bible books" and not others, but it did make lists to determine which books had been accepted by the church from early on (Van Bruggen, 1986, 58).

The canon is a given fact. Nothing was included that should have been excluded and nothing is missing that should have been incorporated.

The Lord's care for his church is not only manifested in the documentation of his Word but also in its preservation through the centuries. There are no historical or theological grounds for the thesis that the canon of Scripture derives its authority from that of the church. We reject the Roman Catholic position that the authority of the canon is sustained and guaranteed by that of the church. The church did not produce Scripture, but received it from God's hand. In this regard it merely had a receptive function.

But there is also a subjective approach that we must reject. According to this view the Scriptures are not accepted as they have come to us, "but only to the extent that they can pass the test of our criticism, or can be received by us on the wavelength of our own experience" (Van Bruggen, 1986, 69; cf. Ridderbos, 1955, 26). Then the "judgment of faith" of the individual or the church becomes the decisive factor, or one seeks a "canon within the canon." This is a canon that is discovered within the Bible by theologians. But it implies a rejection of the canon as canon, because then it can no longer be the canon in the fullest sense of the word.

The canon points beyond itself: God gave it to his church as a standard and guide. And also in the factual recognition of the books of the Bible as canon we recognize the work of God in his church. It is "the Holy Spirit [who] witnesses in our hearts that" it is from God (Belgic Confession of Faith, article 5).

When it says in this article: "because the Holy Spirit witnesses," it is not the case that this testimony is the real basis for the recognition of the divine nature of Scripture. This basis is found in Scripture itself. Bavinck correctly observed: "The canonicity of the Bible books is rooted in their existence. They have authority in themselves, by their own right, because they exist" (*R.D.*, 1:371).

In the French Confession of Faith, which served as a model for our Belgic Confession of Faith, it says "par" (par le tesmoignage: by the testimony). It is therefore possible to interpret the word "because" in article 5 as "by which." Beza already formulated it very carefully as follows: I am instructed by the Holy Spirit by means of Scripture and therefore I believe what I believe, because thus it stands written in the Word of the Lord.[39]

Therefore the basis for the recognition of the canon does not lie in the testimony of the Holy Spirit, but in the trustworthiness (*autopisty*) of the Bible itself. We do not base our faith on the testimony of the Holy Spirit, but on what Scripture itself says (cf. article 5). But the testimony of the Holy Spirit has led to the recognition that these books of the Bible are the Word of God, which is normative for our faith and our lives. In this way the Word of God accomplishes its goal. This is how God achieves his goal with his Word. He sent the same Spirit, through whose power he had provided the Word, to complete his work through the effectual confirmation of the Word (Calvin, *Institutes*, 1.9.3).

Some Literature

M. J. Arntzen et al., *Het gezag van de Bijbel* (the authority of Scripture), 1987.

D. L. Baker, *Two Testaments, One Bible*, 1976.

J. Barr, *Fundamentalism*, 1981².

F. Beisser, *Claritas scripturae bei Martin Luther*, 1966.

G. C. Berkouwer, *Het probleem der Schriftkritiek*, 1938.

G. C. Berkouwer, *Holy Scripture*, 1975.

R. Bijlsma, *Schriftuurlijk Schriftgezag* (scriptural authority), 1959.

J. van Bruggen, *Wie maakte de Bijbel?* (who made the Bible?), 1986.

H. von Campenhausen, *Die Entstehung der christiche Bibel* (the origin of the Christian Bible), 1968.

D. A. Carson, H. G. M. Williamson (ed.), *It Is Written: Scripture Citing Scripture*, 1988.

B. S. Childs, *Old Testament Theology in a Canonical Context*, 1985.

J. A. Cramer, *De Heilige Schrift bij Calvijn* (Holy Scripture according to Calvin), 1926.

K. Dijk, *Het profetische Woord* (the prophetic Word), 1931.

E. E. Ellis, *The Old Testament in Early Christianity*, 1991.

E. Flesseman-van Leer, *Schriftgezag in de oecumene* (the authority of Scripture in ecumenism), 1982.

39. Th. Beza, *Tractationes theologicae*, 1570, 1:503.

J. van Genderen, *Het getuigenis van de Heilige Geest* (the testimony of the Holy Spirit), 1961.

God met ons . . . over de aard van het Schriftgezag . . . (God with us . . . concerning the nature of the authority of Scripture), 1981.

J. van der Graaf (ed.), *De Heilige Schrift*, 1984.

C. Graafland, *Het vaste verbond* (the certain covenant), 1978.

W. de Greef, *Calvijn en het Oude Testament*, 1984.

D. J. de Groot, *Calvijns opvatting over de inspiratie der Heilige Schrift* (Calvin's view regarding the inspiration of Holy Scripture), 1931.

Het hoge Woord (the lofty Word), 1976.

P. H. R. van Houwelingen, *De tweede trompet* (the second trumpet), 1988.

J. de Jong, *Accommodatio Dei*, 1990.

B. Kamphuis, *Klare taal* (clear language), 1988.

J. Kamphuis, *In dienst van de vrede* (in service of peace), 1980.

Klare wijn, Rekenschap over geschiedenis, geheim en gezag van de Bijbel (clear wine, accounting for the history, secret and authority of the Bible), 1967.

E. F. Klug, *From Luther to Chemnitz*, 1971.

W. J. Kooiman, *Luther en de Bijbel*, 1977[3].

J. L. Koole, *De overname van het Nieuwe Testament door the christlijke kerk* (the adoption of the New Testament by the Christian church), 1938.

W. Krusche, *Das Wirken des Heiligen Geistes nach Calvin* (the work of the Holy Spirit according to Calvin), 1957.

H. M. Kuitert, *Verstaat gij wat gij leest?* (do you understand what you are reading?

J. C. S. Locker, *De leer van Luther over Gods Woord* (Luther's teaching regarding God's Word), 1903.

B. M. Metzger, *The Canon of the New Testament*, 1987.

B. J. Oosterhoff, *Het openbaringskaraker van het Oude Testament* (the nature of revelation of the Old Testament), 1954.

J. I. Packer, *"Fundamentalism" and the Word of God*, 1958.

J. Pannier, *Le témoignage du Saint-Esprit* (the testimony of the Holy Spirit), 1893.

A. D. R. Polman, *Het Woord Gods bij Augustinus* (the Word of God according to Augustine), 1955.

A. B. du Preez, *Die dualistiese inspirasieleer* (the dualistic doctrine of inspiration), 1933.

B. Ramm, *The Witness of the Spirit*, 1960.

H. Ridderbos, *Heilsgeschiedenis en Heilige Schrift van het Nieuwe Testament* (the history of redemption and Holy Scripture of the New Testament), 1955.

H. W. Rossouw, *Klaarheid en interpretasie* (clarity and interpretation), 1963.

B. Rothen, *Die Klarheit der Schrift* (the clarity of Scripture), 1, 1990; 2, 1990.

K. Runia, *Karl Barth's Doctrine of Holy Scripture*, 1962.

R. Schippers, *Getuigen van Jezus Christus in het Nieuwe Testament* (witnesses of Jesus Christ in the New Testament), 1938.

J. N. Sevenster, *Rome en de vrije Bijbel* (Rome and the free Bible), 1956.

W. van 't Spijker, *Fundamentele vragen betreffende onze omgan met de Bijbel* (fundamental issues concerning our treatment of the Bible), 1962.

C. Trimp, *Betwist Schriftgezag* (disputed authority of Scripture), 1970.

J. Veenhof, *Revelatie en inspiratie*, 1968.

P. de Vries, *Het onfeilbare Woord* (the infallible Word), 1991.

B. B. Warfield, *The Inspiration and Authority of the Bible*, 1948.

Chapter 4

Concerning God

§ 10. Knowledge of God

10.1. *Knowledge of God is faith-knowledge*

The question as to who God is cannot be separated from the question of who God is to us. Otherwise, thinking about God would lead to theoretical speculation about him, while the objective is to speak of him in faith in line with the creed of the church.

Those who declare that they believe in "a god," or believe that God exists, do not necessarily have a personal relationship with him. But our faith in God gives expression to our personal relationship with him. With the expression "knowledge of God" we do not mean that we as human beings have merely an inkling of him or acknowledge a superior power over us. Rather, with the knowledge of God we mean faith-knowledge.

This is knowledge of God that comes from God himself. With this we mean that it is possible for us to know God and that this knowledge is a gift from him. In theology this was expressed quite early on: God can only be known by God.

Knowledge of God can never mean that God is comprehensible. With our minds we can try to understand things pertaining to this world, but the Bible says of God that he is incomparable (Isa. 40:18) and that his greatness is unsearchable (Ps. 145:3). Elihu says: "Behold, God is great, and we know him not" (Job 36:26). God far exceeds our understanding. God is always greater than we think (*Deus semper maior*). God is God. "We may not form any earthly conceptions of God's heavenly majesty (Heidelberg Catechism, Lord's Day 46).

Like Augustine, who was deeply convinced of the ineffability and incomprehensibility of God and found it easier to say what God is not than what he is, we know that we need not stop here. "Although we cannot say anything profound about God, yet he tolerates the obedient service of the human voice and desires that by means of our words we rejoice in praising Him" (*De doctrina christiana*, 1:6).

God's incomprehensibility does not render knowledge of God impossible. This is then knowledge of a unique nature. Knowledge of God is already a key concept of the prophetic proclamation. In multiple ways the New Testament testifies to the fact that people know God in Christ.

The Old Testament employs the word "*yada*." This knowledge is not the result of research and reflection. It is a familiarity acquired through experience and interaction. "Knowledge signifies communion based on encounter" (De Groot and Hulst, no date, 67). While our word "knowledge" largely signifies intellectual knowledge, its Old Testament counterpart does not indicate being thoroughly informed but rather having a deep, living bond with someone.[1] Thus the poet could say: "Taste and see that the LORD is good" (Ps. 34:8). This knowledge reflects a personal relationship. This relationship must be kept in mind in thinking about God's knowledge of his people and Israel's knowledge of God. In Amos 3:2, God's knowledge of his people is equated with his election of them. Human knowledge of God implies that he is acknowledged by them (Isa. 41:20). Knowledge of God means knowing his ways, not only being aware of them but also following them. Therefore knowing and acknowledging God also includes dispensing justice to the poor and needy (Jer. 22:15–16).

1. Cf. Ph. Kohnstamm, *Schepper en schepping* (creator and creation), *De heilige* (the holy one), 1931, 3:3.

Not knowing and acknowledging God implies guilt toward him who desired to make himself known. Lack of the truth, mercy, and knowledge of God has dire consequences (Hos. 4:1–6).

Knowing God and fearing God go hand in hand. On the basis of Old Testament scholarship it is correct to say: this knowledge of God touches all aspects of human life; it signifies true communion with God and at the same time confidence in faith; it is knowledge of the heart and demands one's love (Deut. 6; Vriezen, *Hoofdlijnen* = main perspectives, 168). There are people who know God. They have encountered him and keep on encountering him; they acknowledge and obey him; they love and honor him.

Just like the Old Testament, the New Testament refers to the distance between God and people. God dwells in unapproachable light, and no human being has ever seen him or can ever see him (1 Tim. 6:16). Although we cannot see God, yet it is possible for us to know him. Has he not sought to reveal himself to us? The evangelist writes: "No man hath seen God at any time; the only begotten Son, which is in the bosom of the Father, he has declared him" (John 1:18). Jesus said: "He that hath seen me hath seen the Father" (John 14:9). God is the way he is.

The meaning of the Greek word "*ginōskein*" has evolved in the direction of intellectual, conceptual knowledge. But New Testament references to the knowledge of God presuppose an Old Testament connotation and imply a knowledge that results from encountering God. It has been said: this knowledge is based on revelation; it reflects a personal relationship, a real personal bond; and it is completely certain, because it constitutes knowledge of the truth.[2] Knowledge and faith go hand in hand. To the extent that they do not coincide, they belong together (cf. John 6:69; 1 John 4:16). Essential knowledge of God is knowledge that is based on revelation and faith. To know God also means to love him (1 John 4:7–8), to live with him, to live in communion with him, to live eternally (cf. John 17:3). To be able to live truly, we must know God.

In the New Testament, knowledge of God has the same practical implication as in the Old Testament. To know the Lord and to keep his commandments are inextricably intertwined (1 John 2:3–6). Through knowledge of him, the Lord bestows upon his people everything that pertains to life and godliness (2 Peter 1:3). "The new man . . . is

2. F. Büchsel, *Theologie des Neuen Testaments*, 1937, 82.

renewed in knowledge after the image of him that created him" (Col. 3:10). The New Testament also refers to growth in the knowledge of God. The apostle prays for this and fights for this (Col. 1:9–10; 2:1–3). Those who know God desire to know him completely and to see him face to face (1 Cor. 13:12).

Knowledge of God is given to us by Christ and the Holy Spirit. "No man knoweth . . . the Father, save the Son, and he to whomsoever the Son will reveal him" (Matt. 11:27). "The things of God knoweth no man, but the Spirit of God. Now we have received . . . the Spirit which is of God; that we might know the things that are freely given to us of God" (1 Cor. 2:11–12). The apostle prays for the believers at Ephesus, "that the God of our Lord Jesus Christ . . . [will] give [them] the Spirit of wisdom and revelation in the knowledge of him" (Eph. 1:15–21).

We shall nevertheless always have to keep in mind that our knowledge of God can never equal God's knowledge of himself. It is knowledge of God on the part of people who are on their way (*theologia viatorum*). "We know in part, and we prophesy in part" (1 Cor. 13:9). The limitation of our knowledge of God reflects the distance between him and us, our insignificance, and our sinfulness. "The riches of God's being—riches that surpass all knowledge—are in fact a necessary and significant component of our knowledge of God" (Bavinck, *R.D.*, 2:56). God is infinitely more and can do infinitely more than we realize (cf. Eph. 3:20). There is a depth of richness, wisdom, and knowledge of God that we cannot fathom. "How unsearchable are his judgments, and his ways past finding out!" (Rom. 11:33). With respect to these words of Paul, Calvin points out that we must learn never to try to get to know more about the Lord than what has pleased him to reveal to us through Scripture. Otherwise we enter a labyrinth from which it would be difficult to extricate ourselves.

God's revelation to us is not exhaustive. Theologically we can also put it as follows: the Author of revelation transcends the act of revelation (Thielicke, *Ev. Glaube* = evangelical faith, 2:41). Therefore God represents much more than we can say about him. But at the same time it is true that he is not hiding behind his revelation. He is exactly the way he makes himself known to us.

God's revelation includes all that God reveals. Christ is the heart of all of revelation as Scripture speaks of it. The objective is to know

God through Christ, i.e., "the light of the knowledge of the glory of God in the face of Jesus Christ" (2 Cor. 4:6).

We have no *adequate* knowledge of God. We do receive *true* knowledge with respect to God. But we know that the Son of God has come and given us understanding so that we may know him who is true; and we are in him who is true, in his Son Jesus Christ. "This is the true God and eternal life" (1 John 5:20).

Doubting the reality of the knowledge of God does not only affect theology, but also the church's faith. Here we need to say something about agnosticism. This is the philosophical postulate of the unknowability of reality to the extent that it eludes direct data capture of controllable experience. According to H. Spencer, the absolute does exist, but is completely unknowable to us. The onset of agnosticism can be detected in the philosophy of I. Kant, who does not deny the existence of a transcendent world, but teaches that the thing itself (das "Ding an sich") falls outside the human ability to know. Religion can be known, but God cannot be known. Positivism and neo-positivism also display agnostic traits, because according to these theories one must limit oneself to ascertaining and explaining phenomena. It is considered to be futile to attempt to go beyond this.

There are surprisingly many people who consider it a waste of time to contemplate the existence of God! This constitutes more practical than theoretical agnosticism. However, it borders on atheism and frequently leads to it. If it does not come to this, it is because man does indeed have the sense that God exists (see § 5.1).

Negative theology is something else again. It teaches—sometimes based on ideas of the church fathers that have been influenced by Neoplatonism—that we can say that God exists, but not what he is like (J. Scotus Erigena). According to mystics, the incomprehensibility of God can be significantly reduced through his knowability (cf. Auer, 1978, 101–6).

We confess that God is incomprehensible or unfathomable *as well as* that we know him (Belgic Confession of Faith, articles 1 and 2). His incomprehensibility does not exclude knowability. "He makes himself . . . known to us by his . . . Word . . . as far as is necessary for us to know in this life, to his glory and our salvation." For this reason our knowledge of him is only partial.

Among theologians who understand what knowledge of God based on Scripture means, Calvin holds an important place. Following in the footsteps of others, he pointed out that knowledge of God and knowledge of ourselves are interdependent and interrelated. Without knowledge of self there is no knowledge of God. But the reverse is also true: without knowledge of God there is no knowledge of self. Man never achieves a clear knowledge of himself unless he has first looked upon God's face. Being aware that there is a God does not necessarily imply knowing God. Neither does it imply knowing a great deal about God. God is actually not known in the absence of religion and piety. Knowledge of God involves respect and trust (cf. *Institutes*, 1.1, 2).

While scholastic theology tends to have a speculative character—according to Thomas Aquinas, sacred doctrine is more reflective than practical—Calvin's[3] emphasis on the knowledge of faith does not result in contemplation without practicality. According to him the main question is how God desires to approach us (*Institutes*, 1.10.2; 3.2.6). The key is the right knowledge of God. This also means that the right relationship with God is essential. These two are one and the same thing. Then the chief goal of human life becomes that we may know God who created us. The answer to the question as to what true and right knowledge of God is, is that he is known in such a way that he is given the honor that is due him (cf. Genevan Catechism, 1–7).

In this manner the essential element of the knowledge of God is clearly brought out. In theology—especially theology in the strictest sense of the word, thinking and speaking about God (*locus de Deo*) —the object is the glorification of God. "Theology's enquiry into God commences with praising him, is accompanied by the church singing his praise, and culminates in doxology" (Kraus, *Syst. Th.*, 280).

According to the Bible, to know God and to give him the honor that is due him, are one and the same thing. People express it with grateful joy and reverent wonder: this God is our God. They sing of it:

> For this God is our God for ever and ever:
> He will be our guide even unto death. (Ps. 48:14)

The Psalms, in which people who know God speak about him, are full of the praise of his name. Psalm 103 is a good example. The psalmists exhort the people to join in doxology:

> I will bless the LORD at all times:
> His praise shall continually be in my mouth.
> My soul shall make her boast in the LORD;
> The humble shall hear thereof, and be glad.
> O magnify the LORD with me,
> And let us exalt his name together. (Ps. 34:1–3)

3. More on this in J. van Genderen, *Geloofskennis en geloofsverwachting* (faith's knowledge and faith's anticipation), 1982, 7–37.

Songs of praise are also encountered in the books of Moses (Ex. 15; Deut. 32) and in the prophetic Scriptures (Isa. 12; Mic. 7:18–20; Dan. 2:19–23). Doxology is not strange to the New Testament either. Angels and people glorify God at the birth of Christ. In the apostolic epistles, references to God and his work invariably culminate in a doxology (Rom. 11:33–36; 1 Tim. 1:17; Jude 24–25), and in the Book of Revelation the songs of praise, thanksgiving, and adoration occupy an important place.

Those who know God are deeply aware that it is through grace that they may know him in Christ as their God and Father. This is expressed in the words, "Now, after that ye have known God, or rather are known of God" (Gal. 4:9), which indicate that it is a knowledge of being known. There is therefore no reason to be proud of our knowledge in faith or our theological acumen. There is nothing in us to be proud of, but we boast in God as we are encouraged to do: "But let him that glorieth glory in this, that he understandeth and knoweth me, that I am the LORD which exercise lovingkindness, judgment, and righteousness in the earth: for in these things I delight, saith the LORD" (Jer. 9:24; cf. 1 Cor. 1:30–31).

There is an increase in the knowledge of God, not only in the personal lives of believers—who may continually encounter God, view life and everything increasingly in God's light and anticipate future perfection—but also in the progression of history. One of Paul's doxologies pertains to "the revelation of the mystery, which was kept secret since the world began, but now is . . . made known to all nations for the obedience of faith" (Rom. 16:25–26). We may anticipate that "the earth shall be full of the knowledge of the LORD, as the waters cover the sea" (Isa. 11:9), and that the words already being fulfilled today will take on yet greater significance: "They shall all know me, from the least of them unto the greatest of them, saith the LORD: for I will forgive their iniquity, and I will remember their sin no more" (Jer. 31:34; cf. Heb. 8:11–12).

10.2. *Natural theology?*

1. *Rome*

We know God from his revelation in his Word and through faith. This we posit over against agnosticism. Rome, however, fights it in a different fashion.

Of fundamental significance is the doctrinal pronouncement made by the Vatican Council of 1870 that God, the beginning and end of all things, can be known with certainty by means of the natural light of human reasoning applied to creation. Those who deny this face excommunication (*DS*, 3004, 3026).

Although these pronouncements actually pertain to the knowability and not the provability of God, the latter is implied. It is therefore not surprising that the pope subsequently adds that God can be known with certainty and also can be proven to exist on the basis of visible causes and their effects. This is declared in the 1910 oath against the heresies of modernism (DS, 3538), but is subsequently replaced by a declaration of allegiance.

The background of this doctrine is "the twofold order of knowledge" adopted by the council of 1870. There is knowledge through reasoning and knowledge through faith. The former belongs to the natural order and the latter to the supernatural order. There are truths about God that are within reach of natural intelligence and there are mysteries that are hidden in God, which transcend created intelligence and which cannot be made known other than through revelation from God. With respect to natural and supernatural knowledge of God, reference is made to Romans 1:20 and 1 Corinthians 2:7–8 respectively (*DS*, 3004ff.).

In essence, this is the teaching of Thomas Aquinas, who viewed knowability of God also as provability. The "five ways" of Thomas became classical (cf. Wentsel, *Dogm.*, 3a:159). His reasoning is based on the validity of the law of causality.

The possibility of a natural knowledge of God and of various proofs for the existence of God rests on the "analogy of being" (*analogia entis*) of God and man. Through the analogy between God's existence on the one hand and the existence of creation on the other hand, man can ascend cognitively from relative existence to infinite existence, "which everyone understands to be God" (Thomas). This doctrine of the knowability of God is furthermore related to the Roman Catholic notion that original sin is not to be viewed as a radical depravity of human nature. Human intelligence has not been completely blinded toward God. The human will cannot be considered to be totally incapable of seeking God and goodness. Otherwise man could never be addressed concerning God, and he could never be exhorted to love God in any form whatsoever.[4]

One seeks in man's nature—with its intellectual and moral capacities—his receptivity and openness to a life by grace, i.e., the capacity for grace. "Grace presupposes nature and perfects it" (Thomas). Thus man progresses gradually from his natural state (Bavinck, *R.D.*, 2:110).

Rome does not deny that difficulties remain when one attempts to find God in this manner. God helps man by means of his revelation by which things not in themselves inaccessible to human reasoning can be known in the present situation of the human race with ease, with certainty, and unaffected by any error (DS, 3005). Nevertheless supernatural revelation is necessary for salvation, for in its absence there is only

4. See J. C. Groot, *Karl Barth en het theologische kenprobleem* (Karl Barth and the theological issue of knowability), 1946, 304.

partial knowledge of God, and with mere natural knowledge of God one lacks the perspective of salvation in Christ.

Since certain theologians attach little value to natural theology, Pope Pius XII warns in the encyclical *Humani Generis* (1950) against "novelties." It is not to be doubted that the human mind without the assistance of revelation and divine grace can demonstrate the existence of a personal God by means of proofs inferred from creation. Within Roman Catholicism there are also other representations of the relationship between nature and grace (cf. Wentsel, 1970) which are only partly consistent with *Humani Generis*, the conciliar pronouncements of 1870, and Thomas Aquinas's system, but we leave these aside and limit ourselves to official Roman Catholic teaching.

We cannot agree with this position of Rome.

a. This perspective is not indicated anywhere in Holy Scripture. Natural knowledge of God, in the absence of faith, does not exist. A supreme being that one would get to know in this way is not the living God of the Bible. Natural theology leads only to a philosophical concept of God.

b. The relationship that exists between God and man, whom he created, cannot be viewed as an analogy between God's existence and man's existence.

c. Knowledge of God by means of reason is inextricably intertwined with the anthropological optimism that permeates all Roman Catholic teaching. Man's natural capacities are overestimated and their consequences underestimated. This leads to a scenario in which the supernatural superstructure is supported by a natural infrastructure which has a side opening toward humanism.

2. *Calvin*

In the connection between "natural knowledge of God" and "natural theology" the term "natural" can have a double meaning in Roman Catholicism: from nature, out of creation, *and* with the assistance of human intelligence that is part of the created order.

Calvin had an entirely different view. Nevertheless, there are those who believe that Calvin also practiced natural theology, considering what he wrote in the first few chapters of the *Institutes*.[5] But is this correct?

5. See E. Brunner, *Natur und Gnade* (nature and grace), 1935². Another view was held by P. Barth, *Das Problem der natürlichen Theologie bei Calvin* (the issue of natural theology in the case of Calvin), 1935.

According to Calvin there is a certain awareness of the Godhead (*sensus divinitatis*). He says that "all men without exception perceive that there is a God and that he is their Creator. But they are condemned by their own testimony, because they have not honored him and have not consecrated their lives to the fulfillment of his will" (*Institutes*, 1.3.1). He also refers to a seed of religion (*semen religionis*), a constant conviction and very strong impression. However, in this way one does not acquire the true knowledge of God: "Although experience testifies that all have received a seed of religion, barely one in a hundred is found to treasure it in his heart; there is no one in which it ripens, let alone that it bears fruit in due time. It is Paul's view that this vague and erring view of the Godhead implies ignorance with respect to God" (1.4.1, 3). According to Calvin, religious awareness is "nothing else than a frightful source of idolatry and of all superstitions" (commentary on John 3:6).

Apart from man's creation after God's image, which implies a relationship with God, our religious awareness is also related to God's revelation in his works. God has revealed himself and daily discloses himself in the whole workmanship of the universe, that men cannot open their eyes without being compelled to see him (1.5.1). But human reason neither approaches, nor strives toward, nor even takes a straight aim at truth, to understand who the true God is or how he wishes to be toward us. Our keenness of mind is pure darkness as far as knowledge of God is concerned (2.2.18, 19). With nature as a guide, no one has ever reached the point of knowing God, according to Calvin. We need Scripture to come to God the Creator (1.6.1).

By way of summary we can say that as human being, man has a religious awareness (*sensus divinitatis*, *semen religionis*, sometimes *persuasio* or *impressio*) that was given to him and that he has retained. He is aware that God exists and that he must deal with him. Since God reveals himself in his works, man is continually reminded of him. There is no knowledge of God in the fullest sense of the word.[6] We cannot prove God's existence intellectually. As far as knowing and serving God are concerned, this Reformer does not expect anything from the capabilities that remain in man. Anything that we can come up with can only be judged negatively and not positively. This implies a cardinal difference with Roman Catholicism. One cannot appeal to Calvin for a natural theology!

3. *Subsequent developments*

Many Reformed theologians went beyond Calvin by teaching that there is an innate as well as an acquired knowledge of God. The former is common to all people and does not require the Bible and faith,

6. Calvin frequently emphasized this by using the word *notitia* instead of *cognitio*. Cf. Weber, *Foundations*, 1:217.

because "the book of nature" and the "book of conscience" provide all the necessary ingredients.

Under the influence of Melanchthon, orthodox Lutheran theologians definitely thought along these lines. Natural theology was treated in isolation. It was considered to be secondary to revealed theology, and yet it was nevertheless believed to constitute its foundation and precondition. In this sense the relationship between natural and revealed theology was reminiscent of that between the law and the gospel.

J. H. Alsted was a Reformed theologian who early on advocated natural theology (*Theologia naturalis*, 1615). According to him there were a number of natural dogmas (*dogmata*) such as: God exists and God must be loved above all else; one must give everyone his due; one should harm no one; and one must place the common good above one's personal interest. According to others, natural theology had more or less the same content.

Natural knowledge of God was defended especially over against Socinians, who taught that man on his own could not know anything about the path to eternal life. In polemics one correctly pointed out that, having been created in God's image, man is a religious being, and that even subsequent to the fall into sin God did not abandon him. But this was not all. Arnold (Arnoldus) held that God could build on what is already present in man by way of natural religion (cf. Schilder, *H.C.*, 1:91–98).

When the philosophy of Descartes (1596–1650), including an innate concept of God, gained ascendancy, Reformed theologians had to refine their natural theology. Some of them positioned themselves antithetically over against this philosophy and maintained that innate knowledge of God in their theological view differed from an innate concept of God in philosophy. Voetius foresaw that in this case one would be able to dispense with revelation.

The dogmatics of J. à Marck is representative of works from the school of Voetius. He also distinguishes between natural and supernatural or revealed theology. In nature one has the book of one's own heart and that of other creatures. In the former case one speaks of innate theology. Since other creatures point us to God as the primary Cause, there is a natural, acquired theology. By means of natural theology man is aware—if only dimly and imperfectly—of God's existence, his spiritual Being and attributes, the works of his creation and providence, God's law and man's own misery. This theology is not per se in conflict with revealed theology, just as a small amount of light does not contradict an abundance of light, but it is always mixed up with erroneous concepts and must therefore concede to revealed theology in the case of any conflict. Philosophy has been viewed as subservient to theology since antiquity.[7]

The above distinction reflects two truths that we encounter in early theological treatises of this type. There are truths that belong to the realm of natural theology and there are supernatural truths: *articuli mixti* and *articuli puri*. The former—which can be known to some extent outside special revelation—include creation, providence, and immortality; the latter include the Trinity, the incarnation, and atonement.

7. J. à Marck, *Het merch der christene Got-geleertheit* (the hallmark of Christian theology), 1741[4], 5–11.

A comparison with Calvin reveals that thus a considerable shift took place, in that an awareness or impression that God exists was interpreted as innate knowledge of God. Furthermore, human speculation about God was given a name, namely acquired knowledge of God. Practitioners of early Reformed dogmatics may have believed that in this way they could more effectively combat atheism, but this requires more than a mere concept of God. Furthermore, there is a striking resemblance to the Roman Catholic concept such as in the bifurcation of the content of faith into two kinds of truth. Views with respect to man and his capabilities differ from those of Rome, but here also too much weight is given to natural knowledge of God including the role of the law, as it is believed that in this way man can discern his sins and culpability in the light of God's righteousness (according to Brakel, *R.S.*, 1:17). It seems as though man in his natural knowledge of God stands waiting in the outer court of the temple for the gate to be opened.

While some theologians thus assigned some limited scope to natural theology, there were others who saw more potential in it. One of them was H. A. Roëll, who envisioned a synthesis of theology and (Cartesian) philosophy. In his inaugural lecture on rational religion (1686) he posited that we have a concept of a Being that is sovereign and perfect. To this Being we owe reason, which is the foundation of natural or rational religion. According to Roëll, reason is infallible. What it teaches and dictates is like a pronouncement of God. Its innate ideas and clear concepts are as conclusive as Holy Scripture, which is a divine microscope that enables us to see what we cannot attain through reasoning. Reason must judge whether or not something has been revealed and what has been revealed. In this sense faith in the mysteries of Christianity rests on the judgment of reason and must be rational.[8]

This view differs substantially from that of J. à Marck, and it is no surprise that the views of Roëll and his sympathizers were not readily accepted. Here reason does not act as *ancilla*, but as *domina*, not as servant but as master. Natural theology became another name for rational theology and became critical of revelation. Rationalism increasingly gained the upper hand.

Natural theology gained momentum in the eighteenth century, because it pretended to meet the requirement—imposed by the Enlightenment—that everything be based on reason. Everything that was natural and rational had to be universally recognized. Furthermore, the term "natural" now had an attraction that it did not have at the time of the Reformation. Everything that was natural was considered to be

8. Cf. J. van Genderen, *Herman Witsius*, 1953, 182–90. Regarding Roëll see J. van Sluis, *Herman Alexander Roëll*, 1988.

good! Man's natural capacities were not questioned. This is how the two centuries following the Reformation witnessed an anthropological shift in thinking. Kant also, with his support for natural theology and rejection of biblical theology, fit in this climate of Enlightenment. It was thought that biblical theologians appealed to unproven authority, while rational theologians treated the Bible and the church's faith with skepticism.[9] Bavinck understood it well: "Natural theology became the real, the scientific and demonstrable theology by which revealed theology was increasingly marginalized and driven from the field" (*R.D.*, 2:78).

4. Canons of Dort

The history of natural theology is quite informative. When Barth objected to collaboration between natural and revealed theology and a bias in favor of natural theology, he did not warn against an imaginary danger. But his criticism of article 2 of the Belgic Confession of Faith was misplaced (see § 5.1).

There is another passage in our confessional documents that could be viewed as debatable. The Canons of Dort refer to the light of nature and some knowledge of God. Some light of nature did remain following the fall into sin; in this way man retained some knowledge of God, of natural things, and of the distinction between what is acceptable and what is not, and also gave proof of some attempt to practice virtue and—ostensibly—to observe good morals.

The question arises whether this knowledge of God and the distinction between what is acceptable and unacceptable reflects a natural knowledge of God and natural morality. And is the light of nature a biblical concept? The Canons of Dort, however, do not cross this boundary. The context proves that this knowledge of God is not a foundation on which to build. At any rate, "some knowledge" is less than unqualified knowledge. What cannot be inferred from translations is clear from the Latin of the original text. There a distinction is made between *cognitio* and *notitiae*, and knowledge is not enhanced by the use of the plural (*notitiae*). It might be considered to read, some notions of God, or, some sense of God. In this way we get closer to Calvin, whose theology appears to be reflected in this chapter of the Canons of Dort. The first few chapters of the *Institutes* are followed by the sixth chapter whose title is: Scripture is needed as Guide and Teacher for anyone who would come to God the Creator. In chapter VI of the second volume it says that we must embrace the preaching of the cross humbly if we desire to return to God our Author and Maker from whom we have been estranged. Thus we read in the Canons of Dort, 3–4.4–6, that man does not use the light of nature in the right way and even abuses it. Whatever it means, it offers no scope for grace. What it cannot achieve and what the law cannot achieve, God does through the power of the Holy Spirit and through the Word of the ministry of atonement. Over against man's own insight and striving there is the

9. A good summary of Kant's point of view can be found in A. D. R. Polman, *Gereformeerd katholieke dogmatiek* (Reformed Catholic dogmatics), 1969, 1:12–19.

work of the Holy Spirit. We need the light of the Word to come to know God, for every other light is inadequate.

10.3. *The problem with proofs*

The foregoing suggests that we can be brief with respect to proofs for the existence of God, which have received a great deal of attention over the centuries.[10] They are of a philosophical nature and could be left to the philosophy of religion. Yet they were not infrequently covered in dogmatics (cf. Bavinck, *R.D.*, 2:77–91).

Proofs for the existence of God (*argumenta Dei*) were once held in high esteem and even played a major role at the time of the Enlightenment, but subsequently fell into discredit as a result of fierce criticism by I. Kant. There was only a single "proof" that met with the latter's approval. However, there is again some talk of rehabilitation. Could it be a renaissance? At any rate, attempts are being made to reconstruct the proofs with the help of modern logic (cf. De Vos, 1971, 3ff.; Hubbeling, 1976, 57–79, 125ff.).

Classical formulations can be found in the writings of Thomas Aquinas, but in addition to his "five ways" there are other arguments that lead to the conclusion that God does exist, such as the ontological proof of God by Anselm, the moral proof of Kant, and the historical proof, or the proof of the consensus of peoples, that already turns up in the works of Cicero and Seneca and that resurfaces in early Reformed theology.

In gauging the strength of these proofs, without going into details, we can confirm that as a rule it is concluded, on the basis of observable reality, that there exists a Being that must be its Source and Goal and which everyone refers to as God (Thomas).

From a theological point of view, the most important presupposition of each proof of God's existence is that man, on his own, through sheer observation and contemplation, can know God. The proofs represent an aspect of natural theology, whose object it is to reflect on the natural knowledge of God. Here natural theology is contrasted with supernatural or revealed theology. It is hereby assumed that man, in his natural capacity, can come to know God without anything having to happen to him or requiring change in him.

We offer the following considerations:

10. For a broad overview of the literature see *TRE* 8:776–84.

1. Proponents of a natural theology are generally positive about the proofs. However, if one rejects natural theology on the basis of principle, one cannot accept the proofs of God's existence as being conclusive, despite the fact that they are employed with the good intention of combating atheism.

2. In addition, we are dealing with the provability of the existence of the First Mover, the First Cause, the Necessary Being, the Highest Good, the Highest Goal, or the Supreme Being. In essence, this is an extremely abstract concept of God. In his *Pensées*, Pascal (1623–62) pointed to the contrast between God as discussed in philosophy and the God of the Bible, the God and Father of Jesus Christ. The God of Abraham, the God of Isaac, the God of Jacob, the God of Christians, is a God of love and consolation. He is a God who fulfills the souls and hearts of his people. He lets them feel inwardly their misery and his infinite mercy (*fragm.* 556). In another fragment Pascal said: "All those who pretended to know God and prove his existence outside Jesus Christ, only offered powerless proofs" (547).

3. In the light of God's revelation, all proofs are superfluous. He proves himself through his words and deeds.

4. Christian thinkers who leave room for proofs of God's existence seek to convince others of this. But the question arises whether faith is really made more attractive through proofs of God's existence that immediately attract serious criticism from philosophy and theology, since they are not proofs in the strictest sense of the word and it is a matter of faith that is not subject to proof.

But do we then have to consider all human efforts to reach God through reason to be in vain? Bavinck, who did not wish to underestimate or scorn these proofs, referred to them as weak proofs but strong testimonies. Others do not consider them to be proofs at all, but mere pointers.

Our human intelligence is unable to prove that God exists. But it definitely cannot be proven that God does not exist. Atheism is an entirely unprovable theory. It is never certain of itself. To those who contemplate the deeper questions of life, there is a great deal more in favor of faith than opposed to it. The so-called proofs have value to the extent that they point out that as human beings we cannot ignore God. Therefore, we do not limit ourselves to the phenomena that we observe, but focus our minds on God to whom the world owes its formation and existence. This is how it can be explained that the arguments for the existence of God, which in themselves are inadequate and problematic, yet make a favorable impression.

§ 11. The revealed names of God

11.1. ***The meaning of God's names***
11.2. ***The Lord is our God***
11.3. ***God as Father***

11.1. *The meaning of God's names*

What does a name indicate? In the Ancient Near East a name did not only serve to distinguish one person from another. A person frequently acted according to his name. A well-known example is Nabal. He was what his name implied: "For as his name is, so is he; Nabal is his name, and folly is with him" (1 Sam. 25:25). Already in the book of Genesis we read of the giving of names with an explicit purpose, such as Eve, Cain, Noah, and Joseph. Names were sometimes changed for a specific reason. Abram became Abraham, Jacob became Israel, and Simon was called Peter. The name Jesus is the supreme example of a name that is much more than a designation. Jesus is what his name says: Savior.

God has given himself names to reveal himself. He is what his name says of him and he is that preeminently. Therefore his name represents him.

He makes his name known to us so that we can call upon him in this way and not in a way invented by people.

When God reveals himself to us in his names, these names are adapted to our understanding. When he calls himself our King and our Father, he speaks to us in a language that we can understand. Calvin, who refers to this as accommodation (*accommodatio*) to our capacity to understand,[11] says: "Only let us remember that [God] condescends to us in order to raise us up to himself" (commentary on Gen. 35:7).

In this context we need to realize that the words we employ on the basis of God's revelation have a content that does not coincide with the content of our human concepts. When we say that God is good, this is not at all the same thing as when we call a human being or

11. Cf. J. de Jong, *Accommodatio Dei*, 1990, 35–43. The views of K. Schilder, who followed in Calvin's footsteps, were summarized in this study (275–82).

another creature good. Theology has adopted a single term to indicate both correspondence *and* differences, namely *analogy*.

In medieval scholasticism, a distinction was made between different kinds of analogy. Especially important was *analogia proportionis*, which subsequently became known as *analogia entis*. This "analogy of being" ascribes being to both God and man: God is and man is. There is a certain analogy between God's Being and that of man, and this enables man to ascend in his thinking from finite being, associated with this world, to God's infinite Being.

The theologian who opposed this *analogia entis* the most strenuously was Barth. He even considered it as an invention of the antichrist. He was correct in the sense that we should not believe that God's Being is analogous to our being. He is also correct in wanting to take only revelation as his starting point. We can agree with Barth that we cannot claim that our words relate to God. But he has every right to claim us and all of our words, and to claim that he is the first, last, and proper object (*Gegenstand*) of our words. He places words at our disposal by the grace of his revelation. The important thing is that we use them in line with their purpose (*C.D.*, 2.1.228–31). So God gives words their actual meaning!

There is analogy in the use of words. God speaks, but he expresses himself in our own language. In this way he ensures that we understand the words of his revelation.

The meaning of God's righteousness cannot be inferred from the concept of justice that applies to this world. When it comes to God's justice or righteousness, we must ask what the Word of God says about them. Then it turns out that God's justice far exceeds our imagination (see § 13.9).

These considerations are not intended to give the impression that while God tells us his name, he seeks to keep himself hidden from us. This is not implied by Exodus 3:14, as we shall see below. Revelation is revelation and not concealment.

We can agree with Vondel (Rey van Engelen = row of angels, speaking in *Lucifer*):

> Thou art known as thou art,
> The splendour and conduit of eternities;
> To whom was this light revealed?
> To whom did the splendour of splendours appear?
> This view is yet a higher bliss
> Than we derive from your grace;
> Which exceeds the limit, and measure
> Of our ability.

This is preceded by lines such as:

> All knowledge of angels
> And speech, weak and incapable,
> Is but sacrilege, and desecration.

Ignoring the context, such words could be interpreted to mean that all knowledge of God, even that of the holy angels, is but desecration. This would be unbiblical. But they are intended as a testimony to the minuteness of creatures over against the greatness of God. The poet therefore also says: "Who can call Thee by Thy name?"[12]

In summary we can say that God reveals himself in his names, that he adapts himself to our understanding, and that he employs words that correspond with our words and yet differ in terms of content.

However difficult it may seem, we shall yet have to speak about God's names in a certain order. In line with earlier dogmatics we can make a distinction between:

- *proper names*, such as God and LORD
- *personal names*, Father, Son, and Holy Spirit
- *characteristic names or names of attributes*, such as the Almighty, the Holy One

God gave himself various names. There are those who think that there actually is no single name that really suits him (Pseudo-Dionysius Areopagita in *De divinis nominibus*). God would be the ineffable one: panonymous and anonymous. This is a Neoplatonic and not a biblical notion!

It has also been taught that all names of God are merely subjective concepts of ours, which do not correspond to reality (Occam), or subjective experiences of our religious consciousness (Schleiermacher). But neither is there a biblical basis for this interpretation of the diversity of God's names.

It is true that we cannot form a concept of the infinite fullness of God's Being unless it reveals itself to us in a continually changing relationship and perspective. The multiplicity of names serves to give us an impression of the all-transcending greatness of God (cf. Bavinck,

12. *De werken van Vondel* (the works of Vondel), 1931, 5:630. Cf. K. Schilder, *Wat is de hemel?* (what is heaven?), 1954^2, 121–24.

R.D., 2:126ff.). In the diversity of his names, God reveals his glory in a multifaceted manner.

On the basis of the revelation that comes to us in his names and deeds, we call God a person. He makes himself known to us, because he wants there to be a personal relationship between him and us. He says in his Word: I; we respond in faith and prayer with: Thou.

We agree with Berkhof that it would represent a denial of his Godhead if we were to refer to him in impersonal terms, such as: Being itself, the ground of Being, or the power of Being (P. Tillich and others). Although God is infinitely more than what we know of human personality, we may ascribe to him "whatever in the world of persons is more than the world of things: self-consciousness, freedom, the ability to enter into fellowship with others, in brief: being a subject" (Berkhof, *C.F.*, 139).

A traditional classification of God's names can be found in the work of Bavinck. After the proper names come the names of God's attributes and then the personal names, the latter under the heading: The Holy Trinity. But here and there in the sections that are devoted to the attributes of God, their biblical-theological content risks being crowded out by metaphysics, which renders the doctrine of God too abstract. Although Bavinck was on his guard against this danger, he did not altogether escape it.

Barth, however, started out with the doctrine of the Trinity, and Weber by and large followed in his footsteps.

One of the reasons why Bavinck, following the discussion of the proper names, first addresses God's attributes is the fact that Scripture teaches us the essence of God prior to his Trinitarian nature, for God's Trinity is not clearly revealed prior to the New Testament (*R.D.*, 2:150). On the other hand, according to him it is also true that love and all other attributes of God really take on life and reality through the Trinity. "Apart from it, they are mere names, sounds, empty terms. As attributes of the triune God they come alive both to our mind and to our heart" (*R.D.*, 2:331). This is precisely a good reason for not waiting with the doctrine of the Trinity until after a general discussion of God's nature. Does the Christian church not confess simultaneously that God is one and that he consists in three persons?

In contemplating the various names of God, it is a good idea to begin by asking who God is according to his revelation. He is the LORD (§ 11.2). He is the Father of our Lord Jesus Christ (§ 11.3). He is the triune God (§ 12). Subsequently we consider how he has revealed himself in his divine glory in a multifaceted manner (§ 13).

11.2. *The* LORD *is our God*

In the Old Testament *the* name of God is Yahweh, also referred to as the *tetragrammaton*, because in Hebrew this name comprises four consonants: YHWH. Early translations sometimes substitute Jehovah, but this deserves no emulation. In a number of well-known translations it is rendered as LORD.

The Septuagint led the way by not leaving YHWH untranslated, but rendering it as Kurios (Lord), although this word was also used for the name *Adonai*. At the Synod of Dort (1618–19), in preparation for a new translation—known to us as the *Statenvertaling* = Authorized Version—it was pointed out that there was no word in the Dutch language to express the power of the name YHWH. Yet they had no desire to leave this name untranslated. Jews came to speak of the name. In the period subsequent to the exile they came to interpret the prohibition to blaspheme the name of YHWH (cf. Lev. 24:16) as a prohibition to pronounce this name. They resorted to paraphrases and, when reading the sacred books, it became customary for them to say *Adonai*.

The name YHWH is a proper name, which was therefore never combined with a possessive pronoun, as for example the word "God." God revealed himself with the words: "I am the LORD thy God, which have brought thee out of the land of Egypt, out of the house of bondage" (Ex. 20:2). The people of Israel confessed: "The LORD our God is one LORD" (Deut. 6:4). Psalm 100 exhorts everyone to acknowledge "that the LORD . . . is God."

Scholars disagree with respect to the derivation of the name YHWH. In reaction to attempts to seek its origin among the Kenites or elsewhere, it was correctly pointed out that beyond Israel no traces have been found of the worship of God by this name.

The name YHWH has to do with the root *hayah*: to be. Some have thought in terms of a causative explanation: he who causes to be, he who causes to live, but there is more support for the rendition: he who is or he who will be. This agrees with the words of Exodus 3:14, which are of fundamental significance: "I am that I am" (*eyeh asher eyeh*). However, etymology does not tell the entire story. The ideas of theologians go in various directions, but one idea does not always preclude the other (cf. Wentsel, *Dogm.*, 3a:266ff.).

1. An ancient interpretation, already encountered in the Septuagint, is: he is the Being One. Although this is far more abstract than the original text, it has not infrequently been accepted. Augustine interpreted it to mean that God is Being itself, immutable Being.

J. à Marck employs: the Be-er (*Weesenaar*). Gispen says: he is who he is, both for the fathers and for Israel, the Being One "from generation to generation," the Constant One.[13] This interpretation of the name is also found in Roman Catholic theology, but is increasingly being abandoned by both Protestants and Roman Catholics.

2. In a second interpretation, the emphasis is placed on the context in which these words occur. It is believed that God did not want to respond to the question as to what his name was and did not want to divulge the secret of his nature. I am who I am. It is simultaneously revelation and concealment. God remains hidden in his revelation (Barth, *C.D.*, 1.1.365, 370). References to Scripture passages such as Genesis 32:30 and Judges 13:18, encountered in Barth's work, do not prove this, however. Although in Exodus 3 Moses did not receive the response that he might have expected, it was indeed a revelation of YHWH to both him and his people. In this passage we also hear how sovereign God is in his acting. This is a recurrent theme in history.

3. To be able to understand the words of Exodus 3:14 and thereby the name, it is necessary to compare it with similar sentences. For example, subsequently God says to Moses: "I will be gracious to whom I will be gracious" (Ex. 33:19). This formulation can express indefiniteness but also intensity, as is the case here. In Exodus 3 there is a connection between verses 12 and 14. Here the Being of YHWH means: to be there, to be present, not to be present in silence, but to be actively involved. He sympathizes with the lot of his people (Ex. 3:7–9). One could translate as follows: I am, who I am, but also: I shall be with you, as I shall be with you. The words apply to both the present and the future.

This response has to suffice for Moses and the people of Israel. The name is an "open name," accompanied by promises. The glory of the name of the Lord shall be demonstrated more and more by his words and actions. The important thing is to know and acknowledge him who is as his name proclaims. The key is to entrust oneself believingly to him who thus reveals himself.

4. There is an element of truth in the view, especially found in Reformed theology, that the name is an indication of God's covenant faithfulness.[14] Is the Lord not the God who wants to be in the midst of his people and wants them to experience his holy presence and

13. W. H. Gispen, *Exodus*, 1932, 1:54.

14. Cf. L. Berkhof, *Reformed Dogmatics*, 1932, 1:31.

redeeming power? This is suggested by the burning bush (Ex. 3:1–12). Through his name the LORD binds himself to his people. He fulfills the promises that he has made. He is the God of Abraham, the God of Isaac, and the God of Jacob. This is his name for ever and this is how he wants to be invoked from generation to generation (cf. Ex. 3:15).

Of great significance is the fact that the LORD subsequently proclaims his own name (Ex. 34:6–7). This proclamation reads as follows: "The LORD, The LORD God, merciful and gracious, longsuffering, and abundant in goodness and truth, keeping mercy for thousands, forgiving iniquity and transgression and sin, and that will by no means clear the guilty; visiting the iniquity of the father upon the children, and upon the children's children, unto the third and to the fourth generation."

Here we are struck by the double aspect, which also occurs in Exodus 20:5–6 and in many other places in the Old Testament—especially in connection with the covenant relationship: he shows mercy to thousands, but he definitely does not consider the guilty to be innocent.

The prophecies of Ezekiel say repeatedly: "And thou shalt know that I am the LORD." This has two aspects: you can depend on me and you have to deal with me. Does it not mean salvation for those who await him, but disaster for those who do not fear him? (cf. Ezek. 36:38; 6:13–14 and other places).

From Exodus 6:2 it need not be deduced that the name YHWH is a completely new name. Yet we may read into it that God did not make known the deeper sense of this name prior to revealing it to Moses. Actually the entire history of revelation is required to fully understand the name.

The New Testament reveals the name of him who seeks to be with his people in the appearance and work of Christ, as well as in the outpouring and continuing work of the Holy Spirit, fulfilling the promises of the covenant in the church, the temple of the living God (2 Cor. 6:16–18).

The name also appears in the final book of the Bible: he is, he was, and he is to come (Rev. 1:4). From a linguistic point of view, this is a proper name without being grammatically declined.

The name of Jesus Christ is the fulfillment, confirmation, and continuation of this name. The name was manifested in him (cf. Miskotte, 1941, 43ff.). The name of the LORD is written out in full in the revelation of God in Christ.

There are other names of God in the Old Testament that accompany *the* name, but can only be understood in the light of that name. It often says: *Elohim*. This is God's most common name. But it should not be inferred from this that Yahweh is an epithet for this name.

Considered in isolation, neither Elohim nor El clearly answers the question as to who God is, because these words could be used for various national gods. But when Yahweh is called El or Elohim, the former name fills the other term with its truth and light. The name Yahweh determines the content of the name Elohim.[15]

Names such as *El*, *Elohim*, and *Eloah* do not say much on their own. In the Semitic world *El* is a general word for a power that is worshiped as a deity. Perhaps its root meaning is: the Strong One. *Eloah* is a poetic form. *Elohim* expresses the fullness of the divine power.

The name *Adonai* says that God is the Sovereign of all and everything. Furthermore, the name *Yahweh Sabaoth* occurs with striking frequency. God is the LORD of Hosts. Does this name indicate that he is the God of battle or the God of the angels? It means at any rate that he is a God of great power. A translation of this name that we encounter in the Septuagint and in the New Testament is the Almighty. It refers in the first place to the manifestation of the power of the LORD in the history of his people, but this name also implies that all earthly and supernatural powers are subject to him.

God is called the Most High (*Elyon*) to indicate his magnificence and majesty (cf. Gen. 14:18–22). The name *Shaddai*, which occurs frequently in Job, is more difficult to explain. In Genesis 17:1 this name probably means Mighty Protector. It is frequently translated as the Almighty.

In summary we can say that many names of God speak of his might, majesty, and dominion. Returning to the first name, we may add that Yahweh, the God who is with his people and who has joined himself to his people so graciously, is the God who manifests this might, majesty, and dominion.

11.3. *God as Father*

Although the name LORD predominates in the Old Testament and also occurs regularly in the New Testament—usually translated as

15. Cf. H. Rosin, *The Lord Is God*, 1955; K. H. Miskotte, *Als de goden zwijgen* (when the gods keep silence), 1956, 103.

Lord—the actual New Testament name of God is Father. There it is not his only name, nor an entirely new name.

The background of the biblical use of the name Father is definitely not to be sought in the idea of the Godhead as father of both human beings and gods, which we encounter in the writings of Homer, among others, or in the ancient Eastern idea that the relationship between the Godhead and the king is that between a father and a son.

In Israeli tradition nothing points to a natural solidarity between God and his people or between God and the king. God is the Father of his people Israel, for in sovereign freedom he has chosen Israel to be his people. In the Song of Moses (Deut. 32:6) it is said: "Is not he thy father that has bought thee? hath he not made thee, and established thee?" Very significant is the prayer: "But now, O LORD, thou art our father; we are the clay and thou our potter; and we all are the work of thy hand" (Isa. 64:8). In Jeremiah 31:9 it says: "I am a father to Israel." This points to a covenant relationship. The LORD promises that he will be a father to the theocratic king (2 Sam. 7:14). This means that he will grant him his favor.

In a number of places, figurative language is used to explain who God is as Father. As a Father he shows compassion on all those who fear him (Ps. 103:13).

We are inclined to think of God's Fatherhood in terms of his love or loving care. Although the idea that he is a caring and loving Father to his people is present in the Old Testament (see in addition to Ps. 103:13 also Ps. 68:6), this name of God reflects primarily that he has authority over those who belong to him. Being his people implies obligations: "If then I be a father, where is mine honour?" (Mal. 1:6).

The God of Abraham, Isaac, and Jacob is the Father of the Lord Jesus Christ. Christ reveals his name to the people whom God has given to him (John 17:6). The name Father now becomes the common name of God (Bavinck, *R.D.*, 2:147ff.). This name is disclosed in all of its riches in the revelation of God as the Father of our Lord Jesus Christ. "Call him thy Father, the crown of his glorious names" (as in the Dutch version of the hymn "Praise to the Lord, the Almighty" by Joachim Neander, 1680, adapted from Pss. 103 and 150).

Jews also referred to God as Father in the time of the New Testament and subsequently as well: Our Father, Our King, or Our Father in Heaven. Nevertheless God was to them primarily the holy and mighty God in heaven (cf. *TDNT*, 5:978–82).

According to Jeremias, the very personal address "my Father" did not occur in Jewish prayers of those days; according to others it did, albeit rarely, which confirms that the word was given a new meaning by Jesus.

When believers call God "Abba," they speak intimately, emboldened by the work of the Lord Jesus as Mediator and led by the Spirit of Christ, who is "the Spirit of adoption" (Rom. 8:15; Gal. 4:6). Jesus put the name "Father" and the prayer "Our

Father who art in heaven" into the mouths of his people (Luke 11:2; Matt. 6:9). In a sphere of familiar interaction the Aramaic word "Abba" was used by small children and older children as well[16] and thus Jesus spoke with his Father (Mark 14:36).

Believers have learned from the Lord Jesus Christ to call God their Father, although they need to keep in mind continually that their relationship with their heavenly Father cannot be equated with the unique relationship between their Lord and his Father. He referred to God as his own Father (John 5:18), and the Jews inferred from this that he identified himself with God. He revealed both inequality and unity by his words: "I ascend unto my Father, and your Father; and to my God, and your God" (John 20:17).

Also in the New Testament the name Father continues to indicate that God has power and authority, but in addition implies especially love and communion, guidance and care. He is our Father in heaven, whose heavenly majesty must not be interpreted in earthly terms. At the same time, we may approach him with "that childlike reverence and trust toward God . . . [who] has become our Father through Christ" (Heidelberg Catechism, Lord's Day 46). Familiarity does not diminish the need for reverence for God and vice versa.

The Father is "the God and Father of our Lord Jesus Christ," whose name is to be blessed and praised (Eph. 1:3). All salvation may be expected from him, and we must direct our lives toward Him. In Christ he is the Father of his children, who cares for them and "give[s] good things to them" (Matt. 7:11), "who hath blessed [them] with all spiritual blessings" and through whom they "have access by one Spirit" (Eph. 1:3; 2:18). John wrote: "Behold what manner of love the Father hath bestowed upon us, that we should be called the sons of God [and so we are]" (1 John 3:1).

Jesus said that "the Father loves the Son, and hath given all things into his hand (John 3:35). This is God's original Fatherhood, which cannot be compared to anything else. The relationship between the Father and the Son is further addressed in connection with the Trinity (see § 12).

We may not start out with what a human father can be to us and then ascribe that to God as our heavenly Father, as though he would be similar in a divine manner: infinitely good, infinitely loving, infinitely

16. J. Jeremias, *New Testament Theology*, trans. John Bowden (London: SCM Press, 1971), 1:61–68.

wise. Then we form a God in our own human image, whereby bitter experiences could well result in displacing this ideal father image. God is *the* Father and not *a* Father. Faith in God the Father is therefore not dependent on our own concepts and images with respect to fatherhood.

We have explained it this way also in light of certain recent views with respect to God. There are feminists who have trouble with the traditionally "male" image of God as Father and who believe they are able to identify feminine and motherly attributes of God.[17]

In Scripture we encounter the comparison between God and a mother who comforts (Isa. 49:15), but nowhere do we find a statement regarding God as mother equivalent to the Bible passages about God as Father. The image of God is not a mirror image of relationships in human society, which are subject to all kinds of change. Even though patriarchy is a thing of the past and fathers no longer occupy a dominant position in their families, this name of God retains validity (cf. Pannenberg, 1988, 1:286), because "Father" is a term from God's revelation that refers to election, the covenant, and the love of God that go out to us through Jesus Christ, his only begotten Son.

Faith in God the Father is continually being obfuscated and eroded. This can give rise to the humanized image of God that we know from the theology of the Enlightenment. God is projected as the good and loving Father of all people and benevolent Providence. The proponents of this view see no necessity for reconciliation of sinners with God, because it is thought that God will treat people with generous benevolence despite their imperfections. The ideas of the Enlightenment continued to affect thinking throughout the nineteenth and twentieth centuries.[18]

The notion is widespread that faith in God the Father implies that he is the Father of all people and that everyone can therefore count on his fatherly care and protection. "We believe and confess God's Fatherhood, Christ's Leadership and the Brotherhood of all people."[19] But there is no support for this idea in the Bible, not even in the words, "Have we not all one Father?" (Mal. 2:10)—for in light of the context we must here think of the covenant of God with his people—nor in Matthew 5:45 (cf. *TDNT*, 5:990ff.).

Stoics taught a universal fatherhood of the Godhead and a brotherhood of all people. But this is an ethical pantheism, which is far removed from the teaching of Scripture.

According to the Bible, God is not just the Father of all people. Only through and in Christ do we come to know him as a conciliate God and a loving Father and to

17. See among others M. Daly, *Beyond God the Father*, 1973; R. R. Ruether, "De vrouwelijke natuur van God" (God's feminine nature), *Concilium* (1981–83): 64–70; C. J. M. Halkes, "Kritische vragen bij het vader-beeld van God" (critical questions concerning the father image of God), in M. H. Bolkestein and H. J. Bolkestein-van Bindsbergen (ed.), *Vrouw zijn in het licht van het evangelie* (being a woman in the light of the gospel), 1982, 148–70; E. Moltmann-Wendel, *Das Land, wo Milch und Honig fliesst* (the land flowing with milk and honey), 1985.

18. Cf. G. Aulén, *Het christelijk godsbeeld* (the Christian concept of God), 1929, 282–95.

19. Cf. A. de Wilde, *Over het Apostolicum* (concerning the Apostles' Creed), 1950, 47.

confess "that the eternal Father of our Lord Jesus Christ . . . is for the sake of Christ his Son my God and my Father" (Heidelberg Catechism, Lord's Day 9).

§ 12. The Trinity

12.1. *The revelation of the triune God in Holy Scripture*

The one name of God unfolds in the Word of God in three names: Father, Son, and Holy Spirit. The church confesses that God has revealed himself in his Word in such a way that these three distinct persons are the one, true, and eternal God (Heidelberg Catechism, Lord's Day 8).

This is the fundamental answer to the question as to who he is whose name we confess when we say: I believe in God. Up to this point, whenever God was discussed in doctrine or dogmatics, the focus was on him, who is the triune God.

In the Old Testament the unity of God is paramount. It is part of God being God that he is the one and only God. "If God is not one, there is no God" (Tertullian).

Yet one cannot say that the doctrine of the triunity of God has no foundation in the Old Testament, as is claimed by both Muslims and Jews. It does lay the groundwork for the trinitarian revelation of God.

The Belgic Confession of Faith points to expressions such as: "Let Us make man" (Gen. 1:26–27; cf. Gen. 3:22). But would this plurality really indicate that God is more than one person? It is not improper to follow Barth in thinking of a "communion in terms of mind and action within God's being" (*C.D.*, 3.1.291–93) or A. van Selms in postulating an exchange of thoughts within the one Being of God, which offers scope for what would subsequently become the doctrine of the Trinity.[20] But it could also mean that God takes counsel with himself and addresses himself.[21]

20. A. van Selms, "Theologie van de filoloog" (theology of the philologist), in *Kerk en theologie* (church and theology), 1959, 129–38.
21. Cf. C. Westermann, *Genesis*, 1974, 1:199–201.

There is more. Proverbs 8:22–31 speaks of God's wisdom in a striking manner. It is represented as a person. Judging by the use of the word "grieve," there is in the prophecies of Isaiah a depiction of the Spirit of the LORD, who is called Holy (Isa. 63:10). He is distinguished from him and yet one with him. The Angel of the Lord or the angel of his presence (Isa. 63:9) is a special manifestation or revelation of God (cf. § 5.2). In Isaiah 9:6 the Messiah is called God: the Mighty God. In the light of the New Testament (Luke 4:18–21), Isaiah 61:1 is also an important verse. Then we read the Old Testament in the perspective of the progression of the revelation and the fulfillment of the prophecies in the new dispensation. "What is latent in the Old Testament is clearly brought out in the New Testament" (Wentsel, *Dogm.*, 3a:307), or as the Belgic Confession of Faith puts it in article 9: "What appears to us somewhat obscure in the Old Testament is very plain in the New Testament."

One can say with Bavinck that the whole New Testament is Trinitarian (*R.D.*, 2:270). The New Testament revelation is in this regard richer and fuller than the revelation of God in the Old Testament. This is directly related to the redemption events of the incarnation of the Word and the outpouring of the Holy Spirit.

In the testimony of the New Testament, one can distinguish four forms. There are a number of passages with Trinitarian formulations (e.g., Matt. 28:19 and 2 Cor. 13:14). Other passages are referred to as triadic in nature (e.g., Eph. 4:4–6 and 1 Peter 1:2). A third type of passage consists of verses in which the three persons are mentioned together, but without a Trinitarian or triadic structure within the text itself (e.g., Mark 1:9–11 and Gal. 4:4–6). Finally, there are Scripture passages in which the relationship among the persons clearly comes to the fore (e.g., John 14:26; 15:26; 16:15). See in this connection Guthrie, *N.T. Theol.*, 112ff.

Those who remember the *loci classici* from earlier dogmatics will miss 1 John 5:7. But the most important manuscripts omit the words that are crucial in this context: "the Father, the Word and the Holy Spirit—and these three are one." The most important argument in support of the genuineness of this text—which can be found in the commentary of S. Greijdanus—is that without these words there is a gap in the train of thought. Admitting that this "Comma Johanneum" fits well into this context does not necessarily imply that it is vital. We should not weaken the Scripture proof that is essential for dogmatics by appealing to a text that in all probability was not part of the original epistle of John.

Many believe that Matthew 28:19 should also be left out. This text (according to Berkhof, *C.F.*, 348) would be "evidently the product of a later reflection." From the point of view of text criticism these words are very solid. Do they constitute an isolated reference in this gospel as is sometimes suggested? One can at least see a connection with Matthew 11:27. Furthermore, following his resurrection Jesus was in a position to teach the apostles a great deal (cf. Acts 1:3). Criticism of the Trinitarian formulation of the command to baptize rests particularly on the unprovable thesis that this Trinitarian confession presupposes a theological refinement that could not yet be part of the gospel.

Matthew 28:19 does not state that baptism should be administered in the names of the Father, the Son, and the Holy Spirit. The name here is the common name that expresses unity of Being (*TDNT*, 5:274). The Father is God the Father. Just as he is a divine person, so are the Son and the Holy Spirit divine persons.

In the epistles of Paul, the place where belief in the triune God is most clearly expounded is: "The grace of the Lord Jesus Christ, and the love of God, and the communion of the Holy Ghost, be with you all" (2 Cor. 13:14). In the case of "the communion of the Holy Ghost" the question is how the genitive case should be interpreted. It can be communion with the Holy Spirit, partaking of the Holy Spirit, but also the communion which is established and granted by the Holy Spirit. In both cases the Holy Spirit is looked upon as a divine person (see Versteeg, 1971, 315–18).

It is unnecessary to discuss or list all texts in which the revelation of the triune God comes to us. However, we must not ignore the fact that faithful contemplation in the church and in theology has paid a great deal of attention to the Gospel of John, and in particular chapters 1, 14–16 and 17. Jesus calls the Father his own Father, and he implies thereby a unique relationship. He says: "I and the Father are one." He refers to the glory that he had with the Father before the world was made (John 5:18; 10:30; 17:5).

Jesus is the Son. What is meant by this is the subject of Christology (§ 29). Historically, the dogma of the Trinity evolved from Christology. At the very least we need to refer to words of Scripture that brought the church to confess that the Son is very God of very God (Nicaea).

When Jesus says: "All things are delivered unto me of my Father: and no man knoweth the Son, but the Father; neither knoweth any man the Father, save the Son, and he to whomsoever the Son will reveal him" (Matt. 11:27), these words—which have sometimes been referred to as Johannine—imply a unity of Being with the Father.[22]

"In the beginning was the Word, and the Word was with God, and the Word was God." He is "the only begotten Son [of the Father],

22. Cf. also G. Sevenster, *De christologie van het Nieuwe Testament*, 1948², 99–102.

which is in the bosom of the Father" (John 1:1–18). In the New Testament, Jesus is called not only the Son of God, but also God (see John 1:1; 20:28; Rom. 9:5; Titus 2:13; 2 Peter 1:1; 1 John 5:20). Those who reflect on this may wonder how this can be consistent with the belief in one God.

Through the testimony of the New Testament, the church is also convinced of the divinity of the Holy Spirit. He is referred to as the Spirit of the Father and the Spirit of the Son (Matt. 10:20; Gal. 4:6). He is a divine person who can be grieved (Eph. 4:30). He makes alive (John 6:63), which is a divine act. He searches all things, even the depths of God (1 Cor. 2:10), which would not be possible if he were not God himself.

The Spirit of truth acts personally. He shows the way, he speaks, and he proclaims (John 16:13–15). The book of Acts shows us repeatedly how the Holy Spirit acts. As a person, he speaks, he gives direction to the apostles and to the church, and he appoints overseers (Acts 20:28).

Divine works are attributed to the Father as well as to the Son and to the Spirit. Creating and re-creating—who can do this except God alone? The Son and the Spirit participate in these works of God, not only in re-creation, but also in creation (Gen. 1:2; John 1:3).

Thus not only the divine names, but also the divine works form the basis for the belief that equal honor belongs to the Son and the Holy Spirit as the Father, and that God is one and his work is one, while we also need to speak of a plurality in God. In the church this is said with words that do not appear in the Bible, but which do have a scriptural foundation: God is one Being and he exists in three persons.

12.2. *The confession of the Trinity in the church*

We must leave it to dogmatic history to describe the course of the controversy that led to the formulation of the Trinitarian dogma. Belief in the triune God, confessed on the basis of revelation, came first; the dogma of the Trinity established by the church came second.

This could not be avoided in view of the heresies that the church had to combat. During the first few centuries of the history of the church there were a large number of views about God that did not agree with what the Word of God said. Here we mention only two main movements: *modalism* and *subordinatianism*, also referred to as

Sabellianism and Arianism, respectively—after their two most prominent representatives.

Modalism or *modalistic monarchianism*, which was widespread in the West, detracted from the threefold nature of the divine persons and taught that the Father, Son, and Spirit were merely modes of appearance of the one divine Being, which was sometimes referred to by Sabellius as the Son-Father. He was thought to show himself sometimes as Father, sometimes as Son, and sometimes as Spirit. As Creator and Lawgiver he would have the appearance of the Father, as Redeemer that of the Son, and as Life-giver that of the Spirit. Those were not three modes of Being, but merely three successive modes of appearance of the one God. Until the incarnation one dealt with the Father, subsequently with the Son, and following the ascension with the Spirit (cf. Courth, 1988, 56ff.).

Church fathers such as Tertullian (d. 220) and Hippolyte (d. 235) realized that in the modalistic view the God of the Bible was no longer recognizable at all. Tertullian stresses the distinction among the persons, while the Father, the Son, and the Holy Spirit are nevertheless one in Being (*substantia*). He uses the term *trinitas* (Trinity).

Opponents of modalism have correctly objected that the Father, who sent his Son, remained to Jesus his Father in heaven, to whom Jesus turned continually, throughout his life on earth. What Paul says in Galatians 4:6 does not mean at all that the Father existed first, then the Son, and then the Holy Spirit. They exist simultaneously. Otherwise Christ would also not be able to say of the Holy Spirit: "Whom the Father will send in my name" (John 14:26).

Subordinationism subordinated the Son and the Spirit to the Father. In the form presented by Paul of Samosata, this is referred to as *dynamic monarchianism* or *adoptionism*. The latter only considered the Father to be God, while Jesus was to him a human being, inspired by the Logos, who was at one with the will of the Father. In subordinationism the Holy Spirit was a power or gift of God.

The subordinationism of Arius (d. 336) did not consider the Son and the Spirit to be of the same Being as the Father either. The Father alone was the only true God, although the Son might be called divine. There was a time when the Son did not exist. He was considered to be the first and most prominent creature of God.

Athanasius (295–373) was the great opponent of the position taken by Arius. In Christ, God himself came to us. Faith stands and falls with the true divinity of the Son. Its denial implies that there is no true communion with God and no true redemption.

Subordination concepts about the Holy Spirit, which surfaced in the church following the confession of the Council of Nicaea that the Son is of one Being with the Father, were opposed by Athanasius and the three Cappadocians. We have in mind the doctrine of the *Pneumatomachians* (or Macedonians—named after Macedonius of Constantinople), of whom Eustathius of Sebasteia was the most prominent representative. According to him the Holy Spirit is of a different nature than the Father and the Son, and one may not give him the same honor. It appears that eventually he called the Spirit a creature.

Against this background it is clear that the church had to take a position not only with respect to the divinity of the Son, but also regarding the divinity of the Holy

Spirit. The building blocks for this position were obtained not only from Scripture but also from the theology of the church fathers.

The first ecumenical council, which met in Nicaea in 325, confessed that the Lord Jesus Christ is "the only-begotten Son of God," which means that he is of the substance of the Father, "God of God, Light of Light, very God of very God; begotten, not made, being of one substance (*homoousios*) with the Father."

More was said about the Holy Spirit by the second ecumenical council (Constantinople, 381) than by that of Nicaea. This is understandable following the position advocated by the Pneumatomachians. In the first place, it was stated that the Spirit is Lord. This is a divine name, an indication of divine glory and divine sovereignty. He brings to life. This has a biblical foundation (cf. John 6:63; 2 Cor. 3:6). He carries out a divine work. The creed of Constantinople says further that the Holy Spirit "proceeds" from the Father. This must have been taken from John 15:26. Like the Son, the Spirit must be seen in unity with the Father. Only this relationship with the Father must be described differently from the relationship between the Son and the Father. This is why the word "proceed" is employed here. The Spirit receives equal honor with the Father and the Son. This is the honor and worship that is due to God alone. Together with the Son, "He is worshiped and glorified." Finally it is confessed that he "spoke by the prophets." These would be the prophets of the Old Testament. The Holy Spirit is the Spirit of revelation, and the Old Testament is to the church also the Word of God.

How all of this must be interpreted is reinforced by a letter from the Synod of Constantinople to the bishops of the West (382). It refers to belief in the name of the Father, the Son, and the Holy Spirit. According to this belief there is a single Godhead, power, and Being of the Father, the Son, and the Holy Spirit, and equal honor, dignity, and eternal dominion. These are three complete hypostases of three complete persons.

Although the crucial councils for the establishment of the Trinitarian dogma were held in the fourth century, belief in the triune God emerged much earlier in the church. The command to baptize had great influence on the development of the doctrine of the Trinity. Belief in the Father, the Son, and the Holy Spirit constitutes the core of the Apostles' Creed and other early baptismal creeds. The Creed of Constantinople (Nicaea-Constantinople) is of the greatest significance from an ecumenical perspective, because it originated in the East and was also accepted in the West (cf. Torrance, 1988, 332–36).

However, specifically in connection with the Creed of Nicaea-Constantinople, a dogmatic difference emerged between the church of the West and that of the East. The addition of the words "and of the Son" to the confession regarding the procession of the Holy Spirit from the Father, i.e., the "*filioque*" in Latin, continues to be an issue. It led to schism in the eleventh century.

The *filioque* reflects the continuing development of the theology of the West and in particular can be linked to the theology of Augustine. This church father, who reflected deeply on the mystery of the Trinity, teaches that the Spirit proceeds from the Father and the Son, although he adds: primarily (*principaliter*) from the Father. The *filioque* is referred to in pronouncements of various synods in Spain, of which that of Toledo (589) is best known. It is also contained in the creed that was named after Athanasius (the *Symbolum Quicumque*). In Rome in 1014 this term was inserted in the text of the creed, for which the Orthodox churches continue to reproach the Western church.

What the Reformers did with the Trinitarian dogma cannot be called a revision and barely a reinterpretation. Luther was of the view that "the high articles of the divine majesty" were not at issue in the conflict with Rome. Neither did he abandon the terminology of the early church, although he realized that these words were not adequate. In the light of Scripture he advocated a "new confession of the ancient faith." The same is true of Calvin. Scripture provided the content for his doctrine and the church the formulas. The doctrine of the Holy Spirit was done greater justice than earlier.[23]

Considering the position taken by the Socinians and other anti-Trinitarians it is not surprising that a number of Reformed confessions go into great depth with respect to this doctrine. A good example is the Belgic Confession of Faith (articles 8–11). It confesses the oneness of God and the distinction of the three persons. The persons are really and truly distinguished from eternity in line with their incommunicable attributes. We need to listen to the testimony of Scripture and pay attention to the work that each of these three persons does for us. Jesus Christ is according to his divine nature the only begot-

23. See J. Koopmans, *Het oudkerkelijke dogma in de Reformatie, bepaaldelijk bij Calvijn* (the dogma of the early church in the Reformation, especially according to Calvin), 1938, 40–44, 66, 88–93, 104.

ten Son of God, one with the Father. The Holy Spirit from eternity proceeds from the Father and the Son. In order, he is the third person of the Trinity, "of one and the same essence, majesty and glory with the Father and the Son."

But over against the confession of the triune God there is also the opposition to this dogma, which cannot be ignored, although we must be brief.

The *Symbolum Quicumque* confesses the catholic belief that we worship one God in threeness and the threeness in oneness, without blending these persons or partitioning their Being. This had to be stated over against monarchianism, which modalistically eliminated the distinction among the three persons or subordinationistically denied the unity of the Father, the Son, and the Holy Spirit.

The anti-Trinitarianism of the Socinians was distinctly subordinationist. One can detect modalism in the work of Servetus.

Old heresies frequently return in new guises. Thus we encounter subordinationism anew in the theology of the Groningen school. Various liberal theologians went further than Arius by viewing Jesus as an eminent human being whose will coincided with God's, and the Holy Spirit as a power emanating from God. Jehovah's Witnesses are particularly fierce critics of this doctrine of the church.

Modalism has fewer adherents, but it is still alive. Schleiermacher gave it new expression (cf. Barth, *C.D*, 1.1.405, 469; Heyns, 1953, 117–31; Moltmann, 1981, 144ff.)

In the twentieth century, Brunner was linked with modalism. Although he did consider it an error on the part of Sabellius et al. that they placed the three names in historical sequence, did he not himself get caught in the trap of modalism? He criticized the classical doctrine of the Trinity as a logical mystery that was presented to the faithful by the church, i.e., a pseudo-mystery that did not originate in biblical teaching itself. The three names had to be mentioned in sequence and not simultaneously. With that he meant "sequentially, as implied by the progression of God's self-revelation." We have the Father through the Son, in the Son, and not the Father beside the Son and the Son beside the Father. We have the Son through the Spirit, in the Spirit, but not the Spirit beside the Son and the Son beside the Spirit. One of Brunner's theses is that there are works of the Father that are not at all works of the Son, e.g., God's wrath. But in this regard Brunner ignored passages such as Revelation 6:16–17.[24]

For theology in the Netherlands, the views of H. Berkhof are of greater relevance. His study *The Doctrine of the Holy Spirit* (1964) implies that he abandoned the

24. Cf. Brunner, *Dogmatics*, 1:205–40; M. Schmidt, "Der Ort der Trinitätslehre bei Emil Brunner" (the place of the doctrine of the Trinity according to Emil Brunner), *Theol. Zeitschrift* (theological journal) 5 (1949): 46–66.

orthodox path that he once walked. He identifies Christ with the Spirit, based on the words: "now the Lord is that Spirit" (2 Cor. 3:17).[25] The Spirit is the ministering Christ or the ministry of the glorified Christ. There are passages that are reminiscent of Brunner: The three names point "to the action of one God and not a static communion of three Persons." "They are the description of a progressive movement of descent in which God reaches ever more deeply to man in his sin and distress." According to Berkhof, the word "Spirit" is essentially a predicate of the nouns God and Christ. "The triune God does not comprise three Persons: He himself is a Person and he meets us in the Son and the latter's Spirit." In Jesus Christ the person of God manifests himself as a human being. In creation the Spirit is the acting person of God and in re-creation the acting person of Christ. Jesus Christ, God, and the Holy Spirit are "three modes to describe God's saving reality."[26] These are definitely modalistic thought processes!

Subsequently Berkhof distanced himself even more from the doctrine of the church. Subordinationist themes also came to play a significant role, especially in his Christology, in which Jesus is presented as the ultimate man, *the* New Man. As far as the doctrine of the Trinity is concerned, Berkhof believes that one should not have to be restrained by an impressive but equally artificial tradition, which in its abstractness threatens faith. The Trinity has been incorrectly viewed as a "divine tête-à-tête." It is, however, an open event, which describes how God, according to his eternal purpose, extends and carries in time his own life so as to share it with man. He says so in a section dealing with the covenant as a "Tri-(u)nity," in which the three names are referred to as the "summary description of the covenantal event." "The Father is the divine partner, the Son the human representative, the Spirit the bond between the two and therefore also the bond between the Son and the daughters and sons whom he draws to the Father" (Berkhof, *C.F.*, 330–37).

It goes without saying that Berkhof thus elicited a great deal of opposition. To make this interpretation of the doctrine of the Trinity acceptable, one must first of all set aside all that Scripture says about the preexistence of the Son and the Holy Spirit. One has to go far in eliminating pronouncements of the Bible. One has to see more in the views of Marcellus of Ancyra and Schleiermacher than in the dogma of the church. It is putting it very mildly when Heyns finds this description of the Trinity—as a continuing and open event focused on man—difficult to comprehend and to accept (Heyns, *Dogm.*, 52).

We have had to come to the realization that in the church and in theology a great deal of conflict has raged with respect to the Trinity. The early church encountered *monarchianism*, which sought to hold onto the unity and sovereignty of God in the face of belief in the triune God. The two chief manifestations of monarchianism, *modalism* and *subordinationism*, have continued to surface in various

25. Regarding this text and various interpretations, see Versteeg, 1971, 308–37; with respect to Berkhof's view, see 318–20.

26. H. Berkhof, *The Doctrine of the Holy Spirit*, 1964, 13–29, 109–21.

forms and variations. Around 1600, the opponents of the confession of the church were referred to not only as anti-Trinitarians, but also as *Unitarians*. In the eighteenth century the latter went so far as to establish a church.

Although the early dogma of the church did express the belief that God reveals himself to us as the triune One, it has been objected that this doctrine is the product of speculative thinking, which employs philosophical concepts of Greek origin. When in the more recent theology the doctrine of the Trinity is rejected, it is frequently replaced by a "trinity of revelation," which is inferred from the history of redemption and is part and parcel of it. Then much of the church's Trinitarian language is obscured behind the functional concepts of contemporary theology.

12.3. *A theological approach to this dogma*

1. *The meaning of the terms* Being *and* person. It is part of the role of theology to assess in the light of Scripture the terms that are employed in the formulation of ecclesiastical dogma and to interpret them in a biblical manner.

Augustine refers to the Trinity as the one God from whom, through whom, and in whom everything exists. In this way the Father, the Son, and the Holy Spirit are each God, and are also together one God. Each of them is the full Being (substantia), and together they are one Being.[27]

Theological reflection falls short of the reality that has been revealed. We cannot have adequate knowledge of the Trinity. Our concepts are inadequate. As far as the conflict about specific words is concerned, Calvin could say: "I could wish they were buried, if only among all men this faith were agreed on: that the Father and the Son and the Spirit are one God, yet the Son is not the Father, nor the Spirit the Son, but that they are differentiated by a peculiar quality" (*propietate quadam*, *Institutes*, 1.13.5).

"And although this doctrine far surpasses all human understanding, nevertheless we now believe it by means of the Word of God, but expect hereafter to enjoy the perfect knowledge and benefit thereof in heaven" (Belgic Confession of Faith, article 9). We stand before a mystery. This was not invented by human beings, as E. Brunner and

27. Augustine, *De doctrina christiana*, 1:5.

others claim, but is implied by God being God. Those who allow themselves to be led by Scripture must say God to the Father, the Son, and the Holy Spirit, and at the same time believe in one God. This means that God exists in these three persons, who are distinguished from each other. Trinity (*trinitas*) is a word that does not occur in the Bible, but that the church began to use because it saw a need for it. Originally Being and person were indeed Greek concepts, but subsequently acquired biblical content.

There is no reason whatsoever to support Brunner in considering these to be fatal and dubious concepts. With God's Being we mean God's divinity. The Son being of one Being with the Father (*homoousios*) means to the Council of Nicaea and to us that he is truly God, just as the Father is truly God.

In the teaching of the church the word "person" has a meaning all of its own. Various definitions have been given, of which we mention those of Thomas Aquinas (a relationship which constitutes a unique manner of being) and K. Barth (manner of being). We can agree with Calvin when he says: "In God's being I call Person a subsistence, which, while related to the others, is distinguished by an incommunicable quality" (*Institutes*, 1.13.6). At any rate, our concept of a person as an individual or an individual personality does not point us in the right direction. Three human persons could never be one human being just as the Father, the Son, and the Holy Spirit are one God.

2. *Being and person; person and person.* The three persons are not three parts of God. We confess of God that he is simple. This implies also that in him there is no compositeness whatsoever. He does not consist *of* three persons, but *in* three persons. The word "triune" captures better who God is than the word "threefold." The Father, the Son, and the Holy Spirit are three persons and simultaneously one God. In each person as well as all three persons we encounter God himself.

Since John of Damascus (d. 749), the term "*perichoresis*" serves to express theologically the intimate communion of the divine persons. It implies that they permeate each other. None of them exists without the other two persons. The Council of Florence (1439) therefore pronounced: "As a consequence of this unity the Father is wholly in the Son, wholly in the Spirit. The Son is wholly in the Father, wholly in the Spirit. The Holy Spirit is wholly in the Father, entirely within the Son" (see also Calvin, *Institutes*, 1.13.19).

A term such as *perichoresis* (*circumincessio*) may some day be replaced by another. But there are indeed grounds for this notion. One can point to the following words of Scripture: "Believe the works: that ye may know, and believe, that the Father is in me, and I in him. . . . I and my Father are one" (John 10:38, 30). In this connection Gregory of Nanzianzus (d. 390) is generally quoted: "I cannot think of the one God without quickly being encircled by the splendour of the three Persons; nor can I discern the three without being straightway carried back to the one God" (see also Calvin, *Institutes*, 1.13.17).

We should therefore not separate the work of the Father, the Son, and the Holy Spirit. The external works of the Trinity are undivided. Although distinctions can be made within God's acts of creation and re-creation, there are no divisions. In everything we deal with the triune God and never one of the three persons alone. Our relationship with God is therefore simultaneously a relationship with the Father, the Son, and the Holy Spirit. Jesus says: "He that hath seen me hath seen the Father" (John 14:9). John writes: "Whosoever denieth the Son, the same hath not the Father: he that acknowledgeth the Son hath the Father also" (1 John 2:23).

3. *The relationships among the persons*. Can we say more about what is unique about each of the three divine persons? Like Augustine, we think in this connection of the interrelationships among the Father, the Son, and the Holy Spirit.

The personal attribute of the Father is his Fatherhood (*paternitas*). This constitutes the relationship to his Son, whom he generates as Father. The Father is never without his Son and the Son is never without his Father. Jesus says: "For as the Father hath life in himself; so hath he given to the Son to have life in himself" (John 5:26). But neither is the Father ever without his Spirit, who proceeds from him. Jesus speaks of "the Spirit of Truth, which proceedeth from the Father" (John 15:26).

Because of their relationship with the Father the other divine persons cannot be separated from him, but are indeed united with him. Viewed in this way, the confession of faith in the Father is already a confession of faith in the triune God.

What is unique about God the Son is that he is generated by the Father (*generatio passiva*). We also refer to this as his Sonship (*filiatio*). In the New Testament the Son is the only begotten Son and the Father's own Son. In addition to John 5:26 we are reminded of Hebrews 1:5, where it says: "I will be to him a Father, and he shall be to me a Son." "Thou art my son, this day have I begotten thee." The church has joined in with these words and has come to speak of the *eternal generation* of the Son. This means that the Father generates him from eternity to eternity. It is a permanent relationship. If this process of generation were not eternal, the Father would not be eternally the Father and the Son would not be the eternal Son of God (cf. Heidelberg Catechism, Lord's Day 13). Then at some point the Father would have become what he is now and similarly the Son. God would then be changeable.

The confession that the Son is generated or begotten, being of one substance with the Father (Nicaea), rejects the view that this generation could solely be ascribed to the will of the Father. As Son of God the Son would then be subordinate to the Father. *Creation* owes its existence to the will of God, but *generation* implies a sharing of divine life.

Here we confront the limit of our thinking. In early theology it is said that the manner of generation is inexpressible to us.

When we think of *filiatio* as the personal attribute of the Son, we have thereby not yet expressed that the Son causes the Spirit to proceed from himself. But we cover this in discussing what is unique about the Holy Spirit. We shall also have to reflect on this more deeply, as we encounter the doctrinal difference between the churches of the occident and the orient (the *filioque*).

It is the personal attribute of the Holy Spirit that he proceeds from the Father and the Son (*processio, spiratio passiva*). In the gospel we read that the Spirit proceeds from the Father (John 15:26). Once again, no analogies can be found. It is something entirely different from being created. Just like the generation of the Son, the proceeding of the Spirit points to a sharing of the same Being. But *generatio* and *processio* cannot be identified with each other and therefore we need to employ different words. We cannot explain what the difference between these two is. That would require definitions to which no human being has access.

Augustine realized that he needed to address not only the relationship of the Father and the Spirit, but also the relationship between the Son and the Spirit. The Reformers were of the same mind.

Jesus says not only that the Spirit of truth proceeds from the Father, but also that he will send him from the Father (John 15:26). When he says elsewhere that he will send the Comforter and that the Father will send him in Jesus' name (John 16:7; 14:26), this refers to the progression of the events of redemption. But we may believe that when the Father and the Son cause the Spirit to proceed or send the Spirit in time, this implies an eternal proceeding of the Spirit from the Father and the Son. These words therefore imply something with respect to the Trinity itself, i.e., the *ontological Trinity*. The fact that in the New Testament the Holy Spirit is called not only the Spirit of the Father, but also the Spirit of the Son, and the Spirit of Jesus Christ, points in the same direction (Matt. 10:20; Gal. 4:6; Acts 16:7). The Spirit of God is the Spirit of Christ (Rom. 8:9).

When in the West during the Carolingian era the *filioque* (and of the Son) came to the foreground, there was a sharp reaction from the East. The Patriarch Photius interpreted the procession of the Spirit from the Father, as confessed by the church, as: from the Father only. He considered the *filioque* to be entirely in conflict with sacred tradition. Tradition is extremely important in Eastern orthodoxy!

In 1439 the Council of Florence made an attempt to accommodate the East (*Decretum pro Graecis*). It agreed to accept a formulation that was not unfamiliar in the East: the Holy Spirit proceeds from the Father *through* the Son. But this did not lead to a rapprochement.[28]

Under the influence of the ecumenical movement, attempts were made to patch up this difference. In 1978 and 1979 theologians from the East and the West spoke at conferences under the auspices of the Commission on Faith and Order of the World Council of Churches. The resulting memorandum ends with the recommendation that the original form of the creed—without the *filioque*—be accepted everywhere as normative. This recommendation met with little support, as H. G. Link pointed out in 1987.[29] There is also a proposal by Moltmann: the Holy Spirit proceeds from the Father of the Son (Moltmann, 1981, 182).

The question can arise whether all this is a matter of semantics or whether a confession with or without the *filioque* would make much of a difference. Is there in the East somewhat of a rigid retention of the tradition of the fathers? Is there in the West on the part of Roman Catholics not a belief in the infallibility of doctrinal

28. Some prominent Roman Catholic theologians considered both traditions to be legitimate and complementary, and in the spirit of Florence were prepared to make a concession to the church of the East (cf. Y. Congar, *Der Heilige Geist*, 1982, 449–53.

29. Cf. L. Visscher (ed.), *Geist Gottes—Geist Christi* (Spirit of God, Spirit of Christ), 1981; H. G. Link (ed.), *Ein Gott—ein Herr—ein Geist* (one God, one Lord, one Spirit), 1987, 15.

pronouncements, and on the part of Protestants the idea that the development that led to the acceptance of the *filioque* was theologically necessary?

The answer is that this concerns the relationship between God the Son and God the Holy Spirit, and therefore also the relationship between Christ's redemptive work and that of the Holy Spirit. Neither is it a matter of secondary importance that the East reproaches the church of the West that the latter teaches a "double origin" of the Spirit. However, the West does not say or mean it this way. On the contrary, it is indeed a matter of a single origin (*principium*, cf. Barth, *C.D.*, 1.1.557). In the East it is thought that the Holy Spirit is not adequately honored when the *filioque* is accepted, because he would then be subordinate to the Son. This would lead to a one-sided christocentric doctrine, for the freedom of the Spirit would be restricted by being bound to the Son.

But the West has said to the church of the East that the independence of the Spirit with respect to the Son has consequences for the work of the Mediator. Then the revelation of the Spirit also has a degree of independence beside that of the incarnate Word, and there are two ways to the Father. Those who go the way of the Son learn to know the Father; those who follow the way of the Spirit will enjoy God (cf. Bavinck, *R.D.*, 2:284).

We need to consider the *filioque* as a further development in pneumatology for which we may be grateful. Just as in the case of other doctrinal questions, the church has gained increasingly more insight. It has understood that the Council of Constantinople did not have the last word. The crux of the matter is whether there are biblical grounds for saying something about the relationship between the Son and the Spirit involving the term *filioque*.

If the Spirit did not proceed from the Son, Christ could not send him or pour him out (John 15:26; 16:7; Acts 2:33). God is exactly as he has made himself known in his revelation in Christ. Therefore we cannot restrict ourselves to the idea that for the sake of his work of salvation the Spirit was sent *in time* by the Son. *Synopsis* points out correctly: "Although the sending of the Holy Spirit in time is not the same thing as the Spirit's eternal procession, this sending is nevertheless rooted in the origin and order of the persons. Just as the Holy Spirit has everything of the Father and the Son, or of the Father through the Son, and therefore acts and works in the same manner, he brings everything back to the Father through the Son" (*Synopsis*, 79ff.).

The significance of the Spirit's procession from the Father and the Son is that the work of the Spirit forms a unity with the work of the

Son, who is our Mediator. Christ works through the Spirit and the Spirit's work is focused on Christ.[30]

We have access to the Father because Christ has secured salvation for us and the Holy Spirit makes us share in it. Scripture says emphatically that one cannot come to the Father except through Christ and that there is no faith in Christ except through the Holy Spirit (John 14:6; 1 Cor. 12:3).

This doctrine therefore has a practical dimension. Jesus says of the Spirit: "He shall glorify me: for he shall receive of mine, and shall shew it unto you" (John 16:14). It is well known how the traditional form for baptism expresses it: "When we are baptized into the Name of the Holy Spirit, the Holy Spirit assures us by this holy sacrament that he will dwell in us, and sanctify us to be members of Christ, applying to us that which we have in Christ." This unity is missing whenever the *filioque* is denied. Thus there emerge two separate avenues in the spirituality of the Orthodox churches (cf. Wentsel, *Dogm.*, 3a:388). Beside the way of Orthodox doctrine there is the road of mystical experience.

Comparable biases can also emerge in the Western churches whenever the significance of the *filioque* is not fully appreciated. One can place the entire emphasis on the salvation earned by Christ and thus fall into objectivism. One can also place the entire emphasis on the application through the work of the Spirit and end up in subjectivism.

In the distinction between the accomplishment of salvation by Christ and its application by the Holy Spirit, we are always conscious of the fact that the Spirit applies everything as the Spirit of Christ. Therefore, although the accomplishment and its application go hand in hand, they do not coincide.

12.4. *The triune God in his works*

The unity of God is manifested by the fact that the three divine persons are inextricably interconnected in their actions.[31] In combating the followers of Arius, Augustine pointed to the words: "What things soever [the Father] doeth, these also doeth the Son likewise" (John 5:19). Creation is not the work of the Father alone, for the other two persons participate in it (cf. John 1:3; Gen. 1:2). Reconciliation is not

30. "The coming of the Spirit was brought about by the work of Christ. The work of the Spirit is focused on the coming of Christ," A. A. van Ruler, *Reformatorische opmerkingen in de ontmoeting met Rome* (Reformational remarks for the encounter with Rome), 1965, 67.

31. Cf. Augustine, *De Trinitate*, 1.4.7.

the work of the Son alone, for the Father and the Spirit also participate in it (2 Cor. 5:19; Heb. 9:14). Sanctification is not the work of the Holy Spirit alone, for this work is also attributed to the Father and the Son (cf. 1 Thess. 5:23; Eph. 5:26).

The external works of the Trinity are undivided (*opera trinitatis ad extra sunt indivisa*). To this key theological statement must be added that nevertheless the distinction among the three persons as well as their internal order remain valid. This distinction focuses on the unique role that is attributed to each of the three persons (*de appropriations*).

We have in mind God's modus operandi in the economical sense. Here one can speak of the economical Trinity, as long as it does not conflict with the ontological or immanent Trinity, which is only too often the case. These two are one and the same thing, for God in his works does not reveal himself to be any different from the way he actually is. The economical Trinity presupposes the Trinity of Being or the immanent Trinity. It goes against Scripture to recognize a Trinitarian modus operandi of God without believing in the triune God.

1. Already in the days of the church fathers reference was made to the various prepositions that are used in the New Testament: out of (*ek*) and through (*dia*) for the work of the Father and the Son (1 Cor. 8:6); through (*dia*) and in or through (*en*) for the work of the Son and the Spirit (Eph. 2:18).[32] Saying that everything proceeds from the Father, is accomplished by the Son, and is perfected by the Holy Spirit is an attempt to describe this distinction.

2. Since the Middle Ages theologians have, from the perspective of appropriation, ascribed power to the Father, wisdom to the Son, and goodness to the Spirit (Thomas Aquinas). Calvin teaches that one must consider the Father to be the beginning of activity and the fountain and wellspring of all things, the Son as the eternal wisdom, and the Holy Spirit as the power and efficacy of that activity (Genevan Catechism, cf. *Institutes*, 1.13.18).

3. Luther provides the well-known triad that we also find in the Heidelberg Catechism: of God the Father and our creation, of God the Son and our redemption, of God the Holy Spirit and our sanctification. Luther says in his Large Catechism: we wish to summarize the entire faith concisely in three main articles corresponding with the

32. See also A. A. van Ruler, *De vervulling can de wet* (the fulfillment of the law), 1947, 182–84.

three persons of the Godhead, on whom is focused everything that we believe. "Faith is briefly summarized as it were in these words: I believe in God the Father who created me, I believe in God the Son who redeemed me, I believe in God the Holy Spirit who sanctifies me" (*BSLK*, 647).

This agrees with what the Belgic Confession of Faith says of the unique work that each of the three persons does for us: "The Father is called our Creator, by his power; the Son is our Saviour and Redeemer, by his blood; the Holy Spirit is our Sanctifier, by his dwelling in our hearts" (article 9).

We conclude by pointing out that Barth prefers to speak of God as Creator, God as Reconciler, and God as Redeemer (*C.D.*, 1.1.441–560). His approach has been followed by some. One can object that the work of the Spirit—by way of appropriation—consists therein that he makes man receptive to the work of the Father in the Son and causes him to become a man for God. This ministry is still best described by the old term of "sanctification" (cf. Weber, *Foundations*, 1:394). In connection with this concept we are reminded of Luther's description: "Therefore sanctification means nothing but taking things to the Lord Christ in order to receive what we could not obtain on our own" (*BSLK*, 654).

12.5. *The significance of the doctrine of the Trinity*

1. Just as God's Trinity is a mystery, we encounter mystery in everything that he does. As far as God's counsel is concerned, we need to admit: "O the depth of the riches both of the wisdom and knowledge of God! how unsearchable are his judgments and his ways past finding out!" (Rom. 11:33). When we reflect on the incarnation, we confess: "Great is the mystery of godliness: God was manifest in the flesh" (1 Tim. 3:16).

2. The doctrine of the Trinity gives us an impression of the richness of God's life. He is not Being itself or the Ground of Existence. Neither is he the Highest Good or the Supreme Being. He is the living God, who is compassionate in himself. In himself he is a God of communion. God is love. Behind his acts of love and grace in time stands his eternal love.

3. Knowledge of the triune God and his work goes hand in hand with the doxology. We bless and praise the God and Father of our Lord Jesus Christ, who chose us in him and graced us in the Beloved. The Holy Spirit seals the believers and is the Earnest of their inheritance. All this is in praise of his glory (Eph. 1:3–14).

4. All of redemption has a Trinitarian character. We need to express that theologically.

Only the Word became flesh, but the incarnation of the Son of God was the work of the triune God, for the Father sent him and he was conceived by the Holy Spirit.

The work of the triune God restores the right relationship with God, which we severed through our sins. Reformed theology developed the doctrine of the covenant of redemption (see § 15.2). The unity of the three divine persons implies that our salvation is assured by the eternal plan of salvation of the triune God.

In the justification of sinners we can recognize the work of the Father, the Son, and the Holy Spirit. "Out of . . . perfect love [God gave] his Son unto death for us and [raised] him for our justification . . . Christ [offered] himself on the tree of the cross and [poured] out his precious blood to purge away our sins . . . [To provide us with] true knowledge of this great mystery, the Holy Spirit kindles in our hearts an upright faith." This is the means whereby we embrace Christ, our righteousness (Belgic Confession of Faith, articles 20–22).

Viewed from a Trinitarian perspective, the church is the people of God, the body of Christ, and the temple of the Holy Spirit.

There is a unique ministry that each of these three persons performs for us. This is what we believe and experience (cf. Belgic Confession of Faith, article 9). "We know ourselves to be children of the Father, redeemed by the Son, and in communion with both through the Holy Spirit" (Bavinck, *R.D.*, 2:334).

5. The Trinitarian dogma may not be termed speculative. It did not arise as a result of speculation, nor does it encourage it. However, in theological and philosophical literature some highly speculative views can be encountered, e.g., those of Hegel and F. C. Baur.

Nor has scholastic theology been able to avoid speculation. In discussing the value that this dogma has for life and referring to the mysticism of the Middle Ages, Bartmann points out that the supernatural life of our souls is a reflection of the threefold life of God. For just as the Son is eternally begotten of the Father, in time he wishes to be born a second time by taking on human nature from Mary, and a third time in the soul of a Christian, now in a spiritual way. Early mysticism referred to this as the birth of God within our soul.[33]

Are there *analogies* to the Trinity? According to Augustine there are "incomparable parables," which he also refers to as traces of the Trinity. The fact that he paid a great

33. B. Bartmann, *Grundriss der Dogmatik* (outline of dogmatics), 1931, 51–53.

deal of attention to this reflects his view of man as image of God and the world as God's creation, in which the invisible things of God can be recognized by the human mind (cf. Polman, 1965, 234–47).

Analogies have been sought in the realms of nature, culture, history, religion, and psychology (cf. Barth, *C.D.*, 1.1.383–89). Calvin was among those who treated these with skepticism. He doubted that it was appropriate to look for analogies in human life. He considered that Augustine's views about the soul as the reflection of the Trinity—because in it reside the understanding, will, and memory—is by no means sound (*Institutes*, 1.13.18; 1.15.4).

A modern form of looking for traces of the Trinity can be recognized in the work of Moltmann, who extended the way in which the Cappadocians compared the three persons, yet one God, with three human beings in some sense participating in a single (human) being. Moltmann pursued a social doctrine of trinity leading toward the development of social personalism. Through the doctrine of the Trinity the church is constituted as a community free from any authoritarian rule. This Trinitarian community can serve as a model for "human," non-patriarchal society (cf. Moltmann, 1980, 192–200).

The question whether this view is a consequence of faith in the Trinity or personal speculation is not difficult to answer, although we appreciate that Moltmann sought to focus on our relationship with the triune God. This is what he means when he speaks of the inviting unity of the triune God.[34]

6. Moltmann says that the unity of the Father, the Son, and the Holy Spirit offers scope for the unity of believers, humanity, and all of creation. He also alluded to baptism in this connection. However, it is better to interpret baptism in the name of the Father, the Son, and the Holy Spirit as the triune God's invitation and obligation to live in communion with him.

The promises and demands that are embedded in baptism are brought to our attention in the traditional liturgy for baptism. "We are . . . admonished . . . [to] cleave to this one God, Father, Son and Holy Spirit; . . . trust in him and love him." This is implied by his covenant with us.

In worship services the church expresses its faith in a Trinitarian confession: the Apostles' Creed or the Creed of Nicaea-Constantinople.

When we are blessed in the name of the triune God, this is frequently done with the words: "The grace of the Lord Jesus Christ, and the love of God, and the communion of the Holy Ghost, be with you all" (2 Cor. 13:14).

The ministry of the Word must proclaim the great works of the triune God in terms of the plan of redemption, the accomplishment

34. J. Moltmann in *Concilium*, 1985, 47–54.

of redemption, and the application of redemption. The absence of Trinitarian preaching would lead to serious biases and would preclude strong spiritual leadership.[35]

Just as in the past, faith in the triune God is expressed in hymns of praise and adoration in which "Thou" is said three times and nevertheless once. The *Te Deum laudamus* is a well-known example of this:

> The Father of infinite Majesty.
> Thine adorable, true: and only Son.
> Also the Holy Ghost: the Paraclete.
> Thou art the King of Glory: O Christ.
> Thou art the everlasting Son: of the Father.

7. From theological and practical points of view, the doctrine of the Trinity is of the utmost importance. Calvin borrowed its structure for his dogmatic work when he gave his *Institutes* its definitive form.

It definitely has no merit to leave a discussion of the Trinity to the end of dogmatics, as is done by some theologians. We see the same thing happening in *Fundamentals and Perspectives of Confession* (1949) and in The New Catechism (1966). We should not wait to the last to call God by the names by which he has made himself known. This could lead to the misunderstanding that we could remain neutral with respect to the doctrine of the Trinity of the Eternal Being. The New Catechism refers to diffidence, but diffidence is called for in all speaking about God and also in speaking to God.

When theology of the doctrine of God does not do justice to "our catholic and undoubted Christian faith" (Heidelberg Catechism, Lord's Day 7, response 22), derailments in the doctrines of Christ and the Holy Spirit can be expected. The doctrine of the Trinity is the theological underpinning of Christology, pneumatology, and soteriology, although from the perspective of the history of dogma, Christology was the cornerstone of the Trinity.

We close this section with a few quotations from Bavinck, which do not lack in terms of clarity (Bavinck, *R.D.*, 2:333, also quoted by Barth, *C.D.*, 1.1.347): "The entire Christian belief system, all of special revelation, stands or falls with the confession of God's Trinity. It is the core of the Christian faith, the root of all its dogmas, the basic

35. Cf. W. Kremer, *Priesterlijke prediking* (priestly preaching), 1976, 23ff.

content of the new covenant. It was this religious Christian interest, accordingly, that sparked the development of the church's doctrine of the Trinity. At stake in this development—let it be said emphatically—was not a metaphysical theory or a philosophical speculation but the essence of the Christian religion itself. This is so strongly felt that all who value being called a Christian recognize and believe in a kind of Trinity. The profoundest question in every Christian creed and system of theology is how God can be both one and yet three. Christian truth in all its parts comes into its own to a lesser or greater extent depending on how that question is answered. In the doctrine of the Trinity we feel the heartbeat of God's entire revelation for the redemption of humanity."

§ 13. God's perfections

13.1. *Introduction*

In God there is a fullness of life that surpasses all human concepts. When we call him the almighty and merciful God and Father of his people, more can be said. He is almighty and merciful, holy and good, eternal and just, and much more. His immeasurable perfection is manifested in the multiplicity of his perfections. If completeness in the enumeration and description of his attributes were required to tell the truth about God, it would be best to remain silent. This problem remains when we try to leave aside theological views and focus on summarizing what the Bible says about God. We realize once again that our knowledge of God is altogether inadequate, but that it is not impossible to arrive at true knowledge of God.

We must consciously avoid taking three particular approaches that have frequently been suggested in the past. The starting point used to be a search for a relationship between human and divine attributes: Man can be wise, but God is the All-Wise (*via eminentiae*); man is mortal, but God is eternal (*via negationis*); man's love owes its existence to God's love (*via causalitatis*). We do not attain God's wisdom or love by inferring it from human wisdom and love, or taking it to be the superlative case of the latter. God's perfections are not the superlatives of human attributes. The only acceptable and reliable approach is that of revelation (*via revelationis*).

All of Holy Scripture could be read as a song of praise about God and his perfections. However, to say it with Calvin, there are certain Scripture passages in which clearer descriptions are set forth to us, wherein his true appearance is exhibited, to be seen as in an image (*Institutes*, 1.10.2). We specifically refer to Exodus 34:6 and Psalm 145, "in which the sum of all God's attributes is so precisely reckoned up that nothing would seem to have been omitted."

More recent theology emphasizes that we know God's attributes or perfections from his acts in creation and re-creation. Thus Miskotte points to Psalm 92:2–5. In these acts we encounter the righteous and merciful God. And the supreme act is the sending of God's Son, the coming of the Messiah, his death and resurrection. In him God is present in the fullness and oneness of his attributes, for he has revealed God's name (Miskotte, 1941, 90–97). More than tended to be the case in earlier Reformed theology,[36] the doctrine of God must reflect how God revealed himself in Christ. Here dogmatics may somewhat resemble a biblical dictionary.

Our confession lists a series of attributes or perfections of God (Belgic Confession of Faith, article 1). This raises the question as to how we should interpret, in the light of Scripture, what is meant by God's simplicity, spirituality, eternity, and whatever else is mentioned.

But has the beginning of this confession article been properly formulated? Does the simplicity of God not also have a philosophical dimension? Not only with respect to this attribute, but also in the case of eternity, infinity, and other predications, it will turn out that theological reflection cannot limit itself to quoting Bible verses in order to explain the meaning of God's pronouncements.

36. See Bremmer's criticism of Bavinck's expositions in *Gereformeerde dogmatiek* (Reformed dogmatics). Bremmer speaks of a mixture of biblical notions and philosophical, mostly Thomistic, themes, R. H. Bremmer, *Herman Bavinck als dogmaticus* (Herman Bavinck as dogmatician), 1961, 196.

To this point words such as "perfections," "properties," and "predications" have been employed interchangeably. The terms "virtues," "attributes," and "qualities" also exist. We are dealing with names of God's Being, which have already been distinguished from the names of his roles and persons (§ 11).

Theology does well not to limit itself to one type of name, because this will always be open to criticism. A property can always be treated as a secondary characteristic, whereas in the case of a virtue the ethical perspective predominates. In following Barth and others we shall prefer to use the term "perfections." In order to make clear that one speaks of essential attributes, it is sometimes said that God *is* his attributes. Man can love, but God *is* love. This means that he is altogether love. Similarly, he is entirely holiness and entirely wisdom. Whatever God is, he is wholly so. One of God's perfections should therefore not be contemplated without keeping in mind the others. There is no contrast between his righteousness and his mercy, or between his holiness and his love.

This unity of all of God's perfections is indeed a reason for never separating or demarcating them from each other, but not to identify them with each other. When we call on God as our omnipotent and merciful God and Father, we do not mean that God's omnipotence is identical with his mercy. He is not the omnipotent *or* merciful God, but he is omnipotent *and* merciful. Precisely by distinguishing his perfections we come to know him increasingly better.

Now the question arises, whether a classification of God's perfections or attributes can be formulated. They have been divided into negative and positive attributes, absolute and relative attributes, or incommunicable and communicable attributes. Roughly speaking, these schemes predominate in the Roman Catholic, Lutheran, and Reformed traditions, respectively, but the differences among them are not major.

The more recent Reformed theology is critical of such distinctions (cf. Honig, *Handboek*, 183–85; Heyns, *Dogm.*, 61).

Communicable attributes actually do not exist. God's holiness used to be listed among the communicable attributes, but—as the Holy One—God is precisely different from all creatures. There is an essential difference between his wisdom and goodness and the wisdom and goodness of people, between everything that pertains to God and all that can be said of people. The subject determines the predicate!

There is no classification scheme that satisfies completely. Therefore we also have reservations with respect to the classifications advocated by Barth and Weber: perfections of divine love and perfections of divine freedom.

There are prayers in which names of God are interrelated, for example when in the prayer of thanksgiving of our classical liturgy for baptism, God is addressed with the words: "Almighty God and merciful Father."

There are examples of this in passages of Scripture in which various names of God's Being are mentioned together. In one of the Psalms it says: "The LORD is gracious and full of compassion" (Ps. 111:4). "Holy and reverend is his name" (Ps. 111:9). In Hosea 11:12, God is referred to as Holy One who is faithful.

H. Berkhof correctly points out the connection between God's *transcendence* and *condescendence*, his exaltedness and his condescension toward us. The latter is not the same as what frequently is referred to as God's immanence (Berkhof, *C.F.*, 113–26).

One could say that in earlier days God's transcendence frequently predominated, while in modern theology his condescendence is highlighted. In this connection it is alarming that this tendency has brought many to reject God's transcendence, which does not only apply to the concept as such but also to its biblical content.[37] Barth sees God's transcendence realized in his immanence. According to Berkhof, the aspect of condescendence predominates. God insists on being the God of humanity. God is man's Partner and man is God's partner. Some go still further by saying that God needs us. In process theology, God is no longer seen to be independent of world developments (cf. Erickson, *Chr. Th.*, 279–81).

The history of the church and theology teaches us to be aware of the great danger of forming an image of God that is contrary to his revelation.

Scripture refers to both God's exaltedness and his nearness. We are completely comfortable with this perspective. In Isaiah we read: "For thus says the high and lofty One that inhabiteth eternity, whose name is Holy; I dwell in the high and holy place, with him also that is of a contrite and humble spirit, to revive the spirit of the humble, and to revive the heart of the contrite ones" (Isa. 57:15). "The heaven is [God's] throne, and the earth is [his] footstool . . . . [He who made] all . . . things . . . [looks] to him that is poor and of a contrite spirit, and trembleth at [his] word" (Isa. 66:1–2). Whenever Daniel prays, the LORD his God is to him "the great and dreadful God, keeping the covenant and mercy to them that love him, and to them that keep his commandments" (Dan. 9:4).

In listening to the Word of God, we must always think of God's transcendence and condescendence at the same time. It is possible to express this by saying that God is holy love. In his holiness he is exalted above us, and in his love he turns himself toward us.

He is holy. Psalm 99 tells us so three times in succession. "Holy, holy, holy, is the LORD of hosts" (Isa. 6:3). This does not only come to us from the Old Testament (see Rev. 4:8). "God is love" (1 John 4:8, 16). "God commendeth his love toward us, in that, while we were yet sinners, Christ died for us" (Rom. 5:8). This does not only come

37. See G. C. van Niftrik, *Het bestaan van God in de kentering van deze tijd* (God's existence in the current turn of events), 1971, 7–16, 84–104.

to us from the New Testament, for God revealed himself also prior to the coming of Christ as a God of love and grace.

H. Berkhof believes that in addition to God's holiness and love, his omnipotence and unchangeableness should not be forgotten, but treated in parallel with his defenselessness and changeableness. Apart from holy love, God is to him also defenseless superiority and changeable faithfulness. He objects to the earlier theology that God's transcendent attributes almost completely overwhelm his condescendent attributes, but the reverse is true in his own case. We do not wish to follow Berkhof in his doctrine of defenseless superiority and changeable faithfulness, because there are no biblical grounds for this.

We follow a less systematic and artificial approach by allowing ourselves to be guided by the Belgic Confession of Faith (article 1), once we have explored God's holy love. As far as God's perfections or attributes are concerned, the most important aspect is to see the biblical concept of these names. Although we cannot ignore earlier and more recent theological views, we treat them with circumspection.

13.2. *God is holy love*

Before all else, we focus on the fact that God is love. Although the Johannine pronouncement, "God is love" (1 John 4:8, 16), gives no definition of God—he also says that God is light—it is one of the most profound statements concerning God.

1. God's love is *incomparable* and *immeasurable*. The Bible does indeed make comparisons, such as the love of a father, a mother, or a spouse (Ps. 103:13; Isa. 49:15; Hos. 1–3), but the incomparability exceeds any comparability. We cannot define God's love by raising our own concept of love to the power of infinity. "The concept of love does not determine what God is, but God determines what love is" (Berkhof, *C.F.*, 129). We must not start out from a human perspective, but from God's perspective. The Father loved his Son from before the foundation of the world. The three divine persons love one another perfectly. Therefore God does not need us to express his love.

It is characteristic of his love to give itself. God gives himself. In his love he seeks communion with us to enrich our lives with his love.

2. God's love is *sovereign love*. If this is not kept in mind, there is a danger that God's love will be humanized. It is love that is grounded in God himself and not on something outside himself.

Hosea 14:4 says: "I will love them freely." A number of liturgies refer to his infinite mercy. With an older expression we can say that God takes reasons out of himself. We did not ask for his love, we did not deserve it, and we cannot earn it. God loves us of his own accord. It is love that comes from one side, love that elects (cf. Deut.

7:7), love that discriminates. God's love reaches out to people who are sinners and enemies of his (Rom. 5:8–10). It is love that knows no boundaries and for which no sacrifice is too great (see 1 John 4:9–11). That is why John says: "Behold what manner of love the Father hath bestowed upon us, that we should be called the sons of God" (1 John 3:1).

3. God's love is *merciful love*. Our word "charity"—just as *misericordia* in Latin—reminds us of the heart. The Old Testament root of this word—the plural of *rechem* (womb)—indicates man's inner being as the seat of tender feelings for others. It refers to God's inner compassion. He is inwardly motivated to regard human beings in need. This is his mercy. He shows *grace* to sinners. This agrees with a well-known expression from the days of the Reformation, i.e., "undeserved favor."

4. God's love is *holy love*. Those who ignore this have a very human concept of God and his love. He is the holy God who loves his creatures. We may never divorce his love from his holiness, let alone contrast it with his holiness.

God's love is divine love that distinguishes itself from all other love in that it is holy love. This implies that although he gives himself, he remains true to himself. He therefore asserts his will in order to condemn, exclude, and annihilate all opposition (cf. Barth, *C.D.*, 2.1.359).

God can also display holy wrath. His love has its ground in him alone, but his wrath is provoked by sin. His wrath is therefore not in conflict with his love. It is the wrath of him who is love. His wrath can be viewed as an expression of his injured love, as a reaction to the scorning of his love.[38] God's wrath has sometimes been called the tip of the flame of his love.[39]

God is love in the giving of himself, but also when he makes claims on us. Precisely because he is love, he desires that we do not live without him, but with him and for him. Otherwise we find ourselves outside the circle of the light of his love, where there is darkness and death. It is irresponsible to despise God's love, which is revealed in Christ. Nothing richer can be imagined than sharing in his love. Scripture says: "We love him because he first loved us" (1 John 4:19). His love for us is the ground and mainspring of our own love, while mutual love

38. Cf. H. M. Ohmann, *Wie kent uw toorn?* (Who knows your wrath?), 1988, 21–33.
39. J. H. Gunning Jr., *Blikken in de openbaring* (glimpses of revelation), 1929², 2:165.

is also our indispensable response to God's love. "Beloved, if God so loved us, we ought also to love one another" (1 John 4:11).

We have seen how God's love and holiness go hand in hand. But what is God's holiness?

In earlier days, God's holiness was frequently described as moral perfection (cf. Doekes, 1960, 102–30). However, we should first of all realize that he is altogether different from all that has been created. "Holy" then refers to the divine. This cannot be equated with numinous, horrible, and fascinating mystery, for the supporting arguments for this are more religious-philosophical than biblical in nature.[40]

"The Holy One says: To whom then will ye liken me, or shall I be equal?" (Isa. 40:25). "I am God and not man; the Holy One in the midst of thee" (Hos. 11:9). God's holiness, exaltedness, and majesty stand in contrast with the insignificance of all creatures, also of the angels who serve him (Isa. 6:2).

In the second place, holy stands in contrast with all that is sinful. God is "of purer eyes than to behold evil, and [can]not look on iniquity" (Hab. 1:13). In the light of God's holiness Isaiah realizes his own sinfulness and that of his people (Isa. 6:5). There is justification for the question: "Who is able to stand before the holy LORD God?" (1 Sam. 6:20).

The holy God wants to see sin eliminated. Since he is holy, he cannot leave sin unpunished (Lev. 10:3). The fact that the atonement of sin is not only necessary but also possible emanates from his holy love. Consequently, a man such as Isaiah can be engaged in his holy service (cf. Isa. 6:7–8).

In the third place, it can be said of God's holiness that he strictly maintains his justice and does not give his glory to anyone else. As the holy God, he is a jealous God (Josh. 24:19). He manifests his holiness in saving as well as dreadful acts. This implies judgment for his enemies, but redemption for his people (Ezek. 28:20–26). As the Holy One, he directs everything toward his glorification (cf. Doekes, 1960, 233).

Precisely for this reason, he demands *and* offers holiness. He commands his people: "Ye shall be holy: for I the LORD your God am holy" (Lev. 19:2; cf. 1 Peter 1:15). He accomplishes their sanctification

40. Here we think especially of the well-known book by R. Otto, *Het heilige* (that which is holy), 1928 (*Das Heilige*, 1917).

through the work of Christ and the Holy Spirit. God who is the source of holiness (*Synopsis*, 6:40) sanctifies his children, because he insists that they live in communion with him and consecrate themselves to his service. In Christ, the holy God has made the sanctification of his people, the atonement of their guilt, and the accomplishment of his will in their midst his own business (cf. Barth, *C.D.*, 2.1.367).

God is the Thrice-Holy One. This supplies us with inexhaustible reasons to sing his praises (Calvin on Isa. 6:3).

13.3. *God is a single and simple spiritual being*

1. *God's simplicity*. The word "simple" occurs in both theology and confession. Scripture itself says that God is one.

We have in mind Deuteronomy 6:4. We could translate: "Hear, O Israel: the LORD is our God; the LORD is one!" Another rendition is: "The LORD is our God, the LORD the only one," or, "The LORD is our GOD, the LORD alone" (cf. De Groot and Hulst, no date, 56–59). It can indicate oneness as opposed to division, or a oneness that stands in contrast with multiplicity.

The latter option undoubtedly makes good sense. In the world various gods are worshiped, but the LORD is the only God. This is a characteristic theme of the entire Old Testament. Moses says to the people: "Know therefore this day, and consider it in thine heart, that the LORD he is God in heaven above, and upon the earth beneath: there is none else" (Deut. 4:39; cf. Deut. 32:39; 2 Kings 19:19; Ps. 18:31; Zech. 14:9). In the book of Isaiah it is brought out convincingly that he is the only God and that therefore all salvation must be sought in him. In Isaiah 44:6 it says: "I am the first, and I am the last; and beside me there is no God" (cf. 45:21–22). In the New Testament he is called "the only true God" (John 17:3), the "immortal, the invisible, the only . . . God" (1 Tim. 1:17). This implies that his revelation is the only true and valid revelation (cf. Wentsel, *Dogm.*, 3a:270).

We can also interpret these words in the former sense. They then tell us that the LORD is one in himself. He is not partly this and partly that. Today he is no different from who he was in the past, and in the future he will be no different from who he is today. Regardless of how he reveals himself, he remains true to himself. He is one and the same in all his words, ways, and works.

We not only confess that our God is the only God (*singularitas Dei*), but also that he is one (*unitas*) and simple (*simplicitas*). The original text of the Belgic Confession of Faith, article 1, says: "Une seule et simple essence spirituelle" (a single and simple spiritual being).

Brunner and others consider the latter to be a speculative doctrine. We admit that one can treat it as an abstraction which is better employed in a theory about God than in a theology focused on the knowledge and worship of God.

When we note how church fathers such as Irenaeus, Athanasius, and Augustine came to speak of the simplicity of God, we see that in this way they were able to place the living God over against the gods of paganism and to combat gnostic conceptions of God.[41]

For a doctrine of God's simplicity we can refer to phrases from the New Testament such as God is Spirit, God is light, God is love (John 4:24; 1 John 1:5; 4:8). This does not mean that he is part Spirit, part light, and part love. As Spirit, he is entirely so. He is altogether light and altogether love. God's love is the loving God himself. He is totally and indivisibly himself in all that he is and has and does. He is one in his manifestation as Creator and as Redeemer. Neither does the distinction among the three divine persons detract from God's oneness.

God is one in the riches of his distinct perfections. What he is, he is totally and completely. What he is, he is simultaneously. What he is, he is in and of himself (cf. Schilder, *H.C.*, 1:480).

There is both a negative and a positive side to this. The former implies that there are no tensions or contradictions within God. He cannot be divided within himself. In him everything is in complete harmony. In the coming of Christ and his work we see the way in which his justice and mercy go hand in hand (cf. Belgic Confession of Faith, article 20). Like Koopmans we cannot agree with the old Dutch hymn that gives the impression that God's wisdom must mediate between his righteousness and his grace:

> Righteousness insisted on punishment,
> Grace pleaded for safe conduct.

41. Concepts from early theology (Anselm, Thomas Aquinas, and Zanchius) were newly interpreted and evaluated by F. G. Immink in his study *Divine Simplicity*, 1987. He interpreted the doctrine of divine simplicity as a logical determination or characterization of God's unique mode of existence, and in particular the absolute independence (*aseitas*) and transcendence of the God of Abraham, Isaac, and Jacob (190–96).

Then God's grace interceded,
And satisfied both.[42]

From the positive point of view, God's simplicity means that God always gives himself as he is. Everything in God is essential to him. Therefore God's counsel must not be considered in isolation. From early dogmatics we know the formulation: God's decree is the decreeing God himself.

As Barth puts it: God himself is simple, so simple that in all his glory he can be near to the simplest perception and also mock the most profound and acute thinking—so simple that he forces everyone to be silent and yet permits and commands everyone boldly to make him the object of their thought and speech (*C.D.*, 2.1.485).

With Miskotte we can say that God's simplicity has practical implications.[43] The *Shema* ("Hear, O Israel"—Deut. 6:4) goes together with: "Thou shalt love the LORD thy God with all thine heart, and with all thy soul, and with all thy might" (Deut. 6:5; cf. Mark 12:29–30). In this way "the confession of the Perfect One is immediately followed by the command of perfect dedication and love" (Wentsel, *Dogm.*, 3a:276).

God's simplicity brings with it that we can always rely on him. "What he does surpassing human understanding, we will not curiously inquire into further than our capacity will admit of; but with the greatest humility and reverence adore the righteous judgments of God, which are hid from us" (Belgic Confession of Faith, article 13). A Dutch poet once remarked:

O Lord, what I understand is exceedingly good,
And what I do not grasp must be equally so.[44]

2. *God's spirituality*. When God is referred to as a spiritual Being (Belgic Confession of Faith, article 1), the word "spiritual" can be interpreted as incorporeal or immaterial, on the basis of tradition. Away with material images or corporeal representations of God! When Scripture says that God has ears and eyes or hands and feet, these are anthropomorphisms, which God utilizes to accommodate us in

42. Cf. J. Koopmans, *De Nederlandse Geloofsbelijdenis* (the Belgic Confession of Faith), 1939, 101. This stanza comes from the collection *Evangelsche Gezangen* (evangelical hymns, no. 125).

43. See H. Miskotte, *Verzameld werk* (collected works), 1990, 9:295–317—originally an inaugural speech, 1945.

44. Revius in his *Over-ysselsche sangen en dichten* (songs and poems of Overijssel—an eastern province of the Netherlands, 1930, 1:17), quoted by K. H. Miskotte, ibid., 37).

his manner of speaking. They imply recognition of our weakness (cf. Calvin, *Institutes*, 1.13.1).[45]

The confession that God is spiritual implies that he is entirely different from everything earthly and human. He is not corporeal and dependent as we are. He is the Giver of life. "God's spirituality points to the essential distinction that exists between God the Creator and Re-creator, and man, his creature" (Gootjes, 1985, 228).

There is yet another approach. "Spiritual" can be considered to be a reference to self-conscience and personality. Sometimes it is understood in terms of God's absolute freedom to act and judge.

There is a tendency to assign a special role to God's spirituality and view it as an indication of Being. But the phrase: "God is Spirit" (John 4:24) does not mean that God is a Spirit. This would assign a categorical significance to the word "pneuma" (spirit) and make it into class concept, which could include other beings. However, Jesus' words are qualifying and not categorizing. It actually says: Spirit is God. We thereby need to think especially of the biblical idea that it is the Spirit who gives life (cf. John 6:63).[46]

13.4. *God is eternal*

1. A primary aspect of God's eternity (*aeternitas Dei*) is that he has not become what he is and will not cease to be what he is. God has life in himself. He has no beginning and no end. This is stated quite clearly in Psalms 90:2 and 102:28. "The everlasting God [is] the Creator of the ends of the earth" (Isa. 40:28). Prior to the existence of the world, God is who he is. From the beginning to the consummation the world and time are sustained and encompassed by the eternity of God (cf. Pannenberg, 1988, 439). When this world no longer exists, God is there and then also is who he is.

2. God's eternity also means that he is elevated beyond all changes of time. The distinction between time and eternity is not quantitative but qualitative. God's eternity is not endless time. With Barth (*The Epistle to the Romans*), one can speak of the infinite qualitative differ-

45. Kuitert pursued an entirely different direction. This led him to refer to God as *theomorph* or human in form, "which does not exclude God's corporealness." His human form would imply nothing but his "manifestation as Covenantal Partner" (H. M. Kuitert, *De mensvormingheid Gods* (God's human form), 1962, 213, 222. For a critical evaluation, see among others Gootjes, 1985, 184–87, 193–99.

46. What is true of God according to this name is, now that the Messiah has come, actually the case in a way that was hitherto unknown. That is how J. R. Wiskerke interpreted the words of John 4:24, *De strijd om de sleutel der kennis* (the battle for the key of knowledge), 1978, 115–17; Cf. Gootjes, 1985, 141.

ence between time and eternity, as long as one keeps in mind that the eternal God seeks to have communion with human beings in time.[47]

Since God is elevated above time, there is no succession of moments to him and thus no past, present, and future as for us. In this connection we can point to the passage: "For a thousand years in thy sight are but as yesterday when it is past, and as a watch in the night" (Ps. 90:4; cf. 2 Peter 3:8). God's eternity is an eternal present, for from his perspective everything is in the present, as was pointed out by Augustine already. He can see time in its entirety, namely our past, our present, and our future.[48]

3. The eternal God has absolute sovereignty over time and everything temporal. Because of his eternity he can enter at any point of history and penetrate each moment of time with his eternity. "In each moment of time beats the pulse of eternity."[49]

Because of this relationship with eternity, life in time is highly serious. In time we encounter the eternal God, who has revealed himself in Christ. Definitive decisions are made. God's eternity does not in the least eliminate our responsibility in time. His eternity is therefore "not a wall, but a door to our prayers."[50]

4. With this we have arrived at the practical significance of the confession that God is the Eternal One.

The fact that he is God "from everlasting to everlasting" (Ps. 90:2) and that he is "the King eternal" (the King of the ages, 1 Tim. 1:17) means that we meet him all the time, however far we go back and however far we look ahead. What is true for the world and time may definitely be said of the life of God's children. It is sustained from the beginning and encompassed by the eternal God, who in Christ is their God and Father.

"Whatsoever God doeth, it shall be for ever" says the Preacher, "and God doeth it, that men should fear before him" (Eccl. 3:14). "Trust ye in the LORD for ever: for in the LORD Jehovah is everlasting strength" (Isa. 26:4). "The word of our God shall stand for ever" (Isa. 40:8) "and endureth for ever" (1 Peter 1:25). His "salvation shall be for ever" (Isa. 51:6). "The mercy of the LORD is from everlasting to everlasting upon them that fear him" (Ps. 103:17). "His praise endureth for ever" (Ps. 111:10). "Unto the King eternal, immortal, invisible, the only wise God, be honour and glory for ever and ever. Amen" (1Timothy 1:17).

47. Barth came back from his earlier views of eternity and time, because at first he did not see the concept of eternity in its biblical totality as pre-temporality, supra-temporality, and post-temporality (*C.D.*, 2.1.635).

48. Augustine, *Confessiones*, 11:13–16. Cf. Polman, 1965, 335–38.

49. H. Bavinck, *Wijsbegeerte der openbaring* (philosophy of revelation), 1908, 23.

50. O. Jager, *Het eeuwige leven* (eternal life), 1962, 520.

13.5. *God is unchangeable; he is faithful and true*

God is unchangeable. There was a time when this was considered to be a very meaningful aspect of the image of God. Church fathers such as Origen, Athanasius, and Augustine, in the face of paganism with its fickle gods whose behavior was always unpredictable, in the face of Gnosticism in its various forms, and in the face of various heresies, maintained emphatically that God does not change.

In the early doctrine of immutability (*immutabilitas Dei*) we recognize a biblical element: God is the Faithful One. But there also is a philosophical aspect: he is immovable. The influence of Aristotle led Thomas Aquinas to a rigid concept of immutability: God is the Unmoved Mover, the First Cause who was not created himself.[51] According to the Reformed theologian F. Junius (1545–1602), God is also the immovable First Mover! This scholastic train of thought can still be recognized in Bavinck's work, although he also draws from the biblical well. According to him, the idea of God itself implies immutability. "He cannot change for better or worse, for he is the absolute, complete, the true being." Not only Scripture testifies of God's immutability, but reflection on this matter also leads to the same conclusion (*R.D.*, 2:156–59).

However, thinking definitely did not bring the Remonstrants, at least not Vorstius, to this conclusion! And in the more recent theology many have been led by the charm of Hegelian dialectics to presume a process of change in God!

It has been pointed out that the doctrine of God's immutability has the merit of erecting a bulwark against a pagan erosion of the concept of God, but that at the same time it leads to an equally pagan rigidity of thought.[52]

If only one thing has become clear in this review of various views, it is that we may not limit ourselves to human contemplation of God, but must ask for the light of the revelation of God himself.

A classical Scripture proof is 1 Samuel 15:29: "Also the strength of Israel will not lie nor repent: for he is not a man, that he should repent" (cf. also Num. 23:19). God remains the same, in contrast with the passing and decay of everything that exists (cf. Ps. 102:26–28). "For I am the LORD, I change not" (Mal. 3:6). The image of the rock stands for invariability. "Ascribe ye greatness unto our God. He is the Rock, his work is perfect" (Deut. 32:3–4).

A clear text in the New Testament is James 1:17. With "the Father of lights . . . is no variableness, neither shadow of turning." Reference is made to "the immutability of his counsel" (Heb. 6:17). "The gift and calling of God are without repentance" (Rom. 11:29).

Reformers such as Luther and Calvin directly follow Scripture in speaking of God's immutability. Luther says (with an appeal to Malachi

51. Cf. P. den Ottolander, *Deus immutabilis*, 1965, 22–28.
52. F. W. A. Korff, *Christologie*, 1942^2, 1:257.

3:6 and Rom. 11:29) that our comfort is that even if we change, we may yet seek refuge with God who is unchangeable. If God would not be faithful to his promise, our faith would come to an end. God has manifested himself in the flesh. It is an immense joy that he is unchangeable and that he cannot deny himself, but keeps his promises. Luther criticizes Erasmus by saying that God works everything in an unchangeable manner and that his will cannot be resisted, changed, or thwarted (WA, 43:458, 461; 18:619). Therefore God's immutability gives comfort, joy, and certainty to believers. One could also refer to it as God's veracity or his faithfulness to his promises.

According to Calvin, God's children may trust that God will remain the same to them in the future. God is not like human beings who weary of their own generosity, or whose resources are spent. He is permanently himself (*Institutes*, 3.20.26). The terms truthfulness and faithfulness are used in the same context. A synonym of immutability is constancy (*Institutes*, 1.17.12).

When Bavinck presents the witness of Scripture, he describes God's immutability also along these lines: he remains who he is. He is who he is. What he says, he will do. He completes what he has begun (*R.D.*, 2:153).

But then we still need to deal with Scripture passages such as Genesis 6:7; Exodus 32:10–14; 1 Samuel 15:11, 35; and other Old Testament texts in which we read of divine repentance.

According to Bavinck, Scripture speaks here in human terms. Others refer to it as an uncharacteristic manner of speaking.

How should we interpret God's repentance? According to the dictionary, the word "repentance" suggests that someone is sorry about the fact that he has done or failed to do something. But God's repentance is different from that of people (see 1 Sam. 15:29). He fulfills his promises and carries out his threats. But he does react to the changing stance of people. Israel's history is replete with this! Whenever he adjusts his actions and thinks better of the judgment that he has announced, this is referred to as repentance, but it should have been anticipated on the basis of his covenant. It is "covenantal non-repentance" (Kamphuis, 1955, 122). In this connection see especially Jeremiah 18:7–10, which refers to God's repentance concerning the evil that he had planned to visit upon Israel, and to his repentance with respect to the good that he had promised. The former emerges when his people repent; the latter when they turn away from him.

God's immutability does not imply a lack of compassion. Otherwise it could not be said that "it grieved him at his heart" (Gen. 6:6). Neither could he be moved by his entreaty (2 Chron. 33:13). It would not be consistent with his words: "Mine heart is turned within me, my repentings are kindled together. I will not execute the fierceness of mine anger, I will not return to destroy Ephraim" (Hos. 11:8–9). When God repents and then does something or refrains from doing something (cf. Ex. 32:10–14), this reflects his living encounter with his people. But in doing so, he is always true to himself.

There is no biblical foundation whatever to portray God as a God who changes when the world changes and who therefore can be encountered especially in those changes—a view known to be held by process theology, as influenced by the philosophy of A. N. Whitehead (d. 1947; cf. Wentsel, *Dogm.*, 3a:173ff.).

Berkhof has correctly pointed out that we come across a Scylla and a Charybdis here: "Before we know it, we fall into the Scylla of the Hegelian God-concept (the absolute Mind realizing itself in the world), even theology has for centuries succumbed to the Charybdis of the Aristotlelian God-concept." But Berkhof himself also makes statements that are more reminiscent of Hegel than the Bible. One example: God's decision "to be together with us involved a process, a process which includes Gethsemane's anguish and Calvary's God-forsakenness" (*C.F.*, 151–54). He has a section titled: "The Changeable Faithfulness." But from a biblical perspective it would have to be God's unchangeable faithfulness!

We hereby also reject the views of A. van de Beek, who goes still further than Berkhof when he discusses these issues under the heading: "God is changeable." He does admit that God's actions are consistent, but holds that the God of the Bible is an emotional, vehement, changeable God, who takes one course today and another tomorrow, who changes his mind from moment to moment. That he continually changes in his judgments, and follows a capricious course through history, can seem frightful, but "what else does one expect in this frightful world in which people must live?"[53] The latter betrays that human experience is Van de Beek's starting point.

If one finds the concept of immutability to be too rigid or too static and therefore has difficulty with this word, there is always the option to adopt Barth's term of "Beständigkeit" (constancy, *C.D.*, 2.1.490). This implies that God does not change from moment to moment.

But it is preferable to emphasize that the main thing is the immutability of him who has compassion for us and who is involved in all that happens. This is the God of the covenant, the God and Father of our Lord Jesus Christ.

Any misunderstanding would be prevented by mentioning God's immutability, truthfulness, and faithfulness in a single breath. Scripture shows us the way in this regard. Reference has already been made

53. A. van de Beek, *Waarom?* (why?), 1984, 252–66.

to the image of the Rock, which implies unchangeable steadfastness (Deut. 32:4). There it also says that he is "a God of truth and without iniquity" and that he is "just and right."

From a theological perspective, God's immutability, his truthfulness, and his faithfulness cannot be separated from each other.

While God's immutability is referred to in a relatively small number of places, his faithfulness and truthfulness turn up time and again throughout the Old and New Testaments. Our word "reliable" is an approximation to Hebrew words that point to steadfastness (especially *ʾemet*). God is a God of *Amen*, "the God of truth" (Isa. 65:16). "The words *chesed* (solidarity) and *ʾemet* (faithfulness, steadfastness) are continually used in combination and actually form a single concept: the steadfast, faithful solidarity which is indissoluble" (Vriezen, *Hoofdlijnen* = main perspectives, 335–39). The LORD is "abundant in goodness and truth" (Ex. 34:6). "Be thou exalted, O God, above the heavens: let thy glory be above all the earth" (Ps. 57:11).

New Testament terms (especially *alèthinos* and *pistos*) represent a confirmation and an extension of what the Old Testament says about God's trustworthiness.

The Father of our Lord Jesus Christ is "the only true God" and his "word is truth" (John 17:3, 17). "God [is] true, but every man a liar" (Rom. 3:4). To believe in Christ is to confirm "that God is true" (John 3:33). Jesus called himself "the truth." He is called "the Amen, the faithful and true witness" (John 14:6; Rev. 3:14).

There are additional statements in the epistles in the New Testament: "Faithful is he that calleth you, who also will do it" (1 Thess. 5:24). "He is faithful that promised" (Heb. 10:23). Their aim is that we shall always allow ourselves to be guided by this God who revealed his truth and faithfulness so perfectly in Christ, and that we shall place our entire trust in him. He means what he says and he does what he says (cf. 2 Cor. 1:20). His people can depend on him in all circumstances. We can rely on him for ever.

13.6. *God's omnipresence*

In early dogmatics God's eternity and omnipresence were frequently distinguished from each other as infinity with respect to time and space respectively. But we understand God's eternity to be more than a matter of infinity. Since the same thing is true with respect to his omnipresence, it is preferable to devote a separate discussion to this aspect rather than infinity.

1. We need to understand in the first place that God's omnipresence (*omnipraesentia Dei*) implies that he is not bound to place and space. Space is not merely a human perspective. It is the mode of existence of creation. Space is an aspect of the structure of created reality. "Behold, heaven and heaven of heavens cannot contain [God]" (1 Kings 8:27).

His omnipresence implies that he fills and controls all places with his presence. He says: "Do not I fill heaven and earth?" (Jer. 23:24). We are nowhere beyond his reach. He is everywhere with his Spirit, his presence, and his hand (Ps. 139:5–10). Omnipresence includes sovereignty, for how could he be present somewhere without ruling there in a divine manner? This is how he upholds and governs everything through his almighty and omnipresent power (Heidelberg Catechism, Lord's Day 10).

2. His omnipresence does not mean that he is present everywhere in exactly the same manner. In heaven he is present differently than on earth (see Isa. 66:1). In heaven everything is filled with his glorious presence. There is a distinction between his presence in the church of Christ and his presence in creation. He is also with them who seek to escape from his presence (cf. Amos 9:2). There is a presence of God that is to be feared.[54] But his nearness brings salvation and peace to his people. "[He] dwell[s] in the high and holy place, with him also that is of a contrite and humble spirit" (Isa. 57:15–21).

In Christ God is present among people in an altogether unique way. "In him dwelleth all the fullness of the Godhead bodily" (Col. 2:9). Christology delves more deeply into this. God lets his children share in his nearness and dwells in the church with his Spirit. "God is present; God is in our midst" (Dutch hymn by Gerhard Tersteegen, 1697–1769). This also will be discussed further below. God will be present everywhere more gloriously than ever, at the fulfillment of what is said in the book of Revelation: "Behold, the tabernacle of God is with men, and he will dwell with them, and they shall be his people, and God himself will be with them, and be their God" (Rev. 21:3).

54. Concerning the question as to how God is present in hell, see K. Schilder, *Wat is de hel?* 1932, 100ff. Schilder said: Everything there spells God's name. The I-He relationship is indeed there, but the I-Thou relationship is lacking. Cf. also H. Vogel, *Gott in Christo*, 1952², 375.

3. God's omnipresence also far exceeds our understanding. "God is in heaven, and thou upon earth" (Eccl. 5:2). Yet "he [is] not far from every one of us" (Acts 17:27). "The LORD is nigh unto all them that call upon him, to all that call upon him in truth" (Ps. 145:18).

A distinction that was made by Augustine is that between the presence of God, whereby he is present everywhere and absent nowhere, and the grace of his indwelling. In this sense God is not everywhere, for then he dwells in those whom he makes his temple (1 Cor. 3:16; 6:19).[55]

13.7. *God's omnipotence*

1. When we reflect upon God's omnipotence (*omnipotentia Dei*) we should not think in terms of the superlative of our human concept of power. This would be power on a grand scale or absolute power, but not divine power. God's omnipotence does not differ in terms of degree, but in terms of essence from everything that we call power.

In his Word he makes himself known as the Almighty. The name LORD of Hosts occurs frequently in the Old Testament (280 times) and is also used in the New Testament. There it says: the Almighty (Rev. 1:8, among other places). The question whether anything would be "too hard" for the LORD (Gen. 18:14; cf. Jer. 32:17–19) refers to God's omnipotence.

2. God's omnipotence is no anonymous power. The Apostles' Creed begins with the words: "I believe in God the Father, the Almighty," or "I believe in God, the almighty Father" (for this translation is also possible). God's omnipotence should at any rate be seen from the perspective of his Fatherhood.

We should not make God's omnipotence into an abstract concept. Therefore we do not refer to it without thinking at the same time of his holy will, his infinite wisdom, and his goodness. Based on the conviction that to God literally everything is possible, nominalism has raised a number of ingenious questions. We contrast this with impossibilities that the Bible itself refers to. God cannot deny himself, he cannot lie, he cannot be tempted by evil (2 Tim. 2:13; Heb. 6:18; James 1:13). God cannot do anything that is in conflict with his essence. But this is not impotence! He is unable to do these things in a mighty way (Augustine). The measure of what is feasible lies within God himself.

3. God manifests his omnipotence in all his deeds. Early Reformed dogmatics perhaps defined God's omnipotence too much from the

55. See Polman, 1965, 320–28.

perspective of creation and the preservation of the world. Barth, however, runs the danger of falling into another extreme. Using as his starting point the witness of Jesus Christ as the very center of history, in terms of which the entire biblical testimony to God's omnipotence is characterized, he seeks to interpret God's omnipotence as power of salvation (cf. *C.D.*, 2.1.522–607, especially 604–7). He has many followers in this regard.

God's power of salvation is undoubtedly a power that must be interpreted as omnipotence. But this does not necessarily imply that his omnipotence is solely power of salvation or—with a variation borrowed from Bonhoeffer—that God's omnipotence is preeminently manifested in the saving power of Christ, who on the cross was unable to save himself. Bonhoeffer wrote the frequently cited words: "God permits himself to be crowded out of the world as far as the cross."[56] Van Ruler correctly observes in this regard: "This divine impotence on the cross actually reflects a divine omnipotence of atonement. The cross does not stand on its own. There is also the resurrection!" (Van Ruler, *Ik geloof* = I believe, 28ff.).

God's omnipotence is indeed always the omnipotence of his holy love. Believers recognize this as the "gracious omnipotence" of him who opened his heart to us in Jesus Christ (cf. Weber, *Foundations*, 1:446–47).

4. Berkhof believes that the Bible only speaks of God's omnipotence in eschatological contexts and that we cannot associate it with the present time (*C.F.*, 146). On the basis of the biblical "story of revelation" one supposedly gains the impression of God's impotence, which Berkhof refers to as his defenselessness. This defenselessness reaches its nadir on the cross, where Jesus is not able to save himself, when God remains silent, and free and rebellious man triumphs over God. However, this is not the defenselessness of God's impotence, but of his superior power. To Berkhof, God is "the Defenseless Superior Power" (*C.F.*, 140–47).[57] The superior power of love will some day melt away all resistance and will then be almighty. "If some day in his fellowship of love with us God will be the almighty, then such is possible only because he is already in himself and from eternity the almighty." Does this imply that God is almighty after all? It is portrayed here that he is so in himself, but that in creation he relinquished some of his power to man, whereby a definite limit was put to the power of God, and that one day he will yet be almighty.

56. D. Bonhoeffer, *Widerstand und Ergebung* (resistance and surrender), republished 1970, 394 (letter of 16 July 1944).

57. This image of God appeals to many. Cf. among others H. Wiersinga, *Verzoening met het lijden?* (reconciliation with suffering?), 1975, 66.

All of this reflects a certain view of the relationship between God and man that we reject. We shall address this below. Here it suffices to say that there is no biblical ground for the notion of a vulnerable superior power of God that is neither impotent nor omnipotent. Theological concepts, however important, should never displace the message of the Bible. In Scripture we can find no support for the idea that God's omnipotence would suffer as a result of man's freedom, because God grants it to him in the first place; neither can man's rebellion diminish it. Van Ruler said: God is superior to man. This is true in three respects: the vicissitudes of life that God apportions to man; God's sovereignty in election and reprobation; and the Spirit's magic wand with which God merely needs to touch a person to turn him into a new human being to the depth of his being, so that he no longer rebels against God (Van Ruler, *Ik geloof* = I believe, 30ff.).

5. God's power is a sovereign power. His omnipotence and his absolute sovereignty—what he can do and will do—cannot be separated from each other. The creation of the world testifies of both his omnipotence and his absolute sovereignty. An exclamation of praise says: "Thou hast created all things, and for thy pleasure they are and were created" (Rev. 4:11).

He works miracles, not primarily to demonstrate what he can accomplish, but who he is. We think of the miracle of creation, but no less of the miracles that are part of the history of redemption. The incarnation of the Word and the resurrection of Christ are miracles performed by almighty God, the God and Father of our Lord Jesus Christ.

Bultmann and many others who attempt to interpret the Christian faith in a modern way start out from a closed causal system, in which there is no room for God's intervention. In the face of such thinking we must cling to the belief that God is omnipotent. Thielicke points out that the real message of the history of miracles is that God remains in control of his world.[58]

The confession of God's omnipotence is also focused on the future. We believe that with him more is possible than has become reality up to now. A still richer manifestation of his omnipotence is anticipated (Beker/Hasselaar, *Wegen* = ways, 1:82).

6. It is almighty God who governs everything. The fact that many do not recognize this, and that it cannot be casually inferred from day-to-day events, is no reason for doubt. The church believes in him who is "almighty God and . . . a faithful Father" (Heidelberg Cate-

58. H. Thielicke, *Ik geloof* (I believe), 1965, 77.

chism, Lord's Day 9). We are conscious of our own weakness and dependence. But we have the confidence that He, "our King, who [has] power over all things, [is] both willing and able to give us all good . . . that thereby . . . his holy Name may be glorified for ever" (Heidelberg Catechism, Lord's Day 52; cf. also Lord's Day 49).

13.8. *God's wisdom and omniscience*

In the Bible, wisdom comprises more than knowledge. It refers to action that is focused on the right goal. God's wisdom (*sapientia Dei*) means that he subjects everything to his purpose. He is the "only wise God" (Rom. 16:27). There is yet another aspect that theology has identified: God's wisdom is a continuing readiness to make decisions (cf. Schilder, *H.C.*, 3:424ff.).

God reveals his wisdom in the creation and preservation of the world (Ps. 104:24; Jer. 10:12), in his guidance through history and the history of redemption (Rom. 11:33), and most of all in Christ, who is called "the power of God and the wisdom of God" (1 Cor. 1:24). "In [Him] are hid all the treasures of wisdom and knowledge" (Col. 2:3). He is the personification of God's wisdom.

God gives wisdom to his people (Prov. 2:6; James 1:5). His Word can make us "wise unto salvation" (2 Tim. 3:15). His Spirit is "the Spirit of wisdom and revelation." The manifold wisdom of God must be made known everywhere through the church (Eph. 1:17; 3:10).

In some passages wisdom and the knowledge of God are mentioned in one breath (Rom. 11:33; Col. 2:3). In the case of people, wisdom and knowledge can be kept apart. One can acquire a great deal of knowledge without becoming wise. But in God's case knowledge and wisdom are inseparable.

God's knowledge (*scientia Dei*) is not based on observation and inference. His "understanding is infinite" (Ps. 147:5). Calvin says: All things are so under his eyes that he truly looks upon them and discerns them as things placed before him (cf. *Institutes*, 3.21.5). He not only sees everything standing before him, he is also always involved. His is an all-encompassing and all-penetrating knowledge. He is the omniscient God. Elihu calls him the One who "is perfect in knowledge" (Job 37:16).

Scripture says: "The LORD is a God of knowledge, and by him actions are weighed" (1 Sam. 2:3). And yet more personally: "O LORD, thou hast searched me, and known me. Thou knowest my downsitting and mine uprising, thou understandest my thought afar off" (Ps. 139:1–2). God's actions are in harmony with his knowledge (cf. Jer. 17:9–10).

God's knowledge surpasses our own understanding (Ps. 139:6). His omniscience must instill terror in those who do not fear him (cf. Jer. 16:17), but it is a comfort to believers that he knows those who are his own and knows what they need (2 Tim. 2:19; Matt. 6:32).

13.9. *God's righteousness*

1. When God's righteousness or justice (*iustitia Dei*) is broached, we are inclined to follow our own concept of what is just. This has also frequently been the case in theology. Usually the following prescription was borrowed from Plato or Aristotle, also encountered in Roman jurisprudence: give everyone his due. Thomas Aquinas followed this tradition by saying that God's justice could be recognized from the fact that he gives everyone what he deserves.

Luther became altogether bogged down in it. This philosophical or scholastic concept of justice blocked his way to an understanding of the message of the Bible. If God's justice implies that he gives everyone what he deserves, he must reward those who do the right thing and punish those who sin and are unrighteous. But how can the psalmists then pray for salvation through God's righteousness? How can Paul say in Romans 1:17 that God's righteousness is revealed in the gospel?

2. We must ask ourselves what Scripture says about God's righteousness. There is an Old Testament term that points to judging righteously and doing justice (*mispat*). The Hebrew word for righteousness that occurs frequently in the Old Testament (*sedaqa*) is sometimes presented as a relational concept. Righteousness and justice are manifested in relationships. Someone is just when he acts as may be expected in his relationship with God and fellow human beings.

God is the Just One. He deals with us as would be expected on the basis of his Word. He keeps his covenant. This cannot be equated with "giving each his due" or "treating everyone the same way." He is called just with reference to his promises, but also in relationship to his demands. He requires from people: "to do justly, and to love mercy, and to walk humbly with thy God" (Mic. 6:8).

God reveals himself in his words and actions as the just God. He is also the just Judge (Ps. 7:11). "For in thy sight shall no man living be justified" (Ps. 143:2). "O Lord, righteousness belongeth unto thee, but unto us confusion of faces" (Dan. 9:7).

According to a number of theologians, the concept of a punishing righteousness of God is alien to the Old Testament. See, however, Psalm 94:2: God punishes the arrogant, because he is Judge of the earth (cf. also Pss. 7:12; 11:5–7; Isa. 5:16; 10:22; 59:16–18; Dan. 9:14). Yet the idea that God's righteousness brings about salvation predominates in the Old Testament (cf. Isa. 46:13). His salvation and righteousness go hand in hand (Ps. 98:2). The word "righteousness" can also be used in the plural as an indication of God's redeeming acts ("righteous acts," 1 Sam. 12:7).

There are Scripture passages that focus on the definitive revelation of God's righteousness. Jeremiah 23:6 announces the coming of him who bears the name, "The LORD our righteousness." In and through him God's righteousness will be achieved and therefore the salvation of his people. The Messiah will establish and sustain his Kingdom with justice and righteousness (Isa. 9:7).

Also in the revelation of the New Testament God is the God of righteousness. He demands righteousness and he grants righteousness.

The apostle Paul objected to Jewish views of his time. We cannot fulfill God's commandments in our own strength. It is wrong to seek God's favor in this way. The aim is the righteousness that is of God and that we can only participate in through faith.

There are various interpretations of God's righteousness as presented by Paul. The first is that of Augustine and the Reformers. To them it is the righteousness with which God clothes people, the righteousness that comes from God and that belongs to him. But there is more to be said for the christological view. God's righteousness is connected with the revelation of God manifested in Christ's death and resurrection, and the salvation that God grants us in consequence. On the basis of this righteousness, the just God declares sinful people to be just.[59]

3. Partly as a result of the greater emphasis on the soteriological character of God's righteousness in more recent biblical research, many focus exclusively on the connection between righteousness and salvation. It is then doubted or denied that God can also be angry. Yet his wrath is an effect of his righteousness and holiness. A. Ritschl (1822–89) denies God's vindictive righteousness. Others cannot believe that his wrath can endure forever. If he is angry at all, his anger will not last and his love will ultimately prevail.

59. Cf. J. van Genderen, *Gerechtigheid als geschenk* (righteouness as gift), 1988, 26ff.

We do not counter this with the traditional concept of righteousness, which emphasizes just rewards, retribution, or exaction. We must allow ourselves to be guided by the notion that God's righteousness implies that he acts in accordance with his Word. And his Word is clear. It tells us that his righteousness does not always redeem or liberate, but sometimes also condemns, requites, revenges, and punishes. It depends on our relationship with him. See Psalm 11:5–7; Isaiah 5:16; and other places in the Old Testament. In the New Testament it is no different (2 Thess. 1:5–8; Rev. 16:5–7).

Neither is it biblical to view God's righteousness as merely a qualification of his love, as advocated by Barth. Then his righteousness is identified with his mercy. God's righteousness, manifested in the judgment of Golgotha, signifies grace to us, because it has made judgment a thing of the past. God's grace is then so all-pervasive that the question arises whether apart from after-pains of the reality of this divine judgment there could still be another judgment in addition to the judgment that Christ underwent (cf. *C.D.*, 2.1.405).

4. Especially in the Reformed confession and in Reformed theology God's righteousness is assigned a prominent place.

- In the first place in the doctrine of sin and its punishment (see Heidelberg Catechism, Lord's Day 4). From a human point of view, it is not easy to accept what Scripture says—neither in the past nor today—but we must learn to agree with God.
- Further in the confession of predestination (see Belgic Confession of Faith, article 16; Canons of Dort, 1). In Romans 9:14, Paul says: "What shall we say then? Is there unrighteousness with God? God forbid."
- The question as to God's righteousness can also emerge in thinking about providence. Reference is made to adoring "the righteous judgments of God, which are hid from us" (Belgic Confession of Faith, article 13).
- The doctrine of atonement through satisfaction quite directly focuses on God's righteousness (see Belgic Confession of Faith, article 20; Canons of Dort, 2).
- We further think of the doctrine of salvation. God is just also when he justifies those who believe in Jesus (Rom. 3:26). Justification is a gracious and judicial act of God (cf. Heidelberg

Catechism, Lord's Day 23). God requires of us to love all righteousness, which is part of our sanctification (cf. Lord's Day 44).

- Finally, there is the doctrine of the last judgment. We anticipate his coming "as Judge from heaven" who first "offered himself for [our] sake to the tribunal of God" (Heidelberg Catechism, Lord's Day 19).

13.10. *God's goodness*

A song praising the goodness of God (*bonitas Dei*) permeates the entire Bible. He alone is good in the strictest sense of the word (cf. Mark 10:18). He is good and does good (Ps. 119:68). It is his nature to do good. Its foundation lies within himself.

The evil nature of people does not prevent God from showing his goodness to them, "for he maketh his sun to rise on the evil and on the good, and sendeth rain on the just and on the unjust" (Matt. 5:45). He "is good to all" (Ps. 145:9), although not everyone is aware of this. Those who share in his favor "taste and see that the LORD is good" (Ps. 34:8; cf. 1 Peter 2:3).

God's goodness is the source of all that is good. "Every good gift and every perfect gift is from above, and cometh down from the Father of lights" (James 1:17). Luther calls him the eternal source of overflowing goodness, from whom comes everything that is good and is called good (Larger Catechism). Calvin refers to the unmerited goodness of God as being immeasurable.

The church confesses God's goodness. "He is . . . perfectly good, and the overflowing fountain of all good" (Belgic Confession of Faith, article 1). He reveals his goodness most richly in Christ. "In his admirable wisdom and goodness [God gave] his Son" to man (article 17). The Lord gives his people "a true assurance of his fatherly goodness" (article 34).

God's goodness means that everything that comes from him is good. It is impossible for him to be the author of evil. Creation is good (Gen. 1). God's "commandment [is] holy, and just, and good" (Rom. 7:12). What God does in the lives of his people is good (Phil. 1:6).

God's goodness also means that everything that is good comes from him. Calvin says: "No drop will be found either of wisdom and light, or of righteousness or power or rectitude, or of genuine truth, which does not flow from him, and of which he is not the cause" (*Institutes*, 1.2.1). Bavinck writes: "No good exists in any creature except that which comes from and through him" (*R.D.*, 2:212).

Let us praise God for his goodness, as Scripture directs us. Not infrequently does it speak in one breath of his goodness and his mercy or lovingkindness (*chesed*). "For the LORD is good; his mercy is everlasting; and his truth endureth to all generations" (Ps. 100:5). "O give thanks to the LORD; for he is good: for his mercy endureth for ever" (Ps. 136:1).

13.11. *God's glory*

Any theological doctrine of God is far surpassed by what God reveals about himself. This does not render our own words false or useless, but does make us aware that we need to listen to the Word of God with an open heart to attain a richer knowledge of him.

This knowledge has implications. God's eternity causes us to number our days (Ps. 90:12). His incomprehensibility encourages us to give him all honor (Rom. 11:33–36). His invisibility teaches us to "walk by faith and not by sight" (2 Cor. 5:7).[60]

The foregoing material may be incomplete in part because the subsequent chapters that deal with God's works will cover what has received little or no attention thus far: God's autonomy in the doctrine of creation; God's long-suffering in his providence; God's grace in election, the covenant of grace, and the doctrine of salvation. His "power, wisdom, goodness, justice, mercy and truth shine forth" brightly in his works (Heidelberg Catechism, Lord's Day 47). At the same time, it is true that there are more perfections of God that stand out in this regard.

We can think of everything that has been left out when we finally focus on God's glory.

God's majesty is expressed in all of his names, but the word "glory" expresses it eminently. It is noteworthy that in the Old Testament, "glory" (*kabod*) can be equivalent to God's name (Ps. 102:16; Isa. 59:19).

God's glory fully reveals all of his perfections (Barth, *C.D.*, 2.1.643). He may be called the Illustrious One (cf. Wentsel, *Dogm.*, 3a:chapters 9–10).

God's glory (*Gloria Dei*) represents the imposing majesty and splendor that are characteristic of him and that he radiates when he reveals himself. A number of passages suggest an overwhelming radiance,

60. See further J. Koopmans, *De Nederlandsche Geloofsbelijdenis* (the Belgic Confession of Faith), 1939, 21.

which indicates that God is present. His glory may appear in the form of a cloud (Ex. 16:10). The Bible makes a connection between God's glory and his holiness, power, greatness, majesty, and luster (Isa. 6:3; Ps. 63:2; Deut. 5:24; Ps. 104:1). It is the glory of his kingship (Ps. 145:11–12).

He reveals his glory in creation, in his acts in the history of his people Israel, and in his dwelling among the people in the tabernacle and the temple. His exaltedness is awe-inspiring, but so is his nearness (cf. Ps. 113:4 and 1 Kings 8:10–11). His glory makes him as unapproachable as a consuming fire (Ex. 24:17). Yet he dwells with his glory in the midst of his people, and this leads to respect and adoration, praise and thanksgiving (2 Chron. 7:1–3). The appearance of his glory is longed for, because it brings salvation (Isa. 60:1–3).

God is "the Father of glory" (Eph. 1:17). The person and the work of Christ are the manifestation of his glory (cf. John 1:14). God's glory is seen and proclaimed upon Christ's arrival (Luke 2:9, 14). The New Testament refers to "the glory of God in the face of Jesus Christ" (2 Cor. 4:6).

Mighty prophecies in the Old Testament testify to the fact that the glory of God has universal dimensions and points to God's great future (see *TWAT*, 4:36–38). "For the earth shall be filled with the knowledge of the glory of the LORD, as the waters cover the sea" (Hab. 2:14). One day everything will be full of the glory of God (Isa. 66:18; Rev. 21:23). At the end of all of God's ways and works stands his glory.

The revelation of God's glory is accompanied by the glorification of his name. Angels and people are invited to bring God the honor that is due to him (Pss. 29:1–2; 66:2). It is sinful not to glorify God in whose hands is our breath and who ordains all of our ways (Dan. 5:23).

Doxology is part of the worship services of the church, and more scope could be given to praise and adoration. Following in Calvin's footsteps, the Reformed tradition came to see the glorification of God as the chief goal of a Christian's life. Is it not our aim to live to the honor of God? (see 1 Cor. 10:31). The first response in the Westminster Larger Catechism is very meaningful: "Man's chief and highest end is to glorify God, and fully to enjoy him forever."

Although the formal doctrine of God it not itself a doxology, the contemplation of God's glory must end in praise, which is the implication of all of his perfections: Soli Deo Gloria. Scripture guides us in this regard:

And blessed be his glorious name for ever:
And let the whole earth be filled with his glory;
Amen, and Amen. (Ps. 72:19)

Blessing, and honour, and glory and power,
Be unto him that sitteth upon the throne,
And unto the Lamb for ever and ever. (Rev. 5:13)

Some Literature

J. Auer, *Gott—Der Eine und Dreieine* (God—one and triune), 1978.

Th. de Boer, *De God van de filosofen en de God van Pascal*, 1989.

L. J. van den Brom, *God alomtegenwoordig* (omnipresent), 1982.

F. Courth, *Trinität. In der Schrift und Patristik* (in the Bible and patristics), *Handbuch der Dogmengeschichte* (handbook of dogmatic history), 2:1a, 1988.

H. Cremer, *Die Christliche Lehre von den Eigenschaften Gottes* (the Christian doctrine of the attributes of God), 1917[2].

L. Doekes, *Der Heilige* (the holy one), 1960.

E. A. Dowey Jr., *The Knowledge of God in Calvin's Theology*, 1952.

J. J. F. Durand, *Die lewende God* (the living God), 1976.

N. H. Gootjes, *De geestelijkheid van God* (the spirituality of God), 1985.

J. de Groot and A. R. Hulst, *Macht en wil* (power and will), no date.

J. A. Heyns, *Die grondstruktuur van die modalistiese triniteitsbeskouing* (the foundation of the modalistic view of the Trinity), 1953.

H. G. Hubbeling, *Denkend geloven* (believing while thinking), 1976.

F. G. Immink, *Divine Simplicity*, 1987.

J. Kamphuis, "Christus en de Geest in de Gereformeerde theologie" (Christ and the Spirit in Reformed theology), *Radix* 15, (1989): 154–80.

J. Kamphuis, *Katholieke vastheid* (Catholic firmness), 1955.

W. Kasper, *Der Gott Jesus Christi* (the God Jesus Christ), 1983[2].

C. Link, *Die Welt als Gleichnis* (the world as a parable), 1976.

H.-G. Link (ed.), *Ein Gott—ein Herr—ein Geist* (one God—one Lord—one Spirit), Beiheft zur Ökum. Rundschau 56 (supplement to Ökum. Review 56), 1987.

K. H. Miskotte, *Bijbelsch ABC* (biblical abc), 1941.

J. Moltmann, *The Trinity and the Kingdom*, 1981.

G. W. Neven (ed.), *Levenslang wachten op U* (waiting for Thee one's entire life), 1988.

G. C. van Niftrik, *Het bestaan van God in de kentering van deze tijd* (God's existence in the current turn of events), 1971.

P. den Ottolander, *Deus immutabilis*, 1965.

J. I. Packer, *Knowing God*, 1974[2].

W. Pannenberg, *Systematische Theologie*, 1, 1988.

J. Patout Burns and G. M. Fagin, *The Holy Spirit*, 1984.

A. D. R. Polman, *De leer van God by Augustinus* (the doctrine of God according to Augustine), 1965.

B. Stein, *Der Begriff* (concept) *K^{e}bod Jahweh*, 1939.

T. F. Torrance, *The Trinitarian Faith*, 1988.

J. P. Versteeg, *Christus en de Geest* (Christ and the Spirit), 1971.

L. Vischer (ed.), *Geist Gottes—Geist Christi* (Spirit of God—Spirit of Christ), Beiheft zur Ökum. Rundschau 39, 1981.

H. de Vos, *De bewijzen van Gods bestaan* (the proofs of God's existence), 1971.

B. Wentsel, *Natuur en genade* (nature and grace), 1970.

Chapter 5

God's Counsel

§ 14. God's all-sovereign counsel

14.1. *Biblical starting points and theological considerations*
14.2. *God's decree and sin*
14.3. *The central place of the plan of salvation*

14.1. *Biblical starting points and theological considerations*

A work on Reformed dogmatics usually contains a chapter about God's counsel or his decrees, specifically focused on predestination.

All of God's actions are based on his counsel or decree. It is therefore necessary to consider what God's counsel is. In this chapter we focus on the belief that in everything, God works according to the counsel of his will (Eph. 1:11).

Early dogmatics employs a single term for God's creating and re-creating work: the outward works of God's essence. They are supported by his decrees. These decrees (*decreta*) are described as God's counsel, whereby the singular underscores the unity of God's decisions. It comprises "God's plan and pleasure" (Wentsel). "We cling to the belief that God in his wisdom and freedom designed a plan for the world and carries out his plans with a firm hand" (Wentsel, *Dogm.*, 2:162ff.).

The Old Testament says: "The counsel of the LORD standeth forever, the thoughts of his heart to all generations" (Ps. 33:11). "There are many devices in a man's heart; nevertheless the counsel of the LORD, that shall stand" (Prov. 19:21). In Isaiah 46:10 it says: "My counsel shall stand, and I will do all my pleasure."

The New Testament employs a range of terms that in our translations are rendered as "counsel," "will," "pleasure," or "purpose." The first of these words reminds us of Ephesians 1:11 and Acts 2:23: "by the determinate *counsel* and foreknowledge of God"; the second term is used in places such as Revelation 4:11: "For Thou hast created all things, and for Thy *will* they are and were created." The word "pleasure" reflects on the one hand the freedom and sovereignty, and on the other hand the graciousness of God's decree: the former element is especially prominent in Matthew 11:26, the latter in Luke 2:14 (cf. *TDNT*, 2:746–51). One of the clearest places in Scripture where the term "purpose" has theological significance is Ephesians 3:11: "according to the eternal *purpose* which he purposed in Christ Jesus our Lord" (cf. *TDNT*, 8:167).

When we employ biblical expressions such as "counsel" and "purpose" or speak about God's decree, we must avoid human connotations. On God's part there is no weighing of pros and cons as in our own approach to decision making. Furthermore, in God's case it is impossible for him to decide and not to act.

Dogmatics refers to God's counsel as being *eternal*, *sovereign*, *wise*, *unchangeable*, and *efficacious*.

1. Ephesians 3:11, which speaks of God's eternal purpose, is particularly significant for the first of these properties. God is the eternal God. Unlike us, he does not distinguish between before and after. It is all simultaneous to him. It is therefore unthinkable that he would ever act outside of his decree.

2. God is sovereign in his decision making, because he is God. His decree is not determined by anything outside himself. His sovereignty, however, is no arbitrariness. He has reasons for willing what he wills, and to will as he wills.

3. God's counsel is wise, for he is the only wise God (Rom. 16:27). What is emphasized by the apostle in Romans 9 and 11—and which is exactly what is being considered in this chapter—concludes in Romans 11:33 with the doxology: "O the depth of the riches both of the wis-

dom and knowledge of God! how unsearchable are his judgments, and his ways past finding out!"

4. God's counsel is unchangeable and efficacious. The Bible refers to the immutability of his counsel (Heb. 6:17). God remains true to himself, and therefore his decrees are sure. What Scripture says about him repenting does not detract from this (cf. § 13.5). The above quotation from Isaiah 46:10 implies that he does everything that pleases him (cf. Ps. 115:3). "The LORD of hosts hath purposed, and who shall annul it?" (cf. Isa. 14:24–27).[1] When the book of God's decrees is opened (cf. Rev. 5:1–10), the events that have been spelled out in it actually materialize (cf. *TDNT*, 1:619).

When we hear of God's eternal purpose (Eph. 3:11), we realize that this purpose of God cannot be separated from the eternal God himself. A well-known statement of earlier days says: God's decree is identical with the decreeing God (*Decretum Dei idem est ac Deus decernens*). What is meant here is that God's decree cannot be viewed in abstraction. It is not a set of specifications that once established, awaits implementation. A comparison with architectural plans, found in the literature (e.g., Erickson, *Chr. Th.*, 346), is not applicable. Schilder points out correctly that God continues to decree his eternal purpose every moment and continuously (*H.C.*, 3:134). In the doctrine of God's counsel we encounter the living God himself who has made and continues to make his decisions.

It is biblical to cling to the belief that God's counsel governs everything. However one translates Ephesians 1:11 ("who works all things according the counsel of his will"; "who establishes everything according to the decree of his will"; "who in everything works according to the counsel of his will"), it always comes down to the all-encompassing nature of God's counsel.

It has sometimes been objected that this only pertains to the fulfillment of God's counsel of salvation. It would be deterministic to hold that God's counsel pertains to everything, including every little thing and sin as well. We do admit that the Greek words (*ta panta*) could be rendered as: all of this (everything referred to). In this connection it may be pointed out that it is indeed a "foundational Biblical notion" that all things in heaven and on earth happen according to the preexistent counsel and intention of God (Ridderbos, *Paul*, 348).

There are a number of additional theological considerations. If God's counsel did not cover everything, the unity of his plan would be violated. Then part of everything that exists and happens would be beyond his control and would be autonomous.

1. See also Isa. 25:1. Cf. W. Werner, *Studien zur alttestamentlichen Vorstellung vom Plan Jahwes* (studies in the Old Testament representation of Yahweh's plan), 1988, 95ff., 145ff.

This is irreconcilable with the confession of God's sovereignty and would therefore be unacceptable to us. The thesis that God's counsel controls everything would be deterministic if it would eliminate human freedom and responsibility. But we remain true to the Bible if we fully honor human responsibility. Although we cannot fathom the relationship between God's sovereignty and our own responsibility, it is certain that the one does not detract from the other.[2]

14.2. *God's decree and sin*

Does God's counsel also pertain to sin? Is it correct to say that it is not biblical to hold that God decreed sin in his eternal counsel? (Woelderink, 1951, 39).

In the first place, sin definitely does not have its origin in the will of God in any way whatsoever. In the second place, it is certain that sin is not a power over which God has no control.

Therefore we can say with Augustine: God's work is so great that in a wonderful and unspeakable manner even what happens against his will does not occur without his will.[3] The rejection and crucifixion of Jesus Christ is the most heinous sin ever committed by mankind, but God's counsel was fulfilled through this event. Even the betrayal by Judas fitted into God's counsel. Jesus himself says: "Truly the Son of man goeth, as it was determined: but woe unto that man by whom he is betrayed!" (Luke 22:22). The book of Acts brings out both aspects (cf. Acts 2:23; 4:27–28).

If it is true that God's counsel is fulfilled through sinful acts of people, can this also be said of the fall into sin itself?

This is a very difficult question and it is important to discuss it with great prudence, especially since there are no explicit Scripture passages to which we can point. If our knowledge is imperfect, it is definitely so in this regard!

Reformed dogmatics decidedly rejects the notion that God was surprised by sin. Some theologians go no further than to state that God knew of it beforehand. Calvin went beyond this, but his contemporary, Bullinger, very definitely did not.[4] In the face of this understanding, the question arises why God did not prevent sin. Did he not permit it to happen? Calvin employed the word "to ordain" (*ordinare*). He wrote: "Accordingly, man falls according as God's providence ordains,

2. Cf. K. Sietsma, *Goddelijke souvereinitiet en menschelijke verantwoordelijkheid* (divine sovereignty and human responsibility), 1941, 62.

3. Augustine, *Enchiridion*, 100.

4. H. Bullinger, *Huysboec* (book for the home), 1566, 139; *Sermonum decades quinque*, 1552, 164–66. Cf. P. Walser, *Die Prädestination bei Heinrich Bullinger*, 1957, 219–21.

but he falls by his own fault" (*Institutes*, 3.23.8). Whatever term one chooses (foresee, permit, or ordain), man's guilt is always affirmed at the same time.

It has happened that a theologian viewed sin so exclusively in the light of God's all-controlling sovereignty that he alleged that God had destined man for sin, and that God desired sin to happen. This was the view of J. Maccovius, who was called to order by the Synod of Dort (1618–19). He was directed to adopt a manner of speaking in accordance with Holy Scripture, plain, clear, and current at orthodox academies (cf. Dijk, 1912, 216).

It is not possible to make transparent how the fall into sin fits into God's counsel. We can speak of the emergence of sin in Paradise to the extent that the Bible sheds light on it, but this does not quite explain its ultimate origin. According to Bavinck, sin is the greatest contradiction tolerated by God in his creation, yet used by him in the way of justice and righteousness as an instrument for his glory (*R.D.*, 3:145).

A. A. van Ruler, who selected the problem of sin in God's counsel as the theme of a lecture, put it more strongly yet: "When one explores all questions in a wholly Christian manner, everything appears to point in the direction of the idea that sin, even sin, is included in God's decree."

However, he distinguishes three possible nuances of the statement that "even sin is part of God's decree." The first one is that sin is included, contained in the decree, i.e., in the totality of God's decrees; that in one way or another it has been incorporated into it; that his decree also pertains to sin and its implications. The second nuance implies that God decided that sin would occur. There is still a third nuance, according to which God desired sin in one way or another (Van Ruler, *T.W.*, 6:49–60).

The inclusion of the words "in one way or another" makes the last nuance sound somewhat less harsh than otherwise would have been the case. It is questionable, however, whether it clarifies anything.

Augustine's careful formulation (reiterated by Calvin in *Institutes*, 1.18.3) is preferable. Sin does not circumvent God's will. God has tolerated (Bavinck) and permitted it. He consciously permitted it and desired to permit it. Although this could perhaps be said, it is better to draw a line in our thinking than to want to penetrate any further.

14.3. *The central place of the plan of salvation*

If God's counsel is his eternal decree concerning all that will be or will happen in time (Bavinck, *R.D.*, 2:372), is it correct to call this counsel as such a counsel of salvation?

We can say that in both his counsel and his actions God aims at the salvation of his people. For God is good. Many would like to interpret God's decree specifically as salvation in Jesus Christ. This reflects Barth's influence. According to him, when the Old and New Testaments speak of what our older theology called the divine decree, they point indirectly or directly to Jesus Christ. We must see Jesus Christ as *the* decree, the one reality of the divine decision. It comprises everything else that God also wills. All these things are subordinate to it, are determined by it, and are focused on it (*C.D.*, 2.1.521). All of God's ways and works are determined by this one fundamental decision of God (*C.D.*, 2.2.92ff.).

Those who consider the world to be an embodiment of the thoughts of God (this expression is from Bavinck,[5] *R.D.*, 1:233; cf. 2:425) cannot accept this, or else they would have to view creation already as a manifestation of salvation in Jesus Christ (cf. § 17.3, subsection 7). The creation of man is an act of God that rests on his counsel or decree (Gen. 1:26). It does not refer to Christ, either directly or indirectly.

One of the sections below will deal with predestination. There we encounter God's counsel as counsel of salvation, for predestination constitutes election in Christ and election to salvation (Eph. 1:4; 2 Thess. 2:13). Without any doubt, the covenant of redemption, which formerly was frequently referred to as the counsel of peace, can be called a counsel of salvation. The heart of what Scripture refers to as God's counsel is his plan of salvation.

§ 15. God's plan of salvation

15.1. *The mystery that has been revealed*

On the basis of God's revelation we speak of his eternal counsel that rules everything. This implies immediately that what the Bible says about our redemption must be seen in the light of his counsel.

Our reflection of God's plan of salvation, however, has a much surer and broader foundation than this theological conclusion can offer. We may start from clear biblical data. These may even be counted among Paul's fundamental structures (terminology suggested by H. Ridderbos). It is indeed characteristic of the apostle that he speaks of the revelation or announcement of the mystery (*mysterion*) that was hid-

5. The term "the idea of the world" (Bavinck, *R.D.*, 2:376, 425ff.) is too close to Neothomism to be of any use to us (cf. R. H. Bremmer, *Herman Bavinck als dogmaticus* (Herman Bavinck as dogmatician), 1961, 328–31.

den or kept secret for a long time (Rom. 16:25–26; Col. 1:26). In Ephesians 3:4–5 this mystery is referred to as the mystery of Christ. Christ is its content (cf. Col. 2:2–3). See also Ephesians 1:9–10 and 2 Timothy 1:9–10.

We may not interpret this mystery as secret teaching. It refers to the mystery of salvation, which already existed within God's counsel before being revealed to people. It was established prior to the ages or ordained from eternity (cf. 1 Cor. 2:7) and is now revealed. This implies more than being made known. It means first of all that it becomes reality in history. As the plan of salvation implemented by God, this mystery becomes the object of proclamation that is focused on the obedience of faith (cf. *TDNT*, 4:813–27; Ridderbos, *Paul*, 44–49).

When Paul writes, "But we speak the wisdom of God in a mystery, even the hidden wisdom, which God ordained before the world unto our glory" (1 Cor. 2:7), he refers to God's mighty plan to save us through Christ and his sacrifice on the cross. Thus it pleased God and thus his wisdom determined it. He had it in mind from eternity. Christ is the core of God's plan of salvation which brings with it glory for believers. The content of this mystery—the mystery of godliness—is according to 1 Timothy 3:16:

> God was manifest in the flesh,
> justified in the Spirit,
> seen of angels,
> preached unto the Gentiles,
> believed on in the world,
> received up into glory.

God's plan of redemption, established before the world was created, provides the foundation for Christ's sacrifice. Peter refers to Christ as the lamb that "was foreordained before the foundation of the world, but was manifest in these last times" (1 Peter 1:19–20).

The entire history of salvation proceeds from God's plan of salvation. This is reflected in dogmatic reflection, when we first focus on "the secret counsel and will of God concerning our redemption" revealed to us in Christ (Heidelberg Catechism, Lord's Day 12), and subsequently see how this plan of God is achieved.

In starting out with God's plan of salvation we do not at all imply that what materializes in time should be considered to be less momentous because everything was already decided beforehand. In the light of God's eternal counsel it has precisely its full importance. The good pleasure of God's will, the intention of him who works all things according to the counsel of his will, indeed stands behind it (cf. Eph. 1:5, 9, 11). The unity of God's counsel and God's acts means to believers that they see the salvation, which they share together with others, as being anchored in God's eternal love in Christ (cf. Eph. 1:5–6).

Everything is to the praise of the glory of God's grace (cf. Eph. 1:6, 12). "Just as the mystery has been prepared by eternal God from eternity, so will also the praise for the revelation of God's mystery be accorded to eternity."[6]

15.2. *The covenant of redemption as divine plan of salvation*

1. *Theological considerations*. God's plan of salvation exhibits the character of a decree of salvation. Everything is determined by God's counsel and therefore everything is under his control.

In Reformed theology, since the beginning of the seventeenth century, it has been the practice—in connection with the doctrine of the covenant, the doctrine of atonement, and the doctrine of predestination—to reflect on the mode of the plan of salvation, which formerly was referred to as the "counsel of peace" and subsequently as the "covenant of redemption" (*pactum salutis*).

B. Loonstra presented in the first part of his dissertation a detailed overview of the treatment of this doctrine. The doctrine of the pact has never been uniform (Loonstra, 1990, 19–184, 347).

Already in the work of church fathers such as Athanasius and Augustine we come across a concept with which many would agree. Over against Arians, who believed they could appeal to a text such as "My Father is greater than I" (John 14:28) as well as other Scripture passages that appear to suggest a subordination of the Son to the Father, they held that a distinction must be made between the eternal Son of God and the Mediator. When the Mediator subjects himself to the will of the Father, this does not imply that the Son of God is subordinate to his Father. The Son himself is fully involved in the preparation for our salvation. He was made Redeemer before time and took upon himself the work of redemption (cf. Loonstra, 1990, 35–38).

Thus, early on emerged what was subsequently referred to as the appointment of the Mediator (*constitutio Mediatoris*). This is based on Scripture. First Peter 1:20 was already quoted in section 15.1. When the apostle says that God chose us in Christ before the foundation of

6. H. Ridderbos, *Aan de Romeinen* (to the Romans), 1959, 355.

the world (Eph. 1:4), he refers to the place of Christ in God's eternal decree. Calvin writes: God turned his eyes upon his Christ (*Institutes*, 3.22.1).

The appointment of the Mediator pertains to both his person and his work. We think particularly of the incarnation of the Word and the surety of Christ.

His surety (*sponsio*) is a matter of great importance. "In this way the Son of God, who has been appointed by the Father to be the Mediator of the covenant, stands surety for two things: in the first place that he will give satisfaction for the sins of all those whom the Father has given to him . . . ; in the second place that he will ensure that those who are incorporated in him will enjoy peace in their conscience and will be renewed from day to day according to God's image."[7] If hereby we take into account what Olevianus in this connection says about the Father's command and promise, we see delineated the doctrine of the covenant of redemption, which involves a covenantal relationship between the Father and the Son (cf. Loonstra, 1990, 75–76).

If one follows Barth in thinking of superior and inferior states within the Godhead, involving commanding and obeying (*C.D.*, 4.1.202–4), one crosses the boundaries of revelation.[8]

When we contemplate the message of the Bible, the question does arise whether the appointment of the Mediator coupled with the implied incarnation and the entire work of atonement rests within a decree of God or reflects a covenant among the three persons. Is it a Trinitarian decree or a Trinitarian covenant?

At times Scripture speaks of the Son as being sent by the Father, and at other times of the coming of the Son. The New Testament says: "But when the fullness of the time was come, God sent forth his Son, made of a woman, made under the law" (Gal. 4:4). "Herein is love, not that we loved God, but that he loved us, and sent his Son to be the propitiation of our sins" (1 John 4:10).

The New Testament also says that "the Son of man came . . . to minister, and give his life a ransom for many" (Mark 10:45). "Lo, I come . . . to do thy will, O God" (Heb. 10:7). These words concerning his being prepared to do the will of God, and to bring the sacrifice

7. C. Olevianus, *De substantia foederis gratuiti inter Deum et electos* (concerning the substance of the covenant of grace between God and the elect), 1585, 23.

8. According to G. C. Berkouwer, *De triomf der genade in de theologie van Karl Barth* (the triumph of grace in the theology of Karl Barth), 1954, 301.

of his life, can be understood as the words of the Mediator, who has already been appointed, but he is also the one who took all of this upon himself in his eternal love. The latter is quite clearly expressed in Philippians 2:5–8. The statement that Christ Jesus was in the form of God and did not think it robbery to be equal with God refers to the preexistence of the Son of God. "He made himself of no reputation and took upon him the form of a servant and was made in the likeness of men." It says: "In the beginning was the Word, and the Word was with God, and the Word was God." "The Word was made flesh" (John 1:1, 14). On the basis of this and other Bible passages we must—in thinking about the appointment of the Mediator—not lose sight of the fact that the Son of God chose to take this route.

Is this made clear enough when we speak of a Trinitarian plan of salvation or decree? Predestination is a decree of God that pertains to people, but when the Son agrees to stand surety for them, this reflects more a covenant between the Father and the Son, which also involves the Holy Spirit.

Against the doctrine of a plan of salvation of God, which may be viewed as a Trinitarian covenant, it has been objected by K. Barth, and prior to him by A. Comrie and others, that the three persons are then portrayed as being too independent of each other. Scholastically interpreted, including stipulations such as a demand issued by the Father and accepted by the Son, this would indeed appear to be the case. The objection becomes more serious when this covenant is described in terms of human relationships and agreements and is more or less depicted as a contract. This concern cannot be alleviated by viewing the life of the three divine persons as a covenantal life (as in Bavinck, *R.D.*, 3:214), for there are no grounds for this. It loses its validity, however, when we no longer need to think of a covenant in which the participants stand over against each other. The Father, the Son, and the Holy Spirit so closely cooperate within this covenant that the redemption of sinners can be ascribed to all three of them jointly, and at the same time to each one of them individually, while taking into account the distinction that exists among them in the economic sense (see § 12.4).

It would therefore not be amiss for dogmatics to reinstate the term "counsel of peace," which has fallen into disuse.

The history of Reformed dogmatics shows that the understanding of Jesus being subordinate to the Father was a key element of this doctrine. Jesus said: "I have power to lay down [my life] and power to take it again. This commandment have I received of my Father" (John 10:18). "I have glorified thee on the earth: I have finished the work which thou gavest me to do" (John 17:4).

Those who confess with the church of the ages that the Mediator is true and eternal God can explain his subordination to the Father and his obedience unto death on the cross (Phil. 2:8) only by seeing him as the Servant of the Lord. When his redeeming work is presented to us in the New Testament, we are faced with the mystery of the Servant of the Lord, which has its foundation in the plan of salvation of the Father, the Son, and the Holy Spirit—as intended in the doctrine of the counsel of peace (cf. Berkouwer, 1960, 170).

We still need to consider the place of the Holy Spirit in the covenant of redemption. Nowhere in the Bible is there explicit mention of the Spirit being subordinate to the Father. Yet the Spirit is sent by the Father. He is also sent by Christ (John 14:26; 15:26). Theologians who consciously avoid mentioning the Holy Spirit in this context do not do justice to the root ideas of the revelation of salvation. The work of Christ cannot be separated from the work of the Spirit, who is also the Spirit of Christ. The Mediator is dependent on the support of the Holy Spirit, but the work of salvation of the Spirit is in turn dependent on the work of Christ (cf. Loonstra, 1990, 346 and 291).

One can follow Dijk (*K.D.*, 195) in saying that the third person took it upon himself to lay the groundwork for the incarnation of the Word, to effect the conception, to complete his work in the sacrifice of Christ (Heb. 9:14), and to impart the righteousness achieved by our Mediator to all those who have been chosen in Christ (Rom. 8:14; 1 Cor. 12:3). Van der Schuit gives the following description of the covenant of redemption: a mutual undertaking of the three divine persons to stand guarantee in the attainment of salvation of those chosen by God for eternal life. He adds that the Father determines the way of redemption, the Son takes the road of obedience as the Servant of the Lord, and the Holy Spirit establishes the work of redemption in the hearts of those who have been marked by God for eternal life. More so than many others, Van der Schuit focuses on the work of the Holy Spirit who turns the covenant of redemption into truth that is known and enjoyed (Van der Schuit, 1982^2, 13ff., 36).

2. *The biblical foundation.* In early theology too much was read into Zechariah 6:13, which refers to "the counsel of peace" between two persons. This does not imply consultation between divine persons (cf. Arntzen, 1983, 68–70).

A recent study says that a number of additional passages—which at one time were frequently employed as scriptural proof for God's plan of salvation—do not contain any direct reference to a *pactum salutis* (Loonstra, 1990, 187–90). Luke 22:29 is one of these. In our view it is possible, however, that theologians such as Cloppenburg, Coccejus, and Witsius were right in appealing to these words of Jesus in the sense of a decree contained in God's eternal counsel, but not a testament as they called it. It says: "And I appoint unto you a kingdom, as my Father hath appointed unto me." For this decree of the Father no specific moment in time can be identified. Sovereignty accrues to Jesus on the basis of God's eternal decree.

Perhaps John 10:36 provides some basis for the doctrine of the *pactum salutis*. Jesus says that the Father has consecrated him and sent him into the world. His mission into the world—a key concept in John's gospel—is here preceded by his consecration by the Father, whereby we may think of him being set apart and destined for his work as Mediator. Was he consecrated at his arrival upon earth or subsequently? It is more likely that his consecration took place prior to his being sent (cf. *TDNT*, 1:111–12; Arntzen, 1983, 72–74).

Among the most prominent proof texts in early and more recent theology, 1 Peter 1:20 must not be overlooked. This text is referred to by W. à Brakel (1635–1711) and J. à Marck (1656–1731) as well as H. Bavinck, J. J. van der Schuit, and J. A. Heyns.

Peter says: "Who verily was foreordained before the foundation of the world, but was made manifest in these last times for you." The verb "foreknow" here means: "foreordain."[9] "Christ's foreordination to his office is nowhere spoken of as unequivocally as here" (Arntzen, 1983, 85). B. Loonstra also interprets this as the prehistoric consecration of the preexistent Christ to his office (Loonstra, 1990, 267).

A passage of Scripture that is relevant not only to predestination but also to the doctrine of the covenant of redemption is Ephesians 1:3–14. God has chosen us in Christ before the foundation of the world (Eph. 1:4). The apostle testifies to the good pleasure that God had purposed in himself (Eph. 1:9). This pericope addresses not only the blessings received by believers from God, but also God's eternal love and pleasure, on which their entire salvation is based. Their predestination, which is from eternity, is a predestination in Christ, which implies that he must be seen as the Mediator of his people or the Head of his church from before the foundation of the world (see § 16.2).

An agreement (*pactum*) or covenant, as Reformed theologians have referred to this, is nowhere mentioned explicitly in Scripture. This

9. *TDNT*, 1:715; L. Goppelt, *Der erste Petrusbrief* (the first epistle of Peter), 1978, 126.

does not mean that this concept is not biblical. Its core is that in God's eternal counsel the Son of God is consecrated to be Mediator and that he has come to complete the work that the Father has given him to do (cf. John 17:4).

The relationship between God the Father and Christ the Mediator was the basis for the elaboration of the doctrine of the covenant of redemption. This was combined with various human ideas on which opinions can vary.

References to the "counsel of peace" or the "covenant of redemption" do not appear in our confessional statements. This is not surprising, for the development of this doctrine did not really begin prior to the seventeenth century, although Olevianus in his thinking went in this direction somewhat earlier.

Although the confessional elements are scarce, they are not unimportant. The Heidelberg Catechism confesses that the Mediator is called Christ, i.e., the Anointed One, "because he is ordained of God the Father, and anointed with the Holy Spirit, to be our Prophet, High Priest and King" (Lord's Day 12). The Canons of Dort say that God appointed him "the Mediator and Head of the elect and the foundation of salvation" (1:7).

In the Bible we find enough direct and indirect support to maintain that this perspective is scripturally sound.

3. *The meaning of the covenant of redemption.*

a. *The counsel of the triune God and our redemption.* The doctrine of the covenant of redemption (the counsel of peace) allows Reformed theology to see our salvation anchored in the depths of the counsel of the triune God. This constitutes a difference with other theological traditions that do not allude to it.

The deeds of the divine persons in time proceed from God's eternal counsel (cf. § 15.1). "The Father is the Origin, the Son the Procurer, and the Holy Spirit the Applier of our salvation."[10] Already in eternity the triune God made our redemption his business. No one persuaded him to do this—we did not even exist—but he was moved within himself to reach out in love toward sinners.

The foundation of our salvation is unshakably secure in God's counsel. The words of Peter quoted above point to this (1 Peter

10. H. Bavinck, *Magnalia Dei*, 1931², 256.

1:20).[11] It has been said correctly: "Motifs of immutability, faithfulness, unshakable foundation, inviolable certainty, and lasting comfort come repeatedly to the fore in the reflection on the '*pactum salut*is'" (Berkouwer, 1960, 165).

It is not surprising that there are theologians who have eloquently expressed their emotions in reflecting on God's plan of salvation by saying: Glory be to the Father, glory be to the Son, glory be to the Holy Spirit.[12]

b. *God's counsel and the Son as Servant of the Lord*. These issues have implications for Christology.

What the New Testament says about the subordination of the Son to the will and the command of the Father and about his obedience (Rom. 5:19; Phil. 2:8; Heb. 5:8) has been totally misunderstood by subordinationism. It is the eternal Son of God who takes the path of the Servant of the Lord. The doctrine of the *pactum salutis* emerged precisely in the reflection on the submissiveness of the Son to the Father (cf. Berkouwer, 1960, 168).

c. *The covenant of redemption and predestination*. The appointment of the Mediator is referred to in the Canons of Dort, 1.7, in the context of predestination in Christ.

However closely connected the *pactum salutis* is with *electio* (predestination), there nevertheless remains a distinction. The question is whether one can go along with G. Vos in saying that in the covenant of redemption the divine persons interact with each other in judicial relationships, while with respect to predestination they act collectively.[13] It is rather the case that by virtue of the *pactum salutis* it is settled who the Mediator is, and what he will do for those whom God predestines to eternal life, and that in predestining people God determines who will share in the salvation that Christ obtains. These are indissolubly linked.

Predestination to eternal life and the covenant of redemption have the same scope. If all people were predestined in Christ, as Barth teaches (see § 16.4), it would be unthinkable that God's eternal plan of salvation would not imply the redemption of all through the work

11. W. Schrage in H. Balz and W. Schrage, *Die "Katholischen" Briefe* (the Catholic epistles), 1973, 77.

12. See among others H. Witsius, *De Oeconomia Foederum Dei*, 1694³, 2:4, 23; W. à Brakel, *R.S.*, 1:263.

13. G. Vos, *De verbondsleer in de Gereformeerde theologie* (the doctrine of the covenant in Reformed theology), reprinted 1939, 25.

of Christ. But if election in Christ may not be interpreted universalistically, the *pactum salutis* that underlies Christ's work of mediation does not imply that all people will be redeemed.

One encounters both the view that the decree of predestination logically precedes the pact and vice versa. Predestination following upon the pact could also fall within the pact. B. Loonstra even sees scope for the decree of election and reprobation within the Messianic pact between the Father and the Son (Loonstra, 1990, 347). However, realizing what reprobation implies, one runs into great problems here (see § 16.7).

We cannot apply our concepts of time and sequence to God's eternal counsel (cf. Van der Zanden, 1949, 45–47). We therefore also leave open the question of sequence since the Bible is silent in this regard. It is sufficient to view the covenant of redemption or the counsel of peace and predestination in Christ from a single perspective.

d. *The covenant of redemption and the covenant of grace.* The doctrine of the *pactum salutis* was developed in the seventeenth century in connection with the overall doctrine of the covenant. This was especially the case with the theology of the covenant. There is indeed an intrinsic connection between this pact and the covenant of grace. The covenant of redemption indeed concerns the appointment of him who as the Mediator is at the center of the covenant of grace.

These two covenants are not infrequently collapsed into one. Kersten does not see a distinction between these two in terms of their nature and essence (Kersten, *R.D.*, 1:233). This view brings with it that the covenant of grace becomes subservient to predestination. However, the difference between the covenant of redemption and the covenant of grace that God in time establishes with believers and their children may not be lost sight of. Otherwise no justice can be done to what the Bible says about God's interaction in time with all those with whom he concludes the covenant of grace (cf. van Genderen, 1983, 55ff.). These few comments must suffice for now, because the covenant of grace is not discussed till later (chapter 11).

Those who ignore the covenant of redemption have difficulty understanding the nature and significance of the old dispensation of the covenant of grace. In line with Zwingli and Calvin, Reformed theology teaches emphatically that Christ's work of mediation already took effect before he appeared on earth. The covenant, of which he is the Mediator, does have two dispensations, but is in essence one. There are clear differences (cf. Calvin, *Institutes*, 2.11), but the Scriptures of the Old Testament also testify to Christ (John 5:39), and the Spirit of

Christ was already at work in the testimony of the prophets (1 Peter 1:11).

What Christ has accomplished has significance for all times, for it proceeds from God's eternal love, which was manifested in the *pactum salutis*. Bavinck writes: "Although Christ completed his work on earth only in the midst of history and although the Holy Spirit was not poured out till the day of Pentecost, God nevertheless was able, already in the days of the Old Testament, to fully distribute the benefits to be acquired and applied by the Son and the Spirit." He says succinctly: "There is one faith, one Mediator, one way of salvation, and one covenant of grace" (*R.D.*, 3:215ff.).

§ 16. Predestination

16.1. *Background*
16.2. *Election by God in Holy Scripture*
16.3. *The Reformed doctrine of predestination*
16.4. *Recent views*
16.5. *Election in Christ*
16.6. *Infralapsarian and supralapsarian views*
16.7. *Election and reprobation*
16.8. *Election and proclamation of the gospel*
16.9. *Election and the assurance of our salvation*

16.1. *Background*

As long as there has been a doctrine of predestination (*electio*), it has engendered a great deal of controversy. We are reminded of the theology of Augustine, who was convinced that the number of the elect was limited; of Calvin, of whom it is well-known that he taught both election and reprobation; of the conflict between the Remonstrants and Contra-Remonstrants, and the frequently criticized pronouncements of the Synod of Dort (1618–19); and finally of the Barthian doctrine of election and reprobation, which evoked numerous reactions.

Especially when it comes to double predestination, whereby it is not overlooked that there is also reprobation, i.e., the antithesis of election, we are confronted with what Calvin refers to as great and difficult questions (*Institutes*, 3.21.1). Over a short period of time (from 1955 till 1977) in three church denominations in the Netherlands gravamina were lodged that viewed double predestination as a problem (see also § 16.7). The first gravamen, coupled with theological developments in the mid-twentieth century, led the Netherlands Reformed Church (NHK) to publish an important document that contained guidelines for the interpretation of the doctrine of predestination (*De uitverkiezing*, 1961). "In grateful obedience to Holy Scripture" and "in agreement with the confession of the fathers," the synod sought to adhere to predestination, but presented this doctrine in such a way that the General Assembly of the Remonstrant Brotherhood could state in 1962 that these guidelines placed the doctrine of predestination in a new light and that far-reaching objections had been raised against the Five Articles Against the Remonstrants (Canons of Dort).[14]

It is not surprising that predestination always engenders a good deal of discussion. According to this doctrine it is God, not man, who decides his salvation. That no one can claim salvation, and that as sinners we deserve that God would pass us by, is a bitter pill to swallow. We need to be won over to be prepared to live by grace only. There are those who are offended by this doctrine.

Furthermore, the danger is not imaginary that the doctrine of predestination is misunderstood. The thought may arise that man must simply wait and see what has been decided with respect to him. This can make people totally passive or even depressive.

It is not clear to all believers how important the doctrine of predestination really is. The Reformed are more aware of this than others. They gladly speak and sing of God's eternal good pleasure.

The document of the Netherlands Reformed Church (NHK), referred to above, expresses the gist of the matter from a practical point of view as follows: "When we confess that we live by predestination, we say two things:

"In the first place there is something humbling, namely that our redemption is not in the least dependent on our own initiative and strength, but rests entirely on God's unwarranted turning towards us; and

"In the second place there is something comforting, namely that our redemption is unshakably certain, since it does not depend on anything of our own, but solely and completely on God's faithfulness" (*De uitverkiezing* = predestination, 1961, 13).

For the earlier literature on the history of this doctrine we refer especially to the two-volume work by A. Schweizer, *Die protestantischen Centraldogmen* (1854–56). A more recent book is that by C. Graafland, *Van Calvijn tot Barth* (1987).

In the first edition of his *Institutes* Calvin discussed predestination in the context of the doctrine of the church, but in 1559 he did so in four chapters of the third book, following the exposition of the doctrine of salvation. C. Graafland considers it possible

14. *Voorbeschikking of verkiezing* (predestination or election), 1962, 110.

that Calvin let the doctrine of salvation culminate in the doctrine of predestination, since from the start it represents its dominant theme and goal (Graafland, 1987, 14). However, this interpretation is open to criticism (cf. Kamphuis, 1989, 16–22).

Judging by the sequence of the articles of the Belgic Confession of Faith—or the French Confession of Faith (1559), designed by none other than Calvin himself—one would have to assign a different place to predestination, i.e., after the doctrine of sin and before the doctrine of Christ. So this is also a distinct possibility. From a theological point of view, however, it is advisable not to leave predestination and all that pertains to God's counsel to the end of the discussion, but to present it in direct relationship with the doctrine of God (cf. Bavinck, *R.D.*, 2:359–61). But one needs to beware of speculation and present nothing but the teaching of Scripture!

Otherwise, according to Calvin, the analysis can be compared to entering a labyrinth from which one can find no exit. As soon as we go beyond the boundaries set by the Word, we lose our way and stumble. The pursuit of an interpretation of predestination different from the one presented to us in God's Word is no less foolish than wanting to travel where there is no road or wanting to see in the dark.

There is still another perspective. Calvin is correct in pointing out that we may not ignore what Scripture teaches, however tempting this may be from certain points of view. Is Scripture not the school of the Holy Spirit? "Let us, I say, permit the Christian man to open up his heart and ears to all of the words of God" (*Institutes*, 3.21.1–3).

16.2. *Election by God in Holy Scripture*

1. *An initial comment*

Subsection 16.2 deals specifically with Scripture passages that are considered to be proofs in the Reformed doctrine of predestination but that are variously interpreted. There is insufficient space to reflect on all Scripture passages that refer to election by God.

There are more references to the New Testament than the Old Testament. This reflects the progression of God's revelation. It is in line with the New Testament to interpret election as election in Christ (Eph. 1:4). The Old Testament does not present it this way.

2. *Election in the Old Testament*

The forms of the verbs used in the Old Testament indicate that election is an act of God in time. God selects persons such as the Levites and a place such as Zion. Most of the time, however, the focus is on the election of the people of Israel.

The basis for this election is not Israel itself, for it is not more numerous or more deserving than other nations. God is guided by his sovereign love and faithfulness (Deut. 7:7–8). The election is a selection *from* among. It says: "The LORD thy God hath chosen thee to be a special people unto himself, above all people that are upon the face of the earth" (Deut. 7:6). "You only have I known of all the families of the earth" (Amos 3:2). In Malachi 1:2 the word "to love" indicates God's selecting love. Its opposite is "to hate."

God chooses his people for life in his service and in communion with him. He chooses them because he desires them to be his covenant people. Israel is therefore referred to as his own people (Deut. 14:2). It is holy: it is consecrated to him and must live in genuine devotion to his service. Election always brings obligations with it. Election implies increased responsibility (cf. Amos 3:2).

When God chooses people, he distinguishes them from others. The opposite of election is reprobation. Sometimes the word means "not chosen" (1 Sam. 16:7–8). However, in numerous places reprobation is directly linked with sin and can be seen to reflect God's judgment (cf. 1 Sam. 15:23; 2 Kings 17:20). The rejection of his people, however, is not total and final (Jer. 31:36–37). The LORD was angry but he "shall yet choose Jerusalem" (Zech. 1:17).

The Old Testament also refers to a remnant by the grace of God (see *TDNT*, 4:196–214). A distinction can be made between the people of Israel and God's elect (Isa. 65:9, 15, 22). These servants of God "shall sing for joy of heart" while others "shall howl" (Isa. 65:14). "Here God's elect are the true people of God, true believers" (Oosterhoff, 1987, 35).

3. *Election in the New Testament*[15]

Like the Old Testament, the New Testament speaks of election to a specific ministry. For example, Christ chooses or selects the apostles. Yet he refers to one of them as a devil (John 6:70). This election is therefore not the same thing as election to salvation (cf. 2 Thess. 2:13).

15. In this section we frequently refer to commentaries that for the sake of brevity will be mentioned only by the names of their authors. They are: L. Goppelt, *Der erste Petrusbrief* (the first epistle of Peter), 1978; S. Greijdanus, *De brief van den apostel Paulus aan de gemeente te Rome* (the epistle of the apostle Paul to the church in Rome), 1933, vol. 2; H. J. Jager, *Enige opmerkingen over Romeinen* (a few comments on Romans), 1978 (completely outside the responsibility of Professor Jager); A. F. N. Lekkerkerker, *De brief van Paulus aan de Romeinen* (the epistle of Paul to the Romans), 1965, vol. 2; L. Morris, *The Epistle to the Romans*, 1988; J. Murray, *The Epistle to the Romans*, 1960, ch. 1–8; F. J. Pop, *De eerste brief van Paulus aan de Corinthiërs* (the first epistle of Paul to the Corinthians), 1965; H. Ridderbos, *Aan de Romeinen* (to the Romans), 1959; A. J. Visser, *De Openbaring van Johannes* (the Revelation of John), 1965; U. Wilckens, *Der Brief an die Römer* (the epistle to the Romans), 1980, Rom. 6–11.

In a unique way Christ is *the* Chosen One (Luke 9:35; cf. Matt. 12:18). In 1 Peter 2:4, 6 he is referred to as a chosen and precious cornerstone. He is foreknown by God from the foundation of the world as the One who redeems his people through his blood (see § 15).

Gospels and Acts. There are those whom God has chosen and preserved (cf. Matt. 24:22–24). Mark 13:20 says emphatically: "for the elect's sake, whom he hath chosen."

Not all those who have been called or invited by him to salvation are predestined. Being called does not necessarily imply being chosen (Matt. 22:14). In the preceding parable heavy emphasis is placed on the responsibility of those who are invited. Not all of them come. Sometimes they seek entry inappropriately. Only coming in response to the invitation or calling is proof of election.[16] In this text, the response to the call of the gospel is viewed in the light of election.

In Acts 13:48 we read that all those who "were ordained to eternal life" came to faith. Being ordained to eternal life is sometimes explained as being called to salvation. All Gentiles to whom salvation was announced according to God's plan came to faith (*De uitverkiezing* = predestination, 31). A similar view is that of Venema (1965, 66): being placed on the way that leads to eternal life, to salvation. Others have thought in terms of a certain predisposition or suitability on the part of those involved. However, this was definitely not the intention. It says that they "were ordained to eternal life." By whom else but God? He has determined who will receive eternal life, and he brings them to faith. Not only do Protestant translations in the Netherlands point in this direction, but also the Roman Catholic Willibrord translation: "and all those who were predestined to eternal life accepted faith."

Epistles. Here not only scattered texts but also entire pericopes demand our attention. First of all, Romans 8:28–30. For those "who are called according to God's purpose" God causes "all things to work together for good" (v. 28). He knows them beforehand. Does this mean only that God knows ahead of time who they are? It has been correctly pointed out that his foreknowledge indeed constitutes election (*TDNT*, 1:715). The subsequent verses (29, 30) also point to predestination, which proceeds by means of calling, justification, and glorification. This salvation is altogether the result of what has been done by God, who predestined his people "to be conformed to the image of his Son" (v. 29). They are the elect and nothing can

16. Cf. H. N. Ridderbos, *Mattheüs*, 1948, 2:113; J. van Genderen, "Roeping en verkiezing" (calling and election), in *Woord en kerk* (word and church), 1969, 114ff.

separate them from the love of God, which is in Christ Jesus, their Lord (Rom. 8:33, 38, 39).

We now come to Romans 9 through 11. There are two contrasting views: 1. an *explanation based on predestination*, whereby the election is the source of eternal salvation (Augustine, Calvin, Greijdanus), and 2. an *explanation based on the history of redemption*, which does not address the salvation or damnation of individuals, but the place of Israel and other nations in God's plan of salvation (Woelderink, 1951; *De uitverkiezing* = predestination, 1961). Berkouwer largely supports the latter view, because at any rate, the redemptive-historical point of view is to him of decisive significance (Berkouwer, 1960, 211). Also according to Ridderbos, the history of redemption predominates. The latter's focus is on the mystery of God's dispensation of salvation to Israel. He is of the view, however, that the redemptive-historical perspective should not be separated from the personal one.

Romans 9:11 refers to God's electing purpose. This is obvious from the statement: not on the basis of works but on the basis of God's call. God's grace has the first and the last word. This is illustrated by the contrast between Jacob and Esau: Jacob I have loved, but Esau I have hated. The former is more than a predilection or a preference for Jacob, and the latter cannot be equated with loving Esau any less or passing him by. Those who merely think in terms of the temporary and historical place of a nation do not do justice to the highly serious matter to which the apostle here refers, i.e., participating in Christ's salvation or not (Venema, 1965, 111ff.). What is said in Genesis 25:23 with respect to two nations is here applied by Paul to persons. Since sin, which according to Malachi explains the rejection of Esau (Mal. 1:4), is not mentioned by Paul, the emphasis shifts to God's sovereign action, which is independent of people.

God is free to have mercy on whom he will (Rom. 9:14–18). The apostle employs the meaningful image of the potter and the clay. Just as the potter is free to do what he will with the clay, so God has the power and the right (*exousia*) to do as he pleases and no one can call him to account.

In Romans 9:22–23, the objects of wrath and mercy stand over against each other. God desires to reveal on one hand his wrath and power, and on the other hand the richness of his glory. The objects of wrath were being prepared for destruction. Some interpret this as saying that God had predestined them to destruction. It is striking, however, that there is no strict symmetry between what is said with respect to the objects of wrath and those of mercy (Morris). God did indeed prepare some for glory, but there is a preparation for destruction or ripening for destruction that the apostle does not say God effects. "Sin itself is a contributing factor" (Greijdanus).

There is a connection between what it says in Romans 9:23 and in Romans 8:29–30. They both represent statements about election (Murray, Lekkerkerker). The context confirms that as in Romans 8 this applies to individuals (cf. Wilckens), for Paul continues with: "Even us, whom he hath called, not of the Jews only, but also of the Gentiles" (Rom. 9:24).

Furthermore, for the doctrine of election it is especially important that the apostle speaks of "a remnant according to the election of grace" (Rom. 11:5). The election is "gracious sovereignty and sovereign grace" (Ridderbos). Here Paul refers to Christians from among the Jews, "the elect," who are distinguished from "the rest" (Rom. 11:7). It does not say that the others have been rejected, but that they have hardened themselves. This hardening may be interpreted as being their own fault, although it is sometimes said of God that he hardens people (Rom. 9:18).

It is worth pointing out that everything that is said about God's grace, his mercy, and his sovereignty in these chapters does not diminish man's responsibility. See especially Romans 11:20–24. Jager has pointed out that it must not be inferred from the image of the potter and the clay that we need to sit back and see whether God will do something to us. Jeremiah's prophecy which compares God's action to that of a potter ends with a call to repentance: "Return ye now everyone from his evil way, and make your ways and your doing good" (Jer. 18:11).

In 1 Corinthians 1:26–31 the word "choose" is used three times. The context makes clear that the action of God's choosing is manifested whenever the call of the gospel takes effect. With respect to the elect the same thing can be said as for those who are called: they only live by what God has given, gives, and will give to them in Christ. The one cannot exceed the other. "Precisely because the church emerges and is sustained by God's saving acts of grace, it can only comprise sinners and beggars. Only then can God show it what his grace means and can achieve" (Pop). Thus only God receives the glory (1 Cor. 1:31).

Several Scripture passages that have served at one time or another as proofs for the doctrine of eternal election are not convincing to everyone, but no one can ignore Ephesians 1:3–4. This verse engenders far less discussion than Romans 9 through 11.

The apostle begins with glorifying and praising God, the Father of our Lord Jesus Christ. In Christ he has granted various spiritual blessings, which are subsequently listed. It all goes back to having been elected in Christ. It says: "He has chosen us in him before the foundation of the world, that we should be holy and without blame before him in love" (Eph. 1:4).

It does not say that God has chosen us because as believers we are in Christ, but that he has chosen us in Christ—not apart from him but in him. What this implies for the doctrine of election will be discussed below (see § 16.5).

The text indicates that election by God precedes the foundation of the world. God chose his people from eternity (cf. *TDNT*, 3:620). He has a purpose for this. It is indicated with the words: "that we should be holy and without blame before him in love."

According to Venema, the expression "before the foundation of the world" indicates the deepest ground and origin of election. Our election derives from the eternal and eternally decreeing God. Venema interprets election in the New Testament primarily as an act of God in history through which people are placed under Christ's ministry of salvation or within his sphere of influence (Venema, 1965, 52–63). It has been appropriately objected to his view that the evidence of prehistorical elements in the Pauline doctrine of predestination cannot be denied (Ridderbos, *Paul*, 347ff.). This is also implied by the words with which the apostolic doxology continues: "Having predestinated us unto the adoption of children by Jesus Christ to himself, according to the good pleasure of his will" (Eph. 1:5), as well as what the apostle says (Eph. 1:9) of the good pleasure that God had purposed in him ("vor aller Schöpfung" = prior to all of creation, *TDNT*, 8:167).

The expressions used in 2 Timothy 1:9–10 point in the direction of election, although the term itself does not appear. It refers to God's "own purpose and grace, which was given us in Christ Jesus before the world began, but is now made manifest by the appearing of our Saviour."

With respect to 1 Peter it has been said that it is the only New Testament Scripture where the term "chosen" constitutes a theme right from the start. In the opening words of this epistle we come across a description of the life of a Christian in terms of grounds, means, and purpose, which takes the fundamental eternal election as its starting point. Furthermore, the three divine persons are referred to in the process (cf. *TDNT*, 4:190).

Christ is the chosen cornerstone and believers are the chosen race, charged with proclaiming God's virtues (1 Peter 2:4–10). There is a clear contrast between this chosen race and unbelievers referred to in 1 Peter 2:8. There is a problem with the final words: "whereunto also they were appointed." What were these people destined to do?

Opinions vary. Some interpret this text to mean that they are destined to stumble if they are disobedient to the Word. This would then not imply predestination. However, the text rather says that those who in disobedience take offense at the Word of Christ are destined to do so. This does sound harsh. However, it should not be detached from its context. First Peter 2:8 does refer to a destiny (cf. *TDNT*, 8:157) that may be interpreted to be a decree and a judgment of God, but in the foregoing the emphasis is on unbelief and disobedience. These are not mutually exclusive perspectives. Goppelt points out that man is responsible for his rejection of the message of salvation, while at the same time there is a blinding by God. It is not impossible that this is a parallel passage to Romans 11:7, where the elect portion of Israel is contrasted with those who have been hardened.

The Book of Life. We still need to consider whether Scripture passages in which reference is made to the Book of Life have significance for the doctrine of election. Until recently, Reformed theologians took it to be almost a foregone conclusion that this book contained the names of those who would inherit eternal life, i.e., the book of God's counsel (cf. Dijk, 1924, 277). Woelderink had strong objections to this view. He believes that heaven's register contains the names of true believers and that new names are continually being added, while some names can also be stricken out.[17]

In the New Testament, the Book of Life is primarily referred to in Revelation (but also in Phil. 4:3, and we come across the same idea in Luke 10:20 and Heb. 12:23). For the eternal future with God it is crucial whether our names are contained in this book. Scripture says clearly that this is not the case for all people (Rev. 13:8; 17:8; 20:15; 21:27). These are the names of the elect—this word occurs in Revelation 17:14—and according to Revelation 17:8, their number was fixed prior to creation (Visser).[18] This does not mean only that God knows

17. The latter is based on Rev. 3:5: "I will not blot out his name out of the book of life" (Woelderink, 1951, 63). The promise that the names of those who overcome definitely will not be blotted out is, however, not the same thing as allowing for the possibility that names could be removed from the Book of Life. It is philologically untenable (cf. *TDNT*, 3:620) that there would be a significant difference between being listed in the Book of Life "since the foundation of the world" (Rev. 13:8) and since *before* the foundation of the world (Woelderink, 1951, 63), especially not if we also consider the form of the verb (*gegraptai*).

18. Even a Remonstrant document states that an "undeniable predestinate flavour" could probably be ascribed to the Book of Life in places such as Rev. 13:8; 17:8 (*Voorbeschikking of verkiezing* = predestination or election, 1962, 78).

beforehand who his people are. He determines it himself. They have been destined by him for eternal life (*TDNT*, 5:281). This implies an unshakable eternal anchorage in God's gracious decree (*TDNT*, 1:619). There is a direct connection between the concept of election, as expressed in the words of the Book of Life, and the perseverance to which believers are called (Rev. 13:8, 10).

The Book of Life is the book of the Lamb (Rev. 21:27). "He who has his name written in it reveals his election in the concreteness of his life of faith on earth" (Berkouwer, 1960, 115).

The eternal salvation of believers is unshakably secure in Christ. It is an unassailable reality in all the vicissitudes of their lives. It is no coincidence that this is mentioned more than once in the book of Revelation!

We admit that the idea that the names of the elect are contained in the Book of Life is open to abuse. One would think that no one could claim to know this, because it remains God's secret. He obviously does not give us access to this book.

Although it cannot be called exegesis that in a Lutheran confession statement Christ is referred to as the true Book of Life in which are listed all those who will be saved (*BSLK*, 1068), there is a close connection between being chosen in Christ before the foundation of the world (Eph. 1:4) and having one's name listed in the Book of Life of the Lamb since the foundation of the world. This book does not refer to the mystery of election but to the certainty of the preservation of the chosen children of God.

4. *Summary*

The Old Testament perspective carries on into the New Testament, but in many respects the latter is more explicit about predestination than the former.

1. When God chooses people, it reflects his sovereign love (Deut. 7:8). It reflects his love and his good pleasure (Eph. 1:5, 11; cf. also Luke 2:14).

2. God has predestined his people in Christ (Eph. 1:4). The Book of Life is the book of the Lamb (Rev. 13:8). We do not see it referred to in the Old Testament, not even when it mentions the Book of Life (Ex. 32:32–33; Ps. 69:28), although the idea of eternal salvation is already alluded to in Isaiah 4:2–3.

3. Although election is known in the Old Testament through the acts of God's choosing, the New Testament refers more than once to election as an eternal decree of God (cf. Rom. 8:29–30; Eph. 1:4). The eternal dimension of election is more clearly stated (Bavinck, *R.D.*, 2:346ff.).

4. Although in the Old Testament personal salvation is never out of the question (cf. Isa. 65), the focus is more on the election of Israel as the people of the covenant. The New Testament puts greater emphasis on personal salvation (Rom. 8:33; 1 Peter 1:2). The Book of Life, which is the book of the Lamb, contains specific names.

5. In the Old Testament God elects not only to his service, but also to communion with him. In the New Testament election definitely does not pertain to a particular ministry.[19] Jesus does choose his twelve apostles (Luke 6:13–16). But the main focus is on election to salvation (Acts 13:48; Rom. 8:29–30; Eph. 1:5; 2 Thess. 2:13). This means being predestined to conformity with the image of Christ (Rom. 8:29).

6. Salvation, which proceeds from election, is granted through grace. It is the "election of grace" (Rom. 11:5).

7. There is a direct connection between election in Christ and the assurance of salvation (Rom. 8:29–39; Eph. 1:3–12).

8. The purpose of election is that we shall be holy and blameless in God's sight (Eph. 1:4). The highest goal is the glorification of God (Eph. 1:12; 1 Peter 2:9–10).

9. God chooses one and not the other. He is free to do so (cf. Rom. 9:11–23). Receiving his mercy is contrasted with being hardened by him (Rom. 9:18). Does the New Testament teach that both election and reprobation are from eternity? A number of texts appear to point in this direction (1 Peter 2:8; Rev. 13:8; 17:8).

16.3. *The Reformed doctrine of predestination*

It is not within our present scope to outline the entire history of the doctrine of predestination. Yet something needs to be said about the teachings of Augustine and Calvin. They not only stand at the beginning,[20] but they are also very clear in terms of their motives.

19. A. Richardson believed that both the New and Old Testaments focused on service rather than privilege (*An Introduction to the Theology of the New Testament*, 1966^3, 275). See Berkouwer, 1960, 319–22, for the rejection of unbiblical contrasts.

20. For Augustine see: Polman, 1936; Nygren, 1965. For Calvin besides Polman see: Otten, 1938; Klooster, 1977; Graafland, 1987, 5–46. For Luther see: Brosché, 1977.

1. *Augustine*

Augustine can be considered to be the father of the doctrine of election. Most church fathers who preceded him emphasized man's responsibility and freedom. Augustine initially did the same thing. In looking back on his life and work, he says that initially he did advocate free will, but that God's grace won out.

The study of Scripture played a crucial role in this reversal. In addition to Romans 9, a passage of Scripture such as 1 Corinthians 4:7 made a deep impression on him. In the conflict with Pelagius and those who did not radically reject the latter's views, he forcefully maintained that we owe everything to God's free grace. Grace is only grace if it is granted through grace. No one is saved except through unmerited mercy and no one is condemned other than through a well-deserved judgment. The elect are predestined to eternal life. God has not chosen us because we believe, but so that we may believe and so that we would be holy and blameless before him (cf. John 15:16; Eph. 1:4). We reencounter this perspective in Calvin and the Canons of Dort.

2. *Calvin*

In his *Institutes* Calvin starts out from the fact that the preaching of the covenant of life does not come to all people without distinction, and that those who hear the gospel do not all respond in the same way. The distinction between faith and unbelief reveals the grandeur of God's judgment. The doctrine of predestination provides answers to questions engendered by this perspective (*Institutes*, 3.21.1).

This is only an introduction to the topic and it would be wrong to interpret it as though Calvin starts out from experience, let alone that it gives the impression that the doctrine of predestination is part of a theology of experience (contrary to Graafland, 1987, 19–22). What can be inferred from a review of numerous Scripture passages in the *Institutes*, and is also attested by Calvin's statements in various discussions, already comes through clearly in his commentary on the epistle to the Romans (1539) in which an outline of his doctrine of predestination can be recognized. Here as everywhere else, Scripture is used to tell the whole story. Whenever words of Augustine come to mind—which happens not infrequently—he quotes them. In many regards there is agreement with what Bucer wrote. The main point is that he is convinced that he replicates the teaching of Scripture (cf. Klooster, 1977, 20–24). This also explains his sharp rebuttals of criticism of his teachings.

In part as a byproduct of polemics, he deeply delves into God's decree to reprobate people. However, the main thing is that the doctrine of double predestination makes us see in our election God's unmerited mercy and glorify his grace (*Institutes*, 3.21.1).

More so than any others, Calvin points to the significance of the apostolic word that God chose us before the foundation of the world (Eph. 1:4). Our election in Christ implies that it is pure grace and that faith in Christ is the way to come to the certainty that we have been chosen by God (cf. Graafland, 1987, 35–41).

The doctrine of predestination has both theological and soteriological aspects. The former focuses on the recognition that God's grace is sovereign grace. The decision about our salvation is in God's hands and not ours. We owe it to him alone and we shall therefore glorify and praise him. The latter implies especially the assurance of salvation that we receive through faith. This is not a temporary certainty, but a permanent one. The certainty of salvation is in essence the certainty of the eternal love of him who chose us in Christ.

It is entirely in line with Calvin that the Canons of Dort (1.14) state that the doctrine of divine election must continue to be taught today in God's church to the glory of God's holy name and to great comfort for his people.

3. *Canons of Dort*

The Reformed doctrine of predestination is contained in article 16 of the Belgic Confession of Faith which closely resembles the corresponding article of the French Confession of Faith (1559), which is largely from the pen of Calvin. But we have this doctrine in elaborated form in the Canons of Dort. It is clear from this confession that its emergence reflects the conflict with Remonstrants (i.e., Arminians). In terms of content, this doctrine is entirely Calvin's. Although differences with Remonstrants received the primary focus, it is not correct to say that as a result the confession of Dort became one-sided. This synod had the firm resolve to let itself be guided solely by the Word of God.[21] Scripture does indeed have the final word, judging by numerous quotations of Bible passages or references to them. It is understandable that the New Testament is quoted more extensively than the Old Testament (see § 16.2).

It can be concluded from *Remonstrantie* (1610), *Contra-Remonstrantie* (1611), and other sources that between the two camps there was more at stake than the doctrine of predestination. Arminius also had a diverging view of justification. But one cannot say that this represented the essential difference between the two factions. The Remonstrants treated all of faith, election, atonement, regeneration, and perseverance from the point of view of cooperation between God's grace and man's free will.

A key statement can be found in the Canons of Dort, 3–4.14: Faith is a "gift of God." God produces in man "both the will to believe and the act of believing also." Therefore God does not await our faith

21. *Acta ofte handelinghen* (acts or proceedings), 1621, 12.

but works it. This is the fruit of election. It is election to faith, not election on the basis of "foreseen faith" (1.9). The canons teach that before the foundation of the world, out of mere grace, God elected to redemption in Christ a certain number of people "neither better nor more deserving than others, but with them involved in one common misery" (1.7).

A number of salient points may be highlighted:

1. One can consider the purpose of chapter 1 of the Canons of Dort to be both concrete and historical.
2. The Synod of Dort does not dwell on varying reactions to the gospel. Everything is viewed from the perspective of God's eternal counsel. There is a decree of both election and reprobation. This is reminiscent of Calvin's line of thinking (*Institutes*, 21.1).
3. All salvation proceeds from election, i.e., election in Christ.
4. The foundation of gracious election is solely God's good pleasure.
5. In time the elect attain assurance of their election from eternity.
6. The effect of all of this is that God's children humbly love God. It does not cause them to be careless.
7. The main point is that the doctrine of election is correctly explained in church, for which it is particularly intended.
8. Reprobation (Canons of Dort, 1.15) remains completely overshadowed by election itself. God has decided to let people go their own way subject to his just judgment and to condemn and punish eternally their unbelief and all other sins.
9. God-fearing parents need not doubt the election and salvation of their children if God removes them from this life in their youth. In this connection reference is made to the meaning of the covenant of grace and God's promises.
10. We adore these mysteries with devout reverence.

G. C. Berkouwer, who once said that he produced his study on God's election (1960) not without hesitation and persistent questions, "distorted" the Reformed doctrine of election (Graafland, 1987, 353). In a well-known article (1963) he signaled a tension between gracious election as the underlying theme of the Canons of Dort and its framework of causality. God's eternal decree to reject some people (1.15)—as well as the corresponding statements in 1.6—would reflect this framework, and one should not have to be held accountable for this without thereby being obliged to submit a gravamen.[22]

A significant objection to this interpretation is that since the Canons of Dort present this doctrine as a unified whole, it does not make sense to separate the underlying theme from its overall framework. When the Synod of Dort decided to list a series of fallacies in chapter 1, it felt that it had adequately interpreted the orthodox doctrine of election and reprobation.

16.4. *Recent views*

1. *K. Barth.* Of all recent views on the doctrine of election, Barth's is the most prominent and influential. He says himself that here he had to leave the framework of theological tradition much more so than in the preceding part of this dogmatics (*C.D.*, 2.2.x).

Through his *Epistle to the Romans* (1922) and especially *C.D.*, 2.2, the doctrine of predestination became the focal point of theological discussion.[23]

A phase in the development of Barth's thinking, which resulted in the definitive formulation of his doctrine, was a shorter work published under the title *Gottes Genadenwahl* (God's gracious election, 1936). It says that predestination is grace within grace. Since God's Chosen One takes upon himself our reprobation, it is thereby canceled.

From the beginning, Barth rejects the view that election involves a specific number of persons. He sees it as an open multiplicity and no *numerus clausus*! God does not distinguish between people and people. We all are subject to God's judgment and may all live by grace. Nevertheless, initially the emphasis is on the *sovereignty* of God's grace, and subsequently more on the sovereignty of God's *grace*. The doctrine of election and reprobation in *The Epistle to the Romans* is marked by universal crisis, while in *Church Dogmatics* the triumph of grace is given prominence.

The doctrine of election is the synopsis of the gospel. Its focus is the selection of divine grace (*Genadenwahl* = election by grace). The simplest form of the doctrine of predestination, which strictly speaking captures the entire dogma, is: Jesus Christ is the electing God and Jesus Christ

22. G. C. Berkouwer, "Vragen rondom de belijdenis" (questions around the confession), in *G.T.T.* 63 (1963): 1–41.

23. Apart from the works of Van Niftrik, Kraus, Weber, and others listed among the literature at the end of this chapter, cf. also G. C. Berkouwer, *De triomf der genade in de theologie van Karl Barth* (the triumph of grace in the theology of Karl Barth), 1954; W. Kreck, *Grundentscheidungen in Karl Barths Dogmatik* (fundamental decisions in Karl Barth's dogmatics), 1978; C. Vermeulen, *Het hart van de kerk* (the heart of the church), 1986. Also, concise but critical, J. van Genderen, "De leer van de verkiezing bij Karl Barth" (the doctrine of election according to Karl Barth), in A. G. Knevel (ed.), *Visie op Karl Barth* (evaluation of Karl Barth), 1987, 41–48.

is the chosen man. Concerning the latter it should be added that he is this in his union with mankind, so that in and with him the others are also elected (*C.D.*, 2.2.103–18). In Jesus Christ God chooses man. The concrete decree of election in Jesus Christ replaces the absolute decree that figures in the traditional doctrine of predestination.

Jesus Christ is not only the elected man; he is also the reprobate man. In this sense there is a double predestination: election and reprobation, grace and judgment. "In the election of Jesus Christ which is the eternal will of God, God has ascribed to man . . . election, salvation and life; and to himself he has ascribed . . . reprobation, perdition and death." Belief in God's predestination means as such: not believing in the reprobation of man. "For man is not rejected. In the eternal decree of his counsel God himself is rejected in his Son. His Son was rejected so that we would not be rejected" (163–68).

Israel and the church reflect reprobation and election respectively. The one church of God must bring out God's judgment in her manifestation as Israel and God's mercy in her manifestation as church. Since God in his only Son bore the rejection incurred by man, the rejection of Ishmael, Esau, Pharaoh, and all of Israel is also characterized as a rejection borne by God himself. Barth reads this into Romans 9:22–23 (195, 226).

The question arises whether according to this christologically based doctrine of predestination all people are saved. There are statements that point in this direction. "The only truly rejected man is God's own Son." He is *the* Reprobate One, precisely because he is *the* Chosen One. Apart from him—from the perspective of his election—no one else is rejected (318, 351). For each one of us God has made a life of rejection into an objective impossibility. Any attempt to live such a life is perilous, but to no avail. Faith in God's promise is the only option and unbelief is precluded (346, 326). In this case one cannot escape the rod of God's wrath, but it is unlikely that one would be struck down by God's sword. According to Barth this is all that we can say. One is not permitted to teach *apokatastasis* or universal atonement because we must respect the sovereignty of God's grace. Neither is it completely out of the question, for one must gratefully accept the grace of divine sovereignty (349, 418).

Those who reject the classical doctrine of predestination usually defend man's freedom to choose. Although God's grace may take the initiative, man also has a role to play and he needs to act in tandem (*synergism*). But according to Barth it is not a question of God and man jointly deciding.

We agree that it is a matter of God's *Gnadenwahl* (gracious election), i.e., the priority and sovereignty of his grace. But it has to be the biblical doctrine of grace.

We shall leave aside for now that Barth's dialectical approach led him to ignore Scripture and to enter into the realm of speculation.

His doctrine is *universalistic* and *objectivistic*. Those are two serious objections—and there are others. Later we shall trace through what it means that election is an election in Christ (§ 16.5), but there is definitely no biblical foundation for the idea that all people are chosen in Christ and that through his Son God has borne the rejection of all. Scripture says: "He that believeth on the Son hath everlasting life: and he that believeth not the Son shall not see life; but the wrath of God abideth on him" (John 3:36).

Barth does not recognize the role of faith that God requires from us according to the Bible. If unbelief is ignored, by considering it to be precluded, it is hard to accept that faith is crucial for partaking of salvation.

The doctrine of predestination says that it is mere grace to accept grace. Faith operates within the sphere of grace. The Word of God does not only say that we are saved by grace (Eph. 2:5), but also: "For by grace are ye saved through faith; and that not of yourselves: it is the gift of God" (Eph. 2:8).

2. *Theology in the Netherlands*. In the Netherlands this doctrine of Barth has been accepted by many. K. H. Miskotte, G. C. van Niftrik, E. J. Beker, J. M. Hasselaar, and others agreed with him to a great extent.[24]

The report titled *Enige aspecten van de leer der uitverkiezing* (some aspects of the doctrine of predestination), produced by well-known Reformed (*Hervormd*) and Remonstrant theologians, is proof of the great influence that Barth had on theology in the Netherlands. One of its premises was that in speaking about election the focus ought to be shifted from the individual to the church and the world. It is said in this report that God elects us to his service as a church. The authors follow Barth in referring to Christ as the Man of God who represents all human beings. This is an objective situation that must be recognized. Then the church can only proclaim that every human being is in Christ and that this proclamation demands faith (*Enige aspecten*, 22, 33, 45).

In Graafland's judgment the real questions, which reflect the old controversy, have been cloaked in a universalistic concept of salvation (Graafland, 1987, 592).

J. G. Woelderink takes an independent position with his well-known paper *De uitverkiezing* (predestination, 1951). Although the Reformed

24. Cf. Miskotte, *V.W.*, 2; Van Niftrik, *Kl.D.*; Beker/Hasselaar, *Wegen* (ways), 2.

perspective is clearly recognizable, the author has a greater appreciation for Barth's view than other Reformed theologians. He even writes as follows: "Barth's key concept is in complete agreement with the gospel and has been derived from it." He judges it to be biblically responsible to see all of God's decrees as proceeding from his eternal love (*De uitverkiezing* = election, 34).

Woelderink fears disdain for sin on Barth's part (37ff.), but his chief objection is the relativization of the decision of faith. "Not until our acceptance of faith are we assured of this electing love of God" (73, 78).

At least as important as Barth's influence is Woelderink's own reaction to the preponderance of a concept of election that overshadows the calling through the gospel and the promise of the covenant.

Woelderink says that God chooses when he calls, and that he calls when he chooses. This choosing act of God is effected through the call (44, 53). Romans 9 deals with divine actions rather than an eternal decree of election and reprobation. Woelderink refuses to acknowledge an eternal decree of God to reprobate people. He cannot accept what is said about this in the Canons of Dort.[25]

From an exegetical point of view his interpretation is weak for Scripture passages such as Matthew 22:14, Romans 9–11, and the texts that refer to the Book of Life. From a theological point of view we must counter that God's actions in time reflect his eternal counsel. This is an insight that we already encounter in earlier Reformed dogmatics.[26]

16.5. *Election in Christ*

In line with words of Scripture (Eph. 1:4; cf. also 2 Tim. 1:9), we speak about election as election in Christ. This is also confirmed by the Reformed confessional statements (Belgic Confession of Faith, article 16; Canons of Dort, 1.7). We highlight this because it is of great significance that the role of Christ in election is well understood.

To us this does not mean the same thing as it did to Barth, to whom the apostolic expression "in Christ" is the basis for a christological doctrine of election with a universalistic thrust.

Neither do we mean the same thing as the Remonstrants. In their conflict with the Reformed tradition they gave a contrived interpretation to the words "chosen in Christ" (Eph. 1:4): He has predestined us, who are in Christ, where the words "in Christ" are equated with believing in Christ, because no one without faith is in

25. Woelderink, 1951, 17–22. See also among others, Trimp, 1954; Graafland, 1987.

26. Cf. *Synopsis*, 24:10; H. Witsius, *De oeconomia foederum Dei cum hominibus*, 1694, 3.4.4.

Christ. This suited the Remonstrant concept of election: God foreknew who would believe in Christ. However, according to Paul, "in Christ" goes with "predestined" and is not a clause modifying "us."

The words of the apostle do not imply that Christ is the grounds or meritorious cause of election. At the Synod of Dort (1618–19) the question did arise whether one could consider him to be the foundation of election (*fundamentum electionis*). Although this synod deliberately avoided this expression, it did consider Christ to be the foundation of salvation (*fundamentum salutis*, 1.7). Whenever Christ is considered to be the foundation or cause of predestination, the idea could arise that Christ (or his work) led God to elect people. It has been correctly pointed out that the Son did not move the Father to love, but that the electing love originated in the Father himself (Bavinck, *R.D.*, 2:401).

It has been suggested that if Christ is not the grounds of election—as K. Barth wants to believe and many others with him—he can only be the means of the implementation of an eternal decree that God established independent of him. This places Christ outside the decree (Van Niftrik, *Kl.D.*, 125). It would be difficult to have to defend all of Reformed theology against such criticism. However, this criticism does not touch the teachings of the church directly. The Belgic Confession of Faith, article 16, and the Canons of Dort, 1.7, imply that Christ is not excluded from the decree of election.[27]

This avoids treating predestination as an abstract concept. From a biblical point of view one cannot speak of predestination without being aware of Christ and his work. Blessed by God the Father in Christ, we are chosen in him and adopted as sons. In him we have been graced and in him we have redemption through his blood. In him we have obtained an inheritance and were sealed with the Holy Spirit (Eph. 1:3–14). The expression "in Christ" opens all stops of the gospel!

Election is not merely a matter of God's sovereign will, for it is God's "gracious election" (Canons of Dort, 1.10). The confession that God has chosen us in Christ from before the foundation of the world is the confession of God's eternal love. This is the electing love that is revealed to us in Christ, and from which all our salvation flows.

If God had not predestined us in Christ, but had made his decree without Christ's involvement, Christ could merely execute it. Would we

27. Graafland (1987, 140–48) inferred from the official Dutch text of the confession documents, published in 1983, an argument in support of his thesis that in the Canons of Dort Christ does not figure in the core of election per se, but clearly "occupies a subsidiary position which does not involve election proper but its execution." What he quotes (from Canons of Dort, 1.7) cannot be considered to be proper proof. Although the text of 1983 offers room for more than one interpretation, and someone could read into it that God has chosen us to salvation in Christ, the original Latin text does not offer any scope for ambiguity. It says in a single sentence that God has chosen His people in Christ, only through grace unto salvation.

then not have to seek the assurance of our election beyond Christ? Then we would have to deal directly with God's secret counsel. Then Calvin would never have been able to say: At any rate I do not refer people to God's secret election to anxiously await their salvation, but I tell them to go directly to Christ in whom our salvation is revealed, which otherwise would have remained hidden in God (*C.O.*, 8:306, 307).

Calvin, who repeatedly pointed to the crucial significance of the expression "in Christ," notes that this name precludes any form of merit (Commentary on Eph. 1:4). Election in Christ implies indeed that it is by God's pure goodness and out of mere grace (Belgic Confession of Faith; Canons of Dort). This is confirmed by the words "before the foundation of the world" employed by the apostle (Eph. 1:4). This election exists since before the world was made; it exists since before we arrived on the scene. It cannot possibly be based on any qualifications of our own. The grounds for our election lie altogether beyond us!

As Calvin says: What could God possibly find in us that would persuade him to elect us? "When Paul teaches (Eph. 1:4) that we are chosen in Christ before the creation of the world, he takes away all consideration of real worth on our part. It is just as if he said: since among all the offspring of Adam, the heavenly Father found nothing worthy of his election, he turned his eyes upon his Anointed, to choose from that body as members those whom he was to take into the fellowship of life (*Institutes*, 3.22.1).

Calvin correctly contrasts the expression "in Christ" with "in us." God chose his people in Christ, for he could not love them other than in him (*Institutes*, 3.24.5).

The apostolic words concerning election in Christ not only are of great importance because they preclude all efforts to seek qualifications within ourselves, but they also explain how we can acquire the assurance of our election. This is eminently stated by Calvin in a frequently cited passage: "If we have been chosen in him, we shall not find assurance of our election in ourselves; and not even in God the Father, if we conceive him as severed from his Son. Christ, then, is the mirror wherein we, and without self-deception may, contemplate our own election" (*Institutes*, 3.24.5).

There is yet another aspect. One can ask oneself how the preposition "in" in the expression "in Christ" (Eph. 1:4) can be described philologically. Is it meant instrumentally: in and through Christ, who is the Mediator? Does it mean: in communion with Christ? Is it comprehensive?

In a somewhat different context Calvin says that we must ascend to the Head, in whom the heavenly Father has gathered his elect together and joined them to him with an unbreakable bond (*Institutes*, 3.21.7).

The one does not preclude the other. Christ is the Mediator whose work is discussed in Ephesians 1. If we have been chosen in him, we are so as human beings who have been given to him by the Father to be his people and to form together the new humanity of which he is the Head. For he has been "appointed the Mediator and Head of the elect and the foundation of salvation" (Canons of Dort, 1.7).

The fact that God has chosen his people in Christ and given them to Christ (see John 17:9–10) brings with it that we cannot interpret election individualistically, as though it only involved predestined individuals in addition to other predestined individuals. Election in Christ implies union with him and with one another, which is essential for the church, which has been chosen to eternal life and which is a communion of saints (Heidelberg Catechism, Lord's Day 21).

It has been correctly pointed out that election in Christ may be seen as the center and the mystery of the biblical message of election (Berkouwer, 1960, 52).

16.6. *Infralapsarian and supralapsarian views*

Infralapsarianism and supralapsarianism refer to different views with respect to the relationship between predestination and the fall into sin (*infra lapsum* = below or after the fall; *supra lapsum* = above or prior to the fall).

The original infralapsarianism that was advocated by Bullinger starts out on this side of the fall into sin. Bullinger did not wish to go back any further and say that God had preordained the fall.

In the same century Beza defended a supralapsarian position. According to him God not only decreed man's fall into sin, but his decree to elect certain people and reprobate others also preceded everything. In this way predestination comes to control everything.

Several Reformed theologians felt attracted to supralapsarianism (W. Perkins, F. Gomarus, J. Maccovius, G. Voetius, A. Comrie, A. Kuyper, G. H. Kersten, C. Steenblok, H. Hoeksema, and others).

A subsequent form of infralapsarianism does teach that God's counsel directs everything, including the fall into sin, although it is preferable to say that God permitted the fall rather than desiring it. However, it does not start out with predestination. When God elects or rejects people, he views them as created and fallen people. In the Netherlands we encounter the infralapsarian view in theologians such as A. Walaeus, S. Maresius, J. à Marck, W. Heyns, J. J. van der Schuit, and W. D. Jonker.

Not infrequently elements of truth and one-sidedness can be recognized in both views. Bavinck says that neither supralapsarianism nor infralapsarianism is able to incorporate the full truth of Scripture and to satisfy theological thinking (*R.D.*, 2:391). Bavinck does nevertheless lean toward infralapsarianism (cf. Jonker, 1989, 69).

Calvin cannot easily be classified in either camp. There are discussions of his concerning predestination that give a supralapsarian impression (*Institutes*, 3.21.5), but his basic tendency remains infralapsarian (cf. Polman, 1936, 377).

More important than the voices of theologians are the pronouncements of churches. It is noteworthy that the vast majority of Reformed confessions embrace the infralapsarian position. This is also true of the Belgic Confession of Faith and the Canons of Dort. At the time of the Dort Synod, Remonstrants made efforts to play out infralapsarians and surpralapsarians against each other (cf. Dijk, 1912, 99–115). There was a proposal to leave the issue undecided, and Gomarus did plead for this. It says a great deal that the infralapsarian view predominates in the canons, although the alternative stance was not condemned with a single word. The difference between the two views is left aside in the Westminster Confession and a number of other confessional statements.

Although it is not a confessional pronouncement, one ecclesiastical decision concerning this doctrinal difference also deserves mention here. The synod of the *Gereformeerde Kerken* in 1905 had occasion to address objections to the teachings of A. Kuyper. According to this synod it is not acceptable to present the supralapsarian view as *the* doctrine of the *Gereformeerde Kerken in Nederland*, but neither to trouble those who have a supralapsarian inclination. Such profound doctrines are to be avoided as much as possible in the pulpit; both preaching and catechetical instruction are to limit themselves to the content of the confessional documents (*Acta*, article 158).

If the difference between infralapsarianism and supralapsarianism merely involved the sequence of God's decrees, we would point out to both camps that God did not sequentially decree one thing and another. Is he not the eternal God (§ 13.4)? What if no chronological but only a logical sequence was intended? Then we would ask how concepts deduced from our own logical thought processes could ever apply to God.

Yet the difference in question is not imaginary. The crux is the question as to how man fits into God's decree. Is he a potentially created human being (supralapsarianism) or a human being seen by God as created by him and fallen away from him (infralapsarianism)?

In the former case creation and the fall into sin represent means to execute double predestination, as sketched by Beza (cf. Graafland, 1987, 47–70). In the latter case God's decree presupposes the creation and man's fall into sin.

From a supralapsarian point of view God directs everything through his decree of predestination, so that the fall into sin becomes a necessary link in his plan. Infralapsarianism has great difficulties with this. It fears an absolutization of God's sovereignty and emphasizes his mercy and justice, both in his counsel and in his deeds.

What does Scripture say? Supralapsarianism seeks support in passages that testify to God's absolute sovereignty, while infralapsarianism "is supported by all the passages in which election and reprobation have reference to a fallen world and are represented as acts of mercy and justice" (Bavinck, *R.D.*, 2:385).

Among these places, Ephesians 1:4 together with its context is of great importance. The apostle says that God has chosen us in Christ. Supralapsarianism cannot do justice to this, for it cannot explain that people who have not yet fallen could be the subject of election in Christ. Does Scripture not present Christ as the Savior of sinners?

A. Comrie believed he found a way out, but his reflections on "the Man Christ" are quite speculative in nature (Graafland, 1987, 242–48).

The implication of supralapsarianism is that election and reprobation are coordinated. This is abundantly clear in Beza's scheme. Precisely this coordination or symmetry is open to much criticism, as we shall see below (§ 16.7). Then it is as though God plans reprobation in the same way as election, while he says in his Word: "I have no pleasure in the death of the wicked" (Ezek. 33:11).

A. Kuyper once pointed out that the one sees the controversy from mountain tops, while the other stands full-square on level ground. Berkouwer was quite correct in wondering whether the latter is not the only place where we can understand anything at all of this mystery of God (Berkouwer, 1960, 369).

The greater reluctance of infralapsarianism with respect to the emergence of sin not only has significance as a warning against the tendency to ascribe everything to God and even to the point of making him in a certain sense the deviser of sin, but it also has the merit of seeking to remain within the limits that the Bible sets to our knowledge. This modesty adorns infralapsarianism.

Barth, who referred to himself as a proponent of a purified supralapsarianism, recognized that it is understandable that the official infralapsarian position was chosen from the point of view of ecclesiastical practicality (*C.D.*, 2.2.131–32). This practical side is a factor to be reckoned with. In Scripture and the proclamation of the Word we are addressed as created and fallen human beings. Similarly, as sinners we encounter the miracle of the electing love of God in Christ.

In connection with this topic we have a strong sense that our knowledge is imperfect and that there remain unanswered questions. Infralapsarianism is particularly convinced of this, and also for this reason has an advantage. The most important thing is that it is closely linked with what Scripture says about election in Christ and adheres to the teaching of the confession, while it serves to unify theology and practice (cf. Van der Schuit, 1937, 28–33).

16.7. *Election and reprobation*

In the Reformed tradition, election and reprobation are frequently mentioned in one breath as two aspects of God's eternal decree. The term "reprobation" (*reprobatio*) is not always used, for the opposite of election can also be expressed differently, for example not elected, bypassed (Canons of Dort, 1.16), or leaving in the fall and perdition (Belgic Confession of Faith, article 15).

When election and reprobation are considered to be equivalent aspects of the concept of predestination, reprobation is viewed as the converse of election and vice versa.

Certain statements made by Calvin (see *Institutes*, 3.21.5, 7) are reminiscent of parallelism. There is a passage in the Canons of Dort that appears to point in this direction: "That some receive the gift of faith from God, and others do not receive it, proceeds from God's eternal decree" (1.6).

Especially theologians who support the supralapsarian view (cf. § 16.6) have a tendency to place election and reprobation side by side. This was done in the sixteenth century by Beza and Perkins, and in the twentieth century by G. H. Kersten and C. Steenblok. In America, the theology of H. Hoeksema is a clear example of this (cf. De Jong, 1954, 113–16). K. Schilder criticizes both supralapsarianism and infralapsarianism (*H.C.*, 3:455–80), but as a rule he speaks in supralapsarian terms and treats election and reprobation as being parallel (cf. Douma, 1966, 298).

In spite of the passage quoted above (1.6), this is not the case with the Canons of Dort. Election and reprobation are described quite differently in the first chapter. In addition, in the conclusion to the Canons of Dort the idea is rejected that reprobation is as much (*eodem modo*) the cause of unbelief and godlessness as election is the source and cause of faith and good works.

Berkouwer (1960, 175–84) and others before him stressed the importance of this consideration for our understanding of predestination. Reprobation is not in the same sense and manner a component of God's decree as election (Bavinck, *R.D.*, 2:395). Election and reprobation may not be coordinated, as if they would take an equal place (Dijk, 1924, 391).

In the Bible election has priority. There is election from eternity, but it is nowhere placed side by side with reprobation from eternity. There is a Book of Life, but we do not read of a book of death. Romans 9:22–23 says with respect to "vessels of mercy" that God has prepared them beforehand unto glory. However, it does not say that God has prepared "vessels of wrath" beforehand unto perdition. The parallel is not perfect.

Election is the source of everything good that leads to salvation. Faith, holiness, and other saving gifts as well as eternal life itself flow forth from it (Canons of Dort, 1.9, with a reference to Eph. 1:4). There is no second source with God from which flow the opposites of these gifts. Faith in Jesus Christ and salvation through him are gifts of the grace of God (Eph. 2:8; Phil. 1:29). "The cause or fault of unbelief is no wise in God, but in man himself" (Canons of Dort, 1.5).

Those who recognize the difference between election and rejection and hold that election does not depend on man himself—since in him there is no merit at all—while reprobation is entirely man's own fault, may nevertheless not detract from God's sovereignty in choosing the one and bypassing or not choosing the other.

Remonstrants taught that faith and perseverance do not only depend on God's electing grace but also on man's free will. Just as unbelief is taken into account in God's decree of reprobation, so man's faith must be taken into account for election. Remonstrants made parallelism and symmetry into a key argument! "Just as faith is a fruit that sprouts from election unto salvation, so unbelief is a fruit that sprouts from the reprobation unto damnation." If the one does not hold, then the other does not hold either. If both perspectives are not joined together, one ends up with a theology that remains lacking in some respect and is crippled (*Schriftelijcke Conferentie* = written conference, 1617, 414).

Theology is not short of critical views of Reformed doctrine. Through the years 1955 to 1977 gravamina were received at three synodical meetings:

1. A. Duetz's gravamen to which the synod of the Netherlands Reformed Church (NHK) responded with guidelines for the treatment of the doctrine of predestination (*De uitverkiezing*, 1961);

2. That of B. J. Brouwer which led to the situation in which the synod of the *Gereformeerde Kerken in the Netherlands* (GK) (1969–70) recognized the right to have objections to passages in the Canons of Dort and to express these openly;

3. That of H. R. Boer, which was rejected by the synod of the Christian Reformed Church in 1980.

A number of serious objections contained in these gravamina and the supporting theological arguments are the following:

a. In referring to the electing God, one may not speak of two categories of predestined people (G. C. van Niftrik);

b. The question concerning the ultimate cause of faith and unbelief, raised by the Canons of Dort, is unwarranted, for it is not focused on God's salvation but represents an attempt to analyze rationally the impenetrable depths of God (J. G. Woelderink);

c. The Canons of Dort ascribe not only faith but also unbelief to an eternal decree of God (A. Duetz);

d. The doctrine of the eternal decree of election and reprobation is a theological construct, and the way in which the Canons of Dort, 1.6, 15, discuss reprobation is contrary to Scripture (B. J. Brouwer);

e. The philosophical-theological concept of the all-inclusive causality of God is of fundamental significance for the doctrine of reprobation from eternity (report of the synod committee of 1969–70);

f. It is an unbiblical, non-Reformed, and unchristian doctrine that there would be an eternal decree of God to reprobate people (H. R. Boer).

What is the alternative? To show another way, while avoiding the synergism of Remonstrants, people follow ever different directions.

- Following in the footsteps of K. Barth, it is not infrequently supposed that all people have been predestined. In themselves reprobate, they are elect in Christ. Although no one is reprobate now, some day there will be those who are (G. C. van Niftrik).
- Election and reprobation are acts of God in time, although the act of election is rooted in his eternal and unchangeable mercy. God chooses when he calls. He calls when he chooses (J. G. Woelderink).
- The question whether all people or only certain people are predestined can be avoided by not treating election of individuals as a starting point, but the election of Israel and the church. Election that does focus on the individual is reflected in the latter being drawn into the church (*De uitverkiezing* = predestination, 1961).

The first option (K. Barth) is definitely to be avoided, but neither do the other paths lead to the full confession of God's free grace.

Much has been criticized in this Reformed doctrine, but on the main points we cannot agree with the critics. We do agree that the Canons of Dort, 1.6, refers to texts that do not support all that is inferred from them. But one should not ignore what is said in the "rejection of errors." One can refer to Romans 9 (cf. Wentsel, *Dogm.*, 2:182; yet more clearly in Douma, 1966, 292). First Peter 2:8 also gives food for thought (see § 16.2). Hereby we do not deny that Scripture says little about reprobation as an eternal decree and much more about reprobation as an act in history (Bavinck, *R.D.*, 2:393–95).

By way of summary, Wentsel says that Scripture principally refers to reprobation as God's reaction to the spurning of his love in the three following manners: as wrath against man with the possibility of a gracious reacceptance in response to repentance; as an irreversible process of hardening; and as definitive rejection in an eschatological sense hereafter. The first event implies that God rejects those who reject him. An example of the second event is Pharaoh, whose heart remained intransigent, while it is said at the same time that God hardened his heart (Ex. 9:7, 12; cf. Rom. 9:17). The Bible clearly refers to definitive rejection by God (cf. Wentsel, *Dogm.*, 2:174–84).

In the confession of double predestination, as maintained by the Synod of Dort (1618–19), the most important question is not whether God's decree to permanently reprobate people is explicitly taught in Scripture. It has to do with the Reformed doctrine of predestination as an indivisible whole.

It is not a universal election, nor an election effected or undone by man himself. It is not only an act of God in time or an option for a nation or the church.

The main point is that God has elected certain people in Christ. This has for them in their lives the implication that they will be called, justified, and glorified, that they believe and that they will live a holy and blameless life in God's sight (cf. Rom. 8:28–30; Acts 10:48; Eph. 1:4). Before they were born, God personally chose them, but there are also people who are hardened (Rom. 11:7). They are not elected (cf. Rev. 13:8; 17:8).

When the synod of the Christian Reformed Church rejected the objections of H. R. Boer, it stated that Scripture indeed teaches a doctrine of election and reprobation, which implies that not all have been elected to eternal life (cf. Boer, 1983, 21). We can go along with this.

As far as the Canons of Dort are concerned, we do not find the essence of this doctrine in 1.6 or in 1.15, which have attracted the most criticism, but in 1.7 and 1.10.[28] The only grounds for gracious election is God's good pleasure. It consists in this: that he has chosen particular sinners out of the whole of sinners to be his possession. When the question arises as to why one was chosen and not another, the answer is: at the bottom of both questions lies God's eternal pleasure (Douma, 1966, 295).

Is it not an issue that God appears to treat people unequally? Does he not do an injustice to people whom he passes by? Can he really make this distinction within his counsel?

28. In this connection we refer to the well-known declaration of the Contra-Remonstrants (1611) that there was a desire on their part to grant the Remonstrants some slack, as long as they would have confessed that God predestined his people without taking into account their faith as a precondition! See *Schriftelijcke conferentie* (written conference), 1617, 43.

If it is really necessary to get to the bottom of this, we refer to the words of Paul which urge the greatest possible caution: "O man, who art thou that repliest against God?" (Rom. 9:14–23).

Furthermore, it can be pointed out that God also makes a distinction through his acts in history. Israel was the people of his choice and no other nation. Those who believe that they can make do with the redemptive-historical declaration of Romans 9–11 must admit that God acts with sovereignty in history by having mercy on some and not others (Rom. 9:18). He determines who will hear the gospel (Acts 16:6–10). The Canons of Dort also remind us of this: "God mercifully sends the messengers of these most joyful tidings to whom he will and at what time he pleases" (1.1–3).

In this first chapter of the Canons of Dort we are repeatedly reminded of the reality on which we are to base ourselves. We have all sinned in Adam, and to God the entire world is punishable. We all find ourselves in the same misery (cf. 1.1, 6–7, 15). As far as God's action is concerned both in time and in his counsel, which is eternal, we confess that he elects and redeems from the fall and perdition, into which they have plunged themselves (Belgic Confession of Faith, article 16). Theology has sought words to capture the connection between the reprobation by God and man's own fault. It has been said: "The decree of reprobation is realized through human culpability" (Bavinck, *R.D.*, 2:396).

It is not true that reprobation accompanies election as shadow follows light. Yet to our eyes reprobation is a shadow that accentuates the light (cf. Douma, 1966, 299). When it is said in the Canons of Dort, 1.15, that some have been bypassed by God's eternal election, then that is how it is intended.

It is grace to receive grace. This is the heart of the doctrine of double predestination. Therefore this doctrine does not give us reason to be pessimistic. "Solely on the basis of justice and merit, we would all have been lost. But since it is a matter of grace, there is hope for the most miserable person" (Bavinck).

We end this section with the well-known words of Bavinck: "No one has the right to believe that he or she is a reprobate, for everyone is sincerely and urgently called to believe in Christ with a view to salvation. No one *can* actually believe it, for one's own life and all that makes it enjoyable is proof that God takes no delight in his death. No one *really* believes it, for that would be hell on earth. But election is a source of comfort and strength, of submissiveness and humility, of confidence and resolution. The salvation of human beings is firmly established in the gracious and omnipotent good pleasure of God" (Bavinck, *R.D.*, 2:402).

16.8. *Election and proclamation of the gospel*

Formulation of a problem. Is the doctrine of predestination a hindrance to preaching? Is it not contradictory to take the glad tidings to all people if not all of them are predestined? This is the problem of particular grace and the universality of the call.

Augustine already encountered this problem (cf. Polman, 1936, 102–6). Luther dealt with it in his conflict with Erasmus. At that time he associated predestination with God's hidden will. However, we may and must hold on to God's revealed will. His Word is reliable. For Luther comments on Genesis 29:9: "But it pleases me to take from this passage the opportunity to discuss doubt, God, and the will of God; for I hear that here and there among the nobles and persons of importance vicious statements are being spread abroad concerning predestination or God's foreknowledge. For this is what they say: 'If I am predestined, I shall be saved, whether I do good or evil. If I am not predestined, I shall be condemned regardless of my works'" (*Luther's Works*, 5:43–50).

Calvin frequently delved more deeply into this in order to respond to opponents such as A. Pighius, G. Siculus, H. Bolsec, and S. Castellio. Through the external preaching all are called to penitence and faith, and yet not all receive the Spirit of repentance and faith. Both are biblical. Since God's mercy is offered to all through the gospel, it is faith—the illumination of God—that distinguishes between pious and impious. Illumination itself also follows God's eternal election as its rule (*Institutes*, 3.24.17).

We recognize Calvin's point of view in the Reformed confession. Remonstrants objected that it implied that the gospel could no longer be taken seriously by everyone. To a large proportion of its hearers the ministry of the gospel became the "fragrance of death."[29] Incidentally, the objective of these Remonstrants was to advocate their view that God presents everyone with the same opportunities, but that it depends on the free will of man himself whether or not he makes proper use of them.

There were Contra-Remonstrants who doubted whether the offer of God's grace in the gospel was indeed so universal. Subsequently, hyper-Calvinists and ultra-Reformed have inferred from the doctrine of double predestination that the gospel cannot be freely proclaimed or that the promise of the gospel is not intended for everyone. H. Hoeksema and C. Steenblok are known for their boldness in making radical statements. According to Hoeksema there is no universal offer of grace, although there is a universal command to repentance and faith. Steenblok says: Away with that universal offer of the promise; away with everyone's right to appropriate the promise.

Preaching, both in terms of audience and content, is here totally dominated by double predestination, which is turned into a closed system (cf. van Genderen, 1983, 14–21).

Barth's opinion is at the other extreme. According to him all people have been chosen in Christ, although many are not yet aware of it. Everyone needs to be told personally that he belongs to Jesus Christ from eternity, and is therefore not reprobated but much rather chosen by God in Jesus Christ (*C.D.*, 2.2.306).

29. According to *Verklaring van Jacobus Arminius* (declaration of Jacobus Arminius, 1608), newly published by G. J. Hoenderdaal, 1960, 87–89.

In addition to the list of objections provided earlier (§ 16.4) there is the possibility that the nature of the proclamation of the Word is altered in the sense that a foregone conclusion is announced and people are no longer faced with their responsibility.[30] The possibility exists that people take note of it and quickly conclude that all is in order.

Certain views of predestination, such as those of ultra-Reformed theologians on the one hand and that of Barth on the other hand, have implications for the proclamation of the Word. Conversely, the notion that nothing ought to stand in the way of the preaching of the gospel to all can lead to difficulties with the Reformed doctrine of predestination as described in the Canons of Dort. This is noticeable within the evangelical movement, but is also present in the works of Woelderink, Berkouwer, and Graafland. This is obvious from *De uitverkiezing* (predestination, 1951) by Woelderink (see § 16.4), while in Berkouwer's case this became more evident in publications subsequent to his dogmatic study *Divine Election*, 1960),[31] and can be recognized in Graafland's *Van Calvijn tot Barth* (1987).[32]

Is it true that the gospel cannot be done justice when the confession of predestination is maintained? We are of the view that predestination and the preaching of the gospel to everyone do not contradict each other. We believe that the Father of our Lord Jesus Christ desires our salvation and ordains it. We are not confronted with God's eternal decree, but we encounter the eternal God who in time comes to us through his Word. Then decisions are made with eternal implications.

In the Bible the proclamation of the gospel is not in the least constrained through the belief that God has "mercy on whom he will have mercy and whom he will he hardeneth" (Rom. 9:18). Jesus said: "It is the Father's good pleasure to conceal things from the wise and the prudent and to reveal them to children." This statement is followed by Jesus' invitation: "Come unto me, all ye that labour and are heavy laden, and I will give you rest" (Matt. 11:25–28). Election and call go hand in hand! Acts contains both the confession, "As many as were ordained to eternal life believed," and the call to faith, "Believe on the Lord Jesus Christ, and thou shalt be saved, and thy house" (Acts

30. Cf. H. Berkhof, *Crisis der middenorthodoxie* (crisis within middle-of-the-road orthodoxy), no date, 38–40; G. C. Berkouwer, *De triomf der genade in de theologie van Karl Barth* (the triumph of grace in the theology of Karl Barth), 1954, 271–75.

31. We mean his well-known article in *G.T.T.* and *Een halve eeuw theologie* (half a century of theology), 1974, 97–148.

32. For Graafland's view see: J. Kamphuis, 1989.

13:48; 16:31). In the midst of the section of the epistle to the Romans in which he testifies to the sovereignty of God's grace, Paul speaks about the significance of preaching (Rom. 10:14–15).

The gospel is intended for everyone. Yet not all share in salvation. God's counsel stands behind the former as well as the latter fact. Therefore the one does not diminish the other.

There is no universal election, but there is indeed a "kerygmatic universality."[33] Calvin can say: "Forasmuch as no man is excluded from calling upon God, the gate of salvation is set open unto all men. Then there is nothing that keeps us back from entering in except our own unbelief" (commentary on Acts 2:21). Bavinck writes that election does not serve to turn off many, but to invite all to the riches of God's grace in Christ (*R.D.*, 2:402).

Election and the preaching of the gospel are therefore not in conflict with each other. From the perspectives of both the Bible and theology they rather reinforce each other.

To save those whom he has chosen in Christ, "God has decreed to give [them] to Christ to be saved by him, and effectually to call and draw them to his communion by his Word and Spirit" (Canons of Dort, 1.7). To arrive where God wants them to be, the chosen believers and the chosen church (see Heidelberg Catechism, Lord's Day 21) need the Word as the means to be used by the Holy Spirit.

After all, election is also an election "to the way of salvation" (Canons of Dort, 1.8). We only encounter God's electing love in Christ through the Word and the preaching of the Word. Election is election in Christ. The call, which comes to us through the gospel, is a call to come to Christ.

In this connection the comment may be made that election and calling naturally go hand in hand, when it comes to calling the elect. What about others? To this we can reply that the fact that God knows his elect does not place any restrictions on the content and the audience of preaching. We are not addressed as elect or non-elect, but as people who depend on God's grace for their redemption. Bavinck points out that in this regard we have nothing to do with the decree of election and reprobation (*R.D.*, 4:36). The message is the same for each one of us: "For God so loved the world, that he gave his only begotten Son, that whosoever believeth in him should not perish,

33. This term has been employed by De Jong (1954, 171) as well as others.

but have everlasting life" (John 3:16). The greatness of God's love is proclaimed to everyone. Everyone is called to faith and everyone is warned against perishing.

The preaching of the gospel has effect because of election. Otherwise it would be fruitless, for no one comes to faith on his own. Preaching, mission, and evangelization are not blocked by the biblical doctrine of predestination. Faith in the electing love of God is rather an incentive to take the message of salvation to everyone! We do not decide for whom it is intended or not. It is up to God to extend his grace to whomever he will.

We may not advocate *universalism* even though it appears to make everything easier. Grace would no longer be seen to be sovereign but would tend to be viewed as a matter of course.

Nothing good can be said about *determinism* either. Then preaching could no longer contain an invitation that is extended to all and has the power to appeal.

The Reformed doctrine of predestination has been the object of fierce criticism especially from the point of view of its perceived implications for preaching. This continues to be the case today. This is no reason to abandon it.

The Canons of Dort already contain the response to criticism from Remonstrants. It is expressed in the following well-considered pronouncements, whose biblical foundations are beyond question: "Moreover, the promise of the gospel is that whosoever believes in Christ crucified shall not perish, but have eternal life. This promise, together with the command to repent and believe, ought to be declared and published to all nations, and to all persons promiscuously and without distinction, to whom God out of his good pleasure sends the gospel" (2.5). "As many as are called by the gospel are unfeignedly called. For God has most earnestly and truly declared in his Word what is acceptable to him, namely, that those who are called should come to him" (3–4.8).

The same canons also give direction for the way in which this doctrine is to be explained: 1. in the church of God, for which it was peculiarly designed; 2. in due time and place; 3. with reverence, in the spirit of discretion and piety, without vainly attempting to investigate the secret ways of the Most High; 4. for the glory of God's most holy name and for the lively comfort of his people (1.14).

16.9. *Election and the assurance of our salvation*

1. *A sure foundation.* Our predestination means that our salvation rests on a gracious choice and decision of God. It has been correctly pointed out that there is one issue that continually preoccupies us, i.e., the question as to where the decision with respect to man's salvation is made. "Is it made exclusively within God himself, in his electing action, *or* within man's freedom to decide, albeit against the *background* of God's initiating grace? Does our salvation depend on God's decision or ours?" Usually a synthesis is sought by attempting to harmoniously combine the two factors of divine grace and human freedom. "This theme of a *synthesis* runs like a red thread through the history of the doctrine of election." There are all kinds of variations within the scope of synthetic synergism (Berkouwer, 1960, 28–29).

One of the most prominent forms of synergism indeed ascribes the initiative to God, but considers it to be man's contribution that God's grace becomes effectual and truly leads to salvation. Calvin already identified it to be an error to view man as God's co-worker, to ratify his election by his consent (*Institutes*, 3.24.3). We agree with Berkouwer that synergism is a theological formulation of the opposition to the sovereignty of God's grace (1960, 47).

This also has serious consequences for the foundation of our salvation. It would no longer have a solid foundation, for human cooperation is and remains an uncertain factor.

Scripture teaches us something entirely different. We are thinking of what traditionally has been referred to as the golden chain of salvation. Our calling, justification, and glorification derive from God knowing us beforehand and having predestined us beforehand to be conformed to the image of his Son (Rom. 8:29–30). This makes clear that God's choice does not follow upon and is not dependent on what we do, but that it precedes our actions and is independent of them.

Here and in the context of Romans 8 and 9 as well as that of Romans 9 and 10 it turns out that justification and election are linked. It is well-known that H. F. Kohlbrugge believed that the Synod of Dort (1618–19) had been tricked by the Remonstrants into losing sight of justification and instead giving prominence to predestination. Graafland (1987, 402, 594–602), Jonker (1989, 112–14), and others agree with Kohlbrugge.

However, one needs to keep in mind that in a direct confrontation concerning justification, it was rejected that man from his side had to meet the prerequisite of faith. The synod objected to this idea through the confession that faith is a gift of

God. Those who believe have been granted faith. This is precisely what the doctrine of election puts into words (see Canons of Dort, 1.5–7).

Faith and justification have everything to do with election, but also with perseverance in faith and sanctification. Synergism and the doctrine of potential apostasy, interpreted as a total and permanent loss of grace and salvation, go hand in hand. Over against this stands the doctrine of the perseverance of the saints (Canons of Dort, 5), which we consider to be the gist of the doctrine of election. Canons of Dort, 1.9, formulates both antithetically and thetically very clearly what the core of the issue is. The thesis is that "election is the fountain of every saving good, from which proceed faith, holiness, and the other gifts of salvation, and ultimately eternal life itself." The apostle testifies: "He hath chosen us in him before the foundation of the world, that we should be holy and without blame before him in love" (Eph. 1:4).

Sanctification is here referred to as the goal of election (cf. Calvin, *Institutes*, 3.23.12). This does not detract from the fact that the highest goal is the glorification of God. Scripture says so explicitly (cf. Eph. 1:12; 1 Peter 2:9–10).

Appealing to the Old Testament, it is frequently argued that election is election to God's service. It is then virtually identified with calling. The idea that God would only predestine for service is not tenable in light of the New Testament (see § 16.2, subsection 4). One could say that the Lord chooses us in Christ to a life of communion with him and in his service.

2. *Assurance of our election.* Election and assurance of salvation are closely linked. A pericope such as Romans 8:31–39 forms one whole with what precedes (Rom. 8:29–30).

Assurance of our election is no other than assurance of our salvation. It is an assurance that we receive only through faith.

Rome teaches that no one can know with unmistakable assurance of faith that he has obtained God's grace. One cannot know whom God has elected other than through special revelation (*DS*, 1534, 1540).

Differences with respect to assurance of election bring us to the core of our conflict with Rome. If our salvation does not depend solely on God's grace, but is in part determined by our disposition and our cooperation, no complete certainty is possible. With its means of grace the church can provide Roman Catholics with a counterweight against permanent uncertainty, but it cannot give believers the guarantee that they have been secured forever. Who is to receive the special revelation that is required to improve on this?

Synergism inherent in the teachings of Rome is encountered among Remonstrants in a slightly different form. It has been said of this that it takes away the sure comfort of true believers in this life, and reintroduces into the church the doubt typically associated with papists. True believers, however, "may and do obtain assurance according to the measure of their faith, whereby they truly believe that they are and ever will continue true and living members of the Church and that they have forgiveness of sins and life eternal" (Canons of Dort, 5, Rejection of errors 5; 5.9).

But does this certainty not lead to carelessness? Judging by the conclusion of the Canons of Dort, the Reformed were reproached for maintaining that the salvation of the elect was not affected by how they lived. This was forcefully denied by the church (see also Canons of Dort, 1.13; 5.12). On the contrary, the certainty of the assurance of election results in humility and true godliness, to ardent love in return to God and steadfast joy in God (see Canons of Dort, 1.13; 5.12). Calvin described it in the same spirit (*Institutes*, 3.23.12).

The way to achieve assurance is clear. We find the assurance of our election in Christ only, for we are chosen in him (see § 16.5). This is why Calvin says: "Christ, then, is the mirror wherein we must, and without self-deception may, contemplate our own election."[34] We have a sufficiently clear and firm testimony that we have been inscribed in the Book of Life if we are in communion with Christ (*Institutes*, 3.24.5).

These splendid statements of the Reformer are found in a specific context. There are believers who doubt their election. This is the most serious and most dangerous temptation with which Satan attacks them.[35] He even tempts them to ascertain it outside the normal way. "Let this be the way of our inquiry: to begin with God's call, and end with it" (*Institutes*, 3.24.4).

Apart from the call, Calvin also sees faith, justification, and sanctification as signs, testimonies, or proofs of election. Elsewhere he advances related ideas (*Institutes*, 3.14.18–19): The Christian's heart focuses entirely on the promise of unmerited righteousness. "But we do not forbid him from undergirding and strengthening this faith by signs of God's benevolence toward him."

From his interpretation of 1 John 3 it is evident that there is nothing left to our worthiness or to the merits of our works. The reality of the new life is seen as flow-

34. See also article 10 of *Confessio Helvetica Posterior* (1566). Here Bullinger followed Calvin.

35. Luther experienced this form of attack very strongly. See among others Brosché, 1977, 159–78.

ing from the mere love of God alone. This is so intended by this passage of Scripture (cf. 1 John 3:1, 14, 16).

This is sometimes referred to as a sideline. Relying merely on the words of the promise would—in view of double predestination—no longer by itself be able to bear the entire burden of the assurance of salvation. "Die Reflexion auf die eigene Subjecktivität" (reflection on one's own subjectivity) supports religious confidence in order to secure or clarify it. This would already be the case with Calvin, but all the more so in pietism.[36]

We encounter here the role of *practical syllogism*,[37] i.e., support for the certainty of salvation is inferred from the work of the Holy Spirit in the renewal of our heart and life. As far as our confession is concerned, in addition to Lord's Day 32 of the Heidelberg Catechism, we refer to Canons of Dort, 1.12. There it is stated that the elect are assured with respect to their eternal election unto salvation, "by observing in themselves with a spiritual joy and holy pleasure the infallible fruits of election pointed out in the Word of God—such as a true faith in Christ, filial fear, a godly sorrow for sin, a hungering and thirsting after righteousness, etc."

This passage has been severely criticized in theology.[38] It should, however, be kept in mind that its background is that according to Remonstrants there is no fruit, no sense and no assurance of election. However, fruits of election do exist; believers can recognize these themselves, and this is important for the assurance of salvation.

This does not make the fruits of election the actual grounds for assurance (cf. Canons of Dort, 5.9–10). In the seventeenth and eighteenth centuries it became common to begin with the marks or the fruits of election. We do not see this only among those who are counted among the Second Reformation and Reformed pietism,[39] but other authors as well.[40]

This reflects a growing interest in subjective experience. But the result is a tendency to look upon ourselves, while it should be pointed out on both biblical and theological grounds that we need to look upon Christ. Calvin says (*Institutes*, 3.24.5): "If we seek God's Fatherly mercy and kindly heart, we must first turn our eyes to Christ, on whom alone the Father's heart rests (Matt. 3:17)."

Some Literature

M. J. Arntzen, *Van eeuwigheid als grond gelegd* (founded from eternity), 1983.

D. L. Baker, *Berkouwer's Doctrine of Election: Balance or Imbalance?* 1981.

G. C. Berkouwer, *Divine Election*, 1960.

36. P. Althaus, *Die Prinzipien der deutschen reformierten Dogmatik* (principles of German Reformed dogmatics), 193ff. This view is shared by many.

37. Regarding the role of *practical syllogism* see among others C. Trimp, *Klank en weerklank* (sound and resonance), 1989, 131–44.

38. Among others by Barth, *C.D.*, 2.2.333–40.

39. See among others W. à Brakel, *R.S.*, 1:247–49.

40. See among others *Synopsis*, 24:42; J. à Marck, *Het merch der christene Got-geleertheit* (the mark of Christian theology), 1741[4], 188.

H. R. Boer, *The Doctrine of Reprobation in the Christian Reformed Church*, 1983.

F. Brosché, *Luther on Predestination*, 1977.

K. Dijk, *De strijd over infra- en supralapsarisme in de Gereformeerde kerken van Nederland* (the conflict about infra- and supralapsarianism in the Reformed churches of the Netherlands), 1912.

K. Dijk, *Om 't eeuwig welbehagen* (for the sake of eternal good pleasure), 1924.

K. Dijk, *Van eeuwigheid verkoren* (chosen from eternity), 1952.

J. Douma, *Algemene genade* (common grace), 1966.

A. Duetz, *Het hart van God—het hart van de kerk* (the heart of God—the heart of the church), 1955.

Enige aspecten van de leer der uitverkiezing. Rapport samengesteld op verzoek van de commissie tot de zaken der Remonstrantse Broederschap en van de generale synode der Nederlansche Hervormde Kerk (some aspects of the doctrine of predestination; report produced at the request of the commission investigating matters pertaining to the Remonstrant Brotherhood and general synod of the Netherlands Reformed Church), 1966.

K. Exalto, *Binnen of buiten* (in or out), 1984.

J. van Genderen, *Verbond en verkiezing* (covenant and election), 1983.

C. Graafland, *Van Calvijn tot Barth*, 1987.

P. Jacobs, *Prädestination und Verantworlichkeit bei Calvin* (predestination and responsibility according to Calvin), 1937.

P. K. Jewett, *Election and Predestination*, 1985.

A. C. de Jong, *The Well-Meant Gospel Offer*, 1954.

W. D. Jonker, *Uit vrye guns alleen* (by free grace alone), 1989.

J. Kamphuis, *Met Calvijn in de impassie?* (with Calvin in limbo?), 1989.

F. H. Klooster, *Calvin's Doctrine of Predestination*, 1977.

G. Kraus, *Voherbestimmung* (predestination), 1977.

B. Loonstra, *Verkiezing-verzoening-verbond* (election, atonement, covenant), 1990.

U. Luz, *Das Geschichtsverständnis de Paulus* (historical interpretation of Paul), 1968.

R. A. Muller, *Christ and the Decree*, 1986.

G. C. Van Niftrik, *Een beroerder Israëls* (a disturber of Israel), 1948.

G. Nygren, *Das Prädestinationsproblem in der Theologie Augustins*, 1956.

B. J. Oosterhoff, *Om de Schriften te openen* (to open the Scriptures), 1987.

H. Otten, *Calvins theologische Anschauung von der Prädestination* (Calvin's theological view of predestination), 1938.

A. D. R. Polman, *De predestinatieleer van Augustinus, Thomas van Quino en Calvijn*, 1936.

Schriftelijcke conferentie, gehouden in s'Gravenhaghe inden Iare 1611, 1617 (conference by correspondence held in The Hague in the years 1611, 1617).

J. J. van der Schuit, *De Dordtsche Synode en het supra-lapsarisme*, 1937.

J. J. van der Schuit, *Het verbond der verlossing* (the covenant of redemption), 1982².

A. Schweizer, *Die protestantischen Centraldogmen*, 2 Tle (vol. 2), 1854–56.

C. Trimp, *Tot een levendige troost zijns volks* (to a living comfort of his people), 1954.

De uitverkiezing (predestination). Richtlijnen voor de behandeling van de leer der uitverkiezing, aanvaard door de Generale Synode der Nederlandse Hervormde Kerk in haar vergadering van 8 november 1960 (guidelines for the treatment of the doctrine of predestination, adopted by General Synod of the Netherlands Reformed Church in its meeting of November 8, 1960), 1961.

C. Veenhof, *Predeking en uitverkiezing* (preaching and predestination), 1959.

H. Venema, *Uitverkiezen en uitverkiezing in the Nieuwe Testament* (to predestine and predestination in the New Testament), 1965.

Th. C. Vriezen, *De verkiezing van Israël volgens het Oude Testament* (the election of Israel according to the Old Testament), 1974.

O. Weber/W. Kreck/E. Wolf, *Die Predigt von der Gnadenwahl* (preaching of election by grace), 1951.

J. R. Wiskerke, *Volk van Gods keuze* (people of God's choice), 1955.

J. R. Wiskerke, *Geroepen volk* (people called), 1967.

J. G. Woelderink, *De uitverkiezing* (predestination), 1951.

H. M. Yoo, *Raad en daad* (decree and deed), 1990.

L. van der Zanden, *Praedestinatie*, 1949.

Chapter 6

God, the Creator of Heaven and Earth

§ 17. The Creator and his work

17.1. *The biblical starting point*

It is a matter of faith that God is the Creator of heaven and earth. This is not an observation or a conclusion that anyone can automatically arrive at by merely using his head. It says in the Apostles' Creed: "I believe in God the Father, the Almighty, Creator of heaven and earth." This belief is based on revelation in the Word of God. The Bible says: "Through faith we understand that the worlds were framed by the word of God, so that things which are seen were not made of things which do appear" (Heb. 11:3).

When it comes to the revelation of God as Creator, one needs to think in the first place of the history of creation (Gen. 1 and 2). Various commentators have pointed out that one should not overestimate the role that the Bible assigns to faith in God as Creator of the universe.

But the danger is great for the significance of faith in the Creator to be underestimated. This is obvious from the widespread disparagement of such faith. In contrast, in light of Scripture's teachings Bavinck went so far as to speak of a preeminent and pivotal place of the doctrine of creation in Holy Scripture (*R.D.*, 2:407). At any rate, we are dealing here with fundamental statements.

Creation is not always an independent theme in the Bible (exceptions being Job 38; Prov. 3:19–20; 8:25–31). The Old Testament usually emphasizes who is the God on whom his people may depend in everything. Salvation is from "the LORD, the Creator of the ends of the earth" (Isa. 40:28) and for whom "there is nothing too hard" (Jer. 32:17). Creation is discussed in all parts of the Old Testament (see passages such as Gen. 14:19, 22; Ex. 20:11; Neh. 9:6; Pss. 8:3; 24:1–2; 33:6, 9; 89:11–12; 121:2; 136:4–9; 146:6; 148:1–6; Isa. 40:21–28; 42:5; 45:12, 18).

Our verb "to create" is a translation of *bara*, which is used in Genesis 1:1 together with versions of "to make" and "to form." In all passages God is the subject of *bara*. He alone can create! In connection with the verb "to create" it is never said that something is created from something else, and through God's creative work always something new results.

The most important New Testament word for the act of creation (*ktizein*) signifies "ein geistiger und willentlicher Vorgang" (a spiritual and deliberate process, *TDNT*, 3:1029). It is an act of God's will (cf. Rev. 4:11), a miraculous act with which nothing can compare. When God creates everything, this means that he calls it into being. "God calleth those things which be not as though they were" (Rom. 4:17). Aside from the verb "to create," use is also made of the verb "to make" (Acts 17:24; Heb. 1:2). A noteworthy place is John 1:1–3. It refers undoubtedly back to "what in Genesis 1 forms the foundation of the Old Testament revelation of God and the Israelite religion: God's creation of heaven and earth."[1]

As is done in the Old Testament (cf. Neh. 9:6), in the New Testament the church appeals to him who created everything (Acts 4:24). Honor and adoration are his due (Rev. 4:11; 14:7).

God reveals his glory, which is manifested in all of his works, also in creation (Ps. 8). Among his perfections, his power and wisdom receive special mention (Jer. 10:12). We think especially of the powerful

1. H. Ridderbos, *Het evangelie naar Johannes* (the gospel according to John), 1987, 1:36.

message contained in Scripture passages such as Job 38 and 39, and Isaiah 40. Knowing him who reveals himself in this way must lead to humility and confidence. By way of summary, N. H. Ridderbos says with respect to the revelation that Yahweh is the Creator of heaven and earth, that it serves to strengthen Israel in the confidence that it is safe within his protection and to encourage it all the more to obey his commandments, but also that thus Israel will be better placed to sing praises to its God (Ridderbos, 1963², 100).

17.2. *An antithetical element*

It is a well-known fact that the words "Creator of heaven and earth" do not occur in the oldest version of the Apostles' Creed. They were subsequently added for specific reasons. In the creeds that emerged in the Orient, it was early on confessed that God is the Maker of all things visible and invisible (there are various versions of this).[2] These words not only have a biblical content, but also have an anti-heretical meaning. This is also true with respect to the confession of God as Creator in the Apostles' Creed.

With this confession the church objects to gnostic views and the teaching of Marcion, who differentiated between the Father of the Lord Jesus and the Creator-Lawgiver. Some gnostics spoke of a demiurge—a concept borrowed from Greek philosophy—who was credited with the creation of the earth. A contrast was seen between the heavenly or spiritual world, and the earthly or material world frequently associated with cosmic powers. One had to liberate oneself from the material world through *gnosis*.

Calvin points out (*Institutes*, 1.14.3) that the first article of faith was probably also intended to reject Manichaeism. The antithesis contained in it is indeed applicable to this gnostic world religion. Only part of existence would be due to God, the God of light: the spiritual world. Physical reality would be the work of an evil power. Here, hope was largely placed in *asceticism*.

Dualistic notions, quite popular in the Hellenist world, thus turned up in various guises, but the church also had to cope with *monism*.

Neo-Platonist philosophers attacked Christian faith in God as Creator of heaven and earth. Over against creation they advocated *emanation*. According to Plotinus, "the One" is the origin of all things. This single being is a source that overflows with eternal necessity, a light that beams into the dark universe. The farther things are removed from their source, the more imperfect they are. It is matter, the most imperfect form of reality, that renders evil possible.

This doctrine of emanation is monistic. Although everything has proceeded from the Godhead, it is characterized by all sorts of gradations. Over against this stands

2. J. N. D. Kelly, *Early Christian Creeds*, 1972³, 196–201.

the teaching of the church: God is not a source, but the Creator. Emanation would imply that from God's perspective there was no alternative. Creation implies that God specifically desired it this way.

Thus both dualistic and monistic views needed to be confronted from early on. Dualism is unacceptable because it gives part of the world a degree of autonomy. But God has created everything and everything is therefore subject to him. Monism is unacceptable because in principle it does not make a fundamental distinction between God and the world. In its higher forms it leads to a deification of the world.

Subsequently *pantheism* and *materialism* needed to be fought. To pantheists the divine is the essence of the world and manifests itself in everything. As a rule they see material reality as being brought about by the spirit (Spirit). To materialists the spirit is a product of material reality. Whenever a cause needs to be identified for certain phenomena, it must be a material cause.

A separate discussion will be required for the confrontation between faith in God as Creator of heaven and earth and *evolutionism* (see § 18).

17.3. *Aspects of creation*

1. *Creation is the work of the triune God.* Creation is the first of God's external works (*opera ad extra*).

The unity of God implies that in his creative work we may not separate what the Father does from what the Son and the Holy Spirit do. "All things originate simultaneously from the Father through the Son in the Spirit" (Bavinck, *R.D.*, 2:423). This formulation goes back to the church fathers, especially Augustine. It partly reflects the use of certain prepositions in the New Testament. All things are *from* the Father—he "is the cause, the origin and the beginning of all things" (Belgic Confession of Faith, article 8); *through* the Son—for "by him all things consist" (Col. 1:17); and *in* the Holy Spirit—for he brings all things to completion. Therefore, when we say that the created world is God's world, this is meant in a completely Trinitarian sense. Everything that has been created bears the mark of the Father, the Son, and the Holy Spirit.

This does not detract from the fact that in an economical sense (cf. § 12.4) the work of creation is ascribed to God the Father. The church leads us in this direction through its confession of faith. Aside from the ecumenical creed we think of the Belgic Confession of Faith: "The Father is called our Creator, by his power" (article 9). "The eternal Father of our Lord Jesus Christ, who of nothing made heaven and earth is for the sake of Christ his Son my God and my Father" (Heidelberg Catechism, Lord's Day 9).

But what does it mean that all things have come into being through his only begotten Son, as confessed in the Creed of Nicaea-Constantinople? Does this mean that the Son is the Mediator of creation?

This is an idea that keeps turning up in theology. Sometimes it remains a vague concept, but at times it involves a great deal more.

The motivation for using this term can be a certain dualism. The Mediator of creation then stands between God and the world. Although Bavinck's doctrine of creation reveals traces of Plato's influence, this definitely is not his intention. He thereby seeks to express that creation and re-creation are interrelated. "The foundations of creation and re-creation are the same. The Logos, who became incarnate, is the one through whom all things were made. The Firstborn from the dead is also the Firstborn of all creatures."[3]

According to Bavinck, in creation God already had re-creation in mind. He even says somewhere that the plan of salvation was incorporated into the plan for creation. Yet creation and re-creation do not coincide in Bavinck's view, as is frequently the case in more contemporary theology (see further subsection 7). It is not a matter of nature and grace becoming fused, with grace being sacrificed to nature or nature to grace.[4]

Bavinck views Christ as the Mediator of both re-creation and creation. Christ has both soteriological and cosmological significance. This is supported by a number of Scripture passages that explicitly state that everything has been made or come into being through the Word or through Christ (see John 1:3; 1 Cor. 8:6; Col. 1:16; cf. also Heb. 1:2).

In this connection we consider the following:

- The Greek preposition *dia* could indeed indicate a mediator, but equally well an effecter. Therefore, on the basis of these texts we need not necessarily think of the Mediator of creation.
- The New Testament refers to Christ as the Mediator between God and men, and the Mediator of the covenant. This places him between God and sinners; he yields himself as a ransom and suffers death (1 Tim. 2:5–6; Heb. 9:15).

3. H. Bavinck, *Wijsbegeerte der openbaring* (philosophy of revelation), 1908, 23. Cf. Bavinck, *R.D.*, 2:423–26.

4. Cf. J. Veenhof, *Revelatie en inspiratie*, 1968, 306–9.

- There is no reason to see in the participation of the Son in the work of creation an analogy to this Mediatorship and therefore to give him the name of Mediator of creation. Neither can it be specified for which intermediary role in creation he could thus be named.
- In light of the cosmic significance of the work of the Lord Jesus Christ—which cannot be ignored in Christology—it does not have to be supposed that he was already Mediator in creation. Behind the coming of our Mediator and his position stands the work of the triune God, which is also the work of the Son of God. When he came into the world, "he came unto his own" (John 1:11). The world was his very own creation, although it became alienated from its origin.[5]

2. *God desired creation.* In view of wide-ranging opinions about creation, an explicit treatment is called for.

We read in Genesis 1 of God's commanding language. "And God said, Let there be light: and there was light" (Gen. 1:3). The Psalms refer back to this (Pss. 33:6–9; 148:5). In a heavenly song of praise it is said: "Thou hast created all things, and for thy pleasure they are and were created" (Rev. 4:11). Therefore the church confesses "that the Father created heaven, the earth and all creatures, when it seemed good unto him" (Belgic Confession of Faith, article 12). Therefore we reject the view that the universe emerged by chance or that nothing more specific can be said about its origin. It is based on a plan of God. At the same time we reject the idea that God was bound to create an object for his love. He did not need creation. Creation is neither the result of chance nor a matter of necessity for God. Those who hold the latter detract from God's *independence*. This must also be pointed out to those who consider creation to be *self-limitation* from God's perspective.

Here we are dealing with an idea—in part developed under the influence of German idealism—which has been further elaborated by theologians such as Brunner, Berkhof, and Moltmann.[6]

5. For the rejection of the idea of a mediatorship of creation see especially Schilder, *H.C.*, 2:83–103. Cf. also Kamphuis, *Aant.* (notes), 41ff. A different point of view is presented in Chul Won Suh, *The Creation-Mediatorship of Jesus Christ*, 1982.

6. Cf. the earlier theology of J. H. Gunning Jr., *Blikken in de openbaring* (glances at revelation), 1929[2], 93, 129ff., which presumed a voluntary self-limitation of God in creation and history.

According to Brunner, one of the subthemes of the doctrine of creation is the independence of creation. In order to make a place for that other reality God restricts himself. The *kenosis* (emptying) begins already with the creation of the world, and reaches its culmination in the cross of Christ. To Brunner, creation implies self-limitation from God's point of view (*Dogmatics*, 2:20, 173).

Berkhof is of the same view. To him creation means that God condescends; that he limits himself; that he provides living and breathing space for the other, which as such is imperfect and even will be rebellious. By setting a world opposite himself, he gives it its own laws and dynamics, which he accepts with all its consequences. In creating man, God gives to the other, who is to be his partner, its own area of freedom and initiative. "In giving this room, with all the attendant consequences, God relinquishes some of his power and makes himself more or less dependent" (*C.F.*, 157–58, 141–42).

Moltmann's reflections concerning God's self-limitation give a strongly speculative impression. Creation would imply self-limitation and self-humiliation from God's perspective. His creating love is always a love that suffers. The redemption of the world and mankind to freedom and community also always involves the process of God's redemption from the suffering of his love.[7]

A thought process such as we encounter here does not stand in isolation. There is a mutual relationship between this view of creation as self-limitation of God, and the relationship between the Creator and the human creature that is described by terms such as "personal correspondence" (Brunner) and "intersubjectivity" (Berkhof). According to Moltmann the transition of God's self-limitation to self-humiliation and suffering directly reflects a form of theopaschitism advocated by him (cf. Wentsel, *Dogm.*, 3a:512–19).[8]

To us it is crucial that the Bible in no way suggests that creation should be viewed as self-limitation or even self-humiliation from God's point of view. Would God make himself more or less dependent, as portrayed by Berkhof? It is precisely proof of his independence that he created everything according to his will and his plan. The existence of creation, therefore, never detracts from God's independence. Neither does man's resistance reduce the Creator's omnipotence to "defenseless supremacy" (see § 13.7).

The immeasurably great difference between the Creator and the created reality is that he alone is *a se*: he exists from himself, by himself, and for himself (cf. Bavinck, *R.D.*, 2:149–53; Wentsel, *Dogm.*, 3a:296ff., 484–98). In earlier Reformed theology this *aseitas* is usually referred to as God's independence (*independentia Dei*). He is dependent on nothing, but everything depends on him. "He is absolutely independent, in his existence, in his attributes, in his decrees, in his deeds" (Bavinck).

7. J. Moltmann, *Trinität und Reich Gottes* (Trinity and God's kingdom), 1980, 75, 123–27; *Gott in der Schöpfung* (God in creation), 1985, 98–105.

8. The influence of cabbalism is clearly recognizable in Moltmann's view. These ideas are not as new as they seem (cf. J. Moltmann, *Trinität und Reich Gottes*, 1980, 40–45, 123–27). More could be mentioned (see Wentsel, *Dogm.*, 3a:512–15).

"Before the mountains were brought forth, or ever thou hadst formed the earth and the world, even from everlasting to everlasting, thou art God" (Ps. 90:2). "Neither is [God] worshipped with men's hands, as though he needed any thing, seeing he giveth to all life, and breath, and all things" (Acts 17:25). "For of him, and through him, and to him, are all things" (Rom. 11:36).

3. *God has created everything from nothing*. What we confess with this (cf. Belgic Confession of Faith, article 12) is not explicitly stated in our Bible, but it is indeed scriptural (cf. Rom. 4:17; Heb. 11:3). The expression "of nothing" occurs in 2 Maccabees 7:28, where a mother says to her son: do you realize that God made these things out of nothing?

Making something out of nothing does seem a good description of creation, but in early times a need was felt to add something to avoid the misunderstanding that "nothing" would be interpreted as "not-being" according to Greek philosophy and that "nothing" would be a negative supposition of created reality. "Of nothing" means that nothing preceded it (*ex nihilo* is at the same time *post nihilum*).

In our time it needs to be emphasized anew that God has created everything from nothing. When Genesis 1 refers to formlessness and emptiness (Hebrew: *tohu wabohu*), this does not imply chaos from which the cosmos emerged. Nevertheless it must be said that the earth had not yet acquired the orderly form that we now know. The earth was an inhospitable abode.[9] The creation of which Genesis 1:1 speaks was not preceded by chaos as the original state. Neither may it be assumed that God would have created chaos.

"Nothing" has a peculiar role in Barth's theology. According to him creation has two aspects: light and shadow. Everything that was created must be thought of as having been subject to this twofold, contradictory destiny, that it is something and not nothing, but something bordering on the nothing, something that is threatened by nothingness and that itself is no match for this threat. However, God makes both of these aspects of creation, its "jubilation" and its "lamentation," his business in the humiliation and exaltation of Jesus Christ. He is the

9. G. Ch. Aalders, *Genesis*, 1949², 1:79, 69–71. Ridderbos has pointed out correctly that the nations among whom Israel dwelled did not know of creation out of nothing. For the conceptions of the various nations, see among others G. Ch. Aalders, 1932, 71–146; C. Westermann, *Genesis*, 1:26–65.

meaning and the goal of creation (*C.D.*, 3.1.375–78; still differently *C.D.*, 3.2.152–57).

In order to understand this as intended one must take into account the structure of Barth's doctrine of creation, which is christocentric. As we shall see (subsection 7), creation and redemption are telescoped together, and Barth's view of nothing is based on this. Everything must fall under this twofold destiny, "indem Alles auf Jesus Christus, auf seinen Tod und seine Aufersthehung hin geschaffen ist" (since everything has been created through Jesus Christ, through his death and his resurrection).

When Barth develops the doctrine of nothing, he proceeds still further along this path. It is the chaos of Genesis 1:2 that the Creator has rejected and to which he has said no, which he has passed by and left behind. It is a reality that he did not seek and did not create, and which represents nevertheless in a certain sense the horizon of his creation and his creatures. Chaos is the wrong, the temptation, and the danger for God's creature. The divine creation of Genesis 1:3 is in the first place a separation of light from darkness. Man's sin, described in Genesis 3, confirms the factual existence of the insignificant. The basis of its existence can only be seen in the sense that God rejects it (*C.D.*, 3.3.352ff.).

God protects his creation from being overwhelmed by meaninglessness, which exists, but only on his left side. It is indeed real, relevant, and active. However, God has already conquered it. Since Jesus Christ is Conqueror, it has come to an end. It is the old reality that has been eclipsed in Jesus Christ. Now the kingdom of meaninglessness with its threatening power is only a sham (*C.D.*, 3.3.360–68).

One could say that Barth superimposes a dialectic scheme on the text of the Bible. With God's yes in Genesis 1, one would simultaneously be able to hear God's no. But the Bible in no way ascribes to God the existence of anything negative, however portrayed—neither as the shadow side of creation nor as a threat to it. This is speculative reasoning.[10] Schilder says: "Spare us this neo-Manichaeism" (*H.C.*, 3:357).

4. *God created everything good.* Those who believe in God's goodness are also convinced of the goodness of his work. Holy Scripture says explicitly that "God saw every thing that he had made, and, behold, it was very good" (Gen. 1:31).

In his exegesis of Genesis 1:31, Calvin points out that this verdict of God must be a rule and example for us, so that no one would dare to think or speak in any other way about God's works.

The goodness of created reality is not limited to a portion of it, contrasted with another part that would be less good and inferior. It is not superfluous to point this out, for there are plenty examples of people who do not easily consider the material and physical realm to be good. A theologian who strenuously objects to such a view is

10. Cf. G. C. Berkouwer, *De triomf der genade in de theologie van Karl Barth* (the triumph of grace in the theology of Karl Barth), 1954, 212–17, 242.

Van Ruler. To him physical reality is creation itself! It is the ultimate "opposite" to God. Physical reality is the pure antipole of God, who is a creating Spirit. Man ought to enjoy all of life and every day again like a juicy peach. Only then, service of the Creator becomes true adoration (Van Ruler, *Ik geloof* = I believe, 40ff.; cf. also Van Ruler, *T.W.*, 5:9–31).

We shall not be able to support every statement made by Van Ruler in this context, but we do understand his reaction. Everything that God has created, without exception, is good as such and ought to be accepted with gratitude (see 1 Tim. 4:4).

Created reality is multifaceted and enormously varied. God created plants and animals "after their kind" (Gen. 1). The goodness of creation is also revealed by the richness of the various forms of life. God has created a well-ordered whole. He repeatedly made separations (Gen. 1:4, 7, 18); he drew boundaries that we may not transgress (cf. Ridderbos, 1963, 88ff.). In this connection the work of Reformational philosophy (philosophy of the cosmonomic idea) may be mentioned, which on the basis of faith in the Creator or Origin of everything observes the various aspects and structures of reality. The laws and norms that God gave to his creatures were not altered by man's fall into sin.[11]

In more recent theology the goodness of creation is frequently denigrated. Those who like Barth teach a shadow or dark side of creation can end up interpreting creation as justification (Barth, *C.D.*, 3.1.366–414). It is a justification of reality through judgment, i.e., the Creator's approval of the good side of creation and his condemnation of the negative side. Above, we found this to be pure speculation (see subsection 3).

We now leave this aside to focus on Berkhof's train of thought. What he says about the goodness of creation (*C.F.*, 166), he subsequently appears to retract again to a significant extent when he proceeds to reflect on the provisional and unfinished state of creation. He has in mind the disharmony that we observe every day—suffering, death, catastrophes, which for centuries were treated under the rubric "consequences of sin." Berkhof is of a different mind.

According to him, the world contains a tragic element. "It is incomplete, unfinished, defective. There is much happiness, true, but this is not without the awareness of its imperfection. There is much sorrow for which no one can be blamed. There is much suffering which no one can remove." Then Berkhof asks: "Why has God (provisionally) wanted something which nevertheless (ultimately) he does not want? The only answer we can give is no answer: apparently it was never God's purpose to call into existence a ready-made and complete world. He evidently wants his cre-

11. See H. Dooyeweerd, *Vernieuwing en bezinning* (renewal and reflection), 1963^2, 41, 58; A. M. Wolters, *Schepping zonder grens* (creation without boundary), 1988, 55–57.

ation to go through a history of resistance and struggle, of suffering and dying." We "may believe that some day it will become clear that all the pains of childbirth and growing up of this world in process of becoming cannot compare with its glorious outcome" (*C.F.*, 174ff.).

But what does it mean then that everything was very good (Gen. 1:31)? To Berkhof this does not mean that it was perfect, but that it suited his purpose, namely, the fellowship between God and man.

Paul's reference to a longing anticipation on the part of all of creation, comparable to birth pangs (Rom. 8:22), supposedly described this provisional state. Here we must disagree with Berkhof. Paul speaks of futility and bondage to decay. Frustration or futility has a beginning and an end (cf. *TDNT*, 4:523). Its beginning is due to a far-reaching event and a divine decree. Romans 8:20 takes us back to Genesis 3:17.[12]

Berkhof does not want to know about the breach caused by man's fall into sin and its consequences. He seeks to combine faith in the Creator of heaven and earth with an evolutionary view of the world. Thus he ends up contradicting the Bible, which calls creation good, by claiming it to be inadequate (defective).

But the qualification "good," repeated six times in Genesis 1, implies definitely more than "suitable for communion with God." It does not say that creation is good in a certain respect. It is not only good in the eyes of people; it is also good in the eyes of God. It is a matter of the highest perfection (Calvin).

We may not trace back to the story of creation what is being viewed as a tragic element or a bitter enigma in this world, as though God would have desired this for the time being. So much happened once he had created everything good! Sin left wounds. What we otherwise would not easily realize, we discover precisely against the background of God's good creation. The world as it exists now does not reflect God's intentions. It is no wonder that the groaning of all of creation accompanies the groaning of God's children and that there is an anticipation of liberation and redemption (Rom. 8:22–23).

5. *The purpose of creation*. The question as to the purpose for which God made the world is indeed answered in that it was created for the sake of man. Some of the church fathers already spoke in this vein. The idea also occurred to Calvin: "Further, God himself has shown by the order of Creation that he created all things for man's sake." Before creating man, God wanted to prepare everything he foresaw would be useful and salutary for him. On the basis of Scripture (Gen. 1:28; 9:2), Calvin says that all things in the whole world are subject to us (*Institutes*, 1.14.22). But this is not the main point. The work

12. Cf. A. F. N. Lekkerkerker, *De brief van Paulus aan de Romeinen* (the epistle of Paul to the Romans), 1962, 1:345ff.

of creation that is described in Genesis 1 is followed by God's resting (Gen. 2:1–4). "The final goal of God's creation is not that there are people, but that there are people at his service.[13] In theological tradition it is a recurring theme that everything must serve to glorify God. And Calvin's doctrine of creation is not in the least anthropocentric. We think of the first few answers of the Catechism of Geneva: 1. What is the chief end of human life? To know God by whom we have been created. 2. On what basis do you say so? God created us and placed us in this world to be glorified in us.

This is a prominent theme in Reformed doctrine. To the extent that it can be said that creation is there for people, it is simultaneously the case that man and the world are there for the sake of God. Everything must be subordinate to his glory. The Belgic Confession of Faith says that God has given "unto every creature its being, shape, form, and several offices to serve its Creator." It says "that he also still upholds and governs them by his eternal providence and infinite power for the service of mankind, to the end that man may serve his God" (article 12).

Man does not stand at the center. This is nowhere the case in the Bible, not even in Psalm 8. The goal is God's glory (Ps. 8:2, 10). "The heavens declare the glory of God; and the firmament sheweth his handywork" (Ps. 19:2). God's "eternal power and Godhead" are revealed in his works (cf. Rom. 1:20).

It is God for whom and through whom all things exist (Heb. 2:10; cf. Rev. 4:11). He intended the world to be his kingdom. As appears from God's creative work, he seeks to reveal his glory and establish his kingdom. In all of his deeds this goal remains the focus. Despite all variety, God's works are one in this regard. It is for this reason that in the Bible his great works of creation, preservation, and governance of the world, and in redemption and consummation, are frequently mentioned in one breath.

We should not restrict ourselves to man and the world, as though creation did not comprise a great deal more. This should make us humble. We think of chapters 38–41 of the book of Job. It has been correctly pointed out that the nonhuman creation everywhere, and especially in the infinite space of the interstellar world where there are no humans, has its own—for us inaccessible—relatedness to God (cf. Berkhof, *C.F.*, 171).

13. B. J. Oosterhoff, *Om de Schriften to openen* (to open the Scriptures), 1987, 68.

If we ignored all of this we could end up viewing man as the center or ultimate goal of creation. Everything that God does would have to serve man. This is only one step removed from saying: God must serve us. But this would be a reversal of the order of creation! We are there because of him and for him.

6. *Creation and providence*. There are verses in which the verb that is rendered "to create" does not refer to the creation of heaven and earth or the creation of man, but to God's acts in history. The words: "They are created now, and not from the beginning" (Isa. 48:7, i.e., "new things," v. 6) are an example of this.

It is therefore not surprising that there are several confessions in which faith in the Creator is linked with the confession of God's providence. In interpreting the first article of the Apostles' Creed it can be said: "As Creator of heaven and earth he rules all of nature according to its kind through his goodness, power and wisdom" (Geneva Catechism).

There is a direct link between creation and the governance of the world, but there is also a distinction. The confession portrays "creation" in the perfect tense, while preservation and governance are presented in the present tense (Heidelberg Catechism, Lord's Day 9).

Genesis 2:2 speaks of both the link and the distinction. God's resting indicates that he does not carry on with the work of creation because he has completed it. It does not imply that he no longer works (cf. John 5:17). God's providence has indeed been described as continuing creation (*creatio continua*). When A. Kuyper and H. Bavinck take this over from earlier theology, they do not intend to ignore the distinction between the two. It is based on God's revelation. "What happens to things as a result of creation is one thing; what happens with them as a result of preservation is another." Creation yields existence, while preservation is persistence in existence (Bavinck, *R.D.*, 2:607–8). Bavinck wants to express that providence constitutes a power of God equally as great, almighty, and omnipresent as creation. But the question may be raised whether the choice of this terminology is sufficiently justified.

This becomes a serious question when we consider the ideas that others associate with this line of thinking. According to Schleiermacher, the doctrine that God sustains the world is entirely equivalent to the doctrine that God is the Creator of the world. The doctrine of providence brings out complete dependence even more so than the doctrine of creation. The Swedish theologian G. Aulén (1879–1978) agreed with this.[14] According to him there is nothing more misleading than to speak of God's work of creation in the perfect tense (*perfectum*). Creation is an ongoing activity of the will of God's love (*creatio continua*).

Thus it continues to be held that everything is dependent on God, but creation is no longer interpreted as creation in the beginning and out of nothing. We must agree with Berkouwer that, especially in light of the way in which modern theological thinking approaches the concept of *creatio continua*, there is every reason to distance ourselves permanently from this concept, because it does in no wise enhance our understanding of God's deeds (Berkouwer, 1952, 64).

Thanks to God's providence there is continuity in God's creation, but this does not mean that God's providence constitutes ongoing creation. We may not identify creation with preservation and governance.

We hereby simultaneously take position over against a certain actualism, which we encounter among other places in *De nieuwe katechismus* (the new catechism, 1966). A few quotations are: "Better than to say: God *has* created, is to say: God *creates.*" "That God is creator means that everything that exists is dependent on him; that everything hinges on him. To fathom God as creator we should not think so much in terms of the beginning, but the present, and the future. He is now in the process of completing things." "God *has* not created the world. He *is* creating the world and he does this in part through us." "Things made by man constitute creation by God" (pp. 309, 573ff., 501).

This interpretation is not based on an exegesis of Scripture. It reflects a new view of the world, which is described as not being static but dynamic. As in the case of P. Teilhard de Chardin (§ 18.3), scope is given to evolution, interpreted as progress for the universe (pp. 12–15). The event of creation is denigrated to a relationship between God and the world, or between God and man.

The authors of *De nieuwe katechismus* say: "The beginning is less important to us than it used to be." They have difficulty with the words "in the beginning" (Gen. 1:1; John 1:1). It is not interpreted as a pure indication of time, but as a matter of order, originality (pp. 309, 574).

Incidentally, an issue is raised by the first few words of Genesis 1: that of the relationship between creation and time (cf. Bavinck, *R.D.*, 2:426–30).

We can view time as a mode of existence of everything that is finite and created. Space can be viewed in a similar manner. Time was created as part of the world and the world in time. Creation is the beginning of the existence of the world and therefore of space, time, and history.

7. *Creation and redemption.* The sequence creation—fall into sin—redemption, which we know from the first few chapters of the book of Genesis and which we find back in the confessions (cf. Belgic Confession of Faith, articles 12–17), has been abandoned by many. This

14. G. Aulén, *Ons algemeen christelijk geloof* (our catholic Christian faith), 1917, 157–64.

reflects a critical treatment of the Bible and doubt with respect to the reality of an initial state of Paradise disturbed by a fall into sin.

The following are well-known pronouncements of Barth: There was no golden age. "The first man was immediately the first sinner" (*C.D.*, 4.1.508).

According to Berkhof, historical criticism dismantled the earlier thought pattern. In the biblical design of creation, the relationship between creation and salvation does not imply a contrast but a prelude. Creation should be viewed as a preamble of and pointer to salvation and a preparation for it (*C.F.*, 172–75).[15]

Kuitert rejects the historical pattern of creation—fall into sin—redemption. According to him, the first few chapters of Genesis should be recast as a "teaching device" or "interpretation tool." Then our evolving world is seen as God's work of creation. Sin is regression in the form of an enigmatic countermovement on our part. Kuitert sees salvation and creation linked in Jesus, whom he views as the completed standard of creation as history. Jesus Christ does away with regression, disturbs the stagnating development of man and the world, and as "the author of our faith" (Heb. 12:2) leads creation to completion.[16]

In more recent Roman Catholic theology, one frequently encounters the same approach as in *De nieuwe katechismus*. The primordial narratives of Genesis 1–11 are viewed as symbolic stories with an eternal message dealing with the most profound elements of our life with God: 1. God creates and permits growth; 2. man is meant for friendship with God; 3. the sinful deeds that are described are symbols of our great sins; 4. but God grants salvation and restoration.[17]

Particularly under the influence of Barth, an amalgamation or blending of creation and salvation has been pursued. According to Barth, the doctrine of creation is governed by two theses: first, creation is the external basis for the covenant and, second, the covenant is the internal basis for creation (*C.D.*, 3.1.98, 230–31). We shall now focus on the latter thesis. The covenant refers to the eternal covenant between God and man. It can be represented by a single name, Jesus Christ, for it has been made in him and is grounded in him. This means that he is the foundation of creation. In this way creation and redemption are one.

This implies more than learning to know God as our Creator, because we may come to know Christ and redemption in him through faith. We encounter the same idea in Calvin's work (cf. Barth, *C.D.*, 3.1.30ff.). Barth is not only concerned with the order of knowledge (the noetic order), but also the order of being (the ontic order). He

15. Cf. in this connection also H. Berkhof, "Schepping en voleinding" (creation and completion), in H. Berkhof, *Bruggen en bruggehoofden* (bridges and bridgeheads), 1981, 37–49.

16. H. M. Kuitert, *Anders gezegd* (putting it differently), 1970, 54–61.

17. *De nieuwe katechismus* (the new catechism), 1966, 307ff.

says that the world is created and sustained by the Baby that was born in Bethlehem, by the Man who died on the cross of Golgotha and rose again on the third day.[18] In the midst of the history of creation in Genesis 1 and 2 we encounter Jesus Christ, and therefore creation is in essence salvation history.

This concept of Barth had tremendous influence among both Protestant and Roman Catholic theologians. Some appear to have been influenced directly, whereas others reveal an affinity.[19]

As far as biblical support for this concept is concerned, the first reference given is usually John 1:1–18. We have already concluded that there is no reason for viewing the Word or the Son as the Mediator of creation (see subsection 1). There is even less justification for interpreting the Word by whom "all things were made" (John 1:3) as Christ in his capacity as Mediator of salvation. It says in the prologue: "The Word was made flesh" (John 1:14), but this did not happen in the beginning. The Word became incarnate only once sin had come into the world, and for this very reason. John 1 first speaks of the Word as existing in the beginning, then about the coming of the Word as the Light of the World, and finally about the glory of the Word incarnate.[20]

Without knowledge of Christ, who is the Word made flesh, and without considering his glory, the evangelist would not have thus referred to the Word in the beginning. But this does not mean that creation by the Word and redemption through the Word incarnate should be identified with each other or thought to coincide in principle.[21] Then there would be no distinction between creation and re-creation. Salvation in Christ would already be implicit in creation. In believing this, one would open the door to the "monism of grace" with far-reaching consequences in the direction of universalism.

For this view, one cannot appeal to the gospel according to John or to Colossians 1:15–23. There the apostle speaks about him who is the firstborn of all creation ("the firstborn of every creature"). He precedes everyone, and all things have their existence

18. K. Barth, *Dogmatics in Outline*, 1949, 58.

19. See B. Wentsel, *Natuur en genade* (nature and grace), 1970, 325–31.

20. We follow here an outline proposed by H. Ridderbos (*Het evangelie naar Johannes* = the gospel according to John, 1987, 1:36).

21. Concerning John 1 see also Ch. de Beus, *Johannes' getuigenis van het Woord* (John's testimony to the Word), 1973; A. Noordegraaf, "De proloog van het Johannesevangelie" (the prologue to the gospel according to John), *TH. Ref.* 18 (1975): 186–221.

in him. This can only be said of the Son of God, whose existence precedes creation. When he is subsequently referred to as the firstborn of the dead, he is considered to be the Mediator and Head of the church. Creation and redemption are interrelated, and Christ's work as Mediator also has cosmic significance. But this does not imply that creation and redemption collapse into one. That he is the firstborn of all creation may not be interpreted à la Barth, even if Christ himself would be the divine decree with respect to all creation (*C.D.*, 2.2.104).[22]

The Bible teaches us to retain the distinction between creation and redemption. Creation is theocentric; redemption, which was necessary on account of sin and made reality through grace, may be called christocentric. Creation does not rest on redemption or on the plan for redemption, but redemption presupposes creation and the fall into sin. Ontologically, creation has priority.

To Barth as well as others the unity of God's work is an important factor. Everything stands in the light of grace. But the unity of God's work is not broken if the redeeming work of Christ does not begin at creation but subsequent to the fall into sin. For there is indeed a unity in his acting prior and subsequent to the fall into sin, implied by the fact that he seeks the salvation of his creatures, which can only be found in communion with him. In addition, the sole aim of all of God's ways and works is his glorification. This is true of both creation and redemption. We recognize these as works of the same God, whom we know as the Father of our Lord Jesus Christ, however, without considering them to be two sides of the same work of God's grace in Christ.[23] Put differently: "If we take a panoramic view of God's plan up to and including the finale of the re-creation of heaven and earth, then creation, redemption, and consummation constitute one mighty, consistent oeuvre" (Wentsel, *Dogm.*, 3a:508).

17.4. *The significance of faith in the Creator*

Reflecting on the various elements of creation, we do not forget that the church's confession does not primarily focus on creation but the Creator. This is true of both the first article of the Apostles' Creed and the explanation given in Lord's Day 9 of the Heidelberg Catechism. The key sentence in the latter is: "The eternal Father of our Lord Jesus

22. On Colossians 1 see also B. Wentsel, *Natuur en genade* (nature and grace), 1970, 333–35.

23. Cf. J. van Genderen, *Verbond en verkiezing* (covenant and election), 1983, 42.

Christ is my God and my Father." The subordinate clause says that it is he who created everything.

For that reason we cannot go along with G. C. van Niftrik, who—incidentally in imitation of G. van der Leeuw[24]—wrote: "Does it really interest you who made this world and whence it comes? The following excites your curiosity: what is the meaning of this world and our lives!" and somewhat further: "I would not start out from Genesis 1. I must begin with John 3:16. And from the perspective of John 3:16 I understand Genesis 1" (*Kl.D.*, 72ff.).

It is of fundamental significance for our faith and our life that God is our Creator and that we are his creatures. With this we confess his sovereignty over us and over all that has been created and our own dependence as well as that of all creatures.

With this we take position over against every deification or idolization of the created world, whether inspired by naturalism, idealism, or materialism.

Ancient *naturalism* worships heavenly bodies and the forces of nature. Israel continually encountered this on the part of Gentile nations. Through faith in the Creator and his work this is cut off at the root level (cf. Gen. 1:14–19). The glorification of race, blood, and territory in the twentieth century was also in essence pagan!

Idealism can be taken far, as in Hegel's philosophy, in which we see where the absolutization of ideas can lead. Then the divine spirit in man and in his thinking comes to himself.

A third form of creature deification is *materialism*, which reduces all phenomena to "energy and matter."

The Bible warns against the sin of honoring "the creature more than the Creator, who is blessed for ever" (Rom. 1:25). Nothing that is part of this world is absolute or autonomous. The entire creation exists by the grace of God.

God is our Creator and we are his creatures. By implication nothing in creation is unimportant.

We hereby take position over against any contempt or disdain of creation. We reject *dualism* of spirit and matter. As though matter were inferior! "For every creature of God nothing [is] to be refused, if it be received with thanksgiving" (1 Tim. 4:4).

24. G. van der Leeuw, *Dogmatische brieven* (dogmatic epistles), 1955^2, 55.

No idolization of any creature, for it is only a creature held in God's hand, but neither any contempt of any creature, for it is a creature of God and he has a purpose for it!

Faith in God as our Creator is for all relationships of the greatest importance.

1. The relationship with God comes first. We can say with Bavinck that creation is the foundation of all religious and ethical life (*R.D.*, 2:407). To say it with Calvin: "How can the thought of God penetrate your mind without your realizing immediately that, since you are his handiwork, you have been made over and bound to his command by right of creation, that you owe your life to him?—that whatever you undertake, whatever you do, ought to be ascribed to him? and that everything that you do must honour him?" (*Institutes*, 1.2.2). We do not belong to ourselves, but to God. Living through him and yet living without him is unlawful and preposterous in the extreme. We do not have our life in our own hands; neither may we take it into our own hands. We are called to serve God.

2. In his explanation of the first article of our faith, Luther indicates that faith in God as our Creator is significant for *relationships with our fellow creatures and other creatures*: "I believe that God has created me together with all other creatures" (*Kleine Catechismus* = short catechism). Those who belong to God also belong to one another. We do not exist on our own! This means that we do not begrudge others place and space, and champion life, especially when it is weak or threatened.

3. The third relationship, which cannot be severed from the first two, is the *relationship with the entire created world*. Man forms part of this, and at the same time he occupies a unique position in it. From Genesis 1:28, which deals with subjugation of the earth and dominion over animals, it has at times been inappropriately inferred that we may make use of everything without restriction. Western thinking, which in this regard has been profoundly influenced by rationalistic philosophy (Descartes), is, however, guilty of a mentality that implies that what can be done may be done. As a result, people have proceeded to exploit nature's treasures selfishly and frequently also without foresight. The marked development of science and technology has contributed to this phenomenon.

Culture has indeed been accurately described as control of nature. But man all too often assumes that he can behave as lord and master, while the Bible always emphasizes his dependence and responsibility. "The earth is the LORD's, and the fullness thereof; the world, and they that dwell therein" (Ps. 24:1). Nature is and remains God's creation and we may not do with it whatever we want. He who "made the world and all things therein, [who] is Lord of heaven and earth" (Acts 17:24), established norms and set limits that we must obey.

We conclude this section by quoting one of Calvin's practical statements: "As often as we call God the Creator of heaven and earth, we should simultaneously bear in mind that the distribution of all that he has created is in his own hand and power, but also that we are his children, whom he has taken under his faithful protection to nourish and educate" (*Institutes*, 1.14.22).

§ 18. Creation and evolution

18.1. *Theories of evolution*

"In the beginning God created the heaven and the earth." And "God created man in his own image, in the image of God created he him; male and female created he them" (Gen. 1:1, 27). What the Word of God says is for believers the answer to the question as to the origin of the world and the beginning of the history of mankind.

But it does not escape our attention that also outside the Bible and the Christian faith thought is given to the question as to where the world and life come from and how the emergence of man must be envisioned.

The most important theory that we encounter is that of evolution. It pertains to the origin of the universe, life on earth, and human life.

The *doctrine of evolution* and *Darwinism* are not exactly the same thing. A precursor of Ch. R. Darwin (1809–82) was J. B. de Lamarck (1744–1829). For that matter, the idea of a development whereby the lower form becomes the raw material for a higher form was already a major theme in Aristotle's philosophy. In more recent philosophy, Hegel and Marx also present ideas involving a process of development, but from a philosophical point of view H. Spencer (1820–1903) had relatively greater significance for the doctrine of evolution. He coined expressions such as the "struggle for existence" and "survival of the fittest," which were subsequently popularized by Darwin.

Lamarck did already have a *theory of descent*, which implied that species could change into others, that man descended from animals, and that changes, becoming hereditary, could be explained on the basis of adaptation to the environment. But proof was lacking. The famous work of the capable researcher of nature Darwin (*On the Origin of Species: By Means of Natural Selection*, 1859) represented a breakthrough. Darwin in turn adopted views of C. Lyell (1797–1875) and T. R. Malthus (1766–1834). Incidentally, he abandoned the authority of Scripture and became an agnostic, as did others in his entourage.

The period of the emergence of Darwinism—which was not limited to biology but became an ideology that influenced psychology and sociology, as well as paleontology and geology—was followed by a time in which criticism of Darwin's hypothesis intensified. It remained to be confirmed by facts, which were, however, definitely lacking. In the meantime Darwinism had become so pervasive that it persisted, although in a modified form (Neo-Darwinism).

The doctrine of evolution exists not only in the form of a scientific theory, but also as an evolutionary mode of thinking. This evolutionism encompasses the past, as well as the present, and the future.

Here we need to say something about the arguments in favor of universal evolution (*macro-evolution*). Its cogency depends on the hypotheses on which it is based! Those who accept the theory of evolution or the evolutionary way of thinking will recognize three categories of proof: 1. that remarkable similarities in structure, function, and development of various forms of life must be explained through common descent; 2. that the laws of genetics demonstrate that forms of life can change into more highly developed forms; 3. that it can be inferred from the fossil record that higher forms of life have developed from lower forms (cf. W. J. Ouweneel in Van der Graaf, 1975, 38).

However, there is plenty of scope for criticism. 1. In the case of similarities, it is not necessary to infer common descent. Simply accepting the existence of analogous blueprints obviates the need for this argument. 2. Variability is observed, and new strains and varieties emerge through breeding techniques and other circumstances. But this does not necessarily imply the transformation of classes and phyla of plants and animals. 3. It has been objected about Darwinism that precisely the essential links are missing in the fossils that have been found. This continues to be the case with respect to the transitional forms among biological phyla. Neither is it possible to identify rising levels within the genus Homo, i.e., man (cf. Ouweneel in Van der Graaf, 1975[2], 37–44).

What Bavinck pointed out in his time continues to be relevant today. In the first place, until now the theory of descent has proved completely unable to make the origin of life somewhat understandable. In the second place, Darwinism has also proved incapable of explaining the further development of organic entities. Transitional forms from one species to another have not been found. Intermediate forms have never been discovered. In the third place, the origin of man is an insoluble problem. In the fourth place, Darwinism fails to provide an explanation of humanness in terms of its psychic and spiritual dimension (*R.D.*, 2:514–20).

This leaves aside the question whether geology, which could be thought of as archeology of the earth, possibly offers evidence in support of the theory of evolution.

The popular view is that geological strata always occur in a certain sequence and that fossils are the remains of lower beings to the extent that they are encountered within lower strata. But geology, which requires long periods of time to explain phenomena, has become dependent on paleontology, and paleontology is almost entirely at the service of the doctrine of evolution. It is presupposed that organic beings have evolved from lower to higher forms, and on this basis the sequence and duration of the formation of sediments is constructed. In turn this sequence of sediments is used as proof for the theory of evolution. This constitutes circular reasoning (Bavinck, *R.D.*, 2:501–5), which in fact proves nothing.

Cosmology is also strongly influenced by the doctrine of macro-evolution.

In the nineteenth century, the theory of Kant-Laplace implied that initially there was a gigantic rotating mist. The sun and its planets would have developed from this mist through condensation. But this was a speculative hypothesis.

In modern physics and astronomy it is nevertheless assumed that this theory is by and large correct. According to the most popular view, which considers the theory of general relativity of A. Einstein (1879–1955) to be a reliable starting point, there was at first a huge explosion or *big bang*. This is supposed to have happened at least ten billion years ago. Some have even come up with an estimate of twenty billion years. Via enormous reactions in rapid succession, a gaseous mixture of hydrogen and helium must have formed. The stellar systems, including our own solar system and within it the earth with its core and crust, owe their existence to condensation and contraction. Expansion is ongoing and one refers therefore to an expanding universe, but it is not known whether this will result in a breakup or a new explosion (Bonting, 1978, 62ff.).

Those who consider how this process is described are surprised that these decisive events must have taken place in seconds or even fractions of a second. "The early universe is a fantastic 'field' for research for physicists and astronomers, where several disciplines converge, but also an area of speculation and fantasy" (H. J. Boersma in *De plaats van aarde en mens* = the place of earth and man, 1987, 38).

No experiment can be devised to demonstrate that it must have happened in this way. The beginning cannot be reached through extrapolation. The entire theory therefore is of a hypothetical nature. There are phenomena that are not well understood with the assistance of the standard model of cosmology, while the objections that have been raised against it are not diminishing. Is the big bang then not a grab bag of unresolved problems?

At any rate, the standard model is surrounded by a shroud of uncertainty (cf. Seldenrijk, 1988, 161). From a scientific point of view it is therefore indeed possible that some day this model will be discarded. Nevertheless, those who believe that there exists a fundamental perspective that, despite all of the uncertainties in scientific cosmology, will probably not soon be abandoned may be right after all. This is the notion of the cosmogenesis: the evolution of the universe including life on earth and human culture (H. R. Plomp in *De plaats van aarde en mens* = the place of earth and man, 1987, 105).

Those who inquire about the cause of the big bang are sometimes told: you have not heard anything about the reason for the big bang because we know which questions may be asked and which not (H. J. Boersma in *De plaats van aarde en mens*, 1987, 58). Sometimes it is recognized that one may ask further questions, although one then arrives in the realm of the philosophy of science.

The philosophy of the standard model is that nothing can be said with certainty with respect to the primary cause, or that it is a matter of chance. This is what evolutionism wants us to believe!

18.2. *Attempts to avoid conflicts*

1. *The concordist theory*. It is understandable that attempts have been made to reconcile as much as possible biblical elements with scientific facts and theories by interpreting the "days" of Genesis 1 as epochs of long duration.

Attempts have been made to limit the number of geological periods to six in order to match them with the six days of creation (G. Cuvier; J. F. Bettex). A variant of concordism is the interperiodistic theory.

It increasingly turned out, however, that no harmony between Scripture and scientific views could be reached in this way. Thus concordism lost the influence it once enjoyed. From an exegetical point of view there are serious objections to the view that the days in Genesis 1 were determined by an alternation of light and darkness.

2. *The restitution theory*. Hereby Genesis 1:1 is separated from Genesis 1:2. The earth would originally not have been "without form and void," but it would have become so as a result of certain causes, perhaps as a result of the fall of the angels. All of the events and phenomena that are usually thought to imply the earth's great antiquity could have preceded "a state of devastation." God subsequently restored everything and prepared earth to serve as a habitation for man.

Like the concordist theory, the restitution theory emerged in the eighteenth century. It has many adherents in North America. The *Scofield Reference Bible* refers at Genesis 1:2 to Isaiah (24:1; 14:9–14) and says that as a result of divine judgment a tremendous change took place. However, not a single proof for this view can be found in these passages. It is a purely speculative theory.

3. *The diluvial theory*. This name has been derived from the *dilivium* (the flood). This was a tremendous catastrophe, which changed the entire surface of the earth and must have resulted in oceans and mountains. According to the Bible, this coincided with the end of people's exceptional longevity. Changes in nature, in the realms of both plants and animals, must have taken place. The flood could have coincided with the ice ages of geology.

The days of Genesis 1 are hereby not considered to have been epochs of thousands of years, but neither as days as we know them now. They may have been days of an exceptional character. On each day of creation far more took place than the sober words of Genesis would lead us to suspect. Bavinck, who like a number of other Reformed theologians leans toward this view, observes that between the moment of creation (Gen. 1:1) and the flood, Scripture offers "a time span that can readily accommodate all the facts and phenomena which geology and paleontology have brought to light in the twentieth century" (*R.D.*, 2:505ff.).

The diluvial theory in a newer form is forcefully defended in circles of the Creation Research Society in North America, comprising hundreds of scientists. Diluvial geology is also supported in the Netherlands, including articles published in the periodical *Bijbel en wetenschap* (Bible and science, 1975). Some well-known names associated with this theory are H. M. Morris, A. M. Rehwinkel, A. E. Wilder-Smith; in the Netherlands, W. J. Ouweneel (cf. Ouweneel, 1978[3], 165–69).

The critical position of more recent creationism over against the popular doctrine of evolution is strong, but those who support it in principle must realize that it is a very challenging undertaking to arrive at an acceptable diluvial geology. Both evolutionists and creationists need to employ numerous hypotheses and speculations in order to develop a view of the history of the earth (Van Delden, 1989[2], 164ff.).

4. *The ideal time theory*. In this theory one does not hold to the letter of the history of creation but only the underlying concept.

One can then say that the six days represent six different perspectives from which the created world is surveyed in order to present a better overview for the limited vision of man. The sequence presented in Genesis 1 is not a historical sequence. It represents only a literary device to dress up the religious truth that the entire world was called into being by the creative word of God (Ott, *Grundriss* = outline, 122).

This theory can give free reign to science, as long as one does not reject the truth that God is the Creator. The ideal time theory drastically reduces the revelation content of Genesis 1. But what basis is there in the Bible passages themselves to think in terms of purely literary elaboration?

5. *The pictorial-day or literary framework theory*. This theory appears to be related to the ideal time theory. It is proposed by A. Noordtzij and N. H. Ridderbos. According to Noordtzij, it points to the creating activity of God in the light of his contemplation of salvation. This explains the grouping of the material in a framework of two sets of three days each.[25] In his study Ridderbos seeks to consider whether Genesis 1 and the results of science are in conflict with each other.

To him, the literary framework theory implies that the inspired author did not mean to provide an exact report of what happened in creation. By narrating an eightfold effort of God, he gives the reader the impression that everything in existence has been created by God. "This eightfold work of God is placed within a literary framework: he allocates it across six days, to which is added the seventh day as a day of rest."

One of the objections to this view is that it does not agree with the Sabbath command (Ex. 20:11), that the days of creation and also the seventh day only form a framework invented by the author. Ridderbos himself realizes that also with the acceptance of his view plenty of problems remain (Ridderbos, 1963², 66, 113–16).

18.3. *Attempts to achieve a synthesis*

1. *J. Lever and his creationism*. Initially it appeared as though the view of J. Lever, professor at the Free University of Amsterdam, represented an effort to avoid conflict between the Bible and science. But in view of the position that he subsequently adopted, we are dealing once again with a synthesis between Christian belief and the doctrine of evolution.

According to Lever the essence of evolutionism, which he rejects on the basis of principle, does not lie in the doctrine of development but in the concept of autonomy. Since he believes that organisms could emerge immanently through the evolution of life from lifeless forms, the crucial difference from a materialistic approach is that he teaches that God desired and directed it this way. There may have been a genetic relationship between man and animals and a genetic continuity of all living organisms (Lever, 1956, 44ff., 169, 184).

In what sense Lever subsequently believed a synthesis to be possible is evident from his paper *Waar blijven we?* (where does this leave us? 1969). Genesis presents us with a religious view as to the nature of this reality, its relativity, and its dependence on God

25. A. Noordtzij, *Gods Woord en der eeuwen getuigenis* (God's Word and the testimony of centuries), 1931², 111–20. Cf. G. Ch. Aalders, 1932, 232–40.

in terms of both origin and existence. Genesis 3 does not at all reflect specific events that took place there and then, but the quintessence, "the most profound problems of every human being, all people, starting with the very first people. Always, from the very beginning, man has experienced the tension between good and evil, and evil has affected his life." Out of a developmental process that lasted billions of years, ultimately a fantastic being was born through whom this earthly reality opened up to God. "The primeval oceans were the spring out of which life could proceed so that the Source of Life could hold the oceans and life in his creative hands" (Lever, 1969, 23, 28, 37, 50).

This strongly resembles the current doctrine of macro-evolution, but it is a doctrine of evolution with a different starting point. Lever indeed begins by saying that God desired and directed everything in this way. This is the essence of his "creationism."

2. *The synthesis of Teilhard de Chardin.* P. Teilhard de Chardin (1881–1955) was an authority in the areas of geology and paleontology. His chef d'oeuvre is *Le phénomène humain* (the phenomenon of man, 1955). He views the universe as a dynamic whole, marked by development and growth from within. On the axis of growing complexity and the corresponding increasing level of consciousness lie the critical points of vitalization, whereby life emerges, and hominization, whereby the consciously thinking human being emerges. The world converges to a new crucial point, the Omega point, which represents simultaneously a culmination and a conclusion. More than once Omega is equated with God or Christ.

This represents a strongly speculative way of thinking. One of the unproven hypotheses, with which the entire structure stands or falls, is that energy has a psychic interior.

To Teilhard evolution is much more than a theory or hypothesis. He refers to it as a light that illuminates all facts, a curve with which all lines must coincide. He advocates a blend of evolutionist and religious ideas, with the result that Christ is portrayed as a cosmic principle. The universe is Christified. Evolution is declared to be holy!

Teilhard's "vision" captivated many.[26] Berkhof even says: in Roman Catholic theology his vision has had the effect of putting all of theology in a different key (*C.F.*, 180).

3. *H. Berkhof and the evolutionary worldview.* An important theologian who accepts the doctrine of evolution and seeks to incorporate it into his dogmatics is H. Berkhof (cf. *C.F.*, 165ff., 178ff., 212ff.).

He holds that the belief that God has created the world does indeed belong to the inner circle of faith, but that the biblical concepts of creation do not. As a result of the historical-critical study of the Bible one has come to see them as being of secondary importance. In our time it is necessary to express our belief in creation in

26. See N. M. Wildiers, *Het wereldbeeld* (worldview) *van Pierre Teilhard de Chardin*, 1960; B. Delfgaauw, *Teilhard de Chardin*, 1964[9]; P. Smulders, *Het visioen van Teilhard de Chardin*, 1964[4]; H. A. M. Fiolet, *Vreemede verleiding* (strange temptation), 1968; A. Szekeres, *Heil en elan* (salvation and elan), 1974.

terms of the evolutionary worldview. This does not seem difficult to Berkhof. After all, the doctrine of evolution transforms what we refer to as nature into a grandiose historical process, culminating in the phenomenon of man and in him leading to a new, open future. "In the Bible creation and history are similarly combined" (*C.F.*, 179). In the meantime, to be able to agree with Berkhof, one needs to engage in a great deal of smoothing over and relativizing!

He assumes that the evolutionary process probably began billions of years ago with a chaotic, gaseous mass. Negative phenomena such as conflict, suffering, death, and natural catastrophes are not purely negative, because they are inextricably intertwined with the positive good of the progress of life. God has caused us to emerge from a nascent world as threatened and challenged creatures. Evolution is constituted by a growing mobility of molecular links. In the phenomenon of man this mobility takes the form of freedom.

With the help of insights that are presented to us through the evolutionary view of the world, Berkhof seeks to formulate elements of the Christian faith in a more comprehensible manner. But those who compare his reflections with what the Bible says about God's good creation and the fall of man into sin, can see the transformation that has taken place here. It is a different view of the world, life, man, sin, and salvation!

18.4. *Over against the doctrine of evolution and evolutionism*

In the discussion of various attempts to avoid a conflict between the Christian faith and data provided by scientific disciplines, it can be seen that no satisfactory solution to the problem has yet been found (§ 18.2).

Attempts to arrive at a synthesis as undertaken by Teilhard de Chardin, Lever, and Berkhof lead to a theologically enhanced doctrine of evolution, which represents a grave danger to our faith (§ 18.3).

Then there remains the option to acquiesce in a dichotomy. Sometimes *the model of two distinct worlds* is applied, i.e., one of faith that begins with creation and another of science that seeks to explain things on the basis of observation. These two worlds are supposed to avoid each other.

On the theological side many, including P. Althaus, E. Brunner, and G. Eberling, focus on personal faith: I believe that God made me. Luther is cited in the process, but in his *Kleine Catechismus* (short catechism) he adds: "samt allen Kreaturen" (together with all creatures). J. Moltmann has correctly observed: "If God is not the Creator of the world, he cannot be my Creator either" (Moltmann, 1985, 51).

There is but a single reality. Of course, the model of the two worlds can be modified into a *model of two languages* (cf. J. van der Veken in H. W. de Knijff, 1989, 30–33). One can say that the various hypotheses and theories deal with information of a scientific nature, while the Bible contains a message that is addressed to us and that demands to be believed and understood. But there is no double truth, is there?

One can still seek a way out in the distinction between accuracy and truth. Whatever can be demonstrated scientifically, and is considered to be accurate, still need not be true in the biblical sense of the word. Biblical truth is so certain that one can completely rely on it (*'emet*), whereas the scientific theories embedded in models must continually be validated.

In addition, science can only subject observable reality to investigation. The regularities that it looks for, and the links that it establishes, fall within the limits of its own field of research. In its totality creation comprises far more than what falls within the scientific horizon. With C. J. Dippel one can refer to this as the physical reality, which is being chiseled out as it were. It is a limited image of reality (Dippel in *Geloof en natuurwetenschap* = faith and natural science, 1:121–232).

Moreover, we are dealing not only with the doctrine of evolution, but also with *evolutionism*. The former is a scientific theory; the latter is a worldview. The idea of evolution as a universal phenomenon has influenced numerous areas. Also in racism, which was characteristic of National Socialistic ideology, the principle of selection played an important role.

The chief trend is materialistic evolutionism which ascribes autonomy to the powers and forces of nature, which does not recognize any underlying blueprint, which refuses to accept any goal-orientation, and which doubts or denies that reality makes any sense.

According to the well-known American paleontologist G. G. Simpson, man is the consequence of an aimless material process. There never was any planning. J. Monod expresses it even more strongly: Man finally realizes that he is alone in the indifferent infinity of the universe from which he has emerged by chance. His fate and his obligation are nowhere spelled out (cf. J. van der Veken in H. W. de Knijff, 1989, 23).

Yet, not infrequently norms or at least behavioral guidelines are inferred from the process of evolution. Ethics would be a product of evolution, and standards would not be permanent. G. G. Simpson considers it highly advisable for man to strive to keep the direction of his own evolution as much as possible under his own control. Otherwise mankind faces a dim future. In general, large families ought to be discouraged by minimizing family support programs. Financial incentives should be offered to parents with superior hereditary traits![27]

27. G. G. Simpson, *De betekenis van de evolutie* (the meaning of evolution), 1962, 204, 219; idem, *Het wereldbeeld van een evolutionist* (the worldview of an evolutionist), 1968, 46, 389.

We must radically reject evolutionism. The issue is whether we live in a world created and governed by God or in a world that evolves of its own accord, in which man as an autonomous being in principle may do whatever he is capable of. Evolutionism, building on the theory of evolution, is not a science itself, but a philosophical view that as faith in evolution is diametrically opposed to the vision of the Christian faith.

Through the conflict with the doctrine of evolution and everything that is associated with it one could forget that there is also a development or evolution that a Christian can accept. This has been pointed out by Schilder, following in the footsteps of others: "A *created* evolution of things could never represent a stumbling block to those who believe in Scripture" (*H.C.*, 3:268).

In the world created by God there is undeniably development, which is apparent from various changes. This is referred to as micro-evolution.

The church and theology must offer scope to biology, astronomy, and other natural sciences to pursue their research. With the words "after his kind," "after their kind," Genesis 1 indicates diversity in the plant and animal worlds that was intended by God, but it does not say that he then created all of the varieties that are extant today. Whether between the creation of heaven and earth (Gen. 1:1) and the first day on which God said: "Let there be light" there was a shorter or a longer day cannot be determined through exegesis. This means that the earth could have been there already a long time before man was created. With Bavinck and others one can make a distinction between "the first creation" (*creatio prima*) and "the second creation" (*creatio secunda*), which has also been referred to as laying the groundwork. For this, God used the days of creation (cf. Bavinck, *R.D.*, 2:479–97). Were God's "workdays" ordinary days? There are varying opinions about this. Ohmann says that we should not make an issue of whether the days of Genesis 1 lasted exactly 24 hours or not. He also refers to epochs or periods that follow upon each other and are contiguous.[28]

In 1949 the Reformed Ecumenical Synod provided guidelines concerning creation and evolution, which deserve to be mentioned. These affirm the historical character of Genesis 1 and 2 (over against K. Barth and others). The description of God's work of creation is given in a form that is intelligible to people. It does not include an adequate representation of this divine act, but it is sufficient to recognize and glorify God as our Creator and Lord.[29]

God desired that the revelation concerning creation would be comprehensible to Israel and to anyone who relies on what he observes. The following observation

28. H. M. Ohmann in A. P. Wisse (ed.), *In het licht van Genesis* (in the light of Genesis), 1986, 94, 97. However, see also Kamphuis, *Aant.* (notes), 42–48.

29. *Acta van de Gereformeerde Oecumenische Synode van Amsterdam*, 1949, article 89.

has been made about this: "We observe the earth on which we find ourselves, with plants and animals, with continents and oceans; above us we observe heaven and the clouds, also the sun, moon, and stars; we observe the distinction and the alternation of light and darkness; and now we are told about all of these things that they have been created by God, and also in which sequence God has created them" (Aalders, 1932, 167).

In Calvin's works we already read that Moses mentions no other works of God than those that show themselves to our eyes (*Institutes*, 1.14.3). He also writes: "Let all those who are so inclined, study astronomy and other occult arts elsewhere" (Commentary on Gen. 1:16).

We can say with Bavinck that creation was a series of awesome miracles that the biblical story portrays to us with a single brushstroke without giving details. Each day's work of creation must certainly have been much grander and more richly textured than Genesis summarily reports in its sublime narrative (*R.D.*, 2:500).

Theology can by no means answer all questions that could be asked with respect to the early history of the world and mankind. We limit ourselves to the Bible, which focuses our attention on fundamental issues. The history of creation also concerns knowledge of God, our Creator; knowledge of the world as his creation, over which he alone is sovereign; and knowledge of man, who was created in his image and whom he addresses in his revelation.

This takes us further than any science that seeks to explain methods and times without starting at the beginning: "I believe in God the Father, the Almighty, Creator of heaven and earth" (Apostles' Creed).

The theory that appeals most to those who start out from the reliability of the Bible is *creationism*,[30] for it recognizes God as Creator of heaven and earth and strives to work scientifically with the *creation model*. Its key ingredients are:

1. That the earth is relatively young, perhaps no older than ten thousand to fifteen thousand years, and at any rate not millions or billions of years.
2. That geological strata were formed under catastrophic conditions.
3. That the main forms of life emerged independently of each other and at approximately the same time.

30. The term "creationism" is variously employed. See above § 18.2, subsection 3 and § 18.3, subsection 1. Here we follow the definition used by W. J. Ouweneel and many other creationists, and not the interpretation given to it by J. Lever.

However, theology ought not to tie itself down to scientific theories and models, however plausible they may seem, for they are by their very nature tentative. The history of creation in Genesis 1 and 2 and the model of creation of creationism do not coincide. If the diluvial model would turn out to be incorrect, this would not affect the reliability of the story of the flood in the book of Genesis (cf. Seldenrijk, 1988, 202).

The universe could be older than most creationists suppose, just as it is far more extensive than could have been imagined in the past. Faith does not stand or fall with this. Following a fruitless fight, theology has abandoned the idea that the earth is the center of the universe (the geocentric worldview). Neither should it be troubled by the fact that the earth is but a speck in the immensity of space. It must, however, maintain that in the light of the Bible the earth is unique.

The first few chapters of Genesis show us what God did to make it the good earth that he gave to man to inhabit and to serve him. This is followed by the history of man's fall and its consequences. "Everything that [God] had made was very good" (Gen. 1:31). But in Genesis 6:12 it says: "God looked upon the earth, and, behold, it was corrupt; for all flesh had corrupted his way upon the earth."

Yet God did not abandon his creation. On this earth Christ completed his work of mediation. Re-creation and renewal do not apply only to mankind but also to the earth (cf. Rom. 8:18–25).

§ 19. The angels as creatures of God

19.1. *The existence of angels*

God is the Creator of all things visible and invisible. It is likely that the invisible reality in the creed of the early church was largely interpreted to be the angels. Our own confessions explicitly refer to the creation of angels (Belgic Confession of Faith, article 12).

Since the Enlightenment the existence of angels has been doubted by many. The heavens were "depopulated" (Kuyper, 1923[2], 7). More recent theology silently ignores angels or shows little interest in them. It is sometimes granted that angels are more than the product of Christian fantasy. The notion of angels is relatively deeply anchored in Christian piety (Ebeling, 1:332). But whereas some wish to take pious experience into account, others object that they do not fit into the modern view of the world. In the study in which Bultmann unveils his program of "Entmythologisierung" (demythologization), he states bluntly that in a world dominated by science and technology one can no longer believe in the world of spirits and miracles of the New Testament.[31]

Barth has a remarkably detailed section dealing with angels (*C.D.*, 3.3.369–531). They are viewed as being strictly functional, almost devoid of ontological contours (correctly pointed out by Berkhof, *C.F.*, 182). One could say that according to Barth the angels exist for the sole purpose of carrying out their assignments. Berkhof believes that from the Bible no doctrine of angels (*angelology*) can be constructed. Should we then keep silent about them? This is also rejected, for it may be explored whether faith in the "one God as being beneficially related to his earthly creation" might point us in this direction. Furthermore, our generation considers it not unthinkable that beings could exist elsewhere and might wish to concern themselves with the earth. Is belief in angels then so strange? But dogmatics cannot go beyond positing the *possibility* of such sublime—remote and simultaneously nearby—realities (*C.F.*, 181–83).

In view of the extent and complexity of the medieval doctrine of angels, it was no great loss that Reformational theology limited itself in this regard to essentials. This was implied by its reliance on the Scriptures. However, there is ample biblical justification for rejecting the position of those who have reservations about the existence of angels. Angels are undoubtedly part of reality.

It is an error, already associated with the Sadducees according to Acts 23:8, to deny the existence of angels. This error was forcefully rejected by the church (Belgic Confession of Faith, article 12).

We do not see the angels if we do not see them in the light of the Bible.[32] As servants and envoys of God they turn up in various places in Holy Scripture. "Angel," derived from its Greek equivalent via Latin (*angelus*), actually means: messenger, ambassador, just like the corresponding word in the Old Testament. Synonyms are: "sons of God" (Job 1:6), "ministers of the Lord" (Ps. 103:21), and "saints" (Dan. 8:13).

The Bible speaks only indirectly about the creation of angels. One can think of Colossians 1:16 and perhaps also of Job 38:7. The "sons of God" (synonymous with "the morning stars"), who "sang" when God created the earth, most likely were meant to be angels. From this it is not infrequently inferred that Genesis 1:1 also refers to the creation of angels. At any rate, there is a close connection between heaven and the angels. They are with God in heaven. They stand near

31. R. Bultmann in H. W. Bartsch (ed.), *Kerygma und Mythos*, 1960⁴, 1:18.

32. In this section we are not dealing with the Angel of the Lord. See what is said about theophany in § 5.2.

him and go from heaven to earth and back to heaven again (Gen. 28:12; John 1:51).

The created world comprises far more than we can see. Thus there is—invisible to us—an immensely large number of angels (Matt. 26:53; Heb. 12:22). In the realm of angels there is a rich diversity. There are cherubs (Gen. 3:24) and seraphs (Isa. 6:2), while reference is also made to the archangel Michael (Jude 9; cf. Dan. 10:13). Another highly placed angel is Gabriel (Luke 1:19; Dan. 8:16).

The angels are "ministering spirits" or spiritual beings (Heb. 1:14). Whenever they appear to people, they have a form that varies according to the service that they perform. In the fine arts they have frequently been depicted as lovely figures, sometimes having wings, but in the Bible they are referred to as warriors of strength (Ps. 103:20; Luke 2:13).

19.2. *The ministry of angels*

1. The Word of God says more about the ministry of the angels than about everything else that we would like to know about the world of angels. The angels abide in God's immediate presence. They laud and praise him in heavenly liturgy (Isa. 6:3). They listen to the sound of his voice and carry out his will (Ps. 103:20). This is clearly demonstrated in the history of redemption, in which angels are the heralds of salvation (Luke 2:10; Matt. 28:5; Acts 1:10–11). They are also interpreters of mysteries (Dan. 8:19; Zech. 1–6; Rev. 17:7). In this capacity they are also referred to as interpreter-angels.

They are at the disposal of Christ (Matt. 4:11; 24:31; 25:31). When in the book of Acts they guide the church of Christ along its way, it tells us that the business of Christ and his church is the business of God who protects and guides his people (cf. Acts 5:19; 8:26).

Can anything more be said about the angels' ministry to "them who shall be heirs of salvation" (Heb. 1:14)? At any rate this can be said, that for this purpose they are continually being sent out, as the original text says. According to Calvin they are dispensers and administrators of God's beneficence toward us. For this he gives examples from the Bible, especially from the Old Testament. The promises of God (Pss. 91:11–12; 34:7) apply first of all to Christ, the Head of the church, and subsequently to all believers. By way of summary Calvin says: "The angels keep vigil for our salvation, they take upon themselves our defense, they direct our ways, and take care that nothing evil will befall us. This ministry of the angels is there through the mediation of Christ as our Mediator. Through him the angels are bound up with the church of Christ and the church with the angels" (cf. *Institutes*, 1.14.6, 12).

2. Are there *guardian angels*? That they exist is a widespread belief, which is least shared by the Reformed. Matthew 18:10 does not say that every child of God has his personal guardian angel, but that the little ones among them have been entrusted to the special care of the angels (cf. Blauw, no date, 108). God's protecting power is also exercised by means of angels.

In Roman Catholicism the doctrine of angels and that of guardian angels plays a much greater role than in Protestantism. The speculations of Pseudo-Dionysius the Areopagite concerning the heavenly hierarchy, of which the ecclesiastical hierarchy would be a reflection, have had a lasting impact. According to Roman Catholic doctrine, everyone who has been baptized has a guardian angel or an angelic protector, who encourages him to do good and will be his defender in the hour of his death.

But this doctrine cannot be inferred from Scripture (neither from Matt. 18:10 nor Acts 12:15). In addition, it is then considered to be the obligation of believers to call upon and worship angels, especially one's guardian angel. A distinction is made between the worship that is due to God only and doing homage to creatures. Yet doing homage has a religious connotation. This is contrary to God's Word (Rev. 22:8–9).

On this score the Reformation has made itself abundantly clear. According to Calvin this constitutes superstition, although—at least in the *Institutes*[33]—he is careful in formulating his opinion with respect to the possible existence of guardian angels.

Those who would see angels as mediators would also ascribe too much autonomy to their ministry, considering that according to the Bible they clearly do nothing on their own initiative. Their assistance constitutes the assistance of God who employs them in his service.

3. According to Scripture the angels also have to *fight* evil powers (Rev. 12:7–8). The epistle of Jude speaks of "angels which kept not their first estate, but left their own habitation" and have been "reserved unto judgment" (Jude 6; cf. 2 Peter 2:4). This refers indubitably to Satan and his followers who rose up against God. This was followed by the temptation and fall of man (Gen. 3; cf. John 8:44), and lasting activity directed against God, Christ, and his church, against which the Bible warns us vigorously (see among other passages Job 2:1–7; Luke 22:31; 2 Cor. 11:14–15; Eph. 6:10–17; 2 Thess. 2:9–10; 1 Peter 5:8; Rev. 2:10).

Thus sin started in the world of the angels, whom God had created good. We do not know what transpired in the falling away of part of

33. Cf. R. Stauffer, *Dieu, la création et la Providence dans la prédication de Calvin* (God, creation and providence in Calvin's preaching), 1978, 194.

the angels. It is frequently supposed that it was pride that took possession of Satan and the angels who chose his side (Bavinck, *R.D.*, 3:36). But over against Satan and his angels stand the elect angels of God (1 Tim. 5:21).

4. The *distinction* between humans and angels is that the Bible nowhere says that the angels were created in the image of God. It is therefore questionable whether angels have been placed higher than man, as earlier theology sometimes taught. Texts such as Luke 20:36 do not offer scope for this idea.

The elect angels have the advantage over us of never having sinned against God. They will also be kept from doing so in the future. In their devotion to God's service they are a shining example to us. The third petition of the prayer that Jesus taught us makes us say: "Grant that we may obey Thy will, which alone is good; that so every one may discharge the duties of his office and calling as willingly and faithfully as the angels in heaven" (Heidelberg Catechism, Lord's Day 49).

Some Literature

G. Ch. Aalders, *De goddelijke openbaring in de eerste drie hoofdstukken van Genesis* (divine revelation in the first three chapters of Genesis), 1932.

G. Altner, *Schöpfungsglaube und Entwicklungsgedanke in der protestantischen Theologie zwischen Ernst Haeckel und Teilhard de Chardin* (belief in creation and the concept of evolution in Protestant theology according to Ernst Haeckel and Teilhard de Chardin), 1965.

H. W. Beck, *Weltformel contra Schöpfungsglaube* (universal law versus belief in creation), 1972.

G. C. Berkouwer, *The Providence of God*, 1952.

J. Blauw, *Gezanten van de hemel* (ambassadors from heaven), no date.

A. de Bondt, *De satan*, no date.

S. L. Bonting (ed.), *Evolutie en scheppingsgeloof* (evolution and belief in creation), 1978.

R. Boon, *Over de goede engelen of De ontmaskering van een pedant ongeloof* (concerning good angels or the exposure of a pedantic unbelief), 1983.

H. A. Brongers, *De scheppingtradities bij de profeten* (the creation traditions according to the prophets), 1945.

G. Crespy, *Het theologische denken van Teilhard de Chardin* (the theological thinking of Teilhard de Chardin), 1966.

S. M. Daecke, *Teilhard de Chardin und die evangelische Theologie*, 1967.

J. A. Van Delden, *Schepping en wetenschap* (creation and science), 1989[2].

J. A. Van Delden (ed.), *Schepping of evolutie?* (creation or evolution?), 1977.

Geloof en natuurwetenschap (faith and natural science), 1965–67, 1 and 2.

J. van der Graaf (et al.), *Evolutie en geloof* (evolution and faith), 1975[2].

J. Hübner, *Theologie und biologische Entwicklungslehre* (theology and the doctrine of biological evolution), 1966.

J. Hübner (ed.), *Der dialog zwischen Theologie und Naturwissenschaft* (the dialogue between theology and natural science), 1987.

H. Kakes, *Waar zijn de engelen nu?* (where are the angels now?), no date.

D. Kempff, *Die skeppingleer van Karl Barth* (the doctrine of creation of Karl Barth), 1949.

H. W. de Knijff (et al.), *Teksten over theologie en natuurwetenschap* (texts concerning theology and natural science), 1989.

A. Kuyper, *De engelen Gods* (the angels of God), 1923[2].

J. Lever, *Creatie en evolutie*, 1956.

J. Lever, *Waar blijven we?* (where does this leave us?), 1969.

C. Link, *Schöpfung* (creation), 1991.

J. Moltmann, *Gott in Schöpfung* (God in creation), 1985.

E. Neubauer, *Grenzen der Wissenschaft* (limits of science), 1972.

G. P. Olbertijn, *Denken over de engelen van God* (thinking about the angels of God), 1986.

W. den Otter, *Harmonie tussen Bijbel en natuur*, 1976.

W. J. Ouweneel, *De ark in de branding* (the ark in the surf), 1978[3].

W. J. Ouweneel, *De schepping in 't geding* (creation at issue), 1981.

De plaats van aarde en mens in het heelal (the place of earth and man in the universe), 1987.

B. Ramm, *The Christian View of Science and Scripture*, 1955.

H. N. Ridderbos, *Beschouwingen over Genesis 1* (reflections on Genesis 1), 1963[2].

L. Scheffczyk, *Einführung in die Schöpfungslehre* (introduction to the doctrine of creation), 1975.

Schepping en evolutie (creation and evolution), 1986.

R. Seldenrijk, *Langs natuurwetenschap en evolutie-theorie* (through natural science and the theory of evolution), 1988.

C. F. von Weizsäcker, *De draagwijdte van de wetenschap* (the scope of science), 1966.

B. Wentsel, *Natuur en genade* (nature and grace), 1970.
A. E. Wilder-Smith, *Herkunft und Zukunft des Menschen* (man's origin and future), 1966.
A. P. Wisse (ed.), *In het licht van Genesis* (in the light of Genesis), 1986.
E. J. Young, *Genesis een* (Genesis 1), 1971.

Chapter 7

God's Providence

§ 20. The development of the doctrine of providence

20.1. *A creed*

The doctrine of providence formerly seemed clear and obvious. There were difficult questions, but points of controversy were overshadowed by widespread agreement. Faith in God indeed included the confession that he preserved and governed the world.

The doctrine of providence was frequently referred to as a mixed article of faith (*articulus mixtus*) that by nature was known to all people at least to some extent (Bavinck, *R.D.*, 2:593).

Synopsis (1625) held that all those who otherwise were devoid of true religion recognized that everything depends on God. The order and cohesion of everything in the world must give the impression that a wise spirit effects, directs, and preserves this order (*Synopsis*, 88).

Early in the twentieth century it was still said that the universal revelation of God on the basis of which this truth is known—however imperfectly and perversely—must be supplemented through special revelation (Dijk, 1927, 8–15). But this author does add what Bavinck (1854–1921) has written: for natural man so many objections can be raised to the idea of God's governance of the world that he can only believe in it with great difficulty. Faith in God's providence is an article of the Christian faith.

Bavinck correctly points out that in Scripture this belief is based much more on God's covenant and promises than on his revelation in nature. Only saving faith prompts us to believe wholeheartedly in God's providence in the world, to see its significance, and experience its consoling power (Bavinck, *R.D.*, 2:594).

The fact that the concept of providence is widely known does not detract in the least from the purely Christian character of what the church believes and confesses when it refers to God's providence.

The term itself does not stem from Christian thought, but from Greek and Roman philosophy. A Stoic such as Epictetus wrote a hymn to providence, and Seneca devoted one of his writings to it. What Seneca says about the Godhead as being the founder and director of everything, who cares for the human race and helps everyone everywhere, resembles what the Bible says about God's governance and care. Yet there are essential differences.

The philosophical doctrine of *pronoia* or *providentia* is impersonal, for it concerns a function of the cosmic mind. While on the one hand there is providence, on the other hand there is fate, i.e., "a necessity out of the perpetual of cause and effect" (cf. Calvin, *Institutes*, 1.16.8).

There is only limited care for the individual, because the interests of the greater whole, of which he forms part, prevail. If one needs to suffer in consequence, one has to resign oneself to this. Although Stoic philosophy has a teleological element, there is no chance of escaping this vicious circle of events.

In the thinking of Augustine and other church fathers, providence takes on a new significance, because they consider it to be implicit in God's creation. This faith in God is accompanied by prayer. This is especially apparent from Augustine's *Confessiones*, in which God's guidance in his life is a prominent theme. In the Stoic scheme, however, prayer is useless, for everything happens the way it has to happen. Augustine speaks of the hidden mystery of God's providence and of God's providence as working in a hidden fashion (*Confessiones*, 5:11, 13).

As far as evil is concerned, it is totally controlled by God, although man continues to be accountable for it. Also by means of the will of creatures, who did what God forbade, God accomplishes his own will.[1]

The term "*providentia*," as the verb from which it is derived, has two meanings: foreseeing and the provision of something. But God's providence does not indicate foreseeing ahead of time what will happen. It means to provide in everything. Calvin says: "God's providence pertains no less to his hands than to his eyes" (*Institutes*, 1.16.4).

1. Augustine, *Enchiridion ad Laurentium*, 100.

The title of this chapter in the *Institutes* is therefore: "God maintains and protects the world created by him and governs all of its parts by his providence." The Belgic Confession of Faith presents the same view.

Are we here only in the forecourt of the sanctuary? In that case the believers who speak in article 13 of the Belgic Confession of Faith would not call themselves disciples of Christ. The same thing could be said with respect to Lord's Day 10 of the Heidelberg Catechism. It is a confession of faith that forms a unity with the confession of Lord's Day 9. "The eternal Father of our Lord Jesus Christ, who of nothing made heaven and earth with all that is in them, who likewise upholds and governs the same by his eternal counsel and providence, is for the sake of Christ his Son my God and Father."

Noordmans has criticized the doctrine of providence as presented in Lord's Day 10 for having been given a universal-religious emphasis. "Is the world after all some sort of model farm, the best-possible that is conceivable, in which one ought not to interpret things too tragically?" (Noordmans, *V. W.*, 2:262, 458). Others go still further and see it as instruction in atheism if we must be patient in all adversity. "This sort of statement keeps little ones small, the poor impoverished, and the sick ill." Belief in providence of this type would stand at the cradle of the movement of freethinkers in the Netherlands (Beker and Deurloo, 1978, 9ff.).

In the days of the Enlightenment this was revamped into a universal religious confession. Many came to view God as bountiful providence.[2]

The way in which the guidance of providence or a higher power was discussed in National Socialistic circles was no longer Christian, although the words sound more or less religious. This is also implied by the fact that providence and fate (Schicksal) were considered to be the same thing. This was already believed by the Stoics!

With the teaching of the church, as articulated in our confessions, we find ourselves in a totally different climate. One should try to imagine where things stood during the age of the Reformation! It is not for nothing that our confessions speak of an "unspeakable consolation, since we are taught thereby that nothing can befall us by chance, but by the direction of our most gracious and heavenly Father" (Belgic Confession of Faith, article 13).

This is a sensitive matter. When someone feels powerless in the face of events or acquiesces in his fate, because he supposes that it has been determined this way by a higher power, this is no longer living out of God's hand in faith, which is the practical side of the confession of God's providence. It is sometimes said that what happens to us is not done to us by people. But this sounds more like an expression of fatalism than a confession of faith.

2. Cf. G. Aulén, *Het christelijk Godsbeeld* (the Christian image of God), 1929, 282–95.

20.2. *Critique of tradition*

1. *A number of motifs*. Although we cannot support every view of God's providence, we should definitely not abandon the correct doctrine of providence, especially considering that there is currently "a crisis of belief in providence."

According to Berkouwer, in this connection three different *motifs* can be distinguished: the scientific motif, the projection motif, and the catastrophic motif.

As far as *science* is concerned we think of the influence of modern science on faith in God. The more one is able to explain natural phenomena, the less one is inclined to support the "hypothesis" of God's preservation and governance. The idea of a closed world is attractive, and the reality of God has faded away in the consciousness of many.

The *projection motif* is encountered on the part of philosophers such as Marx, Feuerbach, and Nietzsche, who came to view religion as a projection of man's own mind. According to Freud, man as a helpless being creates religious images about creation, providence, a moral world order, and eternal life. According to him religion is consequently of an illusory nature. Science will ultimately do away with it altogether. The simple reality is that man must rely on himself instead of God and his providence.

Then there is the *catastrophic motif*, which emerged early on but was reinforced by the terrible events of the twentieth century and the tremendous suffering that they engendered. These include what transpired in Auschwitz, Hiroshima, and elsewhere. Such events appear to deny the reality of God's guidance. Berkouwer writes that it appears as though realism and soberness increasingly captivate the hearts and thus push to the background the noble perspectives of providence and God's hand as an imaginary flight from bitter reality (Berkouwer, 1952, 17–23).

2. *Some more recent views*. In itself it is not strange that a number of theologians consciously build on modern philosophy of life. This frequently implies that they form a new concept of God and his providence. This is at any rate the case with J. Moltmann, H. Wiersinga, and A. van de Beek.

Moltmann interconnects God and reality far more closely than is customary. His argument is focused on the cross of Christ. In the crucified Son of Man, God is known as the human God. In the earlier doctrine of God, referred to by Moltmann as "theism," God cannot suffer and die. But in this modern theology of the cross God and suffering are no longer incompatible. Moltmann is not satisfied with saying that God is found among those who suffer. He believes that all suffering converges in God. All questions as to why are swallowed up in: "My God, my God, why hast thou forsaken me?" (Ps. 22:1; Matt. 27:46; Mark 15:34). Like the cross of Christ,

Auschwitz is experienced by God himself. That is to say, it has been absorbed in the grief of the Father, the surrender of the Son, and the power of the Spirit. History becomes the history of the "crucified" God suffering, fighting, and liberating, with the participation of people.[3]

Like Moltmann, Wiersinga seeks to make us experience the weight of suffering. He immediately refers to the former's work as well as that of Sölle.[4] Today's theology has fewer answers than that of the preceding generation. In the doctrine of providence, life's fate is directly related to God's decree. All suffering is related back to God and serves a purpose. It constitutes retribution as well as education. In modern theology God has become reconciled to suffering. Wiersinga argues over against this that God has not become reconciled to suffering. He suffers more from it and fights harder against it than people do. He suffers as man's partner, but he has more endurance than we do. He sees possibilities of handling, transforming, and eliminating suffering.

According to Wiersinga, his insight into God's sympathy with the suffering of the world asks for a reformulation of the doctrine of God's providence, however deeply rooted it is in the Christian church. Over against our crippled world and over against the specific testimony of the Bible, the doctrine of the providential God must be replaced by a doctrine of the sympathetic God, of his "defenseless supremacy." The God of sympathy turns people into sympathizers. They become mobilized to participate in the impossible and unbearable situations of suffering individuals and groups.[5]

A third approach to the issues associated with the doctrine of providence and especially with the problem of evil is that of Van de Beek. In his book *Waarom?* (why?, 1984), which could be called a theology of history in view of the chapter in which his position is most clearly described (4), he seeks to treat suffering completely seriously. Over against those who believe that they can no longer accept the Reformed doctrine of providence as formulated in the Heidelberg Catechism, Van de Beek shows respect for this confession. This does not ignore the fact that this belief in the providence of God leaves us with a number of important issues, i.e., questions concerning the sense of suffering, the meaning of sin, and the existence of unbelief. Van de Beek believes he is able to make headway with the idea of God's changeability. God clears a path through history with adaptability. Repeatedly he makes unexpected decisions. Continually his guidance takes unexpected turns. But is a changeable God still a God on whom one can rely? God does not revisit any choice that he has made. In Christ he chose for people. The way to the future is the road that the Spirit travels with us, and God makes allowances for the potential risk of failure.

The result is that not only is there no answer to the reason for suffering, but that another question is added. In addition to "why?" we now have the question as to "whereto?'! It is one of the core principles of the doctrine of providence that God guides everything with a strong hand toward his goal. Characteristic of Van de Beek

3. J. Moltmann, *Der gekreuzigte Gott* (the crucified God), 1972, 214, 266, 294, 315; cf. M. Welker (ed.), *Diskussion über Jürgen Moltmanns Buch "Der gekreuzigte Gott,"* 1979.

4. D. Sölle, *Leiden* (suffering), 1973.

5. H. Wiersinga, *Verzoening met het lijden?* (being reconciled with suffering?), 1975, 29, 49–52, 61–66. With his concept of the defenseless supremacy of God, Wiersinga joins Berkhof (*C.F.*, 140–47).

is, however, what he tells about a discussion triggered by his book. A student asked him whether he knew that everything would end all right. He answered this question in the negative.[6]

20.3. *What does Scripture say?*

Holy Scripture describes the work of God's providence very concretely and vividly. "Scripture in its totality is the book of God's providence" (Bavinck, *R.D.*, 2:595).

The way in which the Bible speaks about this work of God varies. Apart from providing (lit. "seeing to it": Gen 22:8), there are words such as "creation" and "renewal" (Ps. 104:30), "caring" (Deut. 11:12; 1 Peter 5:7), "reigning" (Ps. 47:8), and "upholding" (Heb. 1:3). To this may be added what is said about God's thoughts, his eyes, and his hand (Isa. 55:8; Pss. 33:11; 34:15; Deut. 5:15).

His providence concerns everything (Job 38 and 39; Ps. 139:13–24; Prov. 21:1; Isa. 14:26–27; 41:2–4; 45:5–7; Acts 17:24–28). Jesus said to his followers: "Your Father which is in heaven maketh his sun to rise on the evil and on the good and sendeth rain on the just and on the unjust" (Matt. 5:45).

In its psalms Israel praised God for his care for everything that he created and for his special care for his people (see Pss. 33; 34; 65; 104; 145; 146; 147).

The stories of Abraham, Isaac, and Jacob, even that of Joseph and his brothers testify to God's providence. We also think of the book of Esther and Daniel 1–6. This places the history of Israel (cf. Pss. 78; 105; 136; Ezek. 20) as well as that of the church (cf. Acts 4:27–28; 8:26–40; 16:6–10; 20–22) in a higher light.

In his omnipotence, God can thwart the actions of people in order to transform evil into good, as Joseph pointed out: "Ye thought evil against me; but God meant it unto good" (Gen. 50:20). "The LORD bringeth the counsel of the heathen to nought: he maketh the devices of the people to none effect" (Ps. 33:10).

At the center of everything that happens is the history of the death and resurrection of Christ. How mightily God thwarted here the wrong that was committed by people![7] "Ye have taken, and by wicked

6. A. van de Beek, *Waarom?* (why?), 1984, 97ff., 252–68, 294ff.; idem, "Om de levende God" (concerning the living God), in *Nogmaals: Waarom?* (once again: why?), 1986, 121.

7. In the more recent theology this is referred to as "das Gesetz der Umlenkung" (the law of redirection). This expression appears to have been borrowed from E. Stauffer, *Die Theologie des Neuen Testaments*, 1945, 186.

hands have crucified and slain [Him]: whom God hath raised up" (Acts 2:23–24; 3:15). This throws light on all of the work of God's providence.

Questions with respect to God's providence that have arisen in the twentieth century, because people have experienced dreadful things, may be difficult to answer but are by no means new. The Bible shows us how believers in early times had similar problems. We think of the books of Job and Lamentations, and of Psalms such as 44 and 73. There may be those who consider a review of the doctrine of providence desirable, but Auschwitz or whatever tragedy does not give theology the right to advocate revisions that imply abandonment of Scripture's teachings. We may not replace the faith that God is in control by the idea that God sympathizes with us and stands beside us as our partner.

Leaving aside that such broad generalizations are out of place, it is far below the standards of biblical teaching when Wiersinga writes[8] that God is planning to bring about change, and that the fact that God will gain the upper hand helps us to endure and bear our suffering and gives us the energy to pursue our own resistance and victory. This is meant to be a new image of God.

How much of a change is being contemplated—and this is one of the serious objections to this thought process—is apparent from the approach to the question as to how God was involved in the suffering and dying of Christ. According to Wiersinga, this was not part of God's plan of salvation. The "factual cross of the Messiah" does have historical implications as an act that conquers all passivity and calls into being a chain reaction of love.

20.4. *Strongly diverging opinions*

On the basis of what Scripture teaches, pantheistic and deistic views must be totally rejected. It is characteristic of *pantheism* to identify God and the world with each other and of *deism* to separate God and the world from each other.

When pantheism is idealistically inclined, it views the world as subsumed in God and takes everything to be divine. When it has a materialistic tendency, it sees God as subsumed in the world, which leads to complete secularization. Everything is determined by a higher power or by the course of nature: fatalism or determinism.

In the form in which Augustine already combated it, deism employed the image of an architect who no longer enters the house that he has

8. H. Wiersinga, *Verzoening met het lijden?* (becoming reconciled with suffering?), 1975, 53, 60, 95, 84, 112.

constructed, because if he has done his work well, this is no longer necessary. Even better known is the image of the watchmaker who no longer needs to worry about the timepiece that he has made. It runs! In this mode of thinking God is viewed as the Supreme Being who has given the world and mankind enough independence to take care of themselves.

God's intervention in nature, God's hand in history, and God's guidance in human lives are then considered to be unnecessary or even impossible. Deism and atheism do not differ much from each other in practice.

What is withdrawn from God's sovereignty is assigned to the power of fate or chance. This is the only alternative. Bavinck points out that pantheism leads into the embrace of a pagan fate and that deism basically revives the pagan theory of chance (*R.D.*, 2:599–600).

The doctrines of fate and chance or fortune are both indeed of pagan origin. We therefore cannot agree with Berkhof (*C.F.*, 222–23) that the elbow room of creation is so great that chance and fate, though not having the final say, are certainly elements within a totality that ultimately is fully in God's hands.

Fate played an important role in the thinking of Stoic philosophers, and chance in that of Epicurus and his school. When these philosophers argued with the apostle Paul, the latter proclaimed to them that God, who has created the world, preserves and governs everything. He even gives everyone life and breath and everything. He allocates times and the borders of the habitations of the entire human race (cf. Acts 17:18, 24–28).

20.5. *Distinctions*

1. It has become common practice to distinguish between general and special providence; or between general providence (*providentia generalis*) that governs everything, special providence (*providentia specialis*) that applies to man and whereby the relationship between God's decree and our freedom naturally becomes of interest, and very special providence (*providentia specialissima*), i.e., the very special care of God for his children that is directly connected with his electing love.

In view of the emphasis that the Bible places on the very special type of providence, one could reverse the sequence so that very special care of God is assigned first place (see Wentsel, *Dogm.*, 3a:536).

How are God's providence and God's election related? Barth refers to providence as the execution of the decree of predestination (*C.D.*, 3.3.5). Elsewhere he provides the following formulation: God's providence is nothing but God's free grace, and God's free grace in Christ is providence.[9] In light of his doctrine of creation (see § 17.3, subsection 7), it is consistent that in his doctrine of providence his christological focus predominates anew. Just as in this broadened Christology, creation and redemption are merged into one, so are providence and redemption. There are others who hold that providence is part of predestination, whereby predestination is interpreted à la Barth (Beker and Deurloo, 1978, 27–36).

In this connection we point out that God's predestination and providence must be distinguished from each other. Only through faith in God's free grace in Christ can we come to the awareness of his direction of our existence (noetically), but this does not make God's providence (ontically) identical to his free grace (cf. Berkouwer, 1952, 37–38). God's special care for his children derives from the fact that he loves them with an everlasting love, but God's providence reaches much farther than his electing love (cf. Acts 14:16–17).

From a practical point of view, the important thing about God's providence is that we live from the hand of the God and Father of our Lord Jesus Christ. However, not everyone entrusts himself to him.

2. It has traditionally been the practice to discuss preservation, collaboration, and governance in sequence as aspects of God's providence.

Preservation (*conservatio*) means that God maintains everything through his power; governance (*gubernatio*) means that he directs everything to the goal that he has determined. Cooperation (*concursus*) implies that he does justice to the peculiar nature of his creatures and especially the freedom given to man.

We still need to consider whether cooperation should be viewed as a separate aspect of providence (see § 22.1).

§ 21. Preservation

21.1. ***Preservation and our dependence and responsibility***
21.2. ***Preservation and common grace***

9. K. Barth, *The Heidelberg Catechism for Today*, 1964, 62.

21.1. *Preservation and our dependence and responsibility*

"We mean by the providence of God [that through his] almighty and everywhere present power he upholds and governs all things" (Heidelberg Catechism, Lord's Day 10). When we list preservation and governance separately, this constitutes a distinction and not a partition. We are not dealing here with two differently oriented powers.

We may not identify creation and preservation with each other (see § 17.3, subsection 6). Preservation does tell us that God never forsakes or abandons his creation. He continually sustains everything that he has created, and his care extends to all creatures. What in connection with this has been cited from the Old and New Testaments (§ 20.3) speaks for itself.

Calvin reads in Psalm 104:29: as soon as the Lord takes away his Spirit, everything returns to dust. It does not say so literally. Yet it is not incorrect in this context to think of the cosmic work of God's Spirit who indeed also participated in the work of creation (Gen. 1:2). Then we can join Calvin in saying: "It is the Spirit who, everywhere diffused, sustains all things, invigorates unconscious and conscious life in heaven and on earth" (*Institutes*, 1.13.14). God is at work with his Spirit and his power not only in his work of creation but also in the preservation of everything that has been created.[10]

Berkhof seeks to interpret preservation dynamically: "This human world threatens to disintegrate, to destroy itself, to fall. But God stops its fall. He holds his hands under it. That is how he upholds (preserves) it" (*C.F.*, 219ff.). This is true to the extent that this upholding quite soon turns into the preservation of a world subjected to futility (Rom. 8:20) and of a humanity invaded by sin and death (Rom. 5:12). Hereby the question may be raised as to whether this preservation is essentially grace.

Heyns refers to preservation as a gracious act of God. As grace, preservation is also salvation: salvation from destructive sin and insidious evil (Heyns, *Dogm.*, 148ff.). Perhaps grace is interpreted too broadly here.

A second reason for reflecting on this is the controversy surrounding the doctrine of common grace advocated by A. Kuyper (see § 21.2).

The other side of God's preservation is the enduring dependence of all creatures on him. Everything is sustained by him, but everything according to its nature: heavenly bodies, angels, people, animals, plants, inorganic nature.

10. See W. Krusche, *Das Wirken des Heiligen Geistes nach Calvin*, 1957, 15–32. Heyns also points to this aspect of preservation in *Dogm.*, 296–98.

In the confessions as well as theology, reference is made to means that God employs in his wisdom and goodness (cf. Canons of Dort, 3–4.17). This implies that we should not ultimately rely on these means—food, medication, technical aids, manpower, sources of energy, or whatever else—and should not absolutize anything. We should not believe ourselves to be less dependent on God as a result of everything that we receive from him. The Old Testament contains the warning: "Say [not] in thine heart, My power and the might of mine hand hath gotten me this wealth" (Deut. 8:17).

We may not leave unused the means that God has provided to us, believing that God would also be able to help us directly. Healing upon prayer makes an impression. But healing that is God's answer to the prayer of a believer should leave no less of an impression when a physician has been consulted and the prescribed medications have had a favorable effect.

Conversely, it is also the case that we should not be at our wit's end if physicians are powerless. God is not bound to the means at our disposal. Whatever happens, he is the Hearer of prayer.

As Christians we recognize that everything depends on God's blessing. This does not mean that his blessing is only there to crown our own work. The Bible gives priority to God wanting to bless his creatures (Gen. 1:28; 9:1). He has promised his people rich blessings (Deut. 7:12–16). In this light we do the work to which we see ourselves called. Nehemiah says: "The God of heaven, he will prosper us; therefore we his servants will arise and build" (Neh. 2:20). In Isaiah we read that God has a hand in the correct way of plowing, harrowing, sowing, harvesting, and threshing. He grants wisdom for this. "This also cometh forth from the LORD of hosts, which is wonderful in counsel, and excellent in working" (Isa. 28:24–29). We therefore owe him praise and thanksgiving (Ps. 67:5, 7).[11]

The doctrine of providence teaches us how dependent we are, but it in no way diminishes our responsibility. Calvin already made this abundantly clear. God has entrusted to us the care for our lives, has provided us with means and support to sustain life, and also has ensured that we can anticipate dangers; and so that these events do not surprise us, he has made available to us precautionary measures and means.

11. Cf. C. Westermann, *Der Segen in der Bibel und im Handeln der Kirche* (blessing in the Bible and in the actions of the church), 1968; idem, *Theologie des Alten Testaments in Grundzügen* (principles of the theology of the Old Testament), 1978, 88–101.

It is clear that it is our duty to protect the life that God has granted us; to use the means that God puts at our disposal; to not recklessly plunge ourselves into dangers when he helps us to anticipate them; and not to neglect the medications that he provides to us. We are therefore in no way prevented from looking after ourselves within God's will and to regulate all of our affairs (*Institutes*, 1.17.4).

It may be added that our responsibility is not limited to our own lives. The belief that God preserves his creation and cares for all of his creatures persuades us to care for our fellow men and especially for all those who need help. It teaches us to treat with care everything that belongs to God's creation.

In light of objections that have been raised to various human precautions and provisions—taking preventive measures such as installing lightning rods, employing vaccinations, purchasing insurance, and engaging in contracts regarding the future—it is good to realize that the belief that everything comes to us from God's hand should not leave us passive. It is important for us to employ the gifts and possibilities that we owe to the Lord our God and to live in gratitude, patience, and trust out of his Fatherly hand (Heidelberg Catechism, Lord's Day 10).

21.2. *Preservation and common grace*

The term "to conserve" would not adequately describe preservation (*conservatio*). God's action is far more proactive. He has a purpose with sustaining a world that is continually developing and is exposed to evil powers. Preservation and governance should not be separated, and are directly related to each other.

What is the relationship between God and the world, and between God and man in this work of his? Does he offer grace within this relationship?

According to A. Kuyper, who elaborated his view in considerable detail in *De gemene gratie* (common grace, 1902–4), God offers grace to all people by allowing the world to carry on following the fall into sin. This is common grace, which needs to be distinguished from particular grace. It concerns an act of grace that has a negative as well as a positive side. In the first place there is the postponement of the full punishment for sin. Furthermore, the effect of common grace is constant as well as progressive. The aspect of constancy is the arresting and bridling of the curse of nature as well as sin of the heart, whereby there are various gradations. The other effect is progressive, "whereby God, with steady progress, protects human life more and more fully against suffering and brings it to richer and fuller inner development" (2:601ff.).

Kuyper could in part appeal to Calvin (cf. *Institutes*, 2.2.17; 2.3.3), although their emphases diverge. The idea of a steadily richer unfolding of life and culture is characteristic of Kuyper.

The Synod of the Christian Reformed Church stated in 1924 that according to both Scripture and confession, it is certain that apart from God's saving grace there is also a certain favor or grace of God that he grants to his creatures in general and not only to the elect.[12] This has been particularly strongly opposed by H. Hoeksema. According to him there is no common grace. The content of the gospel is not universal either. It is absolutely false that God genuinely offers his salvation to those who have not been predestined.[13]

In recognition of "differences of opinion" in the churches, which were also said to diverge from prevailing doctrines, the synod of the *Gereformeerde Kerken in Nederland* made a pronouncement about common grace in 1942. It said that God does not yet impose his full punishment on the fallen world during this dispensation. He bears it in his patience. He makes his sun rise over evil and good persons and provides heavenly good to all mankind (Matt. 5:45; Acts 14:17). In man there are still remnants of the original gifts of creation and there is some limited light of nature. These remnant benefits not only serve to absolve man of all innocence, but also to temporarily bridle sin in terms of its implications, and to ensure that possibilities originally embedded in creation would still be given a chance to unfold in this sinful world. In this regard God offers both evil and good persons unrestricted goodness, which among us is referred to as "universal grace" or "common grace," but which must indeed be distinguished from saving grace.[14]

This doctrine, quite reminiscent of Kuyper, is particularly disputed by Schilder. He believes that sin and judgment are indeed being restrained, but holds that grace and blessing are not being fully revealed either. There is indeed an unfolding of the gifts of creation, but this reflects nature rather than grace. The continuation of time and the cultural unveiling of the cosmos do not reflect (common) grace either. Neither are they a curse or judgment. They are the *conditio sine qua non* (= the necessary condition) for both sin and grace. They represent their substrate (Schilder, 1953², 60–65).

Kuyper's views are open to criticism. With his doctrine of common grace he believes he is able to explain that the people of the world frequently exceed our expectations and that human life advances astoundingly—a development that has implications both for now and for the kingdom of glory to be established on the new earth (Kuyper, 1902–4, 2:17; 1:461). This leads to strong cultural optimism.

According to Kuyper, culture is built on common grace. Analysis shows that the cultural process is based on the work of the Mediator of creation, while it is stimulated by the Mediator of redemption (cf. Douma, 1966, 267). But Schilder is interested in the obligation, the "common mandate." Since God's Christ conquers the world for God,

12. Scripture passages such as the following are referred to: Psalm 145:9; Matt. 5:44–45; Luke 6:35–36; Acts 14:16–17 and Romans 2:4.

13. See A. C. de Jong, *The Well-Meant Gospel Offer*, 1954, 11–55.

14. *Acta van de voortgezette Generale Synode van Sneek* (proceedings of the extended general synod of Sneek), 1939, article 682.

he turns the work of culture into concrete service of God. This is true of his people. Everything that is not based on faith is sin (Schilder, 1953, 48, 69).

We need to treat the term "grace" or "favor" with care. Isaiah 26:10 is perhaps the only Scripture passage that speaks of grace (favor) as being extended to the wicked. Incidentally, words such as "goodness" and "mercy" are indeed employed more generally (Ps. 145:9; Luke 6:35; Acts 14:17). In addition there is the word "long-suffering" or "patience." "The Lord is not slack concerning his promise, as some men count slackness; but is longsuffering to us-ward, not willing that any should perish, but that all should come to repentance" (2 Peter 3:9). It is true that God's long-suffering is sometimes encountered in a different context (see Rom. 9:22), and Schilder can point out (*H.C.*, 3:219) that God's protection in Scripture can also be protection from judgment (see 2 Peter 2:4, 9; Jude 6). This does not alter the fact that justice must be done to all words of Scripture, including Romans 2:4, which speaks about "the riches of God's goodness and forbearance and longsuffering."

Schilder sees the preservation of the world and mankind as an underlying layer or substrate for two extreme events: the verdict of acquittal and the verdict of banishment (1953^2, 64). He refers to the conservation of the world and the continuity of history and of the cultural scope together with the associated cultural reality (and still more) as being indispensable "for the preparation of the path to heaven as well as for proceeding down the roads which lead to hell" (*H.C.*, 1:373). We do not find this parallelism in Scripture (cf. Douma, 1966, 159–66, 261–63). In this closed thought process we miss that God does not fail to do good, and that the objective of his preoccupation with people is that they will seek him (cf. Acts 14:17; 17:25–27).

Does the covenant that God makes with Noah (Gen. 9) indicate that the preservation of the world and mankind is an act of God's grace? Kuyper takes this covenant as his point of departure. Also according to Bavinck, it is the covenant of God's patience or long-suffering (*R.D.*, 3:218).

Schilder, however, questions a covenant of long-suffering. We grant him that "covenant" in Genesis 9:8–17 can be interpreted as provision (*H.C.*, 4:133ff.). But we cannot go along with Schilder saying: "Day and night will continue and seasons come with fixed regularity—what else is this after all but 'saving' the earth for—fire?" (*H.C.*, 4:141). The covenant with Noah is very closely related to the covenant of grace, although it is not identical with it. The covenant of grace is surrounded by the covenant with Noah—which is sometimes referred to as the covenant of nature (cf. Bavinck, *R.D.*, 3:218, 255).

We far prefer to follow along with Calvin. According to Calvin, general (common) grace means that God, who is the source of everything good, grants various gifts to people, whereby society is sustained (Douma, 1966, 216–22). He has not abandoned mankind to itself. It is a miracle that he is continually preoccupied with a mankind that fell away from him. His goodness and patience do have a limit and a purpose. In terms of his purpose we think of the preservation of life and the progression of time, because in the entire world there needs to be scope for the gospel of his grace and—to employ Schilder's terminology—"nature" becomes God's shop floor, so that he can one day lay his church floor.[15] We therefore also think of the call to repentance, with which this time span is filled. This is the theme of invitation. This is coupled with a critical theme: those who disdain God's goodness cannot be excused (cf. Douma, 1966, 234–36).

We now come to a conclusion. We have objections to the teachings of Kuyper. We also have reservations about Schilder's position. A certain favor or grace of God toward everyone (Kalamazoo, 1924) is an overly abstract and general indication of God's preoccupation with his creatures. In Scripture, God's grace (Isa. 26:10), goodness (Ps. 145:9), and long-suffering (2 Peter 3:9) fit into a definite context. In connection with Romans 2:4, Calvin points out that earthly blessings for those who fear God are signs through which he makes his benevolence known. "However, when he approaches transgressors of his law with equal indulgence, he indeed desires to mollify their obstinacy, but he does not thereby testify that he is already graciously inclined towards them, but rather that he calls them to repentance."

The question as to how God relates to his creatures in preservation cannot be separated from the question as to how they relate to him. This is a personal matter for everyone who is addressed by him. All people receive impressions of God's goodness and patience. Only his children recognize in this his Fatherly favor and grace.

§ 22. Governance

22.1. ***Preservation and governance or preservation, cooperation, and governance?***
22.2. ***God's hand in history***
22.3. ***God's governance through Christ***
22.4. ***God's sovereignty and evil***

15. K. Schilder, *Wat is de hemel?* (what is heaven?), 1954², 187ff.

22.1. *Preservation and governance or preservation, cooperation, and governance?*

With respect to the doctrine of God's providence, there is a respectable tradition that distinguishes among preservation, cooperation, and governance. According to Bavinck, God sustains all things that he has made and works through them in such a way that they in turn cooperate with him as secondary causes (*causae secundae*, *R.D.*, 2:610). In the doctrine of concurrence (*concursus*) God is referred to as the primary cause, while his creatures are secondary causes—no more and no less (over against deism and pantheism respectively).

The portions of his work that Bavinck devotes to this topic do not belong to the most constructive aspects of his dogmatics. He states: "With his almighty power God makes possible every secondary cause and is present in it with his being at its beginning, progression, and end." The effect that proceeds from the two is one and the product is one. The effect and product are *in reality* totally the effect and product of the two causes, but *formally* they are only the effect and product of the secondary cause. It is God alone who supplies to a sinner all of the vitality and strength he or she needs for the commission of a sin. Nevertheless the subject and author of the sin is not God but man (*R.D.*, 2:614–15).

This train of thought fits eminently into the system of Thomas Aquinas. The traditional doctrine of concurrence is in fact the most scholastic element of the doctrine of providence (Beker and Hasselaar, *Wegen* = ways, 2:100).

The intention is clear. It reflects an attempt not to detract whatsoever from God's sovereignty and our accountability. To God we owe the faculties to accomplish something. But how do we use the gifts and powers that he grants to us? For this we are fully accountable.

It is, however, not obvious that God must be regarded as the primary cause, who with his almighty power makes the secondary causes possible, posits them, makes them move into action, and is present in them. When we consider the practical implications of what Bavinck says about the two causes and the single outcome, sin would formally be the outcome of the human cause, but in reality God would be implicated as the primary cause. Apart from the fact that this does not clarify anything, it also goes too far.

It may be objected to this doctrine of concurrence that if God cooperates with us, we also cooperate with him. But this is not in harmony with the relationship between him and us as we know it from his Word.

There is plenty of Scripture support for preservation and governance, but not for God's cooperation with us. Sometimes the term "*concursus*" is translated and interpreted as accompaniment (cf. Beker/

Hasselaar, *Wegen* = ways, 2:99–107), but this does not make any difference.

In the doctrine of providence it must be kept in mind throughout that God sustains and governs all creatures according to their kind. God treats people as people. Then it is unnecessary to imagine a special act of cooperation or accompaniment in addition to preservation and governance as far as man's place and role are concerned.[16]

22.2. *God's hand in history*

1. "Thy kingdom is an everlasting kingdom, and thy dominion endureth throughout all generations" (Ps. 145:13). In this manner it is confessed throughout Scripture that God rules. There are a number of psalms in which this is the central thought (Pss. 47; 93; 95–99). God's governance encompasses the past, the present, and the future. In no phase of history is this divine governance in any real danger of interruption (Berkouwer, 1952, 85). The Song of Moses sings about it: "The LORD shall reign for ever and ever" (Ex. 15:18). His beneficent deeds cause the psalmist to confess: the LORD is King forever (cf. Ps. 146:10: "The LORD shall reign for ever"). His kingship is manifested by his redemptive actions and his ongoing guidance, but also through his verdicts and his judgments.

He is the King of his people Israel. "Sing praises unto our King" (Ps. 47:6). He is also "the King of all the earth" and he reigns over the nations (Ps. 47:7–8). This is also clear from the history of which the Bible speaks (Isa. 45:1–8; Dan. 2:36–45). His kingship is universal (Ps. 103:19). It extends over all creation (Ps. 95:3–5). In Jeremiah we read: "There is none like unto thee, O LORD! and thy name is great in might. Who would not fear thee, O King of nations?" (Jer. 10:6–7).

All that God does has a purpose. He makes everything serve the coming of his kingdom. Therefore "all power is given unto [Christ] in heaven and in earth" (Matt. 28:18). In due time "the blessed and only Potentate, the King of kings, and the Lord of lords" will let us behold the appearance of our Lord Jesus Christ. "The time is at hand" (1 Tim. 6:15; Rev. 22:6–21).

16. See for a critique of the traditional doctrine of collaboration: Berkouwer, 1952, 125–60; Schilder, *H.C.*, 4:214–56.

2. History contains eloquent facts. In the Bible, Israel is continually reminded of its exodus from Egypt. "The LORD hath brought you out with a mighty hand, and redeemed you out of the house of bondmen, from the hand of Pharaoh" (Deut. 7:8).

Not infrequently, the question is raised whether in various poignant and awesome events, devastating disasters, and rescues from great misfortunes, special acts of God can be recognized. What happened in the past can appear as great miracles in our eyes. But are there still miracles today?

In scientific theories there is generally no room for miracles. A science that is aware of its boundaries will, however, be sufficiently modest to admit that it cannot explain everything and should hesitate to declare unexplainable events as impossibilities. C. F. von Weizsäcker states in this regard: contemporary natural science does not consider itself to be qualified to make any statements about the incidence of unique or exceptional events, which escape its methods, experiments, and control, neither about miracle narratives in the Bible.[17]

In our faith-based view of the work of almighty God there is indeed scope for miracles. The creation and preservation of the world are mighty miracles of God. God desired there to be a certain order. This order can be observed by us and laws can be inferred from it. However, God's acts can break through this order and regularity. This proves that he controls everything and that he does what pleases him.

3. How does God have a hand in history? Augustine thought deeply about this in connection with the fall of Rome. In his book *The City of God (De civitate Dei)* he explains that a state that is full of immorality and where egotism and lust for power predominate is bound to fall, but that the future belongs to the city of God. God guides his people to the everlasting Sabbath, the end without end. All of history—not merely a certain segment of it—can be linked with his providence (cf. Andresen, *Handbuch*, 1:432–45).

In the seventeenth and eighteenth centuries, it was customary to compare the Netherlands to Israel. "If anywhere, wondrous God, thy miracles shone, then here, in and around the Israel of thy Netherlands." The focus was on God's dealings with the Netherlands (A. Rotterdam). This could induce a certain sense of superiority, because Israel was the chosen people of God, but it also provided preachers with the opportunity to interpret the setbacks experienced by the Republic as punishments from God for the sins of the people. It was a "prophetic historiography.[18]

17. According to J. M. de Jong, "De opstanding van Christus" (the resurrection of Christ), in *Geloof en natuurwetenschap* (faith and natural science), 1967, 2:110–11), this was pointed out in a discussion.

18. Cf. C. Huisman, *Neerlands Israel*, 1983, 51–85, 129–45.

One needs to be careful in drawing parallels between Israel and one's own nation, for there is a difference between the history of redemption and the history of the world. One's national history is not a history of salvation. Not in every conflict can it be said of the defeated party that God's enemies perish.

We do not always see God's hand in what we experience, but we do believe that all of history—the history of the world as well as the history of God's people—is in his hand. Although this world is the theater of a tremendous battle between the kingdom of God and the realm of the evil one, God's plans do not fail.

Those who lack faith end up with a complexity of factors that determine the course of events, but they do not arrive at the recognition that God reigns. This cannot be directly inferred from the events themselves at any rate.

The believer, however, is convinced that the Lord reigns. The facts that occur to him are not always equally transparent and do not give him this insight. But he considers the acts of people, and definitely of those who "make history," in the light of the Word of God that speaks of good and evil, and of salvation and calamity. Rulers and nations cannot escape their responsibility. We think of the message that came to King Belshazzar: "The God in whose hand thy breath is, and whose are all thy ways, hast thou not glorified" (Dan. 5:23). Prophetic historiography in earlier days sometimes went too far in pointing to the hand of God in history. But "the divine mystery in history" (M. C. Smit) indeed exists.

The interpretation given by G. Groen van Prinsterer is open to criticism as far as its details are concerned. But he is correct when he emphasizes that the history of the world remains an enigma in the absence of Holy Scripture. Through faith we know its content and purpose: the fulfillment of the promise made in Paradise, the victory of the Messiah over the tempter.[19]

As long as we do not lose sight of what God means by his governance, we see the past, the present, and the future in a greater light. But there is hardly a more dangerous abuse of the doctrine of providence than that one seeks to sanction one's own affairs. When Hitler came to power in 1933, "German Christians" made themselves guilty of this (cf. Berkouwer, 1952, 162–64).

4. However, many do not discern that history is in God's hand. In their minds he exists beyond events. He appears to have been mar-

19. G. Groen van Prinsterer, *Handboek der geschiedenis van het vaderland* (handbook of the history of our native land), 1875[4], 1.

ginalized[20] and even entirely sidelined. People do as they like, and are they not in charge?

This can become a temptation for faith. Is everything not ambiguous? In light of shocking developments in one's personal life and in world events, has it not become more difficult to keep believing that God directs everything? Is it not easier to abandon this faith and to assume that he is outside these events and is actually not in a position to do anything about them?[21]

But we cannot surrender the belief that God governs. It is not true that he merely tolerates things. He does act proactively, but in his way and in his time. He does reign.

In Scripture, especially in the last book of the Bible, we are clearly shown how everything is related to the coming of God's kingdom. He governs in such a way that the history of redemption and especially the history of Jesus Christ is at the center of everything that happens. World events will continue to appear unfathomable to anyone who ignores this.

22.3. *God's governance through Christ*

1. Preservation and governance are the work of the triune God. The Son also rules over everything. When Christ says that all power has been given to him in heaven and on earth (Matt. 28:18), this does not, however, mean the divine "power of being" that he has as the eternal Son, but a special power that the Father has conferred on him as Mediator. The word translated as "power" signifies in the first instance: "executive power," "authority."

It is a power not limited to the church of which he is the Head. We should not interpret the difference between world history and church history to be that God rules the entire world and Christ only the church. The exalted Christ stretches out his scepter across the entire length and breadth of life. He is "above all principality, and power, and might, and dominion." God "hath put all things under his feet" (cf. Eph. 1:21–22). He is "the prince of the kings of the earth" (Rev. 1:5).

20. M. C. Smit, *Het goddelijke geheim in de gescheidenis* (the divine secret in history), 1955, 12.

21. This is the thinking of H. S. Kushner, *Als 't kwaad goede mensen treft* (when bad things happen to good people), 1983.

In the vision of Revelation 5, the Lamb takes the scroll from "the right hand of him who sat on the throne." Christ does not receive the scroll for consultation only. He opens it. When he breaks the seals, things transpire of which we read further on. God's judgments come upon the world, but the people of God are protected and preserved. This refers to the execution of the plan of God's counsel. Here we see that executive power is put into the hands of Christ.

Christ reigns on behalf of the Father. He is the "Head of his church, by whom the Father governs all things" (Heidelberg Catechism, Lord's Day 19). Van Ruler says: "God's governance then has the structure, the form, and the nature of Christ's governance" (*Ik geloof* = I believe, 115). This means that in all of history, the history of the church is central and the key is the coming of God's kingdom. Christ must indeed rule as king "till he hath put all enemies under his feet" (1 Cor. 15:25).

The entire world is Christ's domain, although the evil one has made it into occupied territory. Christ gives his church on earth the necessary room and makes the world into the sphere of activity for his church. Groen van Prinsterer could therefore say: "The vicissitudes of persons and nations through all generations and ages are subservient to the formation, maintenance, and glorification of his Church."[22]

2. A. Kuyper, and others after him, taught that there are two kinds of kingship: on the one hand kingship of the world, which emanates directly from God and establishes on earth the authority of governments, and on the other hand Christ's kingship which is not of this world but applies to a different realm. According to Kuyper, government authority therefore falls outside the sovereignty of Christ. A consequence of this is that prayer at a city council meeting should not bear a special Christian character.[23] Incidentally, in Kuyper's extensive writings one can also find various statements concerning Christ's all-encompassing sovereignty. From a biblical perspective it is, however, unthinkable that secular government would not fall under his sovereignty.

According to E. Brunner, state authority including the police, the military, and mandatory laws are needed precisely because Christ does not yet reign. He can indeed claim sovereignty, but its actual implementation is not yet universal. It is only potential, prospective. Brunner resists the idea that Jesus Christ is Lord over the state, which according to G. Dehn, O. Cullmann, K. Barth, and others is connected with a set of beliefs concerning powers, especially those of angels and demons, which is usually

22. G. Groen van Prinsterer, *Handboek der geschiedenis van het vaderland* (handbook of the history of our native land), 1875^4, 1.

23. According to S. J. Ridderbos, *De theologische cultuurbeschouwing van Abraham Kuyper*, 1947, 77ff., 248.

referred to as the christological foundation of the state. We reject this foundation (see further Berkouwer, 1952, 110–20). However, this does not imply that Christ's rule must be restricted to those who confess that Jesus Christ is Lord, as Brunner advocates (*Dogmatics* 2:338–40).

Governments rule by the grace of God and are in his service. But it is possible that they act entirely contrary to his will, become unfaithful to their calling, degenerate, and place themselves at the service of the evil one. They must protect the legal order and practice righteousness in the biblical sense of the word. Referring to Psalm 2:12, Calvin says that kings and rulers must be exhorted "to submit to Christ the power with which they have been invested, that he alone may tower over all" (*Institutes*, 4.20.5).

God, who "rules and governs all things according to his holy will, so that nothing happens in this world without his appointment" (Belgic Confession of Faith, article 13), "because of the depravity of mankind has appointed kings, princes, and magistrates; willing that the world should be governed by certain laws and policies. We believe [this to be the work of] our gracious God" (article 36).

3. Since preservation and governance are a single work of God's providence, somewhat more may now be said about preservation. How should preservation be viewed in the light of re-creation? Does it not point to the consummation of all things?

We may not confuse the preserving and saving grace of God with each other. Yet there is a link between preservation (*conservatio*) and redemption (*servatio*). In the discussion of issues surrounding common grace we saw that the covenant with Noah is not independent of the covenant of grace of which Christ is the Mediator (§ 21.2). Therefore objections must be raised against a synodical pronouncement of the *Gereformeerde Gemeenten in Nederland en Noord-Amerika* (Reformed Congregations in the Netherlands and North America, 1945 [known in North America as The Netherlands Reformed Congregations of the United States and Canada]), which says that common grace is *not* fruit of the atonement earned by Christ, although the Father governs all things through Christ. Common grace must then serve "so that the reprobate as well as the elect are brought forth, preserved, and governed to the glorification of God's righteousness and mercy according to his sovereign pleasure."[24] This has implications for both preservation and governance.

Those who realize how God has revealed himself in Christ and what he has placed in prospect must understand that preservation and governance are related to this as well and not only to predestination.

Thanks to Christ's work as Mediator there is a future. "According to his promise, we look for new heavens and a new earth, wherein dwelleth righteousness" (2 Peter 3:13; cf. Rom. 8:21). The re-creation of what is being preserved by God has everything to do with the work of Christ as Mediator. Therefore we must accept that this also applies to the preservation of what will be re-created by God.

22.4. *God's sovereignty and evil*

1. *The problematic aspect of theodicy.* If God is love, why is there so much misery in the world? If God reigns and he is omnipotent, why does he not prevent this? These questions, which are ancient, are continually raised anew. "Especially since both world wars, the question as to how the presence of so much evil in the world can be reconciled with the existence of an almighty and perfectly good God, has become one of the most central and crucial topics of theological reflection."[25]

It has already been argued that theology can be written off if it fails to incorporate experiences such as Verdun and Auschwitz into a theological framework (Van de Beek, 1984, 217). This is a strong statement, which has not remained unchallenged. Problems do, however, arise and on the basis of a flood of relevant new literature it can be inferred that many are intensely occupied with these matters.[26]

Aside from theology, philosophy has deeply reflected on this. Furthermore, the issue has been put into sharper focus by well-known writers such as F. M. Dostoyevsky, A. Camus, E. Wiesel, and M. 't Hart—to list but a few—and has been significantly broadened. In theology and philosophy, *theodicy* is the current term to indicate this problem. The word actually means: "justification of God."

24. Cf. Hofman, *Ledeboerianen en kruisgezinden* (precursors of the *Gereformeerde Gemeenten*, literally followers of Ledeboer and followers of the cross as opposed to the state in religious matters).

25. G. van den Brink, "Over de (on)mogelijkheid van een theodicee" (concerning the (im) possibility of a theodicy), *Th. Ref.* 32 (1989): 194.

26. Overviews of recent literature can be found in W. Sparn, *Leiden—Erfahrung und Denken* (suffering—experience and analysis), 1980, 247–72; and J. Lambrecht (ed.), *Hoelang nog and waarom toch? God, mens en lijden* (how much longer still and why? God, man, and suffering), 1989[2], 261–86.

In theodicy the focus is on the justification of God's direction, which one attempts to understand, so that despite its enigma it can yet be seen as being holy, good, and just (cf. Berkouwer, 1952, 232).

Theodicy has been advocated in various forms. We limit ourselves to discussing three of these, each of which has its own variants: dualistic, harmonistic, and pluralistic or dialectic theodicy.[27]

In theodicy of the *dualistic* type, one accepts that good and bad like light and darkness always stand next to and over against each other. There is a cosmic battle between these two fundamental principles. This is the gnostic interpretation.

In connection with the doctrine of the Creator and his work we have already radically rejected dualism, because it makes part of the world autonomous (§ 17.2). This detracts from God's sovereignty, while the entire Bible teaches that his kingship rules over everything, as stated in Psalm 103:19. Neither does it make sense to accept dualism in the present context.

A number of recent views are essentially dualistic, such as that of W. Monod (1867–1943),[28] or tend toward dualism. For example, H. S. Kushner says that God started out from chaos and created order where earlier randomness had ruled. But the random nature of chaos, which in itself is evil, persists in those corners of the universe where God's creative light has not yet penetrated. There is an aspect of reality that comprises—in addition to crime—factors such as earthquakes and accidents, and this is independent of God's will and fills him, like us, with anger and sadness. God does not cause those tragedies, but neither can he prevent them. He does help by inspiring people to provide assistance. Kushner does not even shrink from raising the following question at the end of his book: "Are you in a position to forgive and love God, even when you have discovered that he is not perfect and has left you out on a limb?"[29]

This theodicy has the charm of manageability and transparency.[30] The way to the God and Father of our Lord Jesus Christ, however, cannot be observed from this vantage point.

For theodicy of the *harmonistic* type, that of G. W. Leibniz (1648–1716) can serve as a model. The term "theodicy" was coined by him. He sought to combat skepticism by demonstrating that the present world is the best of all possible worlds. Leibniz employed the distinction among metaphysical, physical, and moral evils. The first of these implies imperfection, the second suffering, and the third sin. Physical evil coupled with moral evil must be interpreted as punishment and as a pedagogical tool. But ultimately everything proceeds from metaphysical evil, which is considered

27. There is a tendency to speak of six different models: the retribution model, the planning model, the pedagogical model, the compassion model, the substitution model, and the mystical model. Cf. H. J. M. Vossen and J. A. van der Ven, "Lijden (suffering), religie en communicatie als pastoral-hermeneutisch problem," *Praktische theologie* 17 (1990): 14–18.

28. See J. F. van Royen, *Het vraagstuk (*issue*) der theodicee bij Wilfred Monod*, 1942.

29. H. S. Kushner, *Als 't kwaad goede mensen treft* (when bad things happen to good people), 1983, 53–56, 131, 138.

30. C. Trimp, *Klank en weeklank* (sound and echo), 1989, 99.

to be an imperfection that serves to bring out perfection all the more. Dissonance is resolved in harmony.

With its explanation of evil, this type of theodicy, in which Stoic influence is clearly recognizable, eliminates the gravity of sin. As a rationalistic and optimistic theory it breathes the spirit of Enlightenment.

The same is true of so-called teleological theodicy, which is related to it. It is pointed out that good can come from evil. In this way one sometimes sees a positive side to the necessity of dying, i.e., making place for someone else.

Pluralistic theodicy, which is the most pervasive, is far more complex. Seemingly contradictory aspects of God's actions frequently are here combined, but there remains an element of tension. This theodicy could also be referred to as dialectical theodicy.

In the work in which he develops a modern theology of the cross, Moltmann seeks to achieve more than theodicy, but his sixth chapter comes quite close to it.[31] Moltmann replies to the objection of M. Horkheimer, who considers suffering in this world to be irreconcilable with the belief that God is omnipotent and perfectly good, by eliminating the contrast between God and suffering. God's being is found in suffering and suffering is found in God's being, because God is love. This theology of the cross observes God in the negative and the negative in God. This dialectical approach is panentheistic—neither theistic nor pantheistic. On Golgotha, all suffering became God's suffering, every death God's death.

It is apparent from this theology that it was born under the stress of the suffering of this time. But Moltmann's dialectic is more reminiscent of Hegel's philosophy than the words of Scripture.

Dialectics also plays an important role in Van de Beek's book entitled *Waarom? Over lijden, schuld en God* (why? concerning suffering, guilt, and God, 1984). God's feelings and involvement in what happens are interpreted as changeability on God's part. The issue discussed in this book is the area of tension between God's omnipotence and goodness. God is the almighty one—nothing passes him by. He is also ultimate goodness—there is no darkness in him. This tension, sensed by people, is ultimately rooted in God's heart.

This is one of the reasons why this conception, which actually is a doctrine of a nascent God or of a historical perspective within God, is unacceptable to us (see also § 13.5 and § 20.2).

We have now arrived at the question whether theodicy, in whatever form, really makes sense. A theologian who in this connection takes a critical view is Berkouwer. According to him the essential error of theodicy is the assumption that the world, with what happens in it, speaks its own language. God and his righteousness then no longer stand at the beginning of one's train of thought, but at the end. However, only in the light of God's justice can one speak meaningfully

31. J. Moltmann, *Der gekreuzigte Gott* (the crucified God), 1972, 184–267. Cf. M. Welker (ed.), *Diskussion über Jürgen Moltmanns Buch "Der gekreuzigte Gott,"* 1979.

about this world. Those who screen out this light, grope in the dark (Berkouwer, 1952, 247–49).

When theodicy is merely intended to justify God before the forum of human thinking, this criticism is well-placed. It would be quite presumptuous on our part to believe that we can or need to justify God. We rather depend on him to justify us through grace.

This does not detract from the fact that believers can indeed struggle with questions concerning God's providence. It is for this reason that we shall attempt to pursue the matter further.

2. *Theological considerations concerning the reason for suffering.* A distinction that is required for a discussion of evil is that between the evil of sin and the evil of suffering. In theological literature the latter frequently takes priority, especially since Auschwitz. But sin is the first and the worst evil of all. There is truth in the saying: at the bottom of all questions lies the world's guilt of sin.

Ever since Augustine the following thought process is familiar: God, who created man, desired the latter to love and serve him voluntarily and not through coercion. This implies that man was at liberty to refuse to do this and to opt for evil. Therefore evil cannot be blamed on God, but only on man who abused his free will. This is known as the "freewill defence."

It is a line of reasoning that appears convincing and is valid from a logical point of view, but which—as admitted by a thinker such as A. Plantinga—yet offers cold and abstract comfort to those who are struck by evil. This approach based on the doctrine of creation calls for amplification.

At creation God did not place man at a crossroad, but on the right way. He sought from man a response of love, trust, and obedience. As we know from Scripture, however, the reality is apostasy from God. "By one man sin entered into the world, and death by sin" (Rom. 5:12). God hates and punishes sin. Not only guilt and stain, but also suffering, death, and the dominion of the prince of this world form part of the punishment for sin and its consequences. Man dragged everything along with him in his fall. For this reason creation is no longer what it was when it came out of God's hands. We have caused this incongruity.

When we restate the questions that arise in us from the perspective of this reality, they appear different to us than when we have no eye for this. Schlink says: when we start out from the reality of our sins, the incomprehensible thing is not the evil from which we suffer, but the patience with which God bears with us (*Ök. Dogm.*, 201). The Bible teaches us to take seriously the reality of God's wrath over our sins. This brings us—in a different way than in Moltmann's theology—to the cross of Christ on Golgotha. He "died there for the ungodly" (Rom. 5:6). This precedes all of our questions! It has been correctly pointed out: "Those who start out from Auschwitz start out too far down the road. They should start out from Gethsemane and Golgotha."[32]

The cross and the resurrection demonstrate what God has done about evil. Beyond this lies what he is yet to do.

We cannot ignore Christology here, or pneumatology. How do we think about these profound questions? And what is our relationship with God? The former depends directly on the latter. The important question is whether we find ourselves within the orbit of faith.

The author of Psalm 92 sees what happens to the ungodly and how they are about to perish. He ends with the confession that "the LORD is upright: he is my rock, and there is no unrighteousness in him." When Asaph enters God's sanctuary, he sees the light (Ps. 73). What Job's friends advocated resembled theodicy, but they were reprimanded. Job did not benefit from their theories. He needed an answer from God. When he encountered God everything changed.

A history such as Job's proves that people cannot resolve the problem of evil. It must be brought into God's presence. "Thou beholdest mischief and spite, that thou mayest take it into thy hands" (Ps. 10:14). God's hand is to his children the hand of their Father (Heidelberg Catechism, Lord's Day 10). "Faith does not find the *perspicuitas*, the perspicuity, which it continues to seek, but rather a perspective in the sense of insight (per-spicio = through-sight) and prospect."[33]

Even after Christ's death and resurrection there continues to be evil in a multiplicity of forms. However, one of the axioms of the Christian faith is the certainty that God will have the last word. He says: "Behold, I make all things new" (Rev. 21:5). His kingdom is coming in all of its glory. Precisely the observation and experience of the enormous power of evil, in the brokenness of this life, makes believers long for complete redemption. Those who come out of "great

32. C. Trimp, *Klank en weerklank* (sound and echo), 1989, 102.
33. G. van den Brink, "Theodicee en Triniteit," *Th. Ref.* 33 (1990): 25ff.

tribulation" receive the comfort that "the Lamb shall feed them, and will guide them unto living fountains of waters: and God shall wipe away all tears from their eyes" (Rev. 7:14–17).

It is fine to raise questions about the existence of evil and the sense of suffering. In doing so, however, we should stay within the bounds of God's revelation. The confession leads us in this way (Belgic Confession of Faith, article 13):

"In this world nothing happens without God's sovereign involvement." But what about evil?! "God neither is the author of nor can be charged with the sins which are committed. He orders and carries out his work in the most excellent and just manner, even when devils and wicked men act unjustly." Since there is a great deal that we cannot understand, the Belgic Confession of Faith adds: "And as to what he does surpassing human understanding, we will not curiously inquire into farther than our capacity will admit of; but with the greatest humility and reverence adore the righteous judgments of God, which are hid from us, contenting ourselves that we are pupils of Christ, to learn only those things which he has revealed to us in his Word, without transgressing these limits. This doctrine [of providence] affords us unspeakable consolation, since we are taught thereby that nothing can befall us by chance, but by the direction of our most gracious and heavenly Father; who watches over us with a paternal care" (see also Matt. 10:29–30).

In this article of faith we encounter the words "permission" and "will": we are "persuaded that he so restrains the devil and all our enemies that without his *will* and *permission* they cannot hurt us."

The word "will" could be clarified with Augustine's profound statement, which is cited by Calvin, that even what happens against God's will, in a wonderful and unspeakable manner does not occur without his will (*Institutes*, 1.18.3).

There are things that happen of which we must say that the evil one has a hand in them. When it comes to the devil's part we cannot ignore the word "permission," although it has been objected that this does not explain anything. It indicates that there is a certain amount of scope for what should not be there and that God does not prevent all evil that people do to each other or themselves. On what basis should we expect this from him? However, it does not imply that he lets us do as we please. It is conscious and not passive permission.[34]

Bavinck says of sin that God tolerates and suffers it. "He would not have tolerated it had he not been able to govern it in an absolute holy and sovereign manner" (*R.D.*, 3:64). God does more to sin than to permit it. He hates it, he forbids and hinders it, he condemns and punishes it, and once the measure of sin becomes full, he once and for all puts an end to it. We think of the prophecy: "They shall not hurt nor destroy in all my holy mountain: for the earth shall be full of the knowledge of the LORD, as the waters cover the sea" (Isa. 11:9).

34. Calvin employed this word in his *Institutes* with reservation, but apparently did need it for his sermons. Cf. R. Stauffer, *Dieu, la création et la Providence dans la prédication de Calvin* (God, creation, and providence in Calvin's preaching), 1978, 276ff.

3. *Suffering in the light of the Bible.* In the preceding reflections we already ended up at Christ's cross and resurrection. Those who ignore what God has done in Christ find no way out.

No one has ever suffered like the Man of Sorrows. He was not spared in any way. This illuminates the suffering of those who are his. Precisely when they must suffer, they may find themselves close to their Savior, in his suffering and dying but also in his victory. Nothing will be able to "separate [them] from the love of God which is in Christ Jesus" (Rom. 8:35–39).

There are in the Bible plenty of examples of believers who were profoundly concerned about suffering. They were preoccupied with it before the face of God. The psalms of lamentation frequently contain complaints about the evil committed by people, but even then the psalmists look upon God and say, Why, O God? Lamentations not only refers to enemies, opponents, and persecutors, but also says: "The Lord was as an enemy." It is immediately added that he "is good unto them that wait for him, to the soul that seeketh him" (Lam. 2:5; 3:25). The prophet Habakkuk starts out with: "O LORD, how long . . . ?" He ends with: "Yet I will rejoice in the LORD, I will joy in the God of my salvation" (Hab. 1:2–3; 3:18).

According to Bavinck, suffering serves not only for retribution, but also as testing and chastisement, as reinforcement and confirmation, as witness to the truth and to glorify God" (*R.D.*, 2:618). This statement can be supported from the Bible.[35]

a. The suffering that comes our way can constitute punishment from God. The Bible links punishment with sin. The Old Testament speaks a clear language in this regard. Israel is seriously warned about the curses that will come its way if it does not listen to the voice of the God of the covenant (Deut. 28:15–68). Amos says: "Shall there be evil in a city, and the LORD hath not done it?" (Amos 3:6).

C. S. Lewis wrote a treatise on suffering, *The Problem of Pain* (1947), which appeared in a Dutch translation under the title *Gods megafoon* (1957). He calls suffering God's megaphone in order to wake up a deaf world.

It contains a call to repentance. The same thing is true of the judgments God poured out over his people Israel and the judgments with which the world is threatened according to the book of Revelation. In connection with a disaster in Jerusalem, whereby eighteen people perished, the Lord Jesus says: "Except ye repent, ye shall all likewise perish" (Luke 13:5).

35. What follows here corresponds with sections from J. van Genderen, *Actuele thema's uit de geloofsleer* (current topics in the doctrine of faith), 1988, 55–57, 59ff.

b. But there is also suffering that is not punishment. It can be a means employed by the Lord to instruct his people and to advance them in his school of life. It is then referred to as chastisement or discipline. This is how the book of Hebrews sees it (Heb. 12:11).

c. Sometimes it is more testing than chastisement. An example is the oppression of Israel in Egypt for which there was no obvious basis in terms of Israel's sin. This is even clearer in the story of Joseph and in the life of Job. The people of God are sanctified through suffering. "Tribulation worketh patience; and patience, experience; and experience, hope; and hope maketh not ashamed" (Rom. 5:3–5).

d. Bavinck further mentions strengthening and confirmation. When he is hit hard, Job says: "The LORD gave, and the LORD hath taken away; blessed be the name of the LORD" (Job 1:21). He replies to his wife: "Shall we receive good at the hand of God, and shall we not receive evil?" (Job 2:10). In the midst of his suffering he has a bright prospect: "My redeemer liveth" (Job 19:25). It brings Job closer to the Lord, as appears from the last chapter of the book: "I have heard of thee by the hearing of the ear: but now mine eye seeth thee" (Job 42:5).

e. A further point is that suffering serves as testimony to the truth. In Acts 5 we read of the apostles, who had been imprisoned and flogged, that they were glad "that they were counted worthy to suffer shame for his name" (Acts 5:41). This is the suffering for Christ's sake that the Savior has given to his followers as their prospect. They share in Christ's suffering (1 Peter 4:13–16).[36] Precisely when the church is a church under the cross, the Lord grants comfort and strength. Paul says: "For as the sufferings of Christ abound in us, so our consolation also aboundeth by Christ" (2 Cor. 1:5).

f. Suffering is therefore also glorification of God. Here we think of Paul and Silas, who having been flogged and imprisoned, pray and sing praises to God. The other prisoners listen to them (Acts 16:25).

Even when we see the suffering of believers in the light of the cross of Christ, much can remain incomprehensible and enigmatic. Job did not receive an explanation of the questions that perplexed him, but he did receive indeed a satisfactory reply. Everything changes for the children of God when they listen to the voice of their Father and live out of his hand. For Christ's sake the bitterness is removed from their suffering.

Psalm 22, the psalm of: "My God, my God, why hast thou forsaken me?" is also the psalm of "but" (nevertheless): "But thou art holy, O thou that inhabitest the praises of Israel" (Ps. 22:1, 3). It is a psalm of the bitterest suffering, but also a psalm that ends with a song of praise.

God can be encountered in the sanctuary (Ps. 73:17). Then one surrenders to his leading. The poet of this psalm testifies to surrender, security, and trust, and looks forward to God's glory (Ps. 73:23–28).

Suffering leads to glory. Here come to mind Bible words such as Romans 8:18: "For I reckon that the sufferings of this present time are not worthy to be compared with the glory which shall be revealed in us" (see also 2 Cor. 4:17–18).

Suffering, like evil, does not belong to creation as God willed it. At the completion of his work of re-creation they will no longer be there. Through the suffering of this

36. See W. H. Velema, *Geroepen tot heilig leven* (called to holy living), 1985, 125–27.

life we look forward all the more strongly to the new world where tears and death, mourning, complaining, and pain will be things of the past (Rev. 21:4).

Some Literature

A. van de Beek, *Waarom? Over lijden, schuld en God* (why? concerning suffering, guilt, and God), 1984.

E. J. Beker, K. A. Deurloo, *Het beleid over ons bestaan* (direction for our existence), 1987.

G. C. Berkouwer, *The Providence of God*, 1952.

K. Dijk, *De voorzienigheid Gods*, 1927.

J. Douma, *Algemene genade* (common grace), 1966.

B. W. Farley, *The Providence of God*, 1988.

H. G. Fritzsche, . . . *und erlöse uns von dem Übel* (. . . and deliver us from evil), 1987.

H. Kuiper, *Calvin on Common Grace*, 1928.

A. Kuyper, *De gemeene gratie* (common grace), 3 vols., 1902–4.

J. Lambrecht (ed.), *Hoelang toch en waarom toch? God, mens en lijden* (how much longer and why? God, man, and suffering), 1989[2].

C. H. Lindijer, *Het lijden in het Nieuwe Testament* (suffering in the New Testament), 1956.

B. J. Oosterhoff, *Het koningschap Gods in de Psalmen* (the kingship of God in the Psalms), 1956.

K. Schilder, *Christus en cultuur*, 1953[2].

T. Schneider, L. Ullrich (ed.), *Vorsehung und Handeln Gottes* (providence and acting of God), 1988.

W. Sparn, *Leiden—Erfahrung und Denken* (suffering—experience and thinking), 1980.

R. Stauffer, *Dieu, la création et la Providence dans la prédication de Calvin* (God, creation, and providence in Calvin's preaching), 1978.

W. H. Velema, *Kernpunten uit het christelijk geloof* (key points of the Christian faith), 1978.

J. Westland, *God onze troost in noden* (God, our comfort in need), 1986.

Chapter 8

Man as the Image of God

§ 23. Biblical data

23.1. *Introduction: subject and method*

The question asked in every study of man (anthropology) is: what is man? Three aspects of this question are: where does he come from; what is the meaning of his existence; and what is his future?

Various disciplines deal with these questions. Formerly anthropology was part of philosophy. Psychology also concerns itself with man, albeit especially with his inner life. Sociology focuses on man from the perspective of the social relationships in his life. Social psychology is a combination of the latter two. It is obvious that man also figures prominently in law, medicine, and ethics. It may be said that in these latter three disciplines man is approached somewhat differently than in the preceding disciplines. Jurisprudence and ethics view man primarily as an acting subject; medicine deals with man's health or recovery from illness.

Psychology, sociology, and social psychology do not leave man as acting subject out of consideration. The emphasis, however, is on the desire to acquire knowledge about man from the specific perspective of each of these three disciplines.[1]

What does theology say in its chapter on anthropology? Theology does not seek to be a partner or rival of psychology or sociology. It is even less its intention to provide a complete overview of what the aforementioned disciplines and those not mentioned say about man.

The aim of theology is to determine what can and must be said about man from the perspective of the Bible as God's revelation. This means that we must speak first of all about man as creature of God and more specifically about man as God's image. This latter description differentiates man from all other creatures. This description is the most characteristic of what we can say about man on the basis of the Bible. This chapter will therefore be primarily devoted to a discussion of the biblical notion that man is the image of God.[2]

Here we face a problem. In the Scriptures we come across this notion from two perspectives: from the point of view of creation before the fall into sin, and from the point of view of redemption after the fall into sin.

In Genesis 1–3 we find very fundamental data about man as created by God. However, there is far more to be found in Scripture, i.e., everything that pertains to being the image of God.[3]

Those who are only prepared to address the additional data about man once a discussion of the doctrine of sin and redemption has taken place must split anthropology into two parts, namely, one part dealing with man prior to the fall into sin and another part that follows upon a discussion of sin and redemption. We consider it incorrect and in fact impossible to proceed in this manner. Calvin wrote in this connection: "For although I acknowledge that these are summarizing figures of

1. See J. van Genderen, *Actuele thema's uit de geloofsleer* (current topics in the doctrine of faith), 1988, 106–88, and in general the collection *Wat dunkt u van de mens?* (what do you think of man?), 1970. Consult also Kwant, 1975.

2. A. König has attempted to combine the various images of man to arrive at an "ecumenical anthropology" (1988).

3. In this connection we will not address the question whether the image of God must be understood especially as viewed with reference to Christ. See Bavinck, *R.D.*, 2:533ff.; Van Niftrik 1951; and both studies of G. van Leeuwen (1959 and 1975).

speech, yet the principle is unassailable, that the key element of the renewal of God's image was also the main focus in creation itself" (*Institutes*, 1.15.4). We consider ourselves justified in discussing all biblical data concerning man in the present section.

This chapter on anthropology concerns itself with a number of fundamental aspects of what being human means. We have in mind:

- body and soul in their diversity and cohesion;
- heart and spirit, together with the question whether these two terms indicate the same thing or whether despite their similarity there is nevertheless a difference;
- freedom and constraint. What does it mean that man is free? Is it an absolute freedom? Is his freedom of choice immune from the pernicious influence of sin?
- the meaning of sexuality. A human being is created as man or woman. What significance does this gender distinction have for human experience?
- living together as human beings. How are individuality and sociality related?
- the equivalence of all human beings and at the same time everyone's individuality that makes him different from others and is himself;
- man's place in creation, his dominion over creation, nature, and culture;
- the future of man, individually as well as collectively. How does it end up? This in turn is related to the question: where does man come from and what has happened in the course of history?

Theology examines biblical data about being human in the conviction that these data cannot be ignored by other disciplines—if they are willing to listen to the Bible. This does not limit the field of research of the other disciplines. It is precisely the other way around: in their own fields of research and in the development of their scientific knowledge the other disciplines deal with the same human being as we do here. God has revealed fundamental perspectives concerning man, his origin, essence, and destiny, which any other discipline can ignore only to its own detriment and therefore also to the detriment of the very human being with whom it is concerned.

23.2. *Created by God in his image*

Man occupies a unique place in creation. (a) This is immediately evident in Genesis 1 and 2. In Genesis 1 the account of creation culminates in man. He is the pinnacle of what God accomplishes in the six days of creation. Bavinck points out that in man the spiritual and material worlds are joined together (*R.D.*, 2:511).

It is noteworthy that the creation of man is preceded by God deliberating within himself. We now quote the passage in its entirety because we need to discuss a number of aspects of it in more detail:

> "And God said, Let us make man in our image, after our likeness: and let them have dominion over the fish of the sea, and over the fowl of the air, and over the cattle, and over all the earth, and over every creeping thing that creepeth upon the earth. So God created man in his *own* image, in the image of God created he him; male and female created he them. And God blessed them, and God said unto them, Be fruitful, and multiply, and replenish the earth, and subdue it: and have dominion over the fish of the sea, and over the fowl of the air, and over every living thing upon earth" (Gen. 1:26–28).

The introductory formula in verse 26 is the same as in verses 3, 6, 9, 14, 20, and 24. It points to uniformity in the powerful acts of creation. However, in the earlier verses we do not read of God deliberating within himself.

(b) The special place of man is also brought out in the blessing that God pronounces over him and in the mandate that he gives him. God's deliberation within himself and his addressing man mark the unique position that man occupies among the other creatures. Man is special.[4]

(c) In the third place, the unique place of man is apparent from the fact that in Genesis 2:4b–9 we come across a second account of man's creation. Much has been written about the fact that right in the beginning of the Bible we encounter two creation narratives. B. J. Oosterhoff characterizes the difference as follows:

> "We could say that in Genesis 1 man, the pinnacle of creation, is the top of a pyramid. Everything works towards the crown of creation, man. In Genesis 2 man is more the centre of a circle. Everything is grouped about man. Without man, creation is still empty" (Oosterhoff, 1972, 98).

A great deal of thought has been given to the use of the plural in 1:26. Does this already foreshadow the doctrine of the Trinity? The verse says emphatically that God deliberates within himself. This points to a plurality within God.[5] We cannot see that this formulation would

4. Barth correctly points out that this concerns an act of fellowship between the speaking of God and the one addressed. *C.D.*, 3.1.191.

5. Moltmann speaks of a *pluralis deliberationis*, 1980, 30; also 1985, 224. A. van Selms, *Genesis 1 (POT)*, 1967, 35, reminds us that we find this "self-consultation" on the part of God also in Genesis 3:22 and 11:7. See also the broad discussion in Barth, *C.D.*, 3.1.191, and in § 12.1.

refer to God consulting with his heavenly court. We do not encounter such a notion anywhere else in the Bible. Furthermore, angels would then play a creative role in the creation event. They would form part of the image according to which man is created. Instead, we are dealing with consultation of God within himself. Some believe that here we can still recognize remnants of polytheism. This is out of the question. Genesis 1 shows us God as the Only One in the omnipotence of his speaking (cf. Ps. 33:6; Isa. 55:10ff.).[6]

We now turn to the meaning of "in our image" (*betsalmenu*; from *tsèlèm*) and "after our likeness" (*kidmuthénu*; from *demuth*). Later on in this chapter we will present a concise overview of the various interpretations of these words. In the course of the centuries they have been distinguished from, as well as identified with, one another.

It may be clear in any case that only man receives this special designation. It points to the special relationship in which man is placed relative to God and the other creatures.

A detailed discussion of *tsèlèm* can be found in *THAT*, 2:556–63 (H. Wildberger) and in A. Kruyswijk, *Geen gesneden beeld* (no graven image), 1962, 192–94; of *demuth* in the same place, 195–97. Consult also C. Westermann, *Genesis*, 1:201–3, with references to a great deal of literature; Berkouwer, 1957, 40–42; and Wentsel, *Dogm.*, 3a:especially 592–97.

According to Westermann, *tsèlèm* means sculpture, plastic image, carved pillar, and also idol (Ezek. 7:20; Amos 5:26; Num. 33:52).

Demuth points to equality, image, and copy. Westermann refuses to accept a meaning of *demuth* that would be weaker than *tsèlèm*.

Both words, *tsèlèm* and *demuth*, say the same thing. The difference in nuance may be interpreted to imply that the one complements the other. It concerns a relationship in which something of God is represented, depicted, and made visible. *Tsèlèm* articulates this depiction and *demuth* indicates that this is done correctly. The image matches and resembles what it is meant to depict. We feel comfortable with de Beus's description, 1968, 23: an image that in many respects resembles the person depicted, without being identical with it.

This contradicts all those exegetes (frequently dogmaticians) who think that they can or should demonstrate a rather fundamental difference between image (*imago*) and likeness (*similitudo*). Especially striking is the progression from image by virtue of creation to likeness by virtue of the history that man is to go through. Luther and Calvin broke with this traditional interpretation and cautioned against any

6. This does not mean that we see man as being specifically created in the image of the eternal Son, as De Reuver, 1980, suggests. Kamphuis, 1985, 28ff., correctly attacked this point of view.

similar interpretations that might come along in the future. They equated *imago* and *similitudo*.

Decisive in this connection—one encounters this line of thought in many publications dealing with the image of God—is that the prepositions "in" (*be*) and "according to" (*ke*) alternate in Genesis 1:26 and 5:1. Subsequently, both terms appear separately and alternately: image and likeness in 1:26; image by itself in 1:27; likeness by itself in 5:1; likeness-image in 5:3. In the New Testament: image by itself in Colossians 3:10 and likeness by itself in James 3:9.

Where only one of these two words is used, the context makes clear that we are nevertheless dealing with the notion of Genesis 1:26. Precisely since these two complementary terms are used in essentially the same sense, they can occur by themselves or in any sequence. We may conclude that since both words are completely equivalent, an explanation in terms of a double image, in which the two words are assigned an entirely different content, is out of the question.

We now focus on the meaning, the intent of both words. For this we must consider data from the Ancient Near East.

It will be clear—as pointed out emphatically by Vriezen (*Hoofdlijnen*, 187–89)—that the words "image" and "likeness" in no way detract from the essential difference between God and man. God precedes all of creation. The creation of man and the world is an act of God's power. Precisely because God, as the Eternal One and the Almighty One, stands absolutely above creation and precedes it, he is able to call it into being (see § 17 above). Vriezen points out that although the expression "image of God" does not mention the father-child relationship, it is nevertheless intended. This must reflect "the desire to avoid giving the impression that the relationship between God and man would be a natural one" (189).

While in the Near East, image and likeness are always used in connection with an image of the Godhead *manufactured* by people, in the Bible precisely these words are applied to human beings created by God! Despite similar terminology, there is a radical difference in terms of content. Against the background of the Ancient Near East, we shall have to look for the meaning of "image" and "likeness" in terms of representation. As Kruyswijk states correctly, God "desires to be represented by him" (194). Man enjoys an unparalleled relationship with God. This is disclosed in the fact that he is God's image.

The same applies to *demuth*. Kruyswijk correctly states: "It is not so important whether man is deemed to look like God; likeness implies much rather that in a certain respect he *behaves* like God; that he acts as God's representative on earth and thus displays his image" (197).

With this interpretation we opt to define the image of God as viceroy over creation. We now face the question whether this says it all. Is representation all there is to the image? And what are we to think about man's body? What of his spiritual, moral capacities? Are they part of the image of God or do they fall outside it? In this connection Noordegraaf correctly points out that formerly the essence of man was sought in the attributes given to him, while today the entire emphasis is on relationship (1990, 32). The shift goes still somewhat further, since relationship is now narrowed down to representation. Representation (dominion over creation) fills out and finalizes this relationship (man as responding being). The response to God is also evidenced in dominion over creation.

See further Wildberger, *THAT*, 2:562; Berkhof, *C.F.*, 142, 187; Westermann, *Genesis*, 1981, 2:16ff.; Wolff, 1974[2], 223ff. Schilder puts the emphasis on dominion; see the extensive discussion in Kamphuis, 1985, 20–36 (these pages are not devoted to Schilder alone). See also Berkouwer, 1957, 51–56.

In contrast with past and present one-sidedness, we must do justice to the *many-sidedness* of Genesis 1:26–28. We discover this many-sidedness by unbiased listening to the passage itself. By unbiased, we mean not being bound by various models of interpretation that have been put forward over the centuries.

God created man in his image and likeness. This means man is God's image and likeness. The *image* (from now on we shall only mention this term, although we continue to have both in mind) cannot be incidental to being human! It would be in conflict with the direct formulation of the passage to imagine a two-stage scenario: first man is created by God; next he is made into God's image. By what means would he then be made into God's image? With Schilder and Kamphuis (25ff.), we would be forced to say that the image of God consists solely in the mandate that man receives at his creation. Only those who see it this way can maintain that the image of God is incidental to being human as created by God.

We are of the opinion, however, that in this case dominion over creation would not have been the only content of the purpose clause in verse 26. The image of God would also have been included here. Only then would the passage have forced us to interpret the image of God as the purpose behind the creation of man. Then indeed would the image of God have coincided with and been equivalent to dominion over creation (*dominium*). However, this explanation is in conflict with the passage. As created by God, man *is* the image of God. With Noordegraaf we wish to plead for not falling from one one-sidedness into another.

We are of the opinion that God's image implies the relationship between Father and child. We posit this because we are obliged to do so on the basis of Ephesians 4:24 and Colossians 3:10.

We wish to go still further, however. The image of God does not only encompass the Father-child relationship. It also has an ontic aspect. With this we mean that being human in body and spirit (in contrast with any other creature) is part of the image of God. It is clear from Genesis 1:26 that one cannot think about man as created by God without bearing in mind the notion of the image of God. Conversely, this also means that the image of God is unthinkable without involving this human nature physically created by God. The image of God is not only defined in terms of those qualities that distinguish man from animals (mind, freedom of choice; in short—as they put it formerly—man is a moral, rational being). The image of God encompasses more!

On the other hand, however, the image of God is unthinkable without involving this "substantial" (corporeal) basis. Those who refuse to do so must seek the image in something incidental. Precisely this explanation is in conflict with the simple, clear formulation of verse 26.

Having said this, we can do justice to both other elements in the passage. Verse 27 is especially decisive here. Being male and female is a clarification of being "in the image of God." First it says, "created he him"; then, "created he them." Just as our being corporeal belongs to the image, so does gender differentiation. Man (Adam) is God's image. If one wants to speak of a collectivity here (as Noordegraaf does, 1990, 34), this can only be done in the sense that each member of humanity is God's image. No one excepted! This has, as we shall see, far-reaching consequences for the rejection of every form of discrimination, e.g., on the basis of race, skin color, or social-intellectual status. Every human being is God's image. This is true of man and woman. Woman is not God's image as gender-neutral creature. Neither is man. The image of God is manifested in (implied by) being human. Further specified: also in the differentiation between being male and being female! If a gender-neutral collectivity, i.e., humanity, were to be God's image, gender differentiation would be excluded. Then a significant aspect of human existence (gender differentiation, on the basis of which marriage, procreation, family life—all three enclosed in and through love) would fall outside the image of God. The entire development of humanity would take place outside the notion of the image of God. We are of the opinion that gender differentiation is part of the image of God in the sense that both man in his masculinity and woman in her femininity are God's image. This image also finds expression in the relationship in which they stand to one another; most intensively and exclusively in marriage; more generally, but no less importantly, in their mutual relationship within social contexts and political relationships.

Here lie important building blocks for a biblical ethics of marriage and the equivalent treatment of women and men. On these grounds discrimination against women must be rejected. The contemporary denial of the difference between man and woman, resulting in the recognition of homosexual relations as being equivalent to heterosexual relations, implies an attack on the biblical notion of the image of God.

We return once more to the question whether dominion is the sole purpose of the image of God, or whether it forms an essential part of it. We believe that the image includes dominion among other aspects. One cannot view dominion as incidental to the image. Conversely, the mandate to have dominion cannot be properly explained if it is not implied by being God's image.

In this connection we reiterate that gender differentiation is also part of the image. How could man execute his mandate with respect to creation if he did not procreate? The notion of history, of the historical development of culture, is based on human procreation. In these several respects man is called upon to make God visible. The execution of this task cannot be achieved without the right relationship with God. This is a Father-child relationship. With respect to the image as *dominium*, it is important that J. Kamphuis, in following Schilder, nevertheless says that in determining the content of the image of God we should not restrict ourselves to a single term. The viceroy is a child of God (Kamphuis, 1985, 30ff.; Noordegraaf, 1990, 33). In our judgment, this is essentially a biblical notion. It should indeed be added, however, that being God's image is not incidental to being God's child. On the contrary, being God's image is unthinkable if being God's child does not form part of it, although it is not equivalent to it. It is the child that represents God, his Father, on earth.

All of this gains in significance when we observe God addressing man. The Lord blesses and gives him a mandate. The blessing pertains to man's life as God's image, and precedes the mandate. Being God's image includes among other aspects dominion over the earth. There God seeks to be visible in the obedient, loving service of humans toward each other and toward creation.

In Genesis 1:26–28 we do not find a definition of the image of God. We do find building blocks for a biblical doctrine regarding man as child of God and as viceroy over creation. That we do not have a complete description is also apparent from the fact that elsewhere in Scripture we encounter data that complement the passage referred to. We shall return to this.

We now focus on the dominion of man according to Psalm 8. "Thou hast made him a little lower than the angels, and hast crowned him with glory and honour. Thou madest him to have dominion over the works of thy hands; thou hast put all things under his feet" (Ps. 8:5–6).

Here we do not find the words "image" or "likeness," but indeed their poetical echo. This psalm tells of the glory of the work of God's hands and man's place in it. On the one hand he is puny, small, compared with stars, the heavens, sun, and moon. On the other hand he is more exalted than everything else that has been created. The question is whether *Elohim* here should be translated as "God" or "angels." Especially considering the context, we opt with many others for the rendering "God." Nowhere in the Bible are angels placed in a context of dominion over the earth, and of the related notion of having been created in God's image. It is undeniable that we are dealing with a comprehensive description of the image of God, even though the term is not used.

It is not hard to see where the difference between God and man lies. A "little lower" reflects the fact that God has dominion as Creator, while man derives dominion from his Creator. Man, as image and likeness of God, does not stand beside but above all other creatures. He shares this elevated position with God. He himself, however, stands below God.

23.3. *The breath of life breathed into his nostrils*

"And the LORD God formed man of the dust of the ground, and breathed into his nostrils the breath of life; and man became a living soul" (Gen. 2:7).

This passage covers two perspectives. In the first place, man is formed from the dust of the earth. Man is therefore a corporeal being (see also in this connection 3:19; 1 Cor. 15:47).

Thus man is not only spirit. The corporeal aspect is not incidental or inferior. It is the element from which man has been created. Thus the metaphor of the potter in Isaiah 29:16 has a deep, anthropological significance (cf. Isa. 45:9; Rom. 9:21).

However one wants to think about the specific nature of man, his derivation from dust is part of it. The above passage, however, provides a second piece of information that we need to take into account immediately. This is the spirit of life that is breathed into man's nostrils. The *nephesh* is just as characteristic of man as the fact that he is taken from dust. Still more precisely formulated: the uniqueness of man is that he is dust and at the same time through the *nephesh* a living being. The unity of these two is characteristic of man. In Isaiah 57:16 the Lord recalls that he himself has given the breath of life.

We do not see a contrast between Genesis 1:26–28 and 2:7. The latter verse is an elaboration of the former. Man, who has been created in the image of God, has been formed from dust and been equipped with the breath of life.

From Genesis 2:7 must be concluded that man is absolutely dependent on God, his Creator. When the LORD removes life's breath from man, he returns to the dust from which he has been taken (Gen. 3:19; Ps. 104:29). Striking is what Job 1:21 says: "Naked came I out of my mother's womb, and naked shall I return thither" (see also Eccl. 5:15). This expression points to what in Genesis 2:7 is called "dust of the ground." To return to dust is then the same thing as losing the spirit of life and returning to the mother's womb, the earth. As far as the corporeal aspect is concerned, beginning and end touch one another.

This observation is confirmed by the remarkable statement of Paul in 1 Corinthians 15:49. He writes there that "we have borne the image of the earthy" man. To him, image and earth (dust) are related. But he continues: "we shall also bear the image of the heavenly" man.

Between these two—earthy (earthly) and heavenly—a comparison is made: "as we . . . ."

In this context we discuss briefly the word *nephesh*. *Nephesh* has several meanings in the Old Testament. In Genesis 2:7 it means breath, the principle of life, and thus the life of man: man's existence between birth and death. It is therefore not simply the everlasting soul or the principle of eternity in man. Those who wish to pursue this must take other biblical ideas into consideration.

Nephesh therefore refers to life: Jeremiah 38:16; Psalm 31:13; 35:7. This word further indicates the seat of emotions, such as desires, love, hatred, hunger, and thirst. See Psalm 103:1; Psalm 31:10.

In the third place *nephesh* can also be described as man's subjective side, his "I" or his individual personality. The term can then be translated as "I," although with this translation one does lose the unique character of this word (Ps. 105:18b; Song 5:6).

The fourth meaning is a broadening of the third one: someone, all those who, especially in provisions of the law (Lev. 7:20a; 11:10; 23:30).

Finally, yet more broadly: a living being, man or animal (Gen. 1:20; 2:7; 9:16). In Leviticus 26:11 even God refers to "my soul." We shall have to infer the specific meaning of *nephesh* relating to man from the context; in this particular case from the passage under discussion.

Regarding this passage see Wentsel, *Dogm.*, 3a:589; Becker, 1942, 95. At this point we do not address the relationship between *nephesh* and *psyche*, except to say that the LXX uses *psyche* 755 times as the translation of *nephesh*. Regarding the term "heart," see Oweneel, 1984, 61.

23.4. *Man still God's image after the fall into sin?*

"Whoso sheddeth man's blood, by man shall his blood be shed; for in the image of God made he man" (Gen. 9:6).

This verse indicates that even after the fall into sin man continues to be referred to as God's image. The author goes beyond mentioning the fact. God attaches a consequence. He who kills a fellow human being, i.e., the image of God, forfeits the right to continue to live on earth as God's image. This is the general tenor of this verse. We leave aside what this implies in concrete terms for the ethics of the death penalty.

It is indeed clear that having been created in God's image is and remains a decisive datum. It is the basis of the death penalty. Viewed in this light, this verse strongly reinforces 1:26. In no event can one read it as a weakening of 1:26, no matter what the consequences of sin may be for the image of God.

Even if like Aalders one were to apply the motivation to the entire preceding pericope, it would still not be a weakening of its significance, but rather a reinforcement by broadening the application to so many.[7]

We wish to pass along two comments on this verse from Calvin's commentary: "Since men bear his image, God deems himself to be offended in their person, when someone is killed." Calvin says further that God, the Creator, keeps the purpose of the first creation in mind even though man has become corrupt. However much corrupted through sin, the significance of man's life has not been reduced in value. Man continues to derive his significance from his being created in the image of God.

In spite of sin, we encounter the identification of man as God's image in the New Testament in James 3:8–9: "the tongue . . . therewith bless we God, even the Father; and therewith curse we men, which are made after the similitude of God" (*homoiosis*).

Mussner refers to the "ganze dämonische 'Paradoxie' der Zunge" (entirely demonic paradox of the tongue): we praise God and a few moments later we curse the creature of the same God. This curse strikes at God himself, because people have been created in God's likeness. This having been created in God's likeness is illustrated with countless passages from Jewish commentaries.[8] As far as the intention of this reasoning is concerned, James says here the same thing as in Genesis 9:6. However the consequences of sin for the image of God are described, it is undeniable that man is viewed as God's image. This is especially apparent from the perfect tense of the verb *ginomai*. This perfect tense does not indicate what once happened and has now passed. No, it remains valid. If this were not the case, the statement as argument would lose all of its precision and force. The fact that so many centuries after creation, and the fall into sin in Paradise, the children of Adam are still called God's image, points to continuity in biblical anthropology, despite the discontinuity brought about by sin.

The question then is why the New Testament nevertheless says that man must be renewed according to the image of Christ. Is man, despite the express statements of these three passages, no longer the image of God? How can this be: the image corrupted and yet persisting?

7. G. Ch. Aalders, *Genesis*, 1949², 1:234.
8. F. Mussner, *Der Jacobusbrief*, 1975³, 187ff.

How can one still speak of man as God's image following the fall into sin? Calvin points us in the right direction in his commentary on Genesis 9:6 already quoted. He says that God keeps in mind the purpose of the first creation. Man has been created with particular qualities, in a particular relationship, and with a particular mandate. As a consequence of sin man has rendered impossible the execution of this mandate. Through disobedience and unbelief he has broken the relationship with God. This does not relieve him of his task. He has not become a different creature, e.g., an animal or a plant. He continues to be called to represent God, even though he is no longer able to do so.

The Belgic Confession of Faith speaks of "small remains" of the image of God (article 14). We do not want to look for these in particular qualities that man has retained. Even these qualities (formerly referred to as image of God in the broader sense) have been impaired by sin. The remnant is man himself, addressed in terms of his original calling.

Can we say with Schilder that the image of God is only a matter of the past and of the future? (*H.C.*, 1:312). In this case one can no longer speak of the image of God after the fall into sin and prior to the restoration. Yet the Bible does so. Why? It is because man continues to be addressed in terms of his original calling and purpose, and because restoration does not mean the creation of something from scratch. Restoration means renewal of what has been corrupted.

Recreatio!

We attempt to rephrase the problem of discontinuity and continuity by referring to man as the image of God in an absolutely negative manner (*in a negative mode*).

This indicates radical corruption. This also says that renewal can and must occur if man is to be once again what he originally was and what God has in mind for him. The fact that man is still called God's image points back to the past and to the possibility of restoration. The negative mode can become positive again through the Holy Spirit. What does this require?

Hoekema[9] distinguishes between *structural* and *functional* aspects of man as God's image (1986, 68–73). He uses these terms in lieu of distinctions made by others: image of God in the broader and narrower sense (Bavinck), formal and material (Brunner), substance and relationship (Berkhof). We are of the opinion that "functional aspect"

9. We also refer to the book by Hughes, 1989. It takes the same approach as Hoekema, but at certain points is broader and more penetrating.

represents a too-formal approach, and that the "structural aspect" is equally as affected by sin as the functional.[10]

Hoekema does not say enough about corruption brought about by sin, and also too little about the right relationship. We seek a middle way. We go a bit further than Douma, who holds that the prerequisites for the image of God have remained. These prerequisites, however, are not the image itself. We have the impression that Douma wants to go beyond Schilder. He does consider holiness and righteousness to be part of the image.[11] This is more than just the right execution of the mandate!

Douma also says that his reply to the question whether the unbeliever is still God's image is not an unqualified no. "It is no, but . . . ." (74). He compares man to a temple. Due to sin, man has become an empty temple. One may not, however, speak disparagingly of that temple, or tear it down.[12]

It occurs to us that Douma has the same idea in mind as we do: to find a way between the partly present image of God and its absolute loss so that one can no longer call sinful man the image of God in any sense. What Douma calls the empty temple, we describe as the image of God in a negative mode! A radical renewal is called for.

23.5. *Christ as the image of God*

In 2 Corinthians 4:4, Paul calls Christ the image (*eikōn*) of God. We encounter in this verse also the word "glory" (*doxa*). Paul refers here to the glory of Christ that comes to us in and through the gospel. The gospel is the medium of Christ's glory. Through preaching, the glory of the gospel of Christ begins to radiate. Pop says: "The sentence could end here."[13]

Yet Paul makes a further point. He refers back to Genesis 1:26, where man is called the image of God. Being God's image includes the mandate and authority to represent the one whose image is borne (Pop, 116). Paul calls Christ the image of God in the context of glory. This is to say in any case that he as the image is a pure reflection (and revelation) of God. "In his speaking, acting, and attitude it has become knowable and tangible how glorious God is. He was and gave a pure reflection of this glory" (Pop, 116). With his coming to earth and his work here, Christ is the image of God in the full sense of Genesis 1:26.

10. See Bavinck, *R.D.*, 2:553–54; Brunner, 1941, 521, and *Dogmatics*, 2:56ff.; Berkhof, 1960, 46–48. For a brief summary, see Berkouwer, 1957, 49–59.

11. J. Douma, *De Tien Geboden* (the Ten Commandments), 1985, 1:73n24.

12. Every image falls short. Yet we find the reference to an empty temple not suitable, as though the formal aspect is still completely intact. The building itself has also been affected by sin.

13. F. J. Pop, *De tweede brief van Paulus aan de Corinthiërs* (the second letter of Paul to the Corinthians), 1962^2, 115ff.

Here we encounter anew the image of God in a positive mode. Christ is not put on an equal footing with Adam here. He is linked with Adam (as Paul does in 1 Cor. 15:45–49). In this sense we can say that Paul applies Adamic categories to Christ (Ridderbos, *Paul*, 70–75). What Adam lost through disobedience is revealed to us anew in Christ. Second Corinthians 3:18 implies that out of Christ we are granted the renewal after his image. It is undeniable that the significance of Christ is described to us in terms derived from the creation of man in God's image.

Versteeg (1971, 333) states that Paul's discussion about causing light to be shone in our hearts through the gospel of glory (2 Cor. 4:6, 4) should be understood against the background of Genesis 1:3 where God says: "Let there be light." We would not designate the relationship between Adam and Christ as fulfillment. Fulfillment presupposes that what is being fulfilled would not otherwise be full. Then the creation of Adam as image of God in Paradise would not be complete, not fulfilled without Christ! The latter does take up and carry on what Adam has destroyed through sin. There definitely is a connection and continuation, but through the graceful coming of Christ. Also in Colossians 1:15 Christ is called "the image of the invisible God, the firstborn of every creature." As in 2 Corinthians 4:4 we encounter here the word *eikōn*.

In Romans 8:29 we read: "For whom he did foreknow, he also did predestinate to be conformed to the image of his Son." Here Christ is called *eikōn*. He is the image of God. We will be conformed (*symmorphous*) to him. In this way we will also once again display the image of God. The purpose of God's predestination is conformity to Christ's image! In other words: being once again the image of God, as God had originally created Adam. In this verse we encounter the same eschatological thrust as in Philippians 3:21 and 1 John 3:2.

But not only at Christ's return can we expect a complete renewal. It appears from 2 Corinthians 3:18 that the change takes place already now. The key word in this verse is being "changed" (*metamorphoumetha*) into the image of Christ. Here also we find the image (*eikōn*) and the glory (*doxa*) in juxtaposition. Being his image is manifested in the glory, while the glory pertains to being his image.

We opt, without detailed justification, for the rendering *reflect*. This reflection of God's glory is equivalent to being transformed in the image of Christ. This is an ongoing process, in terms of both time and gradation. As time progresses, we may indeed speak of becoming increasingly glorious (transformed). Paul uses here a Semitic manner of speaking.

This verse shows how the image of God is restored in the faithful. In this regard Christ is both norm and point of reference, because he himself is the image of God. This is an ongoing process under the guidance of the Holy Spirit. With Versteeg (1971, 332) we can say that this developmental process is achieved by the Lord Jesus Christ through the power of the Spirit. Here we see the direct connection between Christ who is the image of God and the restoration of that image in believers.

23.6. *The new man: knowledge, righteousness, and holiness*

In Ephesians 4:24 and Colossians 3:10 we encounter a further clarification of the transformation to the image of Christ. In Colossians 3:10 Paul speaks of "put(ting) on the new man, which is renewed in (full) knowledge after the image of him that created him." Radical renewal is called for to be able to display this original image. The verb "to create" points to an act of divine power. We can hear verses 2:9–10 resonate in this verse. The goal and the measure of this renewal is the original image of God. As in 2 Corinthians 3:18, the verb is put in the present tense (present participle). The process is in motion and continues. The putting on of the new man (cf. Rom. 13:14) points to the responsibility that believers are to exercise in this regard. The "put(ting) off of the old man" underscores this.

The objective of this renewal is knowledge. It points to the totality of the salvation granted in Christ. Here we find an extension of Genesis 1:26. Having knowledge turns out to be part of the image. It is a full, rich knowledge that is a matter of both head and heart (*epignosis*).

The context indicates that this knowledge is centered on Christ. This was obviously not yet the case in Paradise. It is, however, unthinkable that in Paradise true knowledge of God would not have formed part of the image.

In Ephesians 4:24 we encounter to some extent the same thought process; the difference is that here Paul does not speak of knowledge but of righteousness and holiness. "Created after God" recalls the original act of creation. It is worked by God in the putting on of the new man. These qualities of righteousness and holiness contrast with the tendencies of the old man. Righteousness pertains to agreement with God's law. Holiness points to an inner disposition that is good and sound. Both words typify man in his relationship with God. Both are implicit in and form part of the image of God. Man can only represent God on earth and display God's love as long as he lives in the right relationship with God and is obedient to his will. Knowledge, righteousness, and holiness are neither the presupposition nor the prerequisites of the image. They belong to the essence of the image. Precisely the restoration of the image brings these three gifts to light. Although they are not mentioned specifically in Genesis 1:26–28, it is inconceivable that they would not have been part of it. Otherwise redemption would add something to the image that was not originally part of it. On the basis of these passages we may conclude in hindsight that knowledge, righteousness, and holiness already belonged to the image of God in Genesis 1:26.

23.7. *A few conclusions*

1. In Genesis 1 we do not find a scientific description or depiction of man. We find instead an indication of the nature of man as God intended it. Elsewhere we find additional data that must be considered in discussing (the nature of) man.

2. As the image of God, man has the responsibility to represent God on earth. We can also put it this way: to make visible the love of God for mankind and creation.

3. According to Ephesians 4:24 and Colossians 3:10, knowledge, righteousness, and holiness belong indeed to the (restored) image of God. This image exists in the right relationship with God, that of Father and child.

4. This relationship must be reflected in the interaction of people with one another and with creation. Man may rule over creation. He may only do so by reflecting God's love for creation. God's child must conduct himself as the offspring of the King.

5. This dominion is only feasible through the procreation and development of the human race. Gender differentiation is characteristic of man as God's image, and for the task assigned to him.

6. Man, as created by God, is God's image. All gifts received by man pertaining to both body and spirit form part of this. The image is not merely the sum total of these gifts. Man is to use them in relation to God, himself, his neighbor, and creation.

7. The image of God includes a vertical relationship. This vertical relationship must be reflected in horizontal relationships. God's child on earth is his servant on earth. Being child and being servant are complementary. Being servant is realized in the experience of being child of the King.

We reject the notion that the gifts are merely prerequisites for the image, which in this case would be limited to the mandate of an office. We similarly reject the idea that the mandate would fall outside the image, and thus be incidental to the image.

8. The fact that man must be renewed to the image of God by becoming transformed in the image of Christ proves that the original image has been lost.

The fact that both the Old and New Testaments confirm that Adam's descendents have been created in God's image implies that they continue to be addressed in terms of the originally intended image of God. There is simultaneously complete discontinuity and continuity. We formulate this complex situation as follows: sinful man displays the image of God in a negative mode. The fallen child cannot renounce its descent, even though it seeks in every possible way to blot out the memory of the Father. Sin is the refusal to display the image of the Father and to make the image visible in relation to fellow humans and creation.

9. The image includes more than just the relationship to God, or just a mandate on earth. Only one who acts as subject can maintain a relationship. One can, however, not speak of a subject while ignoring the action of the subject. We reject the separation between ontic, structural, substantial aspects on the one hand and functional, relational aspects on the other hand. Both perspectives belong to the image of God. Both have been impaired by sin. Both subsume a calling that remains valid.

10. Christ came as the image of God. Believers are renewed to be conformed to him through the power of the Holy Spirit. This renewal is a dynamic process, which proceeds from glory to glory. It has an eschatological thrust. Perfection is attained on the new earth!

§ 24. Voices from History

24.1. *Irenaeus and Thomas Aquinas*
24.2. *J. Calvin*
24.3. *E. Brunner*

24.1. *Irenaeus and Thomas Aquinas*

1. We first mention *Irenaeus*, in recognition of the great influence of his concepts. In his *Adverses Haereses* (Against Heresies) (185) he deals with the creation of man. His objective is to combat gnosticism.

Man has been created by God. He is carnal, earthly, and of an animal nature. As such, man is the image of God (*imago*). However, he does not yet have the likeness (*similitudo*). He becomes this likeness when he receives the Spirit. The Spirit must unite himself with the soul in the body if there is to be likeness (5.6.1).

Despite the fall into sin, man has retained his nature as a free and rational being. In the background there is the Greek connotation of rationality and freedom to make decisions. This freedom also brings with it responsibility. We would rather refer to this as man's anthropological endowment. This corresponds with the image that man has received at creation (4.3.4). Unbelievers also (continue to) have this image. However, they lack the Spirit originally received by Adam (5.6.1).

Verburg points out that "this depiction is not always reproduced with equal sharpness and balance" (1973, 73). It would not misrepresent Irenaeus to say: man is created after the image of the Word, which subsequently becomes flesh (1.16.1). This image is still incomplete because the Word, after whose image man is created, is as yet invisible. Likeness hinges on the Spirit (5.6.1). The complete man consists of dust that is created after God's image, a soul breathed in by God, and a spirit. The soul is the connection between body and Spirit. The soul belongs to natural man. Man has lost the likeness connected with the Spirit. This was easy since the image was still invisible.[14]

Here one encounters the trichothomistic concept of man held by Irenaeus. The soul is viewed as the transition between image and likeness. In our view the soul should be part of the likeness, but here appears to be identified with the image! At any rate, in this way Irenaeus avoids stating that man loses the image along with the likeness. The former remains intact. However difficult it is to retrace this formulation, one thing is clear: the image is there, without the Spirit. The

14. Verburg, 1973, 73, and the accompanying notes on page 247.

likeness is again restored later through the Spirit of Christ. Prior to the fall into sin the likeness was there, but rather vaguely so. Christ had not yet become flesh. The dichotomy between image and likeness (reminiscent of Greek dualism in anthropology) is here incorporated into the framework of a salvation history progression from creation to redemption, with Christ as the key transition point. Irenaeus's anthropology is characterized by a combination of this dualism with a salvation-historical approach.[15]

2. *Thomas Aquinas*[16] continues the line of Irenaeus's dualism in his *Summa theologica*. According to him, the image of God consists primarily of reason and intellect (1.Q.93.2). Only rational creatures can be the image of God. This covers angels as well. Their rationality is more perfect than that of humans. For this reason they are more the image of God than mankind (1.93.3).[17]

The image of God can be considered from three perspectives. In the first place there is the natural aptitude to know and love God, which is unique to all human beings. It is man's moral nature. The second perspective consists in knowing and loving God in deed and habit (*actu et habitu*). This is still incomplete. This image (*imago*) exists due to conformity (*conformitas*), which is the fruit of grace. In the third place there is the perfect knowledge and love of God. This is the likeness (*similitudo*). This fits in with (the kingdom of) glory. The first image is found in all people, the second in the righteous, the third only in the blessed (1.93.4).

Thomas draws a careful, but nevertheless clear distinction between image (*imago*) and likeness (*similitudo*) (1.93.4).

Man consists of body and soul (1.75.4). The soul is to the body as form is to dust (1.75.5). Man has a threefold soul. He has the first one in common with plants, the second one with animals. The third is characteristic of people. This is the so-called

15. A very detailed image is presented by Andresen (*Handbuch*, 1:83–87). He emphasizes the synthesis of creation and redemption (anthropology and Christology) in the history of redemption. Cf. J. N. Bakhuizen van den Brink, *Incarnatie en velossing bij Irenaeus* (incarnation and redemption according to Irenaeus), 1934, 34, who points out that the redemption perfects that which was incomplete. Redemption is a synthesis that implies at the same time a true development.

16. We have to skip the intervening period. We refer to the study by W. Otto on the anthropology of J. Scottus Eriugena, 1991.

17. We use the edition of Sac. Petri Caramello, produced by Clem St. Suermondt, 1948. We omit the letter Q. (i.e., question; we would use the expression "subject") from these references.

intellectual soul (intellectiva, 1.76.3). This intellectual part of the soul includes the intellect as well as the will (1.77.8; 1–2.80.2). Knowing God is possible only via what he has created (1.2.2). Hence the possibility of theistic proofs (1.2.3). The will is subject to the intellect (1.82.3); Thomas also writes that the seat of the will is the intellect (voluntas in ratione est, 1.87.4).

We will not pursue the description of the human soul in any further detail. Verburg presents a rather comprehensive overview (1973, 85–88).

We nevertheless mention that man is not created under grace. Man has indeed been created good. Nevertheless, the lower powers of man (*vires*) are not subject to reason (1.95.1). As a result of this inner division, reason is not naturally subjected to God. Man needs the gift of supernatural grace. In consequence, as created, man cannot manage without grace! Here we encounter what for Thomas (and the later Roman Catholic theology) was a decisive dichotomy between the natural and the supernatural (i.e., grace). Sin robs man of supernatural grace (1–2.85.1). We should, however, not overlook the fact mentioned earlier, that (supernatural) grace was already required to make the lower passions subject to reason.

In this regard we are struck by a parallel with Irenaeus. The latter also recognized an imperfection in man as created. We referred to this as dualism. Thomas maintains a similar dualism, but he does not see it as part of the history of redemption. Thomas develops it with his distinction between natural and supernatural being (*ontologically*).[18]

Our conclusion is that in this conception grace is dominant. Nature is an independent stratum that cannot manage without grace. This results in a curious duality in Thomas's view of man. This duality is oriented toward connectedness and harmony. Yet this duality is essential. The image of God remains after the fall into sin, to the extent that the image is found in the natural, rational soul of man. By nature man is good, but not altogether so.

Thomas takes an intermediate position, which appeals to many. This has proven to be the case throughout the centuries, and remains so today. Exactly because of this intermediate position, grace—however central—must share its place with the capacities that man possesses by nature. In this way the radical nature of sin is misperceived, and so is

18. Verburg (1973, 92) speaks in this connection of a suspending. In our view the emphasis must be placed on the dualism of nature and grace. Nature needs grace. Grace complements nature. This is a matter of ontology.

the radical nature of grace. The weakening of this radical condition is clearly recognizable in Thomas's conception of man, who despite the fall remains image of God.[19]

24.2. *J. Calvin*

We now turn to Calvin. Of central significance is Calvin's exposition in *Institutes*, 1.15.3, although the image of God is of course also discussed elsewhere in this work as well as in his commentaries.

To Calvin there is no doubt that the real seat of the image of God is the soul. He recognizes that our outward appearance, to the extent that it distinguishes and separates us from nonrational creatures, at the same time more closely joins us to God. The key is that the image of God is spiritual. In opposition to Osiander he points out that the body does not belong to the image in the same way as the soul. The capacities of the soul are the intellect and the heart (1.15.3; 2.2.2) as well as knowledge and the deeper emotions (affections) (commentary on Gen. 1:26). The angels have also been created after God's image. Appealing to Matthew 22:30, he maintains that our highest level of perfection will be attained when we become like them.

Adam was God's image. This points "to the perfection with which he was endowed, when he was strong through correct understanding, had affections that were within the bounds of reason, senses which were all properly interrelated, and through his exceptional gifts genuinely projected the excellence of his Maker" (1.15.3). One cannot really read these last few sentences without seeing a rejection of Thomas in them!

In the subsequent paragraph he says that man has fallen out of this state through sin. However, the image of God in him has not been completely annihilated and destroyed. However, it has been spoiled to such an extent that what remains is a horrible caricature.

In 2.2.12, Calvin says that the natural gifts of man have been corrupted by sin, and that he has been stripped of the supernatural gifts. The image of God in man has thus been deformed (commentary on Gen. 1:26).

19. In his dissertation De Grijs has presented an interpretation of an early publication of Thomas. He suggests that nature is grace by definition. The duality that we refer to has been synthesized by him.

With respect to earthly matters, the intellect has been weakened (2.2.13–15, 22). As far as heavenly matters are concerned, man is no longer capable of anything (good) (2.2.13, 18).[20]

Yet man has the sense that God is the Creator (1.3.1). This seed of religion (*semen religionis*) is supported by what we know of God through creation (1.5.1) and his rule of the world (1.5.7).

This seed in no way leads, however, to the right knowledge of God. Knowledge, righteousness, and holiness have thus been lost.[21]

We will not pursue any further the gradation that can be identified in these surviving remnants. They have been described by Verburg (1973, 96–97). What remains is owed to God's common grace. It never serves to excuse, but precisely to accuse man.[22]

One can definitely not consider these remnants to be a point of contact for grace. In his commentary on Colossians 3:10 and Ephesians 4:24 it becomes clear that only the Spirit can renew the image of God in us. Faith plays a crucial role in this regard.[23]

The recovery of our blessedness consists in renewal through Christ. The latter is also referred to as the second Adam. *Institutes*, 1.15.4, also discusses the well-known passages of Colossians 3:10 and Ephesians 4:24. Calvin concludes that in Paradise the image of God was visible in man in the light of his intellect, in the uprightness of his heart, and in the soundness of all his constituent parts. We have already pointed out (§ 23.1) that these elements, generated by renewal through the Spirit of Christ, also stood out in creation itself.

He considers it unlikely that likeness with God consisted in the dominion entrusted to man. Indeed, this likeness is not to be sought outside of man. It is the innermost essence of the soul (for these two paragraphs see 1.15.4).

Nevertheless, based on his commentary on Genesis 1:22, dominion is still a (minor) aspect of the dignity with which God clothed man.

20. Peters (1979, 88) points out that with his distinction between being before the face of God (*coram Deo*) and being before the face of man (*coram homnibus*), Calvin has succeeded better than Melanchthon in capturing Luther's distinction between *homo theologicus* and *homo mortalis huius vitae*.

21. One can find numerous references listed by Torrance (1951, 102–8), Krusche (1957, 68–76), and Hoekema (1986, 43).

22. See especially the commentary on Ps. 8:5 and also J. Douma, *Algemene genade* (common grace), 1966, 222–28.

23. Hoekema, 1986, points out that in all places where the grace of God is portrayed as indispensable, man's responsibility is repeatedly underscored.

With this we must bring this section to a close. Our conclusion is that Calvin has a vision that runs counter to that of Thomas. Calvin's treatment of the image of God accentuates the necessity of the grace of God (as correctly concluded by Verburg, 1973, 94). He sees fallen man as continuing to be God's image.

Something of the image has survived. This does not, however, diminish man's total depravity. It is a minor point that dominion over creation is part of the image.

In conclusion, it needs to be pointed out that Calvin does not view being male or female to be an essential part of the image of God. Calvin's view of man as the image of God is determined by the honor of God, for which man has been created, and through the grace of God, which restores the image in man.[24]

24.3. *E. Brunner*

Brunner has become known for his distinction between the formal-structural understanding of the image of God that we encounter in the Old Testament, and the substantive-material view that we encounter in the New Testament.

The former focuses on the specifically human—the *humanum*—that distinguishes man from all other creatures. What differentiates him from all other creatures is based on a certain similarity with God. This characteristic cannot be lost. It is not affected by the contrast between sin and faith. Brunner believes that this is referred to in 1 Corinthians 11:7 and James 3:9, while he also recognizes it in Acts 17:28, although the precise term is not used there. In this formal view of the image of God, Brunner focuses on the *humanum*, the *humanitas*. He considers the *humanitas* such an important concept that he finds it worthwhile to distinguish between formal and material views of the image (*Dogmatics*, 2:76).

Brunner finds the substantive-material view in Romans 8:29, 2 Corinthians 3:18, Ephesians 4:24, and Colossians 3:10, and in all those passages that speak of being similar to God or becoming similar to God. Man has lost this similarity through sin. It is only restored by Jesus Christ. The existence of man is then founded on Christ. Renewal through the Holy Spirit is crucial.

24. The reader is referred to the clear overview produced by Schroten, 1956, and also the two essays by Faber on Calvin's view of man (1990, 227–81).

The first view has to do primarily with man's enduring responsibility, while the second view focuses on his being within God's love, being in Christ, and being a child of God.

Luther is thought to have recognized these two aspects by referring to an *imago publica et privata* (*Dogmatics*, 2:76). The church fathers and medieval theologians were aware of this distinction. However, they have split it inappropriately between *tsèlèm* and *demuth*. Since Irenaeus a distinction has been made between "man's natural endowment of reason," i.e., man as rational being, *and* the right relationship with God that has been lost since Adam. This line of thought was retained in the Middle Ages in the distinction between the natural and supernatural (mentioned earlier).

The Reformers justly protested against this distinction. However, from their point of view they were unable to come up with a satisfactory alternative solution, because they utilized a term such as "remnant" of the image of God. It is clear that this is a stopgap solution, because this remnant is of purely quantitative magnitude.

Brunner wants to propose a qualitative distinction. He does this with the Old Testament's structural view and the New Testament's substantive view already mentioned. Man has been placed in an enduring relationship of responsibility. This relationship proceeds by virtue of creation and is independent of the relationship in love toward God (*Dogmatics*, 2:60f., 77).

To the formal image belongs, in addition to responsibility, also terms such as freedom, self-determination, reason. Brunner characterizes this aspect of being human as "responsive actuality" (*Dogmatics*, 2:60). The structure of being human is one of relationship. Man is always man before God, even when he turns away from God.

It is noteworthy that Brunner says that from God's point of view, the distinction between the formal and the material image does not exist. Nevertheless, however inappropriately, it is there (*Dogmatics*, 2:61). With Hoekema (1986, 57) we would say that from God's point of view this distinction *ought* not to exist. We fail to see why Brunner does not formulate it this way. Now the question remains whether God desires this distinction or not. In our view the position that "it should not be there" is the more cogent one, because the dichotomy referred to above is linked by Brunner himself to the distinction between law and gospel (*Dogmatics*, 2:61).

This also generates questions that we would like to direct to Brunner. If this distinction does not exist from God's point of view, is this because Brunner does not see (acknowledge) the state of affairs in Paradise as historical? For Brunner, whence comes sin?

Next we would like to ask how it can be that sin does not impair the formal structure. Is what Brunner calls formal so lacking in content that sin cannot attack and destroy it? Keep in mind that the formal image includes freedom, conscience, and responsibility.

To this we add the question whether the image is not more than relational. In our view the formal image also implies a relationship of being. There is no relationship without being! Even if one wishes to speak of formal, one cannot limit oneself to the relational apart from being, even when one seeks the material image as consisting primarily of love. For love is definitely more than external. Love permeates all being and determines all relationships.

Brunner's distinction reminds us strongly of the distinction in the older Reformed dogmatics between the image of God in the broader and narrower sense (Bavinck, *R.D.*, 2:550).

The Reformed (like Brunner) included in the image of God in the broader sense everything that distinguishes man from beast. To use the old terminology: man as rational-moral being! Bavinck can appreciate this distinction to the extent that he finds that in this sense the Reformed retained the connection between physical and ethical nature (*R.D.*, 2:550). Yet he rejects it, because he finds that the two images are placed side by side too mechanistically. He favors an organic elaboration of this distinction. Besides, he feels that sin has also impaired the image in the broader sense (*R.D.*, 2:553–54).

We have presented Brunner's point of view mostly on the basis of his *Dogmatics*, 2:55–61. One can find a historical review of the *Imago dei* doctrine on 75–78. In his *Dogmatics* one can find a short summary of his comprehensive volume of 1941, in which he also presents a doctrine of sin.

24.4. *K. Barth*

Barth has a completely different view on the image of God compared with all of the theologians discussed so far. The unique and peculiar nature of his view is that he locates the image in the existence of humanity as male and female. He does not see man's dominion over nature as belonging to the image. He considers it to be a consequence of the image (*C.D.*, 3.1.187).[25]

In standing over against each other and at the same time belonging together as man and woman lie man's *Abbildliche* (likeness) and *Nachbildliche* (copy), which correspond to the *Urbildliche* (original) and the *Vorbildliche* (prototype) in God's being (*C.D.*, 3.1.196). The terms in italics are difficult to translate. One could say God is the original image and at the same time the prototype. Man is a copy of God. One finds God's image in him.

25. In his *Unterricht in der christlichen Religion* (education in Christian religion), 2, Zürich 1990, in connection with the image of God Barth still speaks of man as "Gottes direkter Reflex und Statthalter in der Welt" (God's direct reflection and lieutenant in the world). These lectures date from 1924–25 in Göttingen. See 2:9.

Barth's interpretation of the image goes back to the acceptance of a correspondence based on a relationship (*analogia relationis*). Barth rejects any analogy of being (*analogia entis*). He replaces it with an analogy of relationship. Just as God is there for man, man is there for his fellow men. The image lies in the relationship, not of man to God, but of human being to human being (*C.D.*, 3.1.197). The I-Thou relationship within God himself (as in "let us make man"; see footnote 4) finds its creaturely analogy in the relationship between man and woman. We provide a quotation that summarizes the argumentation of many pages:

"He is this first in the fact that he is the counterpart of God, the encounter and discovery in God Himself being copied and imitated in God's relation to man. But he is it also in the fact that he is himself the counterpart of his fellows and has in them a counterpart, the co-existence and co-operation in God Himself being repeated in the relation of man to man. Thus the *tertium comparationis*, the analogy between God and man, is simply the existence of the I and the Thou in confrontation. This is first constitutive for God, and then for man created by God. To remove it is tantamount to removing the divine from God as well as the human from man. On neither side can it be thought away. That it is God's divine and man's human form of life is revealed in the creation of man. God wills and creates man when He will and created the being between which and Himself there exists this *tertium comparationis*, this analogy; the analogy of free differentiation and relation" (*C.D.*, 3.1.185).

In this analogy lies the real content of the image of God. Berkouwer has correctly pointed out that Barth jumps from the relationship between man and woman—mentioned with respect to the creation of man after God's image in Genesis 1:27—to the distinction and relation between man and fellow man (1962, 73ff.). The specific nature of being man and woman is absorbed by the nonspecific sexually differentiated relationship of person to person (*C.D.*, 3.1.185–86).

Barth does discuss at length the meaning of being man and being woman. It is at this point that he seeks the difference of man from animals, despite formal resemblances. Nevertheless Barth evades the issue by moving to the I-thou relationship of man to man. In this connection Berkouwer speaks of an unevenness, and accuses Barth of artificial construction (1957, 73). We question whether unevenness is adequate enough to describe the rather serious accusation of artificial construction.

We recognize the setting up of a series of problems (correctly identified by Berkouwer), especially in the fact that for Barth the image does not embody the relationship with God, but only that of man to man. This can only mean that the image of God is retained despite the fall into sin.

In our view this is the case for two reasons: in the first place because the creation of man is an act of grace![26] Sin has been taken care of beforehand.[27]

The image of God cannot be lost as a result of "the triumph of grace." "The covenant relationship between God and man in Christ is reflected in human solidarity in terms of being there for and with each other (humanity)," according to Wentsel, and correctly so (*Dogm.*, 3a:610).

There is still another reason. The image consists of the relationship of man to man, as a reflection of the relationship within the divine being. Whatever sin brings about, the formal relational nature of the relationship of man to man continues to exist. In this way the image continues to exist, even after the fall into sin.

With Berkouwer (1957, 73), one can appreciate that Barth has linked the relationship of man and woman with the image of God. At the same time it must be pointed out that this relationship—as exclusive content of the image of God—bypasses data in Scripture that are crucial for understanding of the image of God. We refer in particular to Colossians 3:10 and Ephesians 4:24.

Precisely this exclusive and one-sided approach is typical of the *constructivistic* character of Barth's view. The concept of the covenant is here applied to the relationship of man to man! Just as Barth's doctrine of God is determined by the covenant (God is a God who chooses man, and is unthinkable without this choice), so is the relationship of man to man essential to being human. The image of God receives its content from the *analogia relationis*.

24.5. *K. Schilder*

Schilder has become known for his rejection of the distinction between the image of God in the broader and narrower sense. In his view, this distinction is better abandoned. He does not want to "tamper with

26. In connection with this, see *C.D.*, 3.1, especially section 42.1, "Schöpfung als Wohltat" (creation as benefit), and section 42.3, "Schöpfung als Rechtfertigung" (creation as justification); as far as man is concerned, see especially section 44, "Der Mensch als Gottes Geschöpf" (man as the creature of God).

27. In this connection see J. van Genderen, "De leer van de schepping bij Karl Barth," in A. G. Knevel (ed.), *Visie op Karl Barth*, 1987, 49–56.

the distinction between elements which are more or less constitutive in the construction of the *concept* 'image of God'" (*H.C.*, 1:300).

The well-known passages that are used to describe man as the image of God after the fall into sin (Gen. 9:6; Acts 17:28; 1 Cor. 11:7; James 3:9) refer to man in his original state. Although Schilder does acknowledge that there are remnants, he does not consider these to be the image of God in the broader sense.

Schilder distinguishes between the creation of man and his being God's image. In the creation of man lies the prerequisite for being God's image. Being God's image is not given with creation. Being the image pertains to the office that God gave to man. Schilder employs the term *officium* (*H.C.*, 1:293). The image is not a matter of nature or of qualifications, but of office-bearing (*H.C.*, 1:294). Being the image forms part of the living interaction with God as the God of the covenant. It is not a matter of a particular state of affairs, not of ontic and anthropological qualities, but of service *in actu*, and the dynamics of carrying out the service of the office. "For not in *static* splendour, but in *live service in office* is man in a position to reflect God, here below, in his own sphere (*H.C.*, 1:306). What matters in the image is indeed its visibility. "One can *see*, in one way or another, by an image that the person who is portrayed actually exists" (*H.C.*, 1:254).

As God's image, man is summoned to be ruler over other creatures. He is to represent God to the visible reality (*H.C.*, 1:255, 265).

Schilder discusses in great detail the idea that God adapts to what is given and available. God brings to further development what is already there. Thus the talents that God has given to man are brought to greater richness and development in the implementation of the task (*H.C.*, 1:255). The natural gifts must function in accordance with an official mandate (*H.C.*, 1:272).

They do not belong to the image. Berkouwer understands Schilder in this sense that one then "abstracts the gifts from the service mandate" (1962, 54). Schilder does not say this in so many words. In our view it comes down to this, that Schilder sees the image as belonging to the office. Those who place all of the emphasis on the gifts overlook the office! This is Schilder's point of criticism. In this way Schilder sees in the office a *conformitas*—a conformity to God. Man must actually and actively portray God and make him visible through his deeds.

Schilder's conception is permeated by the dynamics of service and portrayal. Schilder definitely recognizes the gifts that man has received from his Creator. He does not wish to detach the image from these gifts (*H.C.*, 1:255). He sees them as a necessary condition for the fulfillment of man's service in office.

Schilder wants to see the image as the living interaction with God in faith and obedience. He resists identifying certain data or structures of human nature as an ontic stratum to be considered as itself the image. The main thing is that man does something with those gifts.

Since man abuses these gifts, we can no longer speak of the image of God. It has been lost. Schilder interprets passages about man as the image of God after the fall into sin as a reminder of God's intention with man. He was "worthwhile." God intended something grand with him (*H.C.*, 1:312).

We believe that we may interpret Schilder as follows: these passages remind us of the office that God bestowed on man, but that he no longer exercises. Since Schilder sees the image as an actual, active, and dynamic relationship, he can no longer speak of remnants since the relationship has been broken. He can only say: this is what man was intended to be. He no longer carries out his office. Schilder speaks of the loss of the image of God. According to him, the calling to office that was there, and which remains, can no longer be called the image of God.

Schilder uses various images to describe the office: vicar, agent, deputy, office bearer-representative, but especially that of viceroy or governor-general in an overseas territory (Kamphuis, 1985, 29, note 62).

Kamphuis goes along with Schilder, but does not want to commit himself to specific terminology. According to him, the terminology that one uses to clarify the scriptural data concerning the image and likeness of God must be kept fluid. His description is "God employs man, not because He is the Absent One, but because He desires to be the Present One *in this mode*, in the mode of human dominion in his service" (1985, 31).

In Genesis 1:26–27, the Father-child relationship is indeed *intended*, but the formulation is *avoided*. Being the child of the heavenly Father is inextricably connected with being the image of God. "Being created as image, man—the son—is placed in the *centre of the world*, for in him the entire world is open *towards God*'" (Kamphuis, 1985, 34). One can speak of a horizontal territory of dominion. At the same time there is a vertical focus on God, as well as a focus on the (eschatological) future. This is how God wants his kingdom to come: man is his child and viceroy on earth. *In this mode of his presence God wants to make his kingdom come* (Kamphuis, 1985, 35). Kamphuis then argues for a systematic treatment of a number of questions dealing with the coming of the kingdom.

We consider Schilder's view to be one-sided. According to him, man's creation precedes his becoming the image of God. The office is added to being human. And the image lies in this incidental aspect. The idea that the image is added after creation contradicts the clear statement of Genesis 1:26.

Furthermore, the question arises as to how Schilder fits in knowledge, righteousness, and holiness. These are indeed prerequisites for the carrying out of the office. One must admit that a proper exercise of the office cannot succeed without them. Yet they are—merely—prerequisites for the office and thus precede it. Here we encounter a definite bias, in an entirely different way, and also in an entirely different context than in the case of Barth. There is a great deal in Schilder's thought process that we can appreciate, if we may consider his view as part of a much greater whole. Within this greater whole his view is important. Of course, the greater whole modifies Schilder's conception. Man is then not only office-bearer, but also child.

It is noteworthy that Kamphuis incorporates this notion into his interpretation of Schilder. In this sense he provides an expansion that is essential and necessary. It would have been correct if Kamphuis had spoken clearly of an expansion or a development of Schilder's view. Kamphuis's view strikes us as even more attractive than that of Schilder. We only doubt that Kamphuis's expansion goes as far as we consider necessary.

24.6. *A few questions by way of summary*

We summarize the problems that have emerged in this concise historical review. We present them in the form of questions.

1. Is it right to distinguish between image on the one hand and likeness on the other? If not, can we then still speak of a formal-structural and a material image of God? Or of an image of God in the broader and narrower sense?

2. What is the significance of the body and of psychic capabilities (responsibility, reason, and anthropological freedom of choice)? Do these gifts form part of the image of God? Or are they prerequisites for being the image of God? In the latter case, the gifts precede the image as a form of equipping. They do not belong to the image!

3. Can we say that the image of God exists, *either* only in being the child of God, with the calling to be conformed to God and Christ, *or* only in interpersonal relations (concentrated as being man and woman within marriage), *or* only in the mandate to have dominion over creation, a mandate that is then understood as an office?

4. Is man even after the fall still God's image? How is it to be explained that the term is still used, while absolute renewal is needed?

5. However the fourth query is answered, the question remains: how extensive is the ruin caused by sin? Only as far as the relationship with God is concerned, or also in additional aspects of the image of God that we have discussed (reason, freedom, responsibility, psychological and physical capabilities)?

6. How do we take into account the unmistakably rational element in the image of God? Does it involve only relationships or more than that?

§ 25. Aspects of humanity

25.1. *Man as body and soul*
25.2. *Man as a religious being*
25.3. *Man as a social being*
25.4. *Man and the environment*

25.1. *Man as body and soul*

1. There are various words that the Bible employs to characterize man as creature. Man is visible in and through his body. It is striking that very little is said about the body in general. We come across references to the body in a number of contexts. See Genesis 25:22; 47:18; 1 Samuel 31:10, 12; Nahum 3:3. See also in the New Testament Matthew 10:28; Luke 12:23; Romans 1:24; 12:1; 2 Corinthians 5:6. We have made a selection from a multiplicity of passages. The word "body" is used more often in the New Testament than in the Old.

The activities of man are often described by making reference to various organs and parts of the body. H. W. Wolff (1974[2], 116–23) provides quite a detailed description of seeing and hearing as forms of communication. In this connection the eyes, mouth, and ears are the most prominent. The word "face" occurs as many as 2,100 times in the Old Testament.[28]

As far as parts of the body are concerned, it is not feasible to provide a complete list. The data are too numerous. A glance at a concordance quite quickly reveals the multiplicity and variety of terms. This is definitely the case with the word "lips." No human activity is as variously described as speaking. "Auf der anderen Seite werden von keinem menschlichen Körperteil so viele veschiedenartige Tätigkeiten ausgesagt wie vom menschlichen Mund mit Lippen, Zungen, Gaumen, Kehle, sofern sie Sprachorgane sind" (on the other hand, of no other human body part is said as much as of the human mouth together with lips, lungs, palate, throat, to the extent that they are organs of speech) (Wolff, 1974², 121; see 116–23). We encounter other words as well: "flesh" (*basar*) (Gen. 2:23–24; Pss. 56:4; 65:2; Jer. 32:27), "heart" (*leb*) (Gen. 8:21; Ps. 78:18; Prov. 15:13; Isa. 1:5), "spirit" (*ruach*) (Gen. 45:27; Judg. 15:19; 1 Sam. 1:15). We have already referred to *nephesh* (see § 23.3).

It is no different in the New Testament. There we encounter "body" (*soma*) (Rom. 12:1; 2 Cor. 5:10; 1 Thess. 5:23). Also the word "flesh" (*sarx*) (Rom. 1:3; Gal. 2:20), "soul" (*psyche*) (Matt. 10:28, 39; Luke 1:46; Rev. 18:13), "heart" (*kardia*) (Matt. 15:18–19; Rom. 2:5; James 4:8), "spirit" (*pneuma*) (2 Cor. 2:13; 1 Thess. 5:23), "mind, spirit" (*nous*) (Luke 24:45; Rom. 12:2; Phil. 4:7). Furthermore we find references to inward and outward man (Rom. 7:22; 2 Cor. 4:16).[29] The multiplicity and diversity of these terms immediately makes clear that one should not consider them as precise scientific references to specific aspects of humanity. In the description of man, the Bible does not aspire to scientific accuracy. The Bible characterizes man in all aspects of his existence, especially in terms of organs and limbs, and by pointing to the inner and outer man. The emphasis is on man, concrete man in the unity of body and soul, of emotions and thoughts, of activities and dialogue with oneself, of acts of commission and omission, of spiritual growth and struggle.

The various terms are congruent with each other and sometimes overlap. They are intended to characterize the whole man, as a being

28. For a discussion of the function of our body parts and organs see O. Betz, *Der Leib als sichtbare Seele*, 1991.

29. For literature on this topic see Ridderbos, *Paul*, 115–21; R. Bultmann, *Theologie des Neuen Testaments*, 1958³, 188–239.

created by God. They always do so from various points of view, thereby to honor man's Creator and to describe the many possibilities that God has offered to man. With Noordegraaf (1990, 51) we can speak in this context of a holistic vision. We prefer this terminology to the designation employed by Heyns, who speaks of man as a unitary being (*Dogm.*, 120). The main thing is that the Bible sees man as created by God in the unity and cohesion of body and soul.

We now present a brief description of the various terms. The reader can turn to other sources for a more detailed treatment.[30]

We emphasize that *nephesh* typifies the whole person in his accountability to God. Hence, the *nephesh* who sins shall die (Ezek. 18:4). There is a wonderful interconnection and transition among the words "soul," "heart," and "flesh" in Psalm 84. The poet here refers to himself in the richly textured variety of biblical language.

In the New Testament we encounter *nephesh* as *psyche*. The latter transcends the existence of the body, which is especially apparent in Matthew 10:28. Apart from killing the body, this verse indicates the possibility of killing the soul in hell. However directly they are connected according to Genesis 2:7, the soul does not coincide with the body.

Matthew 10:28 is indeed a very explicit verse. Ridderbos points out that *psyche* portrays man in his natural and earthly life, which has no subsistence in itself but is subject to death and destruction (*Paul*, 127). In this sense it is virtually synonymous with flesh and blood (1 Cor. 15:50).

First Corinthians 3:1 and 2:14 refer to sinful man. In the latter verse *pneumatikos* (i.e., illuminated and taught by the Spirit) is contrasted with *sarkikos* (carnal). We agree with Pop that "carnal" refers to limitations brought about by sin.[31] Here *psyche* approaches the second meaning of *sarx*, i.e., flesh that has turned away from God.

"Flesh" alludes to man as creature, including his dependence on God (God's Spirit) as well as his fragility. Man has no strength in and of himself. In this connection see especially Isaiah 31:3; 40:6; Psalm 78:39.[32] Sometimes "flesh" does not specifically refer to man's fragility,

30. In addition to the references contained in the previous note, we refer further to Berkouwer, 1962, 200–8; Van Leeuwen, 1975, 55–58; Bavinck, *R.D.*, 2:557–61.

31. F. J. Pop, *Eerste brief aan de Corinthiërs* (first epistle to the Corinthians), 1965, 68ff.

32. Regarding this aspect of man's being see Van 't Veld, 1989.

but to earthly existence overall (Phil. 1:22, 24; 2 Cor. 10:3), although this certainly incorporates the notion of transience, of being limited to this earthly existence.

"Flesh" also has a latent connotation: man in his hostility toward God and his rebellion against him (especially Rom. 8:6–9; Gal. 5:19–21; Rom. 7:14). We see Romans 7:7–12 as a description of the faithful who experience the discord between the Spirit and the flesh in their new state (see Velema, 1988[2], 77–82).

Here we need to alert the reader to the comprehensive emphasis of biblical language, i.e., that "flesh" as a designation refers to man in his attitude toward God. Sin is not localized in the body or in lower, sensual parts of the body, e.g., the reproductive organs. Man is depraved in his totality. (On this topic see especially C. H. Lindijer, 1952.)

Paul also speaks in various ways about *pneuma*. Naturally in Paul's writings *pneuma* frequently refers to the Spirit given to man by God. Typical of that usage is once again Romans 8:5–11, 13–16 and Galatians 5:16–18.

In 2 Corinthians 2:13 *pneuma* is equivalent to *sarx* in 2 Corinthians 7:5. It refers to man in his earthly being. It may be assumed that the inability to find rest also had physical implications.

Pneuma can also refer to a person directly, without any specific thought being given to renewal or guidance by the Spirit (Gal. 6:18; Phil. 4:23). A parallel greeting can be found in Romans 16:24 and Ephesians 6:24. Here *pneuma* refers to man's inner being, as created by God. Like Ridderbos, one can think of this as man in his natural existence (*Paul*, 120–21).

In this connection reference is sometimes made to the threefold description of man referred to in 1 Thessalonians 5:23: spirit, soul, and body. Here we see man described in terms of the unity of his physical and spiritual existence. Paul's focus here is the unity and totality of man's being: man as before God's face (*coram Deo*; cf. Ps. 86:11). We do not see the use of these three words as supporting an anthropological trichotomy. We do find here a very harmonious combination of various terms. They can be used in any combination or order, because they mean the same thing regardless of any variation. Ridderbos correctly refers to a plerophoric mode of expression (*Paul*, 121). In any case, it is not a matter of three distinct components of humanity that could be extracted trichotomistically (i.e., cut up in three parts) and each part considered separately. It is precisely the other way around: this abundance of terms serves to accentuate unity despite all differentiation.

We call the reader's attention to two additional terms. In the first place there is *nous*. In Philippians 4:7 it denotes: the activity of thought, understanding with the mind. In 2 Thessalonians 2:2 it refers to sober understanding and intelligent judgment.

In Romans 12:2 and 1:20 *nous* is closely connected with knowing God and his will. The latter verse has to do with man's receptiveness to take in and react to God's revelation. In Romans 12:2 Paul goes even further. Here he implies with *nous* man's inner self-determination with respect to God's revelation. Ridderbos correctly brings these separate strands together: capacity for being addressed and responsibility with respect to God's revelation (*Paul*, 118). The *nous* is the locus in man through which God addresses him, and where man makes his decisions vis-à-vis God. Thus we recognize both receptive and reactive characteristics of man as standing in God's presence.

Finally there is the word "heart." "Heart" and "mind" are not altogether synonymous, although there are places where both words have more or less the same meaning. The heart is the center of man's inner being. It signifies the person with the ability to think, to feel, and to will. In 2 Corinthians 3:14–15 and Philippians 4:7, "heart" and *nous* (or a derivative) are used as parallel concepts and thus as synonyms.

Nous indicates the person as characterized by thinking and decision making. The heart encompasses affections, desires, and aspirations. It is the locus of these traits. *Nous* lacks the aspects of feeling and volition. It is rather the locus of thinking and decision making, and the determination whether our behavior is responsible. It should not be necessary to point out that when it comes to the heart, the relationship with God (the *coram Deo*) is understood. This is obvious from the similarity between *nous* and the Old Testament concept of heart.[33]

33. We further refer to two studies that analyze the biblical data in a systematic manner: G. Ebeling, "Cognitio Dei et hominus" (especially in connection with Calvin), in *Lutherstudien*, 1971, 221–22; E. Jüngel, "Der Gott entsprechende Mensch" (man in God's likeness), in *Entsprechungen*, 1980, 290–317.

Our conclusion is that the Bible has a highly nuanced, but by no means dualistic, view of man. Neither the intellect, nor the emotions, nor the will typify man in isolation. It is indeed characteristic of man that, equipped with these various capabilities, he is a unified person. We have referred to this as the holistic view of man. It is a consequence of the fact that man belongs to God, i.e., that he lives before God's face and is accountable to him. This unity is so decisive that one cannot ascribe specific consequences to man's several facets as more or less, higher or lower, or more or less distinguished. Since man was created by God as a physical-spiritual being, everything is included, and each aspect has its own function. Every facet contributes to the whole in the way assigned by God (cf. 1 Cor. 12:12–26). The body is not the prison of the soul.[34]

Unfortunately, we cannot deny that in the history of Christian thought about man and the world, the physical side has frequently been underrated. The body has been more closely connected with sin than man's mind. Through the ages, gnosticism has been an enormous threat to the church. Perhaps we should say that although gnosticism has been rejected, it has continued to have influence via the backdoor (we are tempted to say: via the lower half of the door) by way of an underappreciation of the body and matter.

2. When it comes to the *relationship between body and spirit*, we prefer to speak of *a duality* rather than dualism frequently defended and maintained with appeal to the Bible. We prefer to speak of many-sidedness in the biblical use of terms to describe man's existence. When spirit and body are distinguished from each other, man's *psyche* and *pneuma* are captured with a single term (namely, "spirit"), although they are not always identical. Within the term "spirit" a further distinction needs to be made,[35] hence our preference for the term many-sidedness. This way we can accommodate the differences and interrelations, as well as the similarity of the various terms.

We now turn to the fact that Heitink has referred to a growing anthropological consensus. He finds this to be the case especially since the concept "man as a whole" has evolved over time. He takes "man as a whole" to imply the following:

34. Regarding this expression of Plato used by Calvin see: W. H. Velema, *Ethiek en pilgrimage*, 1974, 35.

35. See how W. J. Ouweneel, 1984, 43ff., distinguishes between the psychic (to be distinguished from the perceptive and the sensitive) and the spiritual. Van Peursen, 1956, 148, views the unity of soul and body as residing in the spirit as one's orientation.

- the unity of man, in terms of body, soul, and spirit;
- man as "existing in relationship," in solidarity with the world of which he forms part;
- being human consciously and unconsciously;
- man in development, aiming at self-realization; and
- man with values or convictions according to which he lives.[36]

It is undeniable that in biblical anthropology greater attention is being paid to the aspects that Heitink lists. Like the anthropology of earlier centuries, contemporary biblical anthropology is not detached from its time.

While Heitink acknowledges this gain, at the same time he accuses the Reformation of narrowing the scope of anthropology. We cannot agree with him in this regard. It is Heitink's view that by concentrating on the heart of the gospel (being simultaneously righteous and a sinner: *simul iustus et peccator*), man as creature is hidden behind man as sinner. According to Heitink, this implies an attenuation. He believes he can support this position by referring to a number of confessional statements of the Reformation. He concludes that the Reformation limits itself to the polarity between sin and grace.

Heitink advocates a different polarity, namely that of creation and re-creation. This polarity is broader and encompasses the polarity between sin and grace. He seeks a Trinitarian approach from the point of view: "man as creature," "the man Jesus Christ," "the Spirit and humanity." This threefold perspective replaces that of the Heidelberg Catechism: sin, redemption, and gratitude (1977, 112ff.).[37]

There is insufficient space to pursue the views of Heitink any further. We limit ourselves to a concluding statement, i.e., that Heitink in fact collapses creation and redemption. Jesus as the new man takes the place of the first Adam, who after all never existed. Jesus is simultaneously the first and second Adam. Thus, based on the accomplishments of Jesus, the Holy Spirit can achieve restoration by establishing true humanity. Where the latter is present, there is salvation. Heitink applies the systematic theology of H. Berkhof to the discipline of anthropology. It is obvious that the consensus identified by Heitink would imply a radical revision of the Reformational doctrine of salvation (*soteriology*).

We dispute the accusation made by Heitink. In the confessional documents of the Reformation there are numerous passages that bring out the unity and holistic nature of being human. This indicates that Reformational soteriology does not by definition imply an anthropological diminution of scope. We refer to instances that deal with both body and soul. See Heidelberg Catechism, answer 37, which deals with the redemption of both body and soul through Christ's sacrifice (see further answers 11, 26, and 57). Nowhere in the confessional documents do we encounter contempt for

36. G. Heitink, *Pastoraat als hulpverlening* (pastorate as providing assistance), 1977, 108. See also the surrounding pages. For a critical review of comparisons of the biblical view with images of man in modern philosophy and psychology see Chr. Gestrich, *Die Wiederkehr des Glanzes in der Welt*, 1989, especially 151–59.

37. For the view of man contained in the creeds of the Reformation see Rebel, 1981, 154–203. See a review of this by Klein Kranenburg, 1988, 158ff.

the body merely because it is physical. The explanation of the resurrection of Christ (Lord's Day 22) points in the exact opposite direction.

What is more, the discussion of body and soul falls within the scope of a holistic perspective. Berkouwer correctly points to this framework (1962, 213). Like others, he alludes to the distinction between scientific and nonscientific language. The confessions were not intended to make scientific statements. They did not seek to explain precisely how man is constituted. References to body and soul apply to the entire person. The various descriptions have an anti-dualistic and anti-dichotomistic focus (in the sense of a fundamental separation of body and soul). In the straightforward language of the Bible it is a matter of both body and soul: body as well as spirit (soul). We should be careful not to commit the error opposite to that of the past, namely that results of modern anthropology would have to be biblically calibrated, just as earlier anthropology made use of concepts from then-current philosophical concepts. Heitink's argument tends in this direction. Then all contemporary anthropological insights are put on a par with the biblical image of man. Over against this point of view we maintain that the Bible reveals essential notions about humanity without developing them as a coherent theory for a scientific anthropology.

3. *These essential notions include at any rate*: the unity of body and soul; the holistic nature of our humanity. Our spirit is aware of its conscious and unconscious depths, passions, and suppressed and camouflaged inclinations. We meet pertinent references and elaborations in Proverbs as well as in the words of the Lord Jesus, and also elsewhere in the Bible. Man is a responsible being. He is called to respond to the Word of God and the claims that God makes on him through his neighbors. This responsibility is accompanied by a relationship that calls for a response, which is addressed, realized, constituted, and maintained by way of the address-response event.

In this connection we deliberately raise the relational aspect of our humanity. Hereby we wish to prevent seeing our being human as entirely limited to relationships with others. There is no relationship without being. The "I" cannot maintain a relationship in the absence of another "I" that functions as subject. We wish to focus on this "I" without shortchanging relationship. The notion that the "I" must be formed and developed fits in well with biblical thought. Growth is an essential reality that has a pneumatic and psychological aspect.

With this foundation we have established our position vis-à-vis the captivating and intensive discussion of the 1930s regarding the anthropological insights of the founders (champions) of the philosophy of the law-idea (now called Reformational philosophy).

J. Stellingwerff has gone so far as to describe the history of the Free University of Amsterdam during those pre-war years from the perspective of these anthropological discussions.[38] W. J. Ouweneel recently devoted his dissertation to this ongoing question.[39] Confronted with this discussion, we repeat what we have said regarding Heitink's argument: the Bible does not offer a scientific anthropology, but does furnish relevant building blocks, which taken together we refer to as the biblical image of man. With this position we follow the line of Berkouwer, whose formulations point in the same direction.[40]

In our judgment, the doctrines of sin and grace (hamartiology and soteriology) fit into the framework of creation, renewal, and consummation. Grace does not set creation aside and does not restrain the renewing work of the Holy Spirit, as far as our being human is concerned. It is rather the case that criticism of the one-sided hamartiology and soteriology of the Reformation originates in the view that creation is left unfinished and that Adam is missing from the beginning of history (see H. Berkhof, *C.F.*, 192–207). Jesus takes his place in the midst of history. With his work of re-creation, the Spirit is actually in the process of filling in lacunae in the original creation. Criticism to the effect that the doctrine of creation in the confessional documents of the Reformation would fall short originates in the desire for a *different* doctrine of creation. We believe that, from the perspective of the confessions of the Reformation, it is this alternative doctrine of creation (placed within an evolutionary framework) that falls short. It does not achieve its creaturely completion until the appearance of Jesus, as human being par excellence. All other people receive this completion in the *eschaton*. Meanwhile, mankind is on its way. Redemption here is not restoration of what has been destroyed and lost as a consequence of sin. Here, redemption coincides with the completion of what has been lacking in creation from the beginning.

38. J. Stellingwerff, *De Vrije Universiteit na Kuyper. De Vrije Universiteit van 1905-1955, een halve eeuw geestesgeschiedenis van een civitas academica*, 1990.

39. W. J. Ouweneel, *Christelijke transcentdentaal-antropologie. Een sympathetisch-kritische studie van de wijsgerige antropologie van Herman Dooyeweerd*, 1985.

40. Berkouwer, 1962, chapter 6, "The whole man," 214–33; also chapter 7, "Immortality," especially 255–63.

Consequently, sin and the forgiveness and restoration thus necessitated receive less attention, in favor of the notion of a completion of creation. In essence this completion is the humanization of creation (see especially Berkhof, *C.F.*, 538–39).

In this connection we also wish to refer to Calvin's nomenclature.[41] It is noteworthy that Noordegraaf speaks of some ambivalence on Calvin's part: on the one hand he makes "sharp comments about contempt for earthly life and the body as a prison of the soul," and on the other hand he rejects conscientious asceticism. He brings in S. van der Linde as a witness against our own argument. According to him, Calvin would not have thought in platonic but essentially Israelite terms concerning life in God's creation. He would only have objected to the caricature that we humans have made of earthly life through sin (1990, 56).

Calvin utilizes certain expressions but not to capture the sentiments of his opponents or of sinners, putting them in parentheses, so to speak. He takes over from Plato and others what we consider to be "hard and negative" expressions. We readily agree that in his writing he uses them in a different context. But this does not justify the use of those terms. We have not accused Calvin of Platonism. We have only said that he uses expressions that fall outside the biblical idiom. We end with the conclusion that we entirely agree with Severijn, that soul and body do not exist side by side as a duality but are united in a diunity.[42]

4. Against this background the question whether man has an immortal soul is frequently discussed and answered (see Noordegraaf, 1990, 57). The duality of body and soul, however dependent on each other, offers scope for differentiation. Thus the continuation of the "I" after death could be claimed or proven. That the "I" continues to exist after death seems to us a perfectly biblical thought. See Matthew 10:28; Luke 23:43; Acts 7:59; Philippians 1:23 (cf. Calvin, *Institutes*, 1.15.2). We do wish to point out that the way in which H. Berkhof (1960, 56–58) and De Knijff (1987, 270) speak about duality does not by definition imply that the "I" continues to exist after death. De Knijff is concerned with a distinction in the life of man *here on earth*. The body is that part of the objective world that in all immediacy belongs to our person. The soul is the experience of the person as subject that is anchored in the body (272). We have already reminded the reader that in Matthew 10:28 the word *psyche* is used in a very peculiar way.

41. In this connection see also W. H. Velema, *Ethiek en pelgrimage: over de bijbelse vreemdelingschap* (ethics and pilgrimage: about biblical pilgrimage) (Amsterdam: Ton Bolland, 1974), 27–34.

42. Severijn, 1963, 31. We consider the entire presentation insightful with respect to our topic. See also the paper of Schroten, 1956, 47–62.

One cannot simply infer continued existence after physical death from the emphasis on the duality of soul and body (as opposed to dualism). Continuation reflects the belief that man has been created for eternity (cf. Eccl. 12:5). He does not perish upon death. In connection with duality it is indeed significant that reference is made to the resurrection of the body. This duality will also be there in the future.

It is of great practical significance that we encounter the duality of body and soul in the biblical image of man. This prevents us from despising the body. It stimulates and obliges us to pay attention to the body, as well as the physical aspect of our humanity in, for example, health care, sexual ethics, and all those forms of assistance where the body or the physical aspect of our being is central. Naturally it is hardly our intention to use the emphasis on the duality of body and soul to return to the ranking of higher versus lower aspects of being. The distinction implies diversity. The unity of both protects us from denigrating either one.

Finally, we raise the question whether with Heyns one could object to the following manner of speaking: "I am my body" or "I have a body." According to Heyns, the latter expression is inadequate, although he finds that the former goes too far (Dogm., 121). Heyns raises the same objection to the expressions: "I am my soul" and "I have my soul" (123).

To our thinking the important thing here is the intention behind this expression. No one would believe the expression "I am my body" to imply that being human would be completely accounted for by one's body. This expression conveys on the contrary that our existence is only in part represented by our body. Our body is not a piece of property that we could readily dispense with. Our mode of existence on earth is unthinkable without our bodies. Our body is part and parcel of our being. We are of the opinion that both expressions (being a body and having a body) complement each other. They are helpful as long as *both* are employed. What Heyns senses as going too far in the expression "I am my body" is rectified in the expression "I have a body." The same is true with respect to the soul. It is one-sided to use either the verb "to have" or the verb "to be"—to the exclusion of the other—in connection with soul and body. The duality of body and soul is indeed captured very well by the dual use of the verbs "to have" and "to be" as they belong together and complement each other.

5. In this connection we can also discuss the ancient distinction between creationism and traducianism. The former maintains that the body is procreated via sexual intercourse, but that for the origination of the soul a separate act of creation is required. In this way creationism seeks to emphasize direct and complete dependence on God as

Creator. Traducianism places the emphasis on the union of body and soul. The soul would also find its origin through procreation by means of sexual intercourse. Bavinck points out that traducianists view sin as a blemish that is passed on through physical procreation, whereas creationists place the emphasis on personal moral accountability. The latter believe that this accountability can only be maintained within creationism (*R.D.*, 2:558ff.).

We are of the opinion that both views are based on the same erroneous contrasting of soul and body. One could say that traducianists think monistically and creationists dualistically. We agree with Berkouwer that the interest in the dilemma diminishes as more emphasis is placed on the unity and the totality of man (1962, 307). God creates the entire person. For purposes of such creation—in his divine way—God makes use of the coming together of husband and wife. One will never be able to say that the genesis of a new body is a "natural" consequence of this union, while the soul is added to that developing body at a subsequent point. Neither will one be able to say that soul and body are both produced by the coming together of semen and ovum, without God effecting the mystery of our being in the way of procreation. On the contrary, God creates. Every human being is his creation. In the process God makes use of the coming together of husband and wife. In this way God's creative act *pertains to the entire person.* Our thinking about the origin of the soul should function within these boundaries.[43]

25.2. *Man as a religious being*

1. As a heading, one could also use the expression: *man in relationship with God.* This expression could be defended with reference to the fact that man is God's image. He cannot be God's image without having a relationship with God. The image presupposes this relationship. This is the most fundamental thing that one can say about man as created by God. Man is dependent on God. He is involved with God. His life on earth is unthinkable apart from this relationship. Those who deny this relationship, disregard the origin and the destiny of man. It signifies in fact that all that man is or does is affected by God entering into a relationship with him. All words spoken by man need to

43. On the views of J. Waterink regarding this topic, *De oorsprong en het wezen van de ziel* (the origin and nature of the soul), 1932^2, remains of value.

be supported by the response that he gives to God. They must be the unfolding, the echo, and the consequence of that response.

God created man through his spoken word (Gen. 1:26). As we have seen already, this is true for each creature (see Ps. 33:6). God has addressed man. This is the basis for the address-response relationship. The address that comes to man comprises a command and a promise, a charge and a blessing.

In these concepts Reformed theology has from the beginning recognized the constitutive elements of a covenant. The relationship between God and man is not an arbitrary contact that can easily be broken off. It is not a flash encounter that is quickly forgotten. No, this contact takes place within the context of a promise and a mandate from God's side, and man's obligation to respond. A covenant relationship implies an enduring framework for interaction, with rules and a perspective for growth.

This covenant relationship is presented in Genesis 1, if only in principle, although all of the constitutive elements are present here. A bit later in the Bible we come across an official, explicit establishment of a covenant. Going back to Genesis 1 we already discern the essential elements of a covenant, such as those subsequently established with Noah, Abraham, and Israel. Both mandate and promise, blessing and curse are present.

In the covenant God spells out his plans for man and what he expects from him. Man may claim this promise, but must also fulfill his commitments. A covenant implies for both parties: being bound to each other, and therefore permanence, certainty. From man's point of view, the maintenance of the covenant relationship ensures progress, prosperity, and security. In the foregoing material we have not restricted ourselves to Genesis 1. We have also brought Genesis 2:15–17 into the picture. Here we find the counterpart of 1:28. Genesis 2:18–25 must also be considered in this connection. Here 2:24 is indeed crucial because of the fact that this verse may be called the "magna carta" of the marriage covenant. The relationship of God to man and vice versa becomes a covenant relationship as soon as God addresses man after creation (see Bavinck, *R.D.*, 2:564–86).

Heyns is mistaken when he says that God's word concerning the creation of man represents at the same time his word of mandate (*Dogm.*, 128). We do encounter both within immediate proximity. The one follows upon the other, but they do not coincide.

It is indeed clear that man—as a creature that is addressed (in distinction from plants and animals)—must also be a creature that responds. The covenant idea implies the need for a positive response. The covenant may have been initiated one-sidedly by God, but its proper functioning is assured only when both parties speak and act in line with the nature of the relationship. Man is a full partner once his response has been given. Otherwise the actual practice and experience of the covenant interaction do not yet exist. Man realizes and achieves his destiny when in his response he echoes the Word of God. This is to say that he maintains and preserves the covenant in love and obedience.[44]

Man will have to give his response to God *directly*. This takes precedence over all other words spoken by man on earth. However, man also responds to God in the way in which he deals with God's creation and his fellow human beings. At the same time God demands from man that, in his dealings with his fellow men and in his management of creation, he respond directly to God himself. One should not downplay this latter response as being indirect. After all, it is God himself who demands this response from man. He charges man with responsibility for his fellow men and creation. For this reason, the interaction with others and creation is a manifestation of serving God. It can also be expressed as a way of life within the covenant with God. The vertical dimension of this covenant does not detract from the horizontal breadth of the service within this covenant. Life on earth cannot be anchored more solidly than in the covenant with God. See further § 26.3, subsection 2.

2. The question arises: *Can one still speak of a relationship with God* after man has rebelled against God and turned away from him? Here we draw a parallel with the question whether man continues to be God's image after the fall. We have answered this question by saying: man does, but in a negative mode. The same is true of his relationship with God. Man is inclined to this relationship with God. He cannot undo this structural disposition, even if he breaks this relationship. In man as human being created in relationship with God there is a yearning to fill the empty place resulting from his rebellion against God.

44. In connection with this, see Wentsel, *Dogm.*, 2:108–13, and Van der Zanden, no date, 67–80.

Here we encounter the phenomenon of religion. Today religion is often described as being linked with a different reality.[45] This longing for a relationship with another reality is deeply entrenched in man's soul. He is incomplete within himself, even if there are people who pretend to be strict atheists or without religion altogether.[46]

Van Leeuwen correctly points out that such people are found predominantly in Western culture. He further indicates that the absence of religion, confessed with no matter how much pathos and eloquence, may well run counter to man's makeup as creature (1975, 138).

In any case, it is clear that man (in principle everyone) must answer questions that can never be satisfactorily answered from within his immediate reality. We are referring to questions that reach beyond the horizon of our experience. Various authors point to the new wave of religiosity that is inundating Western culture.[47] This wave is all the more remarkable to the extent that it is not (any longer) focused on the church.

In the 1970s, Roscam Abbing already identified the questions that confront every human being. Man has an inner urge to find answers to these questions in order to get on with life. He also feels challenged from without to obtain these answers. Roscam Abbing mentions questions that play an important role in life. He says that the gospel takes seriously what we humans also find important: my "I," my fellow human beings, history, the world, and our distress. One can consider these five areas as questions that concern every human being, and which he cannot resolve within the limits of his empirical existence. It requires more.[48]

We are also reminded of the five elements listed by J. H. Bavinck when he describes religious consciousness: the experience of totality,

45. This description is used by D. C. Mulder in various places. See "Het einde van de religie?" (the end of religion?), *Rondom het Woord*, no. 3 (July 1971): 13:295ff. See further G. Dekker, *Godsdienst en samenleving. Inleiding tot de studie van de godsdienstsociologie* (religion and society: introduction to the study of the sociology of religion), 1987, especially 61–74. See also K. Runia, *Het evangelie en de vele religies* (the gospel and the many religions), 1990.

46. For an earlier study on various aspects of being human from a liberal perspective, see C. J. Bleeker et al., *Anthropologische Verkenningen* (anthropological explorations), no date.

47. As an example, we mention W. Zijlstra, *Op zoek naar een nieuwe horizon: Handboek voor klinische pastorale vorming* (seeking a new horzon: manual for clinical pastoral training), 1989, 243.

48. P. J. Roscam Abbing, "Waarom geloven in God?" (why believe in God?), in H. Berkhof et al., *Geloven in God* (belief in God), 1970, 195–202.

the awareness of norms, dependence on a higher power, the need for redemption, and guidance for life (1989^2, 12–69).

Bavinck has a greater "religious" focus than Roscam Abbing. At any rate, a comparison of these two lists confirms that people have questions to which answers must come from outside our lives and outside our world.

This religious predisposition needs to be linked with the biblical notion that man has been created in God's image. Even though the relationship with God has been broken, there remains a need for what man has lost through his own fault. This reminds us of the discussion of proofs of God covered in § 10.3.

Man shows traces of awareness that he is insufficient in himself. He is a being that needs to reply to a word that is addressed to him.[49]

The newer anthropology along the lines of Pannenberg, also defended in the Netherlands by Kuitert, points to this fact. In this anthropology the entire vision is developed on the basis of an analysis of being human. Those who accept this reasoning will arrive at God from within man. We maintain that it is exactly the other way around. Since God has created man in relationship to himself, man cannot survive without him, or without whatever he puts in the place of God. Pannenberg's theory confirms that man is a relational being; he needs to live not just in relationship with fellow human beings, but also in relationship with God. In our judgment this is not due to man himself, but his Creator. Even when man does not honor his Creator, he cannot live outside this structure, apart from this relationship.[50]

We need to delve deeper into what man does when he does not want to acknowledge God. J. H. Bavinck gives a fascinating interpretation of what Paul writes in Romans 1:18 about those who unjustly suppress the truth. J. H. Bavinck interprets this statement of Paul with the words: "suppression" and "substitution" (1989^2, 171–80). Man flees from God, because he does not want to live with God. He suppresses everything that comes his way from God. He extinguishes all

49. It is interesting that philosophers make this the starting point of their philosophical contemplation. As examples see H. van Riessen, *Hoe is wetenschap mogelijk?* (how is science possible?) 1981, and H. G. Geertsema, *Horen en zien: Bouwstenen voor de kentheorie* (hearing and seeing: building blocks for the theory of knowledge), 1985.

50. See especially W. Pannenberg's major work, 1983. This is the elaboration of an outline of 1962, *Was ist der Mensch?* (what is man?). See also his *Die Bestimmung des Menschen* (man's destiny), 1978. Regarding this model see also C. A. van Peursen, *Wetenschappelijke openheid en metafysische kwetsbaarheid* (scientific openness and metaphysical vulnerability), 1982. H. M. Barth has compared Pannenberg's anthropology with that of O. H. Pesch, and raised critical questions to both, *Pastoraltheologie* 75 (1986): 399–413.

traces of God. At the same time he replaces what comes from God with something that is part of creation.

Barth speaks in this connection of powers. Among those belonging to earth he mentions: fashion, sports, sex, race, state, and money. He also lists those of the spirit: ideas, trends, and goals that man sets for himself.[51] Equipped with this interpretation, we can expose these powers. In this way we recognize them as substitutes for the knowledge of God. We spoke of traces of God. Man has no full knowledge of God. But he is not entirely without knowledge either. This knowledge is not done justice. It is rejected before it reaches man.

In this connection Calvin's well-known expression "awareness of God" (*sensus divinitatis*) should be used (see *Institutes*, 1.3.1–3; 2.2.18; his commentary on Rom. 1:21; § 10.2 above, subsection 2).

Man does not have this knowledge himself. He is not its source, as though he would invent God. This knowledge cannot be explained outside God's revelation. The Reformed tradition speaks in this connection of general revelation. We summarize it as follows: it is the revelation that reaches every person to a greater or lesser extent. Man is after all man of God, image of God. This means that God concerns himself with man, reveals himself to him (see also § 5.1).

This general revelation is sometimes viewed as the basis for a legitimate and adequate natural theology. This is, however, incorrect. Within the Reformation this general revelation is never seen as a sufficient basis for the right understanding of God. This general revelation occurs outside the grace of God in Jesus Christ. It can therefore never be the ground and origin of the right knowledge of God. No true understanding of God can be gleaned from general revelation. The outcome is negative. This demonstrates man's guilt. It is evidence of God's concern with people that despite all deficiency, there is any knowledge at all (see *D.L.*, 3–4:4).

From the perspective of the Bible we can regard religion in two ways. On the one hand it is evidence of man's high pedigree and at the same time proof of God's ongoing concern with man. On the other hand it is never a basis or point of departure for religious knowledge regarding the true God or the true knowledge regarding the God and Father of Jesus Christ. Religion is not highly rated in the Bible.

51. K. Barth, *Das christliche Leben* (the Christian life), 1976, 363–99; also discussed by A. W. Kist, *Antwoord aan de machten* (response to powers), 1971, 170–77. Kist made use of Barth's unpublished lecture notes.

Barth has altogether his own view of religion. He views it negatively as a product of sinful man. This is because of his concentration on Christ. No revelation precedes or bypasses Christ. Barth does not recognize general revelation. He interprets knowledge of the not (yet) believing person from the perspective of Christ. In this way Barth gives a positive interpretation to what is viewed as negative in the Bible.[52] Paul's negative declarations regarding the knowledge of God in unbelievers are reinforced by what we read in Acts 14:15; 17:23ff. Especially the latter reference, which contains Paul's speech at the Areopagus, indicates that there is no continuum between paganism and God's revelation in Jesus Christ. On the contrary, one can only speak of a divide. Paul emphasizes this divide by referring to the searching of pagans on the one hand and the entirely different nature of the revelation of God in Jesus Christ on the other hand. Here one can use again the description of the image of God, knowledge of God in a negative mode. The negative inherently lacks the power to turn positive. Positivity derives from the revelation of God's grace in Jesus Christ.

It remains noteworthy that Paul proclaims the gospel in dialogue with his audience. This dialogue implies that Paul contrasts the new positive content of God's saving intervention in Jesus Christ with the negative mode of awareness of God. Compared with the negative, the positive is radically new. This dialogue is Paul's missionary approach. This is entirely different from a discussion in which both partners contribute a portion of the truth. H. Jonker employs the term "point of address" for approaching the negative mode of the knowledge of God. We consider this to be a useful term to characterize the condition of discontinuity with respect to God's universal concern with man. Point of address is something different than point of contact.[53]

Yet it always reminds man in his sinful state of his high pedigree and his greatest destiny. Traces can be found of this in man's actions and thought processes, in his being and behavior, but only in a strictly negative mode, and not without a perspective of renewal, restoration, and re-creation.

3. Here *man's freedom* also needs to be addressed. It can only be understood within the framework of his relationship with God. Man has been created as a being that must decide and act. One can also speak of man as a discerning and accountable being.

The questions arise: What is the nature of this freedom? What is its content? Man is by no means free in an absolute sense. This is not

52. For Barth see § 5.1; J. M. Vlijm, no date; and G. C. Berkouwer, *General Revelation*, 1955, especially 2, "Reaction to Karl Barth's Offensive."

53. H. Jonker, *Theologische Praxis*, 1983, 87, 164.

the case, because in many respects man is constrained by boundaries, and is conditioned by heredity and circumstances.

We shall not discuss the issue of *determinism* versus *indeterminism* as topics in anthropology in any detail.[54] Both are correct to a point. In certain respects man is conditioned. This is the correct point made by determinism. It is incorrect in the sense that this would be all there is to say about man. The reverse is also true. Man is a being that must decide for himself and is accountable for this decision, despite being relatively conditioned. This is how God created him. This is how he is constituted.

It is crucial that man can choose in terms of his abilities, his situation, and his constitution. He must choose. He is accountable. One can call this his freedom as an anthropological reality. In this regard he differs from animals, plants, and inanimate matter.

However, this does not exhaust the topic. Man is precisely characterized by the fact that he is God's image. Therefore freedom as an anthropological reality falls within the framework of his relationship with God. Those who consider freedom as an anthropological reality to be everything, remove man from this relationship with God. They thereby deny the essence of human freedom, which is by no means absolute. Man is not a product of himself, but God's creation. For this reason man's freedom cannot be defined outside his relationship with God.

Man's freedom consists in responding to God's purpose for him. God seeks a life of love, lived before his face in joy, happiness, peace, and abundance. This is a life of love and obedience. When man is removed from this bond, he is separated from God his Creator. By absolutizing man's freedom, one perverts it at the same time. This is made clear by the "commandment of life" in Genesis 2:17 (Belgic Confession of Faith, article 14). Disobedience means abusing this freedom and thereby choosing death.

Genesis 3:22 tells us how sin operates. Man decides for himself what is good and evil. He judges and chooses, without paying attention to God's commandment. This knowledge is the negative mode of his freedom. With this knowledge man abused his freedom, because he absolutized it. Here the decision is made concerning man's autonomy. Declaring man autonomous implies making his anthropological free-

54. See Hoenderdaal, 1965, 62–81, and as far as Feuerbach is concerned, Bakker et al., 1972.

dom all-encompassing. In this way the image of God is broken. Man as God's image assumes the right to be God. God says as much to man: "Behold, the man is become as one of us"; i.e., he has positioned himself next to us, on our level. Thus he has relativized the image of God.[55]

Man's freedom functions properly only within the relationship of love and obedience toward God. He is to use his anthropological freedom within the covenant relationship. In this connection see Calvin's commentary on Genesis 2:9.

Freedom is never an end in itself, just as man is not an end in himself. Here lies the principal difference with humanistic and liberal views concerning freedom. It is typical of the latter to consider anthropological freedom as being absolute. They do so because they recognize neither man's relationship with God nor God's claim on man.

The fall into sin implies that man abuses and forfeits his freedom with respect to God. The result is not that he ceases to be man. Anthropological freedom survives only in a negative mode. We have lost our freedom in relationship to God. On this point the Reformation is clearly unanimous.[56]

Man is radically depraved. He who says no to God, and proclaims himself king, becomes enslaved to sin. The freedom that he seeks to acquire and exercise outside God eludes him. He passes into other hands, i.e., those of the devil, sin, and death. He becomes subject to their power. Man cannot liberate himself from this slavery. This is the view of the Reformation with respect to (sinful, fallen) man. Augustine has put the far-reaching event of the fall into sin into words that still hold true today. His way of speaking and his use of words set the trend for the position of the Reformation. The freedom of being able not to sin has become corrupted to not being able not to sin. This is true slavery.[57]

We point out that Jesus raised this "voluntary absence of freedom" in a radical manner in his conversation with the Jews of John 8 (Noordegraaf). Only when the Son sets us free, i.e., liberates us from the slavery of sin, is there true freedom (vs. 36; see also vs. 44). In this

55. In connection with this, see Oosterhoff, 1972, 137–55; Bavinck, *R.D.*, 3:29–36.

56. See the overview by Polman, *Ned. Gel.*, second part., 132ff., and on 120–32 an overview of the thoughts of Luther and Calvin. See also Rebel, no date, 157–74.

57. Noordegraaf expresses it aptly, 1990, 70: "voluntary lack of freedom." For Luther, see, alongside the overview by Polman, *WA*, 18:744, 783; and for Calvin, Krusche, 1957, 89–95.

passage we see how freedom in relationship with God can be attained only through Christ. Man needs to be liberated and renewed to this freedom (cf. Gal. 5:1, 13–23).

In Brunner's works one can read about formal freedom. This notion is related to his doctrine of the image of God (1941, 265). We prefer to speak of freedom as an anthropological concept that distinguishes man from animals and plants that do not know such freedom. This anthropological concept, however, functions completely negatively, even as man has lost the image of God through sin, but continues to be held accountable with respect to his origin and destiny.[58] H. Berkhof views man in terms of the aspects of love and freedom, of guilt and fate (*C.F.*, 183–92, 192–215). By "fate," Berkhof means more than what we describe as being anthropologically conditioned. Berkhof continues to speak of guilt as correlated with freedom. He also speaks of consequences of sin that are characterized as fate. In this connection he utilizes the word "interpersonal." He also uses the term "superpersonal" (*C.F.*, 213). Hence there is not only liberation from guilt but also release from fate (see his eschatology, *C.F.*, 533, where he speaks of the "structural redemption of mankind").[59]

Precisely the notion of freedom brings us to the consideration that man's life must be governed by and filled with love. It is freedom in love and love in freedom. The Lord commands his disciples to love one another (John 13:34). He points to the love of God and one's neighbor as the summation of the law (Matt. 22:37–40). Paul echoes Jesus in Romans 13:9, while James describes this command to love as the royal law that is simultaneously the law of freedom (2:8, 12). For James also, love and freedom go hand in hand.

The relationship with God is one of love for him, for his commandment, and for everything that belongs to him. Freedom can be experienced only from the perspective of love. The reverse is also true: freedom does not come at the expense of love, but precisely adopts the way of love.

We prefer these descriptions to those of H. Berkhof. The latter says: man is made for love (*C.F.*, 188), as though love would be available apart from the functioning of man's heart and apart from relationships. Love qualifies intention and action, disposition and attitude. We would say: man does not thrive outside the sphere of love. When he leaves this sphere, he becomes alienated from God, from his destiny, and from his life's potential. On the basis of the Bible we can maintain

58. *Confessio Helvetica Posterior*, 9, "Der freie Wille und die anderen Fähigkeiten des Menschen" (free will and the other abilities of man), in H. Steubing, *Bekenntnisse der Kirche* (confessions of the church), 1970, 163ff.

59. See Velema, 1988², 151–67.

this position quite strongly, because man is known in relationships and seeks relationships. Love that avoids or even breaks relationships is self-love. Luther bases his well-known description of sin on this idea: sin is being focused on the self, being bent toward the self (*incurvatus in se*). Berkouwer emphasizes that the image of God consists in conforming to Christ. This is the *conformitas* of holiness (1963, 100). It finds its zenith in love. Hence the analogy of love (*analogia amoris*) (1957, 116). Our objection is that for him the image is limited to this. We say: within the image love is essential. Indeed no one can be God's image without living in love. We are called to love, because we have come forth from God's love and have been re-created by it (John 3:16). There is more, however.

In this connection we wish to call attention to two additional points. The first one is the problem of emancipation, which is much discussed in our time, and in terms of which much effort is expended. Entire programs are assembled and developed to emancipate people. However one thinks about this concept, the matter itself is to be positively appreciated within the framework outlined by us. When people experience their freedom in love, they are liberated from loveless bonds of slavery. This includes an authoritarian attitude of men over women. This includes societal relations and discrimination against people on the basis of skin color, gender, or (lack of) social status. Our enumeration remains incomplete.

Love seeks to encourage growth and maturity. Love seeks to serve progress and development. Emancipation based on love with the perspective and within the framework of biblical freedom (to serve God and fellow men) is to be positively appreciated. It is a realization of freedom that is being discussed here.

There is also a movement for emancipation that is driven by the absolutization of anthropological freedom. This movement proceeds at the expense of the Fatherhood of God. It is an attempt to fill the void left by rejecting the Father.

Christians cannot deny that various non-Christian and non-church movements at times have (had) a sharp eye for an unjust absence of freedom. We are thinking of social movements in Europe and the Americas (South and North). Even though it is other than Christians who give leadership in this regard, their criticism may well be valid. Those who live by different principles can also point the finger at sins and wounds. It behooves Christians to pay attention. The main thing is that we plead for emancipation to reflect freedom in love. This cannot avoid recognition of God's claim on us. Emancipation that distances itself from the norms and frameworks established by God leads to a new form of slavery.

In this connection we remind the reader of Noordegraaf's reference to Wentsel's statement regarding a new form of discrimination in which the natural longing for parenthood is suppressed by a desire for power or status. Alternatively, the woman who seeks her life's goal within the family and whose priority is to be the mother of her children is looked down upon (Noordegraaf, 1990, 43). This type of emancipation not only leads to slavery, but is actually a form of the absence of freedom and a perpetuation of the slavery that is combated.

We also refer to the book by Van Gennep, *De terugkeer van de verloren Vader* (the return of the lost Father). Why is the Father said to be lost? Is it because we have lost him or because he himself (just like the son in the parable) got lost? The message of Van Gennep is clear. The Father can and will return only to guarantee the autonomy of his sons and daughters.[60] This means restating the problem in other terms than the way it arose. After all, autonomy is the reason why the children have lost their Father.

One should not reverse matters, however. It is the children's fault that they have lost their Father. If one wishes to use the adjective "lost," it should not be applied to the Father, but the sons.[61]

Freedom in the biblical sense is both a gift and a responsibility. It is unthinkable without the stamp of God's love. In connection with emancipation we need to ask both: Emancipation from what? and, Emancipation to what? The idea of emancipation has the same seductive and deceptive connotation as the term "freedom." It is to be used and practiced only for the good. It can, however, also be a force for evil. Then it is a manifestation of sin, which further activates sin. It is important to discern well.[62]

25.3. *Man as a social being*[63]

1. We wish to cover two specific points. First there is being male and female, i.e., *sexuality*, and next—more broadly—life of people together, i.e., *sociality*.

We already saw how Barth viewed the image of God as entirely captured by man being male and female.[64] We interpret this one-sidedness from the perspective of the strong covenant focus that characterizes Barth's theology. The covenant is seen by Barth as a relationship

60. See for this term F. O. van Gennep, *De terugkeer van de verloren Vader* (the return of the lost Father), Baarn 1988, and the collection *De gelijkenis van de verloren Vader* (the parable of the prodigal Father), 1991, as reaction to it.

61. See the contribution of W. H. Velema, "De plaats van Christenen en kerk in de moderne cultuur" (the place of Christians and the church in modern culture), in the collection of reactions, 138–51.

62. On emancipation and secularization see the article in the collection for J. Verkuyl by H. Berkhof, "Emancipatie, secularisatie en de zending van de kerk" (emancipation, secularization, and missions of the church), now incorporated in H. Berkhof, *Bruggen en bruggehoofden* (bridges and bridgeheads), 1981, 176–88. In this essay Berkhof responds to the inaugural speech of Verkuyl of 1965.

63. A broad treatise on man as historical, cultural, and social being can be found in Niebuhr, 1957, especially 2. Of more recent date are the sketches for anthropology by Thielicke, 1976, and by Pannenberg, 1983, especially parts 2 and 3. A more popular treatment can be found in Noordegraaf, 1981.

64. Barth, *C.D.*,3.1.186; Van Niftrik, 1951, 218ff.

between God and man by virtue of creation through Jesus Christ (see also § 14.3). It is a bold and astute move on Barth's part to make this covenant relationship the exclusive content of the image of God. Husband and wife must reflect this relationship in their marriage covenant. The trouble with Barth's construction shows up particularly in that it is not restricted to being husband and wife within marriage. He transfers it without hesitation to the relationship among people (Berkouwer, 1962, 72ff.). This is not surprising. Relational thinking predominates. Data from creation play a subordinate role for Barth. The covenant relationship predominates. Thus one sees captured in the transition from the husband-wife relationship to the inter-human relationship the entire tension of Barth's theology. Creation (man-woman) is subordinate to the covenant (inter-human).

We have argued for viewing the relationship among human beings, being human with the other, from the perspective of the concept of the image of God. This relationship is then applied to the specific and exclusive relationship between husband and wife within marriage. This relationship is not the one and only application of this concept, but rather like one aspect among others. The totality shows how man represents God on earth.

This implies in the first place that man and woman have equality of worth. We adhere to this term in this context. There is equality of worth despite differences, therefore despite distinctness. The woman is female, the man is male. They differ in terms of their makeup. This does not detract from their equality of worth in any way. Paul honors both points of view when he recalls the sequence of creation: Adam first, then Eve (1 Tim. 2:13), while in Galatians 3:28 he emphasizes the equality of worth of man and woman.

Wentsel says: Scripture knows no discrimination against women (*Dogm.*, 3a:634). We wish to stress especially the fact that man and woman are created as God's image. The non-discrimination principle rests on being the image of God, which includes the cultural mandate.

Wentzel (Dogm., 3a:636ff.) seeks a position between feminism and what we might call fundamentalism. His solution is that a distinction should be made between the general rule (i.e., the arrangements between husband and wife) and its application in the customs of the day (3a:637), or, as Herman Ridderbos puts it: the order as such and its expression in the culture, which varies (*Paul*, 460–63).

Nevertheless Wentsel leaves the reader somewhat in the dark. This becomes clear in connection with the question whether a woman may hold office in the church of

Christ (3a:632–37). In light of his seven considerations toward a solution of the issue, one has to conclude that Wentsel continues to see an essential distinction. This does not, however, lead him to reject women as office-bearers in Christ's church. We do not fathom the practical implications of the distinction proposed by Wentsel. This distinction does not function, at least not adequately.[65]

2. *Equality of worth and inequality* are also expressed in the biblical concept: a helper who is suitable for him: "*ezer*" (Gen. 2:18). Since God himself is called the Helper of Israel (Pss. 121:1–2; 146:5), it is impossible to explain the helper as inferior to the person who is helped. In the latter references it is exactly the other way around.

Being a helper points to a mutually complementary and supporting relationship. In the relationship between God and man God is the only helper. In the relationship among human beings it is different.

In Genesis 2:18 the phrase "a helper who suits him" results in what we have referred to as the "magna carta" of marriage. In the marriage relationship, being a helper to the other comes to be filled with a very exclusive content. It functions through three verb forms: leaving his father and mother, cleaving to his wife, and being one flesh. Oosterhoff has pointed out that "being one flesh" applies to the marital communion between husband and wife in its *totality*, thus not only physically, but also spiritually. Referring to the words of Jesus in Matthew 19:5, Oosterhoff says that the marriage bond is so pervasive that the spouses are no longer two individuals, they "no longer stand beside each other as free and independent persons, but are completely dependent on each other and are entirely joined to each other" (1972, 161).

It is noteworthy that this verse does not refer to offspring. Having children is not explicitly mentioned. It is our view that this means that the sexual relationship of husband and wife is not intended exclusively for procreation (the procreative aspect). Genesis 1:28 does refer to this, whereas Genesis 2:24 does not. If we take the latter verse to be the institution of marriage (it appears in numerous places in the New Testament), sexual intercourse need not take place exclusively to generate offspring. It has its own role in the relationship of husband and wife. Paul alludes to this in 1 Corinthians 7:3. Noteworthy is the complete equality of worth of husband and wife, referred to

65. See the discussion of various points of view of Wentsel. Noordegraaf, 1990, 43, pursues that of M. H. Bolkestein. Informative with respect to this entire issue is also a collection on the Roman Catholic side, Schneider (ed.), 1989.

by Calvin in his commentary on this verse. He explicitly mentions marital faithfulness, but precedes this with: the union (*coniunctio*) of the bed. With this he means undoubtedly that the husband may not rule over his wife's body. They are both bound by mutual (and reciprocal) benevolence.

For a renewed appreciation of Calvin's treatment of sexuality see De Knijff's study, 1987, 174–81. He points out that we may indeed speak of a reformation of ideas about sexuality. This removes any justification for a preference for celibacy. Marriage becomes the normal, indeed pre-eminently religious state of life. This also determines the place of the family. See the splendid summary on pages 180ff.

3. We wish to emphasize that *in his life with others man is called to love.* The command to love, which originates in the Old Testament, reaches its highest, broadest, and deepest revelation in the person and work of Jesus Christ (1 John 4:11).

The foundation of this command to love is God's love revealed to us in Jesus Christ (John 3:16). This is the deepest ground for people living together in love. This includes the relationship between husband and wife, whatever erotic aspects may be involved here. The love of Christ for his church is now the bedrock of the marriage relationship (Eph. 5:25–28). Precisely this love underscores the equality of man and woman within marriage as well as beyond marriage.

Eros is not crowded out or dispelled by love as *agape*. The former is permeated and stabilized by the latter (employing an expression from Noordegraaf, 1990, 106). It is noteworthy that *agape* is to characterize the relationship among people (male and/or female) also beyond the marriage relationship. This also implies how representative the relationship between husband and wife must be for society. The marital relationship is a special case because of the unique and exclusive character of this relationship.

This love does not take the place of mercy and justice. It is not just a kind of first aid that temporarily replaces the two concepts just mentioned. No, this love reveals itself precisely in mercy and righteousness (see Matt. 6:33; 25:31–46). Love adorns mercy and righteousness with luster and glow. These phenomena are put in motion by love.

The church of Christ must put this love into practice in the diaconate. It must do its utmost for its members in particular, but also for those outside the church, as a missionary signal of Christ's church on earth and God's loving involvement with the world.

The church will appreciate all the various forms of assistance outside the church as signs of God's goodness to everyone. This goodness is also experienced and practiced where people do not know or acknowledge God himself in Jesus Christ.

This fact does not prevent us from continually stressing God's love in Christ as the source of all neighborly love and service to each other. It is Christ who—as God's image—makes us conform to his image. Where this evangelical foundation is missing, we can still encounter remnants of God's original intention. The foundation, inspiration, and objective of all such activity remain human. Man must do it. It is for him only. Unfortunately, everything that we have presented in this chapter concerning the *man of God* is then lacking. This brings out its dubious, fragmentary, and temporary nature. We have another, firm foundation. We have a never-diminishing source of inspiration. It is the calling of the Christian and of Christ's church to make good on this—to be once again God's image, also in relation to others, within marriage and beyond, close to home and far away.

4. Another question is whether we can speak legitimately of *loving ourselves*. This question is answered affirmatively in the Bible. In various places the fact of love for oneself comes to the foreground as a reality that is not to be criticized. We refer to Matthew 22:39; Romans 13:9; Galatians 5:14; James 2:8—and all of this based on Leviticus 19:18. The friendship between David and Jonathan is an example of this (1 Sam. 18:1, 3: "Jonathan loved him as his own soul").

It is therefore better to formulate this question as follows: Must one love oneself? Is it a command? In the very least it can be stated that man has a relationship with himself. This is revealed in man's self-consciousness. With Heyns (*Dogm.*, 1978, 134), we are thinking of self-knowledge, self-criticism, self-development, etc., and also of self-acceptance and self-respect. These words indicate that man considers, judges, encourages, addresses, and motivates himself—sometimes also forgets, short-changes, wounds, or even kills himself.

Can one describe this relationship with oneself as an I-thou relationship? It is noteworthy that all these terms are compounds that include "self." Therefore it is not I-you, nor I-thou, but I-myself. Since I am different from everyone else, my self is never a "thou." Consequently every comparison of I-myself with I-thou suffers from paralysis. There is something in the I-myself relationship that differs in a fundamental sense from the I-thou relationship. Yet one can speak of judging oneself; also of obligations to oneself. Self-knowledge presupposes that I can step outside myself, to consider myself, and to defend myself. An animal cannot do this. It has no self-consciousness, only consciousness. Our self-consciousness implies that our responsibility concerns not only others, but also ourselves. He who has responsibility for and toward himself must also be able to explain himself. Actually the highest form of self-knowledge is that you accept yourself as a gift from God's hand. Thus man has responsibility as well as obligations toward himself (see Velema, 1998, 140–50).

This idea is rejected by some because they do not consider love for oneself to be compatible with self-denial and self-sacrifice. As proof they quote Matthew 10:39 and John 12:25.

Yet this objection is incorrect. A person must exercise self-denial with regard to *sinful* self-love. However, as creature of God, man does not have to hate himself. This would even run counter to God's command. Man must hate and fight against sin within himself and his sinful heart. The old nature must be discarded. It is striking that in the Bible, love of oneself is always referred to in the context of loving God and one's neighbor. When our love for ourselves is removed from this relationship and thus rendered absolute, we speak of sinful love of ourselves. This self-love proceeds at the expense of the love of God and one's neighbor.

Moreover it may be said that he who is not himself, who is not an "I," cannot function as an "I" either. He who loves himself more than and at the expense of God and his neighbor is what Luther termed: inclined to himself (*incurvatus in se*). This is an exclusive and egotistical focus on oneself.

What applies to myself applies also to what is mine: talents, family, relatives, possessions, and culture. He who seeks himself in all of these respects, at the expense of others, abuses what God gives. He who receives these as gifts to be enjoyed by himself and to be shared with others makes an honorable use of them. One has to possess something to be able to share it with others. He who retains for himself everything that he has received practices the attitude of *incurvatus in se* and sins thereby. Here the criterion is also whether we wish to be of service with what has been entrusted to us. This demands a balanced stewardship.

The above concept of self-image is an important datum in modern psychology. We consider it crucial for vital self-development, supported by upbringing, education, and formation. It is critical how one thinks and writes about this self-image. In light of the foregoing, we reject an autonomous self-image, as well as the idea that people could achieve their destiny without the grace of the Holy Spirit. On the contrary, it is precisely the power of the Spirit that causes people to find their destiny.

The following events form part of the core of this self-image: through sin we have rebelled against God and have disobeyed his commands, failing in terms of love for our fellow men. A focus on sinful self implies cheating God and one's neighbor. He who has the Spirit and faith in Jesus Christ is a new creation. He may see himself as dead to sin, but alive to God in Christ Jesus. See Romans 6:11. This is not just a theory. For believers this is a pneumatic reality. It comes down to a judgment that man may pronounce upon himself in faith on the basis of his relationship with Jesus Christ.

Unfortunately this pneumatic reality is not the full picture. There is still the remaining and even driving force of sin. Paul writes in Romans 6:12: "Let not sin therefore reign in your mortal body, that ye should obey it in the lusts thereof." It is noteworthy that being dead to sin does not imply that sin is now also in fact dead. If this were the case, it would no longer be a matter of "no longer letting sin reign." The self-image of a believer includes the fact that the pneumatic reality must show its strength in the daily fight against sin.[66]

Hoekema has written about the destruction and the renewal of the image (1986, 104–11). We prefer to employ the terms "old man" and "new man." We are of the opinion that both are present in the renewed man, while we are being called to put off the old man. Our sinful nature must be renounced. Renewal means also that I choose for the good things. See further § 42.2.

25.4. *Man and the environment*

1. In his commentary on Genesis 2:15, Calvin refers to man as a steward. He does so when he speaks of thrift and diligence with respect to

66. For the term "pneumatic reality" see Velema, *Aan Christus gelijkvormig* (conformable to Christ), 1988.

the material goods that God gives us to enjoy. This is characteristic of Calvin's view of stewardship. It comes down to a sober, responsible, and dedicated management of what we have received from God.

This management pertains to the environment and the entire creation: nature and culture. Culture means the cultivation of everything in creation that has been given to us; in the first instance agricultural land. The Latin expression "*colere*" goes beyond this, however. Aside from cultivation and protection it also means adornment and care. Culture can also be understood in a somewhat more limited sense. Then it means civilization, development, refinement of spiritual and moral life, and for each the level achieved, i.e., the current state of civilization.[67] All aspects of human activity fall under cultural engagement in the broadest sense of the word: physical, intellectual, economic, technical, scientific, social, and moral.

In our time much has been at issue and much has been written concerning the relationship of man to the environment. We refer here to the study by Manenschijn, *Geplunderde aarde getergde hemel* (plundered earth, provoked heaven), 1988.

Under the heading of "Noodzakelijke ordening" (required planning), he provides a number of descriptions. Nature refers to what is there outside of man's intervention (97ff.). In this regard one can speak of a *natural environment*, an environment not made by people, which meets the conditions required for living creatures.

There is further the *artificial environment*: the environment fabricated by man to live in (shelter, clothing, equipment, and agriculture).

Finally there is the *social environment*: the institutional side of human life, such as customs, law, morality, and religion. These distinctions significantly expand the terminology used in the Bible. For the more limited terminology of the Bible see the study by Houtman, 1982, and Douma, 1989.

Two givens are decisive for approaching contemporary issues from the perspective of the Bible, and for relating today's questions to the Bible.

There is in the first place the mandate given to man. It is at the same time a right, a privilege granted to rule over fish, birds, and creeping animals (Gen. 1:26–28). We find the poetical echo of this in Psalm 8, as described above. Directly related to this, but terminologically distinct from it, is the calling in Genesis 2:15 to cultivate and safeguard the garden. The three verbs to rule (*radah*), to cultivate (*abad*), and to

67. Van Dale, *Groot woordenboek der Nederlanse taal* (large dictionary of the Netherlands language), 1985[11], 545.

conserve (*shamar*) will have to be read in connection with each other. Ruling has to take place in a context of cultivation and conservation. Both cultivating and conserving belong to ruling.

These three verbs apply to the situation prior to the fall into sin. This means that the subsequent abuse of creation definitely was not subsumed in the mandate given to man by God. This abuse is precisely precluded by legitimate usage. Abuse is illegitimate use of God's good creation.

Work is a mandate that belonged at home in Paradise. It did not emerge for the first time after the fall into sin. Safeguarding is precisely the turning away of forces inimical to God. It means watching over what was well-made by God. The combination of ruling, cultivating, and safeguarding includes performing one's task of being occupied with creation as a child of the King.

For theories that ascribe the exploitation of creation—and therefore the cause of the ecological crisis—to biblical data, see especially the brief but substantial booklet by Schuurman, *Het "technische paradijs"* (technical paradise). He explains lucidly that technicism (definition on p. 12) is the driving force behind the ecological crisis. It should be realized that Christians also allow themselves to be driven by technicism.

In no case can we ascribe the ecological crisis to the application of biblical notions. It is exactly the other way around. Biblical notions are turned around by sinful man into their opposites. This is what causes ecological crises. This is also implied by the fact that *abad* not only means cultivation of the earth, but is also the technical term for serving God. It means making obedient use of creation as a form of serving God.

2. In this connection the question needs to be addressed whether on the basis of these data one can speak of a *cultural mandate*. Precisely in the circle within which it was first employed—K. Schilder and the *Gereformeerde Kerken (Vrijgemaakt)*—objections to this term and its biblical foundation have been raised. We will not discuss all of the counterarguments. The claim that only the mastery of the animal world would be intended implies a denial of the charge found in Genesis 2:15. The idea that Psalm 8 would have nothing to say about this issue—because it would have been exclusively fulfilled in Christ—supposes that this psalm applies only to Christ. This implies, however, an illegitimate narrowing of this psalm.

We do not wish to adopt Schilder's entire conception of culture, although we do wish to confirm that ruling over creation is part of the charge given to man as God's image.

At the beginning of the Bible we come across the mandate given to man to cultivate and safeguard the earth, and to make history by expanding the human race. One cannot expect these early chapters to present an extensive theory of culture. But we can say that we encounter here the essential elements that delineate man's place in creation and his dominion over it. The implementation of this mandate has limits. It remains God's creation, which we may not spoil. Although man as child of the King may be in the center, he is not the norm. He remains subject to God's commandment as norm. Those who seek terms to describe the execution of this mandate should use phrases such as: use with gratitude; develop, take care of and safeguard with respect; i.e., serve God and fellow men.

Certain circles today speak of a *nature mandate*[68] as a correction of the concept of cultural mandate. We have two fundamental objections to this. The so-called cultural mandate is by definition a mandate with respect to nature. Culture stems from nature. Our second objection is the reverse of the one just mentioned: whoever works with nature, cultivates it, seeks to safeguard it, and whatever he does with it, is engaged in cultural work with nature. The contrast between a nature mandate and a cultural mandate is absolutely untenable. The mandate with respect to nature amounts to culture, while culture stems from nature. There is only a single mandate in which both concepts have their own rightful place.

This cultural mandate has yet another aspect. Nature has been given to man to be cultivated. It contains nothing divine. The erstwhile nature worship of ancient paganism has returned in contemporary forms of pantheistic nature mysticism. The New Age movement opposes cold rationalism and treats man and the world as a single whole. Nature is deified. Man is part of it. This fills the vacuum brought about by the abandonment of a personal God, the Creator of heaven and earth, the Father of Jesus Christ. This movement is nothing but the revival of ancient paganism in a typically post-Christian form.[69]

68. F. Pansier, "Cultuurmandaat en de Schrift" (cultural mandate and the Scriptures), in *Cultuurmandaat* (Amersfoortse Studies No. 6), 5–17, which also contains references to other literature.

69. For a critical discussion of this movement see P. J. van Kampen, *De cirkel en het kruis* (the circle and the cross), 1989; J. Verkuyl, *De New Age beweging* (the New Age movement), 1989.

The concept of a mandate with respect to creation gives us the right understanding of nature. It has been created by God. One must bear in mind how according to Genesis the heavenly bodies were created to serve man by controlling the seasons. Furthermore—as we saw in 1:26–28 and 2:15—man is called to cultivate, safeguard, and rule over nature. The difference between man and nature is a definite given in the early chapters of Genesis. One can call it a reflection of the difference between God and man. (See also what we wrote in § 23.2 in connection with Ps. 8).

3. In this connection *secularization* must also be mentioned. At bottom, it is a movement of withdrawal from the sovereignty of God. It is a break with the recognition of God's authority over the world. Of course, one can also speak of secularization in the sense of removal of the sacred aura from creation (de-sacralization) and releasing it from the grip of idolatrous worship to allow it to be creation.

There is, however, more to secularization than just the influence of the Christian faith that leads to de-sacralization of reality. Secularization as fruit of the Enlightenment rejects the sovereignty of God himself, not just the idolatrous worship of creation. It is especially Schuurman who in his publications dealing with the philosophy of culture identifies the spiritual driving force behind science and technology. In this connection he speaks of technicism.

We wish to summarize our judgment in the thesis that secularization elevates man to king of creation in God's place. Consequently the concept of grateful usage is thwarted. It is replaced by a self-centered regime that knows no bounds, precisely what the Scriptures warn against. Undoubtedly there are Christians who, despite the message of the Bible, have yielded to this idolatrous regime. Early evidence of this may be what Noordegraaf (correctly) identifies, namely that Christian theology has usually paid more attention to the notion of cultivation than that of conservation (1990, 49).

In passing, the reader is reminded of Moltmann's suggestion to call man the image of the world (*imago mundi*). He explains this designation in terms of three concentric circles (1985, 196ff.). As the last creature before the Sabbath, man embodies all other creatures. He carries within himself all evolutionary systems. He is the microcosm that represents the macrocosm. As such man represents God in the community of creation. He represents God's glory. Man finds his priestly destiny in that he represents creation to God and God to creation. He may not be completely identified with the creation community, nor be detached from it. According to Moltmann, the *imago mundi* can only be defended in connection with the image of God (*imago Dei*).

We appreciate the responsibility that Moltmann ascribes to man. This responsibility is accompanied by a limitation. We object to the evolutionary framework within which Moltmann, like G. Manenschijn, places his observations. We question whether in this connection one can employ the term *imago* twice, while assigning rather different meanings to it. Is the term *imago mundi* not partly inspired by the evolutionary framework of Moltmann's doctrine of creation? If man is to be *imago Dei* in his rule over creation, he cannot be *imago mundi* at the same time.

We close this section with the term with which we began: "steward." We recognize in it the concept of calling (see Velema, 1988[2], 83–109). This calling offers scope and limitation for man's task. In no way will this calling tolerate man's slavery to the economy, technology, luxury, and capital. Man has been called to rule responsibly.

4. We wish to make two additional points in this connection. The concept of the *pilgrim life* is raised in relation with the cultural mandate.[70] Douma has changed his position to some extent. Although he does wish to retain the concept of the pilgrim life, he no longer places it next to, let alone in contrast with, the cultural mandate (in the sense of *either* cultural mandate *or* pilgrim life). He sees the pilgrim life as a consequence of the cultural mandate. He writes: cultural mandate *and* therefore the pilgrim life (1990, 195). He feels that in retrospect he can yet appeal to Schilder himself.

To us it is critical, however, that the concept of pilgrimage is given by the fact that Jesus has ascended to heaven and from there conducts his work in and through his church on earth. This pneumatological setting is missing in Schilder's theory of the cultural mandate. Schilder returns to the very beginning and on this basis lets man work in creation. The concept of the pilgrim life offers no scope for a yet-to-be-completed program of creation. See the incisive criticism that Douma directs at this programmatic elaboration of creation (1990, 198ff.). When Douma introduces the notion of the pilgrim life in his revised view of the cultural mandate, he thereby incorporates discussions of subsequent years.[71] These, however, are from the post-Schilder era. We

70. See the essay by Berkhof mentioned above (footnote 62). See also G. Dekker and K. U. Gäbler (ed.), *Secularisatie in theologisch perspectief* (1989).

71. Douma, 1989, 50–59, discusses these questions. In his essay "Christ and culture," in K. Schilder, *Aspecten van zijn werk* (aspects of his work), 1990, 169–201, he discusses the subject in summary form.

are of the opinion that the execution of the cultural mandate and the life of the believer as image of God until Christ's return are determined by the pilgrim life. This prevents the programmatic aspect that Douma correctly criticizes in Kuyper and Schilder (1990, 198).

5. The final point is the *future*. We do not mean to present a picture of what will precede Christ's return. It has to do with doing justice to what Paul writes in Romans 8:19–21. Creation itself will be freed from bondage to corruption to the freedom of the glory of the children of God.[72] The destiny of creation is tied to the acts of man. Note that what applies to God's children in the ultimate redemption (glorious freedom) is here ascribed to creation itself. In the consummation of all things it will become apparent how the redemption of people has consequences for creation. After all, as God's image, man has been placed over creation. When man is restored radically and permanently to this image, creation will experience the salutary consequences. Regarding this, see the commentary of Calvin on this passage. The relationship between man and creation, image and salutary dominion, are maintained all the way until the *eschaton*. "He has made us kings and priests unto his God and Father" (Rev. 1:6). This is the perfected state of the image of God (see Rev. 5:10).

In this chapter we cannot elaborate on the eschatology with respect to man. For this, see chapter 15. It is clear that man has an eternal future. Redemption will be definitive. This expectation does not call man away from his place and task on earth. It rather stimulates him. See especially 1 John 3:2–3 and 2 Corinthians 5:6–10.

The calling remains valid. The task is not removed from us. Passages such as 2 Corinthians 3:18, Colossians 3:10, and Ephesians 4:24 (discussed above) show that the renewing work of the Holy Spirit becomes concrete in the fight against sin.

The important thing is that soon we will bear the image of heavenly man. It will not be a mere duplicate of our being human that was given to us at creation. It is as much richer than the creaturely, paradisiacal human being, as the last Adam—the life-giving Spirit—is more glorious than the first man.

72. J. P. Versteeg, "Het heden van de toekomst" (the presence of the future), 1969, and "De toekomst van de schepping" (the future of creation), in *Geest, ambt en uitzicht* (Spirit, office, and outlook), 1989, 117–38, 139–54.

In the New Jerusalem, the Lamb will not disappear. The Lamb is made central there. That we will be conformed to the glorified body of Christ (Phil. 3:21) means that the restoration of the image of God on the new earth will orient us to Christ. Those who with Van Ruler speak of merely a messianic intermezzo cannot do justice to this eschatological, anthropological reality.[73] Our being human is redeemed by Christ. Man remains conformed to him as the image of God—also and especially following Christ's return. Only then will being human be perfect, conforming completely to the image of Christ.

Some Literature

J. T. Bakker et al., *L. Feurbach. Profeet van het atheïsme* (prophet of atheism), 1972.

O. Bardenhewer et al. (ed.), *Bibliothek der Kirchenväter. Eine Auswahl patristischer Werke in deutscher Übersetzung* (library of the church fathers; a selection of works translated into German), 1. und 2. Band, 1912.

J. H. Bavinck, *Religieus besef en christelijk geloof* (religious awareness and Christian faith), 1989².

J. H. Becker, *Het begrip nèfèsj in het Oude Testament* (the nèfèsj concept in the Old Testament), 1942.

H. Berkhof, *De mens onderweg* (man en route), 1960.

H. Berkhof and A. S. van der Woude (ed.), *Wat dunkt u van de mens?* (what do you think of man), 1970.

G. C. Berkouwer, *Man: The Image of God*, 1962.

Ch. de Beus, *De mens als het beeld Gods in the Oude en Nieuwe Testament* (man as image of God in the Old and New Testament), 1968.

E. Brunner, *Der Mensch im Widerspruch* (man in rebellion), 1941.

D. Cairns, *The Image of God in Man*, 1953.

J. Douma, "Christus en cultuur" (Christ and culture), in J. Douma (ed.), *K. Schilder. Aspecten van zijn werk* (aspects of his work), 1990, 169–201.

J. Douma, *Milieu en manipulatie* (environment and manipulation), 1989.

J. Faber, "Imago Dei in Calvin: Calvin's Doctrine of Man as the Image of God in Connection with Sin and Restoration," in J. Faber, *Essays in Reformed Doctrine*, 1990, 251–81.

73. See for this § 41.5.5 and footnote 73 there.

J. Faber, "Imago Dei in Calvin: Calvin's Doctrine of Man as the Image of God by Virtue of Creation," in J. Faber, *Essays in Reformed Doctrine*, 1990, 227–50.

C. Gestrich, *Die Wiederkehr des Glanzes in der Welt* (the return of splendor in the world), 1989.

F. J. A. de Grijs, *Goddelijk mensontwerp* (divine design of man), part 1 and 2, 1967.

A. A. Hoekema, *Created in God's Image*, 1986.

G. J. Hoenderdaal, *De mens in tweestrijd*, 1965.

C. Houtman, *Wereld and tegenwereld* (world and counter-world). *Mens en milieu in de Bijbel*, 1982.

Ph. E. Hughes, *The True Image*, 1989.

J. Kamphuis, *Uit verlies winst* (gain from loss), 1985.

H. W. de Knijff, *Venus aan de leiband* (Venus on the leash), 1987.

A. König, "Rykdom en verskeidenheid. 'n Poging tot 'n ekemeniese antropologie" (wealth and variety: an attempt at ecumenical anthropology), in *'n Woord op sy tyd* (a word in time). *Feestbundel voor* (festschrift for) *Joh. Heyns*, 1988, 77–87.

E. S. Klein Kranenburg, *Trialoog*, De Derde in het pastorale gesprek (Den Haag: 1988).

W. Krusche, *Das Wirken des Heiligen Geistes nach Calvin* (the work of the Holy Spirit according to Calvin), 1957.

A. Kruyswijk, *"Geen gesneden beeld . . ."* (no graven image), 1962.

R. C. Kwant, *Mensbeelden. Filosofie in een pluriforme samenleving* (images of man; philosophy in a pluriform society), 1975.

G. van Leeuwen, *Christologie en anthropologie*, no date.

G. van Leeuwen, *Om mens te zijn* (to be human), 1975.

C. H. Lindijer, *Het begrip sarx bij Paulus* (the concept of *sarx* in Paul), 1952.

G. Manenschijn, *Geplunderde aarde, getergde hemel. Ontwerp voor een christelijke milieu-ethiek* (ravaged earth, provoked heaven; sketch for a Christian environmental ethics), 1988.

J. Moltmann, *De mens* (man), 1972.

J. Moltmann, *Gott in Schöpfung* (God in creation), 1985.

J. Moltmann, *Trinität und Reich Gottes* (Trinity and kingdom of God), 1980.

L. W. Nauta, *De veranderbaarheid van de mens* (the changeability of man), 1973.

R. Niebuhr, *Wezen en bestemming van de mens* (essence and destiny of man), 1, 1951; 2, 1957.

G. C. van Niftrik, *De vooruitgang der mensheid* (progress of man), 1966.

G. C. van Niftrik, *Zie, de mens!* (behold the man!), 1951.

A. Noordegraaf, *Leven voor Gods aangezicht* (living in God's presence), 1990.

A. Noordegraaf, *Medemenselijkeheid* (fellow humanity), 1981.

B. J. Oosterhoff, *Hoe lezen wij Genesis 2 en 3?* (how do we read Genesis 2 and 3?), 1972.

W. Otten, *The Anthropology of Johannes Scottus Eriugena*, 1991.

W. J. Ouweneel, *Psychologie*, 1984.

W. Pannenberg, *Anthropologie in theologischer Perspektive*, 1983.

W. Pannenberg, *Die Bestimmung des Menschen* (the destiny of man), 1978.

A. Peters, *Der Mensch* (man), 1979.

C. A. van Peursen, *Lichaam-ziel-geest* (body-soul-spirit), 1956.

J. J. Rebel, *Pastoraat in pneumatologisch perspektief*, 1981.

A. de Reuver, "De mens naar Gods Beeld" (man in God's image), *Th. Ref.* 23 (1980): 246–60.

M. J. Rouët de Journel S. I., *Enchiridion patristicum. Loci ss. patrium, doctorum scriptorum ecclesiasticorum*, 1958[20].

Th. Schneider (ed.), *Mann und Frau. Grundproblem theologischer Anthropologie*, 1989.

E. Schroten, "De anthropologie bij Calvijn," in *Waarheid, wijsheid en leven (truth, wisdom, and life), feestbundel (festschrift) voor J. Severijn*, 1956, 47–62.

E. Schuurman, *Het "technische paradijs." Om de gebrokenheid van heel de schepping* (technological paradise: about the brokenness of the entire creation), 1989.

J. Severijn, *"Bevestig dat . . ."* (confirm that . . .), 1963; there "Imago Dei," 24–41.

H. Thielicke, *Mensch sein—Mensch werden* (being man, becoming man), 1976.

T. F. Torrance, *Calvins Lehre vom Menschen* (Calvin's doctrine of man), 1949.

B. van 't Veld, *"Gelijk het gras . . ."* ("as the grass . . ."), 1989.

W. H. Velema, *Geroepen tot heilig leven* (called to a holy life), 1988[2].

W. H. Velema, *Wet en evangelie* (law and gospel), 1987.

J. Verburg, *Adam*, 1973.

J. P. Versteeg, *Christus en de Geest* (Christ and the Spirit), 1971.

J. M. Vlijm, *Het religie-begrip van Karl Barth* (Karl Barth's concept of religion), 1956.

Waarheid, wijsheid en leven (Truth, wisdom and life). Collection of studies dedicated to J. Severijn, (1956).

H. W. Wolff, *Anthropologie des Alten Testaments*, 1974[2].

L. van der Zanden, *De mensch als beeld Gods* (man as image of God), no date.

Chapter 9

Sin

§ 26. The origin and nature of sin

26.1. *The place of the doctrine of sin in dogmatics*

1. The expression "it's a sin" is quite typical of the way in which sin is perceived and discussed these days. The word "sin" still forms part of people's vocabulary, but its significance has been substantially eroded. It usually denotes something that is merely unpleasant or a pity. Its deeper biblical significance has disappeared in popular usage.

This reflects not only shallowness but also a degree of disgust or revulsion, which in turn is related to resistance to the gospel on the part of many in our society. Sin is associated with gloom and despair. Those who associate sin with sexual taboos accuse the church of suppressing sexuality. This accusation is usually intended to dismiss sin altogether.

It is not our intention to paint a detailed picture of the way in which sin is viewed today. A concise review is contained in the book by J. Hoek (1988, 9–11). We only wish to highlight two factors: in the first place, it is worth mentioning that the biblical concept of sin has been sharply criticized by feminism. It is believed that women are seriously underappreciated. Preoccupation with sin is thought to have thwarted both self-realization and the gratification of passion. In the second place, reference must be made to a number of modern writers of fiction brought up in Christian homes. Their abandonment of the Christian faith is frequently evidenced by their rejection of the biblical concept of sin, often cloaked in mockery.[1]

Against this background it is therefore noteworthy that the concept of sin has received serious attention in publications such as *Kernwoorden in het christelijke geloof* (key words in the Christian faith) and *Zeven weerbarstige woorden uit het Christendom* (seven troublesome words of Christianity). Regardless of their views, their authors at least recognize that sin deserves recognition as a "key word."

2. Key concepts of the Christian faith such as grace, forgiveness, atonement, redemption, and renewal cannot be explained without reference to sin. This realization presents an immediate methodological problem, i.e., would it not be preferable to *discuss sin preeminently and exclusively from the perspective of grace*? Is sin given too much prominence by being treated in a separate chapter? In view of the biblical message of redemption, would it really be right to discuss sin ahead of the doctrines of the Redeemer and redemption (Christology and soteriology respectively)? Does it isolate sin too much? Do we then not make ourselves guilty of the very nature of sin, namely independence from God, his Word, and his work?

Especially Barth, in radically restructuring dogmatics, refrained from devoting a separate chapter to sin. J. M. Hasselaar followed in his footsteps by refusing to devote a separate, independent chapter (locus) in dogmatics on the doctrine of sin (harmatiology) (1953, 285).

It is surprising that in footnote 8 of chapter 8 on page 355 the latter expresses the view that in describing Barth's anthropology Van Niftrik "appropriately dedicated a chapter to Barth's doctrine of sin." Although sin is not quite treated as a distinct *locus* here, it is at least discussed in a separate chapter.

In reaction to the above objection, we refer to the sequence of *law and gospel* (see § 14.2, subsection 3). The relationship between these two concepts presents us with the same issue. On the basis of the historical sequence of creation, fall, and redemption it is both logical and correct to treat sin as a separate chapter between the doctrines of creation and

1. In his book *Katholiciteit en vrijzinnigheid* (Catholicism and liberalism), 1990, 103, S. W. Couwenberg concurs with Max Scheler, whom he quoted as saying that he hoped soon to be rid of his greatest enemy, namely his preoccupation with sin.

redemption. Furthermore, the absence of a separate chapter on sin in Barth's dogmatics proves that it is only of secondary significance to him. In his view it is eclipsed by the preeminence of grace.[2]

We consider it feasible to discuss sin in a separate chapter prior to the doctrine of redemption, without placing sin on a pedestal and without losing sight of its connection with redemption. The advantage of this approach will become clear in the treatment of the awareness of sin later in this chapter.

3. In this separate chapter *we do not seek to explain sin.*

Especially Berkouwer has shown himself to be a fervent opponent of any attempt to explain sin. He emphasizes that the biblical premise of the doctrine of sin must be that God is neither the author nor the cause of sin ("*Deus non est causa, auctor pecatti.*" *Sin*, 1971, 27 [see Belgic Confession of Faith, article 13]). Berkouwer categorically refuses to speak of a cause (*causa*) of sin. God placed sin under a curse by way of the cross. This clearly reveals the senseless, unwarranted, and lawless nature of sin (*Sin*, 47). God rejects sin absolutely. It does not make sense to speak about God as desiring sin (*Sin*, 54). Consequently Berkouwer completely ignores the relationship between sin and God's counsel. He grants that God employs sin counter to its own intentions, thwarts it, condemns it, and redeems it (*Sin*, 55). Sin is an enigma. Confession of guilt is the converse of the inexplicability of sin.[3]

We now face the question as to what we wish to accomplish with this chapter in the totality of dogmatics, especially considering that the title of the first section is: "The origin and nature of sin." However, it is not our intention to pursue a causal interpretation. What is senseless and completely lawless cannot be explained as making sense. It cannot be a link in a chain of positive factors and developments.

On the other hand, we must say that the Bible refers to the reality and the phenomenon of sin in both a historical and present sense. It places sin within the framework of redemption and the anticipation of a complete liberation from sin.

It is our objective to echo Scripture in retracing the origin of, nature of, and redemption from sin. Berkouwer is right in rejecting a causal explanation of the reality and phenomenon of sin. The question whether there is anything else to be said within the overall message of Scripture will be answered at the end of this chapter.

2. One can see in *Christliche Ethik* (Christian ethics), 1965, 3, by Deen N. H. Soe—who was strongly influenced by Barth—that sin is not discussed until section 32, as the last topic in the main body of the text.

3. See Hoek, 1988, 40ff. Berkhof rejected Berkouwer's alternative—simultaneously confessing and explaining sin—as being artificial (*C.F.*, 202).

26.2. *Biblical data*

1. *We begin* our discussion of the biblical data by starting at the beginning of the Bible, namely in *Paradise.*

Scripture, which we believe to be the authoritative Word of God, testifies with respect to the origin of sin by picturing man as having been created "good" by God, and as having subsequently disobeyed his command in Paradise. See the Heidelberg Catechism, answer 7, and Belgic Confession of Faith, article 14, both of which refer to "the commandment of life."

Paul draws a parallel between Adam and Christ (Rom. 5:12–21). The same parallel figures in Paul's teaching concerning the resurrection (1 Cor. 15:20–22, 45–49).

J. P. Versteeg wrote a significant paper, 1969², 29–70, in reaction to Kuitert's depiction of Adam as merely a teaching device. Various authors have referred to this paper at critical points in their analyses, e.g., Hoekema, 1986, 116, 117; Wentsel, *Dogm.*, 3a:719; Hoek, 1988, 70.

The abandonment of the historicity of Paradise and the fall of Adam and Eve into sin repeatedly proves to have far-reaching consequences for various aspects of the dogmatics. Without pursuing all facets of this issue, we wish to point out that Adam does appear in genealogies as a historical person (Gen. 5:1, 3–5; 1 Chron. 1:1; Luke 3:38). Adam's name turns up in other places as well (Gen. 4:25; Job 31:33; Hos. 6:7). The basis of Jesus' reference to Genesis 1:27 and 2:24 (in Matt. 19:4–6; Mark 10:6–8) is the historicity of Adam as the first human being. See further 1 Timothy 2:13. These references perfectly agree with the passages in Romans 5 and 1 Corinthians 15 referred to above.

In the conclusion of his article, Versteeg points out that treating Adam merely as a pedagogical device rather than a historical person brings with it a particular view of sin, redemption, and the Redeemer (1969, 66–69).

Berkhof distinguishes four clusters of scriptural authority (see § 8.2, subsection 4). In his view, the depiction of Satan belongs to the third or fourth level. Having been derived from contemporaneous depictions as factual information it is not considered to have any normative significance. It merely serves to convey the seductive power of sin. The distinction among levels of scriptural authority appears to us as being completely arbitrary. Furthermore, since depictions of the third and fourth clusters are also used in the first cluster, they also affect the communication of the core message of the Bible.

2. At any rate, in Genesis 3 we learn the following facts regarding the inception of sin in the lives of Adam and Eve.

Man fell into sin through temptation. This implies that evil—the power of sin manifested in antagonism toward God and disobedience against God's command—existed before Adam fell into sin. The very first sin must therefore be ascribed to the devil.

Jesus identifies the serpent with the devil (John 8:44). The latter's work is described as lies and murder. In various places in the Old Testament we also meet the devil as a lying spirit. His temptations are cloaked in lies and entice people to lie (1 Kings 22:22). He incites people to sin (1 Chron. 21:1) and is God's adversary (Job 1 and 2; Zech. 3:1–2). In Revelation 12:9 and 20:2 the devil is called "that old serpent." As far as the disobedience of the unfaithful angels and their judgment are concerned, see Jude 6 and 2 Peter 2:4.[4] See also § 19.2, subsection 3. Referring to Bavinck, Van Houwelingen points out that it is usually assumed that pride drove those angels to apostasy by disobeying God.

The temptation of Adam and Eve involved imagination. Their imagination was aroused by bringing God's prohibition into question. By disputing this prohibition, they gave free rein to their imagination. With the help of the serpent, Satan appealed to the attraction of the forbidden fruit. Imagination and desire reinforce each other (cf. James 1:15).

3. *The fact that man is tempted does not diminish his guilt.* We know that Satan also tempted Jesus (e.g., Matt. 4:1–11; 27:40–44). The same thing is true of people whether they are believers or not (see 1 Cor. 10:12ff.; James 1:13–16; and especially the last petition in the Lord's Prayer, Matt. 6:13). Although temptation can make it harder not to sin, it does not diminish the guilt for the sin committed. Perseverance in loving obedience is demonstrated by resistance to temptation (see James 1:12).

4. Adam's sin consists in *transgression of God's prohibition.* He and Eve were prohibited from eating from the Tree of Knowledge of Good and Evil (Gen. 2:17). Exegetes disagree on practically every aspect

4. Regarding the latter text, see P. H. R. van Houwelingen, *De tweede trompet* (the second trumpet), 1988, 166–68, and Calvin's commentary, to which Van Houwelingen also referred.

of Genesis 2 and 3. It is beyond the scope of this book to compare and contrast every facet of all of the various exegetical positions and findings.

We believe that *knowledge* here refers to determining, ascertaining, and deciding (for a detailed review see Oosterhoff, 1972, 142–51, especially 149). Man is prohibited from deciding for himself what is good and what is evil. He has to accept whatever God decides the distinction to be. He has to submit himself to this rule. This is also confirmed by the fruit that man took. Man appropriated something that is only due God. He claimed equality with God. In Genesis 3:22 God concedes this as a fact without sarcasm or caricature. Man sought to usurp God's position. He reached for God's crown and claimed what was only due God. According to Oosterhoff (1972, 152), man withdrew himself from God's authority and law, sought to stand on his own two feet, and wished to try his own fortune against God's will. God's will had been made known to him through the declared prohibition.

5. Here we encounter *sin in the form of pride* (as in the devil's case) as well as *unbelief and disobedience*. We shall return to these characterizations later. The only thing that needs to be pointed out now is that the punishment for this sin consists in being forbidden to eat from the Tree of Life. This tree signifies and seals man's eternal life in the sense of true spiritual life in communion with God (Oosterhoff, 1972, 130). Since sin results in man's death, he is denied access to the sign of the eternal life that he has forfeited!

6. Sin is *not merely a formal act*. It is not a minor event, such as "just taking a bite out of an apple," as it is sometimes described. It is then thought that everyone stumbles once in a while, at least over a small matter such as this.

On the contrary, the context shows that the key question is whether man recognizes God as God and whether he honors the boundary imposed by God, and that by crossing this boundary man claims equality with God. In fact, the latter implies that he collaborates with the devil in lying (and murdering)! Both trees have sacramental significance. There is a "sacrament" to keep man from evil, by denying him "the sinful pleasure" of the fruit!

This confronts man with a decision with respect to his relationship with God. The test has to be taken to confirm whether man indeed recognizes God as God.

7. Recognition of the boundary imposed by God is intended to be manifested in *spontaneous love and obedience*. This is neither a mere formality nor formalism. It is a matter of life and death. It is an astute insight of the Belgic Confession of Faith, article 14, to speak of "a commandment of life." We consider the expression "commandment of life" to be a true and even essential qualification of the concept of "probationary commandment" first suggested by Augustine. Augustine is right that God tests man. This test is not entirely symbolic. Its aim is the life that God grants upon obedience. Recognizing the boundary is a matter of life and death, death being the consequence of crossing this boundary! Man's sin begins when he crosses this boundary. He takes his life into his own hands (by reaching for the fruit). He wants to decide for himself what is good and what is evil. This implies in fact that what God calls sin, he considers to be good! This is how sin begins and progresses. He who rejects the way and the command of life achieves death instead. When God put Adam to the test, avoidance of death was at stake. He failed, and this is the historical reality of the fall into sin.

8. This beginning is *confirmed in the rest of the Bible*. We are not yet ready to discuss the spread of sin. Instead we focus on the terms used in the Bible to describe sin, of which there is a great variety. Despite common elements, we are struck by numerous nuances. Although we explore various emphases, we never lose sight of the senseless and gloomy phenomenon of sin itself.[5]

We begin with a reminder of the positive meaning of the fear of the LORD. It means wisdom coupled with the avoidance of evil (Job 28:28). It is the key to life (Prov. 4:22; 9:11; 10:11; 14:27). Disobedience means death (Prov. 8:26). Oosterhoff (1972, 154) points out that it is just as though the end of Proverbs 1 was written with the story of Paradise in mind. See 1:29–33.

5. R. Knierim, *THAT*, 1:547, points out that *chata, ra'a, "awoon and pesha"* are to be preferred as formal concepts. They tend to summarize what is involved. *Ra'a* usually occurs by itself. The other three terms tend to turn up as a triad in each other's company.

9. We encounter this same deep contrast in words that denote sin. First of all, there is *to sin* (*chata*) and *sin* (*chattaat*). These terms indicate the missing of a target. It refers to the error described in Proverbs 19:2. Here we encounter sin as violating the order established by God, or—more accurately—opposing someone with whom we have a covenantal relationship (1 Kings 8:46; Jer. 16:10–13). This word is used frequently to describe the sins committed by Israel as a nation (Ex. 32:31; Hos. 4:7; Ps. 78:32).

This particular sin has a dynamic effect. It produces disaster that strikes people contagiously and destructively as a consequence of God's judgment (Josh. 7:11; Hos. 7:1). See especially 1 Kings 13:34. David uses this word in Psalm 51:4. Micah feels himself called and emboldened to denounce Israel's sin in this sense (Mic. 3:8). In the words of the prophets we encounter this very term (Isa. 30:1; 5:18; Jer. 16:18; 17:3). All these places are reminiscent of Israel's apostasy from the God of the covenant. This apostasy is manifested in transgression against the second tablet of the law, and especially the serving of other gods and dependence on (the gods of) other nations on the first tablet.

The next word that we refer to is *awoon*. It means to be crooked, to be wrong, and to depart from the right way. This word expresses evil intent, disloyalty, and inner wrong. It indicates the enmity of the heart. It is noteworthy that two-thirds of its usage appears in Psalms, Job, and Proverbs. We only mention a few passages (Pss. 5:5; 14:4; 36:12; 94:4, 16; Job 31:3; 34:8, 22; Prov. 10:29). This word also reminds us of the disastrous effect of sin! It expresses death and its consequences (Ps. 55:3; Isa. 59:4, 6). In this word we encounter the deepest dimension of sin.

It is typical of the Old Testament that evil intent and disastrous deeds are not kept apart. The depth of sin does not diminish its reach, nor vice versa.

As a third word we mention *pesha*, which means to revolt, to commit revolution, to rebel against legitimate authority. We see the process of this sin described in the Psalms. Paul also refers to this sin in Romans 5:19. We find it expressed in Isaiah 1:2, namely rebellious apostasy from the LORD, the God of the covenant, and especially in Hosea 8:1. In connection with this word we can speak of the vertical dimension of sin, namely pride and presumption, which cause man to collide with the rights and the demands of the God of the covenant. It is not a collision with a peripheral rule, but with the rule of God who seeks the well–being of his people. This is why this type of rebellion is so devastating.

Sin blinds people's eyes and darkens their hearts. This is why it leads to error. *Shaga* means to wander, to be mistaken. This word indicates unintentional sin (Num. 35:15, 22). Although there is no doubt that in 1 Samuel 26:21 Saul does not appeal to his ignorance when he confesses his sin to David, the same verb is used there. See especially the conclusion of this verse.

There is gradation in sin from the point of view of whether one is aware of it or not. There is also gradation from the point of view whether the action is intentional or not. We shall return to this idea later. In this way both ignorance and blindness are the result of sin. Is the consequence of sin in terms of ignorance and in being mistaken not reminiscent of the root of all sin? Those who deny this would have to talk in terms of tragedy rather than sin.

The word *chamaas* refers to sin as an act of violence, especially in the form of injustice perpetrated against a fellow human being. Consider verses such as Zephaniah

3:4, where violence is aimed at the law itself. Jeremiah 22:3, Isaiah 59:6, and Ezekiel 7:23 refer to sin committed against fellow human beings, i.e., bloodguilt that pervades the nation. This word also applies to the deforestation of Lebanon (Hab. 2:17a) and creation itself, including the environment (Gen. 6:11, 13). Psalm 72 portrays the messianic King whose rule will be marked by the antithesis of this violence.

Ra'a is the counterpart of the Hebrew word for good (*tob*). As H. J. Stoebe (*THAT*, 2:796) has pointed out, this word has both profane and theological connotations. When *ra'a* is the consequence of man's actions, it constitutes evil in an active and simultaneously very comprehensive sense. It refers to a destructive act perpetrated against another human being arising from an evil disposition (Ps. 34:17; Prov. 3:7; Deut. 28:20; Isa. 1:16).

Ra'a refers to what is evil and brings disaster. It reflects a harmony of intention and action. This internal evil—so to speak—expresses itself in an act that takes place outside the heart.

The picture in the New Testament is much the same. The most common word for *to sin* is *hamartano*, and the corresponding word for *sin* is *hamartia*. Like the Hebrew word *chata*, it means to miss one's target. In addition we would like to point out that John characterizes sin as lawlessness (*anomia*): 1 John 3:4; 5:17. He refers to the slavery to which the sinner yields and on the basis of which he acts (John 8:34).[6]

Typical of sin is disobedience in terms of transgression of the rule established by God, the breaking of the covenant, the inner opposition to God, and simultaneously the inner depravity of the sinner. Sin causes evil and disaster. It has evil consequences for both fellow human beings and the sinner himself. Sin makes man guilty before God, and takes man prisoner. He loses the freedom given to him by God. Sin chains man to evil. This clearly comes through in the designation of enmity against God (*echthra*, Rom. 8:7). A number of the terms used here will be further clarified below.

26.3. *The nature of sin*

1. Having presented the biblical data, we now turn to a systematic analysis of the nature of sin. In the process of this analysis we shall refer to the foregoing data as well as other Scripture passages.

It may be asked whether one can speak intelligently about the nature of sin separately from a discussion about judgment and atonement. It would be rather one-sided to interpret the biblical data on the nature and manifestation of sin solely from the perspective of atonement. This would imply that only the victory over sin (i.e., the removal of its consequences) would lead us to the core of sin. We want to start at the beginning, and not in the middle, or at the end! The nature of sin can only be revealed in its entirety from the perspective of its onset. In the discussion of God's judgment on sin and the atonement of sin we shall not encounter any other elements than those presented

6. For the New Testament perspective see the overview by Pop, 1972, 613–23.

above. We recall that in the foregoing overview we encountered sin in its reality, i.e., in the vigor of its ruinous act.

We now address the nature of sin. We systematize the biblical data by tracing the interconnections of the breadth, depth, and height of the phenomenon of sin.

2. A key question is whether sin must also be called a *breaking of the covenant*. This is definitely the case for people who live under the covenant of grace. Circumcision and baptism are the sign and seal of the covenant under the old and new dispensations respectively. All sins of its partners imply a breaking of the covenant.

Does this also apply to those who have not been incorporated into the covenant of grace? Is it also true of Adam and all people who lived prior to Abraham, whether or not like Enosh (Gen. 4:26) they knew God and invoked his name?

Here we run into the well-known concept of the *covenant of works*. Those who accept this biblical perspective would have no difficulty in viewing Adam's sin already as covenant breach.

Possible objections to the idea of a covenant of works include not only its name (as though it concerned a labor-wage relationship, cf. a collective labor agreement), but also the fact that Genesis 1–3 does not mention the establishment of an official covenant. Subsequently this does become the case, namely with the establishment of the covenants with Noah (Gen. 9:8–17), Abraham (Gen. 17:1–27 and its preparation in 15:1–21), and Israel (Ex. 24:1–8).

We can say that in the Old Testament *berit* means "a definite recognition of the reality of communion between God and his people (or mankind), the complete recognition of God—the Holy One—who sovereignly establishes and leads this communion, and the definite recognition of the rules of the covenant instituted by God."

This paints the picture of a well-defined communion, established through solemn institution and acceptance, on the basis of an already existing relationship between YHWH and Israel. Its institution must be entirely ascribed to YHWH. Its acceptance by the people reflects their recognition of the position of YHWH as redeemer, protector, and ruler. The covenant comprises the gift and acceptance of God's promises and his commandments. The new communion with its privileges and commitments is cogently summarized in the words: "I shall be your God, and you will be my people" (Loonstra, 1990, 202).

In the Bible there is no detailed description of such a covenant prior to the narrative of Abraham. It is noteworthy that the agreement that God makes with Noah with respect to the continuation of creation is also called a covenant. The core of this covenant is the promise that God will not destroy the earth (again), but will preserve it for mankind. Hence, the rainbow (a phenomenon of creation that appears without human intervention) is the sign from God's side that seals this covenant with mankind.

In other words, the Bible indeed makes reference to a covenant prior to the covenant of grace established with Abraham and Israel.

Now we turn to what the Bible says about God's relationship with the first human being. Genesis 1 portrays creation as including a mandate combined with a promise (see § 23.2). In Genesis 2:17 we read of a prohibition coupled with a sanction, while the Tree of Life reminds us of the blessing of life that man receives if he does not disobey the prohibition (see § 26.2, subsection 5). Although the gift of life is not described with so many words, it can be inferred from the subsequent course of events that man forfeits the blessing of life when he disobeys the prohibition.

In this passage we encounter at any rate a sovereign decree on the part of God as the Creator. There is also the gift of life in communion with God, which is the converse of the threat of death in case of disobedience. The latter is explicitly stated. The former is in fact taken away from man when he is expelled from Paradise, and his descendants are faced with death. It is a matter of man having to acknowledge God by accepting his command and not seeing the sanction of death implemented. God's objective is life in communion with him, hence the "commandment of life." God wants to be the God of Adam and his family. They may belong to him by displaying his image.

Since being God's image implies that the relationship with God is neither arbitrary nor optional, it may be concluded that everything that follows has the character of a covenant, although it does not carry this name. Obedience and the rejection of disobedience are founded on the relationship established in Genesis 1:26–28. We see Genesis 2 as an elaboration of this, rather than the introduction of a new topic. Just as the story of creation is presented twice, so is the relationship between the Creator and man as his creature.

To us this in itself constitutes sufficient grounds for saying that the relationship between God and man is essentially a covenantal relationship. Although all of the elements (ingredients) are present, it does not carry this name. The identification of these elements in Genesis 1 and 2 does not constitute a fabrication on our own part. On the contrary, we merely trace and connect biblical lines. We prefer to speak of a *covenant of life*[7] rather than a covenant of works.

3. There is, however, *an additional aspect that strengthens and completes the foregoing reasoning*. This is *the position of Adam*, which Paul compares to that of Christ. In the next section we shall discuss Romans 5 in greater detail. Here it suffices to say that in a sense Adam occupies as fundamental a position with respect to his people as Christ represents to his people! We cannot speak about Christ's redeeming work without referring to the covenant. It may be concluded that Adam's position in the human race is unthinkable apart from God dealing with mankind through him. This implies a covenantal relationship. God is not dealing with a single human being here. Through Adam, God deals with everyone. The concept of communion, which manifests itself in the life of subsequent generations, is characteristic of the biblical concept of the covenant. According to Romans 5 this element is present when God speaks to Adam about life and death.

We therefore do not hesitate to say that God's relationship with Adam has the character of a covenantal relationship. Just as the explicitly identified covenant with Noah has its own character compared with that with Abraham and Israel, so also the covenant with Adam and his descendants has its own character compared with that of Noah and the subsequent covenant relationships.

We conclude that sin constitutes the breaking of the covenant. This perspective implies that sin does not just represent a transgression of formal rules. It goes deeper. It is directed against the sovereign Creator, who not only creates life, but also wants his people to experience a lasting communion with himself. Therefore sin constitutes opposition to the Creator who commits himself to grant life to man.

Sin is further intensified when it carries on in its rebellion against God who gives his Son Jesus Christ. Sin against the original favor and goodness of God is compounded by the rejection of God's grace. In this way sin does not change in character, but in intensity. It rejects

7. This term is also found in the Westminster Shorter Catechism, Müller, *Bek.*, 644. The study, including a detailed historical review by N. Diemer, *Het scheppingsverbond met Adam* (the covenant of creation with Adam), no date, is quite instructive.

not only God's original goodness but also his grace, which is meant to redeem from man's guilt and the evil consequences of his sin.

4. With the foregoing description we have exposed sin to its very core. But *there is yet more to be said*. Additional aspects can be identified and various nuances can be described. The Bible itself does so by employing a variety of terms.

Having defined "sin" as the breaking of the covenant, the main distinction that remains to be made is the question whether sin should be characterized as unbelief or disobedience. Once this question has been addressed, we shall deal with sin as a *privatio*. Heppe (*Dogm.*, 254), on the other hand, starts out his analysis with this latter term. Nevertheless, in the first segment of his discussion he does focus on the perspective of the law. The focus of his analysis is sin as lawlessness.

Sin is always the sin of man as the image of God. Therefore sin cannot be discussed without bringing it in relationship with God and without involving the sinner in this relationship. He is, after all, God's image.

Sin is indeed *unbelief*. Adam did not believe the word of God that came to him in the prohibition as a word of life. He did not consider it to be true, reliable, or forceful. To Calvin this characterizes sin. "Therefore unbelief was the root of apostasy. This in turn led to ambition and pride, coupled with ingratitude, because Adam, more covetous than warranted, despised the great goodness of God with which he had been blessed" (*Institutes*, 2.1.4).

For this reason Calvin opts for the definition of sin as unbelief and combines this with other characterizations that are its consequences. Earlier he says that Augustine is not incorrect in saying that pride is the beginning of all calamities. Yet Calvin does not end with Augustine.

In this connection it is good to point out that especially the New Testament warns against unbelief (coupled with distrust and doubt; e.g., Matt. 13:58; 17:17; John 20:27; Acts 28:24; Rom. 11:20; 2 Cor. 4:4; Heb. 3:19; Rev. 21:8). *Disobedience* is equivalent to unbelief. It consists in transgressing God's command (Gen. 3:6; Rom. 5:12–21; 2 Cor. 10:6; Heb. 2:2).

It is difficult to choose between these two. Sin is an act of the heart (Prov. 4:23; Matt. 15:18–19; the converse is the beatitude of the pure in heart, Matt. 5:8). He who in his heart chooses against God engages in both unbelief and disobedience. Both are aspects of the same thing. Sinful man rejects the Word of God that calls for faith. He rejects the commandment, which demands obedience.

As a third characterization we mention *pride*, which has also been expressed as being puffed up.[8] It is the antithesis of humility or meekness referred to in both the Old and New Testaments (see especially Phil. 2:3; Matt. 11:29; and many places in Proverbs, e.g., 15:33). For pride, see Proverbs 8:13; 14:3; 15:25. The kings of Babylon personify pride from a global point of view (Isa. 13–14; Jer. 50–51) as does Babylon at the end of time (Rev. 17–18).

It is obvious that sin also consists in hating God and one's neighbor. This hatred is the antithesis of the love commanded by God in his law. See especially Exodus 20:5 and Leviticus 19:17. The fact that hatred is the root of manslaughter is clear from Genesis 4:5–9 and Romans 3:11–16.[9]

5. When we now compare the various characteristics mentioned above, sin *as the breaking of the covenant* stands out. We consider this to be the best overall characterization of sin. It is directly related to the creation of man as the image of God.

The *breaking of the covenant manifests itself in various forms*, namely unbelief and disobedience, but no less in pride and hatred. We do not wish to consider these four characterizations in order of priority or as links in a chain of causation. Each of these four indicates in its own way what the nature of sin is. Man is such a richly variegated creature that a single characterization of sin would not suffice. Those who focus on lovelessness should not forget that it is very closely connected with unbelief. Love cannot exist in the absence of faith, and vice versa. The same is true of pride and disobedience. A disobedient human being seeks to elevate himself above God. Those who seek to elevate themselves above God are indeed disobedient. In this way one can form even more combinations!

These four sins spring from the heart as soon as man breaks the covenant. Conversely, all four of these characterizations imply that the covenant has been breached.

8. See a concise description of numerous aspects by Wentsel, *Dogm.*, 3a:719ff.

9. Berkouwer (1960, 18–27) discusses the nature of sin especially from the point of view of disobedience to the double commandment of love. This reflects his view of the image of God as *analogia amoris* (1957, 122).

Thus we end the characterization of sin. A number of consequences of sin will be discussed in a subsequent section. Our preference is to discuss these there rather than here. This is in contrast with Wentsel's approach (*Dogm.*, 3a:719ff.). For a philosophical discussion of sin and evil, we refer to Plantinga (1974) and Kroesen (1991).

We now return to the characterization of sin by Barth. He uses the terms "pride," "procrastination," and "deceit" (*C.D.*, 4.1.413–78, 4.2.403–83, 4.3.434–61). These terms have been derived from Christ's threefold office: King, Priest, and Prophet. We prefer unbelief to deceit and disobedience to procrastination. Barth's characterization reflects the fact that he does not think of the law as preceding the gospel. He characterizes sin from the perspective of the preeminence of grace. To us this is the reverse order (see Velema, 1987, 3–41, and then *C.D.*, 4.2.4).

Regarding the threefold office of Christ, see Immink, 1990, although he does not discuss the characterizations suggested by Barth.

Berkouwer questions whether these three characterizations are the most appropriate terms to describe sin, and wonders why other equally biblical expressions could not be used instead (*Sin*, 282). He points out that H. Vogel also starts off with the gospel. The latter suggests ingratitude as a Christian characterization of sin. Berkouwer points out that Barth does not infer his three definitions of sin directly from Christ's threefold office, but illustrates them with examples from both the Old and New Testaments. He adds: "From the central perspective of sin vis-à-vis God, all Biblical expressions are no more than rays of a single revealing light that falls on the deep darkness of sin" (*Sin*, 283). We prefer to distinguish between these characterizations of sin and the diffusion of sin into various manifestations that will be discussed below.

A strikingly different approach can be found in Wiersinga's book about sin. The subtitle, "Doom or Deed," indicates the dilemma facing him. He characterizes the view of the Reformed confessions and theology as a form of fatalism. In contrast with the nature of sin as doom he places the emphasis on the nature of sin as deed.

This is not the total picture. He emphasizes the nature of sin as deed in order to open the door to protesting against sin and being liberated from it! He rejects everything associated with the classical doctrine of sin. For example, he ignores the notion of opposition to God on the part of disobedient, rebellious human beings. In fact his position reflects an entirely different perspective. To him sin represents evil encountered in the world, which needs to be fought. To Wiersenga, the classical doctrine of sin implies that one has to put up with it. One has to accept the fact that one is sinful. Sin has become our second nature. He speaks of the naturalization of sin, which leads to neutralization. People no longer do anything about it. They acquiesce in it and live with it. He feels that the concept of original (hereditary) sin is the most fatalistic and eloquent description of this attitude.

Naturalization implies privatization. People lose track of connections and structures. If Wiersema had written his book today, he would of course also have included ecology.

The core of Wiersinga's doctrine of sin is that we can get rid of it. We simply have to resist it. Those who fail to do so commit the worst possible sin, namely complicity and collaboration. Sociological and political offensives need to be mounted against sin. This is necessary because of the collective violence of institutionalized greed. The worst sin is the absence of hope that change is possible. Jesus was without sin, because he did not surrender to disheartening acquiescence. Thus we have indicated a number of perspectives from this book (see also Wiersema, 1978a, 83–86).

It is to be appreciated that Wiersema is prepared to mount a fight against sin and its consequences. This aspect is sometimes overlooked. However, it does not do justice to the biblical perspective to limit our discussion of sin to a consideration of what can be done about it. Self-liberation is then a counterpart of the denial that sin is directed against God. According to Wiersinga it is not the worst thing that we have sinned, but that we do not have the courage and hope to do something about it. We would call this a radicalization of the position of Pelagius.

6. We now focus on the term *privatio boni* (privation of the good). We agree with Berkouwer (*Sin*, 256) that it "may seem strange" that this term has played such an important role in dogmatics.

For Augustine's use of this term see *Enchiridion*, 4:11, and *Confessiones*, 7:8, 22. With respect to Reformed theologians, see Heppe, *Dogm.*, 255, where the term *actuosa privatio* (actualized privation) is used, in contrast with *mera privatio* (mere privation). For references to proofs, see Polanus and Heidegger (262).

The concept of *privatio* is intended to emphasize that sin has no independent existence. It has no essence of its own. It is negatively related to what God says and does. It is not created as such. It is nothing but destruction, and therefore a lie, a rejection of the good word and work of God. Sin has not been created and makes no sense. Its nature is completely, demonically negative.

Despite reservations, Bavinck clearly defends the term *privatio*, "hereby described inadequately" (*R.D.*, 3:136–37), and, "objections against it rest on a misunderstanding" (*R.D.*, 3:140–41).

Berkouwer recalls that Calvin does not hesitate to employ negative terms for sin. "The legitimacy of the privatio concept is revealed by the context" (*Sin*, 260n84).

In our judgment, the characterization *privatio* contains an important element of truth.[10] However, it can only be understood and done full justice so long as it is related directly to the characterizations given above. The negative character of unbelief and disobedience, pride and lovelessness is correctly described as *privatio actuosa*. However, it is important to view *privatio* in the perspective of the relationship of man to God. It is not a matter of a neutral, highly general *negatio*. It comes down to the negatio of man in his relationship with God. This *negatio* constitutes man's *negatio* of God.[11]

We remind the reader of the description of man following the fall into sin as the image of God in a negative mode. *This negative mode can also be described as negatio*, which characterizes sin in its deepest essence.

Here we refer to characterizations of sin given by Bavinck: it is unlawful, irrational, foolish, and preposterous (*R.D.*, 3:70); it is unlawful (*R.D.*, 3:74); it cannot have its own principle and its own independent existence (*R.D.*, 3:138); its objective is the annihilation of everything that is good (*R.D.*, 3:139); it is an incomprehensible mystery and came into the world without motivation (*R.D.*, 3:145).

In all of these descriptions we encounter the characterizations discussed above as root concepts, because they express the foolishness of rebellion against God. Sin does not make sense and rebels against creation. Sin is without reason. It is irrational. It opposes the law and is beyond explanation. Those who despise the good law of God and depart from goodness end up choosing death. This is foolish, senseless, incomprehensible, unjust, and unfathomable. This is the very sin that says no to God and ends in nothingness.

We reject the view that Barth's doctrine of *Das Nichtige* is equivalent to the above characterizations provided by Bavinck (Berkouwer, *Sin*, 281n145). The key difference between Bavinck and Barth is that the former starts out from the situation in Paradise and the latter characterizes sin as *nichtig* (null and void) from the perspective of the preeminence of grace.

10. Berkouwer refers to it as a religious theme, incorporated polemically, 1960, 34.

11. M. Honecker, *Einführung in die theologische Ethik* (introduction to theological ethics), 1990, 52, points out that the distinction between good and evil does not represent the difference between Christian and non-Christian ethics. The difference is that Christian ethics views evil as sin against God (*coram Deo*). It defines evil in relationship to God.

§ 27. The spread and progression of sin

27.1. *The spread of sin*
27.2. *The progression of sin*

27.1. *The spread of sin*

1. *Sin spreads; this is its nature.* It wants to carry on. It is not satisfied with a single act and does not restrict itself to the human being who sins. Sin as rebellion against God is imperialistic and totalitarian. In this sense, it is the negative image of the beneficent rule that God exercises over mankind.

Sin has passed from the domain of angels to Adam and Eve. It has been passing from them as parents to their children. Genesis 3 is followed by Cain's murder of Abel. In this act sinful motives play a role, e.g., jealousy, envy, and hatred, and therefore begrudging the other person his life. This event is only one chapter removed from the story of Paradise.

The further we progress in the Bible, the more we see how sin spreads in terms of breadth and depth, scope, and intensity. We refer to the magnitude of man's evil as depicted in Genesis 6:5, 11–12. At this stage we are not focusing on the passages that are always mentioned in connection with original sin. We merely point to the enormous extent, the universality, the baffling self-evidence of sin as a phenomenon in our history (Pss. 14; 53; 130:3; 143:2; Prov. 20:9; Eccl. 7:20; Gal. 3:22; 1 John 1:8; 5:19). Both Job and David reflect on the sins of their youth (Job 13:26; Ps. 25:7; see also Ps. 58:4 and Isa. 43:27; 48:8; 57:3; Eph. 2:3).

This overview is not complete, but suffices to show that sin is general, universal, and total. Sin has succeeded in taking control of this world and its inhabitants. There is no human being, no situation, and no history in which we do not encounter it. We still need to address gradations of sin and the power of restraint. However, these two facts do not detract whatsoever from the universality of sin. They do make clear that sin does not always and everywhere achieve the maximum possible degree of evil.

2. Having described the universality and extent of sin, we now turn to a discussion of *the question of original sin*. No book about sin leaves this topic untouched.

We begin our discussion of original sin with Augustine. Van Genderen points out that prior to Augustine we encounter little of significance for the doctrine of the church (1987, 33). Augustine was first in exploring this doctrine in its biblical breadth and depth. This was triggered by the position taken by Pelagius. In contrast with the latter, Augustine confessed the radical nature of depravity through sin. It is not correct to ascribe Augustine's negative view of man solely to his Manichaean past. Augustine did not bring into the church from Manichaeism what has been labeled a pessimistic view of man. What he learned there—or actually from a different, dualistic context—he reworked from a biblical perspective. It was especially Paul (Rom. 5:12) who brought him to the confession of the radical depravity of man. Beginning with Augustine, characterizations of sin as pride and love of oneself have been used to gauge sin within the church and theology.

Pelagius focused exclusively on the act of sin. He conceded at most some weakening of our will and ability. In his view, man could save himself, albeit with God's help. He did not see a need for the renewal of our nature, but only of our behavior.

This contrast reveals a divergence of view that has persisted throughout the ages. The concept of original sin supports the radical nature of Augustine's view.

For a dogmatic description of these two positions, including salient references, see the contribution of Mühlenberg in Andresen, *Handbuch* (handbook), 1:445–63, which describes the four phases in the development of Augustine's doctrine of sin and grace. For his view with respect to original sin (including a host of references), see R. Seeberg, *Lehrbuch* (textbook), 2:504–6, and also Leo Scheffczyk, *Handbuch*, 2(3a):204–29, with a summary starting on 224. It remains a blemish on Augustine's doctrine of original sin that he interpreted *concupiscientia* as sexual desire. We are inclined to consider Augustine's biography to be partly responsible for this "derailment." See H. W. de Knijff, *Venus aan de leiband* (Venus on a leash), 1987, 108–11. This author refers to "Augustine's synthesis." With this he means that various themes from the ancient church converged in him.

There are many who object to the term original (hereditary) sin. Berkouwer points out that the expression "original sin" in and of itself cannot possibly provide a comprehensive perspective of the reality of guilt (*Sin*, 532). This formulation of Berkouwer's objection typifies his position. He, after all, considers the core of what is usually referred to as the issue of original sin to be the divine accusation and the human confession of guilt. Briefly, his exploration of various possible scenarios leads to the conclusion that they weaken the reality of guilt, albeit sometimes unintentionally and inadvertently so.

Hoek also raises objections to the term "original sin." He considers the translation of the term *peccatum originale* as *hereditary sin* (in Dutch) to be problematic. He accepts what is meant by it, but finds that the term itself leads to misunderstanding (1988, 73). Berkouwer agrees with him. So does A. van de Beek. The latter says: "If we deny original sin we ignore the aspect of collectivity of the human race, and it becomes a small step to wash our hands in the sovereign innocence of individuality" (1984, 140ff.). We can also mention Wentsel (*Dogm.*, 3a:724–26) and Brunner, although the latter expresses himself very negatively regarding this subject (*Dogmatics*, 2:113–17). This unanimity is remarkable. But it remains a question whether all of these authors mean the same thing, and how they arrive at their conclusions.

A discussion of original (hereditary) sin raises the question whether sin can really be inherited. When one inherits something, it becomes one's property, although one has not put any effort for it. It is a gift. This is the essence of an inheritance; it is something that you receive upon the death of the testator. This does not make any sense in the context of sin! Inheriting sin implies receiving a negative balance. But it is not a personal debt. It is at most an inherited debt, a debt that has been passed on. However, this runs counter to the biblical concept of what it means to be a sinner! One can only be guilty before God through personal sin.

3. These lines describe at the same time the issue of *realism* versus *federalism*. Before clarifying these terms, we remind the reader that a similar issue was encountered in the concepts of creationism and traducianism (§ 25.1, subsection 5).

Realism holds that we must have sinned in and with Adam. Otherwise it would be unjust for God to consider us guilty in Adam. There can only be guilt in the context of actual sin. Our relationship with Adam can only make us guilty if we actually sinned in and with him.

Putting it bluntly, but without ridicule, the question becomes whether we sinned in and with Adam as it were preexistently. This is how Berkouwer formulates the question (*Sin*, 440). Berkouwer calls Schilder's appeal to Hebrews 7 an ancillary line in the doctrine of original sin. Levi would have become subject to the tithe in Abraham. Schilder holds that Levi was indeed already present in Abraham. Berkouwer, however, feels that this genealogical perspective fails to justify an anthropologically realistic principle of preexistence in Abraham (*Sin*, 442–44).

Bavinck qualifies realism with "in a certain sense" (*R.D.*, Bavinck, 3:102), which considerably relativizes realism.

Over against this, *federalism* maintains that God holds all people guilty in Adam and treats them accordingly, not on the basis of actual participation in Adam's sins, but on the basis of attribution of Adam's guilt. The context of the covenant makes all people guilty in view of their relationship with Adam, the head of the covenant.

Berkouwer raises the objection that federalism fails to link punishment with guilt. It is in conflict with God's just judgment to punish imputed guilt. Only the person who sins acquires guilt and needs to be punished. This is also the reason for Barth's great annoyance with the concept of original sin (*C.D.*, 4.1.500ff.).

Federalism cannot escape the implication that Adam's descendants are forthwith considered guilty on the basis of extraneous sin (*peccatum alienum*). Original sin brings with it original pollution. This in fact implies double guilt, even though federalists refuse to admit this: guilt that is imputed immediately (*imputatio immediata*) as a consequence of being included in Adam, *and* the pollution of sin that actually causes us to sin. Federalism recognizes a causal link between (original) sin and original pollution. This (*causally connected*) twin concept implies a strange, original (inherited) guilt (*peccatum alienum*). It implies fatalism and determinism. Man is not considered guilty on the basis of personal sin, but because of the situation into which he is born: as a consequence of the covenant with Adam of which he is part.

In order to retain the concept of personal guilt (*peccatum proprium*), some have proposed to consider *original pollution to be the explanation of original sin*. Personal guilt would then reflect the sinfulness of our nature. Having inherited this nature, we would not really become sinful until the commitment of actual sin. This is an intermediate position between that of Pelagius (sinning by imitation) and the positions presented above. However motivated, both views start with guilt (Berkouwer, 1960, 239–43).

4. Is there *a way out* of this dilemma? Berkouwer rejects both realism and federalism. He emphasizes that one encounters the distinction

between original sin and original pollution neither in article 14 of the Belgic Confession of Faith, nor in Calvin's theology (*Sin*, 472–84, especially 483ff.).

This remark indicates the direction in which Berkouwer looks for a solution. He says that in Romans 5 Paul "focuses on an undeniable cohesion and solidarity in terms of death and guilt, without being prepared to state so theoretically." Paul treats the sin of one as the sin of all. In this connection Berkouwer refers to a *corporate perspective* that does not go as far as federalism or realism (*Sin*, 517–18). At any rate, he feels that the concept of original sin does not produce a global picture of the reality of guilt (*Sin*, 532).

There is solidarity in terms of guilt, although we cannot explain how it comes about. In our view, the divine accusation emphasized by Berkouwer does not imply that solidarity precludes personal sin.

We are inclined to say that Berkouwer must necessarily end up with a combination of corporatism and realism, although he personally does not want to go beyond the corporate perspective. If the corporate perspective is not to detract from the divine accusation, it must be based on the actual commitment of sin, because God's accusation focuses on man's personal sin (*peccatum proprium*). This is the core of Berkouwer's argument with respect to sin. This core also needs to be taken into account in his solution.

If Berkouwer does not wish to somehow relate his corporate perspective with realism, we shall have to conclude that with this concept he only intends to express the universality of sin. This would in fact imply that Berkouwer ignores the essential point of original sin, namely how our sin is related to that of Adam. To be frank, it must be admitted that his reasoning benefits from ignoring this issue. The only thing that matters to him is the divine accusation in terms of actual sins committed. In this case Berkouwer should have stated more clearly that to him (and to others) the concept of original sin merely captures the universality of sin! However, this would rob original sin of its essential core.[12]

5. We now seek to lay out *our own position* based on Scripture. In our first point we saw how widespread sin is (i.e., universal and totalitarian).

We have not yet mentioned the passages that indicate that every human being is depraved and guilty from the beginning of his existence.

12. The following article by Randall E. Otto is of interest, "The Solidarity of Mankind in Jonathan Edwards's Doctrine of Original Sin," *EQ* 62, no. 3 (1990): 205–21. He criticized Edwards's realism on the basis of various arguments. He himself defended solidarism.

At this point we continue to leave aside the most telling passages. In his prayer at the dedication of the temple, Solomon says: "for there is no man that sinneth not" (1 Kings 8:46; see also Ps. 143:2 and Eccl. 7:20). Psalm 130:3 indicates that no one is righteous before God. Job 14:4 says that nothing pure can be produced from the unclean. In Psalm 51:5, David says that he brought guilt with him when he came into the world.

This is correctly pointed out by Hoek (1988, 20). It is not clear to us why he adds that original sin could not be inferred from Psalm 51:5, but that it only provides a building block for what the church implies with the doctrine of original sin, i.e., to underscore the radical nature of sin. A dogma is constructed from considerations based on biblical data. A dogma is never found ready-made in a single Bible verse. Hoek is correct in saying that the essence of what the church confesses in terms of original sin is contained in Psalm 51:5.

N. H. Ridderbos correctly points out that this "is one of the clearest Old Testament passages dealing with original sin" (*K.V.*, 1973, 174).

Kraus interprets Psalm 51:5 as follows: "Der Urgrund, der Wurzelgrund meiner Existenz ist durchwirkt von Verderbnis" (the very ground, the root of my being is permeated with depravity, *Psalmen*, 1961², 387).

To these verses we must add the ones referred to earlier, namely Genesis 6:12; Job 15:14; Psalm 58:4; Proverbs 20:9 and 6. John 3:3–5 indicates that everyone needs to be born again.

Romans 5:12–21 is central to the discussion of original sin. We shall discuss this pericope in some detail, although Berkouwer provides an extensive treatment (*Sin*, 490–519). Berkouwer also refers to 1 Corinthians 15:22. This latter text does not deal explicitly with sin. It clearly does speak of dying in Adam. Berkouwer points to its connection with Romans 5 and wonders whether one could say that whereas Roman 5 speaks about "sinning in Adam," 1 Corinthians 15:22 focuses on "dying in Adam" (*Sin*, 491).

Before we start discussing Romans 5, we have to admit that the verses identified above do not explicitly connect the universality of sin with Adam. However, we believe that Romans 5 (in combination with Gen. 3 and 1 Cor. 15:22) should be interpreted as the root of the biblical concept of the universality of sin.

Although Romans 5 may have particular significance for the doctrine of original sin, the passages listed above should not be left out of consideration. All of them, including Psalm 51:5, elucidate Romans

5, which is the root and foundation of the interpretation of all of the other passages and facts, beginning with Genesis 3.

We shall now make a number of comments on Romans 5:12–21, without providing an exegesis of all facets of this pericope.

1. Romans 5:12 refers to Adam and all of his descendants: "Wherefore, as by one man sin entered into the world, and death by sin; and so death passed upon all men, for that (because) all have sinned. . . ." There has been a great deal of discussion about which term is the better translation: *in whom* or *because* (for that). We agree with many (see Berkouwer, *Sin*, 492ff.) that, whichever translation is used, Paul says *at any rate* that all sinned when Adam sinned.

How this connection ought to be interpreted is not clear from the term *because*. Neither does the term *in whom* entirely explain how all have sinned in Adam.

"In him" must mean "included in him." The term "because" only makes sense if all are subsumed in him. This must be accepted by those who prefer "because." However, this difference in translation is not conclusive.

2. We support Ridderbos's train of thought. He emphasizes that the verb "to pass upon" (the subject being death) as distinguished from "to enter into" (the subject being sin), refers to something that is passed on from one person to many. The principle of "all through one" is manifested among mankind (of which Adam is the beginning) in the death of all (1959, 113ff.).

The continuation of this verse makes clear that it is not a matter of the sinful actions of Adam's descendants or the sinful nature transmitted to them. All of them participate in Adam's sinful deed. This is how both Adam and his descendants brought death upon themselves. "Here the true nature of the connection between 'all' and 'one' finally comes to light." Elsewhere this is indicated with the preposition "in." See 1 Corinthians 15:22: "in Adam" and "in Christ."

Ridderbos adds: "Various attempts have been made to describe this relationship. Keeping in mind what is said elsewhere about the body of Christ (e.g., Rom. 12:5 and 1 Cor. 12:12) it may make sense to speak here also of the corporate unity of Adam and his descendants, which, as the nature of this unity implies, reflects not only physical descent and solidarity, but also the structure of creation and redemption of the human race as ordained by God" (1959, 114).

Although we prefer the translation "because," we reemphasize that the implication of this translation is equivalent to that of "in whom." This is confirmed by the correspondence with 1 Corinthians 15:22.

3. Calvin's reasoning is rather subtle. He interprets the idea that all have sinned as referring to actual sins. At the same time he says that a natural depravity has diffused into all parts of the soul; therefore, all of us are unrighteous and wicked. In this connection he speaks about the corruption that we bear inborn and that we have inherited. This depravity makes us unrighteous.

If we understand Calvin correctly, he sees a direct link between original pollution and original sin. He does not believe that we commit sin as a consequence of original contagion and thus acquire guilt. In this case original guilt would be the consequence of sin spawned by original pollution.

No, being depraved implies that we already stand condemned before God. Calvin emphasizes that we are depraved and guilty as a consequence of our relationship with Adam.

For this interpretation we refer to *Institutes*, 2.1.8: "since we through his transgression have become entangled in the curse, he is said to have made us guilty. Yet not only has punishment fallen upon us from Adam, but a contagion imparted by him resides in us, which justly deserves punishment." He points out that, although Augustine often calls this "another's" sin, nevertheless it is also "peculiar to each." A bit further he mentions that we "have been enveloped in original sin and defiled by its stains." Our nature is "hateful and abhorrent to God. From this it follows that it is rightly considered sin in God's sight, for without guilt there would be no accusation."

We conclude that to Calvin original pollution and original sin are the same thing. They cannot be distinguished from a temporal point of view. One cannot say that guilt proceeds from pollution. Pollution is *de facto* guilt, and vice versa.

That Calvin is of the view that our sinful nature indeed deserves God's judgment, is confirmed by the fact that in his interpretation of verse 12 he includes children in the verdict of death, even if they have not yet sinned. As pointed out by Oosterhoff (1972, 83), Calvin is *not specifically* thinking of children only. However, he does have them in mind as well. Calvin implicates them without any qualification, and does so very emphatically in *Institutes*, 2.1.8 ("guilty themselves, because of sin").

The Belgic Confession of Faith reminds us of the commandment of life. By transgressing it, man "lost all his excellent gifts, which he had received from God" (article 14). "Through the disobedience of Adam original sin was extended to all mankind, which is a depravity of the whole nature and a hereditary disease, wherewith even infants in their mother's womb are infected, and which produces in man all sorts of sin, being in him as a root thereof, and therefore is so vile and abominable in the sight of God that it is sufficient to condemn all mankind" (article 15). Here we read that our inner depravity makes us deserve God's damnation. The same thing is confessed in the Canons of Dort, 3–4.2–3, and in response 7 of the Heidelberg Catechism! See also Polman, *Ned. Gel.*, 2:171–75.

4. These people did not sin in the same way as Adam. Paul says so because they did not have the explicit prohibition that Adam received from God. It is their sinful nature that makes them guilty before God. Calvin speaks of despising oneself for not being able to suppress one's blindness and obstinacy. With this he means our sinful nature and everything that flows from it. Our nature is so depraved that we deserve God's judgment.

It goes against Calvin's clear train of thought to distinguish between our sinful nature that does not deserve God's judgment *and* our sinful deeds that do deserve God's judgment.

We also reject such a distinction. If this distinction were correct, man would still not owe his guilt to his relationship with Adam. He does inherit depravity from Adam. However, he does not become guilty until he actually commits sin.

This approach does not in fact solve the problem. Man's guilt is maintained. Behind sinful deeds lies the sinfulness that man inherits from Adam, without thereby acquiring any guilt. We do not fathom why this approach ignores the depravity all around and inside us.

With this kind of reasoning the point at which Calvin approaches realism is lost. It entirely ignores the element of truth in realism. Incidentally, the same is true of the element of truth in federalism, which is not done justice either.

5. Now we turn to verse 19. How are we to interpret "being made sinners"? Does Paul mean that we are declared sinners, although we are not? In this case "being made" would ascribe something to us that we previously did not have or were not. In this case "being made sinners" would be a synthetic-forensic verdict.

This is unacceptable. It is possible in the case of the imputation of Jesus' righteousness. This is imputed and given to us by grace. However, one cannot possibly be made a sinner by imputation. This would deny sin's nature as transgression and guilt!

Berkouwer is correct in this regard (*Sin*, 500). He points out that the imputation of an offense not actually committed by us perforce raises Greijdanus's questions, which "since 1906 have still not been answered satisfactorily and in which the Biblical perspective cannot be denied" (ibid.).

We interpret "being made sinners" as a pronouncement of God describing real and actual sinners! Mankind indeed has become sinful and guilty in and through Adam. This adds a realistic dimension to federalism. Conversely, this moment of truth of realism is not thinkable without taking into account the perspective of federalism with Adam. The complementary significance of federalism and realism obviates the need to think in terms of preexistent participation in Adam's sin.

In Adam all became corrupt and *ipso facto* sinful. Our being is corrupt in the eyes of God, which implies guilt. This is because Adam's deed was decisive for all. We therefore choose for a combination of representation (federalism) and realism. The fact that all of us are guilty before God reflects the fact that Adam represents us all. This is the profound significance of "one for all" and "all through and in the one"![13]

6. *Does this "explain" original sin?* It depends on one's definition of "explain"! It is well known that Berkouwer is strongly opposed to any possible explanation of original guilt. He says that it is "totally illegitimate to excuse oneself by seeking causality in relationships of communality" (*Sin*, 518). This is, however, far from our intention. Precisely our emphasis on the combination of realism and federalism is intended to deny ourselves all innocence. We can never think or write about original sin in such a way that we ourselves would seek an external cause through pointing to certain relationships. By iden-

13. Stanley E. Porter argued in "The Pauline Concept of Original Sin in Light of Rabbinic Background," *Tyndale Bulletin* 41, no. 1 (1990): 3–30, that Paul in his own way, in complete contrast with rabbis, spoke of the origin of mankind's sin.

tifying this cause we would thereby excuse ourselves. We agree with Berkouwer that such an approach would be absolutely illegitimate.

Pointing to relationships established by the Bible itself is something very different. We would fall short of biblical standards if we shrank from tracing these relationships.

In this connection, the biblical perspective of "one for all" and "all in one" is in our view decisive. We are included in Adam because God has specifically ordained such an interdependent relationship. Adam is not only the first sinner; he is also the origin of all sin. Because of his unique position as head of mankind the sins of all of us lead back to him *and* his sin carries on in all of us!

Many objections can be raised against *the term* original (hereditary) sin! It does not make sense to think of sins as being inherited! *Besides, the term denies that we become sinners not through Adam's death but through Adam's deed.* Sin is in fact passed on to his descendants not upon his death, but already during his lifetime!

The truth that is captured in *the concept* of original sin is that Adam's sin is the origin of all sin and everyone's sin.

The point is not that we inherit a certain amount of sin and add a few sins of our own. This would imply an unacceptable dichotomy. The point is that our sin (being a sinner, committing sin, and being guilty) cannot be contemplated apart from the sin of Adam in his position as our head!

In this context we need to keep in mind both the connection and the distinction between being a sinner and committing sin. Being a sinner does not necessarily imply committing all kinds of sin. On the other hand, committing specific sins must always be traced back to the sinful nature of the one who sins.[14] The use of the term "sin" in the singular is frequently employed in the context of being a sinner.[15]

We reiterate that hereby we do not imply anything that could possibly constitute an excuse for our sins, as though someone else would be to blame for our guilt. No, we have sinned in Adam. There is no excuse.

14. See Brunner, *Dogmatics*, 2:121–24.

15. It appears to us that being a sinner (also characterized by Paul as flesh) epitomizes Paul's doctrine of sin. We do not agree with Ridderbos, 1975, 93, when in this connection he refers to a supra-individual mode of existence in which one shares through the single fact that one shares in the human life context. He thinks too much in terms of spiritual powers. In the process he disputes that our being persons is affected by sin.

There are those who only go so far as to concede a corporate connection without describing the nature of the relationship between us and Adam. They merely indicate that sin is universal, as implied by the term *corporate*.

The problem with this view is that it says nothing about the relationship between Adam's sins and ours. It only goes halfway. We cannot explain this point of view better than to conclude that *corporate does not mean the same thing as representative*.

The depth of what the Bible teaches us, in terms of Adam's sin being the origin of the sins of all of us, is that God has structured our interconnectedness in such a way that together with Adam we have become guilty in terms of the sinful depravity of our nature.

Versteeg is right in objecting to the concept of "a corporate personality" by saying that it leaves no room for representation. The concept of corporate unity implies two-way interaction. Whatever is said of one can be said of many, *and vice versa* (1969[2], 46). The concept of corporate unity only implies universality. It implies that we all do what Adam did, *and vice versa*. What is lacking is the relationship established by God, i.e., the relationship of representation!

This relationship is the focus of the grace revealed in Christ. Its glory is all the greater considering the extent to which his life surpasses the death deserved by Adam and all of us in him.

Death comes to all of us through the transgression of the covenant of life established with Adam (§ 26.3)! The life that Christ obtained changes death to life for all those who belong to him. This is not the whole story. Through grace in Christ all who belong to him receive (new and eternal) life. The structure of "one for all" is the same as that of "all through one." The outcome is all the richer to the extent that the life earned by Christ eclipses the death brought about by Adam!

Finally, the reader should be reminded that above we do not choose between imputed and therefore someone else's guilt (*peccatum alienum*) and our own guilt (*peccatum proprium*). The aspect of imputation is achieved through representation. We are all subsumed in Adam. And *therefore* it is our own guilt. The imputation and the reality of being sinful (being a sinner) go hand in hand. See Canons of Dort, 3–4.2, and Murray, 1959, 42–95.

The new Roman Catholic view of original sin reflects the rather generally shared conviction that sin is universal. We encounter this view in Schoonenberg. He sees original sin as a situation in which all of us find ourselves. He distinguishes between a physical and a more psychological concept of this situation (1962, 151). In his view this concept of *situation* does not deny the reality of original sin. However, reality is explained in a special way. It is described as a situation "marked by an absence of supernatural grace and an incapacity for any kind of love, in which man finds himself as a consequence of the fact that as human being he is born into a world in which the covenant with God has been gambled away in a sinful manner" (1962, 155).

Trooster wrote *Evolutie in de erfzondeleer* (evolution in the doctrine of original sin). The title of his book reflects the fact that he places the doctrine of original sin within the context of evolution. He interprets Romans 5 in such a way that Adam's sin cannot possibly be understood to be that of chronologically the first person (1965, 100). His basic hypothesis is that the end time already exists in primeval time (1965, 74). It is incidentally noteworthy that he starts off by giving a new interpretation to the biblical data. He concludes from his historical review that the traditional presentation of the doctrine of original sin needs to be adjusted with the help of what he calls "the Scriptural perspective." This amounts to a universal state of calamity for mankind in this world, i.e., the mystery of solidarity in sin and disaster from the beginning (1965, 154). However, VanderVelde concludes that the newer view of Schoonenberg and Karl Rahner requires the restatement of original sin as the absence (or theft) of sanctifying grace (*gratia sanctificans*). Another perspective in the Roman Catholic interpretation of original sin is that of the depth dimension of sin. This personal-existential reinterpretation of the doctrine of original sin is also considered to be deficient by VanderVelde (1975, 300–11, and especially 324–26).

7. We summarize the results of our inquiry by way of a number of propositions that constitute our position.

1. Romans 5 and 1 Corinthians 15 imply a decisive relationship between Adam and his descendants.
2. The fundamental character of this relationship is clarified and superseded by the relationship between Christ and his people: one for all—all through one.
3. The parallel ends with this structure.
4. Adam's descendants all share in the guilt *and* the pollution of Adam's sin, which is so real that all of them in fact commit sin.
5. They are not considered to have sinned in Adam in a preexistent fashion.
6. The reality of their guilt is constituted by the fact that Adam represents them and they are subsumed in him.
7. Proposition 6 is a combination of elements of truth in federalism and realism. We stand by the formulation "combination of elements of truth": each perspective on its own leaves unanswered questions.

8. Calvin makes no temporal or sequential distinction between original sin and original pollution.
9. As a consequence of the covenantal relationship (covenant of life), pollution and guilt are one. We are personally held accountable for our guilt in Adam.
10. Realism denies the relationship of federalism between Adam and his descendants. Federalism limits itself to imputation associated with justification, but not with becoming a sinner in Adam.
11. We wish to do justice to both realism and federalism without simply combining them. The element of truth of each must be done full justice, which is only feasible when the two are brought together in a new structure.

27.2. *The progression of sin*

1. Having discussed the biblical data on the relationship between Adam's sin and that of his descendants, we shall now focus on *the destructive process of sin*. The question is how it progresses and what its impact is.

This confronts us with a problem. Sin is in essence lawlessness. It seeks to be autonomous and works autonomously. On the other hand sin is subject to God's judgment. In its progression it is subject to the verdict that God pronounces over sin. Even in its negative mode it remains subject to God's law.

This gives the progression of sin a two-pronged effect. On the one hand it spreads and intensifies its negative impact. On the other hand God executes his judgment over it. He permits it to increasingly achieve its potential, namely to be a destructive force that leads to death. The sentence of death is executed upon and through it. He who rejects the life that God offers to us in love chooses death (Deut. 30:19). It is God's judgment upon sin that death increasingly gains ground. God delivers man up to sin in line with the latter's own wishes. See Romans 1:24, 26 and 28.

Therefore, in the discussion of the progression of sin we come across God's judgment over sin. This judgment as punishment from God will be the focus of the next section. Here we address the progression of sin. Sin is in essence negative (*negatio*, *privatio*). As its essence implies, it can therefore only generate something negative. This is how God executes his judgment over sin.

We now wish to focus on the fact that God allows sin to develop as sin.

2. The first thing that we need to observe about sin is *that it carries death within itself and increasingly brings about death*. One may ask whether the foregoing statement contains a contradiction. After all, dead is dead. Period!

The appalling thing about sin is that it opposes life, that it destroys everything positive. However, it is very persistent in this negative pursuit. Paul refers to this in Ephesians 2:1–2: "And you hath he quickened, who were dead in trespasses and sins; wherein in time past ye walked." It is clear that this state of death is an active event. The entire life of a sinful human being can be described as death. "For to be carnally minded is death" (Rom. 8:6). The progression of sin is in fact the progression of death.[16]

In the next section we shall specifically address physical and eternal death as punishment for sin. Now it suffices to say that sin implies death as a consequence of its negation of the love and the life that God holds out to us. We refer to this as spiritual death, in order to distinguish it from physical and eternal death. This is the loss of a living relationship with God. It sends us increasingly into the clutches of death.

In this light we can also address the question whether it is correct to say that sin punishes itself. Our starting point is that God punishes sin. He establishes the law and also determines the sanction for transgression of his law. In this connection see Velema, *Rechtvaardiging van de straf* (justification of the penalty), 1978, 13–35, on page 21 of which there is a reference to the well-known study by K. Koch concerning the question whether the Old Testament teaches a doctrine of retribution.

The penalty for sin includes that its negative process intensifies. In this sense we can say that the sinner punishes himself. He yields himself to the enslaving power of sin and becomes increasingly its prisoner (Rom. 7:14).

This process does not follow a natural law. It proceeds on the basis of the sanction of God's holy law.

Hoekema proposes to speak of pervasive depravity instead of total depravity (1986, 150). With this proposal it is not at all his intention to deny or soften radical depravity. He fully acknowledges it. However,

16. The Apostle Paul calls this state of death the flesh. See Romans 8:7–8 and Galatians 5:13–26. For other designations see Jeremiah 17:9; Mark 7:21–23; John 5:42; Romans 7:18; Titus 1:15–16.

he seeks to emphasize the fact that sin does not have the same extreme effect on every human being. At the same time pervasive depravity indicates the dynamic process of the inner degradation brought about by sin! We ourselves consider pervasive and total depravity to be complementary terms.

Total depravity expresses that we "are wholly incapable of doing any good, and inclined to all evil" (answer 8 of the Heidelberg Catechism). Hoekema correctly points out that for those for whom this is true an intensification of sin and evil is conceivable.

3. We further refer to Ephesians 4:18: "having the understanding darkened, being alienated from the life of God through the ignorance that is in them, because of the blindness of their heart." One of the worst manifestations of the progression of sin is *darkness, inner blindness*. From the perspective of the Old Testament one can speak of foolishness, which one can find personified in Proverbs 9:13–18, while its deceptions are depicted in numerous places in the book of Proverbs. It is noteworthy that darkening of the mind in Ephesians 4:18 is directly connected with "alienation from the life of God," and a yielding to sin (v. 19; see also Rom. 1:21).

Another manifestation of the progression of sin is *the deceitfulness of our heart* (Jer. 17:9). What constitutes this deceitfulness? It is self-justification through which we excuse ourselves and transfer our guilt to others. This self-justification stands in contrast to the fact that the LORD searches the heart and "tries the reins" (Pss. 139:23; 7:9).

4. Another point is the progression of sin in terms of *Satan's dominion*. We read that he is called "the prince of this world" (John 12:31; 14:30; cf. Eph. 2:2). It is no coincidence that this title also turns up as "the prince of devils" (Matt. 9:34; 12:24).

Satan is the prince of this world. He acquired this dominion through falsehood and robbery, i.e., illegitimately. From this position he offered Jesus dominion of "all the kingdoms of the world and their glory" in the temptation on the mountain (Matt. 4:8–9). Jesus would have acquired this dominion outside the way of the cross, by participating in the devil's deceit and robbery. He would then have belonged to the latter's kingdom. Jesus resisted the devil with an appeal to the command of God to worship and serve him only (v. 10).

In the meantime the title "prince of this world" is an indication that God will not definitively end his stolen dominion until the latter's dethronement (1 Cor. 15:25; Col. 2:15). Although Satan's dominion is illegitimate, God tolerates it. This toleration is sometimes coupled with the handing over of people to sin. Aside from the passages referred to above see also how God hands Israel over to its enemies (Judg. 6–7; 1 Sam. 28–31).

Regarding the power of Satan from which people are (must be) delivered, see also Acts 26:18; Colossians 1:13.

In this connection we finally mention the *futility* to which creation is being subjected (Rom. 8:20–21). Undoubtedly, this passage refers back to Genesis 3:17. The curse upon the earth is due to man's disobedience. The judgment that strikes man also touches creation. The consequences of sin spread across all of created reality. Man is responsible for what goes wrong in nature, either through deliberate action, or indirectly through the curse attracted by him as ruler (steward) of creation.

5. Precisely in light of the foregoing, we also must pay attention to the *gradation and variation of sin.*

Despite the inner dynamic of sin, there is nevertheless also *a certain tempering of sin* as a result of God's goodness. Berkouwer captures this in the title of a chapter titled "Radicality and Gradation" (*Sin*, 285–323). The employment of the term "gradation," which at the same time suggests a certain temporary moderation, does not constitute a denial of radical depravity or the universality of sin. This tempering is not due to sin or sinful man, but God. He permits the goodness of his law to affect life (society). See Romans 2:14–15.

Douma thoroughly discusses the relevant passages. See 1966, 320–24. He deals with Psalm 145:9; Jonah 4:2; Matthew 5:44ff.; Luke 6:35; Acts 14:16–17; 17:30; 1 Peter 3:20; and 1 Timothy 4:10. See also the further treatment of this material on 314–30.

For the effect of general revelation in this sin-restraining process we refer to Berkouwer, *General Revelation*, 197–206, and Wentsel on Calvin, Kuyper, and Schilder, *Dogm.*, 2:226–32.

It is God's goodness that he gives scope to the superior power of his law. The result is a manifestation of humaneness. This does not detract from radical depravity. It demonstrates that God does not permit sin to realize its full potential always and everywhere. Nevertheless, Scripture does speak of the filling up of unrighteousness (Gen. 6:11; Matt. 23:32). The progression of sin is revealingly depicted in James 1:15;

Matthew 24:12 (with the positive counterweight being the increase in faith and love, 2 Thess. 1:3).

A distinction may be made between sins *that are committed inadvertently* and *those that are perpetrated with premeditation* (those with and without uplifted hand, Lev. 4:1–2; 5:15; Num. 15:30). Compare the law of cities designated as places of refuge for those who kill others inadvertently (Num. 35:15). Those who flee there, having committed premeditated murder, have to be put to death all the same (Num. 35:30–31).

Similarly, the judgment of those who know the will of the master will be different from that of those who do not. They will be beaten more severely (Luke 12:47–48). In this connection, think of the city that rejects Jesus' words. The judgment for Sodom and Gomorrah will be more bearable than for such a city (Matt. 10:15; 11:20–24). The people of that city bear greater responsibility. More will be required from those who have received more. This is also true with respect to knowledge and ignorance of the gospel.

Against this background one also needs to read Hebrews 5:2. There the author speaks of the high priest who can be compassionate toward the ignorant and erring (cf. Heb. 9:7).

6. Is this related to the Roman Catholic distinction between *mortal (unforgivable)* and *venial (forgivable) sins*?

The Council of Trent elaborated this distinction for everyday life. Everyday sins, which someone commits repeatedly, do not separate him from grace. However, mortal sins do (*DS*, 899: *peccata mortalia*). It does not say that daily sins must be confessed. However, this is true of mortal sins (*DS*, 917, which rejects Baius's proposition that every sin deserves eternal punishment, *DS*, 1020). The difference between the two kinds of sin is that mortal sin robs a person of sanctifying grace and other supernatural gifts, as well as the bond of love with God.

See H. Brink, *Theol. Woordenboek* (theological dictionary), 1952, and E. Drewermann, "Sünde/Schuld" (sin/guilt), in *Neues Handbuch* (new handbook), 1985, 4:149. The latter reference discusses sin as a loss of the grace of justification and as exclusion from the kingdom of God. The author refers to the paradox that apostasy is part of my existence and therefore is inescapable, and yet must be a free act; otherwise, guilt would be part of God's creation!

Berkouwer reminds us that the Canons of Dort speak of the guilt of death (5.5) [*reatum mortis incurrunt*], although the Reformation does not consider guilt to be unforgivable. The term "forgivable sin" as such cannot be rejected (*Sin*, 305n82). It does have to be rejected as a separate category distinguished from mortal sin! The foregoing makes clear that this distinction is derived from anthropology (see § 24.1).

The distinction between forgivable sin and mortal sin is not designed to capture the biblical concept of gradation in sin. Neither is it intended to do justice to the distinction between faults and crimes used by Calvin, among others (*Institutes*, 4.12.4. Excommunication is an appropriate punishment for a crime; an admonishment or a reprimand suffices in the case of a fault).

From an anthropological perspective this distinction serves to soften certain sins and to regard others as more grave. The mistake made in this connection is that sins are not assessed in the light of God the lawgiver, but in the light of human nature! It is no longer man—who sins before God (*coram Deo*)—whose behavior is being judged. Human nature itself—apart from this relationship—is called to account regarding the consequences of sin!

When the *coram Deo* nature of sin is respected, it is impossible for one sin to lead to a loss of grace and not another. It is a speculative, dualistic anthropology that teaches a view of sin that may be characterized as detached, abstract, and atomistic. The *coram Deo* character of man as the image of God makes it impossible to consider one sin as qualitatively less serious and less blameworthy than another.

It is noteworthy that the biblical gradation of sin and punishment offers no scope for excuse. Berkouwer correctly points out that a greater sin (*comparativus*) reflects greater responsibility in line with superior knowledge and ability (*Sin*, 311). The Roman Catholic distinction minimizes the seriousness of sin. Reformational dogmatics maximizes the seriousness of sin.[17]

Finally, it may be pointed out that this distinction is also related to the Roman Catholic view of the law. This distinction comprises a classification that corresponds to the casuistry that is common in Roman Catholic ethics.[18]

17. See also Heppe, *Dogm.*, 257, for all kinds of distinctions; Müller, *Bek.*, 529, for the Irish articles of 1615, and 557 for those of Westminster of 1647.

18. See B. Häring, *Das Gesetz Christi* (the law of Christ), 1961, 7, and a discussion of a change in the position of Häring, in Velema, *Oriëntatie in de christelijke ethiek* (introduction to Christian ethics, 1990, 95ff.).

In opposing this dismantling of the law into atomistic and isolated commands, we point to texts such as Matthew 5:17, Galatians 5:10, and James 2:11.[19]

7. We still need to address what has been called *the unpardonable sin, namely, the sin against the Holy Spirit*. Relevant Scripture references include Mark 3:28–29: ". . . but he that shall blaspheme against the Holy Ghost hath never forgiveness, but is in danger of eternal damnation." As parallel passages see Matthew 12:22–32 and Luke 11:14–23, with the summary referred to above in Luke 12:10. It is thought that the same sin is meant in Hebrews 6:4–6; 10:26–27; 1 John 5:16. Here we find no explicit reference to blaspheming against the Holy Spirit, but to sin unto death, i.e., deliberately sinning after having acknowledged the truth and falling away after having been enlightened.

The fact that the Bible refers to this sin and its eternal punishment—no forgiveness being possible—frightens many people. Especially people who suffer from depression may fear that they have committed this sin and therefore cannot expect forgiveness.

We shall try to describe this sin very briefly from the point of view of its unpardonable nature. Its uniqueness does not lie in its intentional nature, nor in the fact that it involves blasphemy, for both elements are typical of this sin. Neither is it decisive that it involves the Holy Spirit. All sin is committed against the triune God and is by implication sin against the Spirit!

The sting, the devilish nature of this particular sin is the brutish, deliberate rejection of Christ, having initially been persuaded by the Spirit with respect to the truth of God in Christ. It is committed by someone who has first been enlightened, but nevertheless not only chooses darkness rather than light, but also *calls light itself darkness*. Characteristic of this sin is not only resistance against God. The denial of God's work to the extent that what comes from God is viewed as the work of the devil explains the unforgivable nature of this sin and the inner impossibility of contrition.

We are reminded of the fact that Jesus himself refers to this blasphemy in connection with the Pharisees. We ask ourselves whether the accusation of blasphemy against God in the trial before the Sanhedrin (Matt. 26:65) constitutes the perpetration of this sin. Following the

19. M. Honecker (172n11) pointed out that following Vatican II there is an entirely different approach to ethics, and therefore also to casuistry.

meeting of the Sanhedrin (John 11:53), it is a foregone conclusion that Jesus has to die. His sentence of death is decided before any official accusation has been brought forward. The sentence of death is finally pronounced on the basis of the conviction of blasphemy against God. The fact that the Messiah, sanctioned by the Scriptures, is condemned to death as a blasphemer of God constitutes the rejection of God's work of redemption through him. This is the zenith of all sin. It is the most radical way of ridding oneself of the Redeemer. Here God's Redeemer is pronounced to be the devil. He receives the punishment of a blasphemer of God.

Christ had revealed and manifested himself as Messiah. He was eliminated as a son of the devil. This constitutes rejection of grace in its most extreme, most concentrated form. We see this verdict as the perpetration of the sin against which Christ warns in Matthew 12:32. Those present there are at the point of committing this sin. It is already within their reach, so to speak. In the condemnation by the Jewish council, the members approve the judgment of their president. At this point they surrender themselves to this rejection. He is a devil and must therefore die.

They show themselves to be both stubborn and obstinate in their opposition to Jesus. This results in his sentence of death. This is how they believe they can eliminate him. In fact, they cut themselves off from redemption. Although they hear the appeal in Jesus' preaching that he will judge them as the Messiah, they do not yield themselves to him. They persist in their rejection, especially when they turn the truth of his resurrection into a lie (Matt. 28:13–15).

Blasphemy against the Holy Spirit consists in standing on the side of the devil and declaring God's work to be the work of the devil. The redemptive work of God is interpreted as the work of the devil. This is the worst thing one can do to the message of redemption. It may be asked whether Satan himself, in tempting Jesus to worship him in order to acquire dominion of all of the stolen treasures of the earth, seeks to tempt him into sinning against the Holy Spirit (Matt. 4:8–10). This does not succeed.

In the end Jesus dies as a result of the sin against the Holy Spirit committed by the Sanhedrin.

Here is made clear why there is no way back from this sin. It is after all this sin that identifies the light of redemption revealed in Christ with the darkness brought over this world by the devil. The perpetrators of this sin sell themselves to darkness and seek to extinguish the light. This is the most radical opposition to God, the nadir of sin, because it presents light as darkness. It is not only a repetition of Adam's sin, i.e., deciding oneself what is good and what is evil. It declares the redemption work of God to be the work of the devil. It trips all circuit breakers and causes darkness to be absolute and definitive.[20]

8. We wish to focus on one more aspect of sin. This is the question whether we *should also speak of structural sins*. This concerns structures that are so drastically affected and pervaded by sin that they crush people, impair humanity, and rob people of the freedom to live spiritually and sometimes even physically.

Regarding this terminology see J. Verkuyl, *Verantwoorde revolutie* (justified revolution), 1970, 2:52–54, with references to theologians such as Niebuhr, P. Lehmann, R. Schaull. Douma is very open to this idea (*De onmisbaarheid van de personele ethiek* = the imperative of personal ethics, 1970, 18). He says that when man truly repents, structures also change. When structures change for the better, they do not necessarily imply repentance.

We object to the concept of collective, institutional, and structural sins. Only those who are accountable to God can sin. Those who sin must repent. Structures and institutions cannot do this. It is the responsibility of the people who are accountable for maintaining these structures. The structures need to be changed, i.e., made to serve God's plan for mankind.[21]

We do recognize that certain structures are manipulated by people for their sinful ends to such an extent that these structures end up in the service of sin. They are the manifestation of sin and they promote the dominion of sin. We have no desire whatsoever to deny the connection between sin and these structures. However, these structures do not sin in and of themselves. They have been created and organized by people in such a way that they serve sin! These structures cannot repent. Those who manipulate and control them must repent. When they repent, those structures are "delivered from the bondage or corruption into the glorious liberty of the children of God" (Rom. 8:21). We are prepared to go so far as to say that within certain structures

20. See the pastoral discussion of sin by D. Rietdijk, *De zonde tegen de Heilige Geest* (the sin against the Holy Spirit), 1990.

21. See Velema, 1985, 151–67.

sin has become flesh and blood. The same thing can be said of certain publications and programs in the media. "Sinful structures," however, are not the same thing as "structural sins." Although we accept the former term, we reject the latter.

§ 28. Punishment and knowledge of sin

28.1. *Punishment of sin*

1. *God punishes the transgression of his commandment*. Already in Paradise he announced death as punishment (Gen. 2:17). He repeated this judgment once Adam and Eve had sinned (Gen. 3:19) and subsequently actually executed it. See the genealogy in Genesis 5, which can also be called a death roll.

Death is the most radical punishment for sin. After all, it signifies the end of life. This is true of physical death. It is no less true of death as eternal punishment for sin. We shall revisit this later. We do wish to point out that this sentence of death was not executed immediately upon the sinful acts of Adam and Eve. Had this indeed been the case, then the history of Adam's race would have ended on the day they sinned.

2. The fact that *the announced death penalty is not executed immediately* is viewed by many as a manifestation of grace.[22] We prefer to see it mainly as a manifestation of God's long-suffering. The Lord postpones the execution of the sentence. He forbears sinners. This long-suffering provides scope in history to lay the groundwork for redemption. At this point we cannot address in depth the issue of common grace. It suffices to say that what is referred to as common grace mitigates the verdict of death. It prepares the historical foundation upon which forgiveness, redemption, and renewal of grace can be manifested. This grace—or rather long-suffering—is also manifested in the revelation of God's goodness toward sinners who deserve the

22. See especially A. Kuyper, *De gemeene gratie* (universal grace), 2.1.94; also 1.228ff., 243; 2:86. Cf. Douma, 1966, 21, and S. J. Ridderbos, *De theologische cultuurbeschouwing van Abraham Kuyper* (Abraham Kuyper's theological view of culture), 1947, 31ff.

punishment of death. God's long-suffering has two aspects, namely the postponement of judgment and, in the interim, the manifestation of God's goodness toward those who deserve death.

In Genesis 3 we see something of the pattern of history and can identify the following facets:

The verdict is not immediately executed, but remains in force. Its postponement provides scope for the plan of redemption.

The Redeemer is announced. However, there are two additional factors that will shape the course of history. In connection with the promise of the Redeemer we mention the conflict between his offspring and that of the devil.[23] *History will be marked by conflict between two kingdoms*. Besides, the earth is cursed. People's lives in terms of their work in creation, their interaction with one another, and their relationship with their descendants *lie under a curse*. This does not mean that nothing can be done about the implementation of the curse. God himself works on the redemption of this curse (Gal. 3:13) and mitigates it by showing his goodness and long-suffering.

The curse on the earth and its inhabitants implies, however, that the postponement of death does not exempt mankind from punishment. By means of the curse, God announces his punishment on man and the earth, even though it will not be implemented immediately in its starkest form. The curse represents the initial execution of the verdict over sin. Its full implementation means death.

We recognize two developments in history. In the first place we see the conflict between the seed of the woman and that of the serpent, between the kingdom of light and that of darkness: grace over against sin; forgiveness over against guilt; renewal over against deadly alienation. Subsequently we see the implementation of the curse culminating in death, and its mitigation though God's long-suffering. From both points of view there is struggle and strife. This imbues the history of mankind and everyone's personal life with a dynamic intensity. There is no stagnation but progression. There is also the manifestation of that other force, that of God's forbearance and goodness. The conclusion of these reflections based on Genesis 3 must be that we have to interpret the curse as a preliminary implementation of the punishment pending its culmination in death. *The curse is the precursor of death*.

23. This is the foundation of the two kingdoms. Regarding Augustine's view see J. Oort, *Jeruzalem en Babylon*, 1986, and also W. H. Velema, *Solidariteit en anithese. Een theologische peiling* (a theological analysis), 1978.

It is clear from the first sin that the transgression of God's commandment causes man to deserve the curse. This curse also affects the earth. This reflects man's central place in creation (see § 23.2). There are various forms of punishment.

3. *Why is man punished for sin?* God ordained it so. The question cannot be avoided: why did God ordain it so? We mention God's justice. We read that God hates "all workers of iniquity" (Ps. 5:5). "The LORD will take vengeance on his adversaries, and he reserveth wrath for his enemies" (Nah. 1:2). He "will by no means clear the guilty" (Ex. 34:7; see also Ex. 20:5; Num. 14:18; Deut. 7:9–10). God punishes those who are proud, because he is the Judge of the whole earth (Ps. 7:11; 11:5–7; Isa. 5:16; 10:22; 59:16–18; Dan. 9:14; and also Rev. 16:5–7; see § 13.9).

In all of these passages we encounter God's punishing justice. The Lord is the Holy One who hates sin and resists his opponents (Ex. 15:11–14, Velema, 1988², 26–31). God's justice is also revealed in that he punishes those who transgress his law. He keeps his word. From the point of view of sinners it is a word of judgment (Heidelberg Catechism, Lord's Day 4).[24]

What drives God to judge sinners? The Bible refers to God's vengeance (Ps. 94:1; Isa. 34:8; 35:4; 63:4; Jer. 46:10; 11:20; 20:12). Vengeance and retribution are mentioned in one breath (Deut. 32:35). God's vengeance is always connected with sin. It is not an emotional retaliation driven by vanity. God's vengeance applies to situations in which people have transgressed the rules established by God. God's righteousness (*mispat* = to judge righteously and to do justice; *sedaqa* = relationship) indicates that he acts according to his Word, promises, and threats. God's vengeance is the punishment of the transgression of his commands and the breaking of the covenant.

We have seen that sin comprises unbelief and disobedience, pride and hatred. These violate God's glory and holiness. Man usurps the place that belongs to God alone. He seeks to drive God away from his rightful place in order to occupy it himself. God's punishment is his verdict over this transgression, this insubordination. God created man to bestow upon him a destiny of goodness and love. The rejection of this destiny is a deliberate preference for death (see § 26.2). This

24. Regarding God's wrath as reaction to contempt for his holy love, see H. M. Ohmann, *Wie kent uw toorn?* (who knows your wrath?), 1988, 21–33.

choice of man does not go unpunished.[25] He receives what he asks for by sinning. It is a deliberate choice. He turns away from God. Man cannot reject the glory of life in God's love without punishment. He who rejects this love must face its converse. Vengeance and retribution strike man as a consequence of his proud rejection of God.

It is customary in this connection to say that the purpose of punishment is to redress the justice of God that has been violated by sin (Bavinck, *R.D.*, 3:161). We emphasize that through punishment God upholds his justice. He preserves his justice. He does not yield to man. God is and remains God, even when man rebels against him.

The redress of his justice, in the sense that people submit themselves once again to his commands, takes place in redemption. Then people are restored to their proper place before God and recognize once again his justice.

We believe that Berkhof is wrong when he says that the encounter between God and hostile mankind appears to imply a conflict in God (*C.F.*, 133). Having recognized a conflict, Berkhof needs to come up with a solution, which is that love triumphs (*C.F.*, 134). This constitutes the basis for a favorable outcome for the history of mankind.

It is a misunderstanding to believe that man can bring about a conflict between God's justice and his offended love. If man had not rebelled against God, notions such as God's wrath and retribution would not have had any relevance! It is noteworthy, however, that even before man sins, God already speaks of sanction and punishment. It is true of course that God's wrath is not activated, i.e., does not begin to manifest itself, until after man has sinned. Before man rebels against God, this possibility is already contemplated and is averted by the announcement of punishment. It is true that God's wrath is triggered by man. It represents, however, his reaction to the rebellious, arrogant conduct of man. He is at one with his love. He demonstrates his love in maintaining himself over against rebellious mankind. It is precisely this notion of God maintaining himself that makes it impossible to conceive of a conflict within him. God's integrity does not require him to overcome the wrath within himself, so as to allow his love to triumph and predominate. He is at one with his love and his wrath. Hereby we do not wish to detract from the awe-inspiring nature of God's wrath.

We must say that his love is equally great, awe-inspiring, and holy. The present-day tendency to explain away God's wrath arises from the humanization of God. It is fundamentally the notion of God as partner on which Berkhof bases the entire development of his concept of God and the culmination of the history of God, mankind, and the world (see Velema, 1991, 79).[26] We ourselves confess the unity of

25. Wiersinga completely rejected the concept of God's punishing righteousness. See his *De verzoening in de theologische diskussie* (redemption in theological analysis), 1971.

26. Immink, 1990, 59, aptly raised the question whether Berkhof had changed tracks in anticipation, by eliminating all dynamism from the encounter between God and mankind. This resulted in an interaction between God and mankind that was strongly harmonious in nature.

God's mercy and his justice (Heidelberg Catechism, response 11). See also Immink, 1990, 58ff.

4. With the foregoing, we reject that God's demanding justice facilitates his redeeming justice (Loonstra, 243).

After all, facilitation of God's redeeming justice would imply supporting its deployment and achievement. Redeeming justice dominates and triumphs. For this it requires demanding justice. It must follow the path of demanding justice.

It is not clear to us how the commandment of life and the associated sanction could be seen as aiding redeeming justice.[27] Demanding—i.e., punishing—justice goes into effect when man fails to meet God's demand. It is the punishment for the transgression of God's justice. It is the dark antithesis of the claim that is embedded in God's life-giving justice. After all, it does not bring about salvation, positive reward, or redemption. It brings disaster and death. Man himself invokes it by rejecting God's redeeming justice. By viewing demanding justice as aiding the redeeming justice, one can only indirectly allow for the fact that God maintains himself in his condemnation of sin.

It is important to remember that punishment is also intended to encourage people to respect the law and to prevent transgression. We refer to this as the preventive intent of punishment. See Deuteronomy 13:11; 17:13; 19:20; 21:21.

In this context Bavinck speaks of a twofold purpose of punishment. Punishment applies to both the past and the future. Transgressions already committed need to be remedied. Future transgressions need to be prevented (*R.D.*, 3:161). It may be said that this twofold intent expresses both aspects of justice, namely retribution *and* restoration and healing.[28]

5. We now consider in greater detail the various punishments that we encounter in the Bible. Especially noteworthy are the chapters regarding the curse on disobedience, in contrast with the blessing on obedience (Deut. 11; 27–28; 1 Kings 8; Prov. 8; 9; 16; 17). Numerous passages in the books of the prophets could be mentioned. It is clear that God's punishment strikes people in their physical and historical

---

Berkhof accomplished this by picturing the conflict resolved within God himself. God had to and wanted to overcome the conflict within himself.

27. In adopting the expression *redemptive righteousness*, we use it to indicate the righteousness of God that sought the life, well-being, and welfare of people already before the fall into sin.

28. Velema, 1978, 29–35, and various other places held that the biblical concept of righteousness in criminal law intended both retribution and the return of the offender to society.

existence (through the evil that they suffer at the hands of others). There is a link here with the environment (drought, famine, natural disasters).[29]

The idea that God punishes sin through natural disasters, illnesses, and all kinds of evil that people do to each other is rejected by many today. The best seller by Harold Kushner, *When Bad Things Happen to Good People*, expresses this rejection penetratingly and eloquently. His book demonstrates that this rejection is not restricted to the doctrine of sin. He also sees implications for the doctrine of God, namely, God being helpless in the face of suffering and sympathizing with mankind.

As far as the latter is concerned, we must refer once again to the connection between mankind and the earth in light of man's creation after God's image. Man's stewardship of creation implies that the earth is cursed for his sake. In this connection, see especially Romans 8:19–23. These verses cannot be understood without taking into account the connection with Genesis 1–3.

Without implying that for each natural disaster a particular sin (of a certain nation or a group of people) could be identified, it is clear that Scripture sees a close connection between what happens with respect to nature and the earth on the one hand, and mankind's sins on the other hand. In some cases this connection is very transparent. Abuse of nature and pollution of the environment and the unbridled pursuit of financial wealth at the expense of care and responsibility toward other nations come to mind.[30]

The connection can also be indirect. God holds man responsible for the earth. Everything that goes wrong has to do with the curse that God has pronounced over the earth. This is also true when no special sin by a particular group of human beings is the cause of certain events in the environment, nature, the economy, or agriculture. Just as there is a certain degree of coherence in people's guilt, so there is a connection between the guilt of people and what happens in creation and history. Man's punishment also affects this dominion of creation.

29. Wentsel, *Dogm.*, 3a:728–32, describes in greater detail the implications of the curse for man's dominion.

30. See B. Goudzwaard, *Kapitalisme en vooruitgang* (capitalism and prosperity), 1976; *Genoodzaakt goed te wezen* (forced to be good), 1981; and *Wij rentmeesters* (we as stewards), 1983. Much of this literature as well as the report by the Club of Rome brought together by Meadows (1974) has been discussed by Douma, *Milieu en manipulatie* (environment and manipulation), 1990, 9–34.

In subsection 27.2 we discussed the various ways in which sin progresses. We pointed out that this process itself could also be seen as a punishment of sin. God's punishment is in part that he gives sin free rein. The various ways in which sin progresses also form part of God's punishment. As ordained by God, they are closely integrated with sin itself. This is why we described them in the context of the progression of sin. We shall not repeat them here.

For the sake of completeness, we point out that the punishment of sin was especially manifested in the life, suffering, and death of Christ. He lived and suffered by divine foreordination (e.g., Luke 2:49; 24:7, 26, 44–47; Heb. 5:7–9).

The work of Christ in his humiliation is addressed specifically in section 30. There the foregoing concepts are discussed more concretely in connection with Christ's work. Here we limit ourselves to stating that "Christ hath redeemed us from the curse of the law, being made a curse for us" (Gal. 3:13). The word "curse" brings out sharply the concept of punishment that leads to the judgment of death. The well-known expression *reconciliation through satisfaction* (see Belgic Confession of Faith, articles 21 and 22; Canons of Dort, 2.2–4) is a succinct description of all that we have said about the punishment for sin as it applies to Jesus Christ.

6. *We now address death in greater detail.* It has already been referred to as the antithesis of life, i.e., alienation from God (§ 27.2). We now recall that the Bible describes death as God's judgment over sin (Gen. 2:17; especially also Rom. 6:23 and Heb. 9:27). The Bible clearly identifies sin as the cause of death.

B. van 't Veld concludes from a review of relevant Scripture passages that death is not part of God's good creation (1989, 94). This study is an elaboration of his 1985 dissertation. See also the popular study by J. Hoek, *De dood hoort er niet bij* (death is not part of it). Hoek examines a number of Protestant theologians (Roman Catholics are not covered). Referring to Scripture, he defends the same view that we present here. As in other areas of Reformed theology, Kuitert is the trailblazer with respect to an interpretation that considers death to be a natural phenomenon (1970). He appeals to both Barth and Karl Rahner.

It is important to realize that man could have died in Paradise. This is not to say that he was bound to die there. In the Bible we tend to encounter death in the company of the devil and sin. This begins as early as Genesis 3. To Paul, death is the last enemy that is robbed of its power (1 Cor. 15:26).

Because of secularization, death is now taken for granted and has lost its connotation as enemy of mankind.[31] Death has become integrated with life ("sein zum Tode" = living toward death, Heidegger) or is even considered to be beneficial. Death is given a positive interpretation, in the sense that those who die make room for others and they cease to be a burden; or it is seen as a consequence of the supposition that in the end man is left with only a biological justification to live. When this becomes the sole reason to live, human life ceases to have value (Kuitert, 1989, 50).

Eternal death is described in Revelation 20:14 and 21:8 as the second death (see also Rev. 2:11; 20:6). This death is the execution of the definitive, eternal judgment. We take these pronouncements to mean a condition of eternal perdition. Berkhof's view has become well-known. He believes that there is room to hope that hell will be a form of purification (*C.F.*, 536). In our last chapter we shall go into greater depth concerning the dual end of the history of mankind. It is impossible for us to interpret the biblical perspective in such a way as to predict a favorable outcome for all human beings. The universality of the gospel does not offer any scope for universal redemption. Such an interpretation would do violence to the foundation of the biblical doctrine of sin.

We refer to the popular essays collected under the title *Hemel of hel, onze eeuwige bestemming* (heaven or hell, our eternal destination). H. G. Fonteyn's short book titled *Laatste (on)mogelijkheid over de (on)werkelijkheid van de hel* (final (im)possibility with respect to the (un)reality of hell, 1988) is a popularized version of Berkhof's position.

In that booklet, the triumph of grace is explained as the right to place a question mark behind eternal abandonment by God as an ultimate possibility. The author sees a penultimate possibility, although he recognizes that hell is (must be) the consequence of persistent resistance and indifference. However, this position is not consistent with the perspective of prophets and seers. It implies that night will give way to day. However, up to and including the book of Revelation there continue to be references to eternal darkness. The modern "seers and prophets" who teach the alternative view do not interpret Scripture correctly.

31. The collection of essays edited by Berghmans (1991) is a clear example of this.

28.2. *Knowledge of sin*

1. From early on, the law has been identified as *the key source of knowledge of our sin and misery* (Heidelberg Catechism, answer 3). However, this does not solve all problems.[32]

The law comes to us in the context of the gospel. God gave his law to Israel following the exodus from Egypt. The prologue to the law (*Decalogue*) clearly refers to redemption. Barth points out that the place of this law used to be the Ark of the Covenant, underneath its cover of the mercy seat.[33]

This means that one only had access to this law via the blood of atonement. Those who point to the law as the source of knowledge of sin cannot ignore that God's law is revealed to us in the gospel. We referred to this fact at the start of our discussion. We wish to avoid the idea that references to the law would give a legalistic impression at variance with the gospel. The reference to "the law in the context of the gospel" does not solve or settle all problems. It does provide a fundamental framework for discussion. See § 50.3.

The law is viewed as the key source of the knowledge of our misery in answers 3 and 115 of the Heidelberg Catechism. The law reveals God's will and is normative for the behavior of man. Man is created by God to be obedient to his will and thereby to honor him. This implies that all knowledge of sin could be gauged with the help of God's law. The objective of the law of God is to point positively to the way of life (the covenant of life). At the same time it is the standard for ascertaining man's transgression. In this respect it is particularly revealing. Berkouwer correctly points out that we should not see a conflict between the denoting, edifying function of the law (*usus normativus*) and its exposing, unmasking function (*usus elenchticus*): "It is after all the nature and character of God's law that it exercises *both* functions at the same time and that a single commandment of God simultaneously denotes and rejects sin *and* indicates the way of obedience" (1958, 159).

This unity is intentional on God's part. It is the nature of sin that it separates what God has joined together. Those who reject or resist the normative function of the law remain subjected to its unmasking, accusing function, even if they reject this. God's law remains in force

32. This subsection is based on W. H. Velema, *Wet and evangelie* (law and gospel), 1987.

33. K. Barth, *Gesetz und Evangelium* (law and gospel), 1935. See Velema, 1987, 10–12, which refers to other publications of Barth as well as reactions to his thesis.

in its twofold function. Sin attacks both functions at the same time. We conclude that the law is the standard for gauging all sin.

2. It must be pointed out that *knowledge of sin does not only come about through the law*. In this regard Berkouwer appropriately quotes the words of Bavinck "that true repentance, real sorrow over sin, and genuine return to God and his service definitely come about not only through the law but *also and even more so* through the gospel" (1958, 181). It is noteworthy that Bavinck here makes the comparison (*comparativus*) of "not only, but also and even more so." What could Bavinck mean by this? To our mind he means that the gospel is also a source of knowledge of our misery. Why is this the case? It is because the gospel continues to confront us with the law; it is the good news that Christ has met the requirement of the law. The fulfillment of the requirement of the law comprises a twofold obedience, namely, to fulfill the commandments of God *and* to suffer the curse of the law.[34] See the discussion of the aspects of the work of Christ (§ 32).

Precisely the cross of Christ reveals how serious sin is. It is so serious that only the sacrifice of Christ's life, his death on the cross, accomplishes redemption (Rom. 3:25ff. and Gal. 3:13). The living illustration of our misery is the Man of Sorrows on whom God brings down all unrighteousness, on whom the punishment of sin is laid. "For the transgression of my people was he stricken" (Isa. 53:6–8). To understand the gospel one always needs to approach it through the law. The great thing about the gospel is that the requirement of the law is held up to us as already having been fulfilled through Christ. The suffering of Jesus reveals how heavily the curse of the law weighs down on man *and* that God does not ignore sin. In his suffering, Christ was occupied with the Father. It may be noted that his first (known) and last words pertained to the Father (Luke 2:49; 23:46). He was occupied with his Father's will and law. This is why the gospel also is a source of the knowledge of sin, no less than of redemption. The cross is the revelation of God's love, but also of his holiness and justice (1 John 1:7, 9; 4:10).

34. The fact that Berkhof had no room for the latter is entrenched in the structure of his dogmatics. See W. H. Velema, "Rechtvaardiging en heiliging" (justification and sanctification), in *Weerwoord* (rejoinder). *Reacties op dr. H. Berkhof's christlijk geloof* (reactions to Dr. H. Berkhof's Christian faith), 1974, 174–83.

3. It remains to discuss whether we should consider *the law as the preeminent means whereby knowledge of sin is worked in man.* We encounter this idea in Pietism and a number of representatives of the Second Reformation.[35]

In opposition to this view we identify two clear perspectives. In the first place we recall the fact that Paul declares the law to be "weak through the flesh" (Rom. 8:3). We realize that he uses these words in a different context than we do here. Yet there is a similarity. The undoing through the law is part of true repentance. It may be viewed as the dying of the old nature. If the law on its own (preceding and therefore separate from the gospel) would be able to break a man, it would be an effort on the part of the law. However, the law is unable to change a sinful heart. Works of the law do not please God. It is rather that sinful man tends to employ the law to justify himself. It is impossible for the law by itself to humble man before God.

The law rather leads to hardening in sin. Paul clearly identifies this tendency of the law to multiply sin (Rom. 3:20; 5:20). He recognizes God's judgment in this. Sinful man employs the law to justify himself before God. This is how he multiplies his sins. He abuses the law to this effect.

One should not treat the preaching of the law in isolation. The entire Word of God needs to be preached. This Word comprises both the law and the gospel. No one can preach the gospel while ignoring the accusation of the law. Theologically, the accusation comes first. How can the acquittal be announced before the accusation has been brought forward?

As accusation, the law always precedes the preaching of the gospel and resonates in it. However, by limiting oneself to the accusation, one would fall short of the mandate to preach God's Word. By stopping after the word of the law, one cuts the gospel in half by eliminating its saving and purifying perspective. It causes despair without indicating the way back to God.

4. *It is not up to us to determine precisely how the Holy Spirit convinces man of sin*, righteousness, and judgment (John 16:8). However, it is clear from this verse that the Holy Spirit makes use of the gospel. After all, the sin mentioned is their refusal to believe in Christ (v. 9).

35. See § 50.3, subsection 2, and also Berkouwer, 1958, 183; Velema, 1987, 125, 135.

It does not befit us to prescribe for the Holy Spirit how to do his work. We have the mandate to preach the gospel (as acquittal from the accusation of the law; i.e., in terms of both of these words). For some the accusation through the law will hit home, and for others, the graceful love of God for a sinner. At any rate, both need to be proclaimed: guilt and redemption; punishment and forgiveness; judgment and grace.

It is up to the Spirit to use this as it pleases him. We need not, cannot, and may not systematize the way in which the Spirit brings someone to repentance. There are various examples of how people are brought to the knowledge of sin. Some learn this at the start of their conversion, while others come to see things more sharply as they are led more deeply into their relationship with God. It is always the Spirit who teaches this. He employs the one Word of God, which is explained and proclaimed as both law and gospel.

Velema, *Wet en evangelie* (law and gospel), 1987, discusses the relationship between these two perspectives in greater depth. He also writes extensively about the teachings of Calvin. Calvin emphatically points out that in the Gospels the call to repentance rests on the salvation of the (approaching) kingdom.

Some Literature

H. J. Adriaanse et. al., *God, goed en kwaad* (God, good and evil), 1977.

J. T. Bakker, "Zonde en schuld" (sin and guilt), in G. C. Berkouwer, A. S. van der Woude (ed.), *Kernwoorden in het christelijk geloof* (key words of the Christian faith), 1970, 22–29.

A. van de Beek, *Waarom? Over lijden, schuld en God* (why? concerning suffering, guilt, and God), 1984.

A. van de Beek, "Zonde" (sin), in J. Firet (ed.), *Zeven weerbarstige woorden uit het Christendom* (seven troublesome words in the Christian faith), 44–60.

R. L. P. Berghmans, *De dood in beheer* (death in command), 1991.

G. C. Berkouwer, *Man: The Image of God*, 1962.

G. C. Berkouwer, *General Revelation*, 1955.

G. C. Berkouwer, *Sin*, 1971.

G. C. Berkouwer, A. S. van der Woude (ed.), *Kernwoorden in het christelijk geloof* (key words of the Christian faith), 1970.

J. Douma, *Algemene genade* (common grace), 1966.

P. Eicher (ed.), *Neues Handbuch theologischer Grundbegriffe* (new handbook of theological concepts), 4, 1985.

J. Faber, "Imago Dei in Calvin." Two essays in idem, *Essays in Reformed Doctrine*, 1990, 227–81.

J. Firet, *Zeven weerbarstige woorden uit het Christendom. Zijn zij nog mogelijk?* (seven troublesome words in the Christian faith: do they still make sense?), 1986.

J. van Genderen, "De ontwikkeling van de leer van de zonde" (the development of the doctrine of sin), in A. G. Knevel (ed.), *Zonde* (sin), 1987, 32–39.

J. van Genderen, *Gerechtigheid als geschenk* (righteousness as gift), 1988.

C. Gestrich, *Die Wiederkehr des Glanzes in der Welt* (the return of splendor in the world), 1989.

J. M. Hasselaar, *Erfzonde en vrijheid* (original sin and freedom), 1953.

J. van Heerde, *Zonde dat er zonde is* (it's a sin that there is sin), 1985.

H. J. Heering, *Over het boze. Als macht en als werkelijkheid* (concerning evil: as power and as reality), 1974.

J. Hoek, *De dood hoort er niet bij* (death does not belong), 1983.

J. Hoek, *Zonde: opstand tegen de genade* (sin: rebellion against grace), 1988.

A. Hoekema, *Created in God's Image*, 1986.

Ph. E. Hughes, *The True Image*, 1989.

F. G. Immink, *Jezus Christus, profeet, priester, koning*, 1990.

A. G. Knevel (ed.), *Visie op Karl Barth* (view of Karl Barth), 1987.

A. G. Knevel (ed.), *Zonde* (sin), 1987.

J. Kroesen, *Kwaad en zin: Over de betekenis van de filosofie van Emmauel Levinas voor de theologische vraag van het kwade* (evil and sense: concerning the significance of the philosophy of E. L. for the question of evil), 1991.

H. M. Kuitert, *Anders gezegd* (put differently), 1970.

H. M. Kuitert, *Mag alles wat kan?* (may it be done if it can be done?), 1989.

H. S. Kushner, *When Bad Things Happen to Good People*, 1983.

B. Loonstra, *Verkiezing-verzoening-verbond* (election-atonement-covenant), 1990.

J. Murray, *The Imputation of Adam's Sin*, 1959.

B. J. Oosterhoff, *Hoe lezen wij Genesis 2 en 3?* (how do we read Genesis 2 and 3?), 1972.

A. C. Plantinga, *God, Freedom, and Evil*, 1974.

F. J. Pop, *Bijbelse woorden en hun geheim* (biblical words and their secret), 1972.

H. Ridderbos, *Aan de Romeinen* (to the Romans), 1959.

H. Ridderbos, *Paul*, 1975.

P. Schoonenberg, S.J., *De macht der zonde* (the power of sin), 1962.

S. Trooster, S.J., *Evolutie in de erfzondeleer* (evolution in the doctrine of original sin), 1965.

G. Vandervelde, *Original sin*, 1975.

B. van 't Veld, "*Gelijk het gras . . .*" ("as the grass . . ."), 1989.

W. H. Velema, "Berkhof over hemel en hel" (Berkhof on heaven and hell), in A. G. Knevel, *Hemel of hel. Onze eeuwige bestemming* (heaven or hell: our eternal destination), 1991, 75–82.

W. H. Velema, "Ethiek on invloed van de nieuwere zondeleer" (ethics under the influence of the newer doctrine of sin), in A. G. Knevel (ed.), *Zonde* (sin), 1987, 79–87 (1987a).

W. H. Velema, *Geroepen tot heilig leven* (called to a holy life), 1988².

W. H. Velema, "Het einde van de zonde: vooruitgrijpen of afwachten" (the end of sin: now or later), in A. G. Knevel (ed.), *Zonde* (sin), 1987, 97–105 (1987a).

W. H. Velema, *Rechtvaardiging van de straf* (justification of the punishment), 1978.

W. H. Velema, *Wet en evangelie* (law and gospel), 1987.

J. P. Versteeg, "Is Adam in het Nieuwe Testament een 'leermodel'?" (does the New Testament treat Adam as a pedagogical device?), in *Woord en kerk* (Word and church), 1969², 29–70.

J. A. D. Weima, "The Function of the Law in Relation to Sin," in *Novum Testamentum*, 1990.

H. Wiersinga, *Doem of daad* (doom or deed), 1982.

H. Wiersinga, *Verzoening met het lijden?* (reconciled to suffering?), 1975.

Chapter 10

Christ, the Mediator

§ 29. The person of Christ

29.1. *Person and work*

Faith in Christ is the core of the creed of the church. It is *the heart of the Christian faith*. For this reason Christology is the centerpiece of dogmatics.

This chapter must be seen in the perspective of the preceding chapters. We have in mind the doctrine of revelation because the revelation of salvation is God's revelation in Christ, and the doctrine of man's sin because of which the coming of Christ as Redeemer became necessary. Subsequent chapters must be seen in the perspective of this chapter, namely the doctrine of the covenant of grace of which Christ is the Mediator; the doctrine of salvation, which he obtained; the doctrine of the church of which he is the Head; the doctrine of the means of grace that the Spirit of Christ employs; and the doctrine of consummation, an essential part of which is Christ's return to judge.

Therefore not everything about Christ needs to be covered in the chapter on Christology. There are chiefly two questions that we need to address: Who is he? What is his work?

A common subdivision is: 1. *The person of Christ*; and, 2. *The work of Christ*. The work of Christ is so all-embracing that it is a good idea to treat sequentially the work of Christ in his humiliation (§ 30), the work of Christ in his exaltation (§ 31), and the principal aspects of the work of Christ (§ 32).

The person and the work of Christ cannot be separated. When he says that he is the Good Shepherd, or the Way and the Truth and the Life (John 10:11; 14:6), both aspects are included. Numerous passages of Scripture testify to the glory of his person and the richness of his work. The name "*sotèr*" (Savior) indicates both who he is and what he does. One cannot discuss his person without considering his work, or reflect on his work while ignoring his person.

There have been theologians who paid little attention to Jesus as a person. A. von Harnack (1851–1930) held that only the Father figured in the gospel as Jesus taught it—not the Son. Von Harnack was influenced by A. Ritschl who considered "*Seinsurteile*" (empirically verifiable statements) unimportant in contrast with "*Werturteile*" (value judgments). He considered pronouncements with respect to the divinity of the Son to be too speculative.

Did Melanchthon in his *Loci* (1521) not limit the knowledge of Christ to that of his benefits? In his analysis he appeared to distinguish between the natures of Christ and the benefits of his redemption.[1] It is a fact that Melanchthon rejected scholastic speculations and subtleties that had no practical purpose. However, he did not ignore the teaching of the church. The purport of his words is that the doctrines of Christ and redemption cannot be separated from each other. To speak of Christ means to refer to our Savior and the salvation that we have in him. Various pronouncements of Luther and Calvin imply that the Reformers wished to show who the Lord Jesus Christ is to us.

Jesus once asked: "What think ye of Christ?" (Matt. 22:42). When he was on earth, divergent responses were given to this question. This is still true today.

1. There are those who see him as an example, as though the important thing is what he exemplified to us and not what he accomplished for us!

1. Melanchthon wrote: "Hoc est Christum cognoscere, beneficia eius cognoscere, non, quod isti docent eius naturas, modos incarnationis contueri," *Werke in Auswahl* (selected works), ed. R. Stupperich, 2:1, 7. Cf. Berkouwer, 1954, 102: "To acknowledge Christ is to acknowledge his benefits, not, as is sometimes taught, to behold his natures or the modes of his incarnation."

2. There is the view that he is one of the greatest teachers of mankind. However, what is said to be his teaching is not always what he himself teaches, definitely not when what he says of himself is ignored.
3. In liberation theology it is stressed that he is the champion of the poor and the helper of the oppressed, so that the Messiah is seen as a political figure.
4. It appeals to many to see Jesus portrayed as the human being in whom God manifests his sympathy with people and this world.

The images that people have of Jesus may reflect the spirit that characterizes a particular age.[2] When rationalism dominated, Jesus was primarily seen as a great teacher, and moralism saw Jesus as an example. In the present age he is particularly viewed as a liberator by those who resist powers of oppression.

Now that a variety of dialogue between Jews and Christians has been initiated, many Christians, particularly theologians, allow themselves to be influenced by Jewish views. This is a recent phenomenon (see Vlaardingerbroek, 1989). It has been said of discussions between P. Lapide and J. Moltmann that bridges have been built where many expected deep chasms. In Lapide's view, Jesus is the Son of God only in the sense that all who are led by the Spirit of God are sons of God (cf. Rom. 8:14).[3]

Years ago, Van Ruler made the comment that the modern Christian way of speaking about "Jesus the Messiah" can easily camouflage a curtailment and muzzling of the message of the New Testament and the content of the Christian faith. He warned against the replacement of the Christian perspective with an Israelitic one and the replacement of the latter with a human perspective. The latter case is in essence pure humanization (Van Ruler, *Ik geloof* (I believe), 56ff.

In the encounter between Jews and Christians the question is Jesus' identity. But this is also the point of controversy within Christian theology in the Netherlands and beyond. For example, there is always much to do about Berkhof's Christology, which will be touched on below. In a collection of papers comprising a variety of reactions to his concept, one of the authors points out: "Even when the divinity of Jesus is denied, one can still fully confirm the benefits that God has provided to us in and through his beloved Son Jesus (Flesseman-van Leer, 1985, 94). But we most definitely object to this.

2. M. Kähler sharply criticizes the Leben-Jesu-Forschung (research on the life of Jesus): "Es ist zumeist der Herren eigener Geist, in dem Jesus sich spiegelt" (it is largely the Lord of one's own spirit that is pictured in Jesus), *Der sogenannte historische Jesus und der geschichtliche, biblische Christus* (the so-called historical Jesus and Jesus of the history of the Bible), 1986[2], 57.

3. P. Lapide and J. Moltmann, *De Heer uw God is één* (the Lord your God is one), 1985, 62. To the words of Jesus, "no man cometh unto the Father, but by me" (John 14:6), Lapide added, "except those who are already with the Father, namely the Jews" (52).

If Christ were not the only-begotten Son of God and if both Scripture and confession erred in calling him thus, we would not only treat him differently but also his work. The writings of Berkhof and Flesseman-van Leer demonstrate that they also reinterpret biblical references to salvation.

We hold that the person and work of Christ are inextricably connected. The significance of Christ's work can only be understood when it is seen as the work of this very person. The significance of the person of Christ is manifested in all of his work.

The question that Jesus once asked of his disciples may not be left unanswered: "But whom say ye that I am?" Apostles and evangelists have given the answer that we owe to God's revelation: "Thou art the Christ, the Son of the living God" (Matt. 16:15–16). The church of Christ may not express it differently. The church says so in faith guided by the Word of God.

This does not imply that testimonies to Jesus in non-biblical sources are of no value. We are reminded of what Tacitus, Josephus, and the Talmud say of him. Yet the four Gospels, as records of the earthly life of Jesus, are so to speak "four high mountains of information in rather empty lowland" (Van Bruggen, 1987, 23–37).

Historical and literary criticism has raised objections to the use of the Gospels as sources for information about Christ. These documents are thought to reflect the church's faith rather than reality.

It is clear that their authors wished to do more than merely record history. They were too much involved in the life and work of Jesus. The Gospels are from beginning to end testimonies to their faith in him. What John refers to as the objective of his writing is also the aim of the other Gospels. "They [were] written, that ye might believe that Jesus is the Christ, the Son of God; and that believing ye might have life through his name" (John 20:31). This predilection or emphasis of the Gospels does not detract at all from their authenticity and reliability.

Matthew, Mark, Luke, and John tell us what they personally experienced of the history of Jesus and what they learned as immediate witnesses. "On the basis of a clear, unanimous and trustworthy tradition we may consider the four gospels to have originated within the circle of ear and eye witnesses." One can know Christ in each gospel separately, but even more so in all four combined (Van Bruggen, 1987, 56–58).

29.2. *Names of Christ*

1. *The name Jesus and the name Redeemer.* Dogmatic works frequently include a discussion of the names of the Lord Jesus Christ. Such a discussion can never be as exhaustive as a monograph.[4] At any rate it is necessary to reflect on the names that occur in the New Testament and the creed of the church, i.e., *Jesus Christ, God's only begotten Son, our Lord.* Jesus is also referred to as God in the New Testament. He is the Word that was with God in the beginning (John 1:1). These names are discussed below (see § 29.4).

They have great importance in terms of what they reveal about Christ. He is what his names declare about him.

"Jesus" is the Greek form of *Jeshua*, which in turn is a contraction of *Jehoshua*. In the latter version we recognize the name YHWH (see § 11.2) and the form of a verb that means "to help," "to save," "to redeem," "to bring salvation." In the name Jesus we learn that the LORD redeems.

Two great figures in the Old Testament have the name Joshua, i.e., Joshua the successor of Moses and Joshua the high priest (Zechariah 3). There were contemporaries of Jesus of Nazareth who also had this name, but subsequently the name Jesus began to disappear among Jews, while Christians did not find it appropriate to give or receive this name.

Our Lord received the name Jesus because he saves his people from their sins (Matt. 1:21). This explains first of all from what we need to be redeemed. But the salvation that Jesus grants includes more than this. The traditional saying that he delivers us from the greatest evil and provides us with the greatest good can still be used.

It has been said that the name "*sotèr*" (Savior) was derived from pagan usage. There were indeed all kinds of expectations of salvation and images of redeemers among the nations. However, here we actually encounter an Old Testament perspective. In the Old Testament God is portrayed as the Savior of his people (cf. Luke 1:47). Jesus is the Savior (Luke 2:11) who performs God's redemptive work on earth.

There are those who believe that the biblical name "Savior" refers to the healing miracles of Jesus, but others have correctly pointed out that this name applies to his entire ministry. From the perspective of the Old Testament it is redemption from sin and death both now and in the future (Rom. 3:24; 1 Thess. 1:10; Phil. 3:20–21). Various aspects merge in the apostolic reference to our "great God and our Saviour Jesus Christ; who gave himself for us, that he might redeem us from all iniquity, and purify unto himself a peculiar people, zealous of good works" (Titus 2:13–14).

4. Examples include V. Taylor, *The Names of Jesus*, 1953; O. Cullmann, *Die Christologie des Neuen Testaments* (Christology of the New Testament), 1958[2]. A more critical work was that of F. Hahn, *Christologische Hoheitstitel* (christological titles of sovereignty) 1966[3].

2. *The name Christ and the names Son of Man and Son of David.* The Hebrew name for one who has been anointed (*meshiach*) is rendered in Greek as *Christos*. In the Old Testament priests were anointed, and sometimes prophets also, but in this context we are to think primarily of the anointment of kings. Psalm 2, where the LORD and his Anointed are mentioned in one breath, has been interpreted by Jewish exegetes to refer to the Messiah, i.e., the great Son of David (cf. Edelkoort, 1941, 305–11).

Israel awaited the Messiah as King, partly on the basis of prophecy (2 Sam. 7:12–16). Although there were various messianic notions at the time of Jesus, the Messiah was usually portrayed as a political figure.

It may be for this reason that Jesus did not proclaim himself to be the promised Messiah. People were already about to proclaim him king! On the basis of the fact that Jesus did not present himself as such, many have erroneously concluded that he did not consider himself to be the Messiah. There are sufficient eloquent proofs that he indeed did so, e.g., in his reply to Caiaphas (Matt. 26:63–64).

Jesus did refer to himself in the third person as the *Son of Man*. This also has frequently been challenged in theology. C. Colpe, despite his critical approach, admits that diverse pronouncements of Jesus concerning the Son of Man originated with and applied to himself (*TDNT*, 8:430ff.). Objections to the historicity of other passages are not difficult to refute (see Sevenster, 1948², 91–96; Kim, 1983). The contention that the evangelists would have put these words into Jesus' mouth and that they would have done so on the basis of the "church's theology" is not tenable for the simple fact that this name of Jesus was not at all current in initial Christianity. How can it be explained in the context of this hypothesis that the evangelists employ this title solely when they present Jesus as speaking? (cf. Cullmann, 1958², 158).

The name "the Son of Man" is an Aramaic expression for *human being* and can also indicate *this particular human being* (cf. Kim, 1983, 32–37).

In early Reformed theology this name was associated with Christ's human nature. This interpretation, however, cannot be supported on the basis of Scripture. It is a title that indicates royal rank! Jesus is the Son of Man mentioned in Daniel 7:13.[5] His declaration based on Daniel 7:13 and Psalm 110, during his trial before the Sanhedrin, must definitely be understood to be Messianic in nature. This is when he was accused of blasphemy and condemned to death (Mark 14:61–64).

5. See J. de Vuyst, *Mensenzoon, mensengetal, mensenzielen, mensenmaat* (Son of man, numeral of man, soul of man, measure of man), 1988, 6–12.

The big difference with Jewish Messianic expectations is that according to the New Testament the Son of Man came to redeem his people through his sacrifice (Mark 10:45). In these words of Jesus a clear connection is made with Isaiah 53:10–12. The Son of Man is none other than the suffering Servant of the Lord. Christ's path leads from suffering to glory (cf. Luke 24:26). Now he is seated at the right hand of God (Acts 7:56), because God has given him the dominion to which Daniel's prophecy refers.

As the promised Messiah, Jesus is also the Son of David. This points specifically to his sovereignty. At the announcement of his birth it is said that the Lord God will give him the throne of his father David (Luke 1:32). Jesus is of Davidic descent, but he is also the One in whom is fulfilled the promise given to David (2 Sam. 7:12–16). As David's great Son he is at the same time David's Lord (Mark 12:35–37).

The name Christ points to the continuity between the expectation of the Old Testament and its fulfillment in the New Testament. In Christ the prophetic tradition, the establishment of the priesthood, and the prospect of the messianic king are fulfilled (cf. Pannenberg, *Jesus—God and Man*, 1968, 224–25).

Although the names Messiah and Christ mean the same thing, the latter is given much greater content in the New Testament. By merely referring to "Messiah Jesus" or "Jesus the Messiah" there is a risk of ignoring this. "Jesus is the Christ! He is the Anointed One! He is the Office Bearer! He is the One who comes to perform God's great work on earth, i.e., ultimate redemption" (A. A. van Ruler, *Ik geloof* = I believe, 57).

Especially in the presence of the definite article (as in Luke 24:26 and Rom. 9:5) or when reference is made to Christ Jesus, the name Christ is the designation of his work as Office Bearer. God anointed him with the Holy Spirit (Luke 4:18–19). In the Bible, anointment symbolizes someone's appointment and commissioning. Christ is given a mandate by the Father together with the corresponding authority. According to classical formulation, Christ's office is that of prophet, priest, and king. This will be discussed in § 30.2.

3. *Son of God.* In the Old Testament this name is used for the people of Israel as well as their king in a theocratic sense[6] (regarding the for-

6. Job 1:6 and 38:7 refer to angels.

mer see Hos. 11:1; for the latter 2 Sam. 7:14 and Ps. 2:7). According to the New Testament Jesus is *the* Son of God. He is immediately associated with God.

Could this name also have another origin? In the Hellenistic world great men, rulers, and wise men were called divine and given the title of son of some divinity. According to a certain theory, Hellenistic followers of Jesus would have wished to honor him as a divine being by giving him this name. However, this notion is completely unfounded. There are indeed several passages in which Christ and the Son of God have the same meaning (cf. Luke 4:41; 22:67, 70).

The Messianic perspective sometimes refers beyond itself to the ontological dimension, i.e., a relationship between the Father's being and the Son's being (cf. Korff, 1942^2, 1:137). There are passages in which this name has this additional connotation. This is the case when Christ refers to himself in an absolute sense. He is the Son. Scripture passages such as Matthew 11:27 and 28:19 are of particular relevance in this context. Although questioned by modern Scripture criticism, these are the very words of Jesus, which address the unity of being of the Father and the Son (cf. Sevenster, 1948^2, 101; Cullmann, 1958^2, 294).[7]

Especially in the writings of John and Paul, it is obvious that the unity of the Father and the Son is a unity in terms of being, and that the Son is preexistent. He is with the Father before the creation of the world. The Son is the "only begotten Son of God" (John 1:18; 3:16; 1 John 4:9). It is crucial to believe in Jesus, the Son of God (John 20:31; 1 John 4:15).

A parallel to what John says about "the only begotten Son" of God is Paul's reference to God's "own Son" (Rom. 8:32). We also refer to what is said about the Son in the epistle to the Hebrews (see especially Heb. 1:1–3, 8). God created the world through his Son. In this book of the Bible, the union of the Son with the Father and the divinity of the Son are clearly expressed (cf. Cullmann, 1958^2, 312). Christological titles such as Son of God, Lord, and God refer to the essence of Christ to emphasize the special significance of his ministry. For our redemption we may place our entire confidence in this Christ who carries out the work of God and in his being is closely identified with him (cf. Sevenster, 1948, 256).

7. See also what Ridderbos (*Paulus en Jezus*, 1952, 103) said about the words with which the Father addressed Jesus at his baptism and the transfiguration on the mountain (Matt. 3:17; 17:5).

We totally agree with Van Ruler when he says of the confession that Jesus Christ is the only begotten Son of the Father: "The church did not cast this expression in the hot forge of the formulation of its dogma. It originates in the earliest tradition of Christianity. It comes directly from the gospels, particularly John's" (Van Ruler, *Ik geloof* = I believe, 58).

4. *Lord.* In the *Septuagint*, Lord (*kurios*) is the translation of *Adonai* and the common representation of the name YHWH (see § 11.2). This name indicates power, sovereignty, and authority.

In the Hellenistic world "lord" figured prominently in the imperial cult as a title of divinities and emperors. Domitian was called "lord and god." Paul probably alludes to the frequent use of these names when he writes: "For though there be that are called gods, whether in heaven or in earth, (as there be gods many and lords many,) but to us there is but one God, the Father, of whom are all things, and we in him; and one Lord Jesus Christ, by whom are all things, and we by him" (1 Cor. 8:5–6). The confession that Christ is our Lord can therefore have a polemic connotation. Only he and no one else is our Lord.

The title *kurios* was not borrowed from a Hellenistic environment as W. Bousset, R. Bultmann, and others have contended. It is apparent from the use of the Aramaic word *maranatha*, which occurs in 1 Corinthians 16:22, but must have come from Christians who spoke this language, that Christ was already recognized as Lord in the earliest churches in Palestine. Therefore, Christians used the Old Testament name of God when they referred to Jesus in this way. This is how they confessed his divinity. To God "every knee shall bow, every tongue shall swear. Surely, shall one say, in the LORD have I righteousness and strength" (Isa. 45:23–24). In the New Testament this is said of Christ. It is "to the glory of God the Father" (Phil. 2:9–11).

This name is given its full content when—as in Acts 2:36 and Philippians 2:11—it is given to Christ in his exaltation. He is Lord from the beginning (Luke 2:11), but his glory is especially revealed following his resurrection. Then he says: "All power is given unto me in heaven and in earth" (Matt. 28:18).

Apostolic preaching is the proclamation of Christ as Lord (2 Cor. 4:5). The key to our salvation is the confession that he is Lord and the belief that God has raised him from the dead (Rom. 10:9). "No man can say that Jesus is the Lord, but by the Holy Ghost" (1 Cor. 12:3).

Thus the apostolic church confesses that Jesus is Lord. Those who confirm this in faith accept his lordship, which rules over everything and everyone (cf. Rev. 19:16). Precisely this name implies a personal relationship with Christ, as in Thomas's confession: "My Lord and my God" (John 20:28), which so to speak is the culmination of the entire gospel (cf. Cullmann, 1958, 239). The apostle Paul continually refers to Christ as our Lord.

We see this also in the Apostles' Creed. He is God's only begotten Son, which points to his relationship with the Father. He is our Lord, and this expresses his relationship with us. He is the Son of God and became our Lord. This sequence cannot be reversed.

The common confession contains a personal element. This is explicitly stated in Reformational confessions. Luther says: "I believe that Jesus Christ is my Lord, who redeemed me, a lost and condemned human being, so that I may be his possession and may live under him and serve him in his kingdom" (*BSLK*, 511). Lord's Day 1 of the Heidelberg Catechism may be read as a declaration of the confession: Jesus Christ is my Lord (cf. also Lord's Day 13).

As our Lord he has authority over our lives. Then we belong to him forever. Paul says: "Whether we live therefore, or die, we are the Lord's" (Rom. 14:8). We serve the Lord and we await him (Col. 3:24; Rev. 22:20). "All that Christianity is and all that it has signifies that it belongs to him and he is its Lord" (cf. *TDNT*, 3:1091).

29.3. *Teaching of the church*

1. *The first few centuries*. From the history of the formulation of the Apostles' Creed can be inferred that faith in Jesus Christ, God's "only begotten Son, our Lord," was already confessed by the middle of the second century. There is no indication whatsoever that any other statement preceded it or that there was a controversy about whether it could be expressed in this way.

Following the Apostles' Creed we mention the Creed of Nicaea-Constantinople. The core of this creed is that the Son is of the same substance as the Father or "of one substance with the Father" (in the original text this was indicated with the word *homoousios*). In this important ecumenical symbol the church also stated that the "Lord Jesus Christ, the only-begotten Son of God, [is] begotten of the Father before all worlds; God, of God; Light, of Light; very God, of very God; begotten, not made." "Who for us men and for our salvation came down from heaven, and was incarnate by the Holy Ghost of the Virgin Mary, and was made man."

Thus the ecumenical council of Constantinople in 381 expressed its faith in Christ in a way that agreed with the formulation of Nicaea (325). At this time the church placed its faith conviction—that God's very Son became incarnate to redeem us—over against the false doctrine of Arius and his followers who portrayed Jesus as a creature, albeit God's most important creature (see also § 12.2).

People could be in agreement with the Nicaean Creed, but nevertheless be called to order because of their Christology. This was the case with Apollinaris the Younger (ca. 310–ca. 390) who believed that although Christ was very much human, he was not equal to us in every way, since he did not have a human soul or spirit. There were also others according to whom Jesus' life on earth paled in significance compared with the radiant glory of the Word that manifested himself in the flesh.

There has been a great deal of discussion about the relationship between the divinity and humanity of Jesus. Irenaeus wrote: "He is true man and true God." His contemporary Tertullian introduced new ideas and spoke of the union of divinity and humanity in the one person of Christ (cf. Gilg, 1955, 31–44). For a period of time the Alexandrian and Antiochian schools opposed each other. The former portrayed Christ as God who came to earth cloaked in human nature, and the latter as a human being in whom God dwelled as though in a temple.

The church rejected the views of both Eutyches and Nestorius. Based on the Alexandrian view, the former taught a merging of both natures. The latter, belonging to the opposite school, made statements in which the unity of the person of Christ was not beyond doubt. This dual rejection is implicit in the dogmatic position of the Council of Chalcedon (451), in which the combination of the divine and human natures of Christ is described as follows: "without confusion, without change [in contrast to Eutychianism], without division, without separation [in contrast to Nestorianism]."

There is no reason to refer to these qualifications as being purely negative or abstract. In the view of this council, Christology was not a theoretical or speculative matter. The objective was to safeguard the mystery of the single person of our Lord Jesus Christ who is both God and man, i.e., God who became incarnate.

According to the Creed of Chalcedon, Christ is truly God and truly man, perfect in his divinity and perfect in his humanity, of one being with the Father in his divinity and of one being with us in his humanity. Both natures come together in one person.

This christological dogma has played an important role throughout the centuries. It says that we must continually keep in mind that both the divinity and the humanity of the Savior must be done full justice.[8] The one can never be interpreted as detracting from the other (see also the Creed of Athanasius, *Symbolum Quicumque*).

2. *The Reformation*. With Gilg we can be grateful that the church of our fathers did not struggle in vain to acquire the knowledge of Christ that it required and that we still need in our own time (1955, 99). The church of the Reformation interpreted this dogma of the early church in the light of Scripture and embedded it in all of its teaching. Although its Christology was not new, new emphases were given.

Luther's theology is strongly christocentric. He sees Christ as the heart of Scripture. To him it is impossible to approach God except through Christ. In his testimony to Christ, Luther emphasizes that the key question is, Who is he for me (*pro me*)? In this way he links faith in Christ directly with justification by faith.

He has his own view with respect to Christ's divinity and humanity and their interrelationship. If Jesus had been only human, he would not have been able to save us. Those who deny Christ's divinity abandon the entire Christian faith (*WA*, 40–44). At the same time Luther is very keen on the true humanity of the Mediator. In his preaching he refers very concretely to the real humanity of Jesus who has become our brother. Luther strongly emphasizes the unity of God and man in the person of the Mediator (cf. Lienhard, 1980, 274–82).

Luther's Christology is influenced by his doctrine concerning the Lord's Supper and vice versa. In the controversy surrounding the Lord's Supper he reproaches his opponents who believed they could meet God outside Jesus' humanity; they argued that in the Lord's Supper, Christ is present only in terms of his divine nature. To Luther it is a matter of faith that Christ is also present physically. To him real presence is his presence in terms of both God and man, including his physical presence. After all, Jesus himself says: this is my body.

But can he really be physically present everywhere? Luther propagates the idea that through the incarnation of the Word Christ's human nature acquired the divine attribute of omnipresence.

Although we do respect Luther's intentions, we must reject this particular view. In essence it implies the deification of Jesus' humanity.

The Reformed tradition has always had a problem with this. Calvin rejects this Lutheran view when he writes in a commentary on Luke 2:40: "Although Christ is both God and man in one person, it does not follow, that the human nature received all that was peculiar to the Divine nature." According to him, both divine and human

8. It is for this reason that the Council of Constantinople (680–81) confessed that Christ also had a human will, but that it never opposed his almighty, divine will (*DS*, 556). For the development of the Christology and the dogma of Chalcedon see Grillmeier, 1, 1979, and A. M. Ritter in Andresen, *Handbuch* (handbook) 1:222–83. With respect to the problems that the church faced subsequent to the Council of Chalcedon, we refer to Grillmeier, 2/1 and 2/2 (1986/1989).

attributes belong to the one Mediator. Christ does not need to be physically present in the Lord's Supper in order to cause us to have communion with him. He is truly present in his Spirit and his grace (see further § 53.3).

God made himself our Redeemer in the person of his only begotten Son. If the Mediator had been God alone, he could not have suffered death for us. If he had been man alone, he could not have overcome it (*Institutes*, 2.12.2–3).

Entirely in the spirit of Calvin, Lord's Day 5 of the Heidelberg Catechism says that we need a "Mediator and Deliverer . . . who is a true and righteous man, and yet more powerful than all creatures; that is, one who is withal true God." This is not a theory concerning a mediator figure. We as human beings have no right to determine which qualifications he should meet. Nevertheless, in this context it is asked what significance it has that he is who he is (Lord's Day 6). He is no other than our "faithful Saviour Jesus Christ," whose name is already confessed in the first answer of this doctrinal standard of the church.

29.4. *Christ's divinity*

1. *Critical views and new interpretations.* The church's teaching has not escaped criticism. Since the eighteenth century, numerous objections have been raised against the doctrine of the two natures of Christ in the unity of his person and particularly against the confession that he is true God.

Schleiermacher was prepared to place Jesus in the center, but only as "*Urbild*" (archetype). In the place of the divinity of Christ he referred to the divine in him, which meant the enduring strength of his "*Gottesbewußtsein*" (awareness of God).

Ritschl saw Christ much more as an *example*. He established the kingdom of God as a realm of moral values. When he is referred to as God, this is based on the complete agreement of his will with that of God, and this is a value judgment of the church (cf. McGrath, 1986, 9–58).

Among the many forms of criticism of ecclesiastical Christology that we encounter in liberal theology, the position of G. J. Heering is the most significant. Heering, who subscribed to right-leaning modernism, was prepared to confess the holiness and divineness of Jesus Christ, but the term "divinity" (Godhead) reminded him too much of the second person of the Trinity. "Jesus Christ is a holy Reality; in him God approached us. In him God is near to us."[9]

In attempts to design a modern Christology, dogmatic criticism and a unique interpretation of the Bible go hand in hand. This is particularly the case with Bultmann,

9. G. J. Heering, *Geloof en openbaring* (faith and revelation), 1944², 348ff.

who attracted a great following with his existential interpretation. He approached and analyzed the New Testament in an extremely critical manner. According to him, the New Testament concept of the world and the history of redemption were myths. Modern man has done away with myths. However, they cannot just be eliminated, but must be interpreted. The main thing is kerygma, by means of which we are addressed and placed before the decision whether or not we want to have faith and live by grace.[10]

Bultmann's theology engendered a great deal of opposition and protestation. Thus emerged the Bekenntnis-bewegung "Kein anderes Evangelium" (confessional movement, not another gospel). The Düsseldorf declaration pronounced that the church stands or falls with the confession of Christ: "Wir bekennen das Evanglium, daß der ewige Sohn Gottes in dem geschichtlichen Jesus von Nazareth Mensch wurde und zugleich Gott blieb" (we confess the gospel that the eternal Son of God became incarnate in the historical Jesus of Nazareth and remained God at the same time).[11]

Various perspectives that characterize the development of modern Christology converge in Berkhof's chef d'oeuvre that was published in 1973. Subsequent editions contained refinements that do not constitute fundamental change.

Berkhof favors the earthly approach that emerged strongly with the Enlightenment. Especially after 1960 there emerged (once again) an emphasis on the human world of experience, and many adopted the Synoptic model, thus basing themselves on the historical Jesus and no longer on the incarnation of the Word (the Johannine model), although there frequently were reversals to the classical Trinitarian treatment.

Berkhof's argument, that in Jesus' own time people began to interpret him in terms of their own world of experience, is particularly weak, except to those who believe that the New Testament presents human encounters with Jesus. Verses from Matthew 1 and Luke 1 do not play a role of any significance according to Berkhof.

One thesis that Berkhof retains—despite opposition—is that Jesus' sonship implies that he is preeminently the obedient and therefore beloved covenant partner, although he adds that Jesus becomes the Son as the result of a new and unique act of creation of God (*C.F.*, 286ff.). According to him, a few times Jesus is called "God" in the New Testament on account of the intimate union of God and man in him (in any case in John 20:28; Titus 2:13; 1 John 5:20). "What we have here is a covenantal functionality." Little or nothing remains of Scripture passages that in an unbiased exegesis serve as proof texts for the preexistence of the Son. In Philippians 2, preexistence is not seen to apply to God the Son but to the man Jesus, implying a divine initiative.

However, the apostle says that he was "in the form of God" and "equal with God" (Phil. 2:6).

10. From R. Bultmann's works we mention his well-known *Neues Testament und Mythologie* (1941) as well as a brief summary: *Jesus Christus und die Mythologie*, 1958. Regarding Bultmann and others see J. M. de Jong, *Kerygma*, 1948.

11. See H. Steubing (ed.), *Bekenntnisse der Kirche* (confession of the church), 1970, 310–12.

Colossians 1:15–20 is thought to refer to a cooperating of the historical Jesus with God in the work of creation (cf. *C.F.*, 293–98). How does Berkhof picture this?

According to Berkhof Jesus is a human being, the ultimate covenantal human being, *the* New Human Being, the eschatological human being. "His human 'I' is, out of free will, fully and exhaustively permeated by the 'I' of God; and in virtue of this permeation he becomes *the* representative of the Father." It signifies a new union of God and man, which passes through a history in which humanity is not obliterated but brought to its highest fulfillment (*C.F.*, 291ff.).

Berkhof says of Schleiermacher that he starts out on the human side, portraying Jesus as *Urbild* (archetype) of the true humanity envisioned by God from eternity. However, he does exactly the same thing himself! In this sense his Christology is not new, although to many it has the appeal of something new. According to Beker and Hasselaar (*Wegen* = ways, 3:248ff.), Berkhof's starting point is essentially the same as Schleiermacher's christological starting point, namely that the evangelists portray the Redeemer's self-consciousness as infused with the consciousness of God. Does the name of Jesus Christ then mean more than a sign, symbol, illustration of the mystery of the covenant between God and man?

Berkhof says that Jesus is no dual being. It says after all that "the man Christ Jesus" is "mediator between God and men" (1 Tim. 2:5). We wish to point out that in referring to 1 Timothy one may not ignore the words: "God was manifest in the flesh" (1 Tim. 3:16). In other words, Berkhof refuses to accept the two natures of the Mediator. He does, however, recognize a duality of the structure of the being of Jesus' person: The man Jesus, because of his total obedience even to death, may share in the life and rule of God" (*C.F.*, 291–93). But if this is true, he is a demigod! This is exactly what the early church objected to, as is apparent from its fierce opposition to Arius and the polytheism embedded in his teaching.[12]

Berkhof allows his Christology to be dominated by a scheme of his own choosing. He pictures Christ within a covenantal framework as the human representative over against the Father as the divine partner (*C.F.*, 331–32). This does away with the confession of the Trinity (see § 12.2). However, in the context of the covenant we must

12. Cf. B. Lohse, *Epochen der Dogmengeschichte* (epochs in dogmatic history), 1986[5], 55–57.

keep in mind Christ's mediatorship, which emanates in God's counsel. The eternal Son of the Father became incarnate to be our Mediator (see § 15).

Berkhof's Christology has implications for all of his dogmatics. We shall see in the following subsection that one implication is that one can no longer speak of Christ's true humanity.

Christ's work and salvation through him are also reinterpreted. In light of his view of the new and exemplary humanity of Jesus, it is clear that Berkhof focuses on this new humanity.

E. Flesseman-van Leer is one of those who fully support Berkhof. This is obvious from the work in which she summarizes the contemporary discussion of Christology and provides concise responses to the reactions of other theologians. She is at least as clear and consistent as Berkhof himself. In her work we encounter a denial of Jesus' preexistence in the sense that as God he would have preceded his human life, while also the doctrines of the incarnation and the Trinity fall by the wayside. She does admit that God revealed his love in Jesus, but finds it more important of Jesus "that he and he alone reveals and manifests true humanity" (Flesseman-van Leer, 1985, 85–94).

This is in contrast with what Berkouwer wrote in defense of the christological dogma: in the confession of Christ's preexistence, so far from being a theological construct, the die is cast for the redemption of God, as is attested by the whole New Testament. All the outlines of the apostolic testimony become vague and its message is emasculated, if this confession is abandoned (Berkouwer, 1954, 182ff.).

2. *Biblical starting points and theological considerations.* There are Scripture passages that say about Jesus or quote him as saying that he has been sent by the Father, that he has come to do the will of the Father, and that the Father is greater than he. These are the very passages that have been quoted throughout the centuries by those who deny Christ's divinity—from Arians to Jehovah's Witnesses—and also by theologians such as Heering and Berkhof.

However, one has to hold on to the concept that here we are dealing with the place that Christ occupies as the Mediator and as the Servant of the Lord (cf. Berkouwer, 1954, 184–89). This was already mentioned above in connection with the doctrine of the covenant of redemption (see § 15.2).

In earlier theology it was pointed out that Christ's divinity is revealed in the names that he bears, the divine attributes that he exhibits, the divine works that he performs, and the divine honor that he receives. We share this conviction.

a. *Divine names*. There are those who believe that the doctrine of Christ's divinity rests on only three Scripture passages (John 20:28; Titus 2:13; 1 John 5:20). Berkhof also refers to these passages, but through his interpretation robs them of their force. Bultmann mentions John 1:1 and 20:28, and finds that probably three other places should be considered as well (2 Thess. 1:12; Titus 2:13; 2 Peter 1:1).[13] Grammatically and exegetically, however, there is sufficient certainty with respect to Titus 2:13 and 2 Peter 1:1 (see Cullmann, 1958², 322).

One must read critically the work of those who treat the New Testament critically! Then one discovers how arbitrarily they frequently approach their work. Numerous attempts have been made to interpret John 1:1 in such a way that it ceases to be proof for the divinity of the Word! It cannot be denied that the Word, which according to verse 14 became incarnate, is here referred to as God, while it continues to be distinguished from God ("the Word was with God"). See also Wentzel, *Dogm.*, 1:298.

As we have already seen (§ 29.2), "Son of God" and "Lord" are divine names in various places in the New Testament. So are "the Word" (John 1:1, 14; 1 John 1:1; cf. Guthrie, *N.T. Theol.*, 321–29) and no less "image of God" (Col. 1:15; cf. Phil. 2:6; cf. Wentzel, *Dogm.*, 1:299). In this connection we also have in mind Hebrews 1:3, where the Son is referred to as "the brightness of [God's] glory and the express image of his person."

b. *Divine attributes.* The Son has life in himself, as does the Father who gave it to him (John 5:26). He is preexistent. This preexistence is fundamental to the fourth gospel (see John 1:1–3; 17:5; and other places),[14] but also turns up in Paul's writings as well as Hebrews (Phil. 2:6; Col. 1:15; Heb. 1:2). See particularly Berkouwer, 1954, 162–67, 179–84. It is impossible to transmute everything that Scripture says about the preexistence of the Son into an "ideal preexistence," i.e., a prior existence of the Son in God's mind only.

When Jesus says, "I and my Father are one" (John 10:30), it is not sufficient to think of unity in terms of power or disposition. The Father and the Son are two persons, but in perfect unity.

c. *Divine works.* He grants forgiveness of sins. This is God's prerogative, which the Jews also realized (Mark 2:5–7). Like the Father, he gives life to whom he will. All judgment has been entrusted to him (John 5:21–22). He grants life to all those whom the Father has given to him (John 17:2).

13. R. Bultmann, *Theologie des Neuen Testaments*, 1958³, 131.

14. Cf. Ch. de Beus, *Johannes' getuigenis van het Woord* (John's testimony to the Word), 1973, 158–61.

d. *Divine honor*. Everyone must honor the Son as they honor the Father (John 5:23). Every knee must bow to him, as to God, and every tongue must confess that he is Lord (Phil. 2:11; cf. Isa. 45:23–24). There is no essential difference between the adoration of God and that of the Lamb (Rev. 5:12–13).

Those who reject Christ's divinity must take it that he was deified within the faith of the church. There are theories that attempt to explain this, but the one hypothesis is even more improbable than the other.

There is but one explanation of the faith in the divinity of Christ that lives in the church, namely, the evidence of the revelation of Christ. The Jews desired to kill him, not only because he violated the Sabbath, but also because he referred to God as his own Father, thus making himself equal to God. They wanted to stone him for blasphemy and because he, though human, declared himself to be God. They demanded his death, because he declared himself to be the Son of God (John 5:18; 10:33; 19:7). This is the offense that the gospel speaks of. It is contrasted with the belief that Jesus is the Christ, the Son of God (John 20:31).

Scripture is so clear that a number of theologians belonging to the liberal camp no longer contradict it on this point. Among them is H. de Vos, who holds the view that in the unity of his person Jesus Christ is simultaneously God and man.[15]

G. Sevenster says at the conclusion of his analysis of the Christology of the New Testament that what in modern Christologies is all too often ignored and yet deserves to be emphasized was done more justice in the earlier dogma, namely, that Jesus Christ is to us an object of both faith and adoration (Sevenster, 1948², 363).

In more recent theology Christ's divinity is frequently replaced with the divineness of the man Jesus. "Only a deep alienation from the testimony of Scripture" can explain this (Berkouwer, 1954, 170). At the same time the practitioners of this theology are guilty of the deification of the man Jesus. Barth's judgment is fierce: "If one rejects the Biblical teaching that Jesus Christ is God's only begotten Son and that therefore God's entire revelation and his redemption of men is subsumed in him, and yet speaks of faith in Jesus Christ, one actually believes in a demigod. In this case one has surreptitiously fallen into polytheism."[16]

We are not redeemed by a demigod, but by God himself who came to us in Christ. The Word became incarnate.

"True God" in addition to "true man" is of fundamental significance for the work of Christ. Our salvation depends on it!

15. H. de Vos, *Het christelijk geloof* (the Christian faith), 1948, 191ff.
16. K. Barth, *Credo*, 1946 (1935), 46.

29.5. *Christ's humanity*

1. *Jesus as human being among human beings*. It is consistent with the development of Christology in the church to first focus on the divinity and subsequently on the humanity of the Mediator. The first ecumenical council (Nicaea, 325) confessed that he is true God. It did not add that he is also true man.

The phrase "true man and true God" (*vere homo vere deus*), as an indication of the mystery of his person, emerged first with Irenaeus (*Adv. Haer.*, 4:6–7). Prior to this, Ignatius already emphasized the significance of Jesus' humanity. This reflects not only a conflict with emerging Docetism, but also and primarily the clarity with which the New Testament teaches his humanity.

In the portrayal of Jesus by the evangelists, we never cease to be struck by the characteristics that revealed that he was truly human. He was born in Bethlehem as Mary's first child. There are genealogies that contain names of people to whom he was related. He grew up in Nazareth, just as John the Baptist grew up elsewhere (Luke 2:39–40; cf. 1:80). Just as the young Samuel "grew on, and was in favour both with the LORD, and also with men" (1 Sam. 2:26), "Jesus increased in wisdom and stature with God and man" (Luke 2:52). He was obedient to his parents. He was referred to not only as the carpenter's son, but also as "the carpenter, the son of Mary" (Mark 6:3).

Jesus knew fatigue; he suffered hunger while being tempted in the wilderness and complained of thirst at Golgotha. He could be happy, but also indignant and sad. When Lazarus had died, he wept. In Gethsemane he was sorrowful unto death, and at Golgotha he felt himself abandoned by both God and men.

There is nothing that indicates that the evangelists had trouble portraying Jesus' real humanity. This is true of the entire New Testament. In Acts 1:21 it says "that the Lord Jesus went in and out among us." He fully participated in human life. He was "made of a woman, made under the law" (Gal. 4:4). He "was made in the likeness of men" (Phil. 2:7). Especially in Hebrews, Christ's humanity is clearly portrayed. He shared our flesh and blood and had "to be made like unto his brethren" (Heb. 2:14, 17; see also Heb. 4:15; 5:7–8). The false teaching that denies his incarnation is sharply rejected in 1 John 4: "this is that spirit of antichrist."

"The Word was made flesh" (John 1:14). "Flesh" here indicates man in his creaturely existence manifesting the weakness and dependence, the limitation and transience of human nature following the fall into sin. The glory of the Word, which is God himself, has manifested itself in the flesh.[17]

Jesus is familiar with everything that is part of everyday life, but at the same time he is more than a human being among human beings. He lives in a unique way with his Father, and he always accomplishes the will of him who sent him. Jesus is man the way God intended man to be.

2. *Rejection of views according to which Christ's true humanity is suppressed.* The church confesses not only that Jesus is both God and man, but also that he is true God and true man. The latter word "true" has just as much history as the former. Here we encounter both Docetism and Monophysitism.

From Ignatius's warning against Docetism it can be inferred that his opponents doubted the reality of the history of redemption. He writes about Jesus Christ of the house of David, who was really born of Mary, who ate and drank, who was really prosecuted (condemned) under Pontius Pilate, who was really crucified, who died, and who was really raised from the dead (*Ad Trall.*, 9–10).

Irenaeus fought two main forms of Gnostic Docetism. Some thought that Christ only appeared to suffer. Others considered his entire appearance as unreal (*dokèsis*).

The concept—also advocated by Marcion—that the Son of God came to earth in an incorporeal body was based on dualism. In other words, heavenly and earthly phenomena could not be combined.

In the judgment of church fathers such as Irenaeus and Tertullian, everything was at stake in this conflict (cf. Grillmeier, 1979, 1:212–19, 240–57).

When Docetism is rejected, there can still be Docetic tendencies. According to Apollinaris the Younger, Christ was not like us in every way. Eutyches spoke of a deification of Christ's human nature. Their views were condemned by the councils of Constantinople (381) and Chalcedon (451).

Monophysitism was an important movement. As the name indicates, it held that Christ had a single nature, i.e., that of a god-man. By explicitly referring to two natures of Christ, the Council of Chalcedon (451) left no room at all for Monophysitism. At that time the church did not answer all theological questions that had arisen. This council did not obviate the need for further reflection, but did make an extremely important decision.

A new form of Docetism emerged within the Anabaptist movement. Among both Anabaptists and Mennonites, Christology was influenced by the dualism of nature and grace, creation and re-creation. The Word of God entered into Mary and became

17. Cf. H. Ridderbos, *Het Woord is vlees geworden* (The Word became incarnate), 1979, 8–12.

incarnate in her. According to the Anabaptist view, the Son of God could not have taken on human nature from Mary, because it would have been a sinful nature.[18]

As a result of the conflict with the Anabaptist movement, the christological confession of the Reformed tradition acquired certain emphases. The Son of God did not bring his human nature with him from heaven, but received it through birth from the Virgin Mary. He was "like unto his brethren in all things, sin excepted" (Heidelberg Catechism, Lord's Day 14). Since man's soul was as much lost as his body, he had to accept both in order to be able to redeem both. Thus he truly is our Immanuel, i.e., "God with us" (Matt. 1:23; Belgic Confession of Faith, article 18).

There is also modern Docetism. When Bultmann says that we know little or nothing about the life and personality of Jesus, and that we have no use for a physical Christ, he cannot appeal to Paul's words in 2 Corinthians 5:16. With "knowing after the flesh," Paul means here knowing and judging according to purely human standards. Jesus' true humanity is definitely not of minor significance to the apostle.[19]

In this context, we also need to say something about Berkhof. In his Christology, which we rejected in principle in the previous subsection, "true God" in the church's creed is held to be incorrect, and so is "true man." The human "I" is thought to be completely permeated with the divine. Berkhof portrays a history in which the human Jesus, who started out his role in the covenant as the son of the carpenter of Nazareth, was granted to "share in the life and rule of God . . . because of his total obedience even to death." In this connection Berkhof implies the relative similarity between Adoptionism and Monophysitism (*C.F.*, 292–94).

This implies a gradual deification of the human Jesus, which is not only in conflict with the church's creed, but also contrary to Scripture (cf. Graafland's criticism, no date, 96–100).

3. *Christ as true and righteous human being*. We still need to address the question as to how we should imagine Christ's humanity in comparison with our own. Familiar ecclesiastical terminology is more abstract than the language of the New Testament itself. The concept of "human nature" could be interpreted to mean something that all people have in common. Could Jesus then still have attributes that distinguish him from other people?

Jesus was not only human, but he also had an identity of his own. His body was a body that suited him. He could be recognized by his facial expression and his voice. He had human imagination, human emotions, and a human will. Human beings have their responsibilities, and Jesus was well aware of his responsibility toward God and God's creatures. This was quite apparent from his speaking and acting.

18. See H. J. Wessel, *De leerstellige strijd tusschen Nederlandsche Gereformeerden and Doopsgezinden in de zestiende eeuw* (the doctrinal conflict between Netherlands Reformed and Baptists in the sixteenth century), 1945, 169–202.

19. Cf. J. M. de Jong, *Kerygma*, 1948, 130.

With the confession that the Son of God became human, we do not mean to say that he had to become the ideal man in order to be for us an example of true humanity. This is how he is frequently portrayed in modern theology.

Neither is it sufficient to see in his humanity the possibility of solidarity with us and all people. There is indeed a holy brotherhood between him and his people. If he is "one of us" (Calvin), it is not only to place himself in our situation, but also to take our place. In Calvin's own words: "This is how our Lord appeared as true man. He took the person and the name in order to take Adam's, to present our flesh as the price of satisfaction to God's righteous judgment, and in the same flesh, to pay the penalty that we had deserved" (*Institutes*, 2.12.3).

In the Reformed confession it is said emphatically that Christ was a righteous and sinless human being. "One who himself is a sinner cannot satisfy for others" (Heidelberg Catechism, Lord's Day 6).

It is scarcely necessary to mention Scripture passages that say that the Mediator was without sin (see John 8:46; 2 Cor. 5:21; Heb. 4:15; 7:26; 1 Peter 2:22; 3:18; 1 John 3:5).

But does it not say (in Rom. 8:3) that God sent "his own Son in the likeness of sinful flesh," and thus "condemned sin in the flesh"? It is striking that the apostle expressed it in this way and did not speak of Christ taking on sinful flesh. Despite every similarity between Christ's human existence and ours there remained a distinction in this fundamental sense (*TDNT*, 5:195ff.). We are sinful people—he is not.

There is a tendency in more recent theology to draw Christ deeply into the flesh. This is how it is frequently expressed, alluding to a statement by Luther (*WA*, 10.1.1, 68).

When Kohlbrugge describes what incarnation means to him, he says that flesh pictures man as being totally alienated from God. Flesh is depraved and cursed. The Word took on such flesh and yet remained the innocent and spotless Lamb (in connection with John 1:14; cf. particularly his commentary on Matt. 1). He went so far as to say that Christ adopted sinful flesh. Sin had to expend itself and be eradicated in his flesh.

Kohlbrugge should not be suspected of denying Christ's sinlessness. Although Christ adopted our sinful existence, he remained a holy person. Strong expressions that we cannot quote here were employed by Kohlbrugge to bring Christ as close to us as possible.[20]

20. See more on this in J. van Genderen, "Waarachtig mens, II" (true man), *Homiletica & biblia* 24 (1965): 249–52.

On the basis of what the New Testament says of Christ's temptations, it is sometimes inferred that the possibility existed for him to sin, although this did not in fact become reality.[21]

We maintain that he did not sin and could not sin. The actual sinlessness of the Savior reflects his divine person. His humanity is so united with his divinity that it is unthinkable that he could bring himself to commit sin. He is the holy Son of God, conceived of the Holy Spirit, and always guided by the Spirit. He neither desired to sin nor could sin.

This does not at all detract from the seriousness of the temptations that he endured. His fight with sin was in no way diminished as a result of this. Precisely as a true and righteous human being he suffered from the satanic nature of his temptations, and he experienced more than anyone how dreadful sin is.

29.6. *The unity of the person of Christ*

We confess that the divine and human natures of Christ are united in one person (Belgic Confession of Faith, article 19). However, this does not answer all questions.

Even among those who respect the boundaries drawn by the Council of Chalcedon (§ 29.3), doctrinal differences persist. We recognize this in a comparison of the Reformed view with those of Lutherans and Roman Catholics. There are diverging views of the *communicatio idomatum* (communication of proper qualities).

According to the Reformed view, the person of the Mediator is the subject of the attributes that he has as God and man, and the subject of the works that he performs as God and man. The Lutheran view is different: Not only are the attributes of both natures associated with the one person of Christ, but the divine attributes are also associated with his human nature, which thus is considered to be omnipotent and omnipresent.

Luther reacted sharply to Zwinglian concepts, and Lutheran confessions followed him in this regard. Although Zwingli agreed that Christ suffered for us, he meant that only his human nature suffered for us. Luther wondered whether in this case God could really have redeemed us: "Wo es nicht sollt heißen, Gott ist für uns gestorben, sondern allein ein Mensch, so sind wir verloren" (when it does not say that God died for us, but only that a human being did, then we are lost; *WA*, 50:590; cf. *BSLK*, 1030ff.). In other words, the objection that Luther had to Zwingli's view was of a religious nature.

According to Lutheran theologians, Scripture teaches that Christ's human nature, by virtue of its union with his divine nature, was given majesty, glory, and power. His human nature radiates his divine nature just as red-hot iron radiates heat. During the time of his humiliation this effect remained hidden, but in his state of exaltation

21. See H. Windisch, *Der Hebräerbrief* (the epistle to the Hebrews), 1931, 39ff.

Christ's majesty is also manifested in his human nature. In his adopted humanity he can be present anywhere he wishes. He is also physically present in the Lord's Supper. This omnipresence (*ubiquitas*) of Christ's body is inextricably connected with the Lutheran doctrine of the Lord's Supper (see *BSLK*, 1042–44).

Reformed theologians detected in this view a Docetic element (Bavinck, *R.D.*, 3:309), because it detracts from Christ's true humanity.

Lutheran and Roman Catholic theologians refer to a *perichorese* (interpenetration). Christ's human nature is interpenetrated by his divine nature. Roman Catholicism interprets this as exaltation, glorification, and deification of his human nature. The implication of the concept of interpenetration here differs again from that in Lutheran Christology.

In this connection Rome could refer to certain pronouncements of the sixth ecumenical council (680–81) of Christ's deified flesh and human will (*DS*, 556).

An analysis of the differences between Roman Catholic and Reformational Christology reveals that the former is not an isolated doctrine. Although divine and human spheres can be distinguished in the incarnate Son of God, they interpenetrate each other. All references to the nature of grace can be related to this key concept. Salvation granted to us through Christ's work of redemption is thus portrayed from the perspective of his incarnation.[22]

This has first of all consequences for the position of Mary. If there is only one person who is thought to share in this deification, it is Mary. This is how one can explain Mariological developments in recent Roman Catholicism.

The significance ascribed to this issue is apparent from Hulsbosch's statement concerning the core of the divergence between Roman Catholic and Calvinistic views: "They reject any form of *deification*, either of Christ's human nature or of the believer."[23]

Calvin raised serious objections to the *Lutheran view*. Christ became equal to us in every respect. When the Son of God took on human nature, he did not exalt it beyond the limits set by its creation. The Belgic Confession of Faith speaks along the same lines: "The human nature [has] not lost its properties but remained a creature, [. . .] being finite in nature, and retaining all the properties of a real body" (article 19).

The *Roman Catholic view* is rejected more strenuously in more recent Reformed theology than earlier. This has to do with the further elaboration of the concept of exaltation and deification of Christ's humanity. We refer to the theology of M. J. Scheeben, K. Rahner, A. Hulsbosch, and others. Wentsel points out that Christ here plays the role of prototype of the penetration of the divine nature into the human nature and of the partnership with the divine nature (*Dogm.*, 1:337). A study of Rahner's Christology led to the conclusion that in his theology one finds ever so little of the Mediator and his work of mediation from the perspective of Jesus' humanity.[24]

22. A. Hulsbosch, "De genade in het Nieuwe Testament" (grace according to the New Testament), in *Genade en kerk* (grace and the church), 1953, 47ff., 86, 96.

23. A. Hulsbosch, 23n22.

24. L. Schellevis, *De betekenis van Jezus' mensheid* (the significance of Jesus' humanity), 1978, 97ff. See especially also G. C. Berkouwer, *Conflict met Rome*, 1949², 254–82.

A transformation or deification of Christ's human nature as a consequence of its union with his divine nature is unacceptable.

However, objections have also been raised against the Reformed view. It has been charged with resentment against his human nature. A more serious accusation is that Reformed Christology contains a tendency toward Nestorianism (cf. Korff, 1942², 1:262). However, it is not true that Calvin and his followers—in emphasizing the distinction between both natures—risked divergence from their christological doctrine (cf. Emmen, 1935, 37–45). According to Calvin, Nestorius's heresy was that he devised a double Christ (*Institutes*, 2.14.4).

In reading the Bible, one needs to discern whether things are ascribed to Christ's humanity or his divinity. According to Calvin, when Christ said: "Before Abraham was, I am" (John 8:58), he did not refer to his humanity. Calvin said: "Let this, then, be our key to right understanding: those things which apply to the office of the Mediator are not spoken simply either of the divine nature or of the human" (*Institutes*, 2.14.3).[25] The person of the Mediator is one and his work is one. It is said that he "gave himself a ransom for all" (1 Tim. 2:5–6).

Each nature retains its own properties. Therefore the union of the Word with his human nature does not imply its deification, nor does the union with his human nature imply a humanization of the Word that is with God and that is itself God.

The question may be asked whether the relationship of both natures of Christ can be compared to something else. The creed that is named after Athanasius employs the following image: just as the union of an intelligent soul with flesh constitutes a single human being, so also the union of God and man constitutes a single Christ. Calvin also employed this comparison (*Institutes*, 2.14.1). However, Barth has correctly pointed out that it is invalid (*C.D.*, 4.2.53). There are no analogies.

Concepts have been sought to capture or at least denote the unique character of the union of Christ's divinity and humanity. The consideration that the two natures could not possibly belong to two separate persons led to a denial of the personhood of the human nature. This nature was referred to as anhypostatic (usually rendered as impersonal).

This appears to detract from the integrity of Christ's humanity. We therefore prefer to say that Christ's human nature has its personal existence in the Word that became flesh. For this the term "enhypostatic"[26] was chosen. The important thing is to avoid Docetism by not detracting in any way whatsoever from Christ's human

25. In theology, four types of *communicatio* or announcement eventually came to be distinguished: namely attributes, gifts, works, and adoration (cf. Heyns, *Dogm.*, 249ff.).

26. This term is ascribed to Leontius of Byzantium (sixth century). Schillebeeckx considered it to be a confusion of theological terminology to refer to a human being "in, of and through

nature, and at the same time to guard against Nestorian tendencies by not viewing this nature as being autonomous (cf. Berkouwer, 1954, 312ff.).

Christ's human nature did not have an existence of its own, but this does not make it impersonal, general, or abstract (cf. Schilder, *H.C.*, 3:37–49, 95). It may be referred to as *not-independent*. At no time did it exist by and for itself, but "from the very moment of conception was united with and incorporated in the person of the Son" (Bavinck, *R.D.*, 3:307).

One cannot make the miracle of the incarnation of the Word transparent with the help of images or concepts. The union of Christ's divine and human natures surpasses our abilities to think and speak.

We believe that our Mediator is both true God and true man in *one* person. It also remains a mystery to believing contemplation. It is "a mystery of godliness [that] God was manifest[ed] in the flesh" (1 Tim. 3:16).

§ 30. The work of Christ in his humiliation

30.1. *Introduction*

Christ's work is so rich and multifaceted that both Scripture and the church's confession use different words every time to describe it. Those who isolate and emphasize a single facet—such as his obedience to the will of the Father or his proclamation of the love of God—may well appeal to specific Scripture passages but cannot do justice to the work of Christ overall. History demonstrates that such an approach frequently leads to representations that are one-sided and erroneous.

In the course of time a number of key theological concepts have been devised. "Satisfaction" is one example. Yet we do not use the concept itself as a starting point, but rather what Scripture says about the Mediator and Christ's ministry of mediation.

God" as an "enhypostasis," i.e., a human person subsumed in the "person" of God (*Jezus*, 1975[3], 531). For Schillebeeckx, see Wevers, 1986, 62–71.

Christ is referred to as the "mediator (*mesitès*) between God and men" (1 Tim. 2:5). As mediator, he represents God to men and men to God (*TDNT*, 4:619). He is the mediator of a new or better covenant (Heb. 9:15; 12:24; 8:6). Even when it is not spelled out in so many words, the New Testament identifies him as the only Mediator. He himself puts it this way: "I am the way, the truth, and the life: no man cometh unto the Father, but by me" (John 14:6). Peter says, "There is none other name under heaven given among men, whereby we must be saved" (Acts 4:12).

As Mediator, Christ not only stands between God and us, but he also intermediates. This word assumes that there is a gap that needs to be bridged, a guilt that must be atoned, and enmity that must end.

According to the Old Testament, a mediator can step into the breach for a people who stand guilty before God, through intercessory prayer or the sacrifice of his own life (cf. Ex. 32:30–32; Isa. 53). The Old Testament view of a mediator points to him in whom this mediatorship will find its fulfilment (*TDNT*, 4:615).

Behind Christ's mediatorship stands God's eternal counsel of salvation, i.e., the covenant of redemption (§ 15). Although his work as Mediator commences when he comes to earth, it already manifests its validity and power before he is born. The church confesses that God gave his Son to be "the Mediator and Head of the elect and the foundation of salvation" (Canons of Dort, 1.7). With Bavinck, we can say that the word "Mediator" is eminently suited to describe the place of Jesus' person and the character of his work (*R.D.*, 3:363).

A second term to indicate the unity of the work of the Mediator is Redeemer or Savior (*sotèr*). But the best-known term is Christ. Especially when the New Testament speaks of the Christ or of Christ Jesus, Christ is the name of him whom God anointed. He was anointed with the Holy Spirit to be prophet, priest, and king for his own (Heidelberg Catechism, Lord's Day 12).

Apart from Christ's threefold office (§ 30.2), in this section we need to focus on his twofold state, i.e., his state of humiliation and his state of exaltation (§ 30.3).

30.2. *Christ's threefold office*

1. *Three aspects of a single work*. The "new office" (Calvin on John 1:5) that the Son of God took upon himself is the office of Mediator.

It consists of three components (Calvin, *Institutes*, 2.15.1). Are they three offices, or is it a threefold office? Those who speak of three offices of Christ emphasize thereby the diversity of his ministry, while the expression "threefold office" reminds us particularly of the unity of his ministry. We prefer the latter. It focuses on three facets of the one work of the Mediator.

There is a clear distinction between an office and an occupation, because an office indicates a role in which a person derives authority from his appointment and is accountable to the one who appoints him. To practice an occupation or profession is different from holding an office. An office involves an appointment (cf. Wentsel, *Dogm.*, 3b:69).

For Christ's ministry, to which he was appointed by God, the word "office" is therefore an appropriate term. He says: "I have glorified thee on the earth: I have finished the work which thou gavest me to do" (John 17:4). Of Aaron it is said that he was called to the dignity of the high priesthood. Similarly, of Christ it is said that he "glorified not himself to be made an high priest." It is God who assigned this office to him (Heb. 5:4–6; cf. Heb. 3:2).

Since the second century it has been customary to refer to Christ as Priest and King. This originated with Justin Martyr (ca. 100–165). Eusebius (ca. 265–339) referred to a threefold office, namely, that of High Priest, King, and Prophet.

A doctrine of a threefold office is first encountered in the writings of Calvin. His explanation of the name Christ is: "He was anointed by the heavenly Father to be King, Priest, and Prophet" (Genevan Catechism). His kingdom is a spiritual kingdom. His priesthood alludes especially to his sacrifice. Of Christ as Prophet it is said that he was the messenger and authorized ambassador of God, his Father, to make fully known the latter's will and thereby bring to an end all prophecies and revelations (Heb. 1:2). The *Institutes* contain a more detailed exposition (2.15).

Thanks to Calvin, the doctrine of the threefold office was incorporated in various Reformed confessions. Lord's Day 12 of the Heidelberg Catechism is the best known. This concept was also adopted elsewhere, so that by the seventeenth century it was a common element of Lutheran dogmatics. It is noteworthy that also the *Catechismus Romanus* (1566) was familiar with this scheme. It turns up frequently in more recent Roman Catholic theology (cf. *M.S.*, 3/1, 677–708).

2. *The basis and the significance of the doctrine of the threefold office.* It is generally accepted that Christ holds a threefold office. But what is the scriptural foundation and what is the dogmatic and practical significance of this doctrine?

It has not sprung from a desire for schematization, but from contemplation of what Scripture says. Among the many Scripture passages that mention the name of Christ, there are those that say that he is the promised and expected Messiah (Matt. 1:16; 16:16; Luke 2:11; 24:26; Acts 9:22).

What happened at his baptism in the Jordan had the nature of unambiguous designation and public appointment (cf. John 1:33; Matt. 3:16–17).

There are also relevant passages that speak of "anointing." "The Spirit of the Lord is upon me, because he hath anointed me." He was the Anointed of the Lord—the Lord himself had anointed him (Luke 4:18–21; cf. Isa. 61:1–2; Acts 4:26–27; 10:38; cf. Heb. 1:9). The anointing is a symbolic act that is frequently referred to in the Old Testament. Kings were anointed, as were high priests and other priests, and occasionally prophets (*TDNT*, 9:485–89). This marked the appointment and empowering of those whom God had called to a special task.

The New Testament persuades us to say that the kingly, priestly, and prophetic ministry that God expected from his servants under the old dispensation found their culmination in the kingly, priestly, and prophetic office of Christ (cf. Wentsel, *Dogm.*, 3b:62–82).

Without suggesting that Christ's prophetic ministry predominated, we begin by noting that there is no shortage of Bible passages that persuade us to think of him as our *Prophet*. Deuteronomy 18:15 was an important verse for Jews who awaited the coming of the great prophet of the end times. The New Testament tells us that Jesus is the Prophet whom Moses pointed to by saying that God would raise him up (Acts 3:22). Jesus also compared himself to the prophets. Although he proclaims the Word of God like them, he is more than a prophet. This is clearly brought out in Hebrews 1:1. God reveals himself through Christ's words as well as his deeds. Christ revealed God's name to the people whom God gave to him (John 17:6). He who "is in the bosom of his Father, he hath declared him" (John 1:18).

Christ is *Priest*. The epistle to the Hebrews is permeated with the idea that Christ is the High Priest, i.e., "the Apostle and High Priest of our profession, Christ Jesus; who was faithful to him that appointed him" (Heb. 3:1–2). Christ is a higher priest than Aaron. He is "a priest for ever" (Heb. 7:21, 24). This priest is at the same time the sacrifice. He "was once offered to bear the sins of many" (Heb. 9:28). He is not only "the propitiation for our sins," but also "an advocate [for us] with the Father" (1 John 2:2, 1).

Christ is *King*. Already at the announcement of his birth it is said that he will rule as King and that his kingship will have no end. He is the great Son of David (Luke 1:32–33; cf. 2 Sam. 7:12–16). The prophecy of Isaiah is fulfilled in him and in his kingdom (Isa. 9:5–6). He is given all power in heaven and on earth (Matt. 28:18). His name is "KING OF KINGS, AND LORD OF LORDS" (Rev. 19:16).

In the light of the New Testament, the office of high priest of Israel and that of a king such as David can be viewed as foreshadowing Christ's office. Analogously we can think of Old Testament prophecy as foreshadowing Christ's ministry. This brings out the connection between the Old Testament anticipation of salvation and its fulfillment in Christ.

Christ combines the three offices. He is Prophet in a priestly and kingly manner, Priest in a prophetic and kingly manner, and King in a prophetic and priestly manner (Heyns, *Dogm.*, 270). Restricting this interpretation to one or the other leads to one-sided and unscriptural conceptions, e.g., when he is portrayed rationalistically as teacher, pietistically and sentimentally as sufferer, or politically and civilly as king (cf. Noordmans, *V.W.*, 2:273).

When we make the well-known distinction between the work of Christ in his state of humiliation and that in his state of exaltation (see § 30.3), it implies that he is simultaneously prophet, priest, and king in both states. He is not only prophet when he is on earth and proclaims the gospel himself. Following his resurrection he continues his prophetic work, for through the preaching of the apostles and the proclamation of the Word by office bearers his Spirit—as the Spirit of truth—points the way for the church (cf. John 16:13). His priesthood is not limited to his sacrifice on the cross, for he continues to fulfill his priestly ministry now that he is with God in heaven. He lives forever to intercede for his people (Heb. 8:1–2; 7:25). He is a king whose kingdom is not of this world (John 18:36–37), and he "must reign, till he hath put all enemies under his feet" (1 Cor. 15:25).

In Christ's ministry we do see the prophetic, priestly, and kingly perspectives alternate in prominence, i.e., especially the prophetic perspective in his preaching, the priestly perspective in his sacrifice, and the kingly perspective in his sitting at the right hand of God. This leads to formulations such as Heyns's (*Dogm.*, 270): As Prophet he proclaims redemption, as Priest he obtains redemption, and as King he completes redemption. As Prophet he proclaims the kingdom, as Priest he acquires the kingdom, and as King he prospers the kingdom.

We can describe it slightly differently, but not better than the Heidelberg Catechism in Lord's Day 12: "He is ordained of God the Father, and anointed with the Holy Spirit, to be our chief Prophet and Teacher, who has fully revealed the secret counsel and will of God concerning our redemption; and our only High Priest, who by the one sacrifice of his body has redeemed us, and makes continual intercession for us with the Father; and our eternal King, who governs us by his Word and Spirit, and defends and preserves us in the salvation obtained for us." What is confessed here means therefore that as Prophet he shows us the way of redemption, as Priest he accomplishes our redemption, and as King he preserves us in the redemption.

The focus in Christ's threefold office is our *redemption*. We should therefore not make any attempts to base it on anthropology, as though Christ had to be Prophet, Priest, and King because man was created with a head to know his Creator, with a heart to devote himself to his Creator, and hands to rule to the glory of his Creator (according to Honig, *Handboek*, 485).

It is more plausible to see a connection between the threefold office of the Mediator and the nature of sin. His work consists in redeeming his people from sin (Matt. 1:21), from falsehood and folly, as well as from guilt and the power of sin.

The doctrine of Christ's threefold office can be *polemically* employed against Roman Catholic theology (cf. Berkouwer, 1952, 82–90). There is reason to assume that the word "only" in Lord's Day 12 of the Heidelberg Catechism ("our only High Priest") implies a rejection of the Roman Catholic doctrine of the priesthood and the sacrificial nature of the mass (cf. also Lord's Day 30 and articles 21 and 26 of the Belgic Confession of Faith). We also oppose the doctrine of the vicariate. Christ has no deputy (*vicarius*) who is able to make infallible pronouncements. The prominence that is given to the pope detracts from Christ's kingly office or—as Rome sometimes refers to it—Christ's pastoral office.

In his continuing work Christ does employ people whom he calls to be office bearers. He commissions them, but he never transfers to them the authority that underlies their commission. Ecclesiastical office would otherwise become an independent authority rendered legitimate by Christ!

The doctrine of Christ's threefold office also has *practical implications*. Noordmans has pointed out that this means there is saving power in all that Jesus says, suffers, and does (*V.W.*, 2:275). This enriches and deepens our insight in Scripture. With this we do not mean that all of Christ's words and deeds can be divided up among three offices, but rather that we encounter him always and everywhere in the power of his threefold office. A theologian who emphatically pointed this out was K. Schilder.[27]

Calvin demonstrates in his extensive discussion of this aspect of Christology that the fruit and power of Christ's kingship, priesthood, and prophecy are apportioned to the believers. This is concisely and cogently expressed in the words of the Heidelberg Catechism (Lord's Day 12). The believer says: "I partake of his anointment, so that I may confess his name, dedicate myself to him, and fight against sin and the devil." Among the Scripture passages on which this is based is 1 Peter 2:9, where it says: "But ye are a chosen generation, a royal priesthood, an holy nation, a peculiar people; that ye should shew forth the praise of him who hath called you out of darkness into his marvelous light."

30.3. *Christ's twofold state*

The Apostles' Creed describes Christ's descent as well as his ascent. In the Creed of Nicaea-Constantinople his descent is even more precisely portrayed with the words: "Who for us men and our salvation came down from heaven."

People began to refer to Christ's twofold state (*status duplex*) in the days of the Reformation. Although this doctrine is of Lutheran origin, there is also a Reformed version (already found in the work of Olevianus). It is not surprising that Lutheran theologians distinguish between a state of humiliation and a state of exaltation. As we saw earlier (§ 29.6), Lutheran Christology envisages a sharing of attributes between the divine and human natures that are combined in the person of Christ. Thus his divine attributes such as his omnipresence and omnipotence belong also to his humanity. But why did he then not manifest the omnipresence of his body when he was on earth?

It was then taught that although his human nature did have these divine attributes, he abstained from using them temporarily, i.e., during his state of humiliation or emptying. The incarnation of the Word itself was not viewed as an emptying (*kenosis*), but rather the abstention from employing his divine attributes (not employing them openly, according to a particular school of thought).

This Lutheran doctrine reveals a tendency to deify Christ's human nature (§ 29.6). Within the Lutheran community in the nineteenth century, a theological theory emerged that led to the opposite extreme, namely, the humanization of Christ's divine nature. This is the *kenotic Christology*, which initially attracted a large following in Germany and subsequently in England especially. Also in the Netherlands some were attracted to this view.

27. Cf. K. Schilder, *Christus in zijn lijden* (Christ in his suffering), 1930, 1:5. See also J. J. C. Dee, *K. Schilder: zijn leven en werk* (his life and work), 1990, 1:182–205.

In his incarnation, the Son of God would have completely or partly given up his divine attributes or retained them only in a latent form. An initially prominent theme of this Christology is divine love that characteristically wants to give itself, deny itself, and restrain itself. Sometimes God is viewed as restraining himself already in creation, and even more so in the incarnation. A second theme is a tendency to interpret Jesus' life on earth as a truly human life (cf. Korff, 1942², 1:270–91; Pannenberg, 1968, 325–44).

Kenotic Christology is unacceptable, because the Son of God is imagined to be other than he truly is. It implies a (partial) abrogation of his divinity or a temporary abrogation of his divine existence. We agree with Korff that it is necessary that God really *comes* to us, but that it is also necessary that in coming to us he truly *remains God* (Korff, 1942², 1:290).

The Reformed tradition interpreted the incarnation of the Word as a laying aside or veiling of the divine glory. This notion was based on Philippians 2:7: "But he made himself of no reputation, and took upon him the form of a servant, and was made in the likeness of men." It was combined with another apostolic message: "For what the law could not do, in that it was weak through the flesh, God sending his own son in the likeness of sinful flesh, and for sin, condemned sin in the flesh" (Rom. 8:3).

Being "obedient unto death, even the death of the cross" (Phil. 2:8) goes beyond taking on "the form of a servant." It should therefore be distinguished from it, although it is implied by it and is inextricably intertwined with it. It is a continuing on the same path. It is a description of Christ's humiliation.

Although this Scripture passage is not the only biblical grounds for the doctrine of Christ's twofold state, it does have a great deal to say to us. It is a song of praise that focuses on the person and work of Christ,[28] "who, being in the form of God, thought it not robbery to be equal with God" (Phil. 2:6). The concept of "robbery" is variously interpreted. It probably reflects the idea that one does not hold on to something to employ it to one's personal advantage. The alternative is to renounce something that one possesses. This is what happens in emptying and taking on himself the form of a servant (slave).

This emptying cannot mean that he abandoned himself, but that he yielded up the glory that he had with his Father before the world was created (cf. John 17:5). His life on earth was a life of humiliation. In obedience to God and his law (cf. Gal. 4:4) he accepted even the deepest humiliation, namely, that of death on the cross.

28. Cf. R. P. Martin, *Carmen Christi*, 1967.

In summary we can highlight two aspects:

- He emptied himself. He yielded up the glory that he had before he became man. He was prepared to become equal to men (cf. also Heb. 2:17; 4:15).
- Thus he humbled himself. His humiliation manifested his obedience to the will of God that made him go to the very limit and brought him to the cross.

Following this deep humiliation, God exalted the Mediator to high heaven. It says: "Wherefore God hath highly exalted him, and given him a name which is above every name" (Phil. 2:9). First is explained what Christ did and then what God does.

Exaltation follows upon humiliation. It does not say "subsequently," but "therefore." This link between humiliation and exaltation reflects progression in the acts of God and must be viewed in the light of his plan of salvation. This was already foretold by the prophets (Luke 18:31–33). We particularly have in mind the fourth prophecy of the Servant of the Lord (Isa. 52:13–53:12). Jesus referred to having to suffer to be able "to enter into his glory" (Luke 24:26). When he took upon himself the cross and despised the shame, he had in view the glory that lay ahead of him (cf. Heb. 12:2).

1. This doctrine of Christ's twofold state encountered criticism, namely by Schleiermacher in the nineteenth century, among others, and in the twentieth century by Bultmann. Bultmann believes he discovered a gnostic myth in Philippians 2 (and in 2 Cor. 8:9 and Eph. 4:8–10), which ceases to have validity for us.[29]

In refuting these critics we point out that Scripture offers a great deal more support for this doctrine. The words of Jesus regarding the way of the Son of Man, which through suffering leads to glory (Mark 10:33–34 and other announcements of his suffering), and the clear statements in Luke 24 (vv. 26, 46) have nothing to do with gnosticism; neither does the apostolic preaching as recorded in the book of Acts (see Acts 2:23–24; 17:3). The entire New Testament refers to Christ's suffering and glory (cf. also Heb. 2:9–10; 1 Peter 1:11).

2. Barth gave his own interpretation to the doctrine of the humiliation and exaltation of Christ that implies a fundamental shift. According to him, Christ's humiliation is not abandonment or concealment of divine glory. The glory of the true divinity of Jesus Christ consists precisely in his humiliation. It is "a humility grounded in the being of God" (*C.D.*, 4.1.193).

29. R. Bultmann, *Theologie des Neuen Testaments*, 1958^3, 179.

According to Barth, Christ's one work cannot be divided into successive phases. He does not recognize two successive states but two aspects or manifestations of the reconciliation between men and God in Christ. He sees both natures and both states intertwined. Since Christ is God humiliating himself, he is at the same time exalted man. Redemption consists in the humiliation of God and the exaltation of man. The first theme of Barth's Christology is therefore: "Der Herr als Knecht" (the Lord as Servant); the second theme: "Der Knecht als Herr" (the Servant as Lord). In summary he says: the content of the doctrine of reconciliation is the knowledge of Jesus Christ, who is true God humiliating himself and thus the reconciling God, but also true man exalted and reconciled by God, and who in the unity of God and man is the surety and witness of our atonement (*C.D.*, 4.1.79).

In this way the twofold state of Christ is replaced by two aspects of reconciliation: God humiliates himself and man is exalted. In this dialectic the emphasis is much more on what God does in Christ than the work that Christ does as Mediator between God and men. This has consequences that will be discussed below (see § 32.1). Barth does not recognize any transition from the state of humiliation to the state of exaltation, but perfect simultaneity.

Scripture, however, refers to a progression with a clear point of demarcation. We not only think of the transformation in Philippians 2:8–9, but also announcements of Christ's suffering and apostolic preaching (see the Scripture references under 1).

3. There is both a state of humiliation and a state of exaltation. "State" (*status*) indicates not only a situation but also a judicial position. The key is how the Mediator stands before the Father in these two states. He who is both God and man performs the functions of his office in both humiliation and exaltation.

In his state of humiliation he obtained righteousness for his people and in his state of exaltation he applies it (cf. Heidelberg Catechism, Lord's Day 17). In both states various *stages* or *gradations* can be distinguished. The state of humiliation comprises his humble birth, his suffering and death, his burial, and his descent into hell. The state of exaltation comprises his resurrection, his ascension, his sitting at the right hand of God, and his return to judge.

4. Just like the doctrine of the threefold office, the doctrine of the two states has practical implications. There is a sequence in the aspects that are brought to the fore in preaching. Noordmans points out that this division assists the preaching on the great feast days (*V.W.*, 2:276).

Faith focuses on the way that Christ went when he humbled himself so deeply and when he was exalted so highly. He "was delivered for our offenses, and was raised again for our justification" (Rom. 4:25). He descended to earth to raise us to heaven (Calvin, *C.O.*, 22, 54).

At every stage of his humiliation and exaltation we may inquire about its significance, its benefit, and the comfort that it presents for our lives (cf. Heidelberg Catechism, Lord's Day 11–22). In believing contemplation of the work of Christ in his humiliation and his exaltation we note continually: this was done for us (*pro nobis*), as pointed out in the traditional liturgy for the Lord's Supper.

30.4. *The incarnation of the Word*

1. *The fulfillment of the promise.* The confession that God came to us in the person and work of Christ represents the core of the Christian faith. One can distinguish between God's preparatory coming under the old dispensation and his definitive coming under the new dispensation to which the New Testament testifies (Korff, 1942^2, 2:50). The Old Testament is full of the expectation of the coming Messiah, going well beyond the "Messianic prophecies."

Here we ignore the point of view of those who only accept a historical-critical exegesis of the Old Testament and recognize in it an eschatological expectation but nothing pertaining to Christ. We agree with Edelkoort (1941, 11) that the prophets of ancient Israel associated the ultimate kingship of God with the coming of the Messiah. At the other extreme there is christological exegesis that ignores the historical aspect of the Old Testament in favor of "Christuszeugnis" (witness to Christ). According to W. Vischer, the Old Testament explains what Christ is, and the New Testament who Christ is. Here the redemption-historical perspective is replaced by the circle of witness (cf. Berkouwer, 1952, 101).

Did Messianic expectation emerge late, following the exile, or in the days of the kings, or already in the time of the patriarchs? Or did it originate in Paradise? Did this notion occur to people as a result of certain circumstances or was it preceded by a divine promise of salvation? With Edelkoort (1941, 101–7), we end up at the "mother promise" (Gen. 3:15). From its very beginning the Christian tradition regarded this as "the first gospel," the first announcement of the coming of the Savior[30] (cf. Belgic Confession of Faith, article 17).

Apart from Genesis 3:15, the promises to Abraham (Gen. 12:2–3) and to David (2 Sam. 7:11–16; 23:1–4) are of fundamental significance (cf. Edelkoort, 1941, 158–70). The line of Messianic promises runs throughout the Old Testament, and Messianic expectation is a response of faith.

30. In contrast with the interpretation of this text as "proto-gospel" (see, e.g., G. Ch. Aalders, *De goddelijke openbaring in de eerste drie hoofdstukken van Genesis* = divine revelation in the first three chapters of Genesis, 1932, 513–25; K. Schilder, *H.C.*, 2:276–93), there is another interpretation that emphasizes the continuing conflict between snakes and people (cf. C. Westermann, *Genesis*, 1974, 1:349–59).

Especially in the book of Isaiah there are prophetic pronouncements that find their fulfillment in Christ, such as the prophecy of Immanuel (Isa. 7:14; cf. Matt. 1:23) and the prophecy of the shoot of the stem of Jesse (the King on whom the Spirit of the LORD would rest and through whom would come the kingdom of peace: Isa. 11:1–10; cf. Rom. 15:12). When Isaiah says: "For unto us a child is born, unto us a son is given" (Isa. 9:6), from his prophetic perspective he already sees this child as having come, although it still remains to come. This is how certain God's promise is. One of the special names of the Messiah is: "Mighty God." "In the Messiah God himself comes to man." He comes to redeem. Redemption will be perfect, for he is the Mighty God.[31] The prophetic pronouncement about the Servant of the LORD and particularly that of the Suffering Servant (Isa. 52:13–53:12) must be interpreted in the light of the New Testament as prophecies about Christ (Matt. 8:17; Acts 8:32–35; 1 Peter 2:22–24).

Jesus saw the way that he went clearly spelled out in Scripture. The Scriptures testify of him (John 5:39). He says: "This day is this scripture fulfilled in your ears" (Luke 4:21). "And beginning at Moses and all the prophets, he expounded unto them in all the scriptures the things concerning himself" (Luke 24:27).

Matthew is the evangelist who by means of "fulfillment quotations" indicates numerous connections between what was promised and anticipated in the Old Testament and what was fulfilled in Christ. It is very significant that his gospel starts out with the genealogy that reveals that Jesus, who is called Christ, is the Son of David and the Son of Abraham.[32] While Matthew emphasizes the connection with the history of Israel by going back to Abraham, the genealogy presented by Luke (3:23–38) includes the name of Adam, the son of God. The latter gospel, which has a missionary character,[33] emphasizes the significance of Jesus for all mankind.

"God sent forth his Son, when the fullness of the time was come" (Gal. 4:4). This does not mean that the time was precisely ripe for this or that we can understand why it happened then and not at some other point in time. God determines when the time has come to send his Son (cf. Gal. 4:2, i.e., the point in time determined beforehand by his Father). As in Mark 1:15, the point in time in Galatians is the time of salvation, when the promises of God are fulfilled. The apostle Paul views the coming and the work of Christ as revelation of the fulfilling action of God in history and as the breakthrough of the great time of salvation (cf. Ridderbos, *Paul*, 44).

2. *The miracle of Christ's Birth.* The birth of our Lord Jesus Christ was a real human birth: "And so it was, that, while they were there,

31. B. J. Oosterhoff, *Israëls profeten*, no date, 91.

32. Since Mary was betrothed to Joseph, who descended from David, Jesus was considered to be the latter's son and thus belonged to the family of David.

33. Cf. J. P. Versteeg, *Evangelie in viervoud* (fourfold gospel), 1980, 21–25, 85–89.

the days were accomplished that she should be delivered. And she brought forth her firstborn son, and wrapped him in swaddling clothes, and laid him in a manger; because there was no room for them in the inn" (Luke 2:6–7).

What happened then seems quite ordinary. Yet it is the greatest miracle conceivable. The birth announcement precedes the narrative in Luke 2. Mary is told: "The Holy Ghost shall come upon thee, and the power of the Highest shall overshadow thee: therefore also that holy thing which shall be born of thee shall be called the Son of God" (Luke 1:35). "When as his mother Mary was espoused to Joseph, before they came together, she was found with child of the Holy Ghost" (Matt. 1:18). An angel of the Lord said to Joseph: "That which is conceived in her is of the Holy Ghost" (Matt. 1:20). Therefore the church confesses that Christ "was conceived by the Holy Spirit and born of the virgin Mary."

Not only did the Holy Spirit make Mary's womb fruitful, but his work was also sanctifying and preparatory. This does not mean that this holy conception was the reason for Jesus' sinlessness. As divine person, he was indeed beyond the sin of mankind. He did not emerge from within mankind, but entered into it from outside. "God sent forth his Son, made of a woman" (Gal. 4:4).

The name "Immanuel," which is his by right, implies that in him "God [is] with us" (Matt. 1:23).[34] In Jesus Christ the miracle—that God is with us—became reality.

A key verse in the fourth gospel is: "The Word was made flesh, and dwelt among us, (and we beheld his glory, the glory as of the only begotten of the Father,) full of grace and truth" (John 1:14). The Logos, which belongs to God and is himself God, became flesh (*sarx*). This means that he took on a new mode of existence marked by weakness, vulnerability, and mortality.[35]

The Old Testament refers several times to God as dwelling among his people and manifesting his glory. Now God has come to his people in the Word made flesh. This latter dwelling constitutes a new nearness.

34. Matthew 1:23 quotes Isaiah 7:14, a prophecy incorporating a Hebrew word that can be translated as "young woman." This prophecy may have been fulfilled in the days of Ahaz, so that the birth of the child with the name "Immanuel" then represented a sign. The evangelist used the text of the *Septuagint*, which did not refer to a "young woman" but a "virgin" (*parthenos*). The birth of Jesus threw a new light on Isaiah's prophecy of Immanuel: the light of the fulfillment in him in whom God is with us.

35. H. Ridderbos, *Het Woord is vlees geworden* (the Word became flesh), 1979, 9.

Paul writes that "God sent his own Son in the likeness of sinful flesh" (Rom. 8:3). "Christ came, therefore, in the weak, transitory human state, without sharing in the sin of the human race" (Ridderbos, *Paul*, 65).

The manifestation of God in Christ is a manifestation in the flesh. This is also expressed in the hymn that the apostle introduces with the words: "And without controversy great is the mystery of godliness" (1 Tim. 3:16). The first line says: "God was manifest in the flesh." This referred to the manifestation of Christ in human reality throughout his earthly life and not only in his incarnation.[36]

The great mystery that was then revealed causes us to be astonished at God's plan of salvation and to adore his holy love. The feast of Christ's birth is celebrated with songs of praise!

It was God's pleasure from eternity that this glorious person—Christ—would do this for us and also did this. Whose heart would not melt with joy? In this context, who would not love, praise, and thank him? (Luther, *WA*, 17.2.244ff.).

The incarnation of the Son of God is the incarnation of the Word. "The grace of our Lord Jesus Christ consists in this that, though he was rich, yet for [our] sakes he became poor, that [we] through his poverty might be rich" (2 Cor. 8:9). "Who being in the form of God . . . took upon him the form of a servant" (Phil. 2:6–7).

He "was made of the seed of David according to the flesh" (Rom. 1:3), but this royal house had lost its luster and glory. He came on earth in poverty and not in a palace. As a little child he was laid in a manger, a feeding trough for animals. Joseph and Mary had to flee with him to Egypt when Herod threatened his life. The shadow of the cross fell already on the manger of Bethlehem. An old Christmas song puts it this way:

> Behold him, who is the word, without speaking,
> behold him, who is king, without splendour,
> behold him, who is all, with frailties,
> behold him, who is the light, in the night,
> behold him, who is the good, that is so sweet,
> is rejected, is despised.
> (*Liedboek voor de kerken* = songbook for the churches, 139)

36. See J. P. Versteeg, *Christus en de Geest* (Christ and the Spirit), 1971, 131–75; W. Metzger, *Der Christushymnus 1. Timotheus, 3, 16*, 1979, 62–82.

We can also express it in the words of the traditional liturgy for the Lord's Supper: "He assumed our flesh and blood." This means that he came as near to us as possible. The nature that he adopted was weak and tarnished. "The deeper we draw Christ into nature and the flesh, the more comforting it is to us" (Luther, *WA*, 10.1.1, 68).

According to many, however, the virgin birth of Christ is more a fairy tale than a real miracle, more a great problem than a great mystery of godliness.

Critical reactions date from the days of Rationalism and Deism. A. von Harnack inaugurated a new phase of criticism with his rejection of this article of faith that forms part of the Apostles' Creed. This led in 1892 to the "Apostolikumstreit" (dispute regarding the Apostles' Creed).[37] Since that time there has been a flood of literature dealing with this topic.

We know this dogma, in the form in which it occurs in the *Apostolicum*, from the fourth century. But already by the middle of the second century it said: "born from the Holy Spirit and the virgin Mary." Although this pointed to a supernatural event, it could nevertheless lead to misunderstanding. The difference between the work of the Holy Spirit and the role of Mary is more clearly expressed in the present formulation: "conceived by the Holy Spirit, born of the virgin Mary."

In view of the confession that Christ is the only begotten Son of God, which precedes the article quoted above, no one can hold that his sonship commenced when he came to earth. One can therefore understand that this article was used in the eighth century to combat the view that the man Jesus, son of Mary, was assumed into union with the Son of God through adoption (i.e., Adoptionism).[38] This article also has a role in combating modern Adoptionist theories.

The most important objections to the confession of Christ's conception by the Holy Spirit and birth of the Virgin Mary are the following (cf. among others Brunner, *Dogmatics*, 2:350–56; Pannenberg, *Jesus—God and Man*, 1968, 141–50): 1. The narratives in Matthew 1 and Luke 1 are of a legendary nature; 2. The biological explanation of this miracle detracts from Jesus' true humanity; 3. It implies a disqualification of marriage; 4. It encourages the idealization of virginity and fosters the veneration of Mary; 5. It is a mythological depiction of events which does not appeal to modern Christians and at any rate presents a stumbling block to logical thinking; 6. Faith is not interested in it.

Some of these arguments have been superseded. For example, as far as the second argument is concerned, it is noteworthy that particularly Ignatius, who radically rejected Docetism, wrote the following: he was indeed born of a virgin (*Ad Sm.*, 1); the third argument has not been proven; as far as the fourth argument is concerned, it cannot be blamed on this article of faith that the veneration of Mary has been based on it.[39] It may be pointed out with respect to the fifth argument that there is a

37. Y. Feenstra provided a review in *Het Apostolikum in de twintigste eeuw* (the Apostles' Creed in the twentieth century), 1951, 49–62.

38. See J. N. D. Kelly, *Early Christian Creeds*, 1972^3, 376–78.

39. It is a christological and not a Mariological confession. J. van Genderen has discussed

world of difference between pagan stories about demigods and what the Bible says about the creative power of the Spirit.

As far as the first argument is concerned, we maintain that these chapters deal with a historical fact (cf. Guthrie, *N.T. Theol.*, 365–74), and that they form an essential part of the gospels. We do not know why the remainder of the New Testament is silent in this regard, but it cannot be demonstrated that these facts should also have been mentioned elsewhere. What is said in the opening chapters of Matthew and Luke is definitely not at variance with what we read in the writings of John and Paul.

This particular article of faith pertains to him who is true God and true man. Precisely because he is God, the Holy Spirit uses his power to open this way for his incarnation. He truly became man: he was born as a child of Mary. Paul puts it quite differently than these two evangelists, but what he writes harmonizes with their witness: "When the fullness of the time was come, God sent forth his Son, made of a woman, made under the law" (Gal. 4:4).

One can join Feenstra in saying that those who push the virgin birth to the periphery, and a fortiori reject it, must realize that they are not engaged in an innocent or innocuous game. They play with the gospel of the birth of our Savior that was presented to us in this form and that we only know in this form.[40]

The virgin birth of Christ does have a place in Barth's dogmatics, but only as a sign. He interprets it as an accompanying sign of the revelation of God in the incarnation. It is a miracle of grace that the Son of God unites human nature with himself. Its sign is the setting aside of man. Mankind is only involved in the figure of the Virgin Mary, i.e., in the form of humanity who can only receive, accept, and permit something to be done to her (*C.D.*, 1.2.191).

This implies a disparagement of the significance of the virgin birth (cf. Berkouwer, 1953, 116). Much more than a sign is involved. What we confess concerns the manner in which the Word became flesh.

We agree with Bavinck that the doctrine of the supernatural conception of Christ is of supreme importance (*R.D.*, 3:291).

Christ wished to start out just as we start out, namely, as a child. Yet the fundamental difference between him and us is there already at the beginning of his life on earth.

a. From the very first moment of our lives we are part of humanity consisting of sinners. We must be redeemed—not he. We are all included in Adam—he is not. We fall under God's judgment—he does not. He comes to us to take God's judgment voluntarily upon himself.

b. In and with Adam we have turned away from God. Over against the disobedience of the first man, who is the head of the old humanity, stands the obedience of the Second Adam, who is the Head of the

to some extent the development of Mariology coupled with a growing adoration of Mary in "Nieuwe dogma's" (new dogmas), in A. G. Knevel (ed.), *Maria*, 1988, 45–53.

40. Y. Feenstra, *Geboren uit een maagd* (born of a virgin), 1959, 78.

new humanity (Rom. 5:12–21). God makes an entirely new beginning with him. This is precisely why we need him.

In faith we may say that "he is our Mediator, and with his innocence and perfect holiness covers, in the sight of God, [our] sin wherein [we were] conceived and brought forth" (Heidelberg Catechism, Lord's Day 14).

For us there is no other way back to God but through him, "Who for us men and our salvation came down from heaven, and was incarnate by the Holy Ghost of the Virgin Mary and was made man" (Creed of Nicaea-Constantinople).

3. *The reason for the incarnation and its purpose.* The question why the Word became flesh is thus answered in the church's creed, namely, "for us men and our salvation." It was for our redemption (*sotèria*). This may not be split up into a twofold purpose, namely, first of all "for us men" and secondly "for our salvation." Yet it is the view of no small number of theologians that the reason for the incarnation is not purely soteriological. According to them the incarnation would have taken place regardless of man's fall into sin. Redemption from our guilt and our salvation from perdition can then be viewed as coincidental.

There are various formulations of the question that is addressed here. Would the Son of God have had to become incarnate if sin had not entered into the world? (Osiander, 1550). Is the ground for the incarnation to be found in mankind's need for redemption or in unrelated purposes of God? (Haubst, 1969).

With regard to this issue Duns Scotus and Thomas Aquinas, Osiander and Calvin, J. H. Gunning Jr. and A. Kuyper, G. van der Leeuw and O. Noordmans, H. Berkhof and A. A. van Ruler stand over against each other. According to Berkhof the unique and prophetic union between God and man in the person of Jesus Christ is not just an emergency measure necessitated by sin. Regardless of the fall into sin, this world was from the beginning oriented to his appearance. The term "emergency measure" originates with Van Ruler. He holds that, "The ministry of redemption in Jesus Christ only came about, so that creation could once again exist in the sight of God; it was therefore a single event, an emergency measure in the one counsel and one work of God."[41]

We should not permit ourselves to be guided by human considerations, but by the pronouncements of Scripture. The purpose of the coming of Jesus is explicitly mentioned in numerous places (see Matt. 1:21;

41. Cf. J. van Genderen, "Theologie van de incarnatie of theologie van het kruis" (theology of the incarnation or theology of the cross), *Th. Ref.* 14 (1971): 277–91. See further Wentsel, *Dogm.*, 3b:171–82.

20:28; Luke 19:10; Rom. 8:3; Gal. 4:4–5; 1 Tim. 1:15; Heb. 2:17). John says not only "that God sent his only begotten Son into the world, that we might live through him" but also that he "sent his Son to be the propitiation for our sins" (1 John 4:9–10). There are no biblical grounds for a contrary view.

Those who pursue scenarios that are not supported by Scripture engage in pure speculation. It is wrong to infer from the incarnation for redemption a universal principle of the union of God and man, or the concept of an incarnation that extends to the church.[42] Such a theology of incarnation can be developed in two different directions. One can use it to arrive at a glorification of nature by grace, but also a humanization and secularization of salvation.[43]

Noordmans correctly points out that in the Bible and the creed, the incarnation is the necessary condition for Christ's suffering on the cross. "The Son of God needs his human nature to be able to immerse himself in sin and death, to cover and destroy them in the sight of God. This is how he is our Mediator" (*V. W.*, 2:498–502).

However, redemption may not be restricted to redemption from sin. Our salvation does comprise redemption, forgiveness, renewal, and sanctification, but in Christ we are also granted eternal life (cf. Van Ruler, *T. W.*, 1:164).

30.5. *Christ's suffering and death*

Christ's suffering entails a great deal more than its human witnesses observed. At least three dimensions can be identified.

1. In the first place we think of *what the people who desired his death on the cross did to him*. Their guilt is clearly portrayed by all of the evangelists. It says in the book of Acts: "Ye have taken [him], and by wicked hands have crucified and slain [Him]" (Acts 2:23; cf. 5:30). He was rejected by men and executed. This brings out the nature of man, namely, enmity against God and his Anointed. Jesus knew that he would be put into human hands. The chief priests and scribes would condemn him to death. Gentiles would mock him, spit on him, flog him, and kill him (Mark 10:33–34). He also had to endure a great deal on the part of his own. He was betrayed by one disciple, denied

42. See G. C. Berkouwer, *Conflict met Rome*, 1949^{2}, 272–82.
43. See J. van Genderen (footnote 41), 283–89.

by another, and deserted by all. Those were bitter drops in his cup of suffering.

2. There is yet a deeper dimension in Christ's suffering. *The Father also had a hand in it and God's counsel was fulfilled in it.* It does not go far enough to refer to this as God's foreknowledge, for Christ's suffering and death had a place in his plan. He was "delivered by the determinate counsel and foreknowledge of God" (Acts 2:23).

It is true that people delivered him up, namely, Judas, the Jews, Pilate (Matt. 26:16; 27:2, 26). However, the apostle Paul employs the same word when he writes that God "delivered up" his only Son (Rom. 8:32). What is said of the suffering Servant of the Lord happened to Jesus, i.e., "he was afflicted," "yet it pleased the LORD to bruise him" (Isa. 53:7, 10).

Jesus was continually aware that in his suffering and death he stood before the Father. He accepted the cup out of his Father's hand (Luke 22:42). On the cross he turned to his Father, both in his cry of abandonment and in his committing his Spirit into his Father's hands.

The word "must" occurs repeatedly in the announcements of the passion. This does not mean that it had to happen from the point of view of men but not God, as Wiersinga believes (1971, 169). Neither may this word be robbed of its force by interpreting it as an indication that Jesus had a premonition that his conflicts with the Jews would end in his death.

It had to happen to him because the Scriptures had to be fulfilled (Matt. 26:54; Luke 24:25–27). It was a divine "must" because it resulted from God's plan of salvation. In his suffering and death Jesus oriented himself to the holy will of God as he had done in his entire life and action (cf. *TDNT*, 2:21–25).

3. This brings us to the third dimension. The will of God is at the same time Christ's will. *He accepted his suffering and death consciously and voluntarily*. The Son of Man, of whom is said that he is delivered up, gives himself. He gives "his life as ransom for many" (Mark 10:45). He declares: "I lay down my life, that I might take it again. No man taketh it from me, but I lay it down of myself" (John 10:17–18). His death is a deed. He is no martyr; he is the Mediator.

Christ's entire life was suffering. It already constituted suffering to him that he had to live in a sinful world. To him it was a painful experience to encounter denial and unbelief. He had to say to Jerusalem: "How often would I have gathered thy children together, as a hen doth gather her brood under her wings, and ye would not" (Luke 13:34).

Jesus' suffering was most severe at the end of his life on earth. The people turned away from him—his disciples deserted him—his Father forsook him. There are depths in this suffering that we cannot fathom. Then we think of what happened in Gethsemane and on Golgotha and of the way in which Jesus then put into words what went on in his mind.

Christ's suffering was incomparably severe, because, "He bore . . . the wrath of God against the sin of the whole human race" (Heidelberg Catechism, Lord's Day 15). God's wrath is God's reaction to sin, his holy abhorrence of all that is sinful and of everyone who commits sin. Jesus was willing to experience this wrath.

We must "abhor [ourselves] and humble [ourselves] before God, considering that the wrath of God against sin is so great that he, rather than to leave it unpunished, has punished it in his beloved Son, Jesus Christ, with the bitter and shameful death of the cross." We may thank God for it that he gave us his "only begotten Son for a Mediator and sacrifice for our sins" (liturgy for the Lord's Supper).

If Jesus had been merely human, he would not have been able to perform this ministry of mediation. By the power of his Godhead he was able to bear in his human nature the burden of God's wrath (Heidelberg Catechism, Lord's Day 6).

The Mediator is both God and man. However, we may not infer from this that God suffered when Jesus suffered, let alone that God gave himself up when Jesus gave himself up. Theologians such as Barth[44] and Moltmann[45] do not hesitate to express it this way, but Scripture does not lead us in this direction. It was the Mediator who suffered and died. As Servant of the Lord he completed the work that the Father had assigned him to do (cf. John 17:4).

The biblical message speaks of the greatness of God's love manifested in the sacrifice of his Son. "Herein is love, not that we loved God, but that he loved us, and sent his Son to be the propitiation of our sins" (1 John 4:10). God "spared not his own Son, but delivered

44. See G. C. Berkouwer, *De triomf der genade in de theologie van Karl Barth* (the triumph of grace in the theology of Karl Barth), 1954, 294–324, about the "Passion Gottes" (suffering of God) according to Barth.

45. J. Moltmann, *Der gekreuzigte Gott* (God crucified), 1972. See § 32.1, subsection 5.

him up for us all" (Rom. 8:32). If he did not spare his own Son, he did not spare himself. Our redemption was a matter of blood and tears for our Mediator. Our redemption cost God a great deal.

Jesus "suffered under Pontius Pilate" (Apostles' Creed); he "was crucified also for us under Pontius Pilate" (Creed of Nicaea-Constantinople). Pilate's name is included in the creed of the church not because he was the guiltiest of all. Jesus says: "He that delivered me unto thee hath the greater sin" (John 19:11). Perhaps it was intended to fix the event in time, i.e., Christ's suffering and death can be dated in history. This interpretation was given by Rufinus (345–410) and others. Barth agrees and adds the following perspective: "This time, the time of the world, dated with reference to Pontius Pilate and his like, can but be a time of suffering for the only Son of the Father.[46]

There is more support for another interpretation. Pilate was the representative of the Roman Empire in Judea and his authority as judge had to be recognized. Jesus said to him: "Thou couldest have no power at all against me, except it were given thee from above" (John 19:11). Although the judge pronounced him innocent, he permitted him to be crucified. Mankind committed the gravest possible injustice against him. Yet we agree with Van Ruler that Christianity has always recognized something of the mystery of salvation in this grievously unjust course of events. "Jesus suffered innocently, he died innocently. The great reality of redemption is constituted by the fact that he suffered and died for us, while bearing our guilt" (*Ik geloof* = I believe, 86ff.). He suffered under the judge Pontius Pilate, "that he, though innocent, might be condemned by a temporal judge, and thereby free us from the severe judgment of God to which we were subject" (Heidelberg Catechism, Lord's Day 15).

The Jews did impose Jesus' death penalty, but they delivered him up to the Romans, who were responsible for the execution of this sentence. It became a Roman punishment, i.e., no stoning but crucifixion.

Death by crucifixion was known as the most cruel and most horrible death penalty (*TDNT*, 7:573). The Romans only crucified criminals who were slaves or aliens. However, in the light of the Bible more can be said. Since the suspension of a dead body from a tree was accursed in the sight of God (Deut. 21:23), it can be said of Christ that in his death on the cross he was the target of God's curse. This implies that he underwent the very worst thing that could have happened to him. Paul says: "Christ hath redeemed us from the curse of the law, being made a curse for us: for it is written, Cursed is every one that hangeth on a tree" (Gal. 3:13). This is the basis of the confession: "Thereby I am assured that he took on himself the curse which lay upon me; for the death of the cross was accursed of God" (Heidelberg Catechism, Lord's Day 15).

46. K. Barth, *Credo*, 1946 (1935), 73.

When it is asked why he "had to humble himself even unto death," the answer is that "satisfaction for our sins could be made no otherwise than by the death of the Son of God" (Heidelberg Catechism, Lord's Day 16).

It is in line with God's righteousness and the Word of God (Gen. 2:17) that sin calls for the death penalty. God cannot leave sin unpunished. "For the wages of sin is death" (Rom. 6:23). See further § 28.1.

Why then did Christ, who knew no sin, die? Paul says: God "hath made him to be sin for us" (2 Cor. 5:21). The apostle implies that he was treated as a sinner in our stead, because our sins were imputed to him. The church has confessed from the very beginning "that Christ died for our sins" (1 Cor. 15:3).

He who had to and desired to pay our debt was not spared anything, not even death on the cross. This guarantees the salvation of all his people. This was expressed as follows in the Canons of Dort: "The death of the Son of God is the only and most perfect sacrifice and satisfaction for sin, and is of infinite worth and value, abundantly sufficient to expiate the sins of the whole world" (2.3).

30.6. *Burial and descent into hell*

1. *Christ's burial.* The answer of the Heidelberg Catechism to the question, why Christ was buried, contains an anti-Docetic element: "To prove thereby that he was really dead" (Lord's Day 16). Although this is not incorrect, it is incomplete.

Yet this declaration is important in its incompleteness. The gospels as well as 1 Corinthians 15:3–4 view Christ's death, burial, and resurrection from a single historical perspective. They are facts by which the church of Christ lives. Precisely in the face of doubt about the physical resurrection of Christ, which is shared by many people, it is necessary to realize that the burial and resurrection pertained to the very same Jesus and therefore also to his very own body. Pop puts it this way: "On the one hand Jesus' tomb was the convincing sign and seal of his death and on the other hand it was the historical and geographic spot where God intervened by raising him from death."[47]

The answer of the Heidelberg Catechism is incomplete in the sense that it does not adequately explain that Christ's burial also was part of

47. F. J. Pop, *De eerste brief van Paulus aan de Corinthiërs* (the first epistle of Paul to the Corinthians), 1965, 350.

his work as Mediator. It is a stage in his humiliation. Christ was among the dead. He bore the punishment for sin to the fullest possible extent.

Since he was in the tomb and left it behind, it loses its horror to those who believe in him. Since Christ has died for them, the nature of death changes for them, and becomes a passage to eternal life. The tomb is turned into a waiting room.

2. *Christ's descent into hell.* The words that have usually been translated as "descended into hell," but also as "descended into the realm of death," represent a late addition to the Apostles' Creed. It is not easy to ascertain what its original significance was. Through the centuries there have been different "patterns of interpretation."[48]

a. An old and perhaps the oldest interpretation is the following: Upon his death, Christ went to the place where the dead reside (Greek: *ta katachthonia*). According to one interpretation, in this way he redeemed the believers who preceded his coming and opened to them the gate to the heavenly paradise; according to another interpretation, he descended to the underworld in order to preach the gospel to Gentiles and unbelievers, which implies that following death there remains a possibility to come to repentance.

The Roman Catholic Church was comfortable with the former interpretation (cf. *Catechismus Romanus*). Reformational theology correctly objected that the salvation of the fathers from the centuries prior to Christ was not a function of this type of attention from Christ. The Reformation rejected out of hand the idea of preaching to the dead. Neither does it say so in 1 Peter 3:19–20. Although this passage is admittedly difficult to interpret, we cannot see that it supports universalism, for which many appeal to these words of Peter (cf. Wentsel, *Dogm.*, 3b:222–32). Bolkestein, who gives a clear overview of the most prominent views, also rejects it. He provides a different exegesis, namely, "Christ's sovereignty knows no boundaries. There is no domain on or below earth where he does not reign. He has power even where no man can exercise power, i.e., in the realm of the dead."[49]

b. Appealing to pronouncements made by Luther in a sermon at Torgau, the *Formula Concordiae* says that Christ, following his burial, descended into hell, conquered the devil, destroyed the power of hell, and took away the devil's power. The essence and the comfort of this event is that neither hell nor the devil can imprison or hurt us and all those who believe in Christ (*BSLK*, 1053). In the light of this interpretation, Christ's descent into hell is not a low point in his humiliation, but the beginning of his exaltation.

48. Cf. G. P. Hartvelt, *Patronen van interpretatie*, 1966, 5–10.

49. M. H. Bolkestein, *De brieven van Petrus en Judas* (the epistles of Paul and Jude), 1963, 147. There are Reformed theologians who in connection with Christ's departure (v. 19), in the context of the same Greek word as in verse 22, think in terms of Christ's ascension: his going to heaven was to the spirits in prison a preaching, a proclamation of his victory (according to Bavinck, *R.D.*, 3:479; P. H. R. van Houwelingen, *1 Petrus*, 1991, 130–40).

c. However, in Luther's work we also encounter another view, which corresponds to his theology of the cross. In this context Luther has in mind the hellish pains that Christ endured in Gethsemane and on Golgotha (cf. Du Toit, 1971, 14–25).

This agrees with Calvin's interpretation. According to him the article of faith refers to Christ's struggle with the power of the devil, the horror of death, and the sorrows of hell. He mentions the depth of Christ's abandonment by God and the anguish of his soul, in connection with which he also thinks of "the pains of death" in Acts 2:24 (Catechism of Geneva, 65–70). We encounter this view also in the Heidelberg Catechism (Lord's Day 16): "In my greatest temptations I may be assured, and wholly comfort myself with this, that my Lord Jesus Christ, by his inexpressible anguish, pains, terrors, and hellish agony in which he was plunged during all his sufferings, but especially on the cross, has delivered me from the anguish and torment of hell."

d. Christ's descent into hell is interpreted differently in the Westminster Confession and Larger Catechism. This humiliation did not take place prior to his death, but subsequent to it. He was buried, and until the third day remained in the realm of the dead and in the power of death (cf. Du Toit, 1971, 37ff.)

When we consider these interpretations of Christ's descent into hell in the light of Scripture, we see no basis for the Lutheran doctrine of his descent into hell. When he died, he yielded his Spirit into the hands of his Father.

Those who go along with Calvin and the Heidelberg Catechism recognize in the descent into hell the very deepest humiliation and the bitterest suffering of Christ's soul. In completing his work of redemption, he wished to endure all anguish and pain on his people's behalf. It is a biblical truth that he humbled himself to the very deepest shame and anguish of hell, with body and soul, on the wood of the cross, "when he cried out with a loud voice: My God, my God, why hast thou forsaken me? that we might be accepted of God, and nevermore be forsaken of him" (form for the Lord's Supper).

From a historical perspective, however, this interpretation of the article of faith is not very robust. There is more support for the view of the Westminster Assembly,[50] which several Reformed theologians consider to be consistent with that of the Heidelberg Catechism (e.g., *Synopsis*, 27, 32).

Consequently, the meaning of this article of faith is that Christ not only died but also remained for a time in a state of death or in the realm of the dead. This also was part of his humiliation. He knows

50. A connection could probably be found in some ancient documents. Cf. J. N. D. Kelly, *Early Christian Creeds*, 1972[3], 383.

what it means to be dead, because he has experienced it. However, he was not abandoned to the power of death. Therefore, those who believe in him should not be afraid of it either.

The Apostles' Creed as presented in *De Nederlandse belijdenisgeschriften* (the 1983 text of Netherlands Confessions) says: "He descended into the realm of death." For this idea there is a biblical foundation or at least a biblical precedent in the words of Peter (Acts 2:24–31): Christ "was not left in hell." We may think of Christ's descent into hell as a state of death, in which he existed between his dying and rising again. Herein also he is our Mediator, who bears the punishment of sin to the end, in order to redeem us from it (cf. Bavinck, *R.D.*, 3:416).

§ 31. The work of Christ in his exaltation

31.1. *Christ's resurrection*
31.2. *Christ's ascension*
31.3. *Christ's sitting at the right hand of God*
31.4. *Christ's return*

31.1. *Christ's resurrection*

1. *The reality and certainty of the resurrection*

a. New Testament pronouncements concerning Christ's awakening or resurrection, his ascension or his being taken up into heaven, his sitting at the right hand of God and his sovereignty can all be summed up in the one term "exaltation" (*TDNT*, 8:611). This is not intended to blur the distinctions among his resurrection, his ascension, and his sovereignty. Just as there is a progression in his humiliation, so there is a progression in his exaltation.

In the context of Christ's suffering and death, there is no need to spell out that we are dealing with historical facts. *In the case of his resurrection, however, we must begin with establishing its reality.* Theologically there is a whole set of issues surrounding belief in the resurrection and the event of the resurrection itself (cf. Künneth, 1951^4, 17–61).[51] Nevertheless, even theologians who adopt a skeptical point

51. Cf. W. Marxsen in *Die Bedeutung der Auferstehungsbotschaft für den Glauben an Jesus Christus* (the significance of the resurrection gospel for faith in Jesus Christ), 1967^5, 9–39; F. O. van Gennep in *Waarlijk opgestaan?* (truly risen?) 1989, 9–23.

of view must admit that the belief that Jesus was raised from the dead is one of the earliest events that Christians held to be true (H. J. de Jonge in *Waarlijk opgestaan!* = truly risen! 1989, 31).

The New Testament in its entirety testifies to the resurrection of Christ. It is the climax of each of the four gospels. Although it is invariably presented at the end of each gospel, it can nevertheless be thought of as the starting point for the evangelists. All of them view the entire life and work of Jesus in the perspective of his resurrection. "The resurrection is as it were the prism that brings to light the primary colours of Jesus' life."[52]

For the apostles' preaching, as highlighted in Acts, we refer to 2:22–36; 4:8–12; 10:34–43; 17:29–31. As far as Paul is concerned, there is the magnificent chapter of 1 Corinthians 15, although it does not stand on its own. To him the resurrection is of fundamental significance. Peter starts out with the glorious song of praise: "Blessed be the God and Father of our Lord Jesus Christ, which according to the abundant mercy hath begotten us again unto a lively hope by the resurrection of Jesus Christ from the dead" (1 Peter 1:3). John refers to Jesus Christ as "the faithful witness, the first begotten of the dead, and the prince of the kings of the earth" (Rev. 1:5).

Besides the apostolic proclamation, we have the homologies or confessions of the church of Christ. At times they are brief formulations that express faith, such as in Romans 10:9. At other times we come across lengthier statements such as 1 Corinthians 15:3–5: "For I delivered unto you first of all that which I also received, how that Christ died for our sins according to the scriptures; and that he was buried, and that he rose again the third day according to the scriptures: and was seen of Cephas, then of the twelve."

The resurrection of Christ is part of the fundamental tradition that Paul passes on as he had received it. The words "died" and "rose" stand out. "Seen" goes with "rose" and constitutes its confirmation. The time reference of "the third day" establishes the resurrection of Christ as a fact within known history, although the event of the resurrection itself was not witnessed by anyone.

In the Corinthian church there were those who held that there is no resurrection of the dead. Most likely they considered a physical resurrection to be incredible. Some thought in terms of a spiritual resurrection, which they had already experienced. This is a gnostic

52. K. Runia, *Vragen van deze tijd* (questions of our time), no date, 57.

view. From various tombstone inscriptions it can be inferred that many believed death is final.

In this connection the apostle greatly emphasizes that the resurrection of Christ is of fundamental significance to the Christian faith (see 1 Cor. 15:14–20). In this context the resurrection cannot have been meant to be other than a physical resurrection. The New Testament does refer to a spiritual body—which differs from a physical body (1 Cor. 15:44)—and the glorified body of Christ (Phil. 3:21). Although this body is different, it is his body. The personal identity of the suffering and risen Christ is associated with a physical identity (cf. Vos, 1990, 143ff.). In his new body Jesus was recognizable to his disciples, although he was not always immediately recognized and some initially doubted (Matt. 28:17).

As we shall see later, the appearances of the Savior are of the greatest significance for belief in the reality of his resurrection. This is reinforced by the silent witness of the empty tomb. This also is significant for belief in the reality of the resurrection, as long as it is not viewed in isolation, but seen in the light of the message of the angel and the initial appearances. The empty tomb does not only tell us that Jesus lives, but that his resurrection is a physical resurrection.

b. Since the eighteenth century we have had to deal with numerous theories that detract from the reality of the resurrection.

1. There is a rationalistic explanation that implies that Jesus' death was merely an apparent death. 2. According to the subjective vision theory, following his death the disciples saw him in visions and thought that he was alive. But in fact he was dead and buried. 3. There is also an objective vision theory. Christ supposedly continued to live spiritually and by means of visions to his followers instilled in them the confidence that he lived. He sent them "telegrams from heaven." Such a message from heaven would have been just as miraculous as resurrection from the tomb! The appearances of Jesus, however, should not be treated as visions. 4. Besides these vision theories, the existential interpretation of Bultmann et al. has great influence. According to Bultmann the resurrection of Jesus is not a historic event and its reports are legends. To him "resurrection" means that Jesus' cross made sense. According to others, faith in the resurrection represents a certain interpretation of the experiences that people gained subsequent to Jesus' death. The important thing is to keep the tradition of Jesus alive. Jesus lives on in what the church does and in the message that it brings.[53] We also encounter the notion that Peter and the other disciples had a new experience, and that the sense of freedom exuded by Jesus became so infectious that they subsequently told the story of Jesus of Nazareth as the story of a free

53. W. Marxsen, *Die Sache Jesu Geht Weiter* (the Jesus venture carries on), no date; idem in *Die Bedeutung* (footnote 51), 38.

human being who had set them free.[54] Those who, like H. J. de Jonge, believe that they can only accept what does not conflict with the established order, cannot believe "supernatural interventions in everyday life" and can only see Christ's resurrection as a certain interpretation that Jesus' followers subsequent to his death gave "to his previous living, speaking, acting, and dying." The sense that we are left with today would then be: I also believe that God assigned Jesus a fundamental role in history and wanted him to inaugurate God's sovereignty (H. J. de Jonge in *Waarlijk opgestaan*! = truly risen! 1989, 31–50).

We are continually reminded of Noordmans' remark (1947): "The watershed between the liberal and orthodox camps runs right through all Christian festival days, but particularly the resurrection of Christ" (*V.W.*, 2:94). It is noteworthy that the word "resurrection" continues to be used, while it is given a new interpretation. Here we encounter a more universal phenomenon. The great words of the gospel have an incomparable appeal, i.e., the glitter of gold. Their continued usage confirms the appeal of the truth. However, these words are abused if people do not actually surrender themselves to their appeal (cf. Korff, 1942, 2:266ff.).

In various ingenious ways the fact of the resurrection is replaced by a "resurrection" that is meant to suggest something else. The miracle of the festival is then not the resurrection of Christ, but belief in his resurrection. But if this belief has no basis in an actual resurrection, it is more of an enigma than a miracle!

A very limited concept of what constitutes reality then becomes a hindrance to believing in the reality of the resurrection. In an effort to hang on to some semblance of "resurrection," one gropes for its meaning. In this regard, there are almost as many interpretations as there are modern theologians. But how much meaning is left when the resurrection is no longer seen as reality? How can something that has not really happened still be true?

Barth has pointed out that it amounts to superstition to believe that something can only have actually happened in time if it is "historically" verifiable (*C.D.*, 3.2.446). It may be helpful to distinguish between objectivity or factuality and objectifiability or registrability. Künneth says to Fuchs: the reality of the resurrection is not objectifiable; it cannot be photographed; but it is nevertheless a fact.[55]

It concerns a fact that is without parallel (*sui generis*), i.e., a unique event. This is why the disciplines of history and physics have trouble accepting it. Although one would expect a different attitude on the part of theologians, there are those who believe that God does not—or

54. P. van Buren, *The Secular Meaning of the Gospel*, 1963, 126–34.

55. See the record of the debate held at Sittensen (1964) in E. Fuchs and W. Künneth, *Die Auferstehung Jesu Christi von den Toten* (Jesus Christ's resurrection from the dead), 1973, 67.

cannot—interfere in the course of events. However, those who believe in the revelation of God in Christ have no reason to doubt it. The Lord has been raised indeed.

c. *The certainty of the resurrection has been sought in various ways.* We briefly touch on two theologians who have explored this quest in greater depth, namely Pannenberg and Schillebeeckx.

To W. Pannenberg, modern thinking definitely constitutes a challenge. To establish a firm basis for historical analysis, he believes that one should not start out from the Gospels, but from Paul's experience on the road to Damascus, which has been described as a vision. The notion that the entirely different world that was experienced in this manner could be interpreted as an encounter with someone who had risen from the dead could only be explained in the context of the Jewish expectation of the resurrection of the dead at the end of time. In this way Jesus' resurrection could be viewed as an anticipation of the general resurrection of the dead.

What was valid then continues to be valid today. The credibility of the message of the resurrection depends on the universal question whether a resurrection of the dead is to be expected. According to Pannenberg, this idea makes sense in the context of modern anthropological insights. Although he is not absolutely certain, he considers the resurrection to be indeed highly probable (Pannenberg, 1968, 88ff., 109).

Our view is that our faith cannot be satisfied with a mere probability, not even a probability bordering on certainty, to which a purely historical investigation could perhaps lead us (cf. McGrath, 1986, 174–77). Faith requires absolute certainty. It can only acquire such certainty by basing itself on the testimony of the Bible.

In Schillebeeckx's theology one can recognize another attempt to approach the resurrection from a different angle. His key concepts are experience and its interpretation. The clue to an experience lies within itself. This notion is applied to the "resurrection experience." What leads the disciples to believe that Jesus has risen? A conversion experience centered on the new presence of the risen Jesus in the midst of the assembled church! This conversion experience has been described as a resurrection (Schillebeeckx, 1975[3], 319–24; 1978, 84–94).

According to Schillebeeckx, Christian theology continually draws on two sources: on the one hand the entire tradition of experience of the great Jewish-Christian movement and on the other hand the current, new human experiences of Christians and non-Christians alike (1978, 13). He gives a great deal of weight to these new experiences at the expense of revelation. He emphasizes the resurrection *experience* at the expense of the resurrection itself.

In Rome he had to defend himself before the Congregation for the Doctrine of the Faith. One of the issues was the objective reality of Jesus' resurrection. In his defense against criticism he referred to a passage concerning the significance of Jesus' resurrection for inner salvation, a perspective that he added to what he had written earlier (1978, 85; 1975, 528 a-e).

Schillebeeckx seeks to interpret the festival of Christ's resurrection experience as a conversion experience or as a process of conversion. All Christians would have to undergo this experience. But this interpretation ignores the unique position of those in the New Testament who are referred to as witnesses of the resurrection (see Acts 2:32; 3:15; 10:41–42).

d. When the question is asked, why we believe and confess that the Lord was truly raised, we do not point to historical research or human experience, but to the testimony of Scripture. When the latter is abandoned, doubts continue to have the upper hand.

The New Testament speaks of an empty tomb, the resurrection message delivered by the angels, and the numerous appearances of Christ.

In all of the Gospels the message of Christ's resurrection includes the fact that on the third day following Jesus' death the tomb was found to be empty. One cannot speak of the reality of the resurrection and deny at the same time that Jesus rose from the tomb. It has been correctly noted that the proclamation of the resurrection could not have been maintained in Jerusalem for a single day or a single hour if all those who were implicated had not been convinced that the tomb was empty (cf. Pannenberg, 1968, 103).[56]

Therefore we reject the common view that the reports of the empty tomb were of secondary importance and the thesis that in view of the danger of misconception on the part of the church and outsiders one should no longer speak of a physical resurrection (F. O. van Gennep in *Waarlijk opgestaan!* 1989, 9–23).

Those who were connected with Jesus would not have been convinced that he lives merely on the basis of the empty tomb. Several interpretations would have been possible. But not only the tomb was empty; so were the grave clothes. This is highly significant (cf. Van Bruggen, 1987, 247ff.).

The fact that the tomb was empty and the miracle that Jesus had risen are inextricably connected in the resurrection message: "He is not here: for he has risen, as he said" (Matt. 28:6).

Also in the appearances of Jesus, hearing is coupled with seeing. The word *ophthe*, of which Jesus is the subject, in the dative construction does not mean that he was seen, but that he appeared

56. See also W. L. Craig, "The Historicity of the Empty Tomb of Jesus," *New Testament Studies*, 31 (1985): 39–67.

(cf. *TDNT*, 5:358–62). This word underlines Jesus' initiative in the appearances (Weber, *Foundations*, 2:72). They were manifestations of Jesus and not just visual experiences of people. The women and the disciples did not merely get an impression of him and they did not just see an image of him. They encountered Jesus himself. He showed them the marks of his wounds. He observed mealtime with his disciples. This is how Christ revealed himself in his appearances (see John 21:1, 14). To the apostles he showed himself alive (Acts 1:3).

The reports of the appearances in the gospels are not uniform. This is no reason to question them, as is frequently done. A gospel is not a chronicle of past events. In writing his gospel, every evangelist made choices, which at times reflected his purpose. There are differences in the presentation of the facts. However, a comparative analysis leads to the following conclusion: "This does not reflect after-the-fact construction, but first-hand reporting by people who were dumbfounded by the great event" (Van Bruggen, 1987, 239).

Jesus knew that his appearances were personally needed by his own to raise them to the joy of his resurrection. He took Peter aside. He accompanied the residents of Emmaus to their home. He brought Thomas to the confession: "My Lord and my God!" (John 20:28). The initial appearances represented somewhat of a "crisis ministry" (Vos, 1990, 55). We should especially not lose sight of the redemption-historical dimension. The forty days after Christ's resurrection are a time of transition. Jesus comes and goes. He says to Mary Magdalene: "Touch me not; for I am not yet ascended to my Father" (John 20:17), and he announces his ascension. He prepares his followers for their task in the church and in the kingdom of God.

First the apostles needed to be deeply convinced of the reality of the resurrection, for the church of all time would depend on their testimony. Today no angels come down from heaven with a message of Christ's resurrection, and the appearances are not repeated. But the testimony of the apostles and the church that enfolds them has to suffice for us.

With their authoritative proclamation, the apostles of Christ constitute the foundation of the church. In its confession, the church accepts the apostolic witness of the resurrection.

There is a dazzling certainty in the words written by Paul: "But now is Christ risen from the dead, and become the firstfruits of them that slept" (1 Cor. 15:20). What God has accomplished is presented to us in apostolic preaching in all of its glory and takes effect. Those who accept it in faith truly experience its reality. They are granted to live by the power of the resurrection.

2. *The significance of the resurrection*

a. *Perspectives of Christ's resurrection.* It is significant that the resurrection of Christ is the oldest feast of the church. The first day of the week was quite early celebrated as a special day. It was the day of the Lord (Acts 20:7; 1 Cor. 16:2; Rev. 1:10). Wherever possible, it was then that the meetings of the church were held.

Still today, every Sunday we are reminded of the fact and the lasting significance of the resurrection. But when Paul writes to Timothy: "Remember that Jesus Christ . . . was raised from the dead" (2 Tim. 2:8), he implies that Timothy should keep in mind—throughout his life and in all his work—that Jesus lives. To believers there is no day upon which the light of his resurrection does not fall.

Christians were aware of the connection between Christ's resurrection and the Jewish Passover, which is evident from a second-century sermon by Bishop Melito of Sardes. Its starting point was Exodus 12, which was considered to be fulfilled in Christ: "He is the Pascha of salvation, the Lamb that was sacrificed for you, your ransom, your life, your resurrection, your light, your salvation, your King."[57]

Originally the festival of Christ's resurrection was focused on the commemoration of Christ's suffering, death, and resurrection, but subsequently it was preceded by a period of forty days by way of preparation. The seven weeks after the festival of Christ's resurrection were a period of joy, which culminated in the celebration of Pentecost. It became customary to administer baptism during the night before the festival of Christ's resurrection. The focus was on new life in the light of the redemption brought about by Jesus Christ.

We ought to "take seriously the unique event of Christ's resurrection, the fact that Jesus rose, as well as the significance, the fruit, the purpose of this fact of salvation for the church and the world, for individuals and the community." In this way his resurrection offers a new perspective.[58]

b. *Its theological significance.* The resurrection is a key element of the New Testament proclamation of salvation in Christ. Those who allow themselves to be directed by Scripture realize that the resurrection is of the greatest significance in more than one way.

57. Cf. J. J. Thierry, *Opstandingsgeloof in de vroegchristelijke kerk* (faith in the resurrection in the early church), 1978, 63.

58. See A. Noordegraaf, *Pasen geeft perspectief* (Christ's resurrection offers a new perspective), 1988, 5–14.

Its theological significance comes first. This means that God has manifested himself in the act of raising Jesus from the dead. We usually speak of rising, but the message of his resurrection actually is: Christ has been raised. God has raised him. He "was raised up from the dead by the glory of the Father" (Rom. 6:4). He rose, because he was raised.

In a number of Bible verses God is called the God who raised Jesus from the dead (cf. Rom. 8:11; Gal. 1:1; 1 Peter 1:21). Just as he is the God of the exodus from Egypt, so he is the God of the raising of Jesus. He thus revealed himself more gloriously than ever in the power of his holy love.

The New Testament contains turns of phrase and expressions that indicate that the resurrection of Jesus was an act of God favoring him (cf. Acts 2:24; 5:30). The Father declared his Son—rejected by men and executed—to have been right. The words of Psalm 118:22–23 were fulfilled in him: "The stone which the builders refused is become the head stone of the corner. This is the Lord's doing; it is marvelous in our eyes" (cf. Acts 4:11; 1 Peter 2:6–8).

The raising of Christ constitutes divine approval of the work of the Mediator. In it we hear the Father's "Amen" to the Son's "It is finished."

c. *Its christological significance*. The resurrection is the resurrection of him who was crucified. The angel says to the women at the tomb: "Ye seek Jesus of Nazareth, which was crucified; he is risen" (Mark 16:6). We need to view the cross in the light of the resurrection and the resurrection in the light of the cross (cf. Calvin, *Institutes*, 2.16.13). This means that the commemoration of his sacrifice and the proclamation of his death in the celebration of the Lord's Supper (1 Cor. 11:25–26) apply to his entire work. The Lord, whose death we proclaim as the church, has been exalted and glorified. His resurrection proves that he is God's Son in power (cf. Rom. 1:4).

The resurrection is the first stage in his state of exaltation, but not the only one. There is a progression in his work as Mediator. Paul writes: "It is Christ that died, yea rather, that is risen again, who is even at the right hand of God, who also maketh intercession for us" (Rom. 8:34).

He triumphed over death which came into the world through sin. If he had merely escaped death, its power could have persisted. "But

. . . our Saviour . . . abolished death and brought life and immortality to light through the gospel" (2 Tim. 1:10). This has enormous consequences.

Christ is "the firstborn from the dead" (Col. 1:18; cf. Rev. 1:5). He is the trailblazer who opens the way for all of his people. His resurrection is the great breakthrough of the powers of the kingdom of God.

d. *The soteriological significance.* Jesus says: "I am the resurrection and the life." He wants us to seek and to find life in him. He has life and he gives life, because he is life. With his statement at Lazarus's tomb (John 11:25) he means not only that he will raise his followers from the dead some day. Eternal life is given now already. It is received in communion with him. "Whosoever liveth and believeth in [Him] shall never die" (John 11:26). Paul's words are very meaningful, "Christ . . . is our life" (Col. 3:4), and, "For to me to live is Christ" (Phil. 1:21).

When Christ reveals himself to John with the words, "I am he that liveth, and was dead; and, behold, I am alive for evermore, Amen; and have the keys of hell and of death" (Rev. 1:18), he means: I died for you and I live for you. In Christ the salvation of his people is forever secure. They have life from him, through him, and with him.

Three of the most important aspects of salvation that we owe to Christ's resurrection are justification, renewal, and glorification. These are mentioned in Lord's Day 17 of the Heidelberg Catechism.

In the first place there is *justification* that proceeds from Christ's death and resurrection (Rom. 4:25). He makes us partakers of the righteousness that he obtained for us through his death.

In the second place there is *renewal.* He raises us up to new life by his power, so that believers can be assured that they "are dead indeed unto sin, but alive unto God through Jesus Christ" (Rom. 6:11). Christ "renews [them] through his Holy Spirit after his own image" (Heidelberg Catechism, Lord's Day 32).[59]

In the third place there is *glorification.* Christ's resurrection is a pledge of the resurrection of believers in glory (cf. Rom. 8:11). Their redemption includes their bodies, because Christ's resurrection and that of his own cannot be separated in this respect either. He is "the firstfruits of them that slept" (1 Cor. 15:20), and now his own are not left behind (see 1 Cor. 15:49; Phil. 3:21).

59. See W. H. Velema, *Aan Christus gelijkvormig* (conforming to Christ), 1988.

e. *The ecclesiological significance.* The resurrection is of the greatest significance not only for believers personally, but also for the church as church. The church is the church of the resurrection! Without Christ's resurrection the existence of the church would be an enigma. In the absence of the redemption fact of his resurrection, there would be no church!

On the day of his resurrection the Savior was already gathering his followers. Today he carries on with his work of gathering his church. The King of resurrection gathers his church in the unity of the true faith.

He who has all power commanded all nations to be made his disciples and added the promise: "And, lo, I am with you always even unto the end of the world" (Matt. 28:18–20). This command must be seen in the context of Christology, and in its execution the church is dependent on the Holy Spirit (see John 20:22; Acts 1:8). Then the apostles give their testimony to the resurrection of the Lord Jesus "with great power" (Acts 4:33).

The proclamation of salvation that is given to us in his resurrection culminates in the exhortation to be "always abounding in the work of the Lord" (1 Cor. 15:58). It is the work of the Lord, because he stands behind it and it is done at his command. We may know that it is not in vain in the Lord.

f. *The eschatological significance.* Christ's resurrection is decisive for our future. In him the future has already begun. The beginning of the end has already come, but not all of God's promises have yet been fulfilled. It is not for this life only that we place our hope in Christ (1 Cor. 15:19). Our expectations are well-founded.

Christ's exaltation progresses all the way from its first stage to the final one. He will appear in glory. God will judge the world through him whom he raised from the dead (Acts 17:31).

John writes: "We know that, when he shall appear, we shall be like him; for we shall see him as he is" (1 John 3:2). Everything will become new! There will be new people and a new world, a resurrection of the mortal bodies of the believers and a liberation of creation "to the glorious liberty of the children of God" (Rom. 8:11, 21). "We, according to [God's] promise look for new heavens and a new earth, wherein dwelleth righteousness" (2 Peter 3:13). Earth and heaven will put on a resurrection robe and a Pentecost gown (Luther).[60]

60. Cf. J. Köstlin, *Luthers Theologie*, 1901², 2:348.

31.2. *Christ's ascension*

1. *Ascension as redemption event*

The reason for starting out with the fact of Jesus' ascension is to counter the widely held view that the story of his visible ascension is a fabrication of the gospel writer Luke.

People wonder why Luke did not limit himself to the notion that Jesus was exalted by God, as is done in various New Testament scriptures. There are those who believe that Luke had in mind the Old Testament-Jewish traditions with respect to the taking up into heaven of important figures (Enoch, Elijah, Moses, Aaron). According to others, Luke wanted to use the "image" of the ascension to make Jesus' exaltation understandable, because he and his readers were influenced by the Hellenistic culture in which people were familiar with the taking up of important persons into a higher world (Den Heyer, 1991, 3:127ff.).

Exegetes and systematic theologians who reject the latter explanation nevertheless frequently treat the history of the ascension as Luke's personal interpretation, which is of little significance to theology and means even less to faith.

Among the critics we first of all mention Von Harnack, who felt that the church was wrong in maintaining an article of faith that did not belong to the core of Christ's gospel and at best was an explanation and a teaching device, but represented a stumbling block for many in our own time.[61] Half a century later Bultmann gave a boost to such criticism by arguing that the history of the ascension lost its significance at the same time as antiquity's view of the world.[62]

In the ensuing discussion it was correctly pointed out that the ascension does not depend on a certain view of the world. Brunner, who himself subscribes to the modern concept of the world, says that he does not feel persuaded by secular reasoning to abandon the traditions of the church. To him such reasoning is not at all conclusive, and the main thing is that Luke's unique depiction is in conflict with Paul and John's interpretation that Christ's resurrection constitutes his exaltation (*Dogmatics*, 2:373ff.).

With Brunner and Althaus we agree that scientific objections are not conclusive. Yet Althaus and other Lutheran theologians treat the story of a physical, visible ascension as a legend. It captures the assurance of faith that Jesus was exalted through his resurrection and is now with God (Althaus, *C.W.*, 489ff.).

Roman Catholics are also frequently skeptical with respect to the ascension presented in the New Testament. This can be summarized as follows: "As a result of his resurrection, Jesus is now with the Father. The last appearance story shows this in a symbolic way: ascension" (*The New Catechism*, 1966, 226).

61. A. von Harnack, *Das Apostolische Glaubensbekenntnis* (the Apostles' Creed), 1892, 40.

62. R. Bultmann, "Neues Testament und Mythologie," in H.-W. Bartsch (ed.), *Kerygma und Mythos*, 1960^4, 1:17.

Given this situation it is important to carefully listen to Scripture. Although only Luke describes the ascension, this does not make his testimony less credible. In John 20 it clearly says that the resurrection and ascension cannot be identified with each other. After all, Jesus says: "Touch me not; for I am not yet ascended to my Father" (John 20:17). In several places there are indirect references to the ascension.[63] Other places in Scripture also have a bearing on this topic, e.g., Ephesians 4:10; 1 Timothy 3:16 (the words: "received up into glory"); Hebrews 9:24; 1 Peter 3:22 (see Guthrie, *N.T. Theol.*, 391–401; Wentsel, *Dogm.*, 3b:286–92).

In reading Luke 24 the impression may be gained that the ascension followed virtually immediately upon the resurrection. But this same author refers to the forty days between these two events (Acts 1:3). It is true that the ascension falls within the perspective of the resurrection and marks the final appearance. The ascension, however, is more than a "solemn and majestic final chord" (Van Niftrik, *Kl.D.*, 214). Like the resurrection, Christ's ascension is a redemptive fact. We maintain this also over against Berkhof (*C.F.*, 323ff.).

Already in the first stage of its formulation, the Apostles' Creed contained the confession of the ascension. It makes eminent sense to reflect on the meaning of the words: "He ascended into heaven."

2. *The significance of the ascension*

a. *The christological aspect.* The ascension first of all has significance for Christ himself. Just as he was raised and rose, he was taken up and ascended into heaven. Especially in Luke 24:50–53 there is a doxological moment in the presentation of the event: "praising God." As the exalted Lord, Christ is in heaven, which is filled with the glory of God. "He is crowned with glory and honour" (Heb. 2:9).

The ascension is a new stage in the state of Christ's exaltation. His sitting at the right hand of God is greater than his resurrection (see Rom. 8:34). The ascension occurs in between. The Mediator is exalted to high heaven.

b. *The soteriological aspect.*

1. Jesus departed from his own while blessing them. This departure did not destroy their communion. It should never be forgotten that he departed while he blessed them. When we think of Jesus, we may picture the Savior as bestowing his blessing both then and now. "With respect to his human nature, he is no more on earth; but with respect to his Godhead, majesty, grace and Spirit, he is at no time absent from us" (Heidelberg Catechism, Lord's Day 18).

63. C. Stam, *De hemevaart des Heren in de Godsopenbaring van het Nieuwe Testament* (the ascension of the Lord according to God's revelation in the New Testament), 1950, 24–37.

2. The Heidelberg Catechism asks "what advantage to us is Christ's ascension into heaven? First that he is our Advocate in the presence of his Father in heaven." He is our *Paraclete* (1 John 2:1): our Helper, our Intercessor, and our Advocate. See also Romans 8:34, Hebrews 7:25, and other places that deal with his intercession (*intercessio*).

It is a very essential part of our faith in Christ that he prays for us. He already did so prior to his exaltation. For all those who believe in him, he prays that they may be one in him (John 17:20–21). He prays that the faith of his followers will not fail (Luke 22:32). He entered "into heaven itself, now to appear in the presence of God for us" (Heb. 9:24).

In addition to the Heidelberg Catechism, the Canons of Dort (5.8) and the Belgic Confession of Faith (article 26) also focus on Christ's intercession. The detailed nature of the latter article reflects a conflict with Rome. It remains relevant, especially since two new dogmas of Rome (1854: Immaculate Conception of Mary; 1950: Corporeal Assumption of Mary) imply a highly analogous treatment of Jesus and Mary. It detracts from Christ's work as Mediator that Mary has been accorded far greater honor than can be supported by Scripture. The Reformation rejected any concept of Mary as queen of heaven, co-redeemer, and most powerful intercessor, because it detracts from the unique and exclusive significance of Jesus Christ.[64]

Christ is our only Mediator and Intercessor and we have no access to God except through him. Those who invoke the intervention of certain saints do not place their entire trust in him. We should not seek another mediator, "for there is no creature, either in heaven or on earth, who loves us more than Jesus Christ" (Belgic Confession of Faith, article 26).

Here we can refer to *prayer*, although this may be done in other places as well.[65]

64. More details can be found in J. van Genderen, "Nieuwe ontwikkelingen rond Maria (new developments concerning Mary), in A. G. Knevel (ed.), *Maria*, 1988, 54–61.

65. Calvin discussed prayer in detail in connection with soteriology (*Institutes*, 3.20); Wentsel did so in connection with Christ's ascension (*Dogm.*, 3b:296–325). In the twentieth century Barth, Brunner, Berkhof, and some others paid attention to it in their dogmatics. It can also be defended to deal with prayer as a separate topic in ethics. In the context of this topic see

In this context it is apparent how much we need the Mediator when we approach God in prayer. The prayers of believers are cleansed by his blood; otherwise, they would never be free of uncleanness (Calvin, *Institutes*, 3.20.18). Precisely after the ascension we pray in the name of Jesus, as he desired us to do (see John 16:24). Prayer does not entirely consist in making personal requests. It means to express our dependence on God and our trust in him. It means to adore him. It also means to make intercession for others. Believers rely on the sole intercession of Christ, when they intercede with God for themselves and others. When we are called to continually offer to God the sacrifice of our praise through Christ, this means according to Calvin that our mouths are not pure enough to glorify God's name unless the priesthood of Christ intervenes (*Institutes*, 3.20.27–28). The prayer that Jesus taught us is the example and rule for our prayer (cf. Heidelberg Catechism, Lord's Day 45).

Through Christ, our "only Mediator . . . we call upon the heavenly Father" and are "assured that whatever we ask of the Father in his Name will be granted us" (Belgic Confession of Faith, article 26). Christ's redemption work is the grounds for the hearing of prayers, and through his intercession they find their fulfillment. Then we pray "under the arc of the promise of God's surprising responses" (Wentsel, *Dogm.*, 3b:314).

3. Christ is in heaven as both God and man. He is the Head of his body, the church. In faith we may look up to him who preceded us and—in part because he is now in heaven with our human nature—have the certainty that he as our Head will take us, his members, up to be with him.

In this context we are reminded of his reference to the Father's house with its many mansions, where he went to prepare a place for his followers (John 14:2–3). Heaven, which opened itself to the Mediator, will not remain closed to the people that belong to him. In him believers have a place in the heavenly realms (Eph. 2:6). Now already they are citizens of the kingdom of heaven and from there they expect Christ to come as their Redeemer (Phil. 3:20–21).

4. Christ sent us his Spirit as a pledge. The coming of the Spirit is associated with his departure (John 16:7). What he promised (John 15:26–27), he made come true at Pentecost (Acts 2:33). We may expect of Christ that he will continue to give us his Spirit. Through the power of his Spirit we "seek those things which are above, where Christ" is (Col. 3:1), which does not mean that we turn our backs to earthly reality or neglect our tasks here and now. It does mean that we see everything in a higher light.

L. Doekes, in C. Trimp (ed.), *De biddende kerk* (the praying church), 1979, 43–83; J. Douma in the same volume, 84ff.

c. *The eschatological aspect.* Following Christ's ascension, his ministry of mediation continues. It is focused on the coming of the kingdom of God in all its glory.

The apostles, who stared up to heaven on the Mount of Olives, heard the announcement of the angels: "This same Jesus, which is taken up from you into heaven, shall so come in like manner as ye have seen him go into heaven" (Acts 1:11). The belief that Jesus has ascended to heaven is tone with the belief that he will come again. The church lives during the interval between his ascension and his return, as it says (Titus 2:13), "looking for that blessed hope, and the glorious appearing of the great God and our Saviour Jesus Christ."

During this interval we have to forgo the visible presence of the Lord Jesus. It is, nevertheless, quite apparent that he is there. He blesses us with his gifts from heaven.

He is in heaven while his people are on earth. But it will not remain this way. The distance between heaven and earth, between God's dwelling place and ours, is bridged in Christ. What we believe, we shall also see. We are moving toward a new heaven and a new earth, where God will dwell with people (Rev. 21:1–3). Christ's ascension brings this future closer.

Now that Christ has ascended to heaven, we look up: *Sursum corda*! Lift up [your] hearts! We also look forward and say: *Maranatha*! Come, O Lord!

31.3. *Christ's sitting at the right hand of God*

1. *Christ shares in God's glory and sovereignty*

Following his ascension, Christ sits at God's right hand. The fact that this is the next stage in his exaltation is more apparent from certain revised texts of the Apostles' Creed than the earlier version, which utilized the present participle "sitting." When we now read "and sits"—which stands out following the past participles of the redemption events that precede it—this implies that this *sessio* (sitting of Christ at the right hand of God) has an important place in what we believe and confess.[66] The New Testament frequently makes reference to this, often referring to Psalm 110 (Acts 2:34–35; 1 Cor. 15:25; Heb. 1:13;

66. A view that we completely reject is that of H. Wiersinga, according to whom there is no succession of separate events, but varying concepts of Jesus' glory. Even his humiliation and exaltation are viewed as being one and the same thing. Wiersinga said: "To stand next to people means to sit beside God," *Je kunt beter geloven* (it is better to believe), 1978, 85ff.

and other places. Cf. Cullmann, 1958^2, 230). Both in Psalm 110 and the New Testament it is an image that has been derived from human relationships and that implies the ascription of honor and power. The poet of Psalm 110—a royal psalm—saw the king in a Messianic light (Edelkoort, 1941, 330–40), and the Christian church has appropriately applied these words to Jesus Christ.[67] Various expressions are used: God has placed him at his right hand; the Son has sat down at God's right hand; he is seated at the right hand of God; he stands at God's right hand (cf. Eph. 1:20; Heb. 1:3; Col. 3:1; Acts 7:56).

To our way of thinking the place at someone's right hand is a place of honor (see also 1 Kings 2:19). But against the background of Psalm 110 it is best to think of this in terms of utmost power.

God reigns, but Christ also reigns. This means that Christ reigns on God's behalf and that God reigns through him. For this reason Calvin says: "He reigns in the Father's power and majesty and glory" (*Institutes*, 4.17.18). The Heidelberg Catechism puts it eminently: "By whom the Father governs all things" (Lord's Day 19).

We are reminded of the words of Jesus, "All things are delivered unto me of my Father" (Matt. 11:27), and, "All power is given unto me in heaven and in earth" (Matt. 28:18). Infinite and boundless power! It is an entirely different power than the power that is imposed on the people of this world and is wielded to intimidate them. Power (*exousia*) here means: authority, full power, power that is rightfully his. He is "the prince of the kings of the earth," the "King of kings" and the "Lord of lords" (Rev. 1:5; 19:16).

This article of faith does therefore not merely indicate the place where the Mediator dwells following his ascension. Now that he is seated "on the right hand of the throne of the Majesty in the heavens," he ministers in "the sanctuary" (Heb. 8:1–2). This means that he carries on his work as Mediator in heaven.

Christ, who now sits at the right hand of God, as Head of all that is, has been given to his church, which is his body (Eph. 1:20–23). He is also the Head of the church (Col. 1:18; Heidelberg Catechism, Lord's Day 19). He is therefore the Head of the church as well as the cosmos (Du Plessis, 1962), but there is a difference. The church is his body, while the cosmos is not. His dominion over the church is a qualified dominion. He rules it in love. From the perspective of the church it is a relationship of complete dependence and loving communion.

67. J. de Groot, *De psalmen*, no date, 151ff.

We read in Revelation 5 that the Lamb takes the scroll from the right hand of God. This means that this scroll has been given to Christ, who is the Lamb of God, and that he now holds it in his hands to break its seals. The scroll is like a testament. Opening a testament involves more than just perusing it and ascertaining its content. It also means proceeding to the execution of its provisions. Thus everything that God has determined in his counsel is to be executed. The executive power is assigned to Christ.

He receives this power as the Lamb who stands as it had been slain (Rev. 5:6). It bears the scars of the knife put to its throat. It is mortally wounded but not dead, for it stands there alive. In the symbolic language of the book of Revelation, this means that Christ, who sacrificed himself for his own as the Lamb of God that takes away the sins of the world (John 1:29), has all power. We may contemplate that this power is given to him who loves his own to the end.

From this vision it may not be inferred that the Father has ceded the throne to his Son and that he now withdraws himself. He has not surrendered this power, but has given Christ the mandate to govern the church and the world. Christ does not rule in the Father's stead, but in the Father's name. This is what the Heidelberg Catechism means with the statement that the Father governs all things through him. Van Ruler therefore says: "God rules the world in Christ's way." In this connection he employs a modern image: "The high tension of God's governance passes through the transformer of Christ's work as Mediator of mediation" (*Ik geloof* = I believe, 115).

Some thought has been given to the relationship between God's sovereignty and Christ's sovereignty. Three views call our attention.

1. Although in his subsequent work, A. Kuyper does not deny Christ's all-inclusive sovereign power—defended so eminently in his speech, *Souvereiniteit in eigen kring* (sphere sovereignty), given at the occasion of the opening of the Free University in 1880—he did maintain that there are two kinds of kingship: kingship over the world, emanating directly from God and establishing governmental authority on earth, and Christ's kingship, which is not of this world and rules in a different sphere. *De Gemene Gratie* (common grace, 1902–4) contains an extensive elaboration of this distinction.

2. According to O. Cullmann there is a kingly dominion of Christ, which affects all of creation. Yet Christ's kingdom cannot be identified with God's kingdom. Christ's kingdom has been there ever since his ascension, but God's kingdom is entirely futuristic. When God's kingdom is inaugurated, Christ's kingdom ends with Christ transferring his kingdom to the Father, as explained by Paul in 1 Corinthians 15.[68]

3. A. A. van Ruler has reservations about a temporal division. God's kingdom and Christ's kingdom can only be distinguished in terms of modality. Christ's kingdom is God's hidden kingdom.[69]

68. O. Cullmann, *Königherrschaft und Kirche im Neuen Testament* (sovereignty and the church in the New Testament), 1950³, 11–14.

69. A. A. van Ruler, De *vervulling van de wet* (the fulfillment of the law), 1947, 89. There are additional views, such as those of E. Brunner, who limits Christ's sovereignty to those who truly confess that Jesus Christ is Lord, *Dogmatics*, 2:301.

We must cling to the unity of God's kingdom and Christ's kingdom more so than Kuyper, Cullmann, Van Ruler, and others. The New Testament usually refers to God's kingdom, but sometimes also the kingdom of the Son of his love, or the kingdom of Jesus Christ (Col. 1:13; 2 Peter 1:11). It is "the kingdom of Christ and of God" (Eph. 5:5).

We confess with David: "Thine is the kingdom, O LORD, and thou art exalted as head above all" (1 Chron. 29:11), but neither is there anything that falls outside Christ's realm of power. After all, God has "put all things under his feet" (1 Cor. 15:27). The apostle says the same thing in Ephesians 1:22. In this connection Calvin points out that complete power and sovereignty over everything has been entrusted to him who is the Head of the church.

God's sovereignty is an everlasting sovereignty, and of Christ's reign it is said that "there shall be no end" (Luke 1:33). This is also stated in the Creed of Nicaea-Constantinople.

There was a specific reason for making this statement, because Marcellus of Ancyra taught that the Logos, who proceeded from the Father for the work of creation and the work of redemption, would one day withdraw himself and be subsumed in God (see Andresen, *Handbuch*, 1:157–63). He believed he could base this on Paul's words regarding the subjection of the Son to the Father and the transfer of the kingdom (1 Cor. 15:23–28). He viewed this as the end of Christ's kingship.

The question arises as to how we should interpret this Scripture passage, which a theologian such as Van Ruler interprets to mean that Christ's mediatorship is an intermezzo and that the incarnation will be abrogated in the eschaton (see § 31.4, subsection 2, for a discussion of this concept).

2. *A doctrinal difference*

According to the Lutheran view, the right hand of God means everywhere. It is not a certain place in heaven, but God's almighty power that fills heaven and earth (*BSLK*, 1026). Since he is at God's right hand, he is also physically omnipresent. This is the *ubiquity* that is essential for the Lutheran doctrine of the Eucharist. According to Luther and his followers there is a correlation between Christology and the doctrine of the Eucharist. In this view it is an error that as a consequence of his ascension Christ would physically be in a certain place in heaven, so that in the Eucharist he could and would not be truly and substantially present in his body (*BSLK*, 1013).

The manifestation of this glory and power, which preeminently reveals his omnipresence, reflects Christ's exaltation, but his humanity already possesses the same attributes by virtue of the union of his divine and human natures. This is the Lutheran view of the *communicatio idiomatum* (see § 29.6).

The Reformed have major objections to this view. They agree with the Council of Chalcedon (451) that each nature retains its own attributes. There is indeed exaltation and glorification, but no deification of Christ's human nature. In article 19 of the Belgic Confession of Faith it says: "And though he has by his resurrection given immortality to the same, nevertheless he has not changed the reality of his human nature; forasmuch as our salvation and resurrection also depend on the reality of his body."

As the Heidelberg Catechism says, the Reformed view implies, that "Christ's . . . Godhead . . . is beyond (*extra*) the bounds of the human nature it has assumed, and yet none the less is in this human nature and remains personally united to it" (Lord's Day 18). Here we encounter the "*extra-Calvinisticum*" (cf. Calvin, *Institutes*, 2.13.4; 4.17.30). This label is, however, open to criticism, because in this regard Calvin aligned himself with an entire tradition (cf. Weber, *Foundations*, 2:132, 147).

Lutherans have criticized this Reformed view for not recognizing any benefit from Christ's humanity subsequent to his ascension. We can respond to this charge in the spirit of the epistle to the Hebrews: "We have a great high priest that is passed into the heavens, Jesus the Son of God . . . . [He] was in all points tempted like as we are, yet without sin" (Heb. 4:14–15). This Jesus is now with God as our Mediator. For our sake he became and remained man. Therefore Ursinus, who like Olevianus participated in the discussion of this controversy with Lutheran theologians at the Maulbronn colloquy (1564), stated: "We teach that Christ takes care of his church, sustains and protects it by both his spirit and his will, which are divine and human."[70]

3. *Christ rules not only the church, but also the world*

a. "What profit unto us is this glory of Christ, our Head? First, that by his Holy Spirit he sheds forth heavenly gifts in us, his members; then, that by his power he defends and preserves us against all enemies" (Heidelberg Catechism, Lord's Day 19). This explains the bare essentials.

In connection with the first point we have in mind especially the gift of the Holy Spirit. Although the ascension and Pentecost do not coincide, they are interconnected. When Christ had been exalted at God's right hand and had received the promise of the Holy Spirit from the Father, he poured out the Spirit (see Acts 2:33). There are also spiritual gifts or gifts of grace (charismata) that are bestowed by the Spirit of Christ, and with which believers as members of Christ's body are equipped (1 Cor. 12, 14). Christ, who "ascended . . . that he might fill all things," also "gave some, apostles; and some prophets; and some, evangelists; and some pastors and teachers; for the perfecting of the saints, for the work of the ministry, for the edifying of the body of Christ" (Eph. 4:10–12). Offices and ministries are gifts of the exalted Christ to his church on earth.

70. Z. Ursinus, *Opera*, 1612, 2:521. Cf. K. Schilder, *H.C.*, 4:174–213.

When it comes to the protection of believers, words come to mind concerning preservation by the Lord, such as the promise: "I will also keep thee from the hour of temptation, which shall come upon all the world" (Rev. 3:10). Jesus gives us the assurance that no one will snatch his followers out of his hand (John 10:28). The church does not only receive from him its mandate, but also the scope to carry it out.

There is more. We confess that he is an eternal King, who cannot go without subjects. He is the only Head of the church (Belgic Confession of Faith, articles 27 and 31). This has consequences for church governance. It means at any rate that the church cannot have a single head or a hierarchical structure, as we see embodied in the papacy. It also implies that the church is not a democracy but a Christocracy. We reject everything that is in conflict with the principle that the church is governed by Christ alone.

Concerning the work that he continues to do as Head of his church through his Word and Spirit, it may be said in summary that he gathers and protects his church, bestows upon it his gifts, leads it, and governs it. Calvin writes: "Such is the nature of his rule, that he shares with us all that he has received from the Father" (*Institutes*, 2.15.4). The Scottish Confession (1560) refers to our perspective of the *sessio* as a comfort: "For our comfort he has received all power in heaven and on earth" (11).

b. Christ's sovereignty is not restricted to the church, for it is a *universal or cosmic lordship*. "He is Lord of all" (Acts 10:36). "Every knee should bow . . . and every tongue . . . confess that Jesus Christ is Lord" (Phil. 2:9–11).

It has not yet reached this stage. We do not yet see that all things have been subjected to him (Heb. 2:8). The world that is ruled by Christ is still the world. There is a "prince of this world" (John 12:31), who has turned it into occupied territory and acts as though he has a rightful claim to it. There are people who have been "blinded . . . by the god of this world" (2 Cor. 4:4).

It is not incorrect to say that God's rule reflects toleration (Van Ruler, *Ik geloof* = I believe, 115). However, it must be added that Christ rules militantly. He rules in the midst of his enemies (see Ps. 110:2). In his war against the powers of evil he enlists his people. It is not without reason that the church is referred to as the church militant (*ecclesia militans*).

The question may be asked what we in this world can see of Christ's dominion over everyone and everything. People appear to be in charge. They do as they please. There are powers that we cannot withstand. Van Ruler, however, points out that although in reality there is a good deal of evidence that Christ is in charge, the main thing is that we believe this to be the case—on the basis of the apostolic gospel—and live by such faith (*Ik geloof*, 116). On the one hand there are signs of the sovereignty of Christ restraining the powers of evil; on the other hand there are signs of stubborn opposition to him and his kingdom. This opposition, however, will ultimately come to nothing.

The significance of Christ's sovereignty to us also depends on whether we bow to this King or not. Calvin says (*Institutes*, 2.15.5): "For just as he fulfills the combined duties of King and Shepherd towards the godly who subject willingly and obediently; on the other hand, we hear that he carries a rod of iron to break them and dash them all in pieces like a potter's vessel (Ps. 2:9)."

In reflecting on Christ's glory and sovereignty we need to keep in mind that he wants to be recognized as Head of his church and as King of kings and Lord of lords. This recognition is first of all an inner condition, but also needs to be reflected in the lives of his people, so that they will be grateful and obedient citizens of his kingdom. It is our joint responsibility as Christians to stand up for Christ's kingship and honor the confession—which was the confession of the first Christians in a hostile world—"that Jesus Christ is Lord, to the glory of God the Father" (Phil. 2:11).

31.4. *Christ's return*

1. *The place and significance of the return of Christ.* Christ's return is part of his work in his exaltation. This is discussed not only in Christology but also in eschatology, which addresses the approach of his coming and the question whether it is a matter of one or two returns (the chiliastic view).

Christology and eschatology are closely related. The core of eschatology is the anticipation of Christ's return. Christology is of fundamental significance for eschatology; it is also elaborated and further developed in eschatology.

Here we note first of all that Christ's work as Mediator would not be complete if his sitting at the right hand of God would not culminate in his return. His entire exaltation anticipates his coming in glory. The same is true of his resurrection, his ascension, and his sitting at the right hand of God (see Acts 17:31; 1:11; Matt. 26:64). The book of Revelation shows us how Christ, whose glory was revealed to John (Rev. 1), directs everything toward the ultimate consummation.

Christ's return will bring his preceding work to completion and crown it. It will be the final and highest stage of his exaltation (Bavinck, *R.D.*, 4:685).

The Son of God will come "with power and great glory." "The Lord himself shall descend from heaven with a shout, with the voice of the archangel, and with the trump of God." "Behold, he cometh with clouds; and every eye shall see him" (Matt. 24:30; 1 Thess. 4:16; Rev. 1:7). Acts 1:11: points out that he will be visible, just as he ascended to heaven before the eyes of his disciples. Those who know him will be able to say: it is the Lord.

Christ's return is a *redemption event*. A difference with other redemption events is that we continue to look forward to this event. The Apostles' Creed first uses the past tense in referring to redemption events, then the present tense ("is seated"), and finally the future tense.

Christ himself announced his return. He said: "For as the lightning cometh out of the east, and shineth even unto the west; so shall also the coming of the Son of man be" (Matt. 24:27). The word "coming" (*parousia*) first of all means "presence," but also indicates the beginning of someone's presence, i.e., his appearance or arrival (cf. 1 Cor. 16:17). In the New Testament world, the arrival of a monarch, making an official visit to a certain region, was called a *parousia*. It was not only a great honor to be allowed to receive him, but one could also expect the granting of a variety of privileges. Whenever he made his splendid entry into a city, one could present petitions to him. The announced *parousia* was anticipated with longing. It inaugurated a new era!

This is a picture of what will happen when our King comes. We anticipate his appearance in glory, which will benefit his people. It will inaugurate a new era of unprecedented glory.

There are also other indications of the advent of Christ. It is his appearance, the appearance of his glory (1 Tim. 6:14; Titus 2:13). The New Testament also uses the word "revelation" (2 Thess. 1:7). In addition there is the verb "coming." Thus are fulfilled the prophecies that the Lord will come and that his day will come. In this connection the second coming of the Lord is frequently seen in the perspective of his first coming. This condensed or summary form of speech is also referred to as the prophetic perspective.

The New Testament clearly distinguishes between the first and second comings. "So Christ was once offered to bear the sins of many; and unto them that look for him shall he appear the second time without sin unto salvation" (Heb. 9:28). The coming of Christ that we anticipate is therefore his return. Jesus himself says: "And if I go and prepare a place for you, I will come again, and receive you unto myself; that where I am, there ye may be also" (John 14:3).

The chapter on eschatology will portray Christ's return from the perspective of the consummation of all things and the coming of the kingdom of God in glory. Christology must at any rate mention one of the key aspects of his coming: *He will come to judge*. The full extent of Christ's exaltation is underscored by the fact that the Father has given full jurisdiction to the Son and has given him power to hold judgment because he is the Son of Man (John 5:22, 27). The resurrection of the dead is associated with this judgment (John 5:28–29). The Son of Man comes in his glory and all the angels with him, and he will sit down on his throne of glory. Then the great separation will take place (Matt. 25:31–46).

By the time of his return, the resurrection of the dead, and the final judgment, the glory of the exalted Mediator will have become fully manifested.

The Creed of Nicaea-Constantinople says of Christ's first coming that "for us men and our salvation [he] came down from heaven," and of his second coming that he "shall come again with glory to judge both the quick and the dead." There is a clear difference.

Since this judgment implies that all of us will have to give an account of ourselves, it may be asked whether and to what extent Christ's return to judge really forms part of his work of salvation. All will be judged and many will be condemned (Matt. 25:31–46). The last judgment has two aspects. "The consideration of this judgment is justly terrible and dreadful to the wicked and ungodly, but most desirable and comfortable to the righteous and elect" (Belgic Confession of Faith, article 37). The relationship between man and God in Christ is decisive. The question is how we think of Christ. We shall not need to fear the Judge if he is our Savior.

The Heidelberg Catechism does not ask what we know of the return of Christ, but: "What comfort is it to you that Christ shall come to judge the living and the dead?" The answer reflects a personal element: "I look for [him] as Judge from heaven who . . . before has offered himself for my sake to the tribunal of God, and has removed all curse from me." He "shall take me with all his chosen ones to himself into heavenly joy and glory" (Lord's Day 19).

The church of Christ will therefore look forward to the coming of its Lord and Savior. The Belgic Confession of Faith ends with the words: "Therefore we expect that great day with a most ardent desire, to the end that we may fully enjoy the promises of God in Christ Jesus our Lord."

Then all of God's promises will be fulfilled, also the words that say "that God may be all in all" (1 Cor. 15:28).

2. *The transfer of kingship*. We have already met Van Ruler's view (§ 31.3, subsection 1), that Christ's mediatorship will end upon his return. He believes that all of the implications of the eventual transfer of kingship from the Son to the Father must be taken into account. "It is the ultimate and highest act of the Messiah that he ceases to be the Messiah."[71]

There has been much to do about Paul's words in 1 Corinthians 15 to which Van Ruler refers. Several questions arise. Does Christ remain King forever or not? Will Christ's threefold office come to an end? Will he give up his human nature, so that the incarnation will have been a temporary reality? Van Ruler refers to this as the messianic intermezzo.

Whereas Calvin did not go beyond a few "groping formulations,"[72] we come across drastic pronouncements and daring theses on the part of Van Ruler. He holds "that the incarnation will cease in the eschaton and that then (in God's kingdom) we are left with nothing but the triune God and things in their pure (albeit) redeemed state" (*T.W.*, 1:171).

It is very much the question whether there are any biblical foundations for this view. We read nowhere that Christ will retreat to such an extent that he will give up his human nature, which he has taken on. The Lamb is in the New Jerusalem (Rev. 21:22–23; 22:3). The Lamb will be the lamp of the city of God, which will be lit by the glory of God. His messianic attributes continue in glory.[73] Christ's mediatorship will have no end. He is "our eternal King" (Heidelberg Catechism, Lord's Day 12), "whose kingdom shall have no end" (Creed of Nicaea-Constantinople; cf. Luke 1:33).

There will be a transfer of kingship to God the Father. This reflects the mandate from God that preceded it. In the New Testament there is mention of the Son's subjection as well as his obedience. The divine mandate was completed by the work of Christ in his humiliation. It was finished. Similarly there is a mandate from God for Christ's work in his exaltation, which is moving toward its culmination.

In the present state, Christ's kingdom is characterized by the struggle against the enemies of God and his people. Some day this will change. God's enemies will have perished by then.

71. A. A. Van Ruler, *De vervulling van de wet* (the fulfillment of the law), 1947, 95, 107.
72. G. C. Berkouwer, *De wederkomst van Christus* (the return of Christ), 1963, 2:246.
73. See W. H. Velema, *Confrontatie met Van Ruler*, 1962, 94–101.

Theology has groped for concepts to indicate the distinction between "the present of the future"[74] and the future of the present. Thus it is said that the kingdom of grace is transformed into the kingdom of glory. Bavinck believes that the mediatorship of reconciliation will come to an end. What will remain is the mediatorship of union (*R.D.*, 3:482).

It is doubtful whether one can put it this way, for communion with God will always be founded on redemption. We meet the Lamb. We meet God in Christ.

Christ is and will continue to be the Head of his church. The exalted and glorified Mediator is the Head of the new humanity. He will be so forever. It has been correctly said: "The Son, who became Mediator in the Covenant of grace and achieved redemption, will continue to disseminate the salvation of communion."[75]

The question whether the transfer of kingship to God the Father is part of Christ's work in his exaltation can be answered affirmatively. This "subjection" is a sign that he has completed the work that the Father assigned him to do (John 17:4). When he will stand before the Father together with all of his people, he will have completely fulfilled the words that he spoke: "I will that they also, whom thou hast given me, be with me where I am; that they may behold my glory, which thou hast given me" (John 17:24). All of the work of Christ anticipates the future glory. Paul said: "When all things shall be subdued unto him, then shall the Son also himself be subject unto him that put all things under him, that God may be all in all" (1 Cor. 15:28).

§ 32. Aspects of the work of Christ

32.1. *Atonement (reconciliation)*

1. *Christ's work and our salvation*

In this section we discuss a topic that the Bible speaks about in numerous places, employing a great variety of terminology and imagery. We must seek to safeguard the riches of the biblical message from

74. This expression comes from J. P. Versteeg. See his inaugural speech, *Het heden van de toekomst* (the present of the future), 1969.

75. J. Kamphuis, "Het Lam in het Nieuwe Jeruzalem," in *Almanak van het Corpus Studiosorum in Academia Campensi "Fides Quadrat Intellectum,"* 1987, 214.

limitations inherent in any type of summary. In particular we should not be selective in our treatment of the biblical data, as happens all too often.

The danger is real that our perspective of salvation, which as a human phenomenon can change as we change, is allowed to become normative in our treatment of salvation in Christ. It is then believed that we must redefine what constitutes Jesus' salvation for today's world in a way that appeals to people in their everyday situation. This brings with it a shift in the meaning of salvation in Jesus.[76]

Christology is then a function of soteriology, and soteriology in turn a function of anthropology! One needs to take to heart Pannenberg's warning (1968, 38–49): our personal interest in salvation cannot be the foundation of Christology. Soteriology must be based on Christology and not the other way around. We are focusing on the work of Christ and our salvation in this particular sequence, which may not be reversed.

"Atonement" and "victory," which we consider to be *key concepts*, do not tell the entire story. Indeed a great deal can be associated with them. For example, atonement includes Christ's sacrifice and his obedience unto death on the cross, and Christ's victory includes destruction of the work of the devil, deliverance from the power of darkness, and dominion over all powers.

Whichever aspect is considered, there is always a direct link between the work of Christ and the salvation of his people. He is after all the Mediator and Redeemer of his own in everything that he does. "For us men and our salvation [he] came down from heaven"; he "was crucified also for us under Pontius Pilate" (Creed of Nicaea-Constantinople). The reference "for us" (*pro nobis*) also occurs repeatedly in the Reformational confession statements (see Belgic Confession of Faith, articles 20, 22; Heidelberg Catechism, Lord's Day 16–17; Canons of Dort, 2.2). It says not only "for us" but also "for our sins."

All this is based directly on Scripture. Here we merely cite a number of relevant Scripture passages, but some of them will be discussed below. Jesus "came to minister and to give his life a ransom for many" (Matt. 20:28). His blood was shed "for many for the forgiveness of sins" (Matt. 26:28). He "was delivered for our offenses, and was raised again for our justification" (Rom. 4:25). "Christ died for our sins according to the Scriptures" (1 Cor. 15:3). "God was in Christ,

76. This is the view of H. M. Kuitert in H. M. Kuitert and E. Schillebeeckx, *Jezus van Nazareth en het heil van de wereld* (Jesus of Nazareth and the salvation of the world), 1975, 9, 13–17.

reconciling the world unto himself, not imputing their trespasses unto them" (2 Cor. 5:19). "Christ has redeemed us from the curse of the law, being made a curse for us" (Gal. 3:13). "Christ also hath loved us, and hath given himself for us an offering and a sacrifice to God for a sweetsmelling savour" (Eph. 5:2). "Jesus . . . by the grace of God . . . taste[d] death for every man" (Heb. 2:9). "Christ also hath once suffered for sins, the just for the unjust, that he might bring us to God" (1 Peter 3:18). "God . . . loved us, and sent his Son to be the propitiation for our sins" (1 John 4:10). "Glory and dominion . . . be [unto Christ] who loved us, and washed us from our sins in his own blood" (Rev. 1:6, 5).

It is a perspective that runs throughout the New Testament, but is already apparent in the Old Testament. We have in mind especially the ministry of sacrifice, and the prophecy of the suffering Servant of the LORD (Isa. 53).

However popular the topic of atonement has been through the second half of the twentieth century (cf. van Genderen, 1988, 61ff.), we do not wish to start from more recent theological views, but rather from Scripture (subsections 2 and 3).

Throughout the centuries thought has been given to what it means that Christ did this for us. Does it involve more than our benefit? Does the fact of his dying "for our sins," or "because of our sins," imply that he bore the punishment for our sins and that thus we become reconciled with God? We need to discuss various views and theories (subsection 4).

Furthermore, the question arises whether the message of the Bible that Christ died for us implies that he died for all people. Those who hold this view and emphasize the universality of atonement face a new problem. Does this imply that everyone is saved by him or not? In this respect relative and absolute universalism, the doctrine of universal atonement, and that of universalism diverge. How far does atonement go (subsection 5)?

2. *The testimony of the Old Testament*

The Hebrew word for atonement is *kipper*. The original meaning could be "to cover" or "to wipe away and blot out." This word was usually connected with the role of sacrifices in the cultus.

The bringing of sacrifices is not an attempt to placate God, because he clearly says to Israel that atonement originates with him. "For the life of the flesh is in the blood: and I have given it to you upon the altar to make an atonement for your souls: for it is the blood that maketh an atonement for the soul" (Lev. 17:11). Viewed in this way, atonement is *a gift of God*.

It is sometimes believed that God is only involved as Giver of the sacrifice and as Interested Party (see Wiersinga, 1971, 137, 144), but this is incorrect. The act of sacrifice takes place "before the LORD" (Lev. 4:4–7). Sin must be viewed as sin against God and must be removed out of his sight. Atonement through sacrifice is *not only a gift, but also a demand of God* (see also Heb. 9:22).

According to the law, the great Day of Atonement is the high point of the worship of Israel. Then the high priest must sprinkle the blood of the sacrificial animal on and in front of the mercy seat of the Ark of the Covenant. Another animal is taken into the desert, where it will die. First the high priest must place both of his hands on the head of the male goat and confess all of the sins of the Israelites. He is to place them on the head of the male goat. Away with them! (Lev. 16:21–22). This is not just an ancient ritual, in which the idea of a magical transfer can still be recognized. The possibility of the transfer of sin and guilt, and of substitution, reflects a deep mystery, which finds its fulfillment in Christ. Therefore, according to the Old Testament, the people of Israel did not automatically share in atonement. They had to humble themselves before God (Lev. 16:29–31).

It has been said: "Isaiah 53 represents the most profound spiritual summary of the aspects of atonement; here virtually all lines converge and are fused into a greater whole" (Vriezen, *Hoofdlijnen* = main perspectives, 294).

The question once asked, "Of whom speaketh the prophet this? of himself or of some other man?" (Acts 8:34), continues to engender a good deal of discussion. Both collective and individual interpretations have been given. Does the servant, who is to suffer so much, represent the entire people of Israel or only its faithful segment, or does it refer to a single person and if so, whom? Do these words offer scope for varying interpretations?

Thinking merely of Israel, or a servant of God at the time of the prophet or earlier, does not do full justice to this verse. What is said here of the suffering servant goes far beyond what could be true of Israel or of the prophet himself. Furthermore, its fulfillment in Christ illuminates the deepest meaning of Isaiah 53. The words of this prophecy are employed repeatedly in the New Testament to shed light on the significance of Christ (cf. Wolff, 1984; Guthrie, *N.T. Theol.*, 258–68).

This verse clearly states that God has a hand in the suffering of his servant (Isa. 53:6, 10). This is no popular "dogma of retribution" (contrary to Wiersinga, 1971, 158ff.). The servant presents himself as "an offering for sin" (10). He suffers as a substitute for others, by bearing their punishment and sacrificing his life (5, 8, 12). The bearing of the sins of many, whereby he justifies them, does not merely constitute sympathy as proof of exceptional solidarity (contrary to Wiersinga, 1971, 158). It is on solid grounds that the Dutch Reformed Synod declares in a pastoral letter that the concepts of sacrifice, atonement, transfer of guilt, and substitution are particularly well expressed in the prophecy concerning the Servant of the Lord.[77]

There is an inextricable connection between the Old Testament proclamation of atonement through sacrifice and the substitutionary suffering and death of him who was ordained for this by God, and the New Testament gospel of atonement through Christ.

3. *The testimony of the New Testament*

The Greek of the New Testament has two words for reconciliation. The first one is *katallasso*: "God . . . hath reconciled us to himself by Jesus Christ" (2 Cor. 5:18); the second word is *hilaskomai*: "that he might be a merciful and faithful high priest in things pertaining to God, to make reconciliation for the sins of the people" (Heb. 2:17). These two words are no synonyms. Emphasizing this difference in translation in Dutch is more difficult to achieve than in other languages. In German they speak of *versöhnen* (reconcile) and *sühnen* (expiate, atone); in English, of *reconcile* and *propitiate* or *expiate*; in French, of *réconcilier* and *expier*.

The first word indicates the restoration of a relationship. This comes through clearly in Colossians 1:21–22. The other word is a term that has to do with the cultus and is equivalent to the Old Testament term *kipper*. Just as God himself provided the required sacrifice for sin, in Christ he makes atonement his own responsibility. We agree with Versteeg that the words *katallage* and *hilasmos* together express the single reality of atonement. Reconciliation implies the bringing together of two opposing factions (*katallage*). Atonement is brought about by the sacrifice that covers guilt (*hilasmos*).[78]

It is *reconciliation through satisfaction*. In this way we attempt to describe the core of the biblical doctrine of atonement. It deals with reconciliation with God through the atoning sacrifice of Christ (see Rom. 5:10–11).

Precisely the doctrine of atonement by means of Christ's sacrifice is contested from all sides. Therefore it is more necessary than ever to pay careful attention to what Scripture itself says.

77. *De tussenmuur weggebroken* (the inner wall removed), 1967, 37. There is a great deal of literature with respect to Isaiah 53. Cf. H. W. Wolff, *Jesaja 53 im Urchristentum* (in original Christianity), 1984[4]. See also the commentary by J. L. Koole, *Jesaja II*, 1990, 2:199–274.

78. J. P. Versteeg, *Bijbelwoorden op de man af* (Bible words point-blank), 1982, 31.

There are those who agree with E. Käsemann that Paul's concept of sacrifice has no real significance, or with H. Berkhof that Jesus' death cannot be primarily and exclusively interpreted along the lines of Paul's juridical and cultic concepts but also with "the Johannine concepts of love, obedience, and glorification" (*C.F.*, 311); there are others who recognize no substitution in his sacrifice but merely a countercurrent to dispel bad influences (A. M. Brouwer), or believe that the direction of his sacrifice is manward and not godward, so that it brings about a change in us and not God (H. Wiersinga). See van Genderen, 1972, 17–19.

However, there are relevant Scripture passages that cannot be neutralized or eliminated by theological arguments. In this connection we mention Ephesians 5:2, "Christ also hath loved us, and hath given himself for us an offering and a sacrifice to God for a sweetsmelling savour," and Hebrews 9:14, where it is said that "Christ . . . through the eternal Spirit offered himself." This is stated in a document that undoubtedly presents a doctrine of atonement (cf. Lekkerkerker, 1966, 119). In Paul's case one needs to consider the passages that deal with the blood of Christ (Rom. 3:25; 5:9; 1 Cor. 10:16; 11:25; cf. also Eph. 1:13; Col. 1:14, 20). As far as John is concerned, one also needs to think of the words about "the Lamb of God, which taketh away the sin of the world" (John 1:29); the flesh that Jesus gives for the life of the world (6:51), and the dying of the grain of wheat (12:24). Various places in 1 John and Revelation may be added.

We still need to consider the meaning of 2 Corinthians 5:21 and Galatians 3:13. These words make us stand in awe.

God "hath made him to be sin for us, who knew no sin; that we might be made the righteousness of God in him" (2 Cor. 5:21). This means that God treated Christ as a sinner, because he imputed our sins to him. Through faith we know that this is the reason why sin is not imputed to us (cf. Rom. 4:8). We are declared to be righteous. This constitutes a "wonderful exchange" (Luther).

"Christ hath redeemed us from the curse of the law, being made a curse for us: for it is written, Cursed is everyone that hangeth on a tree" (Gal. 3:13). According to Wiersinga (1971, 35ff.), this is the curse of the Jewish authorities, the defenders of the law, and not the curse of God. However, the verse by itself and the context of Paul's message are clear enough. The apostle means God's law and God's curse (cf. Ridderbos, 1972, 28–32).

Romans 8:3 is also an important reference. God "condemned sin in the flesh." This judgment was carried out in the real, human existence of Christ. This implies that although we should have been condemned by God because of our sins, Christ was condemned in our stead. This constitutes God's righteous judgment. His righteousness is also a punishing righteousness. The apostle refers to this in Romans 3:25, when he says that God, who granted redemption in Christ Jesus, presented him as a "propitiatory sacrifice (*hilasterion*) . . . to demonstrate his righteousness" (cf. Ridderbos, 1972, 28ff.).

Those who believe that these ideas are only found in Paul's writings and to a lesser degree in a few other New Testament epistles, should not forget Matthew 20:28 (Mark 10:45) and Matthew 26:28 (together with parallel passages).

Modern theology frequently doubts whether Jesus ever indicated or even foresaw the significance of his death for salvation. On the contrary, he both expected and foretold that he must die for his people. He came "to give his life a ransom for many" (Matt. 20:28). The term "ransom" occurs elsewhere in the Bible. In Israel it involved a debtor, a creditor, and punishment or equivalent compensation. A ransom could be paid for guilt associated with causing death (Ex. 21:30). When Jesus gives his life as a ransom for many, it is because their lives are at stake. The situation is so serious that nothing less will do. In line with the preposition "for" (*anti*), the entire tenor of Jesus' statement points to the reality of substitution (cf. *TDNT*, 4:343). Jesus' death means the salvation of many, because in his ministry of love he places himself in their stead and gives up his life to atone for their guilt (see further Wentsel, *Dogm.*, 3b:452–56).

The words of Jesus at the institution of the Lord's Supper also refer to his sacrifice. Just as he gives his life as a ransom for many, so is his blood "shed for many for the forgiveness of sins" (Matt. 26:28). The words "for many" refer back to Isaiah 53:11–12. By putting himself in their place and taking upon himself their sins and atoning for them, Jesus establishes the new communion between God and his people. "He reduces the entire proclamation of the gospel, in an extremely concentrated form, to his sacrifice of atonement" (Ridderbos, 1972, 51). This is strikingly captured in our form for the celebration of the Lord's Supper: "we see that he directs our faith and trust to his perfect sacrifice, once offered on the cross, as to the only ground and foundation of our salvation."

In the New Testament there are other words besides *reconciliation*, *sacrifice*, and *ransom* that describe the work of Christ; e.g., it is also referred to as *obedience*.

This is a popular term in more recent theology. To Berkhof, Jesus' obedience to the Father and his solidarity with people are linked with *representation*, which he considers to be a key concept because it involves the core of our salvation. Jesus did not come to earth merely to die. He came to live, but to live in such a way that in this world he was bound to perish. Only in this sacrifice was *the new humanity* that he came to bring perfected and fully manifested. To the very end he maintained his obedience to the Father and his solidarity with unsympathetic and hostile people. His suffering and dying signify his sustained and perfected presence with people for the sake of God and with God for the sake of the people (*C.F.*, 204–312).

Jesus' true humanity—his absolute obedience to the Father and his complete solidarity with the people—benefits us, which, however, according to Berkhof, does not imply that Christ reconciled us with God by bearing the punishment for our sins.[79]

According to Wiersinga, Jesus was the Obedient One, who through his actions became the victim of sin, and people are bound to change when they are confronted with this (1972, 25–32, 41).

The Savior had "to fulfill all righteousness" (Matt. 3:15). His obedience does not merely imply that he wants nothing but what God wants, thus representing God to people, but also that he is "obedient unto death . . . of the cross" (Phil. 2:8). When Paul writes: "For as by one man's disobedience many were made sinners, so by the obedience of one shall many be made righteous" (Rom. 5:19), this is inextricably connected with what the apostle says in the preceding pericope about Christ's dying for the wicked and about our reconciliation with God through his death (Rom. 5:6–11).

Dogmatics came to distinguish between Christ's *active* and *passive obedience*. Although his obedience is indivisible, it does have these two facets. He met the demand of God's law on behalf of his people and bore the punishment for sin. Whereas the former stresses what he did, the latter brings out what he suffered—which does not at all mean that he was passive in this regard and that this was merely done to him.[80]

While centuries ago J. Piscator's concept—that Christ's active obedience was only of indirect significance to us—had to be rejected (cf. van Genderen, 1972, 21), we now need to object to more recent views according to which Christ's suffering and death are no longer seen as fulfillment of God's will, but only as a consequence of his obedience to God. The question then becomes whether his death still has intrinsic significance (cf. Immink, 1990, 12).

79. Cf. W. H. Velema, "Rechtvaardiging en heiliging" (justification and sanctification), in *Weerwoord* (reply), 1974, 175–79.

80. A theologian who greatly stressed the significance of Christ's obedience was K. Schilder. In the process he referred back to the very beginning, i.e., creation, Paradise, and the covenant with Adam. He allowed himself to be guided by Scripture (see Rom. 5:19). Cf. J. J. C. Dee, *K. Schilder*, 1990, 1:201–5.

4. *Various views*

a. *The ransom theory.* A very old representation of the work of Christ is the ransom theory of Origen, Gregory of Nyssa, and other church fathers. The starting assumption is that the devil exercises dominion over the world and that people are under his control. According to some, the evil one has this power only *de facto* [in fact], but according to others also *de jure* [by right]. A sort of "orderly settlement" took place with the devil, in that Christ offered himself as ransom. Then the evil one had to let the people go (cf. Korff, 1942, 2:67).

This has been referred to as a childish theory. It nevertheless contains important biblical themes.

Anselm already pointed out that God does not deal with the devil. He could merely have used his power to liberate men. A serious objection to this theory is also that the reconciliation of man with God is left out of the picture. In general, the early church, especially in the Orient, was more concerned with liberation from the power of evil than atonement for the guilt of sin.

b. *Anselm's doctrine of atonement.* The core of Anselm's theory is the concept of *satisfaction.* In light of the patristic literature, this concept cannot be considered to be new (cf. Korff, 1942[2], 2:69), but prior to Anselm it had not yet been worked out systematically. In his famous treatise *Cur Deus Homo?* (1198), he tried to make transparent in a rational way why the incarnation and satisfaction were necessary. Man's sin constitutes a disturbance of the divine order. It is not giving to God what we owe to him, i.e., withholding from him the honor that is due to him. God owes it to himself to maintain his honor. He cannot just forgive sin. Either his honor must be restored or sin must be punished.

But if God were to execute man's well-deserved punishment, what would happen to his plan for him? Therefore sin is not punished but satisfaction is made. The satisfaction has to have infinite value, because guilt is infinitely great. Only man is required to give satisfaction, but only God can accomplish it. The logical solution to this problem is for God to become man and the God-man to accomplish it. In this regard it is not Jesus' holy life that is decisive, for as man he already owed obedience to God for himself, but his voluntary death. This act of love could not remain unanswered. Since God could not give his Son something that he did not already have, the latter's merit benefits people.

With few exceptions, theologians view Anselm's doctrine with considerable skepticism. It must be granted, however, that he treated the relationship between man and God seriously. Something needed to happen in view of the seriousness of our guilt. However, the gospel of atonement was not done full justice in this scholastic type of reasoning. Anselm failed to see that in his work as Mediator Christ represents his people, and that therefore they are involved in it.

c. *The Reformational doctrine of atonement through satisfaction.* In what follows we still need to focus on the Reformed doctrine of atonement. Here we merely note that the views of the various Reformers did not essentially differ from each other. The Reformational doctrine that we encounter in Calvin's work and in our confession documents is sometimes characterized as Anselmian. However, a substantial difference is that Calvin bases himself on the biblical message that God gave us his Son as Mediator and Surety to give his life for us and to pay our debt. See also the Canons of Dort, 2. 2, which confesses what Christ did for us and in our stead. The teaching of Lord's Days 5 and 6 of the Heidelberg Catechism, which is frequently ascribed to Anselm, nevertheless differs from the theory of this medieval theologian. It is not an artificial framework into which Christ fits as Mediator, but believing contemplation of what has been revealed to us in Christ, who is our faithful Savior (Lord's Day 1 precedes Lord's Days 5 and 6!).[81]

d. *The doctrine of subjective atonement*. The doctrine of atonement through satisfaction has been discredited for various reasons. It was vigorously opposed by the Socinians (see Bavinck, *R.D.*, 3:348ff.), and the influence of their criticism can be recognized in the Remonstrant and Rationalistic views of atonement (cf. Wenz, 1984, 1:87–275). In the nineteenth century, the doctrine of satisfaction, also in its confessional-Reformed form, was rejected by both the Groningen School and modernism.

The doctrine of subjective atonement, which essentially was already held by Abelard (1079–1142), gradually gained ground. We have in mind first of all A. Ritschl. Just as Abelard believed that we are saved by Christ's love, because it engenders counter-love on our part, so Ritschl held in his work, *Die christliche Lehre von der Rechtfertigung and Versöhnung* (the Christian doctrine of justification and atonement, 1888–89³), that Christ redeems us by leading us to put our trust in God. According to the latter, it is a misunderstanding on our part that God is angry with us. Christ liberates us from this, for he teaches us to know the love of God. Atonement is therefore a change in us.

In the Netherlands, G. J. Heering was a champion of the doctrine of subjective atonement. The cross is to him the core principle of God's love. It tells us: "Here died at your hands the Holy One of God." At the same time Christ spreads out his arms in a divine gesture: "I also did this very last thing for you, to open your eyes, to convince you of the love of the Father and to make you kneel down to receive his mercy."[82]

The alternative doctrine of atonement, which H. Wiersinga presented in his dissertation (1971) and in subsequent writings, and which has met with a great deal of resistance, can be viewed as a variation of the doctrine of subjective atonement. According to Wiersinga, satisfaction, merit, and substitution are non-biblical terms and thought processes, which need to be discarded (1971, 202). We are called by the voice of the blood of the Crucified One to repentance and conversion. The first one upon whom it had a shock effect was Judas; the second one was Peter. The initial impact is repentance; the subsequent impact is resurrection to new life. The important thing is effective atonement, a change in people, which radiates to the world (1971, 189–94). "Effective atonement implies change" (1972, 55). One cannot say that Christ brought about atonement; he set it in motion.

While the rightist-modern theologian Heering did admit that Paul had in mind an atoning and substitutionary suffering and death of Christ, he did not consider himself to be bound to this doctrine of the apostle. Wiersinga made attempts to interpret

81. Cf. W. Metz, *Necessitas satisfactionis?* 1970, 168–73.

82. G. J. Heering, *Geloof en openbaring* (faith and revelation), 1944², 363.

Scripture in the spirit of his alternative doctrine of atonement, but it is not difficult to demonstrate that his exegesis is completely incorrect in crucial respects (cf. among others, Ridderbos, 1972).

The theory of subjective atonement turns up in a variety of forms. Its proponents dispute that Christ's sacrifice was required by God's justice or by God's holy wrath at our sins. They argue that Jesus had to die because people wanted this, not because according to God's counsel it was necessary to reconcile us with him. They see Christ as the victim of sin, but deny his sacrifice of atonement.

The synod of the *Gereformeerde Kerken in Nederland* felt obligated to state its view with respect to Wiersinga's doctrine of atonement. In 1976 it declared that in bringing about atonement God ordained that he who was crucified by human hands—in the suffering and death that he underwent—bore in our stead the divine judgment for human guilt. It considered this aspect of the confession of the church to be of such fundamental significance that it could not possibly be diminished or rejected.[83] Nevertheless, it resigned itself to the fact that the consistory having jurisdiction over Wiersinga at this time considered the latter's opinions to be admissible within the scope of the confession (cf. Immink, 1990, 11).

e. *Theopaschitic tendencies in the doctrine of atonement (Barth and Moltmann).* Barth approaches atonement entirely differently from the proponents of a doctrine of subjective atonement. To him the crux lies in what God has done in Christ.

Atonement begins with the covenant: God's eternal covenant with man in Jesus Christ. Atonement is provided in Jesus Christ as God and man, because in him God humbles himself and in him man is exalted (see § 30.3).

In the person and work of Christ we are dealing with God himself. What Christ does is God's own work. Then the humiliation of Jesus Christ as an act of obedience cannot be alien to God himself (*C.D.*, 4.1.193). In various places Barth refers to God's obedience, and interprets the actions and suffering of Jesus Christ as actions and suffering of God himself. He can say that God renounces himself (4.1.246, 72). This has sometimes been referred to as neo-theopaschitism.

Concepts such as substitution and satisfaction appear in this dogmatics in a different context and sense than in Reformational theology. The work of Christ is substitutionary. The Judge is the one who is judged in our place (4.1.211). But did Christ satisfy the demand of God's justice in our stead? Satisfaction is for Barth a problematic concept. He gives it a new meaning by saying: in the suffering of Jesus Christ, in the giving up of his Son to death, God has done that which is satisfactory in the victorious fight against sin (4.1.254).

A noteworthy feature of this doctrine is its inclusive nature. What God did in Christ applies to all people. In Christ the decision was made for all of us and no one can undo it. His death constituted the death of all people: of Christians, but also of Jews and Gentiles, whether they heard and accepted the message or backed away from it. In his own person, in his surrender to death, Christ in fact caused sinful man to disappear 4.1.295ff.). There is no one for whose sin and death he did not die,

83. *Acta van de Generale Synode van Maastricht* 1975/1976, article 189.

whose sin and death he did not remove on the cross! There is no one who has not been sufficiently, totally, definitively justified in him! (4.1.629ff.).

It is a much-debated question whether Barth thus arrived at universalism (*apokatastasis*). One of his last pronouncements in this regard was that although one cannot count on it, one may at least hope for it (4.3.477ff.). We now let this matter rest, but will return to it in the discussion of eschatological questions (see § 57.3).

Because of its strong emphasis on what God has done in Christ and on what he grants us whether we believe it or not, his doctrine makes a very strong *objectivistic impression*. This is one of our objections against it.[84]

We now focus on the *theopaschitic tendency*. God is the subject of reconciliation (2 Cor. 5:19). However, Scripture nowhere speaks about the obedience and suffering of God. He who suffers and dies for our sins is the Mediator, who stands before his Father as the Servant of the Lord. When God executes against him the judgment that we deserved, it does not mean that he executes it against himself. However much the suffering and death of Christ affects God, it is apparent from the words of Paul that God "spared not his own Son, but delivered him up for us all" (Rom. 8:32). But Scripture says nowhere that God gave himself up for us. It is incorrect to infer from the Bible that the work of Christ is the work of God in Christ.

Theopaschitic tendencies are even stronger in Moltmann's teachings. This is apparent from his work *Der gekreuzigte Gott* (the crucified God, 1972), in which he sought to present a Trinitarian theology of the cross, and his subsequent writings, among which should be mentioned in this context especially *Der Weg Jesu Christi* (the way of Jesus Christ, 1989).

His theology of the surrender of Christ, for which he appeals to passages that include the term "delivered up" (gave up), implies that the Father also gave himself up in giving up his Son, although not to the same degree. Jesus experienced death in the forsakenness. The Father, who abandoned him and gave him up, experienced the death of Jesus in the infinite sorrow of love. This is no patripassianism or absolute theopaschitism (Moltmann, 1972, 230; 1989, 195).

Starting with the fact that God was in Christ (2 Cor. 5:19), Moltmann says that Jesus' weakness was also God's weakness and that his suffering was also God's suffering. He calls God's love "*leidensfähig und leidensbereit*" (capable of suffering and prepared to suffer). The suffering of Christ was also the suffering of the Spirit (1989, 194–99).

The divine dimensions of Christ's suffering are solidarity, substitution, and rebirth: Christ is with us and for us, and in him we are a new creation. Substitution does mean that he saves us in a place where we could never stand, but is not to be associated with the notion of an atoning sacrifice. Instead Moltmann teaches emphatically that through his divine suffering God is in solidarity with the people and with all of his creatures (1989, 202–11).

A theopaschitism such as that of Moltmann moves automatically into the realm of universalism. It has a speculative character and lacks a biblical foundation. For the

84. Cf. J. van Genderen in A. G. Knevel (ed.), *Karl Barth*, 1987, 62.

sake of the chosen starting point, namely that God himself was in Christ, Scripture passages dealing with Christ's atoning sacrifice and the work of Christ as Mediator between God and men—in part under the influence of E. Käsemann—are set aside (1989, 209).

Support for theopaschitism has grown since the end of the nineteenth century, especially since the First and Second World Wars.[85] One of the factors that explain this is that one prefers it over the Reformational doctrine of atonement and also over the theory of subjective atonement (B. Wentsel, *Dogm.*, 3b:414; see also 405–22).

It is incorrect to pretend that the alternative of the theology of God's suffering is the notion of God's impassibility. After all, Christ's entire work as Mediator testifies to the fact that God sympathizes with us and is prepared to give up everything for us. The Father does not stay aloof from the suffering and death of his Son, but is completely involved in it. However, Scripture does not permit us to think in terms of the suffering of God, let alone the death of God.

5. *Atonement through satisfaction*

Having discussed various views, we still need to say more about the Reformed doctrine of atonement. A common and useful description of this is *atonement through satisfaction*. A second characterization is *vicarious satisfaction (satisfactio vicaria)*.

Both of these express that satisfaction and substitution are essential elements of the Reformed doctrine. Those who reject this, e.g., Wiersinga (1971, 202), come into conflict with not only Reformed theology but also the Reformed confession, for reconciliation with God through Christ's sacrifice is at the core of both.

"God . . . sent his Son to assume that nature in which the disobedience was committed, to make satisfaction in the same, and to bear the punishment for sin." "Christ . . . presented himself in our behalf before the Father, to appease his wrath by his full satisfaction, by offering himself on the tree of the cross." We are "reconciled to God [through] this sacrifice, once offered." Christ performed his holy works for us and in our stead (Belgic Confession of Faith, articles 20–22). "Satisfaction for our sins could be made no otherwise than by the death of the Son of God" (Heidelberg Catechism, Lord's Day 16). "For our Surety, [he] was made sin, and became a curse for us and in our stead, that he might make satisfaction to divine justice on our behalf" (Canons of Dort, 2:2). We confess with the words of the classical liturgy for the Lord's Supper, "that he has borne for us the wrath of God, under which we should have perished everlastingly . . . and has fulfilled for us all obedience and righteousness of the divine law."

85. See Van Egmond, 1986, especially 22–34; Feitsma, 1956, 15–27.

We cannot say this without saying something about ourselves. Confession of faith is simultaneously confession of guilt. The emphasis on the necessity of satisfaction is related to a deep awareness of the dreadful reality of the wrath of God over our sins. We have not only become alienated from God, so that we must find our way back to him, but because of sin a chasm has opened up that we cannot possibly bridge, a fracture that requires healing. If the relationship between God and us is not restored, we cannot live in communion with him.

God is so good that he wants to reconcile himself with us. This is why he gave his Son, who satisfied the demand that we could not satisfy. "Christ . . . redeemed us from the curse of the law, being made a curse for us" (Gal. 3:13). "Being . . . justified by his blood, we shall be saved from wrath through him" (Rom. 5:9).

We cannot let our guilt be borne by anyone else, but he came to take it over from us, and to pay the penalty for it. Calvin says: "Our burden was placed on him. Therefore faith takes hold of the acquittal in the condemnation of Christ and the blessing in his curse" (*Institutes*, 2.16.6). Luther refers to this as that wonderful exchange, and so does Calvin.[86] We are reminded of the words of our liturgy for the Lord's Supper: "He was innocently condemned to death that we might be acquitted at the judgment seat of God . . . ; [he] has taken the curse from us upon himself that he might fill us with his blessing." Apart from Galatians 3:13, Scripture passages such as 2 Corinthians 5:21 and 1 Peter 2:24 are also behind this thought process.

The adherents of the theory of subjective atonement fear that the Reformational doctrine leads to objectivism. They believe that it should not be said that Christ paid for our sins. A "payment theory" would turn the transfer of guilt into a business transaction.

Our response is that since financial imagery is employed in the New Testament (cf. Lekkerkerker, 1966, 124ff.), the word "payment" cannot be rejected and that it interprets sin as guilt. He gave his life as "a ransom for many" (Matt. 20:28).

By placing himself as human being in our situation and as Surety in our stead, he did not only bear our punishment, so that we might go free, but he also brought us into an unbreakable relationship with himself, so that we are united with him. Therefore, we can say in faith that everything that he has is to our benefit.

86. This theme is actually much older. It occurred already in the epistle to Diognetus (first half of the second century), 9:5.

Against the doctrine of atonement through satisfaction it is frequently objected that apparently Christ had to give satisfaction to the Father. But is God not love and is atonement not initiated by him?

Theology sometimes employs expressions that appear to suggest that Christ persuaded the Father to be gracious to sinners. This idea can also arise as a result of traditional preaching and an experience of faith. It is, however, not Reformed doctrine, but only a caricature of it, to say that God, who was angry, changed his mind as a result of Christ's sacrifice (the so-called *Umstimmung*). In this connection Berkouwer points out: after satisfaction has first been interpreted as a primitive "Umstimmung" (change of mind), the theopaschitic tendency in the new doctrine of reconciliation becomes the great counterpart of the orthodox doctrine of satisfaction (1965, 267).

God's love is not first activated once the demand of his righteousness has been met. When he reconciles the world and us with himself, as Scripture says (2 Cor. 5:19; Col. 1:21–22), the initiative rests with him. It can be seen in the light of his righteousness (cf. Ridderbos, *Paul*, 167ff.) and his love that atonement in Christ is reality (see Rom. 3:25; 1 John 4:10). Simultaneously with the emphasis on the necessity of satisfaction, the church says in its confession that "God . . . in his infinite mercy [gave] his . . . Son for our Surety" (Canons of Dort, 2.2). Those who hold on to this can also speak of the merits of Christ, as is done by the churches of the Reformation (cf. Belgic Confession of Faith, article 22; Canons of Dort, 5.8), because there is confessed what Christ achieved through his sacrifice.

In atonement through Christ, as in Old Testament atonement, there is bidirectional action (Wentsel, *Dogm.*, 3b:445–47). The atoning sacrifice is oriented toward God, and on the basis of this sacrifice of atonement communion with God is bestowed on people. Korff's thesis (1942^2, 2:187) that "the essence of the passion history is aimed at us" was correctly countered by: the quintessence of atonement that emanates from God's love continues in the work of Christ; the quintessence of atonement also runs from Jesus Christ to God (Van der Zanden, 1950, 36).

Substitution fits into a Trinitarian framework, for "Christ offered himself without spot to God through the eternal Spirit" (Heb. 9:14). "Vicarious satisfaction has its foundation in the counsel of the Triune God, in the life of supreme, perfect, and eternal love, in the unshakable covenant of redemption" (Bavinck, *R.D.*, 3:406).

6. *The extent of atonement*

We return to the question as to how far the atonement reaches. Are there grounds for teaching the universality of atonement?

As we pointed out in connection with Barth's view (§ 32.1, subsection 4, point e), we shall leave aside *absolute universalism* or the doctrine of *apokatastasis*. There are, however, a number of Scripture passages that are believed to point in this direction. *Relative universalism* that we usually encounter in the form of the doctrine of *universal atonement* also appeals to these passages. It is especially this form of universalism and the grounds on which it is based that we need to address in this section.

The doctrine of universal atonement finds widespread support. According to Rome, Christ died for all, but not everyone receives the benefit of his death (*DS*, 1523). The Second Vatican Council teaches that through his incarnation the Son of God in a certain sense united himself with everyone. Through his suffering he cleared a path for us. In union with him, a Christian hastens toward the resurrection. The same thing is true of all well-intentioned people, in whose heart grace works in an invisible manner. After all, Christ died for everyone (Rom. 8:32).[87] According to Roman Catholicism, this universalism of salvation is in our time frequently coupled with universalism of revelation (cf. Wentsel, *Dogm.*, 2:91–102; 3b:517–19).

The Remonstrant doctrine of atonement has much in common with the doctrine of Rome, because the possibility-realization scheme captures its essence. The possibility of being saved is given by God's grace in Christ. Whether or not this possibility is realized depends on people's reaction; i.e., free will, which collaborates with grace or not, has the last word. *Remonstrance* (1610) says that Jesus Christ, the Savior of the world, died for all and every human being individually. He obtained atonement and forgiveness of sins for all of them, but only believers enjoy this forgiveness (John 3:16; 1 John 2:2). That Christ died for us means according to the Remonstrant view that it was for our sake and to our benefit, but not in our stead.

Bavinck points out that the difference with respect to atonement is defined incorrectly or at least incompletely when one formulates it exclusively in the question whether Christ died and made satisfaction for all people or only for the elect. According to the Canons of Dort, the real issue concerned the value and power of Christ's sacrifice, the nature of the work of salvation. In this connection he referred to the Canons of Dort, 2.8 (*R.D.*, 3:467).

Methodists who follow in the footsteps of J. Wesley (1703–91) constitute a third important group that teaches universal atonement. There is a difference between the "evangelical Arminianism" of Wesley and the Remonstrant doctrine. Nevertheless, also according to Wesley the decision rests with man.[88]

87. *Pastorale constitutie over de kerk in de wereld van deze tijd* (pastoral constitution concerning the church in the world of this time (Gaudium et spes), no. 22.

88. Cf. Ch. Hodge, *Systematic Theology*, 1888, 2:329–31.

The influence of Methodism is noticeable in the doctrinal position of the Salvation Army and has also influenced various revival movements. At any rate, the Holiness movement and Pentecostalism were clearly influenced by Wesleyan Methodism.

Hypothetical universalism of the school of Saumur deserves separate mention. Figures such as J. Cameron (1580–1625) and M. Amyraut (1596–1664) sought an intermediate position between Calvinism—as subscribed to by the Synod of Dort—and Remonstrantism. This led to a good deal of conflict in France. In Saumur it was taught that Christ died for all, but that this universal atonement only becomes reality for those who believe in him. God first of all ordained universal atonement in Christ. According to a second decree of God, certain people receive faith as a precondition for participation in Christ's redemption. Universal atonement may be preached to everyone, but only some are predestined to receive faith and others not. Amyraut distinguishes a twofold will of God: a will of God that seeks the salvation of everyone, and a will that leads part of mankind to salvation.

From a theological perspective there is a separation here between Christ's work of atonement that is intended for all, and the work of the Holy Spirit who grants faith that is not universal. Amyraut believed Calvin to be on his side, but—also according to Graafland—he is closer to Arminius.[89]

Our first objection to the doctrine of universal atonement is that in this way the work of Christ implies *a possibility for salvation* to everyone, without guaranteeing its reality. Thus the accomplishment and application of salvation are separated from each other, which is not biblical.

Jesus' speaking about his sheep (John 10:27) implies a contrast. Not everyone belongs to his sheep. He offers his life for his sheep; he knows them, and they know him (John 10:14–15). He does not only say that he is prepared to give his life for his own, but also gives us the assurance: "And I give unto them eternal life; and they shall never perish, neither shall any man pluck them out of my hand" (John 10:28).

The inextricable connection between the accomplishment and the application of salvation is also apparent from the words of Paul: "We thus judge that . . . one died for all." The apostle adds: "Therefore if any man be in Christ, he is a new creature" (2 Cor. 5:14, 17). Paul does not mean that Christ died for all without exception, for then they would all have died and risen with him and would all be in Christ. Everyone who is in Christ is a new creation. But not everyone is in Christ.

89. See A. Schweizer, *Die protestantischen Centraldogmen*, 1856, 2:225–503; C. Graafland, *Van Calvijn tot Barth*, 1987, 181–97; F. P. van Stam, *The Controversy over the Theology of Saumur*, 1635–50, 1988.

Our second objection is that when Christ's sacrifice is thought to have been made for all, it is *given a different interpretation* than Scripture proclaims. A theologian such as Korff is of the opinion that according to the New Testament Christ died for all, but that his death did not achieve satisfaction (Korff, 1942[2], 2:201).

Here the atonement achieved by Christ is weakened for the sake of a broad scope for the preaching of the gospel. Whenever atonement is considered to be universal, its content is reduced (Murray, 1955, 74). Atonement then can no longer be atonement through satisfaction. We agree with Bavinck: "If Jesus is truly the Savior, he must also *really* save his people, not potentially but really and in fact, completely and eternally" (*R.D.*, 3:467). Otherwise the center of gravity is shifted from Christ to the Christian. The nature of faith also changes, for it is then no longer receptive with respect to salvation in Christ, but is given a creative role in making salvation effective. Faith then becomes work that needs to be added to the work completed by Christ, who has done everything for us already.

However, the proponents of universal atonement are not unanimous in this regard. There are those who wish to continue to view faith as a gift of God. In this case, the latter objection no longer applies, but other objections emerge. If Christ has reconciled all people with God but the Holy Spirit does not grant faith to all, the work of the Spirit is placed over against that of Christ. Would this not imply a tension or conflict within God?

However, when appropriation of salvation is viewed to be dependent on man, the latter objection remains valid. It implies that God has done his part through Christ's sacrifice, to which man must now add his share. This is an unbiblical representation of the facts.

One of the most serious objections to the Reformed doctrine of atonement is that it threatens the proclamation of the gospel to everyone. The Remonstrants emphasized this very strongly. If atonement is not universal, then there is no gospel for everyone either!

In reaction to this view, the Synod of Dort (1618–19) clearly stated (Canons of Dort, 2.5) that "the promise of the gospel . . . ought to be declared and published to . . . all persons . . . without distinction . . . together with the command to repent and believe." It is not only permitted; it must be done! Freely and joyfully!

It is not, however, the mandate of the church to tell everyone: Christ has died in your place; all your sins have been atoned for and forgiven (cf. Bavinck, *R.D.*, 4:36). The apostolic proclamation is: "God was in Christ reconciling the world unto himself, not imputing their trespasses unto them . . . . We pray you in Christ's stead, be ye reconciled to God" (2 Cor. 5:19–20).

No one may conclude from the gospel of atonement that Christ has reconciled him or her with God, without more ado. This can only be confessed in faith. "I can receive . . . the satisfaction, righteousness and holiness of Christ . . . and apply to myself in no other way than by faith only" (Heidelberg Catechism, Lord's Day 23). This agrees with Scripture. There we continually encounter the first person singular or plural: "I live by the faith of the Son of God, who loved me, and gave himself for me" (Gal. 2:20). "We also joy in God through our Lord Jesus Christ, by whom we have now received the atonement" (Rom. 5:11).

The gospel of atonement has universal significance. It concerns the entire world and is intended for everyone. Christ is "the Saviour of the world" (John 4:42; 1 John 4:14). "The Lamb of God . . . taketh away the sin of the world" (John 1:29; cf. 1 John 2:2). This is why it says in the Canons of Dort: "The death of the Son of God is the only and most perfect sacrifice and satisfaction for sin, and is of infinite worth and value, abundantly sufficient to expiate the sins of the whole world" (2.3).

Universalism of salvation that cannot make do with this kerygmatic universality contradicts the unity of God's work, which includes everything from election unto salvation up to and including the consummation of salvation.

This indivisible unity is, however, not sufficient ground for us to restrict the proclamation of the gospel to those who already share in salvation, as sometimes happens (cf. Wentsel, *Dogm.*, 3b:495ff., 524ff.), when it is feared that emphasizing the universality of the gospel will lead to the doctrine of universal atonement, or at the very least Remonstrant tendencies (see also § 16.8).

There are statements in the New Testament that appear to support universalism. In this connection we mention Romans 5:18; 8:32; 1 Timothy 2:6; 1 John 2:2; and Colossians 1:19–20. There are other Scripture passages that appear to point in the same direction (cf. Bavinck, *R.D.*, 3:465).

Romans 5:18. At first glance this verse appears to be a strong Scripture proof for the doctrine of universal atonement or even for *apokatastasis*. The twice-occurring "all men" is then given the same interpretation: everyone without distinction. But does the second "all men" have the same content and scope as the first? The first instance refers to all of Adam's descendents and focuses on the reality of sin and its consequences (cf. Rom. 5:12). In the second instance the apostle refers to the reality of justification to life. According to him, we can only participate in this through faith. Therefore, "all men" first refers to all mankind and subsequently to the new humanity, i.e., those who are in Christ.[90]

Romans 8:32. God has "delivered up . . . his own Son . . . for us all." "Us all" is equivalent to "us" (31, 34, 35) and to "God's elect" (33). It refers to those of whom the apostle has said in this context that they have been "called according to [God's] purpose," "foreknown" and "predestined to be conformed to the image of his Son" (28–30).

Election, atonement, and redemption extend equally far. Election by God is not a universal election (§ 16); neither can the appropriation of salvation through the work of the Holy Spirit be viewed as being universalistic. Neither is the atonement by Christ a universal atonement. A. Kuyper was correct in making the following statement (in the title of one of his writings): *Grace is particular* (1909²).

1 Timothy 2:6. In view of the context the word "all" can seem universalistically intended (cf. 1 Tim. 2:4). Yet two different interpretations may be considered. First Timothy 2:4 could be interpreted analogously to 2 Peter 3:9: "The Lord . . . is not willing that any should perish, but that all should come to repentance." This has to do with the will of God as we know it from the gospel. It is not God's will or desire that some will be lost. His Word says that he has "no pleasure in the death of the wicked; but that the wicked turn from his way and live" (Ezek. 33:11; cf. also 18:23). There is also a respectable tradition in which—together with Augustine and Calvin—"all" or "all men" is interpreted as: all kinds of people (cf. 1 Tim. 2:1). Salvation is for all categories of people and goes beyond all human divisions and restrictions. The apostle emphasizes this because of Judaist views with which he was continually confronted (cf. Ridderbos, *Paul*, 339ff.).

1 John 2:2. "Christ . . . is the propitiation for our sins; and not for ours only, but also for the sins of the whole world." The efficacy of propitiation (hilasmos) is not restricted to the immediate circle of disciples of Jesus and the believers who enjoy communion with them (1 John 1:1–4). Propitiation reaches far beyond them (cf. Murray, 1955, 82–84).

Colossians 1:19–20. Does it not say there that "it pleased the Father that in [Christ] . . . and through the blood of his cross . . . all things [be] reconciled unto himself'"? This verse, however, does not say that all people or all creatures become reconciled with God. The pericope speaks of Christ's glory and dominion. In this context the focus is on peace through his blood and its significance for everything. This is the cosmic aspect of atonement. It will remove the disharmony under which everything suffers right now. One can think in terms of "eschatological pacification" (Ridderbos, *Paul*, 184).

A different question is who will share in the peace through the blood of the cross. In Colossians 1:13–14 and 21–23 it indicates which people have redemption in Christ and who is reconciled with God through him. There the apostle speaks to believers and on their behalf.

90. See H. Ridderbos, *Aan de Romeinen* (to the Romans), 1959, 121.

Atonement is accompanied by "the ministry of reconciliation" (2 Cor. 5:18). This ministry, which has been assigned to us—as office bearer or otherwise—should be viewed in the perspective of the cosmic sovereignty of Christ. When all power had been given to him, he said: "Go ye therefore . . ." (Matt. 28:18–19).

Atonement is therefore not universal. It does have a broader scope than the hearts of people who have been reconciled with God.[91]

Although "the word of reconciliation" has priority (2 Cor. 5:19), we realize that "the ministry of reconciliation" has a broader scope. People first need to heed the call: be reconciled to God. But subsequently it will affect their lives.

God's love, which has been revealed to us in the atonement by Christ, makes us live in love. Atonement results in peace. Apart from peace with God and inner peace, there is the peace between those who were first separate from each other. This peace is also founded on the atonement (reconciliation) (Eph. 2:14–16). "Those who live out of the atonement (reconciliation), are also called to serve the cause of reconciliation *in the midst of society* and in relationships among people, groups, and nations *and* in the cosmos in which we breathe, on the basis of what God has done for us." Key elements then are recognizing guilt, practicing forgiveness, and seeking ways and means to change unacceptable relationships and situations.[92]

We believe that atonement (reconciliation) has implications. We do not witness all of these yet. Atonement (reconciliation) has broader implications than we sometimes think. Yet a large part of the world does not want to hear of the reconciliation that God gives in Christ. But we anticipate the coming of the kingdom of God, in which the fruit of Christ's work of reconciliation will be fully revealed in a new humanity and a new world.

32.2. *Victory*

The aspect of victory should not be overlooked in a review of Christ's work. Victory implies conflict. Theology that focuses especially on motivation has assigned priority to the theme of conflict and victory,

91. B. Wentsel, *De koers van de kerk in een horizontalistisch tijdvak* (the church's course in a horizontalistic epoch), 2:91.

92. Cf. *Verzoening met God en met mensen. Herderlijk schrijven van de Generale Synode van De Gereformeerde Kerken in Nederland* (reconciliation with God and people: pastoral letter from the General Synod of De Gereformeerde Kerken in Nederland, 1976), 62–68.

because this has tended to receive too little attention except on the part of Luther.

We have in mind the school of Lund, of which G. Aulén (1879–1978) is the best known representative. In his work on the topic of atonement[93] he attempted to go beyond the differences between the positions of Anselm and Ritschl, who held, respectively, an objective doctrine of atonement centered on Christ's sacrifice, and a subjective doctrine of atonement focused on changes in human disposition.

The *Latin approach* (Anselm) places atonement within the framework of the law court; the *ethical approach* (Ritschl) makes atonement a function of what happens within a person. A third approach is *dramatic*. The last approach was advocated by church fathers such as Irenaeus and Origen. Here Christ is portrayed as victor in the battle against the powers of depravity, sin, death, and the devil. This doctrine of atonement, referred to as classical by Aulén, was revitalized and expanded by Luther.

According to Aulén, the Latin theory is legalistic, because a demand for satisfaction is presupposed and Christ's merits are required to bring about man's salvation, which completely depends on Christ's work according to his human nature. In the classical view of Aulén, atonement is a drama in which the actions of God's love and power are crucial.

An abundance of quotations was employed to demonstrate that the dramatic doctrine of atonement predominates in Luther's thinking. *A Mighty Fortress Is Our God* constitutes clear testimony in support of this view. Following in Paul's footsteps, this Reformer added the law and God's wrath to the trio of sin, death, and the devil. Christ also had to redeem us from the law. In him, God's wrath is conquered through a divine work.

These ideas are also supported by the New Testament. The Gospels, Paul and John, Hebrews, and other books all refer to the great conflict between God and the powers of evil. This dualistic-dramatic theme pervades the New Testament.

The discussion triggered by publications of Aulén and a number of other Lutheran theologians—also in Germany and America—focuses on the question whether Luther's interpretation is too one-sided and whether the classic view of Aulén is preferable because it does greater justice to the message of the Bible.

As far as the first point is concerned, we are dealing with a *communis opinio*. In Luther's work one can find numerous pronouncements that appear to support Aulén. But Luther's doctrine of atonement also contains other elements. The dramatic representation hardly takes into account the necessity of atonement of the guilt of sin. Redemption from the power of sin and the evil one receives most of the attention. This is not the case with Luther. He teaches that we first of all owe our justification to the work of Christ. We are liberated from our guilt! Just as fundamental as the content of Luther's hymn is the fact that Luther says with respect to the office and work of Jesus Christ and our redemption in an important document such as the *Smalkaldic Articles* (1537): "The first, chief article is that Jesus Christ, our God and Lord, died

93. G. Aulén, *De christelijke verzoeningsgedachte* (the Christian concept of atonement), Dutch translation 1931. See in this connection H. Alpers, *Die Versöhnung durch Christus* (atonement through Christ), 1964.

for our sins and rose for our justification (Rom. 4:25), that he alone is the Lamb of God that takes away the sin of the world (John 1:29)" (*BSLK*, 415).

More so than many others, Luther was very much aware of the immense seriousness of the conflict between Christ and Satan. He loved graphic depictions[94] and also repeatedly used that of the devil conquered by Christ or put to shame by him, so that he has to release his prey. In this way Luther accepted the ancient ransom theory (§ 32.1, subsection 4).

However, the interpretation of Aulén and his school is not correct, because the conflict with the devil is part of a bigger picture in Luther's body of thought. Christ also conquered for us the law and God's wrath. This tells us that our redemption in the first place applies to our relationship with God.[95] Despite strikingly "classical" elements, there is a clear "Latin" baseline (cf. Alpers, 1964, 184–86).

Aulén's support for the dramatic perspective is directly related to the trouble that he had with the doctrine of satisfaction. However, in light of Scripture, we cannot ignore the significance of Christ's conflict and victory.

In prophecy, the Messiah is also the Mighty God and the Prince of Peace. These names pertain to his government and the kingdom that is established with judgment and justice (Isa. 9:5–7).

Jesus' life was marked by conflict. It is very significant that at the beginning of his ministry he was tempted by the devil. He fought the evil one and his kingdom by casting out demons. The healing of the sick proved his might and compassion. In raising the dead he demonstrated who he was. Conflict escalated when Satan entered into Judas and when he demanded to have the disciples that he might sift them like wheat (Luke 22:3, 31).

It has been said of Jesus' work that it may first of all be characterized as deliverance from the power of Satan. The Gospels reveal the truth of the word: "For this purpose the Son of God was manifested, that he might destroy the works of the devil" (1 John 3:8). Even prior to the great conflict, Jesus was already victor (John 16:33). Paul considered Christ's work as a great, cosmic battle in which the final outcome had already been decided, but which needed to be continued on many fronts (cf. Sevenster, 1948[2], 108ff., 164ff., 235). Christ "spoiled principalities and powers" and "made a shew of them openly," thus "triumphing over them" (Col. 2:15). The context employed the image of the triumphal entry of the field marshal of antiquity. The believers are also called to resist the temptations of the devil (Eph. 6:11). Christ's triumph is also described in an impressive

94. H.-M. Barth, *Der Teufel (devil) und Jesus Christus in der Theologie Martin Luthers*, 1967, 91.

95. Cf. M. van Rhijn, *Ritschl en Luther*, 1946, 72.

manner in the book of Revelation (see Rev. 12:10; 17:14; 19:11–16).[96] The Lamb that will conquer is the King of kings and the Lord of lords (see *TDNT*, 1:341).

All of this should not be treated in isolation, and Christ's coming to destroy the works of the devil should not be contrasted with his coming "to minister and to give his life as a ransom for many" (Matt. 20:28). He destroyed the works of the devil in the way of his ministry and his sacrifice. His ministry and his conflict are fundamentally one and the same thing (cf. Berkouwer, 1965, 335).

When Jesus says, "It is finished" (John 19:30), this also means that the conflict has been settled and that the victory is secure. Calvin writes: "The triumph that Christ obtained on the cross was praised so gloriously by Paul, as if the cross had changed into a triumphal chariot" (*Institutes*, 2.16.6). This is said with Colossians 2:14–15 in mind. This triumph over powers is coupled with the forgiveness of our trespasses through "blotting out the handwriting of ordinances that was against us." The same thing is true of the dethronement of the devil, who exercised power over death, and the sacrifice that Christ made as high priest to atone for the sins of the people (Heb. 2:14–18). Here it says that Christ dethroned him through his death. His priestly surrender and his kingly power cannot be separated from each other.

The resurrection is preeminent proof of his victory. "By his resurrection he has overcome death" and "we also are raised up by his power to new life" (Heidelberg Catechism, Lord's Day 17).

Christ's work has more than one dimension, and so does the salvation that we owe to it: it is reconciliation and redemption through his sacrifice of atonement and through his victory, as the Heidelberg Catechism summarizes it in Lord's Day 1: "With his precious blood [he] has fully satisfied for all my sins and delivered me from all the power of the devil."

It has sometimes been noted that Aulén's unique emphasis might serve as a corrective (cf. Wenz, 1986, 2:468). This would be the case if we were to view the restoration of our relationship with God through atonement as the entire story. However, Christ's work comprises more than this. We also need to be liberated from the power of darkness. After all, we ended up in the grip of the evil one through our own bad

96. Cf. J. de Vuyst, *De Openbaring van Johannes* (the Revelation of John), 1987, 122–33.

choice. We cannot deliver ourselves from the powers that rule over us as tyrants. He does this for us. Through the sacrifice of his life he brings us under his gracious sovereignty.

In Aulén's depiction, the power of God's love is indeed manifested in the work of Christ, but his justice is ignored. For us, however, there is no atonement without satisfaction and no redemption without atonement.

In this regard we do not wish to overlook how much our reconciliation with God and our liberation from the power of the evil one has cost. When in faith we say with Paul that "we are more than conquerors," we are so "through him that loved us" (Rom. 8:37). Precisely in this context Christ is referred to as the one "that died, yea rather, that is risen again, who is even at the right hand of God, who also maketh intercession for us" (Rom. 8:34). There are therefore no grounds for triumphalism. Those who conquer the evil one cannot do so in their own strength, but only "by the blood of the Lamb" (Rev. 12:11).

Another reason why we cannot be too triumphalistic is that the conflict has not yet ended. The evil enemy has been defeated, but he continues to bestir himself.

Barth and others have been reproached for downplaying the latter. We may not detract whatsoever from the confession that Jesus is victor,[97] but there is no doubt that the New Testament very explicitly takes into account the reality of the threat of demons.[98]

Having said this, we need to reflect once again on the consequences of the outcome of the conflict. The assaults of the evil one are attacks of a defeated enemy. The evil powers have forever been constrained. It is just a matter of time before they are definitively annihilated. Soon Christ will have "put down all rule and all authority and power." "All things [have been] put under his feet" and "the last enemy that shall be destroyed is death" (1 Cor. 15:24–27). Then becomes true what was written: "Death is swallowed up in victory" (1 Cor. 15:54).

Christ's curbing of powers is coupled with and related to the conquering power of his gospel. Through his Spirit he transforms the work that is done in his kingdom into a triumphal procession (see

97. Barth agreed emphatically with J. C. Blumhardt: "Jesus ist Sieger" (Jesus is victor), (*C.D.*, 4.3.1, 168–71).

98. See G. C. Berkouwer, *De triomf der genade in de theologie van Karl Barth* (the triumph of grace in the theology of Karl Barth), 1954, 371–81.

2 Cor. 2:14). The church of Christ itself is involved through prayer (Acts 4:24–31).

The Bible repeatedly points to the significance of prayer in spiritual warfare. In this connection we especially have in mind prayers of intercession focused on the progression of God's work on earth and the coming of his kingdom. Through faith we can be sure of victory in the midst of conflict. Christ is Conqueror!

Some Literature

W. J. Aalders, *De incarnatie*, 1933.

H. Alpers, *Die Versöhnung durch Christus* (atonement through Christ), 1964.

A. van de Beek, *De menselijke persoon van Christus* (Christ's humanity), 1980.

G. C. Berkouwer, *The Person of Christ*, 1954.

G. C. Berkouwer, *The Work of Christ*, 1965.

C. Breytenbach, *Versöhnung* (atonement), 1989.

J. van Bruggen, *Christus op aarde* (Christ on earth), 1987.

E. Brunner, *Der Mittler* (the Mediator), 1930[2].

O. Cullmann, *Die Christologie des Neuen Testaments*, 1958[2].

W. S. Duvekot, *Kunnen wij Jezus kennen?* (can we know Jesus?), no date.

A. H. Edelkoort, *De Christusverwachting in het Oude Testament* (the anticipation of Christ in the Old Testament), 1941.

A. van Egmond, *De lijdende God in de Britse theologie van de negeniende eeuw* (a suffering God in British theology of the nineteenth century), 1986.

E. Emmen, *De christologie van Calvijn*, 1935.

M. Feitsma, *Het theopashitisme*, 1956.

E. Flesseman-van Leer, *Wie toch is Jezus van Nazareth?* 1985.

J. van Genderen, *Actuele thema's uit de geloofsleer* (current topics in the doctrine of faith), 1988.

J. van Genderen, *Christus in onze plaats* (Christ in our stead), 1972.

A. Gilg, *Weg und Bedeutung der altkirchlichen Christologie* (approach and sense of the Christology of the ancient church), 1955.

C. Graafland, *Wie zeggen de mensen dat ik ben?* (who do people say that I am?), no date.

M. Green (ed.), *The Truth of God Incarnate*, 1977.

S. K. Greijdanus, *Menschwording en vernedering* (incarnation and humiliation), 1903.

A. Grillmeier, *Jesus der Christus im Glaubern der Kirche* (Jesus Christ according to the faith of the church), 1–2/4, 1979–90.

F. W. Grosheide (ed.), *Christus de Heiland* (Christ the Savior), 1948.

C. Harinck, *De uigestrektheid van de verzoening* (the scope of atonement), 1989.

R. Haubst, *Vom Sinn der Menschwerdung* (on the meaning of the incarnation), 1969.

C. J. den Heyer, *De messiaanse weg* (the way of the Messiah), 3 vols., 1983–91.

F. G. Immink, *Jezus Christus, profeet, priester, koning*, 1990.

M. de Jonge, *Christology in Context*, 1988.

W. D. Jonker, *Christus, die Middelaar* (Christ the Mediator), 1977.

H. Karpp, *Textbuch zur altkirchlichen Christologie* (textbook on the Christology of the ancient church), 1972.

W. Kasper, *Jesus der Christus*, 1975[2].

S. Kim, *The "Son of Man" as the Son of God*, 1983.

B. Klappert (ed.), *Diskussion um Kreuz und Auferstehung* (discussion of the cross and the resurrection), 1971[4].

F. W. A. Korff, *Christologie*, 2 vols., 1942[2].

W. Künneth, *Theologie der Auferstehung* (theology of the resurrection), 1951[4].

A. Kuyper, *De Vleeschwording des Woords* (the incarnation of the Word), 1887.

A. F. N. Lekkerkerker, *Het evangelie van de verzoening* (the gospel of atonement), 1966.

J. Liébaert, *Christologie (Handbuch der Dogmengeschichte* = handbook of dogmatic history, III, Ia), 1965.

M. Lienhard, *Martin Luthers christologische Zeugnis* (Martin Luther's christological testimony), 1980.

E. Lohse, *Märtyrer und Gottesknecht* (martyr and servant of God), 1963[2].

I. H. Marshall, *The Work of Christ*, (1969), 1981.

A. McGrath, *The Making of Modern German Christology*, 1986.

J. Moltmann, *Der gekreuzigte Gott* (the crucified God), 1972.

J. Moltmann, *Der Weg Jesu Christi* (the way of Jesus Christ), 1989.

J. Murray, *Redemption, Accomplished and Applied*, 1955.

K.-H. Ohlig, *Christologie*, 2 vols., 1989.

W. Pannenberg, *Jesus—God and Man*, 1968.

I. J. du Plessis, *Christus as hoof van kerk en kosmos* (Christ as head of church and cosmos), 1962.

C. H. Ratchow, *Jesus Christus*, 1982.

K. H. Rengstorf, *Die Auferstehung Jesu* (Christ's resurrection), 1960[4].

H. N. Ridderbos, *Het Woord is vlees geworden* (the Word has become incarnate), 1979.

H. [N.] Ridderbos, *Zijn wij op de verkeerde weg?* (are we on the wrong road?), 1972.

H. Ristow/K. Matthiae (ed.), *Der historische Jesus und der kerygmatische Christus*, 1962[3].

E. Schillebeeckx, *Jezus, het verhaal van een levende* (Jesus, the story of one who lives), 1975[3].

E. Schillebeeckx, *Tussentijds verhaal over twee Jezus boeken* (story in-between two books about Jesus), 1978.

H. Schroten, *Christus, de Middelaar, bij Calvijn* (Christ, the Mediator, according to Calvin), 1948.

G. Sevenster, *De Christologie van het Nieuwe Testament*, 1948[2].

P. Stuhlmacher, *Versöhnung, Gesetz und Gerechtigkeit* (atonement, law, and righteousness), 1981.

V. Taylor, *The Atonement in New Testament Teaching*, 1958[3].

D. A. du Toit, "*Neergedaal ter helle . . .* (descended into hell)," 1971.

J. Veenhof, *De dubbele Jezus* (the double Jesus), 1985.

J. P. Versteeg, *Evangelie in viervoud* (fourfold gospel), 1980.

J. Vlaardingerbroek, *Jezus Christus tussen Joden en Christenen* (Jesus Christ between Jews and Christians), 1989.

A. Vos, *Het is de Heer!* (it is the Lord!), 1990.

B. Wentsel, *Hij is voor ons, wij voor Hem* (he is for us, we for him), 1973.

G. Wenz, *Geschichte der Versöhnungslehre in der evangelishen Theologie der Neuzeit* (history of the doctrine of atonement in evangelical theology of today), 2 vols., 1984–86.

H. E. Wevers, *Jezus Christus vanwaar komt hij?* (from where is Jesus Christ?), 1986.

H. Wiersinga, *De verzoening in de theologische diskussie* (atonement in theological discussions), 1971.

H. Wiersinga, *Verzoening als verandering* (atonement as change), 1972.

H. W. de Wolff, *Jesaja 53 im Urchristentum* (Isa. 53 according to ancient Christianity), 1984[4].

L. van der Zanden, *De spits der verzoening* (the essence of atonement), 1950.

Chapter 11

The Covenant of Grace

§ 33. The development of the doctrine of the covenant

33.1. *Introduction*

Reformed theologians frequently discuss the doctrine of the covenant of grace prior to the doctrine of the person and work of Christ. For those who think like Kersten, this is a natural thing to do, for it makes it easier to link the covenant of grace with the covenant of redemption. According to Kersten, these two covenants essentially form a single entity. In Christology, which comes next, the focus is then on the salvation of the elect (*R.D.*, 1:233, 259). The question is, however, whether this does justice to the covenant that God establishes with us in time.

We prefer the reverse order, because not only God's eternal plan of salvation, but also the accomplishment of salvation by Christ, form the foundation of the covenant in which God comes to us with his promise of salvation. The various facets of salvation are then discussed within the doctrine of salvation immediately following the doctrine of the covenant (cf. Ten Hoor, *Comp*., 119).

In an introductory section it is useful to briefly trace the origin of the doctrine of the covenant of grace and to sketch a broad outline of its development.

During the era of the church fathers and in the Middle Ages a doctrine of the covenant as such did not yet exist, although some of Augustine's reflections on the subject and the medieval concept of *pactum* did have some influence on its subsequent development.[1] It was not until after the Reformation, however, that the church discovered the richness of the covenant. Here we have in mind especially the Reformed family of churches, for the Lutherans hardly mentioned the significance of the covenant (cf. Vos, 1939, 5). The Reformed, however, were not all on the same wavelength. There were divergent opinions as well as a number of controversies.

33.2. *The emergence of a doctrine of the covenant*

What Luther said in some of his early writings about the relationship between the promise and faith, and about the confirmation of the promise through the testament, pact, or covenant (cf. Bayer, 1971, 161, 255), was indeed of vital importance, but it did not lead to the emergence of a theology of the covenant. For this we must go to Zwingli and Bullinger. In his writings against the Anabaptists, Zwingli vigorously defended the validity of infant baptism. For this he went back to the covenant with Abraham of which circumcision was the sign. God sought to establish a covenant with Abraham and his children, so that he would be their God. In Zwingli's *Fedei ratio* (1530), he says: like circumcision, baptism calls for either confession or covenant, i.e., the promise (Müller, *Bek*., 86). God's promise is the most essential aspect of the covenant of which the sacraments are the visible signs.

This early beginning already shows us that much more is involved in the covenant, such as the unity of the Old Testament and the New Testament, the unity of God's people, and the role of the sacraments.

Surprisingly early a monograph about the covenant was published, which, centuries later, we can continue to read with appreciation: *De testamento seu foedere Dei unico et aeterno* (the only and eternal testament or covenant of God, 1534), by Bullinger. This Zürich theologian saw a direct connection between the covenant that God established with sinful and mortal people and the coming of Christ who bears the name Immanuel—God with us. Bullinger fully emphasized the unity of the covenant. When a new covenant is mentioned (Jer. 31), the focus is not on the substance or essence of the covenant. God's covenant with us includes conditions and stipulations that form part of a bond. First, God shows what he wants to do and what we are to expect from him. Then he spells out what he requires from us

1. B. Loonstra, "De historische wortels van de leer aangaande het verbond" (historical roots of the doctrine of the covenant), *Th.Ref*. 30 (1978): 46–63.

and what we must do. The former constitutes the covenant promise, the latter the covenant obligation. Whoever is guilty of covenant breach is removed from the covenant and the inheritance (Bullinger, 1923, 41–48, 31–36).

In this monograph Bullinger started out from the covenant with Abraham, but in *Der alt Glaub* (the ancient faith, 1529), he went back farther, for he dealt extensively with the fall into sin and the promise of grace. Genesis 3:15 constitutes the first gospel. The patriarchs also were saved by faith in Christ. Bullinger, like Zwingli, had an eye for the history of the covenant. The covenant established with Adam was subsequently renewed with Noah, and next with Abraham. It is one promise, one Savior, and one faith (Bullinger, 1923, 86–101).

Like his predecessors, among whom we must also count Bucer (see W. van 't Spijker in *Rondom de doopvont* = at the baptismal font, 1983, 248–62), Calvin defended the unity of the covenant of grace over against the Anabaptists. It is essentially the gracious adoption (*gratuita adoptio*) as children of God. The covenant with the fathers does not differ in any way from the covenant with us; it is one and the same covenant. There is only a difference in administration or dispensation. There is a progression in the revelation of the salvation of God's covenant (Institutes, 2.10–11; cf. Wolf, 1958; Graafland, 1978, 22–42). Christ also was the foundation of the covenant in the Old Testament. He represents at the same time its fulfillment (*complementum*).

Calvin spoke of ratification of the covenant through the death of Christ as well as ratification through faith. "After all, God's covenant is ratified, when by faith we embrace what he promises" (commentary on Gen. 17:14). This does not mean that the covenant acquires legal validity only when we believe God's promises. It does mean that otherwise the covenant does not achieve its objective in us. "We know, that the promises do not reach their intended effect (*efficases esse*), until we accept them in faith" (*Institutes*, 3.24.17).

This Reformer employed terms such as "condition" and "stipulation." We also encounter the word "ministry" in this context. The faith and obedience that God demands from us are also gifts that he promises to us. The repeated warning against violating and breaking the covenant indicates that the necessary emphasis is placed on man's responsibility

Calvin spoke in a twofold manner about God's children, just as he distinguished a twofold election, a twofold adoption, and a twofold calling. To indicate the distinction involved, he employed the scheme: general-particular. By virtue of the call that comes to them, all descendants of Abraham are considered to be children of God. "In God's innermost sanctuary, however, no others are considered to be children of God, but they in whom the promise is confirmed by faith" (Commentary on Gen. 17:7). Believers are the true children of God. According to Calvin there are promises that accrue only to believers and the elect. By this he meant that their fulfillment is meant for them only (Van der Vegt, no date, 75).

In his doctrine of the covenant he did not ignore predestination, but according to him the covenant was not governed by predestination. While he did take election into consideration in his doctrine of the covenant, he did not allow election to dominate the covenant.

33.3. *Past controversies*

In the latter years of the sixteenth century, there emerged a view of the covenant that was characterized by a sharp distinction between conditional and unconditional aspects of the covenant of grace, which even led to the doctrine of a twofold covenant: the unconditional covenant with the elect (which is actually a testament), in which our role is acceptance, and the conditional covenant (such as God established with the people of Israel), in which the human reaction must be taken into account.

When it became common to speak of a covenant of God with Adam in his state of original righteousness—Ursinus and Olevianus having contributed to this extension of the doctrine of the covenant—some resemblance was seen between this original covenant with man, often referred to as a covenant of nature or a covenant of law, and the Sinaitic covenant (Ex. 19–24). The Decalogue was described as a law of nature or a law of the covenant of works. In connection with this development we refer to W. Perkins in England (*A Golden Chaine*, 1591) and F. Gomarus in the Netherlands (*De foedere*, 1594). See Baker, 1980, 205–7.

The proper covenant of grace then is not the conditional or external covenant, but the unconditional or internal covenant. The former includes the offer of grace and the requirement of faith and conversion, while in the latter God promises faith and eternal life to the elect.

The Westminster Confession (1647) has a chapter dealing with the covenant that contains descriptions of the covenant of works and the covenant of grace. In connection with the covenant of grace, we are struck by a distinction made between what God graciously offers to sinners, while requiring faith on their part, and what he promises to the elect (Müller, *Bek.*, 558ff.). The extent to which the doctrine of election influenced the doctrine of the covenant is especially apparent from the Larger Catechism of Westminster: "The covenant of grace is established with Christ, the second Adam, and in him with all the elect as his seed" (Müller, *Bek.*, 615).

Cocceius (1603–69) made a significant attempt to break with the scholastic way of thinking and present a biblical theology. To him, the covenant and testament of God were the most important theological subject matter. In covenantal theology, of which Cocceius was the most prominent representative, the covenant (*pactum*) between the Father and the Son was firmly ensconced (see Loonstra, 1990, 80–139). Thought was given to the relationships among the various covenants, both the relationship between the covenant of works and the covenant of grace, and that between the covenant of grace and the eternal covenant of redemption (cf. Van Asselt, 1988, 98–123).

Characteristic of Cocceius are his doctrine of the gradual abrogation of the covenant of works and the great difference between the Old Testament and New Testament dispensations of salvation. The conflict between Voetians and Cocceians, which carried on for years, is directly related to this.

33.4. *Current controversies*

Today the question whether or not the covenant of grace is subject to predestination is an important point of controversy. In the doctrine of the covenant are we permitted and obliged to start out with election?

Various authors have identified two views with respect to the relationship between covenant and election, which lead to two different theological approaches (cf. Van Teylingen, no date, 9ff.; Harinck, 1986, 207).

The view that we mention first, because we already encounter it in Bullinger's work and in essence also in Calvin's work,[2] is based on the covenant that God established in time with believers and their children. To them pertain the promises coupled with the demand to be faithful to God's covenant. Faith and conversion can be identified as conditions, but they are at the same time gifts from God. We recognize this train of thought in our own time on the part of theologians belonging to various denominations, such as K. Schilder,[3] J. G. Woelderink (cf. van Genderen, 1983, 82–87), and J. J. van der Schuit (Vander Schuit, 1982[2]).

The second view of the covenant is characterized by the fact that it is placed in the light of election from eternity. Actually the focus is solely on the elect. The most essential aspect of the covenant of grace is then God's unconditional promise of salvation, which by virtue of election is fulfilled in the lives of those who are his. In this connection we can mention the names of Perkins, Witsius, Boston, and Comrie, but there are many others. "The Scottish doctrine of the covenant" (cf. Harinck, 1986) did not remain within the borders of Scotland.

In pursuing this second view one can go in divergent directions. In the Netherlands one can in essence choose between A. Kuyper and G. H. Kersten. Many in the *Gereformeerde Kerken* in the Netherlands followed the former; those in the Netherlands Reformed Congregations in the Netherlands and North America followed the latter. We recognize the impact of this in synodical doctrinal pronouncements, respectively those of 1942–46 and 1931. Those who follow Kuyper either entirely or in key respects view the church not only as the church of the covenant, but also as the assembly of the elect. In the other case this is not generalized but individualized. Wherever signs of election can be identified, the essence of the covenant is present. This makes for significant differences in practice (for more on this see van Genderen, 1983, 8–33).

2. Baker (1980, 193–98) pits Bullinger against Calvin. A. A. Hoekema, whom Baker opposes, better reflects Calvin's covenant doctrine in "The Covenant of Grace in Calvin's Teaching," *C. Chg.* 2 (1967): 133–61.

3. For K. Schilder's covenant doctrine see S. A. Strauss, *"Alles of niks"* (everything or nothing), 1982.

According to the view that we mentioned first—in Jonker's terminology, "the second type or type B," 1989, 91–101—the distinction between election and covenant is continually kept in mind. Within the covenant of grace there is a concretely historical emphasis.[4]

Within the Reformed community, differences of view with respect to the covenant indeed led to a great deal of discussion and conflict, both theologically and ecclesiastically, but the contrast between the Reformed views and modern ideas with respect to the covenant is more profound.

To Barth the covenant is a major theme. It plays a fundamental role in his analysis, as is evident from the second thesis on which his doctrine of the creation is based: the covenant constitutes the inner ground of creation (for the consequences of this thesis, see § 17.3, point 7).

According to Barth, the covenant was not established with particular people—neither with believers and their children, nor only with the elect portion of humanity—but with all people. The covenant signifies that God is with us. This implies that we are with God. Jesus Christ is the content of the eternal will of God, of the eternal covenant between God and man. Before man existed, he was destined in God's eternal will to be a brother to God's Son and a child of God. Every word about Jesus Christ is a statement about all people, an ontological declaration regarding all people, including unbelievers (cf. *C.D.* 4.1.54, 63; 4.2.275). In him the decision was made for all. God's choice goes hand in hand with God's command. It points to the responsibility that comes with the covenant. As covenant partner, man must respond to and live up to what has been said from God's perspective.

Kuitert and Berkhof are Dutch theologians who adopted Barthian concepts, but developed their own approach to the doctrine of the covenant.

According to Kuitert, God's being God should be sought solely in his being covenant Partner. This presupposes a being human that is also characterized as being covenant partner.[5] As covenant partner man has tremendous scope for input, according to Kuitert.[6]

To Berkhof, the covenant is a gracious disposition from God, yet involving two parties who relate to each other as subjects and whose attitude and behavior are mutually co-determinative (*C.F.*, 252).

While Barth proceeds from the idea of a covenant between God and the man Jesus Christ, which is a covenant with all people, Berkhof arrives at the same point by starting out with the covenant with Israel, which plays a vicarious role for all of humanity—"Israel as experimental garden" (*C.F.*, 248ff.). Because of the unfaithful-

4. See report *Breedere omschrijving van de gronden waarop het antwoord van de Synode van 1934 aan de Gereformeerde Kerken rust* (more detailed description of the basis on which rests the reply of the Synod of 1934 to the Gereformeerde Kerken), 1937; also in *Acta van de Generale Synode der Christelijke Gereformeerde Kerk in Nederland*, 1937, 131–70. See also the "*Verklaring van gevoelen*" (explanation of views), 1943; also in C. Veenhof, *Om de "Unica Catholica,"* 1949, 441–46.

5. H. M. Kuitert, *De mensvormigheid Gods* (God's human form), 1962, 228, 233.

6. See W. H. Velema, *Aangepaste theologie* (adapted thology), 1971, 173.

ness of this nation, the covenant fails, but thanks to God's faithfulness there is hope. This dialectic of faithfulness and unfaithfulness can only find its equilibrium via man, who is God's faithful human partner and who by virtue of the perfect covenantal relationship is permeated with the Spirit (*C.F.*, 291ff.). From Jesus a wind begins to blow in our life. He is the one man, who is at the same time the firstfruits. What the Spirit must do to us from Christ as the source is to bring us to voluntary surrender and participation, in order that we may become conformed to the image of the Son (*C.F.*, 328–32).

Like Barth's theology, that of Berkhof tends toward universalism. Israel is seen as the trial grounds of God's relationship to man. When Paul says, "God has concluded them all in unbelief that he might have mercy upon all" (Rom. 11:32), Berkhof applies this to all of humanity. We must think more highly of God's faithfulness than human unfaithfulness (*C.F.*, 536). It has been correctly pointed out that to Berkhof the covenant, in the final analysis, does not constitute a relationship established by God with certain people but the *modus operandi* of God's relationship with all people, and that in Berkhof's analysis election disappears behind the covenant (Jonker, 1989, 178, 186).

We can list a number of characteristics of this new style of thinking about the covenant:

1. The covenant of grace is here the only and original covenant of God with man, because it was never preceded by a state of original righteousness and fall into sin;
2. The doctrine of the covenant takes on a universal tenor because God as partner of the man Jesus is the partner of every human being;
3. Since from a christological perspective man is viewed as God's partner, the implication is that he plays a decisive role.[7]

§ 34. The covenant in Holy Scripture

34.1. ***The Old Testament***
34.2. ***The New Testament***

34.1. *The Old Testament*

1. *General.* The covenant occupies an especially important place in the Old Testament. This is seen by all those who reflect on the relationship between God and people, and who allow themselves to be guided first of all by the Old Testament.

7. The latter is emphasized even more by E. Flesseman-van Leer. See van Genderen, 1983, 88–92.

The etymology of the word *berit* that occurs almost 300 times in the books of the Old Testament is uncertain. The *Septuagint* translates this Hebrew word as *diatheke* (arrangement, testament) and not as a term that denotes an agreement or a treaty. However, is "covenant" indeed the correct rendition of *berit*? This question is raised especially by Kutsch, who prefers "obligation" (1973, 203ff.; *THAT*, 1:339–52). This can then be the obligation that God takes upon himself (*Selbstverpflichtung*) or the obligation that he imposes on man (*Fremdverpflichtung*). In relationships among people there is also indeed a *berit* in the sense of a mutual obligation, but theologically one would have to give up the term "covenant" and the concept of a covenant (*TRE*, 7:399). From a discussion of this view by L. Perlitt and other Old Testament scholars can be deduced that *berit* is a complex concept which has diverse aspects, including at any rate those of promise and demand.

We agree with McCarthy that these more recent views contain elements of truth, but that we have no reason to replace *covenant* with *obligation* (see also M. Weinfeld in *TWAT*, 1:781 f.). *Berit* involves not only obligations, but also a relationship. A covenant that people ratify with each other includes negotiations, a description of the relationship, and a sign or ritual. There are numerous examples of this in the Old Testament.

In the history of the renewal and confirmation of the covenant of the Lord with Israel in the days of Joshua (chapter 24), there is a great deal that is characteristic of a covenant in general.[8] To be valid, the covenant relationship does not need to be expressed in such a solemn fashion. It exists because God says: I will be your God and you will be my people, the so-called *covenant formula*, which sometimes occurs in direct connection with *berit* and sometimes without the covenant being mentioned. The relationship is clearly implied in the words: "I am the LORD thy God" (Ex. 20:2; Lev. 19:3). See in this connection McCarthy, 1981, 16–22.

A covenant by no means always involves equal parties. One person can take the initiative without the other person seeing a need for it, and a superior can impose it on his underling. Such a covenant is sometimes compared to suzerainty treaties of the Ancient Near East.

When God ratifies a covenant with people, the two parties are indeed very unequal. He never says: let us make a covenant, but, "I will establish my covenant between me and thee" (Gen. 17:7). It is his covenant. In its formation this covenant is *unilateral* (coming from one side), which does not take away from the fact that it then immediately takes on two sides and is *bilateral*. Yet it is different than when he confronts people with his law. In the covenant the promise, which accompanies the demand, is primary. God establishes his covenant with insignificant and sinful people. Therefore—after Genesis 1 and 2—it is *a covenant that in its origin and existence testifies to grace*.

Words that describe what God does are: give, establish, ratify, command, and keep; words that indicate what is required of man are: observe, maintain, hold fast to the covenant, and act in accordance with the covenant (see Gen. 17:9; Ex. 19:5; Isa. 56:4; 2 Chron. 34:32). People, however, can forget, forsake, transgress, violate, and break the covenant with their God. The book of Deuteronomy especially contains serious warnings (see 4:23–24; 29:25–28; 31:16–17). The God of the covenant shows

8. On Joshua 24 see especially W. T. Koopmans, *Joshua 24 as Poetic Narrative*, 1990.

his faithfulness and mercy (*'emet, chesed*) to his people. He also expects them to be faithful to him (see Mic. 6:8).

2. *The covenant in the book of Genesis.* God's covenant goes through *history*, and various phases can be distinguished (cf. Francke, 1985, 19–190).

In the Bible the word "covenant" (*berit*) is first mentioned in Genesis 6:18. God says to Noah: "But with thee will I establish my covenant; and thou shalt come into the ark." This is a one-sided arrangement on God's part with a specific purpose and a limited duration. The covenant mentioned in Genesis 9:8–17 is usually referred to as the Noahitic covenant. The promise of this covenant serves the covenant of grace (cf. Francke, 1985, 37–42; Van der Waal, 1990, 36–41). In this connection Schilder points out that all of "nature" becomes God's "work floor" for the laying of his "church floor."[9]

The covenant with Abraham occupies a central position. When God made it with him he first presented his promise: "I will establish my covenant between me and thee and thy seed after thee in their generations for an everlasting covenant, to be a God unto thee, and to thy seed after thee" (Gen. 17:7).

This is not the first promise of salvation. Genesis 3 already tells us that in his grace God reaches out to man who has sinned (cf. Belgic Confession of Faith, article 17) and that he promises him redemption, in Genesis 3:15, a passage of Scripture of which Bavinck says that it contains in substance the whole gospel, the entire covenant of grace (*R.D.*, 3:200). It is a promise that affects all of mankind.

The promise that all "families of the earth [will] be blessed" in or together with Abraham (Gen. 12:3) is essentially messianic in nature and is fulfilled by the coming of Christ, through whom both Jews and Gentiles are saved.[10] The promise to Abraham is subsequently repeated and is then accompanied by a sign. Genesis 15:18 says: "In the same day the LORD made a covenant with Abram."

In Genesis 17 the promise of salvation takes on the form of a covenant. In the promise that he desires to be a God to Abraham and his descendants after him, the Lord gives himself. The covenant continues

9. K. Schilder. *Wat is de hemel?* (what is heaven?)1954, 187f.

10. Cf. A. H. Edelkoort, *De Christusverwachting in het Oude Testament* (the anticipation of Christ in the Old Testament), 1941, 95f.; B. J. Oosterhoff, *De beloften aan de aardsvaders* (the promises to the patriarchs), 1973, 39.

through the generations: Isaac and Jacob receive the very same promise. The sign of circumcision goes with the covenant. All male persons belonging to the household of Abraham must be circumcised, even if they are slaves and of alien descent (Gen. 17:9–14).

3. *The Sinaitic covenant.* We can say with Bavinck that the covenant with the fathers is the foundation and core of the Sinaitic covenant (*R.D.*, 3:220). God's faithfulness toward the patriarchs is mentioned as the motive (Deut. 7:8). There is continuity so that also this covenant with Israel bears the character of a covenant of grace. This is sufficiently clear from the words of Exodus 20:2, although in this phase of the history of the covenant there is a great emphasis on the observance of God's commandments.

Sometimes the distinction between the covenant with Abraham and that with Israel at Sinai is almost turned into a contrast. Thus it is said that although the latter is indeed not a covenant of works, it is presented in a form that is strongly reminiscent of a covenant of works (Aalders, 1939, 179). We can object that the emphasis on what God demands from his people does not take us into the sphere of a covenant of works. In Deuteronomy the central idea is that the people will keep the covenant. Blessing and curse depend on this (Deut. 27–30), but it is the obligation to respond to God's love that carries the covenant (see Deut. 6:4–5; 7:6–8; 30:19–20). The law is the *torah*, which plays a role within the covenant. It provides the instruction that is required to make the people walk in the way of the covenant. The *torah* can be called the rule of the covenant. Just as Abraham is called to walk before God's face when the Lord allies himself with him (Gen. 17:1), so the law that is given to Israel serves the covenant as a further explanation of the statement: "Walk before me and be thou perfect" (cf. Bavinck, *R.D.*, 3:222).

4. *The new covenant.* In connection with the prophecies concerning a new covenant or an eternal covenant, which God is about to establish with his people (Jer. 31:31–34; 32:37–41; Ezek. 37:24–28), the question arises whether this is a covenant other than the covenant made with Israel or whether we must think in terms of a renewal of the covenant.

Some theologians contrast the Sinaitic covenant with the new covenant. The bond with the people of God in the covenant of Sinai is purely external and national; in the new covenant it is purely internal and spiritual. Today we deal with the new covenant. The members of the covenant are members of the invisible church, the living members of Christ (Aalders, 1939, 158f.). An important conclusion is that covenant and election are quantitatively identical. The number of covenant members is identical to the number of the elect. Incidentally, the covenant appears to include illegitimate members, to whom also God has said that he establishes his covenant with them to be their God, but who refuse to acknowledge him as their God. This can be interpreted as a breach of the covenant on their part (Aalders, 1939, 193, 222).

According to Reiling, the prophecy of the new covenant implies that the old covenant no longer exists. It has been breached by the people and there is nothing left to be restored or renewed. The old covenant and the new covenant constitute the same covenant only to the extent that God remains himself. As far as the covenant people are concerned, however, we must speak of two fundamentally different covenants.[11]

While Aalders, Reiling, and others emphasize the discontinuity of the covenant with Israel and the new covenant, others point to continuity. The distinction is not that the old covenant is only external and the new covenant internal. This would constitute an essential difference. It is disputed by L. H. Van der Meiden (1955, 35). The difference lies entirely in the area of the history of redemption (Wiskerke, 1955, 173).

Regarding the relationship between the old (Sinaitic) covenant and the new covenant (Jer. 31), we must keep in mind both the *similarities* and the *distinctions* between them.

a. *It is in essence one covenant of God with his people.* When the covenant first established with Abraham was subsequently ratified with Israel at Sinai, it retained the character of a covenant of *grace.* Jeremiah 31 implies in a surprisingly new manner that God commits himself to extend his grace and faithfulness toward people who do not at all deserve it (cf. in this regard Jer. 31:32). He renews his covenant with his people.

b. *The new covenant is none other than the old covenant.* The law that is to be written in the hearts is the same law that was given earlier. The all-encompassing promise (Jer. 31:33), "I . . . will be their God and they shall be my people," is the same promise of Moses' time ("I . . . will be your God, and ye shall be my people," Lev. 26:12). One may not infer from Jeremiah 31:33–34 that in earlier days the law was not yet written in the hearts or that there was then no forgiveness of sin and knowledge of the Lord. This "internalization"[12] was already promised in the books of Moses (Deut. 30:6). The law was indeed written in the hearts of the godly, and the saints of God stood in the right relationship to him.

c. *The manner in which God deals with his people has not changed in the new covenant.* He grants promises such as those expressed in Jeremiah 31:31–34 not just to those who have been chosen to eternal

11. J. Reiling, *Verbond, oud en nieuw*, 1976, 11f.
12. See E. Malatesta, *Interiority and Covenant*, 1978, 68–77.

life. Just as those in Genesis 17 and Exodus 19, they are promises that require a believing response.

d. *There is nevertheless a clear progression in the history of the covenant*, which is at the same time redemptive history. "Behold, the days come, saith the LORD, that I will make a new covenant" (Jer. 31:31). More blessings can be expected in the future. In essence, what was granted under the old covenant is given to a fuller and richer extent under the new covenant. Thus there is indeed a difference in degree (cf. Vander Meiden, 1955, 41).

e. *As far as the fulfillment of this prophecy is concerned*, some place it after the exile, because the context refers to people returning (Jer. 31:23–25) and because they would then naturally be preoccupied with the law (cf. Neh. 9:38–10:31). In our view the prophecies concerning the new covenant refer more to a new, enduring dispensation of the covenant. This new dispensation came when Christ completed his work as Mediator and when his Spirit was poured out (see Heb. 8:6–13; 2 Cor. 3:6). Believers from among the Jewish people and from the nations of the world are proof that God fulfils his promises (cf. Rom. 9:24–26; 2 Cor. 6:16–18). Thus the church of Christ represents the people of the new covenant.

34.2. *The New Testament*

1. *Covenant and promise*. Concerning the covenant (*diatheke*), the New Testament emphasizes what the Lord gives, demands, and does. Sometimes this Greek term denotes final will and testament (Gal. 3:15; Heb. 9:16–17), but elsewhere it points to the covenant of God with his people, whereby—as in the Old Testament—it is clear that the covenant and the covenantal relationship exist by virtue of his decree.

The New Testament says explicitly that in the covenant God comes to us with his promises. In Luke 1:72 the covenant is analogous to the oath he swore to Abraham and indicates the promise of salvation. The promise is an essential element of the covenant (see Acts 3:25; Rom. 9:4; Gal. 3:16; Eph. 2:12; Heb. 8:6). Galatians 4:24 refers to "two covenants," one of which is characterized by the promise and the other by the law. We hereby think of two distinct covenantal dispensations, that of the covenant with Abraham and that of Sinaitic covenant, the focus being on their actual functionality (cf. De Vuyst, 1964, 64).

2. *The new covenant.* There are various passages that apply to the new covenant (e.g., Luke 22:20; 1 Cor. 11:25; 2 Cor. 3:6; Heb. 8:6–13; 10:15–17).

Jesus' words at the institution of the Lord's Supper (Luke 22:20; 1 Cor. 11:25) are reminiscent of the establishment of the covenant at Sinai. He seals the new covenant with the sacrifice of his life. In Exodus 24:8 the blood of the covenant is the blood of the consecration of the Sinaitic covenant, while the gospel (see Matt. 26:28) speaks of the blood of the consecration of the new covenant. This is the new covenant of Jeremiah 31 (cf. De Vuyst, 1964, 59f.). There is no reference to blood here, but according to Jesus' words the power and certainty of this covenant rest on his sacrifice.

In 2 Corinthians 3:6 the old and new covenants are contrasted. The former is associated with the name of Moses (3:15). It is the covenant of the letter, which points to a certain aspect of the law of Moses, namely that the law kills when its letters remain mere letters and when the law is interpreted legalistically, as Paul's opponents did. The new covenant is characterized as the covenant of the Spirit. This does not preclude the Spirit from being at work already under the old dispensation. Since Pentecost, however, the Spirit dwells in the midst of the church. Through the work of Christ and his Spirit the new covenant surpasses the old covenant in glory. Reference is made to what is passing and what is permanent. Thus the contrast between the old and the new covenants is of a redemption-historical nature.

Hebrews speaks in a different manner about the new covenant. It is contrasted with the first covenant which, coupled with the Levitic priesthood, failed to bring perfection. It is a superior covenant, whose judicial validity rests on better promises (Heb. 8:6). This does not mean that these promises are different, but that they are more effective. The first covenant was not faultless, but it waxed old, for it gave way to the second covenant as foretold in Scripture (Heb. 8:7; 10:15–17). Just as the promises of the new covenant are better, so the calling of the new covenant is stronger and the associated responsibility greater (cf. De Vuyst, 1964, 239ff.).

3. *The people of the covenant.* The key question is how the people with whom God has ratified his covenant will conduct themselves before him? Will they remain faithful to the covenant and love him? (cf. Ex. 20:5–6; Deut. 7:9–10). The Old Testament shows us again

and again that a separation takes place among the people of the covenant. A line of demarcation is also visible within the New Testament dispensation. Paul speaks of this in Romans 9:6 with a focus on Israel. Christ faces everyone with a determination, as already announced in the prophecy of Simeon (Luke 2:34). "Many shall come from the east and west" to receive a place in God's kingdom and share in the salvation first promised to Abraham and his descendants, "but the children of the kingdom shall be cast out" (Matt. 8:11–12). But one can also belong to the kingdom in a deeper sense (Matt. 13:38). The expression "children of the kingdom" can thus be interpreted in two different ways. Jesus says to the Jews: "If God were your Father, ye would love me. . . . He that is of God heareth God's words: ye therefore hear them not, because ye are not of God" (John 8:42, 47). In the prologue to this gospel the enigma of unbelief and the miracle of faith already stand over against each other (John 1:10–13). God's words of warning addressed to Israel as the people of the covenant also apply to the Christian church (see Heb. 3:7–4:13).

In Hebrews, in which the word "covenant" occurs more often than in any other book of the New Testament, the focus is especially on Christ who is the Mediator and Surety of the new covenant and on his sacrifice. His blood is the blood of an eternal covenant (Heb.13:20. See in this connection further § 35.2).

According to the New Testament the new covenant dispensation has a *universal* character, in contradistinction to the old covenant. The covenant is no longer limited to one nation (see Acts 2:17, 39; Rom. 9:24–26; Eph. 2:12, 19). But there is no biblical basis for the notion, which we encounter in the theology of Barth, that the covenant was established with Jesus and therefore with all people (cf. § 33.4).

Thanks to the finished work of Christ and the richer work of his Spirit (John 14:12), the new covenant not only has more glory than the old one, but its scope is also broader.

§ 35. The place of Christ in the covenant of grace

35.1. ***The Old Testament***
35.2. ***The New Testament***
35.3. ***Is Christ the Head of the covenant?***

35.1. *The Old Testament*

There is a striking statement in the prophecies concerning the Servant of the Lord: "I the Lord have called thee in righteousness, and will hold thine hand, and will keep thee, and give thee for a covenant of the people, for a light of the Gentiles" (Isa. 42:6).

The expression "a covenant [for] the people" could mean the mediator of the covenant for the people.[13] "In him the covenant of God with his people finds its personification and guarantee." At the same time it is said of the Servant of the Lord that he will be a light to the Gentiles. His significance extends beyond Israel alone. The prophecy refers to the Messiah, who is the great Son of David, who will bring justice and salvation on earth.[14]

When we read Isaiah 53 in the light of the New Testament—which we are entitled to do by virtue of the unity of the revelation of salvation—we see that this prophecy about the Servant of the Lord is also important in this connection, even though the word "covenant" does not appear in it. When at the institution of the Lord's Supper Jesus speaks of "the blood of [his] covenant, which is shed for many for the remission of sins" (Matt. 26:28), he sees in the sacrifice that he brings the fulfillment of Isaiah 53:12. Of him, who is called the Mediator of the new covenant, it is said that he "was once offered to bear the sins of many" (Heb. 9:15, 28). We must therefore take into account what Isaiah 53 contributes to our understanding of the work of the Mediator of the covenant.

Noteworthy is the promise, meant first of all to comfort the people in exile: "I will make an everlasting covenant with you, even the sure mercies of David" (Isa. 55:3). There is a clear connection with 2 Samuel 7:12–16 and 23:5, the promise given to David in the form of a covenant that his dynasty will last forever. We can interpret Isaiah's prophecy in such a way that God will make a new beginning with the people and with the house of David and that he will manifest his grace and faithfulness in an everlasting covenant. The messianic interpretation merits preference over any other. We can link this with the fact that in Acts 13:34 there is a reference to a fulfillment of this promise in the resurrection of Christ.[15] Both the covenant with Abraham and the covenant with David, which falls within the framework of the covenant of grace, feed the expectation of the Messiah, who is the son of David and the son of Abraham (Matt. 1:1).[16]

In addition, two passages in Ezekiel may be mentioned: Ezekiel 34:21–30 and 37:24–28. These prophecies refer both to the coming of the Messiah, who is a royal figure, here called David, the Servant of the Lord who will be the shepherd of his people, and to the covenant of peace that God will establish with his people.

13. W. Zimmerli, *Grundriss* (outline) *der alttestamentischen Theologie*, 1975, 198.

14. See B. J. Oosterhoff, "Tot een licht der volken" (to a light of the nations), in *De knecht* (servant). *Studies rondom Deutero-Jesaja*, 1978, 161–72.

15. Cf. Aalders, 1939, 127–39; J. L. Koole, *Jesaja II*, 1990, 2:324–28; B. Loonstra, 1990, 102–5, 218 ff.

16. See also Jeremiah 30:21–22; cf. Loonstra, 1990, 204.

The messianic expectation and the anticipation of the covenant that brings peace and salvation will have to go hand in hand on the basis of these promises, although the nature of this connection is not described in detail.

35.2. *The New Testament*

The New Testament refers to Christ as "the mediator of the new covenant" (Heb. 9:15; 12:24) or "the mediator of a better covenant" (8:6) while he is also "the surety of a better testament" (7:22).

The Greek word for mediator denotes someone who mediates between two parties, e.g., in drawing up a contract. A mediator plays a role in the conclusion of a treaty, while he can also render useful services as arbitrator or peacemaker.

References to the Mediator of the covenant are reminiscent of Old Testament experience. The Old Testament mentions mediators who represented God to the people and the people to God (see § 30.1).

Christ is both Mediator and Guarantor (Surety) of the covenant. These are not identical functions, but the difference between the two is not great. A guarantor assumes legal obligations. His liability could exact a heavy price. It could even cost him his life (cf. *TDNT*, 2:329).

As *Mediator* of a new and better covenant, Christ obviates the need for the mediatorship of Moses and Aaron. The temporary nature of their mediatorship already foreshadowed that of Christ. The Mediator of the new covenant "offered himself without spot to God" and "appeared to put away sin by the sacrifice of himself" (Heb. 9:14, 26). Thus he opened for his people the way to God (Heb. 10:19–23).

As *Guarantor*, Christ guarantees the covenant and its realization. It is secure in him (cf. Bavinck, *R.D.*, 3:228). It is guaranteed by him (De Vuyst, 1964, 221). We recognize this notion in a number of ecclesiastical documents. In the Canons of Dort, 2.8, it says that "by the blood of the cross . . . he confirmed the new covenant," and in the Form for the Lord's Supper we read that he "confirmed with his death and shedding of his blood the new and eternal testament, the covenant of grace and reconciliation, when he said: 'It is finished.' "

The covenant is founded in Christ. As we saw, Calvin called Christ the foundation and fulfillment of the covenant (*fundamentum* and *complementum*). Biblically speaking, the latter can be understood in the sense that the covenant promises are fulfilled in and through him.

With regard to the former, the question may be asked whether this is also true of the Old Testament dispensation of the covenant. We hereby take into consideration that the various phases of the history of the covenant nevertheless refer to one and the same covenant. Christ's work of mediation is of fundamental significance for the covenant with Abraham, the covenant with Israel, and the covenant with us (cf. Loonstra, 1990, 294ff.).

35.3. *Is Christ the Head of the covenant?*

In the New Testament Christ is the Head of his church, while somewhere in our confessional statements he is also referred to as "the Mediator and Head of the elect" (Canons of Dort, 1.7).

Earlier theologians sometimes also called him the Head of the covenant, without alluding to any grounds for doing so. This was done much more consciously once it became common practice to speak of a covenant before the fall into sin, i.e., the covenant of works, of which Adam was the head, and following its breach a covenant of grace, of which Christ as the Second Adam is the Head. Several twentieth-century authors emphatically hold that Christ is the (representative) Head of the covenant of grace. This is not an isolated element of their doctrine of the covenant, but has theological and practical implications.

In this connection, Aalders, Polman, and others refer to Romans 5:12–21: "Here Holy Scripture reveals to us in a clear manner that the same position that Adam occupied in the *covenant of works*, is occupied by Christ in the *covenant of grace.*" The covenant of grace is made with Christ and in him with all those who are subsumed in him. "The number of covenant members is equal to the number of the elect" (Aalders, 1939, 175ff., 193).

Polman argues that covenant members do not constitute an aggregation of individuals but a body with Christ as its head. "Just as Adam in Paradise was the representative of all of us, so Christ is the representative head of all who are subsumed in him." Both in the Old and New Testaments Christ is the actual Head with and in whom God establishes this covenant of grace. However, he is not only the Head but also the Mediator of this covenant.[17] See also Honig, *Handboek*, 430.

The thesis that Christ is the Head of the covenant of grace is also vigorously defended by theologians of other church denominations. That he is the Mediator and Surety of this covenant is then usually made subordinate to his headship. "In Romans 5:12–19 Paul deals with two covenant heads" (Kersten, *G.D.*, 1:325).

If Christ is the Head of the covenant of grace, the obvious implication is that it was made with him from eternity. This is indeed how Kersten views it: the covenant of grace is the implementation of the covenant of redemption, which was established from eternity with the elect in Christ, their representative Head of the covenant (1:308).

17. A. D. R. Polman, *Woord en belijdenis* (word and confession), no date, 1:304ff.

According to this view, the covenant of grace *was* established with Christ from eternity and in him with the elect and *is* established in time with the elect when through regeneration and faith they are incorporated into the covenant. God establishes the covenant with Abraham and his spiritual descendants, the elect. The words of Acts 2:39, which indicate for whom the promise is meant, are combined with a specific condition: "As many as the Lord our God shall call." These are the elect. Those who give a different interpretation invalidate the doctrine of the covenant (1:323–28).

This line of reasoning, which Kersten develops in his dogmatic work, can be found already in the "six important statements" concerning the covenant of grace (cf. Moerkerken, no date, 47f.) issued by the Synod of the *Gereformeerde Gemeenten in Nederland* (1931).

The view of Aalders, Polman, and others, who thought that a covenantal doctrine of this type was "unassailable" (Aalders, 1939, 194), was shared by many in the *Gereformeerde Kerken* in the Netherlands for a period of time and left its mark on various important synodical documents (cf. van Genderen, 1983, 8–33).

Is it true that Christ is the Head of the covenant of grace as Adam was the head of the first covenant? Is this the unanimous confession of all those who think along Reformed lines, as Aalders writes?

It is already significant that this notion is nowhere stated in Scripture or in our confessional statements. But what about Romans 5? According to Romans 5:12–21, there is an antithetical parallel between Christ and Adam. It is by no means a perfect parallel (cf. § 27.1).

We must be careful with conclusions drawn from this Scripture passage for the very reason that the term "covenant" is not mentioned. As the Head of all those who belong to him, Christ stands over against Adam and all those who belong to the latter. He is the Head of the new humanity as Adam is the head of the old humanity. He is the Head of the new humanity, because those who belong to him are chosen in him and have been given to him by the Father (Eph. 1:4; John 17:6). This is also how the church confesses it in the Canons of Dort (1.7).

The discussion of this topic brings up the relationship between the covenant and election. We therefore point out that *election and the covenant must be distinguished from each other in more than one respect.*

1. God elects those who are his before the foundation of the world, but he establishes the covenant in time and allows it to run its course through history;

2. Election is God's gracious decision concerning lost people, and the covenant of grace is the blessed relationship that God seeks with believers and their children;
3. The covenant and election are not quantitatively identical. Not all children of the covenant share in the communion with God to which he elects his people.

Based on the above considerations, we conclude that the covenant of redemption and the covenant of grace cannot be identified with each other.

1. In contrast with the covenant of redemption (cf. § 15.2), the parties in the covenant of grace are very unequal: God and sinful man.
2. The covenant of redemption requires of Christ that he bear the punishment and fulfil the law of God for his people. But the covenant of grace requires from us faith and repentance, which Christ does not achieve in our stead (see further van Genderen, 1983, 52–56).

The notion that Christ is the Head of the covenant of grace, and that in essence it only has significance for those who are subsumed in him, has implications. Apart from this there may still be an external manifestation or administration of the covenant, but the promises of the covenant and the seals of the covenant or sacraments, which confirm the promises, are in reality intended for the elect only.

This view brings with it that the full reality of the covenant, the validity of the covenant promises and the authenticity of the sacraments, cannot be maintained for the entire church. It is not surprising that this view encountered major objections and resulted in a good deal of conflict (cf. Kamphuis, 1984, 6f.).

To those who cannot accept that the covenant was made only with the elect, represented by Christ as their Head, it is sometimes pointed out that they do not sufficiently take into consideration the statement of Paul that appears to imply a christological qualification of the children of the covenant: "And to thy seed, which is Christ . . . were the promises made" (Gal. 3:16). One might gain the impression that the words God spoke to Abraham (Gen. 17:7) point only to Christ and believers, according to Paul.

However, the apostle here is not reducing the circle of the children of the covenant for the sake of election. It is not a reduction but a concentration. Paul always starts out from the reality of the promises that God made to Abraham and to all Israel. But Christ is the true seed of Abraham and the real heir to the promises. If these promises are to stand and be fulfilled, then Christ must come, in and through whom God will fulfill his promises of salvation.[18] This notion is not far removed from what the apostle says in another epistle: "For all the promises of God in him are yea, and in him Amen, unto the glory of God by us" (2 Cor. 1:20).

The name of Christ is mentioned in Galatians 3:16 not in order to limit the covenant promises to the elect. This verse does say that only through faith in Christ—and according to the context, not through the works of the law—we share in what God promises us in his covenant. This applies to everyone, no matter who he or she is. "If ye be Christ's, then are ye Abraham's seed, and heirs according to the promise" (Gal. 3:29).

§ 36. The covenant relationship

36.1. ***God's decree lies at the bottom of the covenant relationship***
36.2. ***Promise and demand***
36.3. ***God and his people***

36.1. *God's decree lies at the bottom of the covenant relationship*

The covenant exists because God ordained it so and not because we human beings asked for it.

The establishment of the covenant does not involve any negotiations as in a treaty or covenant that people ratify with each other. *God and man are not partners.* It is for this reason that we object to various modern views of the covenant.

The covenant would be a relationship between God and man if the one would continually allow himself to be influenced by the other's attitude and behavior. God's nature would be such that he would have ordained to need us.[19] If God's nature consists in being a covenant partner and his relationship with man is an integral part of his nature,[20] this not only implies that man is inconceivable without God but also that God is inconceivable without man. Thus one sometimes arrives at a new concept of God: God is then "a rational God who chaperones people in love and faithfulness, and who is also present in creation."[21]

There is a clear tendency to emphasize the reciprocity of the covenant relationship with or without the help of the concept of partnership. However, in the Bible

18. Cf. S. Greijdanus, *De brief van den apostel Paulus aan de Gemeenten in Galatie*, 1936, 224.

19. See Berkhof, *C.F.*, 255; E. Flesseman-van Leer, "Over de tweezijdigheid van het verbond" (concerning the bilateral nature of the covenant), in *Weerwoord* (reply), 1974, 36.

20. See H. M. Kuitert, *De mensvormigheid Gods* (the human form of God), 1962, 228, 265.

21. See C. M. Halkes, "Verbond met heel de aarde en elkaar . . ." (covenant with the entire earth and each other), in *Sleutelen aan het verbond* (fiddling with the covenant), 1989, 162.

the sovereignty of God's grace is primary. This is precisely what is expressed in the Reformed doctrine of the covenant, without at the same time detracting from man's responsibility.

We hereby take into account that God's covenant with his people is unilateral (*monopleuric*) in origin and bilateral (*dupleuric*) in practice. It is intended to be consciously and voluntarily accepted and kept by man in the power of God (cf. Bavinck, *R.D.*, 3:230).

From the moment that we are taken into God's covenant, there is a relationship between him and us. How can this covenant relationship be described?

At the establishment of the covenant with Abraham, God says: "I will . . . be a God unto thee, and to thy seed after thee" (Gen. 17:7). To Israel he says: "I will walk among you, and will be your God, and ye shall be my people" (Lev. 26:12). He says the same in the New Testament (see 2 Cor. 6:16; Heb. 8:10). With these words God commits himself to his people and at the same time he binds his people to himself.

In this relationship God's promise is of primary significance. His earlier promises of salvation are reiterated to Abraham, Israel, and the church in the form of a covenant.

The parties are indeed absolutely unequal: God and man. God is God and man is a sinner. The people with whom God establishes his covenant are always a people that consist of sinners. At the renewal of the covenant in Shechem, Joshua has to say to the people of Israel: "Ye cannot serve the Lord: for he is an holy God; he is a jealous God; he will not forgive your transgressions nor your sins" (Josh. 24:19). At the ceremony for the establishment of the covenant described in Exodus 24, Moses takes blood from sacrificial animals to sprinkle it on the altar and the people with the words: "Behold the blood of the covenant which the Lord hath made with you " (Ex. 24:8). Heb. 9:18–20 says of this that the covenant was not "dedicated without blood." Christ is the Mediator of the new covenant and his blood is "the blood of sprinkling that speaketh better things than that of Abel" (Heb. 12:24). Jesus himself speaks of "the new testament in [his] blood" (Luke 22:20). What is true of the new covenant or the new dispensation of the covenant applies also to the covenant in its Old Testament form, for the new covenant is essentially the same covenant (see § 34.1–2).

In each dispensation, the essence of the covenant that God makes with sinners implies that it is a covenant of grace with Christ as Mediator who binds us to God. As we saw earlier (§ 35.1), the Old Testament already contains elements that point to his work of mediation. Christ's mediatorship and the blood of the atonement are essential aspects of the covenant. In Christ God is with us, but apart from him this is impossible.

The covenant of grace can be described as God's relationship with believers and their children, established by him by grace, and whereby he binds himself to them to be their God and binds them to himself to be his people through Jesus Christ, the Mediator of the covenant. The covenant relationship is therefore a blissful relationship.

36.2. *Promise and demand*

The above description implies that God's promise comes first and yet is not the only element of the covenant. His promise is coupled with his demand, for he not only says that he is our God, but also that we are his people. His promise binds us. He gives himself to us and he desires that we give ourselves to him. The classic Form for Baptism brings this out clearly: when following the explanation of the content of the promise of the covenant as promise of the triune God, we read that we are "admonished and obliged unto new obedience, namely, that we cleave to this one God, Father, Son, and Holy Spirit; that we trust in him, and love him."

In the promise of the covenant of grace, salvation is not only described to us, but is also offered and given to us, so that we have a right to it. It is ours for Christ's sake, i.e., by grace and by right. "We have [it] in Christ" (Form for Baptism).

The promise of the Lord, our God, calls for faith that responds with "Amen" (2 Cor. 1:20). No one can come up with faith as though it were his own contribution to the right relationship with God. But the faith that God demands is also promised to us by him (cf. Heidelberg Catechism, Lord's Day 27) and is worked and confirmed by him (Lord's Day 25). In the covenant of grace God promises what he demands and demands what he promises. His promise and his demand extend equally far. In the covenant of grace there is no balance between promise and demand, but a preponderance of promise. "On the basis of this promise we may expect from the Lord that he will also provide what he demands. Within the covenant God obtains victory upon victory over people's unfaithfulness" (van Genderen, 1983, 62).

The demand of the covenant of grace is preceded and followed, supported and surrounded by the promise. Within this covenant all is grace, including the demand of faith and repentance.

The words "promise" and "demand" do not tell the whole story about God's dealings with his people within the framework of the covenant. In addition to promises and commands there are also threats. Numerous places in the Old Testament speak emphatically about punishment for unfaithfulness and disobedience. The covenant brings both "blessings" and "curses" (see Deut. 28–29). Sometimes reference is made to divine vengeance in the context of the covenant relationship. At the end of the "holiness code," Israel is summoned once more to take the covenant seriously. If Israel breaks the covenant by not listening to God, he will turn his face against the people and discipline them. If they despise his statutes he will despise Israel (Lev. 26:14–18, 30). There is a "sword . . . that shall avenge the quarrel of [his] covenant" (v. 25). This covenant vengeance represents both punishment and a means of discipline that serves to bring the people to "confess" their iniquity and unfaithfulness. Then the LORD will "remember" his covenant with Abraham, Isaac, and Jacob. He will not break the covenant, for he is "the LORD their God" (vv. 40–45).

Under the new dispensation, the responsibility involved in belonging to God's covenant and to his church is even greater than under the old dispensation. This is especially obvious from Hebrews 10:29–31 and 12:25–29. These warnings imply that "on the part of the addressees there is a danger that those who have been sanctified by this blood of the covenant will despise it, so that they break the new covenant from their side and incur God's covenant vengeance" (De Vuyst, 1964, 238).

A covenant implies obligations. Hardly anyone will object to terms such as obligation and covenant obligation, which are also found in earlier theology, but there are some authors who consider the term "conditions" to be troublesome. To prevent the misunderstanding that first certain conditions must be met, some rather do not use this term to be on the safe side. According to others, the covenant with Israel indeed had conditions attached to it, but the promise of salvation of the new covenant is unconditional.

With Bullinger, Calvin, and others we need to be aware of the conditional form of speech that God employs vis-à-vis his people. This strikes us not only in the Old Testament but also in the New Testament. There are plenty of examples (see Rom. 11:22; 2 Tim. 2:12–13; Heb. 3:6; 4:7; Rev. 2:5; 3:20). These are not conditions to be met in order to enter the covenant, but the conditional form of speech that the Lord as the God of the covenant has adopted make it very clear what he expects from his people.

The foregoing implies that we should not view the promise of the covenant as an "unconditional promise of salvation to the elect" (cf. § 33.4).

The juxtaposition of promise and demand indicates that the promise is not *a prediction but a pledge*. Schilder applies this specifically to baptism when he says that here God promises everything but predicts nothing (Schilder, 1946, 60).

The promise must be matched with appropriation. Other terms can be used to describe this, such as granting (receiving) and imparting (partaking), which are derived from our confession (Lord's Day 25 and 20). This means that participation in the promised salvation cannot be ascertained or even presumed when the promise is received.

In the New Testament the promise sometimes denotes the promised salvation (cf. Ridderbos, no date, 8), but there are also numerous places in the Old Testament and a few in the New Testament that imply an unequivocal distinction. Hebrews 3:7–4:13 suggests that, despite the promise of God's rest, it is possible to be left behind. Those who received the gospel first did not enter, due to their disobedience. They could not enter because of their unbelief. We must be serious about entering the rest that God gives and not following the example of disobedience. It is a matter of obtaining what has been promised (Heb. 10:36).

Here we run into important points of difference. For many years the Formula of 1905 was in force in the *Gereformeerde Kerken in Nederland*, which says that the children of the covenant by virtue of God's promise are to be presumed to be born again and sanctified in Christ, until in growing up the opposite becomes apparent from their walk or doctrine. In 1946 the *Replacement Formula* was adopted, which had binding authority until 1959: building on God's promise and in harmony with the teaching of Scripture, the church must view and treat children as those who share in the regenerating grace of the Holy Spirit, unless they manifest themselves to be unbelievers. A footnote was added, indicating that this formula implies presumed regeneration or at any rate presumed election.[22]

We see in this an overstraining of the covenant relationship (cf. Kremer, 1955, 13). The danger of false security is then not imaginary.

It is noteworthy that those who in the doctrine of the covenant proceed from the perspective of election, and the unconditional promise of salvation to the elect, can arrive at an entirely different view of the church, whereby the promise, which belongs to the essence of the covenant, has limited significance because it is only of importance to the elect portion of the church. This is the official view of the *Gereformeerde Gemeenten*, as is apparent from the doctrinal pronouncements of 1931, with the result that God's promises cannot be a pleading ground for the entire church, for believers and for their children.

22. *Acta*, 1905, article 158; *Acta buitengewone* (extraordinary) *Generale Synode*, 1946, article 197.

36.3. *God and his people*

Since the covenant of grace is essentially the same covenant in all dispensations, we may begin with clear scriptural data from the Old Testament to address the question as to with whom the Lord established his covenant.

Genesis 17 as well as the subsequent history of the covenant imply that the covenant endures throughout the generations. God is the God of believers and their children. In Genesis 17 he is the God of Abraham and his entire household.

Abraham's era is followed by that of the Sinaitic covenant. God had said, "But my covenant will I establish with Isaac" (Gen. 17:21), which does not mean that Ishmael stood outside the covenant, but rather that the covenant line would run through Isaac and his descendants.

For centuries Israel enjoyed this privilege while other nations had to forego God's covenant revelations. With this in mind it is impossible to maintain that the covenant is a covenant with all people, because it is established with Jesus Christ. This view of Barth (see § 33.4) is in conflict with Scripture. Those who speak of the universality of the new dispensation in seeking to distinguish it from the old dispensation should not go so far as to teach covenant universalism. The covenant has boundaries.

The question as to with whom God has established his covenant must not be answered differently for the new dispensation than for the old dispensation. It is not established with all people, but neither is it established only with the elect. *It is established with believers and their children.*

For Scripture proof, we refer in the first place to the words of Peter: "For the promise is unto you, and to your children, and to all that are afar off, even as many as the Lord our God shall call" (Acts 2:39). In these words the covenant promise of Genesis 17 resurfaces, but with an extension, in keeping with the inauguration of the new dispensation. They are after all words spoken after the outpouring of the Holy Spirit. Those who are still afar off will come within the reach of the covenant. This does not mean to say that Israel will now fall beyond this reach, or that there are no promises left for the ancient people of God. After Pentecost it is also said: "Unto you first God, having raised up his Son Jesus, sent him to bless you, in turning away every one of you from his iniquities" (Acts 3:26).

In the Old Testament, Israel, as the people of God, is called a holy nation, a holy people (Ex. 19:5–6; Deut. 14:1–2). The New Testament refers to the church, comprising believers and their children, as being holy. A passage of Scripture that is of direct relevance is 1 Corinthians 7:14.

As a nation Israel is holy by virtue of God's sanctifying action. This word denotes their relationship with him. With several earlier Reformed theologians we can speak of covenant holiness.

In 1 Corinthians 7:14 "holy" has the same meaning when children are called holy because the parents are believers or, in the case at hand, because one of them is. With Calvin (*Institutes*, 4.16.6), we must keep in mind that they are heirs of the covenant. In his commentary on this verse he refers to his explanation of Romans 11, where he says that the holiness of the Jews resulted from the covenant (Rom. 11:16).

Israel was a holy nation, but it frequently failed to live up to what God could justly expect from it. The Old Testament repeatedly speaks of a breaking of the covenant.

Among the Scripture passages that could be mentioned in this connection is Jeremiah 3. There Israel is called "backsliding Israel," because it has fallen away from the Lord, and Judah is called "her treacherous sister Judah," because it has been unfaithful to the Lord and has broken the covenant with him. The people, however, are called to repentance: "Turn, O backsliding children, saith the LORD; for I am married unto you" (Jer. 3:14). This focuses on the establishment of the covenant and the covenant relationship. The people are God's people, God's possession.[23]

From what the Old Testament—but also the New Testament—says about the people of God, we infer that there are faithful, but also unfaithful children of the covenant. There are those who receive the promise with a believing heart, but there are also those who do not. Paul says, "They are not all Israel, which are of Israel" (Rom. 9:6). There are branches on the vine that do not bear fruit and are removed (John 15:6). In his commentary on Romans 9:6 Calvin points out that the promise of salvation, given to Abraham, extends to all of his descendants, because it is offered to all without exception. They are heirs to the covenant and children of the promise. At the same time it is true that those in whom the power and the effect of the promise manifest themselves are called children of the promise in the true sense. The distinction that exists does not affect the offer of the promise but its fulfillment. Many reject their adoption with ingratitude. Therefore

23. Cf. B. J. Oosterhoff, *Jeremia*, 1990, 1:141–52.

we must first of all point to the personal responsibility and personal guilt of those who have been accepted into the covenant with God. But we must recognize God's grace in embracing the promise. This means that the "hidden grace" of predestination is limited to a portion of the people.[24]

With Kremer (1955, 19), we can identify various dimensions of the covenant community. To indicate the distinction involved here, terms such as *promissory bond* and *vital communion* have been employed. This is not a doctrine of a twofold covenant, but a distinction between what the covenant as such is and what is accomplished within the covenant. Being within the covenant is not identical to being born again. The essence of the covenant is not communion of life but the relationship of promise. The goal is communion of life: the real, personal, spiritual, active relationship of life between God and believers through Christ, the Mediator of the covenant worked by the Holy Spirit (cf. Ten Hoor, *Comp.*, 178–80, 186f.).

The covenant relationship is not yet what it should be, if this communion of life is absent. The covenant relationship includes the bond and obedience of faith. For believers the covenant of grace entails that God has admitted them into his communion by grace and that for Christ's sake he will always let them share in his favor.

God's promise, which accompanies believers throughout history and which is repeatedly stated in the Old Testament and the New Testament, "I . . . will be your God and ye shall be my people" (Lev. 26:12; Jer. 31:33; Heb. 8:10), has an infinite reach. Revelation 21:3 says after all: "Behold, the tabernacle of God is with men, and he will dwell with them, and they shall be his people, and God himself shall be with them, and be their God." This is followed by: "He that overcometh shall inherit all things; and I will be his God, and he shall be my son" (Rev. 21:7).

In the light of perfect communion with God, of which the book of Revelation speaks with these words and with the help of an abundance of images, we see what God's purpose is in making us his people in the covenant. He seeks a holy people in the deepest sense of the word, a people that belong entirely to him.

24. See also Calvin's commentary on Genesis 17:7, where he makes a distinction between children and children (*duplex filiorum ordo in ecclesia* = a twofold class of sons presents itself to us, in the church), *C.O.*, 23, 238.

The richness that is given in the covenant, in which all is grace, causes us to laud and praise the Lord, our God, following the lead of the authors of the Psalms, which are songs of the covenant:[25]

> But the mercy of the LORD is from everlasting to everlasting
> upon them that fear him,
> and his righteousness unto children's children;
> To such as keep his covenant,
> and to those that remember his commandments to do them.
> (Ps. 103:17–18)

The word "mercy" is a translation of *chesed.* This word indicates how good the Lord is to his people. It is his "*huldvolle Zuwendung*" (respectful, loving care, *TWAT*, 3:69). Precisely to the people of the covenant he shows how great his *chesed* is. This word is frequently interpreted as covenant faithfulness (cf. *TDNT*, 2:479–87; 9:376–87), but this interpretation is increasingly being abandoned.[26]

Moses says to the people: "The LORD, thy God, he is God, the faithful God, which keepeth covenant and mercy with them that love him and keep his commandments to a thousand generations" (Deut. 7:9). See also 1 Kings 8:23; Nehemiah 1:5; Daniel 9:4.

When God shows his mercy, he grants his salvation (Ps. 85:7). The poet of Psalm 25 asks that his God, in whom he trusts, will remember him in his "tender mercies" and his "lovingkindness," and remember him according to his "mercy" (Ps. 25:6–7). This is the psalm that says: "The secret of the LORD is with them that fear him; and he will shew them his covenant" (Ps. 25:14). Psalm 138:2 says: "I will . . . praise thy name for thy lovingkindness and for thy truth; for thou hast magnified thy word above all thy name." Psalm 136 is in its entirety a song of praise to God's mercy.

In this way the God of the covenant receives the love and adoration of his people: "O love the LORD, all ye his saints" (Ps. 31:23).

These songs of praise reach a climax when the promised Savior arrives. In Luke 1 the Greek equivalent of *chesed* is *eleos*, which is usually rendered "mercy." "And holy is his name. And his mercy is

25. Cf. A. Janse, *De heerlijkheid der Psalmen als liederen des verbonds* (the glory of the Psalms as songs of the covenant), no date, 9–16.

26. Cf. on the one hand N. Glueck, *Das Wort hesed*, 1972; W. Baumgartner, *Lexicon in Veteris Testamenti Libros*, 1953, 318; on the other hand *THAT*, 1:600–621; S. Romerowski, "Que signifie le mot *HESED*?" *Vetus Testamentum* 60 (1990): 89–103.

on them that fear him from generation to generation" (Luke 1:49–50; cf. Luke 1:54–55, 72–73).

§ 37. The significance of the covenant of grace

37.1. *The covenant and the church*

In the covenant of grace everything proceeds from the Lord. It is grace to belong to the covenant, and grace to share in the blessings and benefits of the covenant. The covenant with God also means that the covenantal relationship brings with it great responsibilities for us.

The covenant of grace has its own place in dogmatics, but at the same time has implications for other components. Wentsel calls it a key concept that needs to be taken into account in every aspect of doctrine (*Dogm.*, 3a:220–23, 251). At least four types of relationships can be identified.

The covenant and the church are related if only because Christ, the Mediator of the covenant, is also the Head of his church.

As we shall see later (§ 44), the church constitutes the people of God, the people that belong to God. This notion fits well within the framework of the doctrine of the covenant, but also plays an important role in the doctrine of the church. In the old dispensation Israel is both the people of the covenant and the church of the covenant. It shall be "a kingdom of priests, and an holy nation" for the Lord. The basis for this is the covenant, which he made with the people and which the people are to keep (Ex. 19:5–6). In a similar way the church of the New Testament is founded on the covenant together with its promises and demands (see 1 Peter 2:9–10).

The Heidelberg Catechism mentions the covenant and the church in one breath (Lord's Day 27). Here the church is the church of the covenant to which believers and their children belong. But the church and the covenant do not coincide. Of the church it is true that Christ gathers it by his Spirit and his Word (Lord's Day 21). Not all children of the covenant, however, let themselves to be gathered together into the unity of the true faith to be one community of faith in the sense in which the confession speaks of it (Belgic Confession of Faith, article 27).

As far as the church is concerned, just as in the case of the covenant, we may not start out from man. The God of the covenant assigns us a place in the church that we may not abandon when we feel drawn somewhere else.

Behind each reformation of the church there stands the faithfulness of God who remembers his covenant. As was the case with the reformation in the days of Josiah (2 Chron. 34:29–33), every true reformation involves a return to the covenant. He who is the Faithful One does not only require his people to be faithful to him, but also causes them to live faithfully by the promises and demands of his covenant.

37.2. *The covenant and the sacraments*

Baptism and the Lord's Supper clarify and seal the promises of the gospel to us. These promises include all of the promises of the covenant.

Circumcision, which was at one time the sign and seal of the covenant, has found its fulfillment in baptism, which signifies "the circumcision of Christ" (Col. 2:11–12). See also Belgic Confession of Faith, article 34.

If we were not convinced that the covenant promise is for believers as well as their children we would have to question the legitimacy of infant baptism. But the promise is also for the children of the church and therefore they not only "may" be baptized but "ought to" be baptized (Form for the Baptism of Infants).

Those who reject infant baptism demonstrate that they have no eye for the structure of the covenant of grace. Opponents of infant baptism usually ignore, in an individualistic manner, the historical administration of the covenant in the line of successive generations, while stressing from their side the necessity of personal faith.

The unity of the old and new covenants is here also at stake. Through the centuries the covenant of grace constitutes one single covenant, and God's grace has even increased in the new dispensation. Otherwise God's grace would be more obscure and less attested to us than earlier for Israel. One cannot say this without grievously slandering Christ (cf. Calvin, *Institutes*, 4.16.6).

The Lord's Supper, which is the table of the Lord (1 Cor. 10:21), is also called the table of the covenant. It is the meal of the covenant, which is rooted in Christ's sacrifice for the forgiveness of our sins (see Matt. 26:28).

While baptism makes clear that all salvation derives from God's covenant—we *are* baptized, even if we are not infants but adults—in the Lord's Supper we see something of the two-sidedness of the communion of the covenant, which is the Lord's objective in his covenant with us. This is why W. Teellinck and others speak of the renewal of the covenant in the celebration of the Lord's Supper (cf. van Genderen, 1983, 65ff.).

37.3. *The covenant of grace and preaching*

The words of God's covenant must be proclaimed to the church because it is the church of the covenant. In keeping with the character of the covenant as covenant of grace, the promise must be emphasized.

Preaching, which is "the ministry of reconciliation" (2 Cor. 5:18), is also the ministry of the covenant. The call by means of the Word is an essential element in the ministry of the covenant (cf. Heppe, *Dogm.*, 298).

With Trimp one can say that preaching is the central event in God's covenant relationship with us.[27] The main thing is that we are addressed by the Word. Man—as he is, or as he must be, or can become—is not to be the focus of attention. What is of prime importance is who the Lord our God is, what he does, what he grants, and what he asks. Our God desires that we live by his grace and to his honor.

In our view of the covenant, God's promises must be proclaimed to the entire church and not only to a segment of it. Preaching must appeal to the entire church. If the promises of the covenant were there to provide a perspective on things pertaining to the future, we would have to anticipate their fulfillment. Since they are promises of God, they must be received and appropriated in faith.

Preaching the promises is preaching Christ, the Mediator and Surety of the covenant. The proclamation of salvation in Christ must and will find resonance within his church. This proclamation of the promise and the gospel comes to everyone with the command to "repent and believe" (The Canons of Dort, 2.5).

In the church of the covenant we must take into account that not all children of the covenant share in the promised salvation. There are those who do not genuinely repent. The biblical covenant doctrine

27. C. Trimp, *Klank en weerklank* (sound and echo), 1989, 52.

does not lead to an idealistic view of the church! A separation takes place within the people of the covenant, which comes to light in the responses to the call of the gospel of Christ. Preaching must therefore also have a discriminating element.[28]

37.4. *The covenant of grace and the life of faith*

In the covenant the Lord comes first and remains first. *Life of Grace and Covenant of Grace* is the title of a book (Moerkerken, no date). In principle, *Covenant of Grace and Life of Grace* would be a more correct sequence of these words. A life of grace is a life out of God's promises, a life of faith resting on promises, as Brakel called it (*R.S.*, 2:601–38).

God's promises precede our faith and constitute its foundation. The promises focus on faith and faith focuses on the promises. Calvin says that the life of grace begins with the promise, rests on it, and ends in it (*Institutes*, 3.2.29). We must believe what God promises us in the gospel. We have in mind the well-known formulation in Lord's Day 7 of the Heidelberg Catechism (Q&A 22). From the subsequent statement, that the articles of our Christian faith teach us this by way of summary, it is clear that here are not only meant the explicit promises of the gospel, but everything that God wants to give us according to the gospel.

Of ordinary human promises we can say that they are no longer of direct importance to us once they have been fulfilled. With God's promises this is entirely different. He says repeatedly in his Word: this is for you. On the basis of this the believer can say with firm confidence: this salvation is not only given to others, but also to me out of pure grace and only for Christ's sake (cf. Heidelberg Catechism, Lord's Day 7).

We may forever hold fast to the promises of God's covenant, which in Jesus Christ are yea. Only when through him—and this means also through the work of the Holy Spirit—we continually say Amen to this (cf. 2 Cor. 1:20), is there continuity in our life of faith.

Some Literature

G. Ch. Aalders, *Het verbond Gods* (God's covenant), 1939.

W. J. van Asselt, *Amicitia Dei*, 1988.

28. See W. Kremer, *Priesterlijke prediking* (priestly preaching), 1976, 61–68; W. H. Velema, "De toeeigening van het heil in de prediking" (the appropriation of salvation in preaching), in W. H. Velema (ed.), *Delen in het heil* (sharing in salvation), 1989, 57–64.

J. W. Baker, *Heinrich Bullinger and the Covenant*, 1980.

O. Bayer, *Promissio*, 1971.

H. Bullinger, I. *Het eenige en eeuwige testament of verbond Gods*; II. *Het oude geloof* (the only and eternal testament or God's covenant; the ancient faith), Dutch translation by H. A. J. Lütge and G. Oorthuys, 1923.

J. Cocceius, *De leer van het verbond en het testament van God* (the doctrine of the covenant and God's testament), tr. W. J. van Asselt and H. G. Renger), 1990.

L. Doekes, *Der Heilige* (the holy one), 1960.

J. Francke, *Lichtende verbintenissen* (enlightening connections), 1985.

J. van Genderen, *Verbond en verkiezing* (covenant and election), 1983.

C. Graafland, *Het vaste verbond* (the certain covenant), 1978.

C. Harinck, *De Schotse verbondsleer* (the Scottish doctrine of the covenant), 1986.

W. D. Jonker, *Uit vrye guns alleen* (out of free grace only), 1989.

J. Kamphuis, Een eeuwig verbond (an eternal covenant), 1984.

B. Klappert, *Promissio und bund* (promise and covenant), 1976.

W. Kremer, *Enkele opmerkingen over het spreken Gods in de openbaring onder het Nieuwe Testament, bepalend voor de positie der bondelingen in het verbond der genade* (a few remarks about God's speaking in the revelation of the New Testament, applicable to the position of participants in the covenant of grace), 1955.

E. Kutsch, *Verheissung und Gesetz* (promise and law), 1973.

B. Loonstra, *Verkiezing-verzoening-verbond* (election-atonement-covenant), 1990.

D. J. McCarthy, *Treaty and Covenant*, 1981.

T. E. McComiskey, *The Covenants of Promise* (repr.), 1988.

L. H. van der Meiden, *Het nieuwe verbond* (the new covenant), 1955.

A. Moerkerken, *Genadeleven en genadeverbond* (living by grace and covenant of grace), no date.

L. Perlitt, *Bundestheologie im Alten Testament* (theology of the covenant in the Old Testament), 1969.

H. N. Ridderbos, *De belofte van het genadeverbond* (the promise of the covenant of grace), no date.

J. von Rohr, *The Covenant of Grace in Puritan Thought*, 1986.

Rondom de doopvont (around the baptismal font), ed. W. van 't Spijker et al., 1983.

K. Schilder, *Looze kalk* (empty chalk), 1946.

G. Schrenk, *Gottesreich und Bund im älteren Protestantismus vornehmlich bei Johannes Coccejus* (God's kingdom and covenant in early Protestantism, especially according to Johannes Cocceius), 1923.

J. J. van der Schuit, *Het verbond der verlossing* (the covenant of redemption), 1982[2].

E. Smilde, *Een eeuw van strijd over verbond en doop* (a century of strife concerning covenant and baptism), 1946.

S. A. Strauss, *"Alles of niks"—K. Schilder oor die verbond* (all or nothing—K. Schilder on the covenant), 1982.

S. Strehle, *Calvinism, Federalism and Scholasticism*, 1988.

E. G. van Teylingen, *Aard en achtergrond van het geschil in de Gereformeerde kerken* (nature and background of differences within the reformed churches), no date.

Vast en zeker! (definite and sure!), 1974.

W. H. van der Vegt, *Het verbond der genade* (the covenant of grace), no date.

G. Vos, *De verbondsleer in de Gereformeerde theologie* (the doctrine of the covenant in Reformed theology), 1939.

J. de Vuyst, *"Oud en nieuw verbond" in de brief aan de Hebreeen* (old and new covenant in the epistle to the Hebrews), 1964.

C. van der Waal, *Het verbondsmatig evangelie* (the gospel based on the covenant), 1990.

D. A. Weir, *The Origins of the Federal Theology in Sixteenth-Century Reformation Thought*, 1990.

J. R. Wiskerke, *Volk van Gods keuze* (people of God's choice), 1955.

H. Witsius, *Vier boecken van de verscheyden bedeelinge der verbonden Gods met de menschen* (four books on the various dispensations of God's covenants with people, *De oeconomia foederum Dei cum hominibus libri quatuor*, 1694), tr. M. van Harlingen, 1696.

J. G. Woelderink, *Het doopsformulier* (the form for baptism), 1938.

J. G. Woelderink, *Verbond en bevinding* (covenant and experience), 1974.

H. H. Wolf, *Die Einheit des Bundes* (the unity of the covenants), 1958.

Chapter 12

The Doctrine of Salvation

§ 38. Concerning the Term *Order of Salvation*

1. *The content of this chapter has a fixed place in dogmatics.* There is no dogmatic reference book in which concepts such as calling and regeneration, faith and conversion, justification and sanctification are not at least mentioned.

There are, however, differences in the sequence in which these notions are discussed. There are also authors who include additional concepts. Another difference is the name under which all of these concepts are brought together.

We mention a few terms that can be encountered in the literature. Bavinck has an extensive section on the "Order of salvation" (*R.D.*, 3:485–597). Honig chooses as the title for his chapter *Locus de Salute*: "The benefits of the Covenant" (*Handboek*, 14). "The order of salvation" appears as the third introductory section (534–36).

Berkouwer wrote in his first dogmatic study a chapter on "The way of salvation" (1954, 25–36), which is the name he gives to this topic. Hoekema, 1989, 15, follows in his footsteps. He adds that various aspects of this wonderful work of God's grace can be distinguished.

H. Berkhof treats this material under the title "The renewal of man" (*C.F.*, 427–501). On page 467 (i.e., not exactly at the start of his book) he devotes "a few words" to the concept of "*ordo salutis*" commonly employed in Reformational dogmatics.

Heyns calls the chapter in which he discusses the order of salvation "The person and work of the Holy Spirit" (*Dogm.*, 291–328).

Barth discusses the order of salvation highly critically in small print. He even alludes to Bunyan's *Pilgrim's Progress*. His conclusion is that in principle one should not allow oneself to be drawn into this sort of venture (*C.D.*, 4.3.541ff).

E. Herms dedicated his inaugural address in München to the doctrine of salvation. He used the title "The reality of faith" (1982).

C. Graafland wrote an article on the question whether Calvin taught a particular order of salvation (1983).

The issue described above has three aspects. In the first place there is the question as to *what title* should be given to this chapter. Then there is the question *what exactly is meant by the term "order of salvation" (ordo salutis)*. Finally there is the question as to *what topics ought to be covered in this chapter and in what sequence.*

2. In this chapter we encounter the work of the Holy Spirit (*pneumatology*). There is something to be said for including the Holy Spirit in the chapter's title, as Heyns does.

We do not do this for two reasons. The Holy Spirit has already been discussed (§ 12.3–4). Now that we are focusing on the fruits of the work of Christ, it would not be right to explicitly address pneumatology (again). A second objection is that we would then also have to address the cosmological work of the Spirit. This subject has also already been discussed (§ 17.3; § 21.1).

We treat the content of this chapter as the fruit of the work of Christ. His name is Savior (*soter*: Luke 2:11; 2 Tim. 1:10; Titus 1:4; 2:13). What he does for people is referred to as salvation (*soteria*, especially John 4:22; Acts 4:12; Eph. 1:13; Heb. 1:14; Rev. 12:10).

We find this concept so crucial that we have decided to use it in the title of this chapter. The term "benefits of Christ" refer to the same thing. However, in this term we miss the connection with *soter*, *soteria*. The same thing holds for the term "benefits of the covenant." This term is not incorrect. Yet we find "doctrine of salvation" (*soteriology*) more appropriate. This term refers to the title of Christ that reflects both his work and his benefits.

The subject matter of this chapter has also been referred to as the application of Christ's benefits, while Christology focuses on their attainment. The distinction between attainment and application is a good characterization of the difference between the work of Christ and that of the Spirit. Yet this chapter does not only focus on the application of the benefits. It also discusses those benefits themselves. Therefore, it would be less correct to treat this subject under the title "The Holy Spirit." But in this chapter we do find ourselves within the sphere of *pneumatology*.[1]

We are of the view that Calvin formulated the issue appropriately (though somewhat broadly) in the title that he gave to the third book of the *Institutes*, namely, "The way in which we receive the grace of Christ: what benefits come to us from it, and what effects follow." Chapter 1 directly addresses the fact that what is said about Christ benefits us through the secret working of the Spirit. We find that the title of this third book brings together all of the elements that are appropriate and indispensable for the present chapter, namely, the *grace* of Christ, the *way* in which we may share in it, its *fruits*, and its *effects*. These four key words characterize both the content of our chapter and the issues that need to be addressed.

3. What does the term "order of salvation" (*ordo salutis*) mean? We wish to point out that this term actually indicates two distinct but inseparable perspectives. In the first place there is the salvation that Christ has accomplished for his people. In the second place we find that through his Spirit, Christ permits us to share in these benefits acquired by him. Calvin distinguishes between fruits and effects. Although this distinction is correct, it should not give the impression that the effects would not also be fruits.[2]

This is indeed the case. The fruits of Christ's work include the fact that he gives them to us through his Spirit. In the absence of this work of the Spirit these fruits would remain foreign to us. It is necessary for us to be renewed through the Spirit to be able to live with God and to come to know and receive salvation in Christ.

Here we encounter what sometimes is called: Christ for us and in us (*pro nobis et in nobis*). Both aspects figure among the topics to be discussed here.[3] Because of this twofold perspective it is not always clear what is meant by the term "order of salvation."

1. Beker/Hasselaar, *Wegen* (ways), treated this material in part 4.1., which discussed the Holy Spirit, while elements of this theme were also addressed in 5.1.A., "De kerk" (the church, e.g., calling), and 5.2., "De voleinding" (culmination, i.e., faith and hope). The essay by Van Ruler, *T.W.*, 1.175–90, remains relevant for the difference between Christology and pneumatology.

2. These two aspects have been clearly addressed in historical reviews, e.g., R. Seeberg, *PRE* 9, 594, and Faulbusch, 1989^3, 472ff.

3. See Velema, 1989, 41–45, for a more detailed discussion.

Graafland points out that the *ordo salutis* is not only a theological doctrine, but also the way of the experience of faith (1983, 110). At the conclusion of his article he refers to a certain order or sequence in the application of salvation (127). This description refers more to effects than fruits. Nevertheless, Graafland recognizes that Calvin placed Christ and faith as the work of the Holy Spirit so centrally that the order in the application of salvation remains of secondary importance. All the same, "certain elements emerge in Calvin's teachings which subsequently serve as building blocks for the development of a more or less systematized *ordo salutis*. This systemization does not derive directly from Calvin, but was pursued by others with the help of scholastic thought processes which played an important role in Reformed orthodoxy already in Calvin's lifetime but especially after him" (127).

A similar shift in focus took place in Lutheran theology. According to E. Faulbusch, order of salvation becomes a technical term to describe various stages of spiritual life that flow from the work of the Holy Spirit. The working of grace is further described as a process that takes place within the soul. The objective foundation of salvation is thus given a subjective counterweight. This marks the transition to Lutheran orthodoxy. See Velema, 1987, 125–31, for a more detailed discussion.

The question is now what we mean by the order of salvation. We pursue a solution to the issues outlined above in line with the title that we have selected for this chapter. *The fruits of the work of Christ constitute our main focus. Those fruits include the ministrations of the Holy Spirit within us.* We do not start from man and his experiences, the certainty that he seeks, or the way in which he obtains it. The main focus is what Christ as Savior has accomplished for his people and how he applies this to his people. Both fruits and effects belong to the benefits. Especially in light of this distinction it appears incorrect to us to imply a certain chronological order or sequence of experiences with the term "order of salvation." Therefore we do not accept the orthodox interpretation of this term.

Yet we continue to refer to order. We do so deliberately in contrast with the term "way of salvation" employed by others including Berkouwer. The term "way" takes us again in the direction of orthodoxy, as though we were dealing with a way of conversion. Besides, Berkouwer does not want to have anything to do with a structuring of experience along the way of salvation.[4]

4. A. König (1982) totally rejected the concept of an order of salvation. He preferred to see the way of salvation as an experience of salvation through which a sinner becomes a partaker of salvation. This called for a distinction between the way of salvation and salvation itself. O. Weber took exactly the opposite direction. In 8 he discusses the work of the Holy Spirit with as main foci justified man and the man of God (*Foundations*, 2:229–407). The concept of Beker/Hasselaar can be viewed as an intermediate position between Barth and Weber.

We choose the term "order" to indicate that there is an internal coherence among the various benefits. This coherence is clear from passages such as Romans 8:29–30, Mark 1:15, and 1 Corinthians 6:11. All salvation proceeds from election. The Canons of Dort, 1.7, summarizes these benefits, assigning a pivotal place to Christ. All benefits are enjoyed in communion with Christ.

For example, sanctification does not precede justification but follows it, even though it is inextricably intertwined with it. Conversion follows calling, and not the other way round. Perseverance is not the first but the last link in the chain. The key is that the various benefits cannot be treated in an arbitrary sequence. Their interconnections preclude this.

We do not want to turn it into a sequence of experiences, i.e., a chronological order. Our interest is in the theological coherence of the benefits, i.e., the soteriological coherence of the gifts and the ministrations. We do not seek to prescribe an order. Yet we recognize an order when we consider salvation in its internal coherence (see Kremer, 1976, 24ff.). We are convinced that this is the sense in which we could speak of an order of salvation on Calvin's part.

4. *Which topics need to be treated in a doctrine of salvation?* We have already mentioned the most common ones. There are, however, other topics to be addressed.

Dijk (1958[2], 3:414), in referring to others, provides the following list: forgiveness of sins, adoption as children, redemption from the law, hope, love, peace, joy, comfort, approvedness, experience, glorification.

We agree that the topics just mentioned do belong to the fruits and/or ministrations of Christ in us through his Spirit. It would, however, go too far to treat each one of these concepts separately.

We believe that each one of these concepts can be categorized among the main themes mentioned above. We do wish to point out that a number of terms can be discussed in greater detail in connection with sanctification, while they should not be ignored in a discussion of ethics. By way of example we mention freedom, joy, struggle, love, and prayer. The special character of Christian ethics is revealed in a review of these concepts.

Do we need to adhere to a certain framework? Bavinck mentions four groups of benefits: 1. calling, regeneration, faith, and repentance, which prepare man for and enable him to accept the blessings of the covenant; 2. justification as a change in man's status and redemption of his guilt; 3. sanctification as a change in man's condition; and 4. glorification. Subsequently he provides a division of benefits derived from the work of the Holy Spirit (*R.D.*, 3:595).

Dijk employs a partition into three areas: beginning, progression, and completion (1958[2], 3:414). The problem with Dijk's partition is that justification is ignored. We wish to adhere to the usual sequence of: *calling and regeneration; faith and conversion; justification; sanctification; and perseverance*. Glorification may also be mentioned here, but does not need to be discussed in detail, since this is done in chapter 15. It is the fulfillment of all of the foregoing benefits. Perseverance is the perspective of the entire chapter.

§ 39. Calling and Regeneration

39.1. *Call in a general sense*
39.2. *Call to salvation*
39.3. *Regeneration*

39.1. *Call in a general sense*

God proceeds by calling. He creates by calling into being. Wisdom says: "The LORD possessed me in the beginning of his way, before his works of old" (Prov. 8:22). God called Israel into being ("appointed" it, Isa. 44:7).

In Genesis 1 we read that God creates by speaking (vv. 3, 6, 9, 14, etc.). "By the word of the LORD were the heavens made; and all the host of them by the breath of his mouth. . . . For he spake and it was done; he commanded, and it stood fast" (Ps. 33:6, 9).

God's calling is a concentrated, focused form of speaking. We point out that God speaks in various ways, and therefore also calls in various ways (cf. § 5.1). God speaks through creation. See the psalms that speak of God's greatness in nature (Pss. 8:1, 9; 19:1–6; 29:3–9; 147:15). God also speaks through history (Acts 14:16–17; 17:26). Passages such as Romans 1:18–23 and 2:14–15 can only be understood in this light.

We wish to refer to this as *God's call in a general sense*. Heyns speaks in the current context of an impersonal call, while referring to the call that remains to be discussed as a biblical call (*Dogm.*,

304). We prefer to distinguish between the call from the perspective of creation and providence (including history) *and* the call from the perspective of salvation in Jesus Christ.

However brief this subsection may be, we emphasize it for two reasons. In the first place, in calling to salvation, God takes the same approach as in creation and providence. Only the content of the call and its effect vary. In soteriology, calling is not a new theme that has never been discussed before.

We further point out that *the distinction between calling in the general sense and calling to salvation focuses attention on the connection between creation and redemption.* This may be stated more strongly by saying that God's providence is a link between creation and redemption that cannot be ignored. Rather than referring to the call in a general sense as a preparation for the call to salvation, we prefer to see them as being analogous. Heyns qualifies this by adding "in a certain sense" (Dogm., 304). The term "analogy" indicates a connection that we do not explore any further at this point (see instead § 5.1).[5]

39.2. *Call to salvation*[6]

1. *Especially in the New Testament there are many passages that refer to the call to salvation.* The reference that God called his Son out of Egypt (Matt. 2:15 as fulfillment of Hos. 11:1) is an illustration (pre-figuration) of what we read elsewhere about people being called. We could call John the Baptist "John the Caller" (Matt. 3:3 as fulfillment of Isa. 40:3). Jesus characterizes his own work as not having "come to call the righteous, but sinners to repentance" (Matt. 9:13; more detailed in Luke 5:32). He called the twelve disciples to himself (Matt. 10:1). It is in the same spirit that in his epistles Paul presents himself as having been called to be an apostle (Rom. 1:1; 1 Cor. 1:1; and other passages). The invitation to the wedding feast (first in Matt. 22:3; subsequently Rev. 19:9) is characteristic of the relationship between salvation and calling.

5. Beker/Hasselaar, *Wegen* (ways), 5, 42, distinguished between *vocatio generalis* and *specialis*. They called *vocatio specialis* a *vocatio generalis*. The context suggests that this had to do with their christological view of creation.

6. *Synopsis*, 30:2, distinguished between a general and a special call. The latter was also referred to as call to salvation or evangelical call.

We mention a few additional passages that relate calling and salvation, namely, Ephesians 1:4–14; Hebrews 3:1; 2 Peter 1:10; and of course Romans 8:30, which refers to it as a link in the chain of salvation. Without calling there is no participation in salvation.[7] That is God's way of doing things.

2. The central question is *why the call engenders such a varied response*. One person responds in faith and another with unbelief. On the basis of the parable of the sower and the seed it is clearly possible that the call initially engenders a positive response, although no lasting fruit is produced. The latter reflects the seed that falls in stony places (Matt. 13:20–21).

Are the varying responses consistent with a single type of call? Or would the twofold effect be due to a difference in call? In this connection we also need to ask whether the call varies depending on whether we have been elected or not.

The difference, just alluded to, has frequently been described as that between *external* and *internal* calling. The former does not lead to faith. A call that is responded to in faith is an internal call.

Objections to this distinction are obvious. The external call that does not lead to faith could be dismissed as being merely external and as having less value than the internal call. What would be the benefit of an external call? How does its content vary from that of the internal call? Do they really have the same content? And if the content is thought to be different—in view of the difference in outcome—would the external call really be a call in the full sense of the word?

In the issue just raised the relationship between election and calling is of fundamental importance. The fact that there is indeed a connection between the two is evident from Revelation 17:14, where those who have been called are also referred to as those who (believe and) have been chosen. We encounter the same connection in Paul's writings (2 Thess. 2:13–14; 2 Tim. 1:9; Rom. 8:30; Rom. 10:14–15 also plays a role in the relationship between preaching and the freedom of God's grace. See the discussion of these passages by van Genderen, 1969, 109).

7. Pop, *Bijbelse woorden* (words of the Bible), 437, pointed to the direct connection between God's call and the proclamation of the gospel to engender faith.

It is important to point out the connection that the Canons of Dort establish between the proclamation of the promise and election. Neither in Scripture nor in the Canons of Dort do we find any limitation imposed on preaching, and therefore the call to salvation, because of the confession of election. On the contrary, the two belong together because both of them place Christ in the center and originate with the Father. See Canons of Dort, 1.7; 1.3.

This close connection does not imply that they are the same thing. Those who are called are not thereby (*ipso facto*) chosen. The call should not be discussed from the perspective of election. In his mandate to preach the gospel to all nations and to make them his disciples, the Lord Jesus did not refer to election or the elect. Election is nevertheless an essential aspect of salvation in Christ (Eph. 1:3–14).

Nowhere in Scripture or the confessions is there a conflict between the proclamation (doctrine) of election and the call to salvation. Election becomes reality through calling, as formulated by Paul in key passages of his epistles (Rom. 8:29–30; also Eph. 1:4–13, which cannot be understood without viewing the call as the implementation of God's electing purpose).

The Canons of Dort point out correctly that those who are called, are called in all seriousness (3–4.8). Nowhere is the scope of the call limited by election. In a chapter titled "Election is confirmed by God's call," Calvin points out that "we must begin with the call . . . and . . . end with it" (*Institutes*, 3.24.4).

3. *The call is universal.* The call to salvation is not limited. It is in accordance with God's good pleasure that the gospel is proclaimed to all nations and persons without distinction (Canons of Dort, 2.5).

Is it therefore always and everywhere the same call? The data that we have explored so far can in no way be interpreted to imply that the content of the call varies from person to person. The universal scope of the call in no way restricts its content. If the content of the call varied between the elect and non-elect, its universal nature would be diminished.

The question is then what the content of the call is.

In discussing this point we cannot ignore Barth. He holds that we may tell everyone that they have been elected in Jesus Christ from eternity. The call then becomes the announcement of a decision concerning man that has already been made. There are people who are still unaware of this. This ignorance spurs the church to missionary activity. See especially *C.D.*, 3.2.607, which deals with Barth's doctrine of election. We quote a sentence that is very typical of the significance that Barth attaches to the promise: "It is not for his being but for his life as elect that he needs to hear and believe the promise" (*C.D.*, 2.2.321). The distinction between *being* and *living* stands out. We can only conclude that everyone's *being* is in Christ. The proclamation of the promise is required for *living* as a believer.

There is a striking analogy with Kuyper, according to whom proclamation is needed to coax *existence* into consciousness. See Velema, 1957, 119, 158. Obviously, this analogy reflects entirely different frames of reference. We still like to think in terms of an analogy because of the fact that the thesis of each of these theologians is based on speculation.

It is noteworthy that Barth interprets *die Berufung* (the call) as "by which He awakens man to an active knowledge of the truth and thus receives him into the new standing of the Christian, namely, into a particular fellowship with Himself, thrusting him as His afflicted but well-equipped witness into the service of His prophetic work" (*C.D.*, 4.3.481).

For a succinct and simultaneously illuminating review of Barth's doctrine of election, in the context of his emasculation of the biblical content of the call, see van Genderen, 1987, especially 46–48. He characterized Barth's doctrine of election as objectivistic and universalistic.

De triomf der genade in de theologie van Karl Barth (the triumph of grace in the theology of Barth, 1954, 271–78) by G. C. Berkouwer remains the classic, meticulous, and simultaneously critical—in essence dismissive—discussion of Barth's doctrine of election, including criticism of the lack of appellate kerygma (276).

C. Vermeulen (1986) attempted to demonstrate that in Barth's theology there was indeed room for kerygma that calls for faith. It is our view that the former did not succeed in this regard. He has to admit (e.g., 185) that at some point it is no longer possible to sharply distinguish between the work of God the Son and that of God's Spirit. The *proprium* of the Spirit was made to coincide with the presentation of the Messiah. In the resulting pneumatological Christology of the third office, Christ and the Spirit become interchangeable as subjects.

We may offer Christ in the promise of the gospel.

Calvin clearly distinguishes between the promise of the gospel of which Christ is the content *and* receiving the content of the promise through faith.

Calvin speaks of the effectiveness of the promises that only appears when they have found faith in us.

At the same time he adds that the force and peculiar nature of God's promises are never extinguished by our unbelief and ingratitude (*Institutes*, 3.2.32).

This expresses clearly that the call is one *and* what constitutes the call. The call is an invitation to salvation in Christ, to come to him.

The call is an appeal coupled with a "command to repent and believe" (Canons of Dort, 1.3; 2.5; see also 3–4.8).

This appeal comes to everyone in the same fashion and with the same content. Nevertheless the effect varies. Unbelief causes people to eschew the announced salvation (Matt. 13:58; Mark 6:6; Heb. 3:19).[8]

Here we encounter man's guilt as the cause for not receiving salvation, but also God's grace as the source of salvation. There is no symmetry between these two; neither is there between election and reprobation. The Canons of Dort refer to God as the source of salvation and to unbelief as man's fault, in a balanced and evangelical manner that simultaneously recognizes God's sovereignty (3–4.8–10). This is in line with Scripture, which says that "as many as were ordained to eternal life, believed" (Acts 13:48).

In this connection we encounter the well-known words of Matthew 22:14 ("For many are called, but few are chosen"), which employs the expression "to call" (*kalein*).

Various interpretations of this verse have been discussed more broadly elsewhere (van Genderen, 1969, 114ff.). Here it will suffice to state the key idea, which is that the call is universal. There are no exceptions in the call. The reality is, however, that not everyone, indeed very few, respond. A positive response implies election to salvation. This result of the call in no way detracts from the seriousness and earnestness of the call. Those who believe otherwise blunt the force of the equality of all in the face of the call.

Ridderbos, *Mattheüs* (Matthew, K.V.), 1946, 2:113, says that the call does indeed go out to many. However, "in comparison there are only few who demonstrate through repentance and faith to have been predestined by God to inherit salvation." See also § 16.2, subsection 3.

We can draw three conclusions from this verse:

1. Election neither limits nor emasculates the call.
2. The call is meant seriously. Rejection implies guilt.
3. The call does not coincide with election. In the parable of the sower and the seed, the call comes first. Election can only be inferred from the outcome.

See § 16.8 as well as Bavinck, *R.D.*, 2:402–3 on the connection between election and calling.

8. A. C. de Jong, *The Well-Meant Gospel Offer*, 1954, 171–76, refers to kerygmatic universality.

4. In this context we wish to discuss *the distinction between external and internal call (vocatio externa en interna)*. This implies not only that salvation is proclaimed by men, but that via this proclamation the Spirit also establishes communion with Christ (Heppe, *Dogm.*, 404ff.). In its original meaning, this distinction does not imply a differing content of the call. It is not intended to contrast one type of call with another.[9] There is only one call.[10] It identifies a *twofold outcome* of the one call. The Canons of Dort refer to being called "earnestly" and "effectually" (*serio*, 3–4.8, and *efficaciter*, 3–4.10). *Vocatio interna* does not mean that the other call only comes externally, and would therefore be less serious and effective. How could this be if Christ himself is the content of the call? The term *interna* implies that something needs to happen inside the human heart before a positive reaction can take place. Consequently, the direct effect of the *vocatio interna* is regeneration (Heppe, *Dogm.* 407).

In this connection see the article by C. Trimp, "Is de prediking uiterlijk?" (is the proclamation external?), in *Bezield verband* (inspired context), 1984, 220–30. He emphasizes that the expression "external" is meant antispiritualistically, while it calls attention to the work of the Holy Spirit. *Interna* indicates the specific sphere of influence of the Holy Spirit (224). The expression *vocatio externa* is not intended to diminish the significance of the force of the call.

We also refer to the study by Exalto, 1978, in which he argues based on Luther, Calvin, and the confessions that election and calling should not be played off against one another. In view of the numerous references to Luther and Calvin, this is a valuable piece of work.

Weber emphasizes that the proclamation is not a one-time announcement. It does not operate automatically (*ex opere operato*). It can even turn into what in essence it is not, namely, "the savour of death unto death" (2 Cor. 2:16). The proclamation is not ambivalent. The *vocatio interna* makes clear that man pronounces his "yes" in the power of the Spirit. He does not create something new. He receives everything. Weber says that in this connection Calvin speaks of "the latter signs" (*signa posteriora*) that are attestations of election. "Latter" pertains to the signs that belong to election, *Institutes*, 3.24.4. (*Foundations*, 2:501–4, especially 559). See also Niesel, *Die Theologie Calvins*, 1957, 173ff. W. Krusche, in *Das Wirken des Heiligen Geistes nach Calvin* (the work of the Holy Spirit according to Calvin), 1957, takes a different approach, by considering the content of the call as determined by the work of the Holy Spirit (see especially 239–41).

9. *Synopsis*, 30:46, discusses two types of call by distinguishing between an ineffective and an effective call (*tam inefficaci, quam efficaci*).

10. W. J. Aalders, *Roeping en beroep bij Calvijn* (call and vocation according to Calvin), 1943, provides an illuminating analysis of the one call to salvation and the various callings of God in everyday life in Calvin's theology.

In *Wet en Evangelie* (law and gospel), 190n42, we already criticize the way in which Krusche approaches the relationship between the *usus elentichticus* and the Holy Spirit.

We end this subsection by underlining that the call of God is intended seriously and that one can never ascribe its rejection on its external nature. If the call remains external, its content (i.e., Christ himself) is rejected through one's own fault. It is unbelief that prevents the *vocatio* from entering the heart. It is called *interna* in recognition of the Holy Spirit. The Spirit as the Spirit of Christ is also part of the content of the promise that comes to us in the call. Therefore man's unbelief can never be used as an excuse.

39.3. *Regeneration*

1. We encounter the term "regeneration" *in several places in the New Testament*, while its actual, pneumatological content is also found in the Old Testament. Titus 3:5 is of key significance. There Paul says: "he saved us by the washing of regeneration, and renewing of the Holy Ghost." Here regeneration is directly linked with salvation *and* the work of the Holy Spirit. This defines regeneration. It is the fruit of the Spirit and is part of salvation.

Although James 1:18 does not explicitly mention regeneration, it does refer to being born subsequent to our first birth on earth. This regeneration is the same as that to which Jesus refers in John 3:3, 5. He employs the terms of being "born again" and being "born of water and the Spirit." In Titus 3:5 Paul follows these words very closely. James 1:18 refers to "the word of truth" as the means of regeneration. Peter does the same in 1 Peter 1:23.

In John's writings we encounter the expression "born of God" (John 1:13; 1 John 3:9).

Although the word "regeneration" is not mentioned explicitly, we encounter its concept in the following expressions: "quickened together with Christ" (Eph. 2:5); "renewed in the spirit of your mind," in connection with "putting on the new man" (Eph. 4:23ff.; see also Col. 3:10). The following expressions also fit into this context: "new creation" (2 Cor. 5:17); "his workmanship" (Eph. 2:10); "transformed by the renewing of your mind" (Rom. 12:2); and "the inward man is renewed day by day" (2 Cor. 4:16). In the Old Testament we encounter this pneumatic reality as a gift of the new covenant: the writing of the law in the heart (Jer. 31:31–34). Ezekiel refers to this in 36:25–28. There he mentions the cleansing of uncleanness and the new spirit within us as benefits. Deuteronomy 30:6 speaks of the circumcision of the heart.

It is noteworthy that among the passages just referred to there are some that also play an important role in the discussion of (the restoration of) the image of God (see § 23.6).

By way of summary it may be said that—in their interconnectedness—all of these passages permit us to present the following characterizations:

1. Regeneration is part of salvation in Christ.
2. It is specifically fruit of the Holy Spirit; God is its ultimate origin.
3. The Spirit employs the Word as a means.
4. Regeneration implies the total inner renewal of our humanity before God. Regeneration constitutes its beginning, but is not totally restricted to this initial moment. The new life reveals itself subsequently as the fruit of regeneration.

Regeneration is therefore *inner renewal through the Spirit of God, who is apportioned to us as a gift from Christ*. There are additional names for this gift. Regeneration reminds us of the sovereign work that God does in man. It is not surprising that usually regeneration is referred to as the firstfruit of the *vocatio* (*interna*). This is implied by the first few passages referred to above.[11]

2. It is necessary to point out *the difference between regeneration in the narrower sense and that in the broader sense*. Regeneration in the narrower sense signifies the beginning of new life. Just as birth indicates arrival in this world, whereupon life can unfold, there are those who think of regeneration as the beginning of the new life. Others include the subsequent unfolding and maturing of this new life.

Calvin describes regeneration as repentance (*Institutes*, 3.3) and associates it with one's entire life. This is especially the case in 3.3.5. Calvin sees a connection between repentance, and therefore regeneration, with the restoration of the image of God (3.3.9). He places a good

11. In the Reformed tradition, a broad discussion has taken place with respect to the relationship between baptism and rebirth. See §§ 33, 36, 52.

deal of emphasis on the connection between faith and regeneration (3.3), as is also done in the Belgic Confession of Faith, article 24.

In the Canons of Dort we encounter regeneration as the beginning of the new life (3–4.11–12). It is, however, important to keep in mind the practical orientation of 3–4.13: "The manner of this operation cannot be fully comprehended by believers in this life. Nevertheless, they are satisfied to know and experience that by this grace of God they are enabled to believe with the heart and to love their Savior." According to the Canons of Dort, the fruit of regeneration is therefore love toward Christ.

Polman has made clear that one cannot speak of a contradiction between Calvin (and others) and the Canons of Dort. These two views are compatible with each other. They agree that regeneration is the fruit of the Holy Spirit and a gift of God's grace. Regeneration is something that takes place within man (Belgic Confession of Faith., 3.113–20).

In a separate study (1903), Bavinck deals extensively with the relationship between calling and regeneration. In his dissertation titled *Herman Bavinck als dogmaticus*, 1961, Bremmer traces the perspectives of Bavinck's book in considerable detail. Of the no fewer than 12 statements as summary of Bavinck's argument we mention the following: Bavinck adheres principally to the sequence of regeneration and faith. He interprets regeneration to be the granting of the ability to believe. The Word is required to activate this ability. In this regard he follows Kuyper (see Velema, 1957, especially 149–58). Bavinck is aware of the distinction between regeneration in the narrower and broader sense, but follows post-Dort theologians in favoring the former. He maintains that regeneration takes place under and with the Word, but not through the Word. He espouses this sequence and interpretation in opposition to Anabaptists and Remonstrants.

The terminology introduced by Kuyper allows for the possibility that regeneration remains dormant for a long period of time. See Velema, 1957, 152ff., for a discussion of this concept per se and of Kuyper's framework within which it fits.

We consider it correct to use the term "regeneration" to indicate the beginning of new life (as taught by the Canons of Dort, 3–4.11, and especially 12). However, we do not want to restrict this term to its very onset (see Belgic Confession of Faith, article 24). Based on the same reasoning, we consider regeneration to be a ministry of the Spirit under and through the proclamation of the Word. We consider Bavinck's linking up with Kuyper's view to be a step backward rather than keeping pace with Calvin. We do admit that Bavinck is more nuanced in his approach than Kuyper.

3. At the same time this takes care of the difference between *immediate* and *mediate regeneration*. Although Honig positions himself on the side of Kuyper (*Handboek*, 549ff.), he rejects the notion of dormant regeneration. We consider regeneration and the proclamation of the gospel, specifically the call, to be closely and directly related.

The fact that, through his Holy Spirit, God can regenerate little children—who cannot yet reason—does not detract from the clear connection between calling and regeneration as taught by Scripture. We would rather not modify the concept of calling on the basis of a limited interpretation of regeneration. God is sovereign in the work of his Spirit. We must adhere to what his Word teaches us in this respect. Then we are not permitted to interpret the Scripture passages discussed at the beginning of this section as pertaining solely to regeneration in the broader sense, and to associate a relationship other than calling and regeneration with regeneration in the narrower sense.

4. *Regeneration does not alter people physically, but changes their relationships with God and their fellow human beings.* The core of regeneration is the restoration of the image of God. In this way man acquires new knowledge, insights, and affections. His entire nature being affected by sin is cleansed and renewed. Regeneration may be described as a change of heart. In love it is now directed toward God and fellow human beings (Canons of Dort, 3–4.11, 12). This is why Christ is called "our life" (Col. 3:4; see also Gal. 2:20; Phil. 1:21).

This life is conceived and nurtured through the Word (1 Peter 1:23; cf. 1 Cor. 4:15). Growth is characteristic of the new life.[12]

5. Finally, *there is one passage where regeneration is related to the cosmos, i.e., the renewal of heaven and earth* (Matt. 19:28). Van Bruggen, 1990, 369, correctly points out that this concerns the restoration of people and the world. Cosmological reality does not exist without ethnological reality. The world does not exist without the church, and heaven is not without residents. This cosmological, ecclesiastical renewal (with references to Israel) will represent the culmination of the renewal begun in regeneration.[13]

12. See W. H. Velema, *De geestelijke groei van de gemeente* (spiritual growth of the church), 1966, for various aspects of spiritual growth.

13. König (1982), 135, also pointed to the personal dimension in addition to the entire creation. He referred to Romans 8:18ff.

The end of this section is marvelously connected with its beginning. We started out after all with the call in a general sense. Via personal renewal we end up with regeneration in which both the world and God's people are to participate. The breadth of the perspective at the beginning does not narrow toward the end. By concentrating on the Redeemer Jesus Christ we see as our ultimate destiny the renewal not only of the church as the people of God but also of the entire cosmos. Thus in the *ordo salutis* we recognize the broadness of salvation.

§ 40. Faith and repentance

40.1. *Faith*

1. It may be asked *whether faith should have been discussed earlier.* Would it have been preferable to follow the discussion of the call (calling) immediately with that of faith? Since we did not address this question in the preceding section, it is necessary to do so now.

It is true that faith and calling go together. Faith is the positive response of man to the call of the gospel. From this perspective there is something to be said for treating both calling and faith in the same section.

We did not do this, because through the Word and the Spirit the call brings about a complete inner change, which is manifested in faith. Faith does not emerge in the absence of this inner renewal, i.e., regeneration. In the preceding section we emphasized the fact that the call must not only touch but also change the heart. Because of the pneumatic connection between call and inner change, we discussed regeneration in the context of the call.

Section 38 makes clear that we do not discuss the elements of the order of salvation in a chronological sequence based on experience. We discuss the benefits of salvation from a *theological* point of view, i.e., based on the inner connection that we can discern among the gifts of God. From this theological perspective we—and many others who have led the way—consider the discussion of calling and regeneration as a single topic to be eminently justified.

On the basis of article 24 of the Belgic Confession of Faith, which says that "this true faith, being wrought in man by the hearing of the Word of God and the operation of the Holy Spirit, regenerates him and makes him a new man, causing him to live a new life," regeneration could also be discussed subsequent to faith. In this case calling, faith, and regeneration could be discussed in a single section.

Our decision to treat faith and repentance subsequent to calling and regeneration is motivated by the desire to emphasize the aspect of grace in faith. *The human reaction to the call, resulting in faith and repentance, is fruit of the Holy Spirit.* We stress this in the discussion of the call. This is further emphasized by treating regeneration directly after calling. This is not to deny that we confess that we are regenerated through faith. From the formulation used in the Belgic Confession of Faith we can conclude that faith itself is no less fruit of the Holy Spirit. In this sense faith is a fruit of regeneration.[14]

We are justified in employing the two-sided approach outlined here, because we do not seek to describe an experiential sequence, but God's work in us and our work in consequence. In light of the call, there is no regeneration without faith. There is no faith in the absence of regeneration.

2. *What is faith*? Bavinck sees a close connection between faith and the intellect on the one hand, and repentance (conversion) and will on the other hand (*R.D.*, 4:132). This distinction is based on anthropology. We do not agree that anthropology should be the criterion for establishing the significance of faith and repentance in a biblical sense. The meaning of both terms must be inferred from Scripture itself.

At this point we may raise the question whether faith is a universal human attribute that is given special content in soteriology. We raise this question especially in view of the fact that Reformational philosophy in its analysis of reality recognizes a pistic function that is thought to be common to all human beings.[15] In this regard this philosophy follows Kuyper, who distinguishes between faith in a general sense and faith in a special sense, i.e., faith implanted in a sinner. Faith in a general sense is

14. Calvin maintained in various places that rebirth preceded faith. See especially his commentary on John 1:12–13 and Luke 17:13. See further De Groot, 1952, 188–90.

15. We refer to L. Kalsbeek, *De wijsbegeerte der wetsidee* (the philosophy of the law-idea), 1970, especially 130–35, and M. E. Verburg, *Herman Dooyeweerd*, 1989, 175–78. This so-called pistic function was criticized by, among others, J. Douma, *Kritische aantekeningen bij de wijsbegeerte der wetsidee*, 1976, especially 26–32.

thought to be a function of consciousness by means of which man, created in God's image, recognizes God as God (*De Salute*, 98).

By way of objection, we would like to point out that the Bible nowhere refers to man as having a pistic function prior to the fall into sin. Nevertheless, unbelief is referred to repeatedly (Num. 14:11; 2 Kings 17:14; Ps. 78:22, 32; Isa. 7:9; Matt. 13:58; Mark 6:6; Heb. 3:19). As far as Gentiles are concerned, we read about the vanity of their thinking, the dullness of their understanding, and an alienation from the life of God because of their ignorance and the hardening of their hearts (Eph. 4:17–18; cf. Rom. 1:21).

Nowhere in the Bible do we encounter the thought that prior to the fall into sin man had faith that needed to be changed from negative to positive by the grace of the Holy Spirit. Man is created as the image of God (see § 23.2). This includes a relationship with God. This relationship has turned into negation. We do not wish to go beyond this statement. It agrees perfectly with what Paul calls "alienation from the life of God" (Eph. 4:18). This alienation is more profound and contrasts more sharply with the original relationship between man and God than the formulation that man has a capacity to believe that behaves negatively. Sin affects the entire being, the heart. It implies (spiritual) death (cf. § 27.2).

It is not surprising that in the Bible we only read about faith in terms of the restored relationship of man to God, and about unbelief as rejection of the Word of God.

Faith comprises the overall relationship of man to God and the totality of human existence before God. Bavinck points out that the Old Testament "lacks a technical term for what in the Christian religion is now called faith" (*R.D.*, 4:104). If he implies that this technical term only turns up in the New Testament, it may be pointed out that the noun "faith" actually does occur in Habakkuk 2:4, while the corresponding verb turns up in various places (Gen. 15:6; Ex. 14:31; Ps. 116:10; Jonah 3:5). In the passages referred to, we encounter a form of the verb *'aman*.

3. We begin our more thorough discussion of what faith or believing is, by pointing out that *faith is necessary for the correct, restored relationship with God*. This becomes clear in Hebrews 11:6: "Without faith it is impossible to please him" (God). It should be kept in mind that Enoch's faith is referred to as an essential aspect of his walk with God (see also Rom. 3:22; Gal. 3:11). We encounter the same connection with life (with God and in God's presence) in John 20:31: "These

are written, that ye might believe that Jesus is the Christ, the Son of God; and that believing ye might have life through his name."

The scriptural focus of faith on Christ is also encountered in 2 Timothy 3:15. The relationship between faith and Christ is essential (see John 3:16; Acts 3:16; Gal. 2:20; 3:22). An extension of this is that justification comes through faith (Rom. 3:26; 4:5; 9:30; Gal. 2:16; 3:11, 22, 24; see § 41 and Berkouwer, 1954, 187, especially chapter 7).

Faith comes by hearing (Rom. 10:17). This is reflected in the central role of the Scriptures (2 Tim. 3:16). The Spirit employs Scripture and preaching in order to work faith. They form a duality. See Revelation 1:3 and Colossians 4:16. The Scriptures and preaching are the means by which God extends the call to faith.

Now that we have seen that faith is essential for salvation and finds its focus in Jesus Christ, we add that faith is a gift of God (see especially Acts 10:44; 16:14; Phil. 1:29). For the Trinitarian concept of the message of salvation we refer to Galatians 4:4–6. We may indeed use the terms *essential for salvation* and *gift of salvation* to describe faith.

4. *What does faith consist in*? We already saw that faith has to do with life before God's face (John 20:31; see also 11:25–26). Is there more to be said about the activities and components of faith? With this question we have in mind the elements of *knowledge* and *confidence* mentioned in Response 21 of the Heidelberg Catechism.

In Reformed dogmatics there was in this regard initially a difference in emphasis, which subsequently developed into a difference of view. In his well-known explanation, Calvin emphasizes a firm and certain knowledge of God's benevolence toward us. He refers to it as being revealed to our minds and sealed upon our hearts through the Holy Spirit (*Institutes*, 3.2.7).

In his dissertation S. P. Dee (1917, especially 13–44) holds that this definition restricts faith to the intellect. There would seem to be no place for confidence. For a brief discussion of this see Honig, *Handboek*, 517ff. See also Van der Spek, 1942, especially 143–52, and van Genderen, 1982, especially 12–21.

The question emerges whether faith can be described as both knowledge and confidence, and how these two are related. Especially the latter question is anthropologically motivated. It reflects the distinction between the intellect and the will, in the sense that knowledge is associated with the intellect and confidence with the will.[16] See the overview by Bavinck, *R.D.*, 4:112–15 (adopted by Van der Spek, 1942, 145–49).

Melanchthon distinguishes three elements in faith, namely, knowledge (*notitia*), assent (*assensus*), and confidence (*fiducia*). For Luther's view of faith as "nicht bloss Heilsempfang durch den Menschen, sondern Heilsgeschenk im Menschen" (not merely the acceptance of salvation by man, but the gift of salvation to man), being directly linked with Christ, see R. Slenczka, *TRE* 13, 1984, especially 322–24, and W. van 't Spijker, *Luther, Belofte en ervaring* (promise and experience), 1983, especially 189–91.

The discussion of the relationship between knowledge and confidence was carried on in Reformed theology. Emphases varied. It is noteworthy that Heppe does not devote a separate chapter to faith. He treats it in connection with calling (*Dogm.*, 408, 421, 423) and justification (441). The focus of the discussion is on the anthropological question whether one can distinguish between the two psychic functions of knowledge and volition (*cognitio* and *affectus*). Especially Van der Spek refers to this issue in his final chapter (1942, 49).

W. Verboom, *De catechese van de Reformatie en de Nadere Reformatie* (catechetical instruction of the Reformation and the Second Reformation), 1986, analyzes the concept of knowledge employed by Luther, Melanchthon, Calvin, and the Heidelberg Catechism. He recognizes two different perspectives with regard to knowledge in the Heidelberg Catechism (173–83, especially 182). Regarding the role of intellectual knowledge in the position of the Second Reformation see 246–57.

Bavinck describes this historical development objectively and cogently. He explains that many theologians consider faith to consist of the employment of two different capabilities. Melanchthon, who employs three words to characterize faith, encourages theologians to identify still more activities (*actus*) of faith. Turretin distinguishes seven, and Witsius as many as nine. The latter subdivides these activities into three categories, namely preceding, contemporaneous, and subsequent (in terms of the fruit of faith). The acceptance and embracing of Christ is seen as central in all of these activities.

We also refer to Wilhelmus à Brakel. He does not see saving faith as assent to the promises of the gospel, i.e., knowledge, but as confidence. The intellect is not seen to be the seat of faith, but the will (*R.S.*, 1:277–96). "Faith is a heartfelt trust in Christ—and through him in God—in order to be justified, sanctified, and glorified, leaning upon Christ's voluntary offer of Himself and upon His promises that He will perform this to all who receive Him and rely upon Him to that end" (*R.S.*, 2:295).

For a critical discussion of this view we refer to F. J. Los, *Wilhelmus à Brakel*, Leiden 1991[2], 247ff. This author points to the similarity between Brakel and the

16. Buber tried to capture the difference between Judaism and Christianity in the distinction between confidence and faith. See his *Zwei glaubensweisen* (two ways of believing), 1950. Th. C. Vriezen addressed this critically in his Utrecht speech *Geloven en vertrouwen* (believing and trusting), 1957.

Labadists. A sympathetic appraisal of Brakel's view is contained in J. van Genderen, "Wilhelmus à Brakel," in *De Nadere Reformatie* (the Second Reformation), 1986, 178ff. This article points out that Brakel's concept of faith is anti-intellectual. By seeking the essence of faith in confidence of the heart, this concept of faith can differentiate between true and historical faith. Van Genderen points to Brakel's evangelical gentleness. Ames also seeks the seat of faith in the will.

Regarding Brakel, see also W. van 't Spijker, *De verzegeling met the Heilige Geest* (the sealing with the Holy Spirit), 1991, 109–33. In connection with this topic, the author also discusses Brakel's concept of faith (see especially 113–16).

Comrie adopts the classical perspective of three aspects (rejecting Witsius's nine): knowledge, assent, and confidence.[17]

5. In the past, attempts were made to clearly determine the essence of faith. In our view, part of the difficulty encountered in these attempts was that the starting point was man and his psychic abilities. On the other hand it is clear that there was an appreciation for the totality of faith. With this we mean that faith involves man in his totality, that it is a matter of the heart. Faith encompasses much more than mere cerebral acceptance of certain tenets, or intellectual assent to a number of truths.

Once again we call attention to *the relationship between faith and life* (John 20:31). To have faith means *to receive life in receiving the promises of the gospel.* This is how through faith we are born again.

We must abandon the idea that faith consists of a number of independent elements and that by merely combining these one could capture the essence of faith.

Faith is ultimately an act of the heart that involves our entire being, including our intellect, our will, and our emotions. The concept of faith becomes clouded when only one or two of these psychic attributes are thought to be the seat of faith. We believe with our hearts. Through faith we gain a relationship with God, who reveals himself to us through his promise. We cannot believe in him without knowledge of his promise. We are mistaken, however, if we believe that this knowledge constitutes part of faith. Those who divide faith among various attributes of the soul quantify it and rob it of its essence and quality.

We can approach this issue from yet another angle. Sin has been characterized as unbelief, disobedience, pride, and hatred (§ 26.3). Faith means that we are redeemed from sin in all of its manifestations.

17. See the description by Honig, *Alexander Comrie*, Leiden 1991², 211–19. See also Graafland, "Alexander Comrie," in *De Nadere Reformatie* (the Second Reformation), 1986, 327ff.

It constitutes a restoration of our relationship with God, which results in the acceptance of his Word, in the confidence that the content of his promise is ours, and in obedience and humility, so that we recognize our pride as sin and repent from it.

Faith means that man once again becomes man of God and is restored to a positive relationship with his Creator and Redeemer. Through this faith we are renewed and redeemed from the various manifestations of sin (unbelief, disobedience, pride, and hatred). We are re-created in the image of Christ. It is for this reason that faith is focused on Christ.

6. In this light it is understandable that *there is no faith without repentance, inner brokenness, and awareness of guilt*. The last item arises when man is reborn in humility before God.

It is unimportant and impossible to determine precisely how from a psychic point of view these various aspects occur to us chronologically. Faith is an act of the heart. It involves our entire being. It affects all of our psychic attributes. It is possible to distinguish all of the various elements of the one act of faith. We view them as different aspects of the one act of faith. There is place for knowledge, as well as confidence in the God who reveals himself to us, and humility as the counterpart of sinful pride and egocentricity.

Sometimes it is explained that faith puts its trust in the Word of God in order to have communion with the God of the Word. Actually this is a beautiful perspective: the Word of God and the God of the Word, which can never be separated from each other. Rationalists are satisfied with the Word of God (however they may define it). Mystics (of whatever type or affiliation) rely on God apart from his Word. This is in essence spiritualism. The Reformed tradition sees the Word of God as well as the God of the Word as the "object" of faith. Rational understanding is insufficient. Neither is it possible to have a relationship with God apart from knowledge of his Word. This knowledge is embedded in a living relationship with God. Confidence in the truthfulness and reliability of God's promises and therefore in the God of these promises has an important place beside knowledge. At the same time this confidence manifests itself in bowing before God in humility and dependence, and turning away from an unbelieving, disobedient, and proud attitude toward God.

This depiction makes clear that faith and repentance are directly related with each other and must be discussed in the same context.

7. In this light we can also address questions concerning *the assurance of conviction*. In essence faith is characterized by certainty with respect to God's benevolence. This certainty is founded in God himself and the reliability and truthfulness of his Word.

We have in mind the distinction between the act of faith and its object, i.e., the well-known distinction between *fides qua* (faith that believes) and *fides quae* (faith that is believed). In English this is reflected in the distinction between the words *faith* (*fides qua*) and *belief* (*fides quae*). Faith has certainty because of the certainty and reliability of the Word of God and the God of the Word, i.e., not in itself but through him in whom we believe.

Of course, with his *fides qua* the believer can be subject to a variety of experience. He may find himself in difficulty. He can say: "I believe; help thou mine unbelief" (Mark 9:24). Weak faith and little faith remain to be discussed.

This changeability of experience is on the side of the believer. There can be stagnation in the functioning of faith. This is different from declaring faith itself to be uncertain. Those who call faith in essence uncertain or still on the way to certainty, and do not regard certainty as implicit in the *fides quae*, detract from the essence of faith.

We have already pointed out that in the Old Testament, faith is related to the root *'aman*. This word implies certainty and assurance. We frequently encounter the act of faith in the expressions *to trust*, *to expect*. Bavinck extends this list with additional verbs: to serve, to cleave to, to rely on, to lean on, to hope in, and to wait for (*R.D.*, 4:104, with a reference to 3:491ff.). Those who incorporate an element of uncertainty in these verbs rob them not only of their force, but also of their essential content. To identify these verbs with the essence of uncertainty implies attaching a negative sign to them. Certainty derives from the prophetic word (2 Peter 1:19) and the salvation to which it testifies (Rom. 8:16; Heb. 10:19, 22). Salvation leads to personal certainty (Rom. 8:38–39; 1 John 3:14). This certainty is imprinted on our hearts through the gift of the Spirit as a pledge (2 Cor. 1:22; 5:5).

8. Aside from being fruit of the call and gift of God, faith is *also an act of man*. It is for this reason that the call to faith (and repentance)

is continually sounded (Isa. 55:6; Jer. 3:22; Mark 16:16; John 3:16; Acts 2:38–39; 16:31). Against this background it is easy to understand how serious a sin unbelief actually is, and how it makes one guilty before God (2 Kings 17:14, 19; Ps. 78:22; Isa. 7:9; Matt. 13:58; Mark 6:6; Heb. 3:19).

In a context of inter-subjectivity, Berkhof emphasizes the decisive role that we play within the covenant. Those who ignore this fundamental aspect of the act of our faith ignore the reality of the covenant. Berkhof calls faith simultaneously nothing and everything, passive and active, on the one hand purely instrumental, no more than a receiver, and on the other hand a source of inspiration, a center of activity (*C.F.*, 443–49).

We now address *the content and the character of faith*. Does the description of *faith as an instrument* (Belgic Confession of Faith, article 22) have a methodical and mechanical connotation?

Those who believe this are definitely mistaken. The description in article 22 occurs in the context of the righteousness of Christ and communion with him. It refers to faith as an instrument that keeps us connected with Christ in communion with all of his treasures and gifts.

It is confessed above that faith itself does not justify us, because it is only a means (instrument) by which we embrace Christ who is our righteousness. This formulation clearly defines the significance of faith as well as its absolutely non-meritorious character.

Berkouwer writes extensively about the value of faith (1954, chapter 7). He emphasizes that in the exclusion of one's own worthiness, the real nature of true faith is brought out (1965, 189). Faith is not empty. It is not a mechanical instrument. It is the relationship with God in which the believer completely looks away from himself and lives by what God gives him in Christ and for his sake. Although faith has no merit of its own, it is significant. It is indispensable for apprehending the gift of God's grace. Through faith we receive Christ's righteousness. The fact that faith itself is a gift from God indicates that faith has no merit in and of itself. Faith is the way that God himself prepares to let us share in his salvation.

In this connection we do not wish to characterize the relationship between faith and righteousness as a correlation. Correlation implies a relationship of mutual dependence or influence. The completely receptive character of faith makes it impossible to speak of a mutual dependence or influence. The latter implies a bipolar situation, which can also be described as inter-subjectivity. We prefer to (continue to) speak of the relationship between faith and its object, the relationship between the believer and God who manifests himself in his promise, and who wants to be known and acknowledged in faith.

Faith is not meritorious. Neither is it vacuous. It is an instrument to experience communion with Christ. Faith itself is part and parcel of this communion and operates within it.

The fact that faith is not vacuous is also clear from the classical statement by Calvin that although it is true that we are justified by faith alone, faith does not remain alone (*C.O.*, 7:477).

9. We finally wish to indicate *various circumstances in which the believer can find himself*. This has to do with the exercise of faith. The various ways in which a believer can be described reflect the functioning of his faith.

The Lord Jesus speaks of *great faith* on the part of the centurion of Capernaum (Matt. 8:10; Luke 7:9). His faith is marked by the following characteristics: He expects everything from Jesus. He puts his confidence in Jesus' benevolence. He recognizes his own unworthiness and believes in the power of Jesus' Word. These four characteristics together specify the faith that Jesus calls great. It is all the more poignant that such faith is not found on the part of anyone else in Israel at this point in time (Matt. 8:10).

Jesus speaks of *little faith* in connection with Peter, who looks at the waves instead of Jesus (Matt. 14:31), and in a context in which the disciples are surprised by a storm (Matt. 8:24–26). In the latter incident, they get Jesus involved by waking him up. They are more afraid of the storm than confident in his power. We encounter a similar situation in Matthew 17:20. There, "little faith" is due to worry (Matt. 6:30). It is focused on Jesus, but does not give full credit to his Word and power. The smallness of their faith does not imply a limited magnitude (cf. Matt. 17:20). It refers to the smallness of their expectation and confidence. Little faith runs into fences put up by itself, while in his admonishment Jesus breaks through these barriers.

In Mark 9:24 we encounter what we would like to call a *weak faith*. Such a faith is conscious of its own limitations. Weak faith reflects an inner incapacity and helplessness. A weak faith is conscious of its own deficiencies and imperfections. It is not much different from little faith. The latter is unaware of this and therefore needs to be rebuked from outside. In contrast, a weak faith struggles with its own shortcomings.

Frequently reference is made to *refuge-taking faith* as though God would be a final recourse and that seeking refuge with him would be an act of desperation. If nothing else works, maybe this will!

This is not a correct picture. In Scripture God is frequently confessed as a refuge (Pss. 14:6; 46:1; 59:16; 62:7–8; 71:7; 90:1; 94:22; 142:5). With confidence Ruth finds refuge under the wings of the God of Israel. Boaz praises her for her act of faith (Ruth 2:12; cf. Pss. 57:1; 61:4; 118:8–9). In refuge-taking faith, reliance is placed on the certainty that God offers. The fact that reference is made to taking refuge does not imply inner weakness on the part of the believer, but the threat of external circumstances and the trouble that the believer encounters or with which he is confronted. Refuge-taking faith is not an act of desperation, but confident expectation in a difficult, perhaps desperate situation.

Temporary faith, *historical faith*, and *faith in miracles* are essentially manifestations of unbelief. They imply that a personal relationship with God in Christ is missing. They are (external) manifestations without (internal) content.

Faith in miracles accepts the possibility of miracles without believing in the Savior himself and therefore without knowing salvation (see John 6:26, 66; Acts 8:13a). This is a form of superstition, i.e., faith in extraneous matters.

Temporary faith lasts for a while (Matt. 13:21); it does not last indefinitely, because although it has the appearance of faith, it lacks the essence of real faith.

Historical faith mentally accepts the truth of events and concepts (Acts 26:27–28), without having an inner relationship with the God behind them. We recognize in this the individuals of Matthew 7:21–23 of whom Jesus says that although they bear the hallmarks of believers, they lack substance (cf. 2 Tim. 3:5). They have a formal faith without a personal relationship with the God of the Word.

All these phenomena are in essence forms of unbelief. One should be careful not to interpret them as preliminary stages of true faith. This is absolutely not the case in terms of their nature and structure, content and intention. True faith is living faith, i.e., a faith that knows life.

40.2. *Repentance*

1. *Scripture passages pertaining to faith and repentance frequently appear in each other's proximity* (Mark 1:15; the Canons of Dort, 1.3; 2.5). The question may be asked what the difference is between the two. Another question that needs to be answered is what the difference is between regeneration and repentance. Do both words not describe the same thing and could they therefore not be considered to be synonyms with the inner renewal (to be) brought about by the Holy Spirit?

We have already seen that Kuyper relates repentance chiefly with the will and faith with the intellect. Bavinck follows in his footsteps. Honig criticizes both (*Handboek*, 553ff.).

As far as the difference between regeneration and repentance is concerned, it may be pointed out that regeneration is considered to be not only a necessary way to salvation but also part of salvation. However, nowhere do we encounter a command to be reborn. Those who object that such a command (*imperativus*) is unlikely in the case of the passive form of a verb may be reminded that in Ephesians 5:18 we encounter an imperative in the passive form of the verb to fill, i.e., "be filled."

Regeneration is a gift of God, effected by the Holy Spirit. It is brought about by means of the Word and results from the call. The response to the call leads to the two activities that we have described as faith and repentance. Regeneration is a concept that strongly emphasizes the nature of the new life as a gift. Man plays a passive role in it. However, he does not remain so. Faith and repentance manifest themselves in this new life. *There is no repentance without regeneration. Neither is there regeneration that does not manifest itself in repentance.*

Faith and repentance are fruits of regeneration. They are also manifestations of the life that has been reborn. The latter formulation is even more stringent than the former. There is no new life that does not manifest itself in faith and repentance. Reborn life can be recognized from both of these. The root of faith and repentance is regeneration. This root cannot, however, be experienced without being apparent in terms of faith and repentance. This is the manifestation of the work of the Holy Spirit in man. The pneumatic root of this work is regeneration, and man's act of receiving and responding consists of faith and repentance. In this way we have described the true nature of regeneration as a ministry of the Holy Spirit that one receives and undergoes. At the same time we have made clear that this ministry of the Holy Spirit puts man into action. Receiving the ministry of the Holy Spirit cannot occur without the response of the one who is reborn. From a practical point of view, there is therefore every reason to distinguish between regeneration on the one hand and faith and repentance on the other hand. This distinction is encouraged by the language employed by the Bible itself. However, it should never be viewed as a dichotomy.

2. *What is the difference between faith and repentance?* We frequently encounter these concepts together but also on their own. This implies that they cannot be identified with each other. We do not seek the distinction between these two by associating them with different inner, psychic abilities. Those who go this route break up the work of God and deny the all-inclusive nature of both faith and repentance. With this all-inclusive nature we mean the fact that both faith and repentance involve the entire person, and therefore the heart.

On the basis of the Bible we can describe the difference between these two as follows. Through faith man entrusts himself to God, leaning on his promise. Faith is the surrender of one's heart in accepting God's gracious benevolence, declared and shown to us in the gospel of Jesus Christ.

The act of repentance is not different from that of faith. Turning to God is impossible without turning away from sin. Repentance indicates the restoration of the relationship with God across the full spectrum of our existence.

Sin brings separation, in part by exercising dominion over us (see § 27.2). Those who yield themselves to God in confidence are also delivered from the power of sin. This bond is broken. Man turns back toward God with the devotion of his heart and the engagement of his energy.

Repentance implies living once again with God in obedience to his command to be his people on earth. This has two aspects, namely being released from sin and being focused on God in loving obedience and service. These two aspects are indicated as "the mortification of the old man, and the quickening of the new" (Heidelberg Catechism, Lord's Day 33). Therefore, repentance consists especially in obedience and humility, which replace sinful disobedience and pride. Faith consists especially in trustingly surrendering to God and accepting his favor.

Faith and repentance go together. They point to one and the same work of God in us, and one and the same change in our lives in relationship with God. *Repentance cannot proceed without faith. Faith cannot fail to manifest itself in repentance.*

3. The Hebrew word *shub* and its noun *teshubah* indicate respectively "to repent" and "repentance."

The following traits characterize repentance:

1. Repentance consists in listening to God's voice, to go and do what God commands with all our heart and all our soul (Deut. 30:2).
2. Repentance is repentance to God, which manifests itself in directing one's heart to the LORD, to serve him (1 Sam. 7:3). For coming to God not only with our lips but also with all our heart, i.e., wholly, see also Isaiah 29:13.
3. Repentance is coupled with confession of guilt and humiliation. People used to dedicate an entire day to penance. Humiliation was demonstrated by pouring out water and fasting (1 Sam. 7:6).
4. Repentance is always a return from life without God and in disobedience to his commands, to a life with him and in obedience to his Word. Therefore repentance always has two sides, namely, turning away and turning toward, both of which are unthinkable without man humbling himself and confessing his sins (Luke 15:17–20).
5. In principle, repentance is always connected with the promise of grace (1 Sam. 7:3; 1 Kings 8:33–34). Frequently the latter is the foundation of the call to repentance. See Matthew 3:2. In this connection we may think of the interrelationship among guilt, the announcement of judgment, and a call to repentance coupled with the promise of forgiveness (Isa. 41–44:20; see Velema, 1987, 139–42).
6. Especially in Isaiah (41–44:20), Amos (9:11–14), and Hosea (2:14–23; 11:8–11; 14:2–8) the call to repentance from serious apostasy is combined with the announcement of the time of salvation.

7. The LORD himself brings his people to repentance (Hos. 14:4; cf. Jer. 30:17). Notice also how the LORD puts words of guilt and confession on Israel's lips. This also happens in Jeremiah 3:21–25. In Lamentations 5:21 repentance is sought as a gift from God.

Here we shall have to ignore the redemptive-historical context of these passages. Neither can we explore the idea that only a remnant will escape (Isa. 10:20–22).

4. In the New Testament we encounter the concept of "repentance" in the words *metanoia* (22 times) and *epistrophe* (once), and "to repent" in *metanoeo* (34 times) and *epistrepho* (15 times; Pop, *Bijbelse woorden* = biblical words, 76). Both the preaching of John the Baptist (Matt. 3:2, 8) and that of Jesus were characterized by the call to repentance (Luke 5:32).

Salvation and judgment are imminent. In light of the serious nature of both, the call to repentance is proclaimed. It includes confession of sins and the new life that yields fruit commensurate with repentance. Baptism is a sign of forgiveness and renewal (Mark 1:4; cf. Acts 2:38). Luke 3:10–14 describes the concreteness of repentance to God as a response to the preaching of the imminent kingdom (Matt. 3:2–3). John does not merely seek a change in morality, which would be moralism. Baptism for the forgiveness of sins indicates that repentance is a turning toward God, just as in the Old Testament. It provides entry into the imminent kingdom.

The preaching of Jesus that calls for repentance comes from the same perspective and has the same objective (Luke 5:32; 13:3, 5; 15:7, 10; cf. Matt. 11:20; 12:41). Repentance is a prerequisite for entry into the kingdom of heaven (Mark 4:12 for Israel; Luke 24:47 also beyond the borders of Israel).

In the Synoptic Gospels repentance constitutes the content of Jesus' preaching and plays a key role in the kingdom's perspective of salvation. It is not only part of this salvation, but also represents the way to salvation.

We also encounter repentance further in the New Testament as the way to salvation (see Acts 3:19–20; 5:31; 9:35; 11:18, 21; see also 17:30; 20:21; 26:18).

Repentance also applies to remaining sins or sins committed subsequently (2 Cor. 12:21; 2 Tim. 2:25ff.; Heb. 6:6).

This repentance is then especially turning to God through the gospel, i.e., repentance brings knowledge of the light and redeems from the power of Satan (Acts 26:18). Repentance also means turning to the Lord Jesus Christ (Acts 9:35; 11:21).

In 2 Corinthians 7:10 we see the distinction between worldly sorrow and godly sorrow. The former is a form of the previous life that refused to repent. The latter describes sorrow over sin, which expresses itself as a desire to be obedient to God. We encounter here both sides of repentance, namely, confession of guilt, inward sorrow for sin, aversion to concrete sins, and a turning toward God to obey his will. The same is true of Hebrews 6:1, 6, and 1 Peter 2:25.

In *TDNT*, 4:989–1009, Behm points out that the Old Testament *shub* is rendered as *metanoeo*. All of Jesus' teaching is proclamation of the *metanoia*, even when this word is not always used explicitly (1002).

The concept of repentance is a continuous thread in the New Testament (1005). Both Pop (*Bijbelse woorden* = biblical words, 86) and Bertram (*TWNT*, 7:727–28) point out that when both *metanoeo* and *epistrepho* occur in the same verse (Acts 3:19; 26:20), there is a difference. *Metanoeo* would particularly signify an inner disposition (inward sorrow) and *epistrepho* the purpose of repentance. Apart from this, there is little difference between the two.

A distinction is made between initial repentance (Canons of Dort, 3–4.12) and ongoing repentance (Heidelberg Catechism, Lord's Day 33; see also Honig, *Handboek*, 554ff.; and for Kuyper see Velema, 1957, 160ff.). Although this distinction is legitimate, it should not be viewed as a contrast. It displays a remarkable parallel with the reference to regeneration in the narrower and broader sense (§ 39.3, subsection 2).

By way of conclusion we can say the following:

1. Repentance indicates turning *away* from sin and false gods and turning *toward* the living God.
2. Repentance always has a positive focus, which is manifested in obedience to God's commands and in serving him.
3. Repentance is coupled with inner sorrow and confession of guilt. Sometimes there is an element of penance (fasting; days of penitence).
4. Repentance is *elicited through the preaching of the gospel* and is the work of God in the lives of sinful people.

5. In view of the positive character of repentance, it cannot proceed in the absence of faith in God's word (of promise), even though such faith is not always explicitly mentioned.

5. In the Reformed tradition, particularly since Calvin, we encounter two words that describe repentance, namely, *mortificatio* and *vivificatio*. Calvin means with these two words the aversion to sin and the associated sorrow, and a turning toward God with inner joy and obedience to his commands.[18] The Heidelberg Catechism follows the same idea in Lord's Day 33. Its description of repentance employing the terms "mortification" and "quickening" is formulated in the present tense. This implies an ongoing process in the life of a Christian.

Robert C. Doyle published an essay about "The Preaching of Repentance in John Calvin. Repentance and Union in Christ" in the festschrift for D. B. Knox, *God Who Is Rich in Mercy*, 1986, 287–321. He shows that repentance is directly connected with union in Christ. It has an eschatological dimension. It is focused on the life that is to come. He also points to the difference between Luther and Calvin. The former connects inward sorrow particularly with the foregoing proclamation of the law, while Calvin views repentance as an ongoing element of the new life (*Institutes*, 3.3.2), so that *mortificatio* and *vivificatio* apply to one's entire life (as in Lord's Day 33). This view strengthens the focus on the life that is to come, i.e., the eschatological focus of Calvin's doctrine of repentance and penitence.

With these brief historical notes we have also taken a position with respect to the issues concerning sorrow over sin as being brought about primarily by the proclamation of the law, and the new obedience being due chiefly to the preaching of the gospel.

In *Wet en evangelie* (law and the gospel, 1987) we discuss these questions in greater detail, with references to both Luther and Calvin. Our conclusion is that the two should not be played off against each other. It is true that Calvin relates repentance more closely with the preaching of the gospel than Luther does. By assigning a relative independence to the law he avoided the misconception that repentance could only be ascribed to the proclamation of the law. The law is not known except through the gospel. It cannot be proclaimed without the perspective of the gospel. On the other hand, the relative independence of the law

18. The Council of Trent rejected this Reformational position. For an analysis of its decrees and the polemical nature of its decisions see the dissertation by G. J. Spykman, *Attrition and Contrition at the Council of Trent*, 1955. He characterized the pronouncements of Trent with respect to both of these terms as syncretism. In our view it would be synergism.

also ensures that the law is not abrogated in the preaching of the gospel (1987, especially chapter 5). The link between the law and the gospel advocated there has implications for the preaching of repentance and a place in the order of salvation. Repentance as fruit of the preaching of the law and preceding faith in Christ would be a work of the law, which is rejected by Paul in Romans 8:3 as being powerless compared with (the preaching of) the gospel of Jesus Christ.[19]

Barth points out that Calvin describes penitence as "Erweckung zur Umkehr" (the awakening to conversion). Barth refuses to employ the term "penitence," because it evokes associations with momentary events in life or an experience of conversion as in Pietism (*C.D.*, 4.2.566–70, especially 566–67).

Barth wants to apply the expression *mortificatio en vivificatio* to us only indirectly. They pertain directly to Christ (*C.D.*, 4.2.583).

In view of the dissertation by M. den Dulk, *Als twee die spreken. Een manier om de heiligingsleer van Barth te lezen* (as two who speak: a way to interpret Barth's doctrine of sanctification), 1987, we investigated the way in which Barth treats Calvin's concept of *poenitentia* (repentance). We conclude that Barth's alternative formulation of "Erweckung zur Umkehr" (awakening for turning back) represents nothing but a clarification—through the revelation of Christ—with respect to our being in Christ. See "De leer van de heiliging bij Calvijn en Barth" (the doctrine of sanctification according to Calvin and Barth), in *Th. Ref.* 32 (1989): 117–39, especially 124–31.

6. In closing, we point out that with respect to repentance there is room for the adjective *real or true* (cf. Heidelberg Catechism, Lord's Day 33). The LORD continues to call Israel to repent with all their heart and with all their soul, and to seek him. Apparently there is a real possibility that Israel will only partly turn to God (cf. James 1:6–8). Semi-repentance would be equivalent to the various forms of unbelief that we identified above as intellectual faith, faith in miracles, or only temporary faith.

The practical side of repentance will be discussed as part of sanctification.

§ 41. Justification

41.1. *Exploration and definition*

41.2. *Biblical perspectives*

19. C. G. Vreugdenhil emphasizes in his practical-pastoral study *Alles uit hem. Over de orde des heils* (everything from him: concerning the order of salvation), 1990, that repentance cannot precede faith. Repentance takes place as a result of faith, 84.

41.3. *Grace, Christ, faith in the context of justification*
41.4. *Consensus and confrontation*
41.5. *Broader implications*

41.1. *Exploration and definition*

1. With the topic of this section *we reach the heart of the gospel.* The message of the Bible can ultimately be summarized as the justification of the sinner (the ungodly). This does not mean that this topic displaces the person and work of Jesus Christ (Christology) from his central position. It does mean that the significance of Christ for the salvation of the world (soteriology) finds its focus and culmination in the doctrine of justification. It is not surprising that the sixteenth-century conflict erupted and was settled at this juncture. The question whether grace is fully grace or requires man's cooperation in some way is answered in the doctrine of justification.

Why does justification have such a central role in the dogmatics? It reflects the fact that *here is discussed how the relationship between God and man—radically disturbed by sin—is restored.* The relationship between God and man is a key topic in the Christian faith. The Bible indicates three aspects of this relationship, namely, its good beginning, i.e., its original righteousness by virtue of God's creation; its corruption through man's sinful rebellion against God; and its restoration.

These three terms—original righteousness, corruption, and restoration—indicate the height and depth, the length and the width of this concept (cf. Eph. 3:18).

How do I acquire a gracious God? How do I become righteous before God? This is indeed the core question of the Reformation (particularly to Luther). This is correct, as long as the question is not seen as coming from man (anthropocentrically). It must be seen as a question evoked in man by God himself (theocentrically). How does man become once again man of God? How does he regain his status before God, relieved of his guilt and stain? In short: how does the relationship between God and man become "good" again in the biblical sense (cf. Gen. 1:31)?

This question is answered in this section on justification.

Throughout the centuries justification has been a topic of fundamental significance in the Western church. Different emphases were laid in the Eastern church and post-World War II Africa and South

America as the latter have begun to make their own contributions to theological reflection and the formulation of the confession. In the latter case the dominant perspective is life, liberation, and the breaking of a host of taboos.

The fact that the relationship between God and man is viewed juridically (cf. Anselm, *Cur deus homo?*) is ascribed to the mode of thinking of the Near East. This is contextually determined.[20] At other times and in other cultural contexts it may be expressed differently, which shifts the point of gravity of soteriology, namely, away from man's legal position to his destiny. The central issue is then no longer his guilt, but how he will maintain himself and keep his faith in God intact in the midst of so many confusing experiences.

We shall return to this at the conclusion of this section. Then we shall have to face the question whether the doctrine of justification (in its strongly juridical formulation) is contextually/culturally determined, or that we must say that this doctrine is the sine qua non of the Christian faith. In this context the incorporation of a (concise) historical dogmatic overview is inevitable.

2. A discussion of this topic cannot avoid a number of perplexing issues. We shall now list these in arbitrary order. Each one of these will successively be addressed in the subsequent discussion of our topic.

1. Justification occurs for Jesus' sake. How should we view our relationship with Christ in justification? To what extent should Christ be ours (and we his)? Does Christ's righteousness, manifested in us and having transformed us, constitute the ground for our justification, or Christ's righteousness outside of us?
2. In this context, what are the significance, place, and value of faith in justification? Is it indispensable and therefore in some way yet a contribution on our part? And if faith is not a constitutive factor, is it incidental and therefore of lesser significance?
3. The above questions include the relationship between justification and inner change. Does the former precede the latter? If so, is it then right to discuss regeneration and repentance prior to justification?
4. What is the role of the law, *prior to* and *subsequent to* justification? Does justification imply that the law ceases to have significance in the life of a Christian?

20. See for example W. Pannenberg, *Christliche Spiritualität*, 1986, and a discussion of this in Velema, *Nieuw zicht op Gereformeerde spiritualiteit* (new view of Reformed spirituality), 1991, 49–52.

5. Does the New Testament not contain various perspectives, e.g., those of Paul and James?

We attempt to incorporate answers to these questions in the overall discussion of this topic.[21]

41.2. *Biblical perspectives*

1. In this subsection we wish to *call special attention to what the Bible says about justifying and justification.* In this connection we cannot avoid a discussion of Christ's sacrifice and the role of faith. We shall treat these latter aspects systematically in § 41.3. Here we lay the foundation for this discussion, namely, the biblical-exegetical perspective.

We start out with Paul's key statement that a sinner is justified by faith in Jesus (Rom. 3:26). It says even that God justifies him who is of the faith of Jesus. In verse 28 Paul calls this justification *by* faith. It is contrasted with justification based on (deeds of) the law. Righteousness does not come through the law. In verse 21 Paul even says that it is without the law. Therefore there is no righteousness of our own, but only the righteousness that comes from God (Phil. 3:9).

Faith links us with Jesus Christ. This is obvious from the passage quoted. Why is Christ involved? It is because he is the ground for our justification (referred to in *Synopsis*, 33:13 as *impulsiva externa et meritoria*, i.e., the externally moving and meriting cause). There is no justification apart from this relationship with Jesus Christ. We see this especially in Romans 4:25; Christ "was delivered for our offenses, and was raised again for our justification." Justification is by "grace through the redemption that is in Christ Jesus" (Rom. 3:24). We are "justified by his blood" (Rom. 5:9).

The parallel between being justified by blood and by faith is noteworthy. We can only see this duality as a unity when we are in faith linked with him who shed his blood for us. Faith in Christ is therefore faith that lives out of, and draws its strength from, the sacrifice Christ has brought for us.

2. We shall now attempt to combine the above perspectives into a coherent picture.

21. Our discussion closely follows the study by van Genderen, 1988, although it is not a summary of it.

To justify someone means to declare him to be righteous. This verb has juridical and forensic connotations (cf. a verdict in a court of law).

To declare someone to be righteous is the opposite of declaring him to be guilty, i.e., to condemn him, which is obvious from Romans 8:33–34, where justification by God is contrasted with making accusations in order to condemn someone. See also how, in Matthew 12:37 and Romans 5:16 and 18, justification is contrasted with condemnation.

To justify someone means that he is declared not to be guilty, that he is acquitted. To justify someone means saying that he is righteous. This is the essence of this judicial verdict.

3. Nevertheless, something must be added to clarify the evangelical content of justification. This justification is a *gift*. Those who are declared righteous deserve the verdict. They deserve judgment, damnation (Rom. 5:1).

It is for this reason that according to Paul, justification is always characterized by two perspectives. On the one hand justification must be seen in the context of the law, which accuses and condemns us. On the other hand we see Christ who fulfilled the requirements of the law. He took upon himself the curse of the law in order to redeem his people from this curse (Gal. 3:13).

From a biblical perspective justification takes place in a situation in which people are condemned by the law. They can never obtain or claim justification on the basis of their obedience to the law. The law condemns and damns them.

With reference to Romans 3:24 Calvin says that there probably is no other passage of Scripture that reveals the power of righteousness more clearly. It is brought about by God's mercy; its content is the blood of Christ; it is formally received by means of faith based on the Word of God; and finally its chief goal is the glory of divine righteousness and goodness.

On the other hand there is Christ who takes this judgment upon himself and thus brings about the justification that is imputed to the sinner. In Paul's epistles, to justify someone always means *to declare him righteous by imputing to him the righteousness obtained through Christ's sacrifice*. It is for this reason that to justify someone always amounts to reckoning righteousness to him (Rom. 4:5–6). Here faith is reckoned for righteousness. We shall revisit how faith can be reckoned for righteousness.

Here also the imputation of righteousness is contrasted with and is the opposite of reckoning sin. The latter should have been expected and would have been just.

Justifying someone in the sense of not reckoning sin to him and declaring him to be righteous through the imputation of alien righteousness (*iustitia aliena*) then always has the connotation of liberating grace.

Therefore justifying someone means declaring him to be righteous before the judgment seat of God. However, this comes unexpectedly. In this judgment there is an undeserved and unexpected turn of events, because someone who is unrighteous and ought to be condemned is declared righteous.

It is for this reason that Schrenk speaks of "saving justification." It is equivalent to acquittal and implicit forgiveness of sins. Schrenk associates this with the writers of the Synoptic Gospels (Luke 18:14; *TDNT*, 2:215). It is equally true of Paul.

Schrenk reminds us that the forensic use of the verb "to justify" is not explicitly mentioned in every passage. However, it cannot be denied that the idea of judgment, and therefore a judicial act (by God), echoes in every instance. For example, see Romans 3:20 and Galatians 3:11 (*TDNT*, 2:216).

In contrast with Paul who views justification as taking place in the present, the rabbinical tradition associates it with the final judgment. Justification can occur in the present because of its connection with the saving act (*Heilstat*) in Jesus Christ. Here we face the question as to how (the experience of) justification in the present is related to what happened to Christ. Those who concentrate everything in the present threaten objectivity. At the opposite extreme, by over-emphasizing the past (the there and then) one equally risks objectivism. In the latter case the kerygmatic nature of the benefit of justification loses its fundamental significance. It is obvious that with this objection we imply that in the latter case the connection between calling and justification is fatally severed.

4. Justification comprises *the forgiveness of sins* (Rom. 4:5–8). This forgiveness appears to be based in jurisprudence. It is itself an act of God, the Judge. Justification as forgiveness does not violate God's

justice. Here also God demonstrates himself to be the just Judge (Rom. 3:26), although we may immediately add that his righteousness here bears the character of redeeming grace (Rom. 3:24). It is a bestowed, imputed righteousness that does not take our works into account. The works that should have been considered are not taken into account (Rom. 4:6, 8).

From the perspective of grace, justification comprises more than just forgiveness of sins and purely judicial acquittal of guilt. *It combines a change in status* (righteous instead of guilty) *with a positive relationship with God*. Paul characterizes this new relationship with God as peace (Rom. 5:1). It implies reconciliation, i.e., the elimination of a relationship of enmity (Rom. 5:9–10). Peace means reconciliation in the positive sense of the word, i.e., being permitted to share in the salvation that God grants (Ridderbos, 1959, 105).

Viewed in this manner, expressed in juridical terms, justification signifies the restoration of one's relationship with God. It is the declaration whereby a sinner is acquitted of his guilt and whereby he is declared to be righteous, because the righteousness of Christ is imputed to him. This justification implies the restoration of the right relationship with God, i.e., being restored to the position of being a child of his. The latter is not an incidental, but an essential aspect of justification. It is implicit in the peace that is inherent in justification. This peace constitutes atonement for the guilt that brought separation, and a return to the home and life with the Father.

In justification God imparts to the sinner what he had in mind with respect to the covenant of life. Life is granted to him and sonship is declared to him (having a right to and being heir to eternal life, Rom. 8:17). This is all due to God's juridical declaration. The righteousness connected with obedience to the law has been earned by Christ and is imputed to a sinner in justification. This makes him share in the blessing originally intended for the covenant of life, not in the way of works and of his own obedience to the law but in the way of grace through faith in Christ. This covenant of life has now therefore been determined christologically. It is the covenant of grace.[22]

5. Above we focused principally on the New Testament. Van Genderen (1988, 19) reminds us that *the word "justification" rarely occurs in the*

22. For a simple and practical discussion of the relationship between the covenants of life and grace, see E. Fisher, *Marrow of Modern Divinity*, republished in 1978.

Old Testament. He says that its usage is restricted to Psalm 69:27–28; Isaiah 45:25; and possibly Isaiah 1:18.

We may nevertheless refer to the penitential psalms, e.g., Psalm 143[23] and also Psalm 32, which may be viewed as the Old Testament equivalent of 1 John 1:9. Psalm 130 deals with forgiveness of our guilt through grace. Obviously the name of Christ cannot yet be mentioned. This name is also absent in Luke 18:14. However, it may be said that Jesus himself proclaims the justification of the ungodly. He already does so by way of the restoration of the relationship with the Father in the parable of the father who again accepts his prodigal son as his son (Luke 15:11–24).

In Isaiah 53:10–12 justification by God is linked with the suffering Servant of the LORD.

This messianic (christological) interpretation has not gone unchallenged. In this connection Edelkoort speaks of the anticipation of Christ (1941, 424). He does not want to associate the name Messiah with the suffering Servant. The Messiah is, after all, a king. The suffering Servant is not portrayed as a king.[24] We conclude that justification is at any rate part of the suffering Servant's work of salvation.

The salvation that we receive through justification is also encountered in the Old Testament. The relationship to Christ and his sacrifice is not so explicitly present (except in Isa. 53, but still in the shadow of the Old Testament). In the Old Testament we do not encounter the full revelation of justification—as described above—in precisely those terms. However, the concept itself is clearly present.

6. The Old Testament frequently refers to God's righteousness.[25] It is undeniable that this righteousness is also a punishing righteousness. (See passages such as 2 Chron. 12:6; Pss. 7:11; 11:5–7; 94:2; Isa. 10:22; Lam. 1:18; Dan. 9:14). Yet God's righteousness is also referred to in a

23. Kraus, *Psalmen*, 1961², 2:937, points out that Psalm 143:2 announced the *iustficatio impii* (justification of the sinner).

24. For the Servant as Messiah-King, see J. L. Koole, *Jesaja 53*, 1969, including references to the literature. W. Zimmerli wrote in his essay in a festschrift honoring E. Käsemann, *Rechfertigung* (justification), especially with reference to Isaiah 53, "Die Prophetie schaut aus auf die *iustificatio impiorum*" (the prophecy points to the justification of sinners), 582.

25. We refer now already to the overview of the exegetical literature concerning the terms "righteousness" and "justification" provided by H. J. Kraus in *Reich Gottes: Reich der Freiheit* (kingdom of God: kingdom of freedom), 1975, 307–16. The systematic literature will be reviewed in § 41.4.

different way, namely, as a pleading ground for prayers for help and deliverance (Pss. 31:1; 35:24; 71:2; 143:11).

The Lord keeps his Word. Therefore those who anticipate his coming are called blessed. He does as he says (Num. 23:19; 1 Sam. 15:29; Ps. 89:35). This is why his salvation is announced as righteousness (Isa. 46:13). In the announcement of the Messiah the LORD will reveal his righteousness (Jer. 23:6). It is for this reason that God's justice is revealed through the suffering Servant (Isa. 42:1). The Messianic King will judge the poor in righteousness (Isa. 11:1–5).

Against this background we now wish to discuss the expression "God's righteousness" (Rom. 1:17; 3:21). No fewer than five explanations have been offered (sometimes with refinements within a category). Van Genderen (with reference to Rom. 3:21–25; 2 Cor. 5:20–21; Phil. 3:9–10) makes a case for a christological interpretation. Righteousness then means the salvation that God grants us in Christ. Justification is thus identified with salvation. Van Genderen does not consider the label "eschatological" for this view to be entirely clear (1988, 26).

We consider this christological interpretation to be correct. We add that it makes good sense to interpret this view of righteousness as an extension of the Old Testament concept of God's righteousness. Righteousness then denotes salvation in Christ. This christological definition of salvation indicates that the LORD is faithful to his Word. He fulfills what he has promised. He confirms the Messianic name in Jeremiah 23:5. God justifies a sinner through grace and justice (cf. Rom. 3:25–26).

The expression "God's righteousness" then includes all salvation in Christ, which he promises and applies to people by virtue of his justice. We can call this interpretation christological and at the same time redemption-historical. In this righteousness God fulfills his Old Testament promises of salvation. There we saw the contours of this salvation, but now we see its concrete fulfillment. Christ is central in justification. Hence we can speak of God's righteousness in Christ Jesus.

7. A last point that we need to discuss is the question whether James speaks differently about justification than Paul.[26]

Romans 3:28 and James 2:24 are frequently discussed as irreconcilable antitheses. This is partly because both refer to Abraham: Paul for

26. For an overview of the various interpretations see van Genderen, 1988, 27–29.

justification by faith alone, James for justification not by faith alone, but by faith *and* works.

Yet the solution is simpler than many are willing to accept.[27] Paul fights nomism, which relies on works. In that polemical context, good works are not on the radar screen. Nevertheless, Paul also knows that in justification by faith alone, this faith does not remain alone, but works and manifests itself in love (Gal. 5:6). Elsewhere Paul speaks in this connection of the fruit of the Spirit (Gal. 5:22–23).

From James's perspective faith is not a matter of words only. There is more! Living faith bears fruit. Those who limit justification to cold, lifeless words (in contrast with the living words that Moses received, Acts. 7:38) will be rejected.

Mussner (*Der Jakobusbrief* = the epistle of James, 1975, 18) correctly points out that James's focus is not a dilemma between faith and good works, but living faith. He argues against a misinterpretation of Paul's position, be it *bona fide* or *mala fide*. However, Mussner presents a synthesis of faith and works, which amounts to synergism (141).

41.3. *Grace, Christ, faith in the context of justification*

In this subsection we wish to consider these three nouns, which we already encountered in the context of justification. These three terms (where "Christ" refers to both his person and work) are typical of the biblical doctrine of justification. They determine both its connotation and intention. They refer to the life that is concerned with justification.

1. *The grace of God in justification* (Rom. 3:24) *points to the nature of justification as a gift*. This gift dimension is all the more profound because the gift is contrary to what people can expect, what they deserve. God pronounces his curse over those who disobey his law (Deut. 27:26). Also in Romans 5—precisely there!—Paul speaks of God's wrath over sin. (See also the Canons of Dort, 3–4.5).

The perspective of grace in justification cannot be understood without consideration of the law. Grace is extended to trespassers of the law. There is an inner connection between grace and the juridical character of justification. Justification takes place exactly where grace is extended, namely, before God's judgment seat.

27. V. Subilia, *Die Rechfertigung aus Glauben* (righteousness based on faith), Göttingen 1981, 41, refers to a contrast between these two. This would confirm Käsemann's thesis of "die Vielzahl von Konfessionen" (multiplicity of confessions) in the New Testament.

We emphatically present it this way. Some (perhaps even many) believe that grace has nothing to do with the forensic aspect of justification. Grace is God's good favor toward sinners. We fully subscribe to this. However, the revelation of this grace comes to us by way of the law. Only transgressors of the law are in need of grace, i.e., grace in Christ Jesus. God's favor in general is not the same as God's grace in Christ. Grace is the culmination of God's favor toward guilty human beings. It therefore has always the character of something unmerited, of the opposite of what we deserve because of our sin.

We also encounter the forensic aspect of justification in the nature of justification as grace. It is no coincidence that Paul uses the expression "righteousness of God" as being directly connected and contrasted with "the wrath of God," which manifests itself "against all ungodliness and unrighteousness of men, who hold the truth down in unrighteousness" (Rom. 1:17–18).

The aspect of grace in justification does not affect the original order that God established for his relationship with man. On the contrary, it confirms this order. Grace is God's favor toward those who are guilty.

2. This leads to a twofold question: *How can God grant his favor to those who are guilty?* And on the other hand: *How can God be just, if he does not declare sinners to be guilty, but acquits them?*

These questions lead us to Christ as the heart of justification. The preaching of justification would destroy the entire biblical message if it merely said: God nullifies sin. God does not hold people accountable for sin. Those who are guilty are at once declared innocent. This thesis is explicitly rejected in various passages (Ex. 34:7; Num. 14:18; Deut. 7:9–10). The entire law of God including sanctions for trespasses would become null and void if God did not punish sin, i.e., if God would merely declare sinners to be righteous. The covenant of life would then also be null and void. The original relationship between God and man would be broken.

Just ignoring guilt would be unjust. Then God would no longer be faithful to his word that he spoke as threat, curse, and judgment.

3. Paul says that God is not unjust (Rom. 3:25–26) by being "the justifier of him which believeth in Jesus." We must now speak of *the place of Christ in justification and the significance of his work*. We do so in two different ways: first, we are justified for Christ's sake,

and, second, in justification the righteousness of Christ is imputed to us. Christ paid for our sins with his death. See articles 20–23 of the Belgic Confession of Faith; especially article 23 ("our justification before God") is permeated with the thought of substitution and gracious imputation. They converge in justification and represent the reverse of each other. Jesus Christ is "our righteousness . . . imputing to us all his merits, and so many holy works which he has done for us and in our stead" (article 22, Belgic Confession of Faith). See also the Smalkaldic Articles[28] and the Confession of Augsburg.[29]

Jesus Christ is the means of propitiation (Rom. 3:25). Justification takes place through the blood of Christ (Rom. 5:9–10). This blood signifies sacrifice. Without sacrifice (shedding of blood) there is no forgiveness (Heb. 9:22–28). God's punishing righteousness was effected in Christ. He bore the curse of the law (Gal. 3:13). God does not set aside his own justice when he justifies the ungodly. On the contrary, he maintains his justice and his law. This is demonstrated in the cross of Christ (see § 32.1, subsection 5).

This is explained very clearly in 2 Corinthians 5:21: "He hath made him to be sin for us, who knew no sin; that we might be made the righteousness of God in him" (as the culmination of vv. 18–19).

Here the exchange is clearly spelled out. Christ has taken our place, and we receive what he has earned. The acquittal takes place because he bore our sentence.

God's justice, as characteristic designation of his work of salvation in Christ, proves that he is and remains just in the justification of sinners. At the same time it is clear that the righteousness that is imputed to us neither originates in us nor is earned by us. It originates in Christ.

We referred to Christ as the heart and mystery of justification. But from Christ we must return to the Father. He sent and gave the Son. The initiative of justification originates in the heart of God (John 3:16; Rom. 8:32; Gal. 4:4–6).

28. We refer to the second part, its first article, a translation of which may be found in *Lutherse geschriften. Belijdenisteksten van een kerk* (Lutheran documents: texts of a church's confessions), 1987, 208ff.

29. *Augsburge Confessie*, 4, (page 154 in the above source). On the theological purport of this confession with respect to justification, see E. Schlink, *Theologie der luterischen Bekenntnisschriften* (theology of Lutheran confessions), 1483, 134–41, with references to a great deal of (obviously older) literature.

We still need to focus on Romans 4:25: "delivered for our offenses," "raised for our justification." The question is whether justification is here ascribed to Christ's resurrection. We have discussed this verse elsewhere. Our conclusion may be repeated here. Jesus' resurrection confirms his death. In the absence of this confirmation the significance of his crucifixion would have amounted to death. Paul does not say that justification is not due to his death also. He says that justification is unthinkable without his resurrection. One would be hard pressed to find another place in Paul's epistles where the coherence and continuity of Jesus' death and resurrection for salvation is so succinctly and yet so clearly expressed as here (Velema, 1987, 25; see also van Genderen, 1988, 645ff.).

4. *How does a sinner acquire Christ's righteousness?* Is the ground for justification to be sought in man after all? Does man, who takes hold of Christ's righteousness in faith, have grounds and the right in himself to claim justification by God?

In answering these questions we arrive at *the role of faith in justification*. We may summarize this problem in the following questions: If Abraham's faith was counted to him as righteousness and he was justified on this basis (Rom. 4:3–5, reflecting Gen. 15:6; see also Gal. 3:6; and James 2:23), did Abraham then not have a ground within himself for righteousness, namely, his faith that took hold of God's promise? Or did he have this ground in the faith that embraces and appropriates the righteousness of Christ?

The answer to this question is decided by what faith actually is. Faith is no accomplishment, no attribute of man, comparable with merit. It is not a deed that can be credited to him as a good work in fulfillment of the law. It is true that Scripture refers to faith as a "work," namely, in John 6:29 ("the work of God"). Precisely this conversation of Jesus with the Jews reveals the unique character of this work. In accepting God's grace, it stands in contrast to work as personal achievement. The focus of this dispute (John 6:22–59) is whether or not to accept Jesus' offer of the bread of life. For lack of faith this bread passes them by.

That Abraham's faith is counted toward him as righteousness does not mean that faith is ascribed to him as an achievement. With this quote from Genesis, Paul wants to say that the righteousness taken hold of by Abraham in faith is the ground for his justification. Paul does not say this with so many words. He summarizes this perspective by employing the words "by faith" to indicate the righteousness that is taken hold of and appropriated in faith.

Faith is not a creative but a *receptive* act (see § 40.1 and Berkouwer, 1954, 176–79). Therefore faith is not meritorious, but merely the hand that is filled with the promise. Who would dare to claim this extending of the hand—to accept Christ's righteousness—to be an achievement? Besides, as we saw earlier, faith itself is a gift from God, brought about by the Holy Spirit.

The above does, however, imply that *Christ's righteousness must be appropriated for justification to take place*. In justification Christ's righteousness does not remain far from us, nor we from it. It is not the case that in justification Christ's righteousness is counted toward us while it remains far from us. Justification takes place on the basis of what Christ has accomplished (*iustitia aliena* = someone else's righteousness). This righteousness is taken hold of in faith. Faith is an indispensable element in justification. It is not something that is earned or that constitutes a qualification, but it merely accepts the righteousness that is offered to us. No one is justified without faith, apart from faith, or prior to faith.

The verses quoted above point to the inextricable unity of justification and faith. We agree that faith justifies through its content (van Genderen 1988, 68). This is to say, without faith there is no justification, but faith itself is not the ground for justification.

With this statement we have chosen a position in opposition to theologians such as Woelderink and Jager (see Woelderink, especially 210; Jager 1939, 101–5, where he refers to the former). Their objection to the abbreviated manner of speaking means that they in fact seek a qualification in man "somewhere."

5. We refocus on this issue by asking the following: *Is something claimed that in fact does not exist?* Is something fictitious (Woelderink's term, 210) said to be taking place, something that is not real? Does God do "as if"?

We agree with others (Berkouwer, 1954, 84–88; van Genderen, 1988, 68) that this is a completely erroneous representation of the facts. God is not pretending. This would be a denial of the righteousness of Christ.

What matters is *the nature of the relationship*. This nature is described as being "by faith." Faith appropriates, therefore no fiction. Faith is receptive, therefore no merit. It would be in conflict with the nature of faith to say that faith itself—in its active association with Christ's righteousness—would be our subjective righteousness or something along these lines. Those who claim this base justification on something in man himself after all. They fail to appreciate the ex-centric (self-rejecting) nature of faith. Faith entirely appertains to what it receives. What is received by faith may nevertheless be called its property, but then a property that remains marked by its provenance (*iustitia aliena*). Then it may be said that through faith this alien righteousness is my own righteousness.

It is actually similar to the expression of faith, "my God." God is God. He remains himself. He is not at my disposal. He is prepared to be mine, and yet remain himself. The expression "my righteousness" also implies *association without being identical*, *distinction within union*. Precisely in this way faith points to the Other's righteousness. This is how faith accepts the Other's righteousness as intended for oneself. In justification God counts the Other's righteousness toward the one who takes hold of it.

Is this an analytic or synthetic doctrine of justification? Are we justified on the basis of what we have (done) or on the basis of what we are (i.e., the direction of Jager and Woelderink)? The imputation of Christ's righteousness implies that we are dealing with a *synthetic* doctrine of justification.[30] What is imputed does not remain alien. With this statement, the synthetic does not become analytic. We can only go so far as to say that (through faith) this alien righteousness is my own righteousness. This emphasizes not only faith as being necessary for justification but also faith as not being meritorious.[31] Justification involves a gift that becomes our possession, but in such a way that the faith with which we accept it is itself also a gift. Righteousness does not remain far removed or alien, i.e., not beyond us. Although it becomes ours, it remains a gift (as opposed to acquisition through merit). This is precisely what is meant by "through faith."

With this position we want to guard against both the subjectivization and the objectivization of justification. Subjectivization occurs when the event and experience of faith become the foundation of justification. Objectivization occurs when the event (where and when)

30. For the (dogma-historical) significance of these terms see A. J. Venter, *Analities of sinteties?* 1959. Of interest is his thesis 3 that Karl Holl's rejection of the concept of imputation was because he did not give full scope to the substitutionary work of Christ.

31. Unlike E. Böhl, *Dogmatik*, 1887, 483, we would not speak of a "*conditio sine qua non*." The necessary way is not "an indispensable prerequisite." It is significant that Böhl said that when righteousness is imputed to faith, this is a shortened expression for faith in Jesus Christ.

of salvation in Christ becomes the ground for justification, without faith here and now playing a role. One can investigate the past and draw conclusions without in faith taking hold of and appropriating today what happened in the past. In the latter case justification is no more than the announcement in the present of righteousness achieved in the past or—putting it yet more clearly—the announcement that those who hear it are implicated in this past. This is all.

In closing, we wish to put it this way: not the righteous (even though he has become so by grace), but the ungodly is justified. That this ungodly person, who is justified for Christ's sake, indeed (and in part) becomes righteous is a matter of sanctification. Justification is the judgment that God pronounces over the ungodly who takes hold of Christ's righteousness.

Although faith is no prerequisite, it is a necessary condition for salvation, because it is one with it.[32]

6. Against this background we can also discuss the doctrine of *justification from eternity* that is held by some.

This is not the place to review the work of the relevant theologians in detail.

As far as Kuyper is concerned, see *De salute*, 94, 62–64; *E voto Dordraceno*, 1892, 2:340–42; *Het werk van de Heilige Geest* (the work of the Holy Spirit), 1927, 462. For Comrie, see *Brief over de rechtvaardigmaking des zondaars* (letter on the justification of the sinner), 1832, 2, 74–86, 88, 125. See also Honig, *Alexander Comrie*, 232–46.

Comrie refers to various components, and Kuyper to stages. The latter places more emphasis on what happens in eternity and what man becomes conscious of in time. This particular doctrine is typical of Kuyper's entire theological approach.

Comrie refers to the interconnection of the various components. Justification before the judgment seat is a necessary counterpart to justification from eternity. In addition to justification *prior to* faith, he also distinguishes justification *through* faith (*Brief*, 88, 127).

Our chief objection to this view is that there is no biblical support for it whatsoever. In Scripture, justification is always linked with faith. This faith cannot be projected into eternity, not even by differentiating between *potentia* (potency) and *actus* (actuality), as Kuyper and

32. We still refer to the republished *Drie bevindelijke brieven over de rechtvaardigmaking* (three experiential letters about justification) by Johannes van der Kemp, 1991. This document addresses practical questions dealing with justification from a pastoral point of view.

Comrie do. The *potentia* of faith appears in time and does not exist from eternity.

Both theologians wish to emphasize that justification is not dependent on our faith. There are, however, ways to bring out this truth other than by constructing justification from eternity. The essence of justification is the fact that it is God who justifies. Its essence is not our faith. We consider the motivation for Comrie and Kuyper's views to be correct. Their doctrinal elaboration, however, is an artifact that cannot be legitimized on the basis of the Bible.

We list a few additional objections. In the above view the historical event of justification is enervated in favor of what God has decided from eternity to effect in time. History is simply viewed as the unwinding of his decrees. With respect to justification this means that man eventually becomes conscious of what God has already decided in his regard.

The element of truth sought by Comrie and Kuyper is sufficiently captured in the decree that God surrenders his people to Christ. Justification should be seen as part of the implementation of this decree. Stating this is different from saying that justification took place in eternity.

7. With the rejection of justification from eternity we also reject the concept of *justification in the court of conscience*. This refers to the moment when God announces his acquittal to man (Comrie, *Brief*, 128–41.)

We do not encounter this justification before the tribunal of our conscience in Kuyper's writings. In its stead he holds that "justification is potentially appropriated by the elect through the implantation of the potency of faith" (the fifth of nine stages). Subsequently (at the sixth stage) justification is subjectively presented to the conscience of the elect through the preaching of the gospel. The onetime event that is referred to by others as the justification in the court of conscience is referred to by Kuyper as the implantation of the potency of faith (*De salute*, 45).

There are indeed people who for the first time in their lives quite consciously experience God's justification in a very personal and profound way. It is, however, not right to prescribe the experience of a few as a model for all. Others then await this special, overpowering experience, while—for a shorter or longer span of time that precedes it—they keep themselves far from the acceptance of the promise that

Christ will be our righteousness. Faith in this promise is impeded by the thought that justification must first be experienced in a dramatic way before one can speak of Christ as "my righteousness." In this scheme the significance of Christ is then identified with the experience of this single special moment. This actually leaves no room for hesitant contemplation of God's promise and growth for hope in Christ. There is only this indeterminate waiting for that one special moment. All contact with Christ in faith is marked by the liberating force of justification. Assurance of justification is not restricted to a unique form of experience, but characterizes all contact with Christ, who wants to be our righteousness. The danger is that this special (type of) experience is made into a prerequisite for justification. In this way faith is assigned much more than a functional (facilitating) role.

While stressing the importance of faith, we close by restating that one can only experience justification through the preaching of the gospel. In this preaching salvation, including justification, is mediated.

41.4. *Consensus and confrontation*

We now wish to focus on a number of dogmatic developments in the history of the early church and the Reformation as well as contemporary literature. As usual we only review the highlights.

1. The *Eastern church* focuses on different aspects of the Christian faith than the Western church.[33] The deification of man is a key theme in the thinking of Athanasius. "Through the Spirit we share in God and his divine nature." "He became man so that we could become divine."[34] With an appeal to Paul, Athanasius emphasizes the pneumatic nature of redemption. This is not a doctrine of physical redemption.

It is characteristic of John of Damascus to see the image of God restored through redemption. Man shares (once again) in the Deity and returns to Paradise. This is how he gains immortality.[35]

33. One can find an overview in A. Kalles, *Orthodoxie, Was ist das?* 1979, 79–82; K. Ware, *The Orthodox Way*, 1979, 140–77, especially 166–69. The study by F. Normann, *Teilhabe, ein Schlüsselwort der Vätertheologie* ("sharing," a key word in the theology of the Father), 1978, discusses the doctrine of salvation in the ancient church.

34. Athanasius, *De menswording des Woords* (the incarnation of the Word). See also the fragment in *Enchiridion patristicum*, 1958, no. 787. A. M. Ritter provides a clear overview in Andresen, *Handbuch*, 1:178–85, especially 184.

35. Klaus Wessel in Andresen, *Handbuch*, 1:318–25, especially 324, and van Genderen, 1988, 30.

Eastern soteriology does not assign a central role to justification. Regaining life is of fundamental importance.[36] All of this is determined christologically. The new life affects primarily the will. The process of redemption has a synergistic character.

2. A major reason why *Augustine* gained renown was his doctrine of grace. In fact, he has been called "the doctor of grace" (*doctor gratiae*). He emphasized the gift character of grace. This emphasis precedes his conflict with Pelagius. The latter did cause Augustine to add precision to his view and formulation. Mühlenberg (Andresen, *Handbuch*, 1:446) points out that Augustine's personal life affected the development of his doctrine of grace. On the other hand, practical issues did not permit the discussion to die out, not even when Pelagius was condemned. There is an autobiographical element in Augustine's preoccupation with this issue. If we accept Mühlenberg's division of the latter's views with respect to grace into four distinct phases, Pelagius would also be part of Augustine's biography. In our view one can distinguish between internal and external history. Both of these play a role in Augustine's biography and influence the development of his doctrine of grace.

A difficulty in interpreting Augustine is, in short, that to him grace constitutes healing. The latter comprises not only justification, but also restoration, sanctification, and sometimes even deification. Augustine emphasizes the aspect of grace in this process (according to van Genderen, 1988, 32ff.). He sees it as God's work in us, although it does not bypass our will.

In contrast with Pelagius, Augustine emphasizes that man is unwilling. The will of man needs to be changed. Augustine sees this change—as the fruit of grace—take place in people's lives. This is why he thinks in terms of a process that includes both justification and sanctification. The element of grace in this process comes through in the fact that the reward does not apply to works per se, but to the grace that brings them about.[37]

36. Gerald Bray, "Justification and the Eastern Orthodox Churches," in J. I. Packer et al., *Here We Stand: Justification by Faith Today*, 1986, 107, wrote: "In so far as justification was understood at all, it was assimilated with sanctification and the final re-creation of all things in Christ."

37. For an overview of Augustine's doctrine of justification see A. F. N. Lekkerkerker, *Studiën over de rechtvaardiging bij Augustinus* (studies on justification according to Augustine), 1947, with stages of the way of salvation listed on page 13, and numerous passages from Augustine throughout this book. The question remains whether this interpretation was one-sided. The same is true of G. de Ru, *De rechtvaardigmaking bij Augustinus* (justification according to Augustine), 1966. At any rate, one can find numerous references of importance in both studies. One can find even more material in Mühlenberg, Andresen, *Handbuch*, 1:445–63. The work

3. There are important elements in Augustine's doctrine of salvation to which Luther and Calvin refer.[38]

There are also elements that do not have the clarity and internal cohesion achieved by these representatives of the Reformation. One aspect of Augustine's doctrine that lacks clarity is the assurance of salvation. Luther once pointed out that Augustine was the most reliable interpreter of Paul. He subsequently said that although Augustine came closer to the essence of Paul's teachings than all the scholastic theologians, he did not quite grasp it.[39]

It is similarly true of Luther that his personal history affects his theology. He sought to obtain justification by God in all possible ways. Confession and penitence filled his life, while he remained tormented by the question whether his contrition was sufficiently genuine and deep.[40]

Luther learned to understand the biblical term "righteousness" as righteousness to be granted and indeed granted by God, instead of the righteousness obtained by us through pious acts of obedience to the law and works of penitence and contrition.

In the preface to the complete edition of his works, Luther gives an account of this in a flashback (*WA*, 54:185; 5 March 1545. See also *WAT*, 5, 26). It was to Luther as though he had entered the gate to paradise. This discovery is the secret and the core of Luther's Reformation. One can read about the significance of God's righteousness in many studies on Luther. This comes through especially well in Luther's commentary on the epistle to the Galatians.[41]

It is important to conclude that Luther does not isolate the law from the gospel, although he projects a clear tension between them.

---

by A. E. McGrath, *Institutia Dei: A History of the Christian Doctrine of Justification*, 2 vols., 1986, and his *Justification by Faith* published in 1988 are also significant.

38. J. Koopmans, *Het oud kerkelijk dogma en de Reformatie bepaaldelijk bij Calvijn* (doctrine in the ancient church and the Reformation from Calvin's perspective), 1938 (1983^2), especially 94–97.

39. Van Genderen 1988, 35. A helpful essay is that by W. van Loewenich called "Zur Gnadelehre bei Augustinus und bei Luther" (on the doctrine of grace according to Augustine and Luther) in *Von Augustinus zu Luther*, 1959, 75–87, especially 83ff.

40. H. A. Oberman, *Luther, Man Between God and the Devil*, 1989, especially 4:119–58, and W. van 't Spijker, *Luther, belofte en ervaring* (promise and experience), 1983, 1:10–22.

41. This commentary was discussed by J. van Genderen, "Luthers visie op wet en evangelie" (Luther's view of law and gospel), in W. Balke et al., *Luther en het Gereformeerd Protestantisme* (Luther and Reformed Protestantism), 1982, 249–82. See also Velema, 1987, 146–50. The reader is also referred to W. van Loewenich, *Martin Luther*, 1982, 69–102; B. Lohse, *Martin Luther*, 1981, especially 152–60; O. H. Pesch. *Hinführing zu Luther* (introduction to Luther), 1983^2, especially 80–102; M. Brecht, *Martin Luther*, 1983^2, especially 1:285–370. With the page references for the latter three books we have highlighted different facets of Luther's experience.

Justification is the central theme of Luther's theology, i.e., justification by faith. This is contrasted with works. Faith has no merit of its own whatsoever. Having been crushed by the law, he relinquishes all merit. He holds up his empty hand to see it filled by God with Christ's righteousness.

We mention a number of key places in Luther's work in which this doctrine of justification is confessed and described: *WA*, 2, 13; 2, 720–21; 18; 50, 624, 643–44, 766; 56, 269ff., 271ff.

Imputation acquires an increasingly prominent role. We are declared righteous through faith for Christ's sake. No sin, either of the past or still present in our flesh today, is still imputed to us (*WA*, 39, 1, 83). We are not justified because we are righteous; we are righteous because we are declared to be righteous. This justification has implications for our lives.[42]

Elsewhere we have provided a more extensive discussion of the relationship between the law and the gospel in Luther's work (Velema, 1987, 146–50. For a comparison between Calvin and Luther see 150–53).

We point to the certainty of faith as a gift, and not as something we have in and of ourselves. Personal crisis and temptation affect this certainty, but do not obliterate it. The certainty of faith (*certitudo*) persists, although self-assurance (*securitas*) has no right of existence. The latter, after all, reflects pride, contrasted with the *certitudo* as the result of humility.[43]

We finally remind the reader of a well-known theme of Luther's theology: simultaneously righteous and a sinner (*simul iustus et peccator*).[44] The key idea is that sinners are (have been declared to be) completely righteous—while in fact remaining sinners—but in the process of becoming godly and righteous.

Here resurfaces the twofold righteousness. One can also say that the first aspect of righteousness is forensic or juridical (i.e., complete), while the second aspect in terms of impact is effective and partial. Joest disagrees with K. Holl who interprets Luther's doctrine of justification as the outcome of a process. He interprets the declaration of justification as anticipatory and therefore analytic.[45]

42. See Luther's sermon about twofold righteousness, as translated and discussed by J. T. Bakker in idem, *Luther na 500 jaar* (Luther after 500 years), 1983, 30–57 (translated from *WA*, 2:145ff.).

43. For "humility" in Luther's theology see Th. M. M. A. C. Bell, "Das Magnificat verdeutscht und ausgelegt" (the Magnificat translated into German and interpreted), 1521, in Bakker (footnote 42), 78–98.

44. W. Joest, *Gesetz und Freiheit* (law and freedom), 1968^4, especially chapter 2, 55–82.

45. See Holl, *Gesammelte Aufsätze* (collected essays), 1927^4, 1:111–54, especially 124n2. For Holl's view of the discovery of God's righteousness, see also *Gesammelte Aufsätze*, 1928, 3:171–88.

One can say that the doctrine of the *simul iustus et peccator* reflects the characteristic difference between Augustine and Luther.

It is well known that other key themes of Luther's theology are directly related to justification by faith. This is not the place to elucidate this thesis.[46]

In closing we mention that Roman Catholics also recognize Luther's doctrine of justification as a classical doctrine. It opened a new era in the history of the doctrine of grace.[47]

We also mention the once-sensational study by Hans Küng (with a preface by Karl Barth), *Justification*, 1964. This study made a big impact, even though it was not received with unanimous approval. Another approach is taken by O. H. Pesch, *Theologie der Rechtfertigung bei Martin Luther und Thomas von Aquin*, 1967. Pesch also engendered quite a discussion. See also U. Kühn, O. H. Pesch, *Rechtfertigung im Gespräch zwischen Thomas und Luther* (justification in dialogue between Thomas and Luther), 1967 (report on a symposium held in Berlin). For reactions to Küng see van Genderen, 1966, 13–15, and G. Müller, *Die Rechtfertigungslehre* (the doctrine of justification), 1977, 113–16. This book contains many references to the literature. For Pesch see also *Gerechtfertigt aus Glauben, Luthers Frage an die Kirche* (justified by faith, Luther's question to the church), 1982, and written together with A. Peters, *Einführung in die Lehre von Gnade und Rechtfertigung* (introduction to the doctrines of grace and justification), 1981.

Luther also placed justification in the perspective of appearing before the judgment seat[48] of God (eschatologically).[49]

4. *Calvin's* doctrine of justification is fundamentally the same as Luther's.[50] However, we do not want to ignore his teaching, since he has

46. We emphasize this in view of the fact that today—as a consequence of secularization—Luther's doctrine of two kingdoms is given an entirely non-Lutheran interpretation. An important article on this particular topic is J. T. Bakker, "Wereldse heiligheid—Luther over de Bergrede" (secular holiness—Luther on the Sermon on the Mount), in *Geloof dat te denken geeft* (faith that makes one think), festschrift for H. M. Kuitert, 1989, 9–24.

47. According to J. Martin-Palma in *Handbuch der Dogmengeschichte* (handbook of dogmatic history), 3, 5b, 1980, 8. See 7–21, which were dedicated to Luther, with many references to the literature.

48. Peters, 1984, 33, refers to the practice of confession of the Middle Ages as one aspect of the background to this setting. In our view one should give at least as much credit to its scriptural origin. Hartvelt, 1991, 171, refers to this comment and agrees with Peters that this theme was not sufficiently being taken into account in the study of Luther. See the chapter "Die Rechtfertigungslehre als Eschatologie" (the doctrine of justification as eschatology), in W. Härle, E. Helms, *Rechtfertigung*, 1979, 198–221.

49. We also mention H. E. Weber's description of the contrast between the Reformation and Roman Catholic thinking in *Reformation, Orthodoxie und Rationalismus*, 1966; see 1.1:1–64, with a description of the elaboration of the doctrine by Lutherans on 65–130.

50. For the fundamental similarity between these two doctrines, see W. van 't Spijker, *Luther en Calvijn*, 1985, 12–14, with many references to the literature on 5. For Calvin's doctrine of justification see W. Niesel, *Die Theologie Calvins*, 1957², 121–38, and Peters, 1984, 90–105.

strongly influenced the Reformed confession. We wish to present a number of his fundamental theses together with specific references to his work.

Calvin makes the doctrine of justification the core of his reply to Sadoleto (*O.S.*, 1:457–89). He calls justification the main hinge on which religion turns.[51]

Peters says that Calvin places his key observations in the overall summary of his entire exposition, namely, 3.11 of the *Institutes*.[52]

Calvin interprets justification entirely forensically. He interprets justification as the acceptance with which God receives us into his favor and reckons us as righteous. It consists in the remission of sins and the imputation of Christ's righteousness (*Institutes*, 3.11.2). See also his beautiful Trinitarian description of grace leading to righteousness. Christ is portrayed as its foundation (*Institutes*, 3.15.5). Calvin also refers to the order of justification (*ordo iustificationis*, *Institutes*, 3.11.16).[53]

We point out that in the *Institutes*, 3.14.17, Calvin uses different terminology. Here he identifies four causes (*causae*).[54] It cannot be said that this scholastic (Calvin: philosophical) terminology could not be a suitable barrel to hold the clear water of the Reformational doctrine of grace. To the contrary, Calvin employs these four distinctions precisely to display the fullness and multiplicity of the gospel.

W. van 't Spijker emphasizes that in the context of the doctrine of justification we also should keep communion with Christ clearly in mind. We receive twofold grace from communion with Christ, namely, the forgiveness of sins and the imputation of Christ's righteousness. See his essay "Calvijn in gesprek" (Calvin in conversation) in *Congresbundel 1989* (1989 convention papers), Reformatie-studies, 1990, 28–47, especially 39–41. In emphasizing communion with Christ, we shall always have to keep in mind its connotation with faith. In our view this is the special contribution of Calvin's doctrine of the *unio cum Christo*.

51. Translation by W. van 't Spijker, *Teksten uit de Institutie van Johannes Calvijn* (passages from the *Institutes* of John Calvin), 1987, 133. See *Institutes*, 3.11.1 (*O.S.*, 4:182: *praecipuus sustinendae religionis cardo*; by Peters, 1984, 91, translated as "Entscheidende Angelpunkt zur Erhaltung der Religion" [crucial pivot of the preservation of religion]).

52. It should be kept in mind that 3.11 is continued in 3.15, with another offshoot in 3.16–19.

53. Peters, 1984, 93, says that Calvin had only loosely formulated the four components of this order. In our view, the "locker" (loose) nature of this order implies that this was not a matter of a strictly chronological sequence of experiences.

54. In scholastic terminology: the undeserved love of the Father was the active cause (*causa efficiens*); Christ's obedience was the organic cause (*causa materialis*); faith was the formal or instrumental cause (*causa formalis/instrumentalis*); the display of God's righteousness and the praise of his goodness were the objective cause (*causa finalis*).

In the context of perseverance, Berkouwer (1958, 206) correctly points out that if one wants to use the term "causality" here, he must recognize that this causality is religiously qualified in terms of the mystery of redemption, and therefore can be understood and accepted only in faith. This is also true of the *causae* referred to in the present context.

We shall refer below to the unity of justification and sanctification in Calvin's teaching.[55] Here we still mention the union with Christ effected by the Holy Spirit.

Peters (1984, 97) points out that Calvin's conflict with Osiander does not weaken but rather clarifies his reliance on Augustine and Bernard de Clairvaux. The Spirit is the bond of unity. This implies not only a strong union between the elect and Christ, but also a clear rejection of Christ's essence being mingled with theirs (especially *Institutes*, 3.11.5, 6–7).[56]

Here we may mention the issue of the syllogism (*syllogismus*) of faith. We refer to W. H. Velema, "Geloof en handelen" (faith and action), in *Septuagesimo anno*, 1973, 270–98, and Hartvelt, 1991, 193–203, especially from 202, with a focus on more recent literature as well as Weber's earlier thesis. However, Hartvelt does not refer to the current theory-praxis debate. The latter debate may be mentioned in the present context, considering the fact that it assesses the creditability of the gospel in the light of praxis; to some the gospel stands or falls for example with liberation theology. W. D. Jonker, "Kritische verwantschap?" (critical relationship?), in E. Brown (et al.), *Calvijn aktueel?* (is Calvin relevant?), 1982, 83, addressed syllogism in Calvin's work. J. van Genderen's essay in *Ten dienste aan het Woord* (in service of the Word), 1991, 109–26, is also relevant in this context.

5. In the foregoing, reference was made to an element of consensus achieved in confrontation with Roman Catholic thought. The Council of Trent sought such confrontation. It made pronouncements that radically rejected gains made by the Reformation. Trent confirmed the synthesis of God and man in the form of synergism. There had been a vacuum in this respect since the Council of Orange (529).[57]

55. We may already refer to Tj. Stadtland, *Rechtfertigung und Heiligung bei Calvin* (justification and sanctification according to Calvin), 1972, 27ff., 46ff.; R. S. Wallace, *Calvin's Doctrine of the Christian Life*, 1959, 11–100; and W. H. Velema, "Ethiek bij Calvijn" (Calvin's ethics), in D. H. Borgers et al., *Reformatorische stemmen, verleden en heden* (Reformational voices, past and present), 1989, 193–222, especially 198–200.

56. Cf. W. Kolfhaus, *Christusgemeinschaft bei Johannes Calvin* (communion with Christ according to John Calvin), 1939, 24–53; W. Krusche, *Das Wirken des Heiligen Geistes nach Calvin* (the work of the Holy Spirit according to Calvin), 1957, 265–72. For Osiander see M. J. Arntzen, *Mystieke rechtvaardigingsleer* (mystical doctrine of justification), 1956.

57. Berkouwer used this term in his discussion of "De strijd om de genade" (the conflict regarding grace, chapter 4 of his *Conflict met Rome*, 1948).

Its pronouncements describe grace as a relationship of "powers" and "workings," without treating grace as God's favor. According to Berkouwer, justification and acquittal are not addressed. In rejecting the Reformation, Trent filled this vacuum.

One can find the decisions of Trent in *DS*, 1500–1846, with the accompanying papal doctrines in *DS*, 1847–70. The *canones de iustificatione* represented 33 condemnations. They were specifically directed against the Reformation (*DS*, 1551–83).

It is true that no one can be justified in the absence of divine grace. By the same token, however, Trent excommunicates all those who hold that man's free will has been lost or extinguished as a consequence of Adam's sin (canon 5, no. 155). The possibility and necessity of cooperation with God's grace is clearly implied by the condemnation of the latter position (canon 4, no. 1554). It implies being disposed to one's own justification by freely assenting to and cooperating with that said grace (cap. 5, no. 1525). This disposition (*dispositio*), or preparation (*praeparatio*), is followed by justification itself, which is not remission of sins *merely*, but also the sanctification and renewal of the inward man, through the *voluntary* reception of the grace, and of the gifts, whereby unjust man becomes just, and an enemy a friend (cap. 7, no. 1528; italics added).

It is noteworthy that here also is a reference to four causes: the merciful God is the active cause (*causa efficiens*). Christ is the meritorious cause (*causa meritoria*). The glory of God and Christ and eternal life are the objective cause (*causa finalis*). The latter differs from Calvin. The cardinal difference lies in the instrumental cause (*causa intrumentalis*). Here reference is made to baptism and the acceptance of righteousness (we are not just called righteous, but we are in fact righteous) according to the measure allotted by the Holy Spirit *and* everyone's being equipped and collaborating (cap. 7, no. 1529). Here synergism, based on the capabilities retained by man despite sin, is clearly confessed.

The core of these decrees is that justification is an inner renewal, a simultaneous process of sanctification and justification. Righteousness is not seen to be imputed, but acquired through grace and through disposition (*dispositio*) and preparation (*praeparatio*). Justification is seen to increase commensurate with good works. This implies the rejection of both imputation and faith as unmerited acceptance of grace.

The vacuum is filled in with preparation for and collaboration with grace (see also cap. 8, no. 1532, and on good works cap. 16, no. 1545).

Grace is tied to the sacraments. This implies the objectivization of grace, which was strangely complemented with the subjectivization of synergism. This combination robs the believer of his Reformational certainty of salvation (except through special revelation, cap. 9, no. 1533).[58]

One can indeed speak of a confrontation, even to the extent of the terminology that is employed.

For dogma-historical overviews see H. Jedin, *Geschichte des Konzils von Trent* (history of the Council of Trent), 1957, 2:201–68, and W. Dantine in Andresen, *Handbuch*, 2:437–64, with its conclusion on 464 that man must participate in the decision regarding his salvation. He is made partly responsible for this "Mitbestimmung" (co-determination).[59]

6. We shall now address a number of *recent views regarding justification.*

In the introduction to the collection *Rechtfertigung* (justification), 1989, authored by G. Sauter, one finds an overview of changes with respect to the central place of justification in the Christian faith.

He refers to the closing message of the fourth meeting of the Lutheran World Council held in Helsinki in 1963. There it was realized that the question was no longer: "How do I find peace with God?" but "Where are you, God?" Modern man no longer suffers from the wrath of God, but from his absence. Sin is no longer an evil to be overcome, but the senselessness of existence.[60]

Through the answer to the quest for meaning, so we read, the doctrine of justification itself needs to be justified. It is no longer a matter of the justification of the ungodly, but of God's acceptance of man.

This constitutes a radical shift in theology. We characterize this as a shift in focus away from God toward a questioning, searching, and suffering humanity.[61] Its questions need to be answered; its

58. This chapter has as its title "Against the vacuous confidence (*ianis fiducia*) of heretics." See also canon 16, no. 1566.

59. For the more recent views see H. J. Kouwehoven, *Simul justus et peccator in de nieuwe Rooms-Katholieke theologie* ("at once righteous and a sinner" in recent Roman Catholic theology), 1969.

60. See Sauter, 1989, 14ff. See also van Genderen, 1966, 3–5, with references to Helsinki and other literature.

61. In a different context E. Jüngel, *Zur Freiheit eines Christenmenschen* (toward the liberation of the Christian), 1991³, 21n14, referred to a reversal in theological thinking in which man focused on totality, including God. Chr. Gestrich (*Die Wiederkehr des Glanzes in der Welt* = the return of splendor in the world, 1989, 205) opposed this human quest for the meaning of one's life in a curious manner. He characterized the essence of sin as the justification of man's

problems need to be solved. This implies a 180-degree turnaround in dogmatic-existential inquiry.

Luther has been criticized for anthropocentricism in focusing on the question: how do I acquire a gracious God? However, his emphasis on God's righteousness implies that it is impossible to maintain that Luther's theology is based on man. Precisely the opposite is the case. Nevertheless there is plenty of scope for man in Luther's theology, also for questioning man. But the answers come from above. This characterizes Luther's entire theology.

The turnaround that is currently experienced in the appreciation of life and theology (including preaching) is so revolutionary and so far-reaching that it is believed that all of theology needs to be reconstructed to provide questioning man with a satisfactory reply.

We wish to make two additional comments. In the first place, the rapprochement between Roman Catholics and Protestants as far as justification is concerned is partly a result of this radical turnaround. There have always been fundamental differences between Rome and the Reformation (see above). The fact that a rapprochement is currently shaping up reflects in part that man has become the focal point. We are fully aware that this rapprochement does not yet constitute a complete consensus. A great deal remains to be discussed. Yet there are perspectives that point toward a consensus. This is fostered and legitimized by the fact that man's questions form the point of departure for the approach to dogmatics. Furthermore, modern hermeneutics plays an important role in this process.

We refer to the influential collection of papers (also translated into English), *Lehrverurteilungen—Kirchentrennend?* (condemnation of doctrine: causing church divisions?), published by K. Lehmann and W. Pannenberg, (1987[2]). The subtitle is "Justification, Sacraments, and Offices at the Time of the Reformation and Today." Part I contains a document compiled by more than fifty theologians. It outlines positions and lays the groundwork for a possible consensus. It states that churches need to drop previous condemnations of each other as well as mutual misunderstandings and confessional pronouncements. Nevertheless it is clearly stated (1:75) that there remain differences with respect to justification that go beyond mere terminology. One cannot say, however, that these remaining differences affect the essence of justification. Part 2 (1989), which particularly focuses on justification, discusses various aspects and explicit formulations of this doctrine.

---

own existence. This view also involved man's initiative, albeit in a negative mode. God did not give his law prior to the perpetration of sin (207).

Pannenberg concludes that consensus regarding key elements (including the doctrine of justification) no longer justifies separate ecclesiastical action, despite other (minor) points of difference (2:17–31, especially 30).[62]

It is of interest to recall a similar project with respect to morality: O. Bayer (et al.), *Zwei Kirchen—eine Moral?* (two churches, a single morality?), 1986.

D. Lange (1991) discusses contrasting views concerning justification, the Lord's Supper, and ecclesiastical offices on behalf of the faculty at Göttingen. His conclusion is completely contrary to that of the authors referred to above. He speaks of a negative opinion with respect to fundamental issues (134).

A second comment concerning this displacement is that the question needs to be raised as to what extent there is a connection between the relinquishment of justification as central theme and the so-called "Divine eclipse," i.e., the experience of the absence of God.

This is not the place to pursue this in depth. We are of the view that the relinquishment of justification as the central theme in the very least obscures the biblical illumination of the relationship between God and man. With respect to this issue see C. Graafland, *Gereformeerden op zoek naar God* (Reformed in search of God), 1990, and W. H. Velema, *Nieuw zicht op Gereformeerde spiritualiteit* (new perspective on Reformed spirituality), 1990.

7. We draw attention to what *Peter Stuhlmacher* understands God's righteousness to be. He sees it as a manifestation of God's power as Creator. He associates righteousness more with God's action than with its imputation to man. "Wer im Gericht zu seinem Recht kommt, ist Gott der Schöpfer in seiner wirksamen Macht" (the one who is vindicated in judgment is God the Creator in his efficacious power, 1966^2, 239). In his view referring to God, his righteousness, or even his justice is too conventional. He probably means that this manner of speaking has been unduly divorced from God's creative act of salvation.

Only when the overall context of God's liberating justice is kept in mind can justification remain the *shifting* core of theology (1966^2, 240). His conclusion of a review of numerous passages from the Gospels is that Jesus never spoke of God's righteousness. The kingdom of God as the realm of his rule of love constitutes the core of his message (1966^2,

62. We also refer to G. Müller/V. Pfnür, "Rechtfertigung—Glaube—Werke" (justification—faith—works), in *Confessio Augustana. Bekenntnis des einem Glaubens* (confession of a single faith), 1980, 105–38. Berkhof, *C.F.*, 441, also pointed to the growing consensus with respect to justification. He referred to other publications, in part by the same authors. For a practical application of the current view of justification for preaching see A. Beutel (ed.), *Zur Freiheit befreit. Predigten über Rechtfertigung* (liberated to freedom: preaching about justification), 1989.

251). This rule of love demands a response in the form of obedience. Kingly dominion is the perspective within which Jesus displays and proclaims God's love ("übt und ausspricht" = practices and pronounces). This is apparent from the Lord's Prayer (1966², 252).

Through God's righteousness (displayed and confirmed to us in Jesus Christ) man is called to live with God in confidence, liberated from fear, and brought to the joy that is the hallmark of freedom (258).

In this way Stuhlmacher believes he can avoid the existential interpretation of justification advocated by Braun, Bultmann, and Conzelmann (344). According to them, justification is the expression (*chiffre*) of faithful self-knowledge. According to Stuhlmacher as well as his mentor Käsemann (1965²), righteousness indicates the creative action of God.

In this way man attains his destiny after all. The quest for meaning is answered by pointing to God's faithfulness toward his creation. The process of salvation manifests God's righteousness and therefore justification by God. However much this view may be appreciated as a reaction to the existential interpretation of the New Testament à la Bultmann, it does not teach the classical Reformational doctrine of justification.[63]

Stuhlmacher manages to use the current formulation of the problem as his starting point and still make a case for retaining justification as the centerpiece of theology. It is not surprising that he speaks of a *shifting* core.[64] In our view, this shifting nature is characteristic of the concept itself.[65]

8. The blueprint for an anthropocentric doctrine of justification can also be found in the work of *Paul Tillich* (1886–1965). We shall discuss neither his theology nor his biography in any detail, however interesting his biography may be for the development of his theology.

63. See also the overview by D. Lührmann, "Gerechtigkeit III" (righteousness), *TRE* 12:414–20, especially 416.

64. It is noteworthy that O. H. Pesch in *Neues Handbuch theologischer Grundbegriffe* (new handbook of theological concepts), article on "Rechfertigung" (justification), 1985, 3:454, gives a definition of justification in which he consciously combines the newer Roman Catholic and Protestant insights.

65. The collection of essays, Sauter 1989, has had little impact so far. The collection of W. Dantine, *Recht als Rechtfertigung* (justice as justification), 1982, especially the first two essays, 1–58, has had more of an impact. See also his "Die Rechfertigungslehre in der gegenwärtigen systematischene Arbeit der evangelischen Theologie" (justification in contemporary systematic efforts of evangelical theology), *Ev. Th.* (1963): 245–65.

The Courage to Be[66] amounts to having the courage to believe that one has been accepted. All confidence rests on the acknowledgement that one has been accepted. In this context "self-affirmation" also plays an important role. Belief (that one has been accepted) implies self-affirmation. This is referred to as absolute faith. It goes beyond the mystical experience and man's encounter with God. It is the power of being, through which one is accepted. To believe is to state and project that this is true.

In his *Systematic Theology* this idea is related to being once again in Jesus Christ. Through Jesus Christ man turns out to share in this new existence. He is accepted. This removes the alienation from the mainspring of his being. This alienation is the ultimate sin. Sin separates man from being. This means, in fact, separation from oneself. We may believe that we have been accepted by God. This is how we regain ourselves.

Justification means to accept that one has been accepted by God. He is the cause of our being accepted. Faith is only the means to this end.[67]

Absolute faith may indeed be referred to as a gift from God, but it is ultimately nothing more than faith in oneself, the belief that one is permitted to exist and that one is what one is. Self-acceptance is equated with self-affirmation. Here God is not a person who stands across from us. He is the dimension of the depth of our being.

We are called to believe in ourselves and thus to mobilize and engage the power for inner healing and integration that is present in us.

This "theology" is the anthropological foundation of psychotherapy that is widely practiced in America.[68]

When in this context justification is retained, one only holds on to oneself. One is engaged in liberating one's own strengths from inner distortedness in order to save and justify oneself. It is the opposite of the biblical doctrine of justification. It is, however, the basic perspective of all theology that starts out from the reversal in thinking described earlier.[69]

66. We used its German translation, *Der Mut zum Sein*, 1965, especially chapters 2 and 6: "Der Mut sich zu bejahen als bejaht" (the courage to assert oneself affirmed). The similarity between this concept and the idea of Hans Küng, *Existiert Gott?* (does God exist?), 1978, 471–528, is indeed striking, i.e., the yes to reality as an alternative to nihilism.

67. P. Tillich, *Systematic Theology*, 1968, 2:205ff., further elaborated in 3:235–43.

68. W. Zijlstra, *Op zoek naar een nieuwe horizon* (in search of a new horizon), 1989, discusses Tillich especially from the perspective of the ultimate polarity of the self and the world. For Tillich's place in the history of this movement see W. Zijlstra, *Klinische pastorale vorming* (clinical pastoral education), 1969, 1973[2], and D. Stollberg, *Therapeutische Seelsorge* (therapeutic care of the soul), 1970.

69. Against the background of this complete revamping of the doctrine of justification it is noteworthy that J. Sperna Weiland, *Oriëntatie*, 1966, 55, wrote that Luther dominated Tillich's

9. In this context we also wish to mention *Karl Barth*. His views were discussed earlier. In Barth's doctrine of justification we see basic Reformational elements at work within a revised framework. God exercises justice. This implies a conflict with man. The latter cannot exist before God. Here we encounter Barth's main thesis. He starts out from grace. God does not only stand over against man. God stands up for man over against himself. He is the Judge who is condemned in our stead.

We find Barth's doctrine of justification especially in *C.D.*, 4.1.515–642. We quote the main thesis of this section: "The right of God established in the death of Jesus Christ, and proclaimed in His resurrection in defiance of the wrong of man, is as such the basis of the new and corresponding right of man. Promised to man in Jesus Christ, hidden in Him and only to be revealed in Him, it cannot be attained by any thought or effort or achievement on the part of man. But the reality of it calls for faith in every man as a suitable acknowledgement and appropriation and application" (p. 514.)

From the subtitle to this section, "Des Menschen Rechtfertigung" (man's justification), we conclude:

1. That it is a matter of the proclamation of God's justice, in the face of man's injustice.
2. That this justice is the basis for the new justice that man receives.
3. That this justice has been promised to man in Jesus Christ, and while still hidden, ready to be revealed.
4. That man is called to acknowledge this justice in faith, to seize it as his possession, and to confirm it.
5. That the issue is not that man must be justified by faith. The objective and universal justification brought about through the proclamation of God's justice is to be acknowledged, accepted, and experienced by faith.

Those who doubt that the terms "objective" and "universal" are being used correctly here should read *C.D.*, 4.1.295, where Barth says that all have died in Christ's death, whether or not the proclamation of Christ has been received and accepted by them. According to Barth, Christ's death applies to us regardless of the stance we take.

In summary, we state that to Barth justification is the proclamation of God's justice made real in Christ for man and creation. Faith con-

---

thinking. That may superficially appear to be the case. In terms of content, however, one could hardly imagine a greater contrast.

stitutes endorsement of this reality. This completely overlooks the vital inner change through which we renounce our own rights before God and as guilty individuals ask for his forgiveness. Justification is presented as a foregone conclusion. When Barth still refers to (the need for) faith, once justification has been proclaimed, it is no longer the same faith as described in Lord's Day 7 of the Heidelberg Catechism. The proclaimed reality is valid regardless of this faith. We cannot avoid this issue by thinking of faith as a *noetical* (intellectual) entity, without it being required for redemption and salvation (*ontic*, see § 39.2, subsection 3).

10. Neither do we wish to ignore *H. Berkhof's* doctrine of justification. The reason is that his dogmatics has been widely accepted, at least in Dutch-speaking regions. Furthermore, the particular nature of his view of Jesus as the new man, the preeminent covenantal partner, is clearly expressed in his doctrine of justification.

For Berkhof's Christology we refer to van Genderen (§ 29), who explains that Berkhof has broken with the confession of Christ's true divinity (*vere Deus*).

He does refer to atonement. However, this is no longer sought in Christ's vicarious sacrifice in obedience to the law. The heart of redemption is instead sought in the obedience of Jesus—the new man—to God's law and our participation in this.

We get a proper perspective on this view when we consider what Berkhof means by justification. He discusses justification within the context of the covenant. Man has become alienated from God. Conversion is necessary. God's gracious turning toward man calls for man's turning back to God. The terms "justification" and "sanctification" are used to indicate God's turning toward man and man's turning back to God.

Berkhof employs juridical imagery originating with Paul. It is derived from rabbinical Judaism: how is man justified before God? This question in this particular form can no longer be understood by modern man, because it is no longer an issue for him. Forgiveness of sins is a more negative and less comprehensive expression than justification. After all, those who speak in terms of condemnation—as Berkhof did earlier—need to employ the contrasting concepts of justification and acquittal.

The juridical imagery lends itself to express the realities of the covenantal relationship, namely, rights and duties, being guilty and receiving grace, rendering a verdict, and establishing a new relationship. Theology, however, must not restrict itself to this juridical language. It does not leave enough room for love, the inner life, and the surrender, which are integral parts of the covenantal fellowship.

It is for this reason that Berkhof wants to employ different words. "But none of these is as comprehensive as the term 'justification'" (*C.F.*, 437).

Within Christology, Berkhof speaks of humanity—reconciliation—glorification. What is substitution for Christ is justification for us. On account of the work of the substitute, we are called what we are not: righteous (just), children of God, partners in the covenant.

A new mode of existence is imputed to us. "We receive a new name, because the Spirit unites us with the true sonship of Jesus by putting to our account, in the way of imputation, his glorified humanity." "The first time this event happens is when by faith [we] accept this hand. But it is also a constantly recurring event." Justification is *the source of our renewal*. We no longer need to prove ourselves. We are accepted, apart from our "works." We are set before God, with respect to other people and for the future. "Justification imparts to us an unheard-of invulnerability, which at the same time is a source from which we derive strength to fight against sin, to endure, and to serve" (*C.F.*, 437).

Justification is an event that takes place within our experience. Its origin lies outside us, in Christ (*C.F.*, 437). It continues to be given to us, because it has been promised to us.

The above summary indicates that Berkhof's doctrine of justification incorporates classical elements (not analytic but synthetic imputation; we become what we are not) into a new framework, namely, that of the covenantal relationship, with Jesus as the preeminent covenantal partner.

Berkhof maintains the juridical perspective, but revamps it by interpreting justification as the imputation of true humanity. It is not a matter of a judgment of God according to which the righteousness of Christ's sacrifice is imputed to us. It implies an inner change which begins with the promise and is realized in a humanity received for Christ's sake and subsequently experienced and practiced.

Berkhof does admit that in the cross we deal with the consequences of sin (305ff.). Jesus' sacrifice signifies the completion and the revelation of the new humanity that he came to bring (303). Therefore, redemption remains incomplete if it is not realized in a redeemed community and among redeemed human beings who in turn bring about reconciliation among themselves and toward the outside (300).

Berkhof's doctrine of justification represents a combination of synthetic and analytic judgment. Imputation does not exist—has no force—without the realization and experience of the humanity imputed to us. Thus synthetic judgment does not exist without its practical continuation in our lives. This continuation is part of justification. This is why Berkhof combines a synthetically intended doctrine of justification with analytic implications. In a different context Berkouwer points out this very danger, namely, that one starts out synthetically and ends up analytically (1954, 87).

This synthesis (synergism of convenantal partners) is because Berkhof's doctrine of justification lacks a dimension that in the New Testament constitutes the essence of justification. Berkhof fails to appreciate the imputation of the sacrifice of Christ and the acquittal based on it.

According to him, forgiveness comes about through the attribution of Jesus' true humanity, which enables us to make a new beginning. This new beginning is essentially part of justification. However, it requires continuation without which justification is not complete.[70]

It is clear that Berkhof falls outside the Reformational consensus. By critically confronting it, he places himself in opposition to it.

11. Finally *H. Wiersema*. Starting with his dissertation of 1971, this theologian advocates a radical reinterpretation of the Reformed confession. His renovation amounts to new construction. In the context of this chapter (for his doctrine of sin see § 26.3) we limit ourselves to the question whether we are justified by the imputation of Christ's righteousness. We merely mention—while referring to reviews by others[71]—that Wiersinga seeks to completely remove the notion of satisfaction (*satisfactio*) from the doctrine of atonement. Atonement is not focused on God but man. The sacrifice is a ministry of God to men (Wiersinga, 1971, 137ff., concerning the sacrifice and the blood of Christ, 139–55). It is well known that Wiersinga himself speaks of an alternative, and also of an effective doctrine of atonement (1971, 191). See van Genderen, 1972, 17–21. Wiersinga does defend redemption as change (1972), but rejects the justification of the ungodly.

The fact that change is central in his doctrine of atonement and justification has to do with his view of sin (elaborated subsequently). God liberates man who liberates himself. For the liberation from sin, man depends on himself and his relationship with his fellow human beings. God's forgiveness does not become reality to me until a fellow human being forgives me. The entire process of sanctification thus comes to depend on what we ourselves do for others and what others do for us. This is no substitution, but an exchange of place. Man takes God's place. God adapts himself to man. Van Genderen correctly points out that this implies a shift that affects the very foundations of our faith (1988, 66).

12. We now wish *to summarize the results of this review in a few points* in which we highlight differences with the Reformational confession.

70. In the above we have rephrased our 1974 objection to Berkhof's doctrine of justification and sanctification. See *Weerwoord* (reply), 1974, 174–83.

71. J. van Genderen, *Christus in onze plaats* (Christ in our stead), 1972; B. Wentsel, *Hij voor ons; wij voor hem* (he for us; we for him), 1973; and especially focused on exegesis, H. N. Ridderbos, *Zijn wij op de verkeerde weg?* (are we on the wrong path?), 1972.

1. The Reformational content is stripped from justification by replacing the question of guilt by the quest for meaning.
2. Justification is an act of God in which he creatively corrects things and reclaims man. Man's questions are answered at the same time.
3. Barth takes an objectivistic and universalistic approach. Berkhof does exactly the opposite. Jesus' imputed humanity must be put into practice. Wiersinga gives no scope to satisfaction. Man must do it himself, together with his fellow men.
4. In the concepts reviewed we notice that some biblical content is retained. The one retains somewhat more, the other hardly anything.
5. What has disappeared is the dependence of sinful man on Christ's righteousness achieved through his death. This claim has both christological and pneumatological aspects: Christ is surrendered to God's judgment in our stead. The righteousness thus obtained is imputed to us. This is referred to as the wonderful or happy exchange. On the other hand, we do not share in this righteousness without faith. Our empty hands must be filled. At the same time it breaks our heart. The acceptance of Christ's righteousness cannot proceed without an inner turning toward God. This turning toward God has no merit of its own. Just as righteousness is a gift to us, so the Holy Spirit creates in us—through the proclamation of God's righteousness—the faith that says Amen and accepts this righteousness. It remains God's work from the beginning to the end.
6. Changes in the doctrine of justification reflect a shift in the formulation of the problem. It is thought that the Reformation was a contextual event. Our own context demands a thorough recalibration of this key doctrine. Only through recalibration can justification be retained in theology and preaching. At the same time it no longer justifies the division of the church.
7. We consider the biblical foundation of the doctrine of justification—i.e., culpable man having to be acquitted by God—to be indispensable. It is not a matter of the context. It is the text of the gospel.
8. Justification does not remain without consequences in the lives of those who have been justified. Where these consequences do not materialize, justification is denied.

41.5. *Broader implications*

At the conclusion of this section we wish to indicate the broader implications of the biblical concept of righteousness. It is not our intention to provide a detailed picture. Some of these implications figure more prominently in the discussion of other topics. At the same time, we do not wish to ignore these implications. The important thing is that the righteousness which we receive through justification affects all of life. Justification is not an isolated event, as though we could carry on with life without permitting justification to leave its mark. A justified life is a life that is being sanctified by the Spirit of sonship, in freedom, and in anticipation of the future. In conclusion we point to the role of the church in continuing to uphold the gospel of justification through preaching, teaching, and pastoral care.

1. Calvin refers to a *twofold* grace. One would tear Christ apart by separating sanctification from justification, i.e., by presenting sanctification in isolation without indicating that sanctification goes hand in hand with justification. In the following section we shall revisit this inextricable duality in greater depth from the perspective of sanctification. At this point we look at this duality from the perspective of justification.[72]

Calvin says: "Just as Christ cannot be torn into pieces, we cannot separate the two benefits that we receive from him simultaneously and in combination, namely, justification and sanctification. All those, therefore, whom God accepts in grace, he simultaneously grants the Spirit of adoption as children, through whose power he then reforms them into his image" (*Institutes*, 3.11.6).

This passage clearly articulates the inextricable connection between justification and sanctification. Calvin insists that justification in people's lives could not be discussed without referring to the grace of sanctification. Although justification and sanctification are two facets of the same grace, they are one, cannot be experienced separately, and their sequence is irreversible.

2. According to Calvin, *sanctification is brought about by the Spirit of sonship*. Sanctification and sonship belong together. Those who are sanctified do not remain strangers. The Spirit of Christ is the Spirit of adoption as children (Rom. 8:15, 16). Those who are sanctified receive this gift as child of God. We cannot be children of God without the Spirit doing his sanctifying work in us and to us.

72. See Velema, 1985, particularly chapter 3.

3. We see at the same time that *the purpose of sanctification is the restoration of the image of God within us*. There is no sanctification without becoming once again the image of God (see § 23.5). There is no sanctification that is not focused on this restoration.

Justification means receiving a right to eternal life and thus the destiny of the *covenant of life* (see § 26.3). This destiny includes being once again the image of God through the grace of sanctification. Those who limit the destiny of the *covenant of life* to justification, and identify it with justification, ignore the consequences of sin, which would only consist of guilt, but exclude the stain of sin. They also fail to appreciate the scope of redemption, which after all also implies inner renewal. It includes all aspects of soteriology. Soteriology cannot be limited to one or a few of these aspects. Christ has been given to us for wisdom, righteousness, sanctification, and redemption (1 Cor. 1:30). This inner cohesion is also implied by the list of benefits: "Ye are washed, but ye are sanctified, but ye are justified in the name of the Lord Jesus, and by the Spirit of our God" (1 Cor. 6:11; regarding the Spirit see also 1 Cor. 12:13).

The most striking difference between justification and sanctification is that in sanctification we are actively involved as subjects (particularly 1 Peter 1:16; Heb. 12:14), as it is said that we are to perfect our "holiness in the fear of God" (2 Cor. 7:1). On the other hand sanctification is referred to as a gift with God, Christ, or the Holy Spirit performing the action (1 Thess. 5:23; Heb. 13:12; 1 Cor. 6:11).

We can only speak of justification as a gift, never as an assignment. Even when faith is treated as a subject, one will never be able to say that faith justifies a person. As we have seen already, faith is an instrument, no more, no less. As believers we are indeed actively involved in faith, but always in the passive tense of the verb. The subject of justification is and remains God. This is not the case with sanctification. Another difference between justification and sanctification is that the former is perfected in this life, whereas with respect to the latter it must be said that only "after this life we arrive at the goal of perfection" (Heidelberg Catechism, response 115).

We do not address the sequence in which Calvin treats this material in *Institutes*, 3. See Velema, 1985, 55–57; van Genderen, 1988, 97–100. It is clear that Calvin's striking approach to treating repentance and the Christian life (3.3, 7) prior to justification (3.11) has everything to do with the breadth of redemption and the internal unity of the benefits of salvation. However, Calvin has not weakened justification by first discussing (part of) sanctification. He commences volume 3 with an explanation of the work of the Spirit and next discusses faith. All benefits covered in volume 3 reflect the perspectives of *sola fide* and *sola gratia*. We infer the latter from the pneumatological composition of volume 3.

4. We now turn to *Christian freedom*. Calvin treats this as an appendage of justification (*Institutes*, 3.19.1), which contributes considerably to our understanding of justification. That it is an appendage can never mean that it is insignificant. Christian freedom represents—so to speak—the test case for the Reformational content of the doctrine of justification.

We can only understand Christian freedom well when we treat it against the background of the covenant of life. Calvin refers to Christian freedom as comprising three aspects (*Institutes*, 3.19.2–9; in 9 it is referred to as a "spiritual thing").

As a consequence of justification, Christian freedom liberates us from the condemnation of the law. It liberates us from obedience to the law, as though we still lived under the covenant of life. It liberates us from prejudice, narrow-mindedness, and anxiety that mark immature children. Being reborn to the image of God through the Holy Spirit implies an inner awareness of having been called to the service of God across the full spectrum of life and to employ and enjoy the good things and gifts provided by the heavenly Father. They are after all sanctified through the Word of God and through prayer (1 Tim. 4:5). In this context, God's children need to be fully aware that they are still under way and continue to be pursued by various enemies, not least by the devil who "walks about as a roaring lion" (1 Peter 5:8; Rev. 12:13).

Freedom is found in the tension between having been justified and sanctified, and still requiring continuing sanctification, as Paul says: in the struggle between flesh and the Spirit (Gal. 5:13–26). There is the ongoing temptation to abuse our freedom in favor of the flesh. Where this happens, in whatever form or manner, love is lacking and is thwarted. This is (once again) an attack on the image of God. The "murderer (of men) from the beginning" (John 8:44) does not stop trying to murder (once again) the restored image of God. "For to be carnally minded is death" (Rom. 8:6).

This freedom is the opposite of lawlessness (1 John 3:4). It knows itself to be bound to Christ's commandment (John 14:21). Christ is encountered in this freedom. It is the space within which he reveals himself (John 16:22–23). Justification implies the freedom of God's children, a freedom that is focused on the service of God according to his command. Thus man arrives where God desired him to be by virtue of creation. He is no longer child within the framework of the covenant of life. He arrives there by grace, i.e., justification and sanctification. Although the context has changed, the objective remains the same. This is part of the biblical doctrine of justification.

5. We also point to the *eschatological aspect of justification*. Paul refers to this in Galatians 5:5: "For we through the Spirit wait for the hope of righteousness by faith." Righteousness is also an object of hope.

The song of praise, in Revelation 5:10, speaks of priests and kings. As image of God they fulfill their original task with respect to the renewed creation. This priestly kingship and this royal priesthood reflect the culmination of having been bought with the blood of the Lamb and justified by it (Rev. 5:9).

In Revelation the Lamb is at the center.[73] This imagery shows how justification for Christ's sake continues to work in the new heaven and on the new earth. Justification does not only find its fulfillment and culmination in eschatological renewal. The reverse is also true! This culmination never ceases to recall and focus on justification for Jesus' sake. The bride of Christ is only pure because her clothes have been washed in the blood of the Lamb (Rev. 7:14).

Justification is not only the focus of the church throughout the centuries. It carries through into eternity where it is contemplated and extolled with gratitude. In contrast with the construct of justification from eternity we confess that justification bears fruit into eternity. Therefore in line with God's promise, we "look for new heavens and a new earth, wherein dwelleth righteousness" (2 Peter 3:13). This righteousness is the fulfillment of everything that has been discussed in this section.

6. Therefore *justification remains the heart of the message of the church*. We cannot surrender it as a contextual program that has been superseded as a consequence of changes in the inclinations and vicissitudes of life.

The beginning and the end of the Bible as well as the core of the history of redemption are concerned with the gospel of justification. It is the very foundation of salvation, because justification bears fruit into eternity. *This gospel ensures the continuity of the church throughout the ages, namely, its foundation and its future, its origin and its salvation.*

73. See W. H. Velema, *Confrontatie met Van Ruler* (confrontation with Van Ruler), 1962, 94–96.

§ 42. Sanctification

42.1. *Gift of the triune God*

1. Justification is followed by sanctification. There is *a close connection* as well as *a distinct difference* between these two.

The most striking difference is constituted by the fact that justification is done to a sinner, whereas in sanctification he himself is actively involved (cf. § 41.5, subsection 3). We have already pointed out that justification does not happen without faith. The same is true of sanctification. Activity associated with sanctification comprises not only having faith but also being holy and sanctifying oneself. We already read of this in Leviticus 19:2: "Ye shall be holy: for I the LORD your God am holy." These words are quoted verbatim in the New Testament (1 Peter 1:16).

This verse directly links the holiness of the church with the holiness of God himself. His holiness is the source and goal, the ground and reason for their holiness. Since the people belong to God, they must live a holy life. Their holiness reveals the holiness of God.

2. This description is characteristic of the term "holy" as an attribute of the people of God. *Holy means: separated from and separated to.* The Holy God seeks a people that belongs to him and serves him, that observes his commandments and does his will. Since God is holy, his people must also be holy.

Although it is not spelled out, we encounter here the notion that man has been created in God's image. The image of the Holy God can only be manifested in people who may—once again—be called holy. It is characteristic of Calvin's view of sanctification that he sees the restoration of the image of God as its goal.[74]

3. *Sanctification restores the image of God*, so that people who have turned away from God through sin and have become alienated from

74. *Institutes*, 3.3.9. Here Calvin discusses repentance, which he interprets as regeneration.

life with God (Eph. 4:18) may and can once again live in a good and pure relationship with God.

This sanctification targets especially *the stain and power of sin*, which are eliminated through sanctification. The call to sanctification means the call to resist sin and to live in obedience to God's commandments and in love toward him through the power of the Spirit. Justification has to do with man's guilt, his status before God. Sanctification concerns the stain and power of sin. Sanctification means that we are redeemed from these and that we are renewed inwardly according to the image of God so as to live in his honor.

Sanctification touches our internal motivation *and* our external behavior. In sanctification man experiences the restoration of his relationship with God in everything that he does and leaves undone, in both speech and action. Acquittal from guilt and adoption as child of God are manifested in sanctification. It demonstrates that this person belongs to God,that he is oriented toward him in terms of both attitude and behavior.

Sanctification comes from God. It is also oriented toward God. We can characterize sanctification as aversion to sin and resistance to it. This is a key aspect of sanctification. Just as God's holiness goes beyond his rejection and condemnation of sin, so being holy (sanctified) goes beyond merely being liberated from sin. To be holy means to be oriented toward God in the depth of our desires, in the breadth of our interaction with others, and in the height of our aspirations. Sanctification means to truly again live as the image of God. Its essence is to glorify God and serve him in love.

4. There is no doubt that God's holiness implies that he has an aversion to sin and that he punishes sinners (1 Sam. 2:2; 6:20; Zech. 8:17; for the connection between God's holiness and the condemnation of sin see Ezek. 36:20–23).

Nevertheless, there are additional aspects of God's holiness, e.g., his faithfulness to his covenant and the redemption of his people through judgment (particularly Ezek. 36:23; but also Ex. 15:11; Hos. 11:9).

God is the Holy One, i.e., the Unapproachable One (Isa. 6:3; 1 Tim. 6:16). God's way with people is also called holy (Ps. 77:13).

God's holiness signifies the wholly particular and unique nature of Israel's God. His holiness implies that he not only has an aversion to sin, but also reveals his faithfulness to his people. God's holiness does not only comprise judgment but also grace; not only mercy but also condemnation. God is declared to be holy in the way in which he reveals himself, in the way in which he is God. He seeks people who belong to him.[75]

In connection with God's holiness, A. Noordtzij speaks of God's "uniqueness which runs as a golden thread through all of Scripture." He "wants to see the spotless purity of his Being also reflected in a holy people. Therefore Israel's life must follow the divine example. This is not a vague mysticism, but a daily routine which necessitates a particular way of life and arouses certain emotions on the part of believers."[76]

This reference also makes clear that in Leviticus cultic holiness is the external manifestation of the ethical holiness in one's life. "The admonition in [Lev. 19] verse 2 is the epitome of an attitude towards life which is in part cultic and in part ethical and therefore applies to all areas of life. When in the days of the prophets these two are separated, the prophets emphasize their inextricable unity."[77]

One cannot say that the Old Testament demands only cultic holiness and the New Testament only ethical holiness. When the temple disappears, the emphasis shifts more and more toward all of life, with the human heart being the determinative starting point. The internal and external aspects of life should therefore never be played out against each other.[78]

Holiness derives from God and is demanded by him. In addition to the passages already mentioned, we also refer to 1 Thessalonians 4:7–8, where it says that God has called us to holiness and has given us his Holy Spirit. Without sanctification no one can see the Lord (Heb. 12:14; cf. Matt. 5:8).

The right to demand sanctification from his people rests with the Holy One of Israel.

5. However, there is *also a clear relationship between sanctification and Christ.* This is already implied by the fact that we are renewed in the image of Christ.

75. See especially Vriezen, *Hoofdlijnen* (main perspectives, literally "headlines"), 324. C. Westermann and W. Zimmerli consider God's holiness to be less fundamental. Nevertheless, in *Theologie des Alten Testaments* (theology of the Old Testament), the latter refers to God's holiness as "Herrentum" and "Ausschließlichkeit" ("lordship" and "exclusiveness"). See further Velema, 1985, 26–31, together with the associated footnotes. L. Doekes, *Der Heilige* (the Holy One), 1960, is relevant to the dogmatic development of the concept of God's holiness.

76. A. Noordtzij, *Leviticus*, 1940, 193.

77. Ibid.

78. In various reference volumes, one can find broad overviews of what is and can be meant by the adjective "holy."

Sanctification as God's gift to us is founded on the work of Christ. Here is a striking similarity with justification. Christ is given to us for wisdom, righteousness, sanctification, and redemption (1 Cor. 1:30).[79] The link between sanctification and Christ is also expressed in 1 Corinthians 6:11, where the washing away of sins, sanctification, and justification are linked with the name of Christ and the Spirit of our God.

The relationship between sanctification and Christ's sacrifice is expressed in Hebrews 10:10 and 13:12. Sanctification is owed to Christ, who according to the entire epistle to the Hebrews is the fulfillment of the sacrificial ministry of the Old Testament.

It is noteworthy that "by one offering [Christ] hath perfected for ever them that are sanctified" (Heb. 10:14). Therefore, the decisive one-time nature of Christ's sacrifice applies to both sanctification and justification.

Romans 6:19 (as well as 22) discusses sanctification as a calling in some detail: "Yield your members [as] servants to righteousness unto holiness." These verses contain the practical consequence of what Paul writes in 6:4–7. There he refers to the relationship with Christ, i.e., being buried and raised with him, which implies "that the body of sin might be destroyed" so that we "should walk in newness of life."

The mystery of sanctification is Christ's sacrifice. Actually we need to express this yet more clearly, i.e., the secret of sanctification is the claim of faith on the death and resurrection of Christ.

This is of course true of justification. It is no less true of sanctification, albeit in a different manner.

With the latter we mean that *we are indeed sanctified in Christ and must at the same time pursue sanctification.*

With respect to the latter see 1 Thessalonians 4:3–7, Hebrews 12:14, and 1 Peter 1:16. The question is how it is possible that sanctification is presented to us as a gift from Christ, while at the same time we are still to pursue it. We wish (to attempt) to give an answer to this question in the following subsection. This answer cannot be discussed without referring to faith.

6. *The Spirit is also explicitly linked with sanctification.* We have in mind 1 Corinthians 6:11, 2 Thessalonians 2:13, and 1 Peter 1:2 (see

79. For a detailed discussion and for the passages that are about to be referenced see Velema, 1985, 31–34.

also 4:14).[80] For the fruits of sanctification as fruits of the Spirit see Galatians 5:22. See also Ezekiel 36:27 as the conclusion of verses 25 and 26.

7. At the conclusion of this overview we wish to highlight two additional facts. In the first place, *in Calvin's work we do not encounter sanctification as a separate component of the order of salvation.* He addresses sanctification in a number of sections of *Institutes*, volume 3 (see above). Particularly 3.3 (on penitence) is fundamental for Calvin's doctrine of sanctification.

It is noteworthy that the *Leiden Synopsis* does not employ this term either. There we find a chapter on good works, followed by a discussion of Christian freedom (*Synopsis*, 34–35). Nevertheless, the term "sanctification" is frequently used, especially in 3.11.6, but not as a reference to this material.

We further point out that the foregoing implies that Barth treats the data from Scripture in his own way, when he emphasizes that sanctification applies to believers as a community and less so as individuals (*C.D.*, 4.2.513). In this connection Barth says that we do not hear anything about the sanctification that has already been achieved in us (referred to by Weber, *Foundations*, 2:334n1, as "presented very impressively"). We must ("sollen") be holy (*C.D.*, 4.2.416ff.). This blunt pronouncement does not do justice to the scriptural perspective presented above. Barth's one-sidedness reflects his view that Jesus Christ is the Holy One par excellence. "What has happened to him *de facto* has happened to all men *de jure*" (4.2.511). Our sanctification consists in "our participation in his holiness as grounded in the efficacy and revelation of the grace of Jesus Christ" (4.2.517). Weber follows in Barth's footsteps (*Foundations*, 2:329–36), although he expresses himself less extremely. Yet his terminology is quite reminiscent of Barth.

We find it difficult to understand why Weber thinks that the unity between the *indicative* and *imperative* must be understood only pneumatologically, while he says—by way of conclusion based on a quotation from Barth—that the *indicative* and *imperative* are practically indistinguishable (*Foundations*, 2:334). The difference between the two is precisely captured in pneumatology. In accepting this, one cannot treat them as a functional identity. Weber employs pneumatology to legitimize the unity, the functional identity of the two. To us the difference between the two is exactly based on pneumatology.

42.2. *Experienced in faith*

1. It is striking that although Berkouwer does call a book of his *Faith and Sanctification* (1952), he does not refer to faith in any of

80. W. Schrage, *The Ethics of the New Testament*, 1982, 270 f., in discussing passages from 1 Peter, addresses what he refers to as the pneumatic-charismatic character of Christian life.

the titles of the chapters. Instead, he titles chapter 2 "'*Sola Fide*' and Sanctification."

This probably reflects the fact that in Scripture *we do not come across a parallel to the expression "justified by faith."* The complex situation that we described above prevents us from using the explicit formulation "sanctified by faith." We do need to point out that sanctification—as far as its content is concerned, i.e., works—turns up in the warning against dead faith (James 2:14; in the context of 1:26: sins of the tongue; 2:2ff.: ignoring the poor. See also 1 John 3, especially vv. 2, 15, and 18). Nevertheless, we do not encounter the expression "sanctified by faith" in the New Testament. For the scriptural relationship between sanctification and faith we refer to regeneration accompanied by faith (see John 3:5 in connection with 3:16 and article 24 of the Belgic Confession of Faith).

We wish to emphasize that sanctification as gift from God in Christ can only be received and experienced through faith in Christ. This receiving indicates that Christ is our holiness as much as he is our life (Col. 3:4; Phil. 1:21). The passages referred to above (1 Cor. 1:30; 6:11; Heb. 10:14; 12:14) imply that Christ is our holiness and that we are sanctified before God through his sacrifice.

Also in Romans 6:4 Paul points to the same reality of God's grace in Christ. He refers to the dying of our old nature (being crucified with Christ) and the rising of our new nature. Paul uses here different imagery than the author of Hebrews 10, although he means the same thing. It is clear that we can only share in Christ's death and resurrection through faith. See Galatians 2:20–21 as well as Ephesians 2:5–8. *The reality of sanctification is a reality of faith.*

This becomes especially clear in Romans 6:11: "Likewise reckon ye also yourselves to be dead indeed unto sin, but alive unto God through Jesus Christ our Lord." We encounter this verb "reckon it to be" (*logizomai*) also in 3:28 in connection with justification by faith and in 8:18 in connection with eschatological expectation (without faith being explicitly mentioned).

Therefore faith is not only a gift, but also an obligation (Rom. 6:12–23 as imperative based on the indicative of v. 11); the gift of faith calls for the activity of faith. This means that sanctification can only be undertaken in faith. Christ is after all the source and strength, foundation and scope of sanctification. Sanctification can only be experienced and undertaken through a relationship of faith with him.

Therefore *one can never claim that sanctification is entirely our responsibility* while justification is totally God's work. The latter is definitely true. Sanctification is no less God's work, although here we open a different perspective. This other perspective is implied by the nature of sanctification as distinct from that of justification.

Berkouwer devotes his entire book (*Faith and Sanctification*, 1952) to this theme: sanctification not as effort in return (or quid pro quo), but equally much a matter of faith as justification. He refers to Bavinck's expression of "evangelical sanctification" (1952, 21ff., with a reference to *R.D.*, 4:248). It is for this reason that Berkouwer defends Kuyper despite misgivings about certain (anthropological and anthropologizing) formulations of his. In sanctification Kuyper stresses grace at the exclusion of any merit (1952, 89–90).

2. There are a couple of reasons why it is important to stress the relationship between sanctification and faith. *In the first place, it plays a role in the onset of sanctification.* The latter begins *with faith* rather than brokenness of heart. Calvin emphasizes that repentance proceeds from faith and follows immediately upon it (*Institutes*, 3.3.1). This is in contrast with various (contemporary and subsequent) views that separate contrition and faith chronologically, although in reality they belong together.[81]

Although repentance is part of it, it is a matter of faith. It is the fruit of faith and follows immediately after it. This does not deny that impressions of God's holiness and one's own unworthiness can precede faith. Genuine repentance as the dying to sin is the fruit of faith. Sanctification begins with faith. There is no faith without sanctification.

This is how we can understand that Christ's holiness becomes ours, namely, in the same way that Christ's righteousness becomes ours: through faith. Neither Christ's righteousness nor his holiness remain far from us.

When Christ's holiness becomes ours—on the basis of the indicative of salvation (justification and sanctification)—we immediately encounter the imperative: Be holy; strive for sanctification. Put to death your members which are upon the earth!

This fulfillment of the imperative is just as much a matter of faith as the acceptance of salvation in the indicative.[82]

The continuation of sanctification is also a matter of faith, and no less its culmination. This is the focus in the next section on persever-

81. See Velema, 1985, 66–71, and 1987, 134–37.

82. L. Floor emphasized this in an enlightening article, "Die indikatief en die imperatief in die prediking" (the indicative and the imperative in preaching), *Th. Ref.* 17 (1974): 19–33, particularly 26ff.

ance. In Romans 6 one can find the beginning (4–11), the continuation (12–20), and the end (22–23) of sanctification described from the perspective of faith in Jesus Christ. The reverse is true in 1 John 3:2. There sanctification in the lives of those who look forward to the end is viewed from the perspective of fulfillment. It is clear that 1 John 2:28–3:10 describes the reality of faith. For a conclusion to this gospel of salvation, see 5:10–12.

3. This has *far-reaching significance for the battle against the concept and practice of perfectionism*. A conclusive argument against perfectionism—the idea that a believer can live a perfect life—is the fact that one then lives by one's own strength and no longer in faith.

It is well-known that Wesley and his followers, in connection with their perfectionist concept of sanctification, referred to a *second blessing*. This blessing (and stage) follows upon justification. On the basis of this *second blessing* one is able to live without sin. Just as the *second blessing* inaugurates a separate period following that of justification, so faith in that period no longer has the same significance as that during the time of the *first blessing*.

See Hoekema, 1989, 214–25, for an overview of various authors and their inconsistencies. The term "inconsistencies" implies that these authors introduce various extenuating circumstances and distinctions to maintain their theories of perfection, thus diminishing the seriousness of certain sins and at the same time maintaining that they could meet those reduced expectations. In the process they commit two errors. In the first place they diminish the seriousness of sin. In the second place they imply that man can get away with less than full obedience to God's demands. Both God's demands and the evil of sin are belittled. There is a remarkable similarity between this way of thinking and seventeenth-century Roman Catholic casuistry. See W. H. Velema, *Oriëntatie in de christelijke ethiek* (introduction to Christian ethics), 1990, 94–97. Regarding Wesley see also van Genderen, 1988, 101ff.

For an overview of Wesley's doctrine of sanctification see the essay by M. E. Deter, "The Wesleyan View," in *Five Views on Sanctification*, 1987, 11–46. That sanctification is a matter of faith is explained by Wesley in a sermon that is included in Th. A. Langford, *Wesleyan Theology, A Sourcebook*, 1984, 2–10. The text for this sermon is Ephesians 2:8. His view on perfection is found among other places in a sermon on Hebrews 6:1, included in *The Works of John Wesley*, 1972, 5:410–24. See further H. Lindström, *Wesley & Sanctification*, 1980.

We shall now list a number of biblical arguments against perfectionism. The arguments in favor of perfectionism can be found in Hoekema, 1989, 216–20. Our arguments to the contrary all reflect, in one way or another, the fact that perfectionism abandons faith in Christ who is our sanctification in favor of the perspective of doing good works to honor Christ and express our gratitude to him. It abandons the *sola fide* perspective of our works in favor of works of our own, admittedly enabled through grace.

Our arguments against perfectionism are:

1. Perfectionism shortchanges Christ because our sanctification, from beginning to end, is and remains both his gift to us and his work in us.
2. Perfectionism plays down the continuing need for forgiveness for everything that we do. This is precisely what Scripture teaches us to pray for (see 1 Kings 8:46–51; Ps. 130:3; Prov. 20:9; James 3:2; see also the fourth petition in the Lord's Prayer).
3. Perfectionism is in conflict with the portrayal of believers in the Bible, and with the image that Bible authors give of themselves (Rom. 7:13–25[83] and Phil. 3:12–14; further, Job 42:6; Ps. 130:3–4; Dan. 9:15–16; Mic. 7:18–19).
4. Perfectionism is in contradiction with clear pronouncements of Scripture (Rom. 6:12; 1 Cor. 10:12–13; 1 John 1:8–9), and with all of the admonishments that have a universal and lasting significance (Eph. 4:25–32; Col. 3:5–7).
5. Perfectionism obscures the clarity of the contrast between flesh and Spirit (Rom. 8:1–11; Gal. 5:24; James 4:4–10).
6. Perfectionism weakens the longing for the consummation of all things and demands attention for itself and its own struggle.

In response 115 of the Heidelberg Catechism we encounter the necessity of ongoing penitence through the preaching of the law. There the radical nature of grace (*sola gratia*) is clearly confessed in learning to know one's sinful nature, the desire for forgiveness, prayer for the grace of the Spirit, and the longing for the promised perfection.

It is necessary to address 1 John 3:9: "Whosoever is born of God doth not commit sin." This verse can be interpreted to apply to someone who has been born again and is a child of God (M. de Jonge, *De brieven van Johannes* = the epistles of John, 1968, 148ff.). This not sinning

83. For the exegesis of this pericope see Velema 1985, 78–82.

> or not being able to sin is stated in the present tense. It has the sense of continuing with sin, sinning continuously, pretending that nothing has happened. It is impossible for the Christian to live as he did before (Greijdanus, *De brieven van de apostelen Petrus en Johannes, en de brief van Judas* = the epistles of Peter, John, and Jude, Bottenburg, 1929). This does not mean that the struggle between flesh and the Spirit is over. If this had been intended, John would have been in conflict not only with Paul, but also with himself (see 1 John 1:8).

This emphasis on faith also has implications for viewing man from the perspective of flesh and the Spirit.

Hoekema maintains (in appealing to John Murray) that our old nature dies completely in regeneration. Only our new nature remains. He refuses to speak of both an "old self" and a "new self" (1989, 209–14).[84] He appeals especially to Ephesians 4:20–24, which according to him links up with Romans 6:6 where Paul says that our old nature is crucified with Christ. "If any man be in Christ, he is a new creature" (2 Cor. 5:17).

Hoekema does admit that believers continue to sin. According to Ephesians 4:23 and Colossians 3:10, renewal is a process that lasts a lifetime.

We sympathize with Hoekema's intention. It seems to us that he wishes to make clear that the old and the new do not coexist on equal terms. He seeks to make the supremacy of grace also anthropologically transparent. We wish to point out that in Romans 7:17 Paul says that it is no longer he who commits evil, but the sin that dwells in him. In Romans 6:6 he says: "that the body of sin might be destroyed." In this way Paul carefully draws a certain distinction. We nevertheless cannot go along with Hoekema. The implication (and perhaps also the intention) of his position is that the "new self" has nothing old left in it, and therefore is no longer subject to sin. Hoekema does refer to the old nature. However, as far as we can tell, he sees it as being entirely separate from the "new self." We do have a problem with this.

Who has responsibility for the old nature? Is it not man's "self," i.e., his "new self'? It therefore exhibits vestiges of flesh, sin, and the old nature.

Hoekema's distinction reminds us of Kuyper's distinction between core and periphery. Kuyper ends up with the structure of a twofold self. Hoekema does not go so far. He does recognize that the old nature remains, but does not explain how it is related to the "self" (the "new self") and vice versa!

We find that this anthropological distinction obscures more than it clarifies. The issue of the coexistence of the old and the new in one's heart cannot be made anthropologically and terminologically transparent. (We agree with Berkouwer's criticism of Kuyper in 1952, 88ff.) However one wishes to judge this, the combination of a completely "new self" and the old nature that remains yields the impression of a dichotomy in man that detracts from the totality implied by *simul iustus et peccator* (cf. Berkouwer, 1952, 74).

84. See also his *Created in God's Image*, 1986, and *The Christian Looks at Himself* (1975).

42.3. *In relation to the law of liberty*

1. *The life of sanctification is not a life without the law.* In a life that is being sanctified, the law plays a different role than prior to Adam's fall into sin. We saw this already in the preceding section in the reference to Calvin's view of liberty (§ 41.5, subsection 4).

Since the covenant of life has been superseded by the covenant of grace, the law is no longer the way to life. However, it remains valid as the code of conduct between God and man. The difference between the situation prior to the fall into sin and that subsequent to the redemption by Christ has to do with the covenant. Just as the covenant of grace has superseded the covenant of life, so the nature of the obedience that God demands following redemption by Christ has changed. This is not to suggest that obedience to the law is no longer required, or that the law has lost its validity. Just as the law was upheld in redemption (Christ dying under the curse of the law), so it continues to hold following redemption. It is now written in our hearts (Jer. 31:33; cf. Heb. 8:8–12). Obedience to the law is now a matter of the heart, from the perspective of renewed and complete knowledge of the LORD.[85]

Through faith man is filled with knowledge to such an extent that obedience has become completely voluntary (cf. Ps. 110:3). Here one has to take into account the new situation: "I . . . will be their God, and they shall be my people" (Jer. 31:33).

In Paul's epistles we come across expressions that seem to suggest that the law has lost its validity. In Romans 6:14 Paul says that "ye are not under the law, but under grace." Here he means by the law the condemnation of the law, the curse of the law, as he points out in Galatians 3:10 as well. Christ has redeemed us from this curse of the law (Gal. 3:13). This is how Abraham's blessing is extended to the Gentiles.

Nevertheless, Paul also speaks of fulfilling the requirements of the law, i.e., what the law justly demands from us (Rom. 8:4). He says this of those who walk according to the Spirit, as opposed to those who walk according to the flesh.[86] The subsequent verses make clear

85. Cf. J. de Vuyst, *Oud en nieuw verbond in de brief aan de Hebreeën* (the old and the new covenant according to the epistle to the Hebrews), 1964, 137–65, especially 143.

86. See W. Schrage, *Die konkreten Einzelgebote in der paulinischen Paränese*, 1964, 76, 232.

that not submitting oneself to the law is a manifestation of the flesh. Evidently, those who are in the Spirit do obey the law (vv. 7–9).

2. Here we encounter what Calvin refers to as *the third use of the law*. To him it is the most important role of the law. He says that in discussing this aspect of the law he comes closer to its real purpose. Precisely at this point he refers to the Spirit who reigns in the hearts of people. "For he is the best instrument for them, to learn more thoroughly each day the nature of the Lord's will to which they aspire, and to confirm them in the understanding of it" (*Institutes*, 2.7.12). The Decalogue is given to the people who have just been adopted as God's people at Sinai. It is a gift from God who liberated them from Egypt. This implies that grace and the law are not mutually exclusive. This does happen whenever the law is abused by the Jews to achieve their own righteousness. Then it becomes a matter of either-or—*either* the way of the law *or* the way of grace.

In the Old Testament the glory of the law is sung in Psalms such as 19 and 119. Its echo can be found in the writings of Paul (precisely by him, precisely in) Romans 7:12: "Wherefore the law is holy, and the commandment holy, and just, and good."

3. Elsewhere we have explained in detail that *Jesus maintains the law by fulfilling it* (Velema, 1987, 80–86). Jesus summarizes the law in the commandment of love (Matt. 22:37–40). Paul follows Jesus in this regard (Rom. 13:8–10). See also John 13:34 and James 2:8.

We have made clear that love as the fulfillment of the law does not mean that the commandments have been set aside or are considered to be of lesser value (1987, 86–89). The conclusion of all of these passages cannot be that those who are led by the Spirit no longer want to have anything to do with the law.

Precisely the opposite is true. In a fascinating, dialectical manner Paul makes this clear with respect to his own activities as apostle in 1 Corinthians 9:20–21.

We see all of this summarized in the New Testament expression *the fulfillment of the law of Christ* (Gal. 6:2). "The law of Christ" means "the law of God, which is taken so seriously by Christ, that through his word and deed it achieves its full validity" (Velema, 1985, 103). This is the radicalization of the Decalogue through the commandment to love, of which the Lord Jesus in the Sermon on the Mount gives a number of striking examples.

The law, thus understood, is called the law of liberty by (precisely) James (1:25; 2:12). By this he means that this law does not enslave. Obedience to it occurs within the perspective of Christian liberty.

To be the image of God once again is not possible while ignoring the law. Sanctification does not produce autonomous people, but precisely people who exercise their freedom by knowing themselves to be bound by the law. The question as to how the law should be understood falls outside the scope of this section. It calls for hermeneutics of the law.

It is not simple to capture Kohlbrügge's position with respect to the law as guide for gratitude. J. van Lonkhuyzen, *Hermann Friedrich Kohlbrügge en zijn prediking* (Hermann Friedrich Kohlbrügge and his preaching), 1905, 463, writes that Kohlbrügge does not consistently pursue his rejection of the law as a rule of life. "Especially in his later sermons Kohlbrügge places more emphasis on the law as a rule of life." Kohlbrügge's own writings recognize that a Christian must live according to the law. The statement on page 160 of *Vragen en antwoorden tot opheldering en bevestiging van den Heidelbergsche Catechismus* (questions and answers to clarify and confirm the Heidelberg Catechism), 1930 (seventh revised publication), says, "We must ensure total agreement with the law and to this end we must hold onto Christ and his grace . . . and thus we shall walk according to the law as fulfilled by him." On the other hand, increasing emphasis is placed on the fact that we stand guilty before the law and must rid ourselves of all self-righteousness. See, e.g., *De eenvoudige Heidelberger* (the simple Heidelberg Catechism, 1941), 83, 182, and 334, which places the emphasis solely on faith. We refer to the well-known passage in *Schriftauslegungen* (interpretations of Scripture), 1909, 11:108, where the call to mortify the members that are upon the earth (Col. 3:5) is interpreted as considering them to be dead. In the well-known *Hoogst belangrijke briefwisseling met Da Costa* (highly important correspondence with Da Costa, 1880), 1933[4], 46, it is said that the law must be maintained. However, Kohlbrügge does not find in Scripture anything to justify treating sanctification as a special doctrine to follow upon the doctrine of Christ's righteousness. He does offer a doctrine of gratitude and good works. Also in a sermon on Philippians 1:11 (third and fourth groups of twelve, preached in 1846–47), 1911, 445–70, particularly 468, Kohlbrügge speaks positively about the law.

G. Ph. Scheers, *H. F. Kohlbrügge, zijn leven, zijn prediking en zijn geschriften* (H. F. Kohlbrügge, his life, his preaching, and his writings), 1976, 134, writes that Kohlbrügge drastically reduces the significance of the law compared with Calvin, although he does not entirely ignore it. Scheers concludes that "we cannot escape the impression that Kohlbrügge did not quite know what to make of it."

Our impression is that although Kohlbrügge does see a role for the law in a believer's life (as a guide to gratitude), in practice he refers directly to Christ in whom we have everything and who teaches us to love. We do not agree with S. Gerssen, *Grensverkeer tussen kerk en Israel* (border traffic between the church and Israel), that

Kohlbrügge sees justification as part of sanctification. The central role of justification in Kohlbrügge's work renders this view unlikely.

We finally refer to a suggestion offered by Noordmans. He identifies (*V. W.*, 3:523) a number of sharp paradoxes in Kohlbrügge work regarding sanctification. Noordmans (514) points out that it is difficult to say where the new human being ends up in this dispensation "now that his place that he was not permitted to leave was eliminated in Christ."

We indeed recognize a tension here, i.e., as soon as it comes to practical questions Kohlbrügge again refers directly to Christ. See also the overview by van Genderen, 1988, 103–5.

42.4. *By the pattern of imitation*

Sanctification has content. It manifests a pattern. After all, the core idea is the restored image of God. We now attempt to describe sanctification more concretely. It is not feasible to do this here in a comprehensive, exhaustive manner. All admonishment passages in the Gospels and the epistles of the New Testament pertain to sanctification.

1. *We wish to sketch the basic pattern of sanctification.* For this reason we refer to 1 Peter 2:21–24. Christ left his disciples an example so that they would "follow his steps."

Discipleship of Jesus requires treading in his footsteps. Next, Peter mentions a number of instances in which Jesus set the example: "Who did no sin, neither was guile found in his mouth: who, when he was reviled, reviled not again; when he suffered, he threatened not; but committed himself to him that judgeth righteously: who his own self bare our sins in his own body on the tree, that we . . . should live unto righteousness."

In this passage we find a remarkable blend of *what he did for us* and *what he demonstrated to us*. We can refer to this as the inextricable unity of justification and sanctification.

The imitation can never mean imitating him, seeking to resemble him, just to look good. It is not a matter of moralism or external piety to be practiced to gain people's respect.

Imitation as manifestation of sanctification is itself part of salvation. It is not our sovereign response to what Christ has done for us, nor our grateful repayment (if this were possible). Imitation is itself part of salvation, just as sanctification is part of the doctrine (and the order) of salvation. With the foregoing we deduce the consequence of the thesis that the imperative is also a manifestation of the experience of faith. Imitation does not throw us back onto ourselves, but precisely points us to him, in whose immediate presence we remain by following him. We can only display the image of the Redeemer through the power of his work of redemption.

This is clearly implied by John 13:34: "As I have loved you, that ye also love one another." The word "as" refers to both *the example and foundational significance* of Jesus' love.[87] It is impossible to display this love without personally sharing in Jesus' love. His love, culminating in his atoning death (1 John 4:10), is the foundation of our love toward the brethren (and others). It represents its blueprint.

Jesus spoke about following him in a profound way, immediately upon the first announcement of his suffering (note here also the connection between sanctification and salvation): "If any man will come after me, let him deny himself, and take up his cross, and follow me" (Matt. 16:24; cf. 10:38–39).

Since the publication of Bonhoeffer's book *Nachfolge*[88] (discipleship), the concept of discipleship has also become common currency in Protestant theology.[89] Berkouwer summarizes discipleship (imitation) not as a strenuous striving after a moral ideal, but as a life that can only exist in communion with Christ (1952, 147).

The love of Christ is the centerpiece of discipleship and finds its culmination in the redemption of our sins. Behind this lies God's mercy as source. Following Christ implies practicing discipleship. Only those who follow after Jesus can be his pupils. This pupilage consists in both listening to his Word and his teaching, and following in his footsteps.

Thus we arrive at the formulation frequently employed by Paul: be followers of the Lord and of me. It is striking that Paul also considered himself to be an example. He does this consistently in the context of his own following of Christ (1 Cor. 4:16; Gal. 4:12; Phil. 3:17; 1 Thess. 1:6; 2 Thess. 3:7–9).[90] De Boer concludes that Paul's objective is not that the church will imitate him, but that they will imitate Christ

87. R. Schnackenburg, *Das Johannesevangelium* (the gospel according to John), 1976², 3:59ff.

88. D. Bonhoeffer, *Nachfolge* (discipleship), 1971, 10. See on Bonhoeffer, Chr. Frey, *Die Ethik des Protestantismus von der Reformation bis zur Gegenwart* (the ethics of Protestantism from the Reformation till now), 1989, 211–26.

89. In Roman Catholic theology, that was already the case as a result of the book by Thomas à Kempis, *De navolging van Christus* (following Christ). Regarding this book and the concept of discipleship see Berkouwer, 1952, chapter 7, particularly 136–39; also Velema, 1985, 114–30. R. Strunk, *Nachfolge Christi*, 1981, presented a multifaceted discussion of the theme of discipleship. As subtitle he used: "Erinnerungen an eine evangelische Provokation" (reminiscences of an evangelical provocation). The key was a nonconforming attitude to life that had more appreciation for Bonhoeffer than à Kempis.

90. W. P. de Boer's dissertation, *The Imitation of Paul*, 1962, was dedicated to the interpretation of these passages. On pages 50–70 one finds a discussion of the imitation of Christ, and on pages 71–80 the imitation of God.

via him as their spiritual father and teacher (1962, 214). Paul employs this idea to build up believers spiritually. "To hold Christ's example before his followers was to stimulate their participation in the salvation and transformation which was at work in them by virtue of their living union with their Saviour and Lord" (212).

De Boer's conclusion with reference to the following of Christ differs from that of W. Michaelis.[91]

2. De Boer sees *imitation as having a specific content*. He points to the humility, self-denial, self-giving, and sacrifice of Christ's life for the salvation of people (1962, particularly 65–70).

We believe that we can indeed describe the concept of imitation with the help of the characterizations employed by De Boer. However, it should be kept in mind that these descriptions are compressed indications of Jesus' lifestyle and conduct. Peter mentions a number of concrete examples from Jesus' life that fall under this broad characterization.

Imitation means that Christ is manifested in us. The image of God, which we may once again become, *displays characteristics of the Lamb* that will continue to be praised and adored beyond the consummation of all things. In the discussion of sanctification we encounter the significance of Christ for the restoration of the image of God. This significance is both fundamental and illustrative.

We would like to go further than this and associate discipleship with the idea of *being crucified and raised with Christ*, frequently employed by Paul. (We only mention a few passages: Rom. 6:4–6; Gal. 2:19–20; Eph. 2:6; Col. 3:1–3; see also Phil. 3:10–11).[92] We have tried to show that these passages not only refer back to what Christ underwent and did for his people through his death and resurrection. The fact that Paul treats believers as subjects (in the past tense) implies that by coming to faith in the crucified and risen Christ they experience death and resurrection as a pneumatic reality. They are not only involved in faith in what happened long ago. The redemptive significance of Christ's death and resurrection for their salvation brings with it the dying of the old man (*mortificatio*) and the rising of the new man (*vivificatio*). This is characteristic terminology for sanctification. The two elements with which we opened this section—

91. W. Michaelis, *TDNT*, 4:666–74, particularly 668 and 672, where discipleship was understood as obeying someone's commandment.

92. On these passages see W. H. Velema, *Aan Christus gelijkvormig* (conformed to Christ), 1988.

being redeemed from the pollution and the power of sin *and* being molded to serve God in obedience to his command and to live to his honor—are described succinctly in the terms employed by Calvin: *mortificatio* and *vivificatio*.

One can recognize a direct link between the concept of discipleship and these two terms (two aspects of the same thing). Discipleship is experienced and practiced in dying and rising with Christ. The reverse is also true: there is no dying and rising with Christ that is not manifested in discipleship. In this way discipleship as manifestation of sanctification is in its deepest essence connected with Christ. He did not die for his own sins but for those of his people. Through the power of his death and resurrection we die to our sins. This happened once at Golgotha on resurrection morning (succinctly expressed in Rom. 6:11). This is imputed to us, so that it becomes true for us and of us. This is also made real to us through the Holy Spirit.

We may now conclude that the passages that speak of having died and risen with Christ comprise salvation in its totality, i.e., justification and sanctification, referred to by Calvin as a *duplex gratia* (twofold grace). Those who only recognize justification in these passages and leave out sanctification (as described above) ignore the unity of justification and sanctification and the twofold nature of God's grace.

It is clear that the content of these passages can only be experienced and appropriated through the Spirit. They have christological content and a pneumatological element of experience, which belong together.

We would not go along with Heyns in speaking of self-denial as self-expansion (*Dogm.*, 321ff.). It is true that sin encircles our selves. This circle needs to be broken. This is not the same thing as self-expansion. We prefer to speak of achieving our destiny. Following our fall into sin, this can only be realized through letting go and denying ourselves. This is how God permits us to achieve our original destiny. The fact that this takes place through conforming to Christ and following him clearly implies that the covenant of life is no longer an option. Our goal is now attained through Christ as Mediator of the covenant of grace. It is for this reason that he puts his stamp on our sanctification. This is the deep significance and the practical consequence of the evangelical reality that Christ is as much our sanctification as he is our life (Col. 3:4).

Against this background Barth's criticism of Calvin's emphasis on *mortificatio* is not justified. Calvin sought to do full justice to both aspects. Those who read his extensive chapters on (aspects of) sanctification in *Institutes*, 3, cannot argue that he allows *mortificatio* to overshadow *vivificatio*.

We therefore also disagree with Bakker's condemnation of Calvin's doctrine of sanctification (1991, chapter 4, especially 82–88). We find his criticism of Den Dulk's dissertation no less objectionable (*ibid.*, 90). Bakker's entire book, including this portion, is written from the perspective of Barth's "Triomf der genade" (triumph of grace). Those who do not share this Barthian starting point, or emphasize different aspects (e.g., Den Dulk) are criticized. One needs to keep in mind that the key to Barth's objection to Calvin's doctrine of salvation is the latter's doctrine of predestination.[93] Beker/Hasselaar, *Wegen* (ways), 4:72–74, defends Calvin against Barth.

42.5. *The broad contexts of environment and society*

1. We wish to point out that sanctification is not just an interpersonal matter, among persons, or between a person and society as a whole. *Sanctification affects all of life, including life in creation and society*.

We put it this way intentionally, because we view man as appointed by God to be viceroy over creation and in society (see § 23.2).

Recently a case was made to replace this anthropocentric perspective by an ex-centric view of man. Every person must consider the well-being of every creature (i.e., not only fellow human beings): "Help it to thrive." This view is supported by appealing to Levinas. The idea is to strip man's dominion of its egocentric and anthropocentric character. Man must act according to the ethical norm to handle everything the way God has left it to us.[94] This view demands that man be held responsible for everything that has been created. This appeals to us, because this responsibility is included in the mandate given to man as image of God. The question that this view elicits is whether man is equated with all other creatures to such an extent that his unique responsibility with respect to creation is ignored. In Romans 8:20–21 Paul definitely confirms man's supremacy over all of creation.

Sanctification has consequences for the interaction with people for the purpose of managing creation. All environmental issues ultimately question man's execution of his mandate. Does he take an anthropocentric approach, i.e., focused on his own interest, gain, and pleasure, without paying any attention to those who are geographically and

93. Barth, *C.D.*, 4.2.520ff. For a crucial review of Den Dulk's dissertation see W. H. Velema, "De leer van de heiliging bij Calvijn en Barth" (the doctrine of sanctification according to Calvin and Barth), *Th. Ref.* 32 (1989): 117–39.

94. P. Leenhouwers, "Gerechtigheid doen aan heel de schepping" (doing justice to all of creation), in W. Derkse (ed.), *Gerechtigheid en sociale rechtvaardigheid* (justice and social justice), 1991, 63–91. We wonder whether the author correctly appealed to Levinas. Did he not expand the latter's view unjustifiably?

chronologically far removed from him? We do not wish to consider the concept of *dominium*—which we have portrayed as part of the image of God—to be anthropocentric by definition. Man can execute his task anthropocentrically, but this implies a misuse of his mandate. It occurs when man only thinks of himself, i.e., ignores others and the rules that God has given him for his interaction with creation.

We should not only emphasize love toward one's neighbor, but also respect for what God has created and the way in which he has done so. It is ultimately man who is responsible for misuse, transgression, and neglect of the true nature of all that has been created.

With approval, we refer to a publication by Schuurman. In the end of this book (1989, 56) he speaks about normative structures within creation. We also think of rules that must be followed in technology for construction and preservation; in science for the advancement of knowledge; in agriculture for harvesting, tending, and caring; in health management for the prevention and cure of illnesses and compassion and care for mortal humankind; in the economy for responsible stewardship; in politics for service and the promotion of law and public justice.

The conciliatory process inaugurated by the meeting of the World Council of Churches in 1983 seeks to make Christianity and the entire inhabited world aware of the responsibility for creation and the environment.

Both personal and structural aspects can be identified in this regard. In connection with personal sanctification we have referred to self-control, service-orientation, and sharing, as well as the role of the church in emphasizing in the preaching such attitudes as part of sanctification. We have also pointed out that the sequence of presentation in ecclesiastical education and training must move from the sanctification of life to a conciliatory process, not the other way around.[95]

In the second essay (1990, 105–13), it is held that the cross must be kept central if the church is to link the conciliatory process (and the associated topics) with the kingdom of God.

The church is not a political party or a social action group that seeks to deal with environmental issues merely on a horizontal plane. The role of the church is to preach the gospel. Sanctification is part of salvation. This includes responsibility for the environment, individually, together, and in structural social contexts.

Within the perspective of sanctification the church is to take a clear position in terms of clarification and encouragement. There is no direct link between the resolution of environmental issues and salvation. They are only linked through the cross (death and resurrection). The

95. W. H. Velema, 1990, especially 100–104.

responsibility for the environment must be borne from the perspective of Christ's death and resurrection. The same thing is true of society, which is also affected by sanctification.[96]

2. We believe that sanctification *must also influence society*, through individuals as well as societies, groups, and political and social organizations. As far as the latter is concerned, their objective must be to alter structures. We do not mean to say that structures themselves can be converted. Only people, who are responsible for the maintenance and development of structures, can (and must) be converted. However, structures can be sanctified. This is to say, that they represent channels for the service that God wants us to offer to our fellow human beings.

In this context the term *humanization* can be used in the sense of being of service to mankind as desired by God within a perspective prescribed by God (see § 23.7). Those who ignore the latter qualification use humanization in a humanistic and anthropocentric manner.

Sanctification here means that things are assigned the role ordained by God and thus can serve man and his development. This process of sanctification cannot avoid an investigation into what God says about political and social contexts on earth and in creation (*social ethics*).[97]

There are also many good things happening to mankind that are not the result of sanctification as defined here. In all of those activities we see God's general goodness at work. It preserves and sustains, stimulates and intensifies what people do even if they are not aware of any dependence on God's rules and laws.

In this context we would not speak of sanctification. Sanctification is, after all, part of salvation in Jesus Christ. One cannot think of

96. There is a striking similarity between objective sanctification and what Kuyper called "Christian" culture (here used in the broader sense of the word) as the product of universal grace, which is influenced by the Word. See S. J. Ridderbos, *De theologische cultuurbeschouwing van Abraham Kuyper* (Abraham Kuyper's theological view of culture), 1947, 196–98, which concerns Kuyper's view in *De gemeene gratie* (common grace) (4th printing, 2:680). See for this W. H. Velema, "Kuyper's conceptie van de kerk als organisme kritisch bekeken" (Kuyper's concept of the church as organism critically reviewed), *Th. Ref.* 34 (1991): 295–309.

97. An example of an attempt to provide a Reformed social ethics was J. A. Heyns, *Teologiese ethiek* (theological ethics), 2/1, 1984, 2/2, 1989. Evangelicals in England and America are engaged in (areas of) social ethics. See also the observation by Hoekema, 1989, 231n102, with references to the literature. For a historical overview see E. M. van der Poll, *Sociaal reveil. Evangelischen in de samenleving, vroeger en nu* (social awakening: evangelicals in society, in the past and today), 1984. For Wesley's social ethics see M. Marquardt, *Praxis und Prinzipien der Social-ethik John Wesleys* (practice and principles of John Wesley's social ethics), 1986².

those who reject him as sharing in the sanctification brought about by his Spirit. It is nevertheless important for believers to keep their eyes and ears open to what happens on earth as a result of God's general goodness. It may not be denied or ignored.

42.6. *Reward as eschatological perspective*

1. At the close of the discussion of sanctification we still need to address three additional elements, i.e., perseverance, consummation, and reward.[98] Perseverance is discussed in the next section and consummation in § 57.4.

Here we wish to discuss *the reward that the Scriptures associate with the effort involved in sanctification.* We wish to examine this topic because many have trouble grasping it.

On the one hand the concept of reward is not explicitly spelled out as motivation for sanctification.[99] On the other hand it appears difficult to discount the motivation of reward.[100] Heyns (*Dogm.*, 319–24) does not address the notion of reward at all. The same is true of John Murray (1955, 177–324). Although Berkouwer (1952) does not refer to it explicitly, he does touch on it implicitly in a number of places. The same is true of Hoekema (1989, chapter 12). Although the latter does discuss the future, he does not do so from the perspective of reward.

We are all aware of the statement in response 63 of the Heidelberg Catechism that the reward for "our good works . . . is not of merit but of grace." However, we do not do much with it, because we live under the covenant of grace. All that we receive from God—including our good works (Eph. 2:10)—is his gift to us. How could one infer a motive for sanctification from the idea of a reward for such good works? It suggests that we should work hard so that God will reward his own work in us.

"Grace is such an overwhelming and all-encompassing gift, that asking for it cannot increase its magnitude. Seeking grace for God's

98. See also Velema, 1985, chapter 8, "Heiliging en voleinding" (sanctification and consummation), 168–79. Brunner spoke of an eschatological condition in the context of sanctification, *Dogmatics*, 3:304ff.

99. In one thesis of his dissertation *De prediking van Ebenezer en Ralph Erskine* (the preaching of Ebenezer and Ralph Erskine), 986, P. H. van Harten criticized Velema's book of 1985 for not paying sufficient attention to the New Testament concept of reward as motivation for sanctification.

100. See objections to Van Harten's thesis in Velema, 1989a, 109ff.

honour and our own benefit is so overwhelming and life-fulfilling that there is room for nothing additional."[101]

This consideration is also based on the confession of article 24 of the Belgic Confession of Faith: "Therefore we do good works, but not to merit by them (for what can we merit?); nay, we are indebted to God for the good works we do, and not he to us." The confession refers to Luke 17:10. In this verse reward as motivation for good works is squarely rejected.

We are obligated to devote our entire lives to the service of God's praise. The required zeal springs from God's justice and grace, his love and mercy. In addition to these virtues we require no other motives to perform good works. Reward-based motivation as additional incentive would distort our entire relationship with God.

2. Nevertheless *there is a promise of reward*. Bavinck discusses it briefly and cogently (*R.D.*, 4:236ff.). He refers to this reward as "one of the compelling reasons by which believers are exhorted to live a holy life." For the recompense of everyone's works he refers to Romans 2:6–11; 14:12; 1 Corinthians 3:8; 2 Corinthians 5:10; Galatians 6:5; Revelation 2:23; 20:12. "Godliness is profitable unto all things, having promise for the life that now is, and of that which is to come" (1 Tim. 4:8). "God . . . is a rewarder of them that diligently seek him (Heb. 11:6, 26). Other references are 1 Corinthians 9:18; Colossians 3:24; 1 Timothy 6:19; 2 Timothy 4:8; Hebrews 10:35.

Bavinck even refers to passages that speak of a special reward (1 Cor. 3:12–15; 9:16–17), and of gradations in glory (Matt. 10:41; 18:4; 20:16; 25:14). On the basis of these passages (and those referred to earlier) he concludes that there is a close connection between sanctification and glorification. What is sown here is reaped in eternity (Matt. 25:24, 26; 1 Cor. 15:42ff.; 2 Cor. 9:6; Gal. 6:7–8). Without holiness no one will see God (Matt. 5:8; Heb. 12:14). See also *R.D.*, 4:265ff.

In connection with the word "reward" Preisker (*misthos*, *TDNT*, 4:695–706) emphatically points out that the Jewish concept of reward that men could claim is totally alien to the New Testament (722ff., 698ff.).

The New Testament is very clear on the perspective within which good works play a role, i.e., God's work of grace. Those who speculate that they will receive a reward are so hypocritical and egocentric

101. Velema, 1989a, 110.

that they place themselves beyond the grace of God's love (Preisker, *TDNT*, 4:699f.).

J. L. de Villiers (*Die loongedagte in die Nuwe Testament* = the concept of reward in the New Testament, 1957, 53ff.) points out that particularly in the Gospels the concept of reward is linked with (the proclamation of) the immanent kingdom of God.

3. *The reward refers to the fact that the citizens of the kingdom will enter in.* Their sanctified walk of life is a sign and manifestation of the kingdom. All efforts on behalf of this kingdom and all fighting against its opponent(s) will not be in vain.

"Reward" in the New Testament means: *God fulfills what he promises.* It is not senseless to devote oneself to God's cause. Those who devote their best efforts to it will also share in the victory and the glory. On the negative side, the concept of reward implies that a believer cannot and may not live as a citizen of the realm of darkness. On the positive side it says that he who lives and fights in the service of this kingdom does not do so in vain. He will reap its fruit (see also § 57).

One day everyone will say: My faith and my struggle, my love and my prayers have not been in vain. The LORD fulfills his promise. This has been the goal of my faith and life.

The concept of a reward underscores the necessity and the seriousness with which we are called to live holy lives. The reward itself is part of salvation, as we have seen from various perspectives in this chapter. The biblical concept of reward is an encouragement from God to persevere. It is a means along the way to consummation. It is entirely a reward of grace. God sustains his own work. He crowns it. *Sola gratia.*

§ 43. PERSEVERANCE

43.1. *As an aspect of salvation*
43.2. *As a gift from the triune God*
43.3. *Call to watchfulness and prayer*

43.1. *As an aspect of salvation*

1. Perseverance is part of the order of salvation. It can be viewed as *perseverance along the way till the end.* It can also be viewed as the

consummation for which believers are preserved while they are on their way. In other words one can put the emphasis on *what happens along the way* or on *the culmination of the process*! This distinction should not be viewed as a contrast. The way there cannot be separated from its destination, neither the destination from the way there.

We emphasize these two aspects so that we will not lose sight of the dynamic perspective of the doctrine of perseverance. The great temptation is to believe that those who have been justified and live in sanctification automatically attain consummation. In this case one ignores dangers along the way; one plays down temptations; and one draws a link between justification and consummation that is assumed to be a matter of course, i.e., uninterrupted and certain.

At the other extreme we point to today's experience that many detach themselves and leave the church. In turning away from the church they also reject God and his Word. Sometimes these are people who have played a significant role in the church, have served in office, and were considered to be people on whom one could depend. And yet—they turn away and leave the church as well as the Christian faith. Was their faith not genuine? Did they consciously play the hypocrite in their good days? Who would dare to pronounce such a judgment over these people? Who will guarantee that the same thing will not happen to others who still participate completely and enthusiastically? Who will guarantee that the same thing will not happen to us?

The way to consummation is not a statistic. The way there is not unchallenged. Chapter 5 of the Canons of Dort speaks about "the perseverance of the saints." In article 3 we read: "By reason of these remains of indwelling sin, and also because of the temptations of the world and of Satan, those who are converted could not persevere in that grace if left to their own strength. But God is faithful who, having conferred grace, mercifully confirms and powerfully preserves them therein, even to the end."

Two things are pointed out here very clearly: 1. The converted cannot maintain themselves in their own strength; considering their own strength, perseverance is a lost cause. They would have the same experience as Peter on top of the waves (Matt. 14:30). 2. God is faithful. He will preserve them to the end with his power. Perseverance is therefore a matter of God's faithfulness, in the midst of our unfaithfulness (article 4). Article 5 speaks about offending God and grieving the Holy Spirit!

Although perseverance is a gift from God, it does not guarantee sinlessness and is no justification for living a reckless and carefree life. It should not be assumed that having received grace, one could never lose it again. Those who treat the latter as a foregone conclusion of justification, ignore the role of faith. This constitutes a fundamental error. Those who disregard the tension of a relationship of faith, no longer seek their strength in faith, but in themselves or in their own godliness. Then things go wrong, even for a believer.

2. *The Leiden Synopsis associates perseverance with a saving faith* (30:33). The assurance of perseverance is seen to lie in the object of true faith, but also has to be present in the subject; otherwise there would be no saving or justifying faith. For only those who believe (Mark 16:16) and persevere to the end (Matt. 24:13) will be saved.

Is there then double assurance? This is unthinkable. The certainty of the believer is definitely that of the object; and vice versa, the certainty of the object is shared with the believer.

However, where do we seek the ground for assurance? Do we find it via its object in ourselves, i.e., in our faith? Or do we find it in our faith on the basis of the relationship with its object? These are the questions that we seek to answer in this section.

We are dealing with salvation, which exists by the grace of God. This salvation comes from God, is brought about by him, and made effective in us. It is therefore unthinkable that the preservation of salvation would be solely and entirely our own responsibility. After all, this would change the nature of salvation. It would no longer be only a gift but also work on our part.

Whatever is said about people, they can never be the guardians of salvation in such a way that the preservation of salvation is ascribed to them as merit. They are indeed actively involved as subjects, but by way of faith. Everything that has been said in this chapter about faith remains true up to and including the section on perseverance. The role of faith is to receive and honor grace. This is also true of perseverance. It is God's gift. As a gift it forms part of salvation.

We do not want to associate perseverance only with the continuation of sanctified life (Heyns, *Dogm.*, 325) but also with the progression of salvation in the lives of believers, and their continuing in salvation by the grace of God. In this way we distinguish two aspects (gift and calling) without separating them. Their unity reflects the enduring nature of God's grace toward his children. He continues to call. He continues to give.

The perseverance of believers is therefore primarily a gift, i.e., a lasting gift that keeps on being presented. This gift becomes ours in the way of faithfully responding to God's calling.

In perseverance a believer's spiritual strength is not the basis of his assurance! The focus is on the essence of grace. Heyns correctly states: "Just as it is grace to receive grace, it is also grace to continue in grace" (Dogm., 325).

We see this especially in 1 Peter 1:4–5: "To an inheritance incorruptible, and undefiled, and that fadeth not away, reserved in heaven for you, who are kept by the power of God through faith unto salvation ready to be revealed in the last time." It is noteworthy that these two verses are followed by "joy in suffering." Preserving, guarding is not a process without tension.

This passage indicates that preservation is twofold, namely that of the inheritance per se as well as that of those for whom this inheritance is intended. The connection between the two is faith. A closer relationship is not possible. The inheritance is intended for believers. Believers themselves are preserved for the inheritance. They are aware of this and see themselves connected to it through faith.

3. *Faith is not the ground of assurance.* The ground lies in him who has brought about this inheritance and preserves it. Faith is not perseverance per se, which is, after all, an act of God's twofold preservation, namely, that of the inheritance and that of the inheritors. Faith is the way that God takes with the inheritors to enable them to obtain the inheritance. Faith is a claim on this inheritance on the basis of the relationship with him who has prepared this inheritance and who preserves both it and them for each other. Faith is the instrument through which they receive this grace, i.e., the grace of the inheritance as well as preservation of and for the inheritance.[102]

43.2. *As a gift from the triune God*

Upon further investigation it turns out that *this preservation is the work of the triune God.* According to Romans 8:29 election by *God* constitutes the foundation of perseverance. The gifts of grace and

102. All commentaries point out that two different verbs are employed. The inheritance is protected and the inheritors are "put under guard." This latter term has a military connotation.

God's call (referred to in Rom. 8:29–30) are irrevocable (Rom. 11:29). Philippians 1:6 also refers to the completion of the work that God has begun in believers. The endpoint is the day of *Jesus Christ*.

This is referred to in John 10:28. He will not lose any of the sheep that the Father has given to him. No one will snatch them out of his hands. The ground for this certainty is the unity of the Father and the Son (10:30). Continuity is assured by the fact that the Father's work is one with that of the Son, because they are one in their purpose, execution, and completion. Jesus also speaks elsewhere of his work of preservation and that of the Father (John 17:12, 11, 15). He does this in his prayer, just as he preserves Peter through his intercession (Luke 22:32).

We encounter Christ's intercession in numerous places (Rom. 8:34; Heb. 7:25; 8:1; 9:24; 1 John 2:1). Especially Hebrews 7:25 is characteristic. In this verse the salvation of believers turns out to rest not only on Christ's work on earth, but also and no less on his intercession in heaven, i.e., not only on his sacrifice but also on his life, now in heaven. Here it shows how much the perseverance of believers rests on the perseverance of Jesus' intercession. This is not divorced from his work on earth. It constitutes its effectuation in heaven. The well-known conclusion of Romans 8 cannot be viewed in isolation from Christ's intercession! His love is manifested in his high-priestly intercession. Romans 8:38–39 cannot be understood without seeing the connection between John 17:15–17 and Hebrews 7:25. (See article 26 of the Belgic Confession of Faith.)

The Spirit also participates in this ministry of preservation. See especially John 14:16. We read of his intercession, as distinct from that of the Son, in Romans 8:26. The intercession of the Spirit cannot be divorced from his witness in us (Rom. 8:16–17). This ministry of perseverance is also reflected in the sealing ministry of the Spirit (see especially Eph. 1:13; 4:30), as well as in the image of an earnest (2 Cor. 1:22; 5:5).[103] Perseverance is therefore a gift of grace

This is apparent from the confessions. We have already referred to the Canons of Dort, 5.3. See also 5.14. True believers are preserved in grace through such a great power that they cannot be overcome by the flesh. Grace is also referred to in 5.6.

103. For the redemption-historical significance of these images see J. P. Versteeg, *Het heden van de toekomst* (the present of the future), 1969.

Precisely this emphasis on grace precludes the belief in continuity based on man's faith as a deed of his own (as pointed out correctly by Berkouwer, 1958, 30). It is not faith that preserves man. It is the grace of God that is held on to and known in faith.

See also *Confessio Gallicana*, Article 12, where perseverance is placed within the perspective of grace.[104]

The *Erlauthaler Bekenntnis* (Erlauthaler Confession, 1562) explicitly inquires whether one should doubt election, salvation, redemption, eternal life, being child of God, and being heir. The answer is not unclear. The following grounds for certainty are listed in succession: the mission and incarnation of Christ; the revelation of God's will in his Word; the sacraments; the Holy Spirit through whom we are sealed; and finally the commissioning of prophets, apostles, and teachers of the church (Müller, *Bek.*, 328). The key is God's grace in Christ, declared to us in his Word, and sealed to us by his Spirit.

The connection between Christ, his Word, the work of the Spirit, and the impossibility of a final and total fall from grace is beautifully confessed in the Westminster Larger Catechism (1643, Answer 79; Müller, *Bek.*, 622). Especially in the Westminster Confession (1647) we find the same emphasis on the grace of election (chapter 4; Müller, *Bek.*, 551ff.) and the call to humility[105] (at the end of the confession of justification, chapter 11, Müller, *Bek.*, 568ff.), but also in the Canons of Dort.[106]

It is obvious that this confession disagrees with those of the Remonstrants and Trent. This requires no further elaboration.

As far as Lutherans are concerned, Berkouwer notes a greater understanding for the non-speculative nature of this confession.[107] Calvin does not ("practically not," according to Berkouwer, 1958, 78) proceed or reason in terms of neutral causality.[108] He also focuses on the grace of God. See especially *Institutes*, 2.3.9, with the recognition that the Lord completes the good work that he has begun. In this connection he points out that it is the Lord's doing that the zeal and effort do not falter, but proceed even to accomplishment.[109]

104. Müller, *Bek.*, 226. "Car comme c'est Dieu de faire le commencement, aussi c'est à lui de parachever" (for since it is God who makes the beginning, it is also up to him to complete it). See also Article 22, 226ff.

105. Hartvelt, 1991, 131, pointed out that the Canons of Dort were not guided by triumphalism. He did believe that certain pronouncements of supralapsarists and infralapsarists gave Calvinism a bad reputation. Against this background the Canons of Dort must be viewed as normative and to some extent corrective. In our view it would be inappropriate to judge those theologians on the basis of the Canons of Dort.

106. For a broader overview of confessions see Berkouwer, 1958, 33–36.

107. Van Genderen, 1977, 10, points out that Lutherans consider perseverance to be more discontinuous than continuous.

108. In his study *Prädestination und Perseveranz*, 1961, 13, J. Moltmann refers to Berkouwer's study as the only work devoted to the perseverance of faith up to that time.

109. See also Calvin's commentary on Phil. 2:13.

43.3. *Call to watchfulness and prayer*

We now wish to focus on the exhortations and admonishments with which believers are encouraged to persevere to the end, not to stray, or to stop somewhere along the way. We especially have in mind passages that refer to the race track (Phil. 3:12–14; Heb. 12:1–3) as well as the eschatological setting of the admonishment to perseverance in Matthew 24:13.

We think no less of Romans 5:3–5, which describes the chain of perseverance in a different manner. A similar approach is found in 2 Peter 1:5–11 (especially 5–7).

We refer to joy in temptations (trials) mentioned in 1 Peter 1:6–7, as well as James 1:12–15. It is precisely temptation (trial) that steels and strengthens. We also think of Romans 15:4: "For whatever things were written aforetime were written for our learning, that we through patience and comfort of the scriptures might have hope."

We can conclude on the basis of the quoted passages that perseverance is surrounded by admonishment. This admonishment does not ask for a quantitative countereffort on our part, as though the outcome would be satisfying on the basis of a sharing between what God does and what the believer does. Our effort, faith, struggle, and prayer can be nothing but a total focus on the grace and love of God. This comes through very clearly in the call to keep ourselves in the love of God (Jude 20).

Perseverance is perseverance in and through faith. Faith precisely makes us disregard our own qualifications and achievements. Faith does not rest on or appeal to personal achievement. Faith focuses and leans on the grace of God.

How can we enjoy the comfort of perseverance and experience it as a reality? In faith we see grace and cling to it. Thus faith goes the way of assurance through resting in what lies beyond us.

Only those who know grace can believe that they are being held by God and his grace. As soon as we look to ourselves and cut ourselves off from grace, our glorying in perseverance vanishes and we lose its comfort.

Does the confession of perseverance imply a vicious circle and thus a form of self-deception?

Not in the least; grace is radical and total in terms of both duration and quality. We confess this when we say that we believe in the perseverance of the saints.

It is not true that salvation depends on us in this final phase. Salvation is grace from beginning to end. Consummation is also part of this gift. Therefore in faith we speak of the perseverance of the saints. God preserves the inheritance for us and us for the inheritance by admonishing us to pray. This is how he carries on his work till the day of Jesus Christ.

Some Literature

N. T. Bakker, *Miskende gratie* (neglected grace), 1991.

H. Bavinck, *Roeping en wedergeboorte* (calling and regeneration), 1903.

G. C. Berkouwer, *Faith and Justification*, 1954.

G. C. Berkouwer, *Faith and Perseverance*, 1958.

G. C. Berkouwer, *Faith and Sanctification*, 1952.

J. van Bruggen, *Matteüs* (Matthew), 1990.

S. P. Dee, *Het geloofsbegrip bij Calvin* (Calvin's concept of faith), 1917).

K. Dijk, "Heilsorde" (order of salvation), in *Chr. Enc.*, 1958[2], 3:414ff.

A. H. Edelkoort, *De Christusverwachting in het Oude Testament* (the anticipation of Christ in the Old Testament), 1941.

K. Exalto, *De roeping. Een reformatorische bezinning* (calling: a Reformational perspective), 1978.

E. Faulbusch, "Heilsordnung" (order of salvation), in *E.K.L.*, 1989[3], 2:471–74.

J. van Genderen, *Christus in onze plaats* (Christ in our stead), 1972.

J. van Genderen, *De continuïteit van geloof en kerk* (the continuity of faith and church), 1977.

J. van Genderen, "De leer van de verkiezing bij Karl Barth" (the doctrine of election according to Karl Barth) in A. G. Knevel (ed.), *Visie op Karl Barth* (view of Karl Barth), 1987, 41–48.

J. van Genderen, *Geloofskennis en geloofsverwachting* (faith's knowledge and faith's anticipation), 1982.

J. van Genderen, *Gerechtigheid als geschenk* (righteousness as gift), 1988.

J. van Genderen, *Rechvaardiging en heiliging in the theologie van deze tijd* (justification and sanctification in the theology of today), 1966.

J. van Genderen, "Roeping en verkiezing" (calling and predestination), in *Woord en kerk* (word and church), 1969, 97–117.

C. Graafland, "Heeft Calvijn een bepaalde orde des heils geleerd? (did Calvin teach a specific order of salvation?), in *Verbi divini minister. Opstellen voor L. Kievit* (essays in honor of L. Kievit), 1983, 109–28.

D. J. de Groot, *De wedergeboorte* (regeneration), 1952.

G. P. Hartvelt, *Symboliek. Een beschrijving van kernen van christelijk belijden* (symbolism; an interpretation of key concepts of the Christian confession), 1991.

E. Herms, "Die Wirklichkeit des Glaubens. Beobachtungen und Erwägungen zur Lehre vom ordo salutis" (the reality of faith: observations and considerations on the doctrine of the order of salvation), *Ev. Th.* 42/6 (1982): 541–66.

A. A. Hoekema, *Saved by Grace*, 1989.

H. J. Jager, *Rechtvaardiging en zekerheid des geloofs* (justification and assurance of faith), 1939.

E. Käsemann, "Gottesgerechtigkeit bei Paulus" (the righteousness of God according to Paul), in *Exegetische Versuche und Besinnungen* (exegetical experiments and reflections), 1965, 181–93.

A. König, *Heil en heilsweg* (salvation and way of salvation), 1982.

W. Kremer, *Priesterlijke prediking* (priestly preaching), 1976.

A. Kuyper, *De salute* (*Dictaten dogmatiek* = lecture notes on dogmatics), no date, 4.

D. Lange, *Überholte Veruteilungen?* (obsolete condemnations?), 1991.

J. Murray, *Redemption, Accomplished and Applied*, 1955.

A. Peters, *Rechtfertigung* (justification), 1984.

H. Ridderbos, *Aan de Romeinen* (to the Romans), 1959.

G. Sauter, *Rechtfertigung als Grundbegriff evangelisher Theologie* (justification as the fundamental principle of evangelical theology), 1989.

E. Schuurman, *Het "technische paradijs"* (technical paradise), 1989

P. van der Spek, *De geloofsbeschouwing in de Schriftopenbaring door de apostel Johannes* (the view of faith as revealed in Scripture by the apostle John), 1942.

P. Stuhlmacher, *Gerechtigkeit Gottes bei Paulus* (God's righteousness according to Paul), 1966^2.

W. H. Velema, *De leer van de Heilige Geest bij Abraham Kuyper* (the doctrine of the Holy Spirit according to Abraham Kuyper), 1957.

W. H. Velema, "De toeëigening van het heil in de prediking" (the appropriation of salvation in preaching), in idem (ed.), *Delen in het heil* (sharing in salvation), 1989, 41–65.

W. H. Velema, "Ethics and the Reformed Confessions," *Free Reformed Theological Journal* 6, tr. L. W. Bilkes (fall 2002): 8–23.

W. H. Velema, "Ethiek en confessie," in *Een vaste burcht. Feestbundel voor Drs. K. Exalto* (a mighty fortress: festschrift for K. Exalto), 1989, 99–114, 1989a.

W. H. Velema, *Geroepen tot heilig leven* (called to a holy life), 1988[2].

W. H. Velema, "Het conciliair proces en persoonlijke levensheiliging" (the conciliatory process and personal sanctification), and "Het christelijke geloof en het koninkrijk Gods" (the Christian faith and the kingdom of God), in A. G. Knevel (ed.), *Het conciliair proces* (the conciliatory process), 1990, 97–104 and 105–13.

W. H. Velema, *Wet en evangelie* (law and gospel), 1987.

C. Vermeulen, *Het hart van de kerk. De plaats van de Heilige Geest in de theologie van Karl Barth* (the heart of the church: the place of the Holy Spirit in the theology of Karl Barth), 1986.

S. Voolstra, *Vrij en volkomen. Rechtvaardiging en heiliging in Dopers perspectief* (free and complete: justification and sanctification from an Anabaptist perspective), 1985.

H. Wiersinga, *De verzoening in de theologische diskussie* (atonement in theological discussion), 1971.

H. Wiersinga, *Verzoening als verandering* (atonement as change), 1972.

W. A. Wiersinga, *Gods werk in ons* (God's work in us), no date.

J. G. Woelderink, *De rechtvaardiging uit het geloof alleen* (justification by faith only), no date.

Chapter 13

The Church

§ 44. The church in the light of Holy Scripture

44.1. *Introduction*

The Bible contains such a wealth of important data for formulating a scripturally sound doctrine of the church (*ecclesiology*) that we cannot discuss all of them here. There is also a clear difference between the Old and New Testaments. What does the Bible say about the church? To answer this question we need to listen especially to the New Testament. It should not surprise us that what we know of the church of Christ is derived from the New Testament, for the church belongs to him. However, we may not ignore what the Old Testament says. The church of the New Testament is inseparably connected with the congregation or the people of God in the Old Testament.

In some languages the words "church" and "congregation" are used interchangeably. Etymologically the word "church" contains the notion that it belongs to the Lord (*kuriake or kuriakon*). Luther did not like the term "church" and termed it blind and unclear (*WA*, 50, 625). He was not alone in this regard. Already prior to the Reformation the term "Christendom" was used to describe the church of the creed.[1]

In the Netherlands a number of ethical theologians disliked the concept "church." For them the church was the official church, the ecclesiastical institution with numerous rules. According to J. J. P. Valeton, one must not strive for the restoration of the church. The important thing is for the life of God to become increasingly manifest in the church. J. Riemens is of the opinion that the word "church" should have never been coined and that one should have only used "congregation." For him the congregation is the ideal assembly of Christians referred to in the Apostles' Creed (see Honig, *Handboek*, 692–706).

From the point of view of dogmatics there is no reason to differentiate between these two words. In common parlance "congregation" at times refers to the local assembly and "church" to the larger whole. The same distinction, however, may be expressed by using the singular and plural of the word "church."

We cannot avoid that certain words acquire several meanings. The Dutch equivalent of "congregation" can also refer to a civil community, whereas the word "church" can also refer to a church building, a church service, etc. Since our point of departure is what the Bible says, which employs both "congregation" and "church" (in the Old Testament and New Testament respectively), we see no objection to using "church" and "congregation" interchangeably.

44.2. *Old Testament data*

In the Old Testament there is a tendency to restrict the use of the word *am* (people) to Israel and to refer to other nations as *goyyim*. This tendency to distinguish between Israel and other nations through language is even more noticeable in the *Septuagint* (*laos* as opposed to *ethne*). See *TDNT*, 4:29ff.

Inherent in the concept "people of God" is that the people are related to God in a special way. This becomes clear from passages such as Deuteronomy 14:2: "Thou art an holy people unto the LORD thy God, and the LORD hath chosen thee to be a peculiar people unto himself, above all the nations that are upon the earth" (cf. Deut. 26:16–19). The associated obligations for Israel are stated repeatedly: "Ye shall be holy unto me: for I the LORD am holy, and have severed you from other people, that ye should be mine" (Lev. 20:26). Thus the Israelites are the people of God: the people he predestined to this end and with whom he established his covenant. The objective is that they will know, serve, and love him, and that they will remain faithful to him.

1. Cf. J. N. Bakhuizen van den Brink in *De belijdenisgeschriften volgens artikel X van de kerkorde van de Nederlandse Hervormde Kerk* (confessions according to article 10 of the church order of the Dutch Reformed Church), 1966, 242ff.

In reading the Old Testament, one could gain the impression that God intended the privilege of human beings to be his people only for Israel. However, in the prophecies other nations also come into view: "And many nations shall be joined to the LORD in that day, and shall be my people: and I will dwell in the midst of thee" (Zech. 2:11; cf. also Isa. 45:23; 56:6–8).

The Old Testament employs two words for congregation: *qahal* and *eda*. These identify the congregation especially as a cultic community, a congregation assembled for the service of God. The *qahal* is assembled at Sinai and at the dedication of the temple (Deut. 5:22; 1 Kings 8:22). Moreover, the term *qahal* is also mentioned in connection with men going off to war and sometimes also in conjunction with the administration of justice (Dahl, 1963, 2–12), which should not detract from the underlying notion of a religious community.

A number of constitutive elements of Israel congregating for the service of God can be identified: The congregation owes its existence to the fact that the Lord calls it together and therefore is the assembly of the Lord. It assembles all around him. He is in its midst. This is why in the wilderness the people encamp in a circle around the tent of meeting. The Lord reveals himself in the midst of his congregation. It assembles for the cultus and through the ministry of atonement is increasingly sanctified (see *M.S.*, 4.1.41).

The congregation is constituted by the people assembled in God's presence. It is the assembled people of God. It ascribes praise to him (Ps. 22:22, 25). As is apparent from Nehemiah 8:3, women and children also belong to this congregation. We read about those who may and those who may not join the congregation (Deut. 23:1–8). No matter how closely the people and the congregation are associated with each other in the Old Testament, the congregation is nevertheless not identical with the nation of Israel per se (Kritzinger, 1957, 145ff.).

Following the exile we see the congregation assemble in the synagogue. This originally Greek word actually means meeting, as does its Aramaic equivalent. It also denotes the assembled congregation itself as well as the building that accommodates the meetings. The synagogal community is viewed as the local representation of the congregation of Israel as a whole. The synagogue is a house of instruction as well as a house of prayer. The congregation of Israel assembles here as a confessing congregation (cf. Dahl, 1963, 61–72).

44.3. *New Testament data*

1. *The gospels.* In New Testament (koine) Greek the congregation (church) is the *ekklesia*. This word is also used for a public assembly

(see Acts 19:41). Since the Septuagint usually translated *qahal* as *ekklesia*, this common word acquired a biblical content.

Ekklesia occurs remarkably rarely in the gospels (only in Matt. 16:18 and 18:17). It has frequently been wondered whether these words were ever used by Jesus himself. He might only have announced the coming of the kingdom of God and not have thought of establishing a church. According to Küng, Jesus did not institute the church when he was on earth; instead, it should be seen as a post-resurrection phenomenon. Without the earthly Jesus, however, there would be no church, for Jesus did lay its foundation through his preaching and work (Küng, 1967, 92ff.).

Several renowned New Testament scholars answer the question whether Jesus instituted the church in the negative. Yet there is no reason to doubt the authenticity of the Matthew passages.

One of the primary motives for contrasting the kingdom of God and the church is the notion that the gospel proclaimed by Jesus would only pertain to the future kingdom. However, those who recognize that the kingdom of God as taught in the gospels is now already present, as the gracious dominion of God in Christ, consider this contrast to be unwarranted. There is even *a direct relationship between the kingdom and the church.*

It is incorrect to *identify* the church with the kingdom, as was often done in the past. The kingdom of God comprises far more than the church. Neither may we say that the church *replaces* the kingdom, because Jesus who came to usher in the kingdom would only have retained the church. This is a denial of the "abiding eschatological perspective which encompasses the church on all sides in its expectation and ministry" (Ridderbos, 1950, 307).

The kingdom of God is the messianic kingdom. The church of Christ constitutes the people of the Messiah. The Messiah has a people who belong to him, and he came "to save his people from their sins" (Matt. 1:21). The Messiah also has a church that belongs to him and he "will build [his] church" (Matt.16:18). He says to his disciples that "it is [their] Father's good pleasure to give [them] the kingdom" (Luke 12:32). Ridderbos summarizes this by pointing out (1950, 308) that in various respects the church is jostled on all sides and driven by the revelation, progression, and prospect of the kingdom of God (see Ridderbos, 1950, 296–308; Lindijer, 1962, 180–202).

Time and again, using various illustrations, Jesus speaks of the gathering of the people of God that he brings about.[2]

The passages are clear. Christ himself will build his church and guarantee its future. It will be a confessing church (Matt. 16:18). When brotherly relationships are disturbed by sin and admonishments are ignored, it must be reported to the church (Matt. 18:17). It has implications for the church.

Christ charges his apostles (of whom only Peter is mentioned in Matt. 16:18) to make the nations his disciples (Matt. 28:19). Therefore, the gathering of his people is not to remain restricted to Israel. This is not an isolated saying of Christ but corresponds to what is said in other places as well (Matt. 8:11; 21:43; Luke 24:46–47; John 10:16; 11:52).

All evangelists show us how Jesus gathers his church from among the Jewish people. The building of his church has begun! The gathering of disciples per se does not mean that a church is being established as yet, for there were rabbis who also did this. Jesus, however, does not only bind his followers to his teaching, but also and primarily to his person. What characterizes all those whom he calls to communion with him is that they believe in him. As Messiah he speaks about *his* church and as the Good Shepherd about *his* sheep.

Only that portion of Israel that believes in him constitutes the messianic church. With Ridderbos we can say (1950, 306): The people of God are the people of the Messiah. Conversely, those who confess Jesus as the Messiah are the new Israel. "Thus the ekklesia is the communion of those who, as the true people of God, receive the gifts of the kingdom of heaven." The twelve apostles are the representatives of this people of God. The new Israel that Jesus gathers around him comes to stand over against the portion of Israel that rejects him. This rift begins to manifest itself in the gospels (cf. Matt. 12:30; John 9:34; 10:26–27; 16:2).

It has been claimed that the fourth gospel has no room for the church. However, this must be gainsaid. Essential characteristics of the church, namely, its association with Christ, its being guided by his Spirit and Word, are strikingly brought out, among other places in John 10 (the shepherd and his sheep) and John 15 (the vine and the branches). It is important to listen to the voice of Jesus and to follow him, to abide in him, and to bear much fruit. Those who belong to him constitute a confessing community (John 6:68). It is a community where love dwells (John 15:9–17), but which is hated by the world (John 15:18–27).

2. Cf. J. Jeremias, *New Testament Theology*, 1971, 1:167–70.

2. *Acts*. This book of the Bible is of great importance for the knowledge of the church gathered by Christ through his Spirit and his Word. However fundamental the outpouring of the Holy Spirit is, Pentecost does not mark the birth of the church. By then it already exists, for it is the church of Christ that has assembled (Acts 1:14–15). But now it is equipped for the fulfillment of its calling. Through the power of the Spirit it is transformed into a witnessing church. The missionary activity is not a matter of the apostles only, for the entire church is involved in it (Acts 8:4; cf. Van Swigchem, 1955, 38ff.).

It was characteristic of the Christian church that it "continued steadfastly in the apostles' doctrine and fellowship, in the breaking of bread, and in prayers" (Acts 2:42). The context indicates what is meant by this "fellowship." It has both a spiritual and a material side. It is the fellowship (*koinonia*) that the church owes to the Spirit of Christ, who dwells within the church (cf. van Genderen, 1986, 20–22).

The church is led by the apostles and others, among whom the elders occupy a special place (see Acts 15:22–29; 20:28). Thanks to the work of the Holy Spirit, the church grows. "The Lord added to the church daily such as should be saved" (Acts 2:47; cf. Noordegraaf, 1983, 20–77).

The book of Acts describes the progress of the Lord's work to which the church owes its existence. The gospel travels from Jerusalem to Rome! Initially the church is formed by Jews and proselytes who come to faith in Christ and let themselves be baptized, but the borders are crossed and the church of Christ is gathered from among the Jews and the surrounding nations (see Noordegraaf, 1983; idem, *The Church*, 1990, 37–45).

3. *Paul*. If one can speak of an ecclesiology in the New Testament, it can be found in the writings of the apostle Paul (cf. *TDNT*, 3:506). To him also the church is *the people of God* to whom the promises of the Old Testament as well as the warnings addressed to Israel apply (see 2 Cor. 6:16–18; 1 Cor. 10:1–11). Believers from the Gentile world belong to the New Testament people of God (see Rom. 3:29; 9:24–26; Gal. 3:28–29; Eph. 2:11–22).

A new aspect of the church, at least as far as its designation is concerned, is that it is the *body of Christ*. This is a figurative expression, in addition to which the apostle employs other metaphors, such as "God's husbandry," "God's building," "temple of the living God," "habitation of God through the Spirit," and "house of God" (1 Cor. 3:9; 2 Cor. 6:16; Eph. 2:22; 1 Tim. 3:15).

The question as to what is meant when the church is called the body of Christ will be addressed in a subsequent section (§ 46.2, subsection 2). Here it suffices to say that the image of the body is used differently in Ephesians and Colossians than in Romans and 1 Corinthians. In the latter two epistles the focus is on the unity of the church, within which diversity plays a subservient role; in the two other epistles the focus is on the relationship between Christ and the church. For the essence and life of the church it is decisive that he is its Head.

The apostolic reference to the church as the *habitation of God in the Spirit* (Eph. 2:22 and parallels) is also of great significance. It is the place where the Holy Spirit dwells and where he determines everything. There everything can and must therefore be done according to the way of the Spirit. This aspect of the church is addressed in § 46.2, subsection 3.

What Paul writes focuses on the building up of the church, and especially growth in the knowledge of faith, the ministry of love, and the expectation of the kingdom of God. It concerns the work that the Lord does in his church. This is repeatedly confessed and continually prayed for. The Lord engages people whom he calls to perform a task. There are offices and ministries for which he grants the necessary gifts. Charismata (gifts) and offices do not stand over against each another, but were given to the church with a view to harmonious cooperation, which cannot be achieved without an orderly structure of ecclesiastical offices (cf. A. Noordegraaf in *The Church*, 1990, 46–56).

4. *Other New Testament writings*. There is no New Testament book that does not contain data relevant to our image of the church.

Hebrews depicts the church as people of God who are on their way.[3] For passages dealing with being under way and the associated exhortations and admonishments, see Hebrews 4:1–11; 11:13–16; 12:1–13; 13:14. The church is also the "house of God" of which Christ is the great priest or high priest (Heb. 10:21). The urgency of the call to perseverance is reinforced by the approaching day of the Lord (Heb. 10:23–25).

Although the word *ekklesia* does not occur in *1 Peter*, this epistle does make some extremely important statements about believers. We

3. This expression is used here without the connotation given it by E. Käsemann (*Das wandernde Gottesvolk* = the wandering people of God, 1959).

especially have in mind 1 Peter 2:4–10. The church is compared to a building of which Jesus Christ is the "corner stone." The people of God are to "shew forth the praises of him who hath called [them] out of darkness into his marvelous light." First Peter also speaks of believers as "strangers and pilgrims" in this world who "are partakers of Christ's sufferings" and must undergo "the fiery trial which is to try" them (2:11; 4:12–13).

In the first few chapters of the book of *Revelation* we see Christ "in the midst of . . . seven golden candlesticks" (Rev. 1:12–13), which symbolize "the seven churches" (Rev. 1:20) and represent the entire New Testament church. The churches belong together because they belong to one and the same Lord. All churches belong to him, but they indeed do so in all diversity. Ephesus is not Smyrna and Sardis is not Philadelphia! We hear of faith and love, but also of apostasy and threatening dangers. There is a contrast between the church of the Lord and the synagogue of Satan (Rev. 2:9; 3:9), and false teachers are warned against. The church is faced with enmity and oppression from the side of the world, supported by Satan. It is important to persevere to the end, even if this results in martyrdom. The church is the bride of the Lamb and anticipates the wedding. "The Spirit and the bride say: Come" (Rev. 22:17)! Thus the book of Revelation places the church in an eschatological perspective.

5. *The church and the churches.* It is noteworthy that in the New Testament *ekklesia* refers to the church as a whole as well as to the local church or the meeting of the local congregation (cf. Matt. 16:18 with Matt. 18:17; Eph. 3:10 with 1 Thess. 1:1; Col. 1:18 with Col. 4:16), while the plural *ekklesiai* can also indicate the church as a whole (1 Cor. 11:16). This shows that the totality of the church is not the aggregate of a number of components. The church does not resemble an association with local chapters! *Ekklesia is not a quantitative but a qualitative concept* (cf. *TDNT*, 3:505). The small size of a congregation does not diminish its importance (cf. Rev. 3:8). The church is wherever the Lord gathers his people, be it in a certain place, region, country, or the entire world. For both the universal church as well as the regional or local church, the relationship to Christ is decisive. We may hereby think of Jesus' words, "For where two or three are gathered together in my name, there am I in the midst of them" (Matt. 18:20).

Paul sends his first epistle to the Corinthians "unto the church of God which is at Corinth . . . *with* all that in every place call on the name of Jesus Christ our Lord" (1 Cor. 1:2). These words are variously interpreted, but the most probable explanation is: the church of God at Corinth, which lives in fellowship with all those who confess that Christ is their Lord. Part of the new people of God live in the city of Corinth, but they form a unity with all those who belong to this people, wherever they may be (see Van Stempvoort, 1950, 51ff.). A church such as that at Corinth is therefore not viewed in isolation. A federation of local churches, as we know it today, does not yet exist at this early stage, but a mutual bond in Christ is part of being the church from the very beginning.

44.4. *Some key points*[4]

1. The church (congregation) owes its origin and existence to the work of God who assembles it in order to serve him.

2. It is initially gathered from among Israel and subsequently from among both Israel and other nations.

3. The New Testament presents the church in the light of the kingdom of God that has come and is to come. It lives by the gifts of God's kingdom and anticipates the coming of the kingdom in glory.

4. Names such as "people of God," "body of Christ," and "temple of the Holy Spirit" indicate that the church is the work of the triune God. This ensures that it has a future. The designation "body of Christ" speaks of a permanent bond with Christ, who is its Head. He governs it through his Spirit and his Word.

5. Communion with Christ is communion through the Holy Spirit, which leads to mutual fellowship of the members of the church.

6. All offices and ministries are intended for the edification of the church and the equipping for its task.

7. The gifts that the church receives from God go hand in hand with its calling to live in this world as the holy people of God, to witness to its Lord, and to win others for his service.

§ 45. Diversity of opinion

4. Cf. A. Noordegraaf in *De kerk* (the church), 1990, 62.

45.3. *Reformational insights*
45.4. *Views of Dutch theologians*

45.1. *The catholic church and the Roman hierarchy*

The primary characteristic of the concept of the catholic church, which emerged early on, is that the center of gravity shifted toward an episcopal form of church governance.

The significance of the church is great: "Where the church is, there is the Spirit of God; and where the Spirit of God is, there is the church and all grace. The Spirit, however, is the truth" (Irenaeus, *Adv. haer.*, 3.24.1). In connection with the unity of the church, Cyprian (d. 258) emphasized the office of the bishop. The bishop of Rome has primacy, but not legal primacy. Cyprian emphasizes the necessity of belonging to the church: "No one can have God as Father who does not have the church as mother" (*De cath. eccl. unitate*, 6).

According to Augustine (d. 430), the concept of the church is more complicated. The church is primarily a spiritual community, a church of the Spirit, in which love dwells. It is the body of Christ of which all those who are his form part. God alone knows who the true saints are. But there is also the institutional aspect. The church is the place where one partakes of the means of grace and obtains salvation. It speaks with authority (see J. van Oort in *De kerk* = the church, 1990, 65–94).

Within medieval theology, ecclesiology shows only scant development. There are indeed official doctrinal pronouncements, such as those of Pope Boniface VIII (1302) and the Council of Florence (1439). See *DS*, 875 and 1307. What it amounts to is that the power of the pope is enhanced. It has been said, not without justification, that the church became an *imperium* (cf. *M.S.*, 4.1.235).

The decisions and canons of the Council of Trent regarding the sacrament of ordination (1536) imply that the ecclesiastical office is virtually exclusively associated with the administration of the Eucharist and the remaining sacraments. The image of the church is strongly hierarchical: pope, bishops, priests, deacons, and farther down the line, the faithful laity (Schillebeeckx, 1980, 75–80). The Tridentine Confession of Faith (1564) contains a very important passage: "I acknowledge the holy, catholic, and apostolic church of Rome to be the mother and teacher of all churches and I promise and swear true allegiance to the pope of Rome, the successor to the blessed Peter, the prince of the apostles, and the vicar of Jesus Christ" (*DS*, 1868).

In the sixteenth century, the leading Roman Catholic theologians do not doubt that the church exists squarely as the church of which the pope is the head. The church is as visible as the kingdom of France or the republic of Venice (Bellarmine).

Some of the marks of this concept of the church are: 1. The church is the one visible institution of salvation; 2. The clergy stand above the laity, and within the clergy the bishops are the central figures; 3. The entire church is governed by a hierarchy ruled by the pope.

45.2. *Two important councils: Vatican I and II*

Although it was the intention of the First Vatican Council (1869–70) to resolve more issues, circumstances permitted only that the doctrine of the primacy of the pope was finalized. Some key items are: 1. The pope is the supreme judge of the faithful; 2. He holds the highest teaching office; 3. Whenever he speaks by virtue of his office as pastor and teacher of all Christians (ex cathedra) and decrees a doctrine relating to faith or morals for the entire church, he possesses infallibility by virtue of the divine assistance promised to him in Peter. This is considered to be a dogma revealed by God (DS, 3074).

Between the two Vatican councils, ecclesiology could develop, in part because the doctrine of the church remained incomplete. There were various trends (cf. Valeske, 1962, 1–253), but from an official point of view the 1943 encyclical that Pius XII devoted to the church as the mystical body of Christ was of greater importance. The body of Christ was completely identified with the Roman Catholic Church. Christ continues his work through this church, and the Holy Spirit is the soul of the mystical body of Christ, the church.

The Dogmatic constitution *Lumen Gentium* (1964) and other documents of the Second Vatican Council (1962–65) indicate that the doctrine of the church is a main theme. The relationship between the pope and the bishops is crucial.

Already in the first chapter momentous pronouncements are made. The church is a complex reality, comprising both human and divine elements. There is a significant analogy with the mystery of the incarnate Word (cf. no. 52: continuation of the incarnation in the church). As object of faith, the church is found within the catholic church governed by Peter's successor in unison with its bishops. It is concretely present (*subsistit in*) in this very church.

In the second chapter, which deals with the people of God, we find relatively speaking the most biblical ideas, supplemented with typically Roman Catholic notions such as the dependence of the priestly people of God on the sacraments.

The core of *Lumen Gentium* is the chapter on the hierarchical structure of the church, particularly the episcopate. Here tradition speaks the decisive word. The hierarchical structure belongs to the essence of the church. The bishops practice collegiality. Nevertheless, as though not enough is said in this connection about the primacy and infallibility of the pope, a "prefatory explanatory note" is added to this chapter—on the authority of Paul VI himself—in which collegiality among bishops is circumscribed by even more restrictions.

The doctrine of the church concludes with Mariology. With her cooperation and intercession Mary stands at Christ's side and is at the same time presented as a prototype of the church, which loves and honors her as its mother, and is to emulate her. It is at this time that the pope proclaims Mary as mother of the church.

Traditional doctrine predominates in this Vatican ecclesiology, although it incorporates also some ideas from more recent (Roman Catholic) theology. It is a compromise that gave rise to a variety of interpretations.[5]

5. See from a Roman Catholic perspective G. Barauna (ed.), *De kerk in Vaticanum II*, 2 vols., 1986; *Lexikon für Theologie und Kirche, Das Zweite Vatikanische Konzil*, 1966, 1:137–359;

45.3. *Reformational insights*

Rome teaches: Christ is where the church is. The Reformational view is that it is the other way around: the church is where Christ is. Believers are united with Christ and in him also with each other. Where the Word of God is proclaimed and believed, Christ is engaged in gathering his church.[6]

To Luther the church is essentially the community or assembly of believers, even though apart from this spiritual or inner Christendom there is also an outward Christendom to which also hypocrites belong. Among the characteristics of the holy people of God, the proclamation of the holy Word of God has priority. "God's Word cannot exist without God's people and God's people, in turn, cannot exist apart from the Word of God" (*WA*, 50, 629). The primary identifying marks of the church are: the gospel, baptism, and the Lord's Supper. Where the gospel is not present, there is no church either. In his attack upon the visible institution of salvation of Rome, Luther can say that the church and the saints are hidden. This does not detract from the fact that the church is clearly recognizable. In the Smalkaldische Artikelen (1537) he says that a seven-year-old child—praise God—knows what the church is, namely, the holy believers together with the little sheep who hear the voice of their Shepherd (*BSLK*, 459).

This new view of the church is clearly expressed in the Augsburg Confession (Article 7). It is a gathering (*congregatio*; German text: *Versammlung*) of saints, in which the gospel is purely taught and the sacraments are properly administered (cf. for Luther, among others, K. Exalto in *De kerk*, 1990, 95–110).

Calvin's doctrine of the church exerted great influence. In his ecclesiology he incorporates many valuable concepts of his contemporaries, especially Bucer.[7]

---

from a Protestant viewpoint H. Berkhof and A. J. Bronkhorst in *Protestantse verkenningen na Vaticanum II*, 1967; G. C. Berkouwer, *Nabetrachting* (retrospect) *op het concilie*, 1968; B. Wentsel in *De kerk*, 1990, 231–45.

6. Cf. W. H. van de Pol, *Het getuigenis van de Reformatie* (the testimony of the Reformation), 1960, 188f., who says that the cardinal difference between Rome and the Reformation appears nowhere as clearly as in their views on the church.

7. There is a substantial body of literature on Calvin's ecclesiology. See P. J. Richel, *Het kerkbegrip* (concept of church) *van Calvijn*, 1942; A. Ganoczy, *Ecclesia ministrans*, 1968; B. C. Milner, *Calvin's Doctrine of the Church*, 1970; C. Graafland, *Kinderen van één moeder* (children of one mother), 1989; W. van 't Spijker in *De kerk*, 1990, 143–62.

Initially, the church is placed in the light of predestination. The church to which the article of the Apostles' Creed refers comprises the entire number of the elect. Since election is in Christ, it can be said: when we have communion with Christ, we possess a sufficiently clear testimony that we are among God's elect and belong to the church (*Institutes*, 1536, *C.O.*, 1:72–74).

Beginning with the second edition of his magnum opus, the Reformer demands more attention for the visible church. It is the mother of the believers. Since the Scriptures speak of the church in a twofold manner (*bifariam*), Calvin distinguishes between the church from God's perspective (*coram Deo*) and the church as seen by people (*respectu hominum*). For further details see § 46.3.

There are still other descriptions of the church. It is the communion of saints and the people of God, to which also children belong. The church is where Christ rules through his Word and Spirit. But the papacy lacks the legitimate form of a church.

Just how important the church is to Calvin is apparent from the title of the fourth volume of the *Institutes*. Together with the sacraments, the church belongs to the outward means whereby God invites us into communion with Christ and keeps us there.

The Genevan Reformer is also deeply convinced that we must maintain the divinely prescribed order of the church. The Scriptures tell us how to give form to the life of the church.

We leave it by these observations and will return to Calvin's ideas in subsequent sections.

What the Belgic Confession says about the church (articles 27–32) clearly bears Calvin's imprint. Although the phraseology of the Heidelberg Catechism is different, it breathes the same spirit.

45.4. *The views of some Dutch theologians*

1. *A. Kuyper*. In wishing to focus on a number of influential concepts[8] in this subsection, we cannot ignore Kuyper and Schilder, because as Reformed theologians their views had a significant impact on both theology and the church in the Netherlands. One could say that without Kuyper there would have been no *Doleantie* (grievance: 1886 secession from

8. Berkhof (*C.F.*, 348) mentions nine ecclesiologies that have appeared since 1936 as monographs.

the Netherlands Reformed Church, leading to the establishment of the *Gereformeerde Kerk*), and without Schilder no *Vrijmaking* (liberation: 1942 secession from the *Gereformeerde Kerk* in the Netherlands)!

To Kuyper the church is essentially the invisible church. In the traditional distinction between the invisible and the visible church, with which he works, the invisible church is somewhere between the church as *organism* and the church as *institution*. The church as organism has an invisible and a visible side. As far as its invisible nature is concerned, it constitutes the totality of regenerated humanity under Jesus Christ as its new Head. Within this mystical body of Christ there lives an urge to manifest itself visibly. This essence then takes shape in existence. Through the activities of those who have been regenerated, there emerge in society the Christian family, Christian schools, and various Christian organizations and institutions. The institution of the church serves the church as organism through the preaching of the Word that addresses believers in their consciousness. The institution must then not be deformed qua doctrine and governance. Nevertheless, even if all of its institutions are depraved, a church will continue to retain its essence as church, so long as it carries within its bosom a circle of living members.[9]

A striking element of Kuyper's doctrine, which engendered a great deal of discussion, is his theory of the pluriformity of the church.[10] In the visible church there is a transition from uniformity to pluriformity. Pluriformity is a developmental phase to which the church of Christ was bound to come in the visible domain. "The infinite cannot find adequate expression in a single, finite form."[11]

In Kuyper's ecclesiology we recognize too little of what Scripture says about the church. Neither does he pay adequate attention to the teachings of the Reformed confessions.

Kuyper's view had a stimulating impact on the church, the state, and society, and has its merit (cf. C. Trimp in *De kerk*, 1990, 192ff.). But it is not correct that as institution the church stands in the shadow of the "church as organism." This is bound to dilute the concept of the church. The church is not wherever believers meet or where believers are engaged (cf. Heyns, *Dogm.*, 387). Kuyper's theory of pluriformity

9. Cf. W. H. Velema, *De leer* (doctrine) *van de Heilige Geest bij Abraham Kuyper*, 1957, 196–99.

10. Cf. P. A. van Leeuwen, *Het Kerkbegrip* (concept of church) *in de theologie van Abraham Kuyper*, 1946, 209–36.

11. A. Kuyper, *De gemeene gratie* (common grace), 1904, 3:227–34.

has no biblical foundation, but reflects the idealistic mode of thinking with which he was familiar.

2. *K. Schilder.* In contrast with Kuyper, Schilder proceeds from the revealed norms for the gathering of the church for his formulation of the doctrine of the church, which is one of the focal points of his thinking. Whereas Kuyper's conception is marked by strands of idealism, in Schilder's approach the normative perspective predominates.

According to Lord's Day 21 of the Heidelberg Catechism, the church is what it is because Christ gathers it through his Spirit and his Word. This is action in the progressive present tense. This is how he institutes his church. The church is a *coetus* (assembly) and a *congregatio* (terms from the Latin text of Article 27 of the Belgic Confession of Faith). The first word contains an active element (coming together), the second a passive element (being brought together).[12] We must gather together with Christ, as Matthew 12:30 says. It is not our task to remain faithful to our own church as an existing institution, but to be faithful in instituting the church. God's institution is built by obeying God's commandments. "Obedience institutes." On the other hand, one may not acquiesce in the fact that in a given church there are still a few good ministers and a number of true believers; that one therefore should view one's church as one's mother and not abandon it. Even the Roman Catholic institution can say: there are still so many believers among us. That fatal little word "still"![13]

Schilder rejects Kuyper's view of the church on two important points: The established church and the church to be established may not be subordinated to the "church as organism." Kuyper's theory of pluriformity leads to ecclesiastical relativism and acquiescence in church divisions.

Schilder was a champion of the unity of the church, which was a matter dear to his heart. This is precisely why he formulated the issues more sharply than others did. He frequently developed his thoughts in polemic expositions. In doing so, he made statements from which can be inferred that in his view there can only be one true church of Christ in one place at a time and that by biblical and confessional standards the *Gereformeerde Kerken in Nederland* are the only true

12. K. Schilder, *Verzamelde werken, de kerk* (collected works, the church), 1960, 1:155–60.

13. Ibid., 1962, 2:203, 229ff., 189–91.

and legitimate churches in the Netherlands. Christ does not distribute his mandate in one city or village among various churches. There is one *church* around which "sects" establish themselves. "Within the Netherlands I do not know of a single church, outside of the *Gereformeerde Kerk*, which preaches God's Word purely, administers the sacraments properly, and maintains discipline."[14]

The strong emphasis on gathering along with Christ becomes the primary characteristic of the church: "the first priority—law—of the CHURCH."[15] How does this relate to confessional characteristics? Is a fourth mark added? May we take one element and so "overstrain it that it begins to function as a two-edged sword that *must* by definition divide the church of the ecclesiastical Netherlands into one true church *in the midst* of all remaining, false churches?"[16] Moreover, the question arises whether in this approach to the church, the gathering activity of believers does not get much more weight than being gathered and coming together as true believers. The church is, after all, *the assembly of true believers.*

3. *J. C. Hoekendijk.* With Hoekendijk we come across a view of the church that is determined by its position in a non-Christian world, as experienced in mission and evangelism. H. Kraemer (d. 1965) emphasized the function of the church. It must play a witnessing and ministering role in the world. A functional ecclesiology is found especially in the work of J. C. Hoekendijk (d. 1975—taught in America from 1965). The church is of lesser importance than the kingdom and the world. It is a function of the apostolate. The structure of the church must be changed: a division into categories, groups, and home churches instead of parishes. Furthermore, confessional/denominational differences will then retain little if any relevance. This calls for open communication. Appealing to Bonhoeffer, Hoekendijk advocates the notion of a church that exists for others (pro-existence of the church).[17]

The ecumenical movement was strongly influenced by this type of thinking. Hoekendijk indeed had a hand in the report *The Church for Others*, which says that the world may set the agenda for the church. This report had a major impact on the Assembly of Uppsala (1968).[18]

14. Ibid., 1960, 1:187ff., 183, 374.

15. Ibid., 1962, 2:245–50.

16. This point is raised by H. D. J. Smit, who nevertheless considers Schilder's concept of church a monument of ecclesiastical thinking. See "Gehoorzamen: achter Christus aan!" (obediently following Christ!) in J. Douma et al., *K. Schilder*, 1990, 81–89. See also C. Trimp in *De kerk*, 1990, 187–201.

17. See J. C. Hoekendijk, *De kerk binnenste buiten* (the church inside out), 1965, 51, 99f.; "De missionary struktuur van de gemeente (church)," *G.T.T.* 63 (1963): 225–38.

18. See P. van Gurp, *Kerk en zending* (mission) *in de theologie van Johannes Christiaan Hoekendijk* (1912–75), 1989, 246–62. Cf. also K. Runia in *De kerk*, 1990, 252–56.

There is something in Hoekendijk's ideas that appeals to many. He envisions a church that is not static but dynamic, not introverted but extroverted. This is referred to as functional ecclesiology, but in Hoekendijk's case it amounts to functionalism. The church exists solely for the sake of the world. Here we do not find what the Bible says about the church as the assembled people of God and the body of Christ.

According to Berkhof, the weakness of such an ecclesiology is a profound lack of biblical-theological and dogmatic reflection.[19] Berkhof correctly points out that the church's relationship with its Lord is the source of inspiration, content, and norm for turning toward the world.

4. *H. Berkhof.* Berkhof occupied himself a great deal with questions regarding the church, which reflects to some extent his active role in the ecumenical movement. His most important ecclesiological study is his discussion of the new community, a chapter of his magnum opus that precedes a chapter on the renewal of man. A brief introduction is followed by sections on the church as institute, the congregation as the body of Christ, and the people of God as firstfruits. There is an affinity with Barth's three perspectives (*C.F.*, 349).

This ecclesiology is marked by *synthesis*. There is a catholic church type and a free church type, while the Reformed church type is the daughter of the former and the mother of the latter (*C.F.*, 345–46). The key here is the connection between authority and institution on the one hand and community, freedom, and personal decision on the other hand. According to Berkhof, the partial truths of both perspectives need to be combined into a higher synthesis. We must also be prepared to learn as much as we can from the Pentecostal movements.[20]

Berkhof is critical of functional ecclesiology of which Hoekendijk is a proponent, but believes he can integrate a functional approach into his doctrine of the church and also employs various functional concepts. This is the case when he gives priority to the question as to which activities make participation in salvation possible, so that they are as it were "mediating" between Christ and the people (350); when being church is seen as a perpetual movement and as a bridge event (415); and when he calls outreach into the world, whereby the church is the experimental garden of a new humanity, the key mark of the church (419, 422).

He is further of the opinion that ecclesiology should adopt a sociological approach. His doctrine of the church is consistent with this (cf. 348, 386, 392).

Berkhof's ecclesiology is a fascinating construct, which incorporates many Scripture passages. But at critical points he does not give sufficient scope to the authority of the Bible—which in turn is a consequence of his view of Scripture (see § 8.2, subection 4). This is why it can be said of the institutional media that their recognition does not depend on whether or not they are mentioned somewhere in Scripture, though that may be a help and a pointer (393). In harmony with this position it is believed that the Reformational characteristics of the church have lost their critical potency and that turning toward the world must now be seen as the central characteristic that cannot be ignored (413, 422).

19. H. Berkhof, "Tweeerlei (two kinds of) ekklesiologie," *K. en Th.* 13 (1962): 148ff.
20. H. Berkhof, *The Doctrine of the Holy Spirit*, 1964, 68, 93.

§ 46. The Essence of the Church

46.1. *The church as God's work*
46.2. *The church in Trinitarian perspective*
46.3. *The visible and the invisible church*
46.4. *The attributes of the church*
46.5. *The marks of the church*

46.1. *The church as God's work*

The church manifests itself to us as a community or organization of people. As such, it is also a sociological entity that can be described, e.g., as "the church in the modern world." The church bears some resemblance to an association, which holds meetings to which its members are invited. It has something of a foundation or an institution. In view of the existence of church governance and church polity, once could even look for analogies in the area of the state.

However, through an analysis of the phenomenon called church and a comparison of the structures of the church with those of various societal groups, one cannot determine what the church in essence is. We know it from Scripture as *the church of God and the church of Christ*. We must view it in the light of what God does in Christ. The first question, therefore, is not what we observe of the church, but what we believe about it. The church is a matter of faith. This is how the Apostles' Creed puts it (*credo ecclesiam*).

The theological approach to the church stands over against the anthropological approach. Schleiermacher supplies an example of the latter approach: "Die christliche Kirche bildet sich durch das Zusammentreten der einzelnen Wiedergebornen zu einem geordneten Aufeinanderwirken und Miteinanderwirken" (the Christian church constitutes itself through the coming together of born-again individuals for orderly interaction and collaboration).[21] What born-again people desire to do is then decisive!

In an old rhymed Dutch version of the Apostles' Creed we read: "I believe one church, a universal association (*genootschap*), sanctified, and gathered through heaven's message" (1773). "Association," however, is a word that can denote a society that devotes itself to the promotion of, e.g., the arts and sciences. But the church is not a society of like-minded religious people for the purpose of engaging in certain activities; it is not an association one can join if one is qualified or desires to do so. Furthermore, *kerkgenootschap* ("church association" = denomination) is a term based on constitutional law.

Since the church in essence is not an association, we object to Kersten's definition of the visible church. While the invisible church is according to him the assembly of

21. F. D. E. Schleiermacher, *Der christliche Glaube* (the Christian faith), 1836, section 115.

those who are elect and bought with Christ's blood, the visible church is "a voluntary association of believers for the mutual practice of the communion of saints or the mutual sharing of those matters that pertain to salvation" (*Reformed Dogmatics*, 2:467). It is the assembly of those who profess the faith.[22]

As far as Küng's view is concerned, we enter into an entirely different sphere. We do not deny an element of truth in his emphasis on man's responsibility to answer the call of God. However, when he says that there is no church without the fiat of Mary, without the fiat of the men and women called into discipleship (1967, 156), we cannot go along with him, certainly not when we realize that this is the fiat of the Roman Catholic doctrine of grace.

The church points beyond itself. It does not owe its origin to human initiative, or its continued existence to human faithfulness. *The church is God's work*. It is a creation of the gospel (Luther, *WA*, 2:430).

There is indeed a human aspect. The church consists, after all, of people, and these are always people with sins and shortcomings. When in Article 27 of the Belgic Confession of Faith the church is called "a holy congregation of true Christian believers," one can ask the question who the subject of this congregating (gathering) is? Does God bring the believers together or do they come together? Lord's Day 21 of the Heidelberg Catechism formulates it unambiguously: it is the Son of God who "gathers, defends, and preserves" his church.

In the coming together of the church and in all of church life the human factor is unmistakable. If we only take this human element into account, we cannot avoid relativizing the reality that we call church. Above all we must not lose sight of the other side. A divine work can be recognized in the gathering of the church of Christ. This is the miracle of the church! It remains nevertheless an assembly of people, so that we must not *absolutize* the church as we know it, and may not overlook its problems.

46.2. *The church in Trinitarian perspective*

1. *The church constitutes the people of God*. In a full theological view of the church, we see it in the light of the work of the triune God. The relationship with him already finds expression in names such as "the people of God," "the body of Christ," and "the temple of the Holy Spirit": in the first characterization we see especially the relationship with God the Father; in the second the relationship of the church with

22. One should realize that for Kersten, confession of faith means basically confession of truth (see *R.D.* 2:469).

Christ, who is the Son of God; in the third the relationship with the work of the Holy Spirit.

In the Old Testament Israel is called the people of God, because he chose to be the God of this people. In addition to election, we must also think of the covenant and of God's redeeming acts. The LORD bore Israel "on eagles' wings" and made it his "peculiar treasure" (Ex. 19:4–5). He promised this people his salvation and placed them in his service. He says: "I will walk among you, and will be your God, and ye shall be my people" (Lev. 26:12). "And ye shall be unto me a kingdom of priests, and an holy nation" (Ex. 19:6). In the Old Testament the *qahal* is "die in der Anbetung des Herrn geeinigte und zur Anbetung des Herrn vereinigte *Bundesgemeinde*" (the church of the covenant being united in their worship of the Lord and having been gathered together to worship the Lord).[23]

However, Israel was only partly what it was meant to be. It came to the point where God had to say: "Ye are not my people [Lo-Ammi], and I will not be your God." Yet he promises even then: "In the place where it was said unto them, Ye are not my people, there it shall be said unto them, Ye are the sons of the living God" (Hos. 1:9–10).

God himself will take care that there is a people that belongs entirely to him. The prophets proclaim the message that a remnant or remainder of God's people shall be saved through the judgment. A remnant repents (see *TDNT*, 4:194–214). The election of Israel becomes focused on this remainder of Israel. This focus is ultimately narrowed to the Servant of the LORD through whom the new people of God are gathered from Israel and the nations (A. Noordegraaf in *De kerk*, 1990, 23).

In this connection we also remind the reader of the prophecies that relate to the new covenant (see § 34.1, subsection 4). The God of the covenant makes a new beginning and offers the richest promises (see Jer. 31:31–34).

Promises that belong to the new covenant reemerge in the New Testament (cf. Jer. 31:31–34 and Heb. 8:8–12; Ezek. 37:27 and 2 Cor. 6:16).

To the people of God of the New Testament, who are gathered from among both Jews and Gentiles, the following Old Testament promise applies: "I will dwell in them, and walk in them; and I will be their God, and they shall be my people" (2 Cor. 6:16; cf. Joel 2:17). The believers, who are called exiles in dispersion (cf. 1 Peter 1:1), are addressed as "a chosen generation, a royal priesthood, an holy nation and a peculiar people; that ye should show forth [his] praises" (1 Peter 2:9). In them is fulfilled what was said to Israel (Ex. 19:5–6). They

23. E. Stauffer, *Die Theologie des Neuen Testaments*, 1945, 276.

were once not his people; however, now they are God's people (1 Peter 2:10 as fulfillment of Hos. 1:10). Paul applies Hosea's words to those whom God has called, not only from among the Jews, but also from among the Gentiles (Rom. 9:24–26).

The Bible shows us how God from the very beginning had in mind to gather for his name a people from among the Gentiles. This is how Peter and James articulated their insight at a critical moment (Acts 15:14). Those who were once "far off" and "strangers from the covenants of promise . . . are made nigh by the blood of Christ. For he is our peace, who hath made both [Jews and Gentiles] one" (Eph. 2:12–14; cf. Gal. 3:28–29).

It is not an incidental characteristic of the church as the people of God that it is not impeded by borders dictated by nationality, race, or culture. This is essential for the church. Neither is time a dividing factor. The people of God on earth constitute a unity with all those who in the past were his people and in the future will be his people, for the Lord's work of gathering the church is ongoing. We call this the catholicity of the church (see § 46.4, subsection 4).

The people of God are united with Christ. He has sanctified his "people with his own blood" (Heb. 13:12; cf. also Acts 20:28). They are "called unto the fellowship of his Son Jesus Christ our Lord" (1 Cor. 1:9).

Just as of old, by virtue of God's covenant, children were part of the congregation of the covenant (see Neh. 8:3), they are also included in the church of the New Testament. They form part of the holy people of God to whom the promises apply (Acts 2:39; 1 Cor. 7:14; Eph. 6:1).

Apart from the word *ekklesia*, especially in Paul's epistles, we come across several other names that have an Old Testament background and give expression to the fact, that in the congregation of those who confess Jesus Christ to be their Lord, the true people of God are revealed to be the fulfillment of the historical people of God. They are the saints, the elect, the beloved, and those who have been called (cf. Noordegraaf in *De kerk*, 1990, 47).

One people of God. Those who see the New Testament church as the people of God face the question as to how to interpret the relationship between Israel and the church.

Especially since 1945 much thought has been given to this, which is apparent from a continuous stream of publications.[24] A few comments must suffice here.

24. See among others S. Gerssen, *Modern Zionisme en christelijke theologie*, 1978; C. Graafland, *Het vaste verbond* (the certain covenant), 1978; S. Schoon, *Christelijke presentie in de Joodse* (Jewish) *staat*, 1982; H. de Jong, *Handelingen* (Acts) 7, 1985; J. M.. Snoek/J. Verkuyl,

1. The New Testament maintains the position of Israel's redemption-historical priority. See Acts 3:26 and Romans 1:16.
2. The true Israel consists of those who believe in Christ. Those who are "Christ's . . . are Abraham's seed, and heirs according to the promise" (Gal.3:29).
3. It cannot be inferred from the New Testament, not even from the image of the olive tree in Romans 11 (see Vlaardingerbroek, 1989, 68), that those who believe must be incorporated into Israel in order to be the people of God. Through faith they share in the communion with Christ and through him belong to the people of God. The Judaist view that Christians from among the Gentiles must meet the requirement to be circumcised and also in other respects to live in accordance with Israel's rules in order to be part of the people of God, is vehemently fought by Paul (Galatians).
4. There is no biblical basis for H. Berkhof's view that the appearance of Christ has led to two forms and two ways of the people of God (*C.F.*, 266).

Like Berkhof, many end up with two ways. Jews and Gentiles are both portrayed as being on their way to God's kingdom, Jews by the way of the *Torah*, Christians by the way of faith in Christ. Jesus says indeed that "no man cometh unto the Father, but by me" (John 14:6), but the Jews are already with the Father (F. Rosenzweig, P. Lapide, and others).

Some speak openly of two different "ways," others of Israel's unique "way." The latter does not make things any clearer, any more than the notion that suggests that Jews and Gentiles travel together. This may appear to be an attractive solution to the problem. Then it also does not matter if Jews continue to reject Jesus and need not be called so urgently to faith in him.

But one may not forget that Jesus spoke in the midst of the Jewish people about the only way to the Father. If there were another way besides the way of faith in Christ, Paul's struggle for Israel's salvation (Rom. 9–11) would be incomprehensible.

The consequence of the doctrine of two ways, which has broad appeal, especially at a time when religious pluralism or universalism with respect to revelation is widespread, is that the core of the confession of the church of all ages is suppressed or surrendered. The latter is in fact being advocated by a number of quite vocal theologians such as P. van Buren and H. Jansen.[25]

5. In view of the indisputable reality, that those who believe in Christ are the people of God and share in the privileges that the God of the covenant promises to his people, one cannot call the part of Israel that ignores Christ, in a Jewish-orthodox or other manner, the people of God, unless one means by this designation that God has not written off his ancient people of the covenant and that there remain expectations for Israel, as Paul expresses in Romans 11.

Intern beraad in verband met de relatie tussen kerk en Israel (internal deliberation concerning the relationship between the church and Israel), 1988; J. Vlaardingerbroek, *Jezus Christus tussen Joden* (Jews) *en Christenen*, 1989; series as *Verkenning en bezinning* (exploration and reflection, beginning in 1967); *Zicht op Israel* (focus on Israel, beginning in 1983).

25. Cf. P. van Buren, *Discerning the Way*, 1980; H. Jansen, *Christelijke theologie na* (subsequent to) *Auschwitz*, 1–2, 1981–85.

2. *The church is the body of Christ.* This designation of the church we find only in Paul's epistles (Rom. 12; 1 Cor. 12; Ephesians; Colossians).

a. In Romans 12:4–5 and 1 Corinthians 12:12–27 we encounter a metaphor. It is a well-known image that Paul employs. It has to do with the diversity and unity of the many members of one body, among whom no one may consider himself to be exalted above the other. The gifts and potentials that each individual member has received are to be used in mutual service. When one member suffers, all suffer in sympathy. There must be no divisions among them. This is enjoined to the church also in other places (see 1 Cor. 1:10–11; 11:18). It may be compared to what Paul says in Galatians 3:28 about the unity in Christ: "There is neither Jew nor Greek, there is neither bond nor free, there is neither male nor female."

b. The notion that the church is the body of Christ has therefore great significance for mutual relationships. The apostle goes further, however, for he points specifically to the relationship between Christ and his church. In the epistles to the Ephesians and Colossians, Christ is called *the Head of the body.*

The church is not only associated with him; it also belongs to him. It is permanently united with him. This relationship is rooted in redemption history. Just as Christ's people are subsumed in him and have everything in Christ, in him they are one body (cf. Rom. 12:5). He makes his people members of his body. Paul writes: "Now ye are the body of Christ, and members in particular" (1 Cor. 12:27). Of importance in this connection is also being "baptized into one body" and being "made to drink into one Spirit" (1 Cor. 12:13). This is a reminder of baptism and probably an allusion to the Lord's Supper. Baptism testifies to incorporation in Christ, and the Lord's Supper to communion with Christ in which the work of his Spirit can be recognized.

We encounter a peculiar interpretation of the body of Christ on the part of Roman Catholics. Christ lives on in his church, which is united with him in closest communion. It is sometimes referred to as a single divine-human life. Just as the body needs the Head, so the Head needs the body. To distinguish the church from the physical body of Christ, it is referred to as the mystical body. To a certain extent he lives in his church in such a way that it is, as it were, another Christ (*quasi altera Christi persona*). This mystical identity finds expression above all in the Eucharist.[26]

26. See the encyclical *Mystici corporis* (1943) by Pius XII, no. 43, 52, 82–85.

Via the Eucharist a connection is often established between the church and the personal body of Christ. According to Roman Catholic doctrine, Christ is physically present in this sacrament. Those who partake of it share in his body and constitute his body. In this connection reference is made to 1 Corinthians 10:16–17. The body of Christ, with which this mystical identification takes place, is none other than the real, personal body that lived, died, and was glorified, and with which the bread is identified.[27]

For a critique of this view see Ridderbos, *Paul*, 374ff. Those who equate communion with the blood and body of Christ (1 Cor. 10:16) with *being* the physical body of Christ make a leap in thought. The words: "This is my body" signify that Christ surrendered himself to death for those who are his. It is totally absurd, therefore, to identify the church with this physical body.

In 1 Corinthians 10:16–17, the apostle does want to say, however, that communion with Christ at the Lord's Supper is manifested in the unity of the church.

We can concur with what is said by A. Noordegraaf: "As members of Christ, believers constitute one body in him, share the gift of the Spirit, and are called to manifest this unity by employing their spiritual gifts in the richness of the diversity of their gifts" (*De kerk*, 1990, 51).

c. The idea that the church is the body of Christ is elaborated in Ephesians and Colossians in a specific direction. It is strongly emphasized here that *as Head of his body Christ stands above his church, which is subject to him in every way.* In this connection there is no question of any identification of Christ with his church. The word "Head" denotes that he is in charge and that he makes the decisions. The church as his body is totally dependent on him as its Head.

The apostle points out at the same time that Christ "is the saviour of [his] body." He "loved the church and gave himself for it" (Eph. 5:23, 25). He bestows numerous gifts on it (Eph. 4:7–16). The church owes everything to him. From him the whole body receives its divine growth (Col. 2:19). "From [Christ] the whole body [derives its spiritual growth] unto the edifying of itself in love." It is important that, "speaking the truth in love, [we] may grow up into him in all things, which is the head, even Christ" (Eph. 4:16, 15). In this connection see Velema, 1966, 12–16.

d. Christ, who is the Head of his church, has dominion over everything. God "hath put all things under his feet, and gave him to be the head over all things to the church which is his body" (Eph.1:22–23; for a related thought, cf. Col. 1:15–18). He rules his church, but his

27. L. Cerfaux, *La théologie de l'église suivant saint Paul* (theology of the church according to St. Paul), 1948, 202–12.

dominion is not restricted to it. He is the Head of the church and the cosmos (cf. Du Plessis, 1962).

It is of great importance for the church, in view of its task in the world, to take as its guiding principle that all things are subjugated to him, who is its Head and who protects and guides it in love. With his power that he has, he stands behind the task he assigns.

For the relationship between the church and the world, this means that it must go into the world without ever becoming part of it. It may not withdraw itself in Anabaptist shunning, for it has a calling to fulfill here, by testifying to its Lord and living in a holy fashion for him. This involves mutual love, intercessory prayer, and diaconal assistance.

3. *The church is the temple of the Holy Spirit.* A few statements by the apostles provide the biblical basis for this idea. Paul says to the church, "Know ye not that ye are the temple of God, and that the Spirit of God dwelleth in you?" (1 Cor. 3:16). He calls it "an habitation of God through the Spirit" (Eph. 2:22). According to Peter, the believers constitute "a spiritual house" (1 Peter 2:5). But also apart from these Scripture passages there is sufficient reason to reflect on the Holy Spirit and his work within the perspective of the doctrine of the church.

The redemption event of Pentecost already is for the church immediately of decisive significance. Now the prophecy is fulfilled that the Spirit will be "pour[ed] out on all flesh" (Acts 2:17; cf. Joel 2:17).

The word "to pour out" points to an abundant blessing. The expression "upon all flesh" indicates that the restrictions that once applied now fall away. The current cannot be turned back!

The speaking "with other tongues as the Spirit gave them utterance" (Acts 2:4) foreshadows to some extent that the various languages will present no obstacles to the transmission of the gospel of Christ. The nations will hear of the great acts of God in their own languages.[28]

At the outpouring of the Holy Spirit, the apostles receive the power to witness to Christ. This is why Peter stands up together "with the eleven" (Acts 2:14). The Holy Spirit matures and emboldens the church. In the earlier redemption events angels still had to do the speaking, but now the people speak for themselves.

The Spirit of Pentecost causes the gospel to enter into the hearts (Acts 2:37–41), and he transforms the church into a "fellowship" (Acts 2:42–47).

28. Cf. A. A. Hoekema, *Spreken in tongen*, 65.

The Spirit is the driving force behind all missionary activity of the apostolic era. It is he who shows the way and paves the way to the far corners of the earth (cf. Noordegraaf, 1983, 179–82).

Being the temple of the Holy Spirit does not only apply to the church per se. The body of a believer is also called a temple of the Holy Spirit (1 Cor. 6:19). Galatians 4:6 says that the Spirit is sent into the hearts, which means that he controls the inner life of believers. The idea that Christ dwells in our hearts by faith (Eph. 3:17) is mentioned in the same epistle that describes the church as "an habitation of God through the Spirit" (Eph. 2:22). From the Old Testament we know that God wants to dwell among his people. The word "to dwell" indicates that the Spirit is and remains present here. Through his presence he makes the church his dwelling place and his workplace. This makes the church a spiritual reality.

Augustine calls the Holy Spirit the soul of the church, but to him this is a metaphor. In Roman Catholicism this is an ever-recurring theme. "If Christ is the Head of the Church, the Holy Spirit is its soul."[29] Thus he performs his work as an immanent principle. He is "primarily the creator of the church as a sacramental and institutional reality."[30]

What the Second Vatican Council says about this makes a cautious impression: "Christ shares with us his Spirit who causes the entire body to live, to be united, and to act so that the holy Fathers can compare his task with the function fulfilled by the principle of life or the soul within the human body" (*Dogm. Const.*, 1964, no. 7).

We are of the view that the Holy Spirit cannot be called the soul of the church. He is not one with it in the same way that the soul and the body form a unity, and not all acts of the church are acts of the Holy Spirit (see also *M.S.*, 4.1.465ff.). However, one could say that he invigorates the church, enabling it to live, grow, and function.

The church can never manipulate the Holy Spirit. It must be open and receptive toward the Holy Spirit and his work. It is a miracle of God's grace that despite every way in which people grieve him and work against him, he is willing to dwell among and within them.

Wherever the Spirit comes he brings along his gifts. They are intended for the edification of the church. He remains sovereign in their distribution (see 1 Cor. 12:11).

There is a great diversity of gifts. In the Pauline epistles several lists are given (Rom. 12:6–8; 1 Cor. 12:8–10, 28–30). All these spiritual gifts, which the apostle refers to as gifts of grace (*charismata*), are associated with the grace given in Christ (*charis*).

The emergence of *Pentecostalism* (at the beginning of the twentieth century) engendered a great deal of discussion on the meaning of the gifts of the Spirit.[31]

29. *Mystici corporis* (note 26), no. 56.

30. H. Berkhof, *De leer* (doctrine) *van de Heilige Geest*, 1965, 47.

31. From the perspective of Pentecostalism and the charismatic movement one could mention among others: L. Steiner, *Mit folgenden Zeichen* (with following signs), 1954; D. Gee, *Over*

According to Christians who can be considered to be members of this movement or the related charismatic movement, it has to do with an experience of the Spirit that brings spiritual life to a higher level, a filling with the Spirit that goes beyond the renewal of life. One usually speaks in terms of baptism with or in the Holy Spirit. There is a clear tendency—although some are more or less backing away from this—to consider certain spiritual gifts, whereby one thinks in the first place of glossolalia or speaking in tongues, in the second place of prophecy, and sometimes also of the gift of healing, to be so significant that the church and individual believers will be judged accordingly.

We cannot agree with this view. The apostle Paul does not assign to glossolalia the importance it had among the Corinthians, although he does not disapprove of it. Among the gifts he mentions are those that are less spectacular but no less important, such as the ability to help, to administer (1 Cor. 12:28), to serve, to teach, to exhort, to give leadership, and to show mercy (Rom. 12:7–8).

What matters is not the gifts per se, but how they are employed. They are validated through the recognition of Jesus as Lord. They are directed toward the edification of the church. These are the two criteria Paul gives (1 Cor. 12:3; 14:12). Moreover, the apostle shows "a ['yet'] more excellent way" (1 Cor. 12:31; 13). The love of which he speaks is effected through the Spirit and must be seen as "the [first] fruit of the Spirit" (Gal. 5:22). In the absence of love, the available gifts could have no significance to the church.

In view of the church's enrichment and equipment with gifts of the Spirit, in more recent theology it is often referred to as a charismatic church or a church with a charismatic structure (cf. Versteeg, 1985, 19, 22).

In this connection it must not be forgotten that the ecclesiastical offices also belong to the gifts that serve to edify the church. The office bearers are to "equip . . . the saints, for the work of the ministry, for the edifying of the body of Christ" (Eph. 4:11–12). There is no reason whatsoever to place offices and charismata over against each other, nor to think that the charismatic structure of the church renders offices superfluous (cf. Brockhaus, 1972). One may not minimize the charismata in favor of the offices. Neither may one absolutize them at the expense of the offices. The entire New Testament shows the close relationship between offices and charismata (Versteeg, 1985, 41ff.).

Paul says to the elders of Ephesus that they should "take heed unto [them]selves, and to all the flock, over which the Holy Spirit has made

de geestelijke gaven (about spiritual gifts), 1960; K. J. Kraan, *Ruimte voor de Geest?* (room for the Spirit?), 1970; C. van der Laan, *De spade regen* (the latter rain, cf. Joel 2:23; James 5:7), 1989. For an opposite view see N. Bloch-Hoell, *The Pentecostal Movement*, 1964; F. D. Bruner, *A Theology of the Holy Spirit*, 1976; L. Floor, *De doop met de Heilige Geest* (baptism with the Holy Spirit), 1982; W. D. Jonker, *Die Geest van Christus*, 1981.

[them] overseers" (Acts 20:28). This is an important statement, for it implies that those who take this task upon themselves are dependent on the Holy Spirit, and that he gives them everything they need for the discharge of their office.

There is no contrast whatsoever between the Spirit and ecclesiastical office, for the Spirit wants to employ precisely the services of people who are called into office. Thus offices do not come from below but from above, even though the office bearers come from the church itself, and therefore the church itself chooses gifted brethren.

It was mentioned above that the Spirit of Pentecost transforms the church into a fellowship and also causes it to persevere in fellowship. He is the Founder of spiritual and ecclesiastical fellowship. There exist various forms of fellowship, but ecclesiastical fellowship is unique. Our choice or sympathy is not decisive in this connection, but our calling to be members of this church is. *The communion of saints cannot be sought outside the church community*, even though it is not identical with it. In the Apostles' Creed the article that deals with the communion of saints has everything to do with the article on the church.

The biblical idea of communion clearly emerges in the explanation of the communion of saints given in Lord's Day 21 of the Heidelberg Catechism (answer 55): "First, that believers, all and everyone, as members of Christ, are partakers of him and of all his treasures and gifts; second, that every one must know himself bound to employ his gifts readily and cheerfully for the advantage and salvation of other members."

The communion of saints should therefore be seen as a gift and an obligation (more on this in van Genderen, 1986).

4. The people of God, the body of Christ, and the temple of the Holy Spirit: *these three designations capture the essence of the church*. Something still needs to be said about their *interrelationship*.

The body of Christ is the christological characterization of the people of God in the New Testament. The unity of these people is their unity in Christ, in whom they are subsumed and who is their Head. The apostle says: he "gave himself for us, that he might redeem us from all iniquity, and purify unto himself a peculiar people, zealous of good works" (Titus 2:14).

The people of God are not only the body of Christ, but also the temple of the Holy Spirit. The body of Christ is what it is through the

Spirit (cf. 1 Cor. 12:13). "There is one body and one Spirit" (Eph. 4:4). The communion with Christ and the mutual fellowship of believers is established and maintained by the Holy Spirit.

These three designations place the church in the light of the work of the Triune God. They can also be described with the help of various verbs: God the Father elects the church, the Son gathers it, and the Spirit sanctifies it. See Ephesians 1:3–14; 4:4–6; and 1 Peter 1:2. In 1 Peter 1:1–2 it says: "To [the] elect according to the foreknowledge of God the Father, through sanctification of the Spirit, unto obedience and sprinkling of the blood of Jesus Christ."

In the description given in the Belgic Confession of Faith (article 27), the emphasis falls on the work of Christ and the Holy Spirit. With the words "chosen to everlasting life," the Heidelberg Catechism in Lord's Day 21 also points to the work specifically ascribed to the Father.

The threesome of the people of God, the body of Christ, and the temple of the Holy Spirit also turn up in more recent Roman Catholic theology (cf. Küng, 1967, 131–310; *M.S.*, 4.1.152–63). Yet there is an element of truth in Van Ruler's remark that the Reformation reasons along Trinitarian and therefore also along pneumatological lines, while according to Rome the christological perspective predominates.[32]

We also differ substantially from spiritualism. Here ecclesiastical fellowship is rated below and even rejected in favor of spiritual fellowship. This contrast is not biblical. The focus is on the church that Christ gathers through his Spirit and Word. As a variation of Van Ruler's statement one could say: the Reformation reasons along Trinitarian and therefore also along christological lines.

46.3. *The visible and the invisible church*

In his struggle against the hierarchically governed, all-powerful ecclesiastical institution, Luther refers to the church as being spiritual. The church that matters to him is also referred to as being invisible, but even more so hidden. While—as it were—external Christendom constitutes the body, believers constitute its soul (*WA*, 6:297).

Calvin distinguishes between the visible church and the church that is invisible (*Institutes*, 4.1.7). Some Reformed confessions provide descriptions and definitions, e.g., the Westminster Confession.[33]

In this connection we make the following comments:

32. A. A. Van Ruler, *Reformatorische opmerkingen in de ontmoeting met Rome* (Reformational remarks concerning the encounter with Rome), 1965, 7.

33. In Heppe's view, the way in which these concepts "visible and invisible church" are defined leaves something to be desired as far as clarity is concerned (*Dogm.*, 527f.; see also Bavinck, *R.D.*, 4:287–91, 301–7).

1. The distinction between a visible and an invisible church at any rate may not be interpreted as a separation as though there would be two churches.

2. Although we cannot oversee the entire church, this does not make it invisible to us.

3. We may not equate the church as we see it with the church as God sees it. Although not everything that is visible of the church is essential, there is more to the church than what meets the eye.

4. With Bavinck we can say that we are dealing with the same believers, regardless of whether they are viewed from the perspective of the faith that dwells in their hearts and is known with certainty only to God, or in the other case from the perspective of their confession and life, the side that is turned toward us and is observable by us (cf. *R.D.*, 4:306).

5. It is very much the question whether the invisible side of the church can be interpreted as constituting an invisible church. We need to take into account the serious objections Schilder had against this. It is certainly incorrect to seek the essence of the church in what is invisible, as Kuyper did. The church is the assembly of the believers.

6. To prevent thinking in terms of two separate entities, which can lead and also has led to the distinction between an invisible and a visible church, while at the same time doing justice to the intention of the Reformers, we can agree with Calvin who believes that Scripture speaks of the church in a twofold way (*bifariam*). "The church from God's perspective" (*coram Deo)* and "the church from the perspective of people" (*respectu hominum*) can be considered to be two aspects of the church.

7. Calvin's definitions are useful. Sometimes Scripture does indeed mean the church as God sees it, to which only the children of God, the true members of Christ, are admitted. Frequently, however, Scripture employs the name "church" to indicate all those who confess that they serve one God and Christ. There are also hypocrites in this church (according to Calvin even very many hypocrites, who have nothing of Christ but the name and the outward appearance).

8. When Calvin associates the church *coram Deo* with "believing" and the church *respectu hominum* with "revering and keeping communion with" (*Institutes*, 4.1.7), he gives the impression that the church as God sees it is indeed an object of faith, but that the church as we see it is not. However, the New Testament refers to the church

that conducts its meetings under the leadership of its office bearers as the church of Christ. What is important is the belief that he calls it together and brings it together.

9. In our confession documents both aspects are unmistakably present.

Article 27 of the Belgic Confession of Faith refers to the church from God's perspective. It is "a holy congregation of true Christian believers." Article 29 portrays the church from our perspective. As the true church it must be distinguished from various sects and from the false church. There are also hypocrites who do not belong in the church, although outwardly they are part of it.

Although the wording of Answer 54 of the Heidelberg Catechism is not the same as that of Article 27 of the Belgic Confession of Faith, in terms of content they are similar. In Lord's Day 31 we see the concrete church described differently again. In addition to believers there are also others: unbelievers and those who do not sincerely repent. There are those who project themselves as Christians but whose doctrine and life are unchristian.

In the Canons of Dort, the church is "a church composed of believers, the foundation of which is laid in the blood of Christ; which may steadfastly love and faithfully serve him as its Savior . . . ; and which may celebrate his praises here and throughout eternity" (2.9). In the conclusion of the Canons of Dort, however, the church appears in its historical manifestation: as "the Belgic Churches" in which discord had emerged; as "the Reformed Churches" that had had to defend their doctrine.

46.4. *The attributes of the church*

1. *The meaning of the four attributes*

The Creed of Nicaea-Constantinople assigns four predicates to the church. *It is one, holy, catholic, and apostolic.* The Apostles' Creed mentions only holiness and catholicity; the word "one" here is not a numeral but an article.[34]

These attributes tell us what is inherent in the church as church. To be the church it cannot do without any of these attributes. It is its essence to be one, holy, catholic, and apostolic.[35]

34. See J. N. Bakhuizen van den Brink in *De belijdenisgeschriften volgens artikel X van de kerkorde van de Nederlandse Hervormde Kerk* (the confessions according to article 10 of the church order of the Dutch Reformed Church), 1966, 242ff.

35. Some would mention separately the church's immutability and infallibility, which give us six attributes (cf. Bavinck, *R.D.*, 4:323f.). One may question whether this is wise. These attributes fit in well with Rome's ecclesiology, but we would have to give them a different content. We can speak of the *continuity* of the church because it is the continuation of the one, holy, catholic, and apostolic church (see J. van Genderen, *De continuiteit van geloof en kerk* = the continuity of faith and the church, 1977, 17–33).

But is the first attribute, its unity, then such a clear given that it is inherent in the church? And its holiness? These are burning questions that need to be raised from the perspective of the actual ecclesiastical situation and in view of human imperfection.

Calvin says in this connection that the article of faith, which in the first instance refers to the church from God's perspective, which consists of the elect, also pertains to some extent to the outward church (*Institutes*, 4.1.3). The expression "to some extent" (*aliquatenus*) could be interpreted in a minimizing sense, which would be contrary to Calvin's intent. It is well known how ardently he worked for the unity of the church. J. Bohatec even referred to him as the theologian of ecclesiastical unity.[36]

To prevent misunderstanding, it is better to put it differently: As the church of Christ, the church is one, holy, catholic, and apostolic. It is so in all of these respects in order to become increasingly more so. Thus the church is not holy so as to be able to boast in its holiness, but to make it reality. It is to be holy before both God and people.

Just like the individual believer, the church as the assembly of believers does not achieve perfection in this life. There is a great deal lacking in the visibility of its attributes. There are no grounds whatsoever for *triumphalism*. But this may not lead to *defeatism* either, for the church must strive to meet God's highest purpose.

Since the Holy Spirit has been given to the church, it shares in his gifts, and it is what it is. The Spirit is given to it, so that in every respect it will grow toward him who is the Head, Christ, and in this way will become ever more what it is in him: one, holy, catholic, and apostolic church.

It is quite biblical to say that the church must become what it is. We therefore see the attributes of the church *first as gift and then as calling.*

We do not reverse the order by stating that a process is required to become more and more united, holy, catholic, and apostolic in order to be so. Theologically speaking, the gift precedes the calling.

The validity of the statements that the church makes about itself in its confessions does not depend on observation. They are statements of faith which can and must be made based on what God says

36. J. Bohatec, *Calvins Lehre von Staat und Kirche* (Calvin's doctrine of the state and the church), 1937, 637. Cf. W. Nijenhuis, *Calvinus oecumenicus*, 1959.

in his Word about his church and promises to his church, including its mandate.

2. *The unity of the church*

a. *Unity as a gift.* There is a multiplicity of churches, which all differ from each other. One can investigate the causes of ecclesiastical disunity. Church history explains a great deal and yet not everything. In the doctrine of the church we do not start out from what we see around us, although we may not close our eyes to it. We ask again and again what we can say about the church from the perspective of faith.

The first thing is then not that it ought to be one, but that it is one. *It is characteristic of the church to be one.*

This is crystal clear from the perspective of Scripture. We have in mind John 17; Acts 2:41–47; 1 Corinthians 12:4–27; and Ephesians 4:1–6. These passages deal with the *ekklesia* as the one body of Christ. The unity of the church is given in him. He is the Head of the church. Those who belong to him belong together.

One may call this spiritual unity, as long as one does not mean by this that unity is not visible. The unity of the church ought to be visible to everyone.

In connection with the unity of the Christian church, it has been said of the Reformation that it focused on the invisible side of the church (according to Honig, *Handboek*, 719). This is definitely not true of Calvin. He writes not only about the unity of the elect, who are truly one in Christ, but also about the universal church *(ecclesia universalis)* that agrees on the one truth of divine doctrine and is bound by the bond of one and the same religion. "We preserve for the universal church its unity, which devilish spirits have always sought to sunder" (*Institutes*, 4.1.9).

There exist far-reaching differences regarding the nature of the unity of the church.

For Rome, unity is the most essential attribute and at the same time primary characteristic of the church. Peter is the enduring and visible principle and foundation of unity. His primacy continues in that of the pope. This is how the Second Vatican Council put it—following a centuries-long tradition—in the Dogmatic Constitution of 1964 (no. 18).

As is apparent from papal documents, the pope also views himself as the root and origin of the unity of the church. He is as it were its focal point. One can say that to Rome the unity of the church stands or falls with the pope.

It is curious that the constitution of 1964 refers to both the Holy Spirit and the pope as the principle (*principium*) of unity (cf. no. 13 and no. 18). The difference is that as the visible head of the entire church the pope is the visible principle of its unity.

According to Rome, the Reformation violated the unity of the body of Christ. Calvin refuted this accusation in his magisterial reply to a letter from Cardinal Sadoleto, who said of his church that, being united and consenting in Christ, it has been always and everywhere directed by the one Spirit of Christ, so that no dissension can exist. Calvin pointed out that the Spirit cannot be severed from the Word. Only God's truth can be the bond of unity (*C.O.*, 5:393, 410; cf. *A Reformation Debate: John Calvin & Jacopo Sadoleto*, ed. John C. Olin, 41, 60). In the *Institutes* he says that the communion of the church is held together by two bonds, namely, by agreement in sound doctrine and brotherly love (4.2.5). Thus the unity of the church is therefore the unity of faith. Mutual love is a consequence of this.

With Calvin we appeal to Ephesians 4:4–6 in this connection. It is "one body, and one Spirit . . . , one Lord, one faith, one baptism, one God and Father of all."

With the one church of Christ, Rome means the visible church of which the pope is head, but the ecumenical movement has all churches in view.

In its first period the World Council of Churches put the unity of the church above everything else (Amsterdam, 1948; Evanston, 1954). Its point of departure was that, despite our dividedness as churches, unity is given to us in Christ. Real unity within the World Council has consequences for the concrete relationships of churches that exist side by side.[37]

Within circles of the World Council, great emphasis is placed on Jesus' words, "that they all may be one" (John 17:21). Too little thought is paid to the fact that according to John 17 communion with the Father and the Son is the foundation of the unity of believers. What matters is unity in the truth (John 17:17, 19). Those who realize this cannot ignore the problem of liberalism.

There was a time when it seemed as if the World Council, with its influence on the churches, was on its way to establish a world church. Later on the focus shifted to conciliarity as a new concept of unity: an ecumenical, conciliar form of living and witnessing together. Still more important in the development of the World Council is that after the initial emphasis on the unity of the church, the social and political aspects of being the church in the world moved into the foreground (see K. Runia in *De kerk*, 1990, 246–56).

After 1961 the notion emerged that our concern should not only be with the entire church but also with the entire world. The world even dictates the agenda for the church! This is called *secular ecumenism.*

In *New Directions*, an important document of Faith and Order (1967), it is argued that the church should focus its efforts externally

37. Second Assembly of the World Council of Churches, Evanston, 1954, no date, 95.

rather than on internal affairs. "Its existence and its unity are contingent upon its faithful devotion to the world." This was subsequently implemented in terms of a variety of programs (for a brief overview see Andresen, *Handbuch*, 3:533–45). A theologian whose doctrine of the church reflects this spirit is Moltmann. According to him, "unity in freedom" is directed toward the world (1975, 368, 371–73).

This approach involves a very arbitrary way of dealing with Scripture. R. Slenczka says: Responsibility for the world, however one wants to define it further, is viewed as something that is decisive for salvation (in Andresen, *Handbuch*, 3:540). Theologically the world is not the most likely place to find the sought-after unity of Christians (cf. Kuhn, 1980, 214).

b. *Unity as calling*. Since unity has been given to the church of Christ, it is called to put it into practice. "There is one body . . . one Spirit . . . one Lord . . . one God and Father of all." Therefore believers are called to "endeavour . . . to keep the unity of the Spirit in the bond of peace" (Eph. 4:1–6).

This is echoed in the Belgic Confession of Faith. Since the church is "joined and united . . . in the same Spirit," all believers "are in duty bound to join and unite themselves with it; maintaining the unity of the church" (Article 27–28). Since Christ gathers his church "by his Spirit and Word, in the unity of the true faith" (Heidelberg Catechism, Lord's Day 21), it must always be our concern to come together in the unity of the true faith.

It has been said correctly: "Knowing that unity is God's cause, liberates us from overconfidence and despondency. It does not paralyze our activity, but precisely facilitates it."[38]

The view that spiritual unity among believers ought to be sufficient constitutes a hindrance to the quest for church unity. There are those who think that this is all that Jesus had in mind when he prayed for the unity of all of his people.[39]

In his high-priestly prayer, he prays indeed for the spiritual unity of those who are his. But spiritual unity should not only come to expression in personal contacts and gatherings of like-minded people. It must

38. H. Berkhof, *Gods éne kerk en onze vele kerken* (God's one church and our many churches), no date, 21.

39. D. Hedegard, *De oecumenische beweging en de Bijbel* (the ecumenical movement and the Bible), 1959, 33.

precisely be manifested in ecclesiastical life. It is important "that the world may know that" the Father has sent Christ (John 17:23). It is as Schilder expressed it once: "Spiritual unity may come first, but it must also impel institutional unity.[40]

Although ecclesiastical diversity is not in conflict with biblical unity, ecclesiastical divisiveness is.

At this point something needs to be said about the *doctrine of the pluriformity of the church.* This is often a theological justification of the existing situation. It is a theory that has been called suggestive (Berkouwer, *The Church*, 1976, 51).

Kuyper saw the multiplicity of churches as proof of the richness of Christian life and a manifestation of the manifold wisdom of God. This was an inevitable development. He made a virtue out of the vice of divisiveness. The idealism of the nineteenth century left its imprint on his doctrine.

Bearing in mind that divided churches do not just stand beside, but also over against each other, we must reject the doctrine of pluriformity. With their doctrinal statements, churches choose positions over against each other. Therefore this theory would imply pluriformity of the *truth*.

Over against Kuyper and Bavinck (who speaks less idealistically about pluriformity), it has been correctly argued that ecclesiastical divisiveness must above all be seen as a consequence of sin. Besides, discord and strife harm the cause of the church.

Schilder was a theologian who refused to have anything to do with "pluriformitis." This evil will avenge itself in mercilessly progressive relativism.[41]

Today we encounter pluralism more so than the theory of pluriformity.

It is said that there have always been different views with respect to the truth and salvation. After all, people do differ, and so do their insights and reactions. These differences can be best accommodated by having more churches, denominations, or groups.

This point of view opens the door to boundless individualism and subjectivism: an ecclesiastical smorgasbord!

According to others, in the context of increasingly divergent views, one should not seek the solution in increasing the number of churches or groups, but in making room within the church for an increasing number of opinions.

However, this is not a responsible solution to the problem either. A church with so much latitude that practically everything is considered to be legitimate, or at least tolerable, is no longer a "pillar and ground of the truth," which the church of the living God is, according to the apostle (1 Tim. 3:15). It then becomes a being together in the same large church without really being one. Neither is it to be expected that a purely organizational unity promotes unity in the true faith.

40. K. Schilder in *Verzamelde werken, de kerk* (collected works, the church), 1965, 3:129.
41. Ibid., 332.

We make two comments in connection with the present situation in which ecclesiastical divisiveness is rather increasing than decreasing, a situation with which no one can be content.

In the first place, scriptural ecclesiastical unity is worth making sacrifices for. It would be wrong not to be willing to give up anything for this and not to accept any changes. Uniformity is no prerequisite for unity. We do not need to agree with others in every respect to be nevertheless one with them.

Second, being called to unity does not mean that we are obligated to go along with everything that calls itself church or Christian. Biblical unity has its limits (cf. 2 Tim. 2:16–18; 1 John 2:19). Unity may not be pursued at the expense of the truth. True unity is unity in truth. It is the unity that has the Word of God as its norm.

Regarding the first point, it is important to keep in mind that unity as the antithesis of divisiveness does not preclude diversity. In this respect we can learn a great deal from Calvin. He points out that not all articles of true doctrine are of the same sort. Some are so necessary to know that they should be certain and unquestioned by all men as the proper principles of religion. Among the churches there are other articles of doctrine disputed which still do not break the unity of faith. Examples of these could be given. It is not Calvin's intention to support even the slightest error. But as long as sound doctrine is preserved as well as the sacraments instituted by the Lord, one should not lightly leave the church on the basis of one or another slight issue. "If we try to correct what displeases us, we do so out of duty" (*Institutes*, 4.1.12). See also what he wrote to Archbishop Cranmer of Canterbury about his willingness, if necessary, to traverse ten seas for the sake of the holy communion of the members of Christ (cf. Nijenhuis, 1959, 209ff.).

With respect to the second point, we remind the reader of the words of Calvin's contemporary Bullinger, who adopted a cautious point of view. This is what he wrote to Beza in connection with discussions with Lutherans: "We long for a unity which does not in any way conflict with the pure truth as confessed hitherto, that does not bring darkness or doubt into the bright light and clear truth, which by virtue of its sincerity is common and pleasant to all godly people, and therefore is also enduring and firm, and that does not give rise to new schisms" (in *C.O.*, 16:737).

The foregoing is not intended to imply that hardly anything will be visible of the required unity.

We can find it first of all within our own congregation and within our own federation of congregations, in the gathering of our congregation in unison, and especially in the celebration of the Lord's Supper, the sacrament of unity (Augustine), which eloquently expresses that as many as we are, we nevertheless constitute one body (cf. 1 Cor. 10:17).

c. We consider the unity of the church to be first of all God's gift and next our calling. There is yet another aspect: *the prospect.*

Jesus said that "there shall be one fold, and one shepherd" (John 10:16). As surely as he prayed and suffered for the unity of his people, so surely everything is moving toward the perfect unity of "the marriage supper of the Lamb" (Rev. 19:6–16), in which the Lord's Supper finds its fulfillment. As Schilder points out, there the Lamb heads the table and the joy, and there communion is guaranteed and defined in him.[42]

3. *The holiness of the church*

A statement of faith. Those who are not familiar with the language of Scripture and the confession might wonder what the church thinks of itself when it says: "I believe one holy church." According to the dictionary "holy" means: without sin, pure, perfect, exalted, unimpeachable. Is this not too pretentious?

With this we do not mean, however, that everything in the church is done in a holy manner. It is a holiness that, just like the church itself, is an object of faith.

The term applies more to God's acting than our own human qualities. In the Bible "holy," after all, always refers to what belongs to God—set apart from sin and the world and consecrated to his service.

According to the New Testament, the church owes its holiness to its election by God, to God's covenant with his people, to Christ's sacrifice, and the sanctifying ministry of the Holy Spirit (cf. 1 Peter 2:9–10; Eph. 5:25–27; Heb. 10:10; Eph. 2:20–21 and 1 Peter 1:2). There is a holy church in consequence of the work of the Triune God. The people of God are a holy people; the body of Christ is holy; and the temple of the Holy Spirit is holy.

In the language of faith, "holy" does not mean: of high moral standing or practically perfect. What matters is that everything in the church is placed in the perspective of service of God. The holy church is there to hallow his name.

Two views. Rome is very comfortable with the word "holy." According to conciliar pronouncements, there is in this church an unshakeable holiness, which is and ought to be manifested not only in the fruits of grace, which the Holy Spirit works in believers, but also in the striving for perfection in love and the observation of "evangeli-

42. K. Schilder, *Wat is de hemel?* (what is heaven?), 1954, 162.

cal counsels" (celibacy, voluntary poverty, and obedience; Dogmatic Constitution, 1964, no. 39). The latter is usually referred to as higher holiness. In addition there is the so-called heroic holiness of the martyrs and the charismatic holiness of those through whose intervention miracles take place. Of great importance is also that the church has its saints who are entitled to veneration. All of this is sustained by the objective holiness of the church. This holiness is manifested within the church especially through its sacraments.[43]

But is the church that speaks of itself in this manner beyond the reach of sin? The traditional approach to the problem of sin in the church is to distinguish between the sinless church and its sinful members (Schwintek, 1969, 32).

There is no biblical basis for such an abstract view of the church. The reality is different. Revelation 2–3 contain not only warnings for church members, but also reproaches addressed by Christ to the churches themselves.

Today the ascriptions of praise to the holiness of the church have ceased to sound equally loud everywhere. There are those who speak out against ecclesiastical triumphalism. Küng says: The real church is a sinful church. Its members are "called saints" and are not self-made saints (1967, 379, 385).

The Reformational confession statements call the church holy in a different way than Rome. It is "a holy congregation of true Christian believers . . . washed by his blood, sanctified and sealed by the Holy Spirit" (Belgic Confession of Faith, Article 27). This holy church is to be seen as a congregation of saints *(congregatio sanctorum)* or as a communion of saints *(communio sanctorum)*. Thus the saints do not constitute a separate category in the church, for in the New Testament sense of the word the saints are the believers. The holy church is the assembly of the believers and as such it has its faults. To the question whether the holiness ascribed to the church is already perfect, Calvin answers: "Not as long as she battles in this world, for elements of imperfection always remain and will never be entirely removed, until she is united completely to Jesus Christ her Head, by whom she is sanctified" (Geneva Catechism).

Gift and obligation. The church owes its salvation to Christ, who says in his high-priestly prayer: "For their sakes I sanctify myself, that they also might be sanctified through the truth" (John 17:19). Sanctification means being sanctified by the Spirit (2 Thess. 2:13). This is why in the Apostles' Creed the confession of the church, which is holy, follows upon the confession of the Holy Spirit.

The sanctification of the church of Christ becomes visible when it is in the world yet "not of the world" (John 17:14–17). Its Sender sends it into the world, but he keeps it from being swallowed up by the world.

We must guard against the secularization of the church. Then the boundaries between the church and the world become blurred.

43. Cf. Balduinus in *De Katholieke Kerk* (the Catholic Church), no date, 3:1038–93.

Some have argued that in the concrete situation of our world, which is God's world, the church—by speaking out or remaining silent—will contribute to the humanization of life and in doing so represent Christ. This is "conversion towards the world."[44] Frequently the argument made in support of this view is that the church can only make its message credible and effective if as the church it exists for the world and fights for a more humane and a more just society.[45]

But a church that becomes secularized surrenders its holiness. Its holiness is so essential that it then loses its identity.

With respect to the relationship between the church and the world, one should not forget what on the basis of the New Testament must be said about the calling of the church in the midst of its context and especially about the missionary significance of the sanctification of life. The place of the missionary element in the life of the church is, according to Van Swigchem, an essential element or a necessary aspect. "One can say that the *first missionary task* of the church consists herein that it shows those outside the church something of the redeeming and cleansing power of the Holy Spirit in its own life" (Van Swigchem, 1955, 106, cf. 242ff.).

Precisely in the holiness of the church and the sanctification of its members the world must see that the Lord has a people on earth that belongs to him. It points beyond itself, for it testifies to "the praises of him who hath called [it] out of darkness into his marvelous light" (1 Peter 2:9–10).

In addition to secularization we face a phenomenon that we could call *creeping legalism.*

As far as the first few centuries are concerned, we can think in this connection of the Donatists, who saw the priests and especially the bishops as the actual bearers of the holiness of the church.[46]

In the sixteenth century, the holiness of the church was a crucial issue for the Anabaptists. Calvin says of them that they left the lawful church because they were of the opinion that there was no church where life was completely pure and undefiled. The Reformer challenges their views extensively (*Institutes*, 4.1.13–18). He says: if we only wish to permit a church that is perfect in every respect, we would not be left with a single church. He points to the situation in the church at Corinth

44. J. C. Hoekendijk in "Die Welt (world) als Horizont," in *Evangelische Theologie* 25 (1965): 480; H. J. Schultz, *Konversion zur Welt*, 1964.

45. G. Gutierrez, *Theologie van de bevrijding* (liberation), 1974, 191ff.

46. Compare with E. Altendorf, *Einheit und Heiligkeit der Kirche* (the church's unity and holiness), 1932, 137–53.

and the churches of Galatia in Paul's time. A church such as the one in Corinth is to Paul, nevertheless, a church of Christ and a communion of saints. Calvin points out that the article of faith "I believe in the forgiveness of sins" is linked with the one dealing with the church.

Incidentally, not all of his arguments are equally strong. His appeal to the parable of the wheat and the tares is not valid because, according to Matthew 13:36–43, the field is the world, not the church.

Subsequently we encounter ecclesiological perfectionism among the Labadists. J. De Labadie (1610–74) lists thirty characteristics of the church that relate to the holiness of its members. The church must be judged according to the majority of its members, which makes it necessary to distinguish true believers from others.[47]

Writers such as W. à Brakel clearly defended the Reformed position over against this *(R.S.*, 2:60–64). It was a grievance of the Labadists that church discipline was not adequately maintained. There is indeed a connection between discipline and the holiness of the church, but it leads to rigorism if love is lacking.

Also as far as the holiness of the church is concerned, it must become what it is.

The church is holy, but not to the extent that it will be some day. Christ gave himself up for it in order to sanctify it. But the Lord is daily at work in cleansing its spots (Calvin, *Institutes*, 4.1.17). Christ wants to "present it to himself a glorious church, not having spot, or wrinkle, or any such thing; but that it should be holy and without blemish" (Eph. 5:27). The complete fulfillment of this Scripture passage still awaits us. The prospect of perfect holiness is for the church on its way to the future a strong motivation to live in a holy manner before the Lord.

In communion with Christ, the church is holy in order to become more and more so in obedience to him and to be one day perfectly holy through God's grace. The New Jerusalem, the church in its glorified manifestation, is the holy city where nothing impure will enter (cf. Rev. 21:2, 10, 27).

4. *The catholicity of the church*

a. *The concept.* The word catholic, of Greek origin, actually means "related to the whole, general, universal." It is the opposite of partial and separate.

In the New Testament the church is not yet called catholic; but as early as the second century it is. The catholic church at Smyrna is not so much the universal, but rather

47. Compare with G. Oorthuys, *Kruispunten op den weg der kerk* (intersections along the way of the church), no date, 110–17.

the true church, which is linked with the other churches of Christ. The term "catholic" distinguished the church of Christ from schismatics, heretics, and apostate Christians. Augustine, above all in his opposition to the Donatists, placed renewed emphasis on catholicity in the sense of universal. Cyril of Jerusalem (d. 386) already pointed out that the catholicity of the church has several aspects (Berkhof, 1962, 13).

It is important to know everything that the church must uphold to be catholic. Does it refer to the entire geographical world or the members of the entire church in all their diversity? Is it the entire doctrine in which the church must instruct everyone, or all of salvation that is received within the church? In summary we can say that initially it meant the true church, which is simultaneously the universal church, or the universal church that is at the same time the true church.

It is noteworthy that the usual Reformational rendition of the term "catholic" in the Apostles' Creed is: I believe in one (holy) universal, Christian church. "Universal" is too general a rendering of "catholic," for it ignores that catholicity pertains to the entire truth and fullness of salvation. The words "universal" and "Christian" both translate the original term "catholic." Luther was not fond of the word "catholic" and substituted "Christian." This is, however, not a satisfactory rendition of "catholic." Although the term "Christian" was retained, "universal" was usually added. Therefore "universal Christian church" contains a double translation of "catholic." In the text of *De Nederlandse belijdenisgeschriften* (the Netherlands confession statements, 1983), the original term was restored.

During the time of the Reformation the focus was clearly on universality as is apparent from Article 27 of the Belgic Confession of Faith as well as Lord's Day 21 of the Heidelberg Catechism. It is the church that includes all true believers, the church of all times and places.

If the catholic church is the universal church, it would seem that the Roman Catholic Church is in the best position to lay claim to this name (catholic is usually taken to mean Roman Catholic). Dogmatic works state that the church is called catholic especially in recognition of its spatial universality, i.e., in recognition of its spread around the entire globe (cf. Ott, *Grundriss* = outline, 369).

However, there are theologians who consider it to be unspiritual to make the catholicity of the church dependent on numbers. Küng poses the question: how does it benefit a church to be the most dispersed, if in the process it has become unfaithful to its own essence? Catholic is not primarily a static or historical concept. Catholicity means that the church remains essentially the same through all times and in all of its manifestations (1967, 358ff.; cf. Barth, *C.D.*, 4.1.701–12).

Y. Congar's views on catholicity have been especially influential. According to him, fullness and completeness are of key importance. Catholicity is then not understood in a quantitative but in a qualitative sense. The church must assimilate the contributions of nations and cultures, and above all Christian values, including those of Luther and Calvin, which in their case were developed one-sidedly. The Roman Catholic Church has retained its catholicity more so than other churches; even it is not yet fully catholic. This is why more openness is required on its part. There may and must be theological pluralism *(M. S.*, 4.1.494–501). *De nieuwe katechismus* (new catechism) says: "It is not only grievous to see that the Reformation has missed the truth of the catholic church. The latter also shows evidence of having missed the truths of the Reformation." There must therefore be a growing together toward a new catholic, i.e., universal church.[48]

b. *The biblical foundation of catholicity.* The catholicity of the church presupposes the catholicity of the Christian religion. Christianity is universal: There are no boundaries other than those determined by God in his good pleasure. No boundaries of gender or age, social standing or rank, nationality or language! John 3:16 and numerous other Scripture passages speak of this universalism. "A gospel so rich also creates a people of God that no longer can be contained within the boundaries of a nation or a country." The church has a message that is intended for "all nations" (Matt. 28:19). The catholicity of the church becomes visible in the dispensation of Pentecost (see Acts 2:11, 17, 21, 39; 10–11), but is already soon put to the test. Paul comes into conflict with Jewish exclusivism. The Judaist party gains entry in certain places. The apostle sees what is at stake. The issue is the catholicity of the church, freedom in Christ, the universal value of the cross of Christ, the riches of grace, justification by faith alone. Through the unanimous decision of the apostles (Acts 15) the unity and catholicity of the church is secured. It is not surprising that catholicity is emphatically taught especially in the epistles of Paul (see 1 Cor. 12:13; Gal. 3:28; Eph. 2:14–16; Col. 3:11). See in this connection Bavinck, 1968^2, 1–11.

In more recent theology the qualitative aspect of catholicity is more strongly emphasized than earlier. It is important that catholicity be christologically founded. Like others, Berkhof takes in this connection the Pauline notion of fullness and fulfillment as his starting point (1962, 44–68). In Christ there is fullness (*pleroma*). Berkhof interprets the word *pleroma* in Ephesians 1:23 as domain: the church is the domain of him who dominates all things. The church must "be filled with all the fullness of God" (Eph. 3:19). We read in Ephesians 4:13–15 how the apostle envisions this: by growing in truth and love toward Christ who is the Head of his church (Eph. 4:13–15).

c. *The Reformational view.* Like the unity and holiness of the church, the catholicity of the church is both a gift and an obligation. The church is catholic through the work of Christ, who by his Spirit and his Word gathers for himself a church that is elected to eternal life. He gathers

48. *De nieuwe katechismus*, 1966, 382ff.

it from the beginning of the world to the end, and from among the entire human race—which is the quantitative aspect. He gathers it in the unity of the true faith—which is the qualitative aspect (Heidelberg Catechism, Lord's Day 21). Universality and truth go hand in hand here. We find the same two aspects of catholicity in Calvin's description (*Institutes*, 4.1.9): "The church universal *(ecclesia universalis)* is a multitude gathered from all nations; it is divided and dispersed in separate places, agrees on the one truth of divine doctrine, and is bound together by the bond of the same religion."

We object to the Roman Catholic view of catholicity. Here the church is legalistically tied down to specific places, personalities, and institutions (Rome as the ecclesiastical center, the pope, the hierarchy), which is contrary to Scripture. From this perspective this church has no right to the name "catholic." Bavinck says that the name "Roman" or "papal" church expresses its essence much better than "catholic" *(R.D.*, 4:323). We do not surrender the name "catholic," but we are Reformationally catholic.[49] To us this also means that we do not canonize our ecclesiastical regulations.

Besides the Roman view we also reject the sectarian view. Bavinck also warns against various sectarian phenomena (1968, 35–40). In ecclesiastical life there are sometimes sectarian tendencies, against which we must be on our guard. In addition, sects have considerable appeal. Characteristics of sects include absolutization of one's own point of view and isolation. A sect or a group keeps to itself. It has been said of sects: "From their perspective, God's truth, following a brief flaring up at the time of Christ, does not reemerge until their own sect is born."[50]

Being catholic implies that we want to live out of the fullness that is given in Christ, and want to grow toward his fullness, together with all the saints (Eph. 3:14–19). This also means that we fight against one-sidedness of any kind, and strive for multi-sidedness.

When we confess the catholicity of the gospel of Christ, we may not lock ourselves up within our own circle and shut ourselves off from others. We may not exclude churches and Christians whom he does not exclude, but neither may we include those whom he does not include. There are boundaries set by Christ. The church is not a domain where everything goes that people devise.

49. See J. Riemens, *Reformatorisch-Katholiek of (or) Rooms-Katholiek?* 1948.
50. K. Hutten, *Geloof en sekte* (faith and sects), no date, 96.

From this it follows that catholicity may not be replaced by a new concept such as ecumenicity. Catholic and ecumenical cannot be equated. Berkhof says: "Horizontal ecumenicity is born of vertical catholicity." It is indeed tempting, but not right to try to glue together the fragments of ecclesiastical unity with the help of a series of acceptable compromises. Berkhof adds that the thesis that ecumenicity is the goal and fruit of catholicity should also be reversed. Catholicity must also be the goal and fruit of ecumenicity (1962, 110). As long as one keeps in mind which catholicity is involved! See what is said above about "the biblical foundation of catholicity."

We confess the catholicity of the church not only with a view to what constitutes the church from God's perspective, of which Calvin says that there cannot be two or three, but also with a view to the church as we see it. What matters is that the church of which we are members is linked with the entire church, wherever the Lord gathers it.

This catholicity also implies that there may not be any discrimination within the church. It is open to all people who confess the true faith. Differences in culture, race or nationality, position or mentality are of no decisive significance to the church. They constitute no hindrance to the communion of the saints, because they constitute no hindrance to communion with Christ.

The catholicity of the church is visible, but we see far from all of it yet. It also remains continually threatened, so that it is important to watch and pray that God may grant to his church that also in this respect it may become more and more what it is.

Catholicity also has an eschatological perspective. "With its catholic stake in the consummation, the church points beyond itself to the future of the Kingdom" (Beker/Hasselaar, *Wegen* = ways 5:116). This fullness, for which it longs, will be granted to it. We are moving toward one, holy, catholic, and apostolic church of the future. It will be "a great multitude, which no man [can] number, of all nations, and kindreds, and people, and tongues [standing] before the throne [of God] and before the Lamb" (Rev. 7:9).

5. *The apostolicity of the church*

a. *The apostolic foundation.* We usually mention apostolicity last, but not because it is the least important attribute of the church. Apostolicity is so indispensable that whatever else is said about the church, it loses its value in the absence of apostolicity.

The church is called apostolic because it has a special relationship with the apostles and their work. It is defined by the work of the apostles, so that it bears and must continue to bear the imprint of this.

According to Scripture there is a direct connection between the church and the apostles. See Matthew 16:18; Ephesians 2:20; and Revelation 21:14. The apostles occupy a unique place, which rests on the fact that they were ear- and eyewitnesses of what God did in Christ. They were witnesses of the redemption facts. They testified with great power to the resurrection of the Lord Jesus (Acts 4:33; 10:39–42).

An apostle is actually an envoy. The Jews were familiar with the figure of the *shaliach*, the plenipotentiary, who represented his sender or charge giver. The word of the envoy counted as the word of him on whose behalf he spoke. Jesus says of his envoys: "He that receiveth whomsoever I send receiveth me" (John 13:20).

The apostles are not only authorized to be his representatives but they are also enabled to carry out their assignment, because they are guided in a special way by the Holy Spirit. This was promised by Jesus (John 15:26–27; Acts. 1:8).

The apostles laid the foundation of the church. This work was done once and for all. It is unnecessary and impossible to repeat it. It is for this reason that the apostles did not appoint successors.

The church in Jerusalem was not apostolic because it had the apostles in its midst, but because it "continued steadfastly in the apostles' doctrine" (Acts 2:42). The apostolic teaching is the gospel as the apostles proclaimed it in the name of Christ. This was laid down for the church of all time in the apostolic writings, which were accepted as canonical.

The canon expresses for all time the significance of the apostles, with their preaching of Jesus as the Christ and as the Son of God, for the entire church. The church must hold on to this (H. N. Ridderbos in *De apostolische kerk*, 1954, 81). The church must adhere to this. It is for this reason that the apostle Paul says to Timothy: "The things that thou hast heard of me among many witnesses, the same commit thou to faithful men who shall be able to teach others also" (2 Tim. 2:2; cf. 1 Tim. 6:20).

It equally belongs to the task of the apostles to indicate the boundaries between truth and error (Gal. 1:6–9; 1 John 4:1–3). The church can only be the apostolic church if it takes to heart the apostolic admonitions and does not deviate from the truth (cf. A. D. R. Polman in *De apostolische kerk*, 1954, 177–82).

Moreover, the apostles were assigned not only foundational but also constructive work. Besides the apostles, others were provided "for the perfecting of the saints, for the work of the ministry, for the edifying of the body of Christ" (Eph. 4:11–12). Therefore, in this respect the apostles did not stand alone. The work of edifying the church was continued after their deaths by others who were called to this task. They built on the foundation that had already been laid.

b. *Apostolic succession or apostolic doctrine?* Early on there were those in the church who declared: We are the heirs of the apostles. We are the church of the apostles. This reflected the struggle against heresy. The church appealed to its apostolic origin and to the tradition of the apostles that it had preserved. Besides the canon and the rule of faith or rule of truth (a concise summary of the Christian faith, whose formulation was not always the same), there was yet another factor that was considered to be important: the apostolic succession as an unbroken sequence of bishops that went back to the apostles, to which heretics and schismatics could not lay claim, but only the catholic church. This succession (*successio*) involved the laying on of hands. Since the bishops, especially the bishop of Rome, were considered to be successors of the apostles, the church felt secure that it was following in the footsteps of the apostles. This idea surfaced as early as AD 200 (Irenaeus, Tertullian).

What initially was an ancillary line subsequently became the main line. The development of the doctrine of apostolic succession led to the bishop of Rome acquiring primacy. He was viewed as Peter's successor, and his episcopal see came to be called the apostolic see.

Pope Pius IX declared in 1864 that the true church of Christ is characterized by unity, holiness, catholicity, and apostolic succession. Although according to Rome the apostolicity of the church indeed involves more than this, a great deal appears to revolve around apostolic succession.

The apostolic church and the unadulterated apostolic doctrine is found where Peter and his successors are (Ott, *Grundriss*, 372). Thus a legitimate succession of bishops in Rome would guarantee that everything is well with the teaching of the church. Legitimacy and purity coincide, but legitimacy is primary.[51] This implies that it is not the word of the apostles, Holy Scripture, that decides which church is apostolic. Instead, the church, by virtue of an uninterrupted succession of bishops going back to the apostles, decides what is apostolic, what constitutes the doctrine of the apostles (Bavinck, *R.D.*, 4:238). The church is where the pope is. This is where the truth is and this is where salvation is found.

Bavinck offers an extensive refutation of the main theses associated with Rome's position, namely, that there is an apostolic succession on which the church in essence depends, and that the pope is Peter's successor *(R.D.*, 4:344–68). In this connection he makes the incisive comment: "Eternity hangs here on a cobweb."

According to our view of apostolicity, whereby Scripture is the norm for the church, precisely the church that appeals to the apostolic succession has increasingly abandoned the teaching of the apostles. It came to appeal to the authority of the bishops, the pope, and councils. Instead it should have tested all of its pronouncements against the testimony of the apostles.

According to the Reformational view, the church is not dependent on bishops or the pope. It depends on whether the Word of God is

51. G. C. Berkouwer, *De strijd om het Roomsch-Katholieke dogma*, no date, 163.

proclaimed and believed. "The church is where the Word is" (Luther, *WA*, 39.2.176). This is why the Belgic Confession of Faith states, "In short, [the church is true] if all things are managed according to the pure Word of God, all things contrary thereto rejected, and Jesus Christ acknowledged as the only Head of the Church" (Article 29). As we saw, what matters is that we "continue . . . steadfastly in the apostles' doctrine" (Acts 2:42).

The doctrine summarized in the confession is so important for the life of the church because the church can only then be apostolic if it adheres to the teaching of the apostles. One of the ancient confession statements is known as the Apostles' Creed. This is the name of the creed, which we can continue to use although we know that the apostles did not draw it up. Not only do its origins go back to shortly after the time of the apostles, but its articles of faith are entirely in harmony with the teaching of the apostles.

In our time there are frequent requests for a reformulation of the Christian faith. The pros and cons of these proposals continue to be discussed (cf. in this connection Berkouwer, *The Church*, 1976, 278–309). The question is whether Berkouwer sufficiently appreciates the danger that contemporariness and acceptability might win out over continuity. All confessional statements of the apostolic church will have to show clearly that it cleaves to the gospel as proclaimed by the apostles and that it rejects everything that deviates from this.

Although the apostolic foundation has been laid and the church has been built on it, this "spiritual house" remains incomplete (cf. 1 Peter 2:5). The faithful work that has been carried out calls for continuation in the same spirit. There is no continuity of the church without the preservation of its apostolicity!

In the perspective of the book of Revelation we see how the apostolic church moves toward perfection. On the twelve foundations of the walls of the New Jerusalem are inscribed "the names of the twelve apostles of the Lamb" (Rev. 21:14).

c. *Apostolicity and Apostolate.* The term "apostolate" refers not only to the office of the apostles but, since the middle of the twentieth century, also to the church's mission in the world. A theology of the apostolate emerged, with which names such as H. Kraemer, A. A. van Ruler, J. C. Hoekendijk, and F. J. Pop may be associated.

This development reflects acceptance of the notion that the church exists for the world. According to Van Ruler, the apostolate is not a function but the essence of the church. In contrast with Hoekendijk, he holds on to an office-based form of the apostolate.[52] In the church order of the Netherlands Reformed Church (NHK) (1951), the apostolate precedes the confession of the church, partly because of the appeal of the theology of the apostolate.

According to F. J. Pop, longtime director of the institute *Kerk en Wereld* (church and world) in Driebergen, the Netherlands, the modern apostolate distinguishes itself from earlier evangelism in that what now comes first is that the church must show its involvement in Christ's apostolate in its external attitude and service provision. This does include the spoken word, but the sequence is telling.[53]

One can indeed appreciate the missionary zeal and readiness to respond to the current situation of the world. The apostolic or rather missionary activities, however, may not proceed at the expense of the apostolicity of the church.

The essence of the church lies in what it is as a "congregation . . . of believers" (Belgic Confession of Faith, Article 27), or in the words of the Bible, in its existence as the people of God, the body of Christ, and the temple of the Holy Spirit (see § 46.2).

The church today has no other message for the world than it had in the era of the apostles. It was expressed for all time in Matthew 28:19!

46.5. *The marks of the church*

1. *The focus here is on the marks of the true church.* An important reason for assigning a separate place in ecclesiology to the characteristics of the church is the consideration that we must know not only what the church is, but also where it may be found.

We are called to join the church (cf. Belgic Confession of Faith, Article 28), and must therefore, very carefully and with great wisdom, on the basis of God's Word, discern what the true church is (Article 29). This question, which had emerged much earlier in connection with the distinction between the church and various seceded groups, became burningly relevant in the sixteenth century, because the Roman

52. A. A. van Ruler, *Theologie van het apostolaat*, no date, 20, 40.
53. F. J. Pop, *Traditioneel en modern apostolaat*, no date, 41ff.

Catholic Church and the churches of the Reformation disputed each other's right to call themselves the church.

R. Bellarmine thought that with the help of fifteen characteristics he could prove that the Roman Catholic Church is the true church; someone else came up with as many as one hundred characteristics![54] Roman Catholicism usually views the four *attributes* of the church as its characteristics. This church would then be alone in having all of these.

However, the churches of the Reformation did not allow themselves to be denied unity, holiness, catholicity, and apostolicity. For this reason, Roman Catholic theology increasingly emphasized the connection with Rome. According to Pius IX, unity means the unity of which the primacy of Peter and his successors is the principle, the root, and the origin. The essence of apostolicity is apostolic succession (*DS*, no. 2888). The church is Roman. This became the dominant characteristic.[55]

For us, the marks of the true church are: 1. pure preaching of the gospel; 2. pure administration of the sacraments; 3. the exercise of ecclesiastical discipline (Belgic Confession of Faith, Article 29).

The image that is next given of the false church is the exact opposite of that of the true church. It also has characteristics whereby it can be recognized: It ascribes more authority to itself and its ordinances than to God's Word; it does not administer the sacraments as Christ commanded in his Word; it persecutes those who live in a holy manner according to God's Word (cf. J. van Genderen in *De Kerk*, 1990, 289ff.).

The marks of the church have a critical function: on the positive side they show us which church is really the church of Christ; on the negative side, they also make clear which church is not.

In subsequent Reformed theology, the contrast between the true and the false church recedes into the background and the distinction between pure and less pure churches comes in its place. The characteristics of the true church (*ecclesia vera)* become characteristics of the pure church (*ecclesia pura*), and within purity there are yet again gradations (cf. *Synopsis*, 40:37–51).

According to the Westminster Confession (chapter 25), "the purest churches under heaven are subject both to mixture and error; and some have so degenerated, as to become no churches of Christ, but synagogues of Satan."

With a growing number of ecclesiastical fellowships emerging side by side, it appeared increasingly difficult to employ the distinction between the true and false

54. Cf. G. Thils, *Les notes de l'église* (characteristics of the church), 1937, 106–8.
55. U. Valeske, *Votum ecclesiae*, 1962, 101.

church, and sects. The concept of the true church could evoke the notion that there is but one true church. Was the ecclesiastical situation not becoming too complicated to apply it? The opposite of truth is untruth or apparent truth. One could not speak of a church being less true or a church being still less true, but indeed of a church that is pure, less pure, and still less pure; the danger being that the doctrine of the church would be adapted to observed reality, which encourages relativism.

Our confession makes clear that to those who let themselves be guided by the Word of God it will not remain obscure whether we are dealing with the true church or not. Moreover, it is not incorrect to speak of churches that are more or less pure within the parameters of the true church, because not all churches are equally faithful to the Word of God. This is apparent from a comparison of the letters to the seven churches (Rev. 2 and 3).

It is not enough to be a member of the true church, for it is also important to be a true member, i.e., "a living member" of this church (Heidelberg Catechism, Lord's Day 21). These two aspects must not be separated. By having eyes only for the true church as an institution, one paves the way for churchism. By thinking only in terms of true believers and allowing the church to drop out of sight and out of mind, one opens the door to conventicles.[56]

Among the marks of Christians, faith heads the list (Belgic Confession of Faith, Article 29). The lives of believers are described here in terms of their "fight against" sin, and the emphasis is on their "taking their refuge in the blood, death, passion, and obedience of our Lord Jesus Christ."

The marks of the church are not dependent on the marks of Christians. Anabaptists and Labadists saw this differently. Brakel weakened his position over against Labadists when he made the holiness of its church members a characteristic of the church and even assigned it second place following true doctrine corresponding to the Word of God (*R.S.*, 2:34ff.).

The Reformational doctrine of the marks of the church is based on Scripture references such as John 10:27 that are frequently cited in this context. Jesus says: "My sheep hear my voice, and I know them, and they follow me." This clearly expresses that the church is ruled by Christ alone. This is crucial in the pure ministry of the Word, the sacraments, and church discipline.

As pointed out, the marks play a critical role. Among the attributes of the church especially its apostolicity—as understood in the Reformational sense—points in this direction. If a church is based on the

56. Cf. W. van 't Spijker, *De kerk bij Hendrik de Cock*, 1985, 34.

apostolic foundation, this will be manifested in pure preaching of the gospel and everything connected with it.

The marks of the church are not always presented in exactly the same way. According to Luther, the church actually has a single mark: the Word. The extended series of marks that he enumerates at times does not contradict this, for everything he mentions is subordinate to the Word.

Calvin explains that the pure ministry of the Word and pure administration of the sacraments are a pledge and token that a fellowship in which both of these marks are present may safely be regarded as a true church. So long as these remain, the church may never be rejected, even if it otherwise swarms with many faults (*Institutes*, 4.1.12). He does not mention ecclesiastical discipline here, although he deems it very necessary.[57]

The Belgic Confession of Faith sums up the three marks of Article 29 in this one decisive mark: "in short, [the church is true] if all things are managed according to the pure Word of God, all things contrary thereto rejected, and Jesus Christ acknowledged as the only Head of the Church."

The church is subordinate to the Word of God. This conviction is common to the Reformation. Scripture has credibility within itself, but one may not ascribe such *autopistos* to the church.

In Rome's view the church is not subordinate to the Word, and one may not require it to justify itself over against the Word of God. Its legitimacy lies in its existence as the one, holy, catholic, and apostolic church, in its imperishability and infallibility. These attributes possess a demonstrative power both internally and externally. With this, Rome manifests itself as *the* church.

2. *Some illustrations*

a. The three confessional marks are essential for the church of Christ. This is why they could play an important role in the Netherlands in the *Afscheiding* (secession from the Netherlands Reformed Church, 1834) as well as the *Vrijmaking* (liberation, secession from the *Gereformeerde Kerk*, 1944).

b. One can also make improper use of these characteristics. One may not deduce from them that true believers can only be found where the true church gathers. This

57. See J. Plomp, *De kerkelijke tucht* (church discipline) *bij Calvijn*, 1969, 122–28.

was advocated by J. Hoorn: "And therefore: within the assembly of believers all salvation and outside the assembly no salvation whatsoever."[58] The Synod of the *Gereformeerde Kerken in Nederland*, which had to rule on this view, stated that this detracted unacceptably from the scope of Christ's work and from God's mercy in gathering the church.[59]

With respect to the much-discussed passage (Belgic Confession of Faith, Article 28)—that "outside of it" ("this holy congregation" and "assembly") "there is no salvation"—its background should not be forgotten. There is not the least intention to replace the mother church in which all salvation is found by a Reformational church in which all salvation is found. Salvation does not depend on the church. Why then this strong statement? On the part of a number of humanists, but also Zwingli, the notion had arisen that there is indeed salvation apart from faith in Christ. Socrates and Cicero were thought to have attained it. The Scottish Confession (1560) emphatically rejects the view that one can receive salvation apart from faith (Article16).

Since the idea of an implicit or anonymous Christianity, a latent church, or a church outside the church appears attractive to many, it is necessary to keep pointing to the meaning of what the confession says. Apart from the church as the body of Christ, to which we can only belong if we are joined to him in faith, there is not only no salvation to be expected, and there is not only no salvation as a rule, but there is absolutely no salvation (French text of Article 28: "Il n'y a point de salut" = there is definitely no salvation).[60]

c. The marks of the true church may not be surrendered in favor of the notion of *traces of the church* that has gained currency in the Word Council of Churches since the Toronto Declaration (1950). Traces or elements of the true church that can be recognized in other churches, and that are signs pointing to true unity, are the preaching of the Word, instruction in Holy Scripture, and the administration of the sacraments. Church discipline is not mentioned.

We miss here the normative element that finds expression in the Belgic Confession of Faith. Berkouwer can appreciate the fact that in our time one speaks more positively of traces of the church than earlier (*The Church*, 1976, 64–71). But are certain traces of the church (Calvin thought, in the first place, of baptism) grounds for the optimism of the Toronto Declaration?[61]

We cannot agree with attempts to modernize the doctrine of the marks of the church just because both the world and the church change.[62]

58. J. Hoorn, *Een enige kerk de troost van de ware gelovingen* (a single church, the comfort of true believers), 1984, 31.

59. *Acta van de Generale Synode van de Gereformeerde Kerken in Nederland Heemse 1984–1985*, 1, Article 131.

60. Cf. J. van Genderen, *De ware* (true) *kerk*, 1957, 19ff.

61. See J. Faber, *Vestigium ecclesiae*, 1967, 9–13:185, 192ff.

62. See J. Dantine, *Die Kirche vor der Frage nach ihrer Wahrheit* (the church confronted with the question as to its truth), 1980, 129–58 (the church must be there for others and bear social and political responsibility).

d. The danger exists that the characteristics of the true church are employed merely to ascertain whether what is elsewhere presented as a church, is indeed the church of Christ. These characteristics must be applied outwardly as well as inwardly. Is our church in the true sense of the word the church of Christ, and is this manifested in the life of the church and in church relationships?

The true church can become unfaithful and, via a process of degeneration, change into a false church. A church that must be considered a false church can by God's grace nevertheless still come to repentance and reformation.

When a church meets the characteristics of the true church, by this alone already it says to Christians who remain outside its fellowship: do not keep yourself aloof any longer! At the same time, it says to the members of this church that they may not break with it: "All those who separate themselves from the same or do not join themselves to it act contrary to the ordinance of God" (Belgic Confession of Faith, Article 28).

Viewed ecclesiastically as well as personally, nationally as well as internationally, the characteristics of the church are to us signs of recognition.

§ 47. Church governance

47.1. *The office-based ministry*

1. *The basic principle*

When it comes to church governance, the will of Christ is decisive, for he is the Head of his church. The church is not an association that draws up statutes and bylaws and elects an executive committee. The church is not a democracy but a Christocracy.

The order and rules in the life of the church must give expression to the fact that the church is the church of Christ, where, not people, but only he has the final authority. Therefore Calvin begins the chapter of the *Institutes* that deals with the office bearers and their work (4.3.1) with the sentence: "Now we must speak of the order by which the Lord wills his church to be governed." To the Belgic Confession of Faith, it is a matter of faith that the "true church must be governed by that spiritual polity which our Lord has taught us in his Word" (Article 30).

One has indeed sometimes viewed this as a legalistic notion, whereby the Bible is turned into a body of law for church governance. This is an unfair criticism, for how could we otherwise know what the Lord's will is with regard to the governing of his church than by listening to his Word? Nor must we forget that according to the title and the intent of Book 4 of the *Institutes*, communion with Christ is of primary concern. It is in this light that the church and its order are discussed. Knowing Christ is the main focus of the gospel, as Bullinger and Calvin say in a joint confession statement. There is therefore no doubt that the object of the whole spiritual government of the church is to lead us to Christ (*Consensus Tigurinus*, Article 1).

Spiritual order, in the context of our confession, is most closely connected with fundamental statements about Jesus Christ as "the only universal Bishop and the only Head of the Church," "Christ, our only Master" (Article 31–32).

The scriptural foundation of the Reformed theology of church governance is found in Acts 20:28; 1 Corinthians 12–14; and especially Ephesians 4:11–12. Paul's epistles provide numerous guidelines, which are of abiding significance for the organizational upbuilding of the church (cf. Ridderbos, *Paul*, 480). Not in the least we have in mind the Pastoral Epistles, in which several practical directions are to be found. "These were written at the end of Paul's life and contain various instructions which in view of the falling away of the apostolate are of the greatest significance for the church's development over the centuries" (Polman; Belgic Confession of Faith, 4.32). It has been correctly pointed out that in Paul's epistles to Timothy and Titus, compared with his other epistles, the personal and situational elements recede more into the background and that a pattern of stabilized precepts and ordinances develops (Ridderbos, *Paul*, 469).

We therefore disagree with Berkhof, who is of the view that the New Testament does not in the least present a uniform picture with respect to the church's offices, and who wants to interpret their variety as an invitation to give shape to the structure of such offices in our own situation in our own fashion (*C.F.*, 384). Given the amount of leeway implicit in the terms "invitation," "our own situation," and "our own fashion," one can then permit oneself to take a great measure of freedom![63]

The order or manner of governance that applies to the church is called spiritual. After all, Christ rules his church through his Spirit and his Word.

He thereby employs the services of people, whom he engages by calling them and granting them the corresponding gifts through his

63. One can find a comparable statement in the study report of the Synod of the Netherlands Reformed Church (NHK) titled, *Wat is er aan de hand met het ambt?* (what is going on with the office?), 1970, 32.

Spirit. Calvin says: "Although God can accomplish the work without us, he engages us, puny people, as helpers and makes use of us as instruments" (commentary on 1 Cor. 3:9). In the old Form for the Ordination of Elders and Deacons, they are called "men who are of good testimony, endowed with [God's] Spirit." The congregation must "receive [them] as the servants of God" and honor them on account of their offices.

The characteristic New Testament word for the work that is done in the church of Christ is "service" *(diakonia)*. They who perform this service are ministers (*diakonoi*). Our word "deacon" is derived from this. But the biblical term is a designation of many other servants of Christ: the apostle Paul belonged to them (2 Cor. 11:23), as did certain ministers to the saints at Philippi, who must be distinguished from the overseers (Phil. 1:1; cf. 1 Tim. 3:8). There are not only male but also female *diakonoi* (Rom. 16:1–2). In the church, it is expected that everyone will serve others with the gifts of grace bestowed by the Lord (1 Peter 4:10).

This implies that the special work to which the Lord calls people bears the character of ministry, but that not every ministry points to a specific office.

The thesis that there are offices in the church only because developments led to the desire to give firmer shape to certain ministries does not rest on biblical grounds. Scripture says that God appointed certain people in the church. The first of those who are then mentioned are the apostles (1 Cor. 12:28). Christ gave apostles, prophets, pastors, and teachers (Eph. 4:11). The Holy Spirit appointed overseers over the entire church (Acts 20:28). We can say with Van Ruler that the special office originates in actions and gifts of the triune God. "He *uses* also the offices and the office bearers in the work that he himself performs on earth in the hearts and lives of people" (1965, 89ff.).

We are not dealing here only with ministries for which people have received gifts. These are ministries to which people are called by the Lord. In the church we indicate this with the word "office" or, if we wish to speak with two or three words, with "office-based ministry."

In the literature, the following question is raised: *is the office from above or from below?* The answer must be that it is from above. It is not an institution of the church itself. The office bearers do come from within the church, which fully participates in their election, but they are called to step forward from among the ranks of the members of the church.

The roots of the office can be found in the work of Christ, who is "the Chief Shepherd" of the church (1 Peter 5:4). The essence of his work in office is ministry, and in this regard he is "faithful to him that appointed him" (Heb. 3:2). The fact that he came to serve is decisive for the entire office-based ministry in the churches. In going to the uttermost in his ministering love he gave himself as an example (see the context of Jesus' words about the Son of Man coming to serve in Matt. 20:28).

Ministering in the biblical sense of the word, i.e., giving ourselves entirely out of love, we can only learn from him. Those who are chosen to be office bearers are asked whether they will discharge their offices out of love for Christ and his church.[64]

Jesus said to the apostles, "He that heareth you heareth me" (Luke 10:16). He lets himself be represented by them. They are "ambassadors for Christ" and come to the church in his name (2 Cor. 5:20). This places high demands on those who represent Christ. They speak and act in his name only when they fulfill his commission, and their word has authority only when it is in harmony with his Word.

The office bearer derives a certain authority from the commission that he has received. Those who act in the church in an office-based capacity cannot do so under appeal to their own authority, but come as Christ's ambassadors with the authority of the Word of God (cf. Hendriks, 1990, 102ff., 109–14).

The office bearers must be convinced of this so as to let it govern all their actions, but the congregation no less so. It is also important that this authority be accepted. Authority only functions well when it is accepted. This does not become merely functional authority, for as office-based authority it does not have its origin in acceptance or acknowledgment.

Van Ruler uses an image to clarify these relationships. As in a triangle, we must draw "three straight lines: a line from Christ to the church; a line from Christ to the office; and a bidirectional line from the office to the church and from the church to the office.[65]

64. This promise is asked of office bearers in the *Christelijke Gereformeerde Kerken in Nederland* in the Form for Ordination adopted in 1968–69. This form also states that office bearers should look to him who came to minister and who set an example in this by foot washing.

65. A. A. van Ruler, *Bijzonder en algemeen ambt* (special and general ecclesiastical office), 1952, 61.

For a summary of the characteristics of the office we follow Van Itterzon (1974, 55–57):

1. No one can ever simply take up an office on his own.
2. One is appointed to office and receives thereby a commission.
3. The office must project a ministering character, whereby the idea of lording it over others is entirely objectionable.
4. The office has a certain authority precisely in seeking to serve the church.
5. The office has a permanent character within the context of the church.

Among the many writings in which a different view is advocated is that of Dingemans, *Een huis om in te wonen (*a house to dwell in, 1987), in which he is concerned with the form and structure of the church of the future. The title of his response to a number of reactions is a plea for an open church.

Here the "office" is from below. It originates in the church and is a formalized function. There is no room for office bearers who represent Christ. The question is raised whether in this way a power structure is perpetuated! The communal process of communication around the Bible and tradition must determine the form and structure of the church. In this community the office does not have the dominant voice, but "the various voices from the Bible, tradition, and the individual experience of members of the church—each with their own weight—come together" (Dingemans, 1987, 120–28; idem in *De kerk verbouwen* = rebuilding the church, 1989, 178ff.).

The ideas of those who are searching for new forms and structures frequently show affinity with those of E. Brunner, whose book *Das Missverständnis der Kirche* (the misunderstanding of the church, 1951) has an eloquent title. It would, according to him, be in the spirit of the New Testament if the church as a community of brothers and sisters replaced the church as institute with its sacraments and offices (cf. also Brunner, *Dogmatics*, 3:85, 126ff.).

When office bearers serve in accordance with Christ's commission and do not rule, the members of the congregation are not treated as minors. A Reformed church order contains rules to prevent this, and church polity devotes the necessary attention to it. An important datum is the election of office bearers by the congregation, which expresses in whom it discerns the gifts that are required for office. Van Ruler rightly points out that the congregation continuously surrounds the office: with its intercession, with its criticism, with its cooperation, and with its activities, which must be regulated and channeled by the office. The offices are permanently constitutive, for it remains their task to equip the church for ministry till the end of time (1965, 101ff.).

2. *New Testament data*

a. *The apostles as office bearers*. When the apostolicity of the church was discussed (§ 46.4, subsection 5) something was already said about the apostles and their office. The apostolic church is the church that "continue[s] steadfastly in the apostles' doctrine" (Acts 2:42).

The apostles or the Twelve are in the New Testament a category *sui generis* (cf. Acts 6:2; 1 Cor. 15:5), although others are sometimes also called apostles. We have in mind "the messengers of the churches" (2 Cor. 8:23). The twelve apostles have a unique place in the church:

1. They are called by Christ himself, which also applies to Paul (1 Cor. 15:8–9).
2. They are witnesses of the words and deeds of Christ (John 15:27) and have to be specifically witnesses of the resurrection (Acts 1:21–22). Paul too is able to say that he has seen him (1 Cor. 9:1).
3. The apostles are promised the Holy Spirit to guide them into all the truth (John 16:13). This promise is in the first instance meant for them, although it has broader implications.
4. The apostles represent their Sender and can speak and act in his name (Luke 10:16; John 13:20).
5. The church is bound to the testimony of the apostles. The word proclaimed by them must be kept "in memory" (1 Cor. 15:2). The apostles have an authority that surpasses all human authority. This is why Paul can speak words of eternal weight (see Gal. 1:6–10).
6. The apostolic office does not only have significance for a certain century and for certain churches, but for the church of all places and all times.

In addition to laying its foundation, the apostles also build up the church. Not only do they themselves build on this foundation once laid, but others do as well. Paul says: "As a wise masterbuilder, I have laid the foundation, and another buildeth thereon. But let every man take heed how he buildeth thereupon. For other foundation can no man lay than that is laid, which is Jesus Christ" (1 Cor. 3:10–11; see also Eph. 4:11–13).

From the perspective of Scripture, there is so much to be said about the apostles, their calling and equipment, their mission and authority, their place within and vis-à-vis the church, that we need a summary concept such as an office. Lekkerkerker says (1971, 110): "An office in the sense of a special responsibility within the church and in the world, entrusted to someone by the Office Bearer par excellence, and as a consequence of which Christ is brought to others with authority, in the New Testament is in the first instance the role of the apostle."

b. *Ministries or offices of leadership.*

1. *Evangelists* (Eph. 4:11) have a special gift for missionary work. Philip is called "Philip the evangelist" (Acts 21:8).

2. *Prophets* are sometimes mentioned immediately after the apostles (1 Cor. 12:28; Eph. 4:11). New Testament prophecy does not exclusively and not even primarily relate to the future. It constitutes a speaking that edifies, admonishes and encourages, instructs and exhorts (1 Cor. 14:3, 31).

3. In the case of *teachers*, who in 1 Corinthians 12 are listed after prophets, the focus is on competence to teach (cf. Rom. 12:7). Prophets represent more the current aspect, teachers more the traditional aspect of the preaching of the gospel (Ridderbos, *Paul*, 453).

4. There are *pastors and teachers* (Eph. 4:11), who must give spiritual leadership to the church. These are not two separate groups, pastors on the one hand and teachers on the other hand, but individuals who pastorally take care of the church and provide instruction.

5. There are *leaders* (*rulers*, mentioned in Romans 12:8 and in a few other places) who are to perform their tasks with devotion.

6. *Elders*. An examination of the rather voluminous data that pertain to elders (Greek: *presbuteroi*) must indeed lead to the conclusion that these refer to an office.

We know nothing about the origin of this office. There appear to be elders in Jerusalem (Acts 11:30). There probably is a connection between the Jewish council of elders that conducted the business of a synagogue, but did not play a role in worship, and elders of the church. According to Acts 6, seven men were selected to assist the apostles in Jerusalem. This is where tradition has sought the origin of the office of deacon, but the task of these men encompassed more. Later we encounter elders at the side of the apostles (Acts 15:6). It is for this reason that sometimes a connection is laid between the seven men and the elders (see J. P. Versteeg in Koole and Velema, 1982, 19–21).

Paul and Barnabas appointed elders in various locations where the latter had to provide leadership to the church (Acts 14:23). Those who "rule" (Rom. 12:8) and those who "have the rule over" the church (Heb. 13:7, 17) are probably also to be viewed as elders.

Paul says to the elders of the church at Ephesus that the Holy Spirit has made them overseers of the flock (Acts 20:28). In whatever way they were chosen to be elders, it is certain that the Holy Spirit was behind it. It is their task to shepherd the church and to watch over it, which is to say that they must perform pastoral work. They must also be vigilant and protect the church against false doctrine.

Having oversight of the church is not their only responsibility. The requirements for this office also include competence to teach (1 Tim. 3:2) and "sound doctrine" for exhortation and refutation (Titus 1:9). In the case of illness they are expected to offer intercession (James 5:14).

During the apostolic era they had the right to participate in decision-making with respect to important matters (Acts 15:22–23). There was a council of elders (the assembled elders or "presbytery," 1 Tim. 4:14).[66] The expected submission to elders (1 Peter 5:5) implied the recognition of their authority.

The requirements for overseers or elders (1 Tim. 3; Titus 1) also imply that we are dealing with an office. "If a man desire the office of a bishop (overseer), he desireth a good work" (1 Tim. 3:1). It is primarily this office to which Paul entrusts the church in its further upbuilding and development (cf. Ridderbos, *Paul*, 459).

7. D*eacons* are only referred to in Philippians 1 and 1 Timothy 3, but the significance of the diaconate is far greater than can be inferred from these few references. There are clear diaconal perspectives in the Old Testament. The words and deeds of Christ imply that not only eternal salvation can be expected from him, but also help in earthly distress. Although salvation and healing are not equivalent, they are indeed related. The church that belongs to the ministering Savior is a diaconal church. It looks after the brothers and sisters who have no one to help them (Ps. 72:12) and practices neighborly love (cf. W. Steenbergen in Koole and Velema, 1991, 11–28).

Although we cannot say that Acts 6 deals with the institution of the diaconal office, this portion of Scripture is nevertheless of significance for the diaconate, and not only because it speaks of serving at tables (v. 2). A certain group of widows must not be passed over—either in terms of not receiving any help or not having an opportunity to offer help[67]—for the mutual fellowship must not be jeopardized. The seven men are appointed to foster the new community.[68]

66. Cf. B. van Ginkel, *De ouderling* (the elder), 1975, 37.

67. See for this explanation Noordegraaf, 1983, 125–32; Van Bruggen, 1984, 65–77.

68. Cf. F. H. von Meyenfeldt, *De diaken als componist der gemeenschap* (the deacon as assembler of the community), 1955, 36–40.

In the New Testament deacons are placed after the overseers. This does not mean that they are servants or assistants of the overseers. Just like the overseers or elders, the deacons are ministers of the church and servants of Christ himself. They hold an equivalent but not an identical office.

Among the gifts that the Spirit apportions to each one individually as he pleases (1 Cor. 12:11) there are also those directed toward service orientation and the provision of assistance: ministering, giving, showing mercy (Rom. 12:7–8), and helping (1 Cor. 12:28). The fact that these gifts are given to members of the church does not render the office of deacon superfluous. The deacons can and must provide stimulating and coordinating leadership to these efforts, thereby underlining that this is the work of the diaconal church and indeed the work that Christ does through the church, its members, and its office bearers.

The offices and charismata go hand in hand, although at times the emphasis falls more on the charismata and at times more on the offices. It has been said correctly: "Whereas in the earlier epistles the offices are mentioned in the context of the charismatic articulation of the church, in the pastoral epistles the charismata are mentioned in the context of the office-based structure of the church" (*De kerk*, 1990, 55).

3. *Three offices*

Our Reformed confession speaks of three offices, that of ministers or pastors, that of overseers, and that of deacons (Belgic Confession of Faith, Article 30). The Church Order of Dort, in following Calvin, assigned yet a separate role to the office of doctors of theology, but in comparison with the important controversies about ecclesiastical offices this is not a significant difference. Like other topics that deal with church governance, it can be addressed in connection with church polity (cf. Bavinck, *R.D.*, 4:387ff.).

In the sixteenth century it appeared simpler than today to derive these three offices directly from Scripture. Noordmans once said, "One cannot simply take a walk through the churches a few decennia after Jesus' ascension, and then report back what one has seen. For instance: In Jerusalem I saw elders and in Philippi an overseer and deacons etc., and now we know enough to put together a church order" (*V.W.*, 8:435ff.).

Nevertheless, the mention of bishops and deacons, or elders and deacons (1 Tim. 3; Titus 1), is to us an indication that these are two categories of office bearers who are expected to provide leadership to and to take care of the church. It is more difficult, though not impossible (see Bavinck, *R.D.*, 4:344–45), to recognize in the elders who take on the task of preaching and teaching (1 Tim. 5:17), in principle ministers of the Word.

The three offices referred to are the so-called ordinary offices (Honig, *Handboek*, 743), as distinguished from the extraordinary offices such as apostle, prophet, and evangelist (cf. Eph. 4:11). The line of demarcation between these two categories has been questioned, and one may well wonder why the role of evangelist could not be seen as an ordinary office. But in view of the list provided in Ephesians 4:11—with apostles at the beginning and pastors and teachers at the end—the special or extraordinary nature of the office of apostle must at any rate be recognized. This suggests that the office of pastors and teachers can be considered to be an ordinary office, indicating a permanent ministry.

All office-based work equips the church "for the work of the ministry." The division of office bearers—who work together and complement each other—into three distinct categories has a single goal: "the edifying of the body of Christ" (Eph. 4:12).

Office-based ministry in essence, character, and purpose constitutes a unity. This is apparent from the definition of ecclesiastical office as "a God-given commission to provide enduring institutionally-defined service to his church for the purpose of building it up both internally and externally" (Trimp, 1982, 6).

If, like the Belgic Confession of Faith (Article 30), we take as our starting point that the church must be governed in a spiritual manner, there is every support for the consideration of three offices. Such governance is exercised in the preaching of the Word. "Preaching calls for instruction, the administration of the sacraments, the exercise of church discipline, and the ministry of mercy" (Trimp, 1982, 109ff., 211ff.). The proclamation of the Word, which must take priority, calls for office bearers who are competent to teach. There must also be overseers or elders for the oversight of the church and to ensure adherence to sound doctrine and the sanctification of life. This requires joint meetings of the elders (cf. 1 Tim. 4:14), for they bear responsibility—not only personally but also collectively—for the spiritual well-being of the church. There is again another form of leadership required for ensuring that optimal use is made of all gifts in the church that are directed toward helping others. The deacons are there to lead the way in works of charity.

1. Calvin distinguishes between two kinds of deacons: procurators (*procureurs*) and hospitalers (*hospitaliers*). The former administered the funds collected for the relief of the poor. The latter cared for the poor and the sick. In this connection Calvin also referred to widows possibly providing assistance, referring to 1 Timothy 5:9 (cf. *Les Ordonnances Ecclésiastiques*, Article 56; *Institutes*, 4.3.9; 4.13.9).

2. There is a difference of opinion as to whether the apostle had in mind an office-based ministry of widows, or diaconal work performed in close cooperation with deacons.[69] We tend to agree that it cannot be concluded from the relevant New Testament passages that men and women served equally as elders and/or deacons.[70]

3. The three offices that we are familiar with today did not emerge at once. Initially their development took an entirely different direction. In the writings of the apostolic fathers such as Clement and Ignatius, the New Testament terms of overseers, elders, and deacons do occur, but in the second century there already was a tendency to think of the overseer as a single authoritative office bearer. The overseer (*episkopos*) became a bishop, and not long thereafter (in Cyprian's time) the elder (*presbuteros*) had become a priest who stood at the altar when administering the Eucharist, which was viewed as a sacrifice. A deacon came to be viewed as the assistant of a bishop, and later also acquired a role in the liturgy. This is how the following triad of offices emerged: bishop, priest, deacon.

To Rome these are the three orders of the one consecrated office that is transmitted with laying on of hands and prayer. The bishops are the lawful successors of the apostles, and among them the bishop of Rome is the dominant figure. The Second Vatican Council declared, "In the bishops, therefore, assisted by priests and deacons, the Lord Jesus Christ, the Supreme Priest, is present in the midst of the believers" (*Dogm. Const.*, 1964, no. 21). Another document of Vatican II states, "The bishop is to be regarded as the high priest of his flock. The believers' life in Christ as it were is obtained from him and is dependent on him."[71] This is very strong language indeed!

Bavinck says: "The bishop became the high priest, the presbyters became priests, and deacons became Levites" (*R.D.*, 4:388). Reaching back to the Old Testament cultus, with its priests and sacrifices, indeed played a role.

4. Over against the sacramental priesthood, Luther placed the preaching office. The ministry of the Word is the office proper. "It is not the power of the pope or that of a bishop that rules in the church but the Word of God" (*WA*, 2:676). Luther derives the office (*ministerium*) from the general priesthood of believers, but also

69. For the first opinion see E. L. Smelik, *De wegen der kerk* (the ways of the church), 1940, 64–67, and Hulst, 1951, 52–55; for the second see Den Boer (ed.), 1985, 158ff.

70. C. Den Boer (previous footnote), 164.

71. *Constitutie over de heilige liturgie* (constitution regarding holy liturgy), 1963, no. 41.

says: "With his blood Christ has obtained, granted, and instituted it for us for our salvation."[72]

Luther in fact overlooked the New Testament elders and left much of church governance to the secular government. He strongly advocated that Christians should serve their neighbors out of love, but did not think of diaconal arrangements. In Lutheran regions the necessary provisions became the responsibility of the secular government.

Calvin attached just as much significance to the office-based ministry of the Word as Luther did. But Calvin learned above all from Bucer that the church also needed elders. This reflected the need for pastoral care and church discipline, and was implemented in churches that adhered to this vision. We hereby have in mind Noordmans's comment that on the ecclesiastical chessboard Calvin moved the pawn of the elder and checkmated the pope. We already saw that Calvin drew attention to two aspects of diaconal work. Just like Bucer he was a proponent of an independent diaconate, although during his time in Geneva little of this was achieved (cf. W. van 't Spijker in Koole and Velema, 1991, 84–91).

The traditional triad of offices: bishop, priest, and deacon, which became a hierarchical ladder in the case of Rome, under Calvin's strong influence was replaced by the three offices of pastor, elder, and deacon, working together collegially. The sequence in which we usually mention these three offices has nothing to do with a ranking and does not give any office bearer a reason to elevate himself above others.

5. The Christian churches lack unanimity with respect to ecclesiastical offices, and this has given rise to many problems within the ecumenical movement. The Faith and Order declaration on *Baptism, Eucharist, and Ministry* (Lima Report, 1982) constitutes an important attempt to achieve greater unanimity, which engendered reactions from many sides.

This report considers the apostolic or episcopal succession—with the uninterrupted laying on of hands by bishops—to be of the utmost importance for the continuity of the apostolic tradition. The office of bishop is given prominence and that of the elder is missing. The threefold office is the office of bishop, presbyter, and deacon. Churches that do not follow this threefold pattern are asked whether they should not adopt it as it has evolved.

We could respond critically here but prefer to close this subsection with a comment from Bavinck, which, having acquainted ourselves with more recent literature, we still consider to be entirely relevant. He states that by restoring the office of elder and that of deacon alongside that of the minister of the Word, the Reformed captured the concept of Scripture in its purest form and recognized most firmly the rights of the congregation (*R.D.*, 4:388).

47.2. *Some important systems of church governance*

1. *Office and congregation*

There are various systems of church governance. We cannot ignore this in ecclesiology, but it is possible to keep its discussion succinct and

72. Cf. H. Lieberg, *Amt* (office) *und Ordination bei Luther und Melanchthon*, 1962, 108.

refer to church polity. For the sake of brevity, we leave the territorial and collegial systems out of consideration here (see for this Honig, *Handboek*, 747–49, 752).

There appears to be a fundamental difference of view with respect to the relationship between ecclesiastical office and the congregation. In the main there are *three types* of theology of ecclesiastical office, which à la Berkhof we can characterize as follows:

1. The Catholic or high-church type, which regards ordination as a sacrament by which the bearer, in virtue of a special promise of the Spirit, is permanently placed not only opposite but also above the congregation.
2. The classic Reformed type, which positions the office bearer not only opposite but also within the congregation, and circumscribes his authority by the general office of all believers.
3. The free-church or low-church type, which views the office bearer as no more than a functional specialization of the office of all believers, in principle no different from that of the custodian or administrator.

The first type appeals to the authority of the apostles, which is believed to have passed on by means of the apostolic succession to the later bishops; the second appeals to the equality of the *presbuteros* (elder) and the *episkopos* (overseer) in the New Testament; the third appeals especially to the picture of the charismatic church in 1 Corinthians 12–14 (Berkhof, *C.F.*, 383ff.).

In the first case the church is governed hierarchically and the clergy occupies a position of power. The church is where the bishops are. In the third case the starting point lies within the congregation and the church resembles a democracy. The will of the majority of the members of the congregation is decisive.

In the previous subsection (§ 47.1) we opted for the second point of view. With this we do not choose a median between a high-church and a low-church structure, but we follow a different approach in which everything that Scripture says is decisive.

There are two main perspectives here. The offices are given to the church by Christ (cf. Eph. 4:11) and the office bearers come from within the church, which chooses them because it discerns in them the gifts required for office-based ministry (cf. Acts 6:5). These two perspectives reveal yet a third dimension: the interaction between the congregation and the offices.

We reject the Catholic view because it gives the clergy a power that is not rightfully theirs according to the New Testament. The place and the authority of the apostles are unique. The office bearers that the church has now do not stand above it.

We reject the low-church view because the office is not an institution of the congregation and not a function that only needs to exist to ensure a proper functioning of the life of the church.

2. *Episcopalianism*

In this subsection, we briefly discuss three systems that reflect the above-mentioned views with respect to the relationship between ecclesiastical office and the church: the Episcopalian, the Presbyterian-synodical, and the Congregationalist systems. For a more extensive discussion, see W. van 't Spijker in *De kerk*, 1990, 301–38. The papal system, which is a lopsided version of the episcopal structure, is discussed later (§ 48.3).

A church that is characterized by an episcopal organization is the Anglican Church. It is a state church, for since Henry VIII the monarch is recognized as the head of the church, but its most characteristic feature is its episcopal structure. The emphasis is placed on the historical episcopate, with which an important "Roman Catholic" element has been adopted in a church that in terms of doctrine is considered to be Protestant. The Anglican Church is very much attached to its intermediate position, and with its holding on to apostolic succession and its rejection of the supremacy of the pope believes it can play a key role within ecumenism.

The Old-Catholic Church, like the Anglican Church with which it maintains close contact, orients itself toward the undivided church of the early centuries. Besides the unity of the faith and the unity of the sacraments, unity of organization is of the greatest importance. According to Rinkel, the historically developed monarchical episcopacy presents itself with indisputable authority. It objects to domination by the clergy and supremacy of the pope. The bishops are viewed as successors to the apostles. They are called by the church, which ordains them with the laying on of hands and prayer. The continuity and unity of the church are symbolized, maintained, and safeguarded by the episcopate.[73]

3. *The Presbyterian-Synodical System*

As the name implies, this form of church governance has two focal points: the office of presbyter or elder and the ecclesiastical assembly, which one should not think of only as a general synod. For the Reformed vision, which is hereby indicated, it is characteristic that it is focused on the local church, in which beats the heart of the church—but a church that together with other churches forms a federation. In this connection we can point to the New Testament, which refers to both the local congregation and the church of Christ in its totality as *ekklesia* (see § 44.3, subsection

73. A. Rinkel, *Dogmatische Theologie*, 1956, 3:236–42.

5). The church federation is neither a formality, nor a luxury. The broader assemblies have authority without limiting that of the local consistories.

The first article of the Synod of Emden (1571) says that no church may lord it over another church and no office bearer may lord it over other office bearers. The Church Order of Dort says the same thing in a different place (Article 85), but it says so for a reason: No hierarchy! However, independentism is also rejected.

Above the local church with its members and office bearers and above the church with its assemblies stands the Word of God with which Christ rules his church.

In contrast with various national and state churches, the Reformed vigorously hold fast to the principle of the freedom of the church over against the state. They are conscious of their calling vis-à-vis the government.[74]

There exists an important declaration of the Reformed Ecumenical Synod of 1949 concerning the relationship between church and state, of which a number of key issues can be listed here:

1. The government is instituted by God in order to do its part in promoting the maintenance of human life and its development, in accordance with both tables of the law of the Lord.
2. The government is therefore called to protect the preaching of the gospel and the entire sacred service of God with all its God-given means, in order that freedom of conscience to serve God according to his Word be safeguarded and all anti-Christian powers that seek to hinder the exercise of this sacred service may be opposed and impeded.
3. The church shall acknowledge and honor the government in the exercise of the authority and responsibility that God has entrusted to it.
4. The government must refrain from encroaching on the rights and authority of the only King of the church, Jesus Christ (*Acts*, Article 66).[75]

4. *Congregationalism*

According to this system the autonomous congregation bears all ecclesiastical authority. Robert Browne (d. 1633) is generally viewed to be the founder of congregationalism, also called *independentism*, because it is of the view that the congregation is entirely independent of bishops and of any state authority—thus opposing the Anglican Church—and also because it sees itself as being independent of any form of church federation. In his writings Browne advocates the formation of congregations of true believers, who unite within a covenant to serve God. There is room for consultation with and advice from other congregations, but not for the authority of a broader assembly.

In seventeenth-century England, Puritan theologians such as Th. Goodwin and J. Owen were attracted to congregationalism. There is nevertheless a clear difference between this view, in which the church comes into being by the voluntary joining together of confessing Christians, and the Reformed doctrine that the church owes

74. Cf. W. H. Velema, *Het spreken en het preken van de kerk*, 1987.

75. See also the formulation adopted later by the *Christelijke Gereformeerde Kerken in Nederland*, which comes closer to the intention of Article 36 of the Belgic Confession of Faith, *Acta*, 1968/1969, Article 146.

its origin and existence to the church-gathering work of Christ. To the Reformed, the local church is indeed fully the church of Christ, but it is always associated with other churches that are guided by the pure Word of God (Belgic Confession of Faith, Article 29).

In our time, congregationalism has a certain appeal. There are various free churches or groups that show a spiritual and organizational affinity with it. Not long ago renewed attention for this system of church governance was called for by Dingemans, who considers it to be an interesting option with important insights, whereby "the Reformation in turn would have to be purified." He looks for "light" structures for the community of Christ's followers. A democratic tendency and an appeal to the freedom of the Spirit are motifs that clearly come to the fore here (Dingemans, 1987, 124ff., 191–93; idem, *De kerk verbouwen* = rebuilding the church, 1989. 177–87).

§ 48. The authority of the church

48.1. *The power of the keys in the New Testament*
48.2. *The Reformational view*
48.3. *The power of the papacy*

48.1. *The power of the keys in the New Testament*

Following the essence and governance of the church, theologians such as Bavinck and Honig discuss the authority of the church. This can lead to the misunderstanding that the church possesses authority comparable to the authority that is encountered in various forms in this world. The authority that is meant here has the nature of a power of attorney or authorization (*potestas*). "It consists in nothing else, but also in nothing less, than the power of the keys" (Bavinck, *R.D.*, 4:394).

The *power of the keys* is a biblical concept. Christ says to Peter, "I will give unto thee the keys of the kingdom of heaven" (Matt. 16:19). The image is probably not that of a porter who opens and closes a door, but rather that of a custodian or a steward (cf. Isa. 22:22). Someone who controls keys has authority over something (cf. Rev. 1:18). In Matthew 16 the keys of the kingdom indicate the full authority that Christ gives to Peter (see in this connection Trimp, 1982, 138–78).

Christ describes this full authority in terms of "binding" and "loosing." These are terms employed by rabbis and pertain to authoritative pronouncements. It means to declare something to be forbidden or permitted. There are those who think that it also pertains to condemnation or acquittal (cf. *TDNT*, 3:751; Ridderbos, 1950, 12ff.).

The authority to bind and to loose is repeated in Matthew 18:18. There also Jesus says that God will apply the apostolic word as binding in heaven.

In summary we can say that Matthew 16:19 and 18:18 speak of the full authority to make binding pronouncements about entry into the kingdom of heaven (cf. Van Bruggen, 1984, 43). This is comparable to what is stated in John 20:23, albeit in other words: forgiving sins and imputing sins. Decisions are made in time for eternity.

We now come to the question whether the power of the keys was given only to Peter. The Roman Catholic view is well known. Protestants have frequently countered this by saying that with his statement about the building of his church on this rock (*petra*) Jesus meant that the church would be built on Peter's confession: "Thou art the Christ, the Son of the living God" (Matt. 16:16)! This interpretation is not tenable, at least not in this form. Neither is it the case that Peter is personally a rock. By declaring following Peter's confession what we read in Matthew 16:18–19, Jesus establishes a direct connection between Peter as the apostle who confesses his name and the foundation of his church.

However, this does not elevate Peter above the other apostles. This follows already from the repetition of the words about binding and loosing in Matthew 18:18, where the plural is used. In Matthew 16 Peter acts as spokesperson for the apostles. He answers the question intended for all of them, and Jesus also speaks to all of them in his response (Matt. 16:15, 20). The names of all of the apostles are written on the foundation stones of the New Jerusalem (Rev. 21:14). In the first part of the book of Acts, Peter comes to the fore, and one could perhaps think of him as the first among equals (Bavinck, *R.D.*, 4:321), but this does not exalt him above the others.

In view of the context in which we find the word about binding and loosing in Matthew 18:18, we think not only of the apostles but also others who act in Jesus' name.[76]

People may use these keys only to please the Lord, never to please themselves. Pronouncements by office bearers and the church are valid only to the extent that the keys are administered entirely in conformity with his Word. Ecclesiastical authority is always circumscribed and subject to norms. According to Calvin, looking at it from the perspective of people, the power of the keys is not so much a power as ministry

76. Cf. L. van Hartingsveld, *De sleutels van het koninkrijk der hemelen* (the keys of the kingdom of heaven), 63ff.

(*ministerium*), for "Christ has not given this power (*potestas*) actually to men, but to his Word, of which he made men ministers" (*Institutes*, 4.11.1). By viewing it in this way, one can, with the Reformer, call it indeed a sovereign power or authority (*potestas*) with which the pastors of the church—by whatever name they may be called—ought to be endowed. Through the Word of God they may dare boldly to do all things they have been authorized to do (*Institutes*, 4.8.9).

48.2. *The Reformational view*

The churches of the Reformation think altogether differently about the authority of the church and its office bearers than Rome. Power and authority are not alien concepts to Roman Catholicism. There is a hierarchy (holy dominion), an ecclesiastical government, and a pope who wields supreme power.

A common distinction is made between power to administer the sacraments (*potestas ordinis*) and the power of jurisdiction (*potestas jurisdictionis*), which indicates that the regulations of the church are binding and demand unconditional obedience (cf. Bavinck, *R.D.*, 4:417ff.).

According to the Dogmatic Constitution of 1964, the consecration of bishops confers a threefold authority: doctrinal, administrative, and sanctifying power. Thus bishops fulfill the very role of Christ who is Teacher, Shepherd, and High Priest. Their authority can only be exercised in hierarchical fellowship with the pope and the other bishops (Dogmatic Constitution *Lumen gentium*, 21).

The power of the church and its bishops finds its culmination in the pope. According to a pronouncement of Boniface VIII (1302), which has never been retracted by Rome, it is obligatory to believe that for the salvation of every human creature it is necessary to submit oneself to the pope of Rome (*DS*, 875).

The Reformation breathed new content into ancient terms. The authority to administer the sacraments was replaced by the commission to administer the Word and the sacraments. Jurisdiction now consists in the authority to exclude those who are guilty of public sins and to grant them forgiveness if they repent (*BSLK*, 400). On this point there is no essential difference between the Lutheran and Reformed doctrine, as is apparent from a comparison of the Augsburg Confession (1530) and the Heidelberg Catechism (Lord's Day 31). Both confessional documents deal with the power of the keys, which in the Augsburg Confession is described as a power or a mandate. Nevertheless, a difference emerged with respect to the church. What is said in the ecclesiastical documents concerning exclusion from the church or excommunication was not actually implemented by the Lutheran Church. Discipline was generally left to the government, with the consequence that it lost its spiritual character. But the tendency to leave the key of discipline unused is more widespread.

The administration of the keys of the kingdom of heaven is a highly responsible task for office bearers who are called to use them. The weightiness of opening and closing with the two keys is apparent from the expressions employed in the Heidelberg Catechism: According to the "witness of the gospel" proclaimed by men, "God will judge, both in this life and in that which is to come." Through Christian discipline it can come to exclusion "from the Christian church [and] from the kingdom of Christ" (Lord's Day 31).

The Reformed had a different view of ecclesiastical discipline than Anabaptists. For the sake of the holiness of the church the latter were quick to use excommunication, coupled with shunning, based on Matthew 18:17. The Reformed are no less concerned about the holiness of the church, but there are additional reasons for ecclesiastical discipline. Just as Augustine views discipline primarily as being medicinal in nature,[77] so Calvin repeatedly refers to it as a medicine that must be used correctly. He considers the saving doctrine of Christ to be the soul of the church and discipline its nervous system, which underlines how necessary discipline is in his view. What matters is the honor of God, the holiness of the sacraments, the welfare of the church, and the salvation of the sinner (see *Institutes*, 4.12.1–15). These are notions that we also encounter in the Form for Excommunication. It is clear that the purpose of admonition and excommunication is to regain the individual and put him back on the right track (see Matt. 18:15). No excommunication takes place except after obvious hardening of the heart.

According to the Reformational view, comprehensive authority and multifaceted responsibility go hand in hand.

It has become common practice to link the threefold office of Christ and the three offices of minister of the Word, elder, and deacon (cf. Bavinck, *R.D.*, 4:418ff.), reflecting three kinds of ecclesiastical authority. This, however, poses a threat of schematization (see Trimp, 1982, 110–15).

77. See H. B. Weijland, *Augustinus en de kerkelijke tucht* (Augustine and church discipline), 1965, 115.

Pointing to prophetic, priestly, and royal facets of the task, which the church and its office bearers fulfill at Christ's command, makes it easy to plead for the full-fledged deployment of the ministry of mercy.

Otherwise one is faced with the question as to the relationship between the power of the keys—or the power to make authoritative pronouncements—and the deaconate. But we do not have to call this a third key of the kingdom to be able to speak of a Christ-given office-based authority to lead the church in neighborly service (cf. Trimp, 1982, 203–5).

Bavinck wanted the office of deacon to be more highly regarded in his day, namely, as "an independent organ of the priestly mercy of Christ" (*R.D.*, 4:427ff.). Much has changed in this respect. There is indeed an entirely new appreciation for diaconal activity in the church, although theology will have to be aware, in its treatment of the disciplines that deal with various aspects of the church's ministry of mercy, that not all new motives are scriptural (see C. Trimp in *De kerk*, 1990, 453–71; Koole and Velema, 1991, passim).

48.3. *The power of the papacy*

The steadily increasing power of the bishop of Rome reached its zenith when the Vatican Council of 1870 confirmed a tradition that recognized the rightful primacy of Peter and the bishops of Rome as his successors and taught the absolute supremacy of the pope over the entire church. A new dogma was formulated: that of the infallibility of the pope, when as pastor and teacher of all Christians he establishes a doctrine relating to faith and morals (*DS*, 3074).

The Second Vatican Council reiterated that the interpretations of the pope are irrevocable by their very nature and not by virtue of the assent of believers. They are not subject to appeal or any other judgment (Dogmatic Constitution, no. 25). This means that against such an "infallible" pronouncement no higher appeal is possible, neither to ancient tradition, nor to any council, nor to Scripture!

There is a college of bishops, but it cannot act apart from the pope—whereas, the pope can indeed act apart from this college. The highest authority is the pope, alone or together with the bishops. There are plenty of examples of popes acting entirely on their own!

For a fundamental critique of the papacy and the papal system we refer the reader to Bavinck, *R.D.*,4:400–407).[78]

A number of key issues:

78. See also O. Cullman, *Petrus*, 1960; A. J. Bronkhorst and H. A. Oberman in M. van der Plas (ed.), *De paus* (pope) *van Rome*, no date; M. J. Arntzen, *Het primaat van de paus*, no date; P. E. Persson, *Repraesentio Christi*, 1966; K. Blei, *De onfeilbaarheid* (infallibility) *van de kerk*, 1972. Cf. also H. Küng, *Unfehlbar?* (infallible?), 1970.

1. We saw already (§ 48.1) that in Matthew 16 Peter is not placed above the other apostles. It is not true what the Dogmatic Constitution (no. 22) says of Peter: the Lord only appointed Simon to be the church's rock and bearer of the keys, and called him to be the shepherd of his entire flock.
2. It is absolutely not true that apostolic powers were transmitted to subsequent bishops and those of Peter to the popes. In this case Peter would have had to identify his successor and would have had to consecrate him! This apostolic succession is a human invention.
3. In addition to its Head in heaven, the church does not have a visible head in Rome. "Christ [is] the only universal Bishop and the only Head of the church" (Belgic Confession of Faith, Article 31).
4. Since Innocent III (d. 1216), the pope refers to himself as Christ's vicar on earth (vicarius)—as though Christ would permit himself to be replaced in any way! He himself governs his church through his Word and Spirit. He uses people in his service, to whom he assigns tasks, but this constitutes no transfer of authority.

Attempts have been made to make the primacy of the pope more palatable by presenting it as a pastoral primacy. There would be grounds for expecting that sooner or later, the pope would voluntarily surrender authority (Küng, 1967, 558ff.). But papal primacy in the sense of monarchical authority, which the church has no way of restraining, is an essential element of the teachings of Rome.

The papal system (papism) is unacceptable to us, for it constitutes a degeneration of ecclesiastical authority. We do not view the church as a realm in which the most important decisions are made at the top. Jesus says, "One is your Master, even Christ; and all ye are brethren" (Matt. 23:8). Paul does not want to lord it over the faith of the church (2 Cor. 1:24). We reject the primacy of the pope because we hold fast to the absolute authority of the Word of God.

Some Literature

H. Bavinck, *De katholiciteit van Christendom en kerk* (the catholicity of Christianity and the church), 1968.

H. Berkhof, *De katholiciteit der kerk* (the catholicity of the church), 1962.

G. C. Berkouwer, *De kerk* (the church), 1, 1970; 2, 1972.

C. den Boer (ed.), *Man en vrouw in bijbels perspectief* (male and female in biblical perspective), 1985.

U. Brockhaus, *Charisma und amt* (office), 1972.

A. J. Bronkhorst, *Schrift en kerkorde* (Scripture and church order), 1947.

J. van Bruggen, *Ambten in de apostolische kerk* (offices in the apostolic church), 1984.

N. A. Dahl, *Das Volk Gottes* (the people of God), 1963.

De apostolische kerk (the apostolic church), 1954.

K. Dijk, *De dienst der kerk* (the church's ministry), 1952.

G. D. J. Dingemans, *Een huis om in te wonen* (a house to dwell in), 1987.

Dogmatische constitutie over de kerk (Lumen gentium), 1964.

B. Gassmann, *Ecclesia reformata*, 1968.

J. van Genderen, *De gemeenschap der heiligen* (the community of saints), 1986.

A. van Ginkel, *De ouderling (the elder)*, 1975.

A. N. Hendriks, *Die alles in allen volmaakt* (he who perfects everything in everyone), 1990.

A. N. Hendriks, *Met het oog op de gemeente* (keeping the church in mind), 1987.

Huls, *De dienst der vrouw in de kerk* (the ministry of women in the church), 1951.

G. P. van Itterzon, *Het kerkelijk ambt in geding* (ecclesiastical office in question), 1974.

W. D. Jonker, *Mistieke liggaam* (body) *en kerk in die nuwe Rooms-Katolieke teologie*, 1955.

De kerk (ed. W. van 't Spijker et al.), 1990.

De kerk verbouwen (rebuilding the church), 1989.

E. Kinder, *Der evangelische Glaube und die Kirche* (evangelical faith and the church), 1960.

D. Koole and W. H. Velema (ed.), *Uit liefde tot Christus en zijn gemeente* (out of love to Christ and his church), 1982.

D. Koole and W. H. Velema (ed.), *Zichtbare liefde van Christus* (visible love of Christ), 1991.

W. Kreck, *Grundfragen* (basic questions) *der Ekklesiologie*, 1981.

J. D. W. Kritzinger, *Qᵉhal Jahwe*, 1957.

U. Kühn, *Kirche*, 1980.

H. Küng; *Die Kirche*, 1967.

A. F. N. Lekkerkerker, *Oorsprong en funktie van het ambt* (origin and role of ecclesiastical office), 1971.

H. Lieberg, *Amt* (office) *und Ordination bei Luther und Melanchthon*, 1962.

C. H. Lindijer, *Kerk en koninkrijk* (church and kingdom), 1962.

B. C. Milner, *Calvin's Doctrine of the Church*, 1970.

J. Moltmann, *Kirche in der Kraft des Geistes* (church in the strength of the Spirit), 1975.

W. Nijenhuis, *Calvinus oecumenicus*, 1959.

A. Noordegraaf, *Creatura verbi*, 1983.

A. Noordegraaf, *Orientatie in het diakonaat*, 1991.

I. J. du Plessis, *Christus as hoof van kerk en kosmos* (Christ as head of church and cosmos), 1962.

H. Ridderbos, *De komst van het koninkrijk* (the coming of the kingdom), 1950.

J. Roloff, *Apostolat—Verkundigung* (proclamation)—*Kirche*, 1965.

A. A. van Ruler, *Bijzonder en algemeen ambt* (special and general office), 1952.

A. A. van Ruler, *Reformatorische opmerkingen in de ontmoeting met Rome* (Reformational remarks in the encounter with Rome), 1965.

E. Schillebeeckx, *Kerkelijk ambt*, 1980.

R. Schnackenburg, *Die Kirche im Neuen Testament*, 1963.

M. Schwintek, *Die Kirche der Sünder* (the church of sinners), 1969.

K. G. Steck, *Lehre* (doctrine) *und Kirche bei Luther*, 1963.

P. A. van Stempvoort, *Eenheid en schisma in de gemeente van Korinthe volgens 1 Korinthiers* (unity and schism in the church of Corinth), 1950.

D. van Swigchem, *Het missionair karakter van de christelijke gemeente volgens de brieven van Paulus en Petrus* (the missionary character of the Christian church according to the epistles of Paul and Peter), 1955.

C. Trimp, *Ministerium*, 1982.

U. Valeske, *Votum ecclesiae*, 1962.

W. H. Velema, *De geestelijke groei van de gemeente* (the spiritual growth of the church), 1966.

J. P. Versteeg, *Kijk op de kerk* (focus on the church), 1985.

J. Vlaardingerbroek, *Jezus Christus tussen Joden en Christenen* (Jesus Christ between Jews and Christians), 1989.

Chapter 14

The Means of Grace

§ 49. The Holy Spirit and the means of grace

49.1. *The concept of means of grace*
49.2. *Rejection of spiritualism*
49.3. *Command, not delegation*

49.1. *The concept of means of grace*

In the Reformed tradition the term "means of grace" or "means of salvation" reflects its doctrine of the Holy Spirit and his work.

Faith, by means of which we receive Christ and his salvation, is the most important work of the Holy Spirit (Calvin). It did not originate with man—we cannot give it to ourselves; neither can we instill it in others. The question as to where faith comes from is answered in unequivocal terms by the Heidelberg Catechism: It "comes . . . from the Holy Spirit" (Lord's Day 25). What is then said about how faith is worked and strengthened through the preaching of the gospel and the use of the sacraments is no secondary matter. It belongs to its very core and is the point of departure for the present chapter on dogmatics.

In the light of the work of the Holy Spirit, the correspondence between the Word on the one hand, and baptism and the Lord's Supper on the other hand, overshadows all distinctions. They are all means employed by the Holy Spirit to make us partake in communion with Christ. In Calvin's work we read that the Word is the instrument by which the Lord dispenses the illumination of his Spirit to believers (*Institutes*, 1.9.3). The sacraments are additional instruments of God's grace. Apart from organ and instrument, "means" is also a useful term: Is there any other means (*medium*) aside from the Word of God through which God shares himself with us? The answer is that to the preaching of the gospel he has conjoined the sacraments (Geneva Catechism, 309).

At times people have sought to interpret means of grace more broadly, by adding for example interpersonal dialogue and comforting of the brethren (Luther). Both Westminster catechisms list as common external means through which Christ lets us share in the blessings of his work: the Word, the sacraments, and prayer. It has sometimes been advocated to include communion of saints among the means of grace. Aulén refers to the means of grace of personalities, particularly the saints.[1]

A significant departure from the usual point of view is Berkhof's, who excludes preaching, baptism, and communion from the means of grace, replacing them with nine "mediating" elements brought together under ecclesiology. The question then becomes what is instituted by the elements that are essential to the church as transmission (*C.F.*, 350). Berkhof's starting point is participation in the covenantal event, which is the work of the Holy Spirit. The activities that make such participation possible, which are as it were "mediating," are: instruction, baptism, preaching, discussion, Lord's Supper, diaconate, worship service, office, and church order—the latter two instruments are actually intended to facilitate the work of the instruments of transmission. In principle this list remains subject to change. As time goes by, new instruments emerge that serve in a mediating capacity. It is theoretically undeniable that certain means can cease to play a role over the course of the history of the church.

How can we be sure that the Spirit works through these means? In earlier days it was thought that all lawful means had been instituted by Christ, but this has changed in light of the rules currently employed in biblical exegesis. According to Berkhof, the Spirit who derives everything from Christ is able to use ever-new means, and we must revere the multiplicity of his ways (*C.F.*, 393). One person relies entirely on preaching, the other on dialogue, or the celebration of the Lord's Supper. Also in the case of the diaconate, Berkhof leans quite heavily on experience. What is done for victims of disasters, conflicts, and oppression is currently for many people of more "guiding" significance than any of the other means of salvation (*C.F.*, 374).

What Berkhof gains in terms of breadth with the new version of this doctrine, by incorporating psychology and sociology, he loses in terms of depth, for he ceases to do justice to the Word. Whereas he makes preaching follow after instruction and baptism, Reformational theology gives prominence to the Word, the gospel that is preached to us at Christ's command. This is done on solid grounds, namely, in accordance with

1. G. Aulén, *Ons algemeen christelijk geloof* (our catholic Christian faith; translated by J. Henzel), 1927, 322–26.

Matthew 28:19. The experience of certain people at a specific time can never be the chief criterion. Much more accurate is the insight that is expressed in the interpretation of article 10 of *Fundamenten en Perspectieven van Belijden* (fundamentals and perspectives of confession, authored by Berkhof himself in 1949): To us a special promise is attached to the means of salvation, i.e., preaching, baptism, and the Lord's Supper. But God can also employ other means (conversation, books, Christian lives, etc.), which in turn have been formed and nurtured by the means of salvation.

There is much that God can use to achieve his purpose for us, such as being raised by God-fearing parents, Christian education, catechesis, Bible study groups, the conversation and example of believers, and the influence of fellowship within the church. Nothing happens without prayer. But now we focus on the means by which he will work in us according to his own promises "a living faith," "an assured confidence," "peace of conscience," "filial obedience" and "a glorying in God" (cf. Canons of Dort, 1.16). When it comes to the role that the Word and the sacraments play as means of salvation, the important thing is that we can appeal to God's promises.

49.2. *Rejection of spiritualism*

The words "means" and "instrument" focus our attention on the person who employs them, namely, the Holy Spirit.

Th. L. Haitjema sees both Word and sacraments as instruments of the Holy Spirit. In Roman Catholicism the church has so much control over the grace involved in the means of grace that in reality the Holy Spirit is no longer the sovereign enabler and strengthener of faith. Haitjema correctly contrasts this with the fact that the instruments of Word and sacrament can only truly be employed by the third person of the divine Trinity (Haitjema, 1962, 167ff.).

The fact that the Holy Spirit employs the means of grace does not mean that he is limited to them in the same way that we are. We agree with Calvin's statement: "Although God's power is not bound to outward means, he has nonetheless bound us to this ordinary manner of teaching" (*Institutes*, 4.1.5). The crux of this statement is aimed at "fanatical men" who despise public assemblies and deem preaching superfluous. Although this may be due to pride and self-sufficiency, it can also reflect spiritualistic thinking.

According to spiritualists, everything is due to the Spirit. Only internal, not external, experience matters, for the spiritual dimension is internal. How could external means play a role in the work of the Holy Spirit? What is there to be mediated? It is just a matter of awaiting the coming of the Spirit.

According to various spiritualistic views, the Word and sacraments can at best describe and depict grace. They are not means of grace themselves. However, the distinction that is made here between the internal and the external, the spiritual and the material, is completely unbiblical. It is as though the one is the work of God and the other not! This has been decried as an enormous departure from Christianity (Van Ruler, *T.W.*, 3:138).

Over against this spiritual view we have the Reformational conviction that God himself has given us the means of grace and that we are to rely on them. There is an analogy with what God does in his providence. We believe that God gives us life and health. This does not preclude, however, that we require the proper means: food and medicine. Similarly, "grace is conferred by means of admonitions." We would "presume to tempt God by separating what he of his good pleasure has most intimately joined together, . . . to whom alone all the glory, both for the means and for their saving fruit and efficacy, is forever due" (Canons of Dort, 3–4.17).

In connection with Romans 10:17, Calvin points out that God creates faith in us through the ministry of a man. In the *Institutes* (4.16.19) he says that this is the usual approach of the Lord in calling his people. We are to obey the order of God, who has ordained it this way in his wisdom and goodness.

49.3. *Command, not delegation*

The fact that the Word and the sacraments are administered by people in the church does not make them means with which the church or its office bearers can do as they please. "Es geht hier um Herrenmittel, nicht um Kirchenmittel, um seine, nicht um unsere Instrumente" (we are dealing here with means of the Lord, not means of the church; his instruments, not ours).[2]

In a certain sense the means of grace have been placed in the hands of the church, but in the process they have not ceased for a moment to be instruments in the hands of God. The Word has been given to the church, but has not been put at its disposal, for it remains God's Word. Baptism is not carried out at the church's behest, but Christ's. The Lord's

2. H. Vogel, *Gott in Christo*, 1951, 836.

Supper is celebrated by the church, but it remains the Supper of the Lord. What God commands us to do here, is not delegated to us.

Departmentalization of the work of the Holy Spirit into seven sacraments of the church proves that Rome has all too often forgotten this fact. Berkhof writes: "Up to today the Roman Catholic Church in many countries and in numerous circumstances still gives the impression that it is one great repository of the Holy Spirit which is distributed in the form of sacraments" (Berkhof, 1964, 57). Between Rome and the Reformation there are fundamental differences in the doctrine of grace and in the doctrine of the church, and therefore also in the doctrine of the means of grace.

God's gift to his church can simultaneously be viewed as a responsibility. This is obvious from the role of office-bearers in the ministry of the Word and the administration of baptism and the Lord's Supper. The office rests on the foundation of God's call. He himself stands behind it.

The office-bearer is not a functionary of the church. The office does have a home in the church, but it also has a role vis-à-vis the church. The minister preaches the Word of God within the assembled congregation and yet does not do so on its behalf, for the Lord has called and authorized him to do so. When he celebrates the Lord's Supper with them, he does not administer it on the church's behalf, but because Christ has commanded him to do so. When an ecclesiastical assembly hands him the credentials, it does so in the name of the Head of the church. At the ordination of a minister of the Word the congregation is reminded that God speaks to them through him.

The churches therefore have the responsibility to maintain the ministry of the Word and the sacraments. But in the preaching of the Word and the administration of baptism and the Lord's Supper we encounter the Lord himself.

§ 50. The Word as a means of grace

50.1. *The role of the Word*

In church there is an open Bible on the pulpit. The congregation may expect words to be spoken that pass on the message of the Word of

God. In the worship services of the congregation this Word plays a special role in the "ministry of the Word." We do something with the Word. We listen to it individually and collectively. But it is actually the other way around: the Word does something to us. Those who listen well realize: In his Word God speaks to us. God's Word asks for a response from us. It is God's intention that his Word will find entry into our hearts and will be applied in our lives, so that it becomes a "power of God unto salvation" to us (Rom. 1:16).

We reflect here on the role of the Word at a time when a tremendous degradation of language is taking place. Plenty of words are spoken that constitute but hollow phrases. Saying and doing are frequently two entirely different things. Every day we are assaulted by a stream of information, and there is always a demand for the latest news. But are there not things being said in the church that have already been known for a long time, or at least could have been known? Is the church not saying things that everyone knows already or at least could have known? Is it not old news?

In addition, people appear to be more fascinated by images than words. Listening to words is not becoming any easier. And understanding of the Bible and the language that is spoken in the church requires more of an effort than understanding a story about everyday events. Furthermore, we are part of a community obsessed with the ethos of action. In these days we are probably witnessing a degradation of words unknown in earlier times. It is in part for this reason that sermons are being discredited. Does preaching still make sense?[3]

The question is, in what situation are words guaranteed to have some effect, guaranteed to be understood and to come true?

The poet and linguist Heeroma has sought to demonstrate in a unique way how important a role words continue to have in our culture today and should also retain in the church. The poet is bound to express himself in terms of the words of his poem: he exists within his language. "The believer also, a human being before God, exists in a very special way within his language. He lives in terms of words, because he lives by the Word, spoken to him by God, all the while listening and responding." In literature we always deal with words spoken with power. And is this not also the case with the preaching of the Word? The preacher's objectives are not achieved by his own words, but by those other words that are greater than his own. The essential

3. Cf. C. Trimp, *Woord, water en wijn*, 1985, 9–12; K. Runia, *Heeft preken nog zin*? (does preaching still make sense?), 1981.

function of the worship service is to give scope to the Word. And this is unthinkable without vocalized preaching.[4]

Today, statements such as Heeroma's are drowned out by competing views. These come, for example, from the direction of sociology, to the extent that this discipline concerns itself with the renewal of the church, and from the direction of communication theory.

According to these more recent views, it is not the office or the office-based proclamation of the Word that is decisive, but the personal dedication of the preacher and his communication skills. The idea is to broadcast on the correct wavelength, which should be easy to tune in to. It is not expected from the preacher that he will merely pass on the Word of God, but that he will assist the words of the Bible in gaining an audience in an entirely different situation than the one in which they originated. This requires reinterpretation and actualization—quite an art. This may create new opportunities for the old Bible.

Serious objections can be raised against theories in which communication is the key ingredient. The latter view is that it is not just a matter of God addressing us in the Bible, but that man also has something to bring to the Bible and speak along with it. If people in those earlier days could be part of the conversation, why can people today not join in? The key question is, however, whether man—when he is given the opportunity to speak—commences with recognizing the authority of the Word that is spoken. The saying in Romans 10:17, that faith comes from hearing and hearing through the word of Christ, is interpreted by H.-D. Bastian as "Paul's theory of the verbal medium" as though it were not the order instituted by God. In this modern theoretical formulation, the doctrine of the Holy Spirit becomes a forgotten chapter. But how could the Word of God function appropriately apart from the ministry of the Holy Spirit?[5]

There is justification for continuing to revere the role of the Word in God's work of salvation. The Word must accomplish it and the Word shall accomplish it.

Are we saying this on the basis of personal experience? If this were the case, could this not be refuted by the experience of others who are of the opinion that the Word is no longer effective? On the basis of their own experience, numerous people can testify to the power of the Word of God. Yet this is not the theological foundation for the thesis that the Word will remain effective. Sufficient grounds are provided by God's own promises. The following promise comes to mind: "So shall my word be that goeth forth out of my mouth: it shall not return

4. Cf. K. H. Heeroma, *Nader tot een taaltheologie* (toward a theology of language), 1967, 13, 69, 179.

5. Cf. H.-D. Bastian, *Kommunikation*, 1972, 36ff.; C. Trimp, *Communicatie en ambtelijke dienst* (communication and office-based ministry), 1976.

unto me void, but it shall accomplish that which I please, and it shall prosper in the thing whereto I sent it" (Isa. 55:11).

It is not true that the words of scriptural preaching are like so many other words, or just one communication among others. The Word of God is a message addressed to us. Words are spoken through which people will be saved (Acts. 11:14). They call us to communion with Christ and invite us to enter into the kingdom of God. The promise of the gospel must be proclaimed "to all persons . . . without distinction" coupled with the "command to repent and believe" (Canons of Dort, 2.5). God wants Christians to be taught "by the living preaching of his Word" (Heidelberg Catechism, Lord's Day 35). The proclamation of the gospel is the administration of the keys of the kingdom of heaven (Heidelberg Catechism, Lord's Day 31).

According to the New Testament, the Word of God is the message of salvation, the word of grace, the word of truth, the word of life. It is the word of Christ, the word of the cross, the preaching of Jesus Christ and him crucified.

This places high expectations on the preacher and the content of a sermon. Those who minister to the Word will themselves need to be guided by the Spirit. Holy Scripture must be both the source and the norm for preaching. This ensures that the proclamation of the Word of God is indeed the Word of God, as H. Bullinger puts it.[6] In preaching there is a double focus, first of all on Scripture, which is to be expounded according to its own context and intention, and furthermore on the people of our own time to whom Scripture is to be proclaimed.[7]

In the language of the Bible, the speaking and the happening of the Word, God's speaking and his acting through his Word are inseparable, for the Word happens and makes history. The Hebrew "*dabar*" signifies both word and deed. God's Word is his deed. It is a creative power. It is alive and powerful, sharp, penetrating and judging (Heb. 4:12). It is the living and enduring Word of God that is proclaimed as gospel (1 Peter 1:23–25); it is "the ministry of reconciliation" (2 Cor. 5:18).

This is why preaching does not remain without effect. God operates through his Word in a sovereign way. He engages people in his service to pass it on. He works through the power of his Spirit who employs the spoken Word as a means.

6. *Confessio Helvetica Posterior*, 1.
7. Cf. R. Bijlsma, *Schriftuurlijk Schriftgezag* (scriptural authority of Scripture), 1959, 393.

When he speaks in this manner, we may allow ourselves merely to be told: "Speak LORD, for thy servant heareth" (1 Sam. 3:9). This is not the same as keeping silent because he speaks. The Bible is full of reactions of people to the Word of God. The Word demands a believing response. God's yes is to be joined by our Amen (2 Cor. 1:20). Our God is a speaking God and the life of faith is a listening life.

When the Word of God works and takes effect, the worship service becomes an encounter between the Lord and his church around the open Bible and at the baptismal font as well as the communion table. The church responds to the Word through prayer and song. The Word resonates in the hearts of believers and is manifested in lives that are ruled by love toward God and their neighbors.

Why would I go to church? One of the answers to this question given by Van Ruler—although in his view it is not the most important one—is that we go there to receive salvation in all of its forms and variations. The mediation of salvation in Christ is the work of the Holy Spirit in us. But the Spirit engages helpers. In a sermon, God in Christ comes up to us with his grace. When I have to some extent discovered myself to be a sinner, as being lost and in the wrong, it is hard to believe that there is mercy for me. Preaching continually opens up new vistas. The spirit is enriched, and the heart is filled. Those who have once truly tasted something of the mystery of redemption seek to hear the gospel over and over again (Van Ruler, no date, 68–71).

With Trimp we can say that the objective of preaching is the proclamation of the acquittal of sinners through the blood of Christ. This news is both incredible and entirely credible. This message is always "news," because it is ever new. We "know" it well, and yet it continually needs to be reinforced. Faith consists in continually appropriating the promise of the gospel, always entrusting ourselves anew to the God of the promise (Trimp, 1985, 17ff.).

50.2. *Word and Spirit*

1. It is necessary to delve more deeply into the relationship between the Spirit and the Word, when the Spirit uses the Word as a means of grace. *To start off, we therefore enquire what light the Bible throws on this.*

The Holy Spirit speaks to us through Holy Scripture. In Hebrews 3:7 another Scripture passage is quoted with the following introduction: "As the Holy Ghost saith." The Holy Spirit also speaks to us by means of the Word that is proclaimed to us. The word preached by Paul is received by the believers of Thessalonica and taken to be the Word of God, which indeed it is. It is therefore also at work in those who believe. The apostle knows that God calls the Thessalonians through his gospel so that they may obtain the glory of Christ (1 Thess. 2:13; 2 Thess. 2:14).

There are relatively few Scripture passages where the Spirit and the Word are mentioned in one breath. As far as the Old Testament is concerned, we have in mind Isaiah 59:21, which refers to: "My spirit that is upon thee, and my words which I have put in thy mouth." Calvin points out in this connection: The Spirit is joined with the Word, because without the efficacy of the Spirit, the preaching of the gospel would avail nothing, but would remain unfruitful. Therefore the Word may not be separated from the Spirit, as fanatics imagine, who appeal to the Spirit and despise the Word. As far as the New Testament is concerned, apart from the depiction of the Word of God as the sword of the Spirit (Eph. 6:17), we refer to 1 Thessalonians 1:5–6. In Thessalonica it did not remain a matter of words. Paul's preaching of the gospel appeared there "in power and in the Holy Spirit"—power and the Holy Spirit being juxtaposed in various places in the New Testament—and a great deal happened. Reference is made to great fullness (*plerophoria*).

According to O. Procksch (*TDNT*, 4:97 f.), in the Old Testament we find the most profound theology of the Word in Jeremiah:[8] "I will hasten my word to perform it" (Jer. 1:12). It is as irresistible as a fire or as a hammer that pulverizes a rock (23:29). In Isaiah's prophecies it is also depicted as a power emanating from God. It is no magic power, for it accomplishes what pleases him (Isa. 55:10–11). Over against human mortality stands the power of the Word of God that lasts forever (Isa. 40:8). It will be fulfilled (Ezek. 12:25, 28).

In connection with the role of the Word as such, Hebrews 4:12 and 1 Peter 1:23–25 have already been mentioned. According to Hebrews 4 the Word penetrates to the very core, where decisions are made. Rebirth, which is the work of the Holy Spirit who gives life, comes about by means of the living, abiding Word, the gospel of Jesus Christ (cf. also James 1:18). The gospel is a power of God for salvation to everyone who believes (Rom. 1:16), although it does not have the same effect on everyone (1 Cor. 1:18; 2 Cor. 2:15–16). Faith comes from hearing—one can also translate: what has been heard, i.e., the preaching—and hearing through the word of Christ (Rom. 10:17).

When the meaning and power of the Word are thus discussed, it should be kept in mind that the Word does not stand alone. To sepa-

8. Cf. also B. J. Oosterhoff, *Jeremia en het Woord van God*, 1987.

rate God and his Word would be deistic. God remains its subject and therefore it must be said: "See that ye refuse not him that speaketh" (Heb. 12:25). Those who encounter the Word of God, encounter the God of the Word.

Yet there is more to be considered. Acts 7:51 refers to resistance to the Word as resistance against the Holy Spirit. When Lydia pays attention to Paul's message and believes, it is the Lord who opens her heart to it (Acts 16:14–15). The Spirit is the Spirit of wisdom and of revelation to come to know God in truth, and therefore there is an inner enlightenment (Eph. 1:17–18). Whenever the apostle Paul administers the Word, this is administration of the Spirit (2 Cor. 3:8). Thus Paul is the interpreter of believers when he says: "Now we have received, not the spirit of the world, but the spirit which is of God; that we might know the things that are freely given to us of God" (1 Cor. 2:12).

2. *From a historic perspective, the thoughts of Augustine and those of Luther and Calvin are highly relevant.*

It has been said of Augustine that he conceived of the doctrine of the Word of God. According to him the Word does not merely serve as instruction or as new legislation, as was frequently the case prior to him. As a calling from God (*vocatio*) the Word is a demonstration of the grace of God that instills faith.

In Augustine's life there is a clear theological progression. He says that during the first phase of his episcopacy he still believed that following the preaching of the gospel it was within the ability of man himself to accept or reject the word that was preached. But he discovered that Holy Scripture teaches differently. Subsequently, varying perspectives can be identified in the legacy of this church father. Not infrequently he distinguishes between external and internal words. He does so in a sermon (on 1 John 2:27): The sound of our words only goes as far as our ears; the teacher is on the inside. Do not believe that one human being learns anything from another human being. Christ himself speaks to you on the inside, when none of those people are present.

Referring to such statements, it is frequently claimed that he was unable to do full justice to the Word because—under influence of Neoplatonism—he considered it among the "*signa*" and not the "*res*" and could only see it as symbol of the real thing. However, this did not predominate. Augustine was much more guided by what the Bible says about the significance of the word that is preached.

He had to deal with Donatists, who considered the effect of preaching and the sacraments to be a function of the holiness of the office bearers. Could someone who is dead make others alive? Augustine counters by saying that God's work should not be ascribed to people. It is not the role of people, but that of God, to grant growth (cf. 1 Cor. 3:6–7). "In this way the minister plays a role in the ministry and the distribution of the Word and the sacraments, but not in justification and purification." Whether the voice of the Shepherd comes to us through a bad or a good man, what matters is that it is the voice of the Shepherd. When one of the Donatists appeals to John 20:22–23 to prove that human beings have been charged with forgiving sins, Augustine's reply is that forgiveness is granted through them (*per eos*), but not achieved by them (*ab eis*). He holds on to this "*per eos*" when he has to deal with an underestimation of ecclesiastical office. There were those who taught that God could grant his grace without the intervention of people. Augustine combated this view in *De doctrina christiana* (prologue): Paul was sent to Ananias; Cornelius was instructed by Peter, and the Ethiopian court official by Philip. "Let us be on guard against such utterly arrogant and extremely dangerous temptations." The flock of Christ cannot live without the ministry of the Word and the sacraments. The Word of God, read and proclaimed, is daily bread for believers (cf. Polman, 1955).

Various ideas of Augustine resurface in the history of the church and theology. The medieval church had become more and more a church of sacraments, but the Reformation restored the importance of preaching. Luther's translation of Romans 10:17 was: "So kommt der Glaube aus der Predigt, das Predigen aber durch das Wort Gottes" (thus faith comes from the sermon, but preaching comes through the Word of God). Through the Word faith is called into being, sustained, and strengthened.

From Augustine Luther took over the distinction between the external and internal Word. People can bring it to the ear, but not into the heart, for only God does this. The internal Word is God's own speaking through his Spirit. This is the first perspective in Luther's theology: the Holy Spirit acts sovereignly with the Word. There is yet a second perspective: the Holy Spirit binds himself to the (external) Word. On the one hand: the Spirit blows where he wishes and not where we wish. On the other hand: he gives us the Word and therein (*in eo*) the Holy Spirit.[9] The second perspective is especially apparent in the conflict with Anabaptist radicals who felt that they were more consistent than the Reformer. They believed they were on solid ground with an appeal to the Spirit. But the Word and the Spirit cannot be separated. The "enthusiasts" sought to reverse God's order by priding themselves in the claim that they had the Spirit apart from and prior to the Word (Smalkaldic Articles). But the external aspects (preaching and the sacraments) precede, while the internal aspects follow in

9. The resulting tension is brought out by R. Prenter, *Spiritus Creator*, 1954, 109.

consequence. In line with God's order, one first hears the Word. Then the Holy Spirit comes in the same Word and he makes the external internal. Luther can say that the Word brings Christ into our hearts. He has in mind the Word with which the Spirit is connected. It is then, after all, an efficacious Word.

The Word of God consists of both commands and promises, but it is in essence: gospel, promise. Here we encounter the concept of *promissio*, which is so important in the Reformational doctrine of Word and sacrament.

Christ is present in the Word and he comes to us through the Word. We find and possess Christ only in the Word.

The Reformer combats Roman theologians and Anabaptist radicals with a single powerful statement: Christ cannot be presented to us other than through the Word and he cannot be accepted by us other than through faith (*WA*, 40.1.545).

Luther's view of the Word reflects his Christology. Those who doubt both Word and sacrament doubt the incarnation as God's way to us. Spiritualists do so with their passive awaiting of the heavenly voice. In believing receptiveness, we must remain open to God's work through the Word by means of which salvation comes to us. Then the words of God become to us what they are in themselves. Faith unites the soul completely with the Word.

Calvin delved into the relationship between Word and Spirit more so than anyone else. Certain of his pronouncements give the impression that the external and internal perspectives are mutually exclusive. But in connection with John 14:26 he considers outward preaching to be useless, if it is not accompanied by the teaching of the Spirit. God has therefore two ways of teaching. After all, he makes the Word sound in our ears by the mouths of men and addresses us inwardly through his Spirit. Sometimes he does so at the same moment, or else at different times, as he thinks fit (cf. *Institutes*, 2.5.5).

The external and internal perspectives go hand in hand. The Holy Spirit is the internal teacher (*internus doctor*), through whose effort the promise of salvation penetrates our hearts (*Institutes*, 3.1.4).

Calvin had to fight on two fronts. On the one hand, he had to deal with those who despised external preaching; on the other hand, there were those who ascribed everything to preaching itself. The former were spiritualists, while the latter were humanists who believed that they did not need the Spirit and to whom it was not an issue whether man indeed desired and could believe the Word of God. He had a healthy mind and a free will! One could say that the former group played off the

Spirit against the Word and the latter group permitted the Word to obscure the Spirit. Spiritualists misinterpreted 2 Corinthians 3:6 and humanists Romans 10:17.

To spiritualists it should be pointed out that it is not only a matter of the Spirit but also the Word, and that Paul is misrepresented if his epistles are treated as a "dead letter"; humanists need to be reminded that the Spirit can never be ignored in relationship to Word and faith. Both Spirit and Word, both Word and Spirit! The imprint of polemics is never absent in various statements that are characteristic of Calvin's position (cf. Krusche, 1957, 218–33; Balke, 1977², 98ff.).

Calvin writes in *Institutes*, 1.9.1–3, that the church is equally governed through God's Word and Spirit. One needs to pursue the reading of Scripture and listen to it conscientiously, if one wishes to obtain any benefit and fruit from the Spirit of God. For the Lord has bound together the certainty of his Word and Spirit with a reciprocal bond. In combating Rome's teachings, Calvin says that the Spirit wills to be conjoined with God's Word by an indissoluble bond and that Christ professes this concerning the Spirit when he promises him to his church. Calvin was referring to the promises of John 16:7 and 13 (*Institutes*, 4.8.13).

3. What did Calvin and Reformed theology mean with *the Word and the Spirit being conjoined*? It does not have to imply simultaneity. In this case the Holy Spirit would have to work faith in the heart at the very moment that the Word is proclaimed. The conjunction (*conjunctio*) of the Word and the Spirit does not imply that the work of the Spirit coincides chronologically with the preaching of the Word. But this conjunction should not be described either as a mere potentiality ("it could happen"). It is a connection that rests on God's promise that the Word will not return empty to him, but shall accomplish what pleases him and shall succeed in the thing for which he sends it (cf. Isa. 55:11). We may expect in faith that he will demonstrate his power through his Spirit and his Word. This is our prayer: "Rule us by thy Word and Spirit" (Heidelberg Catechism, Lord's Day 48).

When the Word of God is proclaimed in the right manner and nevertheless fails to be a blessing to some, this does not imply that it has not been of significance to them. God has not failed to address them. Paul writes: "We are unto God a sweet savour of Christ," i.e., either a fragrance to life or a fragrance to death (cf. 2 Cor. 2:15–16). The latter is then the consequence of unbelief. Calvin calls it somewhat accidental, for it is the essence of the Word to work salvation. Those who fail to listen to what the Holy Spirit has to say in Holy Scripture, and in the proclamation of the Word to the church, resist the Spirit (cf. Acts 7:51) and reap the judgment of which God's Word speaks. "As the Word of God is efficacious for the salvation of the believers, so it also is abundantly efficacious for condemning the wicked" (Calvin on Isa. 55:11).

Therefore, no one can escape responsibility by saying that everything is subject to the Spirit. Those who hear the Word of God find themselves within the field of influence of the Holy Spirit. The Word does not exist apart from the Spirit. *It is the Word of the Spirit.* The Spirit does not come without the Word. *He is the Spirit of the Word.* Whenever the Word is believed, it is entirely due to the work of the Spirit, who opens the heart to it. Calvin is correct in saying that without the illumination of the Holy Spirit, the Word can do nothing (*Institutes*, 3.2.33). A useful formulation is from Berkhof: "The Word brings the Spirit to the heart and the Spirit brings the Word into the heart" (Berkhof, 1964, 42).

One needs to be very precise here. With spiritualism and mysticism one can easily forget that the Word is the Word of the Spirit. Spiritualism did not only surface during the age of the Reformation, but it also did subsequently, for example among Quakers. To them the key is the spiritual or inner light (*lumen internum*). The divine inner revelations cannot be verified against the external witness of Scripture. They are certain and clear in themselves. Although the Bible is the most eminent literary expression of all religious experience, it is not the source of truth.

There were various earlier Reformed theologians who felt compelled to signal the danger of spiritualism. This proves that its attraction was not insignificant. Well known is the warning of W. à Brakel against various radicals, among whom he counted not only Quakers but also Quietists and Labadists (Brakel, *R.S.* 2:639–99). It is less well known how J. Verschuir treated the relationship between Word and Spirit, when through a book by J. ten Cate he had learned of the revelations that Antoinette Bourignon (1616–80) was said to have received.[10]

A spiritual separation of Word and Spirit is also encountered in circles that Woelderink regards as having "Anabaptist trends." Although this label was widely adopted, it has been correctly pointed out that not everything that Woelderink calls Anabaptist is really Anabaptist.[11]

10. J. Verschuir, *De zegepralende waarheid* (the triumphant truth), 1724, 120–28 (a summary by J. van Genderen, "Johan Verschuir (1680–1737)," in *De Nadere Reformatie en het Gereformeerde Piëtisme* (the Second Reformation and Reformed Pietism), 1989, 210ff.

11. J. G. Woelderink, *De gevaren der Doopersche geestesstrooming* (the dangers of the Anabaptist movement), 1946, 42–58; G. W. Marchal, *J. G. Woelderink*, 1986, 111–22; cf. W. Balke, "Dopers radicalisme in historisch perspectief," *Th. Ref.* 17 (1974): 114ff.

One can see a connection with the spiritual movement that Van Ruler had in mind when he drew the portrait of the ultra-Reformed, who had come to think increasingly one-sidedly about the work of the Holy Spirit. The work of the Spirit does not begin at the point at which he reaches into the heart of a human being! The fact that the Holy Spirit is already fully engaged in dispensing salvation in its fullest measure when the minister of the Word proclaims the Scriptures from the pulpit is completely ignored (Van Ruler, *T.W.*, 3:116–20).

Among Pentecostal groups that emerged in the twentieth century, there is a danger that one allows oneself to be guided not only by Scripture but also by all sorts of prophecies, while it always remains a question whether the Spirit of God is indeed at work or man himself.[12]

However, rationally, one can also fail to do justice to the fact that the Spirit is the Spirit of the Word. When it is maintained that those who read Scripture, and hear it proclaimed, naturally are capable of believing, or that enlightenment of the mind is adequate since volition automatically follows understanding, one ignores the necessity of the inner work of the Holy Spirit. Just as Augustine had to maintain over against Pelagians that God's grace must change man inwardly, the Synod of Dort had to do so over against Remonstrants, and we ourselves must adhere to it over against all those who overestimate man and his capabilities.

Spiritualism and rationalism have in common that they make man independent of God. The former makes man with his religious experiences independent at the expense of the Word of God against which all experience must be gauged. In the latter case man is made independent as a rational-moral being at the expense of the work of the Spirit, which is not judged to be strictly essential. It is noteworthy that the most highly spiritual mysticism (spiritualism) has over and over turned into the most vulgar rationalism (cf. Bavinck, *R.D.*, 1:473ff.). It is remarkable and yet not so surprising. Both movements are in essence subjectivist. The Spirit then tends to become a pseudonym for our personal notions (cf. Berkhof, *C.F.*, 65).

From the Reformed perspective we have reacted to frequently encountered tendencies to separate the Spirit from the Word and the Word from the Spirit. Yet the Reformed position is not based on reaction. This position expresses that we depend on the Word as well as the Spirit. Scripture, after all, says that faith comes from hearing and hearing through the word of Christ (Rom. 10:17), and that the Spirit is received through the preaching of the faith (Gal. 3:2, 5). It also makes clear that receiving the Spirit of God causes us to know what God has given us by grace (1 Cor. 2:12).

The Reformed view of the relationship between the Word and the Spirit is thus described in one of our confessions. The gospel is intended by God "to be a seed of regeneration and food for the soul" (Canons of Dort, 3–4.17). God "not only causes the gospel to be externally

12. K. Hutten, *Geloof en sekte* (faith and sect), no date, 110ff., 120.

preached" and he does not only "powerfully illuminate [the] minds by his Holy Spirit," but he also opens the closed heart and renews the will. "Regeneration" or "renewal" is brought about in us not only through "external preaching" or moral suasion, but also through an evidently supernatural, very powerful, and simultaneously very tender working of the Holy Spirit (Canons of Dort, 3–4.11–12).

4. *There is a difference between the Lutheran and Reformed points of view.* This is frequently explained with the help of the expressions "through the Word" (*per verbum*) and "with the Word" (*cum verbo*). Honig writes: The Holy Spirit pairs up with the Word. He presents this as the Reformed view over against the Lutheran view, whereby the Holy Spirit works through the Word as his instrument (Honig, *Handboek*, 617ff.). It is usually added that according to the spiritualist view, the Spirit works apart from the Word (*sine verbo*).

This characterization of the Lutheran point of view is open to challenge. For example, the Smalkaldische Artikelen (1537), which were written by Luther, state: through and with the external Word (*per verbum en cum verbo*). But we object especially to the exclusive "with" as a description of the Reformed position. This does not at all agree with Calvin's pronouncements and those of the Reformed confession statements (cf. Heidelberg Catechism, Lord's Day 25: "by the preaching of the holy gospel"). For a subsequent period the *Synopsis* (1625) is representative. It says: the Holy Spirit is at work only through (*per*) the external Word and Holy Scripture in the hearts of people unto salvation (2:9). We can agree with Berkouwer when he points out that Scripture itself testifies so emphatically with respect to the power of the Word that one truly need not shy away from the term "*per verbum.*" He refers to passages such as Isaiah 55:11 and Hebrews 4:12. But he adds that one can speak at the same time of "*cum verbo*" to indicate that it is not a matter of an automatic effect of preaching and to stress that the Word can only be accepted in faith through the power of the Holy Spirit. He refers to Luke 24:45 and Acts 16:14.[13]

The use of the terms "*per verbum*" and "*cum verbo*" in this context largely reflects the controversy about the Word as means of grace, known as the Rahtmann controversy (circa 1625). H. Rahtmann, a Lutheran pastor at Danzig, started off with

13. G. C. Berkouwer, *Sin*, 1971, 217ff.

the practical experience that the Word of God has no impact on the lives of many. It is a signpost, but a signpost by itself does not get us there. It is an axe, but an axe needs to be wielded. The divine external word needs to be coupled with the inner enlightenment of the Holy Spirit. This interpretation was strongly opposed. It was associated with spiritualism, which separated Word and Spirit from each other as external and internal perspectives and was thoroughly despised, as Luther did himself. One also saw a connection with Calvinism that teaches that enlightenment through the Holy Spirit is granted to the elect and not to everyone. The judgment of four theological faculties was highly unfavorable to Rahtmann. It was pointed out, among other things, that Scripture *an sich* has the power to feed mankind and satisfy its hunger. Subsequently, Lutheran orthodoxy taught with emphasis that the "*efficacia*" was inherent in Scripture, because the Holy Spirit is associated with it in a hidden manner (Quenstedt, Hollaz).[14]

The concern of the Reformed was that—by referring to the Spirit as being immanent in the Word and the Word as being charged with the Spirit—the Word came to be seen as a magic power. Can the Holy Spirit really be restricted to the Word? He rather lends effectiveness to the Word, because it pleases him and as it pleases him. In this connection Bavinck points out that Lutherans had to resort to man's free will in order to explain the different outcome. The "*cum verbo*" respects the freedom of the Holy Spirit, who invariably works through the Word, but not always in the same manner. There is a subjective activity of the Holy Spirit, which has to be added to the objective Word. This activity cannot be enclosed in the Word. It is not an activity through the Word (*per verbum*), but along with the Word (*cum verbo*), an opening of the heart (Acts 16:14), an internal revelation (Bavinck, *R.D.*, 4:459ff.).

This formulation is not correct, although the intention is clear. Apart from the fact that the term "subjective" is employed improperly, a contrast between *per verbum* and *cum verbo* is invoked which should not be there. The example of Lydia proves rather the incorrectness than the correctness of Bavinck's judgment. Did the Holy Spirit not open Lydia's heart to the Word by means of the Word?

According to Van der Meiden, who also discusses the words of Acts 16, the *per* and *cum* do not contradict each other, although he prefers to speak of the special role of the Spirit with respect to the Word. "The special work of the Holy Spirit takes place with the Word in such a way that he works re-creatively in the elect under the influence and by means of the Word in accordance with the Word, according to God's good pleasure" (Van der Meiden, 1949, 17).

When the relationship between Word and Spirit was raised in official discussions between representatives of the *Christelijke Gereformeerde* and *Gereformeerde (vrijgemaakt* = liberated) churches in the Netherlands, the latter strongly emphasized that the confession refers to the Holy Spirit as working through and not with the Word. It was feared that otherwise the effectual working of the Holy Spirit would be viewed

14. Cf. R. H. Grützmacher, *Wort und Geist*, 1902, 220–61; O. Ritschl, *Dogmengeschichte des Protestantismus* (dogmatic history of Protestantism), 1927, 4:157–72; A. Adam, *Lehrbuch der Dogmengeschichte* (textbook of dogmatic history), 1968, 2:407ff.

as standing on its own. The former asked whether this interpretation adequately allowed for varying effects.[15]

The conviction that Holy Scripture has divine authority is owed to the inner working of the Holy Spirit who, according to a formulation by the Westminster Confession, testifies in our hearts *by and with the Word—per verbum et cum verbo ipso*. The same holds with respect to the question as to how the message of Holy Scripture enters and takes effect. This occurs because the Holy Spirit testifies in our hearts by and with the Word.

Elements for a doctrine of the witness of the Holy Spirit were already present in Reformational theology prior to Calvin. Thus Luther wrote: the Holy Spirit witnesses to our spirit and man comes to the point where he feels that this is the case and abandons all doubt whether it is entirely sure. For the elaboration of this doctrine we must especially look to Calvin[16] (see § 9).

It is not a voice from heaven. The assurance of salvation "is not produced by any peculiar revelation contrary to or independent of the Word" (Canons of Dort, 5.10). *The assurance of the Christian is an assurance based on the trustworthy testimony of the Word, and finds its origin in the witness that the Holy Spirit gives to the heart by means of the Word.*

50.3. *Law and gospel*

1. The Word of God comprises law and gospel. In the law God reveals his will to us. His law encompasses much more than the "ten words" of Exodus 20 (Deut. 5), although the Decalogue is indeed of fundamental significance for the relationship between the Lord and his people. The core of the commandments is the commandment to love (Matt. 22:37–40). The gospel proclaims to us salvation in Christ. It comes to us in the promise of the gospel.

Through Luther the distinction between law and gospel became an important theological theme. It cannot be equated with the distinction between the Old and New Testaments, although it was customary to

15. *Acta van de Generale Synode der Christelijke Gereformeerde Kerken in Nederland*, 1962, 241ff.

16. J. Pannier, *Le témoignage du Saint-Esprit* (the testimony of the Holy Spirit), 1893; S. P. Dee, *Het geloofsbegrip van Calvijn* (the concept of faith according to Calvin), 1918, 114–77; J. van Genderen, *Het getuigenis van de Heilige Geest* (the testimony of the Holy Spirit), 1961.

do so from the early centuries of Christianity till the Middle Ages. The result was that the gospel came to be viewed as a new and more perfect law.

Luther reacted to the legal interpretation of the gospel, which he associated largely with Rome, by contrasting the law and the gospel. At no price could the law be confused with the gospel. Luther defined both the law and the gospel in terms of their roles: The law serves to identify sin and the gospel serves to forgive sin. While the gospel contains the promise of Christ, it is the role of the law to demand, to accuse, and to condemn. According to Luther, this is not the only, but definitely the most important role of God's law.[17]

For the classic Reformed view we refer especially to Calvin. According to this Reformer, the distinction between the law and the gospel is consistent with the unity of the Word of God. In the covenant of grace, demand and promise, law and gospel go hand in hand. *The gospel grants what the law requires.*

The chapter of the *Institutes* that explains that the law is given to foster hope of salvation in Christ until his coming (2.7) presents a threefold role or use of the moral law. One could follow Calvin in referring to the law as *a mirror, a bridle, and a rule*.

a. The law reveals to us God's righteousness and convicts us of our own unrighteousness. Weighed in the balances of the law, our self-righteousness turns out to signify nothing. The law is a mirror in which we behold our impotence, our unrighteousness, and our condemnation.

b. The second role of the law is to ensure that those who do not care about justice and righteousness are not coerced but at least restrained by the fear of punishment. All those who have for some time sojourned in ignorance of God will recognize that they were kept in some fear and reverence of God by the bridle of the law, until they, having been born again of the Spirit, began to love him with their hearts.

c. The third and most important use of the law, which is also the closest to its actual purpose, is operative in believers in whose hearts the Spirit of God already has dominion. To them the law is an excellent instrument to learn every day better and more surely what the will of the Lord is. In this connection Calvin says: there is but a single eternal and unchangeable rule of life.

Like Luther, Calvin defended Christian freedom. The law, as a rule of life, does not detract from this. Believers are free from the curse of the law, which was borne for them by Christ, as well as the yoke of the law, for they obey of their own will.

17. For greater detail see J. van Genderen, "Luthers visie op wet en evangelie" (Luther's view of the law and the gospel), in W. Balke et al., *Luther en het Gereformeerd Protestantisme* (Luther and Reformed Protestantism), 1982, 249–82 (literature on 281ff.).

Furthermore, they have been relieved of the obligations of the ceremonial law, which was fulfilled in Christ (*Institutes*, 2.8.7; 3.19.3–4; 2.7.15–16).

In the use of the law as a mirror, Calvin was more careful than Luther and Melanchthon to avoid a legalistic interpretation, which results in a tendency to turn the law and the gospel into a scheme, so that for our conversion the law must be held up to us and for faith we are referred to the gospel. Thus the law must precede the gospel in order to bring man to sorrow over his sins and contrition before God. Only then would there be room for the comfort of the gospel. To Calvin the preaching of the law is not a chapter of its own that needs to precede the preaching of the gospel (Velema, 1987, 150–59).

Since 1935 discussion on the theme of law and gospel has been less dominated by differences between the views of Luther and Calvin, and more by the position taken by Barth and reactions to it.

Barth reversed the sequence of law-gospel. In summary, he says that the law is but the necessary form of the gospel whose content is grace. Precisely this content requires this form, the form that demands conformity, the form of the law (*Evangelium und Gesetz* = gospel and law, 1935).

It is no coincidence that this document appeared in 1935. In evaluating Barth's position we need to take into account the battle that he waged in those years against views such as those of F. Gogarten, according to which the law (*nomos*) of the German people directly or indirectly was identified with the law of God. Barth saw this as the consequence of the separation of the law and the gospel of Jesus Christ. Like the *Barmen Declaration* (1934), *Evangelium und Gesetz* was directed against the false teaching of "German Christians."[18]

In his explanation Barth referred to two biblical facts. In the first place, the law came 430 years after the promise (Gal. 3:17), and in the second place, the law was placed inside the Ark of the Covenant.

The content of the gospel is God's grace. God's grace is called Jesus Christ and is Jesus Christ. Through him our humanity is justified by God. The law is not a second agent apart from the gospel. The law is the revealed will of God. But where is the will of God revealed? In Jesus Christ! How can the dominion of Jesus Christ be proclaimed without the proclamation as such becoming a demand for obedience? When the law says, Thou shalt be (promise), we change it into, Thou must (demand). This is how we arrive at works of the law, through which we seek to justify ourselves. But then the law is to us the law of sin and death. If the law is the form of the gospel, it cannot as such condemn us. If God in Jesus Christ is for us, who will then be against us? Not even God's own law!

18. Cf. E. Busch, *Karl Barths Lebenslauf* (the life of Karl Barth), 1973, 279.

The treatment of the law and the gospel does not stand in isolation. These theses together with the underlying concepts must be considered to be the inner core of Barth's dogmatics (cf. Barth, *C.D.*, 4.3.370).

We have two critical comments. The first is that the distinction between law and gospel is rather vague in Barth's position. It has nearly been eliminated. By means of an incorrect interpretation of the imperative he allows the demand to be changed into a promise. According to him it is a misunderstanding to interpret the law as God's demand, which we must satisfy. But if the law is no longer a norm, it can no longer condemn us or place us under the curse, while Holy Scripture does emphatically speak such language (Rom. 2:12; Gal. 3:10, 13). In Barth's position we miss the accusatory function of the law.

The second criticism is that his approach to the question at hand reflects his own doctrine of grace, i.e., the "triumph of grace" in his theology. Just as to Luther the heart of the gospel is the promise of the forgiveness of sins and the law must pave the way for this, so in the case of Barth it is the covenant of God with man in Jesus Christ, of which the law can only be the form.[19]

2. In connection with the differences outlined above, it is necessary to explore *the relationship between the law and the gospel* in greater depth. If over against Barth we retain the sequence law-gospel, we do not do so because this sequence can be based on the fact that the Ten Commandments emerge prior to the gospel that we know from the New Testament. Abraham, after all, precedes Moses. Barth appropriately recalls the words of Paul concerning the promise that predates the release of the law on Sinai by centuries (Gal. 3:17). It does not begin with the Decalogue. Even the publication of the law on Sinai serves the progression of the history of God's covenant with Israel. When the Lord announces what he requires of the people of the covenant, he already has said who he is and what he does. See Exodus 19:4–6; 20:2.

There are additional grounds for not following Barth in his reversal of the sequence of law-gospel. At the center of the gospel stands the Mediator who has come to do God's will. Jesus says: "Thus it becometh us to fulfill all righteousness" (Matt. 3:15). Here "righteousness" stands for everything that is demanded by God. The fulfillment of all righteousness definitely includes the divine demand revealed in the

19. Cf. B. Klappert, *Promissio und Bund* (*promissio* and covenant), 1976, 229.

law and the prophets prior to the appearance of both Jesus and John the Baptist. There is no doubt that, according to Paul, the gospel of the coming and the work of Christ is directly related to our being under the law and under the curse of the law. Christ was born under the law and became a curse for us (Gal. 4:4–5; 3:13; cf. also Rom. 8:3–4). The law may not be reduced to a form of the gospel. This would be inconsistent with the interpretation of these mighty words of the New Testament.

There is no contradiction between the law and the gospel, for in the gospel God maintains his law. But the gospel is at the same time the good news that God himself has taken care of the fulfillment of the law.

It is due to the structure of Barth's theology that he places the gospel first. But in the Bible "the first gospel" (*proto-evangelium*, Gen. 3:15) is God's answer to the transgression of his commandment. It is true that the promise to Abraham precedes the commandments of Sinai, but Abraham was not the one with whom God began. This was Adam! The covenant of grace, to which the Decalogue belongs as the rule of the covenant, is not the original covenant of God with man. Theology must keep in mind that man as creature of God finds himself already under the law of God and that the gospel comes to people who are sinners before God. Sin is the transgression of God's holy will. His forgiving and renewing grace presupposes sin; the gospel presupposes the law. In this manner the sequence law-gospel is directly connected with the historical sequence of Paradise-fall into sin-redemption (see Velema, 1987, 38–41).

In the dogmatic sequence the law therefore precedes the gospel, which does not imply that it needs to be the same way in the sequence of personal knowledge of faith. In the covenant of grace, after all, God does not place his demand first. The promise and the demand go hand in hand. He promises what he demands and he demands what he promises. The love that he commands in his law, he works through the gospel of Christ in the hearts. "We love . . . because he first loved us" (1 John 4:19).

In the Lutheran tradition the law and the gospel came to stand over against each other, and the law came first. There is a passage in the New Testament that keeps turning up here: "Wherefore the law was our schoolmaster to bring us unto Christ, that we might be justified by faith" (Gal. 3:24).

According to the earlier exegesis this means that the law had to and has to lead to Christ and make us look forward to the redemption in him; according to the newer exegesis: From the point of view of the coming of Christ and until the time of his arrival the law had the role of pedagogue, but this stage came to an end. Ridderbos is right, however, when he recognizes here more than an indication of time: "It lay in God's intention not only *after* the time of bondage-under-the-law to make the liberty in Christ to dawn, but also *over against* this killing and enslaving operation of the law to make grace to appear the more gloriously in its indispensableness and its richness."[20] Seen in this light, these words of Paul are not merely intended to reflect the purely historical perspective of redemption.

There are actually those of the Reformed persuasion who agree with the Lutheran way of thinking. This was a rather general tendency of the Second Reformation. Th. van der Groe, who was one of the last representatives of this movement or trend, was of the opinion that God's Spirit first works by means of the law and subsequently also through the gospel. The preaching of the law was seen as a preparation for the application of the promises of the gospel. Thus a law-gospel system emerged, and preaching in the spirit of this system had a stifling influence on the church. It is a preaching that brings obligations: first one needs to experience this and then that.[21]

Similarly, in a discussion by A. Moerkerken, the law and the gospel are incorporated in a redemption-historical fashion into the prescribed experience of those who are en route to faith in Christ, of which the law is the first and the gospel the second phase. An appeal to A. Comrie serves to confirm this. God's usual approach is to lead a soul past Sinai to Zion "right by hell, as it were, before being brought to true rest."[22]

Velema correctly objects to this, because an arbitrary starting point is chosen in the history of redemption. One needs to keep in mind that God's work did not begin by giving the law (Sinai). The purpose of the order of salvation is not to repeat the history of redemption. An effort is made to assign negative work to the law, which is imposed as a precondition for the positive work of the gospel. The law would have to be proclaimed and experienced in the absence of the gospel. But this is legalism! (Velema, 1987, 134–37).

The fact that Lord's Days 2 and 6 of the Heidelberg Catechism refer to the knowledge of one's misery based on God's law and the knowledge of the Mediator based on the holy gospel, respectively, may have contributed to the idea that also according to this classic textbook of the church, in practice the law precedes the gospel and

20. H. Ridderbos, *Paul*, 1975, 152–53.

21. Cf. T. Brienen, "Theodorus van der Groe (1705–84)," in Brienen et al., *De Nadere Reformatie* (the Second Reformation), 1986, 294–96; C. Graafland, *Verschuivingen in de Gereformeerde Bondsprediking* (shifts in the preaching of the "Gereformeerde Bond" = Reformed League, a movement within the Netherlands Reformed Church), 1965, 62ff.

22. A. Comrie, *Verhandelingen van eenige eigenschappen des zaligmakenden geloofs* (a discussion of a number of properties of saving faith), 1778^5, 89; A. Moerkerken, *Genadeleven en genadeverbond* (a life of grace and the covenant of grace), 1977, 27.

that the proclamation of the law has a preparatory role vis-à-vis the proclamation of the gospel. However, this is not the intention. Lord's Days 2–4—like Lord's Days 5–6—represent explanations of what has already been confessed in Lord's Day 1. In this respect, the catechism takes an analytic approach.

The Reformed doctrine of the covenant of grace brings with it that the law and the gospel must be interrelated. They are distinguished from each other, but at the same time held together. *No gospel without the law, and no law without the gospel!* It is the one Word of God with both legal and evangelical dimensions. The Holy Spirit employs the entire Word as a tool in his hands and he does not follow any scheme whatsoever. The Word in its entirety is "quick and powerful, and sharper than any two-edged sword" (Heb. 4:12).

3. Reformed theology is familiar with a *threefold use of the law* (*triplex usus legis*):

- First, a civil use (*usus civilis, usus politicus*)—the law is given to bridle sin.
- Second, a pedagogical use (*usus paedagogicus, usus elenchticus*)—the law is there to convict of sin.
- Third, a normative use (*usus normativus, usus didacticus*)—the law serves as a rule of conduct for believers.

The systematic form of the doctrine of the threefold use of the law comes down to us from Melanchthon. His opinion, however, is not shared by all Lutheran theologians. Actually, it has been the subject of a great deal of controversy as to whether those who consciously live by grace continue to be subject to the obligations of the law. For this reason, the *Formula Concordiae* (1577) addresses varying points of view with respect to the third use.

First, the civil or political role of the law is traditionally mentioned first (*primus usus legis*), but the question may be raised how this function of the law can be related to the Word as a means of grace. However, the one is not isolated from the other.

It has been pointed out that the New Testament says nothing about *usus politicus* of the Decalogue. Yet Romans 13:8–10 has to do with the fulfillment of the law, as does Romans 13:1–7. The law of God applies to all aspects of human society—including the state. God's demand to practice justice applies without restriction.

From a dogmatic point of view this use of the law has to do with God's maintenance of the world and common grace, as well as Christ's sovereignty and the sanctification of life.

God's all-encompassing will, which is focused on the coming of his kingdom, can be known from the gospel of salvation in Jesus Christ as well as from the law that God gave, and therefore from the law in all its functions, also when in its political function it teaches us to take the demand for righteousness seriously.

Second, it is biblical to follow Reformational theology in recognizing that the law has a pedagogical role. The Holy Spirit employs the law to disclose sin's sinful nature. Sin is lawlessness or repudiation of the law (*anomia*). The law imparts knowledge of sin. See 1 John 3:4 and Romans 3:20. This does not suggest that knowledge of sin only comes through the law, but that precisely God's law reveals that man is sinful. Ascribing this function to the law (cf. Heidelberg Catechism, Lord's Day 2 and 44) does not preclude that we can acquire awareness of sin through the gospel. The law imparts knowledge of sin, but so does the gospel!

It is the gospel of Jesus Christ and him crucified. If it can be seen anywhere how terrible sin is, it is especially so on Golgotha. There, however, sin is also condemned in the flesh (Rom. 8:3). Since Christ had to die on the cross as a result of God's wrath against sin, we ought to humble ourselves deeply before God (cf. Form for the Administration of the Lord's Supper). When it comes to the knowledge of sin, it is not an issue whether this is from the law *or* the gospel. This knowledge as faith-knowledge is from the entire Word of God, i.e., both the law *and* the gospel. It is objectionable to turn this into a method or system, for we cannot prescribe an approach to the Holy Spirit, who employs the entire Word to make us see who we are before God.

Only when the law and the gospel are proclaimed in relationship with each other is it clear that the law functions within the framework of the covenant of grace. This is how the *usus elenchticus* is done proper justice. An isolated proclamation of the law can in one case lead to despair and in another to moralism.

Precisely in connection with the gospel, this function of the law remains important to believers. Just as question and answer 3 of the

Heidelberg Catechism should not be interpreted as merely a legalistic stage in preparation for the knowledge of sin and misery, so is the knowledge of sin and misery not merely the initial phase on the way of faith, subsequently to be left behind, having received further guidance from the gospel. Here we can refer to the answer of this textbook of the church to the question as to why the Ten Commandments must be preached so strictly if no one in this life can keep them (Lord's Day 44).

Third, the law also has a *normative role*. God's law is always normative, however we interpret it. This role, however, deals especially with the law as the expression of the will of God with respect to the lives of believers. That the law of God is a rule for our lives is clearly stated in the Heidelberg Catechism (Lord's Day 34–44).

Although believers are not subject to the law, they are nevertheless not without the law (*Formula Concordiae*). Judging by Romans 8:4, it cannot be maintained that in Romans 10:4 Paul would mean that the law has ceased to apply to believers, as is not infrequently believed. There is no contradiction in teaching that the law has found its fulfillment in Christ and that in the lives of believers it is fulfilled through the Spirit. This is entirely in line with the message of the apostle Paul.

Keeping the law as norm reflects the new obedience and gratitude for redemption in Christ. It is grateful obedience. If we show ourselves to be grateful for God's benefits (Heidelberg Catechism, Lord's Day 31), this takes concrete shape in a beginning to live according to all of God's commandments. The law then becomes the rule of gratitude.

The significance of the law of God for Christian living is further discussed in ethics.

§ 51. The sacraments as means of grace

51.1. *What are sacraments?*
51.2. *Word and sacrament*
51.3. *The working of the sacraments*

51.1. *What are sacraments?*

In Reformed dogmatics, discussions of baptism and the Lord's Supper are usually preceded by a chapter or a section on sacraments in general. It is important that the doctrine of the sacraments does not become an abstraction of what Holy Scripture says about baptism and the Lord's Supper, or a construct that does not do justice to the biblical data!

The word "sacrament" is not derived from the Bible. It was Tertullian who incorporated it into the language of theology and the church. The Latin word "*sacramentum*" has two main interpretations: 1. security deposited in a sanctuary by two parties involved in litigation; 2. a military oath, i.e., an oath of allegiance to the regimental flag. In both cases it is a religious commitment. Tertullian may have had the second interpretation in mind when he coined the terms "sacrament of the water" and "sacrament of the Eucharist." But there is still another important notion. Like "*mysterium*," "sacramentum" represented the New Testament notion of "*mysterion*" (mystery, secret of salvation) in the old Latin translations of the Bible. The mysteries or sacraments of the Christian faith were actions with a hidden meaning. According to Augustine they were signs that referred to the reality of redemption. The medieval church taught that there were seven sacraments, which were not only signs but also sources of grace (Lyon 1274, Florence 1439, Trent 1547).

Although the Reformation did not come up with a new term, it did give the concept a largely new content: the essential element is God's promise and the sign is simultaneously interpreted as a seal. We recognize this in Calvin's definition of a sacrament: it is an outward sign by which the Lord seals on our consciences the promises of his good will toward us in order to strengthen the weakness of our faith; and we attest our piety toward him before him and his angels as well as before men (*Institutes*, 4.14.1). In the Reformational doctrine of the sacraments a distinction is made between the sign and the object that is signified (*res sacramenti*). According to the Heidelberg Catechism, "sacraments are holy, visible signs and seals, appointed of God for this end, that by the use thereof he may the more fully declare and seal to us the promise of the gospel" (Lord's Day 25). We also encounter the expression "sign and seal" in the Belgic Confession of Faith. From the perspective of the relationship with the covenant of grace, which is apparent in both baptism and the Lord's Supper, it is also helpful to speak of signs and seals of the covenant.

In the twentieth century there were theologians who distanced themselves from the age-old and strong tradition in which the sacraments are seen as means of grace. For example, Barth rejects them out of principle. A certain development can be recognized in his views on baptism and the Lord's Supper. In the last volume of *Church Dogmatics* that he was able to publish (1969) he came to the conclusion that baptism is a response to the one "mystery," the one "sacrament" of the history of Jesus Christ, but not itself a mystery, a sacrament.

Berkhof is of the opinion that it would be well to break with the concept of sacrament, i.e., with the Reformational triad of "Word and sacraments." Berkhof sees baptism and the Lord's Supper as media of transmission or mediating elements that can die off in the course of history. This would be conceivable for the "washing" and the "meal," but is unlikely to happen (*C.F.*, 394).

There is, however, no reason to yield to such probability calculus, and to hold on to what the New Testament says with respect to the lasting significance of baptism and the Lord's Supper. Baptism will be the sign of being a disciple of Jesus till "the end of the world" (Matt. 28:19–20) and Christ's death will be proclaimed at his table "till he come" (1 Cor. 11:26).

We reject the Roman Catholic position with respect to both the number of sacraments and their nature, in limiting ourselves to baptism and the Lord's Supper. Rome maintains seven sacraments (baptism, confirmation, the Eucharist, penance, extreme unction, holy orders, and matrimony), while the Eastern Orthodox Church has seven mysteries. The authority of the church is decisive in determining the number of sacraments.

Compared with such richness, Protestantism may make a paltry impression with its two sacraments. Nevertheless, Bavinck could say that the Protestant Christian possesses infinitely more in baptism and the Lord's Supper than the Roman Catholic in his seven sacraments. There is no additional grace in confirmation, penance, or extreme unction, for through the Word and through baptism and the Lord's Supper we receive everything that we need (*R.D.*, 4:494ff.).

51.2. *Word and sacrament*

In Reformational theology the Word-sacrament sequence is a matter of principle. The Word has priority and the sacrament must be understood on the basis of the Word. This sequence cannot be reversed. We know of no sacraments that are independent of the Word. Their role is to confirm the Word and especially the promises of the Word.

Rome's view is different. There the sacraments are the means of grace par excellence. The celebration of the sacrament is the core of the liturgy, and preaching has mainly a preparatory function. The actual encounter with God takes place at the altar, although the reading of Scripture in the worship service plays a greater role than in the past.

This new insight in the relationship between Word and sacrament broke through in Luther's thinking. The Word has priority. In it God establishes a relationship with us through his promises. One can have the Word or testament without the symbol or sacrament. According to Calvin the role of the sacraments is no different from that of the Word of God, in the sense that they offer and set forth Christ to us and in him the treasures of heavenly grace (*Institutes*, 4.14.17). The Word and the sacraments both point to "the sacrifice of Jesus Christ on the cross as the only ground of our salvation" (Heidelberg Catechism, Lord's Day 25).

The sacraments are means that take second place (*secunda organa*—Calvin). They are not secondary in the sense that they are of subsidiary significance. According to Calvin, to spurn them is to scorn Christ.

The Word is of primary significance. The sacraments add nothing to the content of the Word. What is more, faith is brought about and strengthened by means of the Word, while through baptism and the Lord's Supper it is strengthened but not brought about.

The sacraments are therefore not required because the Word is inadequate or insufficiently clear, but to make us understand the promises of the gospel more clearly and seal them for us (Heidelberg Catechism). God omits no effort to bring us in. He gives himself to us through the Word and he gives himself to us in baptism and the Lord's Supper. We may both hear *and* see who he wants to be to us in Christ. His goodness can be recognized in the duality of Word and sacrament. God takes into account our slowness to understand and our weakness (Belgic Confession of Faith, article 33). He accommodates us through graphic teaching and by offering us a firmer grip. This is the purpose of the sacraments.

In baptism and the Lord's Supper there is a concentration of the promises of the gospel. See the explanation of these promises in our classic liturgical forms. There is also a personal emphasis. When we are baptized and our name is called, when bread and wine are given to us in the Lord's Supper, God tells us that the promised salvation is also for us. The sacraments are there to be received in faith. We then see the mutuality to which Calvin referred in his description of the sacraments. Around the baptismal font and at the Lord's Table we declare piety (*pietas*) toward God.

51.3. *The working of the sacraments*

1. The sacraments are means in God's hand. The church confesses that the sacraments are "visible signs and seals of an inward and invisible thing, by means whereof God works in us by the power of the Holy Spirit" (Belgic Confession of Faith, article 33). The Holy Spirit employs means. This is an old expression, but it remains valid.

Here we encounter two opposing tendencies: *on the one hand, a tendency to separate the Holy Spirit from the sacraments, and on the other hand, a tendency to tie the Holy Spirit to the sacraments.*

We encounter the former tendency among spiritualists and Anabaptists. Spiritualists are only concerned with the inner workings of the Spirit. In the sixteenth century, figures such as S. Franck and C. Schwenckfeld found that sacraments were not required for Christians who are led by the Spirit or that they are only examples and testimonies for our outer nature. In spiritualist views there is no need whatsoever for the Holy Spirit to work through the sacraments.

Anabaptists did seek to maintain baptism and the Lord's Supper as institutions of Christ, for they allowed themselves to be led by the letter of Holy Scripture. But to them they were not means of grace. Baptism was an act of confession, a sign of the obedience of faith; the Lord's Supper was a memorial meal, a proclamation of the death of Christ and a testimony to mutual love and community.

Among spiritualists and Anabaptists, baptism and the Lord's Supper cannot be called means of grace; neither according to Zwingli, although he could say that the sacraments assist faith and refresh the soul. In contrast, the fundamental principle of Calvin's doctrine of the sacraments can be found in the significance that he associates with the work of the Holy Spirit. The Belgic Confession of Faith speaks entirely in Calvin's spirit.

We encounter the second tendency in Rome's position. In scholastic theology the sacraments are referred to as signs and sources of grace (*non solum significant sed causant gratiam*). According to a doctrinal pronouncement of 1439 (Florence), the seven sacraments of the new law encompass grace and grant it to those who receive them worthily (*continent gratiam et digne suscipientibus conferunt*). In 1547 the Council of Trent declared that all true righteousness begins with the sacraments, or is enhanced if it has already begun, or is restored if it has been lost. The doctrine that the sacraments are not essential for salvation, since man is justified by faith only, was condemned. This implied that all justifying or saving grace is sacramental grace. This grace is confirmed by the sacramental act as such (*ex opere operato*). The work of the Holy Spirit is thus tied to the sacraments of the church.

Does "*ex opere operato*" imply as much as automatic? It is an expression from scholasticism by means of which they sought to emphasize the objectivity of the sacraments as much as possible. The effect of a sacrament does not depend on the minister or the recipient. What matters is that it is administered in the prescribed manner. The Reformers had the impression that thus a magic power was attributed to the sacraments. In his rejection of Trent, Calvin says that the sacraments have no magic power that operates independent of faith. The Roman Catholic position was subsequently described by Bavinck as: "The sacrament, accordingly, works physically and magically by virtue of a power granted to the priest by God, as an instrument in his hand" (*R.D.*, 4:468).

It appears to be automatism, but it is more complicated, because human cooperation plays a role. According to Trent there is also a subjective condition: no obstacle is permitted to be placed in its way. This corresponds with the requirement that the sacrament has to be received worthily. The primary factor is divine causality. The secondary factor is human collaboration or worthiness. At any rate, the key is that there should be no resistance or encumbrance. A mortal sin or conscious unbelief would be a hindrance to the efficacy of the sacrament.

Furthermore, this doctrine of the causality of the sacraments is associated with the view that grace is a power that is poured into man (*gratia infusa*). Differences of view with respect to the role of the sacraments have everything to do with differences of view with respect to the nature of grace. Is grace a supernatural reality or is it the unmerited favor of God to which we owe restored communion, forgiveness of sins, and the renewal of life?

According to the Reformational view, sacraments do not resemble channels through which God's grace flows toward us. They cannot be compared to medication that is administered to us. They signify and seal God's promises. The Holy Spirit employs them to strengthen our faith, which is focused on these promises. Calvin says that to seek Jesus Christ in the sacraments we must interpret the signs as means to be led directly to the Lord Jesus to seek our entire salvation in him (Geneva Catechism, 318).

2. Over against the first tendency—separation of the Holy Spirit and the sacraments—we may hold that the Spirit seeks to employ the sacraments as means of *grace*. Over against the second tendency—tying the Holy Spirit to the sacraments—it must be maintained that the Spirit does not transfer his power to the sacraments. They remain *means* of grace.

Over against the former view we point especially to the language of the sacraments (*phraseologia sacramentalis*). See verses such as, "Be baptized, and wash away thy sins" (Acts 22:16), and, "The cup of blessing which we bless, is it not the communion of the blood of

Christ? The bread which we break, is it not the communion of the body of Christ?" (1 Cor. 10:16).

The connection between the sign and what is signified was established by Christ at the institution of the sacraments. He says with respect to the bread and the wine of the Lord's Supper: this is my body; this is my blood. For those who believe, the sign and what is signified go hand in hand. We indicate this by the term "conjunction." This explains the sacramental manner of speaking.

The supporters of the second view believe themselves to be in a strong position by appealing to verses such as Titus 3:5 and Galatians 3:27. In this connection we point out that baptism can indeed be referred to as "the washing of regeneration" (Titus 3:5), but this regeneration and renewal must be ascribed to the work of the Holy Spirit. According to Holy Scripture we are not saved by baptism, but by faith in Christ Jesus. In Galatians 3:27 the believing acceptance of baptism is presupposed. A well-considered statement by Calvin may be cited in this connection: "Therefore, between the Spirit and the sacraments I make the following distinction, namely that the power to work rests with the Spirit, but that the sacraments serve to provide a ministry, i.e., a ministry which in the absence of the Spirit is empty and of no value, but is filled with tremendous power when the Spirit works inwardly and manifests his power" (*Institutes*, 4.14.9).

Luther's view remains to be mentioned. In the beginning of his Reformational endeavors, the immediate connection between promise and faith predominated. He pointed as much to the relationship between sacrament and promise as that between sacrament and faith. To seek the effectual working of the sacraments apart from promise and faith is a vain effort and leads to condemnation.

However, there is another perspective to be found in Luther and in the church closely associated with him. In his conflict with spiritualism (Schwärmer) and Zwingli, Luther came to see the sacraments as bearers of heavenly gifts, which bring with them that to which they testify. The water of baptism is no ordinary water, but pure blood of the Son of God and pure fire of the Holy Spirit. The bread of the Lord's Supper is Christ's flesh. It is full of the Godhead.

The Lutheran position cannot be characterized with a single word. On the one hand the sacraments are to them signs and seals of the promise on which faith focuses, but on the other hand they are vehicles of grace. To us this implies a discrepancy.

There exist therefore important doctrinal differences with respect to the nature and working of the sacraments.

According to the Reformed point of view, the effect of the sacraments does not depend on the sacramental act itself, but on the Holy

Spirit who employs this means. The Spirit is not tied to baptism and the Lord's Supper, but does bestow upon them his blessing.

If the sacraments owe their effect to the work of the Holy Spirit, it does not mean that we need to wait and see what he will do, but that we may expect everything from him in faith. The church prays that God will look in grace upon those who receive baptism, and will incorporate them into Christ through his Holy Spirit. The anticipation of faith is expressed in the classic liturgy for the Lord's Supper: "not doubting that we shall be nourished and refreshed in our souls, with his body and blood, through the working of the Holy Spirit, as truly as we receive the holy bread and drink in remembrance of him."

3. By way of summary, Reformed theology says that the sacraments are *significative* (they are signs), *obsignificative* (they are seals), and *exhibitive* (they are accompanied by an offer or gift).

A clear description of baptism and the Lord's Supper as sign and seal is contained in responses 73 and 79 of the Heidelberg Catechism. As a consequence of the reality of the sacramental gift, baptism and the Lord's Supper have an exhibitive character. Not our faith but Christ's institution makes baptism and the Lord's Supper sacraments. Although unbelievers do not receive what the Lord offers sacramentally, baptism and the Lord's Supper remain true and perfect sacraments. In his speaking through baptism and the Lord's Supper God is as truthful and reliable as in his speaking through the Word. *We refer to this as the integrity or perfection of the sacraments.*

What is said in article 35 of the Belgic Confession of Faith is a good example of this. The godless do take the sacrament—but to their condemnation—but they do not receive the truth of the sacrament. This is to say that the sacrament is also in this case exhibitive: it is a true and perfect sacrament and not a sham. But it brings the godless no blessing, for they do not receive Christ. Christ cannot be separated from his Spirit, and he can only be received by us through faith. It is no coincidence that in the French text of our confession two different verbs are used: *il prend . . . il ne reçoit pas* (he takes . . . he does not receive).

In baptism and the Lord's Supper the Lord thus tells us what he gives to us (cf. Heidelberg Catechism, Lord's Day 25).

The Holy Spirit works through the sacraments when it pleases him. The effect of the sacraments need not coincide with their administration. The *Consensus Tigurinus* (1549), which is important to the doctrine of the sacraments, says: "The benefit of baptism applies to the entire course of life, because the promise that is contained in it remains in force. It can happen sometimes that our participation in the Lord's Supper, as a consequence of our inattention or slowness of understanding, initially has little benefit, but subsequently brings forth fruit" (article 20).

According to Roman Catholic doctrine, the sacraments bring sacramental grace with them. For each of the seven sacraments one can indicate a special grace. There are sacraments that supply grace for the first time or restore it (baptism, penance) and there are those that multiply the grace already received.

Kuyper also refers to sacramental grace. According to him, in baptism there is a separate work of grace of a particular kind, which cannot be equated with any other. This has been correctly objected to from various quarters. One can follow Bavinck in saying that there is not a single grace that is not conveyed by the Word and only by the sacrament (*R.D.*, 4:521).

§ 52. Baptism

- 52.1. ***The institution of baptism***
- 52.2. ***Baptism as a sign and seal***
- 52.3. ***Role and effect of baptism***
- 52.4. ***Differences of view within the Reformed community***
- 52.5. ***Infant baptism***
- 52.6. ***Baptism and profession of faith***

52.1. *The institution of baptism*

If baptism were merely a human or ecclesiastical institution, it would have significance only as the representation of religious concepts or as a venerable tradition, but we would have no defense against those who reject it. Baptism, however, is *an institution of God*. It is biblical to begin with this. It is also typically Reformed to do so (see Belgic Confession of Faith, article 34).

Baptism has been compared with ceremonial purification rites in Israel and with cleansing rituals of other nations. It does have something to do with the *purification rites* in Israel as well as *proselyte baptism*, which in all probability was already practiced in the first century AD. This was a baptism of pagans who were incorporated into the Jewish community. For them it was a great transition, which was sometimes referred to as a new beginning and a new birth.

Christian baptism is directly related to the *baptism of John the Baptist*. John did not begin to baptize on his own initiative, but was charged by God to do so (John 1:33). There is indeed a distinction between the baptism of John and Christian baptism. We may neither contrast nor equate them. John's baptism, which was a "baptism of repentance for the remission of sins" (Luke 3:3), like his preaching, constituted a pointing to Christ. John's baptism spoke of a coming kingdom, and the baptism, as instituted by the Lord Jesus Christ, spoke of the kingdom that had come. In the case of John's baptism the nations can only be seen from afar, whereas Christian baptism offers a broad horizon. It involves all nations (Matt. 28:19).

New Testament baptism was preceded by Old Testament *circumcision*, which represented the sign and seal of God's covenant with his people (Gen. 17). Israel understood too little that what mattered was not the sign itself, but inner renewal and faith. "And the LORD thy God will circumcise thine heart, and the heart of thy seed, to love the LORD thy God with all thine heart, and with all thy soul, that thou mayest live" (Deut. 30:6). Paul spoke similarly of the circumcision of the heart and circumcision as the seal of the righteousness of faith (Rom. 2:29; 4:11).

The passage that is especially important for the connection between circumcision and baptism, Colossians 2:11–12, contains the expression "the circumcision of Christ": the circumcision that pertains to Christ. It is also translated as: Christian circumcision. Here the apostle Paul refers to baptism. This is clear from his words: "You are buried with him in baptism." In communion with Christ, who died for them, believers received salvation, of which circumcision was the first sign and seal. From this we may deduce that its fulfillment in Christ also implies that baptism is the fulfillment of circumcision. This is to say that for us baptism has come in the place of circumcision. Since circumcision has been fulfilled in baptism, it has been abrogated in the new dispensation. For the Israelites circumcision was the sign and seal of the covenant to which they belonged; for us it is baptism (see J. P. Versteeg, "Baptism according to the New Testament" in *Rondom de doopvont* (around the baptismal font), 1983, 15–34, 105–12).

For the institution of baptism our confession refers us to Matthew 28:19. According to some this can no longer be done. Berkhof refers to this verse as a product of subsequent reflection and even thinks of it as fiction (*C.F.*, 357). This is an extreme form of biblical criticism. The authenticity of the text is questioned because the Trinitarian confession is thought to be of a much later date (see in this connection also § 12.1). Apart from Matthew 28, the *Didache* (7.1) also prescribes that baptism has to be administered in the name of the Father and the Son and the Holy Spirit. How can it be explained that the church adopted this form of baptism if the passage under discussion is not authentic?[23]

Matthew 28:19 is found in a specific context. Following his resurrection Christ instructs his apostles and therefore his church to make all nations his disciples. The proclamation of the gospel is to be accompanied by baptism. The Great Commission is at the same time a command to baptize.

Much has been written about the words "in the name of the Father and the Son and the Holy Spirit." It would be a mistake to replace "in the name of" by "on behalf of." Literally it says "into the name," a technical term that is sometimes connected with payment in commerce. The idea is that of charging to an account over which stands the name of the owner (*TDNT*, 1:539). There is more support for an expression that was current among Jewish rabbis (cf. *TDNT*, 5:275–76). In Matthew 28 the interpretation is then: with a view to the relationship with the Father and the Son and the Holy Spirit. We are comfortable with Bavinck's description (*R.D.*, 4:480), which says that the one who is baptized is placed in relationship and fellowship with the God who has revealed himself as Father, Son, and Spirit, and on this basis is now also obligated to confess that name and glorify it.

We are especially reminded of what the Form for Baptism says about the significance of this relationship with God: "God the Father witnesses and seals unto us that he makes an eternal covenant of grace with us. The Son seals unto us that he washes us in his blood from all our sins. The Holy Spirit assures us that he will dwell in us, and sanctify us to be members of Christ, imparting to us that which we have in Christ."

The words of Matthew 28:19 were quite soon used as a *baptismal formula*, although as such they are not. In the apostolic church we also hear of baptism in the name of Christ.

The church treats the Trinitarian formula of baptism as a prerequisite for valid baptism. This is expressly stated by most churches and for a good reason. We have in mind the strange developments that have taken place in the Netherlands with the emergence of modernism. It was found to be in conflict with the principles of Protestantism and freedom of conscience to make certain terminology mandatory for liturgical acts. It would seem Roman Catholic to make the effect of baptism dependent on a certain formula. Baptism has reportedly been conducted in the name of faith, hope, and love. Baptism has also been administered in the name of the Father

23. Cf. Ch. de Beus, *De oud-christelijke doop en zijn voorgeschiedenis* (the old-Christian baptism and its antecedents), 1945, 1:155.

or in the name of God. One minister baptized with the words: "I baptize you with the wish and prayer that you may become a child of God and a disciple of Jesus. Amen." Baptism has also taken place without the use of a baptismal formula at all (see Lekkerkerker, 1963, 102–7).

The struggle about the language and the institution of baptism was indeed a struggle about the essence of the Christian faith. It had to do with the confession of the church of all ages.

Those who see baptism as an institution of Christ must call it necessary. This does not imply that it is a prerequisite for salvation. This is taught by Rome, which also practices emergency baptism, which we reject.

To us baptism is "a holy ordinance of God" (Form for Baptism). We may not disobey Christ, who instituted it for his church. Churches of the Reformed confession therefore warn earnestly against any contempt for holy baptism.

52.2. *Baptism as a sign and seal*

In addition to the words of its institution, the visible aspect also belongs to the essence of this sacrament. This is not water as such, but being immersed in or splashed with water.

The oldest form of baptism is baptism by immersion. It is also the most striking form of administering baptism. This is not to say that in our own current practice of baptism anything essential of this sacrament is lost. In the early Christian church baptism by immersion was not performed either when it involved sick persons or when sufficient water was not available. It says in the *Didache*: "If no flowing water is available, baptize then in other water. And if you cannot do it in cold water, use warm water. And if you have neither, then pour water three times onto the head of the candidate in the name of the Father and the Son and the Holy Spirit" (7.1).

It is incorrect of Anabaptists, Baptists, and certain other groups to turn immersion into a shibboleth, as though this would be the only biblical form of baptism. Over against this we maintain that there is no biblical prescription. Incidentally, there is every support for not merely sprinkling a few drops of water on the head of the person being baptized, but letting the water as it were flow over him or her.

Baptism is a sign and seal of spiritual cleansing through Christ, a cleansing that pertains both to the guilt of sin and its stain. Christ "seals unto us that he washes us in his blood from all of our sins, incorporating us into the fellowship of his death and resurrection" (Form for Baptism). Those who are incorporated into Christ, share in all of the treasures and gifts of Christ, which are summarized in the liturgy as "the washing away of our sins and the daily renewing of our lives." This is in harmony with the New Testament. Paul writes: "But ye are washed, but ye are sanctified, but ye are justified in the name of the Lord Jesus and by the Spirit of our God" (1 Cor. 6:11).

Since baptism refers to incorporation into Christ, it also refers to incorporation into his church (see Acts 2:41; 1 Cor. 12:13) and separation from this world.

Another aspect is the obligation to new obedience. The Form for Baptism says, "We are admonished and obliged unto new obedience, namely that we cleave to this one God, Father, Son, and Holy Spirit": i.e., cleave, trust, and love. "In baptism God places us under his authority on the basis of the finished work of Jesus. Learning to keep all that Jesus has commanded is nothing but accepting orders from him" (J. P. Versteeg in *Rondom de doopvont* = around the baptismal font, 1983, 39). Sharing in communion with God must lead to keeping Christ's commandments. Baptism and the covenant, of which baptism is the sign and seal, obligate us to do this. The Belgic Confession of Faith therefore refers to baptism as God's "mark and ensign."

The churches of the Reformation are positive that baptism is a sign and seal of salvation in Christ. But there are theologians who contest the sacramental character of baptism. The best known among them is Karl Barth. In a short study on baptism he rejected infant baptism as partial baptism, since the candidate is not involved in it as a partner of Jesus Christ deciding and acting in freedom (Barth, 1943). At this time he still treated baptism as a sacrament, but subsequently—in his more extensive study of 1967—he no longer did so. At this point he referred to baptism by the Holy Spirit as being entirely an act of God and baptism with water being entirely a human act (*C.D.*, 4.4.51; cf. Van Binsbergen, 1982, 92).

He was aware that in this way he ran counter to the entire ecclesiastical tradition. The main thesis of the doctrine of baptism is, after all, always that the focus is on what God does. According to Barth what matters is what man does in response to God's work of grace and God's word of grace, and in following Christ (*C.D.*, 4.4.102).

The influence of Barth's theology is widespread. Yet his views on baptism by no means find support everywhere.

It is true that our baptism is simultaneously a confession. Whenever an adult is baptized, he or she must make profession of faith. Publicly he bears testimony to the faith of the church. Also in the case of infant baptism it needs to be pointed out that baptism and faith go hand in hand.

It is clear, however, from the entire New Testament that in baptism man's action is not central. We do not baptize ourselves! We are baptized. Barth views baptism as an ethical event, which is not the case in the Bible, although there it does have ethical implications.

It is not biblical to separate baptism with water from baptism with the Holy Spirit, as Barth does and—in a different way—Pentecostal groups do. How can such a separation be maintained, since according to Matthew 28:19 baptism with water is also in the name of the Holy Spirit? Baptism is baptism within the field of influence of the Holy Spirit.

52.3. *Role and effect of baptism*

An obvious question has to do with the *implication or the beneficial effect of baptism.* Can we really say from a Reformed point of view that baptism brings about or implies something? We confess that God works in us by means of the sacraments "by the power of the Holy Spirit" (Belgic Confession of Faith, article 33). In this ministry of salvation, i.e., God's work to realize our salvation, baptism plays a role. When it comes to the question as to what role this is, opinions diverge among Roman Catholics, Lutherans, Anglicans, and the Reformed—not to mention other views.

Rome treats baptism as a cause of salvation, as an instrumental cause of justification. This justification not only constitutes forgiveness of sin, but also sanctification and renewal of the inner being. Baptism removes sins, not only original sin but also sins that have been consciously committed. Covetousness remains, but this is not a sin in the proper sense of the word. Sanctifying grace and the supernatural virtues of faith, hope, and love are bestowed. Whenever grace has been lost as a consequence of mortal sin, restoration can be achieved through the sacrament of penance (*DS*, 1515, 1529ff., 1542ff.).

It has been objected from the side of the Reformation that thus sacramental grace is made determinative and faith is not focused on the grace that God promises us in his Word for Christ's sake. In addition, various ceremonies take away attention from what should be the focus when the sacrament is administered.

Although much in the Roman Catholic Church is in a state of flux, this doctrine has not been changed. The New Catechism (Netherlands, 1966) says that baptism washes away sins. "Being pure, one starts anew" (288).

As was to be expected from Luther, in the doctrine of baptism he emphasized *the significance of God's promise and the necessity of faith.* In a sermon of 1519 he referred to baptism as a deluge of grace. In the battle against sin one may freely rely on baptism and say: I know that I cannot claim a single pure work as my own, but I was once baptized, through which God, who cannot lie, committed himself not to charge my sins to my account, but to mortify and eradicate them (cf. Bayer, 1971, 254–59).

Different ideas came to Luther when he took up the fight against despisers of this sacrament, who considered baptism as something external. To Luther the water of baptism was not something external, but something divine! It is "divine, blessed, and fruitful water, rich in grace," water that takes away sin, death, and all misery and assists us in achieving heaven and eternal life. How can water do all of this? Luther replied: The water itself does not accomplish this, but the Word of God that is connected with it (cf. *BSLK*, 693–97). In Luther's well-known booklet on baptism it says: God has regenerated you through the water and the Holy Spirit and forgiven all of your sins (*BSLK*, 541). This can be recognized in many Lutheran baptismal liturgies.

In the Anglican Church, it is also taught that rebirth and forgiveness of sin result from baptism. Documents of the ecumenical movement do not express it any differently. In *Baptism, Eucharist, and Ministry (*1982), it is said that baptism makes the baptized person partaker of the communion with the Holy Spirit. Those who have been baptized are no longer slaves of sin, but are free.

Frequently it is taught emphatically that baptism is *effective* in the sense that it works salvation *as such*. The question is whether Scripture says so.

There are relevant passages that do not mention faith. In Titus 3:5 does Paul mean that regeneration comes about through baptism? Is this why he refers to baptism as "the washing of regeneration"?

There are, however, also relevant passages that do not mention baptism, but do mention faith (Rom. 5:1; Eph. 2:8; and similar Scripture passages). Would Paul in one place ascribe to baptism what in another place he connects with faith? Are we saved by baptism or by faith?

To ask this question is to suggest the answer. Scripture passages that mention both faith and baptism (such as Gal. 3:26–27 and Col. 2:12) imply that putting on Christ and being raised with Christ—as referred to in baptism—does not happen without faith. Neither does this cleansing by the washing of water happen without the Word (Eph. 5:26).

But what about Romans 6:3–4? Here Paul says: "Therefore we are buried with him by baptism into death." Although here there is no specific reference to faith, there is to believers. Through their baptism they understand that they have been buried with Christ in his death in order to be raised with him to new life.

We encounter *the Reformed view* very clearly in the works of Calvin[24] and in our own confession statements. Baptism itself is not the washing away of sin. What matters is what the Lord presents and offers to us. This is forgiveness and renewal. The key is that we receive in faith what he offers to us. In this way the matter itself (*res*) is indeed

24. Cf. W. F. Dankbaar, *De sacramentsleer van Calvijn* (Calvin's doctrine of the sacraments), 1941; J. van Genderen, "De doop bij Calvijn" (baptism according to Calvin)," in *Rondom de doopvont* (around the baptismal font), 1983, 263–95.

connected with the sign (*signum*). It is for this reason that the Form for Baptism can speak so positively about the richness of salvation.

Calvin says: We ought to deem it certain and proved that it is Christ who speaks to us through the sign; that it is he who purifies and washes away our sins; that it is he who makes us sharers in his death. "It is not because such graces are bound and enclosed in the sacrament so as to be conferred upon us by its power, but only because the Lord by this token attests his will toward us, namely, that he is pleased to lavish all these things upon us" (*Institutes*, 4.15.14).

The belief that the key is that he will give us all of this comes through very clearly in the Heidelberg Catechism (Lord's Day 26): At the institution of baptism, Christ promises that he will wash us with his blood and Spirit as certainly as we are washed with the water of baptism.

It is precisely for this reason that we are asked to believe that the Lord will and shall do this. Since baptism binds us to him in this manner, it serves to strengthen our faith. It leads us directly to God (Calvin).[25]

Strictly speaking it is not the sacraments themselves—baptism and the Lord's Supper—which strengthen faith. The Holy Spirit does so by means of them. He teaches us through the gospel and assures us through the sacraments that our entire salvation rests on the single sacrifice of Jesus Christ, made for us on the cross (Heidelberg Catechism, Lord's Day 35).

52.4. *Differences of view within the Reformed community*

Already for over a century there has been conflict with respect to the covenant and baptism.[26] According to A. Kuyper, baptism was a seal of something in man: regeneration, the ability to believe, or inner grace, which was presumed in the person being baptized. He did not consider baptizing in the absence of this presupposition to be consistent with the Reformed tradition.

However, we must point out that baptism does not seal what is present or presumed to be present in the person who is baptized, but the promise of the covenant. There is a difference between sealing a promise and authenticating a believer.

As a result of the objections that were raised against Kuyper's teachings, the General Synod of the *Gereformeerde Kerken* (Reformed churches) pronounced in

25. *C.O.*, 51, 528.

26. Cf. E. Smilde, *Een eeuw van strijd over verbond en doop* (a century of conflict concerning covenant and baptism), 1946; C. Graafland, "De doop als spijtzwam in de Gereformeerde gezindte" (baptism as bone of contention within the Reformed community), in *Rondom de doopvont* (around the baptismal font), 1983, 446–96.

1905 that it was not quite accurate to say that baptism is administered to children of believers on the basis of their presumed regeneration. Yet, on the basis of God's promise, children of the covenant ought to be treated as having been regenerated and sanctified in Christ, until in growing up the contrary turns out to be the case as evidenced by their conduct or conversation. This is not the same thing as saying that every child would truly be born again.[27]

Following the conflicts with respect to covenant and baptism, which led to the "*Vrijmaking*" (liberation, secession), a new synodal declaration replaced the pronouncement of 1905: the Replacement formula, which was binding from 1946 till 1959. It says that the church must consider and treat children as those who share in the regenerating grace of the Holy Spirit, unless they reveal themselves to be unbelievers.[28]

However, this blurs the distinction between granting salvation in the promise and sharing in salvation through faith. These are not one and the same thing. Calvin already said that there is a difference between something being offered and receiving it (*Institutes*, 4.17.33). Receiving does not bypass the work of the Holy Spirit who applies to us that which we have in Christ (in the promise). When the difference between promise and appropriation is kept in mind, there will be a discriminating element in preaching. Although the invitation will have precedence, it is biblical that also a warning be heard in the covenant congregation (see 1 Cor. 10:1–11; Heb. 4:13).

Baptism has sometimes been described as an assurance given to the elect and believers that they share in eternal salvation. This is then the full baptism. There is also a right to baptism, to the extent that this is a confirmation of a conditional promise of salvation, which comes to all those who live within the reach of the gospel.[29] This implies that there are two kinds of promises and two kinds of baptism.[30]

The doctrine of the covenant adopted by the *Gereformeerde Gemeenten* (Reformed congregations) in the Netherlands and North America through pronouncements made in 1931 implies that there is a fundamental difference between the promise of salvation, which is intended for the elect, and the offer of grace to the church as a whole.[31] The sacrament can then not be a confirmation of God's promise to everyone who is baptized. Baptism seals the irrefutable truth, which is of comfort to God's people, "that [the] elect are sanctified in Christ, and that [the] elect are also found among little children" (Kersten, *R.D.*, 2:516).

We seriously object to this. It is incorrect to address the demand for faith and repentance to everyone, but to restrict the promises of the Triune God, as they are explained to us in the Form for Baptism, to those who have been elected or regener-

27. *Acta*, article 158. For critique see R. J. Dam, B. Holwerda, C. Veenhof, Rondom "1905" (concerning "1905"), no date².

28. *Acta van de buitengewone Generale Synode* (acts of the extraordinary general synod), 1946, article 197.

29. *Praeadvies van Commissie I inzake de bezwaarschriften* (preliminary advice from Committee I concerning petitions), 1943, 24, 59.

30. For a critique of this view see J. van Genderen, *Verbond en verkiezing* (covenant and election), 1983, 25–32; J. Kamphuis, *Een eeuwig verbond* (an eternal covenant), 1984, 43–106.

31. For a critique of this doctrine see J. van Genderen, *Verbond en verkiezing*, 1983, 9–16.

ated. Those who are baptized in his name could not know whether he really meant them. But their names are indeed mentioned at baptism. The promise of God's covenant and the accompanying demand are intended for them personally.

The views that we have described naturally have practical implications. The doctrine of two types of promises and two types of baptism takes away the certainty of God's covenant and words, and cause both doubt and uncertainty. It confronts everyone with the question whether the promise of salvation is really for them and whether they may plead their case on it. The doctrine of presumed regeneration or presumed election, however, tends to lead to carelessness and false confidence. We cannot presume that everyone who has been baptized will share in the promised salvation—apart from some exceptions.

52.5. *Infant baptism*

1. *Infant baptism under discussion.* Based on the fact that the New Testament does not explicitly refer to infant baptism, many have concluded that it emerged later. This argument never fails to impress.

There are, however, arguments to the contrary.[32] One has been able to ascertain that baptism administered to young children in Asia Minor, Gaul, Rome, North Africa, Egypt, and Palestine around the year 200 was a generally accepted practice. In addition, it does not appear to have been an issue whether or not infant baptism was permissible, which could have been expected to be the case if the church had not received this tradition from the apostles but decided to adopt it in the second century. The testimony of Origen, who was quite familiar with much of the Christian church, particularly in the East, and the church order of Hippolytus of Rome are cases in point. Tertullian objected to it, but not because it was something new to baptize children. He considered postponement to be more beneficial (*De baptismo*, 18).

Subsequently it became customary to postpone baptism. It was then generally believed that all sins that one had committed would be forgiven at or through baptism. Being baptized at a later age made baptism more effective, for then more sins would be removed! This had serious consequences. Augustine quotes the expression: "Let him be; after all, he has not yet been baptized" (*Confessiones*, 1:11). In his works, Augustine emphasized that as a consequence of original sin, baptism is a prerequisite for obtaining salvation. But for him this was not the only argument. He also mentioned apostolic authority and the connection between circumcision and infant baptism (cf. De Ru, 1964, 16–18).

Opposition to infant baptism emerged among Anabaptists. According to them small children could not possibly believe and therefore still stood outside God's holy church. Not only Anabaptists, but also Mennonites, who followed Menno Simons, were opposed to infant baptism. One had to be born again to qualify for baptism.

32. See Aland, 1961; Cullmann, 1958²; Jeremias, 1949²; De Ru, 1964.

Baptists opposed infant baptism because in their view only baptism subsequent to profession of faith and through immersion was in line with the Bible. Other groups opposed to infant baptism frequently give prominence to personal decisions or spiritual experiences. The growing influence of the Pentecostal movement brought with it increased doubt with respect to the correctness of infant baptism. Pentecostal groups particularly value consciously experienced baptism. Baptism with water still needs to be followed by baptism with the Spirit—being filled with the Holy Spirit, especially with the gifts of glossolalia and prophecy. Sometimes there is a direct connection between rejection of infant baptism and a denial of original sin.[33]

Among theologians, Barth is the most prominent opponent of infant baptism.[34] His criticism became gradually more fierce. Initially he felt that the church should revisit the question whether baptism of children was really justified. The order of baptism includes the conscious longing of the candidate to receive the promised grace and the obligation to take up a ministry of gratitude. Baptism not administered in line with this order could nevertheless be valid baptism. Barth did not wish to promote the idea of rebaptism (1943, 24). Subsequently he ceased to view baptism as a sacrament, for he no longer saw an act of God in it, but instead an act of man, a human response to what God has achieved in Jesus Christ. This did not simply invalidate infant baptism, but made it highly questionable (*C.D.*, 4.4.194ff.).

2. *Grounds for infant baptism*. Our confession gives an unambiguous reply to the question whether infants ought to be baptized or not. Lord's Day 27 of the Heidelberg Catechism refers to the covenant and God's promise. Infant baptism indeed stands or falls with this perspective.

God established his covenant with believers and their children (Gen. 17:7). He confirmed the promises and demands of the covenant with a sign and a seal. Under the old dispensation this was circumcision and now it is baptism. Under the new dispensation of the covenant it continues to hold: "For the promise is unto you, and to your children" (Acts 2:39). What follows: "and to all that are afar off, even as many

33. J. E. van den Brink, *De betekenis van de doop* (the meaning of baptism), 1966, 129–32.

34. Cf. among others G. C. Berkouwer, 1947; A. J. van Binsbergen, 1982.

as the Lord our God shall call," is not intended to be a restriction, but indicates that the circle of the covenant will now be much wider.

One cannot reject infant baptism without denying the connection between circumcision and baptism to which Paul refers in Colossians 2:11–12. On the basis of this apostolic message one can say that circumcision achieved its redemption-historical fulfillment in baptism. Neither can one deny infant baptism without diminishing the unity of the old and new dispensations of the covenant. The covenant of grace is in essence one. In both of its dispensations it has one Mediator and grants the same salvation: the gracious adoption as children of God (cf. Calvin, *Institutes*, 4.16.11). If children, who under the old dispensation were counted as children of the covenant, would now be outside the covenant, grace would have been diminished since the coming of Christ!

First Corinthians 7:14 is a Scripture verse that deserves our full attention. Paul says that a woman who has become a Christian, but whose husband is an unbeliever, should not divorce him because of his unbelief: "For the unbelieving husband is sanctified by the wife and the unbelieving wife is sanctified by the [believing] husband: else were your children unclean; but now they are holy." The apostle means that to God and the congregation such a family counts as a Christian family. "When only one of the two parents is a believer, God nevertheless lays through this one believer a claim on the entire family" (J. P. Versteeg in *Rondom de doopvont* = around the baptismal font, 1983, 132). With Calvin and others we think in this connection of the holiness by virtue of the covenant.[35]

The faith of parents is no ground for the baptism of their children, and neither is the faith of the church. Neither should the grounds be sought in the faith of children themselves, as Luther taught, nor in the capacity to believe or regeneration, as A. Kuyper held. Kuyper did not always put it the same way, but as a rule he referred to regeneration as the basis "on which in a spiritual sense rests the reality of the baptism that is administered to a child." This rebirth of those who are baptized is a hypothesis (presumed regeneration).

In the doctrinal statement of 1905 (see § 52.4), the words "regenerated" and "sanctified in Christ" are treated as an extension of each other. This leads automatically to the contestable view that "sanctified in Christ" as mentioned in the first question in the Form for Baptism

35. Cf. Doekes, *Der Heilige* (the holy one), 1960, 172–76, 234.

would mean the same as "regenerated." The Form for Baptism states that in view of our children being "sanctified in Christ . . . therefore, as members of his Church . . . ought to be baptized." In this interpretation of the words "sanctified in Christ," (presumed) regeneration would according to our Form for Baptism be the basis for baptism. Then Kuyper would be right after all!

3. *The chief objections to infant baptism.* The first objection is that in the New Testament we do not read about children that they ought to be baptized or that they were baptized.

It is incorrect, however, to deduce from this that infant baptism was still an unknown practice in the days of the apostles. It is best to compare the church of those days with the church on the mission field. Here also adult believers are baptized in the first instance. But entire families are baptized as well.

The apostles also baptized entire families: the household of Lydia, that of the prison warden (Acts 16:15, 33), and that of Stephanas (1 Cor. 1:16). We do not know whether these were families with small children. At any rate, the word for household (*oikos*) more often includes children than not. Compare Joshua 24:15: "As for me and my house, we will serve the LORD!"

It also needs to be kept in mind that an individualistic way of thinking is foreign to the Bible. A family is a unit. We know that it was customary among Jews to include children in the baptism of proselytes. The rule associated with circumcision and proselyte baptism, namely, that children were included, was not changed by the New Testament, for this is the rule of the covenant of grace. Children are part of it as a matter of principle and they are entitled to being baptized (cf. De Ru, 1964, 170–83).

The second objection is that faith must always precede baptism in terms of sequence.

We must keep in mind, however, that it is not faith that qualifies us for baptism. Among Anabaptists, Baptists, and Pentecostals baptism is more a sign and seal of man's faith rather than God's promise. A characteristic expression is, "I have had myself baptized," while on the basis of the New Testament one would rather say, "I have been baptized." The latter seeks to testify through his baptism that he belongs to the holy church, and the former that he wants to bury his old nature, thereby emphasizing his act of confessing his faith and experiencing its sealing, while Scripture shows us that the sacrament is primarily an act of God. Whether we are baptized as a child or as an adult, God's promise is key. If this were not the case, i.e., that baptism did not depend on God's promise but on our own faith, we would have to doubt our baptism as soon as we would doubt our faith.

But what about Mark 16:16? It says: "He that believeth and is baptized shall be saved; but he that believeth not shall be damned." This verse also can only be properly understood in its context. The preceding verse refers to the preaching of the gospel to all people in the world. For those who hear the gospel it is the case that: "He that believeth and is baptized shall be saved." What follows is its counterpart. Those who seek a universal rule in this text—the rule that faith must always precede baptism—arrive at problematic conclusions with respect to children. If Mark 16:16a implies that they may not be baptized, it follows from Mark 16:16b that they will be condemned. Therefore, one cannot generalize in this manner. Consequently, even to this extent, one must be careful in referring to this verse (see also J. P. Versteeg in *Rondom de doopvont* = around the baptismal font, 1983, 39–42).

There are many opponents of infant baptism who seek to emphasize the necessity of personal faith. But also to those who are convinced that infant baptism is founded on God's covenant with us and our children, faith and baptism go hand in hand. Baptism demands faith! *In the case of both infant and adult baptism, faith is, however, focused on the promise of the gospel of which baptism is the sign and seal.* Calvin says: "In infant baptism, nothing more of present effectiveness must be required than to confirm and ratify the covenant made with them by the Lord. The remaining significance of this sacrament will afterward follow at such time as God himself foresees" (*Institutes*, 4.16.21).

Infant baptism does not stand in isolation. We are baptized in the midst of the congregation. The sign of the covenant is at the same time the sign of incorporation into the church of Christ.

Subsequent to baptism, faith is demanded from all those who have been baptized. In the case of adults, profession of faith is required of them prior to baptism. During baptism, faith is demanded from the praying congregation (Cullmann, 1958[2], 49).

At the end of his discussion of baptism, Calvin says that we feel a strong stimulus to instruct our children in an earnest fear of God and observance of his law, when we consider that immediately from birth he regards and acknowledges them as his children (*Institutes*, 4.16.32).

52.6. *Baptism and profession of faith*

Public profession of faith, which is related to both baptism and the Lord's Supper, is no sacrament, and we need not seek for Scripture proof of its institution. The New Testament does indeed show us how the church of Christ confesses its faith.

The Roman Catholic sacrament of confirmation, which rounds out the grace of baptism, was replaced at the Reformation by instruction in the Christian religion, profession of faith, and admission to the Lord's Supper. Calvin desired that a child of ten years would present himself to the church to declare his confession of faith (*Institutes*, 4.19.13). The obligation to make profession of faith derives directly from baptism (cf. Hendriks, 1986, 47–57). The word "yes" ("I do") of this confession is not the opening word but a response to the Word of God, i.e., to the promise and the demand of the covenant of grace. God spoke the first word. In the prayer of thanksgiving at the conclusion of the baptismal liturgy, it is asked that the baptized candidate acknowledge (confess) God's fatherly goodness and mercy.

It is less felicitous to say that by making public profession of faith someone accepts responsibility or accountability for his baptism. It can give the impression that profession can be viewed as a complement of infant baptism. In our time infant baptism is sometimes referred to as an incomplete baptism, suggesting—with a reference to Calvin's comments concerning the broader significance of infant baptism (*Institutes*, 4.16.21)—that it requires supplementing or completing (Blei, 1981, 120–27). That the Reformer did not mean this is quite apparent from what he said about baptism in connection with his radical rejection of the sacrament of confirmation (*Institutes*, 4.19.8–11).

It is not true that infant baptism is but half a baptism (in opposition to Barth, *C.D.*, 4.4.188). One could indeed say that once we have been baptized we have not "arrived" yet. There is nothing lacking in infant baptism qua baptism, but this baptism—and every baptism—does bring obligations with it!

Profession of faith is also a factor in the proclamation of the Lord's death in the Lord's Supper. Baptism and profession go hand in hand; so do profession and the Lord's Supper.

Those who as children of believing parents are baptized do not become members of the church through baptism. It is more correct to say that as members of Christ's church they ought to be baptized.

A baptized member does not need to make profession of faith in the midst of the congregation in order to be "accepted" as a new member. The church is the assembly of those who believe in Christ. Therefore it is important that all those who belong to it from childhood, through their conscious profession join themselves to those who confess that Christ is their Lord. Our place is among the brothers and sisters who preceded us in confessing his name.

§ 53. The Lord's Supper

53.1. *The Lord's Supper as instituted by Christ*
53.2. *The sacrament of communion with Christ and with each other*
53.3. *Doctrinal differences*
53.4. *The celebration of the Lord's Supper*

53.1. *The Lord's Supper as instituted by Christ*

1. As in the case of baptism, the first question about the Lord's Supper has to do with its institution. We need to know for certain that this sacrament was instituted by Christ. We find the biblical data in Matthew 26, Mark 14, Luke 22, and 1 Corinthians 10–11.

The Lord Jesus Christ instituted the Lord's Supper at the celebration of the Passover. He had instructed his disciples to prepare the Passover. The bread and the wine were the bread and the wine of the Passover meal. Prior to leaving for the Mount of Olives, they sang the final part of the song of praise that was part of this celebration.

There is also a direct connection with the history of redemption. In Bavinck's work we read that the Passover occupied a unique place in the cultic life of Israel. It was indeed a sacrifice, but immediately afterward it turned into a meal. "It is a sacrifice of atonement and a meal of communion with God and with one another" (*R.D.*, 4:543).

The focus was on the notion that God passed over the Israelites—thus sparing their lives for the sake of the blood of the lamb (Ex. 12:13). The lamb was a sacrificial lamb. In Exodus 12:26–27 we read: "And it shall come to pass, when your children shall say unto you, What mean ye by this service? That ye shall say, It is the sacrifice of the LORD's Passover, who passed over the houses of the children of Israel in Egypt, when he smote the Egyptians, and delivered our houses."

The lamb that was slaughtered and whose blood served as a sign on doorposts pointed to him who is the Lamb of God that takes away the sin of the world. Paul says of him: "For even Christ our Passover is sacrificed for us" (1 Cor. 5:7).

The meal that the Israelites had in Egypt during the Passover night was the meal of redemption. In faith they anticipated that the exodus would take place as promised by God. The Passover had to be celebrated every year again to commemorate the Lord's redeeming acts.

Christ linked the bread and wine of the Passover meal with his death: this is my body—this is my blood. It is significant that it was not at an ordinary meal that he made bread and wine into signs and that he did not use the meat, but only the bread and wine. The Lord's Supper is related to the Passover, but is not identical with it. It constitutes its fulfillment. The Passover was both a sacrifice and a meal. Christ himself became the sacrifice and he gave us the meal.

The Lord's Supper therefore does not have the character of a sacrifice. This needs to be maintained especially over against Rome. It is the meal of redemption, which rests on Christ's sacrifice.

The covenant was also mentioned at the institution of the Lord's Supper (Matt. 26:28; Luke 22:20). There is a link with the blood of the covenant that flowed at Sinai (Ex. 24:8). Over against the blood of the consecration of the covenant of Sinai stands the blood with which Jesus consecrated the new covenant. The prophets referred to this new covenant, the covenant in which the Lord would forgive the unrighteousness of his people and no longer remember their sins (Jer. 31:34; cf. Ezek. 37:26). When Jesus calls it a covenant in his blood, this means that the new covenant is ratified through his death.

Without the blood of the covenant there is no communion with God. But now that the blood of the Mediator has flowed, we may be sure that the Lord will let us, who believe in Christ, share in his covenant communion and that we truly share in "the covenant of grace and reconciliation" (Form for the Lord's Supper). From this perspective the Lord's Supper is also referred to as the meal of the covenant. There is a direct connection not only between baptism and the covenant, but also between the Lord's Supper and the covenant. Baptism and the Lord's Supper are signs and seals of the covenant.

2. The Savior instituted the Lord's Supper so that we would remember him (cf. J. P. Versteeg, "The Lord's Supper according to the New

Testament," in *Bij brood en beker* = around bread and cup, 1981, 58–64). Remembrance is more than a memorial. Remembering his death is different from recalling mentally his death.

In the Bible, remembering is contrasted with forgetting. When it comes to what God does, forgetting is an act of unbelief and ingratitude, while remembering is an act of faith and gratitude. At the annual celebration of the Passover, Israel was to remember God's redeeming acts. Today our remembering is focused on the person and work of Christ, because God grants us complete redemption in him.

The proclamation of the death of the Lord (1 Cor. 11:26) also speaks of this remembering. Here Paul uses a word that means "to proclaim." When the church celebrates the Lord's Supper, it openly witnesses to Christ, who is its Lord in heaven. Believers who have assembled for this celebration confess individually and jointly that they owe their lives to the fact that the Lord Jesus Christ died for them.

The Form for the Lord's Supper expresses the remembrance of Christ and the proclamation of his death in a way that can scarcely be surpassed in the moving passage that begins with the words: "Now after this manner are we to remember him by it . . . ."

The grateful remembrance of the reconciliation with God through Christ leads to thanksgiving or praise, which may not be absent in the celebration of the Lord's Supper. There is "joy in God through our Lord Jesus Christ, by whom we have now received the atonement" (Rom. 5:11).

The Lord's Supper also has an aspect of *expectation*. Remembrance and expectation do not constitute a contrast in the Bible, for both perspectives focus on the redeeming acts of God.

The Lord's Supper reaches out to the future, to the consummation of all things. One day it will be fulfilled in the kingdom of God in which everything will be new. It is a foreshadowing of the sitting at the marriage supper of the Lamb (cf. Luke 22:16, 18; Matt. 26:29; Rev. 19:9) and a guarantee of partaking of the eternal kingdom. For this reason it is also a joyful meal, a foretaste of eternal joy.

The proclamation of the Lord's death must continue "till he come" (1 Cor. 11:26). This is more than an indication of a point in time. Through the celebration of the Holy Supper the longing for the return of Christ is reinforced.

According to the *Didache*, at the celebration of the Lord's Supper the early church prayed: *Maranatha*. Most likely this means: Come, our Lord (cf. Rev. 22:20).[36] In the 1971 revision of the liturgical forms of the *Christelijke Gereformeerde Kerken in Nederland*, a sentence was inserted to give yet more emphasis to the aspect of expectation that was already present in the prayer: "With great longing we look forward to the marriage supper of the Lamb at which we shall enjoy communion with him to the fullest extent."

Just as the institution of baptism was simultaneously the command to administer this sacrament, the institution of the Lord's Supper also contains the command: do this in remembrance of me. It is apparent from the way in which this is expressed in the Greek of the New Testament that this means: do not do this once, but repeatedly. The apostle Paul employs the words "as often as" (1 Cor. 11:25–26). It does not say how often. But in apostolic times it definitely must have been celebrated more often than four times per year.

Calvin already pleaded for more-frequent celebration of the Lord's Supper. In his first study of the Lord's Supper he says: "It must be celebrated much more often than is currently the custom for many. For the more our weakness weighs us down, the more frequently we ought to perform what can and will serve to strengthen our faith and to enhance the holiness of life. Consequently, in all well-organized churches the custom ought to be practiced to celebrate the Lord's Supper frequently, as frequently as the congregation can tolerate it."

What this Reformer says with respect to the purpose of the institution of the Lord's Supper has lost none of its value: In the first place the Lord instituted it to seal unto us the promises of his gospel and to give us the certainty and pledge that it contains our true spiritual food, so that we would obtain a true confidence in salvation; in the second place it serves to practice the acknowledgement of his great goodness extended to us; in the third place it encourages us in all holiness and purity, since we are members of Jesus Christ, and especially in unity and brotherly love.[37]

53.2. *The sacrament of communion with Christ and with each other*

1. *The most essential aspect of the Lord's Supper is that it is the sacrament of communion with Christ.* Paul says in 1 Corinthians 10:16: "The cup of blessing which we bless, is it not the communion of the blood of Christ? The bread which we break, is it not the communion of the body of Christ?"

This communion is not in the first instance the fellowship experienced among believers, but sharing in Christ and all his treasures

36. See L. Goppelt, *Theologie des Neuen Testaments*, 1976, 2:348–51.

37. J. Calvin, *Korte verhandeling over het Heilig Avondmaal van onze Here Jezus Christus* (short treatise on the Holy Supper of our Lord Jesus Christ), no date (*Petit traicté de la Saincte Cene*, 1541), 19 and 6.

and gifts. The Lord's Supper is the sign and seal that he grants communion with him.

From Paul's words in 1 Corinthians 10 we return to the saying of the Lord Jesus himself: "This is my body." "This . . . is my blood." What is added—"which is given for you" and "which is shed for you" (Luke 22:19–20)—implies that the focus is on what happened to his body and blood. The words of the institution of the Lord's Supper refer to the sacrifice that he brought for his people. He gave himself up for us and thus he gives himself to us. He assures us: I did this for you. This is what faith clings to. The church that celebrates the Lord's Supper confesses thereby that it lives by the sacrifice of Christ.

Having communion with Christ does not only mean sharing in what he achieved on the cross, but also having communion with the living Lord himself, who is with and near us according to his promise. To share in Christ means at the same time sharing in all of his benefits. Especially the gift of forgiveness of sins is mentioned (Matt. 26:28).

We do not ourselves bring about communion with Christ. Christ establishes this communion and we share in it through faith. The eating of the bread and the drinking of the wine bring out the believing appropriation for which he invites us to his table: "Take—eat—this is my body"—take the cup and "drink ye all of it—for this is my blood of the new testament" (Matt. 26:26–28). The verbs are in the imperative mood. This means that he expects it from us because this is how he has instituted it for us.

2. *Communion with Christ immediately results in mutual fellowship.* This sequence cannot be reversed. It is a fellowship with each other in Christ. This reflects the context of 1 Corinthians 10:16–17.

Where communion with Christ is not known, there is also a lack of true fellowship with each other. Wherever people do not care about each other, there is no real communion with Christ.

This idea of fellowship is manifested in the celebration of the Lord's Supper. The Form for the Lord's Supper emphasizes this in the passage on being one body through brotherly love. There we encounter also the image of grains of wheat and berries. This is not an interpretation of Paul's words: "For we being many are one bread, and one body: for we are all partakers of that one bread." It is nevertheless an ancient theme.

Fellowship with each other is not as well brought out by the Heidelberg Catechism as by the Belgic Confession of Faith: "We are moved by the use of this holy sacrament to a fervent love towards God and our neighbour" (article 35).

In recent years there has been a strong tendency to give a one-sided emphasis to this mutual fellowship. This reflects a focus on the horizontal dimension.

Berkhof is of the view that the nature of the meal and the mutual fellowship coupled with an anticipation of the future should be emphasized more than is the case in most churches. He says: "Fortunately, everywhere a younger generation begins to ask for a new emphasis on the celebration, on the meal, and on the communal aspect" (*C.F.*, 368).

Reference has been made to the merging of the Lord's Supper and the *agape* meal of the early church, i.e., the idea of fellowship associated in the Bible with having meals and sharing bread and wine with each other.

It is then treated as a solidarity meal, to which one would wish to invite everyone. According to Moltmann the messianic meal was open to the world and encouraged solidarity among its participants and with those who suffer hunger in both a physical and spiritual sense. Thus it becomes a manifestation of solidarity with each other. It is a social event, which is of importance in the struggle with all forms of discrimination![38]

However, this changes the nature of the Lord's Supper. It was not instituted to be a meal of solidarity. A transition is made from the communion of saints to the brotherhood of all men, which is not biblical. Christ does not celebrate his Supper with everyone. He wants believers at his table.

But it is definitely true that we may not lose sight of the mutual fellowship or the communion of saints at the Lord's Supper. Otherwise we also fail to understand what Paul says with respect to eating and drinking "damnation" (1 Cor. 11:27–34). In Corinth there were abuses associated with the Lord's Supper. There were fellowship meals or love meals, marked by lovelessness. Yet at the Lord's Supper one pretended that everything was fine. This constitutes celebrating the Lord's Supper unworthily. It is inconsistent with the character of the Lord's Supper as a meal of communion with the Lord and with each other.

In the Form for the Lord's Supper it says that fellowship is more than a matter of feeling. This is eminently captured in the following words: "So shall we all who by true faith are incorporated in Christ be altogether one body, through brotherly love, for Christ our dear Saviour's sake, who before has so exceedingly loved us, and show this towards one another, not only in words but also in deeds." The Lord's Supper tells believers that they belong together. It will have to

38. J. Moltmann, *Kirche in der Kraft des Geistes* (churches in the power of the Spirit), 1975, 282–86.

be apparent not only from their words but also from their deeds that they love each other.

53.3. *Doctrinal differences*

1. *The Roman Catholic doctrine of the Eucharist*
With respect to the Lord's Supper, which is indeed a symbol of unity, because it speaks of communion with Christ and with each other (Augustine), unfortunately great disunity has arisen.

We first focus on the Roman Catholic doctrine of the Eucharist.[39] Quite early the idea of sacrifice crept into the doctrine of the Lord's Supper. This came about because gifts that Christians brought to the love meal and for the frequently associated celebration of the Lord's Supper were referred to as an offering. An offering calls for an altar and a priest! Already Cyprian of Carthage thought that the priest acted on Christ's behalf.

A second theme is that of the change of the bread and the wine as the words of the institution of the Lord's Supper are spoken. Ambrose of Milan already developed a doctrine of this change, but Augustine made a clear distinction between symbol and reality.

The doctrine of *transubstantiation* became a dogma of the Roman Catholic Church in 1215. This church teaches that through divine power the bread really changes into the body of Christ and the wine into his blood. Dispensing only the wafer at communion, and preserving and venerating the host are customs that also emerged in medieval times.

The Council of Trent fixed the entire Roman Catholic doctrine of the Eucharist and condemned the Reformational doctrine of the Lord's Supper. Rome has never revisited this.

The Eucharist is a sacrament and an offering. One receives the sacrament during communion; the offering is made in the Mass liturgy.

The Mass would have been instituted when Jesus said: "Do this in remembrance of me." He would hereby have instructed the apostles and their successors in the priesthood to offer him up. This offering at the altar is identified with his sacrifice on the cross. It is not a bloody but a bloodless offering. It has effect, "for having been appeased by the bringing of this sacrifice, the Lord grants grace and

39. More extensively treated by J. van Genderen in *Bij brood en beker* (concerning bread and cup), 1981, 80–105.

the gift of repentance, and he also forgives serious crimes and sins" (*DS*, 1739–43).

It is an offering of atonement for the living and the dead. For the living: for various needs, which means that for various reasons one can have Masses celebrated in church. For the dead: in recognition of their suffering in purgatory, and serving to shorten its duration. This explains the practice of requiem masses: masses that one can have said for those who have died.

Here we see that the offering is indeed considered to be a sacrifice of atonement, as though the one sacrifice at Golgotha is not sufficient!

Not a few Roman Catholic Christians have difficulty with this ancient doctrine. But over against more recent views, which were also proposed in the Netherlands, in 1965 Pope Paul VI reiterated the doctrine of transubstantiation.[40] The Mass serves to place the sacrifice at Calvary in present reality, to renew and to apply it. We wonder why it would have to be renewed. And is its application in the hands of the church?

Bavinck says of the practice that accompanies this doctrine that the attention of the believer is deflected from Christ and his cross to the priest and his Mass. Even for a minimum of grace the Roman Catholic Christian is dependent on the priest and the church (*R.D.*, 4:574).

But a new theology has emerged that is critical of the traditional version of this doctrine. This explains why the term "transubstantiation" has been avoided in The New Catechism (Netherlands, 1966). An attempt was made to put it differently than in medieval times: "The bread has truly been withdrawn from ordinary human usage and has become the bread that the Father gives us: Jesus himself" (404). Yet we read in this catechism also that Christ remains present when the host is preserved in the "tabernacle" on the altar. The altar retains its central place in the cultus.

The New Catechism, however, did not have the last word. In 1969, by order of the pope, a Supplement appeared that speaks much more in traditional terms. Some said that bread and wine acquire a new significance and a new purpose through the words: this is my body—this is my blood. In this Supplement it says: they acquire this new meaning and this new purpose because transubstantiation has taken place!

2. *Diverging views among the churches of the Reformation*

Luther and Zwingli. The Reformation broke with the idea that the Lord's Supper is a sacrifice. *It is the supper of the Lord* (cf. 1 Cor. 11:20). But Luther, Zwingli, and Calvin nevertheless developed diverging views.

The Lutheran doctrine to a large extent reflects the insights of Luther himself. In 1520 he rejected the Roman Catholic doctrine in his famous

40. In the encyclical *Mysterium fidei.*

treatise on the Babylonian captivity of the church. The denial of the cup to laymen is in conflict with the institution of the Lord's Supper. In the administration of this sacrament the bread remains bread and the wine remains wine. There is no change in substance, but an inner union with Christ and the elements of the Lord's Supper, a union as between fire and iron as in red-hot iron. Luther rejected the idea of a sacrificial Mass, although he retained the term "Mass."

According to the Lutheran doctrine, Christ is physically present in the Lord's Supper. He is not only present in the place where the Lord's Supper is administered, but at the same time in other places. He is also physically omnipresent (the doctrine of ubiquity).

It is understandable that Luther and Zwingli could not see eye to eye. Zwingli could not accept that Christ is omnipresent in his human nature. It was Luther's impression that to Zwingli the Lord's Supper was a memorial meal. He absolutely refused to agree with this.

Calvin transcended this contrast. On the one hand we must lift up our hearts to heaven where Jesus Christ is. On the other hand the Lord's Supper is more than a memorial celebration, for it is the sacrament of communion with Christ.

Luther and Zwingli faced each other in Marburg in 1529. Over against Zwingli, Luther emphasized the word "is" in: "This is my body. It says so!" Any explanation that turns it into a sign or a symbol fails to do justice to the words of the Bible. Out of reaction, Luther made some very extreme statements. He said that he would rather have only blood with the pope than only wine with Anabaptist radicals!

According to Luther, we truly encounter Christ's body and blood in the Lord's Supper, for he is present there. This does not depend on whether we believe this or not. It is objectively true. But this implies that all those who celebrate the Lord's Supper receive the body and blood of Christ, believers unto salvation and unbelievers to damnation. This is how it is expressed in *Formula Concordiae* (1577): the true body and blood of Christ is distributed with the bread and the wine and received by the mouth of all who participate in the sacrament, whether they are worthy or not.

The godless would therefore receive the same elements as the believers. But is it not in conflict with the nature of the Lord's Supper to put it this way? This remains to be addressed.

The Reformed doctrine of the Lord's Supper. The Reformed doctrine of the Lord's Supper is in essence identical to that of *Calvin*. Like Luther, Calvin believed in the real presence of Christ. With Zwingli, he was convinced that it is a matter of faith.

Christ's presence here is not thought of in terms of a bodily but a spiritual presence. The fact that the Lord's Supper is a spiritual experience, and that the Savior is present in terms of his Spirit and grace, does not mean that it is any less real. The spiritual presence of Christ is so real that believers encounter him and experience his communion.

Only through faith do we share in communion with Christ. When we celebrate the Lord's Supper, as the Lord wants us to do, we accept with a believing heart that he suffered and died also for us. After all, he assures us through this sacrament that it is indeed for us. As believers we "become more and more united to his sacred body, by the Holy Spirit, who dwells both in Christ and in us" (Heidelberg Catechism, Lord's Day 28).

What about those who do not believe? The Lutheran view implies that they receive Christ but remain untouched by the working of the Holy Spirit. This would separate Christ from the Spirit, which is impossible, according to Scripture.

It is possible for hypocrites to participate in a celebration of the Lord's Supper, people who go through the motions but fail to repent sincerely. However, they only receive the sign but not what is signified. The Belgic Confession of Faith puts it as follows: "The ungodly indeed receives the sacrament but not the truth of the sacrament, not Christ of whom believers only are made partakers" (article 35). Although God also addresses his promises to them, they reject what is offered to them. Therefore they cannot be excused. Calvin employs here the image of rain falling on rock. Their stubbornness prevents God's grace from getting through to them.

Calvin says beautiful things about the Lord's Supper. It is instituted "to be frequently enjoyed by Christians, so that they would frequently reflect on Christ's suffering, and support and strengthen their faith through such reflection and encourage each other to confess and sing God's praise and proclaim his goodness, and finally thus to nourish their mutual love and witness, considering their bond in the unity of the body of Christ" (*Institutes*, 4.17.44).

These words of the Reformer stress the importance of frequently remembering the suffering of Christ. Precisely in this way the sacrament serves to strengthen faith. After all, Christ's sacrifice is "the only foundation of our salvation" (Form for the Lord's Supper).

We are also reminded that the celebration of the Lord's Supper is important for experiencing the communion of saints. Mutual love is nourished and mutually attested.

Calvin could at times be fierce. We notice this especially in the chapter devoted to the Mass, which he referred to as sacrilege, an obscuring of the enduring validity of Christ's sacrifice on the cross, and a failure to do justice to the all-sufficiency of his work. Calvin saw transubstantiation as a lie and a dreadful error, which violates Christ's majesty. We must seek Christ in heaven and not on the altar. The adoration of bread and wine is pure idolatry.

Much criticism has been aimed at response 80 of the Heidelberg Catechism with its sharp expressions such as "denial of the one sacrifice of Christ" and "an accursed idolatry." In a letter of the General Synod of the *Nederlandse Hervormde Kerk* (Dutch Reformed [state] church or NHK) concerning its relationship to the Roman Catholic Church (1969), it was said that one would have to admit that the well-known words of response 80 no longer applied to the situation described by The New Catechism (Netherlands, 1966).

It has happened that, in light of new developments among Roman Catholics, joint celebrations of the Eucharist were held and that Reformed Christians participated without qualms. But the sacrament of the altar with its sacrifice offered by the priest is not reconcilable with the Lord's Supper as instituted by Christ. There is no in-between position. A joint celebration of the Lord's Supper with the Roman Catholic Church is in principle impossible for a church that seeks to remain true to its Reformational heritage.

53.4. *The celebration of the Lord's Supper*

1. "For whom is the Lord's Supper instituted? For those who are truly displeased with themselves for their sins and yet trust that these are forgiven them for the sake of Christ, and that their remaining infirmity is covered by his passion and death; who also desire more and more to strengthen their faith and amend their life" (Heidelberg Catechism, Lord's Day 30). The original German text employed a somewhat stronger expression (*sollen* = must). One could translate: "Who must come to the Lord's Table?" It may be put this way, because the celebration of the Lord's Supper rests on Christ's command: "Do this in remembrance of me."

In line with 1 Corinthians 11:28—in connection with which Calvin points out that Paul does not say that one should examine others, but oneself—self-examination is judged to be mandatory by our churches. It says so in our Reformed confession as well as in the classic Form for the Lord's Supper.

Some have difficulty with the words of the Form: "Let every one examine his heart whether he also believes this sure promise of God that all his sins are forgiven him only for the sake of the passion and death of Jesus Christ." The question is then whether someone who is not sure of this may celebrate the Lord's Supper. We must pay close attention to how the word "sure" is used in this context. It is not asked whether we believe with certainty or whether we have a sure faith. The key is that we truly believe God's promise to be sure and definite. The crux is not what we believe with respect to ourselves but what we believe with respect to God's promise. The liturgical form itself points out that we must see it this way and not otherwise. After all, it is said further along "that we do not have a perfect faith and that we must daily strive with the weakness of our faith." Nevertheless, "desirous to fight against our unbelief and to live according to all the commandments of God we rest assured that no sin or infirmity which still remains in us against our will can hinder us from being received of God in grace."

This is completely in line with Calvin's pastoral guidance. When we sense an imperfect faith within us and our conscience accuses us of many shortcomings, this should not hinder us from approaching the Lord's Table. The sacrament is precisely intended for such people! "If to stay away from the Lord's Supper we maintain that our faith is still weak and our life imperfect, we would resemble someone who excuses himself from taking medication because he is sick."[41]

The Form for the Lord's Supper says that God will "count [us] worthy partakers of the table of his Son Jesus Christ." But no one can make himself worthy. There are those who believe that they are not worthy to partake of the celebration of the Lord's Supper, because in looking upon themselves they lack the courage. Is the problem that the New Testament and therefore also the Form for the Lord's Supper warn against eating and drinking unworthily and being guilty of profaning the body and blood of the Lord? The apostle Paul speaks in this connection of judgment (1 Cor. 11:27–32).

Eating and drinking unworthily is, however, not the same thing as a deep awareness of one's own unworthiness! Paul means it differently. Since Corinthians treated each other without love and therefore celebrated the Lord's Supper unworthily, it was not a blessing to them. They even brought judgment on themselves. Paul pointed out that there were many illnesses and deaths in their midst and saw this as a chastisement of the church. The Lord was calling them to order. This judgment was serious enough but did not represent *the* judgment, i.e., the last judgment.

There are those who avoid the Lord's Supper in the belief that they would otherwise sin and bring God wrath upon themselves. It is sometimes believed that the fear of the mystery of this sacrament, which was common in the Middle Ages, has to some extent persisted in the Netherlands. The Reformation did give the right interpretation of the Lord's Supper, but periodic serious warnings against participating without thorough self-examination may have instilled fear in many churchgoers. Could abstention from

41. J. Calvin, *C.O.*, 5:445.

the Lord's Supper have been fostered by the Second Reformation? Lekkerkerker is of the opinion that this is indeed the case (1961, 125–31).

2. *According to the Reformed tradition, the children of the church may not yet partake of the Lord's Supper.* W. Musculus (ca. 1600) was of a different view (cf. Bavinck, *R.D.*, 4:583ff.), but he was virtually a lone voice.

The question whether children may participate in the Lord's Supper, however, has emerged anew. According to the Synod of the Gereformeerde Kerken in Nederland (Reformed Churches in the Netherlands or GK), this is permitted if certain conditions are met. A number of congregations of the Nederlandse Kerken in Nederland (Dutch Reformed [state] church or NHK) admit children in the company of their parents, baptized children, and older baptismal members (cf. Hendriks, 1986, 712).

The arguments for the admission of children are in part of a psychological and pedagogical nature. Children take a childlike view of these things. During their subsequently critical phase the situation becomes more difficult. At a young age children do become used to fixed customs and rules more readily and subsequently would also more readily participate in the celebration of the Lord's Supper. But such an argument is far from convincing.

The primary argument is of a theological nature. Children are members of the church through baptism. For this reason they are thought to have a right to join other members of the church at the Lord's Table. In a variety of considerations it is simply assumed that baptized children must be viewed as believing children. This is a too-idealistic representation of the church, which in turn is related to the view that baptism brings about or presumes regeneration (*Doop, Eucharistie en Ambt* = baptism, the Eucharist, and office, 1982, 14ff., 19).

What 1 Corinthians 11 says about self-examination and discerning the body of Christ makes clear that people must be able to give account of what they believe (cf. Hendriks, 1986, 107). Communion and confession of faith go hand in hand.

If children have as yet no place at the Lord's Table, the danger exists that they will feel themselves little involved in its celebration. The younger ones should not be lost sight of. Access to the Lord's Supper should not be made too difficult for them. An example of what was expected in earlier days was the *Kort begrip der christelijke religie voor hen die zich willen begeven tot des Heren Heilig Avondmaal* (brief summary of the Christian religion for those who wish to partake of the Lord's Supper, 1608).

3. *Especially under the influence of the ecumenical movement a number of different liturgical forms for shared communion have emerged.* A distinction is made between open communion, i.e., the admission of all who are present in the worship service, and limited open communion, i.e., the admission of the members of all churches in special circumstances. There is also a distinction between intercommunion, whereby two churches admit each other's members on the basis of a mutual agreement, and inter-celebration, whereby two churches authorize each other's office bearers to officiate at this sacrament. An example of this is the agreement (consensus) with respect to the Lord's Supper, which was established between the Netherlands Reformed Church and the Evangelical Lutheran Church in the Netherlands in 1956, which led to both intercommunion and inter-celebration. This was preceded by a theological dialogue concerning the doctrine of the Lord's Supper.[42]

There is a growing movement that rejects doctrinal agreement as a prerequisite for shared communion. The hope is that ecclesiastical unity will result automatically from shared communion. But with joint services one cannot intimate a union that does not in fact exist. At the same time it needs to be pointed out that it is indeed one of the saddest consequences of ecclesiastical division that communion tables stand apart. It is not our supper. It is the Lord's Table (1 Cor. 10:21). The Lord Jesus Christ wants his people to be one.

4. *As far as the celebration of the Lord's Supper is concerned, there is a variety of local practices.* What matters is that it is the Supper of the Lord, of which we may participate, because he extends his invitation to us. "This feast is a spiritual table, at which Christ communicates himself with all his benefits to us, and gives us there to enjoy both himself and the merits of his suffering and death" (Belgic Confession of Faith, article 35).

The celebration of the Lord's Supper also has church orderly and liturgical dimensions. In the former case we have in mind the connection between the Lord's Supper and ecclesiastical discipline; in the latter case we have in mind varying customs such as being seated at a table or not. In any case there can be no administration of this sacrament in the absence of the ministry of the Word. Our confession says that "we receive this holy sacrament in the assembly of the people of God, with humility and

42. See C. W. Mönnich and G. C. van Niftrik, *Hervormd-Luthers gesprek over het Avondmaal* (Reformed-Lutheran discussion of the Lord's Supper), 1958.

reverence, keeping up among us a holy remembrance of the death of Christ our Saviour, with thanksgiving" (Belgic Confession of Faith, article 35).

Also in hospitals or nursing homes there can be gatherings of (a part of) the congregation with the Lord's Supper administered by a minister. The Lord's Supper is especially comforting to sick and elderly believers.

The theme of comfort is clearly brought out in the old Form for the Lord's Supper. Comfort does not only stand over against sorrow, for it also represents encouragement and certainty. This is why the celebration must include the prayer "that we with true confidence give ourselves up, more and more, unto [the Lord] Jesus Christ."

Some Literature

K. Aland, *Die Säuglingstaufe im Neuen Testament und in der alten Kirche* (infant baptism in the New Testament and in the early church), 1961.

W. Balke, *Calvijn en de Doperse radikalen* (Calvin and the Anabaptist radicals), 1977[2].

K. Barth, *Die kirchliche Lehre von der Taufe* (the ecclesiastical doctrine of baptism), 1943.

O. Bayer, *Promissio*, 1971.

G. R. Beasley-Murray, *Baptism in the New Testament*, 1962.

H. Berkhof, *The Doctrine of the Holy Spirit*, 1964.

G. C. Berkouwer, *Karl Barth en de kinderdoop* (Karl Barth and infant baptism), 1947.

G. C. Berkouwer, *The Sacraments*, 1969.

U. Beyer, *Abendmahl und Messe* (the Lord's Supper and Mass), 1965.

Bij brood en beker (around bread and cup, ed. W. van 't Spijker et al.), 1981.

A. J. Binsbergen, *Van zegel naar antwoord* (from seal to response), 1982.

K. Blei, *De kinderdoop in diskussie* (infant baptism under discussion), 1981.

O. Cullmann, *Die Tauflehre des Neuen Testaments* (the doctrine of baptism of the New Testament), 1958[2].

W. F. Dankbaar, *De sacramentsleer van Calvijn* (Calvin's doctrine of the sacraments), 1941.

W. F. Dankbaar, *De tegenwoordigheid van Christus in het Avondmaal* (Christ's presence in the Lord's Supper), no date.

L. Doekes, *Een heilige natie* (a holy nation), 1980.

Doop, Eucharstie en ambt. Verklaringen van de Commissie voor Geloof en Kerkorde van de Wereldraad van Kerken (baptism, the Eucharist and of-

fice: pronouncements of the World Council of Churches' Committee on Faith and Church Order), Lima, 1982.
K. Exalto, *Het Avondmaal in de praktijk* (the Lord's Supper in practice), 1987.
H. Feld, *Das Verständnis des Abendmahls* (the understanding of the Lord's Supper), 1976.
A. Ganoczy, *Einführung in die katholische Sakramentenlehre* (introduction to the Roman Catholic doctrine of sacraments), 1979.
J. van der Graaf (ed.), *Geijkte woorden* (standard terms), 1979.
C. Graafland, *Volwassendoop—kinderdoop—herdoop* (adult baptism, infant baptism, rebaptism), 1979.
Th. L. Haitjema, *De Heidelberge Catechismus*, 1982.
A. N. Hendriks. *Kinderen aan de tafel van Christus?* (Children at Christ's table?), 1986.
J. Jeremias, *Hat die Urkirche die Kindertaufe geübt?* (did the early church practice infant baptism?), 1949[2].
E. F. Kevan, *The Grace of the Law*, 1964.
P. Knauer, *Der Glaube kommt vom Hören* (faith comes from hearing), 1978.
A. G. Knevel (ed.), *Het Heilig Avondmaal* (The Holy Supper), 1990.
W. Krusche, *Das Wirken des Heiligen Geistes nach Calvin* (the work of the Holy Spirit according to Calvin), 1957.
U. Kühn, *Sakramente*, 1985.
G. N. Lammens, *Tot zijn gedachtenis* (in remembrance of him), 1968.
G. van der Leeuw, *Sakramentstheologie*, 1949.
A. F. N. Lekkerkerker, *De tafel des Heren* (the table of the Lord), 1961.
A. F. N. Lekkerkerker, *Gij zijt gedoopt* (you have been baptized), 1963.
L. H. van der Meiden, *De bijzondere Geesteswerking met het Woord* (the special work of the Spirit through the Word), 1949.
A. D. R. Polman, *Het Woord Gods bij Augustinus* (the Word of God according to Augustine), 1955.
Rondom de doopvont (around the baptismal font, ed. W. van 't Spijker et al.), 1983.
G. de Ru, *De kinderdoop en het Nieuwe Testament* (infant baptism and the New Testament), 1964.
A. A. van Ruler, *Waarom zou ik naar de kerk gaan?* (why would one go to church?), no date.
E. Schlink, *Die Lehre von der Taufe* (the doctrine of baptism), 1969.
J. J. van der Schuit, *Ten dis geleid* (led to the Lord's Table), 1961.

C. Trimp, *Woord, water en wijn*, 1985.

W. H. Velema, *Wet en evangelie* (law and gospel), 1987.

G. Wenz, *Einführung in die evangelische Sakramentenlehre* (introduction to the doctrine of the evangelical sacraments), 1988.

J. G. Woelderink, *Het doopsformulier* (the liturgical form for baptism), 1938.

Chapter 15

Eschatology

§ 54. A BIBLICAL AND THEOLOGICAL ORIENTATION

54.1. *Biblical starting points*

1. Scripture not only shows us what God has done and still does, but also what he will do. He continues and completes everything that he has begun.

In *eschatology* we reflect on the *final, definitive, and ultimate acts of God*, his promises regarding the future and the expectations engendered by these promises. "It does not concern a number of isolated events that are to take place in the future, but a convergence of events in—and based on—the promise of him who himself is the Last One. In Scripture his coming in glory is the actual focal point of the last things" (Berkouwer, 1972, 9ff.).

Christ refers to himself as the Last One (*ho eschatos*): "I am Alpha and Omega, the beginning and the end, the first and the last" (Rev. 22:13). When we speak of the last things (*ta eschata*), we meet him in all aspects of eschatology. Believers expect a great deal, for they await Christ and everything that accompanies him at his coming.

2. The term *eschatology* is used a great deal in our time, but does not have the same content to everyone. The meaning of the word varies from expectations with respect to the future in general to anticipation of the end of the world, time, and everything that is directly connected with this. Most of the time one has in mind a break with existing reality and a new state of affairs that supersedes it (cf. *TRE* 10, 257; E. Noort in *Vervulling en voleinding* = fulfillment and completion, 1984, 25ff.). In biblical eschatology this new state of affairs is not the result of a certain development, which may or may not evolve gradually, but comes about through the acts of God.

Therefore, a clear distinction must be made between eschatology and futurology or prognostication. In futurology it makes a difference whether the future is extrapolated from the present or is contrasted with the present; whether continuity or discontinuity, optimism or pessimism predominates; but such differences become secondary when we focus on the crux of the matter. The key question is whether one pursues a future that is achieved through human planning and activity, or a future that results from God's plan and actions. Anticipation with respect to the future that is based on faith is characterized by a certainty that is altogether lacking in expectations that are based on human inference or speculation (cf. van Genderen, 1982, 43–47).

3. A significant part of God's revelation comes to us in the form of *prophecy* addressed to Israel and the church of Christ. Prophecy does not exclusively pertain to the future, but at a higher level the future has an important place in it. In Hebrews the common expression "in the latter days" does not always refer to the end of time, for it may pertain to a time not further specified (cf. *THAT*, 1:116–18). But there are prophecies with an undeniably eschatological focus. Habakkuk says that the end "will surely come and not tarry"; Malachi says: "Behold, the day cometh, that shall burn as an oven" (Hab. 2:3; Mal. 4:1). At any rate, as the term says, the intent of *apocalyptics* is to unveil the future.

The distinction between prophecy and apocalyptics cannot always be sharply delineated. Apocalyptics is most strongly rooted in prophecy, and conversely apocalyptic themes may be encountered in prophetic literature. An apocalyptic book of the Bible such as Revelation is called "prophecy" (Rev. 1:3). A few characteristics of apocalyptics are: a sharp separation between this world and the future world; the special place of cosmic phenomena; and complex imagery. In the second part of the book of

Daniel, which is a typical example of this, we can point to the role played by world powers, allegorical representations, the symbolism of numbers, the contrast between spiritual and terrestrial authorities, the destruction of godless hegemonies, and the ultimate arrival of the kingdom of God, in which the dead shall rise.[1]

4. It is not easy to systematically summarize the eschatological expectations of the Old Testament, and every classification has its difficulties, but the *main themes* are clear enough.

a. Both redemption and calamity are announced. There are awesome prophecies in which disaster predominates, as in Amos: "Woe unto you that desire the day of the LORD! To what end is it for you? The day of the LORD is darkness and not light!" (Amos 5:18). See also Isaiah 2:10–19; Zephaniah 1:14–18. The day of the Lord has two aspects, for it is at the same time the great day of redemption (TWNT, 2:948ff.). Judgment will not bypass Israel, but a remnant will escape thanks to God's grace. One of the promises of redemption says: "I will also leave in the midst of thee an afflicted and poor people, and they shall trust in the name of the LORD" (Zeph. 3:12).

b. Judgment will be worldwide. Frequently the emphasis falls on the dreadful judgment pronounced over the nations that do not fear God, while God's people will share in the richness of his salvation. However, in the last days salvation will appear to be destined for "the nations" (Isa. 2:1–5; 25:6–7; Zech. 2:11), as was promised already to the patriarchs (Gen. 12:3; 28:14).

c. A glorious future is inaugurated, which is depicted with words and images that far transcend their fulfillment in the well-known history of Israel. We have in mind especially the prophecies of Isaiah regarding the peaceable kingdom, the elimination of death, and the new heaven and new earth (Isa. 11:1–10; 25:6–9; 65:17).

d. There are several promises that link the future of redemption with the appearance of the messianic king (see Isa. 9:6–7; 11:1–10; Zech. 9:10). The prophecy that the rule of the future king will reach from sea to sea, and from the River to the ends of the earth, means that his kingdom will encompass the entire earth.

e. At times it seems as though predominantly earthly blessings are to be expected, e.g., an end to war and disease and exceptional fertility of nature. Yet salvation has a spiritual depth, which is its nucleus. In Isaiah 11:9 this is spelled out in the words: "The earth shall be full

1. B. J. Oosterhoff, *Israels profeten* (Israel's prophets), undated, 160.

of the knowledge of the LORD, as the waters cover the sea." In what Zechariah 2:10–11 foretells, the central thought is that the LORD will dwell in the midst of his people and that many nations will seek communion with him. Now as well as in the future all salvation derives from the fact that the God of the covenant remembers his people in mercy. The name: "I AM THAT I AM" (Ex. 3:14) contains more than we can comprehend. Those who believe in him have great expectations.

f. This expectation of faith needs to be accompanied by great joy, which is frequently alluded to in the Old Testament. Although we limit ourselves to only a couple of Scripture references, there are many more, e.g., Isaiah 25:9: "And it shall be said in that day, Lo, this is our God; we have waited for him, and he will save us: this is the LORD; We have waited for him, we will be glad and rejoice in his salvation"; and Psalm 98, in which all of creation is called upon to rejoice "before the LORD; for he cometh to judge the earth" (vv. 8–9).

5. *The Old Testament and New Testament starting points* do not essentially differ from each other. The perspectives of the Old Testament are extended in the New Testament. The day of the Lord is here also a day of salvation for the faithful, but a day of calamity for others.

Also in the New Testament the basis for these expectations derives entirely from God's revelation. He is the God who is and who was and who is to come (Rev. 1:4). The connection between redemption and the coming of the Messiah is already presented in the Old Testament, but gains in prominence with the progression of the revelation in the intrinsic connection between eschatology and Christology.

Since God has already come to us in Christ and has furthermore promised us that Christ will return in glory, the church finds itself in the interval between fulfillment and consummation. The significance of Christ's resurrection is so great that it may be viewed as the focus of the interpretation of fulfillment and anticipated consummation in the New Testament (A. Geense in *Vervulling en voleinding* = fulfillment and consummation, 1984, 444). The promised resurrection of the faithful must be viewed in light of the resurrection of Christ. It is based on his resurrection (1 Cor. 15).

The ground and guarantee for all that is to come are found in Christ, who completed his work through his death and resurrection. It is the reason why in eschatology we may think of *the future of the present.*[2] At the same time it deals with *the present of the future* (Versteeg, 1969). We await the consummation of what God is doing already here and now through his Spirit. Paul says: "Ourselves also, which have the firstfruits of the Spirit, even we ourselves groan within ourselves, waiting for the adoption, to wit, the redemption of our body" (Rom. 8:23).

We need to move beyond this christological and pneumatological foundation. Our expectation needs to be directed toward the work of the triune God (see Rom. 8:11). "For of him, and through him, and to him, are all things" (Rom. 11:36).

Living during the interval between fulfillment and consummation, or between the initial and ultimate fulfillment of what God has promised, means that believers sense the tension between the *now already* and the *not yet*. This condensed but clear statement has become widely accepted.[3]

Thus we thank God that he has brought us into the kingdom of the Son of his love, praying continually: Thy kingdom come (cf. Hoekema, 1979, 52). The belief that our redemption in Christ has already become reality is connected with the expectation of the complete redemption promised to us. The Lord has given a great deal already, namely, "all things that pertain unto life and godliness" (2 Peter 1:3–4), and yet not all of his promises have been fulfilled. "According to his promise, we look for new heavens and a new earth, where dwelleth righteousness" (2 Peter 3:13).

6. The entire New Testament is replete with eschatological expectation. When we think of the gospels especially the words of Jesus about the last things come to mind (see § 56.1). But there is more to be found, also in the fourth gospel, where some people least expect it (see John 5:24–29; 6:39–54; 14:3; 17:24).

In Paul's epistles there is a great deal of emphasis on what God has already done for us. His promises have been fulfilled through the work of Christ and his Spirit. Yet there is a longing anticipation of what God is yet to do. Present fulfillment does not diminish expectations with respect to the future! On the contrary, fulfillment of God's

2. Actually it is the future of the One who has already come (W. Kreck, *Die Zukunft des Gekommenen* = the future of the One who came, 1961).

3. See Cullmann, 1946, 188; Berkouwer, 1972, 110–39; Kreck, 1961, 77–108; Hoekema, 1979, 14ff.

promises is ground for new expectation. In the epistle that deals with spiritual gifts within the church (1 Cor. 12–14), we find chapter 15 in which the apostle presents mighty eschatological perspectives implied by the resurrection of Christ. This chapter ends with the encouragement to be "always abounding in the work of the Lord." Thus Biblical anticipation has practical implications (see also § 56.3).

54.2. *More recent views*

The fact that the term "eschatology" is used frequently in contemporary theology does not mean that justice is always being done to biblical eschatological expectation. We mention in this connection a few typical representatives of twentieth-century theology. Several schools of thought can be identified.[4]

1. *Consistent eschatology* is a sharp reaction to nineteenth-century views on the kingdom of God, i.e., a realm of moral values to be attained by man (A. Ritschl). Study of the New Testament convinced *J. Weiss and A. Schweitzer* that according to Jesus, the kingdom of God would be a future kingdom, and would imply the end of this world and the beginning of a new one. It would come about through inexorable interventions of God, and not through the efforts of man.

It is thought, however, that Jesus was disappointed in his anticipation of an imminent arrival of this kingdom (see § 56.1, subsection 1) and we would not be able to do much with it either. Schweitzer personally took the liberty to focus on the imitation of Jesus and reverence for life.

2. *Realized eschatology*. The thesis of *C.H. Dodd* is that the *eschaton* in the preaching of Jesus has already progressed from the future to the present, from the sphere of expectation into that of realized experience. For the New Testament writers the *eschaton* has entered history, and the hidden rule of God has been revealed; the Age to Come has come (*The Apostolic Preaching and Its Developments*, 210) (see also § 56.2, subsection 2).

Dodd appeals chiefly to the fourth gospel, in which he believes he reads that life eternal—a major theme of John—is the life of the Age to Come, which is realized here and now through the presence of Christ by his Spirit in the church.

3. In the case of *transcendental eschatology* we think especially of *Barth*, at least his work *The Epistle to the Romans* (1933). He does not want eschatology to be a short and harmless closing chapter in dogmatics. All of Christianity is eschatological. We find ourselves continuously at the boundary of time and eternity and before God's judgment. Partly because of Barth, the word "eschatological" has come to be used

4. Cf. also Holström, 1936; Hoekema, 1979, 288–316; J. Veenhof, "Lehrmeinungen" (points of view), in H. Ott, *Die Antwort des Glaubens* (the reply of faith), 1981[3], 482–87.

in the sense of "decisive." According to him, what matters is not what lies *ahead of* us or follows after time (*post*), but what transcends time (*trans*).

It is true that Barth has retreated from some of these statements, but this does not detract from the fact that his eschatology is more concerned with unveiling what in Christ already is reality than a new reality in which all of God's promises are yet to be fulfilled. The universal aspect is strongly emphasized. In 1959 he said that a Christian should not restrict himself to or dwell on his anticipated personal portion of salvation in Christ. He should not forget that he will only share in this light together with the entire church, all of mankind, and all of creation; and that he may look forward to and approach this light only as part of this great company (*C.D.*, 4.3.932–33).

4. *Existential eschatology*. According to *Bultmann*, eschatological representations in the New Testament have a mythological character and cease to have meaning for modern man. One needs to pursue an interpretation of the New Testament and its message that is relevant for man today and his perception of himself. He needs to discover that he is not of this world (*Entweltlichung*).

This is therefore definitely not a matter of the last things in the temporal sense of the word. The dimension of the future actually disappears completely. What remains is what is called eternity here and now.[5]

5. *Eschatology of hope*. This refers to the eschatology developed by *Moltmann* in his suggestively written *Theology of Hope* (1967), in which he incorporates ideas of philosopher E. Bloch, who had adopted hope as his key principle. In contrast with those who seek to eliminate the future (Bultmann et al.), Moltmann places it front and center, especially as *adventus* (what is coming toward us). This has to do with what is radically new, of which the exodus of the people of Israel and the resurrection of Christ are examples and foretastes.

Moltmann's answer to the question of what the future promised by God denotes is extremely vague. One is to hope for something that does not yet exist. To this is added that the *promissio* (promise) can also be interpreted as a mandate. Hope must be put into practice, whereby our liberating actions must accompany our anticipation of the kingdom of God (more on this in van Genderen, 1982, 55–60).

6. An important antithesis is that between *futurism and actualism*. In interpreting relevant passages of Scripture—especially Old Testament prophecies and the book of Revelation—chiliasts take a futuristic point of view. This frequently results in an exceedingly detailed partition of the future into distinct periods of experience (see § 56.1, subsection 4).

A contrasting view is that no description of the last things is feasible and that the emphasis needs to be placed on proclamation that focuses on the *actual moment*. In this connection we think of P. Althaus and K. Rahner and the influence that they had.[6]

5. See among others R. Bultmann, *Geschichte und Eschatologie* (history and eschatology), 1964^2 [*History and Eschatology* (1957)].

6. Typical of Althaus is the pronouncement: "Die Eschatologie hat Bilder, aber sie gibt kein Bild des Kommenden" (eschatology includes images, but does not provide an image of what

Something along these lines can also be found in Berkouwer (cf. 1972, 216–19, 246–48, 398ff.). When he calls it a fact "that apocalyptic material is not intended to provide a documentary, but is to support the proclamation" (1963, 2:57), we wonder whether there is nothing between a documentary and support for the proclamation.[7]

54.3. *Division*

A partition of eschatology into an individual or personal and a universal or cosmic eschatology is common, but not desirable. Althaus (*C.W.*, 658ff.) says about this that personal eschatology focuses on the end of life of an individual and what lies on the other side of this end, while universal eschatology inquires about the close and consummation of history (cf. also Heyns, *Dogm.*, 393). Our objection to this is that the return of Christ is then made ancillary to universal eschatology.

Bavinck uses a different division, namely, the intermediate phase; the return of Christ; the consummation of the ages. We can agree with this, although for the first aspect we prefer as title: "life after death." In this section of our book we have preceded a discussion of these topics by a presentation of the biblical starting points.

The most important material is thus divided into three further sections. In this context the return of Christ is central. This is also the core of all of eschatology.

§ 55. Ongoing life after death

55.1. *Immortality of the soul?*
55.2. *The intermediate state under discussion*
55.3. *What does Scripture say?*
55.4. *Various conceptions*
55.5. *Life in communion with Christ*

55.1. *Immortality of the soul?*

To many it is a question whether there is ongoing life after death. Yet there is a widespread belief that man, at least in terms of his soul or

---

is yet to come), 1964⁹, 82. To Rahner, eschatology is no "documentary of the future," but a preview based on the state of redemption history determined by the "Christusreignis" (rule of Christ); cf. *Schriften zur Theologie* (theological writings), 1960, 4:401–28.

7. H. Berkhof has made critical remarks about G. C. Berkouwer's eschatology. According to Berkouwer, chronology, prophecy, documentation, and communication would be foreign to the revelation of redemption. In connection with this, see especially J. C. de Moor, *Towards a Biblically Theo-logical Method*, 1980, who points out that Berkouwer seeks a neutral or objective documentation. Berkhof's point of view remains to be discussed (see § 57.3).

spirit, is immortal. This is not a distinctly Christian doctrine. One can recognize it as a universal protest against death and a proof that in the human heart there is an ineradicable yearning for life.

Life after death has frequently been depicted as a shadow image of this life. Ghosts supposedly dwell in the underworld. In Greece, belief in immortal life found a clear expression in various mystery religions that focused on redemption from mortality. Plato, who was influenced by this, contrasted body and soul in *Phaedo*. The thinking soul was immortal, but the body was mortal: a prison for the soul, so that death means release. Although other philosophers doubted the immortality of the soul—there were those who said: "dead is dead"—the Platonic concept was incorporated in both philosophical and theological traditions.[8]

A pronouncement of the Fifth Lateran Council (1513) implies that the soul is immortal. Also a Reformer such as Calvin speaks of the soul being released from the prison of the body (*Institutes*, 3.9.4), but the context differs from that of Plato's dualism (cf. Quistorp, 1941, 55–57). Many Reformed theologians offered rational arguments for the immortality of the soul. According to Bavinck, several proofs are not without value (*R.D.*, 4:593) and according to Honig they have great value, although they do not end all criticism (*Handboek*, 777). The most important proofs are the ontological proof, the metaphysical proof, the anthropological proof, the moral proof, and the proof of the consensus of nations (*e consensu gentium*).

In the days of the Enlightenment immortality was part of the triad: God, virtue, and immortality. Kant criticized the well-known proofs and accepted immortality only as a postulate of practical reasoning. Subsequently, counterarguments by materialism and positivism made some impression, while the more recent view of the unity of body and soul, and strong belief that man is a finite being, have put roadblocks in the way of a revival of the doctrine of immortality.

The Reformed have raised objections to the more recent manner of speaking. There is no inherent or natural immortality and there is no superior part of man that could be considered to be immortal (A. Kuyper, H. Dooyeweerd).[9] When some feared that this view would bring into question the survival of the soul after death, the Synod of the *Gereformeerde Kerken in Nederland* made a pronouncement in this regard (1942). At death the soul continues to exists, either to enjoy salvation in communion with Christ, or to suffer perdition. On the last day believers will receive eternal salvation, but unbelievers will be abandoned to continue to exist in eternal damnation.[10]

The dispute that led the synod to make this pronouncement concerned anthropology. The criticism of traditional views expressed by Althaus, Van der Leeuw, and others was far more invasive, because it concerned eschatology.

8. Cf. H. Wolf, *Onsterfelijkheid als wijsgerig probleem* (immortality as philosophical issue), 1933.

9. For more information see G. C. Berkouwer, *Man: The Image of God*, 1962, 247ff., 255–64.

10. *Acta* (proceedings), article 682.

According to Althaus, to teach the immortality of mankind would be a refutation of death as God's judgment. There is nevertheless a personal relationship with God that cannot be obliterated. Van Leeuwen states the dilemma more sharply than Althaus: There is either immortality or resurrection. Only God is immortal. He gave man the promise of resurrection (Althaus, 1964[9]; Van der Leeuw, 1947[4]).

Since man as creature of God is a unity, we must reject a dualistic representation of the relationship between soul and body in terms of immortal and mortal elements. Those who presume a natural immortality of the soul disregard the seriousness of death, which affects not only the body. We shall have to give full scope to what the Bible says about the transience and mortality of man as a consequence of the sinful rupture of communion with God who is the source of life.

Man's death, however, does not quite mean that he ceases to exist. It is necessary to listen carefully to what Scripture has to say in this regard.

55.2. *The intermediate state under discussion*

We take the intermediate state of man (*status intermedius*) to mean the state of man and especially the believer between the moment of death and the moment of the return of Christ (see Dijk, 1951).

Criticism of the doctrine of immortality of the soul frequently has consequences for the doctrine of the intermediate state. Various examples of this can be given.

1. In the eschatology of *Althaus*, which is shared by many, there is no scope for an intermediate state. According to him we must break with it (1964[9], 154–59).

2. In the Netherlands *Telder's* position has become well known. His first book on the topic (1960), which is more of a testimony than a theological treatise, is intended to be a purgation of "non-Scriptural notions and conceptions" and "unbiblical fantasies and comforting thoughts" from Reformational thinking. Heavenly joy and salvation do not await the believer immediately upon death, but only upon Christ's return. Till then God's children remain in a state of death. Even in death they will not be separated from Christ, but this does not mean that upon death they will already enjoy an "interim salvation of the soul." Telder has objections to the first part of Answer 57 of the Heidelberg Catechism. He would prefer to say that all those who die in the Lord may commit their spirit into the hands of their heavenly Father and may know that in death they will not be separated from Christ. He refers to Romans 8:39 and Philippians 1:23. Cf. Telder, 1960, 143; 1963, 63, 125.

A Telder controversy arose. In the *Gereformeerde Kerken, Vrijgemaakt* (liberated), to which he belonged, his view was condemned as being totally in conflict with the uninterrupted continuation of eternal life during the interval between death and resurrection promised in Scripture and with the first part of Answer 57 of the Heidelberg Catechism, which rests on this promise (see Wiskerke, 1963, 242). The synod of this federation of churches confirmed this pronouncement.[11]

3. A major difference between Telder and *Berkhof* is that the latter ignores what Scripture says. It has to do with indications of a speculative nature, which form part of the legitimate language of the imagination of faith, but do not offer material for a theological doctrine. Berkhof feels that one cannot make any meaningful comments about an in-between time or an intermediate state except for this statement—and that is decisive—that beyond the death line we shall never and nowhere fall out of the hand of our faithful Covenant Partner (*C.F.*, 530ff.).

4. *Barth* goes still further (cf. *C.D.*, 3.2.587–640). He expects no modification and continuation of the life that God gives to his people now, except "die Verewigung gerade dieses unseres endenden Lebens" (rather the immortalization of our finite life, 760). There was a time when we did not yet exist and there comes a time when we will no longer be there. In this sense, man is "diesseitig" (restricted to this side of death). One day he will only have been there, but his finite life will forever remain in God's consciousness. This is eternization.

The idea that our life is finite (*Befristung*) is based on an analysis of human existence. It has been justly objected that this is not the eschatology of the New Testament! With this doctrine of eternization the prospect of eternal life—an essential part of the creed of the church—is lost.[12]

5. *The New Catechism* (Netherlands, 1966, 551–55) teaches emphatically that death is radical. Death is the end of the complete human being as we know him now. But faith in the power of him to whom nothing is impossible encourages us to trust that ultimately we are meant for life. This catechism is vague regarding the "how" of existence after death. There is an attempt to interpret faith differ-

11. *Acta van de Gen. Synode van de Ger. Kerken in Ned. gehouden te Amersfoort-West* (proceedings of the general synod of the *Ger. Kerken in Ned.* denomination in the Netherlands), 1966–67, article 164.

12. See G. C. Berkouwer, *De triomf der genade in de theologie van Karl Barth* (the triumph of grace in the theology of Karl Barth), 1954, 325–44.

ently than was done in the past when it was imagined that the soul would survive separately.

There are also other trends. Althaus himself referred to the danger of a one-sided reaction. One has to admit that the New Testament assumes that the person lives on. In the New Testament one finds the eschatology of heaven as well as that of the last day. It is not amiss that the hymnal contains songs about the resurrection and heaven.[13]

A letter from the Congregation for the Doctrine of the Faith, which was circulated under the authority of the pope in 1979, declares in connection with current theological controversies: "The church affirms the continued existence of spiritual elements endowed with consciousness and volition." The "human self" continues to exist. To refer to this element the church uses the word "soul," which has been accepted through the use of Scripture and tradition.[14]

55.3. *What does Scripture say?*

The question whether Israel knew of a life after death is not infrequently answered in the negative.

In places the Old Testament sounds quite somber, especially in books such as Job and Ecclesiastes (cf. Job 7:21; Eccl. 3:20). In Psalm 115:17 it says, "The dead praise not the LORD, neither any that go down into silence"; in Isaiah 38:18–19, "For the grave cannot praise thee, death cannot celebrate thee: they that go down into the pit cannot hope for thy truth. The living, the living, he shall praise thee, as I do this day."

Life and praise go hand in hand here. Life is there to praise God, and how could this be done in a state of death? The realm of death (*sheol*) refers to the power of death or the place of the dead (cf. De Bondt, 1938, 95–129).

Yet the Old Testament has more to say. Death and the realm of the dead do not have the last word, but the God of the covenant whose power is limitless. "He bringeth down to the grave, and bringeth up" (1 Sam. 2:6). He will redeem his people from the power of death and destruction (cf. De Bondt, 1938, 223).

13. P. Althaus, "Retraktationen zur Eschaologie" in *Theol. Literaturzeitung* 75 (1950): 253–60.

14. Can be found in translated form in *Archief van de kerken* (archive of the churches), 1979, 34:814.

In the tension of faith, pronouncements have been made regarding communion with God that is not broken even by death and in which the godly know themselves secure, also for the future. The poet of Psalm 49 knows that those who trust in themselves will not escape the power of death. This is contrasted in verse 15 with: "But God will redeem my soul from the power of the grave: for he shall receive me." The same faith is expressed in the well-known words of Psalm 73: "Thou shalt guide me with thy counsel, and afterward receive me to glory" (see Ps. 73:23–26). The poet is sure that God has taken him by the hand, and according to his plan directs him to his end. This is the glory: the radiance of God's world.[15] Others translate Psalm 73:24 differently. When they want to read, "Thou restorest me to honour," they do not do justice to the verb *lakach*, which apart from these two psalms is also used in Genesis 5:24 and 2 Kings 2:9, which deal with the taking up of Enoch and Elijah.

Two places in the Old Testament speak without doubt of a resurrection of the dead, namely, Isaiah 26:19 and Daniel 12:2. The latter verse announces a dual resurrection: to "everlasting life or to shame and everlasting contempt."

In Jewish literature of the years leading up to and at the start of the Christian era we see these expectations become more concrete. However, they are not shared by everyone. For further details and variants see Hanhart, 1966, 18–32; Hoffmann, 1969^2, 77–155.

When it comes to the question what the Old Testament says about life after death, one can point to a number of additional places such as Job 19:25–27, but these are variously interpreted. The New Testament is clearer in this regard. For this reason Vriezen points out that this is one of the instances in which the Old Testament calls for "fulfillment" in the New Testament (*Hoofdlijnen*, 442).

In the New Testament the future is portrayed in the light of Christ's resurrection. On the basis of this event in the history of redemption we await the resurrection on the last day. But there also is a continuation of life after death. Jesus declares that the God of Abraham, Isaac, and Jacob "is not a God of the dead, but of the living" (Luke 20:38). He adds: "for all live unto him." This means more than that God continues to remember them and that their relationship with him is imperishable. Calvin's exegesis is more convincing than Telder's

15. See H.-J. Kraus, *Theologie der Psalmen*, 1989^2, 219; *Psalmen*, 1989^6, 2:672ff.

(1960, 73–75): God preserves them alive in his presence in a manner that transcends human comprehension.

Luke 23:43 sheds more light on this ongoing life. Jesus opens the gate of paradise to a man who has been crucified with him. By this is meant the place where God lets the righteous share in his communion after death. Jesus says: With me you will be there today already and not just in the far future (see *TDNT*, 5:770ff.).

What is promised here by Christ is also believed by Paul for himself: "to be with Christ" (Phil. 1:23). This is one of the clearest pronouncements about life beyond this life: having a desire to depart and to be with Christ, which is far better. Paul can call death gain because life to him is Christ (Phil. 1:21).[16] There are those who in this connection do not think in terms of gain for Paul himself, but gain for Christ, namely, for his name and cause and church. But the apostle does not view his death as gain for the church, at least not here. He himself gains by it. A number of exegetes believe that the prospect to which Paul refers is associated with his expectation of martyrdom. Martyrs were to receive this privilege. In 2 Corinthians 5:8 there is a similar thought, although the apostle there uses the word "we." All believers may expect that they will be with Christ. Here, being with Christ is described as moving in with the Lord. This is an indication of life in the immediate proximity of Christ.

These Scripture references are not isolated remarks. What the apostle says here is based on the conviction that believers belong to Christ in both life and death, and even in death cannot be separated from his love (see Rom. 8:38–39; 14:8). The bond with Christ and communion with him are an enduring reality. When believers pass away they do not cease being in Christ.

In this connection we may also refer to Stephen's prayer in which he expresses his faith that upon his death he will live with Christ (Acts 7:59): "Lord Jesus, receive my spirit" (cf. *TDNT*, 5:771; Wiskerke, 1963, 179ff.).

Significant is also what the fourth gospel says about eternal life. We think of Jesus' words: "I am the resurrection, and the life: he that believeth in me, though he were dead, yet shall he live" (John 11:25).

16. Hoffmann (1969², 295) finds in Phil. 1:23 "die Gewißheit, daß der Tod nicht Trennung von Christus, sondern die Gemeinschaft mit ihm bringt" (certainty that death does not bring separation from, but rather communion with Christ).

He who believes in him has eternal life that will not be touched even by death and that one day will be revealed in its full glory.

There is continuity, not the continuity of immortality, but the continuity of eternal life.

The Old Testament intimates that communion with God will not be terminated even at death. The New Testament shows us that this communion is guaranteed in Christ.

In view of these data one cannot maintain that in the New Testament the intermediate state is *terra incognita* [unknown land], and that apart from perhaps Revelation 6:9–11 no other relevant statements can be found (Hanhart, 1966, 224–39). It is rather the case that in addition to so much else, this passage also is of significance to the questions that occupy our attention.

John saw the souls of the martyrs under the altar in heaven. This refers to believers who have life on earth behind them and are longing for the consummation of all things. They have been told that they will have to rest a little longer, until the number of their fellow servants is also full. However, they have already received white robes. This signifies the rest and peace "that they may enjoy in anticipation of complete splendour" (De Vuyst, 1987, 80).

It is then certain that believers enjoy life with Christ during the interval between their death and resurrection.

55.4. *Various conceptions*

1. *Purgatory*. The notion of purification, which is espoused especially but not exclusively by Rome, is ancient. In 1274 a centuries-old tradition was codified in the doctrine of purgatory (DS, 856–59).

There is a direct connection with the Roman Catholic doctrine of grace and penance. The Council of Trent declared: following the receipt of the grace of justification one's guilt is not forgiven to the extent that no scope for temporary punishment remains, to be borne either in this life or in purgatory (*DS*, 1580). Sooner or later this suffering ends and in the meantime one can help these "poor souls" in purgatory through prayers, Masses, and indulgences. In addition to 2 Maccabees 12:42–46, where there is mention of prayers and peace-offerings for the dead, reference is frequently made to 1 Corinthians 3:12–15. However, in more recent theology there is some reluctance to move in this direction. Support for the concept of purgatory comes largely from the church fathers (Ott, *Grundriss*, i.e., outline, 576).

Roman Catholicism has changed to some extent. The souls in purgatory are referred to less frequently. Yet it is considered not only legitimate but also mandatory to pray for the dead, especially during the celebration of the Mass.

The New Catechism (Netherlands, 1966) says in this regard: Formerly people imagined a particular place, a fire, a specific duration, and finally being summoned by an angel, as in a doctor's waiting room. Instead we should seek to regain early Christian simplicity and associate purification with death itself and not imagine a separate, independent state, especially since Scripture barely refers to it. The other side of death may be a form of purification, but it is impossible to specify either place or time (558–60).

It has not become easier to determine what the Roman Catholic doctrine really is. While the new catechism of 1966 is intended to reflect the renewal articulated by the Second Vatican Council, this council itself did not speak of purification at death, but subsequent to death (*post mortem*), and reaffirmed the decrees of Florence and Trent.[17]

As far as the doctrine of purgatory and related matters are concerned, the protest of the Reformation as expressed in the *Confessio Helvetica Posterior* (1566) remains valid: it runs counter to the article of faith: I believe in the forgiveness of sins and life everlasting, as well as complete purification through Christ (article 26). See also Bavinck's sharp criticism: The doctrine of purgatory fosters on the one hand unconcern and on the other hand the uncertainty of the believers. Faith in the sufficiency of the sacrifice and intercession of Christ is thereby weakened (*R.D.*, 4:632–38).

2. *Transmigration of souls*. Transmigration of souls usually means *reincarnation*. It concerns an ancient belief that has resurfaced in new guises and in which interest has strongly increased. Broadly speaking, this has to do with the belief that upon death something of man returns to earth. This also implies that there is something in him now that—prior to this life—was already on earth in one form or another.

The concept of reincarnation originated in India in Hinduism and Buddhism. Reincarnation there is said to obey the law of retribution (*karma*). Man's fate depends on his good or bad deeds. This results in a cycle of countless lives (*samsara*), which is an oppressive thought. One can be liberated from *samsara* through the realization that one's soul is at one with the soul of the world.

It is probably because of Eastern influences that reincarnation plays some role in Greek thinking, at any rate in the Orphic mysteries, among the Pythagoreans, and in Plato's writings. Plato's teachings include the pre-existence of the divine element of the soul and the transmigration of souls. It was not until the nineteenth and twentieth centuries that belief in reincarnation resurfaced: in theosophy, anthroposophy, a number of spiritualist movements, and New Age circles.[18]

Both in the older and newer forms of this doctrine, the law of cause and effect is front and center. When this is coupled with the concept of evolution, it is taken for granted that overall the process unfolds rather favorably. The idea of reincarnation used to be viewed as oppressive, but has now become a rather uplifting idea! An individual's appearance is indeed lost through death, but the higher "self," the soul or the spiritual being of man, takes on a new manifestation. "The energy that lives

17. *Dogmatische constitutie over de kerk* (dogmatic constitution regarding the church, *Lumen Gentium*), no. 51.

18. For this reason spiritualism is sometimes treated separately in dogmatics, cf. Bavinck, *R.D.*, 4:623–25.

inside us is not lost. It reincarnates itself, most likely inside another human being, but possibly also in an entirely different being (plant, angel, divinity), or even on another planet" (Logister, 1990, 38).

We are of the opinion that transmigration of souls, however portrayed, is in total disagreement with the Christian faith. With the words, "For whatsoever a man soweth, that shall he also reap" (Gal. 6:7), the apostle Paul implies nothing of the kind.

We live but once. The gravity of this span of life is balanced with the gravity of death. Scripture says that "it is appointed unto men once to die, but after this the judgment" (Heb. 9:27). Man is a unique creature of God. Whatever makes him the man he is, he is not to surrender to someone else upon death. By claiming or promising an evolution toward a higher and more perfect existence, salvation by the grace of God is dismissed and supplanted. "The whole reincarnation doctrine is a dangerous siren song" (Verkuyl).[19]

3. *Soul sleep*. This view also arose early on. Calvin fought it in a separate study (*Psychopannychia*, 1542).[20] In this work he maintains that the righteous who depart in faith in Christ, live with Christ, and their souls do not sleep. In Reformational doctrine there is no room for the notion that believers would descend into some sort of twilight zone.

The image of survival in a dormant state is still prevalent today. Some support it with reference to biblical concepts such as "being asleep" and "falling asleep," but these terms lack any explanatory content with respect to survival beyond the grave (cf. Ridderbos, *Paul*, 497ff.; Hoffmann, 1969², 186–206).

4. *A new corporality*. Those who have difficulty imagining a soul without a body, sometimes imagine a temporary body that would consist of the most subtle material and would be bestowed upon death. It is sometimes described as an ethereal body.

The New Catechism appears to move in this direction. "Existence after death is already somewhat like the resurrection of the new body." There are those who have a sense that some of the great saints and truly good people continue to be much more vigorously present than others, and that this implies a more advanced state of resurrection. This belief is linked with Mary, who according to Rome has been taken up into heaven in terms of both body and soul. In this respect she would have preceded other believers (554–58). It is not surprising that this line of thought is particularly prevalent among Roman Catholics (cf. Ratzinger, 1978⁴, 95–99).

This view is not in agreement with Scripture either. The new body, referred to in the New Testament, is the resurrected body that will be like the glorified body of Christ and that God will grant to his people once Christ has appeared in glory (see § 57.1).

19. J. Verkuyl, *Antroposofie en het evangelie van Jezus Christus* (anthroposophy and the gospel of Jesus Christ), 1986, 37–43; R. Kranenborg, *Reïncaratie en christelijk geloof* (reincarnation and Christian faith), 1989; W. Logister, 1990.

20. See W. Balke, *Calvijn en de Doperse radikalen* (Calvin and the Anabaptist radicals), 1977², 1989, 23–36.

55.5. *Life in communion with Christ*

According to Reformed doctrine, communion with Christ awaits his people "immediately after this life" (Heidelberg Catechism, Answer 57). This answer contains both an antithetical and a thetical aspect. Antithetically it states that death is not the end and that no purgatory or sleep of the soul awaits us. Thetically it confesses that the believers will soon be with Christ, to whom they belong as members of the body of which he is the Head. Scripture references such as Luke 23:43 and Philippians 1:23, which have already been discussed, are the foundation of this confession.

The fact that the Heidelberg Catechism distinguishes between the soul of the believer being taken to Christ immediately after this life, and the future reunion of body and soul, has attracted criticism. It appears to suggest a scholastic dichotomy. It should, however, not be viewed in this manner. It is much rather an extension of the terminology that was common at the time of the Reformation and that also occurs in the Bible (see Matt. 10:28). It is not the intention of the confession to dictate a specific anthropological terminology. For that matter, we cannot employ anthropological categories to portray life after this present life. This is no reason to doubt the reality of communion with Christ after this life that the Heidelberg Catechism focuses on. This expectation is not anthropological but christological. It clearly expresses the belief "that neither death nor life, nor any other creature, shall be able to separate us from the love of God, which is in Christ Jesus our Lord" (Rom. 8:38–39).

Life in communion with Christ is a life in the Father's house. He is, after all, with his Father. He has given his people the prospect that they too will be where he is (John 14:3). They will be at home with the Father.

Communion with Christ commences in this life and continues in the life after this life. It is an uninterrupted reality. Communion with Christ will soon no longer be disturbed or threatened by sin. Since it will be more splendid than it currently is, Paul can call being with Christ "far better" (Phil. 1:23).

The beginning of eternal joy is here already—perfect salvation will follow hereafter (Heidelberg Catechism, response 58). This eschatological perspective rests on the New Testament notion that the Holy Spirit has been given to us both as firstfruits and guarantee (*aparchè* and *arraboon*). For this reason we may await with certainty what has already been granted to us. Thus we view life after this life in a pneumatological light.

It has been pointed out that the believer's highest joy is that his Savior and Surety awaits him. "After all, the important thing is not the splendour of heaven, but the Saviour in heaven." His longing for us is even stronger than our longing for him. He prays: "Father, I will that they also, whom thou hast given me, be with me where I am; that they may behold my glory" (John 17:24). See Van der Schuit, 1929, 98–100.

Our own confession statements do not attempt to give a description of life between death and resurrection. A number of other Reformed confessions say more. The Westminster Confession states: "The souls of the righteous, being then made perfect in holiness, are received into the highest heavens, where they behold the face of God, in light and glory, waiting for the full redemption of their bodies" (Müller, *Bek.*, 610). According to the *Erlauthaler Bekenntnis* the souls of believers find themselves in Abraham's bosom, in paradise, under the altar Christ, in the refreshment that constitutes eternal life. They are aware that there are still people living on earth, for they anticipate the resurrection in faith, but they know nothing of those who are there and neither pray for them (Müller, *Bek.*, 344, 352).

We can speak of two aspects of life between death and resurrection based on Revelation 14:13 and 6:11–13. *It is a resting and a waiting.* By way of summary, Calvin states: Let us be content with the limits divinely set for us, namely, that the souls of the pious, having ended the toil of their warfare, enter into blessed rest, where in glad expectation they await the enjoyment of promised glory, and so all things are held in suspense until Christ the Redeemer appear (*Institutes*, 3.25.6).

During this interim there is a tension that characterizes the time prior to the return of Christ: "How long?" (Rev. 6:10). Not all of God's promises have yet been fulfilled. Although salvation commences upon the termination of this life, more is to be expected. The end is eternal glory.

Here we return to the opinion that there are two types of eschatology: that of heaven and that of the last day (see § 55.2). Telder says: we await the coming of Christ; there is no second expectation of prior or simultaneous events (1963, 125ff.).

However, there are not two kinds of expectation. The situation between today and the last day is no isolated event for anybody—neither for them who will then be with Christ, nor for those who will not be with him. All are en route to the end of time. The continued existence of man is described in terms of his relationship with

God. Only those who belong to Christ will be with Christ. The Bible says: "He that believeth on the Son hath everlasting life: and he that believeth not the Son shall not see life; but the wrath of God abideth on him" (John 3:36).

The expectation of believers is based entirely on Christ. It looks ahead to always being with the Lord (1 Thess. 4:17) and being with Christ after this life (Phil. 1:23). Our expectation is not focused on salvation in heaven or on glory at the end of time, but on Christ who is our life. He gives us life now, shortly, and always.

To the believer the immediate horizon of the end of his life on earth and the far horizon at the consummation form a single perspective. In the case of a number of Scripture passages it is not clear whether the former or the latter is referred to (see Berkouwer, 1961, 1:61). However, there is indeed a clear difference between 1 Corinthians 15 and 2 Corinthians 5:1–10—which has led to the hypothesis of a development in Paul's eschatology resulting from the delay in the return of Christ (cf. Hoekema, 1979, 123ff.). However, the main factor that explains the difference between these two is the concrete situation that is being addressed in each case (see Hoffmann, 1969², 321–47). At any rate, no conflict can be identified. Otherwise, how could it be said in one and the same apostolic letter, "I have a desire to depart, and to be with Christ; which is far better" (Phil. 1:23), and, "We look for the Saviour, the Lord Jesus Christ; who shall change our vile body, that it may be fashioned like unto his glorious body" (Phil. 3:20–21)?

The enjoyment of the promises of God already belongs to the closer and more immediate horizon. It is a prelude to the enjoyment of the *full* promises of God in Christ together with *all* believers (cf. Heyns, *Dogm.*, 394). Viewed in this manner, the former will not predominate in the doctrine and life of faith. Neither will the expectation of the return of Christ and the fullness of the kingdom of God play a secondary role.

§ 56. The return of Christ

56.1. *The approach of Christ's return*
56.2. *Christ's return as a redemption event*
56.3. *The expectation of Christ's return*

56.1. *The approach of Christ's return*

1. *The approach of his return*

The expectation of the church of Christ is focused on his coming (*parousia*). This is abundantly clear in the New Testament: "The Lord is at hand." "The coming of the Lord draweth nigh" (Phil. 4:5; James

5:8). It is significant that the New Testament simply refers to "the day." It does not merely say that "the end of all things is at hand" (1 Peter 4:7), but also that "the day is at hand," or "the time is at hand" (Rom. 13:12; Rev. 22:10), or that the day approaches (Heb. 10:25). "For yet a little while, and he that shall come will come, and will not tarry" (Heb. 10:37). Jesus says: "I come quickly" (Rev. 3:11; 22:20).

In light of this overwhelming testimony of the New Testament the question has arisen whether the return of Christ should be considered to be imminent. To many this is indeed the case.

At the beginning of the twentieth century there emerged the *consistent eschatological* view, with which especially the name of A. Schweitzer (1875–1965) must be mentioned. He read into the New Testament expectation merely a *Naherwartung* (imminent expectation). But the kingdom of God did not come at the time and in the manner that Jesus and his disciples had imagined. Schweitzer was of the opinion that the entire history of Christianity flowed from the delay of the parousia and the abandonment of eschatology. Subsequently Bultmann claimed that it simply was a fact that Christ's parousia did not take place immediately—contrary to New Testament expectations—but that world history carried on and will continue to do so. Everyone who is in his right mind is convinced of this. These New Testament conceptions belong to a mythical world image that has ceased to be meaningful to modern man.

It is, however, contrary to the New Testament to view the coming of God's kingdom merely as a future event. In one sense it has already come, while in another sense it is still coming!

In opposing the views of Schweitzer and others, Cullmann alluded to the images of D-Day and V-Day, subsequently taken over by many and criticized by some.[21] The triumph of the future is based on decisive developments in history, much more so than could be imagined in any other situation. Those who are certain that God in Christ has acted decisively will fervently look forward to the day when this will become visible to all.

The New Testament indeed does not only speak of expectation but also of fulfillment: "already" and "not yet"; "the present of the future" (Versteeg, 1969) and "the future of the present."[22]

In imitation of Schweitzer, reference has frequently been made to three "time-interval pronouncements" in the gospels. In Mark 9:1 it says: "And he said unto them, Verily I say unto you, That there be some of them that stand here, which shall not taste of death, till they have seen the kingdom of God come with power" (see also Mark 13:30; Matt. 10:23).

Frequently a rather arbitrary approach is followed in treating other Scripture verses, such as Mark 13:10, as having only secondary significance; very little attention is paid

21. O. Cullmann, 1946, 72ff. Cf. Berkouwer, 1972, 74ff.

22. We also think of the title of the book by W. Kreck, *Die Zukunft des Gekommenen* (the future of what has already arrived), 1961.

to the words that no one knows the day and the hour (Mark 13:32; Matt. 24:36–39 and other places); parables that refer to waiting and urge watchfulness are ignored (cf. Matt. 25:13, 19); and one does not know what to make of Luke (Gospel and Acts), who also portrays eschatological expectations (see Luke 21; Acts 1:11; 17:31).

The "time-interval pronouncements" are indeed difficult Scripture verses (Berkhof, 1958, 68), but it is not inconceivable that they purport something different from what is frequently read into them. What is expected within a relatively brief time span is still not always the parousia itself. Mark 9:1 may allude to the resurrection. We need to take into account the telescopic language of prophecy that we also encounter in the Old Testament (see Ridderbos, 1950, 420–32). "Terms suggesting temporal proximity are apparently intended to underscore the certainty of future events" (Baarlink in Baarlink et al., 1984, 124).

This discussion also has implications for certain expressions of Paul, such as 1 Corinthians 15:51 and 1 Thessalonians 4:15–17 (cf. Ridderbos, *Paul*, 492–94). Paul longed intensely for the return of Christ and may have expected that he would live to see this day. He would not have expected the parousia to be delayed for centuries. Here, however, he speaks much more as a spokesman for the church, as in Romans 8:23 and Philippians 3:20–21, where also the word "we" is employed.

We find in the apostle's writings no pronouncements regarding an interval of time, and so the certainty of his expectations with respect to the future is independent of time. "The horizon of expectation is entirely different from a prognosis of time" (Berkouwer, 1972, 93).

The epistles of Paul are indeed strongly influenced by the proximity of Christ's return, but the apostle did not know how close this day really was. He wrote to one church that the day of the Lord comes like "a thief in the night" (see 1 Thess. 5:1–2).

In summary we can say that references to the proximity of the consummation of all things are wrapped up with the critical significance of Christ's death and resurrection. In the midst of history the end is announced. Since the end will come as the consummation of what has begun in Christ, it is—so to speak—placed in the present before our eyes. Perhaps we could speak of a proleptic element in the New Testament anticipation of the future. The great day is approaching!

2. *Signs of the times*

We live in the final days, or to use biblical expressions, "in the last days" and "the last time" (2 Tim. 3:1; 1 John 2:18). This refers to the time interval between Christ's ascension and return, or the time between the redemption event of Pentecost and the consummation during which everything hastens to the end. No one knows how long this time interval will last. Neither can it be deduced from *the signs of the times*.

This term, which occurs in Matthew 16:3, has come to be used in the sense of striking and frequently shocking events that announce in unambiguous language that Jesus Christ is returning (cf. Dijk, 1952, 115).

To us the biblical point of departure is not the expression itself, but the "Synoptic apocalypse" (Matt. 24; Mark 13; Luke 21). Jesus is here replying to a question of the disciples: "Tell us, when shall these things be? and what shall be the sign of thy coming, and of the end of the world?" (Matt. 24:3). To understand his reply, we have to take into account the prophetic perspective. This means that events that follow each other after (long) intervals of time are viewed in a single perspective in recognition of their interrelationships, here the destruction of the temple and the end of the world. It is also referred to as the telescopic nature of prophecy.

It is possible to distinguish three phases in the last things that Jesus discusses in Matthew 24. First there is the beginning of *sorrows* (v. 8), then the *great tribulation* (v. 21), and subsequently everything that has to do with the coming (parousia) of *the Son of man* (v. 27).

In *the first phase* there emerge tempting spirits and false christs. There is mention of wars and rumors of wars, famines and earthquakes, repression, hatred, apostasy, increasing disregard for the law, a growing cold of the love of the majority, but also the preaching of the gospel of the kingdom as a witness to all nations.

In *the second phase* there will be persecution such as has never arisen before. These days will be shortened for the sake of the elect. False christs and false prophets will arise, who will perform great signs and miracles.

In *the third phase* there will be tremendous cosmic signs. Then the Son of man will appear with great power and glory. He will send out his angels to gather his elect from around the entire world.

Based on the character of these signs, three distinct aspects can be distinguished: 1. They call for the end, e.g., the increasing lawlessness (see also 2 Thess. 2); 2. They announce the end, e.g., natural disasters (cf. Heb. 12:26); 3. They prepare for the end, e.g., the preaching of the gospel to all nations (Matt. 24:14).

The report on eschatology presented at the Reformed Ecumenical Synod of 1948 also discusses these signs (*Acta*, 73–85). Two important points are stressed: a. individual incidents should not be *isolated*—

because of their striking nature—from among the overall acting of God; b. the nature of the signs makes it impossible to *pin down* the day of the Lord. They are signals and warnings that concentrate the minds of believers on the approaching advent of Christ.

In connection with the first point we would like to say that there is a danger that spectacular events are viewed as signs of the times, e.g., Kuyper believed that Revelation 9:16–21 was fulfilled during the First World War.[23]

The second point makes clear that one should not interpret these signs as data for a calendar of eschatological events. The kingdom of God does not come in a predictable way (Luke 17:20). Nevertheless, in the course of time many have ventured to make such calculations and predictions. The Montanists expected the end in AD 150 (120 years after the crucifixion of Christ). Medieval Christians thought that the world would end in the year 1000. In the days of Luther someone predicted the date of Christ's return as October 19, 1533 (Bakker, 1964, 94). Adventists held initially that 1844 would be the year of the end. Hal Lindsey also made a prediction that did not materialize, for in the meantime "his" year has already passed (1988). Various sectarian groups have put a great deal of effort into such predictions. With Hutten we can say that these apocalyptical checks issued by sects are not being honored by God. He follows neither their programs for history nor their eschatological calendars. Being sovereign, he goes his own way.[24]

Signs of the times are to be viewed as signals with which Christ tells us that his return is approaching. His future is becoming more and more definite. Although there are warning signals, we may not turn these into a warning system. They have meaning for all times and not only in the last few years of the world's existence. Mark 13 ends with a repeated call for watchfulness!

In the time of the Reformation signs and signals were not ignored. Luther was especially struck by the fact that the Word of God was powerfully revealed (Bakker, 1964, 88–92). That it was the last hour was apparent from the fact that the great adversary, whom he recognized in the papacy, had established himself in God's temple (cf. 2 Thess. 2:4). To Calvin the suffering of the church of Christ had eschatological significance. But there was more, i.e., the increasing

23. A. Kuyper, *Van de voleinding* (regarding the end), 1931, 4:157–60.
24. K. Hutten, *Geloof en sekte* (faith and sect), undated, 107.

preaching of the Word and the growing opposition of the world, false teaching, and the appearance of the power of the antichrist (Quistorp, 1941, 113–23).

We conclude this section with a quotation from the report of the Reformed Ecumenical Synod: "And thus we follow with intense interest the course of events of our time, both the growing concentration of evil and the power of the Kingdom manifested in this world as an irrefutable reality for faith" (*Acta*, 83).

3. *The antichrist*

Apostasy, referred to by Paul in 2 Thessalonians 2, can also be counted among the signs of the times. "That man of sin [will] be revealed, the son of perdition" (2 Thess. 2:3). "He is a product and at the same time an exponent of secularization" (Dijk, 1952, 157).

The name "Antichrist" is encountered in the epistles of John (1 John 2:18, 22; 4:3; 2 John 7). As the name indicates, he is *the adversary of Christ*. This is something different and something more than a "false christ" (Matt. 24:24). The antichrist is not someone who pretends to be Christ, but who puts himself in the place of Christ and in opposition to Christ.

When the New Testament figure of Christ is fully revealed, the Antichrist will also become more visible. There were already portents of the latter's coming even before the appearance of Christ on earth. In this connection we have in mind several prophecies: Isaiah 11:4 (cf. 2 Thess. 2:8; Ezek. 38–39 [cf. Rev. 20:8]; Daniel 7:23–25 [cf. Rev. 13, 17]; Daniel 11:36–37 [cf. 2 Thess. 2:4].

The first New Testament reference is found in 2 Thessalonians. The apostle refers to the lawless one ("that Wicked," 2:8) and the man of lawlessness ("man of sin," 2:3). He does not only transgress the law that God has given, but he also despises it, and does not want to hear of it. Sin, which is in essence *anomia* ("lawlessness," 1 John 3:4), culminates in the figure that is called the *anomos*. In him lawlessness has become flesh and blood. Ridderbos says that therefore the "man of sin" is the last and highest revelation of man (humanity) inimical to God, the human adversary of Christ, in whom the divine work has become flesh and blood (*Paul*, 515). It is a human being who demands divine honor for himself (2 Thess. 2:4).

The words of Paul give the impression that we are dealing with a future person. The "mystery of iniquity" is already at work, but this person still has to reveal himself. His coming is prepared by Satan. When Christ comes, he will destroy him (2 Thess. 2:7–9).

There are parallels between this portion of Scripture and the book of Revelation. The beast of Revelation 13 receives tremendous power from the world of nations (the sea) and Satan is behind it (Rev. 13:1–2). Ten kings give (hand over) their power and might to the beast (Rev. 17:13). The beast lets itself be worshiped, blasphemes God, and makes war against the saints (Rev. 13:4–7).

The number signifying the beast is 666. This mysterious number has always intrigued people and all sorts of interpretations have been given. Since letters of the Greek alphabet may also be used to indicate numbers, it could refer to a *word* that is equivalent to the number 666. In the time of the church fathers it was thought to refer to "Latin" (*lateinos*). Many consider another possibility to be more likely: Caesar Nero (written in Hebrew letters). In the twentieth century, people have wanted to read the name of Hitler into it (cf. Van der Meulen, 1952, 67–76). Berkhof writes: There are tens of explanations, "all possible, few likely, none satisfactory." He prefers to see 666 as a symbol of the highest possible realization of human effort outside the Sabbath of God's work (1958, 111ff.). It is far preferable to view 666 like so many numbers in the last book of the Bible as a symbolic figure. The number six that is here reinforced by six tens and six hundreds could indicate going to an extreme. We can say with De Vuyst (1987, 102) that the number 666 discloses and emphasizes the utterly extreme political presumption projected by the beast. Yet more urgently than in the preceding section (Rev. 13:9–10), believers are challenged to be steadfast and faithful. It is possible that this number means more than this, but this will remain hidden until the beast appears.

A powerful political alliance is formed that bears the mark of Antichrist. The beast that emerges from the sea carries ten horns and seven heads; the horns bear crowns and the heads exhibit blasphemous names (Rev. 13:1). These symbolize his might and dominion, but also project enmity toward God. The kingdom that is characterized by beastly and demonic behavior is referred to as Babylon or the great prostitute (Rev. 17–18). The great Babylon possesses treasures of trade, industry, and culture, but puts believers to death (Rev. 17:6; 18:24). The book of Revelation shows how the beast and the city meet their ruin.

In addition to the beast from the sea, "the political antichrist," there is a beast from the earth, the false prophet (Rev. 13:11–17). It has two horns like those of the Lamb and pretends to be good and even Christian, but its speech reveals it to be devilish. It is in the service of the first beast and makes propaganda for it. This beast will have access to unknown powers and unexpected possibilities. It is a seductive power, fanatical, and intolerant. Revelation 13 sketches a totalitarian regime that employs tools such as terror and boycott.

Finally there are the references in the Johannine epistles. The first instance is 1 John 2:18: "Little children, it is the last time; and as ye have heard that antichrist will come, even now are there many antichrists." The Antichrist denies the Father and the Son; he denies "that Jesus Christ is come in the flesh" (1 John 2:22; 2 John 7). John also calls this the "spirit of antichrist," who is already in the world (1 John 4:3). He envisages false teaching, which is a deadly danger to the church of Christ.

On the basis of these latter passages, some think that the Antichrist is *a phenomenon that occurs in every age*. Traditionally *an appearance was expected in the last days*, based on Paul's letter to the Thessalonians and the book of Revelation.

Berkouwer says that it is the one signal that is sounded repeatedly: *the* Antichrist, many antichrists, the liar, the adversary, the man of lawlessness. "Anti is denoted in numerous forms varying with times, circumstances, and concrete situations" (1972, 271ff.).

In contrast with Berkouwer, Ridderbos places the emphasis on personality traits of the figure in whom lawlessness converges. He raises the question why one must offer resistance to the idea that the power even now manifesting itself will in the future bear the character of a final, decisive defiance concentrated in one person (*Paul*, 517–18).

A conclusive argument against the complete personification of the Antichrist is that the man of lawlessness is a figure who is not yet there and who also cannot yet be there because of the restraining power that keeps him away, or the restrainer who keeps him away (2 Thess. 2:6–7). Who is meant by this *restrainer* that first must be removed?

An initial view, which was already held by Tertullian and which has much support in our days, is that the restrainer is the Roman Empire or the Roman emperor. This is usually generalized to the power of the state, sometimes suggesting a connection between the state and common grace.

A second view, which also goes back to the days of the church fathers and which was also held by Calvin, believes that it is the preaching of the gospel. Berkhof zeroed in on its unstoppable progress and the work of the Holy Spirit in the growth of the church (1958, 122ff.). In this connection one can ask the question whether the preaching of the gospel and its application by the Holy Spirit would ever end.

According to a third view, for which we refer to Th. Zahn (1838–1933) among others, it is the law. Van der Meulen (1952, 65ff.) points out that the coming of the lawless one is held up everywhere the law of God is adhered to. "Since these days are marked by lawlessness, one may and must conclude that, in the absence of repentance, the Antichrist will face enormous opportunities on all fronts."

There is something attractive in this view. But can it be said of the law of God that some day it will be removed?

Many more possibilities have been raised, but one may ask whether it is consistent with this Scripture verse that we can be so specific? We prefer a more global view.

With Velema we may think of the impact of the Word of God on society. This does not mean that some day God himself will remove his Word, but that society rejects his Word, and that within the churches the Word of God is adapted to current thinking.[25]

When 2 Thessalonians 2 and Revelation 20 are compared, a number of similarities strike us. The restraining of the lawless man ends one day and the binding of Satan is terminated (Rev. 20:3). The lawless one will reveal himself in a satanic manner (2 Thess. 2:9–10) and the devil will seduce the nations of the earth (Rev. 20:8). But then Christ appears and he will make him powerless and destroy him (2 Thess. 2:8). Everything ends with the last judgment (Rev. 20:11–15).

Who is the Antichrist? In the early church, believers sometimes thought he was a Nero resuscitated. The medieval pope was sometimes viewed as the Antichrist. Luther was convinced that it was the pope, recalling the words of Paul that the Antichrist would install himself in the temple of God (2 Thess. 2:4). Calvin calls the pope the leader and standard bearer of the godless and abominable kingdom of the Antichrist (*Institutes*, 4.7.25). With exceptions, this is the fairly standard opinion throughout the centuries following the Reformation. Brakel says: to the question as to who the antichrist is, we reply with all Protestants: the pope of Rome (*R.S.*, 2:44). This is explicitly stated in some confession statements, and very clearly so in the Westminster Confession (Müller, *Bek.*, 599). Our own confessions do not address it specifically, although article 36 of the Belgic Confession of Faith refers to the "kingdom of the antichrist."

There is strong objection to the view that the pope is the Antichrist. The Antichrist radically rejects God's revelation, which most definitely cannot be said of the pope, although antichristian aspects of the papacy have indeed been identified.

In history there are forerunners of the Antichrist and his kingdom, but he himself will be far worse. There are reasons to believe that he will turn up during the period immediately preceding the return of Christ. In the meantime we are warned by John with respect to the spirit of the Antichrist, which expresses itself now already in the denial of the confession that Jesus Christ has come in the flesh. All movements controlled by this spirit display an antichristian character. These include the false religions and ideologies that prepare the coming of the Antichrist with increasing refinement and a growing intensity.

The apostle Paul says that "the mystery of iniquity doth already work"; i.e., lawlessness is already at work in secrecy. The culmina-

25. See W. H. Velema, *Kernpunten van het christelijk geloof* (key points of the Christian faith), 1978, 112–16.

tion of this is the appearance of the lawless one, to be destroyed by Christ. Precisely the appearance of the Antichrist will indicate that Christ will come soon (2 Thess. 2:7–8).

We cannot say ahead of time who the Antichrist is and when he will appear. However, we can observe that the battle between the kingdom of God and the kingdom of the evil one is heating up. Therefore we must be aware that the Antichrist is on his way. The information that the Scriptures provide in his regard is—for the believers who will witness his appearance—sufficient to be able to recognize him. At that time perseverance will be required more than ever before! (Cf. Rev. 13:10).

4. *Chiliastic representations*

a. *Introduction.* Chiliasm is the doctrine of a millennium of peace, which is to precede the return of Christ to judge and during which he is to reign as king on earth. The term has been taken from the Greek language (*chilioi* = 1000). Another name for chiliasm is millennialism, which is of Latin origin (*mille* = 1000).

Chiliasm is actually of Jewish origin. It occurs in apocalyptic writings such as 4 Ezra, 2 Baruch, and 1 Enoch. There is probably a connection between serious oppression of the Jewish people and the development of the expectation of an earthly period of salvation with the Messiah as king and Jerusalem as center, when God's promises will be fulfilled. According to one source the duration for this temporary kingdom would be 400 years, and according to another 1000 years.[26]

Chiliasm is a phenomenon that takes many forms. The two main movements are *premillennialism* and *postmillennialism*, also known as prechiliasm and postchiliasm. Currently *dispensationalism* is the most important chiliastic version.

The difference here is whether the return of Christ will occur prior to (*prae*) or following (*post*) the millennium. Some of the authors, who take the contrary view, hardly consider the latter option to be true chiliasm (Ouweneel, 1988, 1:110).

We first briefly review the post-chiliastic view, and subsequently discuss the alternative view, which demands most of our attention.

26. Cf. H. Bietenhard, *Das tausendjährige Reich* (the kingdom of 1000 years), 1955, 37–43.

b. *Postmillennialism (postchiliasm)* believes that the coming of Christ will be preceded by a long period during which God will richly bestow spiritual and material blessings.

The expectation of a period of blossoming of the church and of conversion and restoration of Israel, held by many Puritans and figures of the days of the Second Reformation, is sometimes considered to be an early form of postmillennialism. J. Edwards (1703–58) saw the "Great Revival" of the eighteenth century as a forerunner of the millennium that would materialize as an answer to prayers by means of the spreading of the gospel. In the United States this notion was combined with political ideas. This country was expected to play a role in the implementation of God's plan for the world.

L. Boettner expects the return of Christ following a golden age of spiritual growth, the duration of which might be much longer than a thousand years. The Spirit of God will do his work in the hearts of people and the changes in individual lives would be accompanied by social, economic, political, and cultural progress. Sin will not be banned completely, but will be reduced to a minimum. Christ will return to a thoroughly Christian world, possibly following a limited manifestation of evil.

Boettner refers to Scripture verses such as the following: The desert will blossom (Isa. 35:1). Godliness has promise of life both in the present and the future (1 Tim. 4:8). "But seek ye first the kingdom of God, and his righteousness; and all these things shall be added unto you" (Matt. 6:33). See Boettner in Clouse (ed.), 1980[4], 115–41.

In many respects the expectation with regard to the future contained in a book by Berkhof (1958, 143–50) follows along these same lines. In Revelation 20 there is much that remains unclear, but the following minimal conclusion is definitely justified: "John expects that following the demise of the antichrist a long and happy period will ensue, in which the boundaries between heaven and earth will fade, the downtrodden will reign, the suffering church of Christ will be publicly put in the right, and a restored Israel will be the centre of the world." Having subsequently become somewhat more subdued, Berkhof still speaks of a future with on the one hand an anti-Christian world dictatorship, but on the other hand a universal and voluntary acceptance of the evangelical structural rules as the only hope of saving a viable human existence (*C.F.*, 518–20).

According to Boettner and others, postmillennialism places a strong emphasis on the universality of Christ's work of redemption. However, it bypasses the seriousness of certain words of Scripture. Confronted with this optimistic description of the future, we are reminded of the question asked by Jesus: "Nevertheless when the Son of man cometh, shall he find faith on the earth?" (Luke 18:8). We are also not of the view that great tribulation is a thing of the past. For more criticism see Hoekema, 1979, 177–79.

c. *Premillennialism or prechiliasm* is the true chiliasm that is encountered the most. Dispensationalism is also sometimes called chiliasm, but needs to be discussed separately.

The most important *characteristics* of chiliasm are:

First, there will be a millennium of peace on earth, inaugurated by an initial coming of Christ and an initial resurrection, based on Revelation 20:5.

Second, this first resurrection is a resurrection of believers only, prior to the millennium, and that following this period there will be a second resurrection, of unbelievers.

Third, numerous prophecies remain unfulfilled, and must be interpreted as literally as possible; they will be fulfilled during the millennium when—following his appearance and following the restoration of Israel—Christ together with his people will rule the nations in a visible manner.

Fourth, Satan will be bound during this time, to be released subsequently when he will seduce the nations, but then to be consumed by fire from heaven.

In comparison with former days, "chiliasm" tends to be discussed in somewhat more generalized terms. However, the mere adoption of minor aspects of a chiliastic concept by certain authors—we have in mind representatives of the Second Reformation—does not make them chiliasts (cf. Meeuse, 1990, 68). One could at most speak of partial chiliasm. An example is Witsius's expectation that there will not only be a conversion of the people of Israel, but also a conversion of many other nations. They "shall even go up from year to year to worship the King, the LORD of hosts, and to keep the feast of tabernacles" (Zech. 14:16). When the threat of Gog and Magog has been removed, the Lord will come in judgment (cf. van Genderen, 1988^{2}, 37–44).

Zechariah 14 plays an important role in chiliasm (cf. Berkhoff, 1926, 109; De Heer, 1934, 347–50); the conversion of Israel and Gog and Magog also always have a place in the picture of the future, but their expectations are then worked out in a periodization that Witsius, Brakel, and their followers do not accept. According to Brakel, the idea that at the beginning of the millennium Christ would physically descend from heaven to earth to rule openly has too much of an earthly connotation (*R.G.*, 3:325ff.).

d. *Dispensationalism* is a radical form of chiliasm. It is built on the foundation laid by J. N. Darby (1800–1882). The term "dispensationalism" or the doctrine of dispensations describes it well, since it teaches that there are seven different dispensations in which man is tested with respect to his obedience to the will of God. It is presented in the notes in the margins of *The (New) Scofield Reference Bible*, which is authoritative among dispensationalists.

We now trace the chief *tenets* of this doctrine.[27]

27. A prominent dispensationalist is J. F. Walvoord, whose system is outlined by H. R. van de Kamp, *Israël in openbaring* (revelation), 1990, 32–40.

Its basis is formed by a literal interpretation of prophecies in the Old Testament. In addition, the portrayal of the future is strongly influenced by a succession of dispensations. Of crucial significance is the clear separation of Israel and the church. The coming of the kingdom is postponed because of the unbelief of the Jews for whom it was originally intended. God made a detour by granting salvation to the church. However, the dispensation of the church is only an intermezzo and will soon come to an end.

The resurrection of believers and the rapture of the church occur at the first coming of Christ. This is stated in 1 Thessalonians 4:13–17 and 1 Corinthians 15:51–52.

While the raptured church celebrates the wedding feast with Christ, a remnant of Israel will put their faith in Jesus as the one-time promised Messiah. These are the 144,000 "which were sealed" (Rev. 7:1–8). Through their witness many from among the nations are converted. But then the enemies of God and his people will assemble for a fearsome assault, namely, the battle of Armageddon.

Christ returns to establish his kingdom on earth and to defeat and destroy all of his enemies. He establishes his throne in Jerusalem and rules visibly for a thousand years—usually interpreted literally. This is primarily a Jewish kingdom, although the other nations will also share in its blessings. It will be a time of prosperity and peace, a golden age such as the world has never yet experienced. People will live longer than ever. "The earth shall be full of the knowledge of the LORD, as the waters cover the sea" (Isa. 11:9).

In Jerusalem the temple is rebuilt, which will be the center of worship in this kingdom of peace. Sacrifices will be made to commemorate that Christ died for us—sacrifices to atone for sin will no longer be necessary.

Under Christ's government there will continue to be people who will not bow to him. With Satan as their commander they will turn themselves against the encampment of the saints, but Christ will bring all opposition to an end. At this point he will hand the kingdom over to his Father.

Although the tendency to indicate concretely how the Scriptures will be fulfilled is characteristic of all chiliastic movements, it is most pronounced among dispensationalists. A well-known author such as Hal Lindsey with his calculations and predictions goes further than many another. Although he admits that no one can know the day and the hour of the (first) coming of Christ, he does take it that his generation will experience the event.[28] According to him Scripture points continually to the United States, the European Community, Russia, and China. To Lindsey the Bible resembles a book of puzzles (see Boersma, 1977²).

e. *Critical comments*. First, there is a reference to reigning as kings with Christ over a period of a thousand years (Rev. 20:4), but it does not say that this will take place on the earth. There are indeed references to thrones (Rev. 20:4) and thrones in heaven (cf. Rev. 4:4; 11:16). When the question is asked where the souls are of those who

28. H. Lindsey, *Op weg naar het einde der tijden* (en route to the end of time), 1984², 178ff.

have been beheaded for their faith (Rev. 20:4), we need to think of heaven (Rev. 6:9).

In chiliastic thinking the verb form *ezesan* ("they lived," Rev. 20:4) needs to be translated as "they became alive," which suggests a physical resurrection. But in connection with the time frame of this verse, another translation is feasible: they lived and ruled as kings for a thousand years. Considering the significance of prayers in the book of Revelation, "reigning as kings with Christ" could be interpreted to mean answering prayers (cf. De Vuyst, 1987, 125).

Second, one of the most important arguments for chiliasm is the relative position of Revelation 20:1–10 (right after Rev. 19, which refers to the appearance of Jesus in glory). This argument is based on a chronological interpretation of this book which is not tenable, and that chiliasts themselves also depart from when it is to their advantage, namely, by referring to certain sections as inserts, digressions, or lengthy clauses (cf. Ouweneel, 1990, 2:61ff., 145). Those who study the book of Revelation are struck by numerous parallels, recurrent themes, and an underlying perspective focused on the end of time. They are "visions of the consummation of all things."[29]

Third, the victory of Christ is already a fact, and at the same time the binding of Satan is not merely a thing of the future. For a parallel see Colossians 2:15. The objective of the binding of Satan for a thousand years—a long period by historical standards—is to prevent him from continuing to seduce the nations. In connection with other Scripture references (Matt. 24:14; 28:18–20; Luke 10:18) we may think of the coming of the kingdom of God by means of the preaching of the gospel. Satan, however, has not yet completely left the scene. When he is released "for a short time" he will try to mobilize the nations against God and his Anointed One (Rev. 20:1–3, 7–8). This brings to mind the time of the Antichrist or a period in which the antichristian spirit reigns supreme and the antichristian power advances (see § 56.1, subsection 3).

But the evil one still appears to be able to do as he likes. Is he then really bound? This question could definitely have arisen in John's time! However, he is shown the heavenly perspective of what happens on earth. The martyrs and the other opponents of the evil one

29. Cf. W. Hendriksen, *Visioenen der voleinding* (visions of the end), 1952 (original title: *More Than Conquerors*, 1949[5]).

and his realm are not dead, but alive. They are "blessed and holy" (Rev. 20:6).

At various times beginning and end dates have been associated with the period of a thousand years. However, historical reality needs to be viewed from an eschatological perspective. It is an "illumination of history from the point of view of the as-yet-hidden triumph of the Lord who is coming" (Berkouwer, 1972, 313). Only, in Berkouwer's view, very little remains of the temporal references given in Revelation 20:3–5. We are of the opinion that overall the book depicts a process that prepares us for the end.

Fourth, neither Revelation nor other places in Scripture refer to a twofold coming of Christ. Christ's discourse concerning the last events points in an entirely different direction. The rapture of the church prior to the commencement of the millennium is not taught by the passages quoted by chiliasts (see Boersma, 1977^2, 215–22).

Fifth, do Old Testament expectations largely apply to the coming millennium? What is pictured for us from a prophetic perspective in terms of earthly images and Old Testament idioms does not necessarily apply to earthly relationships. The New Testament shows us the further implications and the spiritual depth of the old words of prophecy. According to Revelation 21–22, these prophecies are fulfilled in the realm of glory. The New Testament is focused on the return of Christ and the eternal kingdom of God and not on a temporary final phase in the form of an interregnum.

There is a danger that the anticipation of a millennium as a preliminary state of bliss eclipses the expectation of the eternal kingdom of peace.

The biblical message, as understood in our confessions, leaves no room for chiliastic notions. Besides, there are ecclesiastical pronouncements that oppose chiliasm. See Dijk, 1933, 165–67.

Sixth, in addition to the objections that we have raised against chiliasm per se, there is more to say when it comes to *dispensationalism*.

The latter does not sufficiently take into account that prophecies are not always fulfilled to the letter. In the case of biblical images with respect to the future the question should be raised: what thoughts and expectations have they evoked so far and what are they telling us today?[30] Prophecy usually does not become entirely clear until it is

30. Cf. J. de Vuyst, "Enkele hermeneutische opmerkingen over apokalyptische stoffen" (a number of hermeneutical remarks about apocalyptic material), in J. van Genderen et al. (ed.),

fulfilled. Those who keep this in mind will be more careful and less rash in their statements.

In this doctrine of dispensationalism, schemes are devised that seriously hinder understanding of the message of the Bible.

We especially have in mind the contrast postulated here between Israel and the church. Christ, who is the Head of the church, is portrayed as about to become the king of Israel. The promises for Israel are interpreted to be of an entirely different nature from those for the church. This also involves distinct mandates. Israel would be destined for the earthly realm and the church for the kingdom of heaven. With this different kind of salvation for Israel, the unity of salvation would be split up into a fundamental dichotomy.

There is also a fundamental difference with respect to the church.[31] According to the dispensationalist doctrine there was no church prior to Pentecost, although there were believers. This separation between Israel and the church is in conflict with the unity of the people of God, which is so significant in the New Testament (see John 10:16; Gal. 3:27–28; Eph. 2:18).

We cannot concur with the idea that in the dispensation of the church God would make a detour to return to Israel and that the church would need to be taken up into heaven—evacuated, in the words of Lindsey—because God would want to concentrate his attention on Israel. It is after all the case that from the beginning God has sought to gather a church from among all nations. The New Testament says so (see Acts 15:14) and demonstrates this very clearly.

Seventh, in what follows, we shall investigate whether Israel has indeed such a central position as chiliasm and dispensationalism would want us to believe.

Here it suffices to say that all those who share the expectation that Israel will experience a spiritual reformation are not necessarily chiliasts.

5. *Is there sufficient reason to place Israel at the center?*

Since the middle of the twentieth century the Jewish nation—what in this connection we refer to as Israel—has indeed stood in the center of

---

Ten dienste van het Woord. Opstellen aangeboden aan prof. dr. W.H. Velema (in support of the Word: essays in honor of Professor Dr. W. H. Velema), 1991, 200–202.

31. Chiliasts also consider the difference in view with respect to the church to be a definite and fundamental difference. See J. G. Fijnvandraat/A. Maljaars/W. J. Ouweneel, *De kerk onder de loep* (the church under the magnifying glass), 1979, 6–13.

attention. This is reflected in the theological literature. The increased attention for Israel is obvious in light of the terrible events that took place under the Nazi regime and the establishment of a Jewish state in 1948.

Article 17 of *Fundamenten en perspectieven van belijden* (fundamentals and perspectives of confession)—the draft for a new confession for the Netherlands Reformed (state) Church (1949)—is already evidence of this. On the one hand it says that Israel was temporarily rejected by God when it rejected him as its king, and that among the nations it represents a sign and reflection of God's judgment; on the other hand its continuation as a nation as well as the conversion of individuals is viewed as a harbinger and pledge of Israel's ultimate reacceptance. The concept of "harbinger" also plays a role in the work of Berkhof (1958, 142ff.). According to him it can be concluded from Revelation 20 that a restored Israel will be the center of the world during the prolonged and blessed period following the demise of the Antichrist (1958, 147).

In chiliastic movements the pattern of expectations is that the conversion of Israel would be the final sign so to speak that Israel will once again become "the instrument of redemption" and that Jerusalem will become the center of government. See Bietenhard, 1955, 125ff.; De Heer, 1934, 192; Ouweneel, 1990, 2:226.

Although these thought processes have been reinforced by recent events affecting Israel as a nation, they were not triggered by these, but have been around much longer.

While chiliasm clearly distinguishes between Israel and the church, and references to fundamental differences are not uncommon, earlier authors frequently did combine the conversion of the Jews—coupled with a return to their homeland—with a blossoming of the church and unusual fertility of the earth (cf. Brakel, *R.G.*, 3:138, 322–24).

The view of Israel and its future becomes quite different when not only "missions among the Jews" are radically abandoned, but also the preaching of the gospel among the people of Israel is replaced by encounters in the form of dialogues or conversations and through support of Israel. This is done on the basis of a religious pluralism, whereby every religion is considered to be a way to God, or it is believed that Israel and the church can choose paths that, however different, both lead to the kingdom of God. There is also the view that they are en route together[32] (see in this connection § 46.2, subsection 1).

Thus there are various anticipations of the future in which Israel is assigned an important or even central role.

To those who base themselves on the Scriptures, Romans 11:26 is a key verse. There it says: "And so all Israel shall be saved." This word of Scripture is, however, variously understood. There is even a menu of views, four of which we briefly discuss here.[33]

32. Cf. S. Schoon, *Geworteld in Israël* (rooted in Israel), 1982, 81–85.

33. Regarding these four views, see J. P. Versteeg, "Kerk en Israel volgens Romeinen 9–11" (church and Israel according to Romans 9–11) in *Th. Ref.* 34 (1991): 151–69.

a. *These words indicate the preservation of the church.* Calvin says in his commentary that he applies the name "Israel" to the entire people of God. Some day the redemption of God's entire Israel will be realized: in such a way, however, that the Jews will take first place.

We can be brief in this regard. Serious objections can be raised against this exegesis, which continues to be encountered today. The context refers to the people to whom Paul himself belongs (Rom. 9:3). In view of Israel's unbelief he struggles with the question whether God has abandoned his people (Rom. 11:1–2).

b. *These words indicate the redemption of Israel in the last days.* This explanation is found in a large number of commentaries. Once the full number of Gentiles has been saved, all of Israel will be converted. Nevertheless, "all Israel" does not necessarily mean "every Israelite." This view is prevalent not only among exegetes, but also among theologians in general (see Honig, *Handboek*, 819–21). According to Berkhof, the reacceptance, if even only of the last generation, signifies the reacceptance of Israel in terms of all of its generations (1958, 137).

It may be objected that Paul did not write in Romans 11:26: And thereupon. . . , but: "And in that way . . ." (cf. Bavinck, *R.D.*, 4:670). The connection with the preceding thought is not temporal in nature. It has to do with God's way of acting and not the moment in time when all of Israel will be redeemed. Just as the flow of grace was first transferred from (unbelieving) Israel to the Gentiles, now it needs to return from believing Gentiles to unbelieving Israel. Romans 11 does not imply that Paul was thinking of "a conversion of Israel at one point in the eschatological end time" (see Ridderbos, *Paul*, 356–59). It is significant that three times in a row the apostle emphatically writes "now" (Rom. 11:30–31) and that the content of these words corresponds to that of verse 26. It is a qualified "now" (cf. *TDNT*, 4:1112–23), which does not mean once, at the end of time, but now that the time of God's mercy has come for all, Jews and Gentiles alike.

c. *The words signify the redemption of Israel in Paul's own time or shortly thereafter.* H. M. Matter criticizes those who still expect a special future for Israel more sharply than many others. He holds that both the fullness of the Gentiles and the redemption of all Israel were realized during the first four centuries of the history of the church.[34] According to Berkouwer, Paul did not focus on the far future of Israel, but Israel of his days (1972, 346ff.).

In this way the "now" of the New Testament is not done full justice either. Even if it refers to the end of time, it is a simple indication of time as in: now and not later on.

d. *The words signify the redemption of Israel between the first and second comings of Christ.* For this view, which we encounter with minor variations on the part of Bavinck, Ridderbos, and Versteeg, we refer to the parallel between Romans 11:12 and 15 on the one hand, and verses 25 and 26 on the other hand. What Paul first refers to as the inadequacy ("diminishing," v. 12) or the rejection ("casting away," v. 15) of Israel, is subsequently referred to as a partial hardening ("blindness in part," v. 25). This is contrasted first with "the fullness of the Gentiles" (v. 25) or their acceptance ("the receiving of them," v. 15) and then "all Israel" (v. 26). When the fullness of the Gentiles commences (v. 25), they share totally in the bliss of the kingdom of God. Would Israel rank behind them? Are the apostasy and hardening of that people permanent? Certainly not, for Israel also will fully share in the promised salvation. It has sometimes been pictured as the undulatory movement (cf. Ridderbos, *Paul*, 360): from Israel to the nations and from them back to Israel (see Rom. 11:30–32). Christians from among the Gentiles may not consider themselves more eminent than Israel. They are to abide in God's mercy. For Israel there is hope, if it does not remain in its unbelief. The apostle looks forward to this (Rom. 11:17–24).

From all of this it cannot be concluded that according to God's plan for the end of time Israel will be the special focus. It may be said that it will become clear that God has not written off Israel. In his faithfulness he keeps remembering this people.

"There is a remnant according to the election of grace" (Rom. 11:5, 7), of which Paul and other Jewish believers are part. This is the concept of a remnant that we know from the prophecies of the Old Testament (*TDNT*, 4:209–14). It does not matter how large this remnant is in terms of numbers. A certain portion represents the entire

34. H. M. Matter, *De toekomst van Israël in het licht van het Nieuwe Testament* (the future of Israel in light of the New Testament), 1953, 44.

nation. In this remnant Israel lives on as the people of God. The fact that it is a remnant indicates the seriousness of the situation. But the remnant's existence raises expectations.

In our view, Romans 11:26 should not be interpreted as a proof in Scripture for a conversion of Israel *en masse* in the last days. Yet it is noteworthy that Paul in Romans 11 first speaks of a remnant and an elected portion, while everyone else's heart has been hardened, whereas subsequently he uses words such as "fullness" and "all Israel." Therefore, it is possible that Romans 11:26 is "now" initially fulfilled, and that some day it may turn out that the ultimate fulfillment is much more comprehensive.

If there are insufficient grounds to anticipate a wholesale spiritual restoration of Israel in the ultimate or penultimate phase of world history, then we should not interpret it as an eschatological sign.

A national restoration of Israel, however amazing and delightful, should not be interpreted as a sign that the day of Christ is approaching, for otherwise the New Testament would not have kept silent about it. The promise to this nation will be fulfilled in the kingdom of Christ.[35]

What Scripture says about Israel is no justification for us to put this nation at the center in one way or another. However, for the preaching of the gospel among the people of Israel it presents not only a strong incentive but also a hopeful perspective.

56.2. *Christ's return as a redemption event*

1. *Redemption* event. Here we can build on what has already been said about the parousia or return of Christ within the framework of Christology (§ 31.4). There the coming of Christ was called a redemption event.

The New Testament speaks explicitly of the expectation of redemption (*soteria*) as a consequence of his coming and of the expectation of Christ as Savior (*soter*). It says that "Christ was once offered to bear the sins of many; and unto them that look for him shall he appear the second time without sin unto salvation" (Heb. 9:28). Paul writes: "From whence also we look for the Saviour, the Lord Jesus Christ: Who shall change our vile body, that it may be fashioned like unto his glorious body" (Phil. 3:20–21).

35. Cf. B. J. Oosterhoff, *De beloften aan de aartvaders* (the promises to the patriarchs), 1973, 44.

The same thing is put in other words when the apostle says, "When Christ, who is our life, shall appear, then ye shall also appear with him in glory" (Col. 3:4), and when he writes, "He shall come to be glorified in his saints, and to be admired by all them that believe" (2 Thess. 1:10). With Ridderbos (*Paul*, 532) we may interpret this in such a way that his coming means for believers that they will share in his glory and that they will be amazed—in reverence and adoration—at the glory with which he himself is clothed. Paul mentions the parousia of our Lord Jesus Christ and our gathering together to him in one breath (2 Thess. 2:1).

In many places Scripture makes a direct connection between the redemption that is already reality in this life, and the salvation that will be revealed in the last days (cf. Rom. 8:23; 1 Peter 1:3–5). Believers are told: "Rejoice, inasmuch as ye are partakers of Christ's sufferings; that, when his glory shall be revealed, ye may be glad also with exceeding joy" (1 Peter 4:13).

Fulfillment and expectation go hand in hand. Paul writes to the church in Corinth: "In everything ye are enriched by him, in all utterance, and in all knowledge; even as the testimony of Christ was confirmed in you: so that ye come behind in no gift; waiting for the coming of our Lord Jesus Christ: who shall also confirm you unto the end, that ye may be blameless in the day of our Lord Jesus Christ" (1 Cor. 1:4–9). The connection between what has *already* become reality, and what is *not yet* there, but will certainly come—characteristic of the New Testament—is very clearly stated in 1 John 3:2: "Beloved, now we are the sons of God, and it does not yet appear what we shall be: but we know that, when he shall appear, we shall be like him; for we shall see him as he is."

The first and second comings of Christ are inextricably connected with each other. In his first coming to earth lie the ground and guarantee for his return. Since "the grace of God that bringeth salvation to all men" has appeared in Christ, we look "for that blessed hope, and the glorious appearing of the great God and our Saviour Jesus Christ" (Titus 2:11–13). In Titus 2:14 and in other places a connection is made with his surrender and sacrifice (see also Heb. 9:28). Of him who loves us and has redeemed us from our sins with his blood, the book of Revelation says: "Behold, he cometh with clouds; and every eye shall see him" (Rev. 1:7). In the chapter on Christology it has already been pointed out that the entire exaltation of Christ points to his coming in glory and that his return will complete his preceding work (§ 31.4, subsection 1).

The return of Christ is also considered to be a redemption event in the church's confession. In the Belgic Confession of Faith, the redemption expectation of believers is described in various turns of phrase. They will be crowned with glory and honor. The Son of God will confess their names before God, his Father (Matt. 10:32), and his chosen angels, and God will wipe all tears from their eyes (Rev. 21:4). "And for a gracious reward the Lord will cause them to possess such a glory as never entered into the heart of man to conceive" (article 37). According to the Heidelberg Catechism, the consolation that is imparted by the return of Christ includes that "He will take me up into the heavenly joy and glory together with all of the elect" (Lord's Day 19).

Scripture gives us no precise description of the *manner* of his coming. It is indeed not easy to reproduce in our own words what was expressed in prophetic-apocalyptic language with the aid of symbols and images that formed part of the worldview of those days. But this does not make the coming of Christ less certain to us.

a. *He comes unexpectedly*. The image of a thief in the night, which is used in the New Testament, indicates the suddenness and the unpredictability of his coming (see Matt. 24:34, 44; 1 Thess. 5:2; 2 Peter 3:10). It contains an alert to be watchful.

Jesus said that it will be like the days of Noah and Lot. The days of Noah were characterized with the words, "They did eat, they drank, they married wives, they were given in marriage," and in the days of Lot, "they did eat, they drank, they bought, they sold, they planted, they builded" (Luke 17:26–30). In other words, people just go about their business and do not see the end coming. They pay attention to everything, but do not regard God. And suddenly it happens!

It will be unexpectedly sudden to everyone, but not unanticipated by everyone. "The Lord's coming will be unexpected, but it will not be un-expected. . . . The suddenness and incalculability demand constant vigilance and preparation" (Berkouwer, 1972, 85). The closing of the parable of the ten bridesmaids is: "Watch therefore, for ye know neither the day nor the hour wherein the Son of man cometh" (Matt. 25:13). The Belgic Confession of Faith says that it will occur "when the time appointed by the Lord (which is unknown to all creatures) is come" (article 37).

b. Our confession says also *that he will come corporally and visibly*. This agrees with the words of the angels spoken at his ascension: "This same Jesus, which is taken up from you into heaven, shall so come in like manner as ye have seen him go into heaven" (Acts 1:11). All of mankind will see him appear, and his coming will make a profound impression (Matt. 24:27; Rev. 1:7).

c. The return of Christ is a "coming in a cloud *with power and great glory*." He will "come in his glory, and all the holy angels with him" (see Luke 21:27; Matt. 25:31). The clouds surround him, which is an indication of his divine splendor. The angels stand at his disposal, because he is also Lord of the angels (see also 2 Thess. 1:7). Everything must bow to him and all tongues confess: "Jesus Christ is Lord, to the glory of God the Father" (Phil. 2:10–11).

d. His coming will be coupled with *tremendous signs*, which implies that all of creation is involved. "The sun shall be darkened and the moon shall not give her light, and the stars shall fall from heaven" (Matt. 24:29; Luke 21:25). Calvin notes in this connection that we cannot predict how this will be, but that this will become apparent when these words are fulfilled.

e. *Christ comes to end all opposition* (1 Cor. 15:25). The book of Revelation shows us the total victory of the Lamb over all of his enemies. This leads to the final triumph. Satan and all evil powers will be eliminated. Christ is the Lord of lords and the King of kings (Rev. 17:14; 19:11–16).

f. *Christ comes to judge*. He has the power and the mandate to judge (John 5:27; Acts 17:31). At his coming the great separation will take place (2 Thess. 1:5–10). When he comes, his *reward* will be with him, "to give every man according as his work shall be" (Rev. 22:12).

g. The return of Christ is not only tied to the last judgment, but also the *resurrection of the dead* (1 Cor. 15:23, 52). As Mediator, Christ will hand the kingdom over to his Father (1 Cor. 15:23–28). In this connection see § 31.4, subsection 2.

Everything will be characterized by fulfillment and completion. With Korff we can say: faith knows Jesus Christ as the one who *came* in the humiliation of his historical appearance; as the one who *is there now* in his present exaltation and with whom it is connected through the Holy Spirit; but also as the one who *will come* again some day in glory.[36]

36. F. W. A. Korff, *Christologie*, 1942^2, 2:362.

2. The redemption *event*. We call the return of Christ a redemption event for biblical reasons. The foundations of our faith are shaken when the reality of the coming of Christ, awaited by us, is attacked. This happens in modern theology in a variety of ways. Without trying to be complete, we provide the following examples.

a. *C. H. Dodd* has defended the view that the New Testament anticipation of the kingdom of God has already been realized through faith and the church. The powers of the kingdom already operate here. A future kingdom is no longer expected. In the spiritual realm of this kingdom, what has been or is yet to be is irrelevant. As far as biblical references to the future are concerned, they only say that the kingdom comprises more than what appears in present reality. Since eschatology has already been achieved, a return of Christ is no longer to be expected.

There is so much material in the Scriptures to be drawn on to reject this interpretation that we shall leave it aside completely (see Hoekema, 1979, 293–97).

b. *R. Bultmann* considers it mythology that Christ has ascended and will return on the clouds of heaven to complete redemption, and that then the resurrection of the dead and the last judgment will take place. To believers, the future would already have become reality.

The Bekenntnisbewegung "Kein anderes Evangelium" (confession movement "no other gospel"), in its *Verklaring van Düsseldorf* (declaration of Düsseldorf) addressed to Bultmann and his supporters, has correctly explained that it is a false teaching that the expectation of the return of Jesus Christ is senseless and that only this world reflects reality.[37]

c. Besides the influence of Dodd and Bultmann, which can be recognized in various new studies, there is that of Barth, who views the future as the disclosure or the unveiling of what is already the case today. He says: Jesus Christ is the essence of our future. The future will not bring another turn of events in history, but the revelation of what is today.[38] The crucial events of the arrival, death, and resurrection of Christ will be fully revealed to everyone, just as they became understood by the disciples over the first few days after Easter (cf. Blei, 1986, 93–101).

If this were true, the return of Christ would have been much more depicted as a disclosure of what is invisible now or an unveiling of what is still hidden from many, rather than a coming or return of Christ. It involves a new reality (cf. Heyns, *Dogm.*, 407ff.).

d. The reality of the return of Christ pales in significance when it is discussed in The New Catechism (Netherlands, 1966): Christ will not be fully revealed until the perfection of our lives in the new creation. "He does not come back, because he is already with us. His presence is then perfected" (228). In this connection it is pointed out that the word "return" does not occur in the New Testament. We agree that the source word "parousia" means arrival in the New Testament. But the arrival of him who originally came to earth and then ascended to heaven *is* his second coming or return. The New Testament emphatically says so (see John 14:3; Heb. 9:28). It

37. H. Steubing (ed.), *Bekenntnisse der Kirche* (confession of the church), 1970, 311.
38. K. Barth, *Creed*, 1964, 106; *Dogmatics in Outline*, 1949, 155.

involves a new appearance of Christ, which needs to be distinguished from his initial coming to earth and his coming in the Spirit.

e. *Berkhof* follows the same lines as this catechism, when he describes the presence of Christ as a process, of which the crop is to be harvested shortly (1967, 44). Subsequently he calls the return of Christ the image that denotes "that some day Christ will be revealed in our experiential world as its secret and foundation, and that that revelation will not happen as the unfolding of imminent forces, but as a new encounter-event, in which mankind will meet on its way as liberators the Son and in him the Father" (*C.F.*, 526).

Here we merely raise the question, What can then remain of our confession that Christ "will come to judge the living and the dead" (Apostles' Creed)? See further § 57.2.

56.3. *The expectation of Christ's return*

1. *A tense expectation.* Eschatological expectation permeates the entire New Testament. In the apostolic days, the anticipation of Christ's parousia could not possibly be characterized as a wait-and-see attitude, but rather a sincere yearning for that day. This is very clearly captured in expressions such as: "Looking for and hasting unto the coming of the day of God" (2 Peter 3:12). The suspense is also apparent in Romans 8:18–25. The anticipation of the coming of the Son of God is as much part of conversion as of the service of God (cf. 1 Thess. 1:10). It should not, however, turn into an anxious expectation. Paul does not want the imminent coming of the day of the Lord to cause the Thessalonians to lose their cool or feel uneasy (2 Thess. 2:1–2).

A wonderful future is already beginning to take shape in the present. The outward appearance of the world is in the process of disappearing. Time is short. This has implications for everyday life (see 1 Cor. 7:29–31). The apostle does not mean to say that ordinary things of life should be ignored, but against the background of relatively minor matters he points to things of real consequence.

The book of Revelation is replete with anticipation. It begins with an announcement of the return of Christ and ends with his promise and the prayer for his coming (Rev. 1:7; 22:20). This prayer is a response to his promise. "The Spirit and the bride say: Come!" (Rev. 22:17). Here the Spirit is mentioned first, because it is he who prompts them to prayerfully anticipate Christ's return in faith.

In this connection we have in mind the word "Maranatha" (1 Cor. 16:22), which also occurs in the *Didache* (10, 6) where it is a prayer for the celebration of the Lord's Supper. Most probably it means: Come, our Lord (cf. Rev. 22:20).[39]

It is entirely in agreement with what Christ intended with the institution of his Supper, that prayer for his return be included (1 Cor. 11:26). Receiving the bread and the cup, we remember that redemption is anchored in the past, proclaim that it is experienced in the present, and anticipate that it will be consummated in the future.[40]

We concur with Van Niftrik (*Kl.D.*, 234) as far as some key consequences of the belief in the return of Christ are concerned: 1. immense peace in the face of world and life events; 2. an aversion to all false consolation offered by people who suggest that things will take a turn for the better some day; 3. a profound understanding of the times since we know that world history hastens toward the judgment; 4. watchfulness: "We are called to erect signs that point to the coming Kingdom in this world and in our lives. It needs to be obvious from our lives that we put all of our hope into God's future."

There are times when the future plays only a minor role in the experience and thinking of Christianity. People can be so absorbed with the present that longing for the coming of Christ is crowded out. However, the church then becomes secularized. The influence of materialism is a factor that should not be ignored (cf. Hoekema, 1979, 110). The theological influences that we signaled in the preceding subsection suffer in consequence.

Contrary tendencies can also be identified. Preoccupation with the last days can cause Christians to lose touch with the world and to neglect their present calling. Furthermore, various sects have developed a questionable apocalyptics of their own.[41]

According to Barth, eschatology has fallen short of the expectations raised by the theology of the Reformation (*C.D.*, 2.1.632). This criticism, however, is both unreasonable and incorrect. In the first place, the emphasis was more on the Scriptures, justification, the church, and the Lord's Supper. In the second place, the Reformers placed eschatology in a new, more biblical context. The return of Christ is viewed as comforting (Heidelberg Catechism, Lord's Day 19) rather than threatening as in the Middle Ages, when Christ was primarily viewed as Judge. Luther recounted that in his youth he had a terrible fear of the last day. Later in life it was for him "der liebe jüngste Tag" (the dear last day).[42] Calvin says that the people of God need not fear the coming of Christ in judgment. "Let us not hesitate to long for the coming of the Lord, as the happiest thing of all" (*Institutes*, 2.16.18; 3.9.5).

A Scripture passage that had a big impact on Luther, Calvin, and other Reformers is Luke 21:28: "Look up and lift up your heads; for your redemption draweth

39. Cf. *TDNT*, 4:466–72; L. Goppelt, *Theologie des Neuen Testaments* (theology of the New Testament), ed. J. Roloff, 1976, 2:348–51.

40. J. P. Versteeg, "Het Avondmaal volgens het Nieuwe Testament" (the Lord's Supper in the New Testament), in W. van 't Spijker et al. (ed.), *Bij brood en beker* (bread and cup), 1980, 64.

41. See K. Hutten, *Geloof en sekte* (faith and sect), undated, 101–8.

42. See U. Assendorf, *Eschatologie bei Luther*, 1967; J. T. Bakker, *Eschatologische prediking bij Luther* (eschatological preaching according to Luther), 1964.

nigh." The remarkable expression "with uplifted head" in the Heidelberg Catechism (Lord's Day 19) probably also recalls this verse. The intensity with which the coming of the Lord was expected in those days is marvelously expressed in article 37 of the Belgic Confession of Faith, the concluding sentence of which states: "Therefore we expect that great day with a most ardent desire, to the end that we may fully enjoy the promises of God in Christ Jesus our Lord."

This is the place to recall the question: why no parousia feast? J. Overduin, who raised this question, says: "May the Spirit of God persuade the church to believe and hope, anticipate, and watch to such an extent that it desires and demands an annual parousia feast."[43]

2. *An active anticipation.* Christ's return is to us not only a comfort but also an incentive. The anticipation makes us both watchful and industrious. Concerning the latter see the parable of the talents and the pounds (Matt. 25:14–30; Luke 19:11–27), while the remark "watch therefore" loses none of its gravity (Matt. 24:42; 25:13). Considering 1 Thessalonians 5:1–11, we can also say that the anticipation makes us equally watchful and capable to defend ourselves. The Christian's ability to defend himself includes being equipped with faith, love, and hope, which are needed for spiritual warfare, the *militia christiana.*

The consummation of all things, which we expect, calls for sanctification. In turn, sanctification, which is achieved in this life, calls for consummation.[44] The literature frequently refers to the biblical connection between eschatology and ethics. The theme of sanctification features importantly in this relationship, not only in the writings of Paul (see 1 Thess. 3:13; 5:23; Phil. 1:9–10; Titus 2:11–14), but also in other New Testament books (see Heb. 10:24–25; 1 Peter 4:7–11; 2 Peter 3:11–14; 1 John 3:2–3; Jude 20–21; Rev. 22:11). First Corinthians 15, which is replete with eschatological perspectives, ends with the invitation: "Therefore, my beloved brethren, be ye stedfast, unmovable always abounding in the work of the Lord, forasmuch as ye know that your labour is not in vain in the Lord." This means also very concretely: participating in the collection for the congregation in Jerusalem (1 Cor. 16:1–4).

The execution of our mandate in the meantime requires knowing why the time is given to us. We mention two relevant, but very different opinions, namely, those of Berkhof and Aalders.

Berkhof believes that Christ's victory is becoming visible in history and rejects what he calls pessimism with respect to Christian culture (1958, 163ff.). In his chief

43. J. Overduin, *Het onaantastbare* (the inaccessible), 1975, 151.
44. See W. H. Velema, *Geroepen tot heilig leven* (called to a holy life), 1988², 168–70.

work he keeps referring to advance and progress with optimism, despite struggle (*C.F.*, 515–17).

Aalders objects: "We definitely live in a post-Christian world with apocalyptic traits." He sees the progression of events over time as a process of dying.[45]

The one focuses on the horizontal perspective and the other on the vertical perspective of eschatology. However, both views are one-sided.[46]

Our starting point is the "already now" and the "not yet," referred to earlier. The kingdom of God has come, but it is not yet present in its full glory. Aside from signs of the lordship of Christ, there are also signs of opposition to him and his kingdom. This is not going to improve.

A Scripture passage that is of immediate importance to our deliberations is 2 Peter 3. This does not only refer to scornful remarks of outsiders, but also to questions raised within the church. When Peter responds to this, he first says that God's concept of time differs from ours. Next he points to God's purpose for this time. It is a time full of God's patience. The end has not yet come, because God does not wish that any should perish, but that all will come to repentance. However, God's patience is not without limit and therefore neither is time. Everything is focused on the day of the Lord who is to come. This makes the call to repentance still more urgent!

What is said in 2 Peter 3:9 with respect to God's purpose for the time in which we live may be related to what we read in the New Testament about Christ's command "that repentance and remission of sins should be preached in his name among all nations, beginning at Jerusalem" (Luke 24:47; cf. Matt. 28:19).

Those who look forward to the coming of Christ recognize his task for them. Those who carry out their task, do so in the expectation of his coming.

§ 57. Consummation

57.1. ***Bodily resurrection***
57.2. ***The last judgment***
57.3. ***Definitive separation and eternal punishment***

45. W. Aalders, *Burger van twee werelden* (citizen of two worlds), undated, 174; idem, *Schepping of geschiedenis* (creation or history), undated, 34. Regarding the contrast between the view of Aalders and that of Berkhof (as well as many others), W. Aalders, *Een correctie op de tijd* (a correction for this time), 1985, 13–21.

46. Cf. in this connection W. H. Velema, *Christen zijn in deze wereld* (being a Christian in this world), 1974, 7–25; idem, *Geroepen tot heilig leven* (called to a holy life), 1988[2], 151–67.

57.4. *Eternal life*
57.5. *The new heaven and the new earth*

57.1. *Bodily resurrection*

1. Christ's return is directly connected with the last judgment and the resurrection of the dead. This resurrection is the first event that follows upon his return (cf. Bavinck, *R.D.*, 4:692).

There will not only be a resurrection of believers, but also a general resurrection, "a resurrection of the dead, both of the just and unjust" (Acts 24:15). In passages such as Daniel 12:2, John 5:28–29, and Revelation 20:12–15, a clear distinction is made between "the resurrection of life" and "the resurrection of damnation." In Scripture the focus is on the resurrection of believers, similarly in the creed of the church, although article 37 of the Belgic Confession of Faith also speaks with great emphasis of the judgment faced by the ungodly and wicked who in the process will rise and become immortal.

For believers the word "resurrection" brings to mind the resurrection of Christ, but for others it is a judicial act of God and Christ. The dead, and those who live to witness the coming of Christ, together will be called to appear before the Judge (cf. Dijk, 1953, 87–89).

The Heidelberg Catechism calls "the resurrection of Christ . . . a sure pledge of our blessed resurrection" (Lord's Day 17). Van Ruler says: "The resurrection of Christ is the sign, the beginning, the origin, and the ground of the resurrection of the dead."[47]

The resurrection of the dead is a miracle of God that far transcends our imagination and understanding. Many view it with skepticism and unbelief, which also was the case in the past.

According to Acts 23:8 the Sadducees did not believe in it; in Athens some ridiculed the idea (Acts 17:32). Paul needed to ask the Corinthians sharply: "How say some among you that there is no resurrection of the dead?" (1 Cor. 15:12). Probably this does not refer to a rational criticism of the possibility of resurrection, but a spiritualistic or gnostic view (cf. Versteeg, 1971, 4–24).

Since the Enlightenment, criticism of this article of faith has increased significantly. Some find it simply incredible, while others seek a *new interpretation*. Not so long ago a view emerged within Roman Catholicism in connection with the difficulties and possibilities of the new dogma of the bodily assumption of Mary into heaven (1950). This dogma came to be viewed as a model for our own resurrection, in part to reduce opposition to this dogma within the ecumenical community. In *Neues*

47. A. A. van Ruler, *De dood wordt overwonnen* (death is conquered), undated, 38.

Glaubensbuch (new book concerning faith, 1973), resulting from collaboration between Roman Catholic and Protestant theologians, it says: "The individual resurrection takes place at the time of death and in death" (542). We have several serious objections to this. 1. Scripture offers no grounds whatsoever for the 1950 dogma and the conclusions drawn from it. 2. The resurrection would then take place on the day of our death rather than the last day, which runs counter to Scripture. 3. This leads to a significant reduction in eschatology, since now the resurrection is interpreted to mean that man simply finds his history back in God (cf. M.S., 5:881–85; Ratzinger, 1978[4], 92–99).

There is no shortage of biblical grounds for the expectation of the resurrection, although we cannot imagine how it will be.

It is a much-discussed question whether the Old Testament already testifies to it. Sometimes death seems to be the irrevocable and definitive end. However, we have already seen that according to the Old Testament it is not death that has the final word, but God, who is the God of life (see § 55.3). It even says that he will destroy death for good (Isa. 25:8).[48]

The New Testament shows us that the resurrection of Christ is essential and all-encompassing when it comes to the foundation of the expectation of the resurrection of believers. In this connection we have in mind principally 1 Corinthians 15 (but also Rom. 8:11; 1 Cor. 6:14; 2 Cor. 4:14; and other places). The Lord Jesus refers to himself as "the resurrection, and the life" (John 11:25). His resurrection and that of his people are inextricably intertwined. He is "the Firstfruits of them that slept," and this has consequences for his people (1 Cor. 15:20–23). He is "the Firstborn from the dead" (Col. 1:18; cf. Rev. 1:5). "Both references do not merely state that Christ is chronologically the beginning of the resurrection, but also that the beginning made by him is fundamental and opens the way for the 'many brethren' who belong to this Firstborn" (Ridderbos, *Paul*, 538).

The resurrection of believers should also be seen as the completion of the re-creative work of the Holy Spirit. Their bodies, which now already are the temples in which he dwells, will be made alive. Paul says: "But if the Spirit of him that raised up Jesus from the dead dwell in you, he that raised up Christ shall also quicken your mortal bodies by his Spirit that dwelleth in you" (Rom. 8:11).

48. With respect to Job 19:25–29 opinions are much divided. Some recognize in it no more than the reflection of the hope in the resurrection (cf. P. J. Van Leeuwen, *Het christelijk onsterfelijkheidsgeloof* (the Christian belief in immortality), undated, 42ff. De Bondt (1938, 192–204) not only thinks of a blissful seeing of God, but also of a blessed resurrection.

This is how the triune God vouches for the resurrection of his people.

2. The New Testament discusses both the fact and the manner of this resurrection (1 Cor. 15: respectively 12–34 and 35–49). Paul first makes clear that everything is at stake: the resurrection of Christ, the truth of preaching, and the entire Christian faith. Next he replies sharply to the objection that something like this should be unthinkable: "Thou fool!" (vs. 36). The image of a seed serves to demonstrate that the nature of what will be should not be measured against what dies. We are dealing with the vitalizing power and omnipotent sovereignty of God. In contrast with the mortality, shame, and weakness of this life, there is resurrection to immortality, glory, and power. A natural body is sown and a spiritual body is resurrected.

The new body will conform to the glorified body of Christ (Phil. 3:21). Paul's statement that we will be changed points to both continuity and discontinuity. We shall be there, but different from now. "Flesh and blood cannot inherit the kingdom of God" (1 Cor. 15:50). The way man is right now, he cannot enter this kingdom and for this reason he will have to undergo this great change.

From the image of the grain of wheat it has sometimes been deduced that there is a germ of life that is preserved by God (Kuyper) or an "organic mold" that remains (Bavinck). However, from a human point of view it is impossible to make transparent what passes from the old body to the new body. The mystery of continuity does not lie within our human essence, but in the life-giving Spirit.

In this connection Bavinck notes that *cremation* cannot be rejected as limiting God's omnipotence and preventing resurrection. However, it is of pagan origin and in conflict with Christian morality. We entrust bodies to the earth and let them rest till the day of resurrection (*R.D.*, 4:694–98).

The resurrected body will be a *spiritual* (pneumatic) body (1 Cor. 15:44). This does not mean that the physical is absorbed by the spiritual as imagined by Origen (see Boliek, 1962, 62ff.). Neither should we define it as a body controlled by our spirit—as though this were not now the case—nor as an invisible body. From the context it may be concluded that it will be a body that corresponds to re-creation through the Spirit and which he not only inhabits but also rules. Through the stamp that the Spirit puts on his entire existence, the redeemed and sanctified human being will serve God with everything that he is and has (cf. Versteeg, 1989, 123ff.).

We await "the redemption of our body" (Rom. 8:23), which completes redemption. We are redeemed from sin and all of its consequences, including death, which "is swallowed up in victory" (1 Cor. 15:54–57).

Those who are Christ's belong to him completely. He exerts his property rights, including those that pertain to their bodies. Those who bore the image of the first man, will forever bear the image of the second, heavenly Adam (see 1 Cor. 15:49). It involves the complete restoration of the image of God, the completion of the work now already begun by the Holy Spirit (see Calvin on 1 Cor. 15:49).

Finally we consider the question whether "resurrection of the flesh" (Dutch version of the Apostles' Creed) is such a felicitous expression. Many objections to it have been raised (see a summary by Berkouwer, 1961, 192–95).

The Bible speaks of the resurrection of the dead or resurrection from the dead. But it is not necessarily unbiblical for the church to use its own language.

From a historical point of view the formulation of the Apostles' Creed is solid enough. With this Justin, Tertullian, Irenaeus, and others placed the emphasis on the identity of our present body and the resurrected body. In this way they rejected all Docetic and gnostic views (see Boliek, 1962, 24–30).

Yet one can raise the question whether in our own time this expression is sufficiently transparent. Recommendations that have been made include the following: *resurrection of man, resurrection of the person, or resurrection of the body*. The first two expressions, however, could lead to a disregard of the bodily aspect of the term, which would not adequately capture Christian expectation (see Van Ruler, *Ik geloof* = I believe, 152–55).

"Resurrection of the body" (English version of the Apostles' Creed) and "bodily resurrection" are indeed good variants of the words of the creed. Their use would not at all detract from the intention of the confession. We adhere to the way in which the New Testament expresses it (see Rom. 8:11; Phil. 3:21; 1 Cor. 15:44).

57.2. *The last judgment*

1. Christ comes again "to judge the living and the dead" (Apostles' Creed). The formulation of this article of faith agrees with Scripture (see 2 Tim. 4:1; 1 Peter 4:5). In the Old Testament the Day of Judgment is announced as "the great and the terrible day of the LORD" (Joel 2:31, a prophecy that is quoted in Acts 2:20). The New Testament contains a large number of pronouncements regarding the final judgment (see Floor, 1979).

God who is the Judge of all (Heb. 12:23) has given all judgment to the Son (John 5:22, 27). In this way God will judge through him.

Christ will judge in his name. This is part of the work of the exalted Mediator (see § 31.4).

The reality of the last judgment does not preclude that at the end of our lives a decision will be made. "He that believeth not is condemned already" and "the wrath of God abideth on him" (see John 3:18, 36). The last judgment is the public and definitive confirmation of this.

The view that a judgment is no longer to be expected cannot be based on a statement to this effect contained in the fourth gospel. This has frequently been done. Although there is a critical milestone in the present, there is also a critical milestone yet to be expected (see John 5:29; 12:48).

There is no basis for Schiller's suggestion that the world's history constitutes already its judgment. It is a fact revealed by history—if we only take notice—that God's judgments fall upon this world. Indeed, what is sown will already be harvested in this life (cf. Gal. 6:7). This does not contradict that history is not the judgment, but cries out for the final judgment. The book of Revelation is replete with this. Not everything is set right in the present. However, believers know from the Word of God that he will pronounce judgment and do justice.

Therefore the anticipation of the final judgment does not in the least contradict the execution of God's judgments at the time that precedes the end of the world.

Van Ruler also points out that the final judgment is not the only judgment. But on the last day all books will be opened. "Then each person is confronted with what he has done with himself, his neighbour and God's good and beautiful creation." All of us will have to admit that everything is as it is read from these books. Our consciences are turned inside out. They are objectified in the final judgment (*Ik geloof*, 122ff.).

We should not imagine the final judgment too humanly as a process involving accusation, questioning, and sentencing. We are dealing with a Judge who is omniscient.

Questions remain. For example, what does Paul mean in 1 Corinthians 6:2–3? Will believers be expected to concur with the judgment of angels? Does this mean that, in one way or another, angels will participate in the judgment process? On the other hand there also is a role for the angels in the execution of the last judgment (Matt. 13:49–50).

To be convinced of the gravity of the final judgment, it is not necessary to know precisely how everything will happen.

The deepest reality and disposition of our lives will be revealed at the last judgment. Paul says: "For we must all appear before the judgment seat of Christ; that every one may receive the things done in his body, according to that he hath done whether it be good or bad" (2 Cor. 5:10). "Therefore judge nothing before the time, until the Lord come, who both will bring to light the hidden things of darkness, and will make manifest the counsels of the hearts: and then shall every man have praise of God" (1 Cor. 4:5).

We are called to give an account. According to Van Ruler, this also means that we as doers of our deeds and bearers of our lot will be taken seriously (*Ik geloof*, 125).

Responsibility varies according to the extent of revelation (cf. Matt. 11:20–24). This judgment will cover everything. We read in the gospel: "Every idle word that man shall speak, they shall give account thereof in the Day of Judgment" (Matt. 12:36). We shall not be able to hide anything. "All things are naked and opened unto the eyes of him with whom we have to do" (Heb. 4:13). The sins of believers will also come to light, but as forgiven sins for which they will not be condemned (cf. Hoekema, 1979, 259).

2. When God asks whether a person's life has corresponded to his purpose for it, *the relationship to God in Christ will be decisive* (see Luke 12:8). Whoever believes in Christ is not condemned, but those who do not know God and do not obey the gospel of Christ are to be punished (John 3:18; 2 Thess. 1:8).

But does Scripture not also refer to works? There is a recompense in accordance with works (Matt. 16:27; Rev. 22:12).

Faith is important, because we are justified by faith and not by works. However, it is not contradictory to say that works are also important, for what is important is a living faith and a faith without works is dead (cf. James 2:17).

Faith is expressed in works. Although they are not meritorious, they are necessary. Good works are fruits of faith, just as faith is the root of good works. Therefore the Lord does not ignore our works. Scripture says: "For God is not unrighteous to forget your work of labour and love, which you have showed toward his name, in that ye have ministered to the saints, and do minister" (Heb. 6:10).

In this connection reference is frequently made to Matthew 25:31–46. It would be wrong to consider the acts of love, which this Scripture passage addresses, in isolation. The "righteous" are those who did what is right in the eyes of God. However, they could not have done these things without the grace through which they entered into the right relationship with God. These works fall within the framework of grace. When the King says: "Come ye blessed of my Father, inherit the kingdom prepared for you from the foundation of the world," it is clear that this Kingdom was prepared for them before they were able to perform any good work.

3. In medieval times there was great fear for the coming of judgment and a silent fear of Christ appearing as Judge. At that time horrors of the final judgment were portrayed with glaring colors, and little remained of biblical expectation.

Although the Reformation did not detract whatsoever from the awe-inspiring gravity of this judgment, it viewed this component of Christ's work in the light of the gospel that says that "God sent not his Son into the world to condemn the world; but that the world through him might be saved" (John 3:17). As Judge he is no different than as Savior. When we look to him in faith, we do bow down as sinners before God's just judgment, but we know that Christ was condemned to free us from the severe judgment of God that was to fall on us (Heidelberg Catechism, Lord's Day 15).

The New Testament speaks of "boldness in the Day of Judgment" (1 John 4:17). In the Heidelberg Catechism the return of Christ to judge is seen as comforting (Lord's Day 19). Calvin calls it a wonderful consolation for believers that the judgment rests with Christ. "How could our Advocate condemn his own clients?" (*Institutes*, 2.16.18).

It is also comforting that God's righteousness will triumph over all iniquity. Justice is an aspect of salvation. God's children look forward to God setting things right and granting them justice. We are reminded of the prayer: "How long, O Lord, holy and true, dost thou not judge and avenge our blood on them that dwell on the earth?" (Rev. 6:10). Calvin says: Then Christ will openly ascend the judgment seat to establish a perfect order in heaven and on earth, to tread his enemies under his feet and to assemble his believers to partake of everlasting and blessed life. Then there will be a visible manifestation of the reason why the kingdom was given to him by the Father (commentary on Matt. 25:31).

4. The announcement of judgment must constrain unto faith and repentance (see Matt. 3:10; Acts 10:42–43; 17:30–31).

There is also strong incentive to sanctification. The Lord asks the question as "to what extent our behaviour has been marked and permeated by the Spirit on the basis of the salvation wrought by Christ" (Van Ruler, *Ik geloof*, 122). First Corinthians 3:12–15 says that the fire of God's judgment purifies the lives of his people. Their sanctification will be judged by God and it will be revealed whether they have built wisely on their foundation, Jesus Christ.[49]

49. Cf. W. H. Velema, *Geroepen to heilig leven* (called to a holy life), 1988[2], 168ff.

It has been pointed out that Scripture encourages us to rejoice in hope (Rom. 12:12), but that it also says: "Rejoice with trembling" (Ps. 2:11). There is fear that sanctifies joy, and gladness that tempers fear.[50] What matters is that we approach the encounter with Christ in faith. Only then will we be able to say that "we expect that great day with a most ardent desire, to the end that we may fully enjoy the promises of God in Christ Jesus our Lord" (Belgic Confession of Faith, article 37).

57.3. *Definitive separation and eternal punishment*

1. In a Scripture passage such as 2 Thessalonians 1:5–10, the coming of Christ in glory is directly linked with the relief that awaits his people, and the punishment for those who do not know God and do not obey the gospel of Christ. On this day Christ will be glorified in his saints, but others will be separated from the presence of the Lord and suffer eternal damnation.

Thus the final separation takes place. We find the same contrast portrayed elsewhere in the Bible, namely, in connection with the preaching of the gospel (John 3:36; 1 Cor. 1:18), the bodily resurrection (Dan. 12:2; John 5:29), the judgment (Matt. 25:31–46; 2 Peter 3:7–13), and the consummation of all things (Matt. 13:40–43; Rev. 21:7–8). There is not only eternal life, but also eternal punishment (Matt. 25:46).

The teaching of the church includes the last judgment with its various consequences. In 1215 a pronouncement was made that this judgment leads to either eternal glory with Christ or eternal punishment in the company of the devil (*DS*, 801). The Augsburg Confession (1530) says that Christ will grant the believers and the elect eternal life and eternal joy, but that he will condemn the unbelievers and the devils to be tormented without end (article 17). In the Heidelberg Catechism, heavenly joy and glory is contrasted with eternal damnation (Lord's Day 19; cf. Belgic Confession of Faith, article 37). Either heaven or hell awaits us in the end.

2. It is difficult for mankind—and certainly modern man—to accept this. In more recent theology there is growing opposition to the idea, and the view that hell does not exist or will be completely empty is gaining support.

We mention a number of objections that have been raised against the doctrine of absolute separation and punishment forever.

50. J. Overduin, *Het onaantastbare* (the inaccessible), 1975[3], 164.

- It is psychologically unthinkable. Eternal bliss would be disturbed by pity for those who are lost.
- It is in conflict with God's love.
- Because of the triumph of God's grace in Christ, which is immutable and has universal validity, perishing is an inconceivable possibility.
- It is not fair that sin that has a limited and temporary character is followed by eternal punishment.
- The term "eternal" does not always mean "endless," because in the Bible it can also indicate a long time.
- Aside from Scripture passages that appear to indicate both eternal salvation and eternal damnation, there are also passages that suggest that redemption is universal.

3. There are a number of additional views:

- *absolute universalism*, or—to use an older term—the doctrine of the final restoration of all things (*apokatastasis*)
- *conditional universalism*
- *conditional immortality*

a. In the case of *absolute universalism* we have in mind first of all of the theology of Origen, whose view was condemned by the church. Having been subjected to a process of purification, all rational beings, including fallen angels, would ultimately return to God, so that the end would resemble the beginning. A prominent advocate of this type of universalism is Schleiermacher. According to him the distinction between those who die as believers or unbelievers comes down to the distinction between those who are admitted to the kingdom of Christ sooner or later. For additional names see Wentsel, *Dogm.*, 3b:690–93.

b. *Conditional universalism* teaches that upon death there is still a possibility to come to faith and repentance. Redemption is universal, so long as its prerequisite is still met. This view was initially prevalent among rationalists of the eighteenth century, but subsequently gained widespread appeal. A theological ethicist such as Muller supports it with the argument that pagans and others who were bypassed by the gospel need to be given the choice that is implied by John 3:36. Given the will of God (1 Tim. 2:4) and the unique significance of Christ (Acts 4:12), such an opportunity ought to be provided following the earthly dispensation. However, Muller finds no basis for the view that all would end up recognizing Christ.[51]

c. The doctrine of *conditional immortality* teaches not only that faith is a prerequisite for immortality, but also that unbelievers will cease to exist. Since they will be annihilated, there will be no eternal damnation. This view was held by Socinians, but

51. P. J. Muller, *Handboek der Dogmatiek* (manual of dogmatics), 1908[2], 234.

has also had followers since then (cf. Althaus, 1964^9, 188ff.). Kohnstamm leaned in this direction, rejecting both universalism and eternal punishment. The same is true of Rinkel, but the latter's statements are more guarded.[52]

d. Although the idea of an *open end* cannot be identified with the foregoing positions, it deserves mention. Althaus is of the opinion that one may not force a choice between a dual outcome and universalism (1964^9, 192–96). In the face of all attempts to give a simple answer to the question regarding man's eternal future and to paint a straightforward picture of the end, he holds up the word of Jesus that calls for a decision now: "Strive to enter in at the straight gate" (Luke 13:24). According to Brunner, no answer should be given to the question whether there is perdition or universalism. Pronouncements about both are true only when taken together, and this togetherness is understood only if we are participants and no longer spectators (*Dogmatics*, 3:422–24).

e. The *views of Barth and Berkhof* cannot be ignored here.

There are places in *Barth*'s work where he rejects *apokatastasis* and other instances where he inclines toward it. The latter is the result of his desire to give the broadest possible scope to the work of God in Jesus Christ. This divine decision cannot be undone as a result of human decisions. In both the doctrine of election and that of redemption, the universality of grace is firmly emphasized (see § 16.4, subsection 1). According to Barth the ungodly will not escape the rod of divine wrath, but it is expected that God's sword will leave them untouched. Although the punishment of eternal damnation would match the gravity of godlessness, the readiness of the Son of God to suffer in the place of men saves them from this end (cf. *C.D.*, 2.2.319, 289ff.). By what took place on Golgotha, Christ caused sinful man to disappear (cf. *C.D.*, 4.1.296). At a later stage Barth returned to the issue of *apokatastasis*. What he had written earlier came down to saying that although one cannot take it for granted because of the *sovereignty* of God's grace, one could hope for it because of the sovereignty of God's *grace* (cf. 2.2.386). He expressed himself more clearly when he said that we do not have the right not to be open to it. The reality of God's grace commands us to hope and pray for it (4.3.477ff.). Therefore, strictly speaking, Barth does not teach absolute universalism. However, it is in line with his expectations.

Berkhof finds that New Testament passages with a universalistic tenor appear to contradict passages that refer to eternal rejection. The former tend to be found in the New Testament epistles, and the latter in Matthew. These groups of passages should, however, not be considered in isolation, but presented in succession. There is a penultimate and an ultimate truth. To Berkhof this means that we may hope that rejection has a limit and that hell is merely a purifying process, although he realizes that to many this may sound strange and heretical. It is reminiscent of the theology of Barth that he says that although he does not wish to belittle the gravity and consequences of human rejection of God, he does want to think just a bit more highly of God's acceptance of recalcitrant people. "God takes seriously the responsibility of our decision, but yet more the responsibility of his love. The darkness of rejection and

52. Ph. Kohnstamm, *Schepper en schepping* (Creator and creation), 1931, 3:399–403; A. Rinkel, *Dogmatische Theologie*, 1956, 4:262–65. Subsequently J. Bonda called the end of created existence a possibility that should not be written off, but should not be considered a point of departure (*Het heil van de velen* = the salvation of many, 1989, 136ff.).

godlessness can and may not be ignored, but cannot be eternalized either. In God's name we hope that hell will be a form of purification" (*C.F.*, 536).

It has been pointed out that Berkhof's view reflects his entire theology. His selective treatment of Scripture, his doctrine of God, and his doctrine of creation and sin all lead in this direction. "The Partner-God owes it to himself and to mankind that everything will turn out all right at the end. This is a predictable outcome right from the start." See W. H. Velema in Knevel (ed.), 1991, 75–82.

4. We now respond to a number of objections to the doctrine of eternal punishment (see subsection 2).

a. The psychological objection is weak. It is usually accepted that no expectation of the future can be based on human feelings. But the will of the redeemed people will also completely coincide with the will of God.

b. God's love is a holy love. Since God is love, he cannot bear that his love is rejected and despised. The Lord Jesus Christ himself, in whom God fully revealed his love, spoke with emphasis about eternal judgment. Apart from Matthew 13:41–42 and 25:41–46, see also Matthew 8:12 and 10:28. "It is the greatest love that threatens the most severe punishments" (Bavinck, *R.D.*, 4:709).

c. In Barth's view faith pales in significance and the consequences of unbelief disappear in the light of the triumph of God's grace. "The gravity of the announcement of hell collapses under the pressure of universalism, although this is masked by his dialectics" (J. Kamphuis in Knevel [ed.], 1991, 73). Use is made of the image of a storm at sea, in which people appear to perish. They only do not realize that the water is too shallow in which to drown (cf. Brunner, *Dogmatics*, 1:351).

d. Neither God's love and grace nor his justice can be gauged with human measures (see Wentsel, *Dogm.*, 3b:673–77). We should be careful not to criticize God's justice on the basis of our own concept of fairness. "Is there unrighteousness with God? God forbid" (Rom. 9:14). We may not think lightly of sin and its punishment (see § 28.1).

e. It is indeed important to discern among references to "eternity." Sometimes it does indicate a very long time, but frequently it means: everlasting and indefinite. Matthew 25:46 has the latter meaning (eternal life versus eternal punishment). This damnation is forever; this is also clearly stated in other places (see 2 Thess. 1:9; Rev. 14:11; 20:10; and cf. *TDNT*, 1:209–10).

f. There are indeed passages that appear universalistic. A few of these have been discussed already (§ 32.1, subsection 6) in connection with the scope of atonement. In the Bible, words such as "all" and "world" do not always indicate all people without exception or the entire world including every individual. Not infrequently "all" has a categorical scope. For example, the context makes clear that Paul's second phrase "all men" in Romans 5:18 indicates all those who belong to Christ. God's salvation is universal in scope, but this does not imply that everyone will share in it forever.

Here we still wish to comment on the manner in which Berkhof treats Scripture passages. His approach reveals a definite predilection for associating one pronouncement with the penultimate and another with the ultimate. What is more, he views judgment and eternal life as projections of current experience with God in Christ and the Spirit on the screen of the future (1967, 65). Projections of Matthew, Paul, and other authors differ from each other and theology has a choice! Instead we should base ourselves on the entire revelation that God has given to us. Otherwise our expectation is not well-founded!

5. A consequence of universalism, which has strong appeal in our time, is that the call to faith and repentance loses its urgency. There is no support whatsoever in Scripture for either absolute or conditional universalism.

The words of Paul that one day God will "be all in all" (1 Cor. 15:28) would appear to remove all doubt with respect to a redemption of everything and everyone.[53] But in the same epistle the apostle refers to those who perish (1 Cor. 1:18).

In its own way, conditional universalism detracts from the gravity of the decision that is made in this life. Nowhere in the Bible do we find an indication that following this life there will be possibilities for coming to faith and repentance.

Neither is the doctrine of conditional immortality based on the Scriptures. Suffering "everlasting punishment" (Matt. 25:46) and being far "from the presence of the Lord" (2 Thess. 1:9) do not mean the same thing as being destroyed and ceasing to exist.

To those who think of an open end or a double truth, it should be pointed out that we may not leave open to question anything that is explicitly taught in Scripture.

The matter is not settled by personal considerations and feelings, but by the authority of the Word of God, which is unambiguous in its

53. That is the opinion of W. Michaelis, *Versöhnung des Alls* (atonement of the universe), 1950, 123ff.

pronouncements. Therefore we concur with Van Oosterzee (1817–82) that we cannot and may not do anything other than unconditionally submit to the written Word of him who cannot lie and offer him the full honor of faithful obedience.[54]

6. We need not trouble ourselves to paint a picture of *hell*, which is the place of the definitive execution of God's judgment. The Bible employs more images than concepts. Fire is an image of undergoing God's wrath; outer darkness is an indication of abandonment by God; being outside (Rev. 22:15) implies the exclusion from communion with God and his people; and weeping and gnashing of teeth denote remorse and self-reproach.

Restraint and caution are definitely in order here, but it is questionable whether in the New Testament we only encounter "an apparent ultimatum that is inextricably connected with" the proclamation of the gospel (Berkouwer, 1973, 413ff.). There is no objective information without struggle and without faith! In this connection Berkouwer quotes the words of Jesus: "Strive to enter in!" This certainly is the gist of the answer that he gives to the question: "Lord, are there few that be saved?" But at the same time he says "that many will seek to enter in, and shall not be able" (Luke 13:23–24; cf. Matt. 7:13–14).

Berkouwer is right in his sharp rejection of the preaching of judgment in which the gospel is not also sounded. Schilder also objects to this, and yet he wrote a book about hell in which he says: "Let fear not lead to disregard!" The theme of damnation should not be removed from the context of everything that God has taught, including his grace, his love, his mercy, his justice, the Christ, the history of redemption, and its consummation. The message of hell should be heard *in the light of the cross*. This includes an invitation to yield, not to God's wrath but to his love.[55]

On the other hand the gospel takes on its full significance in the light of justice and judgment.[56] It is, after all, the gospel of the coming and the work of the Son of God, "Jesus, [who] delivers us from the wrath to come?" (1 Thess. 1:10).

57.4. *Eternal life*

1. In this chapter on eschatology we refer to eternal life as life in eternal glory. This is what Matthew 25:46 places over against "everlasting punishment" and what Romans 6:23 contrasts with death as "the wages of sin."

54. J. J. van Oosterzee, *Christelijke Dogmatiek* (Christian dogmatics), 1876², 2:568.

55. K. Schilder, *Wat is de hel?* (what is hell?), 1932³, 27ff., 210ff.

56. W. Kremer, *Priesterlijke prediking* (priestly preaching), 1976, 137; W. Kremer, "The Judgment in the Preaching," tr. L. W. Bilkes, *Free Reformed Theological Journal* 9 (Fall 2005): 54.

In the New Testament this expression does not always have the same meaning. Especially in the fourth gospel there are places that imply that eternal life starts here and now. Jesus says: "Verily, verily, I say unto you, he that heareth my word and believeth on him that sent me, hath everlasting life, and shall not come into condemnation; but is passed from death unto life" (John 5:24; cf. John 3:36; 6:47). "And this is life eternal, that they might know thee the only true God and Jesus Christ whom thou hast sent" (John 17:3). Eternal life is like the kingdom of God: it is and it comes.

Eternal life is—both now and later—life in fellowship with God that is not threatened by death (cf. Weber, *Foundations*, 2:668). This is life indeed! It is not only life that lasts forever, but also qualitatively different from life in this world where sin reigns.

There is an inseparable connection between eternal life here and now and eternal life in the eschatological sense. This is the complete fulfillment of communion with God in Christ, which is already reality for those who believe in him, and which is mentioned in the Apostles' Creed and the Creed of Nicaea-Constantinople. In the latter creed it is referred to as "life in the world to come," which means the same thing as the coming age (Mark 10:30; cf. *TDNT*, 1:204–7).

It means being always with the Lord (1 Thess. 4:17); sharing in the glorification of Christ (Rom. 8:17), and receiving the heavenly inheritance (1 Peter 1:4). "There remaineth therefore a rest to the people of God" (Heb. 4:9), a resting from labors, whereby the works of believers follow them (Rev. 14:13). "They are called unto the marriage supper of the Lamb" (Rev. 19:9). Then God will dwell with his people; his servants "shall see his face; and his name shall be on their foreheads" (Rev. 21:3; 22:4). There will be no more tears, no death, no trouble, and no night (Rev. 21:4, 25). The servants of God "shall reign as kings for ever and ever" (Rev. 22:5).

2. What the Bible says about eternal life far transcends our imagination. It has not yet been revealed "what we shall be" (1 John 3:2). We shall nevertheless attempt to summarize what has been revealed to us.

According to Bavinck, in following a certain tradition, contemplation (*visio*), understanding (*comprehensio*), and enjoyment of God (*fruitio Dei*) make up the essence of future blessedness (*R.D.*, 4:722). The question is whether we can concur with this.

The concept "*comprehensio*" cannot be accepted, because we do not find grounds in Scripture for the expectation that people will be able to *comprehend* God, although we may think in terms of a knowledge of God much richer than now.

The New Testament says that God's servants will "see his face" (Rev. 22:4). Roman Catholic theology takes this to mean seeing God in his essence (*visio Dei per essentiam*), which is made possible through the elevation of man to supernatural status. Seeing God would be more or less perfect depending on man's merits (*DS*, 1305). We must reject this thinking about seeing God—so important to Rome—because of its context of the Roman Catholic doctrine of grace and merits.[57]

For that matter, it is a question how man could see God who is "invisible" (1 Tim. 1:17). The apostle Paul speaks of seeing "face to face" and a knowing as we are known (1 Cor. 13:12). This seeing and knowing will rest on revelation. We shall know God eternally from his revelation. His name will then be visible everywhere (cf. Schilder, 1954, 139, 160).

The concept of "enjoying God" (*fruitio Dei*) is quite prevalent in the writings of Augustine, and is reminiscent there of Psalm 34:8: "Taste and see that the LORD is good." Sometimes his words have a mystical flavor and we recognize rapture and ecstasy in them. Calvin uses the expression in an eschatological context. The Lord will give himself to be enjoyed by the elect (*Institutes*, 3.25.10). By this we mean that he will grant his communion to be fully experienced.

There is a description of eternal life that we can indeed take over and expand. It consists in knowing and serving, glorifying and praising God (Bavinck, *R.D.*, 4:727). Both *knowledge* and *service* of God now are still imperfect, but will then be perfect (1 Cor. 13:12). This is what the children of God, who serve him here uprightly but not perfectly, long for. The way of sanctification is also the path to seeing God (cf. Heb. 12:14).[58] Then "his servants will serve him" (Rev. 22:3). The love of God has reached its summit, and love for one another follows suit. Faith and hope do not abide—love does (1 Cor. 13).

In the holy city of God there is no temple to be found anymore. "For the Lord God Almighty and the Lamb are the temple of it" (Rev. 21:22). A separate temple will no longer be necessary, because consecration to God will dominate everything and all of life will have become service of God (cf. Schilder, 1954, 115ff.).

Eternal life also includes *glorifying and praising* God. We are thinking of the songs of praise that appear in the book of Revelation. Life in communion with God now already finds expression in songs of praise and thanksgiving, but then they will be more numerous and

57. Cf. Wentsel, *Natuur en genade* (nature and grace), 1970, 28–33, 364–90.
58. See W. H. Velema, *Geroepen tot heilig leven* (called to a holy life), 1988², 43ff.

purer. Everyone's life will be a song of praise. All that has breath, praise the Lord!

Perfect salvation (blessedness) will be an extension of the eternal joy that the believer feels in his heart today, and the eternal Sabbath begins already in this life (Heidelberg Catechism, Lord's Day 22 and 38).

Eternal life, eternal salvation (blessedness), *and eternal glory* are all terms that are used side by side. As far as salvation (blessedness) is concerned, everyone's measure will be filled, but this does not preclude differences in degrees of glory. Variations in the degree of glory are not a matter of rewards that are earned. They are a special grace with which God crowns his own work.

When life in communion with God is fully achieved, the communion of saints will also be perfect. We hear of "a great multitude, which no man can number, of all nations, and kindreds, and people, and tongues, standing before the throne and the Lamb" (Rev. 7:9). This implies that there will be a great variety of people who nevertheless will be one in the adoration of God and Christ.

Not infrequently the question arises whether we will *see and recognize* each other again.

We agree with Schilder that seeing and recognizing each other are not the right terms, because they have an earthly connotation. Knowing will be different: richer, deeper, purer, and more intensive than on earth. There will be "pneumatic" interaction, far surpassing current experience. Each human being becomes an open letter from Christ to the others (1954, 124–30).

3. One of the interpretations of the last article of the Apostles' Creed is Barth's (see also § 55.2, subsection 4).

According to him human life is limited in that it has both a beginning and an end. Death is not abnormal. This finite life will neither be destroyed nor continued. It will be eternalized, i.e., it will remain present to God forever. As it was for its limited, temporary duration, so it shall be forever in God's sight (*C.D.*, 3.2.554, 623ff.; 3.3.89ff.). The fact that Barth means a disclosure of what has been is implied by what he wrote subsequently (4.3.927–28): Those whom God calls out of their temporal existence and ministry he takes into the light of his consummating revelation at the coming of Christ. Then their concluded existence will be illuminated, having and maintaining its own light, and bearing witness to God in this renewed form in which it is conformed to the image of the Son of God. God places man's temporal existence and all its contents to eternal light and therefore into eternal life.

Being forever alive in the mind of God differs substantially from what the Bible teaches us to expect: eternal life in communion with God in a new world. Barth does refer to a victory over death, but he has no room for the glory of resurrected life that will be bestowed on the children of God in communion with him who has said: "I am the resurrection, and the life; he that believeth in me though he were dead, yet shall he live" (John 11:25).

57.5. *The new heaven and the new earth*

1. In the creed, the expectation of faith culminates in the confession of eternal life. In addition, we may also expect a renewal of the earth. Eschatology has *cosmic implications*.

There is a future for those who belong to God—there is for them also a future in bodily terms. In this connection we need to think of the earth on which he will dwell. Here also we need to base ourselves on Scripture so as not to fall into human fantasies and speculations.

According to God's promise "we look for new heavens and a new earth, wherein dwelleth righteousness" (2 Peter 3:13). This promise occurs already in the Old Testament (see Isa. 65:17; 66:22). John saw the new heaven and the new earth in a vision (Rev. 21:1).

The promise of Isaiah 11:6 is repeated in Isaiah 65:25. Isaiah 11 pictures eschatological peace to be brought in by the Messiah. Among the images that express how everything will be, there are some that remind us of Paradise (Rev. 22:1–2). Other images were taken from the history of redemption, such as the New Jerusalem. The history of redemption is complete when God dwells with his people without any further threat of separation. Sin and death will be things of the past.

"In the beginning God created heaven and earth" (Gen. 1:1). "And I saw a new heaven and a new earth" (Rev. 21:1). The end dovetails with the beginning but far surpasses it. Everything becomes new, not in the usual sense that something new simply replaces something old, but through a miracle of God it stays forever new. In Revelation 21:5 the word "new" (*kainos*) means: "the epitome of the wholly different and miraculous thing which is brought by the time of salvation" (*TDNT*, 3:449).

2. We do not expect that this world will be destroyed to make room for a new world. The idea of *annihilatio* (obliteration) occurs in old Lutheran theology—more so than in the Reformed tradition. Reference has sometimes been made to Scripture passages such as 2 Peter 3:7–12.

It cannot be denied that there will be discontinuity. However, the Scriptures also indicate that there will be a certain continuity. We have in mind especially the words of Paul regarding the release of creation from bondage to decay (Rom. 8:21). There is a regeneration (Matt. 19:28), a restoration, and a removal of uncertainty (Acts 3:21; Heb. 12:27). Therefore Reformed dogmatics usually speaks of a renewal that is simultaneously a cleansing and purification. Christ will "burn this old world with fire and flame to cleanse it" (Belgic Confession of Faith, article 37).

God neither gives up on his creation nor allows it to perish. Continuity is not a function of something durable in the world itself, but signifies that God does not abandon the work of his hands.

We look forward to the completion of creation. Re-creation is the restoration and renewal of creation and not a second creation.

Neither should the events of the future be seen as a mere overhaul or renovation, because the changes will be radical and fundamental. The glory of the new heaven and the new earth will far transcend the former.

There is both continuity and discontinuity (cf. Versteeg, 1989, 118–22). God's creation will be renewed, cleansed from all entrenched evil, and transfigured, but through the judgment. The present world approaches its end, but it will not be written off. *God's creation has a future.*

This expectation does not diminish but enhances our concern for the world in which we live. It is God's world and its future rests in his hands and not those of mankind.

3. In Revelation 21–22, Scripture clearly lays out how the latter things are related to the former.

In creation heaven and earth belonged together, but became separated in consequence of sin. The restored harmony will be through the redemptive work of Christ (cf. Col. 1:20).

The Bible portrays heaven as God's dwelling place and earth as given to mankind (see Ps. 115:16). Heaven is filled with God's glory. It is also the realm of his love.

The history of redemption shows that despite the sin of mankind God comes to them in Christ because he wants to see the relationship restored. That he will once again dwell among men (Rev. 21:3) implies that all disharmony will have been removed. God will connect his dwelling place to that of mankind and live "under one roof" with them. Nevertheless, as Occupant he will dominate (cf. Schilder, 1954, 114). There is no temple in the New Jerusalem (Rev. 21:22). This also implies that God will be with his people everywhere, and they with him.

In Revelation 21–22, the beauty and perfection of the New Jerusalem is portrayed in telling images. To us this is unimaginable and yet recognizable. A biblical term for this future is "*glory.*" The glory of God illuminates the city. The heavenly glory is shared with earth.

When God dwells there, righteousness will also dwell there (2 Peter 3:13). What a difference with the present world, which is full of unrighteousness!

The expectation of the new heaven and the new earth is no escape from the reality in which we now live, but much more an incentive for us here and now to focus on this great future. See 2 Peter 3:11–14.

One of the biblical images is that of a wedding. A wedding is a feast. The wedding feast of the Lamb is the greatest feast of all. Christ will be there as the Lamb. His sacrifice for his people will always be kept in mind.

In the realm of glory God will be "all in all" (1 Cor. 15:28). This is the ultimate goal of God's acts. "For of him, and through him, and to him, are all things: to whom be glory for ever. Amen" (Rom. 11:36).

Some Literature

P. Althaus, *Die letzten Dinge* (the last things), 1964⁹.

H. Baarlink et al. (ed.), *Vervulling en voleinding* (fulfillment and completion), 1984.

J. T. Bakker, *Eschatologische prediking bij Luther* (eschatological preaching of Luther), 1964.

H. Berkhof, *Christus de zin der geschiedenis* (Christ the significance of history), 1958.

H. Berkhof, *Gegronde verwachting* (well-founded expectation), 1967.

A. M. Berkhoff, *De Wederkomst van Christus* (the return of Christ), 1926.

G. C. Berkouwer, *The Return of Christ*, 1972.

H. Bietenhard, *Das tausendjährige Reich* (the millennium), 1955.

K. Blei, *Christelijke toekomstverwachting* (Christian anticipation of the future), 1986.

Tj. Boersma, *De Bijbel is geen puzzelboek* (the Bible is no book of puzzles), 1977[2].

L. Boliek, *The Resurrection of the Flesh*, 1962.

A. de Bondt, *Wat leert het Oude Testamanent aangaande het leven na dit leven?* (what does the Old Testament teach about life beyond this life), 1938.

R. G. Clouse, (ed.), *The Meaning of the Millennium*, 1980[4].
O. Cullmann, *Christus und die Zeit* (Christ and time), 1946.
K. Dijk, *De toekomst van Christus* (the future of Christ), 1953.
K. Dijk, *Het einde der eeuwen* (the end of the ages), 1952.
K. Dijk, *Het tijk der duizend jaren* (the millennium), 1933.
K. Dijk, *Tussen sterven en opstanding* (between death and resurrection), 1951.
L. Floor, *Het gericht van God volgens het Nieuwe Testament* (the judgment of God according to the New Testament), 1979.
J. van Genderen, *De verwachting van een duizendjarig vrederijk* (the expectation of a millenium of peace), 1988[2].
J. van Genderen, *Geloofskennis en geloofsverwachting* (faith's knowledge and faith's anticipation), 1982.
K. Hanhart, *The Intermediate State in the New Testament*, 1966.
J. de Heer, *Het duizenjarig vrederijk* (the millennium of peace), 1934.
A. A. Hoekema, *The Bible and the Future*, 1979.
P. Hoffmann, *Die Toten in Christus* (the dead in Christ), 1969[2].
F. Holström, *Das eschatologische Denken der Gegenwart* (eschatological thinking of the present), 1936.
O. Jager, *Het eeuwige leven* (eternal life), 1962.
A. G. Knevel (ed.), *Hemel of hel—onze eeuwige bestemming* (heaven or hell—our eternal destination), 1991.
W. Kreck, *Die Zukunft des Gekommenen* (the future of the one who came), 1961.
A. Kuyper, *Van de heiligmaking, van de heerlijkmaking en van het rijk der heerlijkheid* (on sanctification, glorification, and the realm of glory), 1935.
G. van der Leeuw, *Onsterfelijkheid of opstanding* (immortality or resurrection), 1947[4].
W. Logister, *Reïncarnatie* (reincarnation), 1990.
C. J. Meeuse, *De toekomstverwachting van de Nadere Reformation in het licht van haar tijd* (the anticipation of the future of the Second Reformation in the light of its time), 1990.
R. J. van der Meulen, *De Antichrist*, 1952.
R. J. van der Meulen, *De openbaring in het laatste Bijbelboek* (revelation in the last book of the Bible), 1948.
J. Moltmann, *Theologie der Hoffnung* (theology of hope), 1964.
G. C. van Niftrik, *De hemel* (heaven), 1972.

W. J. Ouweneel, *De openbaring van Jezus Christus* (the revelation of Jesus Christ), 1, 1988; 2, 1990.

H. D. Preuss (ed.), *Eschatologie im Alten Testament* (eschatology in the Old Testament), 1978.

H. Quistorp, *Die letzten Dinge im Zeugnis Calvins* (the last things in Calvin's testimony), 1941.

J. Ratzinger, *Eschatologie—Tod und ewiges Leben* (eschatology—death and eternal life), 1978[4].

H. Ridderbos, *De komst van het koninkrijk* (the coming of the kingdom), 1950.

K. Schilder, *Wat is de hemel?* (what is heaven?), 1954[2].

J. J. van der Schuit, *Achter het gordijn des doods* (beyond the curtain of death), 1929.

E. Staehelin, *Die Verkündigung des Reiches in der Kirche Jesu Christi* (the preaching of the kingdom of God in the church of Jesus Christ), 1–7, 1951–64.

B. Telder, *Sterven . . . en dan?* (death . . . and then?), 1960.

B. Telder, *Sterven . . . waarom?* (death . . . why?), 1963.

S. H. Travis, *Christian Hope and the Future of Man*, 1980.

S. H. Travis, *Christ and the Judgment of God*, 1986.

J. P. Versteeg, *Christus en de Geest* (Christ and the Spirit), 1971.

J. P. Versteeg, *Geest, ambt en uitzicht* (Spirit, office, and prospect), 1989.

J. P. Versteeg, *Het heden en de toekomst* (the present and the future), 1969.

Vervulling en voleinding (ed. H. Baarlink et al.), 1984.

G. Vos, *The Pauline Eschatology* (1930), 1979.

J. de Vuyst, *De Openbaring van Johannes* (the Revelation of John), 1987.

J. R. Wiskerke, *Leven tussen sterven en opstanding* (life between death and resurrection), 1963.

Index of Scripture

Romans

Index of Subjects and Names